CONSUMER PRICE INDEXES, MAJOR EXPENDITURE CLASSES, 1929–81 (1967 = 100)

Year or month	All items	Food	Housing	Apparel and upkeep	Transportation	Medical care	Entertainment	Other goods and services	Energy[4]
1929	51.3	48.3	—	48.5	—	—	—	—	—
1933	38.8	30.6	—	36.9	—	—	—	—	—
1939	41.6	34.6	52.2	42.4	43.0	36.7	—	—	—
1940	42.0	35.2	52.4	42.8	42.7	36.8	—	—	—
1941	44.1	38.4	53.7	44.8	44.2	37.0	—	—	—
1942	48.8	45.1	56.2	52.3	48.1	38.0	—	—	—
1943	51.8	50.3	56.8	54.6	47.9	39.9	—	—	—
1944	52.7	49.6	58.1	58.5	47.9	41.1	—	—	—
1945	53.9	50.7	59.1	61.5	47.8	42.1	—	—	—
1946	58.5	58.1	60.6	67.5	50.3	44.4	—	—	—
1947	66.9	70.6	65.2	78.2	55.5	48.1	—	—	—
1948	72.1	76.6	69.8	83.3	61.8	51.1	—	—	—
1949	71.4	73.5	70.9	80.1	66.4	52.7	—	—	—
1950	72.1	74.5	72.8	79.0	68.2	53.7	—	—	—
1951	77.8	82.8	77.2	86.1	72.5	56.3	—	—	—
1952	79.5	84.3	78.7	85.3	77.3	59.3	—	—	—
1953	80.1	83.0	80.8	84.6	79.5	61.4	—	—	—
1954	80.5	82.8	81.7	84.5	78.3	63.4	—	—	—
1955	80.2	81.6	82.3	84.1	77.4	64.8	—	—	—
1956	81.4	82.2	83.6	85.8	78.8	67.2	—	—	—
1957	84.3	84.9	86.2	87.3	83.3	69.9	—	—	90.1
1958	86.6	88.5	87.7	87.5	86.0	73.2	—	—	90.3
1959	87.3	87.1	88.6	88.2	89.6	76.4	—	—	91.8
1960	88.7	88.0	90.2	89.6	89.6	79.1	—	—	94.2
1961	89.6	89.1	90.9	90.4	90.6	81.4	—	—	94.4
1962	90.6	89.9	91.7	90.9	92.5	83.5	—	—	94.7
1963	91.7	91.2	92.7	91.9	93.0	85.6	—	—	95.0
1964	92.9	92.4	93.8	92.7	94.3	87.3	—	—	94.6
1965	94.5	94.4	94.9	93.7	95.9	89.5	—	—	96.3
1966	97.2	99.1	97.2	96.1	97.2	93.4	—	—	97.8
1967	100.0	100.0	100.0	100.0	100.0	100.0	100.0	100.0	100.0
1968	104.2	103.6	104.0	105.4	103.2	106.1	105.7	105.2	101.5
1969	109.8	108.9	110.4	111.5	107.2	113.4	111.0	110.4	104.2
1970	116.3	114.9	118.2	116.1	112.7	120.6	116.7	116.8	107.0
1971	121.3	118.4	123.4	119.8	118.6	128.4	122.9	122.4	111.2
1972	125.3	123.5	128.1	122.3	119.9	132.5	126.5	127.5	114.3
1973	133.1	141.4	133.7	126.8	123.8	137.7	130.0	132.5	123.5
1974	147.7	161.7	148.8	136.2	137.7	150.5	139.8	142.0	159.7
1975	161.2	175.4	164.5	142.3	150.6	168.6	152.2	153.9	176.6
1976	170.5	180.8	174.6	147.6	165.5	184.7	159.8	162.7	189.3
1977	181.5	192.2	186.5	154.2	177.2	202.4	167.7	172.2	207.3
1978	195.4	211.4	202.8	159.6	185.5	219.4	176.6	183.3	220.4
1979	217.4	234.5	227.6	166.6	212.0	239.7	188.5	196.7	275.9
1980	246.8	254.6	263.3	178.4	249.7	265.9	205.3	214.5	361.1
1981	272.4	274.6	293.5	186.9	280.0	294.5	221.4	235.7	410.0

Note: Data beginning 1978 are for all urban consumers; earlier data are for urban wage earners and clerical workers.

Source: Department of Labor, Bureau of Statistics.

THE
ECONOMY
TODAY

THE ECONOMY TODAY

SECOND EDITION

BRADLEY R. SCHILLER
The American University

RANDOM HOUSE
New York

Second Edition
98765432

Copyright © 1980, 1983 by Random House, Inc.

Library of Congress Cataloging in Publication Data

Schiller, Bradley R., 1943–
    The economy today.

    Includes bibliographical references and index.
    1. Economics. I. Title.
HB171.5.S292 1983   330   82-23123
ISBN 0-394-33106-0

Manufactured in the United States of America

Design by Betty Binns Graphics/Martin Lubin

Charts by Rino Dussi

Cover design by Leon Bolognese

Cover Art by Ronald F. Hall

PREFACE

The economy today often seems out of control. In just the last ten years, the economy has been hit by three major recessions, recurrent bouts of double-digit inflation, sky-high interest rates, and unprecedented deficits in the federal budget. These repeated setbacks have undermined people's confidence. According to public-opinion polls, relatively few Americans believe that either the president or Congress is willing or able to control the economy. Even fewer people believe that economists can control the economy. A seemingly endless string of bad forecasts together with highly vocal squabbles about how the economy really works have undermined the credibility of the economics profession. Indeed, economic forecasters now have no more credibility than fortune tellers (see the public-opinion poll on p. 329).

In the midst of this economic instability the concept of economic "fine tuning" looks like a historic relic. Yet, it wasn't that long ago that leading economists asserted substantial confidence in their ability to achieve the economic goals of society. And, with inflation well under control and unemployment rates falling, the public and the politicians believed those claims. No such confidence exists today.

The Economy Today may not raise economists' standing in public-opinion polls. But it is designed to explain how things so often go wrong. The text goes beyond straightforward explanations of economic theory to descriptions of the constraints on decision making and implementation. These constraints include mundane measurement problems as well as goal conflicts between competing political forces. The constraints also include the implementation delays associated with congressional deliberations and executive action. Last but not least, the text confesses that economists don't have all the answers.

The Economy Today does not try to inculcate resignation and despair. On the contrary, it attempts to demonstrate how economic policy can move us closer to our economic goals, even if we cannot reach all of them simultaneously. The path to *optimal* (not perfect) policies is constructed out of theoretical principles as well as institutional constraints. This path is found by examining diverse theories of how the economy works, each time seeking insights into specific policy problems. This eclectic approach emphasizes the need for flexibility in policy design in response to (changing) institutional and behavioral realities. Calling for modest expectations and activism, the text is guided by the maxim that it is better to be approximately right than dead wrong.

UNDERSTANDING ECONOMIC GOALS

To appreciate the importance of the policy decisions Congress and the president make, one must understand the nature of our economic problems. Students in particular must understand not only what unemployment *is*, for example, but also *why* it is a serious sociopolitical problem. The same is true of inflation. The ability to define and measure inflation is not enough. Students must also know *why* inflation is regarded as a serious problem, and by whom. Then the search for economic explanations of unemployment and inflation begins to look interesting and important.

The text tries to satisfy this need by devoting three chapters to major economic problems. In the macro section unemployment and inflation each receive full, chapter-length treatment. In the micro section the distribution of income is highlighted as the core economic problem. The discussion in these chapters is highly institutional and reaches beyond economics to the social, psychological, political, and historical dimensions of what we call "economic" problems. The unemployment rate, for example, is not a mere statistic in these chapters but an economic force that depresses incomes, pushes some families into poverty, threatens family relationships, increases social tensions, and even shortens life expectancy. Inflation is viewed in similar terms, with historical references to the Chinese experience of 1948–49 as well as to more familiar and recent examples (German hyperinflation and the U.S. experience from 1978 to 1980). Chapter 29 emphasizes the trade-off between the goals of equity and efficiency in income-distribution policies. The intent of all these chapters is to stimulate interest in learning more about economics and in acquiring tools for solving important problems. The chapters on economic problems should play a pivotal role in establishing a goal-oriented framework for macro and micro theory. They may be read first or as an introduction to specific topics.

POLICY THEME

The relevance of economic theory is emphasized throughout the text. Economics is taught through the mechanics of the economy. *Every* chapter contains a discussion of an actual economic problem. Most chapters are, in fact, developed around a specific economic problem, drawn from the pages of newspapers, magazines, the *Economic Report of the President,* or statements of the president and his advisers. This approach strives to make economics "come alive," so that students see a real purpose in learning economic principles.

THE MACRO CHAPTERS

The basic fiscal and monetary chapters offer several features. From the beginning the stabilization problem is discussed in the context of changing expectations and inventory adjustments. Shifts of the consumption and investment functions are viewed as commonplace rather than rare. Recent changes in bank practices (e.g., automatic transfers and sweep accounts) are explained and linked to definitions of the money supply.

Of particular importance is the way the controversy between Keynesians and Monetarists is handled. The efficacy of fiscal and monetary policies is evaluated from both Keynesian and Monetarist perspectives. The discussion in Chapter 12 not only summarizes the views of each theory but also highlights their different policy implications. The summary tables on page 279 should be particularly helpful to students in assessing the policy significance of the Keynesian-Monetarist debate.

Chapter 13 is devoted to supply-side perspectives, a third basic view of how the economy works. The chapter focuses on the aggregate-supply curve and the forces that can shift it. All major supply-side options are surveyed, not just the more recent versions of "supply-side" tax cuts.

Like most texts, this book threatens to confound students who think they see answers for all of today's economic problems. This threat is particularly acute in *The Economy Today,* which tries to relate policy and theory so closely. To meet such a threat—to respond to the nagging and skeptical question of how economists can be so right when the economy is so wrong—the text presents an entirely new type of chapter. Chapter 14 offers a direct confrontation between economic theory and economic policy. It summarizes the apparent potential of theory to solve our economic problems. It then examines the historical record and identifies the measurement, design, and implementation obstacles that continue to frustrate our policy intentions. The dependence of policy decisions on economic forecasts (along with their spotty records) is emphasized. The political forces that help to shape economic policy are also discussed. The chapter may provide an invaluable bridge between theory and policy. It should certainly encourage more modest expectations for economic performance.

THE MICRO CHAPTERS

The emphasis on real-world applications is apparent in the micro chapters as well. From the very beginning the policy significance of basic principles is stressed. The introduction to competition

(Chapter 21), for example, is developed around the actual experiences of the pocket-calculator industry. The rapid rate of entry by firms into this industry, the unrelenting pressure on prices and profits, and the series of truly spectacular cost and product innovations are used to illustrate competitive forces at work. By following the decline of calculator prices from $200 (in 1972) to under $6 (by 1982) students should develop a keen appreciation of what competition is all about. The dynamics of a competitive market are further illustrated by video games, personal computers, and Atlantic City casinos. (An appendix to Chapter 21 shows the same kind of competitive forces in agriculture and assesses the consequences for farm technology, employment, prices, and income.)

The competitive dynamics of the electronics industry provide the foundation for analysis of alternative market structures. By assuming various barriers to entry and other noncompetitive practices, the calculator industry is transformed into a monopoly (Chapter 22), and an oligopoly (Chapter 23); then its current structure of monopolistic competition (also Chapter 23) is examined. In each case, direct comparisons of behavior and outcomes in alternative market structures are highlighted. The implications for our economic welfare, antitrust activity, and government regulation are emphasized. The AT & T and IBM antitrust cases are used to illustrate the different principles at work.

Chapter 24 provides another unique chapter for an introductory text. No new theory is presented in this chapter. Instead, it surveys the actual behavior of familiar U.S. firms. Firms possessing substantial market power (high market share) are first identified by name. The concentration ratios used here refer to individual product markets (e.g., tennis balls), not the more traditional (and much less meaningful) industry classifications (e.g., rubber products). The noncompetitive practices of these and other firms are then described, in considerable detail and illustrated with many news clippings. Wrigley's gum, Levi's jeans, Coors beer, and Wonder bread are among the products discussed. This chapter should add color to the more theoretical discussions of market structure contained in Chapters 21–23.

Considerable space is devoted to labor markets. Again, both competitive and noncompetitive behavior are described. Unionism and employer power (monopsony) are portrayed as significant influences on market outcomes. Specific unions (the Baseball Players Association, the United Mine Workers, the UAW) and employers are identified, and their behavior assessed. Labor-market outcomes (wages and employment) are seen as the result of both competitive forces and institutional barriers. Of special interest here are applications to robotics and the high salaries of some college football coaches.

THE ISSUES CHAPTERS

In addition to the policy emphasis in the core theory chapters, separate and more detailed discussion of selected economic issues are provided. In the macro section Reagan economics, the continuing problem of energy shocks, and the productivity slowdown all receive chapter-length attention. The Reagan administration's policies are discussed in terms of both its original supply-side expectations and its later compromises with Keynesian and Monetarist perspectives. Chapter 15 ends with the contrasting views of James Tobin and Arthur Laffer on "what went wrong."

In Chapter 16 energy shocks are assessed in terms of both short-run instability and long-run economic costs. At the end of this chapter students should not only know a bit more about the dimensions of the energy crisis but also be more skilled in utilizing economic principles. The productivity problem is examined in Chapter 17 in the context of the various sources of growth as well as the potential limits to productivity and growth.

The issue chapters in the micro section are also a blend of institutional detail and applied theory. Basic principles are illustrated explicitly. Externalities are portrayed as the core of our pollution problems (Chapter 30). Both labor-supply theory and experiments with the negative income tax are used to assess the problems and potential of welfare reform (Chapter 31). And marginal productivity theory is contrasted with the theory of "comparable worth" and the perspectives of "radical" economists in the discussion of discrimination in Chapter 32. It is the blending of theory and policy that distinguishes these chapters.

INTERNATIONAL TOPICS

The final section of the text focuses on international subjects. International trade and finance receive substantial attention, in recognition of their growing influence on our economic performance. In each case the motivations for trade and finance are discussed at length. The market mechanism is then related to those motivations. Finally, the sources of resistance (both micro and macro) to free trade and finance are identified as constraints on policy decisions. In the process, David Ricardo's theories and vested economic interests are both viewed as important determinants of trade flows. One story about Franco-American trade in wheat and wine weaves through the trade and finance chapters, helping to drive home the intrinsic relationships of trade and finance.

Chapter 35 examines the economic problems of less developed countries. The problem of economic development is related to both traditional measures of income and more general "human needs." The constraints on economic growth are then discussed, with an eye toward identifying an optimal growth strategy. The role of external financing (and its limitations) is given special emphasis.

The final chapter of the text provides a detailed look at the purposes and mechanics of socialist planning. Students are asked to meet the challenge of planning head-on, as the superplanner in a newly established socialist order. We begin with basics (production possibilities), then assemble tools for resolving the questions of WHAT, HOW, and FOR WHOM. The actual experiences of the Soviet Union and China are used to illustrate both the challenge of planning and alternative responses. The chapter (and the text) concludes with a comparative assessment of U.S., Soviet, and Chinese performance.

WHAT IS NEW IN THIS EDITION

Users of the first edition of *The Economy Today* will have already spotted some of the major changes in this edition. Altogether, about 40 percent of the text is completely new or extensively revised. Some of the major changes include, in sequence:

Introduction

The concept of opportunity cost is illustrated by the Reagan defense build-up. There is a more ex-plicit treatment of increasing opportunity costs and growth (Chapter 1).

Money and banks

The effects of the Monetary Control Act of 1980 on money-supply measures and Federal Reserve regulation are fully incorporated into the text (Chapters 10–11).

Monetarism

The Monetarist perspective is presented in more detail, and critical elements of the Keynesian-Monetarist controversy are highlighted (Chapter 12).

Supply-side economics

The aggregate-supply curve is introduced and used as the focus of various supply-side perspectives (Chapter 13).

Reagan economics

The theoretical basis for Reagan's policies is described, along with later compromises. The causes of the 1981–82 recession are analyzed (Chapter 15).

Growth and productivity

The sources of productivity and economic growth are examined, especially in relationship to the recent slowdowns in both rates (Chapter 17).

Demand and elasticity

The determinants of demand are introduced earlier. More space is devoted to the distinction between shifts of and movements along the demand curve. Elasticity is discussed and illustrated more fully (Chapter 18).

Costs and production functions

Money costs are explicitly related to the production function (Chapter 19).

Economic profits

The constrasting profit concepts of the public,

accountants, and economists are explicitly compared (Chapter 20).

Industry structure and behavior

Dozens of new illustrations of market behavior are provided. These include price fixing (the Arkansas milk producers, Cleveland supermarkets), monopoly patents (Prince tennis rackets), product differentiation (designer jeans), as well as intense competition (video games, personal computers) (Chapters 21–24).

Monopoly

Profit-maximization computations are introduced; a new policy section contrasts the IBM and AT & T antitrust cases (Chapter 22).

Rent, interest, and profit

Discussions of rent controls and computations of present discounted values for returns to capital are included (Chapter 28).

Workfare vs. welfare

The conflict between the provision of income transfers and work incentives is examined, with an emphasis on the 1981 welfare reforms and "workfare" experiments (Chapter 31).

Economic development

An entirely new chapter on the problems and prospects of less developed countries, with illustrations from Haiti, Ethiopia, and Senegal, is included (Chapter 35).

PAPERBACKS

In this edition the text is also available in paperback splits. The macro half contains chapters 1–17 and 33–36. The micro half contains Chapters 1–3 and 18–34.

STUDENT LEARNING AIDS

It is hoped that the style and approach of *The Economy Today* will motivate students to learn economics. Motivation is not enough, however. A text must also "teach" basic principles. In this regard, the core theory chapters of the text cover the standard topics of macro and micro theory, in a familiar order. The learning process is reinforced by the following features.

Textual learning aids

To facilitate comprehension and retention, each chapter contains the following learning aids:

CHAPTER PREVIEW Each chapter begins with a narrative introduction to the content and purpose of the chapter. Each preview highlights basic questions to be answered and relates them to previous chapters.

RUNNING GLOSSARY Definitions of key terms are provided in the margins, to facilitate retention and quick review. Definitions are repeated in successive chapters where they are relevant, in recognition of the fact that students do not remember basic terms after only one "lesson." All of these terms are compiled into a complete glossary, with chapter references, at the end of the book.

FULLY ANNOTATED GRAPHS AND TABLES *All* graphs and tables in the text are accompanied by self-contained captions. These reinforce the in-text discussions and facilitate quick review. In addition, the content of related schedules and graphs are explicitly synchronized with the aid of labeled rows (in schedules) and dots (on graphs). The demand schedule and curve in Chapter 2 illustrate this feature. Color is used in tables and graphs throughout to highlight new or important concepts.

SELF-CONTAINED EXAMPLES The text makes considerable use of shaded boxes to illustrate key points of the text. Some of these are designed to highlight a basic concept (e.g., *ceteris paribus*). Others are illustrative digressions and include newspaper and magazine clippings, public-opinion polls, or short summaries of related material. The use of shaded boxes clearly distinguishes all of this material from the flow of the basic text.

POLICY IMPLICATIONS Every theory chapter contains a brief discussion of a specific policy implication. These sections reinforce the basic theoretical presentations by underscoring the use of the principles introduced in the chapter.

NARRATIVE SUMMARIES   Chapter summaries highlight basic points and principles in brief, sequenced paragraphs.

KEY-TERM REVIEW   Each chapter ends with a list of key terms for quick review. These lists include all terms contained in the running glossary of the chapter.

DISCUSSION QUESTIONS   Four or five discussion questions are provided at the end of each chapter. These relate directly to basic principles covered in the chapter and can be used for student review, class discussion, or homework assignments.

NUMERICAL PROBLEM   Each chapter concludes with one numerical problem. This tests the student's ability to solve typical exam-type problems. Answers are in the *Instructor's Resource Manual*.

Study Guide

There are several supplements available to accompany the text itself. From the student's perspective, the most important of these is the *Study Guide*, prepared by Professors Lawrence Ziegler at the University of Texas (Arlington) and Michael Tansey at Rockhurst College. Each chapter of the *Study Guide* contains these features:

QUICK REVIEW   Key points in the text chapter are restated at the beginning of each *Study Guide* chapter. The reviews are parallel to and reinforce the chapter summaries provided in the text.

LEARNING OBJECTIVES   The salient lessons of the text chapters are noted at the outset of each *Study Guide* chapter. These objectives focus the student's study and help to assure that key points will not be overlooked. New to this edition, the objectives are keyed to the exercises in the *Study Guide* to help reinforce learning.

KEY-TERM REVIEW   Early in each chapter the students are asked to match definitions with key terms. This relatively simple exercise is designed to refresh the student's memory and provide a basis for subsequent exercises.

TRUE-FALSE QUESTIONS   Twenty or so true-false questions are provided in each chapter. These questions have been class-tested to assure their effectiveness in highlighting basic principles.

MULTIPLE-CHOICE QUESTIONS   Approximately fifteen multiple-choice questions per chapter are also provided. These questions allow only one answer and also focus on basic principles.

PROBLEMS AND APPLICATIONS   Each chapter of the *Study Guide* contains one or two real-world problems. These problems require the student to complete graphs, tables, or simple algebraic solutions.

COMMON ERRORS   In each chapter of the *Study Guide,* errors that students frequently make are identified. The basis for those errors are then explained, along with the correct principles. This unique feature is very effective in helping students discover their own mistakes.

ANSWERS   Answers to *all* problems, exercises, and questions are provided at the end of each chapter. These answers make the *Study Guide* self-contained, thus allowing students to use it for self-study.

INSTRUCTOR'S AIDS

We have tried to make the learning process easier for teachers as well as students. To this end, Professors Virginia Owen and Alan Dillingham (Illinois State University) have prepared an *Instructor's Resource Manual.* In addition, Professor Michael Ellis (North Texas State University) has compiled a completely new *Test Bank* of 1,850 multiple-choice questions.

Instructor's Resource Manual

The purpose of the *Instructor's Resource Manual* is to provide a ready source of lecture and discussion material for classroom teaching. To this end, it offers a variety of material, including:

CHAPTER OUTLINE   The first section of each chapter briefly summarizes the material under the text's major headings. Instructors can duplicate this section for students as an aid in studying.

TEXT EXPANSIONS The second section of each chapter highlights subjects that often require special attention, giving many interesting examples for classroom discussion.

CONTROVERSIAL ISSUES The third section of each chapter, "Take a Stand," describes a controversial issue associated with the theory presented in the text. Chapter 2 of the text, for example, discusses the basic elements of supply and demand. The *Resource Manual* discusses the pros and cons of regulating the price of natural gas, drawing on the text and a recent news article. No resolution of the issue is offered. "Take a Stand" is intended to start a classroom discussion or to form the basis for essay-type questions.

NEWS UPDATE The fourth section of each *Resource Manual* chapter provides a summary and analysis of a recent economics event. The core of the "News Updates" is drawn from *The Wall Street Journal, Business Week,* or similar publications. The news summary is supplemented by a brief analysis that ties the story directly to the content of the text.

SUPPLEMENTARY RESOURCES The final section in each chapter serves two separate functions. First, it provides a list of audio-visual and printed materials that can be readily obtained for class use. Second, it provides references for additional lecture material or student assignments.

Test Bank

A completely new *Test Bank* was prepared for this edition. The *Test Bank* includes: 36 chapter tests of approximately 50 multiple-choice questions per chapter, totaling 1,850 questions. Each question has been classified according to its level of difficulty. There are three levels. The first requires the simple recall of facts, names, or definitions. The second level of question is analytical, requiring greater comprehension and an understanding of functional relationships. The third level, the most difficult, demands a thorough comprehension of theory and a high degree of analytical reasoning.

About half of the *Test Bank* questions are cross-referenced directly to the learning objectives in the *Study Guide.* Two prepared midterms and two comprehensive final examinations, total-

ing 300 question, are also available in the *Test Bank.* The entire *Test Bank* is available on computer tape.

Overhead transparencies

Over 100 of the key tables and graphs in the text have been reproduced as overhead masters. These are made available to users by the publisher.

A COMPLETE TEACHING PACKAGE

We have tried to assemble a complete teaching package for classroom use. In the process we have introduced several unique text features, including the chapters concerned with economic problems; the liberal use of news stories and other supplementary materials; the use of a running glossary; and an explicit, simultaneous introduction to both theory and institutions. In the *Study Guide* we have introduced the "Common Errors" section and a greater emphasis on learning basic definitions. The *Instructor's Resource Manual* features the "Take a Stand" section, as well as "News Updates." We have tried to present all of the material in a lively manner that stimulates student interest.

Have we succeeded in producing a new and effective teaching package? We hope so. The real test will be administered by students who use this text. Success will be measured in terms of increased student interest in and understanding of the economy today.

ACKNOWLEDGMENTS

The second edition of *The Economy Today* has been improved by the suggestions of many users and reviewers. Walter Johnson, Carl Austermiller, and Walter Nicholson were particularly generous with their time in reviewing the text in its various stages. In addition to them, I would like to thank publicly all of the reviewers of both the first and second edition, including:

Carl Austermiller, *Oakland Community College*
Charles Berry, *University of Cincinnati*
Robert Berry, *Miami University*
Neil Browne, *Bowling Green University*
Conrad Caligaris, *Northeastern University*

Philip Caruso, *Western Michigan University*
James Cochrane, *University of South Carolina*
Robert Costrell, *University of Massachusetts*
Steven Cox, *Arizona State University*
David Denslow, *University of Florida*
Michael Ellis, *North Texas State University*
Herbert J. Eskowitz, *Northeastern University*
Donald Farness, *Oregon State University*
Roger Frantz, *San Diego State University*
David Gay, *University of Arkansas*
John Gilliam, *Texas Tech University*
Edna Gott, *Texas Tech University*
William Gunther, *The University of Alabama*
William Haller, *University of Rhode Island*
Upton Henderson, *Central State University*
Walter Johnson, *University of Missouri*
Bruce Kutnick, *Northeastern University*
Charles Leathers, *The University of Alabama*
Patrick Lenihan, *Eastern Illinois University and
    State University*
Alan Mandelstamm, *Virginia Polytechnic
    Institute*
Henry McCarl, *The University of Alabama in
    Birmingham*
Mary McCarthy, *Eastern Michigan University*
Herbert Milikien *American River College*
Dan Morgan, *University of Texas at Austin*
Walter Nicholson, *Amherst College*
Martha Olney, *University of California,
    Berkeley*

Kent Olson, *Oklahoma State University*
Virginia Owen, *Illinois State University*
Martin Perline, *Wichita State University*
Arthur Peterson, *Middlesex County College*
David Spencer, *Washington State University*
Michael Tansey, *Rockhurst College*
Robert Thomas, *Iowa State University*
Michael Watts, *Purdue University*
Lawrence Ziegler, *University of Texas at
    Arlington*

In addition to the reviewers' advice, this book has benefited greatly from the assistance and encouragement of many people. Foremost among these is Paul Shensa, who marshaled all the resources and people required to create this teaching package. Elaine Romano was one of those people and did a meticulous job of editing the entire package. My own efforts were invaluably assisted by Anita Janks, who never hesitated to go the proverbial extra mile, and several research assistants, including Franklin Armstrong, Colin Gibson, Kati Ho, and Ann Levin.

BRADLEY R. SCHILLER
The American University
October 1982

CONTENTS IN BRIEF

CONTENTS

ALTERNATIVE COURSE OUTLINES

The core theory chapters of the text (Chapters 7–13 for macro, 18–28 for micro) are designed to be read in sequence. There is considerable flexibility with respect to the sequencing of other chapters, however. The chapters on problems (Chapters 5, 6, and 29) are particularly flexible and are typically used at the beginning of the course or interspersed as the topics of unemployment, inflation, and the distribution of income are more formally introduced. One-semester courses may focus on only one or two of these chapters.

The following chart indicates suggested content for full-year courses and shorter courses with a macro or micro emphasis. Boxes in color indicate "core" material, open boxes indicate optional material.

Chapter	Full-Year Courses	Short Courses Macro	Short Courses Micro
Section I: Basics			
1 An Overview	■	■	■
2 Supply and Demand	■	■	□
3 The Public Sector	■	■	□
4 National-Income Accounting	■	■	
Section II: Macroeconomics			
Part A: Major Problems			
5 Unemployment	□	□	
6 Inflation	□	□	
Part B: Policy Options: The Keynesian Approach			
7 Aggregate Demand	■	■	
8 Potential Instability	■	■	
9 Fiscal Policy	■	■	
Part C: Policy Options: The Monetarist Approach			
10 Money and Banks	■	■	
11 The Federal Reserve System	■	■	
12 Monetary Policy	■	■	
Part D: Policy Options: The Supply-Side Approach			
13 Supply-Side Policy	■	■	
Part E: Current Policies			
14 Theory and Reality	□	□	
15 Reagan Economics	□	□	
16 Energy Shocks	□	□	
17 Growth and Productivity: Sources and Limits	□	□	

BASICS

CHAPTER 1
AN OVERVIEW

Public-opinion polls suggest that Americans worry more about the economy than anything else. The outlook for jobs, prices, taxes, government spending, and interest rates is always at the forefront of public concern. A Gallup poll taken in April 1982 illustrates this concern. When asked what the country's most important problem was, 44 percent of the population cited unemployment. Almost everyone else worried about other aspects of the economy, such as inflation (24 percent), high interest rates (11 percent), and budget cuts (7 percent).[1] Very few people cited noneconomic problems. Even more remarkable is the response to a Gallup poll taken in October 1943. That poll asked people what they thought the greatest problem facing the country would be in the year ahead. At that time the nation was deeply involved in World War II. Nevertheless, most Americans thought jobs and economic readjustment would be our greatest problems. Little concern was expressed for the prospects of peace.[2]

For many people, of course, concern for the economy goes no further than the price of gasoline or the fear of losing a job. Many others, however, are becoming increasingly aware that their job prospects and the prices they pay are somehow related to national trends in prices, unemployment, and economic growth. Although few people think in terms of price indexes, graphs, or economic cy-

[1] *The Gallup Poll*, April 25, 1982.
[2] George H. Gallup, *The Gallup Poll: Public Opinion 1935–1971* (New York: Random House, 1972), vol. 1, p. 410.

cles, most have learned to recognize the importance of certain economic phenomena. And that is why so many people worry about such abstractions as unemployment rates, inflation, and economic growth.

Despite the widespread concern for the economy, few people really understand how it works. You can hardly blame them. For one thing, the very dimensions of the economy tend to obscure its relevance. The annual output of our economy is now measured in trillions of dollars. For those of us who rarely see a $100 bill, it is difficult to comprehend such figures. The significance of billion-dollar changes in output is easily lost on people who are trying to figure out how to pay this month's rent.

Despite the seeming irrelevance of "the economy," it is very much a part of our everyday lives. We spend much of our lives working to produce the goods and services that flow from our factories and offices. We spend a good part of the remaining time consuming those same goods and services. And during much of the time left over, we worry about what to produce or consume next. Even such simple things as reading this book, going to school, and lying on the beach can be described as economic activities.

Interest in the workings of the economy will develop only as we begin to see some immediate stake in its performance. The loss of a job, for example, can rivet one's attention on the causes of unemployment. A tuition increase may start you thinking about the nature and causes of inflation. And high rents can start you thinking about the demand for housing in relation to its supply.

What we seek to determine, then, is not simply whether we are involved in the economy—a fact nearly everyone can accept with a shrug—but more important, how we are involved and where our interests lie. How can we reduce pollution, eliminate poverty, improve the quality of life? How can we provide jobs for everyone who wants to work? How can you increase your income? To answer such questions, we need to understand the relationship between the workings of the economy and our individual pursuits. We also need to know how our individual and collective actions help shape the course of economic events. To this end, later chapters will focus on two key questions: (1) How does the economy function, and (2) How do our private and public actions affect the course of economic

"Meaningless statistics were up one-point-five per cent this month over last month."

Drawing by Dana Fradon; © 1977 The New Yorker Magazine, Inc.

events? Of special interest will be the potential for public policy to improve the performance of the economy. Each chapter of the text concludes with a section on policy implications.

THE ECONOMY IS US

It may be useful to begin our study of the economy by recognizing a very basic relationship, namely, that *the economy is us.* "The economy" is simply an abstraction that refers to the sum of all our individual production and consumption activities. What we collectively produce is what the economy produces; what we collectively consume is what the economy consumes. In this sense, the concept of "the economy" is no more difficult than the concept of "the family." If someone tells you that the Jones family has an annual income of $22,000, you know that the reference is to the collective earnings of all the Joneses. Hence, when someone reports that the nation's income exceeds $3 trillion per year—as it now does—we should recognize immediately that the reference is to the sum of our individual incomes. If we work fewer hours or get paid less, family income and national income are both reduced. Hence to understand the economy is to understand our own economic behavior, both individually and collectively.

The same relationship between individual behavior and aggregate behavior applies to specific outputs as well. If we as individuals insist on driving cars rather than walking or taking public transportation, the economy will produce millions of cars each year and consume vast quantities of oil. In a slightly different way, the economy produces and consumes billions of dollars of military hardware to satisfy our desire for national defense. In each case, the output of the economy reflects the collective efforts and demands of the 230 million individuals who participate in the economy. In these very tangible dimensions, the economy is truly us.

We may not always be happy with the output of the economy, of course. But we cannot deny the essential relationship between individual and collective action. If the highways are clogged and the air is polluted as a consequence of our transportation choices, we cannot blame someone else for our predicament. If we are disturbed by the size of our military arsenal, we must still accept responsibility for our choices (or nonchoices, if we failed to vote). In either case, we continue to have the option of reallocating our efforts or rearranging our priorities. We can create a different outcome the next day, month, or year.

THE NATURE OF ECONOMIC CHOICE

Because individual decisions directly affect the economy, it is important that we understand the nature of our choices. Why, for example, do we choose private cars, instead of public buses, or more armaments instead of more swimming pools? Why, indeed, don't we choose both, in sufficient quantities to satisfy all our desires?

One basic constraint on our production and consumption choices is a scarcity of resources. In order to produce anything, we need resources, or factors of production. **Factors of production** are the inputs—land, labor, and capital (buildings and machinery)—we use to produce final goods and services (output). To produce this textbook, we needed paper, printing presses, a building, and lots of labor. To produce the education you are getting in this class, we need not only a textbook, but a classroom, a teacher, and a blackboard as well. Without factors of production, we simply cannot produce anything.

Unfortunately, the quantity of available resources is limited. We cannot produce everything we want in the quantities we desire. Resources are scarce, relative to our desires. This fact forces us to make difficult choices. The building space we use for this class cannot be used to show Charlie Chaplin movies at the same time. Your professor cannot lecture (produce education) and repair a car simultaneously. Likewise, the more labor and machinery used to dig holes in the ground for missiles, the less is available to dig holes for swimming pools. Hence the more missiles we build, the less of other goods and services we can produce at the same time. This classic "guns vs. butter" problem is illustrated in the accompanying news clipping. The article indicates some of the goods we could have produced with the resources allocated to production of military goods.

Opportunity costs

The dilemma of guns vs. butter typifies our economic problem. *Because our resources are limited, we are compelled to choose among goods and services.* Even the time you spend reading this book illustrates the problem. The labor time you devote to reading this book reduces the amount of time you have for other activities. You could be sleeping, watching television, or using your time in

factors of production:
Resource inputs used to produce goods and services; for example, land, labor, capital.

Looting the Means of Production

SOUTH WELLFLEET, MASS.— . . . The way that an economy uses its capital—its production resources— is a crucial determinant of its productivity and economic well-being.

The United States has "achieved" its present state of industrial deterioration by assigning to the military economy large quantities of machinery, tools, engineers, energy, raw materials, skilled labor, and managers. . . .

This looting of the means of production on behalf of the military economy can only be accelerated as a consequence of the unprecedented size of the war budgets advocated by the Reagan Administration.

The vital resources that constitute a nation's capital fund cannot be enlarged by waving a budgetary wand. Neither can manufacturing facilities be multiplied by ever richer subsidies to the managers of military industry. Basic machinery, skilled labor, engineers and scientists—all are finite in number and difficult to increase.

The concentration of capital on the military portends sharply diminished opportunity for a productive livelihood for most Americans. Clearly, a choice must be made as to where these resources will be used.

The accompanying list of trade-offs illustrates the kinds of choices that the Reagan Administration and the Congress are now making with their budget and tax plans, intended or not.

—Seymour Melman

Seven percent of the military outlays from fiscal 1981 to 1986	$100 billion	the cost of rehabilitating the United States' steel industry so that it is again the most efficient in the world
The cruise-missile programs	$11 billion	the cost of bringing the annual rate of investment in public works to the 1965 level
Two B-1 bombers	$400 million	the cost of rebuilding Cleveland's water-supply system
The Navy's F-18 fighter program	$34 billion	the cost of modernizing America's machine-tool stock to bring it to the average level of Japan's
Two nuclear-powered aircraft carriers	$5.8 billion	the cost of converting 77 oil-using power plants to coal, saving 350,000 barrels of oil per day
The cost overrun, to 1981, of the Army's UH-60A helicopter program	$4.7 billion	the annual capital investment for restoring New York City's roads, bridges, aqueducts, subways and buses
One nuclear (SSN-688) attack submarine	$582 million	the cost of 100 miles of electrified rail right-of-way

opportunity cost: The most desired goods or services that are forgone in order to obtain something else.

some other way. The true cost of reading this book, then, is the most enjoyable activity you could have pursued in the same amount of time but had to sacrifice in order to complete this reading assignment. As long as you continue to read this book, you are sacrificing the *opportunity* to use your time in other ways. This sacrifice is your **opportunity cost** of reading these pages.[3] Similar costs are associated with all activities.

Opportunity costs exist in all situations where available resources are not abundant enough to satisfy all our desires. In all such situations, we must make hard decisions about how to allocate our scarce resources among competing uses. Because our wants and desires generally exceed our resources, *everything we do involves an opportunity cost.*

Opportunity costs are relevant not only to personal decision making, but also to the decisions of an entire economy. Consider the guns vs. butter dilemma again. The news clipping indicates that the production of a nuclear attack submarine uses land, labor, and capital worth $582 million. That same quantity of resources could build 100 miles of electrified railroad (or thousands of other things). But those resources cannot be used to produce *both* goods at once. Hence, if we choose to build the sub, we forsake the opportunity of building an additional 100 miles of railroad. Forgone railroads become the *opportunity cost* of building more nuclear attack subs. If we make the opposite choice—that is, build more railroads and fewer subs—then the forgone subs would be the opportunity cost of the additional railroads. The opportunity cost of anything is the forgone alternative.

economics: The study of how best to allocate scarce resources among competing uses.

The concept of opportunity cost is basic to economic decision making. Indeed, **economics** itself has often been defined as the study of how to allocate scarce resources so as to attain the greatest satisfaction. The study of economics focuses on "getting the most from what we've got"—on making the *best* use of our scarce resources. In these terms, reading this book right now represents the *best* use of your time if it ultimately yields greater satisfaction (from higher grades, if nothing else) than any other use of the same time. Production of additional nuclear submarines represents the *best* use of society's resources only if the additional subs are more highly valued than any other goods or services that could be produced with the same factors of production.

PRODUCTION POSSIBILITIES

The opportunity costs implied by our every choice can be easily illustrated. Imagine for the moment that labor (workers) is the only factor of production used to produce either submarines or railroads and that no other goods are desired. Although other factors of production (land, machinery) are also needed in actual production, ignoring them for the moment does no harm. Let us assume further

[3] By the way, if you continue reading, we can conclude that you expect the benefits of doing this homework to exceed their opportunity cost, and thus that doing your homework will be "worthwhile."

that we have a total of 1,000 workers (labor) available in a given year, and that they can be used to produce either subs or railroads. Our initial problem is to determine how many subs or railroads can be produced in a year under such circumstances.

Before going any further, notice how opportunity costs will affect our answer. If we choose to employ all 1,000 of our workers in the production of nuclear submarines, then no labor will be available to build railroads. In this case, forgone railroads would become the opportunity cost of a decision to use all our resources in the production of submarines.

We still do not know how many submarines could be built with 1,000 workers or exactly how many railroads would be forgone by such a decision. To get these answers, we must know a little more about the production process involved; specifically, how many workers are required to build a nuclear sub or a railroad.

For the sake of convenience, we shall assume that 200 workers are needed to build either a submarine or a small railroad in a year. As we have only 1,000 workers available, the *maximum* number of subs we *could* build in one year is five. But we would then have no labor available for the production of railroads. Hence a decision to produce five subs per year implies a choice of no new railroads. In other words, the opportunity cost of five subs is the five railroads that could have been built with the same amount of labor, but were not.

Table 1.1 summarizes the hypothetical choices, or **production possibilities,** that we confront in this case. Row *A* of the production-possibilities schedule shows the consequences of a decision to produce submarines only. With 1,000 workers available and a labor requirement of 200 workers per sub, we can build a *maximum* of five subs per year. By so doing, however, we use up all our available resources, leaving nothing for railroad construction. If we want more railroads, we have to cut back on submarine construction: this is the essential choice we must make.

The remainder of Table 1.1 describes the full range of choices that confront us. By cutting back the rate of sub production from five to four subs per year (row *B*), we reduce labor use from 1,000 workers to 800. The remaining 200 workers are then available for other

production possibilities: The alternative combinations of final goods and services that could be produced in a given time period with all available resources and technology.

TABLE 1.1 PRODUCTION POSSIBILITIES SCHEDULE (for one year) So long as resources are limited, their use entails an opportunity cost. In this case, resources (labor) used to produce nuclear submarines cannot be used to produce railroads at the same time. Hence forgone railroads are the opportunity cost of additional subs. If all of our resources were used to produce subs (row A), no railroads could be built.		Submarines				Railroads	
	Total available labor	*Number × of subs*	*Labor needed per sub*	*Total = labor required for subs*	*Labor not used for subs*	*Labor needed ÷ per rail- road*	*Number = of potential railroads*
A	1,000	5	200	1000	0	200	0
B	1,000	4	200	800	200	200	1
C	1,000	3	200	600	400	200	2
D	1,000	2	200	400	600	200	3
E	1,000	1	200	200	800	200	4
F	1,000	0	200	0	1000	200	5

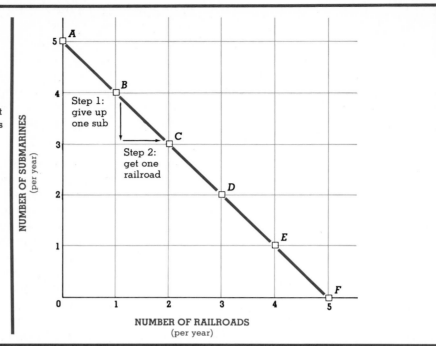

FIGURE 1.1 A LINEAR PRODUCTION-POSSIBILITIES CURVE

A production-possibilities curve describes the various combinations of final goods or services that could be produced in a given time period with available resources and technology. It represents a "menu" of output choices an economy confronts. Point *B* indicates that we could produce a *combination* of four submarines and one railroad per year. By giving up one sub, we could produce a second railroad, and thus move to point *C*. Points *A, D, E,* and *F* illustrate still other output combinations that could be produced. This curve is a graphic illustration of the production-possibilities schedule provided in Table 1.1.

uses, including railroad construction. If we in fact employ these workers to lay rails, we can build one new railroad per year. In this case, we end up with four new subs and one new railroad per year. What is the opportunity cost of that railroad? Clearly it is the one additional submarine that we could have built but did not, in order to make factors of production (labor) available for railroad construction.

As we proceed down the rows of Table 1.1, the nature of opportunity costs becomes apparent. Each additional railroad built implies the loss (opportunity cost) of one nuclear submarine. Likewise, every sub built implies the loss of one railroad.

These trade-offs between railroads and submarines are illustrated in the production-possibilities curve of Figure 1.1 Each point on the curve depicts a particular combination of railroads and submarines that we could produce if we so chose, using all available resources (labor in this case) and technology.

Notice in particular how points *A* through *F* in Figure 1.1 represent the choices described in each row of Table 1.1. At point *A,* we are producing five subs per year and no railroads. As we move from point *A* to point *B,* we are decreasing submarine production from five to four subs per year, while increasing railroad construction from zero to one. This is precisely what Table 1.1 depicts. A production-possibilities curve, then, is simply a graphic summary of production possibilities, as described in Table 1.1. The purpose of the table and the graph is to illustrate the hard choices we must make among alternative goods and services—and the implied opportunity costs of each choice.

In summary, the production-possibilities curve illustrates two essential principles:

- There is a limit to the amount we can produce in a given time period with available resources and technology. (Scarcity is a fact of life.)
- We can obtain additional quantities of any desired good only by reducing the potential production of another good. (Opportunity costs are always present.)

Increasing opportunity costs

Although Figure 1.1 illustrates the principles of scarcity and opportunity costs, it depicts an overly optimistic view of our production possibilities. When we reduce the rate of output of one good in order to get more of another, we have to reallocate factors of production from one industry to another. In order to get more railroads, for example, we have to take workers out of nuclear submarine construction and put them to work laying rails. No magic wand is available to transform nuclear subs into railroads. Instead, the rails must be laid with the same factors of production that would otherwise be used in submarine production. As a consequence, *our ability to alter the mix of output depends in part on the capability of factors of production to move from one industry to another.*

As we contemplate the possibilities of moving resources from one industry to another, two issues arise. First, can the resources be moved? Second, how efficient will the resources be in a new line of production?

In our example, it is probably safe to assume that workers can move from submarine construction to railroad construction. We have made this kind of move after every war. But it is also likely that some efficiency will be lost in the process. Workers who have been constructing submarines for several years will probably not be as adept at building railroads. As a result, we will not be able to "transform" subs into railroads so easily. Instead, we may discover that sooner or later more than 200 former submarine workers will be required to construct one railroad. That is, the opportunity cost of one new railroad will be more than one potential sub.

One reason for this higher opportunity cost is the different skills required for submarine and railroad construction. Both industries need welders, for example. But in railroad construction a weld must be secure, not necessarily airtight. The welds on nuclear subs, on the other hand, must be completely airtight, or the sub may never resurface. So when we start to move welders out of nuclear submarine construction and into railroad development, we will move the worst welders first. That will minimize our losses in submarine production while increasing our output of railroads. As we continue moving labor from sub production to railroad construction, the remaining sub builders are likely to be the least adept at laying rails or the most adept at building subs. If we nevertheless continue to shift resources, one of two things will probably happen. Either we will get less railroad output for each additional worker employed in rail construction or we will sacrifice more sub output for each worker taken out of submarine construction. In either case, we are likely to get

TABLE 1.2 INCREASING OPPORTUNITY COSTS

Resources are not perfectly adaptable from one industry to another. As a consequence, we are unlikely to get one additional railroad for every sub given up. Instead, opportunity costs increase. Notice that we get two railroads for the first sub given up (row A to row B) but only one railroad for the second sub given up (row B to row C). The third sub is "transformed" into only 0.8 railroad. These increasing opportunity costs bend the production-possibilities curve outward, as in Figure 1.2.

		Submarines				Railroads	
	Total labor available	Output of subs	× Labor needed per sub	= Total labor required for subs	Labor not used for subs	Potential output of railroads	Change in output
A	1,000	5	200	1,000	0	0	
B	1,000	4	200	800	200	2.0	> 2.0
C	1,000	3	200	600	400	3.0	> 1.0
D	1,000	2	200	400	600	3.8	> 0.8
E	1,000	1	200	200	800	4.5	> 0.7
F	1,000	0	200	0	1,000	5.0	> 0.5

fewer railroads for each potential sub given up. The opportunity cost of railroads increases as more railroads are produced.

Increasing opportunity costs are illustrated in Table 1.2. We still have 1,000 workers available, all of whom are initially employed in submarine production (row A). When we cut back submarine production to only four per year (row B) we release 200 workers for railroad construction, as before. Now, however, those first 200 workers are assumed to be capable of producing two railroads (rather than only one, as in Table 1.1).

This high rate of submarine-to-railroad transformation does not last long. When sub production is cut back from four to three per year, another 200 workers are made available for railroad construction (row C). But now railroad output increases by only one, from two to three roads per year. Hence we are getting fewer railroads for each sub given up. The opportunity cost of railroads is increasing.

This process of increasing opportunity costs continues. By the time we give up the last sub (row F), railroad output increases by only 0.5. Hence we get only half a railroad for the last sub given up.

Increasing opportunity costs alter the shape of the production-possibilities curve. The linear "curve" in Figure 1.1 suggested that factors of production could be moved effortlessly from one industry to another. In reality, such transformations are more difficult, and the production-possibilities curve will usually bend outward, as in Figure 1.2.

Figure 1.2 is based on Table 1.2. Suppose that we start out again at point A, using all our labor to produce five nuclear submarines per year, leaving no resources for railroad construction. We then decide (Step 1) to reduce the rate of submarine construction in order to free resources for railroad production. According to Table 1.2, we can produce two railroads per year with the labor initially taken out of submarine production. Thus Step 2 takes us to point B, where we produce four subs and two railroads per year.

Suppose that we continue to alter the mix of output by reducing the rate of submarine construction further, from four to three subs per year (Step 3). How many additional railroads can we produce with the released labor? According to Table 1.2, we can obtain only

FIGURE 1.2 A CURVED (NONLINEAR) PRODUCTION-POSSIBILITIES CURVE

The production-possibilities curve bends outward—is actually curved—because resources are not perfectly adaptable from one industry to another. As a consequence, the opportunity costs of a good increase as more of it is produced. In this case, we get two railroads (Step 2) by giving up the fifth submarine (Step 1). When we give up the next sub (Step 3), however, we get only one additional railroad (Step 4). Each additional railroad "costs" more submarines.

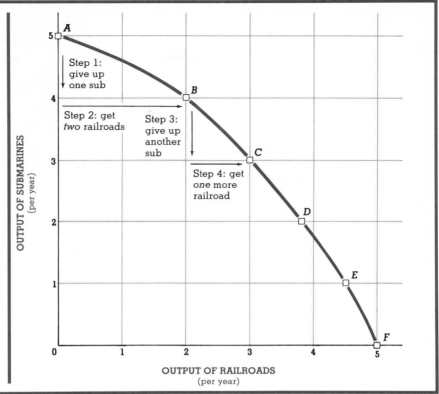

law of increasing opportunity costs: In order to get more of any good in a given time period, society must sacrifice ever-increasing amounts of other goods.

one more railroad per year with the additional labor (Step 4). Hence the opportunity cost of a railroad has risen. The newest (third) railroad "cost" one sub, whereas we earlier obtained *two* railroads by forgoing one sub (i.e., one railroad previously cost only half a nuclear submarine).

Nonlinear production-possibilities curves like the one in Figure 1.2 are so universal that they have become a basic "law" of economics, the **law of increasing opportunity costs.** According to this law, we must give up ever-increasing quantities of other goods and services in order to get more of a particular good.

The law of increasing opportunity costs is not based solely on the limited versatility of individual workers. In most production processes, some amount of land and capital works with labor. If they had to, railroad workers could lay rails with picks, shovels, and sledgehammers. The construction of nuclear submarines requires much more capital, of far greater complexity. Hence the productivity of workers moved from the railroad industry to nuclear submarine construction depends on how much capital equipment we supply them with. With little capital—or the wrong kind of capital—they won't be able to produce many nuclear submarines. Accordingly, our ability to alter the mix of output does not depend on the talents of individual workers alone. It also depends on the adaptability of land and capital and the availability of each in the right proportions.[4]

[4] A more complete discussion of the basis for increasing opportunity costs (diminishing returns) is provided in Chapter 19.

"There's no such thing as a free lunch."

Drawing by Dana Fradon; © 1975 The New Yorker Magazine, Inc.

Points inside and outside the curve

Points *X* and *Y* in Figure 1.3 illustrate two additional combinations of submarines and railroads. One of these combinations is unattainable, however, while the other is undesirable. Consider point *X*, which represents a combined output of five submarines and two railroads per year. Point *X* is clearly better than point *A*, because it includes just as many subs and two more railroads. It appears, in other words, that by moving from point *A* to point *X* we could get two additional railroads *without* giving up any potential submarines. Unfortunately, point *X* lies *outside* our production possibilities and thus is beyond our grasp. In order to produce five nuclear submarines per year, we have to use *all* our available resources and technology, leaving none to produce railroads. Hence we cannot have five new submarines every year *and* two new railroads; point *X* represents an unattainable output combination. In fact, ***all output combinations that lie outside the production-possibilities curve are unattainable with available resources and technology.***

Point *Y* represents a very different situation. At point *Y*, three submarines and two railroads are being produced each year. This output combination is easily attainable with our available resources and technology. But if we produced at point *Y*, we would be wasting resources. Either some labor is completely idle (unemployed) or workers are not employed efficiently (underemployed). This is evident from the fact that we could produce at point *C*, with one more railroad and no fewer submarines each year. Or we could move to point *B* and have one more sub and no fewer railroads. By choosing to stay at point *Y*, we would be forsaking the opportunity to use all

FIGURE 1.3 POINTS INSIDE AND OUTSIDE THE CURVE

Points outside the production-possibilities curve (e.g., point X) are unattainable with available resources and technology. Points inside the curve (e.g., point Y) represent the incomplete use of available resources. Only points on the production-possibilities curve (e.g., A, B, C) represent maximum use of our production capabilities.

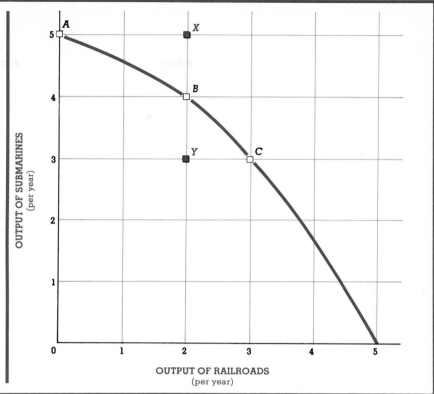

OUTPUT OF SUBMARINES (per year)

OUTPUT OF RAILROADS (per year)

our resources to the fullest, in effect giving up potential output for nothing in return. So long as either more submarines or more railroads (or any other good) are desired, it is wasteful to leave workers idle when they could be producing one of those goods. Thus point Y, and ***all points inside the production-possibilities curve, are undesirable because they imply the waste (nonuse) of available resources.*** The full significance of such unemployment, for both individuals and the economy, is discussed in Chapter 5.

Growth and technology

The production possibilities illustrated in Figure 1.3 are not fixed for all time. As time passes, we will acquire more resources and improve our knowledge of how to use them. Fifty years ago, no one even knew what a nuclear submarine was. Advances in both nuclear technology and submarine design since that time have made nuclear submarines both feasible and familiar. In other words, our technology has improved. As a result, we can produce more subs today than we could fifty or even five years ago, with the same quantity of resources.

Over time, the quantity of resources available for production has also increased. Each year our population grows a bit, thereby enlarging the number of potential workers. Our stock of capital equipment has increased even faster. In addition the *quality* of our labor and capital resources has improved, as a result of more education (labor) and better machinery (capital).

FIGURE 1.4 INCREASING
PRODUCTION POSSIBILITIES

A production-possibilities curve is
based on *available* resources and
technology. If more resources or better
technology become available,
production possibilities will increase.
This is illustrated by the *shift* from
PP_1 to PP_2.

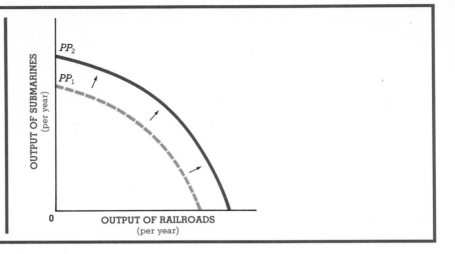

economic growth: An increase
in output (real GNP); an
expansion of production
possibilities.

All of this adds up to an ever-increasing capacity to produce
goods and services. This is illustrated in Figure 1.4 by the outward
shift of the production-possibilities curve. Before the appearance of
new resources or better technology, our production possibilities
were limited by the curve PP_1. **With more resources or better technology, our production possibilities increase.** This greater capacity
to produce is represented by curve PP_2. This outward shift of the
production-possibilities curve is the essence of **economic growth.**
As we shall see in later chapters (especially 17 and 19), much of our
recent growth has come from continuing improvements in technology.

HOW CHOICES ARE MADE

However promising the prospects for growth may be, we still have to
contend with our current production constraints. At any point in
time there is still a limit to how much we can produce. The fact that
those limits may expand in future years does not make our current
choices any easier. Each year we still have to choose some mix of
output that is consistent with our existing production possibilities.
Choosing WHAT to produce is one of our most important economic
decisions.

Our menu of choices is illustrated by the prevailing production-possibilities curve. Because those points that lie *outside* the
production-possibilities curve are unattainable and those *inside* the
curve are undesirable, only those points on the curve represent our
immediate choices. But which of these many points should we
choose? What goods and services should the economy produce?

Although the consequences of alternative output choices can be
illustrated with a production-possibilities curve, the curve itself says
nothing about the reasons for choosing one combination of goods
and services over another. Why do we choose fewer railroads and
more nuclear submarines? Or, for that matter, why do you choose—
and it is a choice!—to do more homework and get less sleep? If we

are really to understand economic outcomes, we have to know more than just what the choices (and associated opportunity costs) are. We also have to know how we, individually and collectively, make such choices.

The market mechanism

market mechanism: The use of market prices and sales to signal desired outputs (or resource allocations).

The actual choices individual consumers and firms make are expressed for the most part in market purchases and sales. The use of the **market mechanism** to express your desires is as familiar as grocery shopping. If you desire ice cream and have sufficient income, you simply buy ice cream. Your purchases act as a signal to producers that ice cream is desired. By expressing the ability and *willingness to pay* for ice cream, you are effectively telling ice cream producers that their efforts are going to be rewarded. If enough consumers feel the same way you do—and are able and willing to pay the price of ice cream—ice cream producers will produce more ice cream.

The same kind of interactions influence the choice we must make between houses and cars. There are many alternative combinations of houses and cars that we *could* produce. But we must choose only one. How do we express our preference? Consumers may express their preference for houses simply by purchasing houses, that is, by expressing a willingness to pay for such output. Similarly, consumers who would prefer to see more new cars can express their desires by buying cars. In this way, the debate over cars versus houses boils down to a question of who is willing and able to pay the most for the available factors of production. If potential homeowners are willing to pay more for our limited resources than are potential drivers, then more houses will be supplied. Why? Simply because suppliers will provide those products that offer the highest profit.

Thus *the essential feature of the market mechanism is the price signal.* If you want something and have sufficient income, you buy it. If enough people do the same thing, the total sales of that product will rise, and perhaps its price as well. Producers, seeing sales and prices rise, will be inclined to increase production. To do so, they will attempt to purchase a larger share of our available resources, and use them to produce the goods we desire. No direct communication between us and the producer is required; market sales and prices convey the message and direct the market, much like an "invisible hand." Although producers and sellers have a variety of reasons for offering their wares, and consumers have myriad motives for buying, prices are used as a common means of communication. It is this price or market mechanism that translates the disparate interests and desires of our 230 million selves into a producing and consuming whole. From this perspective, the price system is a very efficient method of communication.

MARKET IMPERFECTIONS   The details of the price system are reserved for Chapter 2. Before looking at those details, we should note some potential problems associated with the market mechanism. The first of these problems concerns equity. Use of the price system presumes allegiance to certain standards of fairness. In particular, reliance on prices as a mechanism for distributing goods and resources implies that we believe such a distribution is "fair." For example, goods and services distributed through the market mechanism go disproportionately to those with the greatest ability to pay. Whether this system of allocation is "fair" depends on how one views the distribution of wealth and income and the nature of the goods to be divided up. It is at least conceivable that the efficiency of the price system may conflict with standards of equity or fairness, necessitating difficult policy choices. Medical and legal assistance provided for the poor, not to mention public schools, illustrate departures from the price mechanism prompted by our concern for equity.

Another problem that strikes at the very heart of the market mechanism is that some very valuable things are not priced. Clean air, for example, is something nearly everyone (smokers and non-smokers alike) considers precious. Nevertheless, it is difficult to imagine how we could *buy* clean air, much less reserve the cleanest air for those who are most eager and able to purchase it. Air, unlike video tapes or soap, cannot be packaged and marketed. Hence to leave the quality of the air we breathe to the determination of the market mechanism is like tightening one's own noose. The final outcome is foreseeable, but not necessarily desirable. Just breathing in New York City, Los Angeles, or Chicago can be dangerous to your health. The economic forces that actually *encourage* pollution are discussed in Chapter 30.

Clean air is not alone among unpackageable and unmarketable goods. On the contrary, the list of such goods is long, including such diverse products as national defense, traffic congestion, and the vibrations from your next-door neighbor's stereo. In every such case, some sort of interactions among us operate outside the market mechanism: benefits or costs are being exchanged without direct payment. These kinds of interactions are referred to as **externalities.**

externalities: Costs (or benefits) of a market activity borne by a third party; the difference between the social and private costs (benefits) of a market activity.

Externalities violate the basic market dictum that everything must be packaged, marketed, and exchanged for a negotiated price. Consequently, the production and consumption of such goods must often be controlled by other mechanisms. These mechanisms may be public laws (such as those against pollution), taxes (to pay for common defense), or threats against neighbors (to muffle their stereos). In almost all cases, we seek to alter market choices by intervening directly in the production or consumption process. The nature of externalities, and policy responses to them, are discussed at length in Chapters 3 and 30.

Planned economies

Although the United States relies heavily on the market mechanism to make basic economic decisions, there are alternative ways of making the same kinds of choices. One such alternative is centralized decision making, as practiced in such socialist countries as the Soviet Union, China, and Cuba. In socialist economies, the decisions of government planners substitute for the decisions of individual consumers and business firms. For example, we rely on the decisions of millions of individual consumers and a few automobile companies to determine how many American cars will be produced each year.

By contrast, the level of automobile production in the Soviet and Chinese economies is determined by the decisions of government planners.

Countries that rely heavily on centralized decision making for resolution of basic economic questions are referred to as "planned" or "command" economies. Countries that rely primarily on market behavior to make basic economic choices are often referred to as "market economies."

The mixed economy

The U.S. economy is not a purely market economy, of course. As we have already noted (and can observe daily), the government often intervenes in the market to control externalities (antipollution laws and penalties) and to redistribute income (through income taxes and transfer payments). The use of both market-directed signals and nonmarket directives is the hallmark of a **mixed economy** like our own.

mixed economy: An economy that uses both market and nonmarket signals to allocate goods and resources.

Our heavy reliance on the market mechanism is based on its efficiency in allocating resources and goods in accordance with consumer preferences. At the same time, our apparent commitment to government intervention reflects the judgment that market outcomes are not always best. The market mechanism is only a means to an end, not an end in itself. When we find the mechanism or the outcomes incompatible with our visions of the good and proper life, we can and do seek to change them. Such considerations explain why we formulate public policies to reduce unemployment, to slow the rate of inflation, to foster economic growth, and to redistribute incomes. If the market mechanism could itself ensure fulfillment of these goals, economic policy would be unnecessary, and possibly counterproductive.

We should not embrace market interference too hastily, however. We have no assurance that public policy is *capable* of improving our economic performance or that such policy will be properly implemented at the appropriate time. That is to say, nonmarket signals are imperfect, too. Accordingly, we cannot assume that all our economic problems are attributable to the market mechanism or that public policy will always provide a solution. On the contrary, experience has taught us that the truly difficult part of economic policy making is deciding whether or not to interfere with market outcomes. Further, if we decide to interfere, we still have to determine just what kind of action is likely to bring about desired results. This continuing dilemma will be emphasized throughout the remainder of this book. In the final chapter, we shall also examine how planned socialist economies resolve the same dilemma.

WHAT ECONOMICS IS ALL ABOUT

Understanding how various economies work is the basic purpose of studying economics. We seek to know how an economy is organized, how it behaves, and how successfully it achieves its basic objectives. Then, if we are lucky, we try to discover better ways of attaining those same objectives.

Ends vs. means

Economists do not formulate an economy's objectives. Instead, they focus on the *means* available for achieving given *goals*. In 1978, for example, the U.S. Congress identified "full employment" as a major economic goal. The Congress then directed future presidents (and their economic advisers) to formulate policies that would enable us to achieve full employment.

Other major economic goals of our economy include:

- Price stability
- Economic growth
- An equitable distribution of income

In each case, the goal itself is formulated through the political process. The economist's job is to help design policies that will allocate the economy's resources in ways that best achieve these goals. The nature and significance of our major economic goals are discussed in Chapters 5, 6, and 29; the rest of the book is concerned with the means available for attaining them.

Macro vs. micro

The study of economics is typically divided into two parts: macroeconomics and microeconomics. Macroeconomics focuses on the behavior of an entire economy—the "big picture." In macroeconomics we worry about such national goals as full employment, control of inflation, and economic growth, without worrying about the well-being or behavior of specific individuals or groups. The essential concern of **macroeconomics** is to understand and improve the performance of the economy as a whole.

Microeconomics is concerned with the details of this "big picture." In microeconomics we focus on the individuals, firms, and government agencies that actually comprise the larger economy. Our interest here is in the behavior of individual economic actors. What goals do they have? How can they best achieve them with their limited resources? How will they respond to various incentives and opportunities?

A primary concern of macroeconomics, for example, is to determine the impact of aggregate consumer spending on total output, employment, and prices. Very little attention is devoted to the actual content of consumer spending or its determinants. Microeconomics, on the other hand, focuses on the specific expenditure decisions of individual consumers and the forces (tastes, prices, incomes) that influence those decisions.

The distinction between macro- and microeconomics is also reflected in discussions of business investment. In macroeconomics we want to know what determines the aggregate rate of business investment and how those expenditures influence the nation's total output, employment, and prices. In microeconomics we focus on the decisions of individual businesses regarding the rate of production, the choice of factors of production, and the pricing of specific goods.

The distinction between macro- and microeconomics is a matter of convenience. In reality, macroeconomic outcomes depend on micro behavior and micro behavior is affected by macro outcomes. Hence one cannot fully understand how an economy works until

macroeconomics: The study of aggregate economic behavior, of the economy as a whole.

microeconomics: The study of individual behavior in the economy, of the components of the larger economy.

one understands how all the participants behave and why they behave as they do. But just as you can drive a car without knowing how its engine is constructed, you can observe how an economy runs without completely disassembling it. In macroeconomics we observe that the car goes faster when the accelerator is depressed and that it slows when the brake is applied. That is all we need to know in most situations. There are times, however, when the car breaks down. When it does, we have to know something more about how the pedals work. This leads us into micro studies. How does each part work? Which ones can or should be fixed?

Our interest in microeconomics is motivated by more than our need to understand how the larger economy works. The "parts" of the economic engine are people. To the extent that we care about the welfare of individuals in society, we have a fundamental interest in microeconomic behavior and outcomes. In this regard, we examine the goals of individual consumers and business firms, seeking to explain how they can maximize their welfare in the economy. In microeconomics, for example, we spend more time looking at which goods are produced, who produces them, and who receives them. In macroeconomics we tend to focus only on how much is produced, or how many people are employed in the process.

Theory and reality

The distinction between macroeconomics and microeconomics is one of many simplifications we make in studying economic behavior. The economy is much too vast and complex to describe and explain in one course (or one lifetime). Accordingly, we focus on basic relationships, ignoring annoying detail. In so doing, we isolate basic principles of economic behavior, then use those principles to predict economic events and formulate economic policies. What this means is that we formulate theories, or *models*, of economic behavior, then use those theories to evaluate and design economic policy.

Because all economic models entail simplifying assumptions, they never *exactly* describe the real world. Nevertheless, the models may be useful. If our models are *reasonably* consistent with economic reality, they may yield good predictions of economic behavior. Likewise, if our simplifications do not become distortions, they may provide good guidelines for economic policy.

Our theory of consumer behavior assumes, for example, a distinct relationship between the price of a good and the quantity people buy. As prices increase, people buy less. In reality, however, people *may* buy *more* of a good at increased prices, especially if those high prices create a certain "snob appeal" or if prices are expected to increase still further. In predicting consumer responses to price increases, we typically ignore such possibilities by *assuming* that the price of the good in question is the *only* thing that changes. This assumption of "other things remaining equal (unchanged)" (in Latin, **ceteris paribus**) allows us to make straightforward predictions. If instead we described consumer responses to increased prices in any and all circumstances (allowing everything to change at once), every prediction would be accompanied by a bookful of exceptions and qualifications.

ceteris paribus: **The assumption of "everything else being equal," of nothing else changing.**

Although the assumption of *ceteris paribus* makes it easier to formulate economic theory and policy, it also increases the risk of error. Obviously, if other things do change in significant ways, our predictions (and policies) may fail. But, like weather forecasters, we continue to make predictions, knowing that occasional failure is inevitable. In so doing, we are motivated by the conviction that it is better to be approximately right than to be dead wrong.

Policy

Politicians cannot afford to be quite so complacent about predictions, however. Policy decisions must be made all the time. And a politician's continued survival may depend on being more than approximately right. Economists can contribute to those policy decisions by offering measures of economic impact and predictions of economic behavior. But in the real world, those measures and predictions will always contain a substantial margin of error. That is to say, economic policy decisions are always based on some amount of uncertainty. Even the best economic minds cannot foretell the future.

Even if the future were known, economic policy could not rely completely on economic theory. There are always political choices to be made. The choice of more submarines or more railroads, for example, is not an economic decision. Rather it is a sociopolitical decision based in part on economic trade-offs (opportunity costs). The "need" for more subs or more railroads must be expressed politically. Ends versus means again. Political forces are a necessary ingredient in economic policy decisions. That is not to say that all "political" decisions are right. It does suggest, however, that economic policies may not always conform to economic theory. In Chapter 14 we shall explore the interaction of policy and theory, highlighting those forces that contribute to disappointing economic performance.

Controversy

One last word of warning before you go further. Economics claims to be a science, in pursuit of basic truths. We want to understand and explain how the economy works without getting tangled up in subjective value judgments. This may be an impossible task. First of all, it is not clear where the truth lies. For over 200 years economists have been arguing about what makes the economy tick. None of the competing theories have performed spectacularly well. Indeed, few economists have successfully predicted major economic events with any consistency. Even annual forecasts of inflation, unemployment, and output are regularly in error. Worse still, there are never-ending arguments about what caused a major economic event long after it has already occurred. In fact, economists are still arguing over the causes of the Great Depression of the 1930s!

The most persistent debate in economics has focused on the degree to which the government can improve the economy's performance. Two hundred years ago, Adam Smith convinced most of the world that the economy worked best when it was left alone. In the throes of the Great Depression, the British economist John Maynard Keynes forced people to rethink that conclusion. He convinced people that active government intervention in the marketplace was the only way to ensure economic growth and stability. For nearly 30 years his theory dominated the economics profession and public policy. A decade of disappointing economic performance ended Keynes' overwhelming dominance. The 1970s were fraught with repeated recessions, slow growth, and high inflation. "Supply-siders" and "monetarists" laid much of the blame on Keynesian theory. Specifically, they argued that we got into economic trouble because we permitted too much government intervention. Excessive government intervention had stifled the market mechanism, they claimed; Keynes' call for active government policy had to be rejected. This view has had a formative influence on the policies of the Reagan administration.

In part, this enduring controversy reflects diverse sociopolitical views on the appropriate role of government. Some people think a big public sector is undesirable, even if it improves economic performance. But the controversy has even deeper roots. There are still important gaps in our understanding of the economy. We know how much of the economy works, but not all of it. We are adept at identifying all the forces at work, but not always successful in gauging their relative importance. In point of fact, we may never find an absolute truth, because the inner workings of the economy can change over time. When economic behavior changes, our theories must be adapted.

Modest expectations

In view of all these debates and uncertainties, you should not expect to learn everything there is to know about the economy today in this text or course. Our goals are more modest. We want to develop a reasonable perspective on economic behavior, an understanding of basic principles. With this foundation, you should acquire a better view of how the economy works. Daily news reports on economic events should make more sense. Congressional debates on tax and budget policies should take on more meaning. Who knows? You may even develop some insights useful for running a business or planning a career.

SUMMARY

▪ Scarcity is a basic fact of economic life. Available resources (factors of production) are scarce in relation to our desires for goods and services.

▪ Scarcity necessitates difficult choices. Factors of production (resources) used to produce one output cannot simultaneously be used to produce something else. Accordingly, we must forsake the opportunity to produce alternative goods or services when we choose to produce something else.

▪ A production-possibilities curve illustrates the kinds of opportunity costs an economy confronts. It shows the alternative combinations of final goods and services that could be produced in a given time period with available resources and technology.

■ The bent shape of the production-possibilities curve reflects the law of increasing opportunity costs. This law states that increasing quantities of any good can be obtained only by sacrificing ever-increasing quantities of other goods.

■ Production possibilities expand (shift outward) when additional resources or better technologies become available. This is the essence of economic growth.

■ The market mechanism facilitates the actual choice of output combinations. Consumers indicate their preference for specific outputs by expressing an ability and a willingness to pay for desired goods. Their actual purchases act as signals to producers, who in turn assemble factors of production and produce the desired outputs.

■ The market mechanism does not work efficiently when externalities exist, that is, when market interactions between two parties impose costs or benefits on third parties. Market outcomes may also conflict with accepted standards of equity. In both cases, some kind of nonmarket intervention is often desired.

■ A mixed economy relies on a combination of market signals and nonmarket intervention to allocate goods and services. The critical problem for both economic theory and public policy is to determine the mix of market and nonmarket directives that will best fulfill our social and economic goals.

■ The study of economics focuses on the broad question of resource allocation. Macroeconomics is concerned with allocating the resources of an entire economy to achieve aggregate economic goals (e.g., full employment). Microeconomics focuses on the behavior and goals of individual market participants.

Terms to remember

Define the following terms:

factors of production	market mechanism
opportunity cost	externalities
economics	mixed economy
production possibilities	macroeconomics
law of increasing opportunity costs	microeconomics
economic growth	*ceteris paribus*

Questions for discussion

1. What opportunity costs did you incur in reading this chapter?

2. If you read four more chapters of this text today, would your opportunity costs (per chapter) increase? Explain.

3. How does the concept of opportunity cost help explain the maxim "There is no such thing as a free lunch"?

4. If all consumers desire clean air, why doesn't the market mechanism produce it?

Problem

POTENTIAL WEEKLY OUTPUT COMBINATIONS, USING ALL RESOURCES

	Pianos	Stereos
A	10	0
B	9	1
C	7	2
D	4	3
E	0	4

Assume that the schedule at the left describes the production possibilities confronting an economy. Using the information from the table:

(a) Draw the production possibilities curve. Be sure to label each alternative output combination (A thru E).

(b) Calculate and illustrate on your graph the opportunity cost of producing one stereo per week.

(c) What is the cost of producing a second stereo? What accounts for the difference?

(d) Which point on the curve is the most desired one? How will we find out?

(e) What would happen to the production-possibilities curve if additional factors of production became available? Illustrate.

APPENDIX
USING GRAPHS

Economists like to draw graphs. In fact, we didn't even make it through the first chapter without a few graphs. The purpose of this appendix is to look more closely at the way graphs are drawn and used.

The basic purpose of a graph is to illustrate a relationship between two things, or *variables*. Consider, for example, the relationship between grades and studying. In general, we expect that additional hours of study time will lead to higher grades. Hence we should be able to see a distinct relationship between hours of study time and grade-point average.

Suppose that we actually surveyed all of the students taking this course with regard to their study time and grade-point averages. The resulting information can be compiled in a table such as Table A.1.

According to the table, students who don't study at all can expect an F in this course. To get a C, the average student apparently spends eight hours a week studying. All those who study sixteen hours a week end up with an A in the course.

These relationships between grades and studying can also be illustrated on a graph. Indeed, the whole purpose of a graph is to summarize numerical relationships.

We begin to construct a graph by drawing horizontal and vertical boundaries, as in Figure A.1. These boundaries are called the *axes* of the graph. On the vertical axis we measure one of the variables; the other variable is measured on the horizontal axis.[1]

In this case, we shall measure the grade-point average on the vertical axis. We start at the *origin* (the intersection of the two axes) and count upward, letting the distance between horizontal lines represent half (0.5) a grade point. Each horizontal line is numbered, up to the maximum grade-point average of 4.0.

The number of hours each week spent doing homework is measured on the horizontal axis. We begin at the origin again, and count

[1] The vertical axis is often called the Y-axis; the horizontal axis the X-axis.

TABLE A.1 HYPOTHETICAL RELATIONSHIP OF GRADES TO STUDY TIME

Study time (hours per week)	Grade-point average
16	4.0 (A)
14	3.5 (B+)
12	3.0 (B)
10	2.5 (C+)
8	2.0 (C)
6	1.5 (D+)
4	1.0 (D)
2	0.5 (F+)
0	0 (F)

FIGURE A.1 THE RELATIONSHIP OF GRADES TO STUDY TIME

The upward (positive) slope of the curve indicates that additional studying is associated with higher grades. The average student (2.0, or C grade) studies 8 hours per week. This is indicated by point *M* on the graph.

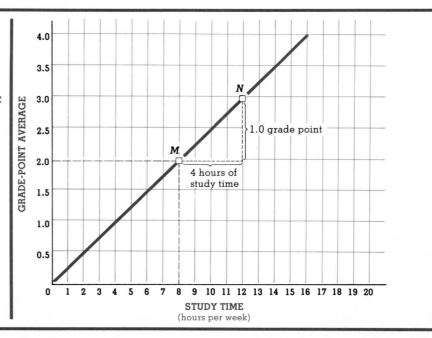

to the right. The *scale* (numbering) proceeds in increments of one hour, up to twenty hours per week.

When both axes have been labeled and measured, we can begin to illustrate the relationship between study time and grades. Consider the typical student who does eight hours of homework per week and has a 2.0 (C) grade-point average. We illustrate this relationship by first locating eight hours on the horizontal axis. We then move up from that point a distance of 2.0 grade points, to point *M*. Point *M* tells us that eight hours of study time is typically associated with a 2.0 grade-point average.

The rest of the information in Table A.1 is drawn (or plotted) on the graph in the same way. To illustrate the average grade for people who study twelve hours per week, we move upward from the number 12 on the horizontal axis until we reach the height of 3.0 on the vertical axis. At that intersection, we draw another point (point *N*).

Once we have plotted the various points describing the relationship of study time to grades, we may connect them with a line or curve. This line (curve) is our summary. In this case, the line slopes upward to the right, that is, it has a *positive* slope. This slope indicates that more hours of study time are associated with *higher* grades. Were higher grades associated with *less* study time, the curve in Figure A.1 would have a *negative* slope (slope downward from left to right).

Slopes

The upward slope of Figure A.1 tells us that higher grades are associated with increased amounts of study time. That same curve also tells us *how much* grades tend to rise with study time. According to point *M* in Figure A.1, the average student studies eight hours per week and earns a C (2.0 grade-point average). In order to earn a B (3.0 average), students apparently need to study an average of twelve hours per week (point *N*). Hence an increase of four hours of study time per week is associated with a one-point increase in grade-point average. This relationship between *changes* in study time and *changes* in grade-point average is expressed by the steepness, or *slope,* of the graph.

The slope of any graph is calculated as:

$$\text{Slope} = \frac{\text{vertical distance between two points}}{\text{horizontal distance between two points}}$$

In our example, the vertical distance between points *M* and *N* represents a change in grade-point average. The horizontal distance between these two points represents the change in study time. Hence the slope of the graph between points *M* and *N* is equal to

$$\text{Slope} = \frac{3.0 \text{ grade} - 2.0 \text{ grade}}{12 \text{ hours} - 8 \text{ hours}} = \frac{1 \text{ grade point}}{4 \text{ hours}}$$

In other words, a four-hour increase in study time (from eight to twelve hours) is associated with a one-point increase in grade-point average (see Figure A.1).

Linear vs. nonlinear curves

In Figure A.1, the relationship between grades and studying is represented by a straight line, that is, a *linear* curve. A distinguishing feature of linear "curves" is that they have the same (constant) slope throughout. In this case, it appears that *every* four-hour increase in study time is associated with a one-point increase in average grades. (By how much do grades tend to rise when study time increases from twelve to sixteen hours? Show this relationship in Figure A.1.) Were the relationship between study time and grades not constant, the line in Figure A.1 would be curved rather than straight; it would be a nonlinear curve.

Causation

Figure A.1 itself does not guarantee that your grade-point average will rise by one point if you study four more hours per week. In fact, the graph drawn in Figure A.1 does not prove that additional study ever results in higher grades. The graph is only a summary of empirical observations. It says nothing about cause and effect. It could be that students who study a lot are also smarter to begin with. If so, then less able students might not get higher grades if they studied harder. In other words, the *cause* of higher grades is debatable. At best, the empirical relationship summarized in the graph may be used to support a particular theory (e.g., that it pays to study more). Graphs, like tables, charts, and other statistical media, rarely tell their own story; rather, they must be "interpreted" in terms of some underlying theory or expectation.

SUPPLY AND DEMAND

E very country must make certain choices about the dimensions of its economy. The United States makes them, the Soviet Union and China make them, even smaller countries such as Burundi and New Zealand make them. Not only are the basic questions always the same, but they are also quite simple:

- WHAT goods and services should the economy produce?
- HOW should they be produced?
- FOR WHOM should they be produced?

Although the questions asked are strikingly similar, the ways countries go about resolving these questions and the choices that result vary widely. In the People's Republic of China and the Soviet Union, these questions are answered for the most part by the government. In the United States, a great deal of decision-making authority is vested in individual workers, consumers, and business people. Each of these people enters the decision-making process by participating in the **markets** for factors of production and final products.

The U.S. economy is not a purely market economy, of course. As we noted in Chapter 1, many production, consumption, and income-distribution questions are decided outside the market mechanism.[1] Income taxes, public-welfare programs, and state univer-

market: Any place where individuals buy or sell resources or products.

[1] Nor are the Soviet and Chinese economies purely "command economies"; both permit some market-type activity. Accordingly, most economies are really "mixed," that is, a unique combination of market and nonmarket activities. The Soviet and Chinese economies are discussed further in Chapter 36.

sities, for example, did not emerge from private production and consumption decisions made in the marketplace. Nor are the regulatory activities of the Food and Drug Administration, the Public Health Service, or the Environmental Protection Agency maintained by market decisions. These economic decisions and activities are handled collectively in the political arena, outside the marketplace. Nevertheless, a great deal of economic activity in the United States is fashioned by decisions that individuals and firms make in the marketplace. Thus, if we know how the market mechanism operates, we can understand a lot about the way the U.S. economy works. We begin in this chapter by looking at the purpose of market transactions, then examine the nature of the decisions that emerge.

MARKET PARTICIPANTS

Over 230 million individual consumers, nearly 12 million business firms, and tens of thousands of government agencies participate directly in the U.S. economy. Fortunately, we can summarize much of this activity by classifying market participants into three distinct groups—consumers, business firms, and government agencies—and analyzing their goals and behavior.

Their goals

Individual consumers, business firms, and government agencies participate in the market in order to achieve certain goals. Consumers strive to maximize their own happiness by purchasing the most satisfying bundle of goods and services with their available incomes. For their part, businesses try to maximize profits by using the most efficient combination of resources to produce the most profitable products. Finally, government agencies are assigned the responsibility of maximizing the general welfare by using available resources to produce desired public goods and services and to redistribute incomes. That is not to say that government agencies are always faithful to this responsibility. Narrow bureaucratic concerns and vested economic or political interests can easily substitute for maximization of the general welfare. In every case, however, it is reasonable to assume that government activity (like private market activity) is directed toward a specific goal.[2]

Their constraints

The tendency of all participants in the economy to try to maximize something, be it profits, private satisfaction, or social welfare, is not their only common trait. Another element common to all participants is their *limited resources*. You and I cannot buy everything we desire; we simply don't have enough income. As a consequence, we must make *choices* among available products, always hoping to get the most satisfaction for the few dollars we have to spend. Likewise, business firms and government agencies must decide how *best* to use their limited resources to maximize profits or public welfare.

[2] We shall explore these issues further in Chapters 3 and 14.

Specialization and exchange

Our desire to maximize the returns on our limited resources leads us to participate in the market, buying and selling various goods and services. Our decision to participate in these exchanges is prompted by two considerations. First, most of us are incapable of producing everything we desire to consume. So we must rely on others to supply us with some desired goods and services. Second, even if we *could* produce all our own goods and services, it would still make sense to specialize, producing only one product and trading it for other desired goods and services.

Suppose you were capable of growing your own food, stitching your own clothes, building your own shelter, and writing your own textbooks. Even in these idyllic circumstances, it would still make sense to decide how *best* to expend your limited time and energy, and to rely on others to fill in the gaps. If you were *most* proficient at growing food, you would be best off spending your time farming. You could then exchange some of your food output for the clothes, shelter, and books you desired.[3]

Our economic interactions with others are thus necessitated by two constraints:

- Our absolute inability as individuals to produce all the things we need or desire
- The limited amount of time, energy, and resources we possess for producing those things we could make for ourselves

Together, these constraints lead us to specialize and interact. Most of the interactions that result take place in the market.

MARKET INTERACTIONS

Figure 2.1 provides a summary of the kinds of interactions that occur among market participants. Note first of all that we have identified three separate groups of participants, each containing many individuals. In the rectangle marked "Consumers" we have grouped all 230 million consumers in the United States. In the "Business firms" box we have grouped all of the various business enterprises that buy and sell goods and services. The third participant, "Governments," includes the many separate agencies of the federal government, as well as state and local governments.

The two markets

factor market: Any place where factors of production (e.g., land, labor, capital) are bought and sold.

A second feature of Figure 2.1 is its identification of two kinds of markets, product markets and factor markets. In **factor markets,** factors of production are exchanged. Specifically, market participants buy or sell land, labor, or capital that can be used in the production process.[4] When you go looking for work, for example, you are making a factor of production—your labor—available to producers. The producers will hire you—purchase your services in the

---

[3] A more formal proof of the basis for specialization and exchange—the theory of comparative advantage—is provided in Chapter 33.
[4] Factor markets are also called "*resource markets*"; "resources" and "factors of production" are often used synonymously.

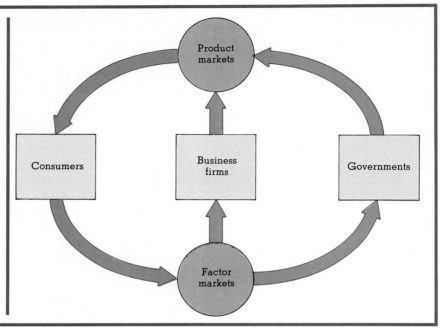

FIGURE 2.1   MARKET INTERACTIONS

Market participation is motivated by the desire to maximize personal utility (consumers), profits (business firms), or the general welfare (governments). Business firms participate in markets by supplying goods and services to product markets and purchasing factors of production in factor markets. Individual consumers participate in the marketplace by supplying factors of production (e.g., their own labor) and purchasing final goods and services. Federal, state, and local governments also participate in both factor and product markets.

product market: Any place where finished goods and services (products) are bought and sold.

factor market—if you are offering the skills they need at a price they are willing to pay. The same kind of interaction occurs in factor markets when the government seeks to employ workers or any other factors of production (land, machinery) that are available.

Interactions within factor markets are only half the story, of course, as both Figure 2.1 and everyday experience quickly confirm. At the end of a hard day's work consumers enter the grocery store (or bar) to purchase desired goods and services, that is, to buy *products*. In this context, consumers again interact with business firms, this time purchasing goods and services those firms have produced. These interactions occur in **product markets.**

In addition to business firms, governments also supply goods and services to product markets. The consumer rarely buys national defense, schools, or highways directly; instead, such purchases are made indirectly, through taxes and government expenditure. In Figure 2.1, the arrows running from the government through product markets to consumers serve to remind us, however, that all government output is intended "for the people." In this sense, the government acts as an intermediary, buying factors of production and providing certain goods and services consumers desire.

In Figure 2.1 the arrow connecting product markets to consumers emphasizes the fact that consumers, by definition, do not supply products. To the extent that individuals produce goods and services, they do so within the government or business sector. An individual who is a doctor, a dentist, or an economic consultant functions in two sectors. When selling services in the market, this person is regarded as a "business"; when away from the office, he or she is regarded as a "consumer." This distinction is helpful in emphasizing the role of the consumer as the final recipient of all goods and services produced.

Locating markets

Although we may speak of two kinds of markets, it would be a little foolish to go off in search of the product and factor markets. Neither a factor market nor a product market is a single, identifiable structure. The term "market" simply refers to any place where an economic exchange occurs—where a buyer and seller interact. The exchange may take place on the street, in a taxicab, over the phone, in the mail, or through the classified ads of the newspaper. In some cases, the market used may in fact be quite distinguishable, as in the case of a retail store, the Chicago Commodity Exchange, or a state employment office. But whatever it looks like, *a market exists wherever and whenever an exchange takes place.* The market is simply a place or medium where buyer and seller get together; which market they are in depends on what they are buying or selling.

Money and exchange

While Figure 2.1 is a useful summary of market activities, it does neglect one critical element of market interactions: money. Each of the arrows depicted in the figure actually has two dimensions. Consider again the arrow linking consumers and product markets. It is drawn in only one direction because consumers, by definition, do not provide goods and services directly to product markets. But they do provide something: money. If you want to obtain something from a product market, you must offer to pay for it with money (typically, cash or check). Thus consumers *exchange* money for goods and services in product markets. This basic exchange of money for goods is depicted in Figure 2.2.

The same kinds of exchange occur in factor markets. When you go to work, you are exchanging a factor of production (your labor) for money, typically a paycheck. Here again, the path connecting consumers to factor markets really goes in two directions, one of real resources, the other of money. Notice in Figure 2.2 that consumers receive wages, rent, and interest for the labor, land, and capital they bring to the factor markets. Indeed, nearly every market transaction

---

FIGURE 2.2 MARKET EXCHANGES

Most market transactions involve an *exchange* of real goods or resources for money (income). When products or factors of production flow in one direction, income flows in the other. *Note:* government revenues are typically not obtained directly from product sales, but instead indirectly from taxes (see Chapter 3).

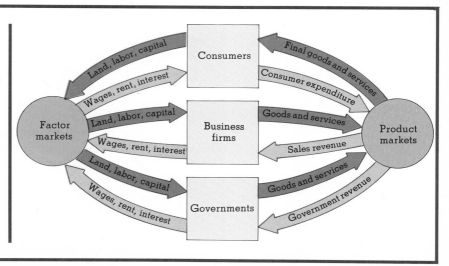

involves an exchange of money for goods (in product markets) or resources (in factor markets).[5]

Supply and demand

supply: The ability and willingness to sell (produce) specific quantities of a good at alternative prices in a given time period (*ceteris paribus*).

demand: The ability and willingness to buy specific quantities of a good at alternative prices in a given time period (*ceteris paribus*).

Because all market transactions actually have two dimensions, it is convenient to have names for both. We call these dimensions—the two sides of each market transaction—**supply** and **demand.**

Whether one is on the supply side or the demand side of any particular market transaction depends on the nature of the exchange, not on the people or institutions involved. Consumers may both demand goods and services and supply labor or other resources. As noted earlier, we are *supplying* resources to the market when we look for a job, that is, offer our labor in exchange for money. By contrast, we are *demanding* goods when we shop in a supermarket, that is, when we are prepared to offer money in exchange for something to eat. Business firms may *supply* goods and services in product markets at the same time that they are *demanding* factors of production in factor markets.

MARKET FORCES

Although the concepts of supply and demand are useful for explaining what's happening in the marketplace, we are not yet ready to summarize the zillions of transactions that are occurring daily in both factor and product markets. Recall that *every market transaction involves an exchange and thus some element of both supply and demand.* Then just consider how many exchanges you alone undertake in a single week, not to mention the transactions of the other 230 million or so consumers among us. Clearly, the daily volume of market transactions is staggering; to keep track of so much action, we will need to summarize the activities of many individuals.

Individual demand

We can begin to understand how market forces work by looking more closely at the behavior of a single market participant. Let us start with Tom, a sophomore at Clearview College. Tom is currently experiencing the torment of writing a paper for his English composition class. To make matters worse, Tom's professor has insisted on *typed* papers, and Tom cannot type with his fingers much better than he can write with his toes. Under the circumstances, Tom is desperate for a typist.

Although it is apparent that Tom has a strong *desire* for a typist, his *demand* for typing services is not yet evident. *A demand exists only if someone is willing and able to pay for the good,* that is, exchange money for a good or service in the marketplace. Is Tom willing and able to pay for typing?

Let us assume that Tom has some income and is willing to

[5] In the rare cases where one good is exchanged directly for another, we speak of *barter* exchanges.

TABLE 2.1 TOM'S DEMAND SCHEDULE		Price of typing (per page)	Quantity of typing demanded (pages per semester)
A		$5.00	1
B		4.50	2
C		4.00	3
D		3.50	5
E		3.00	7
F		2.50	9
G		2.00	12
H		1.50	15
I		1.00	20

A demand schedule indicates the quantities of a good a consumer is able and willing to buy at alternative prices (*ceteris paribus*). This demand schedule indicates that Tom would buy five pages of typing per semester if the price of typing were $3.50 per page (row D). If typing were less expensive (rows E–I). Tom would purchase a larger quantity.

opportunity cost: The most desired goods or services that are forgone in order to obtain something else.

demand schedule: A table showing the quantities of a good a consumer is willing and able to buy at alternative prices in a given time period (*ceteris paribus*).

spend some of it to get his English paper typed. Under these assumptions, we can claim that Tom is a participant in the *market* for typing services.

But can we say anything about his demand? Surely Tom is not prepared to exchange *all* his income for the typing of a single English paper. After all, Tom *could* use his income to buy more desirable goods and services; to give up everything for the typing of just one paper would imply an extremely high **opportunity cost.** It would be more reasonable to assume that there are *limits* to the amount Tom is willing to pay for any given quantity of typing. These limits will be determined by how much income Tom has to spend and how many other goods and services he must implicitly forsake in order to pay for typing services. If the price of typing exceeds these limits, Tom may end up typing all or part of the paper himself.

We assume, then, that when Tom starts looking for a typist, he has in mind some sort of **demand schedule** like that described in Table 2.1. According to row *A* of this schedule, our tormented English compositionist is willing and able to pay for the typing of only one page per semester if he must pay $5 per typed page. At such an outrageous price, he will have only the first page of his paper typed professionally and will peck out or print the remaining pages himself. That way, the paper will make a good first impression, and Tom won't have to sacrifice so many other goods and services for his paper.

At lower prices, Tom would behave differently. According to Table 2.1, Tom would get more pages typed if the price of typing were less. At lower prices, he would not have to give up so many other goods and services for each page of professional typing and would be more *willing* to have his paper typed. The reduced opportunity costs implied by lower typing prices increase the attractiveness of professional typing. Indeed, we see from row *I* that Tom is willing to have 20 pages per semester typed professionally—an entire paper—if the price per page is as low as $1.

Notice that the demand schedule doesn't tell us anything about *why* this consumer is willing to pay specific prices for various amounts of typing. Tom's expressed willingness to pay for typing may reflect a desperate need to finish his paper, a lot of income to spend, or a relatively small desire for other goods and services. All the demand schedule tells us is what the consumer is *willing and able* to buy, for whatever reasons.[6]

Also observe that the demand schedule doesn't tell us how many pages of typing the consumer will *actually* buy. Table 2.1 simply states that Tom is *willing and able* to pay for one page of typing per semester at $5.00 per page, for two pages at $4.50 each, and so on. How much typing he purchases will depend on the actual price of typing in the market. Until we know that price, we cannot tell how much typing will be purchased. Hence ***"demand" is an expression of consumer buying intentions, of a willingness to buy, not a statement of actual purchases.***

demand curve: A curve describing the quantities of a good a consumer is willing and able to buy at alternative prices in a given time period (*ceteris paribus*).

A convenient summary of buying intentions is provided by the **demand curve,** a graphical illustration of the demand schedule. The demand curve in Figure 2.3 tells us again that this consumer is willing to pay for only one page of professional typing per semester if the price is $5.00 per page (point *A*), for two if the price is $4.50 (point *B*), for three pages at $4.00 a page (point *C*), and so on. Once we know what the market price of typing actually is, a quick look at the demand curve tells us how much typing this consumer will buy.

Ceteris paribus

The demand curve in Figure 2.3 has only two dimensions—quantity demanded (on the horizontal axis) and price (on the vertical axis). This seems to imply that the amount of typing demanded depends *only* on the price of typing. This is surely not the case. A consumer's demand for any product depends on a variety of forces, including:

- □ Tastes (desire for this and other goods)
- □ Price (of this particular good)
- □ Income (of the consumer)
- □ Other goods (their availability and price)
- □ Expectations (for income, prices, tastes)

If Tom didn't have to turn in a typed English composition, he would have no taste (desire) for typing services and thus no demand. If he had no income, he would not have the ability to pay and thus would still be out of the typing market. Other goods shape the opportunity cost of typing, while expectations for income, grades, and graduation prospects would all influence his willingness to buy typing services.

If demand is in fact such a multidimensional decision, how can we reduce it to only two dimensions? This is one of the most common tricks of the economics trade. To simplify their models of the world, economists focus on only one or two forces at a time and *assume* nothing else changes. We know a consumer's tastes, income, other goods, and expectations all affect the decision to buy typing services. But we want to focus on the relationship between quantity demanded and price. That is to say, we want to know what

---

[6] Some of the economic, sociological, and psychological forces that influence consumer desires are discussed in Chapter 18.

FIGURE 2.3 A DEMAND CURVE

A demand curve expresses the quantity of a good a consumer is willing and able to buy at alternative prices. Each point on the curve refers to a specific quantity that will be demanded at a given price. If, for example, the price of typing were $3.50 per page, this curve tells us the consumer would purchase five pages per semester (point *D*). If typing cost $3 per page, seven pages per semester would be demanded (point *E*). This particular curve is based on the demand schedule in Table 2.1.

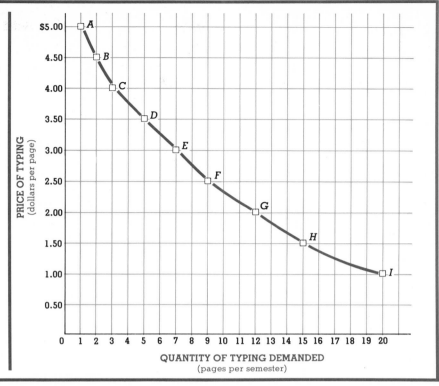

PRICE OF TYPING (dollars per page)

QUANTITY OF TYPING DEMANDED
(pages per semester)

ceteris paribus: The assumption of "everything else being equal," of nothing else changing.

independent influence price has on consumption decisions. To find out, we must isolate the one determinant, price, and assume all other determinants of demand remain unchanged. Formally, this assumption is referred to by the Latin expression ***ceteris paribus*** ("all other things remaining equal").

The *ceteris paribus* assumption is not as farfetched as it may seem at first. In the short run, people's tastes, income, and expectations do not change very much. Also, the prices and availability of other goods remain fairly constant. Hence a change in the *price* of a product may be the only thing that prompts a change in quantity demanded.

Other determinants of demand *do* change, of course, particularly as the time frame is expanded. Accordingly, the demand schedule and curve remain unchanged only so long as these other influences are constant. Were Tom's income to increase, he might be willing to buy *more* typing at every price. In this case, the entire demand curve would have to be redrawn. Such *shifts* of the demand curve are examined later in this chapter.

Market demand

What we can say about demand for typing on the part of one harassed English major we can say about the demand of all other market participants. That is to say, we can identify the demand for typing services associated with every student at Clearview College (or, for that matter, with all 230 million consumers in the United States). Some students, of course, have no need or desire for profes-

Dentists Urged to Go Back to Using Gold

When the price of gold zoomed up, dentists cut back sharply on their use of the precious metal for bridges, inlays and crowns. . . .

And that has set off a sharp debate in the dental profession. Health issues are involved along with economies. While gold's price soared, dentists wanted cheaper materials, and foundries turned out hundreds of alternative alloys from silver and from base metals such as nickel, chrome and cobalt.

Are the substitutes as good as gold? Or risky? Dentists are trying to resolve those questions.

A Cautious Stand

The American Dental Association says in a cautious comment that the best of the new alloys are "as satisfactory as gold, although no long-term studies have been made as to relative durability."

The new alloys are substantially cheaper. Though the price of gold has fallen to $415 an ounce or so from the high of $875, which it reached for only a day in January 1980, gold reconstructive work on a tooth can add $100 or so to a dental bill.

In 1980, the 136,000 dentists in the U.S. used 341,000 ounces of gold, less than half the 706,000 ounces they used in 1978. "That's a fast drop," says Louis Calisti, director of dental-care management at Boston University's Goldman School of Graduate Dentistry.

—Roger Lowenstein

market demand: The total quantities of a good or service people are willing and able to buy at alternative prices in a given time period; the sum of individual demands.

sional typing and are not willing to pay anything for such services: they do not participate in the typing market. Other students have a desire for such services but not enough income to pay for them; they, too, are excluded from the typing market. A large number of students, however, not only have a need (or desire) for typing services but are also willing and able to purchase such services, either because their incomes are sufficient or because typing prices are comparatively low. How much income is "sufficient" and what price is regarded as "low" will depend on the attitudes, experiences, and opportunity costs of each person.

What we start with in product markets, then, is many individual demand curves. Can we make enough sense out of these curves to say anything in general about the market demand for typing services at Clearview College? What we really need is some way to add up all the individual demand curves to produce a single **market demand** for typing.

Fortunately, it is possible to combine all the individual demand curves into a single market demand for typing services, and the aggregation process is no more difficult than simple arithmetic. In fact, simple arithmetic is all that's needed, once you know the buying intentions of all consumers. Suppose you would be willing to buy one page of typing per semester at a price of $8 per page. George, who is desperate to make his English essays at least *look* good, would buy two at that price; and I would buy none, since I only grade papers, and needn't type the grades. What would our combined (market) demand for typing services be at that price? Clearly, our individual inclinations indicate that we would be willing to buy a total of three pages of typing per semester if the price were $8 per page. Our combined willingness to buy—our collective market demand—is nothing more than the sum of our individual demand schedules. The same kind of aggregation can be performed for all consumers, leading to a summary of the total market demand for typing services at Clearview College.

What is nice about a market-demand concept is that it permits us to ignore some of the idiosyncrasies of our friends and neighbors.

With thousands of students at Clearview College, the typing market is large. Accordingly, we don't have to consider whether George's roommate will move out if he starts doing his own typing, or whether you will buy more typing if you win the state lottery. Regardless of the personal virtues that you, George, and George's roommate possess, the market demand for typing services will be little affected by these great moments in your lives. In so large a market, the demand for typing services tends to be more stable and predictable than the demands of the separate individuals who participate in that market. In still larger markets—say, the total U.S. market for typewriters—the predictability of market demand is important to the business people and bureaucrats who make output and price decisions.

We cannot completely ignore the factors that mold and shape the buying habits of individual consumers, however. First of all, we are likely to be as interested in the welfare and happiness of specific individuals as in the dimensions of the whole market. Second, and more important for the purposes of economic forecasting or policy formulation, we must recognize that if enough consumers change their buying intentions, then the market demand will change. Hence, if we want to change the market demand for typing, we have to know what motivates individual consumers of typing services.

Market supply

market supply: The total quantities of a good that sellers are willing and able to sell at alternative prices in a given time period (*ceteris paribus*); the combined willingness of all market suppliers to sell.

Everything we have said about market demand applies with equal force to the concept of market supply. **Market supply** is simply the total quantity of a good that *all* potential sellers are *willing* and *able to sell* at alternative prices. Thus the market supply of typing services at Clearview College is the number of typed pages all professional typists at Clearview, taken together, are prepared to produce (type) per semester, at various prices. Similarly, the "supply of labor" is equal to the amount of labor willingly supplied each year by millions of individual workers at particular wage rates. The "supply of automobiles" is equal to the number of cars produced per year at various prices by General Motors, Ford, and other automakers. The "supply of wheat" is the number of bushels willingly brought to market each year at various prices by a million farmers.

Like market demand, *market supply is an expression of sellers' intentions, of the ability and willingness to sell, not a statement of actual sales.* My next-door neighbor may be *willing* to sell his 1972 Ford Pinto for $8,000, but it is most unlikely that he will ever find a buyer at that price. Nevertheless, his *willingness* to sell his car at that price is part of the *market supply* of used cars. The significance of these various intentions for market prices and sales is examined next.

THE ACTION IN PRODUCT MARKETS

We can use the concepts of market supply and market demand to determine the quantity of goods and services that will be exchanged in each market. The same concepts can be used to determine the

TABLE 2.2   THE MARKET DEMAND SCHEDULE FOR TYPING

Market demand represents the combined demands of all market participants. To determine the total quantity of typing demanded at any given price, we add up the separate demands of the individual consumers. Row G of this schedule indicates that a *total* quantity of 39 pages per semester will be demanded at a price of $2 per page.

	Price per page	Quantity demanded (pages per semester)				Total demand
		Tom +	George +	Lisa +	Me =	
A	$5.00	1	4	0	0	5
B	4.50	2	6	0	0	8
C	4.00	3	8	0	0	11
D	3.50	5	11	0	0	16
E	3.00	7	14	1	0	22
F	2.50	9	18	3	0	30
G	2.00	12	22	5	0	39
H	1.50	15	26	6	0	47
I	1.00	20	30	7	0	57

price at which the goods and services will be bought and sold. Consider, for example, the interplay of supply and demand in the Clearview College typing *market*. As we noted earlier, not all students will desire typing services; even fewer will be able and willing to purchase such services. Nevertheless, so long as *some* students are willing and able to pay for typing, we can speak of a *demand* for typing. We can then use arithmetic to construct a market demand curve based on the willingness to pay expressed by all persons.

The market demand curve

Table 2.2 provides the basic market demand schedule for a situation in which only four people participate on the demand side of the market. Figure 2.4 illustrates the same market situation with demand curves. The four individuals who participate in the market demand for Clearview College typing obviously differ greatly, as suggested by their respective demand schedules. Tom has to turn in several papers each semester, has a good income, and is willing to purchase typing services. His demand schedule is portrayed in the first column of Table 2.2 (and is identical to the one we examined in

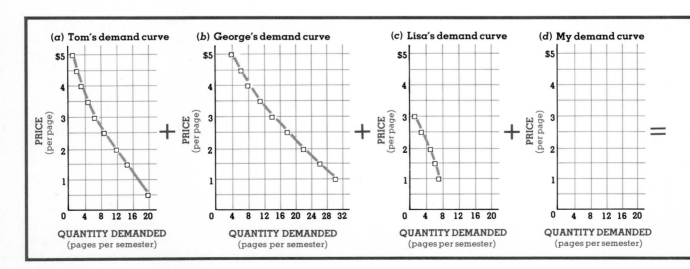

(a) Tom's demand curve   (b) George's demand curve   (c) Lisa's demand curve   (d) My demand curve

Table 2.1). George, as we already noted, is desperate to improve the appearance of his papers and is willing to pay for typing services, even at relatively high prices. His demand schedule is summarized in the second column under "Quantity demanded" in Table 2.2. The third consumer in this market is Lisa. She has a very limited budget and can do her own typing if she must, and so is not willing to buy any typing at higher prices. As prices drop below $3.50 per page, however, her demand schedule indicates that she will get some of her work professionally typed. Finally, there is my demand schedule (the fourth column under "Quantity demanded" in Table 2.2), which confirms that I really don't participate in the local typing market.

The differing personalities and consumption habits of Tom, George, Lisa, and me are expressed in our individual demand schedules and associated curves, as depicted in Table 2.2 and Figure 2.4. To determine the *market* demand for typing from this information, we simply add up these four separate demands. The end result of this aggregation is, first, a *market* demand schedule (the last column in Table 2.2) and, second, the resultant *market* demand curve (the curve in Figure 2.4*e*). These market summaries describe the various quantities of typing that Clearview College students are *willing and able* to purchase each semester at various prices.

How much typing will be purchased each semester? Knowing how much typing Tom, George, Lisa, and I are willing to buy at various prices doesn't tell you how much we are actually going to purchase. To determine the actual consumption of typing services, we have to know something about prices and supplies. What is the price of typing in this market, and who sets it?

The market supply curve

To understand how the going price for typing is established, we will focus on the activities of the three people who offer typing services at Clearview College. None of these three entrepreneurs is willing to type for less than $1 a page; they reason that their leisure time is worth more than that. As a consequence, no typing services are

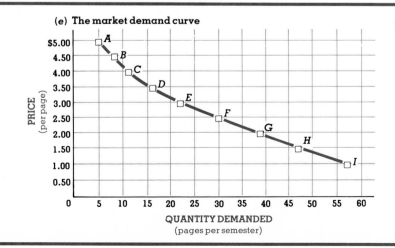

(e) The market demand curve

PRICE (per page)

QUANTITY DEMANDED
(pages per semester)

FIGURE 2.4   CONSTRUCTION OF THE MARKET DEMAND CURVE

The market demand curve expresses the *combined* demands of all market participants. At a price of $3 per page, the total quantity of typing demanded would be 22 pages per semester (point *E*): 7 pages demanded by Tom, 14 by George, and 1 by Lisa.

TABLE 2.3   THE MARKET SUPPLY SCHEDULE FOR TYPING SERVICES

Market supply represents the *combined* willingness to sell of all individual sellers (producers). In this case, the total quantity supplied to the market at alternative prices depends on the ability and willingness of three individual sellers to sell. If typing can be sold at $4 per page (row *h*), a total of 130 pages per semester will be offered.

| | Price per page | Quantity supplied (pages per semester) | | | Total market |
		Don +	Lynn +	Terry =	
j	$5.00	46	54	48	148
i	$4.50	45	51	44	140
h	$4.00	44	47	39	130
g	$3.50	39	43	32	114
f	$3.00	34	32	24	90
e	$2.50	25	23	14	62
d	$2.00	17	15	7	39
c	$1.50	11	9	0	20
b	$1.00	6	4	0	10
a	$0.50	0	0	0	0

available at prices under $1 per page. Prices must be at least high enough to compensate sellers for their opportunity costs, in this case, the leisure or study time given up in order to type.

At a price of $1 per page, two typists are able and willing to forsake some leisure or study time and offer typing services. As row *b* of Table 2.3 indicates, Don is *willing* to type six pages per semester if the price is only $1 per page. Lynn is able and willing to type four pages per semester at that price. Clearly there won't be much professional typing activity at Clearview College if the price for typing is only $1 per page.

At higher prices per page, typing becomes more attractive. As prices rise above $1 per page, typists are receiving more income for the leisure or study time they give up; that is, the *relative* attractiveness of typing improves. Accordingly, when the price of typing is $2 per page (row *d*), it is not surprising that a third typist enters the market. At this higher price, both Don and Lynn are also willing to supply larger quantities of typing, as their demand schedules indicate.

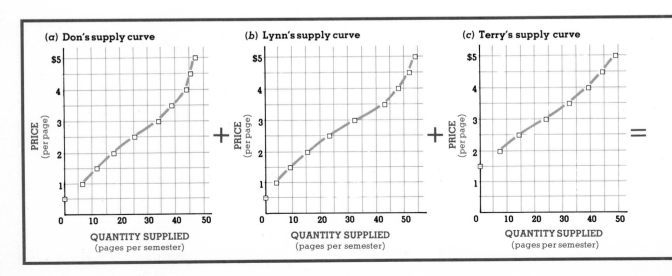

(a) Don's supply curve   +   (b) Lynn's supply curve   +   (c) Terry's supply curve   =

If typing services could be sold at very high prices, Don, Lynn, and Terry would be willing to sacrifice substantial amounts of leisure time for their typing. Hence the quantity of typing supplied to the Clearview College market would rise.

The various inclinations of Don, Lynn, and Terry are reflected in their respective supply schedules. We can combine these schedules into a single *market* supply schedule in the same way that we constructed a market demand schedule. Table 2.3 details the quantity of typing that Don, Lynn, and Terry would be able and *willing to sell* at various prices. Figure 2.5 illustrates this information with supply curves. Notice how each point on the supply curve corresponds to a particular row of Table 2.3. As should be apparent by now, the market supply curve is conceptually the same kind of thing as an individual's (or firm's) supply curve, except that it includes the behavior and intentions of more people (or firms).

EQUILIBRIUM

We can now determine the price and quantity of typing being sold at Clearview College without going to the campus and interviewing all the students. A market supply curve and a market demand curve are all we require. All we need do is bring the two curves together, as in Figure 2.6. The market supply curve expresses the *ability and willingness* of Don, Lynn, and Terry to sell typing at various prices. The market demand curve illustrates the *ability and willingness* of Tom, George, Lisa, and me to buy typing at those same prices. When we put the two curves together, we see that **only one price and quantity are compatible with the existing intentions of both buyers and sellers.** This **equilibrium** occurs at the intersection of the two curves. Once it is established, typing will cost $2 per page. At that price, Don, Lynn, and Terry will sell 39 pages of typing per semester—the same amount that Tom, George, and Lisa wish to buy at that price.

equilibrium price: The price at which the quantity of a good demanded in a given time period equals the quantity supplied.

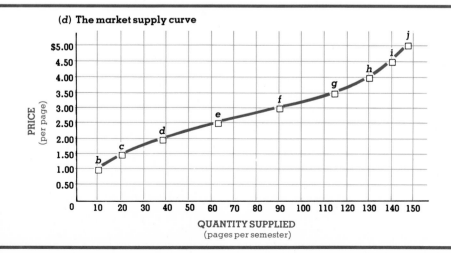

(d) The market supply curve

PRICE (per page)

QUANTITY SUPPLIED
(pages per semester)

FIGURE 2.5   CONSTRUCTION OF THE MARKET SUPPLY CURVE

The market supply curve indicates the *combined* sales intentions of all market participants. If the price of typing were $2.50 per page (point e), the *total* quantity of typing supplied would be 62 pages per semester. This quantity is determined by adding together the individual responses (supply curves) of Don, Lynn, and Terry.

FIGURE 2.6 THE TYPING MARKET

The equilibrium price and quantity are determined by the intersection of the market supply and demand curves. The equilibrium price is the only price at which the quantity demanded equals the quantity supplied. In this case, the equilibrium price is $2 per page. At that price, 39 pages of typing are supplied and demanded per semester.

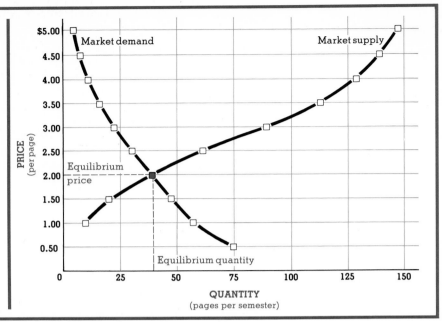

An important characteristic of the equilibrium price is that it is not determined by any single individual. Rather it is determined by the collective actions of many buyers and sellers, each acting out his or her own demand or supply schedule. It is this kind of impersonal price determination that gave rise to Adam Smith's characterization of the market mechanism as "the invisible hand." In attempting to explain how the market mechanism works, the famed nineteenth-century economist noted a certain feature of market prices. The market behaves *as if* some unseen force (the invisible hand) were examining each individual's supply or demand schedule, then selecting a price that assured an equilibrium. In practice, of course, the process of price determination is not so mysterious; rather it is a simple process of trial and error.

Surplus and shortage

market surplus: The amount by which the quantity supplied exceeds the quantity demanded at a given price; excess supply.

Suppose for the moment that Don, Lynn, and Terry believed that typing could be sold for $2.50 per page rather than the equilibrium price of $2.00, and offered it only at this higher price. From the demand and supply schedules depicted in Table 2.4 (themselves taken from Tables 2.2 and 2.3) we can readily foresee the consequences. At $2.50 per page, Don, Lynn, and Terry would be offering more typing services than Tom, George, and Lisa were willing to buy at that price. Thus a **market surplus** of typing services would exist, in the sense that more typing was offered for sale (supplied) than students cared to purchase at the available price.

As Table 2.4 indicates, at a price of $2.50 per page, a market surplus of 32 pages per semester exists. Under these circumstances, Don, Lynn, and Terry would be spending many idle hours at their typewriters, waiting for customers to appear. Their waiting will be in vain, because the quantity of typing demanded will not increase

TABLE 2.4 MARKET DEMAND AND SUPPLY

Only at the equilibrium price of $2 is the quantity demanded equal to the quantity supplied. At higher prices, a market surplus exists—the quantity supplied exceeds the quantity demanded. At prices below equilibrium, a market shortage exists.

Price per page	Quantity supplied (pages per semester)		Quantity demanded (pages per semester)
$5.00	148		5
4.50	140		8
4.00	130	**market**	11
3.50	114	**surplus**	16
3.00	90		22
2.50	62		30
2.00	39	equilibrium	39
1.50	20	**market**	47
1.00	10	**shortage**	57

until the price of typing falls. That is the clear message of the demand curve. The tendency of quantity demanded to increase as price falls is illustrated in Figure 2.7 by a movement along the demand curve from point *X* to lower prices and greater quantity demanded. As we move down the market demand curve, the desire for typing does not change, but the quantity people are able and willing to buy increases. Indeed, a basic implication of the downward-sloping demand curve is that *one can stimulate sales of a product by lowering its price.*

A very different sequence of events would occur if someone were to spread the word initially that typing services were available at only $1.50 per page. Tom, George, and Lisa would be standing in line to get their papers typed, but Don, Lynn, and Terry would not be willing to supply the quantity desired at that price. As Table 2.4 confirms, at $1.50 per page, the quantity demanded (47 pages per

FIGURE 2.7 MARKET SURPLUS OR SHORTAGE

Only at the equilibrium price ($2) is the quantity demanded equal to the quantity supplied. At higher prices (e.g., $2.50), the quantity supplied will exceed the quantity demanded. This imbalance is called a market surplus (excess supply). At lower prices, a market shortage (excess demand) will exist; the quantity demanded will exceed the quantity supplied.

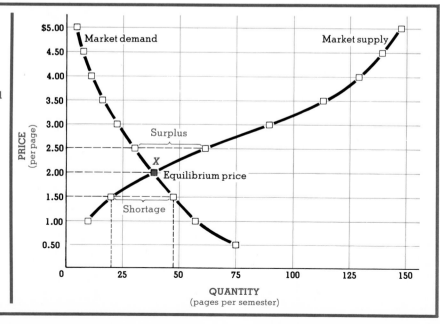

Fed up with the food fight

Forced to queue endlessly for supplies, the Poles are boiling

It is 4 a.m. The sun will not rise for almost three hours, but already the line has begun to form in front of the austere, dimly lit shop. A panel truck pulls up to the rear entrance, and two burly workers, their white smocks spattered with red stains, deliver their precious cargo: a day's supply of meat. Within three hours, the choicest cuts—pork chops, ham, boneless beef—will be gone. The late arrivals will have to make do with sausage, soup bones or chicken. Or perhaps nothing at all. . . .

The government officially maintains that the average Pole spends four hours queuing up each day. That estimate drew derisive laughter from most shoppers. Says one retired woman: "I spend half my time in lines. I do all the shopping for my daughter and her family." Indeed, the elderly are one of the Polish family's most valuable assets, since they have more free time for waiting in line. . . .

With the state-run supply system on the verge of collapse, most Poles must turn to alternate sources for food and other scarce items. Those with friends or relatives abroad may get some of what they need via parcel post. Others resort to barter: a mechanic might trade two quarts of motor oil to a salesgirl for a pound of coffee; in Silesia, the miners are reportedly trading coal to farmers for meat. For exorbitant prices, or hard Western currency, almost anything can be gotten on the black market. Sample prices: blue jeans, $180; one pint of vodka, $24.

More affordable to the average Pole are the so-called free markets, which the government traditionally has ignored. These extralegal bazaars are operated as private enterprises by farmers or nimble entrepreneurs who offer abundant quantities of fruits and vegetables at prices slightly higher than the state stores. A free-market egg costs about 40¢, for example, compared with 30¢ for one in a state store. The more wealthy city dweller may drive out into the country and buy meat directly and illegally from a farmer. One Gdansk bureaucrat admits that he and a neighbor buy whole pigs and then salt the meat down in barrels. Such stratagems have become so common that the government last month prohibited the sale of meat outside state stores. Reason: farmers were refusing to sell their pigs to the government at the official price of $1.30 per lb. when they could get half again as much from individuals.

---

market shortage: The amount by which the quantity demanded exceeds the quantity supplied at a given price; excess demand.

semester) would greatly exceed the quantity supplied (20 pages per semester). In this situation, we may speak of a **market shortage,** that is, an excess of quantity demanded over quantity supplied.

When a market shortage exists, not all consumer demands can be satisfied. In other words, some people who are *willing* to buy typing at the going price ($1.50) will not be able to do so. To assure themselves of sufficient typing, Tom, George, Lisa, or some other consumer may offer to pay a *higher* price, thus initiating a move up the demand curve of Figure 2.7. The higher prices offered will in turn induce Don, Lynn, and Terry to type more, thus ensuring an upward movement along the market supply curve. Thus a higher price tends to call forth a greater quantity supplied, as reflected in the upward-sloping supply curve. Notice, again, that the *desire* to type has not changed; only the quantity supplied has responded to a change in price.

What we observe, then, is that ***whenever the market price is set above or below the equilibrium price, either a market surplus or a market shortage will emerge.*** To overcome a surplus or shortage, buyers and sellers will change their behavior, that is, the prices charged or paid and the quantities demanded or sold. Only at the *equilibrium* price will no further adjustments be required. The equilibrium price is the only price at which the amount consumers are willing to buy equals the amount producers are willing to sell. We can count on market participants to find this equilibrium.

Business firms can discover equilibrium market prices in the same way. If they find that consumer purchases are not keeping up with production, they may conclude that their price is above the equilibrium price. They will have to get rid of their accumulated inventory. To do so they will have to lower their price (by a Grand End-of-Year Sale, perhaps) or convince consumers (via advertising) that they have underrated a most indispensable product. In the happy situation where consumer purchases are outpacing production, a firm might conclude that its price was a trifle too low and give it a nudge upward. Or it might expand production facilities. In any case, the equilibrium price can be established after a few trials in the marketplace.

SHIFTS IN DEMAND

We can anticipate that the collective actions of buyers and sellers will quickly establish an equilibrium price for any product. We should not regard any particular equilibrium price as permanent, however. The equilibrium price established in the Clearview College typing market, for example, was the unique outcome of specific demand and supply schedules. Those schedules themselves were based on our *ceteris paribus* assumption of "all other things remaining equal." Specifically, we assumed that the "taste" (desire) for typing was given, as were consumers' incomes, the price and availability of other goods, and expectations. But any of these other deter-

CETERIS PARIBUS: MOVEMENTS VS. SHIFTS

A demand curve is constructed on the assumption that all determinants of demand other than price are given (i.e., constant). It tells us how the quantity demanded of a good will change in response to a change in the price of that good. The demand curve is a reliable predictor of consumers' behavior so long as underlying tastes, incomes, costs of other goods, or expectations do not change. As long as *ceteris paribus* (other things remain equal), the quantity demanded will move up or down the demand curve in response to changes in price.

But other things do not remain equal forever: tastes, incomes, and opportunity costs do change. When they do, the entire demand curve will *shift* to a new position. As a consequence, the quantity demanded of a good may change even if the price of the good does not.

The quantity demanded of a good may change, then, in response to one of two factors:

- A change in the price of that good, which causes a movement along the existing demand curve
- A change in underlying tastes, income, other goods, or expectations, which causes a *shift in the demand curve*

On the supply side, too, changes in the quantity supplied may result from movements along an existing supply curve or shifts of that curve. We thus distinguish between "changes in supply" (a shift) and "changes in quantity supplied" (which result from a movement or shift).

FIGURE 2.8 A SHIFT IN DEMAND

A rightward shift of the demand curve indicates that consumers are willing to buy a larger quantity at every price. As a consequence, a new equilibrium is established (point *Y*), at a higher price and greater quantity. A shift of the demand curve occurs only when the assumption of *ceteris paribus* is violated.

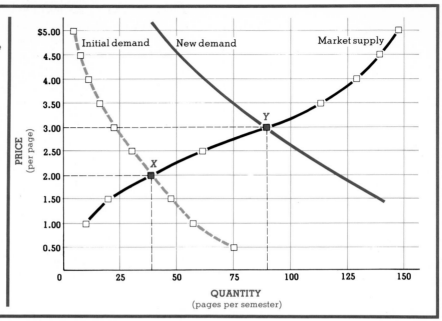

shift in demand: A change in the quantity demanded at any (every) given price.

minants of demand could change. When they do, the demand curve has to be redrawn. Such a **shift in** the **demand** curve will lead to a new equilibrium price and quantity. Indeed, *the equilibrium price will change whenever the supply or demand curve shifts.*

We can illustrate how equilibrium prices change by taking one last look at the supply and demand curves that characterize the Clearview College typing market. Our original supply and demand curves, together with the resulting equilibrium (point *X*), are depicted in Figure 2.8. Now suppose that the professors at Clearview begin assigning additional papers and homework, all of which must be typed. The increased need (desire) for typing services will affect market demand. Tom, George, and Lisa (but not I) are suddenly willing to buy more typing at every price than they were willing to before. That is to say, the *demand* for typing has increased. We can represent this increased demand by a rightward shift of the market demand curve, as illustrated in Figure 2.8.

Note that the new demand curve intersects the (unchanged) market supply curve at a new price (point *Y*): the equilibrium price is now $3 per page. This new equilibrium price will persist until either the demand curve or the supply curve shifts again.

The kinds of price changes we are describing here are quite common. Indeed, equilibrium prices change as often as significant changes occur in the behavior of buyers or sellers. A few moments in a stockbroker's office or a glance through the stock pages of the daily newspaper should be testimony enough to the fluid character of market prices. If thousands of stockholders decide to sell IBM shares tomorrow, you can be sure that the market price of that stock will drop.

In any large market, of course, a change of outlook on the part of any single buyer or seller may have little effect on the market. Were I to sell my two shares of IBM stock, the market price could probably withstand the onslaught, since thousands of shares are exchanged every day. In a product market with many buyers and sellers, many people have to change their behavior at the same time and in the same way before market prices are affected. On the other hand, if there are only a few buyers or sellers, then the action of any one of them may have a significant impact on market prices and sales.

THE ACTION IN FACTOR MARKETS

Once the action in product markets is understood, the action in factor markets begins to look familiar. Indeed, the factor and product markets function in much the same way with the same participants; only the goods and services being exchanged differ. In the factor market, the things being exchanged are intended for use in production processes. Land, timber, machinery, oil, and labor are salient examples of basic resources, although we might also include steel, grains, coal, and other resources that are bought primarily for production purposes.

Because factor markets operate like product markets, the analysis of product markets can be duplicated to explain what's happening in factor markets. The largest factor market is the one for labor. Its behavior is discussed in Chapters 25—27.

POLICY IMPLICATIONS: LAISSEZ FAIRE

The action in the marketplace is intriguing in that so much can happen with no fixed program or direction. The flows of goods and services moving between consumers and businesses in our examples are completely determined by the independent choice made by each buyer or seller. The prices at which goods and services are exchanged are also determined by the interactions of many independent individuals. Moreover, the individual participants need not be familiar with the way the **market mechanism** works. They have only

market mechanism: The use of market prices and sales to signal desired outputs (or resource allocations).

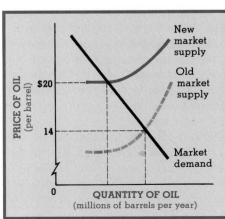

PRICE OF OIL (per barrel)

$20

14

0

QUANTITY OF OIL (millions of barrels per year)

New market supply

Old market supply

Market demand

A SHIFT IN THE SUPPLY OF OIL

In 1979 the Organization of Petroleum Exporting Countries (OPEC) announced that it was no longer willing to sell oil for the existing price of approximately $14 per barrel. Henceforth, OPEC decreed, oil would be supplied to the market only at prices above $20 per barrel. This change in the willingness to sell implied a *shift* of the market supply curve, leading to higher prices and smaller sales. The impact of this shift on the world economy is discussed in Chapter 16.

to follow their own inclinations, buying and selling resources or products as their own incomes and desires dictate.

The highly mechanical nature of the market mechanism has some advantages. First of all, all the participants in our markets can do their own thing and we will still see some sort of coherent action. That is to say, a distinct set of prices, a distinct volume and distribution of products, and a recognizable volume and distribution of resources will be generated by the forces of market supply and demand. In that sense, the market is able to resolve the basic questions of WHAT to produce, HOW to produce it, and FOR WHOM it should be produced with no guidance from external forces.

Not only is some distinct set of economic outcomes generated in the marketplace, but all participants in the market have been able to maximize their respective profits or satisfactions. This is not to say that Tom, George, Lisa, and the rest of the students in our imaginary typing market are in a constant state of euphoria as a result of their market activity. It does mean, though, that each person has got as much satisfaction or profit as is attainable from the resources he or she possesses. Tom and George, for example, would be happier if they had more income or if the price of typing were lower. Given small allowances and their inability to alter market prices, however, the buying and consuming choices they have made represent the best they can do under current conditions. In other words, this is an *optimum* situation. How do we know? Because Tom and George and everybody else in our little drama have had (and continue to have) absolute freedom to make their own purchase and consumption decisions. And also because we assume that sooner or later they will make the choices they find most satisfying.[7]

Accordingly, the market mechanism suggests a situation in which the economy can function and in which all individuals can achieve some satisfaction. What is especially noteworthy is that society's scarce resources end up being devoted to the production of goods and services in greatest demand. This demand is expressed by the *willingness* of market participants to pay for various goods. Moreover, the output gets distributed on the same basis. That is to say, FOR WHOM is determined by the amount of purchasing power each individual is willing and able to give up in order to acquire particular goods.

These features of the market mechanism can be translated readily into policy guidelines. In a word, these features suggest that individuals and the marketplace should be left alone to pursue their own interests. From this perspective, there is no need or justification for market intervention on the part of government or any other body. The price mechanism alone permits people and businesses to achieve the greatest amount of satisfaction possible; government intervention might only disrupt that outcome.

This particular policy implication is the foundation of the **laissez faire** doctrine, the doctrine of "leave it alone." Since its development by Adam Smith in 1776, it has had a profound impact on the way the economy functions and what government does (or doesn't do). Laissez faire continues to be a major plank in what is

laissez faire: The doctrine of "leave it alone," of nonintervention by governments in the market mechanism.

---

[7] The dynamics of individual choices are discussed in Chapters 18–25.

commonly regarded as the conservative platform of American politics.

One cannot dispute the mechanical precision with which the market mechanism works. Prices do in fact serve to allocate goods and factors of production in accordance with people's expressed market wishes. We can note, however, that the fulfillment of individual pursuits does not always create as much satisfaction as might be attainable. As we observed earlier (and will discuss further in Chapter 3), many public goods will not be produced in the absence of some collective, even coercive, effort. Yet nearly everyone obtains some satisfaction from public goods, be they national defense, highways, police officers and fire fighters, or the administration of justice. Hence, if everyone does his or her own thing exclusively, each individual and society as a whole may be getting less satisfaction from available resources than might otherwise be the case.[8]

Someone who has little income available with which to obtain goods or services may also be disenchanted with the doctrine of laissez faire. In a laissez faire world, the amount of food, shelter, and entertainment you can get is limited by the amount of income you possess. If you have little wealth or talent to begin with, you are not going to get much satisfaction or profit, no matter how cleverly you deploy your resources. On the other hand, if you inherited particularly good genes or fortunes, you are likely to reap a good deal of satisfaction and profit in the market. Hence those persons who possess more things to exchange ("dollar votes") are treated better in the market.[9]

Finally, those who possess significant control over productive resources are in a position to alter market outcomes in their own interest. If only one individual owns all the typewriters on campus, then the market supply of typing will be determined by that person's willingness to supply. It will not be determined by the interactions of a lot off independent producers. In such a case, the single producer is likely to tip the scale of profits and satisfaction in his favor.

The way the market treats various individuals and groups is the subject of many subsequent chapters. We shall also consider how various configurations of wealth and power may affect the way the economy works, the kinds of goods we produce, the resources we use, and the incomes we receive. Knowing how things work does not completely answer the question of how things *should* work. That will remain a question for individual and collective resolution.

SUMMARY

■ Individual consumers, business firms, and government agencies participate in the marketplace by offering to buy or sell goods and services or factors of production. Participation is motivated by the

---

[8] The problem of *externalities*, noted in Chapter 1, is further explored in Chapters 3 and 30.
[9] This particular feature of market economies has been a prime consideration in the rejection by socialist economies (especially China and the Soviet Union) of the market mechanism in favor of centralized planning. The economics of planned economies are discussed in Chapter 36.

desire to maximize utility (consumers), profits (business firms), or the general welfare (government agencies).

■ All interactions in the marketplace involve the exchange of either factors of production or finished products among consumers, businesses, and government. Although the actual exchanges can take place anywhere, we may say that they take place in product markets or factor markets, depending on what is being exchanged.

■ People who are willing and able to buy a particular good at some price become part of the market demand for that product. All those who are willing and able to sell that good at some price are part of the market supply. Total market demand or supply is the sum of individual demands or supplies.

■ The quantity of goods and services or factors of production that is actually exchanged in each market will depend on the behavior of all buyers and sellers, as summarized in market supply and demand curves. At the point where the two curves intersect, an equilibrium price—the price at which the quantity demanded equals the quantity supplied—will be established.

■ A distinctive feature of the equilibrium price and quantity is that it is the only price-quantity combination that is acceptable to buyers and sellers alike. At higher prices, sellers supply more than buyers are willing to purchase (a market surplus); at lower prices, the amount demanded exceeds the quantity supplied (a market shortage). Only the equilibrium price clears the market. At that price, everyone who is willing to buy may do so, and everyone who wants to sell at that price may do so.

■ Should either market supply or demand change (shift), a new equilibrium price will be established. Supply and demand curves shift whenever the assumption of *ceteris paribus* (unchanged income, tastes, etc.) is violated.

■ The market mechanism is a device for establishing prices and product and resource flows. As such, it may be used to answer the basic economic questions of WHAT to produce, HOW to produce it, and FOR WHOM. Whether or not these answers are accepted—and laissez faire prevails—will depend in part on our views of the underlying distribution of incomes ("dollar votes") and the prevalence of externalities.

Terms to remember

Define the following terms:

market
factor market
product market
supply
demand
opportunity cost
demand schedule
demand curve
ceteris paribus

market demand
market supply
equilibrium price
market surplus
market shortage
shift in demand
market mechanism
laissez faire

Questions for discussion

1. In our story of Tom, the nontypist confronted with a typing assignment, we emphasized the great urgency of his desire for typing services. Many people would say that Tom had an "absolute need" for typing, and was therefore ready to "pay anything" to get his paper typed. If this were true, what shape would his demand curve have? Why isn't this realistic?

2. If Tom were to type the paper himself, would his opportunity costs thereby be eliminated (and typing thus become a "free" good)?

3. How were the basic economic questions of WHAT to produce and FOR WHOM decided in the Clearview College typing market?

4. Word-processing machines make typing easier and improve the appearance of the final product as well. How have word processors altered the supply and demand for typing services?

5. Can you explain the practice of "scalping" tickets for major sporting events in terms of market shortages? How else might tickets be distributed?

Problem

Given the following data, (1) construct market supply and demand curves and identify the equilibrium price; and (2) identify the amount of shortage or surplus that would exist at a price of $4:

Participant	Quantity demanded or supplied (price or per week)				
	$5	$4	$3	$2	$1
A. Demand side					
Al	1	2	3	4	5
Betsy	0	1	1	1	2
Casey	2	2	3	3	4
Daisy	1	3	4	4	6
Eddie	1	2	2	3	5
Market total	—	—	—	—	—
B. Supply side					
Alice	3	3	3	3	3
Butch	7	5	4	4	2
Connie	6	4	3	3	1
Dutch	6	5	4	3	0
Ellen	4	2	2	2	1
Market total	—	—	—	—	—

CHAPTER 3

THE PUBLIC SECTOR

Not all goods and services produced in the economy pass through product markets, at least not in the conventional way. On the contrary, a vast array of goods and services is produced in the *public sector,* by federal, state, and local governments. These goods are not sold directly to consumers, but instead are paid for through taxes. Among such goods and services are national defense, public schools, highways, courts of law, fire fighters, and sanitation workers. The production of goods in the public sector accounts for nearly one-fifth of our total output.

In view of the public sector's substantial contribution to total output, we cannot begin to know how the U.S. economy answers the basic questions of WHAT to produce, HOW to produce it, and FOR WHOM to produce it until we examine the nature and dimensions of public-sector activity. The purposes of this chapter are, first, to describe the general dimensions of public-sector activity, then to determine why we rely on governments rather than on the market mechanism for so much production. As we shall see, much of what the government produces cannot be produced efficiently by the private sector.

FEDERAL EXPENDITURE

In fiscal year 1983 the federal government spent nearly $800 billion. We can begin to appreciate the dimensions of public-sector activity by looking at the ways in which all this revenue is spent.

The federal budget

fiscal year (FY): The twelve-month period used for government accounting purposes; begins October 1 and ends September 30.

A complete accounting of federal expenditures is contained in the federal budget. At the beginning of each year, the president, with the assistance of the Office of Management and Budget (OMB) and the many agencies of the federal government, prepares a statement of desired expenditures for the next **fiscal year,** which begins on October 1. The president then submits this budget to Congress for review and approval. After amending the proposed budget to its own liking, the Congress returns it to the president, with authorization to begin spending federal money. In February 1982, for example, President Reagan submitted his proposed fiscal year 1983 (FY 1983) budget to Congress. The Congress then reviewed his proposals, revised them, and ultimately gave the president permission (budget authorization) to spend nearly $800 billion in the fiscal year beginning October 1, 1982.

The complete budget of the U.S. government is a document over four inches thick and weighing nearly five pounds. A brief summary of its contents is provided in Table 3.1.

Expenditures on goods and services

Much of the federal budget is devoted to the purchase of goods and services. In FY 1983, for example, the federal government spent over $200 billion on national defense, nearly $20 billion on transporta-

---

TABLE 3.1 PROJECTED FEDERAL EXPENDITURES, FISCAL 1983 (billions of dollars)

The federal government spent nearly $800 billion in fiscal 1983. Half of this ($407 billion) was for goods and services. The rest represents transfers to individuals ($276 billion), general aid to state and local governments ($6.7 billion), and interest payments ($96 billion). All of these expenditures influence our collective answers to the questions of WHAT, HOW, and FOR WHOM to produce.

Expenditures	Amount
A. *Goods and services*	
National defense	$221.1
Transportation	19.6
Education, training, and social services	21.6
Commerce and housing	1.6
International affairs	12.0
Science, space, and technology	7.6
Energy	4.2
Natural resources and environment	9.9
Agriculture	4.5
Community and regional development	7.3
Administration of justice	4.6
Health	78.1
Veterans' services	10.0
General government	5.0
Total purchases of goods and services	$407.1
B. *Income transfers*	
Social security	$175.6
Federal employees' retirement benefits	21.1
Public assistance	42.5
Unemployment insurance	22.6
Veterans' benefits	14.4
Total income transfers	$276.2
C. *General aid to state and local governments*	6.7
D. *Interest* (net)	96.4
E. *Total expenditures*	$786.4

Source: Fiscal 1983 estimates. Office of Management and Budget.

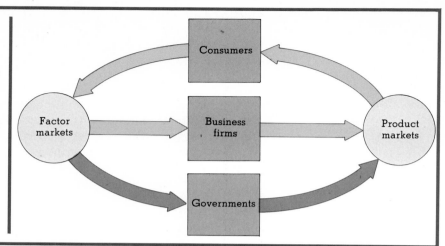

FIGURE 3.1 GOVERNMENT IN THE MARKETPLACE

The public sector is a major participant in both factor and product markets. Federal, state, and local governments hire labor, capital, and land in factor markets. They use these resources to produce goods and services for consumers (taxpayers).

intermediate goods: Goods or services purchased for use as input in the production of final goods or services.

tion, and over $4 billion on the administration of justice (Table 3.1). In many cases—for example, the purchase of new weapons—these expenditures look just like any other purchases in product markets. In reality, however, the government itself typically *produces* the good or service in question. The judges and clerks who comprise the federal judicial system, for example, are employed by the U.S. government to "produce" $4.6 billion worth of "administration of justice." Similarly, the 2 million men and women who serve in the armed forces are employed to "produce" national defense. Although the federal government directly pays for such goods and services, the government's basic role is really to produce these outputs for the use of consumers.

The role of government as a producer of final products is emphasized in Figure 3.1 by the heavy arrows connecting the government and consumers to the product market. Even in those cases where the federal government appears to be buying a final product, such as a new weapons system, such **"intermediate goods"** are simply used to produce something else, such as "national defense." What consumers receive as a finished product is national security, not a new weapons system.

In order to produce all the goods summarized in Table 3.1, the federal government must have access to factors of production. These resources may be purchased directly in factor markets, as in the case of labor employed in the armed forces or the halls of justice. Or they may be purchased indirectly, as when the government pays a building contractor to build a highway or government building. In either case, *expenditures of the federal government imply vast command over our available resources and thus our decisions on* WHAT *to produce and* HOW *to produce it.* An indication of how many of our resources the public sector commands is provided in Table 3.2. The resource shown here is labor. What we see is that the public sector *directly* employs one out of every six workers and indirectly hires another 8 million. These workers are not available, therefore, for the production of private goods.

Income transfers

Although the federal government is the single largest participant in U.S. product and factor markets, expenditures on goods and services account for only half of the federal budget. A large fraction of the budget represents **income transfers** to individuals. Transfers are income payments for which no current services or goods are exchanged.

The most familiar income transfers (and the second largest single item in the U.S. budget) are social security benefits. More than 36 million Americans receive social security checks every month. Most of these individuals are retired; others are either disabled or the children of workers who died before retirement. As Table 3.1 indicates, over $175 billion was spent on social security benefits in fiscal 1983.

Individuals are eligible for social security retirement benefits after reaching a certain age (62 or 65) and having worked a minimum number of years. The benefits themselves are paid for by taxes imposed on those who are still working. Thus social security retirement benefits transfer income from those who are currently working to those who are retired. By altering the distribution of income in this way, ***income transfers help determine*** FOR WHOM ***our output is produced.*** In this case, the income transfers help to ensure that retired individuals will continue to receive some of our current output.

Welfare benefits and unemployment insurance benefits also alter the distribution of income (and output). In the case of welfare benefits, income is transferred to those who are poor in order to enable them to purchase a greater quantity of goods and services.[1] Unemployment benefits serve the same income-transfer purpose but are distributed to those who are unable to find work, regardless of their other income or wealth. In all of these cases, the income transfers are not paid in return for any current product or service. Rather, they represent an explicit attempt to alter the distribution of income, and hence of access to goods and services.

State-local aid

The third expenditure category depicted in Table 3.1 is "General aid to state and local governments," an expenditure that totaled $6.7 billion in 1983. But this figure is a gross understatement of actual aid

[1] The welfare system is examined in detail in Chapter 31.

TABLE 3.2 EMPLOYMENT RESULTING FROM GOVERNMENT PURCHASES, 1980
(in millions of persons)

The public sector directly employs nearly one out of every six workers. The jobs of another 8 million people are directly dependent on government purchases. State and local governments account for most of this employment.

Government	Direct employees	Indirect employees (in private sector)	Total
Federal	4.2	3.5	7.7
State and local	12.1	4.5	16.6
Total	16.3	8.0	24.3

Source: *Employment and Training Report of the President,* 1981.

categorical grants: Federal grants to state and local governments for specific expenditure purposes.

because one-fifth of federal expenditures for goods and services are made through state and local governments. For example, Table 3.1 indicates that the federal government spent nearly $10 billion on natural resources and environment. But one-fifth of this amount was simply given to local communities for the construction of sewage treatment plants. The local governments actually purchased or built the sewage plants; the federal government only provided the necessary revenue. Accordingly, control over WHAT to produce was maintained by the federal government, but local governments exercised some judgment on HOW to produce it.

This "strings-attached" nature of most federal aid is the distinguishing feature of **categorical grants.** Funds bestowed on state and local governments in the form of categorical grants have to be used for specific purposes. If a city government needs street lighting but federal grants are available only for sewage treatment or job training, the city must choose between one of the latter or do without federal aid. Categorical grants cannot be shifted from one use to another.

In fiscal 1983 the federal government gave over $80 billion to state and local governments in the form of categorical grants (including those for welfare benefits, Medicaid, schools, and highways). These intergovernmental transfers appear in the federal budget (Table 3.1) as expenditures on the specific items Congress instructed state and local governments to buy.

The $6.7 billion that does appear in the FY 1983 federal budget as "general aid to state and local governments" represents a different kind of federal assistance. Since 1972, some federal aid to state and

How U.S. aid pie gets divvied up

A new report on federal aid to state and local governments discloses some prime targets for President Reagan's program to reduce government spending.

The study shows the distribution, state by state, of some 90.1 billion in Washington's tax dollars for job-training plans, urban and community-development grants, highway construction, child-nutrition programs, medicaid and other purposes in 1980.

For an idea of just how heavily state and local governments rely on federal aid—

	Per Capita Aid
Alaska	$1,114
Vermont	690
South Dakota	634
Wyoming	620
Montana	609
New York	539
North Dakota	524
New Mexico	507
Rhode Island	500
Massachusetts	498
West Virginia	481
Hawaii	474
Oregon	464
Maine	461
Mississippi	459
Delaware	459
Maryland	433
Georgia	430
Wisconsin	427
Michigan	420
Nevada	413
Idaho	410
Arkansas	408
Minnesota	406
Alabama	402
Washington	400
U.S. AVERAGE	**398**
Kentucky	398
Illinois	388
Utah	386
New Jersey	379
Pennsylvania	375
New Hampshire	375
Connecticut	369
California	367
Louisiana	367
Tennessee	366
Oklahoma	347
Nebraska	346
Kansas	343
Missouri	342
South Carolina	339
Colorado	339
Iowa	337
Virginia	329
North Carolina	325
Ohio	316
Arizona	302
Indiana	290
Florida	289
Texas	274

revenue sharing: Federal aid to state and local governments without stringent restrictions on its use.

local governments has been given with few or no strings attached.[2] Such **revenue sharing** is typically given for a very broadly stated purpose ("block grants" or "special revenue sharing") or for no stated expenditure purpose at all ("general revenue sharing"). In either case, state and local governments not only get to dip into the federal treasury but acquire some independent influence on the mix of output, that is, the issue of WHAT to produce. The recipients of general revenue sharing include all 50 states and more than 38,000 cities, counties, towns, townships, Indian tribes, and Alaskan native villages.

In 1982 President Reagan proposed a further departure from categorical grants. His "New Federalism" would turn over revenue *sources* to the states, not just a share of collected revenues. In the process, the states would acquire more direct control over the level and contents of their budgets.

Interest

interest: payments made for the use of borrowed money.

The last major expenditure category in the federal budget consists of **interest** payments. Federal expenditures usually exceed federal revenues. As a consequence, the U.S. government must borrow money to finance its purchases. Like all borrowers, the U.S. government pays interest on its debts. At the beginning of 1983 the total debt of the U.S. government was over $1 trillion, requiring interest payments of over $96 billion in fiscal 1983.[3]

STATE AND LOCAL EXPENDITURE

Although the federal government exercises substantial influence over the basic issues of WHAT to produce, HOW to produce it, and FOR WHOM, state and local governments also have a role to play. There are 80,171 government units in the United States, most of them at the state and local levels. To some extent, the power of state and local governments to alter the mix of output or distribution of income is easily overlooked. The fragmented nature of such decision making makes the size of individual state and local expenditures relatively small. City, school-district, and township budgets are calibrated in millions of dollars, not billions; even state budgets rarely exceed the billion-dollar level by any significant amount. By contrast, the federal budget is measured in hundreds of billions of dollars. From this perspective, public power at the national level appears to dwarf power at state and local levels.

The forest, in this case, is definitely obscured by the trees. When the fiscal activities of the 50 states, 3,000 counties, 18,000 cities, 17,000 townships, 21,000 school districts, and 21,000 special dis-

---

[2] Once before, in 1837, the federal budget surplus was so large that $28 million was distributed to the states, with no restrictions attached. But this no-strings-attached bonanza came to a halt when the depression of 1838 wiped out the federal surplus. The State and Local Fiscal Assistance Act of 1972 made "revenue sharing" a more permanent feature of the government budget.
[3] The public debt and its impact on the economy are discussed further in Chapter 9.

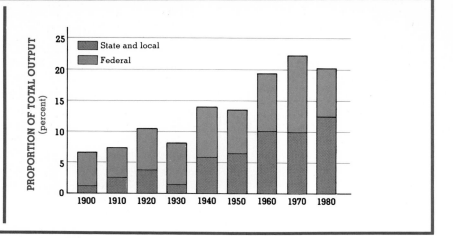

FIGURE 3.2 DIRECT PUBLIC PURCHASES OF GOODS AND SERVICES

The government share of total expenditures in the economy has been relatively constant since World War II (at 20 percent). Within the public sector, state and local governments have acquired increasing control over the decisions of WHAT, HOW, and FOR WHOM to produce. By contrast, the federal share of total expenditures on goods and services has actually declined.

Source: U.S. Census Bureau; Office of Management and Budget.

tricts are combined, a very different perspective on state and local power is achieved. ***In terms of direct purchases of goods and services, state and local outlays exceed federal outlays.*** State and local governments also employ far more people than does the federal government (Table 3.2). This phenomenon should not come as a great surprise—after all, you see a traffic cop or state college professor more often than you see a census taker or Washington bureaucrat.

The aggregate size of state and local budgets and employment rolls is sufficient introduction to the potential of these government units to influence WHAT is produced, HOW it is produced, and FOR WHOM. As Figure 3.2 illustrates, this state and local influence is growing, whereas the share of the federal government in total output has fallen since 1960. If the "New Federalism" results in more state and local autonomy, these trends will accelerate.

How the money is spent

opportunity cost: The most desired goods or services that are forgone in order to obtain something else.

In the light of so much state and local spending—so much influence on output, employment, prices, and the distribution of income—it seems reasonable to ask what we are getting from all this expenditure. **Opportunity costs** are involved here. The resources now commanded by state and local governments could be put at the disposal of the federal government or even at the disposal of the private sector (us taxpayers). Our collective answers to the questions of WHAT, HOW, and FOR WHOM would surely be changed in either case. What kinds of goods and services are purchased or provided by state and local governments?

Table 3.3. provides an overview of the content of state and local expenditure. Education accounts for 40 percent of state and local budgets. State governments tend to split their school expenditures between higher education (state colleges and universities) and state aid to local school systems. For their part, local governments focus nearly all education expenditures on elementary and secondary school systems. States devote other large portions of their resources to highways and welfare programs. At the local level, noneducation expenditures tend to be concentrated on police protection, health services, fire protection, and streets.

TABLE 3.3 STATE AND LOCAL EXPENDITURES, FISCAL 1980

Most direct state expenditures (excluding transfers to local governments) are for education, welfare programs, and highways. Local governments also spend more on education than anything else.

Expenditures	State governments (in millions)	Percent	Local governments (in millions)	Percent
Education	$35,251	25.3	$97,960	44.6
Highways	20,661	14.1	12,650	5.6
Public welfare	33,242	23.0	12,310	5.5
Health and hospitals	15,666	10.9	16,507	7.0
Natural resources	4,124	2.8	1,385	0.6
Housing and urban renewal	331	0.2	5,731	2.5
Airports	360	0.2	2,141	0.9
Social insurance	2,001	1.3	7	—
Interest	6,763	4.7	7,984	3.5
Police, courts, prisons	6,272	4.3	13,668	6.0
Fire protection	—	—	5,718	2.5
Sanitation and sewage	—	—	12,880	5.8
Other	19,047	13.2	34,680	15.5
Total	$143,718	100.0	$223,621	100.0

Source: U.S. Department of Commerce.

TAXATION

Whatever we may think of any specific government expenditure, we must recognize one basic fact of life: we pay for government spending. In real terms, the cost of government spending can be measured by the private goods and services that are forsaken when the public sector takes command over factors of production. Factors of production used to produce national defense or schools cannot be used at the same time to produce private goods or services.

The opportunity costs of public spending are not always apparent, as we don't directly hand over our factors of production to the government. Instead, we give the government part of our income in the form of taxes. Those dollars are then used to buy factors of production or goods and services in the marketplace. Thus *the primary function of taxes is to transfer command over resources (purchasing power) from the private sector to the public sector.* When we pay taxes, we give the public sector increased control over WHAT to produce, HOW, and FOR WHOM.

Federal taxes

As recently as 1902, much of the revenue collected by the federal government came from taxes imposed on alcoholic beverages. The federal government did not have authority to collect income taxes. As a consequence, *total* federal revenue in 1902 was only $653 million.

INCOME TAXES All of that has changed. The Sixteenth Amendment to the U.S. Constitution, enacted in 1913, granted the federal government authority to collect income taxes. The government now collects over $300 *billion* in that form alone. In fact, although the federal government still collects taxes on alcoholic beverages, the

TABLE 3.4 FEDERAL REVENUES, FISCAL 1983 (in billions of dollars)	Source	Amount
	Individual income taxes	$304.5
Taxes transfer purchasing power from the private sector to the public sector. The largest federal tax is the individual income tax. The second largest source of federal revenue is the social security tax.	Social security taxes	222.5
	Corporate income taxes	65.3
	Excise taxes	41.7
	Other	32.1
	Total	$666.1

Source: Office of Management and Budget estimates.

progressive tax: A tax system in which tax rates rise as incomes rise.

individual income tax has become the largest single source of government revenue (see Table 3.4).

In theory, the federal income tax is designed to be **progressive,** that is, to take a larger *fraction* of high incomes than of low incomes. In 1982, for example, tax rates imposed on single taxpayers ranged from as little as 14 percent of incomes of under $3,000 to 50 percent on incomes in excess of $100,000. Thus an individual with a very high income not only was supposed to pay more dollars in taxes, but was also expected to pay a larger *fraction* of his or her income in taxes.[4]

The progressive nature of the federal income tax is designed to distribute the tax burden on the basis of *ability to pay*. It has had another and largely unintended effect, however. During periods of inflation, all incomes tend to rise. As they do, people are pushed into higher tax brackets and end up paying higher tax rates. In the proc-

[4] In reality, however, the federal income tax is not nearly so progressive as it appears, because the tax laws include myriad provisions that permit individuals to "shelter" income that otherwise would be taxed at very high rates. The federal income tax system is discussed further in Chapter 29.

"I can't find anything wrong here, Mr. Truffle . . . you just seem to have too much left after taxes."

GRIN AND BEAR IT by George Lichty. © Field Enterprises, Inc., 1978. Courtesy of Field Newspaper Syndicate.

bracket creep: The movement of taxpayers into higher tax brackets (rates) as nominal incomes grow.

ess, the federal government gets an increasing share of total income. This phenomenon, often referred to as **bracket creep,** was partly overcome by the Economic Recovery Act of 1981. That act indexed tax *rates* to inflation, beginning in 1985. Thereafter, federal income tax rates will be adjusted downward when inflation pushes incomes up. This will prevent the federal government from automatically increasing its share of total output when prices and incomes rise.

SOCIAL SECURITY TAXES The second major source of federal revenue is the social security tax. As we noted earlier, people now working transfer part of their earnings to retired workers by making "contributions" to social security. There is nothing voluntary about these "contributions," however, because they take the form of mandatory payroll deductions.[5] In FY 1983 each worker paid 6.7 percent of his or her wages to social security and employers contributed an equal amount.[6] As a consequence, the government collected over $220 billion.

CORPORATE TAXES The federal government taxes the profits of corporations as well as the incomes of consumers. But there are far fewer corporations than consumers and their profits are small in comparison to total consumer income. In fiscal 1983, the federal government collected less than $70 billion in corporation income taxes, despite the fact that it imposed a tax rate of 46 percent on corporate profits.

EXCISE TAXES The last major source of federal revenue is excise taxes. Like the early taxes on whiskey, excise taxes are sales taxes imposed on specific goods and services. The federal government taxes not only alcoholic beverages ($10.50 per gallon) but also gasoline ($0.04 per gallon), cigarettes ($4.00 per thousand), telephone service (1 percent), and a variety of other goods and services. Such taxes not only discourage production and consumption of these goods—by raising their price, and thereby reducing the quantity demanded—but also raise a substantial amount of revenue.

State and local revenues

State and local governments also levy taxes on consumers and businesses. In general, cities and other local units of government depend heavily on property taxes—taxes levied on the value of homes and other real property. State governments, on the other hand, rely heavily on sales taxes (see Figure 3.3). Although nearly all states and many cities also impose income taxes, effective tax rates are so low (averaging less than 2 percent of personal income) that income tax revenues are much less than sales and property tax revenues.

One feature of state and local tax structures is important to note. State and local taxes tend to be **regressive;** that is, they take a larger share of income from the poor than from the rich. Consider a 4-percent sales tax, for example. It might appear that a uniform tax rate

regressive tax: A tax system in which tax rates fall as incomes rise.

[5] Not all workers participate in social security; government employees, for example, may instead choose a separate public retirement system.
[6] This tax rate is imposed on the first $32,400 of income; both the tax rate and the income ceiling increase each year.

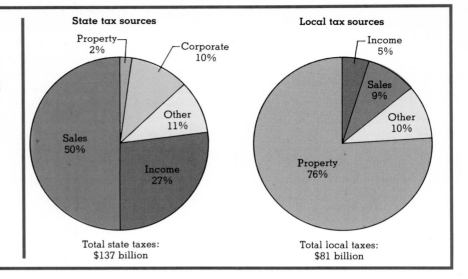

FIGURE 3.3 STATE AND LOCAL TAX SOURCES

State governments get half of their tax revenue from sales taxes. By contrast, local governments depend heavily on property taxes.

Source: U.S. Department of Commerce.

State tax sources

Property 2%
Corporate 10%
Other 11%
Sales 50%
Income 27%

Total state taxes: $137 billion

Local tax sources

Income 5%
Sales 9%
Other 10%
Property 76%

Total local taxes: $81 billion

like this would affect all consumers equally. But this is not the way it works. People with lower incomes tend to spend most of their income on goods and services. Thus most of their income is subject to sales taxes. By contrast, a person with a high income can afford to save part of his or her income and thereby shelter it from sales taxes. A family that earns $20,000 and spends $15,000 of it on taxable goods and services, for example, pays $600 in sales taxes when the tax rate is 4 percent. In effect, then, they are handing over 3 percent of their *income* ($600 ÷ $20,000) to the state. By contrast, the family that makes only $6,000 and spends $5,800 of it for food, clothing, and shelter pays $232 in sales taxes in the same state. Their total tax is smaller, but it represents a much larger *share* (3.9 versus 3.0 percent) of their income.

Local property taxes exhibit the same feature. They are regressive, because poorer people devote a larger portion of their incomes to housing costs. Property taxes directly affect housing costs. Hence a larger share of a poor family's income is subject to property taxes. According to the Advisory Council on Intergovernmental Relations, a family earning $50,000 a year devotes only 2.5 percent of its income to property taxes, whereas a family earning $5,000 pays out 4.6 percent of its income in property taxes.[7]

FEDERAL AID   State and local governments also get substantial revenue from nontax sources. The federal role in distributing money to state and local governments has already been noted. In 1983 federal grants and revenue sharing provided over one-fifth of all state and local revenues. But federal aid is slowing. In fact, federal grants to state and local governments have begun to decline, reversing an upward trend of many decades. The New Federalism, to be discussed in a moment, would reduce federal grants still further.

[7] State lotteries are also regressive, since lower-income people spend a higher fraction of their income on lottery tickets. Fifteen states use lotteries to raise revenues.

user charge: Fee paid for the use of a public-sector good or service.

USER CHARGES   The third major source of state and local revenues consists of **user charges.** The tuition that college students (or their parents) pay for attending a state university or community college is a familiar user charge, and generates billions of dollars in state and local revenues. But tuition fees never cover the full costs of maintaining public colleges. Part of the costs of providing higher education are borne by all state taxpayers, whether or not they attend college. Public hospitals and highways are financed in the same way, with users paying part of the costs directly and all taxpayers paying the remaining costs through state and local taxes. Hence user charges are not identical to market prices, because they are not intended to cover the full costs of supplying a particular good.

FUNCTIONS OF THE PUBLIC SECTOR

In view of the large share of our income we give to federal, state, and local governments, we have the right to ask what purposes are served by such a large public sector. The high opportunity cost attached to all this public activity should be evident to taxpayers, in the form of the income (and implied access to goods and services) given up to finance public expenditures. Do we need such a large public sector? Can't the private sector produce the same goods and services, maybe even at less cost? What economic functions does the public sector fulfill?

Public goods

market mechanism: The use of market prices and sales to signal desired outputs (or resource allocations).

In Chapter 2 we emphasized the unique capability of the **market mechanism** to signal consumer demands for various goods and services. By offering to pay higher prices for some goods, we express our collective answer to the question of WHAT to produce. However, the market mechanism works efficiently only if the benefits of consuming a particular good or service are available only to the individuals who purchase that product.

Consider doughnuts, for example. When you eat a doughnut, you get the satisfaction from its taste and your fuller stomach, that is, you derive a private benefit. No one else reaps any significant benefit from your consumption of a doughnut: the doughnut you purchase in the market is yours alone to consume. Accordingly, your decision to purchase the doughnut will be determined by your anticipated satisfaction as well as your income and opportunity costs.

Most of the goods and services produced in the public sector are different from doughnuts—and not just because doughnuts look, taste, and smell different from nuclear submarines. When you buy a doughnut, you effectively exclude others from consumption of that product. If Dunkin' Donuts sells a particular pastry to you, it cannot supply the same pastry to someone else. If you devour it, no one else can. In this sense, the transaction and product are completely private.

The same exclusiveness is not characteristic of national defense. If you buy a nuclear submarine to patrol the Pacific Ocean, there is no way you can exclude your neighbors from the protection your

public good: A good or service whose consumption by one person does not exclude consumption by others.

submarine provides. Either the submarine deters would-be attackers or it doesn't. In the former case, both you and your neighbors survive happily ever after; in the latter case, we are all blown away together. In that sense, you and your neighbors either consume or don't consume the benefits of nuclear submarine defenses *jointly*. There is no such thing as exclusive consumption here. The consumption of nuclear defenses is a communal feat, no matter who pays for them. Accordingly, national defense is regarded as a **public good** or product, in the sense that consumption by one person does not preclude consumption of the same good by another person. By contrast, a doughnut is a private good, because once I eat it, nobody else can have it.

THE FREE-RIDER DILEMMA   The "communal" nature of public goods leads to a real dilemma. If you and I will *both* benefit from nuclear defenses, which one of us should buy the nuclear submarine? I would prefer, of course, that *you* buy it, thereby providing me with protection at no direct cost. Hence I may profess no desire for nuclear submarines, secretly hoping to take a **"free ride"** on your market purchase. Unfortunately, you, too, have an incentive to conceal your desire for national defenses, and neither one of us may step forward to demand nuclear submarines in the marketplace. As a consequence, we will both be defenseless.

free rider: An individual who reaps direct benefits from someone else's purchase (consumption) of a public good.

Police and fire protection also exhibit this free-rider phenomenon. If your neighbors pay for improved police and fire services, you will benefit from their purchases even if you don't contribute a penny. Would-be burglars are apt to be deterred from both your house and your neighbors' houses by the presence of more police on the street. By the same token, your house is in less danger of fire if your neighbor's house is protected. In both these cases, your neighbors are unable to confine all the benefits of their expenditure to themselves. Consumption of these goods is nonexclusive—that is, public. Even streets and highways have the characteristics of public goods. Although we could theoretically restrict the use of streets and highways to those who paid for them, a toll gate on every corner would be exceedingly expensive and impractical. Here again joint or public consumption appears to be the only feasible alternative.

To the list of public goods we could add the administration of justice, the regulation of commerce, and the conduct of foreign relations. These services—which cost tens of *billions* of dollars and employ thousands of workers—provide benefits to everyone, no matter who pays for them.

The free riders associated with public goods upset the customary practice of paying for what you get. If I can get all the highways, defenses, and laws I desire without paying for them, I am not about to complain. I am perfectly happy to let you pay for the services while all of us consume them. Of course, you may feel the same way. Why should you pay for these services if you can consume just as much of them when your neighbors foot the whole bill? It might be regarded as selfish or unseemly not to pay your share of the cost of providing public goods, but you would be better off in a material sense if you spent your income on doughnuts, letting others pick up the tab for public services.

Because the familiar link between paying and consuming is broken, public goods cannot be peddled in the supermarket. People are reluctant to buy what they can get free, a perfectly rational response for a consumer who has limited income to spend. Hence, if public goods were marketed like private goods, everyone would wait for someone else to pay. The end result might be a total lack of public services. Accordingly, we cannot rely on the market mechanism to allocate resources to the production of such goods, no matter how much they might be desired.

The failure of the market mechanism to signal the desire for public goods necessitates some form of nonmarket payment mechanism. Passing the hat would be one way, but a highly unstable means of support, as most churches and charities will attest. Compulsory taxation elicits a more dependable response and is the more traditional means of payment. Recognizing that everyone benefits from public services, we require everyone to help pay the bill.

WHAT to produce

The nonmarketability of public goods not only requires the presence of governments but complicates production decisions as well. Our basic economic problem is to allocate resources to their most desired uses. But now there is no obvious way to decide WHAT to produce. Consumers do not have the opportunity to buy public goods directly. As a result, they cannot reveal their preferences in the same way that they do for private goods, through the mechanism of market demand.

In addition to deciding *whether* to produce specific public goods, we must also decide how much of any public good to produce. Dunkin' Donuts and other private producers choose the level of output that maximizes profits. A clear and concise set of decision-making rules is available for them. But what about government? If public goods can't be peddled in the supermarket, then they don't have any market price. Hence output levels cannot be determined by market sales. Instead, decisions on what to produce in the public sector must be guided by objectives and rules other than those that apply to private producers. What are the relevant guidelines and how are they expressed?

BALLOT-BOX ECONOMICS The traditional method for communicating consumption desires for public goods is through the ballot box. If you are concerned about the size of the military establishment or upset about the conduct of foreign relations, you have the option of expressing your feelings by electing different public officials. You could also demonstrate in the streets, withhold taxes, or mobilize others to some form of protest or affirmative action, but these forms of expression can land you in jail. As a consequence, public investment and production decisions are likely to be influenced by voting patterns. Some people have even suggested that the variety and volume of public goods are determined by the most votes, just as the variety and volume of private goods are determined by the most dollars. Thus governments choose that level and mix of output (and related taxation) that seem to command the most votes.[8]

Sometimes the link between the ballot box and output decisions is very clear and direct. State and local governments, for example, are often compelled to get voter approval before building another highway, school, housing project, or sewage plant. *Bond referendums* are direct requests by a government unit for the authority and purchasing power to expand the production of particular public goods. In 1980, for example, governments sought voter approval for $2.9 billion of new borrowing to finance public expenditure. Eighty percent of those requests were approved.

Although the direct link between bond referenda and spending decisions is important, it is more the exception than the rule. Bond referenda account for less than 1 percent of state and local expenditures. As a consequence, voter control of public spending is much less direct. Although federal agencies must get authorization from Congress for all expenditures, consumers get a chance to elect new congressmen only every two years. Much the same is true at state and local levels. Hence voters are in the position of dictating the general level and pattern of public expenditures but have little direct influence on everyday output decisions. In this sense, the ballot box is a poor substitute for the market mechanism.

Even if the link between the ballot box and allocation decisions were stronger, the resulting mix of output might not be optimal. A "democratic" vote, for example, might yield a 51 percent majority for approval of new local highways. Should the highways then be built? The answer is not obvious. After all, a large minority (49 percent) of the voters have stated that they don't want resources used in this way. If we proceed to build the highways, we will make those

---

[8] In the absence of unanimity, this means that some people will end up paying for public goods and services they do not want. The majority will thus benefit at the expense of the minority, a familiar consequence of democratic rule. Is there any other way to share the costs of public goods and services?

BALLOT-BOX ECONOMICS: A SAMPLING OF 1980 BOND REFERENDA

□ **Arizona: Phoenix-area residents approved $30 million to build new flood-resistant highway bridges.**

□ **California: Voters approved $285 million for the expansion of state and local parks.**

□ **Maine: Voters said no to funds for improved court facilities but agreed to spend $7 million for energy conservation and school buildings.**

□ **New Jersey: Voters approved $350 million to improve the state's water supply.**

□ **New York: Voters approved $500 million for new prisons.**

□ **Rhode Island: Voters approved $88 million for sewage treatment facilities.**

□ **Texas: Voters rejected a plan to set aside surplus tax revenues for water projects.**

□ **West Virginia: Voters rejected a request for $750 million to improve state highways.**

people worse off. Even the voters who voted *for* the highways may end up worse off, depending on how the benefits and costs of the highway are distributed and what other opportunities exist. The basic dilemma is really twofold. We do not know what the real demand for public goods is, and votes alone do not reflect the intensity of individual demands. Moreover, real-world decision making involves so many choices that a stable consensus is impossible.

BENEFIT-COST ECONOMICS   It is sometimes suggested that benefit-cost analysis provides a way out of this public-choice dilemma. The principles of benefit-cost analysis are straightforward. A public project is desirable only to the extent that it promises to yield some benefits (or utility). But all public projects involve some costs. Hence a project should be pursued only if it can deliver a satisfactory *ratio* of benefits to costs. Otherwise we would not be making very good use of our limited resources. In general, we would want to pursue those projects with the highest benefit-cost ratio. They will maximize the amount of utility we get from the resources we devote to the public sector.

Although the principles of benefit-cost analysis are simple enough, they are deceptive. How are we to measure the potential benefits of improved police services, for example? Do we simply estimate the number of robberies and murders prevented, calculate the worth of each, and add up the benefits? And how are we supposed to calculate the worth of a saved life? By a person's earnings? value of assets? number of friends? And what about the increased sense of security people have when they know the police are patrolling in their neighborhood? Should this be included in the benefit calculation? Some people will attach great value to this service; others will attach little. Whose values should we use?

When we are dealing with (private) market goods and services, we can gauge the benefits of production by the amount of money consumers are willing to pay for some particular output. In the case of public goods, however, we must make crude and highly subjective guesstimates of the benefits yielded by a particular output. Accordingly, benefit-cost analyses are valuable only to the extent that they are based on broadly accepted perceptions of benefits (or costs). In those cases, however, voting systems work well, too. In practice, consensus on the value of benefits is hard to reach, and benefit-cost calculations are subject to great controversy.[9]

Externalities   Although the free-rider phenomenon explains most public-sector activity, it does not explain all government expenditure. The government also regulates much private-sector production and consumption, particularly as they relate to the environment. The Environmental Protection Agency, for example, sets "clean air" and "clean water" standards that force private consumers and producers to limit their pollution. How is such governmental regulation to be explained?

[9] The *Study Guide* accompanying this text contains a detailed application of benefit-cost economics.

externalities: Costs (or benefits) of a market activity borne by a third party; the difference between the social and private costs (benefits) of a market activity.

The explanation for many governmental restrictions on HOW to produce lies in the phenomenon of **externalities.** Externalities are the costs or benefits of a market activity borne by a third party, that is, someone other than the immediate producer or consumer. When you go for a drive in your car, for example, you pollute the air with your car's emissions. All of the people who breathe that air are harmed by your consumption. In this respect, they suffer indirect, or "spillover," costs from your market activity.

Externalities represent a "market failure" in the sense that they are not reflected in market prices. When you drive your car, you pay only for gasoline and car maintenance; you do not pay for the health damage inflicted on others by the noise and pollutants your car emits. In this sense, the market mechanism fails to signal the true costs of driving. Specifically, the market price of driving understates its social cost, and you end up driving too much (the lower the price, the greater the quantity demanded). Moreover, the third parties who suffer from your pollution have no means of collecting medical costs from you.

To redress this inequity, the government must intervene in the marketplace and limit either your driving or the kind of car you drive. As a result, the government has established a regulatory bureaucracy (Environmental Protection Agency) to set and enforce pollution standards.[10] This kind of government regulation also occurs in medicine (Food and Drug Administration), job safety (Occupational Safety and Health Administration), air travel safety (Federal Aviation Administration), and auto liability insurance (state insurance commissions).

Externalities may also be beneficial. Education, for example, enriches not only the individual who goes to school but also the student's community. Basic literacy assures a better-informed electorate and a more viable democracy. Higher education often stimulates scientific and humanitarian discoveries that improve the well-being of millions of people. Educators also like to think that educated people make better neighbors! In these respects, the *social* benefits of education generally exceed the *private* benefits reaped by those who attend school: education generates beneficial externalities.

Goods and services that exhibit substantial external benefits fit our definition of *public goods.* A public good is one whose benefits cannot be captured by the purchaser(s) alone; all benefit if one benefits. Hence public goods, by definition, yield externalities.

FOR WHOM to produce

Although the free-rider phenomenon and externalities explain most public-sector production and regulatory activity, they do not explain all government expenditure. Government budgets are used to alter the market's answers to the questions not only of WHAT to produce and HOW, but also FOR WHOM. The power to alter the distribution of goods and services lies in the income-redistribution activities of governments. As we observed in Tables 3.1 and 3.3, government

[10] The mechanisms used to control pollution are discussed at length in Chapter 30.

budgets include substantial *income transfers*. On what grounds can these transfers be justified?

In our discussion of the market mechanism (Chapter 2), we observed that the market distributes goods and services according to people's *ability and willingness to pay*. But our ability to pay depends on the amount of income we have to spend. As a consequence, the market mechanism tends to answer the basic question of FOR WHOM to produce by distributing a larger share of total output to those with the most income. Although this result may be efficient, it is not necessarily equitable. Individuals who are aged or disabled, for example, may be unable to earn much income, yet still are regarded as "worthy" recipients of goods and services. In such cases, we use income transfers as a mechanism for altering the distribution of income and thus changing the market's answer to the basic question of FOR WHOM goods are produced.

To some extent, public income-redistribution efforts can also be explained by the theory of public goods. If the public sector did not provide help to the aged, the disabled, the unemployed, and the needy, what would they do? Some might find a little extra work, but many would starve, even die. Others would resort to private solicitations or criminal activities to fend off hunger or death. This would mean more beggars and muggers on the streets. In nearly all cases, the general public would be beset with much of the burden and consequences of poverty and disability, either directly or through pangs of conscience. Because the sight or knowledge of hungry or sick neighbors is something most people seek to avoid, the elimination of poverty creates some satisfaction for a great many people.

But even if the elimination of poverty were a common objective, it could be accomplished by individual action. If I contributed heavily to the needy, then you and I would both be relieved of the burden of the poor. We could both walk the streets with less fear and better consciences. Hence you could benefit from my expenditure, just as was possible in the case of national defense. In this sense, the relief of misery is a *public* good. Were I the only taxpayer to benefit substantially from the reduction of poverty, then charity would be a private affair. As long as income support substantially benefits the public at large, then income redistribution is a *public good*, for which public funding is appropriate. There is therefore an *economic* rationale for public income-redistribution activities. To this rationale one can add such moral arguments as seem appropriate.[11]

Stabilization

Another major function of public-sector expenditure is to stabilize the economy. The federal government, in particular, attempts to stabilize the total volume of spending in the economy at a level that is consistent with our production possibilities. That is to say, the federal government uses its vast tax and expenditure powers to help

[11] Current income-redistribution efforts do not benefit the poor alone. The middle class receives a large share of income transfers, particularly from social security. Further discussion of income-redistribution policies is contained in Chapters 29 and 31.

keep the economy producing at some point on its production-possi-bilities curve. The mechanisms used for this purpose and their im-pact on the U.S. economy are the subject of Section II of this book (Chapters 7—13).

POLICY IMPLICATIONS: TAXPAYER REVOLT

If we think only of the goals of public goods, externalities, and in-come redistribution, or of the need for economic stabilization, nearly all public-sector activity appears to be justified. Yet in recent years taxpayers have expressed increasing reluctance to support public-sector activity. The hallmark of the "taxpayer revolt" was Califor-nia's Proposition 13, which was overwhelmingly accepted by Cali-fornia voters in June 1978. Proposition 13 forced local governments in California to reduce property taxes by an average of nearly 60 percent. In 1980, voters in Massachusetts approved Proposition 2½, which put an upper limit of 2.5 percent on local property tax rates. Missouri and Montana also passed limits on tax rates. At the national level, Congress approved the Economic Recovery Act of 1981, which reduced federal tax rates by 25 percent and indexed future tax rates to inflation.

At first blush, the tax revolt appears to be just another expres-sion of people's understandable reluctance to part with their in-come. The origins and impact of that revolt may go much deeper, however. The taxes people pay are used by governments to purchase scarce resources. As a consequence, fewer resources are available for the production of private goods and services. The more policemen or schoolteachers employed by the public sector, the fewer workers available to private producers and consumers. Similarly the more typewriters, pencils, and paper consumed by government agencies, the fewer accessible to individuals and private companies. In other words, ***everything the public sector does involves an opportunity cost.***

When assessing government's role in the economy, then, we must consider not only what governments do, but also what we give up to allow them to do it. The theory of public goods tells us only

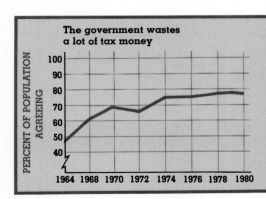

The government wastes a lot of tax money

PERCENT OF POPULATION AGREEING

100
90
80
70
60
50
40

1964 1968 1970 1972 1974 1976 1978 1980

RISING DOUBTS ABOUT GOVERNMENT WASTE

Question: **Do you think that people in government waste a lot of the money we pay in taxes, waste some of it, or don't waste very much of it?**

Source: PUBLIC OPINION © American Enterprise Institute for Public Policy Research, 1981. Reprinted with permission.

FIGURE 3.4 PRIVATE VS. PUBLIC GOODS

The public sector of the United States has grown as production possibilities have expanded. In 1973 we produced at point A, devoting one-fifth of our output to the public sector. In 1983 we produced at point D, with more public *and* private goods. The public sector continues to claim approximately one-fifth of total output.

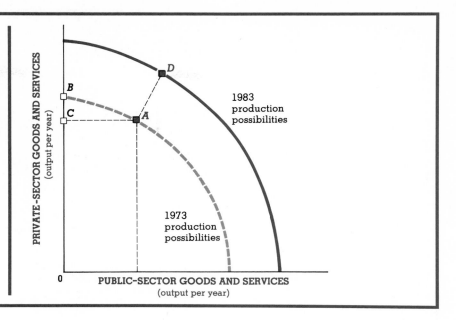

PRIVATE-SECTOR GOODS AND SERVICES (output per year)

PUBLIC-SECTOR GOODS AND SERVICES (output per year)

production possibilities: The alternative combinations of final goods and services that could be produced in a given time period with all available resources and technology.

what activities are appropriate for government, not the proper *level* of such activity. National defense is clearly a proper function of the public sector. Not so clear, however, is how much government should spend on tanks and aircraft carriers. The same is true of environmental protection or law enforcement.

The concept of opportunity costs puts a new perspective on the whole question of government size. Before we can decide how big is "too big," we must decide what we are willing to give up to support the public sector. A military force of 2 million men and women is "too big" from an economic perspective only if we value the forgone private production and consumption more highly than we value added strength of our defenses. The government has gone "too far" if the highway it builds is less desired than the park and homes it implicitly replaced. In these and all cases, the assessment of bigness must come back to a comparison of what is given up with what is received.

The consequences of an expanding public sector are illustrated by the **production-possibilities** curves in Figure 3.4. In any year, our resources and technology set *limits* to the quantity of public and private goods we can produce. In 1973 we chose a mix of output like point A, devoting 20 percent of our resources to public-sector output. The opportunity cost of those public-sector goods and services was the *private* goods and services we could have produced in that year but chose not to, as represented by the line BC.

Over time, the quantity of available resources and our technology have increased, expanding our production possibilities. The public sector, however, has expanded as well. Accordingly, we have moved from point A to point D, producing more public and private goods alike, but still devoting one-fifth of our resources to the public

WHO WASTES MORE?

Of every tax dollar that goes to the federal government in Washington, D.C., how many cents of each dollar do you think are wasted?

And how many cents of each tax dollar that goes to the government of this state do you think are wasted?

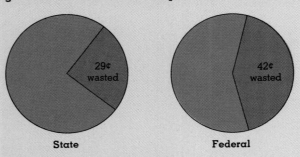

State   Federal

Source: Gallup poll, conducted September 18–21, 1981. Reprinted with permission from National Journal's *Opinion Outlook Briefing Paper*, February 12, 1982 (*N* = 1,546).

sector. Indeed, the relative size of the public sector has remained fairly constant for nearly 20 years. The taxpayer revolt suggests that people either expected the government's share of output to *decline* as total output grew or are disappointed with the quality of the additional public services provided. In either case, taxpayers are clearly stating that they do not believe the additional public-sector goods produced are as valuable as the additional private-sector goods and services given up. This is the essence of the charge that the government is "wasting" the taxpayer's income.

The New Federalism

To a large extent, President Reagan's proposals for a "New Federalism" was a response to these voter frustrations. The basic goal of the New Federalism is to shift more tax and spending decisions back to state and local governments. Both revenue sources and program responsibilities would be turned back (see box). These shifts would serve several purposes. As we noted earlier, "ballot-box economics" is a very imperfect mechanism for deciding WHAT to produce. By moving tax and spending decisions closer to the voter, the New Federalism could increase the effectiveness of ballot-box decision making. Most voters also believe that local governments are less wasteful of tax dollars than the federal government. If that's true, the New Federalism might reduce the costs of producing specific public goods. Last but not least, there is an underlying expectation that the New Federalism will reduce the public sector's share of total output. State and local governments are likely to cut back or eliminate services that were once financed with federal tax dollars but now depend on local financing.

Critics of the New Federalism have emphasized the same point. Some functions are distinctly *national*, they argue. If they are turned over to the states, there will be a strong temptation to "beggar thy

**A SHIFT OF
RESPONSIBILITIES:
THE NEW FEDERALISM**

In his 1982 State of the Economy message to Congress, President Reagan proposed a major shift in the respective roles of federal, state, and local governments. Arguing that "a wide range of federal activities can be more appropriately and efficiently carried out by the states," he proposed:

■ *A swap.* The federal government would assume all costs and responsibility for Medicaid. In exchange, the states would take full responsibility for food stamps and welfare (AFDC). In 1982 the federal government paid roughly 60 percent of AFDC and Medicaid costs and all food-stamp costs. All three programs were administered by state and local governments.

■ *A turnback.* The federal government would abandon 61 specific grant programs, allowing the states to pick them up. These would include education and training programs, child nutrition, social services, noninterstate highways, mass transit, community development, and vocational education.

■ *A trust fund.* For the first eight years of the turnback, states would receive federal revenues from a trust fund. The fund itself would be financed from federal excise taxes and windfall profits taxes on oil. The federal taxes and trust fund would be eliminated by 1991, leaving states free to impose their own taxes.

neighbor" by cutting back local spending. Welfare is a classic example. The extent of poverty is more a reflection of national economic forces than of state or local circumstances. In this sense, the number of people who apply for welfare aid is beyond state and local control. By denying aid, however, states can encourage poor people to go elsewhere in search of assistance. Thus the New Federalism may encourage states to shirk their share of national responsibilities. The basic problem here is the free-rider dilemma that afflicts all public goods. The solution requires a careful sorting out of state, local, and federal responsibilities.

SUMMARY

■ Federal, state, and local governments all participate extensively in the economy, thereby helping answer the basic questions of WHAT to produce, HOW to produce it, and FOR WHOM. Altogether, the public sector absorbs roughly one-fifth of total resources and output.

■ For the most part, government production activities focus on public goods. These are goods and services that benefit consumers generaly, no matter who pays for them. Unlike private goods, public goods (e.g., national defense) cannot be packaged and sold to individual consumers, because consumption by one person does not preclude consumption of the same good by another.

■ The public-goods nature of most government activities complicates the question of WHAT to produce. Production decisions cannot be made on the basis of dollar votes (market demand), as public goods encourage free riders to conceal their demand for public goods. Instead, public production decisions are usually made in the political arena, via general elections and specific tax and spending referenda. Benefit-cost analysis can also be used to guide public production decisions, but it requires difficult and often highly subjective estimates of related benefits and costs.

▪ The presence of harmful externalities also necessitates government intervention. Where the costs of a market activity are borne in part by third parties, the market mechanism fails to signal the true social cost of that activity. In such cases, the government intercedes to alter consumption and production patterns.

▪ Governments also redistribute incomes. Public income transfers are essentially a mechanism for altering the market's answers to the question of FOR WHOM to produce. By taking income from some people in the form of taxes and bestowing it on others, the government alters our access to goods and services.

▪ Guidelines for choosing the right mix and level of government activity can be constructed from the concept of opportunity costs. The transfer of resources from the private sector to the public sector is accomplished through the imposition of taxes. In assessing the level of those taxes, we must compare the benefits of public-sector production with those obtainable from the private production or consumption that must be given up to support it.

▪ The New Federalism entails a shift of both revenue sources and program responsibilities from the federal government to the states.

Terms to remember

Define the following terms:

fiscal year	bracket creep
intermediate goods	regressive tax
income transfers	user charges
categorical grants	market mechanism
revenue sharing	public good
interest	free rider
opportunity cost	externalities
progressive tax	production possibilities

Questions for discussion

1. Why should taxpayers subsidize public colleges and universities? What benefits do they receive from someone else's education?

2. If you abhor tennis, should you be forced to pay local taxes that are used to build and maintain public tennis courts? What if you don't like national defense; should you be able to withhold the part of your taxes that pays for it? What would happen if everyone followed this rationale?

3. Could local fire departments be privately operated, with services sold directly to customers? What problems would be involved in such a system?

4. In what ways do governments affect our collective answer to the basic question of HOW to produce? Can you give specific examples?

Problem Suppose that the following table describes the spending behavior of individuals at various income levels.

Income	Total spending	Sales tax	Sales tax paid as percent of income
$ 1,000	$ 1,000	_____	_____
2,000	1,800	_____	_____
3,000	2,400	_____	_____
5,000	3,500	_____	_____
10,000	6,000	_____	_____
100,000	40,000	_____	_____

Assuming that a sales tax of 10 percent is levied on all purchases, calculate:

(a) The amount of taxes paid at each income level
(b) The fraction of income paid in taxes at each income level
Is the sales tax progressive or regressive in relation to income?

CHAPTER 4

NATIONAL-INCOME ACCOUNTING

national-income accounting: The measurement of aggregate economic activity, particularly national income and its components.

T he economy is so vast that we may be pardoned if we occasionally lose sight of some of the action and forget a few details here and there. But *somebody* has to keep track of all the action in product and factor markets if we are ever going to know what's happening in the economy. How, for example, are we going to know whether we're producing enough goods and services—or, for that matter, the *right* goods and services—unless someone keeps track of our annual output? By the same token, how can we decide whether we can afford another fleet of missiles, more subway systems, or a modernized railroad system unless we know how much output we can produce and how it is now being used? And finally, how would we know when unemployment or inflation were serious problems unless someone were measuring changes in employment or prices?

It is convenient, of course, to ignore all such measurement problems, especially since they tend to be unexciting. But if we avoid measurement problems, we severely limit our ability to understand how the economy works or how well (or poorly) it is performing. We also limit our ability to design appropriate policies for improving economic performance.

The measurement of aggregate economic activity—**national-income accounting**—serves two basic functions. First, it enables us to identify economic problems and gauge their severity. The Great Depression provided an object lesson in how important such information can be and provided much of the impetus for the development of national-income accounts. In fact, it was during the depression that our national-income accounting system was first developed, largely through the efforts of Simon Kuznets (who later received a Nobel Prize for his work) and the Commerce Department.

The second function of national-income accounting is to provide an objective basis for evaluating policy. If national-income accounts allow us to measure the severity of a problem, they can also be used to determine how effective public policy has been in finding a solution. With national-income accounts, we can put to a statistical test any claims made for "sound and decisive action to combat inflation" or "unprecedented growth in consumer incomes," or other such assertions.

An additional benefit of national-income accounts is that they can be used as a framework to hold together all the separate pieces of our economic puzzle. They show quite clearly how factor markets relate to product markets, how output relates to income, and how consumer spending and business investment relate to production. They also show how the flow of taxes and government spending may alter economic outcomes. Thus national-income accounts help us not only to measure the economy but also to understand its functioning.

MEASURES OF OUTPUT

National-income accounting is focused primarily on the nation's output of goods and services. The array of goods and services we produce is truly massive, including everything from professional baseball to guided-missile systems. All of these things are part of our total output; the problem is to find a summary measure.

Itemizing the amount of each good or service produced each year will not solve our measurement problems. The resulting list would be so long that it would be both unwieldy and meaningless. We could not even add it up, since it would contain diverse goods measured in a variety of units (e.g., packages, pounds, quarts). Nor could we compare one year's output to another's. Suppose that last year we produced 3 billion oranges, 2 million bicycles, and 700 airplanes, whereas this year we produced 5 billion oranges, 4 million bicycles, and 600 airplanes. Which year's output was larger? Itemizing all our outputs would not only be tedious but leave a good many questions unanswered as well.

Gross national product

To facilitate our accounting chores, we need some mechanism for aggregating our annual output data into a more manageable summary. The mechanism we use is prices. ***Each good and service produced and brought to market has a price. That price serves as a measure of value for calculating total output.*** Consider again the problem of determining how much output was produced this year and last. There is no obvious way to answer these questions if all output is accounted for in physical terms alone. On the other hand, once we know the price of each good, we can readily calculate the *value* of output produced in a given time period and thus measure

TABLE 4.1 THE MEASUREMENT OF OUTPUT	*Output*	*Amount*

TABLE 4.1 THE MEASUREMENT OF OUTPUT

It is impossible to aggregate all output in *physical* terms. Accordingly, total output is measured in *monetary* terms, with each good or service valued at its market price. GNP refers to the total market value of all goods and services produced in a given time period.

Output	Amount
A. *Last year's output*	
In physical terms	
Oranges	3 billion
Bicycles	2 million
Airplanes	700
Total	?
In monetary terms	
3 billion oranges @ $0.06 each	$180 million
2 million bicycles @ $50 each	100 million
700 airplanes @ $1 million each	700 million
Total	$980 million
B. *This year's output*	
In physical terms	
Oranges	5 billion
Bicycles	4 million
Airplanes	600
Total	?
In monetary terms	
5 billion oranges @ $0.06 each	$ 300 million
4 million bicycles @ $50 each	200 million
600 airplanes @ $1 million each	600 million
Total	$1,100 million

gross national product (GNP): The total market value of all final goods and services produced in a given time period.

each year's economic performance. The total dollar value of final output produced each year is what we refer to as our **gross national product (GNP).** GNP is simply the sum of all final goods and services produced for the market in a given time period, with each good or service valued at its market price.

Table 4.1 illustrates the use of prices to value total output. If oranges are $0.06 each, then the *value* of orange production last year was $180 million ($0.06 × 3 billion). In the same manner, we can determine that the value of bicycle production was $100 million and the value of airplane production was $700 million. By adding up these figures, we can say that the value of last year's production— last year's GNP—was $980 million (top half of Table 4.1).

Now we are in a position to compare one year's output to another's. The bottom half of Table 4.1 shows that the use of prices enables us to say that the *value* of this year's output is $1,100 million. Hence *total output* has increased from one year to the next. Thus the use of prices to value market output allows us to summarize our output activity, and to compare the output of one period with that of another.

GNP accounting can also provide a basis for comparing one country's economic performance with another's. Suppose you wanted to know how the Soviet economy compared with our own in terms of total annual output. Here again, endless lists of specific outputs would be of little use, as the Russians' production of some goods (for example, caviar, furs, oil) would certainly be greater than ours, and vice versa. Moreover, differences in the annual outputs of various goods and services would still have to be "added up" somehow. Which leads us back to prices as a common basis for valuation. By adding up the annual *value* of Soviet and American outputs, we can determine which economy is larger.[1] As Table 4.2 indicates, the annual GNP of the United States is twice as large as the Soviet GNP. In fact, our economy is so big that it produces one-fourth of total world output.

GNP PER CAPITA   International comparisons of total output are even more vivid in *per capita* terms. **GNP per capita** relates the total value of annual output to the number of people who share that output; it refers to the average GNP per person. The United States contain only 5 percent of the world's population, yet we produce 25 percent of the world's output. Our production per capita (per person) thus greatly exceeds that of other countries. Table 4.2 indicates that per capita GNP in the United States is more than four times as large as the world average.

GNP per capita is commonly used as a measure of a country's standard of living, because it suggests the amount of annual output available to the average person. Per capita GNP is only a statistical phenomenon, however, and should not be interpreted as a measure of what every citizen is getting. In the United States, for example, millions of individuals have access to far more goods and services than our average per capita GNP. Similarly, millions of others get by with much less. Although per capita GNP is twice as high in Kuwait as in the United States (see Table 4.2), we cannot conclude that the typical citizen of Kuwait is better off than the typical American. All these figures tell us is that the average citizen of Kuwait *could* have more goods and services each year than the average American *if*

GNP per capita: Total GNP divided by total population; average GNP.

[1] International GNP comparisons are complicated by differences in economic structures, price systems, and international exchange rates. Consequently, all such comparisons are rough approximations. Some of the problems of GNP accounting are discussed in the following pages.

TABLE 4.2 GNP: SOME INTERNATIONAL COMPARISONS

The U.S. economy is the world's largest, as measured by the value of annual output. On a *per capita* basis, we also rank near the top. International comparisons are crude approximations because of differences between countries in the use of prices and markets.

Country	Total GNP (in billions of dollars)	GNP per capita (in dollars)
United States	$ 2,582	$10,610
Soviet Union	1,212	4,040
Japan	1,153	8,730
Germany	828	12,200
United Kingdom	443	7,390
China	283	260
Sweden	112	12,250
Saudi Arabia	100	9,960
Kuwait	30	20,250
Ethiopia	4	120
World total	$10,156	$ 2,430

Source: *World Bank Atlas,* 1981 (1979 and 1980 data).

GNP were distributed in the same way in both countries. ***Measures of per capita GNP tell us nothing about the way GNP is actually distributed or used; they are only a statistical average.*** When countries are quite similar in structure, institutions, and income distribution, however—or when historical comparisons are made within a country—per capita GNP is a rough and ready measure of relative standards of living.

NONMARKET ACTIVITIES   Although the methods for calculating GNP and per capita GNP are straightforward, they do create a few problems. For one thing, our GNP measures exclude most goods and services that are produced but not sold in the market. This may appear to be a trivial point, but it isn't. Vast quantities of output never reach the market. The most common example is the services of housewives—the homemaker who cleans, washes, gardens, shops, and cooks is contributing to the output of goods and services. But because she is not paid a market wage for these services, her efforts are excluded from the calculation of GNP. At the same time, however, we do count the efforts of those workers who sell services identical to the homemaker's in the marketplace. This seeming contradiction is explained by the fact that a homemaker's services are not sold in the market and therefore carry no explicit, market-determined value.

The exclusion of homemakers' services from the GNP accounts is particularly troublesome when we want to compare standards of living over time or between countries. In the United States, for example, women have demonstrated an increasing tendency to hire domestic help and leave the house to find outside employment. As a result, much housework that was previously excluded from GNP statistics (because it was unpaid family help) is now included (because it is done by paid help). In this respect, our historical GNP figures not only are incomplete but may exaggerate improvements in our standard of living.

Homemaking services are not the only output excluded. If a friend helps you out on your homework, the services never get into the GNP accounts. But if you hire a tutor or engage the services of a term-paper-writing agency, the transaction becomes part of GNP. Here again, the problem is simply that we have no objective way to determine how much output was produced until it enters the market and is purchased. The Commerce Department does, however, *estimate* the value of some nonmarket activities (for example, food grown by farmers for their own consumption, the rental value of home ownership) and includes such estimates in GNP calculations.

INTERNATIONAL ACTIVITY   Another difficulty in computing GNP arises from the international activities of U.S. firms. Multinational firms that operate in many countries may count all sales and profits in their domestic reports. This practice exaggerates the amount of productive activity actually occurring in the United States. To remedy this problem, we also compute gross domestic product (GDP), which includes only market transactions originating in the United States.

THE UNDERGROUND ECONOMY

GNP statistics are supposed to measure all market sales of goods and services. But many market transactions escape the notice of national-income accountants. A few examples:

☐ *Illegal drug trade.* The Drug Enforcement Administration estimates that illegal drug sales in the United States exceed $6 billion per year. None of this market activity is reported to either the Internal Revenue Service or the Commerce Department.

☐ *Cash income of domestic help.* Babysitters and other domestic help are often paid for their market services in cash. They may prefer cash payments for several reasons. First, cash income may escape both income and social security taxes. Second, cash income may escape the notice of public-welfare and unemployment-compensation administrators. Finally, cash payments reduce the paperwork of both employees and employers.

☐ *Cash income of other self-employed workers.* Other self-employed workers have similar incentives for not reporting cash income. Self-employed carpenters, dentists, electricians, and doctors all have the opportunity to be paid in cash.

☐ *Tips.* Waiters, waitresses, taxicab drivers, and other service workers typically receive tips in cash. The Internal Revenue Service attempts to estimate the amount of tip income an individual can expect, but the opportunity to evade some taxes remains.

☐ *Sales revenue of small businesses.* Business firms also have tax incentives for not reporting cash income. Street vendors, bars, sandwich shops, and other small businesses that deal in cash have the opportunity to avoid reporting income.

No one knows how much activity takes place in the "underground economy." Because it deals only in cash, there are no records on which to base GNP estimates. Professor Peter Guttman of New York's Baruch College guesses the underground economy may amount to as much as 10 percent of reported GNP. Estimates by Professor Edgar Feige of the University of Wisconsin are even higher—as much as 27 percent of reported GNP. Whatever its true dimensions, the underground economy represents economic activity that is not included in our GNP statistics.

VALUE ADDED Even when we focus on domestic market activity we encounter problems in calculating GNP. A very basic problem arises from the fact that the production of output typically involves a series of distinct stages. Consider the production of bread, for example. In order for bread to reach the supermarket, the farmer must grow some wheat, the miller must convert it to flour, and the baker must make bread with it. This chain of production is illustrated in Table 4.3.

Notice that each of the four stages of production depicted in Table 4.3 involves a separate market transaction. Were we simply to add them up, we would come to the conclusion that the value of a loaf of bread was $1.75 and increase GNP accordingly. But that figure is clearly in error. The market value of a loaf of bread—and thus its value to consumers—is only $0.75, as evidenced by the fact that the supermarket sells it to consumers at that price. Accordingly, we cannot simply add up all market transactions if we want to know the value of the economy's output. Instead, we want to focus on the

TABLE 4.3 VALUE ADDED IN VARIOUS STAGES OF PRODUCTION	Stages of production	Value of transaction	Value added
	1. Farmer grows wheat, sells it to miller	$0.12	$0.12
The value added at each stage of production represents a contribution to total output. Value added equals the market value of a product minus the cost of intermediate goods.	2. Miller converts wheat to flour, sells it to baker	0.28	0.16
	3. Baker bakes bread, sells it to supermarket	0.60	0.32
	4. Supermarket sells bread to consumer	0.75	0.15
	Total	$1.75	$0.75

intermediate goods: Goods or services purchased for use as input in the production of final goods or services.

value added: The increase in the market value of a product that takes place at each stage of the production process.

value of *final* goods and services, and exclude **intermediate goods** from our calculation.

We can arrive at a more accurate measure of *final* output in either of two ways. We could simply include in our calculations only the final transactions in the production process; that is, only sales to consumers. This method poses some difficulty, however, as we would have to know who purchased each good or service in order to know when we had reached the end of the process. Such a method of calculation would also exclude any output produced in stages 1, 2, and 3 of Table 4.3, but not yet reflected in stage 4.

An alternative approach to calculating GNP is to count only the **value added** at each stage of production. Consider the miller, for example. He does not really contribute $0.28 worth of production to total output, but only $0.16. The other $0.12 reflected in the price of his flour represents the contribution of the farmer who grew the wheat. By the same token, the baker *adds* only $0.32 to the value of output, as part of his output was purchased from the miller. By considering only the value *added* at each stage of production, we do not count twice the *intermediate* goods and services that producers buy from other producers, which are then used as inputs. As Table 4.3 confirms, we can determine that value of final output by summing up the value added at each stage of production. (Note that $0.75 is also the price of bread.)

Real vs. nominal GNP

Although prices serve as a convenient measure of market value, they can also distort our perceptions of real output. Imagine what would happen to our calculations of GNP if all prices were to double from one year to the next. Suppose, for example, that the price of oranges, as shown in Table 4.1, rose from $0.06 to $0.12, the price of bicycles to $100, and the price of airplanes to $2 million each. How would such price changes affect this year's GNP? Obviously, they would lead to a doubling of the *value* of final output. GNP would thus rise from $1,100 million to $2,200 million per year.

But such an increase in GNP clearly does not reflect an increase in the quantity of goods and services available to us. We are still producing the same quantities shown in Table 4.1; only the prices of those goods have changed. Hence changes in GNP brought about by changes in the price level can give us a distorted view of economic

nominal GNP: The value of final output produced in a given period, measured in the prices of that period (current prices).

real GNP: The value of final output produced in a given period, measured in the prices of another period (constant prices).

reality. Surely we would not want to assert that our standard of living had improved as the result of the recorded increase in GNP from $1,100 million to $2,200 million.

In order to distinguish increases in the quantity of goods and services from increases in their prices, we must construct a measure of GNP that takes into account price-level changes. We do so by distinguishing between real GNP and nominal GNP. **Nominal GNP** is simply the value of final output at current prices, whereas **real GNP** is what the value of output would have been if prices had not changed. To calculate real GNP, we are effectively pricing goods and services at prices of an earlier year.

REAL VS. NOMINAL GNP

Suppose that we want to determine how much better off the average American was in 1980, as measured in terms of new goods and services, than people were during the Great Depression. To do this, we would compare GNP per capita in 1980 with GNP per capita in 1933.

In 1933 the nation's GNP of $56 billion was shared by 126 million Americans, yielding a *per capita* GNP of $444. By contrast, 1980's GNP was $2,626 billion, and it was shared by 225 million people, giving us a per capita GNP of $11,671. Hence it would appear that our standard of living in 1980 was 26 times higher than the standard of 1933.

But this increase in *nominal* GNP vastly exaggerates our material well-being. The average price of goods and services—the *price level*—increased by 700 percent between 1933 and 1980. The goods and services you might have bought for $1 in 1933 cost $7 in 1980. In other words, we needed a lot more money income in 1980 to buy any given combination of real goods and services.

In order to compare our *real* GNP in 1980 with the real GNP of 1933, we have to adjust for this tremendous jump in prices (inflation). We do so by measuring both years' output in terms of *constant* prices. Since prices went up, on average, sevenfold between 1933 and 1980, we simply divide 1980's *nominal* output by seven. The calculation is:

$$\frac{\text{Real GNP in 1980}}{\text{(in 1933 prices)}} = \frac{\text{nominal 1980 GNP}}{\dfrac{1980 \text{ price level}}{1933 \text{ price level}}}$$

By arbitrarily setting the level of prices in 1933 at 100 and noting that prices have increased sevenfold since then, we can calculate:

$$\frac{\text{Real GNP in 1980}}{\text{(in 1933 prices)}} = \frac{\$2{,}626 \text{ billion}}{\dfrac{700}{100}}$$
$$= \$375 \text{ billion}$$

With a population of 225 million, this left us with real GNP per capita of $1,667 in 1980—as measured in 1933 dollars. This was still nearly four times the per capita GNP of the depression ($444), but not nearly so great an increase as comparisons of nominal GNP suggest.

FIGURE 4.1 CHANGES IN GNP: NOMINAL VS. REAL

Increases in nominal GNP reflect higher prices as well as more output. Increases in real GNP reflect more output only. To measure these real changes, we must value each year's output in terms of common base prices. In this figure the base year is 1972. Notice how *real* GNP declined in 1974, 1975, and 1980, although *nominal* GNP continued to rise. In recent years, nominal GNP has risen much faster than real GNP as a result of rapid inflation.

Source: *Economic Report of the President,* 1982.

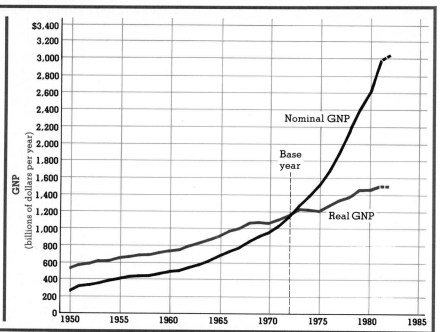

inflation: An increase in the average level of prices of goods and services.

production possibilities: The alternative combinations of final goods and services that could be produced in a given time period with all available resources and technology.

Net national product

Note, for example, that in Table 4.1 prices are unchanged as we go from last year to this year. In this case, this year's *nominal* GNP is equal to this year's *real* GNP, as expressed in last year's prices. But if all prices were to double, as we conjectured before, this year's nominal GNP would rise to $2,200 million, whereas *real* GNP, valued at last year's prices, would remain at $1,100 million. Thus **the distinction between nominal and real GNP is important whenever the level of prices changes.**

Because the price level increases nearly every year, the distinction between nominal and real GNP must be made when the economy's performance is evaluated over time. In calculating real GNP, we can use any year's prices as a base, as long as we consistently value output at the level of prices prevailing in that year. Figure 4.1 illustrates how nominal and real GNP have changed since 1950. Real GNP is calculated here on the basis of the level of prices prevailing in 1972. (Note that real and nominal GNP are identical in that year.) The dollar value of output produced each year has risen considerably faster than the quantity of output, reflecting persistent increases in the price level—that is to say, **inflation.**

Notice in particular that the continuing inflation of the 1970s tends to obscure the actual *declines* in real output that occurred in 1970, 1974, 1975, and 1980. Although the *value* of final output continued to rise in those years, the annual production of goods and services was falling: nominal and real GNP moved in opposite directions.

Although changes in real GNP from one year to the next tell us how much the economy's output has grown, they may exaggerate the growth of **production possibilities.** Recall that our production possibilities depend on the quantity of land, labor, and capital available and our knowledge of how to use those factors of production—our technology.

Unfortunately, we use up some of our capital—our plant and equipment—in the process of producing goods and services. As a consequence, it is possible for GNP to rise at the same time that our production possibilities are shrinking. Under such circumstances, the higher standards of living we attain today will be at the expense of our future well-being. Such binges may provide some temporary enjoyment but are clearly contrary to our long-run interests.

What we want to do, then, is determine how much of our GNP is attributable to the fact that we are using up ("consuming") our capital. To do so we simply subtract from GNP an estimate of our capital consumption, an estimate referred to as **depreciation.**[2] This calculation leaves us with **net national product (NNP),** or the amount of output we could consume without reducing our stock of capital and therewith next year's production possibilities.

The distinction between GNP and NNP has some direct implications for our mix of output. If we are going to maintain our production possibilities, it is evident that we must at least replace the capital we consume. This means that at least some of each year's output will have to consist of newly produced plant and equipment, that is, **investment** goods. Indeed, our total production of new plant and equipment—that is, our *gross* investment—must at least match our depreciation.[3] If we fail to allocate at least that much of our output to investment, our stock of capital and production possibilities will shrink.

The distinction between GNP and NNP is thus mirrored in a distinction between *gross* investment and *net* investment. **Gross investment** is positive as long as some new plant and equipment is being produced. But *our stock of capital—our total collection of plant and equipment—will not grow unless gross investment exceeds depreciation.* In other words, the *flow* of new capital must exceed depreciation or our *stock* of capital will decline. Whenever gross investment does in fact exceed depreciation, we say that **net investment** is positive.

Notice that net investment can be negative as well; in such situations we are wearing out our plant and equipment faster than we are replacing it. Clearly, if net investment continued to be negative for enough years, our capital stock would diminish to the point where we would be left with very little capital. We would thus be much less able to produce goods and services.

THE USES OF OUTPUT

Our recognition of investment as a basic means of maintaining or expanding our production possibilities helps focus attention on the

depreciation: The consumption of capital in the production process; the wearing out of plant and equipment.

net national product (NNP): GNP less depreciation.

investment: Expenditures on (production of) new plant and equipment (capital) in a given time period, plus changes in business inventories.

gross investment: Total investment expenditure in a given time period.

net investment: Gross investment less depreciation.

---

[2] The terms "depreciation" and "capital consumption allowance" are used interchangeably. The depreciation charges firms commonly make, however, are determined in part by income tax regulations, and may thus not accurately reflect the amount of capital consumed.

[3] Investment figures in the GNP accounts also include residential construction and changes in business inventories of final goods and services. Business inventories are discussed in Chapter 7.

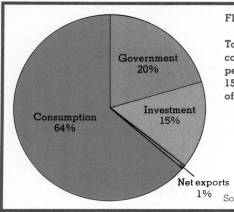

FIGURE 4.2 THE USES OF GNP

Total GNP amounted to $2.922 billion in 1981. Nearly two-thirds of this output consisted of private consumer goods and services. The next largest share (20 percent) of output consisted of public-sector goods. Investment goods made up 15 percent of GNP. Finally, because exports exceeded imports, nearly 1 percent of GNP was used abroad.

Source: *Economic Report of the President*, 1982.

uses to which GNP is put. It is not just the total value of annual output that concerns us, but also the use that we make of it. ***The GNP accounts also tell us what mix of output we have selected, that is, society's answer to the question of*** WHAT ***to produce.***

The major uses of total output conform to the three sets of market participants we encountered in Chapter 2, namely, consumers, business firms, and government. Those goods and services received and used by consumers are called consumption goods. They range all the way from breakfast cereals to massage parlors and include all goods and services consumers purchase in product markets. As Figure 4.2 confirms, nearly two-thirds of all our annual output is devoted to the production of consumption goods. By contrast, in the Soviet Union and China, just over half of GNP is composed of consumption goods.

Investment goods are another potential use of GNP. As we noted earlier, investment goods are the plant, machinery, and equipment that we produce. Like consumption goods, their production entails the use of resources, and thus they compete with consumption goods for our production decisions. Resources used to produce buildings or machinery cannot simultaneously be used to produce television sets or tape decks (opportunity costs again). Approximately 15 percent of our total output is allocated to investment goods.

The third major user of GNP is the public sector. Resources used by federal, state, and local governments to police the streets, teach classes, write laws, and build highways are unavailable for either consumption or investment purposes. Instead, these resources are allocated to the government sector. At present, all levels of government combined absorb approximately one-fifth of our annual output.

Finally, we should note that some of the goods and services we produce each year are used abroad rather than at home. That is to say, we **export** some of our output to other countries, for whatever use they care to make of it. Thus GNP will be larger than the sum of our own consumption, investment, and government purchases to the extent that we succeed in exporting goods and services.

International trade is not a one-way street. While we export some of our own output, we also **import** goods and services from

exports: Goods and services sold to foreign buyers.

imports: Goods and services purchased from foreign sources.

other countries. These imports may be used for consumption (Scotch whiskey, Japanese stereos), investment (German ball bearings), or government (French radar screens). Whatever their use, imports represent purchases of goods and services that were not produced in the United States.

The GNP accounts subtract imports from exports. The difference represents *net* exports. In 1982 the value of exports was $24 billion more than the value of imports. This implies that we shipped, on balance, nearly 1 percent of our total output to other countries. Net exports thus represent a fourth use of output.

What we end up with, then, is a simple equation expressing the components of GNP:

$$GNP = C + I + G + (E - M)$$

where C = consumption goods
I = investment goods
G = government goods
E = exports
M = imports

MEASURES OF INCOME

There are two sides to national-income accounting. The first side focuses on *output*, as we have done thus far. But there is another side to economic activity, and thus to the national-income accounts as well. This second side focuses on *income* flows rather than output flows. Here we are less concerned with the amount we produce each year than with the income that is generated in the production process and the way that income is distributed.

We have already observed (Figure 2.2) that every market transaction involves an *exchange* of money for a good or resource. Moreover, the *value* of each good or resource is measured by the amount of money exchanged for it (its market price). Hence **the total value of market incomes must equal the total value of final output,** or GNP. In other words, one person's expenditure always represents another person's income.

The equivalence of output and income is not dependent on any magical qualities possessed by money. Were we to produce only one product—say, wheat—and pay everyone in bushels and pecks, total income would still equal total output. Clearly, people could not receive in income more wheat than we produced. On the other hand, all the wheat produced would go to *someone*. Hence one could say that the production possibilities of the economy define the limits to real income. The amount of income actually generated in any year depends on the production and expenditure decisions of consumers, firms, and government agencies.

Table 4.4 shows the actual flow of output and income in the American economy during 1981. Total output is made up of the familiar components of GNP—consumption, investment, government goods and services, and net exports. The figures on the left side of Table 4.4 indicate that consumers spent $1,858 billion, business people spent $450 billion on plant and equipment, governments spent $590 billion, and net exports were $24 billion. Our total output value (GNP) was thus nearly $3 trillion in 1981.

TABLE 4.4 THE EQUIVALENCE OF OUTPUT AND INCOME, 1981
(in billions of dollars)

The value of total output must equal the value of total income. Why? Because every dollar spent on output becomes a dollar of income for someone.

Output		Income	
Consumer goods and services	$1,858	Wages and salaries	$1,772
Investment in plant, equipment, and inventory	450	Corporate profits	203
		Proprietors' income	114
Government goods and services	590	Farm income	30
		Rents	70
Exports	367	Interest	215
Imports	(343)	Sales taxes	251
		Depreciation	322
		Adjustments*	(55)
Total value of output	$2,922	Total value of income	$2,922

* Necessary because of sampling, rounding, and other errors in the national accounting system. Such adjustments ensure statistical equivalence of output and income flows.

Source: *Economic Report of the President,* 1982.

The right-hand side of Table 4.4 indicates who received the income generated from these market transactions. Every dollar spent on goods and services provides income to someone. It may go to a worker (as wage or salary) or to a business firm (as profit and depreciation allowance). It may go to a landlord (as rent), to a lender (as interest), or to government (as sales or property tax). None of the dollars spent on goods and services disappears into thin air.[4]

National income

While it may be exciting to know that we collectively received $3 trillion of income in 1981, it might be of more interest to know who actually got all that income. After all, there are not only 230 million pairs of outstretched palms among us, but millions of businesses and government agencies also competing for those dollars and the goods and services they represent. By charting the flow of income through the economy, we can see FOR WHOM our output was produced.

Our annual income flow originates in product-market sales. Purchases of final goods and services create a flow of income to producers and, through them, to factors of production. But a major diversion of sales revenues occurs immediately, as a result of depreciation charges made by businesses. As we noted earlier, some of our capital resources are used up in the process of production. For the most part, these resources are owned by business firms that expect to be compensated for such investments. Accordingly, they regard some of the sales revenue generated in product markets as reimbursement for wear and tear on capital plant and equipment. They therefore subtract *depreciation charges* from gross revenues in calculating their incomes. Depreciation charges reduce GNP to the

[4] Not all of the national income, however, is accounted for by the U.S. Department of Commerce. The "Adjustments" figure in Table 4.4 includes income that eluded the statisticians at the Commerce Department, as well as miscellaneous transfer payments. For current estimates of national income statistics, consult the annual *Economic Report of the President* or the bimonthly *Survey of Current Business.*

level of NNP before any income is available to current factors of production.

Another major diversion of the income flow occurs at its point of origin. When goods are sold in the marketplace, their purchase price is typically encumbered with some sort of sales tax. Thus some of the income generated in product markets disappears before anyone really gets a chance to touch it. These *indirect business taxes*, as they are called, are not considered part of national income because they do not represent payment for contributions to current output. But they do account for a large part of the income spent in the marketplace.

Once depreciation charges and indirect business taxes are subtracted from GNP, we are left with **national income,** the total income earned by the factors of production that have contributed to current production. As Table 4.5 illustrates, our national income in 1981 was $2,344 billion, or roughly $600 billion less than GNP.

national income (NI): Total income earned by current factors of production; GNP less depreciation and indirect business taxes.

Personal income

National income is the income received not only by households (consumers) but also by corporations. Theoretically, of course, all the income received by corporations represents income for their owners—the individual consumers who hold stock in the corporations. But the flow of income through corporations to stockholders is far from perfect. First, corporations must pay taxes on their profits. Accordingly, some of the income received on behalf of a corporation's stockholders goes into the public treasury rather than private bank accounts. Second, corporate managers typically find some urgent need for cash. As a result, part of the profits are retained by the corporation rather than passed on to the stockholders in the form of dividends. Accordingly, both *corporate taxes* and *retained earnings* must be subtracted from national income before we can determine how much income flows into the hands of consumers.

TABLE 4.5 THE FLOW OF INCOME, 1981
(in billions of dollars)

Consumers end up with approximately 70 percent of total income (GNP). The remainder is received by governments and businesses. This table shows how the income flow is distributed.

Income flow	Amount
Gross national product (GNP)	$2,922
Less depreciation	(322)
Net national product	2,600
Less indirect business taxes	(256)
National income *(NI)*	2,344
Less corporate taxes	(76)
Less retained earnings*	(50)
Less social security taxes	(239)
Plus transfer payments and net interest	425
Personal income *(PI)*	2,404
Less personal taxes	(388)
Disposable incomes *(DI)*	2,016

* Retained earnings are net of inventory valuation changes and depreciation.

Source: *Economic Report of the President,* 1982.

personal income (PI): Income received by households before payment of personal taxes.

Still another deduction must be made for *social security taxes.* Nearly all people who earn a wage or salary are required by law to pay social security "contributions." In 1981 the social security tax rate for workers was 6.65 percent on the first $29,700 of earnings received in the year (see Chapter 3). Workers never see this money, because it is withheld by employers and sent directly to the U.S. Treasury. Thus the flow of national income is reduced considerably before it becomes **personal income,** the amount of income received by households, before payment of personal taxes.

Not all of our adjustments to national income are negative, however. Households receive income in the form of transfer payments from the public treasury. More than 36 million people receive monthly social security checks, for example, and another 15 million or so receive some form of public welfare. These income transfers represent income for the people who receive them, and thus an increase in personal income. Accordingly, our calculation of personal income is as follows:

- national income
  less corporate taxes
    retained earnings
    social security taxes
  plus transfer payments
- *equals* personal income

Disposable income

disposable income (DI): After-tax income of consumers; personal income less personal taxes.

The total flow of income *generated* in production is significantly reduced before it gets into the hands of individual consumers. But we have not yet reached the end of the reduction process. We have to set something aside for personal income taxes. To be sure we don't forget about our obligations, Uncle Sam and his state and local affiliates usually arrange to have their share taken off the top. Personal income taxes are withheld by the employer, who thus acts as a tax collector. Accordingly, to calculate **disposable income**—the amount of income consumers may themselves spend (dispose of)—we reduce personal income by the amount of personal taxes.

THE FLOW OF INCOME

Figure 4.3 illustrates how the various measures of output and income relate to each other. In 1981, for example, we started in the product markets with nearly $3 trillion of gross national product (GNP). Of this amount, $322 billion represented depreciation charges, which flowed directly into business firms. Governments siphoned off another $256 billion in the form of indirect business taxes, leaving factors of production with $2,344 billion of national income (NI).

Once national income enters the factor markets, it is distributed in several directions. Most of it goes to consumers, as payment for the labor, land, and capital they supplied to the market. But some of it also goes to business firms, in the form of profits. And a very large chunk ($239 billion in 1981) goes to the government sector, as social security taxes.

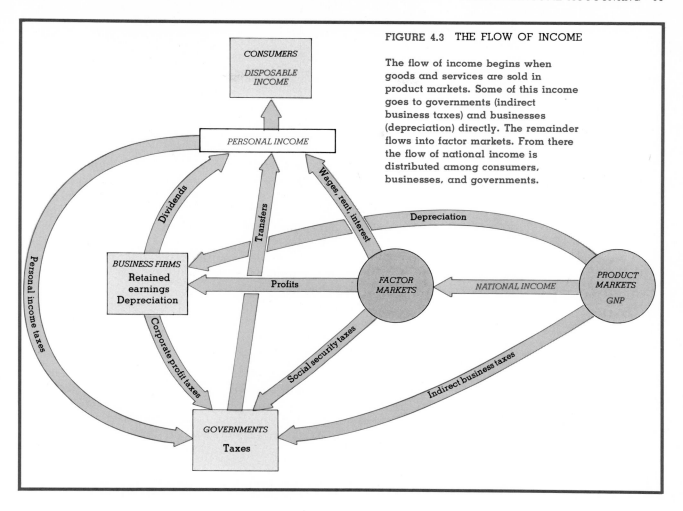

FIGURE 4.3 THE FLOW OF INCOME

The flow of income begins when goods and services are sold in product markets. Some of this income goes to governments (indirect business taxes) and businesses (depreciation) directly. The remainder flows into factor markets. From there the flow of national income is distributed among consumers, businesses, and governments.

The profits that businesses receive are split up among consumers, governments, and the businesses themselves. Government taxes corporate profits, while consumers get their share in the form of dividends. What remains in the business sector is retained earnings, along with depreciation allowances.[5]

The personal income received by consumer households comes from three directions. Most of it comes directly from factor markets, as wages, rent, and interest. But consumers also receive dividends from corporations and transfer payments (social security and welfare benefits and the like) from the government.

Finally, we have observed that consumers must pay taxes on their personal income. Once taxes are paid, consumers end up with disposable income. Thus total income (GNP) ends up being distributed in the following way:

- To CONSUMERS, in the form of disposable income
- To BUSINESS, in the form of retained earnings and depreciation allowances
- To GOVERNMENT, in the form of taxes

[5] These two forms of income are frequently referred to as "business savings."

Income and expenditure

The annual flow of income to households, businesses, and government is part of a continuing process. Households rarely stash their disposable income under the mattress; they spend most of it on consumption. This spending adds to GNP in the next round of activity, thereby helping to keep the flow of income moving.

Business firms also have a lot of purchasing power tied up in retained earnings and depreciation charges. This income, too, may be recycled—returned to the circular flow—in the form of business investment.

Even the income that flows into public treasuries finds its way back into the marketplace, as government agencies hire police officers, soldiers, and clerks, or buy goods and services. Thus *the flow of income that starts with GNP ultimately returns to the market in the form of new consumption (C), investment (I), and government (G) purchases.* A new GNP arises, and the flow starts all over again. In Section II of this book we will examine in detail these *expenditure* flows, with particular emphasis on their ability to keep the economy producing at its full potential.

POLICY IMPLICATIONS: THE QUALITY OF LIFE

Money, money, money—it seems that's all we talk about. Why don't we talk about important things like beauty, virtue, or the whole quality of life? Do the GNP accounts—either their output side or their income side—tell us anything about these essential dimensions of existence? If not, why have we spent so much time examining them?

All of the economic measures discussed so far in this chapter are important indexes of individual and collective welfare; they tell us something about how well people are living. They do not, however, capture the completeness of the way in which we view the world about us or the totality of what makes our lives satisfying. A clear day, a sense of accomplishment, even a smile can do more for a person's sense of well-being than can favorable movements in the GNP accounts. Or, as Professor John Kenneth Galbraith has put it, "In a rational life-style, some people could find contentment working moderately and then sitting by the street—and talking, thinking, drawing, painting, scribbling, or making love in a suitably discreet way. None of these requires an expanding economy."[6]

The emphasis on economic outcomes arises not from ignorance of life's other meanings but from the visibility of the economic outcomes. We can ascertain the size of GNP or changes in the price level with relative ease. It is not so easy to gauge individual happiness, much less to ascertain the status of our collective satisfaction. We may all realize that well-being arises from both material and intangible pleasures, yet we are compelled by the elusiveness of those intangibles to rely on measures we can see, touch, and count. As long as those material components of our environment bear some positive relation to our individual and collective well-being, they at least serve a useful purpose.

[6] Cited in Leonard Silk, *Nixonomics*, 2d ed. (New York: Praeger, 1973), p. 163.

"The way I look at it, there's a price tag
on everything. You want a high standard of living,
you settle for a low quality of life."

The Dig U.S.A. Series: *The Good Life U.S.A.*, New York, Bantam Books, 1973.

Serious problems in the emphasis on material outcomes arise when the relation between those outcomes and our collective welfare is disrupted. If increased automobile production raises congestion and pollution levels, the rise in GNP occasioned by those additional cars is a misleading index of society's welfare. Indeed, in such a case, the rise in GNP might actually mask a *decrease* in the wellbeing of the population. Exclusive emphasis on measurable output would clearly be a mistake in such a situation.

What is true of automobile production might also be true of other outputs. Increased development of urban areas may cause a loss of social welfare if that development occurs at the expense of space, trees, and relative tranquillity. Increased mechanization on the farm may raise agricultural output but isolate and uproot farmers. So, too, increased productivity in factories and offices might contribute to a sense of alienation. These ill effects of increased output need not occur; but if they do, indexes of output tell us little about social or individual well-being.

All this does not suggest that the national-income accounts are useless or irrelevant. Rather, these points help to underscore the fact that *social welfare* and *economic welfare* are not synonymous. The GNP accounts certainly tell us whether our economic welfare has increased, as measured by the quantity of goods and services we demanded in the marketplace. What they don't tell us is how highly we value additional goods and services, relative to nonmarket phenomena. Nor do they even tell us whether important social costs were incurred in the process of production. These judgments must be made outside the market; they are social decisions.

SUMMARY

▪ National-income accounting is the measurement of our annual output and income flows. The national-income accounts provide a basis for assessing our economic performance, for designing public policy, and for understanding how all the parts of the economy interact.

▪ The most comprehensive measure of our output is gross national product (GNP). This is the total market value of all final goods and services produced during a given time period. In calculating GNP, we include only the value added at each stage of production; that is, the contribution to final output made at each stage. This procedure eliminates the possibility of double counting, of exaggerating the value of GNP because business firms buy intermediate goods from other firms and include the associated costs in their selling price. For the most part, only marketed goods and services are included in GNP.

▪ Because the market value of output depends on both the price and the quantity of goods we produce, increases in GNP may occur solely as a result of higher prices. To distinguish such changes from changes in the quantity of output, we call the value of output expressed in *current* prices "nominal GNP." We call the value of output expressed in *constant* prices (typically, the prices of some previous, or *base,* year) "real GNP."

▪ Each year some of our capital equipment is worn out—consumed—in the process of production. Hence GNP is larger than the amount of goods and services we could consume without reducing our production possibilities. The amount of capital used up each year is referred to as depreciation.

▪ By subtracting depreciation from GNP, we derive net national product (NNP). The difference between NNP and GNP is also equal to the difference between *gross* investment—the sum of all our current plant and equipment expenditures—and *net* investment—the amount of investment over and above that required to replace worn-out capital.

▪ All the income generated in market sales (GNP) is received by someone. The sequence of flows involved in this process is:

GNP
less depreciation
equals NNP
less indirect business taxes
equals national income *(NI)*
less corporate taxes
    retained earnings
    social security taxes

plus transfer payments
equals personal income *(PI)*
less personal income taxes
equals disposable income *(DI)*

■ The incomes received by households, business firms, and governments provide the purchasing power required to buy the nation's output. As that purchasing power is spent, further GNP is created and the circular flow continues.

Terms to remember

Define the following terms:

national-income accounting   net national product
gross national product   investment
GNP per capita   gross investment
intermediate goods   net investment
value added   exports
nominal GNP   imports
real GNP   national income
inflation   personal income
production possibilities   disposable income
depreciation

Questions for discussion

1. The manuscript for this text was typed by my wife. Had I hired a secretary to do the same job, GNP would have been higher, even though the amount of output would have been identical. Why is this? Does this make sense?

2. GNP in 1979 was $2.41 trillion. It grew to $2.63 trillion in 1980, yet the quantity of output actually decreased. How is this possible?

3. If gross investment is not large enough to replace the capital that depreciates in a particular year, how large is net investment? What happens to our production possibilities?

4. Can we increase consumption in a given year without cutting back on either investment or government services? Under what conditions?

5. What happened to real and nominal GNP last year?

[handwritten: GNP – CCA – IBT / NI]

Problem

(a) Calculate national income from the following figures:

Consumption	$200 billion
Depreciation	20 billion
Retained earnings	12 billion
Gross investment	30 billion
Imports	40 billion
Social security taxes	25 billion
Exports	50 billion
Indirect business taxes	15 billion
Government purchases	60 billion
Personal income taxes	40 billion

[handwritten: 200 – 20 – 15]

(b) If there were 80 million people in this country, what would the GNP per capita be?

(c) If all prices were to double overnight, what would happen to the values of real and nominal GNP per capita?

MACROECONOMICS

As we noted in Chapter 1, the subject of economics is usually divided into two parts: *macro-* economics and *micro*economics. **Macroeconomics** deals with the behavior of the economy as a whole, while microeconomics studies the behavior of the individuals who participate in the economy. In other words, half of economics (macroeconomics) looks at the completed puzzle, while the other half (microeconomics) examines each of the pieces.

macroeconomics: The study of aggregate economic behavior, of the economy as a whole.

Although macroeconomics is more abstract than microeconomics, it gets most of the public's attention. The front page of virtually every major newspaper frequently carries stories on inflation, unemployment, interest rates, and the federal budget. Stories on microeconomic behavior, on the other hand, are usually buried in the back pages or the "local news" sec-tion.

The preeminence of macroeconomics is easily explained. A rise in the inflation rate potentially affects all consumers and businesses. By contrast, an increase in the price of potatoes affects only some people, and even for them the impact is likely to be small. The same is true of government spending. When President Reagan cut the growth of government spending, he affected thousands of specific programs and millions of consumers; that was big news. By contrast, cutbacks in a single government program involve much less expenditure and affect far fewer people; such ac-tions rarely get mentioned on the evening news.

MACRO GOALS

Our purpose in studying macroeconomics is twofold. First, we want to understand how the macroeconomy works. Then we want to determine how we can change its behavior. The necessity of changing its behavior is apparent from our record of macroeconomic instability. Our economic history is peppered with **recessions**—years in which total output fell and millions of workers lost their jobs. The worst of these economic declines—in the 1930s—was so devastating that it became known as the Great Depression. More recent recessions have been less severe and shorter-lived, but have still left millions of Americans out of work. Figure II.1 illus-

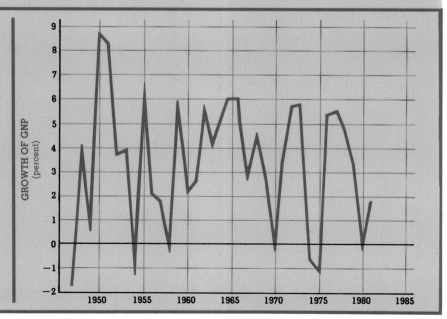

FIGURE II.1 ANNUAL CHANGES IN TOTAL OUTPUT

The U.S. economy has grown tremendously over time. Growth has been uneven, however, with frequent "booms" (high growth rates) and occasional "busts" (negative growth rates). The record of growth before 1947 was even more erratic and included several depressions.

Source: *Economic Report of the President,* 1982.

trates the boom-and-bust character of our economic growth.

recession: A decline in total output (real GNP) for two or more consecutive quarters.

Another recurrent macroeconomic problem is **inflation.** On average, prices increase virtually every year. In some years, however, the price level rises exceptionally fast. In the process many consumers find they can no longer afford the goods and services they had planned to buy. For their part many businesses discover they cannot afford to continue producing goods at the prices they were charging. All market participants are upset by the added uncertainty imposed by volatile prices.

inflation: An increase in the average level of prices of goods and services.

Figure II.2 provides a quick summary of our recent experience with inflation. Two things

are evident in the graph. First, the price level has risen significantly in every one of the last ten years or so. Second, the *rate* of inflation has been very erratic, accelerating sharply in some years (e.g., 1974, 1979, 1980) while slowing down in others (e.g., 1972, 1976, 1981).

In view of our record of price and output instability, the goals of macroeconomic policy are fairly evident. We want greater macroeconomic *stability*. Specifically, we want steady economic growth, with fewer recessions and less inflation.

The U.S. Congress has given the president explicit instructions on these goals. In the Full Employment and Balanced Growth Act of 1978, Congress decreed the goals of macroeconomic policy to be (1) full employment, (2) price stability, and (3) continued economic growth. Moreover, it set a timetable for achieving these goals. By 1983 the economy was to reduce the unemployment rate to only 4 percent and the rate of inflation to 3 percent. The act further re-

quired the president to submit regular reports on our progress toward these goals.[1]

Congress did not tell the president exactly how to attain these goals, and for good reason. Presumably, if we knew how to achieve full employment, price stability, and continued economic growth, we would have done so long ago. In reality, no one is sure how to attain all these goals simultaneously. As a consequence, the annual progress reports submitted by presidents to Congress typically explain why the timetable for attaining economic stability will have to be revised once again. The delays began, in fact, with the very first progress report. In his 1980 report, President Carter

[1] Before the enactment of this legislation, the Employment Act of 1946 was the most explicit statement of congressional intent. That act, however, only called for "maximum employment . . . consistent with other needs and . . . considerations of national policy." The 1946 act established the president's Council of Economic Advisers but did not require the president to develop and report on specific plans for attaining this goal.

FIGURE II.2   ANNUAL CHANGES IN PRICES

Prices have risen virtually every year. The rate of inflation has not been steady, however. In some years (e.g., 1961) price increases were negligible or prices actually fell (1949, 1954). In others (e.g., 1974, 1979) the rate of inflation was very high.

Source: *Economic Report of the President,* 1982.

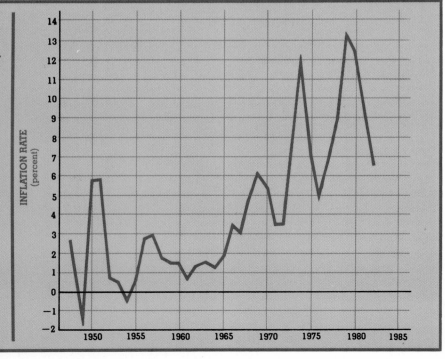

noted that "the goals of a 4 percent unemployment rate and 3 percent inflation by 1983 are no longer practicable." He pushed the timetable back to 1985 for full employment and to 1988 for price stability.[2] President Reagan stretched the timetable even further.

We have not failed completely, of course. Despite occasional flops, we have had more economic stability in the last 40 years than at any other time in history. Moreover, we have managed to find jobs for a steadily increasing number of workers. In the process, we have achieved ever-higher standards of living.

We are determined to do better, however. In poll after poll, American consumers express their desire for greater price stability and less unemployment than we have so far achieved. Congress and the president respond to these wishes by continuously formulating new economic strategies. President Kennedy promised to "get America moving" again; President Johnson offered a Great Society. President Ford declared he would "Whip Inflation Now" (WIN), while Ronald Reagan promised a "New Beginning."

The policy tools available for attaining our economic goals have been the same each time. These tools include:

- *Fiscal policy:* changing the levels of government spending or taxation
- *Monetary policy:* changing the amount of money available
- *Supply-Side policy:* reducing barriers to increased production and employment

What has differed from one administration to another (and from one year to another within a single administration) is the way those tools are used. The

[2] *1980 Economic Report of the President* (Washington, D. C.: Government Printing Office, January 1980), pp. 93–94.

Kennedy administration, for example, relied heavily on fiscal policy to increase the demand for goods and services. The Carter administration took the same tack. The Reagan administration used fiscal policy also but emphasized its effects on incentives for increased production. In addition, Reagan encouraged monetary restraint and vigorously pursued other Supply-Side policies.

ALTERNATIVE APPROACHES

In the following chapters we shall examine both our macroeconomic problems and our policy tools more closely. We shall look first at the nature of unemployment (Chapter 5) and inflation (Chapter 6) and the social consequences of both these problems. Then we shall try to explain how these problems emerge and how they might be solved. As might be expected, the explanation for these macroeconomic problems is to be found in the dynamics of supply and demand. Because we rely largely on market forces to determine WHAT to produce, HOW to produce it, and FOR WHOM, it is not surprising that those same forces are responsible for economic problems that emerge. But concluding that "supply and demand" explain our economic ills is hardly a complete diagnosis. To be of use to policy makers, the diagnosis must be more complete. Is it "demand" that causes unemployment and inflation, or is "supply" the culprit? Or is it some combination of these two market forces?

Here is where economists begin to take sides. Some explain our ills exclusively in terms of problems of demand; others stress supply . Even when there is agreement about which side to blame, there are controversies about just which elements of demand or supply really matter. In the following

chapters we shall examine three competing diagnoses and their attendant policy prescriptions: the Keynesian, the Monetarist, and the Supply-Side approaches.

The Keynesian approach
Our search for the causes of unemployment and inflation will begin in Chapter 7 with the explanation developed by John Maynard Keynes. The Keynesian explanation focuses on the *demand* for goods and services. From a Keynesian perspective, insufficient demand causes unemployment and excesssive demand leads to inflation. On the basis of this diagnosis, Keynes urged policy makers to manipulate the level of aggregate demand by changing the level of government expenditure or taxation. The Keynesian approach took hold during the Great Depression and has been a basic component of macroeconomic policy ever since.

The Monetarist approach
As important as the Keynesian perspective has been, it is neither the only one nor necessarily the best. Another diagnosis of our economic ills emphasizes the role of money. This "Monetarist" perspective asserts that changes in government spending or taxation have little or no impact on the aggregate demand for goods and services. What really matters, Monetarists argue, is the amount of money circulating in the economy. If there is "too much money chasing too few goods," prices will rise. If there is too little money in relation to the goods and services available, some output may remain unsold and unemployment may result. This Monetarist challenge to Keynesian economics is examined in Chapters 10–12.

The Supply-Side approach
In recent years some economists have asserted that the emphasis of both Keynesians and Mone-

tarists on the *demand* side of the economy is misplaced. What holds back production and pushes up prices, they argue, are constraints on the *supply* of goods and services. Businesses that could produce more are discouraged from doing so by high taxes, environmental restrictions, health and safety regulations, untrained labor, and a never-ending flow of governmental red tape. "Supply-Siders" argue that the only way to achieve more employment and less inflation is to "get government off our backs and out of our pockets." We shall examine the theoretical basis for these Supply-Side conclusions in Chapter 13.

Eclectic policies

These differing diagnoses of our economic problems are bound to confuse not only students but policy makers as well. Which approach should Congress and the president follow? Should they rely on changes in government spending and taxes, changes in the money supply, or a variety of Supply-Side initiatives to cure our economic ills? The answer is hardly obvious. Each theory has its own proponents, and all of them seem totally convinced that their policy prescriptions are right.

As a practical matter, every recent administration has used a variety of policy tools. This eclectic approach to policy reflects several considerations. First of all, it is apparent that economists themselves are far from agreeing on a single diagnosis of our economic ills. Second, no single policy approach has ever been shown to be fully effective. Third, all three approaches—the Keynesian, the Monetarist, and the Supply-Side—offer useful insights, even if none of them is totally convincing.

Current policy

Our exploration of macroeconomics will conclude with a look at current economic policy. As we shall see, the Reagan administration initially espoused a narrow Supply-Side program but soon adopted an eclectic mixture of Keynesian, Monetarist, and Supply-Side policies. We shall also look at the institutional factors that limit the effectiveness of *any* policy decision. These factors include our inability to diagnose (measure) problems until they are acute, and an often slow-moving and combative Congress. These and other real-world limits on economic policy making are examined in Chapter 14. The macro section concludes with discussions of "oil shocks" (Chapter 16) and economic growth and productivity (Chapter 17). In the latter chapter, both the sources and limits of growth are examined.

MAJOR PROBLEMS

CHAPTER 5

UNEMPLOYMENT

Jobs are important. Jobs provide workers not only with income but also with social status and a sense of fulfillment. For the economy as a whole, jobs represent the use of our scarce labor resources to produce desired goods and services. Hence both individual workers and the general society gain when people work. For these reasons, a major goal of economic policy has been to foster "full employment," to ensure that everyone who seeks a job can find one.

We have often fallen far short of our full-employment goal. Our worst failure was the Great Depression. In the 1930s, millions of men and women were unable to find jobs—any jobs—for months, even years. For many of these people, prolonged unemployment meant the loss of their life savings, their homes, even their physical and mental health. More recently, our economy has again experienced substantial unemployment. While not nearly so serious as the Great Depression, the recessions of the mid-1970s and early 1980s left millions of individuals and families jobless. Our output of goods and services was reduced by billions of dollars.

The purpose of this chapter is to develop a clearer sense of what unemployment is all about and who suffers from it. This discussion may help explain why "full employment" is regarded as a major economic goal. In later chapters we will study the causes of unemployment and the policy options available for achieving full employment.

THE LABOR FORCE

To get a sense of what our unemployment problem is all about, we need to clarify the concept of "full employment." **Full employment does not mean that everyone has a job.** On the contrary, we can have "full employment" even when you are going to school, people are in the hospital, children are playing with their toys at home, and older people are enjoying their retirement. We are not concerned that *everybody* be put to work, but only with ensuring jobs for all those persons who are ready and willing to work, and who desire and seek jobs.

Our first concern, then, is to distinguish between those individuals who are ready and willing to work and those individuals who, for institutional or personal reasons, are not available for employment. The **labor force** consists of everyone over the age of 16 who is actually working plus all those who are not working but are actively seeking employment. Individuals are also counted as employed in a particular week if their failure to work is due to vacation, illness, labor dispute (strike), or bad weather. All such persons are regarded as "with a job but not at work." Also, unpaid family members working in a family enterprise (farming, for example) are counted as employed. **People who are neither employed nor actively seeking work are not counted as part of the labor force;** they are referred to as "nonparticipants." In 1980 less than half of our population was in the labor force, as Figure 5.1 shows.

Note that our definition of labor force participation excludes most household and volunteer activities. A woman who chooses to devote her energies to household responsibilities is not counted as part of the labor force, no matter how hard she works. Because she is neither in paid employment nor seeking such employment in the marketplace, she is regarded as outside the labor market (a "non-

labor force: All persons over age 16 who are either working for pay or actively seeking paid employment.

FIGURE 5.1 THE CIVILIAN LABOR FORCE, 1980

Less than half of the total U.S. population participates in the civilian labor force. The rest of the population is too young, in school, at home, or otherwise unavailable.

Unemployment statistics count only those participants who are not currently working but are actively seeking paid employment. Nonparticipants are neither employed nor actively seeking employment.

Source: U.S. Bureau of Labor Statistics.

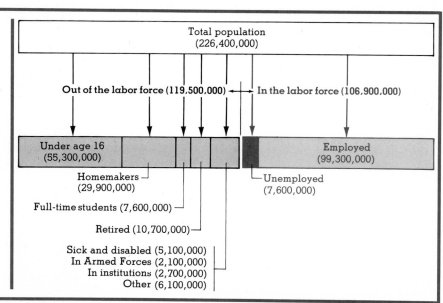

participant"). Only if she decides to seek a paid job outside the home, and engages in active job search, would we say she is "entering the labor force." Students, too, are typically out of the labor force until they leave school and actively look for work, either during summer vacations or after graduation.

Production possibilities

The distinction between our labor force and our total population can be illustrated by production-possibilities curves. As we first saw in Chapter 1, there is a limit to the quantity of goods and services an economy can produce in any time period. In general, our *production possibilities* are limited by two factors:

- ☐ Resources
- ☐ Technology

Figure 5.2 illustrates the limits to our production of any two goods (here called simply "consumption goods" and "investment goods"), given some level of resources and technology. With all of our resources devoted to the production of consumption goods, we could produce the amount 0B of such goods in a year. By devoting all our resources and technology to the production of investment goods, we could produce 0A of such goods. In the more likely situation that we chose to produce some of both goods, we could have any combination of goods represented by the curve AB.

Although resource availability and technological know-how clearly limit our potential GNP, production has other constraints as well. In particular, the size of our labor force is much smaller than the total number of bodies in the country. In fact, we have imposed very strict limits on the amount of labor that may be used in production. Small children are not allowed to work, for example, no matter how much they or their parents yearn to contribute to total output.

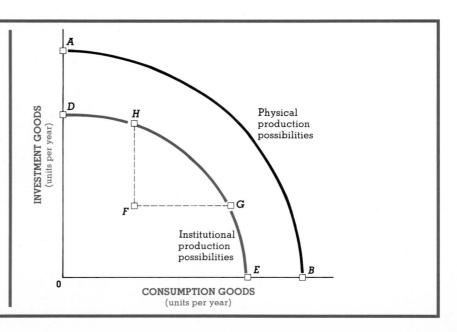

FIGURE 5.2 PHYSICAL VS. INSTITUTIONAL PRODUCTION POSSIBILITIES

Our physical production possibilities express the maximum output that could be produced if all of our resources and technology were employed. We impose limits on the use of resources and technology, however. These limits are reflected in our smaller institutional production possibilities.

Yet we could definitely produce more output this year if we put all those little bodies to work. In fact, we could produce a little more output this year if you were to put down this book and get a job. To the extent that small children, students, and others are precluded from working, both the size of our labor force (our *available* labor) and our potential output shrink.

Constraints are also imposed on the use of material resources and technology. We do not cut down all the forests this year and build everybody a wooden palace because we want to preserve a little greenery and save some wood for future years. Therefore, the federal government limits each year's tree harvest on public lands. The federal government also restricts the use of nuclear technology. In both cases, concern for environmental protection and conservation constrains the use of resources or technology and limits annual output. For the same reasons, we restrict the use of land, water, and air and discourage the use of potentially hazardous chemicals and production processes. These restrictions are known as institutional constraints.

In assessing the limits to total output, then, we must consider not only the physical limitations of resources and technology, but also the institutional constraints imposed on the use of those inputs. Accordingly, we can identify the **physical production possibilities** of society as those that would exist in the absence of institutional constraints. The **institutional production possibilities** are those that incorporate social constraints on the use of resources. Although the dimensions of either definition will be altered as resources, technology, and social constraints change, a distinct physical or institutional limit will exist at any point in time.

Our institutional and physical production possibilities are illustrated in Figure 5.2. Our physical production possibilities are represented by the curve *AB*, which is based on resource and technology constraints only. Our institutional production possibilities are smaller, because they also reflect restrictions on the use of both resources and technology. Thus the institutional production-possibilities curve *(DE)* always lies *inside* the physical production-possibilities curve *(AB)*. The institutional production-possibilities curve is the immediate focus of economic policy.

We cannot move beyond our institutional production-possibilities curve without altering our resources, technology, or social constraints. Any of those things can change, however. New resources are discovered, technology improves, and social constraints change. During World War II, for example, many restraints on labor use were relaxed, and factories were run twenty-four hours a day. This change in our mode of production shifted the institutional production-possibilities curve outward, permitting us to produce a larger quantity of goods and services.

physical production possibilities: The alternative combinations of final goods and services that could be produced in a given time period within the limits imposed by resources and technology.

institutional production possibilities: The alternative combinations of final goods and services that could be produced in a given time period within the limits imposed by resources, technology, and social constraints on their use.

Unemployment

In the short run (with given resources, technology, and social constraints), our immediate problem is not to expand production possibilities but simply to attain them. We cannot reach points beyond the institutional production-possibilities curve, but we can easily end

unemployment: Labor force participants are unable to find jobs; people actively seeking paid employment.

unemployment rate: The proportion of the labor force that is unemployed.

up somewhere inside that curve. *To reach a point on the institutional production-possibilities curve, our entire labor force must be employed.* But there is no guarantee that a job will be available for everyone who is ready and willing to work. On the contrary, the essence of our unemployment problem is that we do not make full use of all our available labor! Some labor force participants cannot find jobs and remain **unemployed.**

In 1980 an average of 7.6 million persons were counted as unemployed at any time. As Figure 5.1 suggests, these unemployed individuals accounted for 7.1 percent of our total labor force. Accordingly, the average **unemployment rate** in 1980 was 7.1 percent.

MACRO CONSEQUENCES: LOST OUTPUT

The impact of unemployment on our gross national product (GNP) is illustrated in Figure 5.2. If we fail to employ our entire labor force, we will not produce as much output as our institutional production possibilities (curve *DE*) permit. Instead, we will end up somewhere *inside* our institutional production-possibilities curve. In every such case (e.g., point *F*) we are clearly not producing as much output per year as we could, even after institutional constraints are taken into consideration.

Notice in Figure 5.2 that we *could* be at point *G*, producing more consumption goods and no fewer investment goods than are available at point *F*. By not fully employing our labor force, then, we are forsaking an annual flow of consumer goods equal to the distance *FG*. Similarly, we could get more investment goods each year, with no fewer consumption goods, if we were to produce at point *H* rather than at point *F*. Here again, our failure to utilize our entire labor force results in lost output. This lost output amounted to roughly $200 billion in 1980 alone, or approximately $900 worth of goods and services for every U.S. citizen.[1]

Although the prospect of another $900 worth of goods and services may sound exciting to many of us, some people might question whether maximum production is really a desirable goal. After all, what's the difference whether we produce $3.0 trillion or $3.2 trillion? We've already glutted the streets with cars and the air with pollution. Why worry whether or not we are fully utilizing production possibilities?

Resource utilization is of vital concern to society for two reasons. First of all, as long as private or public needs remain unfilled, we have a social use for all our resources. Maybe we do have enough cars on the streets already, but what about other goods and services? Do we have enough parks, schools, and clean rivers? If not, then we could use some of our idle resources to produce these things. *By not using all our resources—not fully utilizing our institutional production possibilities—we are forgoing potential output.* Even if we

---

[1] This estimate is based on our definition of "full employment," to be discussed shortly.

felt (and few people do) that all our private and public needs had been met, we could still use our factors of production to aid the rest of the world. The average standard of living on the rest of this planet is only one-fourth as high as our own. Whether we actually use our resources for these purposes is a question of resource allocation and depends on private and public decisions we make in the marketplace. Should those decisions fail to use all our resources, however, we are effectively saying that unmet domestic or international needs are of no value or concern. Few would accept this implication.

MICRO CONSEQUENCES: PEOPLE OUT OF WORK

A second dimension of society's concern for full employment relates to the effects of unemployment on specific individuals. The term "labor" refers not simply to another factor of production but to *people*. Not using all our available labor means that somebody is without a job. That may be all right for a day or even a week, but if you need some income to keep body and soul together, prolonged unemployment can hurt. The same is true for plant and equipment, or land. If available machinery or farmland is not used, then somebody's income is going to be in jeopardy. If the company or farm loses a lot of income, it may shut down, throwing still more people out of work. To the extent that society as a whole cares about the welfare of individuals, the full utilization of our productive resources—*full employment*—is a desirable social goal.

The immediate impact of unemployment on individuals is the loss of income associated with working. For workers who have been unemployed for long periods of time, such losses can spell financial disaster. Typically, an unemployed person must rely on a combina-

UNEMPLOYMENT BENEFITS

In 1981, 11 million people collected unemployment benefits averaging $100 per week. But don't rush to the state unemployment office yet—not all unemployed people are eligible. To qualify for regular weekly unemployment benefits you must have worked a substantial length of time and earned some minimum amount of wages, both determined by your state. Furthermore, you must have a "good" reason for having lost your last job. Most states will not provide benefits to students (or their professors!) during summer vacations, to professional athletes in the off-season, or to individuals who quit their last jobs.

If you qualify for benefits, the amount of benefits you receive each week will depend on your previous wages. In most states the benefits are equal to about one-half of the previous weekly wage, up to a state-determined maximum. The maximum benefit in 1981 ranged from $90 in Alabama, Georgia, and Mississippi to a high of $215 in Ohio.

Unemployment benefits are financed by a tax on employers, and can continue for as long as 26 weeks. During periods of high unemployment, the duration of benefit eligibility may be extended another 13 weeks.

tion of savings, income from other family members, and government unemployment benefits for financial support. After these sources of support are exhausted, public welfare is often the only legal support left.

Not all unemployed people experience such a financial disaster, of course. College students who fail to find summer employment, for example, are unlikely to end up on welfare the following semester. Likewise, teenagers and others looking for part-time employment will not suffer great economic losses from unemployment. Nevertheless, the experience of unemployment—of not being able to find a job when you want one—can still be painful. In addition to the implied income loss, many unemployed people also experience important social and psychological problems. Failure to find a job can suddenly make one feel useless, bitter, and confused. Psychologists have observed that many unemployed people feel discarded by the very social institutions in which they had once placed their trust. This sensation is not easily forgotten, even after one has finally found employment.

It is difficult to measure the full impact of unemployment on individuals. A study for the U.S. Congress, however, provides some frightening suggestions. The author of the study estimated that a prolonged one-point increase in the national unemployment rate— say, from 6 percent to 7 percent—leads, on average, to:

- □ 920 suicides
- □ 648 homicides
- □ 20,240 fatal heart attacks or strokes
- □ 495 deaths from liver cirrhosis
- □ 4,227 admissions to mental hospitals
- □ 3,340 admissions to state prisons[2]

Although these estimates are subject to serious statistical qualifications, they underscore the notion that prolonged unemployment

[2] Harvey Brenner, "Estimating the Social Costs of National Economic Policy: Implications for Mental and Physical Health, and Criminal Aggression," study prepared for the Joint Economic Committee, U.S. Congress (Washington, D.C., October 1976).

Recession Taking Toll in Mental Illness Rate

DETROIT (AP)—In Michigan, perhaps the state hardest hit by recession, the high unemployment rate is triggering increases in "cry for help" calls—increases that mental health experts say may only be just beginning.

Michigan residents are exhibiting symptoms of a problem that is growing nationwide—emotional problems created or aggravated by economic woes.

"It's almost axiomatic that when people are without jobs and their income is down, you're going to see an increase in depression and some overtly dangerous behavior," said James Kipfer, executive director of the Mental Health Association in Michigan. . . .

"The problems that lead people to come to our agencies don't happen the day after one is laid off," said Mel Ravitz, executive director of the Detroit Wayne County Community Mental Health Board.

"It's at some point after people have been out of work a while, after they've experienced the effort to seek re-employment, after creditors are calling their family, when hospitalization coverage ends.

"When all of that ends, and people see no break in the clouds, people begin to yell at each other, abuse each other, experience increasing feelings of pressure and frustration." . . .

In June, police in Detroit and the Port Huron area handled four cases in which unemployed people barricaded themselves with guns inside their homes and threatened neighbors. Two confrontations resulted in suicides.

Washington Star, July 7, 1980, p. A4.

poses a real danger to many individuals. Thomas Cottle, a lecturer at Harvard Medical School, stated the case more bluntly: "I'm now convinced that unemployment is *the* killer disease in this country— responsible for wife beating, infertility, and even tooth decay."

German psychiatrists have also observed that unemployment can be hazardous to your health. They estimate that the anxieties and other nervous disorders that accompany one year of unemployment can reduce life expectancy by as much as five years. In 1981 nearly 600,000 Americans had been unemployed longer than twelve months, and an additional 600,000 had been unemployed for more than six months.

MEASURING UNEMPLOYMENT

The macro and micro losses resulting from unemployment clearly make it a serious policy concern. To keep policy makers informed of just how serious the problem is at any time, the Census Bureau provides monthly estimates of the number of people unemployed. These estimates are obtained by interviews in 65,000 households across the country each month. All persons interviewed are asked whether they are working that week (*employed* members of the labor force). If they are not working, they are asked if they have been actively seeking employment (*unemployed* members of the labor force).[3] On the basis of these responses, the Census Bureau, together with the U.S. Department of Labor, estimates the size of the labor force, as well as the proportion that is unemployed.

The monthly unemployment figures indicate not only the total amount of unemployment in the economy, but also which groups are suffering the greatest unemployment. Typically, teenagers just entering the labor market have the greatest difficulty finding (or keeping) jobs and are most likely to be unemployed. As a result, the average unemployment rate for teenagers is often three times larger than the adult unemployment rate (see Figure 5.3). Blacks and women also suffer a much higher rate of unemployment than do white males. Thus the losses resulting from unemployment are not borne equally.

Discouraged workers

discouraged worker: An individual who is not actively seeking employment, but would look for or accept a job if one were available.

Although the monthly estimates provided by the Census Bureau are an important measure of unemployment, they do not fully capture the dimensions of the problem. When unemployment persists, job seekers become increasingly frustrated in their efforts to secure employment. After repeated rejections, job seekers often get so discouraged that they give up the search and turn to their families, friends, or public welfare for income support. When the census interviewer asks whether they are actively seeking employment, such **discouraged workers** are apt to reply no. Yet they would like to be working, and

---

[3] Recall that an individual is counted as employed if he or she is on strike, on paid vacation, or absent from work because of illness or bad weather. Among the unemployed are those workers waiting to be recalled from layoff and persons waiting to start a new job within 30 days.

FIGURE 5.3 UNEMPLOYMENT ISN'T EXPERIENCED EQUALLY

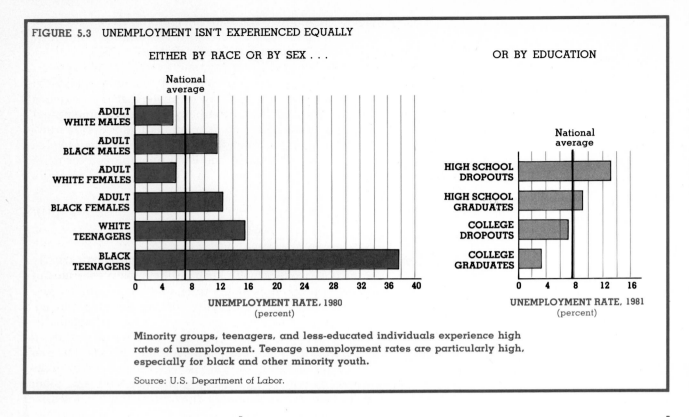

Minority groups, teenagers, and less-educated individuals experience high
rates of unemployment. Teenage unemployment rates are particularly high,
especially for black and other minority youth.

Source: U.S. Department of Labor.

they would probably be out looking for work if job prospects were
better.

Discouraged workers are not counted as part of our unemployment problem because they are technically out of the labor force.
The Labor Department estimates that in 1980 more than 1 million
individuals fell into this uncounted class of discouraged workers.

Underemployment

underemployment: People
work part-time although they
seek full-time jobs or are
employed at jobs below their
capability.

Not everyone can afford to be a discouraged worker, of course. Many
people who become jobless have family responsibilities and bills to
pay: they simply cannot afford to become "discouraged." Instead,
they are compelled to take some job—any job—just to keep body
and soul together. The resultant job may be part-time or full-time
and may pay very little. Nevertheless, any paid employment is sufficient to exclude the person from the count of the "unemployed,"
though not from a condition of **underemployment**.

Underemployed workers represent available labor resources
that are not being fully utilized. They are part of our unemployment
problem, even if they are not officially counted as unemployed. In
1980 over 4 million workers were underemployed in the U.S. economy. The extent of underemployment grew even further in the recession of 1981–82.

The phantom unemployed

Although discouraged and underemployed workers are not counted
in official unemployment statistics, some of the people who are
counted probably should not be. Many people report that they are

Copyright 1974 LOS ANGELES TIMES. Reprinted with permission.

actively seeking a job even when they have little interest in finding employment. To some extent, public policy actually encourages such behavior. For example, most adult welfare recipients are required to look for a job, even though many welfare mothers would prefer to spend all their time raising their children. Their resultant job search is likely to be perfunctory at best, including perhaps only one trip to the state employment office. Similarly, most states require recipients of unemployment compensation to provide evidence that they are looking for a job, even though some recipients may prefer a brief period of joblessness. Here again, reported unemployment may conceal labor force nonparticipation.

A HARDSHIP INDEX   In recognition of the limitations of current unemployment statistics, President Carter established a National Commission on Employment and Unemployment Statistics. He instructed the commission to review our measures of unemployment. In 1979 it recommended a variety of changes in the way statistics on unemployment are collected and interpreted. In addition to these statistical adjustments, the commission also recommended development of a new "hardship index." The commission recognized that many unemployed, discouraged, and underemployed individuals suffer

10 million people without jobs— who they are

Exceptionally high unemployment is sending shock waves through the U.S.—causing hardships for millions of Americans, damaging the economies of entire regions, deepening government deficits and endangering President Reagan's popular support.

After a slight downturn a month earlier, the nation's jobless rate jumped upward in February to 8.8 percent of the work force—nearly matching the post–World War II high in 1975 of 9 percent. In all, the number of jobless approached 10 million.

Not included in the unemployment tally are 1.2 million more jobless people described by government analysts as "discouraged workers," who have given up looking for work, as well as 5.6 million "underemployed" who hold part-time, low-paying jobs because they cannot find full-time work.

Hardest hit by the jobless spiral are blue-collar workers, blacks and teenagers. The heaviest concentrations of unemployment are in the auto, steel and construction industries clustered in factory towns of the upper Midwest, the timberlands of Washington and Oregon and some manufacturing centers in the industrial Northeast. The impact is devastating for these local economies, which must adjust to less retail spending and reduced tax revenues.

"We have a more severe unemployment problem now than we've had since the Great Depression," declares Charles Killingsworth, economist at Michigan State University and a member of the National Council on Employment Policy.

Reprinted from *U.S. News & World Report.* Copyright © 1982 U.S. News & World Report, Inc.

Note: Unemployment rates are for nonfarm workers aged 14 and older (1900–60) or 16 and older (1961–82).

FIGURE 5.4 THE UNEMPLOYMENT RECORD

Unemployment rates reached record heights during the Great Depression. The postwar record is much better than the prewar record, even though "full employment" has been infrequent.

Source: U.S. Department of Labor.

substantial economic losses. Others, including the phantom unemployed, bear minimal losses. To distinguish between these two groups, the commission recommended that an individual's earnings be compared to his or her family's needs. Individuals whose earnings are too low to satisfy the economic needs of their families would be counted as "hardship" cases. These low earnings could result from any combination of unemployment, low wages, and discouragement. Such an index would improve our understanding of the microeconomic losses associated with unemployment but would not replace unemployment statistics.

THE HISTORICAL RECORD

Figure 5.4 provides a historical summary of unemployment in the United States. The exceptionally high unemployment rates in the middle of the graph are a vivid reminder of the realities of the Great Depression, when as much as one-fourth of the labor force was unemployed. The hard lesson taught by the Great Depression—and enshrined in modern economic theory—is that high rates of unemployment can arise and persist in the absence of effective public policy. In recognition of this possibility, Congress has instructed the president to pursue economic policies that will help ensure full employment. The Full Employment and Balanced Growth Act of 1978 (the Humphrey-Hawkins Act) instructs the president to ensure "fulfillment of the right to full opportunities of all individuals able, willing, and seeking to work."

The means for moving the economy closer to our institutional production possibilities, including a broad array of monetary, fiscal, and other policies, are discussed in detail in Chapters 7 through 13. Before looking at the potential of economic policy, however, we need to have a clearer notion of what we mean by "full employment."

DEFINING FULL EMPLOYMENT

Our historical record demonstrates that we have never completely eliminated unemployment. Since 1900, the lowest unemployment rate we have attained is 1.2 percent, and that was in 1944, when the economy was mobilized for war production. Other industrialized countries have had somewhat more success in maintaining low unemployment rates (see Figure 5.5), but none have reached zero unemployment. In view of this record, it has been suggested that "full employment" should not be understood as "zero unemployment," but rather as some *low* (nonzero) level of unemployment.

At first blush, the abandonment of zero unemployment as a national goal might look like an artful attempt to rationalize our historical failures. But there are reasons for believing that zero unemployment is neither possible nor desirable.

Seasonal unemployment

seasonal unemployment: Unemployment due to seasonal changes in employment or labor supply.

Seasonal variations in employment conditions are one persistent source of unemployment. Some joblessness is virtually inevitable as long as we continue to grow crops, build houses, or go skiing at certain seasons of the year. At the end of each of these "seasons," thousands of workers must go searching for new jobs, experiencing some **seasonal unemployment** in the process.

Seasonal fluctuations also arise on the supply side of the labor market. Teenage unemployment rates, for example, rise sharply in

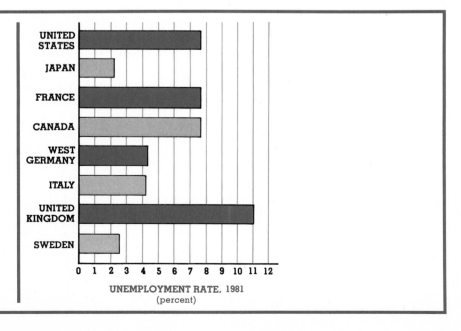

FIGURE 5.5 UNEMPLOYMENT RATES IN MAJOR INDUSTRIAL COUNTRIES, 1981

Many other countries have had more success than the United States in reducing unemployment.

Source: *Economic Report of the President,* 1982.

UNEMPLOYMENT RATE, 1981
(percent)

the summer as students look for temporary jobs.[4] To avoid such unemployment completely, we would either have to keep everyone in school or ensure that all students went immediately from the classroom to the workroom. Neither alternative is likely, much less desirable.[5]

Frictional unemployment

There are other reasons for expecting a certain amount of unemployment. Many workers have sound financial or personal reasons for leaving one job to look for another. In the process of moving from one job to another, a person may well miss a few days or even weeks of work without any serious personal or social consequences. On the contrary, job seekers who end up in more satisfying or higher-paying jobs as a result of their job search will be better off, and so will the economy.

The same is true of students first entering the labor market. It is not likely that you will find a job the moment you leave school. Nor should you take any job just because it's available. If you spend some time looking for work, you are more likely to find a job that you like. The job-search period gives you an opportunity to find out what kinds of jobs are available, what skills they require, and what they pay. Accordingly, a brief period of job search for those persons entering the labor market may benefit both the individuals involved and the larger economy. The unemployment associated with all of these kinds of job search is referred to as **frictional unemployment.**

frictional unemployment:
Brief periods of unemployment experienced by people moving between jobs or into the labor market; not related to basic demand or supply inadequacies.

Three things distinguish frictional unemployment from other kinds of unemployment. First, we assume that enough jobs exist for those who are frictionally unemployed; that is, there is adequate demand for labor. Second, we assume that those who are frictionally unemployed can perform the available jobs. Third, we assume that the period of job search will be relatively short. Under these conditions, frictional unemployment resembles an unconventional game of musical chairs. There are enough chairs of the right size for everyone, and people dance around them for only a brief period of time.

No one knows for sure just how much of our unemployment problem is frictional. Indeed, many observers have noted that the amount of "friction" in the system is sensitive both to the level of economic activity and to political interests. Most economists agree, however, that friction alone is responsible for an unemployment rate of 2 to 3 percent. Accordingly, our definition of "full employment" should allow for at least this much unemployment.

Structural unemployment

Not all unemployment is frictional, however. For many job seekers the period between jobs may drag on for months or even years be-

---

[4] The school calendar was originally designed to accommodate the demand for agricultural labor during the harvest months. Since then, however, agricultural employment has declined sharply.

[5] Seasonal variations in employment and labor supply not only create some unemployment in the annual averages, but also distort monthly comparisons. Unemployment rates are always higher in February (when farming and housing construction come to a virtual standstill) and June (when a mass of students go looking for summer jobs). The Labor Department adjusts monthly unemployment rates according to this seasonal pattern, and reports "seasonally adjusted" unemployment rates for each month. Seasonal adjustments do not alter *annual* averages, however.

cause they do not have the skills that employers require. Imagine, for example, the predicament of coal miners when their mines are mechanized. If they have worked in the mines for 10 to 15 years, they are unlikely to have developed other occupational skills. They may be first-rate miners, but they stand little chance of filling job openings for computer programmers. In this case, there may be as many vacant jobs in the economy as job seekers, but the unemployed coal miners will not be able to fill any of them. Hence we say that the coal miners are **structurally unemployed.**

Teenagers from urban slums also suffer from structural unemployment. Most poor teenagers have an inadequate education, few job-related skills, and even less work experience. From their perspective, almost all decent jobs are "out of reach." As a consequence, these teenagers, many of whom are black or from other minority groups, remain unemployed far longer than can be explained by frictional forces.

Structural unemployment thus violates the second condition for frictional unemployment: structural unemployment is analogous to a musical chairs game in which there are enough chairs for everyone, but some of them are too small to sit in.

Structural unemployment is clearly a more serious concern than frictional unemployment and is incompatible with any notion of "full employment." But there are still other forms of unemployment. **Cyclical unemployment** occurs when there are simply not enough jobs to go around, when the number of workers demanded falls short of the number of persons in the labor force. This is not a case of mobility between jobs (frictional unemployment) or even of job seekers' skills (structural unemployment). Rather, it is simply an inadequate level of demand for goods and services, and so for labor to be used in the production process. Cyclical unemployment thus resembles the most familiar form of musical chairs, in which the number of chairs is always less than the number of players.

The Great Depression is the most striking example of cyclical unemployment. The dramatic increase in unemployment rates that began in 1930 (see Figure 5.4) was not due to any increase in "friction" or to a sudden decline in workers' skills. Instead, the high rates of unemployment that persisted for a *decade* were due to a sudden decline in the market demand for goods and services. How do we know? Just notice what happened to our unemployment rate when the demand for military goods and services increased in 1941!

THE FULL-EMPLOYMENT GOAL

In later chapters we will examine the causes of cyclical unemployment and explore some potential policy responses. At this juncture, however, we have at least established some perspective on the goal of full employment. In particular, we can say that our goal is to avoid as much cyclical and structural unemployment as possible, while keeping frictional unemployment within reasonable bounds.

As guidelines for public policy, these perspectives are admit-

---

structural unemployment:
Unemployment caused by a mismatch between the skills (or location) of job seekers and the requirements (or location) of available jobs.

Cyclical unemployment

cyclical unemployment:
Unemployment attributable to a lack of job vacancies; unemployment that results from an inadequate level of aggregate demand.

tedly vague. It is easier, for example, to define structural and cyclical unemployment than to measure them with precision. As many economists have observed, what appears to be structural (or even frictional!) unemployment often vanishes when the demand for labor increases. Similarly, it is easier to advise policy makers to seek the "lowest possible" level of cyclical unemployment than to specify what that level is. As a consequence, we end up agreeing that "full employment" is something more than zero unemployment, but without a more exact numerical goal.

The first attempt to define "full employment" more precisely was undertaken in the early 1960s. At that time the Council of Economic Advisers decided that a 4 percent level of unemployment was both possible and consistent with our other economic goals (price stability in particular). A few years later there was some embarrassment as well as applause when the national unemployment rate fell below this benchmark.

The 1970s brought about not only sharply higher unemployment rates but also increasing doubts about the economy's ability to attain 4 percent unemployment. Between 1956 and 1979 the proportion of teenagers in the labor force increased from 6 percent to 9 percent, thereby contributing to increased frictional and structural unemployment. During the same period of time, the proportion of adult women in the labor force grew from 29 percent to over 38 percent. Many of these women were entering the labor force for the first time—or reentering it after long periods of homemaking. As a consequence, frictional and structural unemployment increased still further. Because of this, the Council of Economic Advisers estimated that a 4.9 percent rate of unemployment should be regarded as **"full employment"** (or, alternatively, "high employment"). In the council's view, that was the rate of unemployment that would not contribute to higher rates of inflation.[6]

The U.S. Congress provided an alternative definition of "full employment" in 1978. According to the Full Employment and Balanced Growth Act of 1978 (commonly called the Humphrey-Hawkins Act), our national goal is to attain a 4 percent rate of unemployment. The act also requires a goal of 3 percent inflation. The act stipulated that both goals were to be met by 1983. There was an "escape clause," however. In the event that both goals could not be met, the president might alter the timetable for achieving "full employment." In the interim, higher "provisional" definitions of unemployment might be used. Most popular definitions of full employment now converge around 5 percent.

full employment: The lowest rate of unemployment compatible with price stability; variously estimated at between 4 and 6 percent unemployment.

The GNP gap

full-employment GNP: The total market value of final goods and services that could be produced in a given time period at full employment; potential GNP.

By defining "full employment" as 5 percent unemployment, we imply that only 95 percent of our labor force can be employed without causing other economic problems (particularly inflation). Accordingly, we define **full-employment GNP** as the annual value of final goods and services that could be produced at "full employ-

[6] The effects of very low unemployment rates on inflation are discussed in Chapter 13.

"I don't <u>like</u> six-per-cent unemployment, either. But I can live with it."

Drawing by Lorenz; © 1974 The New Yorker Magazine, Inc.

GNP gap: The difference between full-employment GNP and actual GNP.

ment," that is, with 5 percent unemployment. Full-employment GNP is the market value of our institutional production possibilities.

By comparing full-employment GNP with actual GNP, we can calculate the implied loss of goods and services associated with our failure to attain full employment. This loss is referred to as the **GNP gap.** As we noted earlier, the GNP gap in 1980 amounted to $200 billion, or approximately $900 per person. Figure 5.6 illustrates the dimensions of the GNP gap for recent years.

SUMMARY

■ To understand the dimensions of unemployment, we need to distinguish the labor force from the larger population. Only people who are working (employed) or spend some time looking for a job (unemployed) are participants in the labor force. People who are neither working nor looking for work are outside the labor force.

■ The distinction between the labor force and our larger population is mirrored in a distinction between institutional production possibilities and physical production possibilities. Institutional production possibilities express the rate of annual output we could attain if we fully and efficiently employed our entire labor force and heeded social constraints on the use of resources and technology. Physical production possibilities express the maximum output that could be produced if the entire population were put to work and no constraints were imposed on the use of either resources or technology.

FIGURE 5.6 ACTUAL AND
POTENTIAL GROSS NATIONAL
PRODUCT . . .

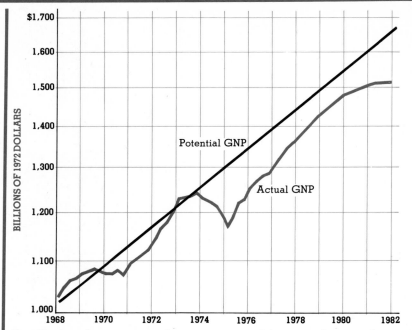

Note: The vertical axis is measured in ratio terms; equal distances indicate equal percentage changes rather than equal absolute changes.

AND HOW ECONOMISTS
CALCULATE IT

Multiply 95% of the normal labor force (which is considered full employment) by the normal hours of work per year by normal productivity. The GNP gap is determined by subtracting actual gross national product from potential GNP.

Potential GNP = $\begin{bmatrix}\text{95\% of normal}\\\text{labor force}\end{bmatrix} \times \begin{bmatrix}\text{normal hours of}\\\text{work per year}\end{bmatrix} \times \begin{bmatrix}\text{normal}\\\text{productivity}\end{bmatrix}$

GNP gap   = potential GNP − actual GNP

Source: Council of Economic Advisers.

■ The macroeconomic loss imposed by unemployment is reduced output of goods and services. The microeconomic losses to those individuals actually out of work include lost income, heightened insecurity, and even reduced longevity.

■ Unemployment is distributed unevenly; blacks, teenagers, and the less educated have much higher rates of unemployment. Also bearing these losses are discouraged workers—those who have stopped looking for work but still want a job. The same losses are experienced by underemployed workers—those who are working at part-time or menial jobs because they cannot find full-time jobs equal to their training or potential.

■ There are four types of unemployment: seasonal, frictional, structural, and cyclical. Because some seasonal and frictional unemployment is both inevitable and even desirable, full employment is not defined as zero unemployment. Instead, full employment is often defined as an unemployment rate of 5 percent or more.

■ The GNP gap—the difference between actual output and our potential output at full employment—measures the loss of goods and services implied by our failure to maintain full employment.

Terms to remember

Define the following terms:

labor force
physical production possibilities
institutional production
  possibilities
unemployment
unemployment rate
discouraged worker
underemployment

seasonal unemployment
frictional unemployment
structural unemployment
cyclical unemployment
full employment
full-employment GNP
GNP gap

Questions for discussion

1. Is it possible for unemployment rates to increase at the same time that the number of employed persons is increasing? How?

2. As increasing numbers of women enter the labor force, what happens to (a) institutional production possibilities? (b) physical production possibilities? (c) unemployment rates?

3. President Reagan and his advisers have suggested that our definition of "full employment" should be an unemployment rate in excess of 5 percent, in large part because the proportion of teenagers and women in the labor force has increased. What was the basis for this suggestion? Do you agree?

4. Can you identify three institutional constraints on the use of resources (factors of production)? What has motivated these constraints?

Problem

The unemployment rate in 1982 reached 10 percent. Using the Council of Economic Advisers' definition of "full employment":

(a) Determine how far we were from full employment in 1982.

(b) Calculate the GNP gap under the assumption that each unemployed worker could produce $25,000 of goods and services.

CHAPTER 6

INFLATION

Inflation is America's greatest worry. That, at least, is the message conveyed by public-opinion polls. Nearly two-thirds of the persons surveyed by the Gallup poll in 1981 said that the cost of living was the most serious problem (economic or otherwise) confronting the nation. Nearly 90 percent of those interviewed believed that prices would rise at a faster rate in the year ahead. These sentiments were not unique to 1981. In virtually every major public-opinion poll since 1940, Americans have expressed an overriding fear of inflation.

It is difficult to explain this great fear of inflation in terms of our historical experiences. By international standards the U.S. economy has experienced relatively low rates of inflation. In the 1970s the U.S. inflation rate averaged around 7 percent—far below the inflation rates of Japan (9.1 percent), Great Britain (13.3 percent), Mexico (16.7 percent), Israel (35 percent), Chile (163.2 percent!), and most of the other countries shown in Table 6.1. Moreover, only *once*—and then only briefly—have we experienced really extreme inflation. And that was during the Revolutionary War (1775–83), when prices more than *doubled* in a single year (see p. 278). Other countries—including Germany in the 1920s and Hungary and China in the 1940s—have experienced much worse hyperinflation, with prices actually doubling *every week*.

Despite our comparatively mild experiences with inflation, fear of rising prices has had a major influence on U.S. economic policy. Every American president since Franklin Roosevelt has expressed a

TABLE 6.1   INFLATION AROUND
THE WORLD

The rate of inflation in the U.S.
economy is quite low by international
standards. Many countries continue to
grow and prosper despite much
higher rates of inflation. What is it,
then, that makes inflation so feared?

Country	Annual inflation rate (average, per year)
Argentina	146.0
Israel	35.4
Mexico	16.7
South Korea	12.6
Great Britain	13.3
Kenya	12.2
Japan	9.1
France	9.1
Egypt	8.3
Canada	7.8
United States	7.2
Venezuela	8.1
West Germany	5.1

Source: International Monetary Fund.

determination to keep prices from rising. President Reagan has been
no exception. Indeed, in his first State of the Union address to Congress, Reagan warned that continuing inflation threatened to "put an
end to everything we believe in and to our dreams for the future."

The purpose of this chapter is to examine the nature of inflation.
Why is inflation so feared? How does it affect individual consumers,
workers, and businesses? Is it a real threat to our economy? As we
will discover, inflation is a serious problem, but not for the reasons
most people cite.

WHAT IS "INFLATION"?

**inflation: An increase in the
average level of prices of
goods and services.**

Most people associate **inflation** with price increases on specific
goods and services. The economy is not necessarily experiencing an
inflation, however, every time the price of a cup of coffee goes up.
We must be careful to distinguish the phenomenon of inflation from
price increases for specific goods. *Inflation is an increase in the
average level of prices, not a change in any specific price.*

Suppose you wanted to know the average price of fruit in the
supermarket. Surely you would not have much success in seeking
out an average fruit—nobody would be quite sure what you had in
mind. You might have some success, however, if you sought out the
prices of apples, oranges, cherries, and peaches. Knowing the price
of each kind of fruit, you could then compute the average price of
fruit. The resultant figure would not refer to any particular product,
but would convey a sense of how much a typical basket of fruit
might cost. By repeating these calculations every day, you could
then determine whether fruit prices, *on average*, were changing. On
occasion, you might even notice that apple prices rose while orange
prices fell, leaving the *average* price of fruit unchanged.

The same kinds of calculations are made to measure inflation in

deflation: A decrease in the average level of prices of goods and services.

the entire economy. We first determine the average price of all output—the average price level—then look for changes in that average. A rise in the average price level is referred to as inflation.

The average price level may fall as well as rise. A decline in average prices—a **deflation**—occurs when price decreases on some goods and services outweigh price increases on all others. Although we have not experienced any general deflation since 1940, general price declines were frequent in earlier periods.

Relative prices vs. the price level

relative price: The price of one good in comparison with the price of other goods.

Because inflation and deflation are measured in terms of average price levels, it is possible for individual prices to rise or fall continuously without changing the average price level. We already noted, for example, that the price of apples can rise without increasing the average price of fruit, so long as the price of some other fruit (e.g., oranges) falls. In such circumstances, **relative prices** are changing, but not average prices. An increase in the relative price of apples, for example, simply means that apples have become more expensive in comparison with other fruits (or any other goods or services).

Changes in relative prices may occur in a period of stable average prices, or in periods of inflation or deflation. In fact, in an economy as vast as ours—where literally millions of goods and services are exchanged in the factor and product markets—relative prices are always changing. Indeed, relative price changes are an essential ingredient of the market mechanism. Recall (from Chapter 2) what happens when the market price of typing services rises relative to other goods and services. This (relative) price rise alerts typists (producers) to increase their output, cutting back on other production or leisure activities. To the extent that the increase in the *relative* price of typing expresses increasing consumer demand for this product, such changes in the mix of output are desirable.

A general inflation—an increase in the average price level—does not perform this same market function. If all prices rise at the same rate, price increases for specific goods are of little value as production signals. In less extreme cases, when most but not all prices are rising, changes in relative prices do occur, but are not so immediately apparent. Table 6.2 reminds us that some prices do fall even during periods of general inflation.

MICRO CONSEQUENCES OF INFLATION

We must distinguish between average prices and relative prices if we are to understand the true consequences of inflation. Popular (and presidential) opinion notwithstanding, it is simply not true that everyone is worse off when prices rise. Although inflation makes some people worse off, it makes other people better off. Some people even get rich when prices rise! The micro consequences of inflation are reflected in redistributions of income and wealth, not general declines in either measure of our economic welfare. These redistributions occur because people buy different combinations of goods and services, own different assets, and sell various goods or services

TABLE 6.2 PRICES THAT HAVE FALLEN	Item	Early price	Later price
Inflation refers to an increase in the *average* price level. It does not mean that *all* prices are rising. In fact, many prices fall, even during periods of inflation.	Long-distance telephone call (3-minute rate, coast to coast)	$ 20.70 (1915)	$ 0.35 (1982)
	Pocket electronic calculator	200.00 (1972)	6.50 (1982)
	Digital watch	2,000.00 (1972)	9.50 (1982)
	Computer time (memory time), per minute	18.00 (1967)	4.00 (1979)
	Polaroid camera (basic black and white)	100.00 (1963)	19.00 (1979)
	Panty hose	2.16 (1967)	1.29 (1982)
	Penicillin (100 tablets)	5.74 (1967)	4.19 (1976)
	Ballpoint pen	0.89 (1965)	0.29 (1982)
	Transistor radio	55.00 (1967)	15.00 (1982)
	Video recorder	1,500.00 (1977)	1,000.00 (1982)
	Personal computer (basic 4k)	599.00 (1979)	399.00 (1982)
	Microwave oven	400.00 (1972)	250.00 (1982)
	Contact lenses	275.00 (1972)	115.00 (1982)

(including labor). The impact of inflation on individuals therefore depends on how the prices of the goods and services each person buys or sells actually change. In this sense, *inflation acts just like a tax, taking income or wealth from some people and giving it to others.* This "tax" is levied through changes in prices, changes in incomes, and changes in wealth.

Price effects

Price changes are the most familiar of inflation's pains. If you have been paying tuition, you know how the pain feels. In the last few years the average cost of tuition has increased rapidly. In 1970 the average tuition at public colleges and universities was $350 per year. Today the average tuition exceeds $700. At private universities, tuition has also more than doubled in the last ten years, to over $4,000. You don't need a whole course in economics to figure out the implications of these tuition hikes. To stay in college, you (or your parents) must forgo increasing amounts of other goods and services. You end up being worse off, since you cannot buy as many goods and services as you were able to buy before tuition went up.

The effect of tuition increases on your economic welfare is reflected in the distinction between nominal income and real income. **Nominal income** is the amount of money you receive in a particular time period; it is measured in current dollars. **Real income,** by contrast, is the purchasing power of that money, as measured by the quantity of goods and services your dollars will buy. If the number of dollars you receive every year is always the same, your *nominal income* doesn't change—but your *real income* will fall when tuition increases.

nominal income: The amount of money income received in a given time period, measured in current dollars.

real income: Income in constant dollars; nominal income adjusted for inflation.

Suppose your parents agree to give you $6,000 a year while you're in school. Out of that $6,000 you must pay for your tuition, room and board, books, and everything else. The budget for your first year at school might look like this:

First Year's Budget

Nominal income	$6,000
Consumption	
Tuition	$3,000
Room and board	2,000
Books	300
Everything else	700
Total	$6,000

After paying for all your essential expenses, you have $700 to spend on clothes, entertainment, or anything else you want. That's not exactly living high, but it's not poverty.

Now suppose tuition increases to $3,500 in your second year, while all other prices remain the same. What will happen to your nominal income? Nothing. Unless your parents take pity on you, you will still be getting $6,000 a year. Your nominal income is unchanged. Your *real* income, however, will suffer. This is evident in the second year's budget:

Second Year's Budget

Nominal income	$6,000
Consumption	
Tuition	$3,500
Room and board	2,000
Books	300
Everything else	200
Total	$6,000

You now have to use more of your income to pay tuition. That means you have less income to spend on other things. You will have to cut back somewhere. Since room and board and books still cost $2,300 per year, there is only one place to cut—the category of "everything else." After tuition increases, you can spend only $200 per year on movies, clothes, pizzas, and dates—not $700, as in the "good old days." This $500 reduction in purchasing power represents a *real* income loss. Even though your *nominal* income is still $6,000, your *real* income is only $5,500. You have $500 less of "everything else" in your second year than you had in the first.

Although tuition hikes reduce the real income of students and their families, nonstudents are not troubled at all by such price increases. A nonstudent with $6,000 of nominal income could continue to buy the same goods and services she was buying before tuition went up. In fact, if tuition *doubled*, nonstudents really wouldn't care. They could continue to buy the same bundle of goods and services they had been buying all along. In other words, increases in tuition reduce the real incomes only of people who go to

Allowances Stay Flat, Candy Rises— and Kids Lose Their Innocence

---

Hurt by Inflation, Children Work, Save and Grumble, Just Like Their Parents

Lauren Krzywkowski is fed up with inflation. She's working as hard as ever, she says, but has less to show for her efforts. To supplement her meager wages, Miss Krzywkowski has begun to seek out odd jobs. "They need it, I do it," she says.

Kelly Collins is feeling the pressure, too. She has been on a fixed income for three years. When asked about inflation, she shakes her head and says glumly, "It's depressing." Common enough sentiments, these. Except for one thing: The ages of the beleaguered citizens are, respectively, 12 and 14. If schoolyard chatter is any indication, inflation has joined thunderstorms, low grades and neighborhood bullies among kids' most dreaded adversaries.

"It's hard to be a kid today because you've got a lot to worry about, including money, which is one of the biggest problems," explains Miss Krzywkowski, a seventh grader in Cleveland. She says the $1-a-week allowance she usually gets is insufficient to buy the snacks and other things she enjoys. "I wish I was back in the good old days when you could go to the store with 10 cents and have a field day," she says.

No Small Problem

Many parents undoubtedly believe that the problem of "kidflation" is child's play. "In a lot of ways, adults don't give that much import to kids' items going up in price, because the items are discretionary," says Charlotte Baecher, editor of Penny Power, a magazine published by Consumers Union for those aged eight to 12. But many kids themselves feel quite harassed by increasing prices. So do manufacturers who vie for the estimated $45 billion that children aged six to 16 spend annually.

Discretionary Income

Although the government doesn't keep such statistics and private research is very limited, there are indications that the buying power of children has shrunk significantly over the past five years. Because even dime and quarter increases in the cost of children's items often mean huge leaps in terms of percentages (and weekly allowances), "kidflation" in some cases has outpaced the adult variety.

Based on conversations with over 50 children, this newspaper compiled a "market basket" of 15 items frequently purchased by children, then determined from manufacturers approximately what has happened to the retail prices of those items. While the resulting "Kiddie Consumer Price Index" isn't scientific, and prices may vary from city to city, it offers some insight into what the younger generation is up against.

KIDDIE CONSUMER MARKET BASKET

	1975	1979	1980
1. Chicago White Sox general admission ticket	$2.00	$2.00	$3.00
2. Jack & Jill Soap Bubbles	.29	.45	.45
3. Wham-O Regular Frisbee	.97	1.26	1.29
4. MAD magazine	.50	.75	.75
5. Vending machine 12-oz. canned soft drink	.20	.35	.40
6. Wrigley's chewing gum (7-stick pack)	.15	.20	.25
7. Hershey's milk chocolate candy (per 1.05 oz.)	.15	.22	.25
8. Marvel comic book (per 18 editorial pages)	.25	.40	.41
9. McDonald's hamburger, small fries and 12-oz. soft drink	.80	1.18	1.39
10. Arista record album	6.98	7.98	8.98
11. Crayola crayons (8 crayons)	.25	.35	.45
12. Duncan Imperial Yo-yo	1.29	1.49	1.79
13. Milky Way candy bar (per ounce)	.083	.137	.122
14. Drumstick (ice cream with chocolate and nuts)	.20	.30	.35
15. Topps chewing gum football trading cards (cost per dozen)	.18	.20	.25
Kiddie Consumer Price Index	14.29	17.27	20.13
Consumer Price Index	166.3	229.9	258.4

—Dean Rotbart

college. Likewise, when the prices of candy, gum, and comic books rise, little kids are hurt the most.

There are two basic lessons about inflation to be learned from these sad stories:

Not all prices rise at the same rate during an inflation. In our example, tuition increased substantially while other prices remained steady. Hence the "average" rate of price increase was not

TABLE 6.3 NOT ALL PRICES RISE AT THE SAME RATE

The average rate of inflation conceals substantial differences in the price changes of specific goods and services. The impact of inflation on individuals depends in part on which goods and services are consumed. People who buy goods whose prices are rising fastest lose more real income. In 1981, college students were particularly hard hit by inflation.

Item	Price change, 1980–81 (percent)	Item	Price change, 1980–81 (percent)
Food		**Bus fares**	+ 28.5
Steak	− 2.1	**Bicycles**	+ 5.0
Chicken	− 8.1	**College expenses**	
Fish	+ 3.7	Tuition	+ 12.8
Apples	+ 30.0	Textbooks	+ 14.6
Sugar	− 33.4	**Other**	
Coffee	− 11.6	Beer	+ 5.8
Transportation		Cigarettes	+ 7.6
New cars	+ 6.8	Jewelry	− 1.4
Used cars	+ 20.3	**Average inflation rate**	+ 8.9

Source: U.S. Bureau of Labor Statistics.

representative of any particular good or service. Typically, some prices rise very rapidly, others only modestly, and still others not at all. Table 6.3 illustrates some recent variations in price changes.

Not everyone suffers equally from inflation. This follows from our first observation. Those people who consume the goods and services that are rising faster in price bear a greater burden of inflation; their real incomes fall more. Other consumers bear a lesser burden, or even none at all, depending on how fast the prices rise for the goods they enjoy.

We conclude, then, that the price increases associated with inflation redistribute real income. In the example we have discussed, college students will end up with fewer of the goods and services they desire after an inflation gets under way. Other consumers can continue to purchase at least as many goods as before, perhaps even more. Thus output is effectively *redistributed* from college students to others. Naturally, most college students aren't very happy with this outcome. Fortunately for you, inflation doesn't always work out this way.

Income effects

The redistributive effects of inflation are not limited to changes in prices. On the contrary, as we observed in Chapter 4, changes in prices automatically influence nominal incomes also.

If the price of tuition does in fact rise faster than all other prices, we can safely make three predictions:

□ The real income of college students will fall, relative to nonstudents (assuming constant nominal incomes).

□ The real income of nonstudents will rise, relative to students (assuming constant nominal incomes).

□ The *nominal* income of colleges and universities will rise.

This last prediction simply reminds us that someone always pockets higher prices. What looks like a price to a buyer looks like income to a seller. If students all pay higher tuition, the university will take in more income. To the extent that the nominal incomes of colleges and universities increase faster than average prices, they actually *benefit* from inflation. That is to say, they end up being able to buy *more* goods and services (including faculty, buildings, library books, and so on) after a period of inflation than they could before. Their real income has risen. Whether one likes this outcome or not may depend on whether anyone in the family works for the university or sells it goods and services.

On average, people's incomes do keep pace with inflation. Again, this is a direct consequence of the circular flow: what one person pays out someone else takes in. Hence, if prices are rising, incomes must be rising, too. Notice in Figure 6.1 that average wages have pretty much risen in step with prices. From this perspective, it makes no sense to say that "inflation hurts everybody." On *average*, at least, we are no worse off when prices rise, since our (average) incomes increase at the same time.[1]

No one is exactly "average," of course. In reality, some people's incomes rise faster than inflation while others' increase more slowly. Hence the redistributive effects of inflation also originate in varying rates of growth in nominal income. If everyone's income increased at the rate of inflation, inflation would not have such a large redistributive effect. In reality, however, nominal incomes increase at very different rates.

[1] In fact, average incomes have usually risen even faster than prices, because of increasing output per worker. Thus average real incomes have increased significantly over time. In those years when wages did not keep up with prices, taxes were to blame.

FIGURE 6.1 NOMINAL WAGES AND PRICES

Inflation implies not only higher prices but higher wages as well. What is a price to one person is income to someone else. Hence inflation cannot make everyone worse off. Since 1967 nominal hourly wages have actually increased a bit faster than prices, due to gains in real output per worker (productivity).

Source: *Economic Report of the President,* 1982.

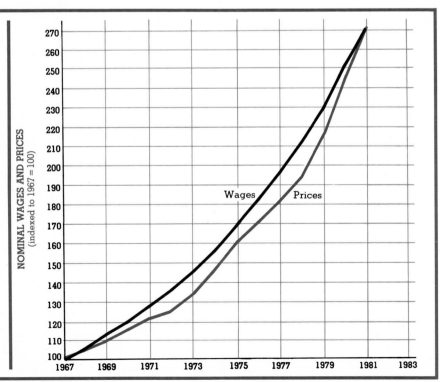

As Table 6.4 indicates, schoolteachers, bureaucrats, and welfare recipients have not been very successful in the competition for nominal income. As a consequence, their real incomes have fallen. By contrast, workers who have successfully negotiated higher (nominal) salaries as prices rose managed to stay ahead of inflation. Older people who depend largely on social security benefits have also been helped by inflation, despite popular belief to the contrary.

Wealth effects

The same kind of redistribution occurs between those who hold some form of wealth and those who do not. Suppose that on January 1 you deposit $100 in a savings account, where it earns 5 percent interest until you withdraw it on December 31. At the end of the year you will have more nominal wealth ($105) than you started with ($100). But what if all prices have doubled in the meantime? In that case, your $105 will buy you no more at the end of the year than $52.50 would have bought you at the beginning. In other words, inflation in this case reduces the *real* value of your savings, and you end up worse off than those individuals who spent all their income earlier in the year!

Inflation also tends to redistribute wealth from people who rent homes or apartments to those who own them. The market prices of homes tend to increase at least as fast as the pace of inflation. Hence the real value of homeownership is not diminished by inflation. On the contrary, the real value of houses and condominiums usually increases during an inflation. By contrast, people who rent homes or apartments usually discover that inflation forces them to spend a larger fraction of their incomes on housing costs (rent); thus their real incomes fall.

TABLE 6.4 THE REAL STORY OF INCOME

Nominal incomes rose greatly during the 1970s, largely as a result of inflation. In the process real incomes were redistributed. People whose nominal incomes rose faster than inflation enjoyed gains in real income. Others, such as schoolteachers, bureaucrats, and welfare recipients, suffered losses in real income, despite increased nominal incomes.

	Nominal income		Change in real after-tax income
	1970	*1980*	
Gainers			
Steelworker	$ 8,653	$23,336	+ 24%
Social security recipient	2,387	6,145	+ 21%
Autoworker	8,844	20,520	+ 6%
Coal miner	9,693	22,666	+ 6%
Postal worker	8,120	18,344	+ 6%
Senior stenographer	6,247	13,876	+ 4%
Losers			
Typist	$ 4,717	$ 9,161	− 9%
Chief accountant	18,780	41,092	− 7%
Accountant	10,686	21,299	−11%
Teacher	9,269	17,264	−15%
Federal bureaucrat	11,065	19,910	−17%
Welfare recipient (AFDC)	2,198	3,357	−28%

Sources: U.S. Social Security Administration and *U.S. News & World Report*, March 30, 1980.

The real story of wealth

How investments have fared over the past decade:

STOCKS

Common stocks have lost ground to inflation in the 1968-78 years.

The record: $10,000 invested in stocks in 1968 would be worth about $10,310 today. Value in 1968 dollars, $5,460.

FARMLAND

Well-located land in most parts of the country has been an effective hedge against the deteriorating dollar in recent years.

The record: An investment of $10,000 in farmland in 1968 would be worth about $28,800 today. Value in 1968 dollars, $15,249.

A HOME

As a general rule, people who have owned a house in the past 10 years have seen it rise sharply in market value.

The record: Each $10,000 invested in a new home in 1968 would be worth on the average about $22,200 on today's market. Value in 1968 dollars, $11,758.

A BOND

Corporate or government bonds suffered because the fixed rate of interest doesn't change with inflation.

The record: Bonds of 10-year maturity bought at par for $10,000 in 1968 are now worth $10,000 when cashed in. Value in 1968 dollars, $5,297.

AN OFFICE BUILDING

The rapid rise in construction costs in the past decade has enhanced the value of many office buildings.

The record: For every $10,000 invested in an office building in 1968, today's value would be $21,580. Value in 1968 dollars, $11,430

COLLECTABLES

Money put into tangible assets — antiques, art objects, collectors' items — has tended to appreciate more than most other forms of investment.

The record: A study by Salomon Brothers shows these compound annual rates of growth in the last decade: Chinese ceramics, 19.2%; gold, 16.3%; stamps, 15.4%; coins, 13%; diamonds, 12.6%; silver, 9.1%. Annual rate of rise in consumer price index, 6.8%.

Reprinted from *U.S. News & World Report*, October 2, 1978. Copyright © 1978 U.S. News & World Report, Inc.

By altering relative prices, incomes, and the real value of wealth, then, inflation turns out to be a mechanism for redistributing incomes. The mechanics of the process are simple:

- People whose nominal incomes are rising faster than the rate of inflation end up with a larger share of total income.
- People who prefer goods and services that are increasing in price least quickly end up with a larger share of real income.
- People who own assets that are increasing in real value end up better off than others.

On the other hand, people whose nominal incomes do not keep pace with inflation end up with smaller shares of total output. The same thing is true of those who enjoy goods that are rising fastest in price or who hold assets that are declining in value. In this sense, inflation acts just like a tax, taking income or wealth from one group and giving it to another. But we have no assurance that this particular tax will behave like Robin Hood, taking from the rich and giving to the poor. Most important, it is a tax that is not subject to sociopolitical controls; it is a capricious tax.

Social tensions

Because of its redistributive effects, inflation also increases social and economic tensions. Tensions between labor and management, between government and the people, and among consumers may overwhelm a society and its institutions. As Gardner Ackley of the

INFLATION'S IMPACT

In recent years the rate of inflation has been in the range of 8 to 10 percent. President Reagan set a goal of reducing inflation to around 5 percent. Would an inflation reduction of this magnitude really make much difference? One way to find out is to see how a specific sum of money will shrink in real value over the next ten years. Here's what would happen to the real value of $1,000 from January 1, 1983, to January 1, 1993, at four different inflation rates:

PURCHASING POWER OF $1,000 AFTER INFLATION

Year	Annual inflation rate			
	5 percent	7 percent	8 percent	10 percent
1983	$1,000	$1,000	$1,000	$1,000
1984	952	935	926	909
1985	907	873	857	826
1986	864	816	794	751
1987	823	763	735	683
1988	784	713	681	621
1989	746	666	630	564
1990	711	623	584	513
1991	677	582	540	467
1992	645	544	500	424
1993	614	508	463	386

University of Michigan has observed, "A significant real cost of inflation is what it does to morale, to social coherence, and to people's attitudes toward each other." "This society," added Arthur Okun of the Brookings Institution, "is built on implicit and explicit contracts. . . . They are linked to the idea that the dollar means something. If you cannot depend on the value of the dollar, this system is undermined. People will constantly feel they've been fooled and cheated."[2] This is how the middle class felt in Germany in 1923 and in China in 1948, when the value of their savings was wiped out by sudden and unprecedented inflation.

Despair   Even in less extreme situations, it's not too hard to see how unsettling inflation can be. With prices changing all the time, a person's comfortable habits are easily upset. People are compelled to cope with a whole new dimension of uncertainty. Should they continue to save part of their incomes, even though the real value of savings is falling? Should they be shopping for different goods and services, at different stores? How can you boost your income to keep up with inflation? All these worries seem to accumulate quickly when prices start to rise rapidly. Psychotherapists report that such "inflation stress" leads to more frequent marital spats, increased pessimism, diminished self-confidence, and even sexual insecurity. In addition, some people turn to crime as a way of solving their inflation stress.

[2] Quoted in *Business Week*, May 22, 1978, p. 118.

"DO I HAVE YOUR ASSURANCE THAT PRICES WILL NOT BE INCREASED BEFORE WE ARE SERVED?"

Money illusion

money illusion: The use of nominal dollars rather than real dollars to gauge changes in one's income or wealth.

Even those people whose nominal incomes "keep up" with inflation often feel oppressed by rising prices. People feel that they *deserve* any increases in wages they receive. When they then discover that their higher (nominal) wages don't buy any additional goods, they feel cheated. They feel worse off, even though they have not suffered any actual loss of real income. This is a phenomenon economists call **money illusion.**

MACRO CONSEQUENCES OF INFLATION

Although redistributions of income and wealth are the primary consequences of inflation, inflation has *macro*economic effects as well. Inflation can alter the rate and mix of output by changing consump-

How inflation brings out the criminal urge

Struggling to maintain their lifestyles despite double-digit inflation and the deepening recession, a growing number of middle-class Americans are turning to crime.

Normally law-abiding citizens, aware of the lenient treatment usually accorded to white-collar criminals, are engaging in a wide range of larceny and fraud that includes—

■ Passing bad checks.

■ Embezzling funds and stealing goods from employers.
■ Shoplifting.
■ Cheating on taxes.
■ Luring friends and neighbors into illegal pyramid schemes.
■ Defrauding insurance companies.

At the same time, some businessmen caught in a crunch by the nation's economic woes are bilking customers and other businesses and plotting bankruptcy fraud.

While nonviolent white-collar crimes always hold the allure of quick and easy cash, they become especially tempting when times are bad, most crime experts believe. Money pressures can cause "a breakdown in moral behavior," asserts Saul Astor,

president of Management Safeguards, Inc., a New York–based security company.

Most of the people trying crime for the first time don't fit the normal profile of the white-collar criminal, says Astor. "They're not evil. They are earning less in real dollars and paying more for energy, more for rent, more for food. They wonder, how the hell do you cut back?"

. . . Experts predict that more middle-class Americans will take the plunge into crime in months ahead unless inflation and other nagging economic problems ease up.

—David Pike

tion, work, saving, and investment behavior. In the process, our macroeconomic profile will take on a new and possibly unwelcome appearance.

Uncertainty

One of the most immediate consequences of inflation is uncertainty. When the average price level is changing significantly in either direction, economic decisions become increasingly difficult. Should you commit yourself to four years of college, for example, if you are not certain that you or your parents will be able to afford the full costs? In a period of stable prices you can at least be fairly certain of what a college education will cost over a period of years. But if prices are rising, you no longer can be sure how large the bill will be. Under such circumstances, many individuals may decide not to enter college rather than risk the possibility of being driven out later by rising costs.

The uncertainties created by changing price levels affect production decisions as well. Imagine a firm that is considering building a new factory. Typically the construction of a factory takes two years or more, including planning, site selection, and actual construction. If construction costs or prices change rapidly during this period, the firm may find that it is unable to complete the factory, or to operate it profitably. Confronted with this added uncertainty, the firm may decide to do without a new plant, or at least to postpone its construction until a period of stable prices returns.

Inflation need not always lead to a cutback in consumption and production. On the contrary, the uncertainties generated by inflation may just as easily induce people to buy *more* goods and services now, before prices rise further. In their haste to beat inflation, however, consumers and producers may make foolish decisions, buying goods or services that they will later decide they don't really need or want.

Whichever response consumers and producers make—decreasing or increasing their rate of expenditure—the economy is likely to suffer in the end. In general, ***people shorten their time horizons in the face of inflation uncertainties.*** If consumers and producers postpone or cancel their expenditure plans, the demand for goods and services will fall. Eventually our production of goods and services will fall as well, and we will end up somewhere inside our (institutional) production-possibilities curve, stuck with a GNP gap and attendant unemployment.

On the other hand, market participants may increase their rate of expenditure in the face of inflation. The motivation here is to "beat inflation" by buying goods now, before prices rise further. The resultant frenzy may push prices up still faster. This kind of panic buying can lead to economic disaster. Ultimately the government will have to take strong action against accelerating inflation. It may cut back on its spending or raise taxes. Such actions will tend to depress the rate of total expenditure and possibly the rate of production as well. This potential sequence of events reinforces the view that inflation represents a major threat to full employment.

Speculation | Inflation threatens not only to reduce the level of economic activity but to change its very nature. If you really expect prices to rise, it makes sense to buy goods and services or factors of production now for resale later. If prices rise fast enough, you can make a handsome profit. These are the kinds of thoughts that motivate people to buy houses, precious metals, commodities, and other assets. But such speculation, if carried too far, can detract from the production process. If speculative profits become too easy, few people will engage in production; instead, everyone will be buying and selling existing goods. People may even be encouraged to withhold resources from the production process, hoping to sell them later at higher prices. As such behavior becomes widespread, production will decline and unemployment will rise.

Shortened time horizons | Even people who don't speculate may find their productive activities disrupted by inflation. If prices are rising exceptionally fast, people must buy basic necessities as quickly as possible, while they can still afford them. This phenomenon reached extreme proportions during the German hyperinflation of 1923, when prices were doubling every week. Confronted with skyrocketing prices, German workers could not afford to wait until the end of the week to do their shopping. Instead, they were paid twice daily and given brief "shopping breaks" to make their essential purchases. In this case, the rate of expenditure on goods and services actually increased as a result of

Inflation and the Weimar Republic

At the beginning of 1921 in Germany, the cost-of-living index was 18 times higher than its 1913 prewar base, while wholesale prices had mushroomed by 4,400%. Neither of these increases are negligible, but inflation and war have always been bedfellows. Normally, however, war ends and inflation recedes. By the end of 1921, it seemed that way; prices rose more modestly. Then, in 1922, inflation erupted.

Zenith of German Hyperinflation

Wholesale prices rose fortyfold, an increase nearly as large as during the prior eight years, while retail prices rose even more rapidly. The hyperinflation reached its zenith during 1923. Between May and June 1923, consumer prices more than quadrupled; between July and August, they rose more than 15 times; in the next month, over 25 times; and between September and October, by ten times the previous month's increase.

The German economy was thoroughly disrupted. Businessmen soon discovered the impossibility of rational economic planning. Profits fell as employes demanded frequent wage adjustments. Workers were often paid daily and sometimes two or three times a day, so that they could buy goods in the morning before the inevitable afternoon price increase. The work ethic suffered; wage earners were both more reluctant to work and less devoted to their jobs. Bankers were on the phone hour after hour, quoting the value of the mark in dollars, as calls continuously came in from merchants who needed the exchange rate to adjust their mark prices.

In an age that preceded the credit card, businessmen traveling around the country found themselves borrowing funds from their customers each stage of the way. The cash they'd allocated for the entire trip barely sufficed to pay the way to the next stop. Speculation began to dominate production.

As a result of the decline in profitability, in the ability to plan ahead, and the concern with speculation rather than production, unemployment rose, increasing by 600% between Sept. 1 and Dec. 15, 1923. And, as the hyperinflation intensified, people found goods unobtainable.

Hyperinflation crushed the middle class. Those thrifty Germans who had placed their savings in corporate or government bonds saw their lifetime efforts come to naught. Debtors sought out creditors to pay them in valueless currency. The debts of German government and industry disappeared. Farmers, too, profited, for, like farmers elsewhere, they were debtors. Nevertheless, the hyperinflation left a traumatic imprint on the German people, a legacy which colors their governmental policy to this day.

—Jonas Prager

inflation, but the rate of production fell. The same kind of frenzy occurred in China during 1948–49. The Nationalist Chinese yuan declined precipitously in value, and market participants rushed to spend their incomes as fast as they could. No one saved income, or even tried to.

In general, then, we expect inflation to alter market behavior. The rates of saving and investment will tend to decline when people shorten their time horizons and face the future with less confidence. This reduced level of saving and investment will in turn retard economic growth. People may also cut back on their job-seeking efforts or work, because they conclude that the extra dollars just won't matter much. This cutback in the supply of labor will further retard the economy's growth.

Bracket creep

bracket creep: The movement of taxpayers into higher tax brackets (rates) as nominal incomes grow.

Another reason savings, investment, and work effort decline when prices rise originates in the federal tax system. Federal income tax rates are progressive; that is, tax rates are higher for larger incomes. The intent of these progressive rates is to redistribute income from rich to poor. However, inflation tends to increase everyone's income. In the process people are pushed into higher tax brackets, and confront higher tax rates. The process is referred to as **bracket creep.**

Bracket creep implies a growing public sector. When taxpayers move into higher tax brackets, the government ends up with a larger share of total income. Hence inflation implies a redistribution of income from the private to the public sector.[3]

Though the government seems to fare well because of bracket creep, in fact, inflation stress tends to create a political backlash. As the public-opinion polls show, voters are quick to blame the government for inflation. If the administration does not put a stop to inflation, the voters will turn to someone who promises to do so.

ANTICIPATED INFLATION

Although inflation can have serious consequences for our economic welfare, its impact need not always be so harsh. Modest rates of inflation—particularly if they are constant, and thus predictable—may actually stimulate output. If producers are certain that prices will continue to rise at a moderate rate, they have an incentive to produce output now (at lower costs) for sale later (at higher prices). In effect, a little bit of inflation acts as a guarantee of some profits.

Unfortunately, there is always the danger that prices will not continue to rise at the steady anticipated rate. If the rate of inflation changes, profit and production calculations will be upset. Even if steady inflation were to persist for some time, more and more people would begin to expect rising prices. Those people would then act to protect their own interests through speculation and increased demands for wages and profits. As they did so, the possibility that a

[3] The Economic Recovery Tax Act of 1981 indexed tax rates to inflation, beginning in 1985. This indexation will restrain future bracket creep.

little inflation would evolve into a big inflation would increase greatly.

Even high rates of inflation are not necessarily disruptive. As we saw in Table 6.1, many other countries do grow and prosper despite much higher inflation rates than ours. Apparently they have adjusted to persistently increasing prices. Indeed, some economists argue that all of the costs of inflation result from price increases that are *unanticipated*. If we all knew which prices were going to rise, and by how much, we could make appropriate changes in our market behavior. From this perspective, there would be no uncertainty, no profit to speculation, and no cause for despair. Inflation would not even redistribute incomes or wealth, since everyone would foresee changes in relative prices.

Theoretically, there is reason to believe that a fully anticipated inflation would do little real harm. In practice, however, not everyone has the ability or energy to make all the required adjustments in market behavior. Also, there is no way to foresee completely all average and relative price increases. As a consequence, inflation is likely to benefit those who have the best information and the greatest ability to adapt their market behavior.

MEASURING INFLATION

In view of the macro and micro consequences of inflation, the measurement of inflation serves two purposes: to gauge the average rate of inflation and to identify its principal victims. Until we know how fast prices are rising and which groups are suffering the greatest loss of real income, we can hardly begin to design appropriate public policies.

Consumer Price Index

Consumer Price Index (CPI): A measure (index) of changes in the average price of consumer goods and services.

inflation rate: The annual rate of increase in the average price level.

The most common measure of inflation is the **Consumer Price Index (CPI).** As its name suggests, the CPI is a mechanism for measuring changes in the average price of consumer goods and services. It is analogous to the fruit-price index we discussed earlier. The CPI does not refer to the price of any particular good, but rather to the average price of all consumer goods.

By itself, the "average price" of consumer goods is not a very useful number. Once we know the average price of consumer goods, however, we are able to observe whether that average *rises*, that is, whether inflation is occurring. Moreover, by observing the extent to which prices increase, we can calculate the **rate of inflation.**

We can get a better sense of how inflation is measured—and how it affects the distribution of income—by observing how the CPI is constructed. The process begins by identifying a "market basket" of goods and services the typical consumer buys. For this purpose, the Bureau of Labor Statistics periodically surveys a large sample of families to determine what goods and services consumers actually buy. Figure 6.2 summarizes the results of the most recent survey, conducted in 1972–73. At that time, 30 cents out of every consumer dollar was spent on housing (shelter and utilities), 19 cents on food,

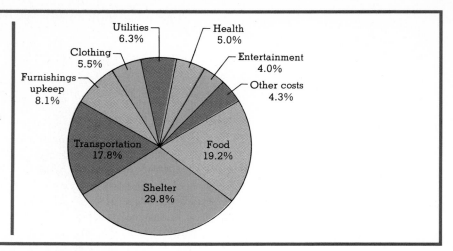

FIGURE 6.2   THE MARKET BASKET
1972–73

To measure changes in average prices, we must first know what goods and services consumers buy. This diagram, based on consumer surveys, shows how the typical urban consumer spends each dollar.

Source: U.S. Bureau of Labor Statistics, based on 1972–73 Consumer Expenditure Survey.

(Pie chart labels:)
Utilities 6.3%
Health 5.0%
Clothing 5.5%
Entertainment 4.0%
Furnishings upkeep 8.1%
Other costs 4.3%
Transportation 17.8%
Food 19.2%
Shelter 29.8%

and another 18 cents on transportation. Only 4 cents of every consumer dollar was spent on entertainment. Each of these broad categories contains, of course, a tremendous variety of goods and services, and the survey attempts to identify them as well. The details of the survey show, for example, that private expenditures for reading and education accounted for only 1.4 percent of the typical consumer's budget, less than was spent on alcoholic beverages and tobacco. It also shows that we spent 8.5 cents out of every dollar on fuel to drive our cars (4.2 cents) and heat and cool our houses (4.3 cents).

Once we know what the typical consumer buys, it is relatively easy to calculate the average price of a market basket. The Bureau of Labor Statistics actually goes shopping in various cities across the country, recording the prices of the items that comprise the typical market basket. This shopping survey is undertaken every month, in eighty-five areas, and at a variety of stores in each area.

As a result of its surveys, the Bureau of Labor Statistics can tell us what's happening to consumer prices. Suppose, for example, that the market basket cost $100 in 1980, and that one year later the same basket of goods and services cost $110. On the basis of those two shopping trips, we could conclude that consumer prices had risen by 10 percent in one year, that is, that the rate of inflation was 10 percent per annum.

In practice, the CPI is usually expressed in terms of what the market basket cost in 1967.[4] For example, the CPI stood at 257 in January 1982. In other words, it cost $257 in 1982 to buy the same market basket that cost only $100 in the base year, 1967. Thus prices had more than doubled over that period of fifteen years. Each month the Bureau of Labor Statistics updates the CPI, telling us how the current cost of that same basket compares to its cost in 1967.[5]

[4] The Bureau of Labor Statistics is changing the base year to 1977. A new CPI series will be published in 1983 or 1984.
[5] Since January 1978 the Bureau of Labor Statistics has actually been computing two CPIs, one for urban wage earners and clerical workers and the second and larger one for all urban consumers (about 80 percent of the population). A third index, which uses rent rather than ownership costs of shelter, was introduced in 1983. The "urban/rental" index is most commonly cited.

THE NEW CPI: TREATING SHELTER COSTS AS RENT, NOT OWNERSHIP

Housing costs represent one of the largest expenditures for the average American household. For people who don't own their own homes or apartments, these costs are reflected in rent payments. For homeowners, the costs of housing include separate outlays for mortgage payments, taxes, insurance, and maintenance. For both renters and owners, changes in housing costs have a major impact on real incomes.

Up until 1983, the CPI treated houses just like all other consumer goods—as though they were consumed in the year they were bought. The basic measure of housing costs used in the CPI referred to *purchase* costs. Changes in housing costs were based on the purchase prices of new homes. As a consequence, changes in the CPI were very sensitive to interest rates (a high portion of ownership costs) and house prices. There were three problems with this procedure. First, the data on new home purchases were not representative of all U.S. consumers. Fewer than 10 percent of all U.S. households buy a house or condo in any given year. Second, homeownership is a mixture of financial investment and current consumption. Homeowners can ultimately resell their homes; renters "consume" their entire rent. Third, new types of mortgages and other financial mechanisms for buying houses made traditional contracts increasingly unrepresentative.

Because of these problems, the U.S. Bureau of Labor Statistics switched procedures in 1983. Since January 1983, rental costs have been used as the basic measure of housing costs in the CPI. Raw data on rents are collected in surveys, just like other price components of the CPI. One effect of this switch to rental costs has been to make the CPI less erratic, as rents do not fluctuate as much as house prices and interest rates. The switch has also made the CPI more representative of the average consumer: everyone pays rent, either explicitly or implicitly. Finally, the switch has reduced the measured rate of inflation in recent years of high interest rates.

Producer Price Indexes

In addition to the familiar Consumer Price Index, there are three Producer Price Indexes (PPIs). The PPIs keep track of average prices received by producers. One index includes crude materials, another covers intermediate goods, and the last covers finished goods. The three PPIs do not include all producer prices, but primarily those in mining, manufacturing, and agriculture. Like the CPI, changes in the PPIs are identified in monthly surveys.

Over long periods of time, the PPIs and the CPI generally reflect the same rate of inflation. In the short run, however, the PPIs usually increase before the CPI, because it takes time for producers' price increases to be reflected in the prices that consumers pay. For this reason, the PPIs are watched closely as a clue to potential changes in consumer prices.

The GNP deflator

The broadest price index is the GNP deflator. The GNP deflator covers all output, including consumer goods, investment goods, and government services. Unlike the CPI and PPIs, the GNP deflator is not based on a fixed "basket" of goods or services. Rather, it allows the contents of the basket to change with people's consumption and investment patterns. The GNP is therefore not a pure measure of price change. Its value reflects both price changes and market responses to those price changes, as reflected in new expenditure patterns. Hence the GNP deflator typically registers a lower inflation rate than the CPI.

Cost-of-living adjustments

For many consumers, changes in a price index are more than a matter of idle curiosity. Many people's incomes depend on changes in the CPI. *Real* income, of course, is always affected by changes in consumer prices. But in a more immediate sense, the size of many paychecks (nominal income) is directly tied to the CPI. Steelworkers, for example, get a raise of $0.01 per hour every time the CPI increases by 0.3 points. In such years as 1980, when the CPI rose by 23.1 points, such raises can be substantial (over $1,000 per year in this case). These raises come about because the workers' wage contracts include a **cost-of-living adjustment (COLA)**, which *automatically* adjusts their nominal wages to changing prices.

cost-of-living adjustment (COLA): Automatic adjustments of nominal income to the rate of inflation.

The objective of the COLA is to maintain the workers' *real* wages in an inflationary period. In private industry, those workers with COLA adjustments seldom have full protection against inflation; the adjustments are only partial. Retired workers are even worse off; they seldom get any inflation adjustments in their private pensions.

Federal transfer payments are more completely indexed to inflation. Social security benefits, for example, go up automatically whenever the rate of inflation exceeds 3 percent. Retired government workers (who do not receive social security benefits) get similar protection. As a result of such inflation protection, a 1 percent increase in the CPI triggers close to $2 billion of additional federal expenditure. All told, the Bureau of Labor Statistics estimates that over half of American families now find some part of their nominal income pegged to the Consumer Price Index (see Table 6.5).

TABLE 6.5 PERSONS COVERED BY COST-OF-LIVING ESCALATOR CLAUSES, 1980

Some 65 million people are at least partially protected from inflation by automatic cost-of-living agreements. Their (nominal) wages or income transfers are automatically increased when prices rise. These adjustments help preserve their real incomes.

Group of recipients	Number
Social security	35,300,000
Supplemental security	4,188,000
Federal civilian retirees	1,712,000
Military retirees	1,308,000
Railroad retirees	1,006,000
Disabled coal miners	416,000
Pensioned war veterans	2,167,000
Postal workers	659,000
Union members under major agreements	5,400,000
Other workers (small unions or nonunion)	2,200,000
State and local-government workers	350,000
State and local-government retirees	1,100,000
Food stamps	20,200,000

Source: *U.S. News & World Report,* June 9, 1980, p. 56.

TABLE 6.6 THE CONSUMER PRICE
INDEX, SELECTED YEARS, 1800–1981
(1967 = 100)

Before World War II, the average level
of prices rose in some years and fell
in others. Since 1945, prices have
risen continuously. The Consumer
Price Index has more than doubled
since 1967.

Year	CPI for all items	Year	CPI for all items	Year	CPI for all items	Year	CPI for all items
1800	51.0	1900	25.0	1945	53.9	1970	116.3
1825	34.0	1913	29.7	1950	72.1	1975	161.2
1850	25.0	1920	60.0	1960	88.7	1980	258.4
1875	33.0	1933	38.8	1967	100.0	1981	281.5

Note: Data from 1913 forward reflect the official all-items Consumer Price Index, which used the pre–1983 measure of shelter costs. Estimated indexes for 1800 through 1912 are drawn from several sources.

Source: U.S. Bureau of Labor Statistics.

THE HISTORICAL RECORD

U.S. inflation rates

Table 6.6 summarizes our experience with inflation since 1800, as measured by the Consumer Price Index. In this case, the base year for pricing the market basket of goods is 1967, and the price has arbitrarily been set at $100 for that year. Notice that the same market basket cost only $51 in 1800. Consumer prices doubled in 167 years. But also observe how frequently the price level *fell* in the 1800s and again in the 1930s. These recurrent deflations held down the long-run inflation rate. Because of these periodic deflations, average prices in 1945 were at the same level as in 1800! By contrast, prices have quintupled since 1945.

Figure 6.3 provides a more convenient summary of our recent inflation experience. In this figure we have simply transformed annual changes in the CPI into percentage rates of inflation. Note in Table 6.6, for example, that the CPI jumped from 258.4 in 1980 to 281.5 in 1981. This 23.1-point jump in the CPI translates into an 8.9 percent rate of inflation (23.1 ÷ 258.4 = 0.089). This inflation rate is represented by point A in Figure 6.3. The inflation rates for the rest of the years have been calculated in the same way.

A quick look at Figure 6.3 confirms that deflations are pretty much a thing of the past; only in the early 1930s did the price level drop substantially. Since that time, prices have risen at least a little nearly every year, and sometimes (1947, 1974, 1979, 1980) by very large amounts. Of particular concern are the generally higher rates of inflation that marked the 1970s and early 1980s.

The resulting redistributions

As we observed earlier, not everyone suffers equally from high rates of inflation. Insofar as individuals are concerned, it is important to look not only at the *average* increase in consumer prices, but also at the various components of that average. Markedly varying rates of inflation are associated with specific groups of goods and services. In 1981, for example, when the average inflation rate was 8.9 percent, coffee prices actually fell. Accordingly, a person who subsisted entirely on coffee would have experienced an increase in real income in 1981, despite the general inflation taking place. Reading down the list of specific items in Table 6.3 provides further insights

FIGURE 6.3   HISTORICAL PRICE CHANGES

During the 1920s and 1930s, consumer prices fell significantly, causing a
general deflation. Since the Great Depression, however, average prices have
risen almost every year. But even during this inflationary period, the annual
rate of price increase has varied widely.

Source: U.S. Bureau of Labor Statistics.

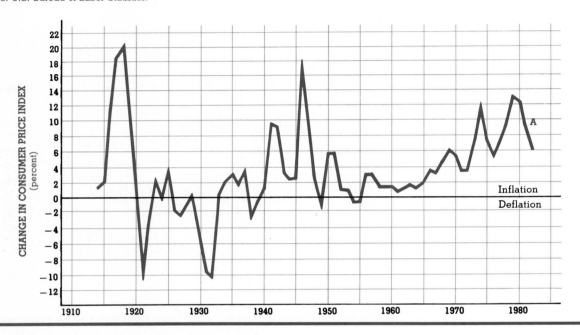

into the way inflation redistributed real incomes in 1981. People
who ate a lot of steak or chicken made out better than those who ate
fish. And sugar became relatively cheaper than apples, bringing
smiles to children and dentists.

As for transportation expenses, the relative advantage of bicycles increased in 1981, as bicycle prices rose less than both bus fares
and autos. As a result, the real incomes of bicycle purchasers rose in
relation to those of people who bought motor vehicles.

This variation in price changes serves to drive home our basic
point: inflation redistributes income. The redistribution occurs as a
result of two phenomena:

- Not all prices rise at the same rate in an inflation.
- Not everyone buys (or sells) the same basket of goods and services or holds the same assets.

THE GOAL: PRICE STABILITY

In view of the inequities, anxieties, and real losses caused by inflation, it is not surprising that price stability is a major goal of eco-

nomic policy. As we observed at the beginning of this chapter, every American president since Franklin Roosevelt has decreed price stability to be a foremost policy goal. Unfortunately, few presidents (or their advisers) have stated exactly what they mean by "price stability." Do they mean *no* change in the average price level? Or is some upward creep in the CPI consistent with the notion of price stability?

A numerical goal

price stability: The absence of significant changes in the average price level; officially defined as a rate of inflation of less than 3 percent.

An explicit numerical goal for **price stability** was established for the first time in the Full Employment and Balanced Growth Act of 1978. According to that act, the goal of economic policy is to hold the rate of inflation under 3 percent.

Why did the Congress choose 3 percent inflation rather than zero inflation as the benchmark for price stability? Two considerations were important. First, Congress recognized that efforts to maintain absolutely stable prices (zero inflation) might threaten full employment. Recall that our goal of "full employment" is defined as the lowest rate of unemployment *consistent with stable prices.* The same kind of thinking is apparent here. The amount of inflation regarded as tolerable depends in part on the effect of anti-inflation strategies on unemployment rates. After reviewing our experiences with both unemployment and inflation, Congress concluded that 3 percent inflation was a "safe" target.[6]

Quality changes

The second argument for setting our price-stability goal above zero inflation relates to our measurement capabilities. Although the Consumer Price Index is very thorough, it is not a perfect measure of inflation. In essence, the CPI simply monitors the price of specific goods over time. Over time, however, the goods themselves change, too. Old products become better as a result of *quality improvements.* A television set costs more today than it did in 1955, but today's TV also delivers a bigger, clearer picture—and in color! Hence increases in the price of television sets tend to exaggerate the true rate of inflation: part of the higher price represents more product.

The same is true of automobile tires. Although tire prices have risen greatly over time, their durability has increased even faster. As a result, the price *per mile* for use of tires has fallen since 1935.

The problem of measuring quality improvements is most apparent in the case of new products. The minicomputers and word-processing machines found in many offices and homes today did not exist when the Census Bureau last conducted its survey of consumer expenditure (1972–73). How should their prices be treated? Ultimately a new survey will be taken, and minicomputers will be included. In the meantime, however, the real incomes of consumers will be influenced by goods the CPI does not yet include. Hence there is a significant (though unmeasured) element of error in the

[6] The nature of the trade-off between unemployment and inflation is discussed in Chapter 13, along with available policy options for changing it.

CPI insofar as it is intended to gauge changes in the average prices paid by consumers. The goal of 3 percent inflation allows for such errors.

TYPES OF INFLATION

In no year since 1965 have prices risen less than 3 percent. Some of the reasons for our failure to attain price stability will be discussed at length in later chapters. At this point, however, it is convenient to identify the major types of inflation that occur.

Demand-pull inflation

demand-pull inflation: An increase in the price level initiated by excessive aggregate demand.

The most familiar form of inflation is called **demand-pull inflation.** The name suggests that demand is pulling up the price level, and this is pretty much what happens. If the demand for goods and services increases faster than production, there simply won't be enough goods and services to go around. Prices will rise as consumers try to outbid each other for the available supply. In the process, the price level will move up and we will be saddled with an inflation.

Consumers are not the only potential villains in a demand-pull story, of course. As we observed in Chapter 2, there are three sets of market participants, and all of their dollars look alike. Thus a surge in aggregate demand can come about through increased spending by consumers, by business firms, or by government agencies.

Cost-push inflation

cost-push inflation: An increase in the price level initiated by an increase in the cost of production.

Increased spending is not the only possible explanation for rising prices. There are two sides to every market, and changes in supply conditions can also raise prices. In 1979, for example, the Organization of Petroleum Exporting Countries (OPEC) sharply increased the price of oil. For domestic producers, this action meant a significant increase in the cost of producing goods and services. Accordingly, domestic producers could no longer afford to sell goods at prevailing prices. They instead had to raise prices. The result was a **cost-push inflation.**

Not all cost-push inflations have such dramatic beginnings. A more common source of cost-push inflation is an increase in labor costs, often resulting from aggressive labor-union bargaining.

Profit-push inflation

profit-push inflation: An increase in the price level initiated by attempts of producers to raise profit margins.

The third form of inflation is called **profit-push inflation,** and its origins should now be evident. If producers decide they want higher incomes, they may try to attain them by raising profit margins. They can increase profit margins by raising product prices faster than costs. The result is a rising price level, that is, inflation.

In reality, it is often impossible to distinguish among these three types of inflation. All we see are rising prices. As prices continue to rise, demand-pull, cost-push, and profit-push forces interact, making the "cause" of inflation difficult to find. But a distinction among types of inflation is useful in alerting us to the kinds of actions that can start an inflation rolling. It also helps us to design effective anti-inflation policies.

SUMMARY

▪ Inflation is an increase in the average price level. Typically it is measured by changes in a price index such as the Consumer Price Index (CPI).

▪ Inflation imposes both macro- and microeconomic costs. At the micro level, inflation redistributes income by altering relative prices, income, and wealth. Because not all prices rise at the same rate and because not all people buy (and sell) the same goods or hold the same assets, inflation does not affect everyone equally. Some individuals actually gain from inflation, while others suffer a drop in real income.

▪ At the macro level, inflation threatens to reduce total output because it increases uncertainties about the future and thereby inhibits consumption and production decisions. Fear of rising prices can also stimulate spending, forcing the government to take restraining action that threatens full employment. Rising price levels also encourage speculation and hoarding, which detract from productive activity.

▪ Fully anticipated inflation reduces the anxieties and real losses associated with rising prices. However, few people can foresee actual price patterns or make all the necessary adjustments in their market activity.

▪ The goal of price stability is defined as an inflation rate of less than 3 percent per year. This goal recognizes potential conflicts between zero inflation and full employment, as well as the difficulties of measuring quality improvements and new products.

▪ There are three major types of inflation. Demand-pull inflation is caused by excessive aggregate demand. Cost-push inflation is caused by increases in the cost of production. Profit-push inflation is caused by efforts of producers to increase their profits by raising prices.

Terms to remember Define the following terms:

inflation	Consumer Price Index (CPI)
deflation	inflation rate
relative price	cost-of-living adjustment (COLA)
nominal income	price stability
real income	demand-pull inflation
money illusion	cost-push inflation
bracket creep	profit-push inflation

Questions for discussion 1. Why is inflation called a "capricious tax"?

2. Can you identify any groups of people who are particularly helped or hurt by inflation? Explain.

3. Does an increase in the price level automatically lower society's real income? Explain.

4. Would it be advantageous to borrow money if you expected prices to rise? Why, or why not? Provide a numerical example.

Problem | Social security legislation mandates an increase in monthly retirement benefits any time the rate of inflation exceeds 3 percent in a single year. The increased benefits are proportional to the rise in the CPI. If the inflation rate is less than 3 percent, no automatic increase in benefits occurs.

What happens to the real incomes of social security beneficiaries both during and after a year in which the inflation rate is (*a*) 2.5 percent; (*b*) 3.5 percent; (*c*) zero?

PART B

POLICY
OPTIONS:
THE
KEYNESIAN
APPROACH

CHAPTER 7

AGGREGATE DEMAND

In the 1930s as many as 13 million Americans were out of work. They were capable people and eager to work. But no one would hire them. As sympathetic as employers might have been, they simply could not use any more workers. Consumers were not buying the goods and services already being produced. Employers were more likely to cut back production and lay off still more workers than to hire any new ones. As a consequence, the "army of the unemployed" first created in 1929 continued to grow for nearly a decade. In fact, it was not until the outbreak of World War II that enough jobs could be found for the army of the unemployed, and even most of these "jobs" were in the armed forces.

The Great Depression of the 1930s was the springboard for the Keynesian approach to economic policy. Observing the growing ranks of unemployed persons and the reluctance of employers to hire them, John Maynard Keynes, a British economist, concluded that the fault lay on the *demand* side of product markets. People simply were not able and willing to buy all the goods and services the economy was capable of producing. As a consequence, producers had no incentive to increase output, and therefore no need of additional labor. So long as the demand for goods and services was inadequate, unemployment was inevitable.

In this and the next two chapters we shall examine Keynes' explanation for macro instability and the policy responses he advocated. The relationship of spending desires to productive capacity is the immediate focus of this chapter. We seek to determine how much spending will occur at various rates of output, particularly at full-employment GNP. For this purpose, we will largely ignore the behavior of individual market participants (the subjects of *microeconomics*) and instead focus on the collective or *aggregate* behavior of groups of market participants (*macroeconomic behavior*). What sort of market behavior leads to unemployment, inflation, or inadequate economic growth?

THE CIRCULAR FLOW REVISITED

full employment: The lowest rate of unemployment compatible with price stability; variously estimated at between 4 and 6 percent unemployment.

full-employment GNP: The total market value of final goods and services that could be produced in a given time period at full employment; potential GNP.

The problem of achieving **full employment** and price stability can be visualized as a problem of reaching our (institutional) production-possibilities curve (Figure 5.2). That curve expresses the various combinations of final output that could be produced in a given time period if our labor force and other resources were fully and efficiently employed. In other words, our institutional production-possibilities curve depicts the rate of **full-employment GNP.**

Our goal, of course, is to produce exactly that much output each year. If we attempt to produce more than our full-employment capacity allows, inflation will result. On the other hand, if the rate of production is less than full-employment GNP, our productive capacity will be underutilized and some workers will be unemployed. Accordingly, we conclude that *full employment with price stability can be attained only if the actual rate of production equals full-employment GNP.*[1]

Derived demand

At first it might seem rather easy to attain full employment. After all, it simply means that we have to put 95 percent of all labor-force participants to work.[2] But the task is not quite that simple. Attainment of full employment is a question not only of *supply* (the available workers) but of *demand* (the employers who hire them) as well. Employers have to be willing to hire all those workers. Accordingly, to explain the origins of unemployment and inflation, we must determine why employers at times fail to hire all available workers, and at others want more workers than are available.

We can get a fairly good sense of the way these problems arise by taking another look at the circular flow of income. As we observed in Chapter 2, there are both factor markets and product markets. Labor is sold in factor markets and purchased by employers (private firms or government agencies). But the amount of labor that employers are willing to purchase (demand) in any period depends on what is happening in *product* markets. That is to say, **business firms hire workers only if the goods and services such workers produce can be sold in product markets.** Firms will demand more

[1] Producing at a rate equal to full-employment GNP is a necessary but not sufficient condition for full employment and price stability. *Demand-pull inflation* and *cyclical unemployment* are eliminated, but other forms of inflation or unemployment may exist, as we shall see.
[2] Recall that the official definition of "full employment" allows for 5 percent unemployment.

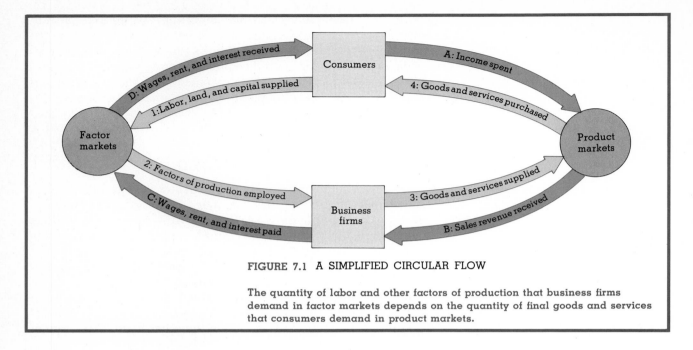

FIGURE 7.1 A SIMPLIFIED CIRCULAR FLOW

The quantity of labor and other factors of production that business firms demand in factor markets depends on the quantity of final goods and services that consumers demand in product markets.

derived demand: The demand for labor and other factors of production results from (depends on) the demand for final goods and services produced by these factors.

labor only if the demand for the goods and services such labor produces is sufficiently strong. In this sense, we say that employers have a **derived demand** for labor, that demand being derived from demands for final goods and services.

The principle of derived demand can be visualized in the circular flow of income, as shown in Figure 7.1. Notice again that we have both product markets and factor markets. But we now ignore the government (it will rise again!) and foreign trade, leaving domestic consumers and business firms as the only market participants. Consumers supply labor to the factor market by going out and looking for jobs; they supply land and capital by offering to sell or rent these factors as well. This supply of resources is illustrated by Step 1 on the inner loop of Figure 7.1.

The role of business firms in factor markets is to hire available workers and other factors of production (Step 2) to produce goods and services (Step 3). The goods and services themselves will later be sold to consumers in product markets (Step 4), thus completing the circular flow.

While the inner loop of Figure 7.1 focuses on the flow of goods and factors between consumers and businesses, the outer loop summarizes the flow of *income* that accompanies each market transaction. Consumer expenditures on goods and services (Step A) generate sales revenue (receipts) for business firms. Business firms use their sales revenue (Step B) to hire labor, land, and capital (Step C). The resultant wages, rent, and interest represent income to consumers (D). In fact, all of the income spent in product markets ends up as income for market participants. This recycled income may be used to finance further consumer purchases (A again). And so the flow continues.

Or does it? What guarantee do we have that the demand for final goods and services (Step A) will continue at a rate strong enough to allow employers to hire all available labor (Step C)? *All we know for sure is that product-market sales will generate income of equal value.*[3] *We do not know whether all this (recycled) income will be spent again.* If sales drop below the rate of full-employment GNP, there won't be enough income (or incentive) to continue employing all available labor. The result will be job layoffs and increasing unemployment.

The principle of derived demand thus provides a first look at the origins of unemployment and inflation. In particular,

- If the demand for final goods and services at full employment *equals* the rate of full-employment GNP, producers will have enough income and incentive to employ all available workers.
- If the demand for final goods and services at full employment is *less* than the rate of full-employment GNP, producers will not have enough income or incentive to employ all available workers. Unemployment will result.
- If the demand for final goods and services at full employment exceeds the rate of full-employment GNP, producers will seek to hire more labor than is available. Inflation will result.

Aggregate demand

aggregate demand: The total value of all final goods and services demanded in a given time period at alternative income levels; total spending.

Consumer spending is clearly a critical determinant of our ability to attain full employment, price stability, and continued economic growth. Also important are the rates of investment spending, government spending, and exports (sales to foreigners). Together these expenditures comprise aggregate demand. Specifically, **aggregate demand** is the total value of final goods and services market participants are willing and able to purchase in a given period at alternative levels of income. It represents the collective expenditure decisions of the millions of individuals, businesses, and government agencies that participate in product markets.

If we want to know whether our entire labor force can be employed, we must determine whether aggregate demand at full employment will be equal to the rate of full-employment GNP. To do so we need to look at the components of total spending. How much will consumers desire to spend on goods and services? How much will business firms desire to spend on plant and equipment? How much will government agencies spend? How much will all this spending add up to? Will it be enough to provide a job for everyone who wants to work? Will total spending exceed our ability to produce?

CONSUMPTION

We begin our analysis of aggregate demand by looking at the behavior of consumers. Consumer expenditures account for two-thirds of total spending in the economy, and are thus the largest single com-

---

[3] GNP accounting also emphasizes the equivalence of the value of total output and the value of total income (see Table 4.4).

consumption: Expenditure by consumers on final goods and services.

ponent of aggregate demand. Our intent here is to determine what factors influence the *rate* of **consumption,** and thus our potential for achieving full employment.

Consumption decisions are influenced by a variety of forces, including income, prices, interest rates, and expectations. Most studies of consumer behavior, however, have found that income alone is an adequate predictor of consumer spending. The rate of consumer spending is directly and closely related to the amount of income consumers have to spend.[4]

disposable income (DI): After-tax income of consumers; personal income less personal taxes.

Disposable income is the key concept here. As we noted in Chapter 4, disposable income is the amount of income consumers actually take home. This is the share of total income remaining after all taxes have been paid, transfers (e.g., social security benefits) have been received, and depreciation charges and retained earnings have been subtracted (see Figure 4.3). **Disposable income** represents the amount of income consumers can actually choose to spend or not spend (save) in a given time period.

Consumption vs. saving

saving: That part of disposable income not spent on current consumption; disposable income less consumption.

As a rule, the more income a person receives in a given period, the more he or she spends. But most people don't spend *every* dollar they receive. On the contrary, most people manage to **save** some fraction of their disposable income in each period, however small that fraction may be. By forgoing some current consumption, savers accumulate purchasing power for consumption in later periods. Typically the savings earn interest (in the bank) or dividends (in the stock market), and thus generate additional income in the future. Thus by forgoing some consumption now, consumers may be able to consume even more in the future.

Our principal interest here is to determine how consumers divide up their disposable income between current consumption and saving. In this regard, we ask two separate questions:

- What fraction of *total* disposable income is spent on consumer goods and services?
- What fraction of *added* disposable income is spent on consumer goods and services?

The first question reflects an interest in past patterns of consumption; the second question is concerned with consumer responses to *changes* in income. As we shall discover, this distinction is critical.

The average propensity to consume

average propensity to consume (APC): Total consumption in a given period divided by total disposable income.

The proportion of *total* disposable income spent on consumer goods and services in a given time period is referred to as the **average propensity to consume *(APC).*** To determine the *APC,* we simply observe how much consumers spend in a given time period out of that period's disposable income. In 1980, for example, total disposable income amounted to $1,774 billion, out of which consumers

---

[4] Recall that in Chapter 2 we also simplified the explanation of consumer demand for a specific good by focusing on the two-dimensional relationship between quantity demanded and price. Here we are focusing on the two-dimensional relationship between total consumption and total income.

spent $1,670 billion and saved only $104 billion. Accordingly, we may calculate the average propensity to consume as

$$APC = \frac{\text{total consumption}}{\text{total disposable income}}$$

For 1980, this works out to:

$$APC = \frac{\$1,670 \text{ billion}}{\$1,774 \text{ billion}} = 0.941$$

In other words, consumers spent, on average, 94 cents out of every dollar received.

The marginal propensity to consume

marginal propensity to consume *(MPC)*: The fraction of each additional (marginal) dollar of disposable income spent on consumption; the change in consumption divided by the change in disposable income.

The fact that the average propensity to consume was 0.941 in 1980 does not imply that all consumers spent exactly 94 cents out of each dollar received. Nor does it imply that any given consumer allocated each dollar of income identically. The *APC* is simply an *average* that summarizes the behavior of millions of consumers, each responding to his or her own income. With different incomes, consumers might have spent more or less out of each dollar.

It is particularly important to observe how the choice between consumption and saving is affected by *changes* in income. For this purpose, we may formulate a second measure of consumption behavior, the marginal propensity to consume. The **marginal propensity to consume *(MPC)*** tells us how much consumer expenditure will change in response to change in income.

To calculate the marginal propensity to consume, we have to observe how consumers respond to *changes* in income. In the extreme case, we could ask how consumer spending in 1980 was affected by the *last* dollar of disposable income. That is, how did consumer spending change when disposable income increased from $1,773,999,999 to $1,774,000,000? If consumer spending increased by $0.90 when this last $1.00 was received, we would calculate the marginal propensity to consume as:

$$MPC = \frac{\text{change in consumption}}{\text{change in disposable income}}$$
$$= \frac{\$0.90}{\$1.00} = 0.9$$

Notice that the *MPC* in this case is lower than the *APC*. Suppose we had incorrectly assumed that consumers would always spend 94 cents of every dollar's income. Then we would have expected the rate of consumer spending to rise by 94 cents as the last dollar was received. In fact, however, the rate of spending increased by only 90 cents. In other words, consumers responded to *increases* in their income differently than past averages implied.

No one would be upset if our failure to distinguish the *APC* from the *MPC* led to an error of only 4 cents in forecasts of consumer spending. After all, the annual rate of consumer spending in the U.S. economy now exceeds $2 trillion! However, policy decisions are rarely calibrated in single dollars. Typically, policy decisions in-

MPC VS. APC . . .

The marginal propensity to consume (MPC) is the *change* in consumption that accompanies a *change* in disposable income; that is,

$$MPC = \frac{\Delta C}{\Delta Y_D}$$

But we may also be interested in the proportion of *total* disposable income that is spent on consumption. This is referred to as the *average* propensity to consume, and equals $\frac{C}{Y_D}$.

. . . AND MPS VS. APS

The marginal propensity to *save* (MPS) is the fraction of each additional (marginal) dollar of disposable income *not* spent—that is, saved. This is summarized as:

$$MPS = \frac{\Delta S}{\Delta Y_D}$$

MPS equals $1 - MPC$, since every additional dollar is either spent (consumed) or not spent (saved). The *average* propensity to save equals $\frac{S}{Y_D}$.

volve billion-dollar changes in income. When we start playing with those kinds of dollars—the actual focus of economic policy makers—the distinction between APC and MPC is significant, as we shall see.

Like the APC, the MPC may change. The marginal propensity to consume is itself determined by a variety of social, psychological, and economic factors. People who have very little income often spend every additional dollar they get; their MPC is very close to 1.0. By contrast, people with high incomes may have difficulty finding new ways to spend additional income; their MPC may be low. As a consequence, if we redistributed income from the rich to the poor, our collective MPC might rise. At any time, however, only one MPC prevails, and we use it to characterize the behavior of consumers.

THE CONSUMPTION FUNCTION

Knowing what the MPC is at any time allows us to predict consumer responses to changes in income, and thus to predict the direction and magnitude of aggregate demand. Suppose that the rate of consumer spending was *completely* determined by current income, and the marginal propensity to consume was some unknown value, denoted by the letter b. In this case, we could say that $C = bY_D$, that is, that the rate of consumer spending (C) depended on the level of disposable income (Y_D) and the marginal propensity to consume (b). Hence the equation $C = bY_D$ would tell us exactly how much consumer spending (C) would take place at various income levels (Y_D).

In reality, consumption is not *completely* determined by current income. In extreme cases, this is evident. Most people who have no income in a given period continue to consume goods and services, using savings or credit to finance their purchases. More generally, we observe that people's current consumption decisions are influenced by expectations of future income, accumulated savings, the availability of credit, and ingrained habits, as well as current income. To allow for this possibility, we expand the equation $C = bY_D$ to

$$C = a + bY_D$$

where a is the rate of consumer spending not dependent on current income. The amount of consumption indicated by a is often referred to as *autonomous* consumption. This is the rate of consumer spending determined by forces other than current income. In theory, this amount of consumption would take place even if Y_D equaled zero. This expanded equation—with both autonomous and income-dependent consumption—is called the Keynesian **consumption function.**[5]

consumption function: A mathematical relationship indicating the rate of consumer spending that will take place in a given time period at various income levels.

An individual function

To see how the consumption function works, imagine an individual who has no monthly income. How much will that person spend? Obviously he must spend *something*, otherwise he will starve to death. At a very low rate of income—in this case zero—the rate of consumer spending depends less on current income than on basic survival needs, past savings, and credit. The a in the consumption function expresses this autonomous rate of consumption; we shall assume it is $50 per month. Thus we may say that the monthly rate of consumption expenditure in this case is:

$$C = \$50 + bY_D$$

Notice that we have said nothing about how our unlucky consumer is going to pay for his basic consumption of $50 per month. For the moment, all we care about is how much he ends up *spending*; that is, how much he will contribute to aggregate demand. And we know it will be a minimum of $50 per month.

Now suppose that our friend finds a job and begins to earn $100 per month. How will his spending be affected? Surely, we anticipate that his rate of spending will increase, because the $50 per month he had been spending provided very few goods and services. Now that he is earning a little income, our friend will certainly want to improve his life-style. That is to say, ***we expect consumption to rise with income.***

But by how much? To predict changes in aggregate demand, we have to be more specific about the influence of additional income on consumer spending. In this case, assume that he increases his consumption by $75 per month when his disposable income rises from zero to $100 per month.[6] His *marginal propensity to consume*, then,

---

[5] The consumption function can be expanded to include other determinants of consumer spending. Keynes focused on disposable income (Y_D) only.

[6] We are assuming that the $100 he "earns" is equal to his disposable income. (We earlier assumed that there is no government, and therefore no taxes.)

is 0.75—$0.75 of each additional $1.00 of income is spent on consumption.

Knowing how much this consumer spends when his income is zero and also how he responds to increases in income, we can write his consumption function as:

$$C = \$50 \text{ per month} + 0.75\,Y_D$$

With this equation, we can predict exactly how much our friend will spend per month at various income levels. According to this equation, our friend's *total* consumption will be $125 per month when his income is $100 per month. This is indicated in row *B* of Table 7.1. This consumption consists of his basic survival package ($50 per month) plus the added $75 of goods and services each month that are financed by his sudden prosperity.

Our friend's rate of consumption still exceeds his income. According to row *B* of Table 7.1, he is now spending $125 per month but taking in only $100 of income. The other $25 is still being begged, borrowed, or withdrawn from savings. Without peering further into our friend's personal finances, we may simply conclude that he is **dissaving** $25 per month. Dissaving occurs whenever current consumption exceeds current income.

If our friend's monthly income continues to rise, he will stop dissaving at some point. Perhaps he will even start saving enough to pay back all the people who have sustained him throughout these difficult months. Figure 7.2 shows just how and when this will occur.

The black line in the figure, with a 45-degree angle, represents all points where consumption and income are exactly equal $(C = Y_D)$. Recall that our hapless friend currently has an income of $100 per month. By moving up from the horizontal axis at $Y_D = \$100$, we see all the consumption possibilities he confronts. Were he to spend exactly $100 on consumption, he would end up on the 45-degree line, at point *F*. But we already know he doesn't stop there. Instead, he proceeds further, to point *B*. At point *B* the consumption function lies above the 45-degree line, so consumption exceeds income; dissaving is occurring.

dissaving: Consumption expenditure in excess of disposable income; a negative saving flow.

TABLE 7.1   A HYPOTHETICAL CONSUMPTION SCHEDULE (in dollars per month)

The rate of consumer spending (C) is directly related to current disposable income (Y_D). As income rises, so does consumption. The marginal propensity to consume indicates by how much consumption will increase with each added dollar of income. In this case, consumption increases by $75 whenever income increases by $100 (e.g., from row B to row C). The marginal propensity to consume equals 0.75.

	Disposable income (Y_D)	Consumption at zero income	+	Additional spending	=	Total
A	$ 0	$50		$ 0		$ 50
B	100	50		75		125
C	200	50		150		200
D	300	50		225		275
E	400	50		300		350
F	500	50		375		425

Consumption ($C = \$50 + 0.75\,Y_D$)

FIGURE 7.2 A HYPOTHETICAL CONSUMPTION FUNCTION

The consumption function indicates how much a consumer will desire to spend at various income levels. Point B, for example, indicates that this consumer will desire to spend $125 per month when his income is only $100 per month. The difference between income and consumption equals (dis)saving.

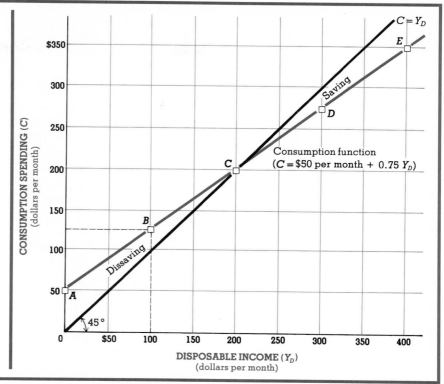

Observe, however, what happens when his disposable income rises to $200 per month (Table 7.1, row C). His rate of consumption increases further, to a comfortable but hardly ostentatious level of $200 per month. Two things are noteworthy. First, his marginal propensity to consume is still 75 percent, as his spending has increased by $75 per month in response to another $100 increase in monthly income. Second, he is no longer dissaving but is now breaking even. Point C lies on the 45-degree line, indicating that current consumption equals current income. Should he be so fortunate as to experience still further increases in income, he will actually begin saving (not spending all his income). To the right of point C, the consumption function always lies below the 45-degree line.

The experiences of our consuming friend can be summarized in an equation (as before), a schedule (Table 7.1), or a graph (Figure 7.2); all of them tell the same story. Take another look at the equation. It says that a consumer will spend something each month (the amount a) even when disposable income (Y_D) equals zero. This is confirmed in Figure 7.2, where the consumption function crosses the vertical axis: at that point (A), monthly income equals zero, yet consumption equals $50 per month.

Now recall what happens when income rises. We have observed that our friend's marginal propensity to consume is 0.75. Thus, if disposable income equals $100 per month, consumption (C) equals $50 + 0.75($100) = $125 per month. This is confirmed in row B of Table 7.1 as well as by point B in Figure 7.2. Thus all versions of the consumption function tell the same story. Any one of them can be used to predict how much consumers will spend out of any given income. We will make most use of the graphic consumption function, as drawn in Figure 7.2.[7]

The aggregate function

We need not dwell any longer on the perils and hardships of this one consumer. Nor do we want to. Our immediate interest is not in the eating and spending habits of any particular consumer but in the behavior of consumers as a class. From this perspective, we can ignore the idiosyncrasies and aspirations of individuals and focus on aggregate (total) consumption.

Repeated studies of consumers suggest that there is nothing very remarkable about the individual we have been studying, except perhaps for his ingenuity during hard times. The consumption function we have constructed for him can be used for the total of all consumers simply by changing the numbers involved. Instead of dealing in hundreds of dollars per month, we now play with hundreds of billions of dollars per year. But the basic relationship is the same. That is to say, we still assume (and can observe) that the rate of consumption spending depends on disposable income, as in Figure 7.2.

The actual relationship of U.S. consumer spending to disposable income is depicted in Figure 7.3. Notice the use of the 45-degree

[7] The slope of the consumption function is equal to the value of the *MPC*, that is, $\Delta C \div \Delta Y_D$.

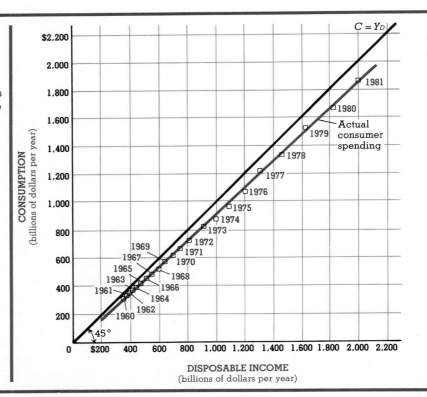

FIGURE 7.3 U.S. CONSUMPTION AND INCOME

The points on the graph indicate the actual rates of U.S. disposable income and consumption for the years 1960–81. By connecting these dots, we can approximate the long-term consumption function. Over time, the average propensity to consume has been around 0.9.

FIGURE 7.4 SHIFTS IN THE CONSUMPTION FUNCTION

The willingness of consumers to spend their current income is affected by their confidence in the future. If consumers become more optimistic, autonomous consumption may increase from a_1 to a_2. This change will shift the entire consumption function upward. It is also possible for b to change; thus changing the slope of the consumption function as well.

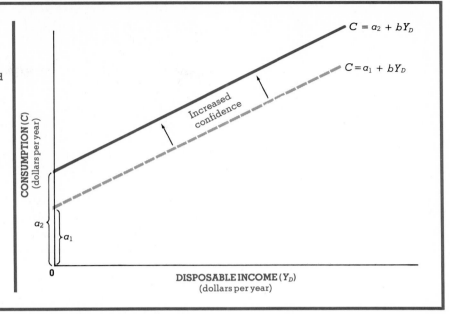

line again. At all points on this line consumption and income are equal. Actual consumer spending lies below the 45-degree line, however, indicating that American families tend to save some fraction of their income.

Expectations and shifts: an important digression

Although consumption generally depends on current income, we should not conclude that all individual consumption functions are identical or that the aggregate consumption function never changes. What is true is that most consumption functions are of the form $C = a + bY_D$. But the values of a and b can and do change. When consumers are optimistic about the future, they tend to spend more, often by borrowing or using credit (apparently in the belief that the proverbial rainy day will never come). Thus increased optimism can lead to more autonomous spending, as reflected in a larger value for a. The size of a may also increase if consumers expect higher prices later and rush to the stores to "beat inflation" (see Chapter 6). Notice what happens to the consumption function when these things happen. In Figure 7.4, the consumption function is initially at $C = a_1 + bY_D$. When consumer confidence increases, autonomous consumption rises to a_2. The new consumption function is therefore $C = a_2 + bY_D$. The consumption function has *shifted* upward; more consumption will occur at every rate of income.

Were consumers to become more pessimistic, the consumption function would shift downward rather than upward. Thus a ***surge in consumer confidence will shift the consumption function upward; a bout of pessimism will knock it down.*** The slope of the consumption function may change as well if the MPC responds to changes in consumer confidence. As the accompanying news article indicates, such changes in consumer confidence can and do occur.

Confidence in Economy Reaches Low

Last month consumer confidence in the economy was lower than at any other time in the 15 years that American families have been surveyed.

Consumer confidence has been battered by a recession, high unemployment and soaring interest rates. Consumer expectations about the future are declining too, although the Conference Board, a nonprofit business research organization that conducts the surveys, said hopes for the future are higher than they were during either the 1974 or 1980 economic slowdowns.

The Conference Board said that 47 percent of U.S. households called current economic conditions "bad," up from less than 46 percent in February. In March 1981, only 31 percent of the 5,000 families surveyed called conditions bad.

"In rating present business conditions, pessimists now outnumber optimists by nearly 5 to 1," said a board spokesman.

Furthermore, the Conference Board said, consumers are scaling back their buying plans, after families raised their buying sights in February.

Until there is a recognizable upswing in consumer buying, one that will impel manufacturers to step up production, the nation will remain in a recession.

The research organization said that buying plans fell for "all of the major items covered: automobiles, homes, appliances and even carpeting." Only 7.5 percent of the families plan to buy cars, compared with 7.8 percent in February, while 2.9 percent plan to buy homes, down from 3.2 percent in February.

—James L. Rowe, Jr.

The Washington Post, Washington, D.C. Copyright © 1982 The Washington Post.

LEAKAGE FROM THE CIRCULAR FLOW

Our basic objective in this chapter is to determine whether the rate of total expenditure at full employment will equal the value of full-employment GNP, thereby minimizing problems of inflation and unemployment. With the aid of the consumption function, we can begin to assess the difficulties of achieving this desired outcome.

Suppose for the moment that we were fortunate enough to be producing at the rate of *full-employment GNP,* which we shall assume to be $2 trillion per year. At this rate of output, we would be generating an equivalent amount of income, as every dollar spent on production ends up in someone's pocket (see Chapter 4). In Figure 7.5 we designate this level of annual income as Y_F (income at full employment). For simplicity, we shall continue to assume that there is no government—and thus that there are no taxes—and that *all* income is received by consumers. Under these assumptions, disposable income (Y_D) and GNP are identical. Thus we can relate the rate of consumer spending directly to total output.[8]

Some inkling of potential problems in maintaining full employment should already be evident. What we have demonstrated is that consumers do not spend all of their income, but instead they save some fraction of it. If all income is not spent, the movement of income around the circular flow (Figure 7.1) is not continuous; on the contrary, the circular flow leaks. Saving is a primary cause of such leakage.

Total output at full employment

If we are receiving $2 trillion worth of income at full employment (Y_F), then $2 trillion worth of output is being produced. In fact, the total value of income is always equal to the value of output. This

[8] Notice that we are also ignoring depreciation, retained earnings, and transfer payments. Taxes and other complications will be introduced in Chapter 8; in the meantime, these assumptions simplify the analysis without changing our basic conclusions.

basic equivalence is illustrated by the 45-degree line in Figure 7.5. This line is now identified as total output. All it does is convert numbers on the horizontal axis into identical numbers on the vertical axis. Thus the horizontal axis of Figure 7.5 tells us not only how much income will be available for spending, but also the value of goods and services that will be for sale in product markets. If we produce $2 trillion of income, point S_F reminds us, $2 trillion of goods and services will be supplied to the market. What the 45-degree line doesn't tell us is how much output will be *demanded*. To determine the value of goods *demanded* when the economy is producing at Y_F, we need to look at aggregate demand, part of which is represented by the consumption function.

Consumer spending at full employment

The consumption function tells us how much consumers will desire to spend in a given time period at alternative income levels. Hence we can use it to predict how much consumer spending will take place at full employment.

Suppose that the aggregate consumption function is $100 billion per year + $0.75Y_D$, as illustrated in Figure 7.5. With the aid of this function, we can determine the rate of expenditure consumers desire to maintain when total annual income equals Y_F. When we substitute $2,000 billion for Y_D, we observe what the annual rate of consumer spending at full employment (C_F) is:

$$C_F = \$100 \text{ billion} + 0.75 \ (\$2,000 \text{ billion})$$
$$= \$1,600 \text{ billion}$$

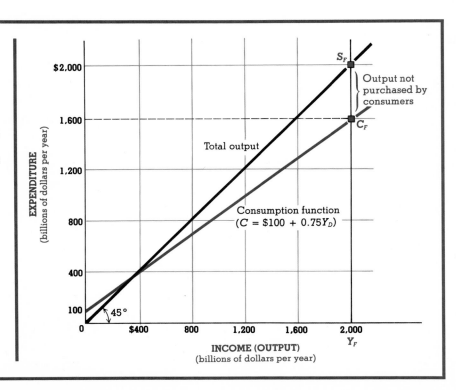

FIGURE 7.5 THE AGGREGATE CONSUMPTION FUNCTION

To determine how much output consumers will demand at full-employment output (Y_F), we refer to the aggregate consumption function. In this case, the amount C_F (equal to $1,600 billion per year) will be demanded at full-employment output ($2,000 billion per year).

We find the same conclusion in Figure 7.5 by moving up from point Y_F on the horizontal (income) axis to the consumption function and noting the value of consumer spending ($1,600 billion) at that juncture.

The message relayed by the consumption function is straightforward. If business firms produce goods and services at the rate of $2 trillion per year (and that much income), consumers will demand only $1,600 billion per year. In short, the rate of production at Y_F ($2,000 billion per year) will exceed the rate of consumer expenditure ($1,600 billion per year). Unless someone else purchases the remaining output ($400 billion per year), producers will start cutting back on production. As production is cut back, people will be thrown out of work.

Consumer saving at full employment

leakage: Income not spent directly on domestic output, but instead diverted from the circular flow; for example, saving, imports, taxes.

The failure of consumers to maintain a rate of expenditure equal to the rate of full-employment output is attributable to their desire to save. People want to put aside some fraction of their current income for future use. What we want to emphasize here is that *consumer saving represents income that does not return directly to product markets as expenditure on final goods and services.* In this sense, consumer saving represents **leakage** from the circular flow (see Figure 7.6).

In our example, this leakage is substantial; at full-employment GNP, consumers desire to save $400 billion per year (recall that $S = Y - C$). This saving reduces the rate of expenditure below the rate of production and raises the specter of increasing unemployment. Unless other market participants (such as investors and government) offset this leakage with purchases of their own, the shortfall in consumer spending will be reflected in growing stocks of unsold goods and services. This accumulation of unwanted inventories in stores and warehouses will ultimately lead to job layoffs.

Notice that imports as well as savings represent leakage from the circular flow. If consumers buy imported goods rather than do-

---

FIGURE 7.6 LEAKAGE

Income saved or spent on imports does not return directly to the circular flow. As a consequence, the total value of goods demanded in a given time period may be less than the value of goods produced. So long as the rate of production exceeds the rate of desired expenditure, undesired inventories will accumulate.

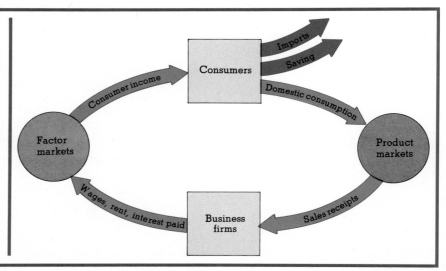

Car Makers Plan 21% Output Cut for 2nd Quarter

Firms' Hopes of Exceeding 1981 Output This Year Are Said to Be Dimming

DETROIT—U.S. automakers are losing hope that they will be able to build more cars this year than they did in 1981.

With output already trailing last year's depressed levels, the automakers are planning sharply lower production for the second quarter and don't expect significant improvement until much later in the year, when they will be hard pressed to make up lost ground.

In the next three months, sources say, domestic manufacturers expect to assemble 1.6 million autos, down 21% from the more than two million cars produced in the second quarter of 1981. Third quarter output is tentatively scheduled to about equal the year-earlier's 1.4 million cars, the sources added.

Such schedules would leave the companies' output almost 900,000 cars below last year's level heading into the fourth quarter, with little prospect of making up the difference.

"We're counting on a little spurt in the fall, but not that big a one," an analyst at one auto company says.

The soft output schedules reflect manufacturers' rising pessimism about the near-term outlook for sales, which have remained disappointing despite extensive rebate programs. With few signs of improvement in the national economy, some sources now say sales of domestically produced autos might total only 6.1 million for the year, compared with 6.2 million in 1981.

—John Koten

---

investment: Expenditures on (production of) new plant and equipment (capital) in a given time period, plus changes in business inventories.

mestic goods, some current income flows out of the domestic economy. As a consequence, domestic producers may end up with unsold output. The consequences of such leakage are potentially the same as those that occur as a result of sonsumer saving. Income taxes are another form of leakage, as we shall demonstrate in Chapter 9.

INVESTMENT

Although leakage from the circular flow is obviously a potential source of unemployment problems, we should not conclude that the economy will sink as soon as consumers start saving some of their income. Consumers are not, after all, the only ones who buy goods and services in product markets; business firms and government agencies also contribute to aggregate demand. So do foreigners who buy our exports. So before we run out in the streets screaming, "The circular flow is leaking!" we need to take a look at what other market participants are doing.

Business firms purchase new plant and equipment for the purpose of expanding or improving their output capabilities; such purchases are called *fixed investment*. Firms also acquire inventories of goods that can be used to satisfy consumer demands; such expenditures are called *inventory investment*. Both forms of **investment** represent a demand for output, and are therefore counted as part of aggregate demand.[9]

Because investment spending represents a demand for current output, it might compensate for the leakage created by consumer saving. But how much investment will take place? Will it be large enough to offset the leakage due to consumer saving (and imports),

[9] Residential construction is also counted in investment statistics, even though houses are a consumer good. The durability of housing motivates this accounting decision.

thereby boosting the rate of total expenditure up to the rate of full-employment GNP?

Expectations

There are several theories about what determines the rate of desired investment spending, but two explanations are most common. First, we recognize that a firm's desire to invest reflects its *expectations* of future sales and profits. Investment decisions are influenced less by *current* income levels than by expectations of *future* income and sales. Surely no firm would want to purchase new plant and equipment unless its managers were convinced that people would later buy the output produced by that plant and that equipment. Nor would a producer want to accumulate larger inventories of goods if he thought sales were going to decline. Thus favorable expectations of future sales are a necessary condition for investment spending.

No one is entirely sure what shapes investors' expectations, however. Essentially, it is a question of confidence in the future course of economic events. Whatever raises investor hopes for economic growth and increased sales will stimulate additional investment. Favorable tax or budget policy, new inventions, or unanticipated sales increases can all raise investor expectations. On the other hand, an unwelcome event—a coal strike or an oil shortage, for example—may shake investors' faith in the course of economic events. Whatever the reasons, expectations are as uncertain as the future itself, and are not easy to predict.

Machine Tool Orders Plunged During February

Fall Was 20% from January and 42% from Year Ago; Producers' Outlook Glum

The widening recession is causing makers of durable goods to further curtail investment in machinery and equipment.

Orders for machine tools, which are machines used to shape most metal parts from oil-drilling bits to car fenders, fell 42% in February to $163.9 million from $280.1 million a year earlier, the National Machine Tool Builders' Association reported.

February orders were down 20% from $205.2 million in January. Except for the holiday-influenced $151.8 million of December, last month's orders were the lowest since April 1976, when orders were $148.6 million.

Machine tool producers find little to be optimistic about because practically all of the major industries that use machine tools have cut purchases. Oil-field equipment producers, who continued to be major buyers in late 1981 after many other businesses had cut orders, also have curtailed spending, machine tool executives say.

Ordering by the auto industry, which was weak most of last year, became worse this year, machine tool officials say. Cash flow of the auto makers is reduced by slow sales and the need to discount to sell cars at all.

February orders were only about one-third of the order rate of two years earlier, association figures show. And the slowdown has hit all major types of machines. Orders in February for lathes, milling machines, machining centers, grinders, boring mills and other machines to shape metal by cutting were down 42% from a year earlier. Orders for metal-forming presses and other machines to shape metal parts with pressure were down 40%. . . .

Before machine-tool orders rebound, however, there will have to be a reduction in interest rates, industry executives agree. "If a company has the cash flow, they can order equipment," says George J. Becker, president of Giddings & Lewis Inc., Fond du Lac, Wis. "But they're playing a touchy game if they have to go out and borrow at 16% to 20% interest rates when the business outlook is this uncertain." Furthermore, he says, the real interest rate, the stated rate minus the inflation rate, is so high that it encourages businessmen to keep money in short-term investments instead of investing in equipment.

—Ralph E. Winter

FIGURE 7.7 INVESTMENT DEMAND

The rate of desired investment depends on expectations, the rate of interest, and innovation. A *change* in expectations will *shift* the investment-demand curve. With given expectations, a change in the rate of interest will lead to *movements* along the existing investment-demand curve. In this case, an increase in investment beyond $300 billion per year (point *A*) may be caused by lower interest rates (point *B*) or improved expectations (point *C*).

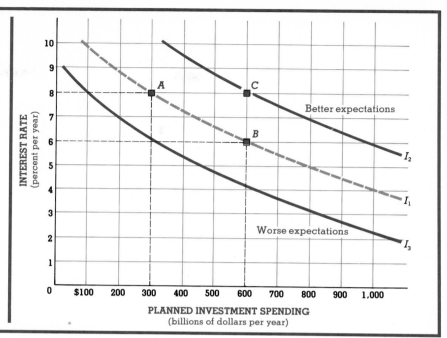

Interest rates

The second major determinant of desired investment spending is the rate of interest. Business firms often borrow money in order to purchase plant and equipment. Naturally, they will be concerned about the cost of such borrowing, as reflected in the rate of interest they have to pay. The higher the rate of interest, the costlier it is to invest. Accordingly, we anticipate a lower rate of investment spending at higher interest rates, more investment at lower rates (*ceteris paribus*).

Figure 7.7 summarizes the influence of expectations and interest rates on investment demand. The curve I_1 tells us how much investment spending business firms will want to undertake at various interest rates, given some fixed set of expectations about future sales and profits. Within this context, we see that lower rates of interest lead to higher rates of investment (compare points *A* and *B*).

Curves I_2 and I_3 illustrate the impact on investment demand of a *change* in expectations. If investors suddenly foresee improved prospects for sales and profits, they will be more eager to invest. Hence they will borrow more money at any given interest rate and use it to buy plant and equipment. This increased willingness to borrow is illustrated by a rightward *shift* of the investment curve to I_2 (that is, greater investment at any given interest rate). On the other hand, should investors' faith in the future be shaken, expectations will worsen and the investment curve will shift to the left (I_3).

Technology and innovation

The demand for investment goods may shift for other reasons as well. When scientists learned how to miniaturize electronic circuitry, an entire new industry of electronic calculators, watches, and other goods sprang to life (see Chapter 21). In this case, the demand for investment goods shifted to the right as a result of improved technology (the miniaturized circuits) and imaginative innovation (the use of the new technology in pocket calculators). More recently, technological advances and cost reductions have stimulated an investment spree in personal computers and video games.

Investment at full employment

Because the demand for investment goods is so heavily influenced by expectations, interest rates, technology, and innovation, it is *not* very sensitive to current levels of income. This is in marked contrast to the demand for consumer goods, which we asserted was directly determined by the level of current income.

As long as investment spending is *not* sensitive to the rate of current income, the investment function may be drawn as a horizontal line in Figure 7.8, which has current income on the horizontal axis. Notice that the rate of investment spending assumed to occur is $300 billion per year, regardless of the level of total income. Remember our earlier assumption that the rate of desired investment spending depends on expectations, the rate of interest, and technology, but *not* on the current level of income.

To determine the desired rate of investment at full employment (or any other rate of output), we must refer back to Figure 7.7, check the current rate of interest, and see how much investment businesses desire to undertake.[10] For the moment we will assume that the rate of interest is 8 percent, and thus that the desired rate of investment spending is $300 billion per year (point A in Figure 7.7).

[10] This is a turn that real-world policy makers often miss, since they seldom have such a detailed map to follow. More on this in Chapter 14.

FIGURE 7.8 AGGREGATE DEMAND

Desired consumer and investor expenditure at full-employment output (Y_F) may not equal total output. In this case, $C_F + I_F$ is $100 billion per year less than full-employment output. As a consequence, producers will accumulate unwanted inventories if they maintain full-employment output.

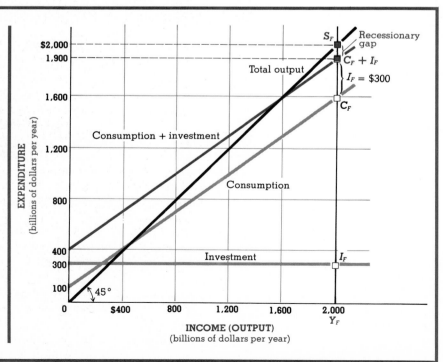

AGGREGATE DEMAND AT FULL EMPLOYMENT

Consumption and investment

Figure 7.8 also tells us how much *combined* consumer and investor spending will occur at every rate of output. Consider the rate of full-employment GNP again. From the consumption function, we know that consumers will want to spend the amount C_F ($1,600 billion per year) at the output level Y_F ($2,000 billion per year). Now we know that investors will want to spend the additional amount I_F ($300 billion per year). By simply adding these two quantities, we can determine the *combined* demand of consumers and investors at full employment. It is C_F plus I_F, or $1,900 billion per year. If we perform the same kind of addition at other income levels, we can quickly confirm that the "consumption plus investment" line expresses the total value of goods and services demanded by consumers and investors at alternative rates of output (income).

Government spending and exports

Consumption and investment are not the only forms of spending, as any taxpayer or traveler knows. As we observed in Chapter 3, government expenditures on goods and services represent over 20 percent of total spending and far exceed investment spending. Purchases by foreigners (exports) of the goods and services we produce also represent a significant fraction of total demand. Hence our analysis of aggregate demand will not be complete until we have examined the determinants of these additional sources of demand. But we can simplify our analysis by ignoring government expenditure and exports for the moment. We will simply pretend that consumers and investors are the only participants in the product market. This has the advantage of illustrating how a completely *private* economy would function, without government purchases or foreign trade.[11] We shall reconsider the expenditure decisions of government and foreigners in the next chapter.

POTENTIAL INSTABILITY

Assuming for the moment that consumers and business firms are the only purchasers of the goods and services produced—that government agencies and foreigners do not exist—we may say that the combined expenditure desires of consumers and investors represent the (private) *aggregate demand* for goods and services. The question now is how aggregate demand compares to total output at full employment.

   As we noted earlier, the total output curve in Figure 7.8 represents the value of total output at every rate of income. The 45-degree angle of this curve indicates that the value of output is always equal to the value of income. It doesn't tell us how much will be spent, however. To determine that, we must look at the aggregate demand

---

[11] A second advantage of this simplification is that it allows us to ignore the distinction between net national product (NNP) and disposable income *(DI)*, since the two concepts differ primarily as a result of taxes and public transfers.

TABLE 7.2   A RECESSIONARY GAP
(all figures in billions of dollars per year)

The recessionary gap is measured at the full-employment level of income. At this level (Y_F), consumers and investors desire to spend less than the economy produces. This difference ($100 billion) between full-employment output and expenditure is called the "recessionary gap."

At income (output) of:	Consumers desire to spend:	+	Investors desire to spend:	=	Total private spending
$ 400	$ 400		$300		$ 700
800	700		300		1,000
1,200	1,000		300		1,300
1,600	1,300		300		1,600
$Y_F = 2,000$	1,600		300		1,900

A recessionary gap

recessionary gap: The amount by which the rate of desired expenditure at full employment falls short of full-employment output.

$(C + I)$ curve. ***Only where the aggregate-demand curve intersects the total-output curve will total expenditure equal total output.***

From Figure 7.8 we see that this is clearly not the case at full employment. On the contrary, aggregate demand at Y_F falls short of total output. At full-employment output (Y_F), the rate of production is S_F ($2,000 billion per year); the rate of expenditure, however, is only $C_F + I_F$ ($1,900 billon per year). The difference, the amount by which the total value of goods supplied at full employment exceeds the total value of goods demanded, is called the **recessionary gap.**

In our example, the recessionary gap amounts to $100 billion per year. This gap is also seen in Table 7.2, which shows the amount of income consumers and investors desire to spend at alternative income (output) levels. At the full-employment rate of production Y_F, consumers desire to spend $1,600 billion per year and investors desire to spend $300 billion, leaving $100 billion worth of goods unsold.

An inflationary gap

inflationary gap: The amount by which the desired rate of expenditure at full employment exceeds full-employment output.

We will not always be burdened with a recessionary gap, of course. A gap emerged here only because we picked too low a level of investment and because we have totally ignored government spending and export sales. Under other circumstances, total spending desires at full employment might actually *exceed* full-employment output, leaving us with an **inflationary gap.**

Desired vs. actual investment

Our purpose here is not to show that an imbalance will necessarily exist between the desired rate of expenditure at full employment and the rate of production. We only wish to show that such an imbalance is possible. When a recessionary gap emerges, producers are unable to sell all the goods they had hoped to. The unsold goods pile up on producers' shelves as additional inventory. This additional inventory gets counted as part of investment spending, because our definition of investment spending includes changes in business inventories. But this additional inventory is clearly *undesired*, as producers had planned on selling these goods. Hence we distinguish between *desired* (or planned) investment and *actual* investment. *Desired* investment represents purchases of new plant and equipment plus any desired changes in business inventories. By contrast, *actual* investment represents purchases of new plant and equipment plus *actual* changes in business inventories, desired or otherwise.

If actual investment at full employment equals desired investment, producers' plans have been fulfilled. No imbalance exists between the rates of expenditure and production at full employment. By contrast, **a recessionary gap implies that producers' expectations have not been fulfilled: actual investment exceeds desired investment and excess (undesired) inventories are piling up.** The existence of an inflationary gap, on the other hand, implies that desired investment at full employment exceeds actual investment, and that inventories are being depleted faster than producers desire. By observing changes in producer inventories, then, we may detect potential imbalances in product markets.

Desired investment vs. desired saving

Imbalances between the rates of expenditure and production are also reflected in differences between desired saving by consumers and desired investment by producers. In particular, a recessionary gap implies that desired saving exceeds desired investment. In our illustration of aggregate demand, we observed (Figure 7.7) that consumers desire to spend only $1,600 billion per year at full-employment output ($2,000 billion). By implication, then, they desire to save (not spend) $400 billion per year. This $400 billion represents leakage from the circular flow. We also observed that desired producer investment spending in this case amounts to only $300 billion per year, not enough to compensate for the leakage represented by consumer saving. From this perspective, **a recessionary gap emerges because desired investment is less than desired saving at full employment.** [12] As a consequence, producers will be unable to

---

[12] A graphic analysis of the imbalance between desired saving and desired investment is contained in the *Study Guide*.

Business outlook

Inventories: supply still exceeds demand

The liquidation of inventories, which began last December, continued at a rapid clip in January, but demand fell even faster, widening the imbalance between stocks and sales.

The biggest imbalance between inventories and sales is accumulating at the factories, which account for more than half of all manufacturing and trade stocks.

Manufacturers' inventories had been rising throughout last summer, and although they were cut $4.2 billion from November to January, that cut represented only about half of the buildup that occurred during the early stage of the recession.

The present squeeze-down in stocks is being forced by the substantial shrinkage in demand. Since last June, factory shipments have fallen continuously, tumbling more than 8%.

Retailers, who have been faced with sluggish consumer demand since last June, appear to have their stocks under a bit more control.

One notable exception: dealer inventories of autos. Even with large rebates continued into early March, auto sales of domestic models stood at an annual rate of only 5.6 million units—well below February's poor rate of 6.3 million.

If sales do no better for the rest of the month, production cutbacks—from an already modest April level—will be needed to clear out overloaded car lots.

sell all the goods they have produced at the prices they expected. As undesired inventories accumulate, producers are likely to reduce the rate of production and lay off workers, sending us down the long road to unemployment.

POLICY IMPLICATIONS: CYCLICAL UNEMPLOYMENT, DEMAND-PULL INFLATION

The emergence of an imbalance between the desired rate of total expenditure at full employment and the rate of production threatens our economic goals. If the desired rate of expenditure at full employment is less than the rate of production, some workers will not be needed and unemployment will spread. Such an imbalance—a recessionary gap—is the origin of **cyclical unemployment.**

When the desired rate of expenditure at full employment exceeds the rate of production, a very different problem emerges. In this case, consumers and investors begin to compete with each other for the goods and services available. Production cannot be expanded beyond full-employment GNP without exerting upward pressure on prices. As a consequence, the competition for available goods and services drives prices upward, setting in motion a **demand-pull inflation.**

Although unemployment and inflation may arise from other causes (to be examined later), the potential imbalances we have described here go a long way toward explaining many of our economic problems. How serious these problems become depends on how producers, workers, and consumers respond to the initial imbalance between the rate of expenditure at full employment and the rate of production. Classical economists thought the economy would adjust quickly to a recessionary gap, setting in motion forces that would close it. Keynesian economists, however, drawing from the lessons of the 1930s, have suggested that a recessionary gap may cripple the economy so severely that it cannot recover on its own. In Chapter 8 we shall consider these two views in more detail, as we examine how the economy responds to both recessionary and inflationary gaps.

SUMMARY

■ The Keynesian explanation of macroeconomic instability focuses on aggregate demand, that is, the desired rate of total spending at various income levels. When the rate of desired expenditure at full employment is not equal to the rate of production (full-employment GNP), either unemployment or inflation results.

■ The rate of desired consumer spending (C) at any income level can be calculated from the consumption function $C = a + bY_D$. The marginal propensity to consume (b) in this function tells us what

cyclical unemployment: Unemployment attributable to a lack of job vacancies; unemployment that results from an inadequate level of aggregate demand.

demand-pull inflation: An increase in the price level initiated by excessive aggregate demand.

fraction of added disposable income will be spent on goods and services. What is not spent is saved.

▪ A potential imbalance between total expenditure and total output first arises because consumers save some of their income, creating a leak in the circular flow. To offset the leak in the circular flow created by consumer saving, we need additional spending from somewhere else.

▪ Business-investment expenditures represent an injection into the circular flow that might offset saving leakage. Business firms purchase new plant and equipment and accumulate inventories of goods and services; all such investment spending is part of aggregate demand.

▪ We have no assurance that desired investment at full-employment GNP will equal desired consumer saving. On the contrary, the rate of desired investment spending depends on sales expectations, interest rates, and technology, and may differ from the rate of desired saving.

▪ A recessionary gap emerges whenever the level of aggregate demand at full employment is less than full-employment GNP. In a completely private and closed economy (no government or foreign trade), a recessionary gap will appear whenever desired saving at full employment exceeds desired investment. The gap will appear as an increase in unsold goods and services (undesired inventories) and may lead to cutbacks in production and employment.

▪ An inflationary gap emerges when the rate of desired expenditure at full employment exceeds the rate of output, setting the stage for demand-pull inflation.

Terms to remember

Define the following terms:

full employment	**consumption function**
full-employment GNP	**dissaving**
derived demand	**leakage**
aggregate demand	**investment**
consumption	**recessionary gap**
disposable income	**inflationary gap**
saving	**cyclical unemployment**
average propensity to consume	**demand-pull inflation**
marginal propensity to consume	

Questions for discussion

1. What factors besides current income might influence consumer spending? How would changes in these factors affect the consumption function?

2. Are current sales really ignored in investment decisions? How might changes in current sales affect expectations or the rate of desired investment? Illustrate graphically.

3. Why do imbalances in the rates of expenditure and production at full employment arise? How might they be avoided?

Problem | Assume that the consumption function is $C = \$150 + 0.8Y$, that desired investment is $500, and that no other forms of expenditure exist.

(a) Complete the following table (all numbers in billions of dollars per year):

At income of:	C	+	I	=	Private aggregate demand
$ 500	$550		$500		$1,050
700	____		____		____
1,000	____		____		____
1,200	____		____		____
1,500	____		____		____
2,000	____		____		____

(b) If full employment is $2,000, how large is the recessionary or inflationary gap?

(c) Illustrate the gap on a graph.

CHAPTER 8

POTENTIAL INSTABILITY

An imbalance between the desires of consumers and the desires of producers can lead to economic instability. As we observed in Chapter 7, if the rate of desired expenditure (aggregate demand) at full employment is not equal to the rate of production, the threat of either cyclical unemployment or demand-pull inflation will arise. But the amount of unemployment or inflation that results and the length of time it lasts depend on the way the economy responds to recessionary and inflationary gaps. If the gaps are closed quickly, the resulting unemployment or inflation will be of little lasting significance. But if such gaps persist, either the unemployment rate or the inflation rate may remain high for substantial periods of time.

The objective of this chapter is to analyze the way the economy adjusts to recessionary and inflationary gaps. Our analysis will emphasize the Keynesian view of the adjustment process. To highlight its distinctive characteristics, however, we shall contrast it with views generally held before Keynes developed his own explanation. These earlier views are usually referred to as Classical theory. The Classical theory of the adjustment process concluded that recessionary gaps and their resulting unemployment would be short-lived. The Keynesian theory of the adjustment process, on the other hand, suggests that a recessionary gap will lead to prolonged periods of unemployment unless deliberate steps are taken to close it. Classical and Keynesian perspectives on the adjustment to an inflationary gap will also be compared.

ADJUSTING TO A RECESSIONARY GAP: THE CLASSICAL VIEW

Classical economists recognized that aggregate demand might not equal total output at full employment. But they argued that the resulting **recessionary gap** would set in motion forces that would quickly close it. In other words, *Classical economists thought the economy would "self-adjust," ensuring a prompt return of full employment.* From their perspective, there was no real stabilization problem.

recessionary gap: The amount by which the rate of desired expenditure at full employment falls short of full-employment output.

Flexible interest rates

The principal source of Classical optimism was the belief that the desires of consumers and investors would be brought into harmony by a flexible rate of interest. Recall our earlier assumption that consumers desire to spend only $1,600 billion per year at full employment ($2,000 billion per year), leaving $400 billion earmarked for desired saving (see Table 8.1). This rate of saving exceeds desired investment ($300 billion per year), leaving us with a recessionary gap.

We earlier argued, however, that the rate of desired investment was influenced by the rate of interest. In particular, we asserted that producers' desire to invest $300 billion was determined by the set of expectations reflected in the investment demand function (Figure 8.1) and an 8 percent rate of interest. The rate of interest may change, however. If it does, the desired rate of investment spending will change, too. Indeed, if the rate of interest were to drop to 7 percent, the rate of desired investment would increase to $400 billion per year (point D in Figure 8.1), so long as producer expectations did not change. Might the rate of interest actually drop this much, thereby stimulating more investment and helping to close the recessionary gap?

The Classical economists argued that this is exactly what would happen. As consumer savings piled up in banks and other financial institutions, lenders would lower the rate of interest in the hope of attracting additional borrowers. As interest rates fell, business firms would come rushing forward with loan applications, hoping to get money for new plant and equipment or larger inventories. Accordingly, the rate of desired investment would increase whenever "sur-

TABLE 8.1 AN INITIAL RECESSIONARY GAP
(in billions of dollars per year)

The consumption and investment schedules tell us how much people desire to consume and businesses to invest at various rates of income (output). In this case, consumption and investment desires at full employment (Y_F) fall short of full-employment output. Desired consumption and investment spending at Y_F amounts to only $1,900 per year, $100 short of full-employment output.

At output (income) level of	Consumers desire to spend	Consumers desire to save	Investors desire to invest
$ 400	$ 400	$ 0	$300
800	700	100	300
1,200	1,000	200	300
1,600	1,300	300	300
$Y_F =$ 2,000	1,600	400	300

FIGURE 8.1 THE CLASSICAL VIEW OF INVESTMENT

Classical economists emphasized the influence of interest rates on investment. If interest rates fell far enough, any desired rate of investment could be attained. In this case, a drop in interest rates from 8 percent to 7 percent stimulates an additional $100 billion in investment. This additional investment closes the recessionary gap.

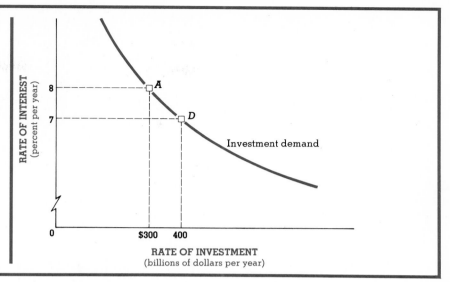

plus" savings accumulated. *From the Classical perspective, changes in the rate of interest serve to equalize desired saving and desired investment,* thereby closing a recessionary gap.

It is evident that if desired investment spending were to respond so quickly and completely to a recessionary gap, the gap would disappear. In our case, consumer spending at full employment ($1,600 billion per year) plus the higher rate of investment spending ($400 billion per year) would completely absorb full-employment GNP.

Flexible prices and wages

Although a flexible interest rate would appear to be a sufficiently powerful force to close recessionary gaps, the Classical economists pointed to still another mechanism of "self-adjustment"; flexible prices and wages.

Assume again that a recessionary gap has emerged at full employment and that $100 billion worth of excess inventories are accumulating (Table 8.1). How will businesses respond to their overflowing shelves and warehouses? Will they simply let the goods pile up? Or will they try to get rid of the excess (undesired) inventories by reducing prices? By reducing prices, business firms might stimulate sales. After all, consumers do love a bargain, and they are likely to respond positively to an "inventory sale."

Producers may thus respond in one of two ways to the appearance of undesired inventories. They may cut back the rate of production, thereby increasing unemployment; or they may cut prices, thereby stimulating sales. In the latter case, the quantity of consumer goods demanded increases and there is no immediate need to cut back production or lay off workers. Hence *the Classical economists assumed that flexible prices would ensure that the quantity of goods demanded at full employment equaled the quantity supplied by producers.*

The price mechanism must work in factor markets, too. If workers were willing to accept lower wage rates, production costs would fall. Lower costs would in turn permit producers to offer goods at lower prices, thereby stimulating sales. In fact, unless wages and other production costs were reduced, it would be unrealistic to assume that producers would lower their prices and maintain full production for very long.

Naturally, no worker would want to accept a cut in wage rates. But the Classical economists noted that the emergence of cyclical unemployment would intensify the competition for jobs. Those workers who became unemployed would then offer their services at reduced wages. This increasing willingness to work at lower wage rates would compel employed workers to accept lower wages or risk unemployment themselves. Hence all wage rates would fall somewhat and full employment would be restored.

Say's Law

Say's Law: Supply creates its own demand.

The faith of Classical economists in the ability of the economy to adjust to a recessionary gap was founded on the twin pillars of flexible interest rates and flexible prices and wages. The flexible interest rates would spur investment spending; flexible prices and wages would spur consumer spending and reduce production costs. Indeed, their faith in these adjustment mechanisms was so strong that their guiding principle was Say's Law. In essence, **Say's Law** — named after the nineteenth-century economist Jean Baptiste Say — decreed that "supply creates its own demand." If $2,000 billion of output per year is produced at full employment, all this output will be sold because:

☐ $2,000 billion of income has been generated.

☐ Interest rates, prices, and wages will all adjust to ensure that all of this income is spent on goods and services.

THE HISTORICAL RECORD

The historical record seemed to justify faith in Say's Law. Although the nineteenth century and the first 30 years of the twentieth century were punctuated with recurrent recessions, these recessions were relatively short-lived (see Figure 8.2). Moreover, in almost every case, prices, wages, and interest rates *had* responded quickly to imbalances between desired investment and saving, thereby closing the recessionary gaps that had first caused cyclical unemployment.

The massive and prolonged unemployment that began in 1930, however, could not be ignored. In the early stages of the Great Depression, the stabilization problem appeared to be no different from that of earlier periods of unemployment, and the Classical economists assured people that full employment would soon be restored. But unemployment grew and persisted, despite falling interest rates, prices, and wage rates. By 1932 the national unemployment rate had risen to 25 percent. In fact, the unemployment rate stayed above 15 percent for almost a decade, despite the fact that average prices fell by over 20 percent and interest rates dropped substantially as well.

FIGURE 8.2 INFLATION AND UNEMPLOYMENT, 1900–40

In the early 1900s prices responded to both upward and downward changes in aggregate demand. Periods of high unemployment also tended to be brief. In the 1930s, however, unemployment rates rose to unprecedented heights and stayed high for a decade. Falling wages and prices did not restore full employment.

Source: U.S. Bureau of the Census, *The Statistics of the United States*, 1957.

THE KEYNESIAN VIEW

The Great Depression effectively destroyed the credibility of Classical economic theory. As John Maynard Keynes pointed out in 1935, Classical economists

> were apparently unmoved by the lack of correspondence between the results of their theory and the facts of observation;—a discrepancy which the ordinary man has not failed to observe. . . .
>
> The celebrated optimism of [classical] economic theory . . . is . . . to be traced, I think, to their having neglected to take account of the drag on prosperity which can be exercised by an insufficiency of effective [aggregate] demand. For there would obviously be a natural tendency towards the optimum employment of resources in a Society which was functioning after the manner of the classical postulates. It may well be that the classical theory represents the way in which we should like our Economy to behave. But to assume that it actually does so is to assume our difficulties away.[1]

Keynes went on to alter the basic assumptions of Classical economic theory and lay the groundwork for an alternative theory of the adjustment process. He emphasized the role of expectations in investment decisions, and the depressing effects of falling prices and wages on aggregate demand. In so doing, he demonstrated the possibility, indeed the likelihood, that cyclical unemployment would result and persist when aggregate demand was determined exclusively by private expenditure decisions.

[1] John Maynard Keynes, *The General Theory of Employment, Interest and Money* (London: Macmillan, 1936), pp. 33–34.

FIGURE 8.3 BAD EXPECTATIONS MAY OVERWHELM LOWER INTEREST RATES

If worsened expectations shift the entire investment demand curve (I_1) to the left (to I_2), lower interest rates may not result in more investment. In this case, we move from point A to point L, rather than to point D.

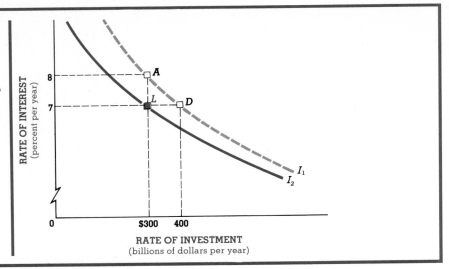

RATE OF INTEREST (percent per year)

RATE OF INVESTMENT (billions of dollars per year)

Expectations

Keynes accepted the Classical argument that an excess of desired saving would tend to lower the rate of interest. But he suggested that a lower interest rate would not be an adequate incentive for additional investment. After all, businesses buy new plant and equipment and accumulate desired inventories only if they expect increased sales. Yet a recessionary gap implies that they are not even able to sell their current output. Why, then, should business firms want to *expand* their production or sales capacity? Keynes argued that it was more reasonable to anticipate that sales expectations will drop when a recessionary gap emerges. Further, this loss of confidence will overwhelm any investment stimulus resulting from a lower interest rate.

Keynes' view of investment decisions is reflected in our earlier distinction between *shifts* of the investment function and movements along any particular investment demand curve. **If expectations worsen, the entire investment function may shift to the left,** implying a *lower* rate of investment at any given rate of interest. Notice in Figure 8.3, for example, that worsened expectations shift the investment function from I_1 to I_2. As a result of this shift, the rate of desired investment spending remains at $300 billion per year (point L) despite a reduced interest rate. In other words, the Classical assumption that lower interest rates will drive us from point A to point D is upset by a leftward shift of the investment function. This shift leaves us at point L.

The Keynesian emphasis on expectations suggests that the Classical economists' first line of defense against cyclical unemployment may be breached. If expectations worsen in response to a recessionary gap, we have no assurance that desired investment spending will rise to the level of desired saving at full employment. Indeed, the rate of investment may actually *decline* once sales start dropping. Even if interest rates continue to fall, expectations may continue to worsen as well, constantly frustrating the effort to close the recessionary gap. This was evidently the case in the Great Depression.

Businessmen Cut Back on Investment

Plagued by high interest rates, collapsing markets and fast declining profits, businessmen are slashing their plans to invest in new plants and equipment, jeopardizing a key element of the Reagan economic program.

A Commerce Department survey released yesterday showed businesses plan to invest 2.4 percent less this year than they did in 1981, after adjustment for inflation. The new survey indicates a sharp reversal in business spending plans since the start of the year.

Most private forecasters expect the actual cutbacks in investment will turn out to be even larger than shown by the survey.

—John M. Berry

The Washington Post, Washington, D.C., June 11, 1982. Copyright ⓒ 1982 The Washington Post.

Total U.S. investment fell abruptly from $16 billion in 1929 to only $1.4 billion in 1933, despite a steep decline in interest rates (to a low of 1.5 percent!).

Inflexible wages and prices

Since a flexible interest rate will not necessarily equalize desired saving and investment, the hope that the economy can self-adjust depends on the second line of defense, flexible prices and wages. This second line of defense does not look very promising, however. To begin with, prices and wages are not easily reduced. Many producers are unwilling to lower product prices in the face of a short-run decline in sales. Moreover, they have no assurance that wages and other factor costs can be reduced to compensate for lower product prices. On the contrary, not only do workers typically respond angrily to any suggestion of wage reductions, but labor unions and other employee organizations have often secured contracts that prohibit such reductions. Accordingly, we cannot rely on wage and price reductions to restore full employment, because such reductions may never take place.

Declining purchasing power

The Keynesian critique of the Classical adjustment process goes beyond the observation that prices and wages do not tend to fall in a modern economy. Indeed, Keynes argued that even if prices and wages did fall in response to a recessionary gap, such wage and price reductions would not restore full employment. On the contrary, such wage and price reductions might actually aggravate the unemployment problem by reducing disposable income.

THE MULTIPLIER PROCESS

Suppose for the moment that the economy is chugging merrily along at full employment when a recessionary gap of $100 billion per year suddenly appears (Table 8.1). As undesired inventory begins to accumulate, producers respond either by reducing wages and prices or by cutting back on production (laying off workers). In either case, disposable income will be reduced. Those consumers who end up with less income will not be able to purchase as many goods and services as they did before. As a consequence, the total value of goods and services demanded will fall further, leading to still larger

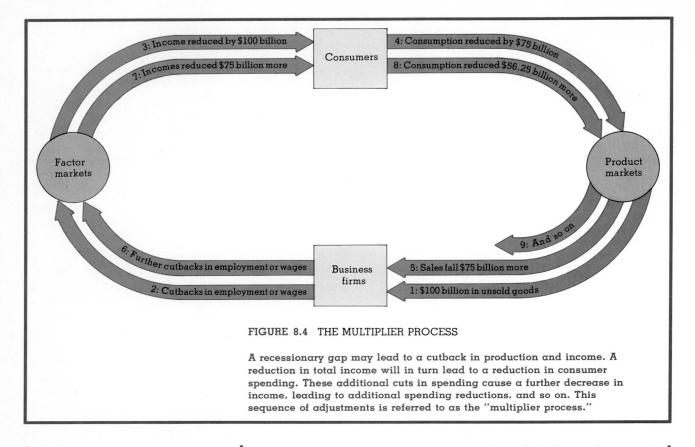

FIGURE 8.4 THE MULTIPLIER PROCESS

A recessionary gap may lead to a cutback in production and income. A reduction in total income will in turn lead to a reduction in consumer spending. These additional cuts in spending cause a further decrease in income, leading to additional spending reductions, and so on. This sequence of adjustments is referred to as the "multiplier process."

consumption function: A mathematical relationship indicating the rate of consumer spending that will take place in a given time period at various income levels.

marginal propensity to consume (MPC): The fraction of each additional (marginal) dollar of disposable income spent on consumption; the change in consumption divided by the change in disposable income.

stocks of unsold goods, more job layoffs, and further reductions in income. It is this sequence of events—called the multiplier process—that makes a recessionary gap so frightening.

We can see the multiplier process at work by watching what happens to the $100 billion gap as it makes its way around the circular flow (Figure 8.4). At first (Step 1) the only thing that happens is that unsold goods appear (in the form of undesired inventories). Producers adjust to this problem by cutting back on production and laying off workers or reducing wages and prices (Step 2). In either case, consumer incomes, mostly wages, fall by $100 billion per year shortly after the recessionary gap emerges (Step 3 in Figure 8.4).

How will consumers respond to this drop in disposable income? Earlier we asserted that consumer spending depends on consumers' disposable incomes. Hence *if disposable income falls, we expect consumer spending to drop as well.* In fact, the **consumption function** tells us just how much spending will drop.

According to the function we examined in Chapter 7,

Annual consumption = $100 billion + (0.75)income

The **marginal propensity to consume** in this function equals 0.75. Therefore, we anticipate that consumers will reduce their spending by $0.75 for every $1.00 of lost income. In the present example, the loss of $100 billion of annual income will force consumers to reduce their rate of spending by $75 billion per year (0.75 × $100 billion). This drop in spending is illustrated by Step 4 in Figure 8.4.

The multiplier process does not stop here. A reduction in consumer spending quickly translates into more unsold output (Step 5). As additional goods pile up on producers' shelves, we anticipate further cutbacks in production, employment, and wages (Step 6), in accordance with the principle of **derived demand.**

As consumer incomes are further reduced by job layoffs and wage cuts (Step 7), more reductions in consumer spending are sure to follow (Step 8). Again the marginal propensity to consume (*MPC*) tells us how large such reductions will be. With an *MPC* of 0.75, we may expect spending to fall by another $56.25 billion per year (0.75 × $75 billion).

derived demand: The demand for labor and other factors of production results from (depends on) the demand for final goods and services produced by these factors.

The multiplier

The multiplier process continues to work until the reductions in income and sales become so small that no one's market behavior is significantly affected. We need not examine each step along the way, because all the steps begin to look alike once you've gone around the circular flow a few times. We can foresee how large an impact the multiplier process will ultimately have. Each time the multiplier process works its way around the circular flow, the reduction in spending equals the previous drop in income multiplied by the *MPC*. Accordingly, by pressing a few buttons on an electronic calculator we can produce a sequence of events like that depicted in Table 8.2.

The impact of the multiplier is devastating. The ultimate reduction in aggregate demand and output resulting from the initial recessionary gap is not $100 billion per year but $400 billion! Even if one is accustomed to thinking in terms of billions and trillions, this is a huge drop in demand, and thus in GNP. What the multiplier process demonstrates is that the dimensions of an initial recessionary gap greatly understate the severity of the economic dislocations that will follow in its wake.

The ultimate impact of a recessionary gap can be determined by

Polaroid to Cut Work Force 6%, by 1,000 Jobs

Outlook for Sales Weakens; Consolidation of Certain Operations Is Considered

CAMBRIDGE, MASS.—Troubles are worsening at Polaroid Corp.

Just two weeks after reporting a 45% drop in nine-month net income, the instant-photo company said Friday that it will cut its worldwide work force by 6%, or 1,000 people.

The step was taken after Polaroid concluded that the vital Christmas sales will be weaker than expected, and the new year will be bleaker than the company previously anticipated.

Polaroid previously has said that retailers, wary about the economy and high interest rates on inventories, have been cutting back orders of Polaroid products since September. The retailers were said to have found shoppers hesitant to buy instant-photo equipment, including cameras and film. Many people consider instant cameras to be luxury items. A single Polaroid photo, for example, costs around 80 cents, more than twice the price of finished photos from conventional cameras.

As yet, Polaroid said it doesn't expect conditions to improve much during 1982. "Despite our collective efforts, current world-wide economic conditions are having an adverse effect on our business," Mr. McCune said. "We don't yet foresee a major improvement in world-wide economic conditions.

"Accordingly, I have asked the members of our senior management team to re-examine their 1982 budget and to reduce our spending plans to a more appropriate level," he said.

TABLE 8.2   THE MULTIPLIER CYCLES

The circular flow of income implies that an initial change in income will lead to cumulative changes in consumer spending and income. Here, an initial income loss of $100 billion (first cycle) causes a cutback in consumer spending in the amount of $75 billion (second cycle). At each subsequent cycle, consumer spending drops by the amount $MPC \times$ prior change in income. Ultimately total spending (and income) falls by $400 billion, or $1/(1 - MPC) \times$ initial change in spending.

Spending cycles	Amount (billions of dollars per year)	Cumulative decrease in aggregate demand (billions of dollars per year)
First cycle: recessionary gap emerges	$100.00	$100.00
Second cycle: consumption drops by $MPC \times$ $100	75.00	175.00
Third cycle: consumption drops by $MPC \times$ $75	56.25	231.25
Fourth cycle: consumption drops by $MPC \times$ $56.25	42.19	273.44
Fifth cycle: consumption drops by $MPC \times$ $42.19	31.64	305.08
Sixth cycle: consumption drops by $MPC \times$ $31.64	23.73	328.81
Seventh cycle: consumption drops by $MPC \times$ $23.73	17.80	346.61
Eighth cycle: consumption drops by $MPC \times$ $17.80	13.35	359.96
.	.	.
.	.	.
.	.	.
Nth cycle and beyond		400.00

multiplier: The multiple by which an initial change in spending will alter aggregate demand after an infinite number of spending cycles; $1/(1 - MPC)$.

computing the change in income and consumption at each cycle of the circular flow, for an infinite number of cycles. This is the approach shown in summary form in Table 8.2. The entire computation may be simplified considerably, however, by use of a single figure, the multiplier. The **multiplier** tells us the extent to which the rate of total spending will change in response to an initial change in the flow of expenditure. The multiplier summarizes the sequence of steps described in Table 8.2.[2]

In our example, the initial change in spending occurs with the appearance of the recessionary gap ($100 billion per year) at full-employment GNP ($2,000 billion per year). Table 8.2 indicates that this gap will lead to a $400-billion reduction in the rate of total spending. Using the multiplier, we arrive at the same conclusion by observing that:

Total change
in spending = multiplier $\times$ initial change in spending

$$= \frac{1}{1 - MPC} \times \$100 \text{ billion per year}$$

$$= \frac{1}{1 - 0.75} \times \$100 \text{ billion per year}$$

$$= 4 \quad \times \$100 \text{ billion per year}$$

$$= \$400 \text{ billion per year}$$

[2] The multiplier summarizes the geometric progression $1 + MPC + MPC^2 + MPC^3 + \ldots + MPC^n$, which equals $1/(1 - MPC)$ when n becomes infinite.

THE PERIOD MULTIPLIER

The actual impact of a recessionary gap depends on two basic things: (1) the size of the MPC and (2) the amount of time that elapses. The larger the MPC, the larger the multiplier. But the full impact of the multiplier will not be felt until we have gone around the circular flow an infinite number of times. In a short period of time—say, one year—we will not travel that far, but will go through only two or three spending cycles. Hence the shorter the period of time (the fewer the number of spending cycles) or the smaller the MPC, the smaller the cumulative change in aggregate demand. For policy makers who are more concerned about next year's election than about the millennium, such a distinction is critical. The *period multiplier* is the value of the multiplier over a finite period of time. It tells us how large multiplier effects will be in a finite period of time. From Table 8.2 we can see how multiplier effects grow with the passage of time and accumulation of spending cycles.

In other words, *the cumulative decrease in aggregate demand ($400 billion per year) resulting from the appearance of a recessionary gap at full employment is equal to the gap ($100 billion per year) multiplied by the multiplier (4).* More generally, we may observe that the larger the fraction (MPC) of income respent in each round of the circular flow, the greater the impact of any change in spending on cumulative aggregate demand.

Plants Plan December Shutdowns as the Recession Spreads Rapidly

It looks as if 1981 will end with a whimper.

From the iron ore mines around Lake Superior to the furniture plants at the southern Appalachians, there will be a lot of shutdowns and short workweeks this month as companies adjust to the rapidly spreading recession. Some plants won't run at all in December, and many will be open only 10 or 15 days.

"It's been a tough year for durable consumer goods, and orders have slowed even more lately," says Henry Timnick, chaiman and chief executive of Stanley Interiors Corp., Stanleytown, Va., a producer of furniture and draperies. "All over the United States, manufacturers are waiting for interest rates to come down some more and for consumer confidence to return." While they wait, they're curtailing production.

Spreading Rapidly

The shutdowns indicate that the recession is spreading very rapidly, but not necessarily that it will be exceptionally deep or prolonged. Prompt action to halt or even avoid inventory buildup could shorten any downturn—if consumers start buying again.

No government statistics measure how many mines, mills and factories will close extra days during December, but a check by The Wall Street Journal shows that the shutdowns will be widespread. The hard-hit auto, truck, farm equipment and construction machinery industries, which ordinarily close plants for the final week of the year, will take a lot of extra time off this year, as will a number of their suppliers. Other businesses, from lumber mills to appliance makers, will lock their doors for additional days or weeks, too.

. . . The plant closings also are evidence of how fast the slump has spread since it began in September. "The economy just fell off a cliff" is a common boardroom comment these days. Retail sales dropped 1.5% in October on top of a 0.1% slip in September. Unemployment in October rose to a six-year high of 8%. Plant operating rates fell to 76.9% of capacity, from just under 80% for much of 1981. Order rates dropped even faster. Durable goods orders in October dropped 8%, the Commerce Department reported. Previously planned production schedules started to produce a buildup of finished goods at the factories.

"We adjusted production to lower levels but before we could react, our inventories were too high," says Ronald Fountain, treasurer of White Consolidated Industries Inc., a producer of household appliances and industrial equipment. "As a result, we're taking an additional week of downtime in December at many of our appliance plants," he says, shutting down two weeks instead of the usual one week. General Electric Co., hit even harder, has halted major appliance production at its Appliance Park facility in Louisville for all of December.

—Ralph E. Winter

FIGURE 8.5 ADJUSTMENT TO EQUILIBRIUM

A recessionary gap indicates that the rate of desired expenditure at full employment $(C_F + I_F)$ falls short of full-employment output $(S_F = Y_F)$. The resultant excess output leads producers to reduce the rate of production to Y_e. The rate of production continues to fall until expenditure desires (aggregate demand) are in balance with the rate of output. The equilibrium rate of output occurs at point E.

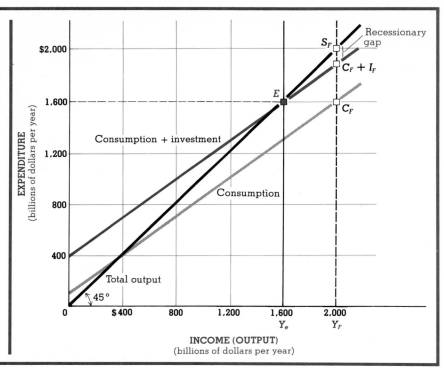

EQUILIBRIUM GNP

The multiplier process underscores the importance of avoiding a recessionary gap. As illustrated again in Figure 8.5, consumption plus investment spending at full employment $(C_F + I_F)$ was less than full-employment income (point S_F). A gap existed between the value of total output and the value of goods *demanded*. As a consequence of that gap, production cutbacks began, and the recessionary process got under way.

We now know that such reductions will continue until GNP has fallen by $400 billion per year (the multiplier times the initial gap). That is to say, GNP will fall from its initial full-employment level of $2,000 billion per year (Y_F) to $1,600 billion (Y_e). Notice the unique character of this particular level of income. At Y_e, desired consumption and investment spending are exactly equal to total income (point E). In other words, the rate of desired expenditure equals the rate of production at Y_e. ***At the equilibrium rate of income there is no longer any cause for further changes in output, because everything produced is being sold.*** This is also illustrated in Table 8.3. At an income level of $1,600 billion per year, desired consumer and investor expenditures total $1,600 exactly.

There is only one rate of **equilibrium GNP,** and it occurs where the aggregate demand curve $(C + I$ in this case) intersects the total output curve (at point E). That is to say, there is only one rate of output at which the total value of goods demanded equals the total value supplied.

What brings supply and demand into harmony at this rate of

equilibrium GNP: The rate of output at which the rate of desired expenditure (aggregate demand) equals the rate of production (aggregate supply).

TABLE 8.3 EQUILIBRIUM GNP
(in billions of dollars per year)

There is only one rate of output at which aggregate demand equals total output. That equilibrium (Y_e) occurs at an output rate of $1,600 billion per year in this case. At equilibrium, desired saving equals desired investment. At all other rates of output, aggregate demand and output are not balanced, and the economy will expand or contract.

	Output (income) level	Consumers desire to spend	Consumers desire to save	Investors desire to invest	Economy
	$ 400	$ 400	$ 0	300	expands
	800	700	100	300	expands
	1,200	1,000	200	300	expands
Y_e	1,600	1,300	300	300	stabilizes
Y_F	2,000	1,600	400	300	contracts

output is the fact that desired investment by producers exactly equals desired saving by consumers. At an income level of $1,600 billion per year, consumers desire to spend $1,300 billion, and desire to save the remaining $300 billion (see Table 8.3). We also noted that business firms desire to invest $300 billion per year. Hence desired investment exactly equals desired saving. As a consequence, no excess (undesired) inventories accumulate, and producers have no incentive to reduce output further.[3]

At equilibrium (Y_e), producers have no incentive to expand production either, because they are just selling as much as they produce, without depleting desired inventories. By contrast, if GNP were less than $1,600 billion per year, desired investment would exceed desired saving (see Table 8.3). In this case, inventories would drop below desired levels, and producers would want to increase output up to the equilibrium level.

Equilibrium GNP vs. full-employment GNP

Although equilibrium GNP implies a certain measure of stability in the rate of output, it is not necessarily a *desirable* rate of output. Indeed, the equilibrium output we end up with in this case is considerably smaller than our full-employment potential. At Y_e we are producing only $1,600 billion of output per year, rather than $2,000 billion. We are stuck at some point *inside* our production-possibilities curve, with a high rate of unemployment. Moreover, there is no obvious relief in sight, as the equilibrium at Y_e equates the desires of consumers and producers. There is no incentive for producers to hire more labor or to increase output.

Equilibrium GNP will not always be less than full-employment GNP. If the consumption and investment functions were to shift upward, equilibrium GNP would move closer to full-employment GNP, and possibly even exceed it (in which case we would confront an inflationary gap). It is evident, however, that equilibrium GNP *might* be less than full-employment GNP, resulting in persistent **cyclical unemployment.**

cyclical unemployment: Unemployment attributable to a lack of job vacancies; unemployment that results from an inadequate level of aggregate demand.

[3] We are assuming here that desired investment remains at $300 billion, despite falling sales. This may be wishful thinking. If investors' expectations worsen greatly, both desired investment and equilibrium GNP will decline.

FIGURE 8.6 AN INFLATIONARY GAP

An inflationary gap indicates that the desired expenditure at full employment $(C_F + I_F)$ exceeds full-employment output (Y_F). This excessive demand at full employment leads to an equilibrium rate of output (Y_e) that exceeds the economy's productive capacity (Y_F). As a consequence, the higher nominal income at Y_e ($2,400 billion per year) implies inflation rather than higher *real* income.

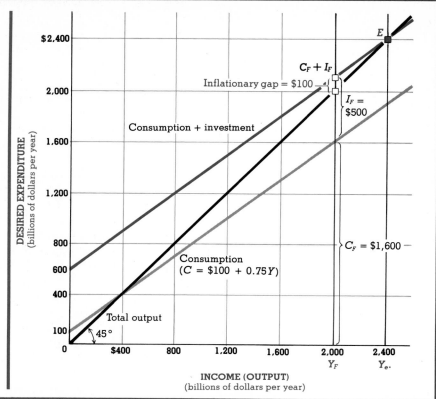

ADJUSTING TO AN INFLATIONARY GAP

Imagine for the moment that consumers desire to spend $1,600 billion per year at full-employment GNP ($2,000 billion per year), but that business firms now desire to invest $500 billion rather than only $300 billion per year, as before (Table 8.3). As a result, the rate of desired expenditure at full employment ($2,100 billion per year) exceeds the rate of full-employment production by $100 billion (see Figure 8.6). How will the economy adjust to this imbalance?

The Classical view

inflationary gap: The amount by which the desired rate of expenditure at full employment exceeds full employment output.

The Classical economists recognized that the economy could not produce output in excess of its production possibilities; hence an **inflationary gap** cannot be closed by an increased rate of production. If an inflationary gap is to be closed, the rate of desired expenditure at full employment will have to be reduced. But what mechanisms will lower the rate of expenditure?

RISING INTEREST RATES   The Classical economists argued that a flexible rate of interest could discourage investment spending as well as encourage it. In particular, a higher rate of interest, by raising the cost of investment, would discourage businesses from buying new plant and equipment or adding to inventories. If the rate of interest increased sufficiently, the rate of desired investment would fall to a level compatible with desired saving.

Will the rate of interest rise as required? The Classical economists said it would. ***The existence of an inflationary gap implies
that desired investment exceeds desired saving*** (see Figure 8.6).
Thus the flow of income into capital markets (banks and other financial institutions) will not be large enough to satisfy the desires of
would-be investors. As investors start competing for scarce savings,
they will bid up the interest rate. Hence the expenditure desires that
initially created the inflationary gap will force interest rates up,
thereby altering investment plans and closing the gap.[4]

RISING PRICES AND WAGES   The Classical economists also noted that
the existence of an inflationary gap implies upward pressure on
prices, that is, **demand-pull inflation.** Such inflation will itself set in
motion forces to reduce the rate of expenditure and therefore close
the gap.

The Classical economists argued that higher prices for goods
and services would dampen consumer enthusiasm and lead to less
spending. In addition, higher wage rates, if attained, would raise
production costs and therefore make continued production less profitable. The Classical economists argued that this combination of
higher prices and wage rates, together with higher interest rates,
would lower the rate of expenditure and close the inflationary gap.
Inflation, therefore, would soon disappear as the economy "self-
corrected."

**demand-pull inflation: An
increase in the price level
initiated by excessive
aggregate demand.**

The Keynesian response

Keynes' response to the Classical view is predictable. It emphasizes
the role of expectations on investment and the impact of higher
prices and wages on disposable income. According to Keynes, the

[4] Higher interest rates may also discourage consumer expenditures (especially on new
houses and other large purchases). The impact of higher interest rates on the mix of
output is discussed in Chapter 12.

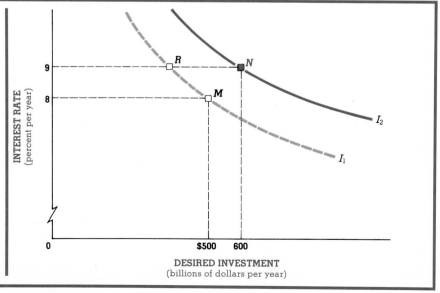

**FIGURE 8.7 INCREASED
EXPECTATIONS MAY OVERWHELM
INCREASED INTEREST RATES**

Classical economists assumed that
higher interest rates would reduce the
rate of investment. This assumption is
illustrated by the move from point *M*
to point *R*. Keynes argued, however,
that improved sales expectations
might shift the investment demand
curve to the right. At point *N*, the rate
of investment is higher, despite a rise
in interest rates.

DESIRED SAVING VS. ACTUAL SAVING: THE PARADOX OF THRIFT

Suppose that the economy is in full-employment equilibrium, with the rate of desired expenditure equal to $2,000 billion per year (higher than our previous example). At this equilibrium, consumers are spending $1,700 billion per year and saving $300 billion per year while investors are spending $300 billion per year. These relationships are illustrated in Figure a.

Suddenly, however, consumers decide they want to save a larger fraction of their incomes. They may foresee harder times ahead, or simply desire to accumulate more savings for later expenses (e.g., college tuition). Whatever the motivation, the impact of this increased desire to save must be reflected in a reduced rate of consumption at full employment (C_F^*). Because every dollar of disposable income is either consumed or saved (by definition), a greater desire to save results in a downward shift of the consumption function. Specifically, if consumers decide to save $400 billion per year at full employment, rather than only $300 billion, consumption at full employment must drop from $1,700 billion per year to only $1,600 billion. This is illustrated in Figure b.

If consumption drops, what will happen to sales and output? As unwanted inventories accumulate, producers cut back on production and lay off workers. Consumer incomes fall, and the economy continues to contract until a new and lower equilibrium is reached. At the new equilibrium, we observe that:

□ Income has been reduced (from $2,000 billion per year $[Y_F]$ to $1,600 billion per year $[Y_e]$).

□ Consumption has been reduced (from $1,600 billion per year $[C_F^*]$ to $1,300 billion per year $[C_e]$).

□ Desired saving has been reduced (from $400 billion per year $[Y_F - C_F^*]$ to $300 billion per year $[Y_e - C_e]$).

Indeed, desired saving is once again equal to desired investment (unchanged at $300 billion per year), as it must be in equilibrium.

economy might not "self-adjust" to an inflationary gap; instead, inflation might persist.

HIGH EXPECTATIONS   If the rate of desired expenditure is higher than the rate of production, firms are selling everything they produce and some of their desired inventory as well. Such buoyant sales tend to raise producers' expectations for *future* sales, and thus shift the investment demand curve to the right (see Figure 8.7). With higher expectations, businesses will not be deterred so easily from their investment plans by a higher rate of interest. Indeed, if expectations improve significantly, the rate of desired investment may even *increase*, despite rising interest rates. Notice in Figure 8.7 that the rate of desired investment expenditure rises from $500 billion (point M) to $600 billion per year (point N) despite an increase in the interest rate. Here again, ***Keynes emphasized that changes in expectations may overwhelm changes in the interest rate as a determi-***

What has happened here? An attempt by consumers to increase the rate of saving (lower the rate of consumption) at full-employment equilibrium creates a recessionary gap. The gap leads to a lower equilibrium output, less income, and a resumption of the initial rate of saving. Hence an attempt to save more results in less income and no more saving! This "paradox of thrift" is explained by the impact of reduced consumer demand on production decisions and income, as illustrated by the multiplier process. The paradox is that an attempt by consumers to increase the rate of saving may lead to less income and no additional saving.

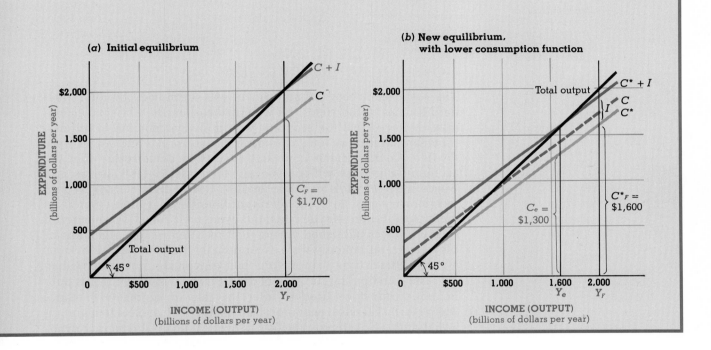

(a) Initial equilibrium

(b) New equilibrium, with lower consumption function

nant of desired investment. As a consequence, interest-rate changes may not lead the economy back to full-employment equilibrium.

HIGHER INCOMES The second line of the Classical defense against continuing inflation must be abandoned, too. Higher prices and wage rates increase disposable income and thus encourage more consumer spending, not less. As illustrated in Figure 8.6, the excessive rate of expenditure at full employment (Y_F) amounts to $100 billion per year. As this expenditure enters the circular flow, it creates an equivalent amount of income. Consumers, in turn, will use this added income to purchase additional goods and services, as indicated by the marginal propensity to consume (MPC). This process gets repeated until the multiplier finally propels the economy to the new equilibrium at Y_e^* in Figure 8.6. At Y_e^* the rate of desired expenditure is $2,400 billion per year, far in excess of the economy's output capability ($2,000 billion per year). But there is no incentive to reduce the rate of desired expenditure, because everyone is spending as much as he or she desires at that income level: Y_e^* represents an *equilibrium* situation.

Notice that this new equilibrium rate of output (Y_e^*) exceeds full-employment output (Y_F). By definition, however, *real* output, valued at constant prices, cannot exceed full-employment output. Hence the higher *nominal* value of Y_e^* must reflect increased prices. Indeed, the inflationary gap implies that people want to spend more than the economy can produce. As consumers compete against each other for available goods and services, they push prices up, resulting in demand-pull inflation and higher nominal incomes.

POLICY IMPLICATIONS: GOVERNMENT INTERVENTION

The Keynesian theory of adjustment was formulated by John Maynard Keynes in the 1930s. As we noted earlier, the Classical economists believed that the economy would always rebound to full employment, at least as long as interest rates or prices and wages were flexible. Keynes' major contribution was to demonstrate that the economy might not self-adjust even when interest rates, prices, and wages were all (downwardly) flexible. Rather than self-adjust to a recessionary gap, an economy might flounder in a high-unemployment equilibrium. Keynes' insights were well timed. His theory of stagnation was published during the Great Depression, when unemployment rates not only were exceptionally high but persisted so for a much longer time than anyone had previously thought possible.

The principal implication of the Keynesian message is that public policy must be used to alter the rate of aggregate demand. Whereas the Classical economists advised policy makers to maintain a wait-and-see posture in the face of cyclical unemployment. Keynes argued that policy makers would have to take explicit action to restore the nation's economic health. Even if the economy might eventually self-adjust in a Classical manner, Keynes argued, the costs of waiting for the adjustment were too great. *At best*, Keynes felt, self-adjustment was a long-run phenomenon. Such a long-term horizon was inappropriate for public policy, however. As he bluntly put it: "In the long run we are all dead."

Keynes' prescription for ending the Great Depression was simple: increase the rate of public spending. Without such an increase, Keynes argued, the rate of production would continue at a low level, leaving millions of workers unemployed. Keynes' advice was largely ignored and the Great Depression persisted until the outbreak of World War II, when aggregate demand surged and the depression ended.

The policy implications of Keynes' recessionary-gap analysis also apply to inflationary gaps. In this case, a wait-and-see attitude on the part of policy makers might leave the economy burdened with persistent demand-pull inflation. The alternative? To force reductions in the rate of desired expenditure, either by cutting government spending or by increasing taxes on consumers and businesses.

The Keynesian call for increased government participation in product markets has been heeded. In Chapter 3 we saw that government expenditures on goods and services absorb one-fifth of annual output. In Chapter 9 we shall examine the impact of changes in government spending and taxes on output, employment, and prices.[5]

SUMMARY

▪ The seriousness of a recessionary or inflationary gap depends on the way the economy responds to an imbalance between the rate of desired expenditure at full employment and the rate of full-employment production. Classical economists argued that the economy could self-adjust to full employment. Thus any cyclical unemployment or demand-pull inflation caused by an imbalance would be temporary.

▪ The two mechanisms of Classical self-adjustment were thought to be:

(a) Flexible interest rates (to equate desired savings and investment)

(b) Flexible prices and wages (to equate the quantity demanded and the quantity supplied)

▪ Keynes argued that these mechanisms might not work, because:

(a) Changes in expectations have more influence on investment spending than changes in interest rates.

(b) Prices and wages rarely fall.

(c) Changes in prices or wages alter disposable incomes and therefore the rate of consumer spending.

As a consequence, the economy will not self-adjust to full employment, but may instead end up at an equilibrium GNP lower or higher than the rate of full-employment production (with stable prices).

▪ The multiplier indicates the cumulative change in total spending that follows an initial change in the flow of expenditure; it equals $1/(1 - MPC)$. The multiplier reflects the fact that a reduction in the rate of expenditure will reduce disposable income, leading to further reductions in consumer spending, which further reduce income, and so on.

▪ The Keynesian theory of the adjustment process suggests that the economy may not self-adjust to either inflation or unemployment. On the contrary, if persistent cyclical unemployment or demand-pull inflation is to be avoided, the government may have to play a direct role in altering the rate of desired expenditure (aggregate demand).

[5] Unemployment and inflation may occur together and for reasons other than excessive or inadequate expenditure at full employment; these possibilities are discussed in Chapter 13. Also, government expenditure and taxation are motivated by reasons other than stabilization requirements (see Chapter 3).

Terms to remember | Define the following terms:

recessionary gap

Say's Law

consumption function

marginal propensity to consume
  (MPC)

derived demand

multiplier

equilibrium GNP

cyclical unemployment

inflationary gap

demand-pull inflation

Questions for discussion | 1. Suppose that the rate of interest were to fall to zero. Can you think of any reasons business firms might have for *not* increasing the rate of investment at such a low rate of interest?

2. Why might consumers continue to buy a great many goods and services when prices are rising?

3. In 1982 auto workers accepted reduced wages, hoping thereby to increase employment. Is such a strategy likely to succeed? What would happen if all workers did the same thing?

4. How can an economy escape an equilibrium that is above or below full-employment GNP?

Problem | Assume that all expenditure is summarized in the following consumption and investment functions:

$C = \$200$ billion per year $+ 0.80\ Y_D$
$I = \$300$ billion per year

Use this information to answer the following questions:

(a) Identify the equilibrium rate of output.

(b) Compute the size of the recessionary gap when full-employment GNP equals $2,800 billion.

(c) What is the value of the multiplier?

(d) What would happen to equilibrium GNP if the rate of investment increased to $350 billion per year?

(e) Illustrate your answers on a graph.

CHAPTER 9

FISCAL POLICY

The Keynesian theory of instability leads directly to a mandate for government policy. From a Keynesian perspective, an insufficiency of aggregate demand causes unemployment; an excess of aggregate demand causes inflation. Since the market itself will not correct these imbalances between aggregate demand and our productive capabilities, something else must. That something else is the federal government. Specifically, the federal government must increase aggregate demand when it is too low and decrease aggregate demand when it is excessive. By balancing aggregate demand and full-employment GNP in this way, the federal government can achieve our macro goals of full employment, price stability, and sustained growth.

In this chapter we shall examine some of the Keynesian tools the federal government *can* use to alter economic outcomes. In particular, we shall look at the potential of taxes and government expenditure to alter the level of aggregate demand. We first want to see how changes in taxes or government spending might alter aggregate demand. Then we shall examine some of the limitations of this policy approach.

THE NATURE OF FISCAL POLICY

The First Article of the U.S. Constitution empowers Congress "to lay and collect taxes, duties, imposts and excises, to pay the debts and provide for the common defense and general welfare of the United

States." It was not until 1915, however, that the Sixteenth Amendment to the Constitution extended that power to include income taxes. And it was not until the 1930s that the use of income taxes to achieve macroeconomic goals was seriously considered. Today things are different. In exercising its tax powers, the federal government now collects and spends over $700 billion each year, an amount equal to 20 percent of GNP (see Chapter 3). When we speak of **fiscal policy,** we are referring to these public tax and expenditure activities. More particularly, fiscal policy is the use of public taxation and expenditure powers to alter macro economic outcomes.[1]

Although fiscal policy can be used to pursue any of our economic goals, we shall begin our study by exploring its potential to ensure full employment. We shall then look at its impact on inflation. Along the way we shall also observe the potential of fiscal policy to alter the mix of output and the distribution of income.

fiscal policy: The use of government taxes and spending to alter macroeconomic outcomes

FISCAL POLICY TO ACHIEVE FULL EMPLOYMENT

As we observed in Chapters 7 and 8, the circular flow of income leaks. The most important form of such leakage in a completely private economy (with no government) is consumer saving. Consumers do not return all of their income directly to the circular flow, but instead save some fraction of it. Unless enough additional expenditure is injected into the circular flow to make up the shortfall in consumer spending at full employment, a **recessionary gap** will emerge.

In the Classical view of the world, it was assumed that desired investment spending would always equal desired saving at full employment, and therefore close any recessionary gap that arose. Keynes asserted, however, that the rate of desired investment might *not* equal the rate of desired saving at full employment. Were this to happen, a recessionary gap would exist, and the economy would begin to wind down to a lower rate of equilibrium output (Y_e in Figure 9.1), with persistent cyclical unemployment.

recessionary gap: The amount by which the rate of desired expenditure at full employment falls short of full-employment output.

Maintaining full employment

Figure 9.1 not only illustrates how a recessionary gap emerges, but also provides some fairly obvious clues about how to prevent one. If a recessionary gap results from a deficiency of aggregate demand, then the logical thing to do is to increase that demand. The government can do this by purchasing available goods and services, that is, by increasing its own rate of expenditure. The potential of such expenditures to fill the gap is suggested by the curve marked $C + I + G$.

The consumption and investment functions of Figure 9.1 are identical to those we used in Chapters 7 and 8. The economy is

[1] Recall that state and local governments also impose taxes and purchase goods and services (see Chapter 3). Their role in fiscal policy will be examined later in this chapter and in Chapter 14.

FIGURE 9.1   THE FISCAL POLICY OBJECTIVE

A major objective of fiscal policy is to close inflationary and recessionary gaps. In this case, a recessionary gap of $100 billion exists in the absence of government spending. (The gap equals Y_F minus [$C_F + I_F$]). In the absence of any other changes, this gap would push the economy into the recessionary equilibrium Y_e. By spending $100 billion, however, the government increases aggregate demand and eliminates the recessionary gap. Notice that total spending at full employment ($C_F + I_F + G$) now intersects the total-output curve at full employment (Y_F).

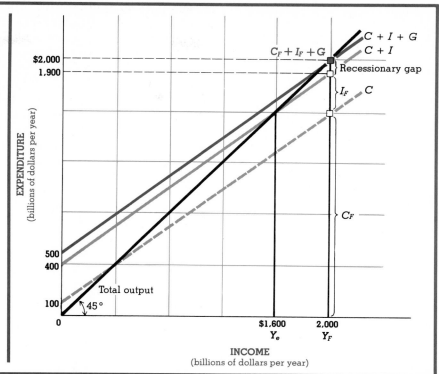

assumed to be at full employment (Y_F) initially, with a GNP of $2 trillion ($2,000 billion). Consumer spending is determined by the function

$$C = \$100 \text{ billion per year} + (0.75)Y$$

Thus desired consumption at full employment (C_F) equals $1,600 billion per year. Investments of $300 billion per year ($I_F$) are dictated by producers' expectations of sales and profits, as well as by the prevailing rate of interest. In sum, the rate of private expenditure at full employment ($C_F + I_F$) totals $1,900 billion per year, leaving a recessionary gap of $100 billion per year.

To close the recessionary gap, we need to boost aggregate demand at full employment by $100 billion per year. The government can do this by entering the market to purchase airplanes, highways, schools, courthouses, public toilets, or whatever else we deem useful. We can illustrate such expenditures by adding a third layer to our aggregate-demand function, as in Figure 9.1.

The line $C + I + G$ represents *total* domestic spending at full employment; it includes $1,600 billion of annual consumption (C_F), $300 billion in annual investment (I_F), and an added $100 billion per year in government purchases of goods and services (G).[2] Since that rate of expenditure equals the rate of full-employment production, no recessionary gap will emerge, and the economy will chug merrily

[2] We are still ignoring imports and exports; international trade is discussed in Chapter 33.

along at full employment. (Y_F is now the equilibrium rate of output.) In this case, *an injection of government spending helps offset the leak created by consumer saving,* thus maintaining aggregate demand at the rate of full-employment output.

PAYING FOR GOVERNMENT EXPENDITURE   Notice that we haven't said anything about how the government is going to finance this expenditure. If the government gets the required $100 billion by imposing taxes on consumers and investors, then the stimulus of government spending will be offset in part by reduced consumption and investment. If, on the other hand, the government *borrows* the money from the private sector, less credit may be available to finance consumption and investment, again creating an offsetting reduction in private demand. In either case, government spending may "crowd out" some private expenditure. For the moment, however, we will ignore these problems and assume that the government's expenditure of $100 billion per year does not reduce private consumer or business spending. Keynes made the same assumption. We shall reconsider this assumption in Chapters 10 through 12, when we look at the way money markets work. As we shall see there, the degree of assumed "crowding out" is a focal point of controversy between Keynesians and Monetarists.

Attaining full employment

If an increase in government spending will not reduce private spending, then the potential of increased government expenditure to close a recessionary gap is evident. Unfortunately, we have no assurance that such spending will take palce or that it will get there in time. Economic policy might not come to our timely rescue for many reasons. For example, we might not realize that a recessionary gap is forming until it is too late. Or perhaps Congress will be on vacation ("in recess") when we need authorization to spend the money. Maybe a presidential election is approaching, and no one is keeping an eye on the economy. Whatever the reason—and we shall discuss these and more in Chapter 14—it is surely possible that the economy will slide into a recession before effective action is taken. Indeed, our experience with unemployment problems (Chapter 5) provides convincing evidence of that possibility.

Let us imagine a different economic dilemma. Suppose now that the economy has already contracted and that we are stuck in a recessionary equilibrium (Y_e in Figure 9.1). In that case, **equilibrium GNP** is simply too low. Such a situation was typified by the Great Depression, but also resembles more recent recessions.[3] The problem then becomes one of *achieving* full employment rather than just maintaining it.

equilibrium GNP: The rate of output at which the rate of desired expenditure (aggregate demand) equals the rate of production (aggregate supply).

Recall our assumption that total output (and income) at Y_e is only $1,600 billion per year, or $400 billion less than our full-employment potential (see Figure 9.1). In such a situation what should the government do? Should it go into the market and buy

---

[3] A recession is officially defined as a decline in real GNP for two consecutive quarters. The distinction between a recession and a depression is one of magnitude, depressions being severe and extended recessions.

FIGURE 9.2 STIMULUS TO THE CIRCULAR FLOW OF INCOME

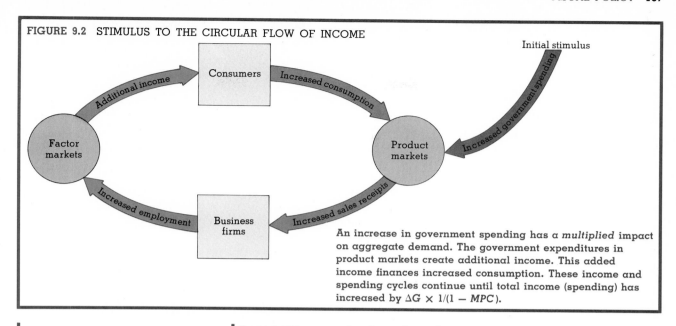

An increase in government spending has a *multiplied* impact on aggregate demand. The government expenditures in product markets create additional income. This added income finances increased consumption. These income and spending cycles continue until total income (spending) has increased by $\Delta G \times 1/(1 - MPC)$.

multiplier: The multiple by which an initial change in spending will alter aggregate demand after an infinite number of spending cycles; $1/(1 - MPC)$.

marginal propensity to consume (MPC): The fraction of each additional (marginal) dollar of disposable income spent on consumption; the change in consumption divided by the change in disposable income.

$400 billion worth of goods and services per year? Or will a much smaller increase in the rate of expenditure bring about the same result?

THE MULTIPLIER   Actually, a much smaller increase in the rate of expenditure is all that is required, thanks to the multiplier. ***An increase in the government's rate of expenditure implies an increase in disposable income,*** as someone must receive the dollars the government spends. From the consumption function, we know that an increase in disposable income will lead to an increase in consumer spending. As this additional consumption enters the product markets, it creates income for other people (Figure 9.2). As this process continues, the *cumulative* increase in income grows larger and larger. Ultimately, the total change in GNP brought about by an initial increase in the rate of expenditure will be much larger than the amount initially spent. The **multiplier** summarizes this process.

Suppose that the government decided to spend $100 billion per year on a new fleet of cruise missiles. How would this decision affect aggregate demand? In the first instance, such an expenditure would clearly increase aggregate demand by $100 billion. This is only the beginning of a very long story, however, as Table 9.1 reminds us. The people who build cruise missiles will be on the receiving end of a lot of income and will be in a position to increase their spending accordingly. How much they actually increase their consumption will depend on their **marginal propensity to consume.**

If the *MPC* of aerospace workers is 0.75, we expect their collective spending to increase by $75 billion (three-fourths of $100 billion per year). Now we have $100 billion of government spending *plus* $75 billion of additional consumption. This brings the *cumulative* increase in aggregate demand to $175 billion per year, already much larger than the initial increase in government spending.

TABLE 9.1 THE MULTIPLIER PROCESS AT WORK

Purchasing power is passed from hand to hand in the circular flow. The *cumulative* change in aggregate demand that results from a new injection of spending into the circular flow depends on the *MPC* and the number of spending cycles that occur. The limit to multiplier effects is established by the ratio $1/(1 - MPC)$. In this case, $MPC = 0.75$, so the multiplier equals 4. That is to say, aggregate demand will ultimately rise by $400 billion per year as a result of an increase in G of $100 billion per year.

Hypothetical spending cycles	Amount (billions of dollars per year)	Cumulative increase in aggregate demand (billions of dollars per year)
First cycle: government buys $100 billion worth of missiles	$100.00	$100.00
Second cycle: missile workers have more income, buy new boats ($MPC = 0.75$).	75.00	175.00
Third cycle: boat-builders have more income, spend it on beer ($0.75 \times \$75$)	56.25	231.25
Fourth cycle: bartenders and brewery workers have more income ($56.25 billion), spend it on new cars ($0.75 \times \$56.25$)	42.19	273.44
Fifth cycle: auto workers have more income, spend it on clothes ($0.75 \times \$42.19$)	31.64	305.08
Sixth cycle: apparel workers have more income, spend it on movies and entertainment ($0.75 \times \$31.64$)	23.73	328.81
•	•	•
•	•	•
•	•	•
Nth cycle and beyond		400.00

Table 9.1 summarizes the rest of the multiplier story; in each cycle, someone's income and spending increases. When the story is over, the cumulative increase in the rate of expenditure (aggregate demand) will total $400 billion per year. Thus the multiplier effects generated by the increased government spending are large enough to propel the economy from the recessionary equilibrium at Y_e ($1,600 billion per year) to the economy's full-employment potential at Y_F ($2,000 billion per year).

Figure 9.3 provides a graphic summary of the multiplier process. When we introduce $100 billion of government expenditure at Y_e, the rate of expenditure (aggregate demand) is suddenly much larger than the current rate of production (compare points D and S). Producers respond to this imbalance by hiring more workers and producing more missiles. In so doing, they set off a chain of multiplier effects that includes repeated increases in consumption. Accordingly, as the economy expands, the rate of consumption increases. By the time we reach full employment, consumption has increased from $1,300 billion per year at Y_e to $1,600 billion per year at Y_F. Thus the *cumulative* increase in aggregate demand includes $100 billion per year in increased government expenditure *plus* $300 billion per year in additional consumption.

FIGURE 9.3 AN EXPANSIONARY STIMULUS

An increase in spending at Y_e creates an imbalance between the rate of expenditure (D) and the rate of output (S). As producers expand the rate of output (hire additional factors of production), they create additional income. This additional income finances increased consumption. Total output and expenditures continue to increase until a new equilibrium (E) is attained at Y_F.

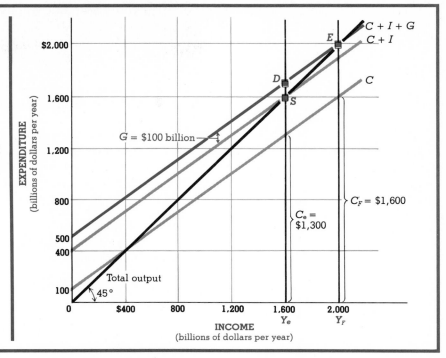

THE DESIRED STIMULUS The multiplier adds a lot of punch to fiscal policy. Every *new* dollar of expenditure injected into the circular flow has a multidollar impact on equilibrium income. While such leverage is often desirable, it also suggests that fiscal-policy mistakes tend to be magnified. For instance, too small an initial expenditure can leave the economy in a deep recession; too large an initial stimulus can rapidly lead to excessive aggregate demand and inflation.

If we were fortunate enough to know the exact dimensions of aggregate demand, as in Figure 9.3, we could easily calculate the desired increase in the rate of government spending. At our recessionary equilibrium (Y_e) the economy is $400 billion short of full-employment GNP. But we require an initial stimulus of only $100 billion per year to get to full employment. This amount is exactly equal to the recessionary gap that would exist at full employment with our initial aggregate-demand function. Thus to determine the appropriate size of the initial stimulus (increased government

Boosting Japan's growth

With an eye on the upcoming elections and a promise that Japan will realize 7% real growth in gross national product in fiscal 1978, Prime Minister Takeo Fukuda is pushing for an additional $13.2 billion in government spending to bolster the economy. The supplement will include appropriations for loans for 73,000 housing starts; $7.1 billion for public works, social welfare, and educational projects; and vessels for the maritime agency. The new plan is $2.6 billion more than a similar package approved a year ago that failed to provide enough stimulus to reach a GNP growth goal of 6.7%.

spending in this case), we simply look at the consumption and investment functions. At full employment (Y_F), they show how large a recessionary gap exists. Once we increase spending by that amount, the economy will follow our lead, propelled by the multiplier process.

In the first case we looked at, the problem was to keep a recessionary gap from emerging. We maintained full employment by increasing government spending by the amount of the *anticipated* gap. No change in the aggregate level of spending actually occurred. Increased G compensated for an expected shortfall in C and I.

In the second case, a gap had already emerged, and the economy was in a recession at Y_e. In this case, the additional government spending altered the initial equilibrium rate of aggregate demand. This stimulus set the multiplier in action. Total output grew by $1/(1 - MPC) \times$ recessionary gap. Hence **the amount of initial stimulus required to restore full employment is always equal to the size of the recessionary gap.**

Unfortunately, our information about the dimensions of aggregate demand is rarely so perfect. As a consequence, we often end up guessing the size of the recessionary gap (anticipated or actual) and hoping our guesses are not too far off. This is another reason economic policy is not always on target. We'll discover other reasons in Chapter 14.

ALTERNATIVES TO GOVERNMENT SPENDING

Although the right level of government expenditure is capable of moving the economy to its full-employment potential, increased G is not the only way to get there. The increased demand required to raise output and employment levels from Y_e to Y_F could emerge from C and I as well as from G. It could also come from abroad, in the form of increased demand for our exports. In other words, any Big Spender would help, whether from the public sector or the private sector. Of course, the reason we are initially at Y_e instead of Y_F in Figure 9.3 is that consumers and investors have chosen not to spend as much as is required for full employment.

Consumer and investor decisions are subject to change. Moreover, fiscal policy can help stimulate such changes, thereby creating an alternative to G as an instrument for achieving full employment. Insofar as the rate of output is concerned, it doesn't matter where the increased spending comes from, as long as it comes at the right time and in the right amount.

The ability of fiscal policy to alter directly the expenditure decisions of consumers and investors emerges from the revenue side of the federal budget. Congress has the power not only to spend but also to tax. By using its power to raise or lower taxes, Congress can materially change the rate of consumption and investment expenditures.

Taxes and consumption

The primary impact of taxes is to reduce disposable income at any given rate of output. Up to now, we have ignored the distinction

FIGURE 9.4 TAXES AND
CONSUMPTION

Taxes lower disposable income and
consumer spending at all levels of
output. In this case, consumer
spending at full employment (Y_F)
drops from $1,600 per year (point M,
before the introduction of taxes) to
$1,300 billion per year (point N, after
taxes are imposed). The consumption
function shifts downward.

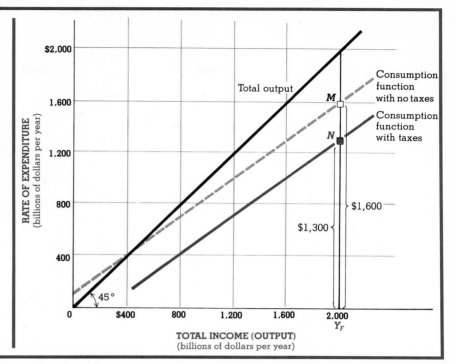

between disposable income and GNP, implicitly assuming that neither government nor business saving (depreciation and retained
earnings) existed (see Chapter 4). Now the government has entered
the picture, however, and with it have come taxes on income, property, sales, and many other things (see Chapter 3). As a consequence,
we now have to distinguish more carefully between the amount of
income we produce (total output) and the amount consumers have
available to spend **(disposable income).**

It remains true that the rate of consumer spending is directly
related to disposable income, that is,

$$C = a + bY_D$$

But disposable income (Y_D) is no longer equal to total income (Y).
Instead, the government taxes total income, leaving consumers with
less than they had before. As a consequence, consumers spend less
at every rate of *total* income. Hence, ***taxes lower the amount of
consumer spending that takes place at any given rate of output
(GNP).***[4]

The general impact of taxes can be illustrated with a downward
shift of the consumption function, as in Figure 9.4. Before the introduction of taxes consumers desired to spend $1,600 billion per year
at full employment, as indicated by point M. Once they start paying
taxes, however, consumers can no longer afford to spend so much:
the rate of consumption at full employment drops to $1,300 billion
per year (point N). Similar reductions in consumer spending occur

disposable income: After-tax
income of consumers; personal
income less personal taxes.

[4] We are still ignoring business taxes, retained earnings, and depreciation here (see
Chapter 4). Our purpose is to assess the impact of taxes on consumer spending.

FIGURE 9.5 A TAX CUT

A tax cut shifts the consumption function upward, pushing up aggregate demand as well. With reduced taxes, consumers have more disposable income at every rate of output. As they spend it, they set off the multiplier process, moving the economy from Y_e to Y_F.

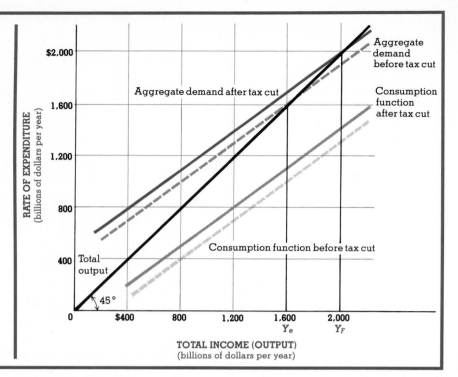

at all other levels of output, shifting the consumption function downward.[5]

The government's power to tax us gives it another instrument for altering the rate of desired expenditure. As we have just observed, an increase in taxes reduces disposable income and consumer spending. By the same token, *a reduction in taxes—a tax cut—can be used to increase disposable income and consumer spending.*

The use of tax cuts to achieve full employment is illustrated in Figure 9.5. Suppose again that the economy has contracted to the recessionary equilibrium represented by Y_e. At Y_e, total output is only $1,600 billion per year, $400 billion short of full-employment output. To achieve full employment, aggregate demand must be increased. Earlier we had increased government spending (G) to achieve this objective; now we want to increase consumer spending (C) instead. A tax cut is our weapon.

But how much of a tax cut is required? We already demonstrated that an initial increase in spending of $100 billion per year (at Y_e) is sufficient to propel the economy to full employment, thanks to the multiplier process. Hence we want to encourage consumers to increase their spending at Y_e by this amount. How large a tax cut is required to stimulate $100 billion more of consumer spending?

If your answer is $100 billion, you have forgotten the marginal propensity to consume. *Changes in consumer spending (C) are*

[5] In practice, income taxes may also change the slope of the consumption function. The example used here ignores this added complication, without misrepresenting the general impact of taxes.

smaller than changes in disposable income (Y_D) because consumers save some of their income. Accordingly, if we reduce taxes by $100 billion, disposable income will increase by the same amount. But consumption will rise by *less* than $100 billion. If MPC = 0.75, consumer spending will initially rise by only $75 billion in response to a $100 billion tax cut, and our policy objective will not be attained. Therefore, we must reduce taxes by *more* than $100 billion.

The appropriate size of the tax cut can be calculated from our definition of the marginal propensity to consume. Since

$$MPC = \frac{\Delta C}{\Delta Y_D}$$

and we know both MPC (0.75) and the desired change in C ($100 billion), the desired change in disposable income must be

$$\Delta Y_D = \frac{\Delta C}{MPC} = \frac{\$100 \text{ billion}}{0.75} = \$133 \text{ billion}$$

To increase Y_D by $133 billion, we simply cut taxes by $133 billion. Consumers will then increase their rate of spending by $100 billion (0.75 × $133 billion); they will save the remaining $33 billion. As the added spending enters the circular flow, it will start the multiplier process, ultimately increasing total spending (income) by $400 billion per year. This process is illustrated in Figure 9.5.

Taxes and investment

A tax cut may also be an effective mechanism for increasing investment spending. As we observed in Chapter 7, investment decisions are guided by expectations of future profit, particularly after-tax profits. If a cut in corporate taxes raises potential after-tax profits, it

How stimulative is fiscal policy?

Tax cuts and defense spending will boost the economy in midyear

The Administration is forecasting that a solid economic recovery will begin sometime in the second quarter and gain momentum as the year rolls on because it is convinced that its fiscal policy is stimulative. And most private economists agree that the massive tax cuts and increases in defense spending, which kick in at midyear, will turn the economy around. The tax cuts alone are expected to pump about $47 billion into the economy at an annual rate, most of it in the second half of the year, after the first of two 10% cuts in income tax rates begins July 1. Increases in defense spending will start earlier and add less, but still at a $25 billion annual rate. And beginning July 1, the economy will also get a boost of about $14 billion to $15 billion in additional Social Security payments as a result of cost-of-living adjustments.

According to the conventional budget arithmetic this injection of cash will more than offset further cuts in government spending at federal, state, and local levels, as well as the increase in Social Security taxes that began in January. . . . The consensus estimate is that the federal stimulus, most of which comes in the second half, will amount to about $15 billion. "There is no question that it is a stimulative fiscal policy, which is not a bad idea when you have almost 9% unemployment," says Alan S. Blinder of Princeton University. . . .

A moderate increase in defense spending in the first half of the year could do a lot to prevent the recession from worsening. Economists say every defense dollar spent more than offsets a comparable cut in transfer payments. Economic studies have shown that the so-called multipliers, which measure the economic impact of government spending and taxes, are higher for defense and other kinds of direct government purchases than for transfer payments or even tax cuts. "Expenditure cuts are concentrated in transfer payments, which have the effect of tax changes," explains Blinder. "Defense purchases have a stronger multiplier."

should encourage additional investment. Once an increase in the rate of investment spending enters the circular flow, it has a multiplier effect on aggregate demand, similar to that which follows an initial change in consumer spending. Thus tax cuts for consumers or investors provide an alternative to increased government spending as a mechanism for stimulating aggregate demand.

Tax cuts designed to stimulate C and I have been used frequently. In 1963 President John F. Kennedy announced his intention to reduce taxes in order to stimulate the economy, citing the fact that the marginal propensity to consume for the average American family at that time appeared to be exceptionally high. His successor, Lyndon Johnson, concurred with Kennedy's reasoning. Johnson agreed to "shift emphasis sharply from expanding Federal expenditure to boosting private consumer demand and business investment." He proceeded to cut personal and corporate taxes by $11 billion. President Johnson proclaimed that "the $11 billion tax cut will challenge American businessmen, investors, and consumers to put their enlarged incomes to work in the private economy to expand output, investment, and jobs." He added, "I am confident that our private decision makers will rise to this challenge."[6] They apparently did, because $C + I$ increased by $33 billion in 1963 and by another $46 billion in 1965 (in part as a result of multiplier effects, of course).

President Carter followed these examples by proposing a $25 billion tax cut in 1978. The objective of this tax-cut proposal was to stimulate private consumption and investment, thereby moving the economy closer to full employment. A second motive for the income-tax cut was to avoid the reduction in disposable income resulting from an increase in social security taxes, beginning January 1, 1979. By the time Congress acted on his proposals, however, the unemployment rate had fallen significantly and the rate of inflation was rising. Thus Congress chose to cut taxes by only $18 billion.

The largest tax cut in history was initiated by President Reagan in 1981. The Reagan administration persuaded Congress to cut personal taxes by $250 billion over a three-year period and to cut business taxes by another $70 billion. We will study the nature and impact of these tax cuts in Chapter 15.

FISCAL POLICY TO ACHIEVE PRICE STABILITY

Fiscal policy will not always be used to *increase* aggregate spending, of course. Just as the expenditure decisions made by consumers and investors may result in deficient aggregate demand, so too may they result in *excessive aggregate demand*. The potential for such an occurrence is illustrated here by Figure 9.6a. Note that aggregate private expenditure $(C + I)$ at full employment (Y_F) is now larger than total output. The excess demand represented by the difference between aggregate demand and total output at full employment is an **inflationary gap.**

Figure 9.6b also illustrates an inflationary gap, but one to which

inflationary gap: The amount by which the desired rate of expenditure at full employment exceeds full-employment output.

[6] *Economic Report of the President,* 1964, p. 6.

FIGURE 9.6 AN INFLATIONARY GAP MAY RESULT FROM . . .

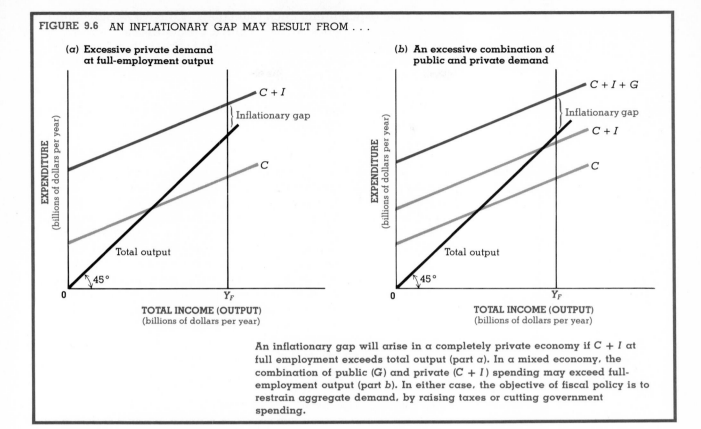

(a) Excessive private demand at full-employment output

(b) An excessive combination of public and private demand

An inflationary gap will arise in a completely private economy if $C + I$ at full employment exceeds total output (part a). In a mixed economy, the combination of public (G) and private (C + I) spending may exceed full-employment output (part b). In either case, the objective of fiscal policy is to restrain aggregate demand, by raising taxes or cutting government spending.

government spending has contributed as well. In fact, excessive aggregate demand could have surfaced because we earlier overestimated the size of a recessionary gap and introduced too much government spending and/or overly large tax cuts! Whatever the reason, we should recognize that government spending can be just as much a source of macro instability as either investment or consumption.

Once an inflationary gap appears, goods, and services will start selling faster than they can be produced at full employment. The existence of inventories makes such selling possible, at least for a while. But as inventories are depleted, there is no longer any way to satisfy the excessive demand with goods and services. Accordingly, prices will start to rise as market participants try to outbid each other for available goods.

In situations where excessive aggregate demand threatens to erode price stability or is already doing so, the objective of fiscal policy is to decrease total spending rather than to increase it. In this sense, fiscal policy is a two-edged sword, which may be used either to stimulate or to suppress aggregate demand.

Government cutbacks

The means available to the federal government for restraining aggregate demand emerge again from both sides of the budget. The difference here is that we use the tools in reverse. We now want to reduce government spending rather than increase it, in order to restrain the rate of total expenditure. Such reductions will have negative multiplier effects analogous to the positive effects that accompany increased government spending. If we cut G by $10 billion per year, for example, sales and income will drop by a like amount initially. But the income and spending reductions will accumulate as the cut in G makes its way around the circular flow. Ultimately, income and expenditure will drop by $10 billion times the multiplier (see Table 9.1).

Tax increases

By the same token, tax increases rather than tax cuts are appropriate to encourage a lower rate of spending. With less disposable income and after-tax profits, consumers and business firms are likely to spend less. In 1968, for example, the economy was rapidly approaching full employment and Vietnam War expenditures were helping to drive up prices. Congress responded by imposing a 10 percent surtax (temporary additional tax) on income, which took more than $10 billion in purchasing power away from consumers. Resultant multiplier effects reduced spending in 1969 by over $20 billion and thus helped restrain price pressures. In 1978 some restraint on aggregate demand again seemed necessary, and Congress increased social security payroll taxes, a move that reduced workers' take-home pay and thus their consumption expenditures.

THE CONCERN FOR CONTENT

Insofar as the aggregate rate of expenditure in the economy is concerned, it would appear not to matter how the government spends its revenue or whom it taxes. The important thing is that the right amount of money be spent at the right time. In other words, insofar as our stabilization objectives are concerned, the content of aggregate demand is of secondary interest, the level of demand being the only thing that counts.

But it does matter, of course, whether federal expenditures are devoted to military hardware, urban transit systems, or tennis courts. Our economic goals include not only full employment and price stability but also a desirable mix of output, an equitable distri-

---

THE FISCAL POLICY OBJECTIVE

Equilibrium GNP: The rate of output at which the rate of desired expenditure (aggregate demand) equals the rate of production. The conditions for equilibrium are:

- □ In a private economy: desired I = desired S
- □ In a mixed economy: desired $I + G$ = desired $S + T$

Full-employment GNP: The total value of final goods and services that could be produced in a given time period at full employment; potential GNP.

The fiscal policy objective: To make equilibrium GNP equal to full-employment GNP.

bution of income, and adequate economic growth. These other goals are directly affected by the content of aggregate demand. The relative emphasis on, and sometimes exclusive concern for, stabilization objectives—to the neglect of related GNP content—has been designated by Professor Joan Robinson as the "Second Crisis of Economic Theory." She explains:

. . . The first crisis arose from the breakdown of a theory which could not account for the *level* of employment. The second crisis arises from a theory that cannot account for the *content* of employment.

Keynes was arguing against the dominant orthodoxy which held that government expenditure could not increase employment. He had to prove, first of all, that it could. He had to show that an increase in investment will increase consumption—that more wages will be spent on more beer and boots whether the investment is useful or not. He had to show that the secondary increase in real income [the multiplier effect] is quite independent of the object of the primary outlay. Pay men to dig holes in the ground and fill them up again if you cannot do anything else.

There was an enormous orthodox resistance to this idea. The whole weight of the argument had to be on this one obvious point.

The war was a sharp lesson in Keynesism. Orthodoxy could not stand up any longer. Governments accepted the responsibility to maintain a high and stable level of employment. Then economists took over Keynes and erected the new orthodoxy. Once the point had been established, the question should have changed. Now that we all agree that government expenditure can maintain employment, we should argue about what the expenditure should be for. Keynes did not *want* anyone to dig holes and fill them.[7]

The alternatives to paying people for digging and filling holes in the ground are enormous in scope and are only suggested by the summary of federal expenditures provided in Table 3.1. It is abundantly clear that, with over $700 billion to spend in fiscal 1983, the federal government had great influence not only on prices and employment, but also on the degree to which our other goals were fulfilled. The same kind of influence exists every year.

The kinds of expenditures and taxes that are appropriate at any given time depend on the values and perceived needs of society, and no structured blueprint can be provided in an economics textbook. We can, however, highlight two major issues.

Public vs. private spending

Fiscal policy can be directed toward private expenditure ($C + I$) or toward public expenditure (G). To bolster aggregate demand, the government can increase its own spending program or use the tax system to stimulate private expenditure. In either case, aggregate demand will rise, but with markedly different implications for the content of GNP. If G is increased, the public sector grows relative to the private sector. In this case, the government increases its influence over the dimensions of our economic and social welfare. If C and I are stimulated, the result will be exactly the opposite. The share of government purchases in total expenditure has actually

[7] Joan Robinson, "The Second Crisis of Economic Theory," *American Economic Review,* May 1972, p. 6.

risen dramatically over time, from only 2 percent in 1902 to over 20 percent in 1982.

We have no objective standard for determining how large the public sector should be. Ultimately it boils down to a question of whether specific public goods are more desired than specific private goods (see the discussion of the "taxpayer revolt" in Chapter 3). And the question of desirability is inherently subjective. We might also note, however, that some people believe individual freedom and substantial economic activity on the part of government are inherently inconsistent. Thus they attach a low or even negative benefit to public-sector activity. Milton Friedman, for one, believes that as the government increases its control over the economy, individuals lose their freedom to pursue their own economic and political goals.[8] President Reagan had much the same thing in mind when he urged Congress to "get the federal government out of our pockets and off our backs" by cutting taxes, government spending, and regulation. On the other hand, some people argue that freedom is not fully attained until government takes control of the production process, guarantees everyone access to the basic necessities, and thereby frees people from economic worry.

Output mixes within each sector

In addition to choosing whether to increase public or private spending, fiscal policy must also consider the specific content of spending within each sector. Suppose we determine that stimulation of the private sector is preferable to additional government spending as a means of promoting full employment. We still have many choices. We could, for example, cut corporate taxes, cut individual taxes, or reduce excise taxes, all measures that have been taken at one time or another. Each alternative implies a different mix of consumption and investment and a different distribution of income. Accordingly, the specific policy instrument chosen will influence a variety of economic goals.

The same is obviously true of public-sector expenditures. Once an appropriate level of public expenditure is chosen, we still have to decide what to spend it on, and even who should spend it.

WHO MAKES FISCAL POLICY?

The general outlines of fiscal policy are reasonably easy to describe. When it comes to specific choices about the level, direction, or content of taxes and expenditures, however, the going gets pretty rough. Fiscal planners must pursue a variety of goals and take into account the probable consequences of any action (or inaction) on each one. They must then weigh the alternatives in terms of values and opportunity costs and design the optimal set of policy actions.

[8] Milton Friedman, *Capitalism and Freedom* (Chicago: University of Chicago Press, 1962). For a very different view, read John Kenneth Galbraith's *The Affluent Society* (Boston: Houghton Mifflin, 1958), or his *Economics and the Public Purpose* (Boston: Houghton Mifflin, 1973).

Discretionary fiscal spending

fiscal year (FY): The twelve-month period used for government accounting purposes; begins October 1 and ends September 30.

As we saw in Chapter 3, the president and Congress jointly make our basic fiscal-policy decisions. Each year they put together the federal budget, which details anticipated revenues and expenditures for the following **fiscal year.** The entire budget is not recreated each year, however. As the Brookings Institution staff has noted, "To pretend that a $700 billion federal budget is freshly put together each year is an exercise in self-delusion. From one year to the next, most of the changes that occur in budget expenditures are 'built-in'; that is, they result from decisions made in previous years."[9] The fiscal 1983 budget (Table 3.1), for example, contained provisions for $175 billion for social security benefits to retired and disabled persons. These benefits represented a commitment first established in 1935 and reaffirmed every few years since. It also contained provisions for $14 billion in veterans' benefits, $96 billion for interest payments on the national debt, and many billions more for completion of projects begun in previous years. Short of repudiating all prior commitments and restructuring our politicoeconomic system, there is little that Congress or the president can do to eliminate these kinds of expenditures in any given year. ***To a large extent, current revenues and expenditures are the results of prior decisions.*** That portion of the budget that is subject to current decision making is referred to as discretionary spending (or nonspending). Expenditures that are built into the annual budget process are called "uncontrollables."

discretionary fiscal spending: Those elements of the annual federal budget that are not determined by past legislative or executive commitments.

That is not to say that the ability of fiscal policy to alter economic outcomes in a given year is negligible. It is much smaller, however, than one might infer from the size of the federal budget. Most observers of the budget process conclude that only one-fourth of the budget in any year represents **discretionary fiscal spending.** Even President Reagan's initial and unprecedented attacks on the federal budget left most of the budget unscathed.

Built-in stabilizers

Although the existence of uncontrollable expenditures in the budget limits the range of current fiscal policy, such expenditures often contribute to increased economic stability. Consider unemployment insurance benefits. The unemployment insurance program, established in 1935, provides that persons who lose their jobs will receive some income (an average of $100 per week) from the government (see Chapter 5). In 1980 total unemployment insurance benefits nearly doubled, not because Congress or the president consciously redirected federal expenditures, but simply because more people were unemployed in 1980 than in 1979. Hence these benefits provided an **automatic stabilizer** by increasing federal outlays at a time when aggregate demand was too low to employ our available resources fully. Welfare benefits, which jumped by nearly $2 billion in the same year, constitute a similar kind of stabilizer. Neither change in outlays required congressional or executive action; they occurred *automatically* in response to changing economic conditions.

automatic stabilizer: Federal expenditure or revenue item that automatically responds countercyclically to changes in national income; for example, unemployment benefits, income taxes.

The most important automatic stabilizers occur on the revenue

[9] Charles L. Schultze et al., *Setting National Priorities: The 1973 Budget* (Washington, D.C.: Brookings Institution, 1972), p. 464; figures have been updated.

side of the federal budget. Income taxes, in particular, constitute an important stabilizer, because they move up and down with the value of spending and output. When aggregate demand rises and incomes increase, income taxes siphon off some of the increased purchasing power. This helps to counteract any inflationary pressures that might emerge. Progressive income taxes are particularly effective stabilizers, as they siphon off increasing proportions of purchasing power when aggregate demand is rising, and decreasing proportions when demand and output are falling.

POLICY IMPLICATIONS: BALANCING THE BUDGET

The use of fiscal policy to alter the level of GNP is commonly referred to as the *stabilization function* of the federal budget. The basic objective of such activity is to stabilize economic expenditure at a rate that is consistent with the goals of full employment and price stability, a rate represented by Y_F in our figures. In pursuit of that objective, the federal budget will sometimes be used to increase aggregate demand and at other times to restrain it.

Budget surpluses and deficits

From a Keynesian perspective, the pursuit of stable economic growth implies that federal expenditures and receipts will not always be equal. In the face of a recessionary gap, for example, the government has sound reasons both to cut taxes and to increase its own spending. By reducing tax revenues and increasing expenditures simultaneously, however, the federal government will throw its budget out of balance. This will lead to **deficit spending**, a situation in which government spending exceeds tax revenues. The size of the deficit is equal to the difference between expenditures and receipts.

deficit spending: A situation wherein government expenditures exceed government revenues.

To pay for deficit spending, the government must borrow money, either directly from the private sector or from the banking system. In either case, the United States Treasury issues (sells) bonds that increase the public debt.[10]

There are also occasions when government revenues will exceed government expenditures, thereby giving rise to a **budget surplus.** Such a surplus might arise as a result of tax increases coupled with reductions in government spending.

budget surplus: An excess of government revenues over government expenditures.

To balance or not to balance?

From a Keynesian perspective, budget deficits and surpluses are a routine feature of fiscal policy. However, there has been growing opposition to budget imbalances, particularly to budget deficits. Public-opinion polls have shown that a majority of the American

[10] Recall that such borrowing may "crowd out" private consumption or investment. The mechanics of government borrowing and its potential impact on the private sector are discussed in Chapters 11 and 12.

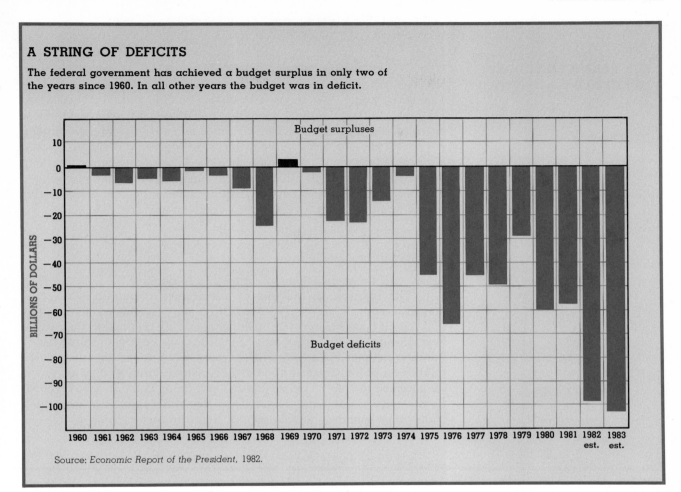

A STRING OF DEFICITS

The federal government has achieved a budget surplus in only two of the years since 1960. In all other years the budget was in deficit.

Source: *Economic Report of the President,* 1982.

people want the federal government to balance its budget. Most consumers seem to believe that if consumers have to balance their budgets, the federal government should, too.

The public demand for a balanced budget has led to a variety of proposals for *requiring* balanced budgets. The most far-reaching of these is the proposed constitutional amendment to compel balanced budgets. According to this amendment, the federal government would have to limit expenditures to the amount of revenue received. No deficit spending would be permitted, except in national emergencies. By 1982, 32 states had passed resolutions demanding a constitutional convention to draft a balanced-budget amendment. If 34 states were to call for a convention, Congress would be forced to oblige.

WHY BALANCE? The persistent demand for a balanced budget reflects several concerns. First, there is genuine worry that the federal government will never be able to repay its accumulated debts. Since 1960, the federal budget has shown a surplus in only two years. In

THE BALANCED-BUDGET MULTIPLIER

There are occasions when a balanced budget will be appropriate, or at least when changes in government spending (G) need to be balanced by equivalent changes in taxes (T). One should not assume, though, that such budget balancing has no effect on the level of aggregate demand. On the contrary, even an equal rise in government expenditure and taxes tends to increase aggregate demand. To see how this curious result comes about, suppose that the government decided to spend $50 billion per year on a new fleet of communications satellites, and to pay for them by raising income taxes by the same amount. Thus

Change in $G = +\$50$ billion per year
Change in $T = +\$50$ billion per year
Change in budget balance $= 0$

How will these decisions affect aggregate demand?

The increase in the rate of government expenditure directly boosts aggregate demand by $50 billion per year. But what about the increased taxes? How will consumer spending respond to the resultant drop in disposable income? According to the consumption function, consumer spending will decrease when taxes go up, but not dollar for dollar. Instead, the rate of consumption will diminish by a *fraction* of the tax increase, that fraction being equal to the marginal propensity to consume (*MPC*). Thus the initial reduction in annual consumer spending equals *MPC* × $50 billion.

all other years, the budget was in deficit. As a result, the outstanding debt of the United States government is now over $1 trillion.

A second source of opposition to deficit spending is the growing size of the public sector. Despite rhetoric to the contrary, Congress never seems able to reduce federal spending. New programs are continually being added to the list of federal responsibilities, while old ones keep growing. To stop this growth, balanced-budget advocates urge that we cut off the *source* of funding. Specifically, those who prefer a smaller public sector want to turn off its principal engine of growth—deficit spending.

Finally, there is a strong conviction that excessive government spending is a principal cause of inflation. In public-opinion polls, one out of three Americans blames federal spending for inflation. If the government were forced to balance its budget, the inflationary pressure generated by deficit spending would be eliminated.

WHY NOT BALANCE? The arguments for a balanced budget have a lot of appeal. However, they are not convincing. In fact, they can be quite dangerous. Were the government forced to balance its budget

The reduction in consumption is therefore less than the increase in government spending, implying a net increase in aggregate demand. The *initial* change in aggregate demand brought about by this balanced-budget expenditure is:

Initial increase in government spending = $50 billion
Initial reduction in consumer spending = $MPC \times$ $50 billion
Net initial change in aggregate demand = $(1 - MPC)$ $50 billion

Like any other changes in the rate of spending, this initial increase in aggregate demand will start a multiplier process in motion. The *cumulative* change in aggregate demand will be much larger, as indicated by the multiplier. In this case, the cumulative (ultimate) change in aggregate demand is:

$$\text{The multiplier} \times \text{initial change in spending per year} = \text{cumulative change in aggregate demand}$$

$$\frac{1}{1 - MPC} \times (1 - MPC)\$50 \text{ billion} = \$50 \text{ billion}$$

Thus the balanced-budget multiplier is equal to 1. In this case, a $50 billion increase in annual government expenditure combined with an equivalent increase in taxes increases equilibrium income (ultimately) by $50 billion per year.

at all times, it could no longer use fiscal policy to achieve our economic goals. By balancing its budget at all times, the government would lose its ability to close inflationary or recessionary gaps. *Whether any given level of deficit, surplus, or public debt is appropriate depends on the stabilization results achieved and the uses to which the attendant purchasing power has been put.* There is no compelling reason to achieve a balanced budget in any given year, decade, or century.

Consider again the implications of a recessionary gap. In the absence of any fiscal response by the government, the economy might stagnate in a recessionary equilibrium. Are we to wait for a Classical self-adjustment, as was done in the 1930s? Or should the government unbalance the budget and stimulate the economy with deficit spending?

Much of the opposition to deficit spending is really directed at the performance, not at the principles of fiscal policy. The theoretical argument for occasional deficits or surpluses is compelling. This argument does not justify *all* deficits or surpluses, however. In Chapter 14, we shall look more closely at the decisions (and mistakes) of actual fiscal policy.

Pro and con: A constitutional ban on red ink?

Yes—the U.S. must "balance what it produces with what it spends"

Interview With
Edmund G. Brown, Jr.

Governor Of California

Q Governor Brown, why do you favor a constitutional amendment prohibiting deficits in the federal budget?

A I believe that the time has come for this nation to balance what it produces with what it spends.

Q Many economists argue that such a ban would impose a straitjacket on government. How do you answer that?

A The resolution pending before the California Legislature provides for exceptions in the event of national emergency such as war, a national disaster or a serious condition of unemployment. Those are matters that can be worked out as the concept is developed and refined.

My own judgment is that governments have great difficulty in controlling spending. An external force is necessary.

Q What about a time when—with no national emergency or unusual unemployment—the economy is poised on the brink of recession? Would spending cuts required by such an amendment bring on recession?

A Many economists think the economy is now headed for a recession after years of deficit spending. So I would turn the question around and ask those who propose that we deficit-spend year in and year out, even at the peak of the business cycle: What is the explanation for the recurring recessions that are sweeping this country and harming those least able to afford recessions—the poor, minorities, the elderly and people on fixed incomes?

I'm not unaware of the need for appropriate stimulus. But I believe that a balanced budget can be constructed in such a way that the investments required to make this a great country can be made—and will be made—by the people. The problem is that, instead of borrowing for capital investment in productive assets, we are borrowing to pay current expenses. No state or corporation can long do that.

I would also point out that California is in the forefront across the broad spectrum of social and labor programs, and yet we've been able to do it with a balanced budget.

Q Critics of the balanced-budget plan argue that cutting spending or increasing taxes when the economy is weak simply slows the economy, reduces revenues and widens deficits—

A That's the conventional wisdom. It deserves consideration in the drafting of a constitutional amendment. But what concerns me is that this theory has been so distorted that deficit spending continues in periods of great economic boom and high job creation, which is where we are today.

No—"There are many occasions in which deficits are appropriate and necessary"

Interview With
Gardner Ackley

Chairman, President's Council of Economic Advisers, 1964–68; Now, Professor of Economics, University of Michigan

Q Professor Ackley, why do you oppose a constitutional amendment requiring a balanced federal budget?

A First, because there are many occasions in which deficits are appropriate and necessary; and, second, because there are many occasions in which deficits are unavoidable.

Q You don't believe that deficit spending has been a major cause of our inflation?

A There have been many occasions when deficits were inappropriate and did contribute to inflation. There are many other occasions in which deficits were appropriate and had no inflationary consequences.

Q If there are times when deficits cause inflation, why not have a constitutional ban on them?

A Because under some circumstances the attempt to eliminate deficits—through cutting expenditures or raising taxes—would only aggravate the unsatisfactory circumstances of the economy and might not succeed in eliminating the deficit.

Think about the middle 1930s, for example, or about 1975. If we had tried to avoid a deficit by raising taxes or cutting expenditures or both, we would mainly have further depressed the economy, but we probably would not have been able to eliminate the deficit.

Q Why?

A Simply because the effect of cutting expenditures or raising taxes is to reduce the level of economic activity and reduce tax collections. In such cases, efforts to balance the budget would not merely be self-defeating but disastrous to the economic well-being of the entire country.

Q Do you believe government spending can be brought under control without a constitutional amendment?

A I don't know what "bringing government spending under control" means. As a percentage of gross national product—GNP—federal spending shows no rise over any reasonable period. It fluctuates when the growth of output slows or increases as a result of recessions and booms, but there's been no trend in it in recent years. Also, it's a lot lower than in other countries whose economic health seems to be admired by the promoters of this idea.

May I also add that those other countries have considerably larger deficits than ours—repeatedly. Any hope that merely eliminating deficits will improve our economic performance is just a dream.

SUMMARY

■ The Keynesian explanation of macro instability requires the government to balance aggregate demand with the economy's full-employment potential. To do so, fiscal policy is used to increase the rate of total spending in the face of a recessionary gap and to restrain the rate of total spending when an inflationary gap appears.

■ To stimulate aggregate demand, the government may choose to increase its own rate of spending. Alternatively, it may reduce taxes on consumers and businesses, leaving them with more income to spend.

■ To restrain aggregate demand, the government may reduce its own rate of spending. Or it may increase taxes, thereby reducing the income and spending of the private sector.

■ Any initial change in the rate of spending will have a multiplied impact on aggregate demand and output. An increase in the annual rate of government spending, for example, will result in more disposable income, which will be used to finance further consumer spending.

■ Changes in government spending and taxes will also alter the content of GNP, and thus influence WHAT to produce. Fiscal policy affects the relative size of the public and private sectors, as well as the mix of output in each sector.

■ Fiscal policy is formulated annually by the president and Congress. Each year's receipts and expenditures, however, are substantially determined by uncontrollables that reflect fiscal decisions and commitments of earlier years. Only a modest portion of any year's budget represents discretionary spending that results from current decisions.

■ An important feature of some uncontrollable receipts and expenditures is that they respond countercyclically to changing economic conditions and thus operate as automatic stabilizers. Income taxes and unemployment benefits are examples.

■ The federal budget is the primary vehicle for implementing fiscal policy. It therefore often shows a deficit or surplus, depending on the condition of the economy and the direction of fiscal policy.

■ The appropriateness of budget deficits and surpluses depends on the need of the economy for stimulus or restraint. Even a balanced change in the budget (change in G = change in T) has some positive impact on the rate of spending, however, because consumers reduce their spending by less than the amount of taxes.

Terms to remember | Define the following terms:

fiscal policy
recessionary gap
equilibrium GNP
multiplier

marginal propensity to consume
 (MPC)
disposable income
inflationary gap

fiscal year   **deficit spending**
discretionary fiscal spending   **budget surplus**
automatic stabilizer

Questions for discussion

1. Would a constitutional amendment that would require the federal government to balance its budget (incur no deficits) be desirable? Explain.

2. Will $20 billion per year spent on housing have the same impact on the economy as $20 billion spent on interstate highways? Explain.

3. Do fiscal-policy makers really need to know the magnitudes of the *MPC* and multiplier? Could they get along as well without such information?

4. "Zero-based budgeting" refers to a situation wherein each year's budget starts from zero, that is, all spending is discretionary. Is this possible? Give some examples.

Problem

Suppose the economy is producing at full employment ($2,000 billion per year), but facing an inflationary gap of $100 billion per year. The spending desires of market participants are:

C = $400 billion per year + 0.5Y
I = $300 billion per year
G = $400 billion per year
There is no foreign trade (imports or exports)

Under these conditions, describe three fiscal-policy options the government could take to close the inflationary gap. Explain the effects of each.

THE FULL-EMPLOYMENT BUDGET

Keynesian theory offers us some fairly straightforward guidelines for combating cyclical unemployment or demand-pull inflation with fiscal policy. Unfortunately, it is not always evident whether these guidelines are being followed and thus whether policy makers can be blamed or praised for changes in economic performance. President Nixon, for example, blamed the poor economic results of his first two years (1969–70) on private spending decisions and fiscal policies that had been carried out by his predecessors as far back as 1965. When 1972 turned out to be a relatively good year for the economy, however, he attributed the economy's performance to his own "sound and forceful Government policy."[1] President Carter, too, was reluctant to acknowledge the role of government policy when economic performance was poor but eager to emphasize it when the economy performed well. He claimed full credit for reducing unemployment in the period 1977–79. In his final Economic Message to Congress, however, he blamed "underlying inflationary forces built up over the past 15 years" for the upsurge in inflation that helped defeat him in 1980.

The difficulty in isolating the impact of fiscal policy stems from the dynamics of the marketplace. In the real world, everything is changing at once, and there is no way to stop all the action so that economists can measure repercussions of a specific fiscal action. At the same time that the consequences of, say, a tax cut are reverberating through the economy, other consumer, investor, and even government actions are also influencing economic outcomes. These forces may either buttress or counteract the intended impact of the tax cut. Accordingly, the economic outcomes that follow a tax cut may occur in spite of or as a result of conscious policy. It is this kind of market interdependence that allows politicians (and economists!) to have their cake and eat it too, as conditions merit.

One way to gauge the independent impact of fiscal policy is to analyze closely the actions taken, rather than just to observe the final economic outcomes. We know, for example, that if the government deliberately seeks to increase aggregate demand, it is likely to cut taxes, increase federal outlays, or both. Such actions will lead to a larger budget deficit (or smaller surplus). Accordingly, an increase in GNP that follows on the heels of an increased budget deficit might be attributed to the wisdom of fiscal policy.

Unfortunately, even this simple test of policy intent and impact is obstructed by the interdependence between the budget and the economy. The automatic stabilizers noted earlier tend to make the budget balance responsive to economic conditions. In a recession, for example, a budget deficit might emerge because tax receipts diminish and unemployment-compensation benefits increase. Such a deficit would reflect the state of the economy, not deliberate fiscal policy. Hence the resulting deficit could not be regarded as the cause of later prosperity. ***Actual budget deficits and surpluses are a poor gauge of fiscal policy because they may arise from economic conditions as well as active policy.*** Table A.1 illustrates the impact of economic conditions on the budget balance.

In view of the ambiguities attached to budget balances, a better standard for measuring fiscal policy is clearly needed. To distinguish the impact of the budget on the economy from the impact of the economy on the budget, economists have formulated a more sophisticated concept of the budget balance. This concept is referred to

[1] *Economic Report of the President,* 1973, p. 3.

TABLE A.1 THE BUDGET IMPACT OF INCREASED UNEMPLOYMENT AND INFLATION
(in 1983 dollars)

Changes in economic conditions alter the federal budget balance. When unemployment increases, the budget deficit grows. When inflation accelerates, the budget deficit shrinks. To discern the true intentions of fiscal policy, we must abstract from these effects. The full ("high") employment budget serves this purpose.

Source: Congressional Budget Office.

A. When the unemployment rate increases by 1 percentage point:

1. Government spending *(G)* automatically increases for:
   - Unemployment insurance benefits
   - Food stamps
   - Welfare benefits
   - Social security benefits
   - Medicaid

   Total increase in outlays: +$11 billion

2. Government tax revenues *(T)* automatically decline for:
   - Individual income taxes
   - Corporate income taxes
   - Social security payroll taxes

   Total decline in revenues: −$17 billion

3. The deficit widens by $28 billion

B. When the inflation rate increases by 1 percentage point:

1. Government spending *(G)* automatically increases for:
   - Indexed retirement and social security benefits
   - Higher interest payments

   Total increase in outlays: +$5 billion

2. Government tax revenues *(T)* automatically increase for:
   - Progressive income taxes
   - Corporate income taxes
   - Social security payroll taxes

   Total increase in revenues: +$16 billion

3. The deficit shrinks by $11 billion

---

full-employment budget: The federal revenues and expenditures that would exist at full employment under prevailing fiscal policy.

as the **full-employment budget.** Rather than comparing actual outlays to actual receipts, *the full-employment budget compares the outlays and receipts that would occur if the economy were at full employment.*

The full-employment-budget concept excludes from consideration reductions in revenue or increases in spending occasioned by less than full levels of output and (taxable) income. Those reductions are the result of economic conditions, not fiscal policy. Consider what happened to the federal budget in 1980. In 1979 the federal deficit amounted to $28 billion. In 1980 the deficit more than doubled, to nearly $60 billion. At first glance it would appear that the government was desperately trying to stimulate economic activity with expansionary fiscal policies. But this was not the case. The primary reason for the larger 1980 deficit was increased unemployment. The rate of unemployment jumped from 5.8 percent in 1979 to an average of 7.1 percent in 1980. As a result, government outlays increased and revenues fell (see Table A.1).

Fiscal policy in 1980 was expansionary, but not nearly so much so as the actual change in the deficit indicates. The full-employment-budget deficit increased by only $16 billion (rather than $32 billion, as in the actual budget). This increase represented explicit expansionary policies. In general, *changes in the full-employment-budget balance are the basic measure of fiscal-policy actions.* If the full-employment balance is increasing (a larger surplus or a

FIGURE A.1 THE IMPACT OF FISCAL POLICY IN THE 1930s (all figures in 1947 prices)

During the Great Depression the federal budget was in deficit. But those deficits were the consequence of reduced tax revenues caused by high unemployment rates and low incomes. Fiscal policy was not expansionary. On the contrary, the full-employment-budget surplus was increasing in 1932, 1933, and 1937.

Source: Adapted from E. Cary Brown, "Fiscal Policy in the Thirties: A Reappraisal," *American Economic Review*, December 1956, Table 1.

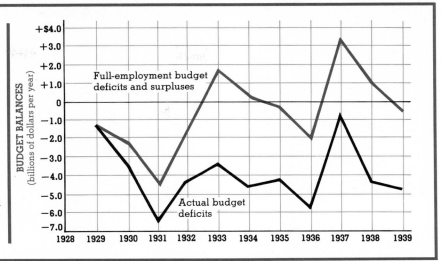

smaller deficit), then fiscal policy is exerting a restraining force on aggregate demand. If the full-employment balance is declining, then fiscal policy is exerting a stimulative effect on aggregate demand.

Fiscal policy in the Great Depression

Use of the full-employment-budget concept can be illustrated by our experiences during the Great Depression. During the 1930s, the federal budget was in a deficit position each year. Many observers have regarded those deficits as the results of good Keynesian economics. The efforts of the Roosevelt administration appear quite timid, however, from the perspective of the full-employment-budget concept. The actual deficits reflected in large part reductions in tax revenues, especially during the early 1930s. Between 1929 and 1932, federal expenditures rose only $200 million. As a result, the full-employment-budget balance actually *increased* from 1931 to 1933 (see Figure A.1), thereby restraining aggregate demand at a time when producers were desperate for increased sales. Only when the full-employment-budget deficit was expanded tremendously by wartime expenditures did fiscal policy have a decidedly positive effect. Federal defense expenditures jumped from $2.2 billion in 1940 to $87.4 billion in 1944!

By distinguishing between the full-employment budget and the actual budget, we can evaluate fiscal policy more accurately. If the full-employment budget has a growing deficit (or declining surplus), the government is stimulating aggregate demand. Whenever the full-employment-budget deficit is shrinking (or the surplus is growing), the government is trying to restrain demand and output. The size of any changes in the full-employment budget will, of course, still be a measure of the intensity of such efforts.

POLICY OPTIONS: THE MONETARIST APPROACH

CHAPTER 10

MONEY AND BANKS

Sophocles, the ancient Greek playwright, had very strong opinions about the role of money. As he saw it, "Of evils upon earth, the worst is money. It is money that sacks cities, and drives men forth from hearth and home; warps and seduces native intelligence, and breeds a habit of dishonesty."

In modern times, people may still be seduced by the lure of money and fashion their lives around its pursuit. Nevertheless, it is hard to imagine an economy functioning without money. Money affects not only morals and ideals, but also the way an economy works.

The purpose of this and the following two chapters is to examine the role of money in the economy today. We begin by studying the nature and creation of money. In the next chapter we shall look at how the Federal Reserve System controls the amount of money created. Finally, in Chapter 12, we shall look at the implications for monetary policy, another approach to macroeconomic stability.

THE USES OF MONEY

To appreciate the significance of money for a modern economy, imagine for a moment that there were no such thing as money. How would you get something for breakfast? If you wanted eggs for breakfast, you would have to tend your own chickens or go see Farmer Brown. But how would you pay Farmer Brown for his eggs? Without

Poles Survive Collapse of Currency by Using Own System of Barter

KARTUZY, Poland—Marietta Dzoitek will wake up long before dawn at least one day this week and wrap herself in three thick layers of clothing. She will slip quietly out the front door, so as not to disturb her sick mother, and go out into the bitter cold to wait in line for hours outside the neighborhood newspaper kiosk.

Miss Dzoitek—a frail, 31-year-old hospital switchboard operator—will say little or nothing to those around her as she waits for the shop to open: Conversations in lines these days too often end in arguments.

She complains but endures the tedium for the reward at the end—cigarets to use as barter. If she is lucky, she'll be able to buy four of the 12 packs her ration coupons entitle her to each month. She'll go through the same sort of ritual later in the week to buy her monthly half liter of vodka.

Miss Dzoitek herself rarely smokes or drinks, but such goods have taken on special significance in Polish society. "Tobacco and alcohol are the best currencies nowadays," Miss Dzoitek says wanly. "Money no longer matters."

Stock in Trade

This small northern town of 15,000, just 20 miles from the Baltic coast and 70 miles from the Soviet border, is surviving on barter. So, indeed, is all of Poland. If one has the right item to trade, he can bypass some of the other exasperating and ubiquitous lines and the frequently empty shop shelves.

This month, Miss Dzoitek wants to use her vodka and cigarets to buy toothpaste, washing powder, and coffee. She also hopes to persuade a nurse to help find medicine, otherwise unobtainable, to treat her mother's asthma. . . .

Finance minister Marian Krzak has warned: "The devolution of Poland into a barter society is our greatest problem. We must stop cigarets from becoming money and money from becoming nothing."

The Worthless Zloty

Indeed, the Zloty, Poland's monetary unit, is one of the few things in Kartuzy that isn't in short supply. More than one-third of Polish wages aren't matched by goods in shops, and that gap grows every day. Incomes have increased more than 25% in the past year, but the supply of consumer goods has dropped by nearly as much. A general flight from money is taking place, and as a result the most desired and least available products— spirits, cigarets, sugar, meat, washing powder, to name a few—have become the means of exchange.

—Frederick Kempe

---

barter: The direct exchange of one good for another, without the use of money.

money, you would have to offer him goods or services that he could use. In other words, you would have to engage in primitive **barter**—the direct exchange of one good for another—in order to get eggs for breakfast. You would get those eggs only if Farmer Brown happened to want the particular goods or services you had to offer, and if the two of you could agree on the terms of the exchange.

The use of money greatly simplifies market transactions. It's a lot easier to exchange money for eggs at the supermarket than to go into the country and cut hay or lay sod every time you crave some eggs. Our ability to use money in market transactions, however, depends on the grocer's willingness to accept money as a *medium of exchange*. The grocer sells eggs for money only because he can use the same money to pay his help and buy the goods he himself desires. He, too, can exchange money for goods and services. Accordingly, money plays an essential role in facilitating the continuous series of exchanges that characterize a market economy.

Money has other desirable features. The grocer who accepts your money in exchange for a carton of eggs doesn't have to spend his income immediately. On the contrary, he can hold onto the money for a few days or months, without worrying about its spoiling. Hence money is also a useful *store of value,* that is, a mechanism for transforming current income into future purchases.[1] Finally,

---

[1] Recall, however, that the purchasing power of money will diminish if prices rise. In other words, inflation reduces the desirability of money as a store of value (see Chapter 6).

common use of money serves as a *standard of value* for comparing the market worth of different goods. A dozen eggs is more valuable than a dozen onions if it costs more at the supermarket.

The great virtue of money is that it facilitates market exchanges and specialization in production. In fact, efficient division of labor requires a system whereby people can exchange the things they produce for the things they desire. Money makes possible this system of exchange. But where does the money come from in the first place? Who determines how much will be available? These are the questions we seek to answer in this chapter.

THE MONEY SUPPLY

Before trying to answer a lot of complicated questions about the role of money, we should first decide what money is. Everything from fishhooks to bullets has been used as money at one time or another. Even today, the concept of money includes more than the dollar bills and coins in your pocket or purse. Most people realize this when they offer to pay for goods with a check rather than cash. People do distinguish between "cash" and "money," and for good reason. The "money" you have in a checking account can be used to buy goods and services or to pay debts, or it can be retained for future use. In these respects, your checking account balance is as much a part of your "money" as are the coins and dollars in your pocket or purse. In fact, if everyone accepted your checks (and if the checks could also operate vending machines and pay telephones), there would be no need to carry cash.

money: Anything generally accepted as a medium of exchange.

There is nothing unique about cash, then, insofar as the market is concerned. ***Checking accounts can and do perform the same market functions as cash.*** Accordingly, we must include checking account balances in our concept of **"money."** The essence of money is not its taste, color, or feel, but rather its ability to purchase goods and services.

THE ESSENTIAL CHARACTERISTICS OF MONEY

Anything that serves all of the following purposes can be thought of as "money":

☐ *Medium of exchange:* is accepted as payment for goods and services (and debts)

☐ *Store of value:* can be held for future purchases

☐ *Standard of value:* serves as a yardstick for measuring the prices of goods and services

Items that have actually been used as money have included beads, shells, stones, furs, fishhooks, grain, cattle, and cigarettes. In the early days of colonial America, first Indian wampum, then tobacco, grain, fish, and furs were used as money. Throughout the colonies, gunpowder and bullets were frequently used for small change. The first paper money issued by the federal government consisted of $10 million worth of "greenbacks," printed in 1861 to finance the Civil War.

Transactions accounts

To determine how much money is available to purchase goods and services, we need to do more than count up all our coins and currency—we must also include our checking account balances. Traditionally, checking accounts were maintained only at large commercial ("full service") banks. However, the Monetary Control Act of 1980 made it possible for many kinds of banks to offer "checking" accounts. Many people hold deposits, for example, in Negotiable Order of Withdrawal (NOW) accounts or Automatic Transfer of Savings (ATS) accounts. Both types of accounts serve the same basic function as regular checking accounts. They permit depositors to spend their deposit balances easily, without making a special trip to the bank to withdraw funds. NOW accounts permit depositors to write checks—negotiable orders of withdrawal—against their accounts directly. ATS accounts, on the other hand, require a depositor to maintain both a checking account and a savings ("time-deposit") account. But the bank will automatically transfer funds from your savings account to your checking account if you write too many checks. Hence you can spend your savings account just as easily as your checking-account balance. An advantage of NOW and ATS accounts is that they pay interest on unused balances; regular checking accounts do not pay interest on your balance.[2]

Credit unions and savings banks also offer the convenience of traditional checking accounts. A depositor may now "spend" funds maintained in a credit union by writing a credit-union "share draft," a piece of paper that looks just like a check. The same is true of many deposits held at mutual savings banks. Because all such deposits can be used directly in market transactions (without a trip to the bank), they are often referred to as "transactions accounts."[3] The distinguishing feature of all **transactions accounts** is that they permit direct payment to a third party, without requiring a trip to the bank to make a special withdrawal.

transactions account: A bank account that permits direct payment to a third party (e.g., with a check).

The money supply

Because all transactions accounts can be spent as readily as cash, they are counted as part of our money supply. Adding transactions-account balances to the quantity of coins and currency held by the public gives us one measure of the amount of "money" available, that is, the basic **money supply.** The basic money supply is typically referred to by the abbreviation $M1$.

money supply ($M1$): Currency held by the public, plus balances in transactions accounts.

Figure 10.1 illustrates the actual composition of our money supply. The first component of $M1$ is the cash people hold (currency in circulation outside of commercial banks). Clearly the cash we carry around in our pockets is a small part of our money supply: most "money" consists of transactions deposits. This is not so surprising. People generally prefer to use checks or credit cards rather than cash for large market transactions. The credit card purchases are themselves later paid for by check, typically through the mail. Hence checks turn out to be more convenient than cash, because they eliminate trips to the bank. Also it is much safer to carry checks (or credit cards) than cash. Lost or stolen cash is gone forever; checkbooks and credit cards are easily replaced, at little or no cost.

---

[2] This situation may change. The Monetary Control Act of 1980 allows banks much more discretion in the 1980s.

[3] They are also called "checkable deposits."

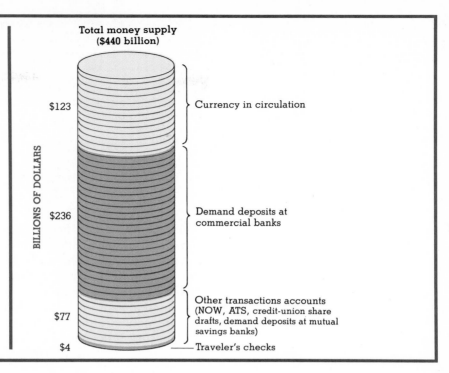

FIGURE 10.1 COMPOSITION OF THE BASIC MONEY SUPPLY (M 1)

The money supply (M 1) includes all cash held by the public plus balances people hold in transactions accounts (e.g., checking, NOW, ATS, and credit-union share-draft accounts). Cash is a relatively small part of our money supply.

Source: *Federal Reserve Bulletin*, February 1982.

Total money supply
($440 billion)

BILLIONS OF DOLLARS

$123 — Currency in circulation

$236 — Demand deposits at commercial banks

$77 — Other transactions accounts (NOW, ATS, credit-union share drafts, demand deposits at mutual savings banks)

$4 — Traveler's checks

demand deposit: Checking-account balance.

Figure 10.1 indicates that the largest type of transactions account in M 1 consists of conventional checking accounts at commercial banks. Balances held in regular checking accounts are often called **demand deposits,** because they can be converted into cash "on demand" or used to pay for goods and services directly. Although other transactions accounts now offer this same convenience, they are usually referred to by their specific names (e.g., NOW accounts).

The last component of our basic money supply consists of traveler's checks issued by nonbank firms (e.g., American Express). These, too, can be used directly in market transactions, just like good old-fashioned cash.

Other money measures

Transactions accounts are not the only substitute for cash. Even a conventional savings account can be used to finance market purchases. This use of a savings account usually requires a trip to the bank for a special withdrawal. But that is not too great a barrier to consumer spending. Some savings banks even make that trip unnecessary by offering computerized withdrawals and transfers from their savings accounts, some even at supermarket service desks. Others offer to pay your bills if you phone in instructions.

Not all savings accounts are so easily spendable. Many savings accounts require a minimum balance to be kept in the bank for a specified number of months or years; early withdrawal results in a loss of interest. Such accounts are called "certificates of deposit" rather than passbook savings. Funds held in certificates of deposit cannot be transferred automatically to a checking account (like passbook savings balances) or to a third party (like NOW-account bal-

'Sweep' Accounts Debuting Here

The latest innovation in banking, the "sweep" account, combining an interest bearing checking account with a money market fund, is headed this way.

The concept was pioneered several years ago by Merrill Lynch for its affluent customers and offered by other money market funds and bank trust accounts as well. In recent months, however, several hundred banks and a few savings and loans from San Diego, Calif., to Bridgeport, Conn., have begun offering the accounts to individuals with a few thousand dollars in their accounts.

In a "sweep" account, customers must usually meet a minimum deposit requirement. Each account is automatically tallied or "swept" by computer each night and any funds above the minimum threshold amount are transferred into the money market account, which pays more than twice the interest rate of the checking account. If a customer's balance falls below the threshold amount, funds are removed from the money market account and redeposited in the checking account. . . .

—Nancy L. Ross

ances). As a result, certificates of deposit are seldom used for everyday market purchases. Nevertheless, such accounts still function like "near money" in the sense that savers can go to the bank and withdraw cash if they really want to buy something.

Another popular way of holding money is to buy shares of money-market mutual funds. Deposits into money-market mutual funds are pooled and used to purchase interest-bearing securities (e.g., Treasury bills). The resultant interest payments are typically higher than those paid by banks. Moreover, the deposits made into the funds can often be withdrawn immediately, just like those in transactions accounts. In recent years of high interest rates, substantial deposits have moved out of regular transactions accounts into these money-market mutual funds.

Additional measures of the money supply have been constructed to account for the possibility of using money-market mutual

TABLE 10.1 ALTERNATIVE MEASURES OF THE MONEY SUPPLY

Measures of the money supply are intended to gauge the extent of purchasing power held by consumers. But the extent of purchasing power depends on how accessible assets are and how often people use them. The various money-supply measures reflect variations in the liquidity and accessibility of assets.

Measure	Components
M1	Currency in circulation outside of commercial banks
	Demand deposits at commercial banks
	NOW and ATS accounts
	Credit-union share drafts
	Demand deposits at mutual savings banks
	Traveler's checks (nonbank)
M2	M1 plus:
	Savings accounts
	Time deposits of less than $100,000
	Money-market mutual funds
	Overnight Eurodollars
M3	M2 plus:
	Time deposits larger than $100,000
	Repurchase agreements
L	M3 plus other liquid assets, for example:
	Treasury bills
	U.S. savings bonds
	Bankers' acceptances
	Term Eurodollars
	Commercial paper

funds and various other deposits to finance everyday spending. These other money-supply measures are noted in Table 10.1.

The several measures of the money supply reflect a lack of clear distinction between money and other assets. What we want to know is how much readily available purchasing power consumers have, since this will affect their ability to purchase goods and services. But purchasing power is an elusive concept. If people are ready and willing to make frequent trips to the bank or to convert other assets into cash, our concept of money will be very large. For the time being, however, we shall focus on $M1$, since it is the most spendable form of money and is the core of all other money-supply definitions. We shall also refer to all depository institutions as "banks," even though there are important distinctions among them.

WHAT IS A BANK?

The roughly 40,000 depository institutions ("banks") in the United States fall into four general categories: commercial banks, savings and loan (S&L) associations, mutual savings banks, and credit unions. In years past there were important distinctions between these types of banks. But the Monetary Control Act of 1980 permits much greater flexibility in banking services. Hence the following distinctions may well be eliminated in the mid-1980s:

Commercial banks: The nation's nearly 15,000 commercial banks provide a full range of banking services, including savings ("time") and checking accounts and loans for all purposes. They hold nearly all demand deposits. Commercial banks also hold nearly half of total savings deposits, despite the fact that they offer a slightly lower interest rate on savings accounts than do other types of banks. Commercial banks also have authority to transfer savings balances to checking balances automatically at a depositor's request.

Savings and loan associations: Savings and loan associations were begun in 1831 as a mechanism for pooling the savings of a neighborhood in order to provide funds for home purchases. This is still the basic function of such banks. The nearly 5,000 S&Ls channel virtually all of their savings deposits into home mortgages.

Mutual savings banks: Mutual savings banks are much like S&Ls. The primary difference is that they were originally intended to serve very small savers (e.g., the Boston Five Cents Savings Bank). They can also use their deposits for a wider variety of purposes, including investment in bonds and "blue chip" stocks. Almost all of the 575 mutual savings banks are located in only five states (New York, Massachusetts, Connecticut, Pennsylvania, and New Jersey).

Credit unions: A credit union is a cooperative savings and loan society formed by individuals bound together by some common tie such as a common employer or labor union. Typically credit-union members hold relatively small savings accounts, but enjoy access to the pooled savings of all members. Most credit-union loans are for consumer purchases and usually are in small amounts. Although there are close to 22,000 credit unions in the United States, they hold less than 5 percent of total savings deposits.

Fed to Report Monetary Base

The Federal Reserve Board has begun to publish weekly data on a money supply figure many economists believe is the best indicator of the Fed's inflationary behavior.

The Fed will report the monetary base, which is composed of currency in the hands of the public and bank reserves in the hands of the Fed. Previously, this information was reported only by the Federal Reserve Bank of St. Louis, which has long advocated its use. . . .

Harris Bank of Chicago economist Beryl W. Sprinkel, one of the advocates of the monetary base, said, "It's important because it is less distorted by technological change in banking and the disintermediation that is occurring."

For example, the rise of automated transfers from savings to checking accounts has resulted in a decline in M1 as people move checking account deposits into savings. Also, the Fed's Regulation Q, which puts a ceiling on savings account interest, has caused many people to withdraw funds from savings accounts to buy into money-market mutual funds and other interest-rate-sensitive securities, he said.

© Chicago Sun-Times, 1979. Article by Bill Barnhart, reprinted with permission.

CREATION OF MONEY

Once we have decided what money is, we still have to explain where it comes from. Because transactions deposits are the largest part of our money supply ($M1$), we shall answer this question by looking at the origins of such deposits. How do people acquire transactions deposits (checking-account balances, NOW balances, etc.)? How does the total amount of such deposits—and therefore the money supply of the economy—change?

Deposit creation

Most people assume that all transactions-account balances come from cash deposits. But this is not the case. There are other, perfectly legal ways to achieve a positive balance. The easiest way is simply to *borrow* money from your bank. If the bank thinks there is a good chance you will repay the loan, it will lend you money. That is, it will create a transactions deposit for you that you would not otherwise have. ***In making a loan, a bank effectively creates money, because transactions-account balances are counted as part of the money supply.*** And you are free to spend that money, just as if you had earned it yourself.

To understand the origins of our money supply, then, we must recognize two basic principles:

- Transactions-account balances are the largest portion of our money supply.
- Banks can create transactions-account balances by making loans.

deposit creation: The creation of transactions deposits by bank lending.

In the following two sections we shall examine the process of **deposit creation** more closely. What we want to determine is how banks actually create deposits and what forces might limit the process of deposit creation.

BANK REGULATION The deposit-creation activities of banks are regulated by the government. The most important agency in this regard is the Federal Reserve System (the "Fed"). The Fed puts limits on the amount of bank lending, thereby controlling the basic money supply. These limits take the form of reserve requirements that force banks to hold reserves rather than use them to support loans. The structure and functions of the Fed are discussed at length in Chapter 11. In this chapter we focus on the process of deposit creation itself.

A monopoly bank

Suppose, to keep things simple, that there is only one bank in town, University Bank. Imagine also that you have been saving (not spending) some of your income by putting loose change into a piggy bank. Now, after months of saving, you break the bank and discover that your parsimony has yielded $100. You immediately deposit this money in a new checking account at University Bank. How will this deposit affect the money supply?

Your initial deposit will have no immediate effect on the money supply ($M1$). The coins in your piggy bank were already counted as part of the money supply, because they represented cash held by the public. ***When you deposit cash or coins in a bank, you are simply changing the composition of the money supply.*** The public (you) now holds $100 less of coins, but $100 more of transactions deposits. Accordingly, no money is created by the demise of your piggy bank (the initial deposit).

University Bank is not in business just for your convenience, however. On the contrary, University Bank is in business to earn a profit. To earn a profit on your deposit, University Bank will have to put your money to work. This means using your deposit as the basis for making a loan to someone who is willing to pay the bank interest for use of money. If the function of banks were merely to store money, they would not pay interest on their accounts or offer free checking services. Instead, you would have to pay them for these services. Banks pay you interest and offer free (or inexpensive) checking because they can use your money to make loans that themselves earn interest.

Typically, a bank does not have much difficulty finding someone who wants to borrow money. Many firms and individuals have expenditure desires that exceed their current money balances, and are eager to borrow money. The question is, how much money can a bank lend? Can it lend your entire deposit? Or must University Bank keep some of your coins in reserve, in case you want to withdraw them?

To answer this question, suppose that University Bank decided to lend the entire $100. What would happen? In this case, assume that University Bank agrees to lend $100 to Campus Radio. Campus Radio wants to buy a new antenna but doesn't have any money in its own checking account. Hence it wants to borrow $100 from University Bank. When University Bank agrees to lend Campus Radio $100, it does so by crediting the account of Campus Radio. Instead of giving Campus Radio $100 cash, University Bank simply adds $100 to Campus Radio's checking-account balance. That is to say, the loan is made with a simple bookkeeping entry.

This simple bookkeeping procedure has important implications. When University Bank lends $100 to the Campus Radio account, it "creates" money because transactions deposits are counted as part of the money supply. Moreover, Campus Radio can use this new money to purchase its desired antenna, without worrying that its check will bounce.

Or can it? Once University Bank grants a loan to Campus Radio, both you and Campus Radio have $100 in your checking accounts to spend. But the bank is holding only $100 of reserves (your coins). In other words, the increased checking-account balance obtained by Campus Radio does not limit your ability to write checks. There has been a net *increase* in the value of transactions deposits, but no increase in bank reserves.

What happens if Campus Radio actually spends the $100 on a new antenna? Won't this "use up" all the reserves held by the bank, and endanger your check-writing privileges? The answer is no.

Consider what happens when Atlas Antenna receives the check from Campus Radio. What will Atlas do with the check? Atlas could go to University Bank and exchange the check for $100 of cash (your coins). But Atlas probably doesn't have any immediate need for cash. Atlas may prefer to deposit the check in its own checking account at University Bank (still the only bank in town). In this way, Atlas not only avoids the necessity of going to the bank (it can deposit the check by mail), but also keeps its money in a safe place. Should Atlas later want to spend the money, it may simply write a check. In the meantime, the bank continues to hold its entire reserves (your coins) and both you and Atlas have $100 to spend.

FRACTIONAL RESERVES   Notice what has happened here. The money supply has increased by $100 as a result of deposit creation (the loan to Campus Radio). Moreover, the bank has been able to support $200 of transactions deposits (your account and either the Campus Radio or Atlas account) with only $100 of reserves (your coins). In other words, **bank reserves are only a fraction of total transactions deposits.** In this case, University Bank's reserves (your $100 in coins) are only 50 percent of total deposits. Thus the bank's **reserve ratio** is 50 percent rather than 100 percent.

reserve ratio: The ratio of a bank's reserves to its total transactions deposits.

The ability of University Bank to hold reserves that are only a fraction of total deposits results from the fact that people use checks for most transactions, and there is no other bank. Accordingly, reserves are rarely withdrawn from this monopoly bank. In fact, if people *never* withdrew their deposits and *all* transactions accounts were held at University Bank, University Bank would not really need any reserves. In this most unusual case, University Bank could continue to make as many loans as it wanted.

A multibank world   In reality, many banks are available, and people both withdraw cash from their accounts and write checks to people who have accounts in other banks. In addition, bank lending practices are regulated by the Federal Reserve System. **The Federal Reserve System requires banks to maintain some minimum reserve ratio.** This reserve requirement directly limits the ability of banks to grant new loans.[4]

---

[4] The role of the Federal Reserve System in regulating banks and their reserves is discussed in Chapter 11.

The potential impact of Federal Reserve requirements on bank lending can be seen readily. Suppose that the Federal Reserve had imposed a minimum reserve requirement of 50 percent on University Bank. Such a requirement would have prohibited University Bank from making any further loans. After University Bank lent $100 to Campus Radio its reserve ratio was 0.5. Any further loans would increase the bank's demand deposits but not its reserves. Hence the reserve ratio would fall below 50 percent if additional loans were made. By requiring a minimum reserve ratio of 50 percent, the Fed prohibits such loans. Thus a minimum reserve requirement directly limits deposit-creation possibilities. It is still true, however, as we shall now illustrate, that the banking system, taken as a whole, can create multiple loans (money) from a single deposit.

AN ILLUSTRATION   The process of deposit creation in a many-bank world with a required reserve ratio is illustrated in Table 10.2. In this case, we assume that legally required reserves must equal at least 20 percent of transactions deposits. Hence when you deposit $100 in your checking account, University Bank must hold at least $20 as **required reserves.**[5]

required reserves: The minimum amount of reserves a bank is required to hold by government regulation; equal to required reserve ratio times transactions deposits.

excess reserves: Bank reserves in excess of required reserves.

The remaining $80 the bank obtains from your deposit is regarded as **excess reserves.** These reserves are "excess" in the sense that your bank is *required* to hold in reserve only $20 (equal to 20 percent of your initial $100 deposit). The remaining $80 of reserves are not required, and may be used to support additional loans. Hence the bank could lend $80 initially. In view of the fact that banks earn profits (interest) by making loans, we assume that University Bank will try to use its excess reserves by making additional loans.

To keep track of the changes in reserves, transactions deposits, and loans that occur in a multibank world we shall have to examine the balance sheet, or "T-account," that banks themselves use. On the left side of the balance sheet, a bank lists all its assets. Assets are things the bank owns or is owed by others. These assets include cash held in a bank's vaults, IOUs (loan obligations) from bank customers, reserve credits at the Federal Reserve (essentially the bank's own deposits at the central bank), and securities (bonds) the bank has purchased.

On the right side of the balance sheet a bank lists all its liabilities. Liabilities are things the bank owes to others. The largest liability is represented by the transactions deposits of the bank's customers. The bank owes these deposits to its customers and must return them "on demand."

The use of balance sheets is illustrated in Table 10.2. Notice how the balance of University Bank looks immediately after it receives your initial deposit (Step 1 of Table 10.2). Your deposit of coins is entered on *both* sides of University's balance sheet. On the left side, your deposit is regarded as an asset, because your piggy bank's coins have an immediate market value and can be used to pay off the bank's liabilities. The reserves these coins represent are divided into

[5] The reserves themselves may be held in the form of cash in the bank's vaults but are usually held as credits with one of the regional Federal Reserve banks.

TABLE 10.2   DEPOSIT CREATION

Excess reserves (Step 1) are the basis of bank loans. When a bank uses its excess reserves to make a loan, it creates a transactions deposit (Step 2). When the loan is spent, a deposit will be made somewhere else (Step 3). This new deposit creates additional excess reserves (Step 3) that can be used for further loans (Steps 4, etc.). The process of deposit creation continues until the money supply has increased by a multiple of the initial deposit.

Step 1:   You deposit cash at University Bank

University Bank

Assets		Liabilities		Change in transactions deposits	Change in M1
Required reserves	$ 20.00	Your demand deposit	$100.00	+ $100.00	$ 0.00
Excess reserves	80.00				
Total	$100.00		$100.00		

Step 2:   Bank makes a loan to Campus Radio

University Bank

Assets		Liabilities			
Required reserves	$ 36.00	Your account	$100.00	+ 80.00	+ 80.00
Excess reserves	64.00	Campus radio account	80.00		
Loans	80.00				
Total	$180.00		$180.00		

required reserves ($20, or 20 percent of your deposit) and excess reserves ($80).

On the right side of the balance sheet, the bank reminds itself that it has an obligation ("liability") to return your deposit when you so demand. Thus the bank's accounts balance, with assets and liabilities being equal. In fact, *a bank's books must always balance, because all of the bank's assets must belong to someone (its depositors or its owners).*

University Bank wants to do more than balance its books, however; it wants to earn profits. To do so, it will have to make loans, that is, put its excess reserves to work. Suppose that it lends $80 to

Step 3: Campus Radio buys an antenna

University Bank				Eternal Savings				Change in transactions deposits	Change in M1
Assets		Liabilities		Assets		Liabilities			
Required reserves	$ 20.00	Your account	$100.00	Required reserves	$16.00	Atlas Antenna account	$80.00	$ 0.00	$ 0.00
Excess reserves	0.00	Campus Radio account	0.00	Excess reserves	64.00				
Loans	80.00								
Total	$100.00		$100.00		$80.00		$80.00		

Step 4: Eternal Savings lends money to Herman's Hardware

University Bank				Eternal Savings					
Assets		Liabilities		Assets		Liabilities			
Required reserves	$ 20.00	Your account	$100.00	Required reserves	$ 28.80	Atlas Antenna account	$ 80.00	+ 64.00	+ 64.00
Excess reserves	0.00	Campus Radio account	0.00	Excess reserves	51.20	Herman's Hardware account	64.00		
Loans	80.00			Loans	64.00				
Total	$100.00		$100.00		$144.00		$144.00		

	.		.		.		.	.	.
	.		.		.		.	.	.
	.		.		.		.	.	.

Nth step: Some bank lends $1.00   +   1.00   + 1.00

Cumulative change

	Bank reserves	Transactions deposits	Money supply
	+$100.00	+$500.00	+$400.00

Campus Radio.[6] As Step 2 in Table 10.2 illustrates, this loan alters both sides of University Bank's balance sheet. On the right-hand side, the bank creates a new transactions deposit for (credits the account of) Campus Radio; this item represents an additional liability (promise to pay). On the left-hand side of the balance sheet, two things happen. First, the bank notes that Campus Radio owes it $80 ("loans"). Second, the bank recognizes that it is now required to hold $36 in *required* reserves, in accordance with its higher level of

[6] Because of the Federal Reserve's assumed minimum reserve requirement (20 percent), University Bank can now lend only $80 rather than $100, as before.

transactions deposits ($180). (Recall we are assuming that required reserves are 20 percent of total transactions deposits.) Since its total reserves are still $100, $64 are left as *excess* reserves. Note again that ***excess reserves are reserves a bank is not required to hold.***

CHANGES IN THE MONEY SUPPLY   Before examining further changes in the balance sheet of University Bank, consider what has happened to the economy's money supply during these first two steps. In the first step, you deposited $100 of cash in your checking account. Because our definition of the money supply includes both cash and transactions deposits, this initial transaction did not change the value of the money supply. Only the composition of $M1$ was affected ($100 less cash held by the public, $100 more in transactions accounts).

It is not until Step 2—when the bank makes a loan—that all the excitement begins. In making a loan, the bank automatically increases the total money supply by $80. Why? Because someone (Campus Radio) now has more money (a transactions deposit) than it did before, and no one else has any less. And Campus Radio can use its money to buy goods and services, just like anybody else.

This second step is the heart of money creation. Money effectively appears out of thin air when a bank makes a loan. To understand how this works, you have to keep reminding yourself that money is more than the coins and currency we carry around. Transactions deposits are money too. Hence ***the creation of transactions deposits via new loans is the same thing as creating money.***

MORE DEPOSIT CREATION   Suppose again that Campus Radio actually uses its $80 loan to buy an antenna. The rest of Table 10.2 illustrates how this additional transaction leads to further changes in balance sheets and the money supply.

In Step 3, we see that when Campus Radio buys the $80 antenna, the balance in its checking account at University Bank drops to zero, because they have spent all their money. As University Bank's liabilities fall (from $180 to $100), so does the level of its required reserves (from $36 to $20). (Note that required reserves are still 20 percent of its remaining transactions deposits.) But University Bank's excess reserves have disappeared completely! This disappearance reflects the fact that Atlas Antenna keeps *its* transactions account at another bank (Eternal Savings). Thus when Atlas deposits the check it received from Campus Radio, Eternal Savings does two things. First it credits Atlas's account by $80. Second, it goes to University Bank to get the reserves that support that deposit.[7] The reserves later appear on the balance sheet of Eternal Savings as both required ($16) and excess ($64) reserves.

Observe that the money supply has not changed during Step 3. The increase in the value of Atlas Antenna's transactions-account balance exactly offsets the drop in the value of Campus Radio's

[7] In actuality, banks rarely "go" anywhere; such interbank reserve movements are handled by bank clearinghouses and regional Federal Reserve banks. The effect is the same, however. The nature and use of bank reserves are discussed more fully in Chapter 11.

transactions account. Hence ownership of the money supply is the only thing that has changed.

In Step 4, Eternal Savings takes advantage of its newly acquired excess reserves by making a loan to Herman's Hardware. As before, the loan itself has two primary effects. First, it creates a transactions deposit of $64 for Herman's Hardware and thereby increases the money supply by the same amount. Second, it increases the required level of reserves at Eternal Savings. (To how much? Why?)

THE MONEY MULTIPLIER

By now it is perhaps obvious that the process of deposit creation will not come to an end quickly. On the contrary, it can continue indefinitely, just like the income multiplier process of Chapter 8. Indeed, people often refer to deposit creation as the money-multiplier process, with the **money multiplier** expressed as the reciprocal of the required reserve ratio.[8]

The money-multiplier process is illustrated in Figure 10.2. When a new deposit enters the banking system, it creates both excess and required reserves. The required reserves represent leakage from the flow of money, since they cannot be used to create new loans. Excess reserves, on the other hand, can be used for new loans. Once those loans are made, they typically become transactions deposits elsewhere in the banking system. Then some additional leakage into required reserves occurs and further loans are made. The process continues until all excess reserves have leaked into required reserves. Once excess reserves have completely disappeared, the total value of new loans will equal initial excess reserves multiplied by the money multiplier.

Notice how the money multiplier worked in our previous example. The value of the money multiplier was equal to 5, since we

money multiplier: The maximum multiple by which transactions deposits (money) can be created from any given level of excess reserves; equal to $1 \div$ required reserve ratio.

---

[8] The money multiplier ($1/r$) is the sum of the infinite geometric progression $1 + (1 - r) + (1 - r)^2 + (1 - r)^3 + \cdots + (1 - r)^\infty$.

FIGURE 10.2 THE MONEY-MULTIPLIER PROCESS

Part of every new transactions-account deposit leaks into required reserves. The rest—excess reserves—can be used to make loans. These loans, in turn, become deposits elsewhere. The process of money creation continues until all available reserves are required.

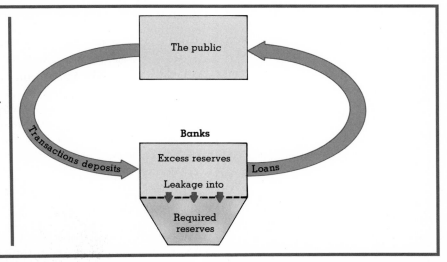

assumed that the required reserve ratio was 0.20. Moreover, the initial level of excess reserves was $80, as a consequence of your original deposit (Step 1). According to the money multiplier, then, the deposit-creation potential of the banking system was:

$$\underset{(\$80)}{\text{Excess reserves}} \times \underset{(5)}{\text{money multiplier}} = \underset{\text{creation }(\$400)}{\overset{\text{potential}}{\text{deposit}}}$$

To the extent that all the banks fully utilized their excess reserves at each step of the money-multiplier process, the ultimate increase in the money supply was in fact $400 (see the last row of Table 10.2).

Excess reserves as lending power

While you are working your way through Table 10.2, notice the critical role that excess reserves play in the process of deposit creation. A bank can make loans only if it has excess reserves. Without excess reserves, all of a bank's reserves are required, and no further liabilities (transactions deposits) can be created with new loans. On the other hand, a bank with excess reserves can make additional loans. In fact, *each bank may lend an amount equal to its excess reserves and no more.* As such loans enter the circular flow and become deposits elsewhere, they create new excess reserves and further lending capacity. As a consequence, *the entire banking system can increase the volume of loans by the amount of excess reserves multiplied by the money multiplier.* By keeping track of excess reserves, then, we can gauge the lending capacity of any bank, or, with the aid of the money multiplier, the entire banking system.

Table 10.3 provides a summary of the entire money-multiplier process. In this case, we assume that all banks are initially "loaned up," that is, without any excess reserves. The money-multiplier process begins when someone deposits $100 in cash into a transactions account at Bank A. If the required reserve ratio is 20 percent, this initial deposit creates $80 of excess reserves at Bank A, while adding $100 to total transactions deposits.

If Bank A uses its newly acquired excess reserves to make a loan that ultimately ends up in Bank B, two things happen. Bank B acquires $64 in excess reserves (0.20 × $80) and total transactions deposits increase by another $80.

The money-multiplier process continues with a series of loans and deposits. When the twenty-sixth loan is made (by bank Z), total loans grow by only $0.30 and transactions deposits by an equal amount. Should the process continue further, the *cumulative* change in loans will ultimately equal $400, that is, the money multiplier times initial excess reserves. The money supply will increase by the same amount.

POLICY IMPLICATIONS: THE IMPORTANCE OF BANKS

The bookkeeping details of bank deposits and loans are rarely exciting and often confusing. But they do demonstrate convincingly that banks can create money. This implies that banks must have some

TABLE 10.3 THE MONEY MULTIPLIER AT WORK

The process of deposit creation continues as money passes through different
banks in the form of multiple deposits and loans. At each step, excess reserves
and new loans are created. The lending capacity of this system equals the money
multiplier times excess reserves. In this case, initial excess reserves of $80 create
the possibility for $400 of new loans.

	Change in transactions deposits	Change in total reserves	Change in required reserves	Change in excess reserves	Change in lending capacity
If $100 in cash is deposited in Bank *A*, Bank *A* acquires	$100.00	$100.00	$ 20.00	$80.00	$ 80.00
If loan made and deposited elsewhere, Bank *B* acquires	80.00	80.00	16.00	64.00	64.00
If loan made and deposited elsewhere, Bank *C* acquires	64.00	64.00	12.80	51.20	51.20
If loan made and deposited elsewhere, Bank *D* acquires	51.20	51.20	10.10	41.00	41.00
If loan made and deposited elsewhere, Bank *E* acquires	41.00	41.00	7.20	32.80	32.80
If loan made and deposited elsewhere, Bank *F* acquires	32.80	32.80	6.60	26.20	26.20
If loan made and deposited elsewhere, Bank *G* acquires	26.20	26.20	5.20	21.00	21.00
• • •					
If loan made and deposited elsewhere, Bank *Z* acquires	0.40	0.40	0.10	0.30	0.30
Cumulative, through Bank *Z*	$498.80	$100.00	$ 99.76	$ 0.24	$398.80
• • •	• • •	• • •	• • •	• • •	• • •
And if the process continues indefinitely	$500.00	$100.00	$100.00	$ 0.00	$400.00

Thus the additional lending potential of the banking system brought about by a $100 cash deposit is:
money multiplier × initial change in excess reserves, or 1/0.20 × $80 = $400.

---

direct influence on economic activity, because all of our market
transactions involve the use of money. The purpose of this final section is to determine the role of the banking system in the circular
flow of income and expenditure.

Banks and the circular flow

What we have demonstrated in this chapter is that banks perform
two essential functions:

- Banks transfer money from savers to spenders by lending
  funds (reserves) held on deposit.

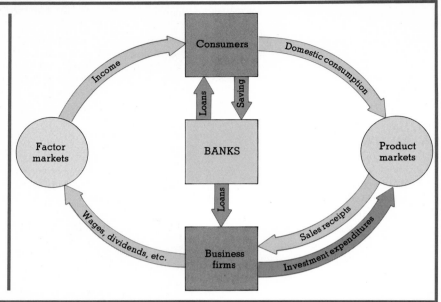

FIGURE 10.3 BANKS IN THE CIRCULAR FLOW

Banks help to transfer income from savers to spenders. They do this by using their deposits to make loans to business firms and consumers who desire to spend more money than they have. By lending money, banks help to maintain any desired rate of aggregate expenditure.

- The banking system creates additional money by making loans in excess of total reserves.

In performing these two functions, banks change the size of the money supply, that is, the amount of purchasing power available for buying goods and services.

Figure 10.3 provides a simplified perspective on the role of banks in the circular flow. As before, income flows from product markets through business firms to factor markets and returns to consumers in the form of disposable income. Consumers spend most of their income but also save (not spend) some of it.

The leakage represented by consumer saving is a potential source of stabilization problems, particularly unemployment. If additional spending by business firms, foreigners, or governments does not compensate for consumer saving at full employment, a recessionary gap will emerge, creating unemployment (see Chapters 7 and 8). Our interest here is in the role the banking system can play in encouraging such additional spending.

Suppose for the moment that *all* consumer saving was deposited in piggy banks rather than depository institutions (banks) and that no one used checks. Under these circumstances, banks could not transfer money from savers to spenders by holding deposits and making loans.

In reality, a substantial portion of consumer saving *is* deposited in banks. These and other bank deposits can be used as the basis of loans, thereby returning purchasing power to the circular flow.[9] In fact, the primary economic function of banks is not to store money but to transfer purchasing power from savers to spenders. They do so

[9] Business savings and government deposits also enter the banking system and become sources of bank lending, but we will ignore these complications here, at no loss to the principles of deposit creation.

by lending money to businesses for new plant and equipment, to consumers for new homes or cars, and to government entities that desire greater purchasing power. Moreover, because the banking system can make *multiple* loans from available reserves, banks don't have to receive all consumer saving in order to carry out their function. On the contrary, ***the banking system can create any desired level of money supply if allowed to expand or reduce its loan activity at will.***

Constraints on deposit creation

There are three major constraints on the deposit creation of the banking system. The first of these constraints is the willingness of consumers and businesses to continue using and accepting checks rather than cash in the marketplace. If people preferred to hold cash rather than checkbooks, banks would not be able to acquire or maintain the reserves that are the foundation of bank lending activity.

The second constraint on deposit creation is the willingness of consumers, businesses, and governments to borrow the money that banks make available. The chain of events we have observed in deposit creation depends on the willingness of Campus Radio to borrow $80, of Herman's Hardware to borrow $64, and so on. If no one wanted to borrow any money, deposit creation would never begin. By the same reasoning, if all excess reserves are not borrowed (lent), deposit creation will not live up to its theoretical potential.

The third major constraint on deposit creation is the Federal Reserve System. As we have observed, the Federal Reserve System may limit deposit creation by imposing reserve requirements. These and other tools of monetary policy will be discussed in Chapter 11.

SUMMARY

■ In a market economy, money serves a critical function in facilitating exchanges and specialization, thus permitting increased output. "Money" in this context may refer to any medium that is generally accepted in exchange.

■ The most common measure of the money supply (M1) includes both cash and balances people hold in transactions accounts (e.g., checking, NOW, and ATS accounts).

■ Banks have the power to create money simply by making loans. In making loans, banks create new transactions deposits, which become part of the money supply.

■ The ability of banks to make loans—create money—depends on their reserves. Only if a bank has excess reserves—reserves greater than those required by federal regulation—can it make new loans.

■ As loans are spent, they create deposits elsewhere, making it possible for other banks to make additional loans. The money multiplier (1 ÷ required reserve ratio) indicates the total value of deposits that can be created by the banking system, on the basis of an initial increase in excess reserves.

■ The role of banks in creating money includes the transfer of money from savers to spenders as well as deposit creation in excess of deposit balances. Taken together, these two functions give banks direct control over the amount of purchasing power available in the marketplace.

■ The deposit-creation potential of the banking system is limited by government regulation. It is also limited by the willingness of market participants to hold deposits or borrow money.

Terms to remember

Define the following terms:

barter	deposit creation
money	reserve ratio
transactions account	required reserves
money supply ($M1$)	excess reserves
demand deposit	money multiplier

Questions for discussion

1. Does money have any intrinsic value? If not, why are people willing to accept money in exchange for goods and services?

2. Does the fact that your bank keeps only a fraction of your account balance in reserve make you uncomfortable? Why don't people rush to the bank and retrieve their money? What would happen if they did?

3. If there were no minimum reserve requirement, would banks lend out an infinite amount of money? What considerations might inhibit their lending activity?

4. If all banks heeded Shakespeare's admonition "Neither a borrower nor a lender be," what would happen to the circular flow?

Problem

Suppose there are no excess reserves in the banking system when the king of Guime withdraws $10 million from his numbered Swiss account and deposits it in his checking account at the Bank of America. Assuming a reserve requirement of 25 percent, show how this transaction and subsequent lending activity will affect:

(a) The balance sheet of Bank of America, before and after it uses its added lending capacity

(b) The level of reserves and demand deposits in the entire banking system, before and after the banks use their new lending capacity

(c) The money supply, before and after the banking system uses its added lending capacity

CHAPTER 11

THE FEDERAL RESERVE SYSTEM

T he ability of banks (depository institutions) to create money was demonstrated in Chapter 10. In making loans, banks create transactions deposits that are counted as part of the money supply (M1). Banks are not permitted to create an unlimited supply of money, however. As we noted earlier, bank lending practices are regulated by the Federal Reserve System. The "Fed" not only limits the volume of loans that the banking system can make from any given level of reserves, but also can alter the amount of reserves in the banking system. Thus the Federal Reserve System maintains control over the supply of money.

The objective of this chapter is to describe the Federal Reserve System in more detail, with particular emphasis on the tools the Fed uses for altering the supply of money. The use of these money and credit controls is referred to as **monetary policy.**

The potential of monetary policy to alter economic outcomes will be examined in Chapter 12. There we shall look at the way changes in the supply of money may alter the rate of unemployment, the rate of inflation, or both. We shall also look at the arguments between Keynesians and Monetarists about whether and how monetary policy is an effective tool for stabilizing aggregate demand. For the time being, however, we shall just focus on the tools available for implementing monetary policy.

monetary policy: The use of money and credit controls to influence macroeconomic activity.

STRUCTURE OF THE FED

In the absence of any government regulation, the supply of money would be determined by individual banks. Moreover, individual depositors would bear all the risks of bank failures. In fact, this is the way the banking system operated until 1914. The money supply was subject to abrupt changes, and consumers frequently lost their savings in recurrent bank failures.

A series of bank failures resulted in a severe financial panic in 1907. Millions of depositors lost their savings, and the economy was thrown into a tailspin. In the wake of this panic, a National Monetary Commission was established to examine ways of restructuring the banking system. The mandate of the commission was to find ways to avert recurrent financial crises. After five years of study, the commission recommended the creation of a Federal Reserve System. Congress accepted the commission's recommendations and President Wilson signed the Federal Reserve Act in December 1913.

Federal Reserve banks

The core of the Federal Reserve System consists of 12 Federal Reserve banks, located in the various regions of the country. Each of these Federal Reserve banks acts as a central banker for the private banks in its region. In this role, the Fed banks perform many critical services, including:

- *Clearing checks between private banks.* Suppose the Bank of America in San Francisco receives a deposit from one of its customers in the form of a share draft written on the New York State Employees Credit Union. The Bank of America doesn't have to go to New York to collect the cash or other reserves that support that draft. Instead, the Bank of America can deposit the draft (check) at its account with the Federal Reserve Bank of San Francisco. The Fed then collects from the Credit Union. This vital clearinghouse service saves the Bank of America and other private banks a great deal of time and money. In view of the fact that over 30 billion checks are written every year, this clearinghouse service is an important feature of the Federal Reserve System.

- *Holding bank reserves.* Notice that the clearinghouse service of the Fed was facilitated by the fact that the Bank of America (and the New York Employees Credit Union) had their own accounts at the Fed. As we have noted before, banks are *required* to hold some minimum fraction of their transactions deposits in reserve. Nearly all of these reserves are held in accounts at the Federal Reserve banks. Only a small amount of reserves is held as cash in a bank's vaults. These accounts at the Fed provide greater security and convenience for bank reserves. They also enable the Fed to monitor the actual level of bank reserves.

- *Providing currency.* Before every major holiday there is a great demand for cash. People want some "pocket money" during holidays and know that it is difficult to cash checks on weekends or holidays, especially if they are going out of town. After the holiday is over, most of this cash is returned to the banks, typically by the stores, gas stations, and restaurants that benefited from holiday spending. Because banks hold very little cash in their vaults, they turn to the Fed to meet these sporadic cash demands. A private bank may simply call the regional Federal Reserve bank and order a supply of cash, to be delivered (by armored truck) before a weekend or holiday. The cash will be

FIGURE 11.1 STRUCTURE OF THE FEDERAL RESERVE SYSTEM

The broad policies of the Fed are determined by the seven-member Board of Governors. The 12 Reserve banks provide central-banking services to individual banks. The Federal Open Market Committee directs Federal Reserve transactions in the money market. Various committees offer formal and informal advice to the Board of Governors.

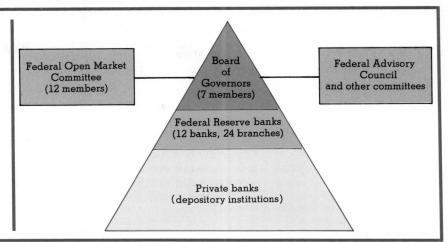

deducted from the bank's own account at the Fed. When all the cash comes back in after the holiday, the bank may reverse the process, sending the unneeded cash back to the Fed.

■ *Providing loans.* The Federal Reserve banks may also loan reserves to private banks. This practice, called "discounting," will be examined more closely in a moment.

Member banks

Before the Monetary Control Act of 1980, only 5,700 commercial banks were "members" of the Federal Reserve System, and thus subject to its regulations and services. Now, however, all banks are subject to reserve requirements established by the Fed. All banks can also use the services the Fed offers. Although the distinction between member banks and nonmember banks still exists, it is of little significance for monetary policy.[1] Accordingly, all private banks that are subject to Federal Reserve reserve requirements may be regarded as members of the Federal Reserve System.

Board of Governors

At the top of the Federal Reserve System's organization chart (Figure 11.1) is the Board of Governors. The Board of Governors of the Fed has broad responsibility for the behavior of the regional Federal Reserve banks, as well as for the formulation of general Fed policy. The Board, located in Washington, D.C., consists of seven members appointed by the president of the United States and confirmed by the Congress. Board members are appointed for 14-year terms and may not be reappointed after serving a full term. Because of their exceptionally long appointments, the Fed's governors tend to be relatively immune to short-term political considerations. Many people regard this immunity as a desirable feature, as it keeps control of the nation's money supply beyond the immediate reach of "politicians" (especially members of Congress, elected for two-year terms). The

[1] The nominal distinction continues because only member banks can vote in the elections of regional Federal Reserve bank directors. This distinction has more political than economic significance.

political independence of the Fed, however, has been a subject of intense controversy, as we shall see.

The president selects one of the governors to serve as chairman of the Board. In July 1979 President Carter appointed Paul Volcker to the Board and designated him as the new chairman. Chairman Volcker may continue to serve as the chief spokesman and principal architect of monetary policy until his term expires in 1993.

Federal Open Market Committee

The fourth major component of the Fed is the Federal Open Market Committee (FOMC). The FOMC is responsible for Federal Reserve transactions in the money market. As we shall see, it plays a critical role in determining the level of reserves held by private banks. The membership of the FOMC includes all seven governors and five regional Reserve bank presidents. The Federal Open Market Committee meets in Washington, D.C., every four or five weeks throughout the year.

MONETARY TOOLS

money supply (M1): Currency held by the public, plus balances in transactions accounts.

Our immediate interest is not in the administrative structure of the Federal Reserve System but in the way the Fed can use its powers to alter the **money supply.** The levers of Fed power include:

- Reserve requirements
- Discount rates
- Open-market operations

Reserve requirements

required reserves: The minimum amount of reserves a bank is required to hold by government regulation; equal to required reserve ratio times transactions deposits.

We have already emphasized the need for banks to maintain some minimal level of reserves. As we noted in Chapter 10, the Fed requires private banks to keep some stated fraction of their deposits "in reserve." **Reserves** are held either in the form of actual vault cash or, more commonly, as credits (deposits) at a regional Federal Reserve bank. ***By changing the reserve requirement, the Fed can directly alter the lending capacity of the banking system.***

Recall that the ability of the banking system to make additional loans—create deposits—is determined by two factors: (1) the amount of excess reserves banks hold and (2) the money multiplier. Both of these factors are directly influenced by the Fed's required reserve ratio.

excess reserves: Bank reserves in excess of required reserves.

money multiplier: The maximum multiple by which transactions deposits (money) can be created from any given level of excess reserves; equal to 1 ÷ required reserve ratio.

Suppose, for example, that banks hold $100 billion of transactions deposits and total reserves of $30 billion. Assume, too, that the minimum reserve requirement is 20 percent. Under these circumstances, banks are holding more reserves than they have to. Only $20 billion of reserves are *required* to meet Federal Reserve regulations (0.20 × $100 billion); the remaining $10 billion are **excess reserves.**

The existence of excess reserves implies that banks are not fully utilizing their lending powers. With $10 billion of excess reserves and the help of the **money multiplier,** the banks *could* lend an additional $50 billion.

OTHER BANK REGULATORS

The Federal Reserve System is not the only public institution that regulates banks. Other important regulatory institutions include:

- *State banking commissions* Long before the Federal Reserve System was established (1914), individual states regulated banks. Even today these commissions determine who may open a bank within a state's borders. They also establish rules for lending, other services, and accounting for state-chartered banks.

- *Comptroller of the Currency* Permission to open a national bank (rather than a state-chartered bank) must be received from the Comptroller of the Currency. The comptroller not only controls national bank charters, but also polices the behavior of national banks.

- *Federal Deposit Insurance Corporation (FDIC) and Federal Savings and Loan Insurance Corporation (FSLIC)* The FDIC and FSLIC insure individual depositors against the loss of their funds. Should a bank fail, the FDIC and FSLIC stand ready to repay the bank's customers for their losses up to a maximum of $100,000 per account.

- *Federal Home Loan Bank Board (FHLBB)* The FHLBB regulates savings banks, savings and loan associations, and other depository institutions not formerly members of the Federal Reserve System.

- *National Credit Union Administration Board* This board regulates credit unions much the same way the FHLBB regulates savings banks.

- *Depository Institutions Deregulation Committee* This committee was established to implement the mandates of the Deregulation and Monetary Control Act of 1980. Its membership includes the heads of the other banking agencies. Its basic mandate is to eliminate unnecessary regulation and make the banking industry more competitive.

The potential for additional loans is calculated simply, as:

Excess reserves × money multiplier = additional lending capacity of banking system

or, in this case,

$$\$10 \text{ billion} \times \frac{1}{0.20} = \$50 \text{ billion of additional lending capacity}$$

That is to say, the banking system could create another $50 billion of money (transactions-account balances) without any additional reserves.

A simple way to confirm this—and thereby check your arithmetic—is to note what would happen to total deposits if the banks actually made further loans. Total deposits would increase to $150 billion in this case (the initial $100 billion plus the new $50 billion), an amount that could be supported with $30 billion in reserves (20 percent of $150 billion).

But what if the Fed doesn't want the money supply (M1) to in-

TABLE 11.1 THE IMPACT OF AN INCREASED RESERVE REQUIREMENT	Required reserve ratio	
	20 percent	25 percent
1. Total deposits	$100 billion	$100 billion
2. Total reserves	30 billion	30 billion
3. Required reserves	20 billion	25 billion
4. Excess reserves	10 billion	5 billion
5. Money multiplier	5	4
6. Additional lending capacity	$ 50 billion	$ 20 billion

An increase in the required reserve ratio reduces both excess reserves (row 4) and the money multiplier (row 5). As a consequence, changes in the reserve requirement have a substantial impact on the lending capacity of the banking system.

crease this much? Maybe prices are rising and the Fed wants to restrain rather than stimulate the rate of total expenditure in the economy. Under such circumstances, the Fed would want to restrict the availability of credit (loans). Does it have the power to do so? Can the Fed reduce the lending capacity of the banking system?

The answer is clearly yes. **By raising the required reserve ratio, the Fed can immediately reduce the lending capacity of the banking system.**

The impact of an increase in the required reserve ratio is summarized in Table 11.1. In this case, the required reserve ratio is increased from 20 to 25 percent. Notice that this change in the reserve requirement has no effect on the amount of initial transactions deposits in the banking system (row 1 of Table 11.1) or the amount of total reserves (row 2). They remain at $100 billion and $30 billion respectively. What the increased reserve requirement *does* affect is the way those reserves can be categorized. Before the increase, only $20 billion in reserves were *required*, leaving $10 billion of *excess* reserves. Now, however, banks are required to hold $25 billion (0.25 × $100 billion) in reserves, leaving them with only $5 billion in excess reserves. Thus the immediate impact of an increase in the reserve requirement is a reduction in excess reserves, as illustrated in row 4 of Table 11.1.

There is a second effect also. Notice what happens to the money multiplier (1 ÷ reserve ratio). Previously it was 5 (1/0.20); now it is only 4 (1/0.25). Consequently, not only are excess reserves reduced, but their lending power is diminished as well.

The full impact of a change in the reserve requirement is conveyed, then, by two distinct phenomena:

- A change in excess reserves
- A change in the money multiplier

These changes lead to a sharp reduction in bank lending power. Whereas the banking system initially had the power to increase the volume of loans by $50 billion ($10 billion of excess reserves × 5), it now has only $20 billion ($5 billion × 4) of additional lending capacity, as noted in the last row of Table 11.1.

Changes in reserve requirements are a powerful weapon for altering the lending capacity of the banking system. The Fed uses this power sparingly, so as not to cause abrupt changes in the money supply and severe disruptions of banking activity. From 1970 to 1980, for example, reserve requirements were changed only twice, and then only by half a percentage point each time (for example, from 12.0 to 12.5 percent). The reserve requirements effective in 1982 are described in Table 11.2. Note that reserve requirements increase with the size of a bank's deposits.[2] These different reserve requirements reflect a desire to give smaller banks a competitive advantage by providing them with a higher ratio of loan capacity to deposits.

The discount rate

Banks have a tremendous incentive to maintain their reserves at or close to the minimum established by the Fed. Money held in reserve earns no interest, but loans and bonds do.[3] Hence a profit-maximizing bank seeks to keep its excess reserves as low as possible, preferring to put its reserves to work. In fact, banks have demonstrated an uncanny ability to keep their reserves close to the minimum federal requirement (see Figure 11.2).

With banks continually seeking to maintain minimum excess reserves, the possibility of their occasionally falling short of reserve requirements is apparent. A large borrower may be a little slow in repaying a loan, or the rate of deposit withdrawals and transfers may exceed expectations. At such times a bank may find that it doesn't have enough reserves to satisfy Fed requirements.

Banks could assure continual compliance with reserve requirements by maintaining large amounts of excess reserves. But that is an unprofitable procedure, as we have noted. Fortunately, at least from a profit-seeking banker's point of view, there are alternatives.

THE FEDERAL FUNDS MARKET   To begin with, a bank that finds itself short of reserves can turn to other banks for help. If a reserve-poor bank can borrow some reserves from a reserve-rich bank, it may be able to bridge its temporary deficit and satisfy the Fed. Reserves borrowed by one bank from another are referred to as "federal funds" and are usually lent for extremely short periods, usually overnight. Although trips to the federal funds market—via tele-

[2] The amount of deposits subject to a 3 percent reserve ratio automatically increases each year by 80 percent of the growth in total transactions deposits.
[3] Legislation that would require the Fed to pay interest on bank reserves is frequently proposed. Like all other activities of the Federal Reserve System, the practice of not paying interest on reserves can be ended by Congress.

TABLE 11.2 FEDERAL RESERVE REQUIREMENTS, 1982

The Fed's reserve requirements vary with bank size. Smaller banks are allowed to maintain lower reserve ratios. Smaller banks thus have a competitive advantage; they enjoy a larger lending capacity per dollar of deposits.

Value of transactions accounts	Reserve requirement (percent)
$0–26 million	3
Over $26 million	12

Source: Federal Reserve System.

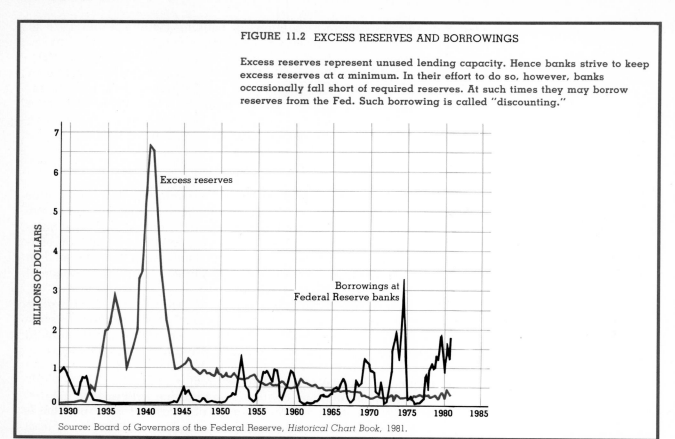

FIGURE 11.2 EXCESS RESERVES AND BORROWINGS

Excess reserves represent unused lending capacity. Hence banks strive to keep excess reserves at a minimum. In their effort to do so, however, banks occasionally fall short of required reserves. At such times they may borrow reserves from the Fed. Such borrowing is called "discounting."

Source: Board of Governors of the Federal Reserve, *Historical Chart Book*, 1981.

phone and computer—will usually satisfy Federal Reserve requirements, such trips are not free. The lending bank will charge interest (the "federal funds rate") on its interbank loan.[4] The use of the federal funds market to satisfy Federal Reserve requirements also depends on other banks' having excess reserves to lend.

SALE OF SECURITIES Another option available to reserve-poor banks is the sale of securities. Banks use some of their excess reserves to buy government bonds, which pay interest. If a bank needs more reserves to satisfy federal regulations, it may resell these securities and deposit the proceeds at the regional Federal Reserve bank. Its reserve position is thereby increased. This option also involves distinct costs, however, both in forgone interest-earning opportunities and in the possibility of capital losses when the bond is offered for quick sale.

DISCOUNTING A third option for avoiding a reserve shortage lies in the structure of the Federal Reserve System itself. The Fed not only establishes certain rules of behavior for banks but also functions as a central bank, or banker's bank. Banks maintain accounts with the

[4] An overnight loan of $1 million at 12 percent interest (per year) costs $329 in interest charges plus any service fees that might be added. Banks make *multi*million-dollar loans in the federal funds market.

discounting: Federal Reserve lending of reserves to private banks.

discount rate: The rate of interest charged by the Federal Reserve banks for lending reserves to private banks.

regional Federal Reserve banks, much the way you and I maintain accounts with a local bank. Individual banks deposit and withdraw "reserve credits" from these accounts, just as we deposit and withdraw dollars. Should a bank find itself short of reserves, it can go to the Fed's "discount window" and borrow some reserves. This process is called **discounting.** Discounting means the Fed is lending reserves directly to private banks.

The discounting operation of the Fed provides private banks with an important source of reserves, but not without cost. The Fed, too, charges interest on the reserves it lends to banks, a rate of interest referred to as the **discount rate.**

The discount window provides a mechanism for directly influencing the size of bank reserves. *By raising or lowering the discount rate, the Fed changes the cost of money for banks and therewith the incentive to borrow reserves.* At high discount rates, borrowing from the Fed is expensive. In addition, high discount rates often signal the Fed's desire to restrain the money supply and an accompanying reluctance to lend reserves. Low discount rates, on the other hand, make it profitable to acquire additional reserves and to exploit one's lending capacity to the fullest. Low discount rates also indicate the Fed's willingness to support credit expansion.

Open-market operations

Reserve requirements and discount-window operations are important tools of monetary policy. But they do not come close to open-market operations in day-to-day impact on the money supply. *Open-market operations are the principal mechanism for directly altering the reserves of the banking system.* Since reserves are the lifeblood of the banking system, open-market operations are of immediate and critical interest to private banks and the larger economy.

PORTFOLIO DECISIONS   To appreciate the impact of open-market operations, you have to think about the alternative uses for idle funds. Just about everybody has some idle funds, even if they amount to just a few dollars in your pocket or a minimal balance in your check-

Discount Rate Cut from 14% to 13% by Fed

WASHINGTON (AP)—The Federal Reserve Board reduced its basic discount rate for borrowing by member banks from 14 percent to 13 percent yesterday in the first significant easing of the Fed's grip on the nation's credit supply in more than a year.

Spokesmen for the hard-pressed housing and auto industries—and even for the Reagan administration, which publicly supports a tight credit policy—have been suggesting such an easing would be welcome.

In the past two months, Federal Reserve governors had reduced a surcharge the Fed tacks onto loans made to big and frequent bank members.

But the reduction in the actual discount rate—the basic interest charged member banks—was the first since the Fed began raising the rate in September, 1980.

The new action will not by itself allow banks to suddenly make large amounts of credit available to individual Americans or to corporations. But it should at least make a bit more credit available by lowering the banks' borrowing costs.

The current national economic weakness—particularly in the interest-sensitive areas of housing and auto sales—has been largely blamed on record-high interest rates. And those high rates have been blamed in turn on the Federal Reserve's tight credit policies.

Baltimore Sun, October 31, 1981. Reprinted by permission of the Associated Press.

portfolio decision: The choice of how (where) to hold idle funds.

bond: A certificate acknowledging a debt and the amount of interest to be paid each year until repayment; an IOU.

ing account. Other consumers and corporations have great amounts of idle funds, even millions of dollars at any time. What we're concerned with here is what people decide to do with such funds.

People (and corporations) do not hold all their idle funds in transactions accounts or cash. Idle funds are also used to purchase stocks, build up savings-account balances, and purchase bonds. These alternative uses of idle funds are attractive because they promise some additional income in the form of interest, dividends, or capital appreciation (e.g., higher stock prices). Funds tied up in bonds, stocks, or savings accounts are not so readily accessible, however, so they do entail some loss of convenience. Deciding where to place idle funds is referred to as the **portfolio decision.**

The open-market operations of the Federal Reserve focus on the portfolio choices people make—whether they deposit idle funds in transactions accounts or purchase government bonds. In essence, the Fed attempts to influence this choice by making bonds more or less attractive, as circumstances warrant. They thereby induce people to move funds from banks to bond markets or vice versa. In the process, reserves either enter or leave the banking system, thereby altering the lending capacity of banks.

THE BOND MARKET   To understand how open-market operations work, we have to take a closer look at the bond market. Not all of us buy and sell bonds, but a lot of consumers and corporations do: daily volume in bond markets exceeds $40 million. What is being exchanged in this market, and what influences decisions to buy or sell?

In our discussion thus far, we have portrayed banks as intermediaries between savers and spenders. Banks are not the only mechanism available for transferring purchasing power from nonspenders to spenders. Funds are lent and borrowed in bond markets as well. In this case, a corporation may borrow money directly from consumers or other institutions, issuing a bond as proof of its promise to repay the loan. A **bond** is simply a piece of paper certifying that someone has borrowed money and promises to pay it back on some future date. In other words, a bond is nothing more than an IOU. In the case of bond markets, however, the IOU is typically signed by a giant corporation or a government agency rather than a friend. It is therefore more widely accepted by lenders.

Because most of the corporations and government agencies that borrow money in the bond market are well known and able to repay their debts, their bonds are actively traded. If I lend $1,000 to General Motors on a ten-year bond, for example, I don't have to wait ten years to get my money back. I can resell the bond to someone else at any time, and that person will collect the face value of the bond (plus interest) from GM when it is due. The actual purchase and sale of bonds takes place in the bond market. Although a good deal of the action occurs on Wall Street in New York, the bond market has no unique location. Like other markets we have discussed, the bond market exists whenever and however bond buyers and sellers get together.

yield: The rate of return on a bond; the annual interest payment divided by the purchase price.

open-market operations: Federal Reserve purchases and sales of government bonds for the purpose of altering bank reserves.

BOND YIELDS People buy bonds because bonds pay interest. If you buy a General Motors bond, GM is obliged to pay you interest during the period of the loan. For example, an 8 percent 1990 GM bond in the amount of $1,000 states that GM will pay the bondholder $80 interest annually (8 percent of $1,000) until 1990. At that point the initial $1,000 loan will be repaid.

The **yield** paid on a bond depends on the promised interest rate (8 percent in this case) and the actual purchase price of the bond. If you pay $1,000 for the bond, then the yield (interest payment ÷ purchase price) is equal to the interest rate printed on the bond. But what if you pay only $900 for the bond? In this case, the interest rate remains at 8.0 percent, but the *yield* jumps to $80 ÷ $900, or 8.9 percent.

Buying a $1,000 bond for only $900 might seem like too good a bargain to be true. But bonds are often bought and sold at prices other than their face value. In fact, a principal objective of Federal Reserve open-market activity is to alter the price of bonds, making them more or less attractive, as conditions merit.

OPEN-MARKET ACTIVITY The basic premise of open-market activity is that participants in the bond market will respond to changes in bond prices and yields. As we have observed, the less you pay for a bond, the higher is its yield. Accordingly, the Fed can induce people to buy bonds by offering to sell them at a lower price (e.g., a $1,000, 8 percent bond for only $900). Similarly, the Fed can induce people to sell bonds by offering to buy them at high prices. In either case, the Fed hopes to move reserves into or out of the banking system. In other words, **open-market operations** entail the purchase and sale of government securities (bonds) for the purpose of altering the flow of reserves into and out of the banking system.

Suppose, for example, that the Fed wants to increase the money supply and therefore desires to provide private banks with additional reserves. To do so it must persuade people to deposit a larger share of their financial assets in banks and hold less in other forms, particularly government bonds. If the Fed offers to pay a high price for bonds, it will effectively lower bond yields. Hence the attractiveness of holding bonds will be reduced. If the price offered by the Fed is high enough, people will sell some of their bonds to the Fed and deposit some or all of the proceeds of the sale in their bank accounts. This influx of money into bank accounts will directly increase bank reserves.

A VARIETY OF INTEREST RATES

The interest rates paid on bonds vary with the creditworthiness of the borrower. A corporation or government agency with an impeccable record of repaying debts and bright prospects for the future (a "triple-A" borrower) will be able to borrow money at a relatively low rate of interest. By contrast, New York City and Fly-by-Nite Corp. must often pay high interest rates. Hence at any time a variety of interest rates are available in the bond market, depending on the creditworthiness of the borrowers.

Banks, too, offer a variety of interest rates, rather than only one. The basic *prime rate* is the rate of interest charged by commercial banks for short-term loans to their most creditworthy corporate customers. Above the prime rate is a multitude of others, reflecting the purposes of loans (automobile, mortgage, personal, commercial), their duration (one week, one year, several decades), and the risk of nonpayment (default) associated with a particular customer. Accordingly, when we speak of "the" interest rate, we are referring to an average of the many rates charged. As the figure below illustrates, however, they all tend to move together.

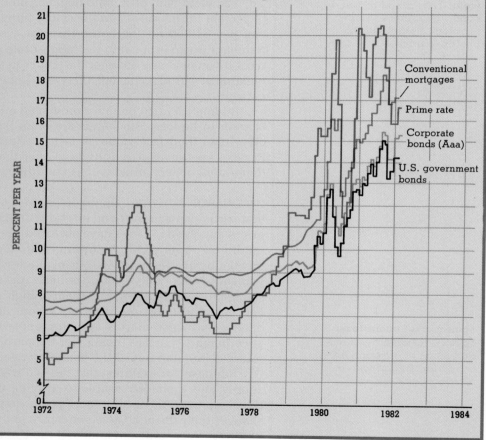

Figure 11.3 illustrates the dynamics of open-market operations in more detail. Notice that when the Fed buys a bond from the public, it pays with a check written on itself. The bond seller must deposit the Fed's check in his bank account if he wants to use part of the proceeds or simply to hold the money for safekeeping. The bank, in turn, deposits the check at a regional Federal Reserve bank, in

FIGURE 11.3 AN OPEN-MARKET PURCHASE

The Fed can increase bank reserves by buying government securities from the public. The Fed check used to buy securities (Step 1) gets deposited in a private bank (Step 2). The bank returns the check to the Fed (Step 3), thereby obtaining additional reserves. To decrease bank reserves, the Fed would sell securities, thus reversing the flow of reserves.

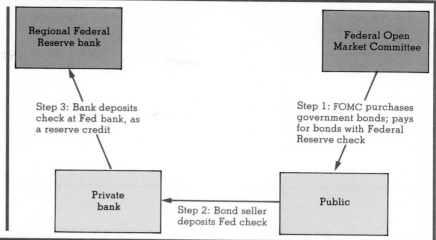

exchange for a reserve credit. The bank's reserves are increased by the amount of the check, and the bank's lending capacity expands accordingly. Thus **by buying bonds, the Fed increases bank reserves.** These reserves can be used to expand the money supply still further, as banks put their acquired reserves to work making loans.

Should the Fed desire to slow the growth in the money supply or even reduce its absolute size, it can reverse the whole process. Instead of offering to *buy* bonds, the Fed in this case will endeavor to *sell* bonds. If it sets the price sufficiently low—so that bond yields are sufficiently high—individuals, corporations, and government agencies will convert some of their transactions deposits into bonds. When they do so, they write a check, paying the Fed for the bonds.[5] The Fed then returns the check to the depositor's bank, taking payment through a reduction in the bank's reserve account. The reserves of the banking system are thereby diminished, as is the capacity to make loans. Thus **by selling bonds the Fed reduces bank reserves.**

To appreciate the significance of open-market operations, one must have a sense of the magnitudes involved. The volume of trading in U.S. government securities exceeds $13 billion per day. The Fed alone owned $125 billion worth of government securities at the beginning of 1983, and bought or sold an average of $200 million worth daily. Thus open-market operations involve tremendous amounts of money and, by implication, potential bank reserves. Each $1 of reserves represents something like $8 of potential lending capacity (via the money multiplier). Thus open-market operations can have a profound impact on the money supply.

INCREASING THE MONEY SUPPLY

The three major monetary policy tools are reserve requirements, discount rates, and open-market operations. The Fed may use these tools individually or in combination to change the money supply. In

[5] In actuality, the transaction is handled through middlemen (bond dealers), but their presence doesn't alter the flow of funds.

TABLE 11.3 ASSUMED
FINANCIAL STATISTICS OF
THE BANKING SYSTEM

The table's figures indicate that the
banking system is "loaned up": there
are no excess reserves. To increase
the lending capacity of the banks, the
Fed may (1) lower the required
reserve ratio, (2) reduce the discount
rate, or (3) buy bonds held by the
public.

Item	Amount
Cash held by public	$100 billion
Transactions deposits	240 billion
Total money supply (*M*1)	$340 billion
Required reserves	$ 60 billion
Excess reserves	0
Total reserves of banks	$ 60 billion
U.S. bonds held by public	$460 billion
Discount rate	7 percent

this section, the use of each tool to attain a specific policy goal is illustrated.

The policy goal in this case is to increase the money supply from an assumed level of $340 billion to $400 billion. In surveying the nation's banks, the Fed discovers the facts shown in Table 11.3. On the basis of the facts presented in Table 11.3, it is evident that:

□ The banking system is "loaned up." Because excess reserves are zero, there is no additional lending capacity.

□ The required reserve ratio must be equal to 25 percent, because this is the current ratio of required reserves ($60 billion) to total deposits ($240 billion).

Accordingly, *if the Fed wants to increase the money supply, it will have to pump additional reserves into the banking system or lower the reserve requirement.*

Lowering reserve requirements

Lowering the reserve requirement is an expedient way of increasing the lending capacity of the banking system. But by how much should the reserve requirement be reduced?

Recall that the Fed's policy objective is to increase the money supply from $340 billion to $400 billion, an increase of $60 billion. If the public is not willing to hold any additional cash, this entire increase in the money supply will have to take the form of added transactions deposits. In other words, total deposits will have to increase from $240 billion to $300 billion. These additional deposits will have to be *created* by the banks, in the form of new loans to consumers or business firms.

If the banking system is going to support $300 billion in transactions deposits with its *existing* reserves, the reserve requirement will have to be reduced from 25 percent to:

$$\frac{\text{Total reserves}}{\text{Desired level of deposits}} = \frac{\$60 \text{ billion}}{\$300 \text{ billion}} = 0.20$$

At the moment the Fed lowers the minimum reserve ratio to 0.20, *total* reserves will not change. The required reserves of the banking system, however, will drop to $48 billion (0.20 × $240 billion) and excess reserves will jump to $12 billion. These added excess reserves imply an additional lending capacity of:

$$\underset{\substack{\text{Excess reserves}\\ \text{(\$12 billion)}}}{} \times \underset{\substack{\text{money multiplier}\\ \text{(5)}}}{} = \underset{\substack{\text{additional}\\ \text{lending}\\ \text{capacity}\\ \text{(\$60 billion)}}}{}$$

If the banks succeed in putting all this new lending power to work—actually make $60 billion in new loans—the Fed's objective of increasing the money supply will be attained.

Lowering the discount rate

The second monetary tool available to the Fed is the discount rate. We have assumed it was 7 percent initially (see Table 11.3). If the Fed lowers this rate, it will become cheaper for banks to borrow reserves from the Fed. The banks will be more willing to borrow (cheaper) reserves so long as they can make additional loans to their own customers at higher interest rates. The profitability of discounting depends on the *difference* between the discount rate and the interest rate the bank charges its loan customers. The Fed increases this difference when it lowers the discount rate.

There is no way to calculate the appropriate discount rate without more detailed knowledge of the banking system's willingness to borrow reserves from the Fed. Nevertheless, we can determine how much reserves the banks *must* borrow if the Fed's money-supply target is to be attained. The Fed's objective is to increase transactions deposits by $60 billion. If these deposits are to be created by the banks—and the reserve requirement is unchanged at 0.25—the banks will have to borrow an additional $15 billion of reserves ($60 billion divided by the money multiplier).

Buying bonds

The Fed can also get additional reserves into the banking system by buying U.S. bonds in the open market. As Table 11.3 indicates, the public holds $460 billion in U.S. bonds, none of which are counted as part of the money supply. If the Fed can persuade people to sell some of these bonds, bank reserves will surely rise.

To achieve its money-supply target, the Fed will offer to buy $15 billion of U.S. bonds. It will pay for these bonds with checks, written on its own account at the Fed. The people who sold the bonds will deposit these checks in their own transactions accounts. As they do so, they will directly increase bank deposits and reserves by $15 billion.

Is $15 billion of open-market purchases enough? Yes. Note that the $15 billion is a direct addition to transactions deposits, and therefore to the money supply (M1). The additional deposits bring in $15 billion of reserves, only $3.75 billion of which is required (0.25 × $15 billion). Hence the new deposits bring in $11.25 billion of excess reserves, which themselves create an additional lending capacity of:

$$\begin{array}{c} \text{Excess reserves} \\ \text{(11.25 billion)} \end{array} \times \begin{array}{c} \text{money multiplier} \\ \text{(4)} \end{array} = \begin{array}{c} \text{additional} \\ \text{lending} \\ \text{capacity} \\ \text{(\$45 billion)} \end{array}$$

Thus the $15 billion of open-market purchases will eventually lead to a $60 billion increase in $M1$ as a consequence of both direct deposits ($15 billion) and subsequent loan activity ($45 billion).

DECREASING THE MONEY SUPPLY

All of the tools used to increase the money supply can also be used to decrease it. To reduce the money supply, the Fed could:

- Raise reserve requirements
- Increase the discount rate
- Sell bonds

On a week-to-week basis the Fed does occasionally seek to reduce the total amount of cash and transactions deposits held by the public. These are minor adjustments, however, to broader policies. A growing economy needs a steadily increasing supply of money to finance market exchanges. Hence the Fed rarely seeks an outright reduction in the size of the money supply over any significant period of time. What it does do is regulate the *rate of growth* in the money supply. When the Fed wants to slow the rate of consumer and investor spending, it restrains the *growth* of money and credit. Although many people talk about "reducing" the money supply, they really are talking about lowering its rate of growth.

POLICY IMPLICATIONS:
THE MONETARY CONTROL ACT OF 1980

Control of the money supply implies a great deal of power over the economy. In recognition of such power, the Communist revolutionary Lenin once remarked that the best way to destroy a society is to destroy its money. If a society's money became valueless, it would no longer be accepted in exchange for goods and services in product markets. As a consequence, people would resort to barter, and the economy's efficiency would be severely impaired. Adolf Hitler attempted to use this weapon against England during World War. II. His plan was to counterfeit British currency, then drop it from planes flying over England. The sudden increase in the quantity of money, together with its suspect origins, was expected to render British currency valueless as a unit of exchange.

Control of the money supply is important in times of peace as well. Even in peacetime, the quantity of money in circulation will influence its value in the marketplace. Moreover, access to credit (bank loans) is a basic determinant of actual expenditure. Consequently, control over the money supply implies an ability to influence our macroeconomic performance.

| Declining control in the 1970s | Before 1980 the Fed's control of the money supply was far from complete and actually weakening. The Fed did not have authority over all banks. Only one-third of all commercial banks were members of the Federal Reserve System and subject to its regulations. In addition, all savings and loan associations and other savings banks remained outside of the Federal Reserve System. These banks were subject to regulations of state banking commissions and other federal agencies (the Federal Home Loan Board, for example), but not to Federal Reserve requirements. As a consequence, a substantial quantity of money and near-money lay beyond the control of the Fed. |

The limits to Federal Reserve authority became more significant when nonmember banks began to offer automatic transfers, NOW accounts, and other new transactions accounts (see Chapter 10). These changes in bank behavior made it easier for people to spend funds that lay outside of the Fed's regulatory authority. As a result, the Fed's control over the money supply diminished.

| New power in the 1980s | In order to increase the Fed's control of the money supply, Congress passed the Financial Institutions Deregulation and Monetary Control Act of 1980. Commonly referred to simply as the Monetary Control Act, the new legislation called for a complete restructuring of the U.S. banking system. Its principal objectives are (1) to extend the Fed's control of the money supply and (2) to encourage greater competition in the banking industry. |

The Monetary Control Act subjects *all* commercial banks, S&Ls, savings banks, and most credit unions to Fed regulation. All such banks now have to satisfy new (and lower) Fed reserve requirements. All banks also enjoy access to the Fed's discount window. These reforms (to be phased in over a period of seven years) obliterated the distinction between member and nonmember banks and greatly strengthened the Fed's control of the money supply.

Other important changes brought about by the Monetary Control Act include:

Banking Challenges Fed Goals

WASHINGTON — Fast-moving changes in banking are making it harder to control the nation's money supply and could even necessitate a "reevaluation" of the Fed's growth targets, Anthony M. Solomon, president of the Federal Reserve Bank of New York, said Monday.

Since banking innovations are likely to continue, Solomon told a meeting of the Allied Social Science Associations, the Fed increasingly will have to make allowances for them in setting and pursuing money targets.

"Perhaps in the longer run," he said, "even the very viability of money stock targets is at stake."

Solomon noted the recent rapid growth of money market mutual funds and other accounts that pay market-related interest rates. He also cited newer "sweep" accounts, in which money is automatically transferred as needed from investment to checking accounts.

These and other innovations, Solomon said, have caused different parts of the money supply to grow at different rates. . . .

Thus, the Fed's money policy appears "tight" by one measure and "easy" by others, Solomon said, and this is confusing to the public.

In addition, Solomon said, greater use of accounts in which interest rates follow the market is changing the relation between interest rates and the holding of money. When rates rise there now is less incentive for people to shift to other investments, since the rate their money earns goes up, too. . . .

Reprinted by permission of United Press International.

■ *NOW accounts:* As of January 1, 1981, all banks were permitted to offer interest-bearing checking accounts (called negotiable order of withdrawal [NOW] accounts).

■ *Interest-rate ceilings:* All ceilings on interest rates paid for deposits are to be phased out by 1985.

■ *New lending powers:* Federally chartered S&Ls and savings banks were permitted to make more consumer loans, offer credit cards, and invest in commercial paper as of January 1, 1981. Over time, all banks will have greater opportunity to provide "full service."

■ *Fed services:* The Fed began to charge fees for the services (e.g., check clearing) it previously provided at no cost to member banks.

The thrust of the Monetary Control Act is thus twofold. On the one hand, it promotes greater competition in the banking system by permitting greater price and service flexibility. On the other hand, the act tightens the Fed's control of the nation's financial reserves, thereby permitting greater control of the money supply.

The Fed's increased control of the money supply has been greeted with mixed emotions. As noted earlier, the Fed enjoys considerable independence. Members of the Board of Governors are elected for long terms and cannot be reappointed. Hence they are relatively insulated from the political process. In fact, the only explicit constraint on decisions of the Fed lies in the ability of Congress to write new banking legislation. Even this constraint is relatively weak, however, since Congress is not equipped to formulate and monitor the fine details of monetary policy and is unlikely to develop new banking legislation except in times of relative crisis.

Although the political independence of the Fed is often thought to be a virtue, it also has its drawbacks. The Fed's Board of Governors may not always share the goals of the president or Congress. Or

Regan, Volcker Fail to Budge on Fed Policy

———

SAN FRANCISCO, Oct. 7—Treasury Secretary Donald Regan and Federal Reserve Board Chairman Paul Volcker remained steadfast today in their differences over monetary policy. . . .

Volcker said he was unmoved by any suggestion that the Fed should loosen its policies. Volcker emphasized repeatedly his view that previous attempts to conquer inflation have failed because "those efforts were not pressed strongly enough, or long enough, to turn the tide."

A "sense of retreat would not only aggravate the present problems, but could set back the prospects for restoring growth and stability for years to come," Volcker said. "Let me not leave any lingering questions in your minds. The Federal Reserve has no intention of backing away from its commitment to reduce inflation by restraining and disciplining the process of money creation. We intend to see it through."

Another time he said, "Clearly we have not won the battle yet."

Enter Regan. Last week, the Treasury secretary told The Post the current "flat period" in the economy may be a recession and that therefore, "a change has to be made" by the Fed in its money-supply reins to permit economic growth. Regan repeated that message today.

Regan said he is not advocating "easy money." But, when asked by a reporter if he had been misquoted, Regan stuck by his earlier statements to The Post, in which he called for the Fed to aim at slightly more rapid money-supply expansion. . . .

Subsequently, when asked how the administration would "insist" that the Federal Reserve loosen its money-supply reins, Regan said he would use "verbal power," leaving the impression that the two officials remained somewhat at odds despite efforts to emphasize agreement.

—William H. Jones

The Washington Post, Washington, D.C., October 8, 1981. Copyright © 1981 The Washington Post.

it may have different views about how best to achieve common goals. In such cases, the Fed's monetary policies may impede other government policies. With its control of the money supply, the Fed can enforce its will, even if Congress and the president object. In Chapter 12 we shall take a further look at these potential policy clashes.

SUMMARY

- The Federal Reserve System controls the nation's money supply by regulating the loan activity (deposit creation) of private banks. The core of the Federal Reserve System is the 12 regional Federal Reserve banks, which provide check clearance, reserve deposit, and loan ("discounting") services to individual banks. Private banks are required to maintain a minimum reserve ratio, in the form of vault cash or reserve deposits at one of the regional Federal Reserve banks.

- The general policies of the Fed are determined by its Board of Governors. The seven governors are appointed for 14-year nonrenewable terms, and are thus relatively immune to short-term political considerations. The Board's chairman is selected by the U.S. president and confirmed by Congress. The chairman serves as the chief spokesman for monetary policy. The general policies of the Fed are carried out by the Federal Open Market Committee (FOMC), which directs open-market sales and purchases of U.S. bonds.

- The Fed has three basic tools for changing the money supply. By altering the reserve requirement, the Fed can immediately change both the quantity of excess reserves in the banking system and the money multiplier that limits banks' lending capacity. By altering discount rates (the rate of interest charged by the Fed for reserve borrowing), the Fed can also influence the amount of reserves maintained by banks. Finally, and most important, the Fed can increase or decrease the reserves of the banking system by buying or selling government bonds; that is, by engaging in open-market operations.

- When the Fed buys bonds, it causes an increase in bank reserves (and lending capacity). When the Fed sells bonds, it induces a reduction in reserves (and lending capacity).

- The ability of the Fed to control the money supply was strengthened by the Monetary Control Act of 1980. That act subjects all banks to the reserve requirements of the Fed and permits them to offer more banking services.

Terms to remember | Define the following terms:

monetary policy	discount rate
money supply (*M*1)	portfolio decision
required reserves	bond
excess reserves	yield
money multiplier	open-market operations
discounting	

Questions for discussion

1. Why do banks want to maintain as little excess reserves as possible? Under what circumstances might banks desire to hold excess reserves? (Hint: see Figure 11.2.)

2. Why do people hold bonds rather than larger savings-account or checking-account balances? Under what circumstances might they change their portfolios, moving their funds out of bonds into bank accounts?

3. What is the current price and yield of U.S. Treasury bonds? Of General Motors bonds? (Check the financial section of your daily newspaper.) What accounts for the difference?

4. Why might the Fed want to increase the money supply?

Problem

Assume that the following figures describe the condition of the commercial banking system.

Total reserves:	$200 billion
Transactions deposits:	$800 billion
Cash held by public:	$100 billion
Reserve requirement:	0.20

(a) How large is the money supply (M1)?

(b) Are the banks fully utilizing their lending capacity? Explain.

(c) What would happen to the money supply *initially* if the public deposited another $50 billion of cash in transactions accounts? Explain.

(d) What would the lending capacity of the banking system be after such a portfolio switch?

(e) How large would the money supply be if the banks fully utilized their lending capacity?

(f) What steps could the Fed take to offset that potential growth in M1?

CHAPTER 12

MONETARY POLICY

The Federal Reserve System has the power to control the nation's money supply. How important is this power? Can changes in the money supply affect the rate of total output or prices?

Virtually all economists agree that "money matters," that is, that monetary policy can affect our macroeconomic performance. There are sharp disagreements, however, about just *how* money matters. For example, do changes in the money supply affect prices and output directly, or do monetary impacts depend on interest-rate movements? In either case, how effective is monetary policy compared to other macro tools (e.g., fiscal policy)?

Debates over the effectiveness of monetary policy typically entail a confrontation between Keynesian and Monetarist economists. Monetarists assert that monetary policy directly affects macroeconomic performance and that it is more powerful than fiscal policy. Keynesians argue just the opposite. They see monetary policy as being less direct and less important than fiscal policy.

In order to assess this debate—and therewith the role of monetary policy—we shall start by taking a closer look at *money markets*. Like all other markets, the money market has two sides: supply and demand. So far, we have looked at only one side of the money market, by describing the factors that determine the *supply* of money. Now we have to look at the *demand* for money. We have to determine why people are willing to hold (demand) money balances, and how the quantity of money held (demanded) changes in response to its price. As we shall observe, the demand for money is really no different in concept from the demand for apples, typing services, or anything else. Money *does* have a price, and people tend to demand more of it at lower prices than at higher prices.

Once we have observed how the money market works, we shall examine the impact of monetary policy more closely. Specifically, we shall seek to determine:

- How changes in the money supply alter money market outcomes
- How money market outcomes affect the level and content of GNP

As we shall see, the Monetarist and Keynesian answers to these questions differ.

MONEY MARKETS

Interest rates

interest rate: The price paid for the use of money.

When we think of markets, we envision goods or services being exchanged at some price. The same is true of money markets. In this case, the "good" being exchanged is money, and its price is the **interest rate.**

People who borrow money realize that the interest they pay is the price for using someone else's money. Even people who don't borrow money, however, are implicitly paying this price. We all make a basic portfolio choice: we either hold our money or put it to work. ***People hold (demand) money* (M1) *by keeping cash in their wallets or maintaining positive balances in their transactions accounts.*** Money held in this form earns little or no interest. By contrast, money used to buy bonds or simply lent to someone else is likely to earn a higher rate of interest. The choice, then, is to hold (demand) money or to use it. This is the basic **portfolio decision** first encountered in Chapter 11.

portfolio decision: The choice of how (where) to hold idle funds.

The nature of the "price" of money should be apparent: People who hold *cash* are forgoing an opportunity to earn interest. So are people who hold money in checking accounts that pay no interest. In either case, forgone interest is the opportunity cost (price) of money people choose to hold. How high is that price? It is equal to the market rate of interest.

Money held in interest-paying transactions accounts (e.g., NOW accounts) does earn some interest. The rate of interest paid, however, is typically quite low. In this case, the opportunity cost of holding money (M1) is the *difference* between the prevailing rate of interest and the rate paid on transactions-account balances. As is the case with cash and regular checking accounts, opportunity cost is measured by the *forgone* interest.

The demand for money

demand for money: The quantities of money people are willing and able to hold at alternative interest rates *(ceteris paribus).*

Once we recognize that money does have a price, we can easily formulate a demand for money. As is the case with all goods, the **demand for money** is simply a schedule (or curve) showing the quantity of money demanded at alternative prices (interest rates).

Why would people ever want to hold money and thereby forgo the opportunity to earn interest? Why do you carry cash around?

Why do you keep a positive balance in your checking account? Are you missing an opportunity to amass a small fortune in interest payments? Are there any good reasons for doing so?

TRANSACTIONS DEMAND   Even people who have mastered the principles of economics do hold money, and for several good reasons. The most obvious is the desire to buy goods and services. In order to transact business in product or factor markets, we need money, in the form of either cash or a positive checking-account balance. Even when we use credit cards, we are only postponing the date of payment by a few weeks or so. Accordingly, we recognize a basic **transactions demand for money.**

transactions demand for money: Money held for the purpose of making everyday market purchases.

PRECAUTIONARY DEMAND   Another reason people hold money is their fear of the proverbial rainy day. A sudden emergency may require money purchases over and above normal transactions needs. Moreover, such needs may arise when the banks are closed or in a community where one's checks are not accepted. Also, future income is uncertain and may diminish unexpectedly. For these reasons, people tend to hold a bit more money (cash or transactions deposits) than they anticipate spending. This **precautionary demand for money** is the extra money being held for precautionary purposes, that is, as a safeguard against the unexpected.

precautionary demand for money: Money held for unexpected market transactions or for emergencies.

SPECULATIVE DEMAND   People also hold money for speculative purposes, so they can respond to financially attractive opportunities. This represents a **speculative demand for money.** Suppose you were interested in buying stocks or bonds but had not yet picked the right ones, or regarded their present prices as too high. In such circumstances, you might want to hold some money so that you could later buy a "hot" stock or bond at a price you think attractive. Thus you would be holding money in the hope that a better financial opportunity would later appear. In this sense, you would be *speculating* with your money, forgoing present opportunities to earn interest in the hope of hitting a real jackpot later.

speculative demand for money: Money held for speculative purposes, for later financial opportunities.

THE MARKET DEMAND CURVE   These three motivations for holding money combine to create a *market demand* for money. The question is, what shape does this demand curve take? Does the quantity of money demanded decrease sharply as the rate of interest rises? Or do people tend to hold the same amount of money, regardless of its price?

People do cut down on their money balances when interest rates are very high. At such times, the opportunity cost of holding money is simply too high. This explains why so many people moved their money out of transactions deposits (M1) and into money-market mutual funds in 1980–82, when interest rates were extraordinarily high (Chapter 11). Corporations are even more careful about managing their money when interest rates rise. Better money management requires watching checking-account balances more closely and even making more frequent trips to the bank, but the opportunity costs are worth it.

FIGURE 12.1 MONEY-MARKET EQUILIBRIUM

All points on the market demand curve represent the quantity of money people are willing to hold at a specific interest rate. The equilibrium interest rate occurs at the intersection (E_1) of the money-supply and money-demand curves. At that rate of interest people are willing to hold as much money as is available. At any other interest rate (e.g., 9 percent), the quantity of money people are *willing* to hold will not equal the quantity available, and people will adjust their portfolios.

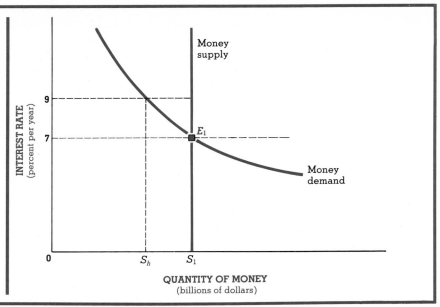

QUANTITY OF MONEY
(billions of dollars)

The total market demand for money is illustrated in Figure 12.1. Like nearly all demand curves, the market demand curve for money slopes downward. The downward slope indicates that ***the quantity of money people are willing and able to hold (demand) increases as interest rates fall*** (ceteris paribus).

Equilibrium

Once a money-demand curve and a money-supply curve are available, the action in money markets is easy to follow. This action is summarized in Figure 12.1. The money-demand curve in Figure 12.1 is assumed to reflect existing demands for holding money. The money-supply curve has been drawn at an arbitrary level of S_1. In practice, its position will depend on Federal Reserve policy (Chapter 11), the lending behavior of private banks, and the willingness of consumers and investors to borrow money.

equilibrium rate of interest: The interest rate at which the quantity of money demanded in a given time period equals the quantity of money supplied.

The intersection of the money-demand and money-supply curves (E_1) establishes an **equilibrium rate of interest.** Only at this interest rate is the quantity of money supplied equal to the quantity demanded. In this case, we observe that an interest rate of 7 percent equates the desires of suppliers and demanders.

At any rate of interest other than 7 percent, the quantity of money demanded would not equal the quantity supplied. Look at the imbalance that exists, for example, when the interest rate is 9 percent. At that rate, the quantity of money supplied (S_1) exceeds the quantity demanded (S_h). All the money (S_1) *must* be held by someone, of course. But the demand curve indicates that people are not *willing* to hold so much money at that interest rate (9 percent). Hence people will adjust their portfolios by moving money out of cash and transactions deposits into bonds, money-market mutual funds, or other interest-earning assets. This will tend to lower interest rates (recall that buying bonds tends to lower their yields). As interest rates drop, people will be willing to hold more money. Ultimately we will get to E_1, where the quantity of money demanded equals the quantity supplied. At that equilibrium, people will be content with their portfolio choices.

CLOSING A RECESSIONARY GAP: THE KEYNESIAN PERSPECTIVE

Money and interest rates

monetary policy: The use of money and credit controls to influence macroeconomic activity.

The equilibrium rate of interest is subject to change, of course. In fact, Keynesian economists assert that the principal effect of **monetary policy** is to alter the equilibrium rate of interest. As we saw in Chapter 11, the Federal Reserve System can alter the money supply through changes in reserve requirements, changes in the discount rate, or open-market operations. By implication, then, the Fed can alter the equilibrium rate of interest.

Figure 12.2 illustrates the potential impact of monetary policy on the equilibrium rate of interest. Assume that the money supply is initially at S_1 and the equilibrium interest rate is 7 percent. The Fed then increases the money supply to S_2 by lowering the reserve requirement, reducing the discount rate, or, most likely, purchasing additional bonds in the open market. The impact of this expansionary monetary policy is evident. If the market demand for money is unchanged, the larger money supply will bring about a new equilibrium, at E_2. At this intersection, the market rate of interest is only 6 percent. Hence by increasing the money supply, the Fed tends to lower the equilibrium rate of interest. Or, to put the matter differently, people are *willing* to hold larger money balances (M1) only at lower interest rates.

Were the Fed to reverse its policy and reduce the money supply, interest rates would rise. You can see this result in Figure 12.2 also

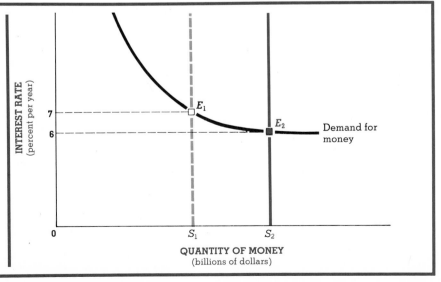

FIGURE 12.2 CHANGING THE RATE OF INTEREST

Changes in the money supply tend to alter the equilibrium rate of interest. In this case, an increase in the money supply (from S_1 to S_2) lowers the equilibrium rate of interest (from 7 percent to 6 percent).

INTEREST RATE (percent per year)

QUANTITY OF MONEY (billions of dollars)

FIGURE 12.3 THE KEYNESIAN VIEW
OF MONETARY POLICY

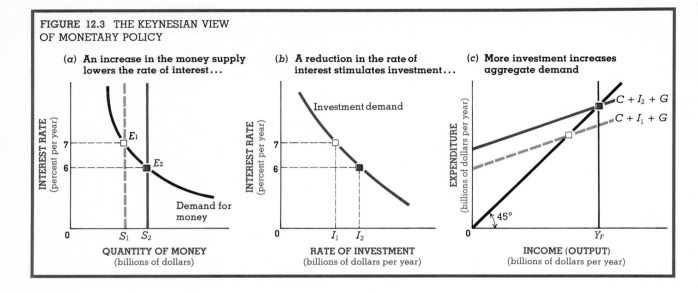

(a) **An increase in the money supply lowers the rate of interest...**

INTEREST RATE (percent per year)

7 — E_1

6 — E_2

Demand for money

0   S_1 S_2

QUANTITY OF MONEY
(billions of dollars)

(b) **A reduction in the rate of interest stimulates investment...**

INTEREST RATE (percent per year)

Investment demand

7 —

6 —

0   I_1 I_2

RATE OF INVESTMENT
(billions of dollars per year)

(c) **More investment increases aggregate demand**

EXPENDITURE (billions of dollars per year)

$C + I_2 + G$

$C + I_1 + G$

45°

0   Y_F

INCOME (OUTPUT)
(billions of dollars per year)

by observing the change in the rate of interest that occurs when the money supply shrinks from S_2 to S_1.

Interest rates and spending

A change in the rate of interest is not the end of this story. The ultimate objective of monetary policy is to alter the macroeconomic dimensions of the economy, particularly the rate of aggregate expenditure. Hence the next question is how changes in interest rates affect consumer, investor, and government spending. In this case, we presume that what the Fed wants is to increase the level of aggregate demand at full employment, so as to close a recessionary gap. For monetary policy to succeed, a lower rate of interest must encourage more borrowing and expenditure by consumers, businesses, or government agencies.

Will lower interest rates encourage spending? In Chapter 7 we observed that investment decisions of business firms are sensitive to the rate of interest. Specifically, we demonstrated that lower rates of interest reduce the cost of buying plant and equipment, making investment more profitable. Accordingly, we anticipate that a lower rate of interest will result in a higher rate of investment spending, as shown in Figure 12.3b.

The increased investment spending brought about by lower interest rates represents an increase in aggregate demand. This increase is illustrated in Figure 12.3c by an upward *shift* of the aggregate demand function. If the shift is large enough, it will close the assumed recessionary gap and bring the economy closer to full employment. Thus, *from a Keynesian perspective, the Fed's objective of stimulating aggregate demand is achieved in three distinct steps:*

- *An increase in the money supply*
- *A reduction in the interest rate*
- *An increase in aggregate spending*

Lower interest rates might also stimulate consumer spending. Houses, cars, and other expensive goods are often purchased with borrowed money. Accordingly, both the availability and the cost of loanable funds may influence consumer expenditures.

Even government spending may be affected by changes in the rate of interest. State and local governments are particularly sensitive to money-market conditions and may postpone planned expenditures when interest rates are too high. When the supply of money is expanded, however, both the availability of loanable funds and their cost improve.

Policy constraints

Figure 12.3 demonstrates that monetary policy can be an effective mechanism for altering the rate of total expenditure. Monetary policy does not always succeed so easily as Figure 12.3 implies, however. From a Keynesian viewpoint, the effectiveness of monetary policy depends on two distinct phenomena:

- The sensitivity of interest rates to changes in the money supply (Figure 12.3*a*)
- The sensitivity of aggregate spending to changes in interest rates (Figure 12.3*b*)

THE LIQUIDITY TRAP The possibility that interest rates may not respond to changes in the money supply is illustrated by the liquidity trap. When interest rates are low, the opportunity cost of holding money is cheap. At such times people may decide to hold all the money they can get, waiting for income-earning opportunities to improve. Further increases in the money supply will be absorbed readily, without reducing interest rates. At this juncture—a phenomenon Keynes called the **liquidity trap**—further expansion of the money supply has no effect on the rate of interest. This situation is portrayed by the horizontal section of the money-demand curve in Figure 12.4.

liquidity trap: The portion of the money-demand curve that is horizontal; people are willing to hold unlimited amounts of money at some (low) interest rate.

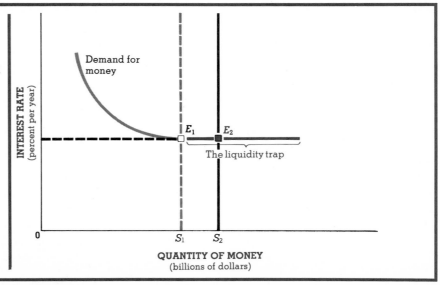

FIGURE 12.4 A LIQUIDITY TRAP CAN STOP INTEREST RATES FROM FALLING

If people are willing to hold unlimited amounts of money at the prevailing interest rate, increases in money supply will not push interest rates lower. A liquidity trap prevents interest rates from falling.

Demand for money

INTEREST RATE (percent per year)

E_1 E_2

The liquidity trap

0   S_1 S_2

QUANTITY OF MONEY (billions of dollars)

What happens to interest rates when the initial equilibrium falls into this trap? Nothing at all. Notice that the equilibrium rate of interest does not fall when the money supply is increased from S_1 to S_2 (Figure 12.4). People are willing to hold all that additional money without a reduction in the rate of interest.

EXPECTATIONS   Even if we are able to avoid a liquidity trap, we have no assurance that aggregate demand will increase as expected. Investment decisions are motivated not only by interest rates but by *expectations* as well. During a recession—when unemployment is high and the rate of spending low—corporations have little incentive to expand production capacity. With little expectation of future profit, investors are likely to be unimpressed by "cheap money" (low interest rates), and may decline to use the lending capacity that banks make available. Investment demand that is slow to respond to the stimulus of cheap money is said to be inelastic, because it will not expand. Consumers, too, are reluctant to borrow when current and future income prospects are uncertain or distinctly unfavorable. Accordingly, even if the Fed is successful in lowering interest rates, there is no assurance that lower interest rates will stimulate borrowing and spending.

The possibility that investment spending may *not* respond to changes in the rate of interest is illustrated in Figure 12.5 by the vertical portion of the investment-demand curve. Notice that a reduction in the rate of interest from 7 percent to 6 percent does *not* increase investment spending. In this case, businesses are simply unwilling to invest any more funds. As a consequence, aggregate demand does not rise. The Fed's policy objective remains unfulfilled, even though the Fed has successfully lowered the rate of interest. Recall that the investment-demand curve may also *shift* if expectations change. If expectations worsened, the investment-demand curve would shift to the left and might result in even *less* investment at 6 percent interest (see Figure 8.3).

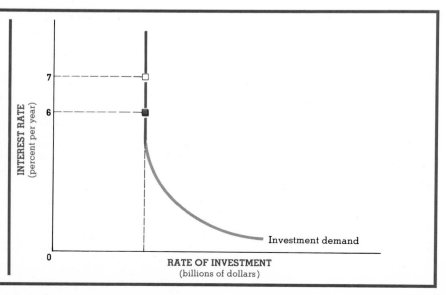

FIGURE 12.5 INELASTIC INVESTMENT DEMAND CAN ALSO IMPEDE MONETARY POLICY

A lower interest rate will not always stimulate investment. If investors have unfavorable expectations for future sales, small reductions in interest rates may not alter their investment decisions. Here the rate of investment remains constant when the interest rate drops from 7 to 6 percent.

CLOSING AN INFLATIONARY GAP: THE KEYNESIAN PERSPECTIVE

Like fiscal policy, monetary policy is a two-edged sword. At times it will seek to increase the rate of desired expenditure; at other times it will try to restrain it. When an inflationary gap threatens, the objective of monetary policy is to reduce the rate of desired expenditure at full employment. A reduction in expenditure will restrain aggregate demand to the dimensions of our production possibilities.

Money and interest rates

The mechanics of monetary policy designed to combat demand-pull inflation are similar to those used to fight cyclical unemployment; only the direction is reversed. In this case, we seek to discourage spending by increasing the rate of interest. The Federal Reserve can push the rate of interest up by selling bonds, increasing the discount rate, or increasing the reserve requirement. All of these actions tend to reduce the money supply, and thus establish a new and higher equilibrium rate of interest.

Interest rates and spending

The ultimate objective of a restrictive monetary policy is to reduce the rate of desired expenditure, of course, not just to raise interest rates. Will it succeed?

The effects of an expansionary policy have been illustrated in Figure 12.3. When the Fed's monetary policy is restrictive, we expect higher interest rates to curb investment and consumer spending. At higher rates of interest, many marginal investments will no longer be profitable. Likewise, many consumers will decide that they cannot afford the higher monthly payments associated with increased interest rates; purchases of homes, cars, and other consumer durables will be postponed. As a result, the aggregate-demand curve will shift downward to close the inflationary gap and a more desirable equilibrium will be established.

Policy constraints

Although the potential impact of restrictive monetary policy is evident, its success is not assured either. We have seen that low sales and profit expectations may overwhelm low interest rates in the investment decision during recessionary periods. Similarly, high sales

Corporate, Consumer Expectations Seen as Cause of Interest-Rate Surge

Nobody believes that inflation is licked. Worried over even higher future interest rates, business—especially big business—is borrowing all the money it can, at today's relative bargains, to finance goods that it can't even sell. That's why short-term interest rates are still heading upward, deterring consumer spending and threatening to make the nation's sluggish economic recovery even more lethargic. . . .

The bankers and economists say there's not much question that high interest rates have discouraged consumers, especially would-be buyers of high-priced goods such as houses and new automobiles. The professionals think that the high rates will keep dragging the economy well into next year.

Consumer Expectations

E. Peter Gillette Jr., president and chief executive of Northwestern National Bank of Minneapolis, says, "Until the consumer begins to perceive that inflation is subsiding and that interest rates are coming down to acceptable levels, he will be reluctant to make major commitments to autos and housing, two important elements in the economy today."

John Wilson, director of economic policy research at Bank of America, San Francisco, says, "The $64 question is whether current interest-rate levels are high enough to drag us back into a quarter or two of zero or negative growth. I think they will. "Industries are saying, 'To heck with the cost of funds, we're concerned about availability and rates several months out, so we're going to borrow now.'"

Earlier this year the widely anticipated recession was seen as the cyclical cure for inflation, by reducing consumer demand, and for high-interest rates, by reducing demand for loans. But the bankers and economists generally say that, because of persistent inflationary expectations, the recession failed to work its magic. "The financial markets want inflation wrung out," says Thomas S. Johnson, executive vice president of Chemical Bank, New York.

"Deep-Seated Fear"

Mr. Kellner in New York suspects that the prospects of a federal tax cut, increased defense spending and a worsening federal-budget deficit are behind the continued fear of inflation. "The fact that business borrowing continues without a letup as the prime rate reaches 18½% is a sign of a deep-seated fear of inflation," he says.

and profit expectations may negate the impact of high interest rates during an expansionary period.

The expectations that may frustrate restrictive monetary policy are of two sorts. First, there are the expectations of future sales and profits. If sales expectations are high, higher interest rates alone may not discourage continued investment. Second, there are expectations of inflation. If people think prices (and interest rates) will continue to rise in the future, then "high" interest rates now will not deter borrowing or spending.

A MONETARIST PERSPECTIVE

The Keynesian perspective on monetary policy suggests that money does indeed matter. But the effects of monetary policy are indirect and subject to substantial limitations. Changes in the money supply affect macroeconomic outcomes only through the intermediary of interest rates. Moreover, the impact of interest-rate changes may be muted by contrary expectations.

True Monetarists think this explanation of monetary policy is unduly complex. They also think the Keynesian perspective understates the potency of monetary policy.

The equation of exchange

equation of exchange: Money supply *(M)* times velocity of circulation *(V)* equals level of aggregate demand *(P × Q).*

income velocity of money *(V)*: The number of times per year, on average, a dollar is used to purchase final goods and services; *PQ ÷ M.*

Monetarists assert that the potential of monetary policy can be expressed in a simple equation called the **equation of exchange.** It is written as

$$MV = PQ$$

where M refers to the quantity of money in circulation and V to its **velocity** of circulation. Total sales are the product of the average price (P) of goods times the quantity (Q) of goods sold in a period.

Suppose, for example, that there are only two participants in the market and that the money supply consists of one crisp $20 bill. What is the limit to the value of aggregate demand in this case? If you answer "Twenty dollars," you have not yet grasped the nature of the circular flow. Suppose I begin the circular flow by spending $20 on eggs, bacon, and a gallon of milk. The money I spend ends up in Farmer Brown's pocket, because he is the only other market participant. Once in possession of the money, Farmer Brown may decide to satisfy his long-smoldering desire to learn something about economics and buy one of my books. If he acts on that decision, the $20 will return to me and I will be in a position to buy more food. When I do so, Farmer Brown will again take possession of the $20 and be able to decide whether to buy another text.

As long as we keep using this $20 bill to buy goods and services from each other, we can continue to do business. Moreover, the faster we pass the money from hand to hand during any period of time, the greater the value of sales each of us can register. If the money is passed from hand to hand eight times, then I will be able to sell $80 worth of textbooks and Farmer Brown will be able to sell $80 worth of produce during that period, for a total nominal output of $160. Thus the quantity of money in circulation and the velocity with which it travels (changes hands) in product markets will always be equal to the value of total output and income. The relationship is summarized as $MV = PQ$. In this case, the equation of exchange confirms that $20 × 8 times per year = $160 per year, the value of total sales (P × Q).

Notice that the identity of MV and PQ says nothing by itself about which dimensions of the economy will change. All we can say with certainty is that if either the velocity of money (V) increases or the money supply (M) is increased, we may anticipate an increase in the nominal value of annual ouput (PQ). But we don't know whether prices (P) or the quantity of output (Q) or both will increase. That will depend on how the supply side of the economy responds to a change in spending. In our illustration, an increase in V or M could stimulate Farmer Brown and me to produce more output, raise our produce and textbook prices, or some combination of these responses.

Monetarists use the equation of exchange to simplify the explanation of how money matters. There is no need, they argue, to follow the effects of changes in M through the money markets to interest rates and further to changes in aggregate spending. The basic consequences of monetary policy are evident in the equation of exchange. The two sides of the equation of exchange must always be in balance. Hence *if* **M** *increases, then either prices* **(P)** *or output* **(Q)** *must rise, or* **V** *must fall.*

Stable velocity

Monetarists assert that the velocity of money (V) is unlikely to fall when M increases. How fast people use their money balances depends on the institutional structure of money markets and people's habits. Neither the structure of money markets nor people's habits are likely to change when M is increased. Indeed, Monetarists assert that V tends to be very stable (predictable) over long periods of time. Accordingly, an increase in M will not be offset by a reduction in V. Instead, the impact of an increased money supply will be transmitted to the right-hand side of the equation of exchange. That means ***aggregate demand must rise if the money supply* (M) *grows and* V *is stable.***

Money-supply focus

From a Monetarist perspective, then, there is no need to trace the impacts of monetary policy through interest-rate movements. Indeed, interest-rate changes and the response of consumers and investors to interest rates are irrelevant to the Monetarist perspective. This perspective leads to a fundamentally stronger role for monetary policy.

From a Keynesian perspective, the Federal Reserve Board must manipulate interest rates to increase or decrease aggregate demand. Changes in the money supply are appropriate only insofar as the desired interest rates are achieved.

A Monetarist perspective leads to a wholly different strategy for the Fed. Because interest rates are not part of the Monetarist explanation of how monetary policy works, the Fed should not try to manipulate interest rates. The Fed should instead focus on the money supply itself. Monetarists also argue that the Fed cannot really control interest rates well, since they depend on both the supply of and the demand for money. What the Fed *can* control is the supply of money.[1] This Monetarist approach was adopted by the Fed in 1979.

Policy constraints

At first glance, the argument between Keynesians and Monetarists seems unduly abstract. After all, they agree that changes in the money supply will influence aggregate demand. The only debate appears to be over the mechanisms for achieving this objective. Keynesians point to interest-rate movements and shifting expenditure functions as key mechanisms. Monetarists point to a mysterious "black box" named MV = PQ. Both concede, however, that aggregate demand responds to changes in M.

In reality, however, the debate goes much further than quibbling over mechanisms. True Monetarists assert that monetary policy will not alter the rate of real output in the long run. From a Monetarist

---

[1] Even this proposition is hotly debated. The availability of many different kinds of money (M1, M2, M3, etc.) and the ease of moving funds between them makes control of "the" money supply very difficult. Many Monetarists, including Milton Friedman, argue that only long-run (e.g., year-by-year) control is possible.

Changing Direction: Why Fed Shifted from Interest Rates to Money Supply

WASHINGTON—The Federal Reserve Board, frustrated for months in its effort to halt inflation, is going to try a new strategy. . . .

Here is an explanation of the new approach:

Simply put, the central bank said it plans to pay less attention to the price of money—that is, interest rates—and focus more directly on the supply of money.

In the past, bankers, financial markets, the press and everybody else with an interest in interest rates watched the Fed's manipulation of the federal funds rate, or the price banks charge each other to borrrow funds for short periods of time.

Until last weekend, the Fed had concentrated on this rate in an effort to control the money supply.

. . . Over the weekend, the Fed announced a new approach. Instead of inching up the federal funds rate in hopes of controlling the money supply, it will control the money supply more directly and let the rate climb where it may.

The central bank will still be buying and selling securities in an effort to regulate the money supply. But it will be watching bank reserves, rather than the funds rate, as it does so. The Fed takes daily readings on the adequacy of bank reserves and because they represent a relatively fixed portion of the money supply, it can control the money supply by controlling the reserves.

As a result, there probably will be volatile swings in what was once a relatively stable federal funds rate. It will make life more difficult for lenders of money who key their rates to the federal funds rate.

And it will greatly complicate things for those who were used to reading great significance into each move of the federal funds rate.

But it should give the Fed a better grip on the money supply, something the central bank believes it urgently needs to curb inflation. . . .

—Greg Conderacci

perspective, money matters only because it influences prices. Output decisions, they assert, are relatively unaffected by changes in the rate of inflation or the money supply.

THE REAL RATE OF INTEREST   Consider again the options for controlling demand-pull inflation. This is a situation where the value of goods and services demanded at full employment exceeds the economy's full-employment capacity. The objective of policy is to reduce aggregate demand.

From a Keynesian perspective, the way to do this is to shrink the money supply and drive up interest rates. But Monetarists argue that nominal interest rates are already likely to be high. Furthermore, if an effective anti-inflation policy is adopted, interest rates will come *down*, not go up.

To understand this Monetarist conclusion, we have to distinguish between *nominal* interest rates and real ones. Nominal interest rates are the ones we actually see and pay. When a bank pays $5\frac{1}{2}$ percent interest on your bank account, it is quoting (and paying) a nominal rate.

Real interest rates are never actually seen and rarely quoted. These are "inflation-adjusted" rates. Specifically, the **real rate of interest** equals the nominal rate *minus* the anticipated rate of inflation.

Recall what inflation does to the purchasing power of the dollar: as inflation continues, each dollar purchases fewer goods and services. As a consequence, dollars borrowed today are of less real value when they are paid back later. The real rate of interest reflects this inflation adjustment.

Suppose you lend someone $100 at the beginning of the year, at 8 percent interest. You expect to get more back at the end of the year

real rate of interest: The nominal rate of interest minus anticipated inflation rate.

than you start with. That "more" you expect refers to real goods and services, not just dollar bills. Specifically, you anticipate that when the loan is repaid with interest at the end of the year, you will be able to buy more goods and services than you could now. This expectation of a *real* gain is at least part of the reason for making a loan.

Your expected gain will not materialize, however, if all prices rise by 8 percent during the year. If the inflation rate is 8 percent, you will discover that $108 buys you no more at the end of the year than $100 would have bought you at the beginning. Hence you would have given up the use of your money for an entire year without any compensation. In such circumstances the *real* rate of interest turns out to be zero.

The market rate of interest, then, really has two components. The first component is the real rate of interest. The second is an inflation adjustment. If the real rate of interest were 4 percent and an inflation rate of 9 percent was expected, the nominal rate of interest would be 13 percent. If inflationary expectations worsened to, say, 10 percent, the nominal rate would climb to 14 percent.

Monetarists argue that the real rate of interest is low and fairly stable. If the nominal rate of interest is high, this is likely to reflect bad inflationary expectations. That is to say, ***Monetarists see high nominal rates of interest as a symptom of inflation, not a cure.*** Indeed, high nominal rates may even look cheap if inflationary expectations are worsening faster than interest rates are rising.

Consider the implications of all this for monetary policy. Suppose we want to close an inflationary gap. Monetarists and Keynesians alike agree that a reduced *M* will deflate aggregate demand. But Keynesians rely on a "quick attack" on high interest rates to slow consumption and investment spending. Monetarists, by contrast, assert that consumers and investors need to be convinced that the Fed will continue a tight money policy long enough to really slow the rate of inflation. Then and only then will their inflationary expectations recede. When inflationary expectations diminish, nominal interest rates will begin to fall. Therefore, ***Monetarists emphasize steady and predictable changes in the money supply.***

Money Is Free!

"Money's not tight, it's cheap. It's free!"

So says one of our most articulate friends along Wall Street. The point is that short-term interest rates, horrendous as they are, are below the short-term inflation rate, horrendous as it is. The August numbers showed a six-month inflation rate of 9.4%, for example, while six months earlier the prime interest rate was 8.0%. If you borrowed and paid back in cheaper dollars, you got your money for free.

We relate the quote because we have the impression a lot of folks in Washington don't realize how those of us out here in the real world look at these matters. In particular, the observation ought to be of interest to the Federal Reserve's Open Market Committee, which meets today to set money growth targets for both the next two months and the next year.

Out here in the real world, folks know free money when they see it. That is why interest rates will not go down, nor the dollar recover meaningfully, until inflation is reduced. And the longer the Fed delays in starting to curb money growth, the higher price the nation will have to pay before inflation is ultimately brought under control.

Closing a recessionary gap

The link between anticipated inflation and nominal interest rates also constrains expansionary monetary policy. The Keynesian cure for a recession is to expand M and lower interest rates. But Monetarists fear that an increase in M will lead—via the equation of exchange—to higher P. If everyone believed this would happen, then an unexpectedly large increase in M would immediately raise people's inflationary expectations. Nominal interest rates would go up, not down, when the money supply was increased!

From a Monetarist perspective, expansionary monetary policies are not likely to lead us out of a recession. On the contrary, such policies might double our burden by heaping inflation on top of our unemployment woes. The rate of real output and employment is more dependent on structural characteristics of the economy than on changes in the money supply.[2] All monetary policy should do is ensure a stable and predictable rate of growth in the money supply.

[2] In the extreme version of this argument, there is a "natural" rate of unemployment that is impervious to either monetary or fiscal stimulus. This argument will be examined in Chapter 13.

"NOT WORTH A CONTINENTAL": THE U.S. EXPERIENCE WITH HYPERINFLATION

The government of the United States had no means to pay for the Revolutionary War. Specifically, the federal government had no power to levy taxes that might transfer resources from the private sector to the public sector. Instead, it could only request the states to levy taxes of their own and contribute them to the war effort. The states were not very responsive, however: state contributions accounted for only 6 percent of federal revenues during the war years.

To pay for needed weapons and soldiers, the federal government had only two other options, either (1) borrow money or (2) create new money. When loans proved to be inadequate, the Continental Congress started issuing new paper money—the "Continental" dollar—in 1775. By the end of 1779, Congress had authorized issuance of over $250 million in Continental dollars.

At first the paper money enabled George Washington's troops to acquire needed supplies, ammunition, and volunteers. But soon the flood of paper money inundated product markets. Wholesale prices of key commodities skyrocketed. Commodity prices *doubled* in 1776, in 1777, and again in 1778. Then prices increased *tenfold* in the next two years.

Many farmers and storekeepers refused to sell goods to the army in exchange for Continental dollars. Rapid inflation had taught them that the paper money George Washington's troops offered was nearly worthless. The expression "not worth a Continental" became a popular reference to things of little value.

The states tried price controls and even empowered themselves to seize needed war supplies. But nothing could stop the inflation fueled by the explosive increase in the money supply. Fortunately, the war ended before the economy collapsed. After the war, the U.S. Congress established a new form of money, and in 1787 it empowered the federal government to levy taxes and mint gold and silver coins.

Source: Sidney Ratner, *The Evolution of the American Economy* (New York: Basic Books, 1979).

Then people could concentrate on real production decisions without worrying so much about fluctuating prices.

THE CONCERN FOR CONTENT

Monetary policy, like fiscal policy, may affect more than just the *level* of aggregate demand. We must give some consideration to the impact of Federal Reserve actions on the content of GNP if we are going to be responsive to the "second crisis" of economic theory.[3] Because monetary policy relies heavily on interest-rate changes to influence spending decisions, its effects on one group or industry may be very different from its effects on another. Investment decisions that are highly sensitive to interest rates are obviously more susceptible to monetary policy than others. The construction industry, especially the residential housing market, stands out in this respect. The sensitivity of housing costs to interest-rate changes forces the construction industry to bear a disproportionate burden of restrictive monetary policy. Accordingly, when the Fed pursues a policy of tight money—high interest rates and limited lending capacity—it not only restrains aggregate demand but reduces the share of housing in that demand. The utility industries, public works projects, and state and local finances are also disproportionately affected by monetary policy.

In addition to altering the content of demand and output, monetary policy affects the competitive structure of the market. When money is tight, banks must ration available credit among loan applicants. In that situation, large and powerful corporations reap great benefits from their decided advantage over smaller firms, because banks will be hesitant to incur their displeasure and lose their business. Thus General Motors and IBM stand a much better chance of obtaining tight money than does the corner grocery store. Moreover, if bank lending capacity becomes excessively small, GM and IBM can always resort to the bond market and borrow money directly from the public. Small businesses seldom have such an alternative.

POLICY IMPLICATIONS: FISCAL VS. MONETARY POLICY

Keynesians and Monetarists clearly have very different views about the efficacy of monetary policy. They also disagree about the effectiveness of fiscal policy. Indeed, ardent Monetarists contend that changes in government spending or taxes really have no impact on the level of aggregate demand. From their perspective, *only* money matters. At the other extreme, ardent Keynesians have countered by asserting that money doesn't matter, that fiscal policy alone can solve our macroeconomic problems.

[3] See the quotation from Joan Robinson in Chapter 9, calling attention to the exclusive focus of economists on the *level* of economic activity (the "first crisis"), to the neglect of content (the "second crisis").

At this juncture, any further arguments between the Keynesian and Monetarist perspectives might seem hopelessly confusing. By examining these extreme positions, however, we may find a good way of summarizing all that we have learned about both monetary and fiscal policy. This summary also highlights the key issues that must concern actual policy makers.

The policy levers

The equation of exchange provides a convenient summary of the differences between Keynesian and Monetarist perspectives. There is no disagreement about the equation itself: aggregate spending $(M \times V)$ must equal the value of total sales $(P \times Q)$. ***What Keynesian and Monetarist economists argue about is which of the policy levers—M or V—is likely to be effective in altering aggregate spending.*** Monetarists point to changes in the money supply (M) as the principal lever of macroeconomic policy. Keynesian fiscal policy must rely on changes in the velocity of money (V), because tax and expenditure policies have no direct impact on the money supply.

Crowding out

The extreme Monetarist position that *only* money matters is based on the assumption that the velocity of money (V) is constant. ***If V were constant, changes in the level of aggregate demand could come about only through changes in the money supply.*** There are no other policy levers on the left side of the equation of exchange.

Think about an increase in government spending designed to increase aggregate demand. How does the government pay for this fiscal-policy initiative? Monetarists argue that there are only two ways of paying for this increased expenditure (G). The government must either raise additional taxes or borrow more money. If the government raises taxes, the disposable income of consumers will be reduced and private spending will fall. On the other hand, if the government borrows more money to pay for its expenditures, there will be less money available for loans to private consumers and investors. In either case, more government spending (G) implies less private spending (C or I). Thus *increased* G effectively **"crowds out"**

crowding out: A reduction in private-sector borrowing (and spending) necessitated by increased government borrowing.

U.S. Share of Borrowing Expected to Hit 56%

More than half the money raised in U.S. credit markets this year will be borrowed by the federal government, as the private sector draws in its horns and the government's borrowing needs swell, according to new estimates from the Office of Management and Budget.

This will be the first year in which the government's share of the total funds raised in U.S. credit markets tops the 50 percent level—56 percent, according to the estimates. In fiscal 1981 it totalled 34.8 percent, the OMB said, and the new estimates show it dropping back to 46 percent for fiscal 1983. However, that figure assumes that Congress cuts next year's deficit to just over $100 billion.

A major reason for the large anticipated jump in the government's share of credit markets is that the budget office forecasts a big drop in total funds raised in the U.S. markets, from $408 billion in fiscal 1981 to $368 billion in the current fiscal year. This is presumably a result of today's deep recession, which discourages individuals and businesses from borrowing more than they have to.

Another is the sharp rise in the federal deficit, which the administration says has come largely because of unforeseen developments in the economy.

—Caroline Atkinson

some C or I, leaving aggregate spending unchanged. From this viewpoint, fiscal policy is ineffective, except in changing the mix of output. Only changes in M (monetary policy) can influence the level of output.

Milton Friedman, formerly of the University of Chicago, champions the Monetarist view with this argument:

I believe that the state of the government budget matters; matters a great deal—for some things. The state of the government budget determines what fraction of the nation's income is spent through the government and what fraction is spent by individuals privately. The state of the government budget determines what the level of our taxes is, how much of our income we turn over to the government. The state of the government budget has a considerable effect on interest rates. If the federal government runs a large deficit, that means the government has to borrow in the market, which raises the demand for loanable funds and so tends to raise interest rates.

If the government budget shifts to a surplus, that adds to the supply of loanable funds, which tends to lower interest rates. It was no surprise to those of us who stress money that enactment of the surtax was followed by a decline in interest rates. That's precisely what we had predicted and what our analysis leads us to predict. But—and I come to the main point—in my opinion, the state of the budget by itself has no significant effect on the course of nominal income, on inflation, on deflation, or on cyclical fluctuations.[4]

The Fiscalist counterargument is, of course, that the alleged constant velocity of money is a Monetarist's pipe dream. Indeed, the extreme Fiscalists argue that the velocity of money is so volatile that changes in V can completely offset changes in M, leaving us with the proposition that money doesn't matter.

The liquidity trap illustrates the potential for V to change. Keynes argued that people tend to accumulate money balances—slow their rate of spending—during recessions. A slowdown in spending implies a reduction in the velocity of money. Indeed, in the extreme case of the liquidity trap, the velocity of money falls toward zero. Under these circumstances, changes in M (monetary policy) will not influence aggregate demand. On the other hand, increased government spending (fiscal policy) can stimulate aggregate demand by putting idle money balances to work (thereby increasing V). Changes in fiscal policy will also influence consumer and investor expectations, and thereby further alter the rate of spending.

How fiscal policy works: two views

These different perspectives on fiscal and monetary policy are summarized in Tables 12.1 and 12.2. The first table evaluates fiscal policy from both Keynesian and Monetarist viewpoints. The central issue is whether and how a change in government spending (G) or taxes (T) will alter macroeconomic outcomes. Keynesians assert aggregate demand will be affected as the velocity of money (V) is altered. Monetarists say no, because they anticipate an unchanged V.

If aggregate demand isn't affected by a change in G or T, then fiscal policy won't affect prices (P) or real output (Q). Thus Monetar-

[4] Milton Friedman and Walter W. Heller, *Monetary vs. Fiscal Policy* (New York: Norton, 1969), pp. 50–51.

TABLE 12.1 HOW FISCAL POLICY MATTERS: MONETARIST VS. KEYNESIAN VIEWS

Monetarists and Keynesians have very different views on the impact of fiscal policy. Monetarists assert that changes in government spending (G) and taxes (T) do not alter the velocity of money (V). As a result, fiscal policy alone cannot alter aggregate spending. Keynesians reject this view, arguing that V is changeable. Tax cuts and increased government spending, for example, increase the velocity of money.

Do changes in G or T affect:	Monetarist view	Keynesian view
1. Aggregate demand?	No (stable V causes crowding out)	Yes (V changes)
2. Prices?	No (aggregate demand not affected)	Maybe (if at capacity)
3. Real output?	No (aggregate demand not affected)	Yes (output responds to demand)
4. Nominal interest rates?	Yes (crowding out)	Maybe (may alter demand for money)
5. Real interest rates?	Yes (nominal interest rates but not prices change)	Yes (real growth and expectations may vary)

ists conclude that fiscal policy is not a viable tool for combating either inflation or unemployment. By contrast, Keynesians believe V will change and that output and prices will respond accordingly.

Insofar as interest rates are concerned, Monetarists recognize that nominal interest rates will be affected (read Friedman's quote again), but that *real* rates won't be. This is because real interest rates depend on real output and growth, both of which are seen as immune to fiscal policy. Keynesians see less impact on nominal interest rates and more on real interest rates.

What all this boils down to is this: fiscal policy, by itself, will be

TABLE 12.2 HOW MONEY MATTERS: MONETARIST VS. KEYNESIAN VIEWS

Because Monetarists believe V is stable, they assert that changes in the money supply (M) must alter aggregate demand. But all of the monetary impact is reflected in prices and nominal interest rates; *real* output and interest rates are unaffected.

Keynesians think V is variable and thus that changes in M might *not* alter aggregate demand. If monetary policy does alter demand, however, Keynesians expect all outcomes to be affected.

Do changes in M affect	Monetarist view	Keynesian view
1. Aggregate demand?	Yes (V stable)	Maybe (V may change)
2. Prices?	Yes (V and Q stable)	Maybe (V and Q may change)
3. Real output?	No (rate of unemployment determined by structural forces)	Maybe (output responds to demand)
4. Nominal interest rates?	Yes (but direction unknown)	Maybe (liquidity trap)
5. Real interest rates?	Maybe (depends on real growth and expectations)	Maybe (real growth may vary)

effective only if it can alter the velocity of money. *How well fiscal policy works depends on how much the velocity of money can be changed by government tax and spending decisions.*

How monetary policy works: two views

Table 12.2 provides a similar summary of monetary policy. This time the positions of Monetarists and Keynesians are reversed, or nearly so. Monetarists say a change in M must alter aggregate demand ($P \times Q$) because V is stable. Keynesians assert that V may vary, so they aren't convinced that monetary policy will always work. The heart of the controversy is again the velocity of money. Monetary policy works so long as V is stable, or at least predictable. *How well monetary policy works depends on how stable or predictable V is.*

Once the central role of velocity is understood, everything else falls into place. Monetarists assert that prices but not output will be directly affected by a change in M. This is because the right-hand side of the equation of exchange contains only two variables (P and Q), and one of them (Q) is assumed to be insensitive to monetary phenomena. Keynesians, by contrast, are not so sure prices will be affected by M, or that real output won't be. It all depends on V and the responsiveness of P and Q to changes in spending.

Finally, Monetarists predict that nominal interest rates will respond to changes in M, although they are not sure in what direction. It depends on how inflationary expectations adapt to changes in the money supply. Keynesian economists are not so sure nominal interest rates will change, but are sure about the direction if they do.

Is velocity stable?

Tables 12.1 and 12.2 provide many insights into how fiscal and monetary policies can and do work. As we have emphasized, the velocity of money plays a key role in the debate over the relative effectiveness of these two policy levers. The critical question appears to be whether V is stable or not. Why hasn't someone answered this simple question and resolved the debate over fiscal vs. monetary policy?

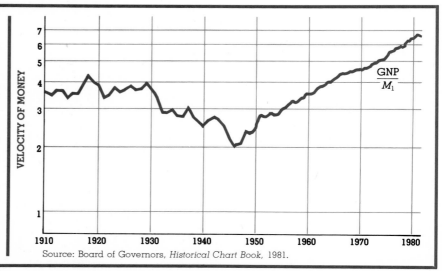

FIGURE 12.6 INCOME VELOCITY OF MONEY
(annually, 1910–60; seasonally adjusted, quarterly, 1960–80)

The income velocity of money (V) equals GNP divided by the supply of money. During the Great Depression the velocity of money fell sharply. Since World War II, however, V has been increasing.

Source: Board of Governors, *Historical Chart Book*, 1981.

How velocity can fool the money watchers

The money supply now commands greater attention than any other economic statistic. Congressmen, businessmen, and money managers eye the money numbers as they do no other figures coming out of Washington, some lining up at the Dow Jones ticker on Thursday at 4:00 P.M. to get the weekly money supply numbers, much like horseplayers trying to get the latest race results. The implication is that control of the money supply leads to stabilization of the economy. And tracing the growth of money yields good forecasts of output, prices, and interest rates.

Yet, just as the money supply achieves superstar status, serious questions are being raised about whether money-watching works, either for forecasters or policymakers.

For money to tell the whole story, or even a good part of it, the rate at which money turns over—its velocity—must be reasonably stable or predictable. If velocity is stable, controlling the money supply is an effective tool for influencing the growth of the gross national product, at least in the long run. But if velocity rises, a given amount of money will support a larger volume of economic activity, so there is no longer a simple relationship between money growth and GNP.

Velocity is a concept that economists have used since Irving Fisher (1867 to 1947), probably America's greatest monetary economist, developed the theory at the turn of the century that the supply of money determined the level of national income. Fisher assumed that velocity was reasonably constant. Today's economists know that velocity is in an upward trend. For example, in the first quarter of 1968 GNP reached $837.3 billion and the narrowly defined money supply, M_1, averaged $189.1 billion. So velocity, or the turnover rate, came to 4.42. But by 1973 velocity had risen to 5.04.

Indeed, since World War II velocity has looked predictable, increasing at about 3% a year. But suddenly in the past two years it has risen at almost twice that rate, and the GNP increased at 24% over that period, double the rate of increase in the money supply. Arthur F. Burns, chairman of the Federal Reserve, expects yet another sharp spurt in velocity, and he is basing Fed money policy on that assumption.

However, few economists agree on just where velocity will end up. The critical issue, therefore, is whether the Federal Reserve can make sound decisions on how much money is adequate to support economic growth without either sending interest rates soaring or reigniting inflation.

THE LONG RUN, THE SHORT RUN To understand the persistence of the debate over V and thus over the question of whether fiscal or monetary policy "works"—we must distinguish between the long run and the short run. The velocity of money (V) turns out, in fact, to be quite stable over long periods of time. And on that basis, the extreme Monetarist view that only money matters makes sense. In the short run, however, economic parameters are not so stable. The velocity of money may fluctuate considerably over a period of a few months, or even years, while still evidencing a longer-run stability (see Figure 12.6). Fiscal enthusiasts argue that these short-run changes in V are important for economic welfare—that is, that people care about what happens to their jobs, income, and prices *this* year. Moreover, government tax and spending policies can help counteract any undesirable changes in V.

IS *V* PREDICTABLE? The Monetarists offer one last observation. They concede that velocity just *might* fluctuate in the short run. But they argue that short-run changes in the velocity of money are *unpredictable*. Accordingly, both fiscal and monetary policies are subject to considerable uncertainty. Under these circumstances, Monetarists argue, policy makers are just as likely to fail as to succeed if they attempt to alter aggregate demand in the short run. The only safe course is to focus on the long run. And in the long run, of course, V is fairly constant, so that fiscal policy is rather ineffective. Monetarists therefore conclude that monetary policy is preeminent. Furthermore, monetary policy should seek to ensure long-term stability and not try to counteract short-run problems of cyclical unemployment or demand-pull inflation, since short-run outcomes are so uncertain.[5]

Economic policy would be most effective, of course, if it incorporated the insights of both the Monetarists and the Fiscalists. The simple equation relating M, V, and PQ is sufficient indication that both monetary and fiscal policy can be effective, because it is possible to change either M or V. Couple that with the fact that both M and V have varied over time, and it is clear that a policy synthesis must strive to coordinate policy weapons. Of course, monetary policies and fiscal policies could be used to cancel each other out, leaving everyone dissatisfied. A much more intelligent course of action would be to combine monetary and fiscal policies in such a way as to approach more closely all of our economic goals. This is what a policy synthesis is all about. The issue is not really whether monetary policy is more effective than fiscal policy or vice versa. We must seek the *combination* of policies that is best suited to deal with a specific set of problems in a specific economic context. That kind of debate may be less exciting, but it is also more likely to contribute to improvements in economic performance.

SUMMARY

▪ The essence of monetary policy lies in the Federal Reserve's control over the money supply. By altering the money supply, the Fed can determine the amount of purchasing power available.

▪ The Fed controls only one side of the money market. The demand for money is also important. This demand reflects desires to hold money (in cash or transactions deposits) for transactions, precautionary, and speculative purposes. The interaction of money supply and money demand determines the equilibrium rate of interest.

▪ From a Keynesian perspective, the impact of monetary policy on the economy occurs in three distinct steps. First, the money supply is changed. Second, changes in the money supply alter the equilibrium rate of interest. Third, changes in the interest rate alter the rate of investment expenditure, and perhaps consumer and government expenditure as well.

▪ For Keynesian monetary policy to be fully effective, interest rates must be responsive to changes in the money supply, and investment spending must be responsive to changes in interest rates. Neither condition is assured. In a liquidity trap, people are willing to hold unlimited amounts of money at some low rate of interest. The interest rate will not fall below this level as the money supply increases. Also, investor expectations of sales and profits may override interest-rate considerations in the investment decision.

▪ The Monetarist view of monetary policy is simpler, and builds on the equation of exchange ($MV = PQ$). Monetarists assert that the

---

[5] The potential for "fine-tuning" the economy—for trying to make small short-run adjustments in economic performance—will be examined further in Chapter 14.

velocity of money (V) is stable, so that changes in M must influence GNP (P × Q).

▪ Monetary policy attempts to influence total expenditure by changing M, and will be fully effective only if V is constant. Fiscal policy attempts to influence total expenditure by changing V, and will be fully effective only if M does not change in the opposite direction. The controversy over the effectiveness of fiscal versus monetary policy depends on whether the velocity of money (V) is stable, or instead is subject to policy influence.

▪ The velocity of money is more stable over long periods of time than over short periods. Keynesians conclude that this makes fiscal policy more powerful in the short run. Monetarists conclude that the unpredictability of short-run velocity makes *any* short-run policy risky.

Terms to remember

Define the following terms:

interest rate	monetary policy
portfolio decision	liquidity trap
demand for money	equation of exchange
transactions demand for money	income velocity of money (V)
precautionary demand for money	real rate of interest
speculative demand for money	crowding out
equilibrium rate of interest	

Questions for discussion

1. What proportions of your money balance are held for transactions, precautionary, and speculative purposes? Can you think of any other purposes for holding money?

2. Why do high interest rates so adversely affect the demand for housing and yet have so little influence on the demand for strawberries?

3. If the Federal Reserve banks mailed everyone a brand-new $100 bill, what would happen to prices, output, and income? Illustrate with the equation of exchange.

4. Suppose that the chairman of the Fed's Board of Governors wanted to reduce the rate of total expenditure (to fight inflation) and the president wanted to increase total expenditure (to fight unemployment). What kind of action would each take? What effects would their combined actions have on GNP?

5. Monetarists argue that the money supply may grow too fast if the Fed focuses on interest rates as a mechanism for stimulating demand. What problems do they see?

Problem

Suppose the Federal Reserve decided to purchase $10 billion worth of government securities in the open market. What impact would this action have on the economy? Specifically, answer the following questions, using graphs where appropriate. Note and explain any differences in the answers of Monetarists and Keynesians.

(a) How will M1 be affected initially?

(b) How will the lending capacity of the banking system be affected if the reserve requirement is 25 percent?

(c) How will banks induce investors to utilize this expanded lending capacity?

(d) How will aggregate demand be affected if investors borrow and spend all the newly available credit?

(e) Under what circumstances would the Fed be pursuing such an open-market policy?

(f) How could those same objectives be achieved through changes in the discount rate or reserve requirement?

POLICY OPTIONS: THE SUPPLY-SIDE APPROACH

CHAPTER 13

SUPPLY-SIDE POLICIES

Although Keynesian and Monetarist economists seem to disagree on most aspects of macroeconomic policy, they have one basic trait in common: they both focus on the *demand* side of the economy. To the extent that they regard either fiscal or monetary policy as effective, they see its impact transmitted through changes in aggregate demand. Indeed, from a simple Keynesian perspective, demand creates its own supply, that is, the supply side of the macro-economy is assumed to respond automatically to changes in demand. Monetarists take a less extreme position. Monetarists do not think actual production is greatly affected by changes in expenditure, but they do expect prices to respond automatically to shifts of aggregate demand.

Supply-Siders have a very different view of the world. They start on the **supply** side of markets, rather than on the demand side. They emphasize that an assortment of government policies *directly* affects the ability and willingness of business firms to produce goods and services. Government policies also affect the ability and willingness of individuals to participate in the production process. In other words, the supply of goods is itself subject to government policies. Demand-side policies are neither necessary nor sufficient to attain our macro goals.

The most familiar supply-side policies are the tax cuts initiated by the Reagan administration. In fact, those tax cuts are often thought of as the entire scope of supply-side economics. However, the supply-side perspective has a much longer history and covers a much broader array of policy options. Many of these options are

supply: The ability and willingness to sell (produce) specific quantities of a good at alternative prices in a given time period (*ceteris paribus*).

designed to reduce structural barriers to increased output and employment. These structural policies include deregulation, education and training, and reduction of discriminatory barriers. Also legitimately part of the Supply-Side perspective are controls that limit the ability of workers and firms to increase wages and prices. Some Supply-Siders reject some or all of these policy options. Nevertheless, *the common element in all supply-side policy options is the attempt to alter supply behavior independently of changes in demand.* The basis for these various policy options will be discussed in this chapter. In Chapter 15 we shall look at President Reagan's unique version of supply-side economics.

SUPPLY RESPONSES TO DEMAND-SIDE POLICIES

equation of exchange: Money supply (M) times velocity of circulation (V) equals level of aggregate demand (P × Q).

The origins of supply-side theory are reflected in the **equation of exchange.** As we noted in Chapter 12, the equation

$$\underset{\substack{\text{(money} \\ \text{supply)}}}{M} \times \underset{\substack{\text{(velocity} \\ \text{of money)}}}{V} = \underset{\text{(prices)}}{P} \times \underset{\substack{\text{(quantity} \\ \text{of output)}}}{Q}$$

summarizes market activity. The left side of the equation measures total expenditure; the right side reflects the value of goods sold. Because every dollar spent on output represents a dollar's worth of goods sold, the two sides of the equation are always equal.

Demand-side options

In Chapter 12 we used the equation of exchange to illustrate how fiscal and monetary policies work. Both operate on the demand side of the equation—that is, the left side. Monetary policy attempts to change the money supply (M), while fiscal policy focuses on changes in the velocity of money (V). In either case, the objective of policy is to alter the rate of inflation (P) or the rate of output (Q). In other words, *the tools of demand-side macroeconomic policy are on the left side of the equation of exchange; the targets of macroeconomic policy are on the right side.*

Although fiscal and monetary policies can alter the level of aggregate demand, they have no direct influence on P (prices) or Q (the rate of output). Suppose, for example, that we want to stimulate aggregate demand so as to reduce unemployment. By increasing M and/or V we can increase total spending. But we do not know whether prices (P), real output (Q), or both will go up. Our *objective,* of course, is to increase output (Q) and thus reduce unemployment. All we can guarantee, however, is that the value of the right-hand side of the equation of exchange will rise; we cannot guarantee which component will increase. It *could* happen that prices (P) would increase rather than output (Q). We would then be left with our original unemployment problem *plus* a new inflation problem.

The same kind of dilemma could confront efforts to stop inflation. Suppose that we were experiencing significant inflation at full employment. Under such circumstances, the appropriate macro re-

The Great Divide

Courtesy of C. P. Houston in the *Houston Chronicle.*

sponse would be to restrain aggregate demand by reducing the rate of growth in M or V. Such efforts, however, ensure only that the value of the right-hand side of the equation will fall; they don't tell us whether prices, real output, or both will decline. We hope that average prices (P) will rise more slowly, bringing a halt to inflation. But it is at least *possible* that the rate of output (Q) may fall instead, leaving us with our original inflation *plus* a new unemployment problem.

Stagflation

Supply-side concerns originate in this recognition that fiscal and monetary policies may fail to attain their goals. ***The effectiveness of demand-side macro policies depends on the price and output responses of market participants to changes in aggregate demand.*** Those responses may be inadequate or even perverse. For example, producers may raise prices (P) rather than output (Q) in response to expansionary demand-side policies. Conversely, producers may reduce output rather than prices in response to restrictive fiscal and monetary policies. Moreover, the government itself may contribute to increases in prices or wages.

In all these cases, we may compound our problems rather than solve them if we rely on demand-side policies. Specifically, our attempts to reduce unemployment may increase the rate of inflation. Likewise, attempts to control inflation may so diminish aggregate demand that unemployment increases. These perverse responses all lead to **stagflation,** a condition in which we suffer from both inflation and unemployment at the same time.

stagflation: Simultaneous presence of substantial unemployment and inflation.

The Phillips curve

Phillips curve: A historical (inverse) relationship between the rate of unemployment and the rate of inflation; commonly expresses a trade-off between the two.

That micro behavior does not always respond as desired to macroeconomic policies is evident from the historical record. Consider, for example, our experience with unemployment and inflation during the 1960s, as shown in Figure 13.1. This figure shows a **Phillips curve** indicating that prices (P) generally started rising before the objective of expanded output (Q) had been completely attained. In other words, inflation struck before full employment was reached.

The Phillips curve was developed by an English economist, A. W. Phillips, as a summary of the relationship between unemploy-

---

FIGURE 13.1 THE PHILLIPS CURVE FOR THE 1960s

In the 1960s it appeared that efforts to reduce unemployment rates below 5.5 percent (point C) led to increasing rates of inflation (points A and B). Inflation threatened to reach unacceptable heights long before everyone was employed.

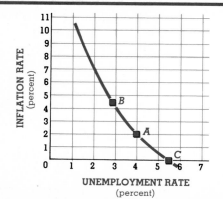

THE DISCOMFORT INDEX: A MEASURE OF STAGFLATION

Stagflation is a situation in which both unemployment and inflation are "too high." But how should the extent of stagflation be measured? And how can we determine whether our stagflation problem is getting better or worse?

The measurement problem results from the fact that we are interested in *two* separate ills: inflation and unemployment. If one goes up while the other goes down, is our economic welfare unchanged? If government policies succeed in bringing down the rate of inflation but not the rate of unemployment, are we better off?

To answer these questions, Arthur Okun proposed a *single* measure of stagflation. He called it the "discomfort index." The discomfort index is simply the *sum* of our inflation and unemployment rates. If the rate of inflation is 9 percent and unemployment is at 7 percent, the discomfort index is 16. Lower values indicate an improvement in our economic welfare; higher values a worse situation. The graph below shows how the level of discomfort increased in the last decade or so.

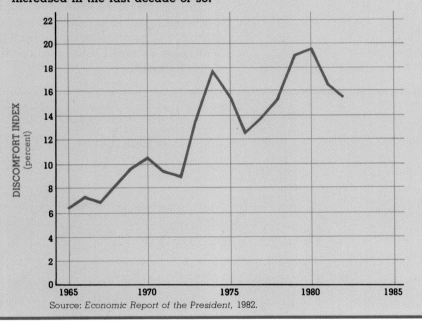

Source: *Economic Report of the President*, 1982.

ment and inflation in England for the years 1826–1957.[1] The Phillips curve was raised from the status of an obscure economics graph to that of a policy issue by the discovery that the same kind of relationship apparently existed in other countries and at other times. Professors Paul Samuelson and Robert Solow of M.I.T. were among the first to observe that the Phillips curve was a reasonable description of U.S. economic performance for the years from 1900 to 1960. For the post–World War II years in particular, Samuelson and Solow noted that an unemployment rate of 4 percent was likely to be accompanied by an inflation rate of approximately 2 percent. This rela-

[1] A. W. Phillips, "The Relationship between Unemployment and the Rate of Change of Money Wage Rates in the United Kingdom, 1826–1957," *Economica*, November 1958. Phillips' paper studied the relationship between unemployment and *wage* changes rather than *price* changes, but most later formulations (and public policy) focus on prices. This is discussed later in this chapter.

tionship is expressed by point *A* in Figure 13.1. By contrast, lower rates of unemployment were associated with higher rates of inflation, as at point *B*. Alternatively, complete price stability appeared attainable only at the cost of an unemployment rate of 5.5 percent (point *C*). Observations such as these led many economists to conclude that a seesaw kind of relationship existed between inflation and unemployment: when one went up, the other fell. Full employment with price stability looked unattainable.

A WORSENING TRADE-OFF? If the Phillips curve shown in Figure 13.1 was a bad dream, more recent experiences have been a real nightmare. Notice in Figure 13.2 that our unemployment and inflation experiences in the 1970s and early 1980s all lie above and to the right of the earlier Phillips curve (PC_1). These experiences suggest that the Phillips curve has *shifted* to the right—first to PC_2, then again to PC_3, and further to PC_4. These shifts have left us with a much greater stagflation problem than we had in the 1960s. Earlier it seemed possible to achieve 4 percent unemployment with relatively little (2 percent) inflation (point *A*). Now, however, it appears that the inflation rate will jump through the roof before we get close to full employment.

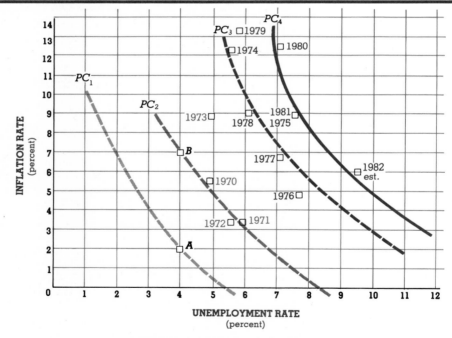

FIGURE 13.2 SHIFTS OF THE PHILLIPS CURVE

In the 1960s it appeared that 4 percent unemployment was compatible with 2 percent inflation (point *A*). In the early 1970s a much higher rate of inflation (point *B*) appeared to be consistent with 4 percent unemployment. In the late 1970s and early 1980s a 4 percent unemployment rate looked completely unattainable at tolerable rates of inflation. The worsening trade-off is expressed by the rightward shifts of the Phillips curve, from PC_1 to PC_4.

Source: *Economic Report of the President*, 1982.

FIGURE 13.3 THE AGGREGATE-SUPPLY CURVE

Supply-side economists emphasize that the rate of output responds to economic incentives, including prices. At higher prices, the incentive to produce is greater, *ceteris paribus*. Also, the cost of production tends to increase as the economy approaches capacity. For both these reasons, the aggregate-supply curve slopes upward to the right.

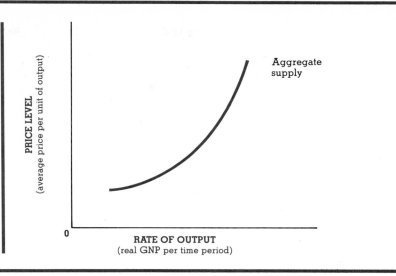

Our experience with stagflation in the 1970s and early 1980s hardly invites optimism about the prospects of achieving full employment and price stability at the same time. On the contrary, the most recent Phillips curve (PC_4) appears to offer us only three alternatives, none of which is desirable. According to curve PC_4, we must either (1) accept very high unemployment rates in return for relative price stability, (2) accept very high inflation rates in return for full employment, or (3) learn to live with "moderate" amounts of both unemployment and inflation.

AGGREGATE SUPPLY

Not everyone is prepared to accept such awful choices. Supply-side economists in particular argue that demand-side theorists are confronted with these awful choices only because they have ignored the supply side of the economy. Specifically, Keynesians and Monetarists have forgotten a basic principle of economics, namely, that the quantity supplied increases when prices rise. **Supply is a behavioral relation, not a fixed quantum.** Hence when we implement policies to get more output (reduce unemployment) we should not be surprised that prices typically rise (more inflation).

The aggregate-supply curve

aggregate supply: The total quantity of final goods and services supplied to the market at alternative price levels in a given time period (*ceteris paribus*); total output.

What underlies supply-side perspectives, then, is a fairly conventional-looking supply curve. The curve slopes upward to the right, as in Figure 13.3. Thus **aggregate supply** behaves much like the supply of any particular good or service (see Chapter 2). In this case, however, we are dealing with the *average* price level, not the price of any single good. And we are gauging *total* output of goods and services, not the output of a single good. The aggregate-supply curve in Figure 13.3 says that a higher price *level* will stimulate more total output.

FIGURE 13.4 THE KEYNESIAN SUPPLY CURVE

In the simple Keynesian model, the rate of output responds fully and automatically to increases in demand until full employment (Y_F) is reached. If demand increases from D_1 to D_2, equilibrium GNP will expand from Y_o to Y_F, without any inflation. Inflation becomes a problem only if demand increases beyond capacity—to D_3, for example.

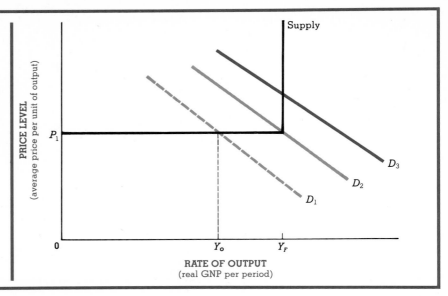

THE KEYNESIAN VIEW That the rate of output should be responsive to prices might seem fairly obvious. But it was not part of the Keynesian or Monetarist explanations of macro instability. Keynes developed his model in the depths of the Depression, when prices were generally falling. Inflation was a remote problem. As a consequence, inflation became a problem in the Keynesian model only when aggregate demand at full employment exceeded the economy's productive capacity. Up until that point, increases in demand affected only the rate of output. The underlying aggregate-supply curve was implicitly thought to be horizontal, as in Figure 13.4. This horizontal supply curve implies that output can and will respond automatically to changes in demand without any effect on price levels until capacity is reached. At capacity Y_F, further increases in demand lead directly to higher prices (inflation). Notice in Figure 13.4 that a rightward shift of the demand curve from D_1 to D_2 increases output, but not prices. By contrast, a further shift of demand to D_3 increases prices, but not output.

THE AGGREGATE-DEMAND CURVE Notice that the aggregate-demand curve in Figure 13.4 does not look like our early ones. Our earlier graphs of aggregate demand had income on the vertical axis and output on the horizontal axis. That was because Keynes emphasized the relationship of *income* to spending. He wanted to show how spending would respond to changes in income (output). To do so, he used our *ceteris paribus* assumption and assumed that prices were constant.

Now we are focusing on the relationship of *prices* to spending decisions. To do so, we now hold income constant. With a given level of nominal income, we expect consumers and investors to demand more goods when the price level falls. This increase in quantity demanded results from the fact that falling prices imply rising *real* income and wealth. A dollar held in the bank increases in *real* value when prices fall—it will buy more goods than it could at higher prices. As the purchasing power of the dollar increases, consumers and investors are likely to demand more goods. This expectation is illustrated by the downward-sloping aggregate-demand curve in Figure 13.4. The thing to remember is that prices are now on the vertical axis.

natural rate of unemployment: Long-term rate of unemployment determined by structural forces in labor and product markets.

THE MONETARIST VIEW The simple Monetarist view of aggregate supply is unrealistic, too. In the Monetarist model, the long-run **"natural" rate of unemployment** is fixed at Y_F by structural forces in the economy. This is illustrated by the vertical supply curve in Figure 13.5. In this model, changes in aggregate demand affect prices only. Hence an increase in the money supply that shifts demand from D_4 to D_5 will cause inflation. Restrictive monetary policies, on the other hand, will lead to lower prices. In either case, the rate of real output (Y_F) is unchanged.[2]

THE SUPPLY-SIDE VIEW Supply-side economists reject both the Keynesian and Monetarist views of aggregate supply, and for good reason. There is no law that requires firms to produce as many goods as possible to satisfy consumer demands. Nor is there a law that requires everyone to work for these firms, up to the limits of their physical and mental abilities. Rather, we permit workers and firms to make their own supply decisions. Not surprisingly, those decisions tend to reflect selfish interests. Workers tend to offer more labor only at higher wages. Likewise, firms offer to produce more goods and services only if they expect higher prices and profits. As a consequence, the quantity of goods and services offered to the market tends to be responsive to economic incentives, including prices. In other words, *the aggregate-supply curve slopes upward,* as in Figure 13.3.

[2] Recall that Monetarists tend to focus on long-run outcomes. They agree that short-run changes in Q are possible, but neither predictable nor deliberately attainable.

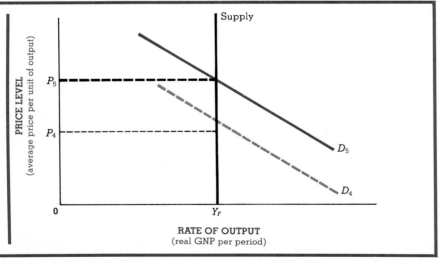

FIGURE 13.5 THE MONETARIST SUPPLY CURVE

Monetarists assert that changes in the money supply affect prices but not output. They regard aggregate supply as a fixed quantum, at the long-run, "natural" rate of unemployment (here noted as Y_F). Accordingly, a shift of demand (from D_4 to D_5) can only affect the price level (from P_4 to P_5).

PRICE LEVEL
(average price per unit of output)

P_5

P_4

Supply

D_5

D_4

0

Y_F

RATE OF OUTPUT
(real GNP per period)

FIGURE 13.6 SHIFTS OF
AGGREGATE SUPPLY

The objective of supply-side policies
is to shift the aggregate-supply curve
to the right. Such shifts imply less
inflation and lower unemployment for
any given state of aggregate demand.
Thus supply-side economists see the
possibility of overcoming stagflation.

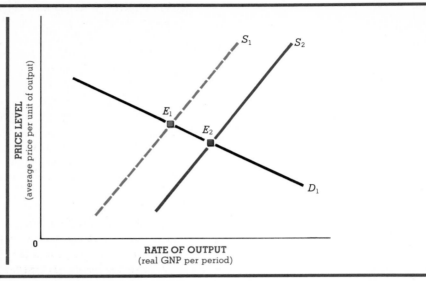

Supply shifts

The upward slope of the aggregate-supply curve explains why
prices rise before full employment is reached. It also helps explain
the more general trade-off between unemployment and inflation, as
reflected in the Phillips curve (Figure 13.2). But that is not the end of
the story. Having demonstrated the existence of an aggregate-supply
curve, supply-side economists are quick to point out that its position
is not permanent. On the contrary, aggregate supply—like aggregate
demand—can be *shifted*. And it is these shifts that hold the potential
for improving our macroeconomic performance.

The potential of supply shifts to improve macro outcomes is
illustrated in Figure 13.6. Suppose we are initially at the equilibrium
E_1, with too much unemployment and too much inflation. What can
we do? Demand-side economists would have us meddle with the
demand curve. But a rightward shift of the demand curve would
aggravate inflation and a leftward shift would increase unemployment. On the other hand, *a rightward shift of the supply curve
would both reduce inflationary pressures and increase employment (output).* Rightward shifts of the aggregate supply curve thus
have the potential to overcome stagflation.

Policy options

The next question, of course, is how to shift the aggregate supply
curve. The supply-side economists look for clues on the right-hand
side of the equation of exchange. That is to say, they focus directly
on the targets of macro policy—price and output behavior. They
look for forces that influence the supply-side response to changes in
demand. Why doesn't output (Q) respond quickly and fully to a
change in demand? Why does inflation (P) rather than output often
increase when demand is increased? What role do government policies play in these response patterns? What kinds of new policies
would improve the supply-side response?

To answer these questions, supply-side economists have developed a small laundry list of alternative policy options. They include:

□ Supply-side tax cuts
□ Deregulation
□ Elimination of structural bottlenecks
□ Wage and price controls

A KEYNESIAN VIEW OF SUPPLY-SIDE ECONOMICS

The contrasting perspectives of Keynesians, Monetarists, and Supply-Siders are usually illustrated with graphs like those in Figures 13.3 to 13.5. The distinguishing feature of these graphs is that they emphasize the relationship of *prices* (on the vertical axis) to output (horizontal axis). Income is assumed to be constant.

The Keynesian model examined in Chapters 7 through 9 uses different graphs. Keynes assumed prices were constant and focused instead on the relationship of spending (vertical axis) to output and income (horizontal axis). The "Keynesian cross" that symbolizes this model is drawn again in Figure *a* below. The economy is assumed to be producing at Y_1 initially, far short of its full-employment GNP (at Y_F). From a Keynesian perspective, the economy needs an injection of new demand that will shift the aggregate-demand curve upward. In Figure *a*, this stimulus comes from a tax cut that shifts aggregate demand from $(C + I + G)_1$ to $(C + I + G)_2$.

The risk of such fiscal stimulus is that inflation will accelerate. As the economy is pushed from Y_1 to Y_2, the economy approaches "full" employment. Capacity constraints begin to increase inflationary pressures; stagflation results.

Supply-Siders argue that the Keynesian notion of "full-employment" GNP is too restrictive. Reductions in marginal tax rates will increase work effort and investment. This increased supply will enlarge our productive capacity. This is illustrated in Figure *b* by the rightward shift of the capacity constraint from Y_F to Y_{F*}. This increased capacity implies that demand and output can be increased with less inflationary pressure.

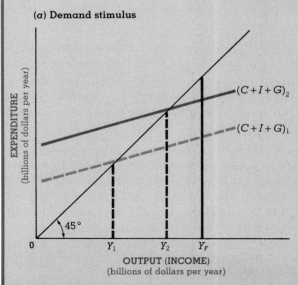

(a) Demand stimulus

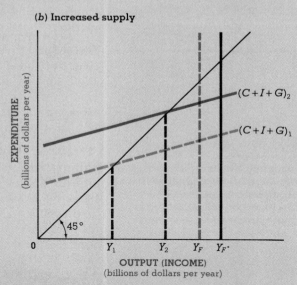

(b) Increased supply

All of these policies have the potential to change supply decisions *independently* of any changes in aggregate demand. If they are effective, they will result in a rightward shift of the aggregate-supply curve. They hold out the promise, then, of an *improved* trade-off between unemployment and inflation. If Supply-Siders are right, then the Phillips curve depicted in Figure 13.2 can be shifted to the left, giving us both lower inflation and lower unemployment.

SUPPLY-SIDE TAX CUTS

The most renowned supply-side policy option for improving the inflation-unemployment trade-off are supply-side tax cuts. Tax cuts, of course, are a staple of Keynesian economics. But Supply-Siders view tax cuts in a wholly different way than the Keynesians. *In Keynesian economics, tax cuts are used to increase aggregate demand.* By putting more disposable income in the hands of consumers, Keynesian economists seek to increase expenditure on goods and services. The rate of output is expected to increase in response. From a Keynesian perspective the form of the tax cut is not very important, so long as disposable income increases.

Supply-side economists have a different view of taxes. Taxes not only determine disposable income but also affect the incentives to work and produce. High tax rates destroy the incentives to work and produce, so they end up reducing total output. Low tax rates, by contrast, allow people to keep more of what they earn and so stimulate greater output. *The direct effects of taxes on the supply of goods are the concern of supply-side economists.*

Marginal tax rates

marginal tax rate: The tax rate imposed on the last (marginal) dollar of income.

Supply-Siders are particularly interested in marginal tax rates. The **marginal tax rate** is the tax rate imposed on the last (marginal) dollar of income received. In our progressive income-tax system (see Chapter 29), marginal tax rates increase as more income is received. Hence Uncle Sam takes a larger share out of each additional dollar earned.

LABOR SUPPLY The marginal tax rate influences the financial incentive to *increase* one's work or production. *If the marginal tax rate is high, there is little incentive to work more or expand production:* Uncle Sam will get most of the added income. Low marginal tax rates, on the other hand, permit people to keep most of the income that results from additional output.

investment: Expenditures on (production of) new plant and equipment (capital) in a given time period, plus changes in business inventories.

INVESTMENT High marginal tax rates discourage not only work effort, but **investment** as well. Business investment is motivated by the desire for profits. Firms buy new plant and equipment only if they think the resulting output will be profitable. But the profitability of an investment depends in part on taxes. If Uncle Sam imposes a high tax rate on business profits, the payoff to investors will be diminished. Consequently, **high business taxes also discourage investment.** With less new investment the economy's productive capacity will be smaller—and more costly.

For Supply-Siders, the Focus Is Incentives

For the past 15 years, Keynesian demand-management policies have been applied to the U.S. economy. They have left an empirical track record—one of progressively worsening economic performance with rising rates of inflation and unemployment. Keynesians have attributed the failure of their policy to Arab oil lords, unions, big business and to a mystical and worsening "underlying rate of inflation," which they believe is independent of fiscal and monetary policies.

The culprit, however, is demand-management itself, which puts monetary policy on the roller coaster and pushes taxpayers higher in the progressive income tax system.

Keynesian economics uses the government's budget as its tool for managing the economy. Unemployment requires a budget deficit to increase total demand or spending in the economy. Inflation requires a budget surplus to reduce total demand in order to relieve pressures on the price level. In practice, this approach produced deficits every year for the past decade.

In an unemployment year, the policymakers would calculate the size of the "fiscal stimulus" or budget deficit required to bring spending up to the full employment level. For the deficit to actually add to spending, the Federal Reserve had to accommodate it with a monetary expansion. Otherwise, the government's borrowing would drive up interest rates and choke off the demand it was trying to stimulate. In effect, it was a policy of fighting unemployment by printing money.

The monetary expansion would push up the inflation rate, and soon the Federal Reserve would be under pressure to cool down the economy by tightening up on the money supply and raising the interest rate. The government's revenues (but not spending) would decline as the economy soured, and this time the budget would unintentionally go into deficit. . . .

The demand-managers didn't realize it, but their problems were created by mixing together demand stimulus with supply disincentives. The inflation that accompanied the demand stimulus eroded the real value of business' depreciation allowances and pushed taxpayers into higher marginal tax brackets.

In 1965, the highest tax bracket encountered by a median income family of four was 17 percent. That means the family got to keep 83 cents of an additional dollar earned. A family with twice the median income encountered a top bracket of 22 percent. . . .

When Social Security and state income taxes are added in, the disincentives are even harsher. Today a median income family that resides in Maryland is in the 40 percent marginal tax bracket; one that resides in New York is in the 44 percent bracket. After 15 years of demand-management, ordinary people are now in tax brackets that once applied only to the rich. Little wonder output has stagnated while inflation has roared.

Under President Reagan's proposals, the median income family will be in the 23 percent federal bracket in 1984. That doesn't turn the tax clock all the way back to 1965, but it is a big step in the right direction.

Demand-side economists don't understand the importance of this step. To them, the function of a tax cut is not to restructure incentives but to increase demand. Thus, over the last decade when they cut taxes, they focused on lowering the average tax rate on existing earnings (through such means as larger personal exemptions and standard deductions) and allowed the marginal tax rate on additional or new income to rise. As a consequence, today for the majority of the population the incentive to produce additional income is the lowest in our history, and the personal saving rate is the lowest in anyone's memory.

—Paul Craig Roberts

The Washington Post, Washington, D.C., April 13, 1981. Copyright © 1981 The Washington Post.

Tax-induced supply shifts

tax rebate: A lump-sum refund of taxes paid.

Supply-Siders conclude that *a reduction in marginal tax rates will shift the aggregate-supply curve to the right,* as in Figure 13.6. The increased supply will come from two sources: more work effort and more investment. This increased ability and willingness to produce will reduce the rate of unemployment. The additional output will also help reduce inflationary pressures. Thus we end up with less unemployment *and* less inflation—that is, less stagflation.

From a supply-side perspective, the form of the tax cut is critical. **Tax rebates,** for example, are not advocated by supply-siders. Rebates are a one-time windfall to consumers, and have no effect on marginal tax rates. As a consequence, disposable income rises, but not the incentives for work or production. Rebates directly affect only the demand side of the economy.

To stimulate *supply,* tax *rates* must be reduced. These cuts can take the form of reductions in personal income-tax rates or reduc-

TWO THEORIES FOR GETTING THE ECONOMY MOVING

Keynesians and Supply-Siders both advocate cutting taxes to reduce unemployment. But they have very different views on the kind of tax cuts required and the impact of any cuts enacted.

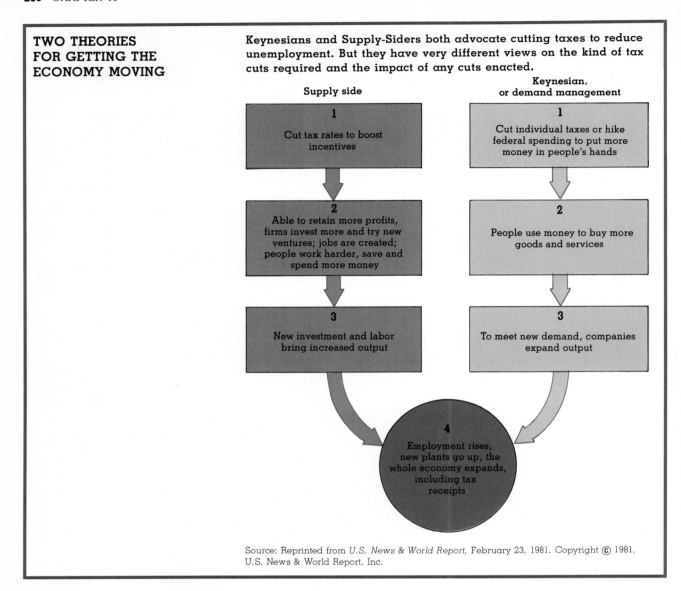

Supply side

1 Cut tax rates to boost incentives

2 Able to retain more profits, firms invest more and try new ventures; jobs are created; people work harder, save and spend more money

3 New investment and labor bring increased output

Keynesian, or demand management

1 Cut individual taxes or hike federal spending to put more money in people's hands

2 People use money to buy more goods and services

3 To meet new demand, companies expand output

4 Employment rises, new plants go up, the whole economy expands, including tax receipts

Source: Reprinted from *U.S. News & World Report*, February 23, 1981. Copyright © 1981, U.S. News & World Report, Inc.

---

saving: That part of disposable income not spent on current consumption; disposable income less consumption.

tions in the marginal tax rates imposed on corporations and other businesses. The various business tax reductions undertaken in 1981 are discussed in Chapter 19.[3]

ENCOURAGING SAVING   Supply-side economists also favor tax cuts that directly encourage consumer **saving.** New investment competes

[3] The supply-side tax cuts undertaken by the Reagan administration were designed to do more than just increase production incentives. It was also hoped that the resulting supply shift would be so great that total government tax revenues would increase, despite lower tax rates. If these hopes were realized, supply-side tax cuts would reduce not only inflation and unemployment but federal budget deficits as well! The basis for this expectation—illustrated in the Laffer curve—will be examined in Chapter 15.

Searching for a Policy for More Saving

Few causes hold as much appeal in Congress today as the desire to boost savings. During the past decade battles over tax legislation frequently focused on closing "loopholes" or redistributing wealth. Now legislators are competing to offer new breaks to savers. More than 100 bills have been introduced this year to provide incentives to save more.

The savings bandwagon began on Main Street and Wall Street with complaints that Americans aren't saving enough to finance necessary investment in housing and new productive capacity. "Personal saving is an essential link to corporate capital formation," the Securities Industry Association told the Senate Finance Committee in May. "A low level of savings precludes a high level of capital investment and severely limits productivity gains."

To help make its case, the association compared the personal savings rate as a percentage of disposable income, the ratio of real investment to gross national product after inflation and 1979 gains in manufacturing productivity in six industrial countries. The result highlights how much the U.S. lags:

	Savings	Invest	Product
Japan	20.1%	23.5%	8.3%
France	15.6%	16.3%	5.4%
United Kingdom	15.1%	15.4%	2.2%
West Germany	14.5%	15.6%	5.2%
Italy	23.8%	14.4%	8.7%
U.S.	5.6%	10.9%	1.5%

Such comparisons, which raise concern about the U.S. ability to compete abroad and to maintain living standards at home, have generated support for new savings incentives.

directly with consumption for scarce factors of production. At full employment, a greater volume of investment is possible only if the rate of consumption is cut back. In other words, additional investment requires additional saving. Hence **supply-side economists favor tax incentives that encourage saving as well as greater tax incentives for investment.** This kind of perspective contrasts sharply with the Keynesian emphasis on stimulating consumption.

In the last few years Congress has greatly increased the incentives for saving. First, banks were permitted to increase the rate of interest paid on various types of savings accounts. Second, the tax on earned interest was reduced. And finally, a new form of tax-free saving was created. Individual Retirement Accounts (IRAs) permit consumers to put $2,000 of their income away in a savings plan each year before any taxes are imposed. Consumers can thus reduce the tax rate on part of their income to zero simply by saving. Such incentives encourage more saving and less consumption. If Supply-Siders are right, such incentives also encourage investment and growth.

DEREGULATION

Taxes are not the only way the government alters supply decisions in factor and product markets. The government also intervenes directly in supply decisions by regulating employment and output behavior. In general, such regulations limit the flexibility of producers to respond to changes in demand. Government regulation also tends to raise production costs. The higher costs result not only from required changes in the production process but also from the expense of monitoring government regulations and filling out endless government forms. Murray Weidenbaum, first chairman of Reagan's Council of Economic Advisers, estimated that federal regulation added $126 billion to the cost of goods and services in 1980. These added costs of production shift the aggregate-supply curve to the

Multibillion-dollar price tag

If just the basic federal regulations were compiled into a book, a shelf 15 feet long would be needed to hold the 60,000 pages of fine print.

This year, the Government will spend 3.5 billion dollars for its regulatory programs—a 21 per cent increase over last year's total.

Federal departments and agencies send out over 9,800 forms and receive 556 million responses a year. To fill out these forms, businesses spend an estimated total of 20 billion dollars. The total annual cost of regulation for consumers? Official estimates range from 60 to 130 billion dollars. President Ford put the price at $2,000 per family.

For large companies, the cost of compliance is enormous. Du Pont estimates that it has to spend almost 5 million dollars a year to fill out Government reports. General Motors places the costs of meeting federal, State and local regulations at 2.2 billion dollars for the two years 1974 and 1975.

Businesses are not the only ones affected by federal rules. Colleges and universities also have to pay handsome sums to meet government requirements. The Southern Association of Colleges and Schools report that it costs some colleges 50 cents to administer every dollar they receive from the Government.

At the University of North Carolina at Greensboro, the computer center was tied up for six months trying to handle the rules laid down by the Department of Health, Education and Welfare.

The expense is just one annoyance. Another problem is conflicting rules from different agencies. The Environmental Protection Agency, for example, wants the steel industry to cover coke-oven hoods to prevent emissions from escaping. The Occupational Safety and Health Administration, on the other hand, opposes hood coverings because they would increase the concentration of coke-oven emissions inhaled by the workers.

left. The net result is to increase the rate of inflation and reduce the rate of output. Some of the ways the government regulates factor and product markets are noted below.

Regulation of factor markets

derived demand: The demand for labor and other factors of production results from (depends on) the demand for final goods and services produced by these factors.

MINIMUM WAGES Minimum-wage laws are one of the most familiar forms of factor-market regulation. The Fair Labor Standards Act of 1938 required employers to pay workers a minimum of 25 cents per hour. Over time, Congress has increased the coverage of that act and the minimum wage itself repeatedly. In 1983 the minimum wage was $3.35 per hour.

The goal of the minimum-wage law is to ensure workers a decent standard of living. But the law has other effects as well. By prohibiting employers from using lower-paid workers, it limits the ability of employers to hire additional workers. As a consequence the principle of **derived demand** cannot be exploited fully. Firms faced with increased demand for their products cannot hire labor below the minimum wage, so they must use more expensive labor and/or raise prices instead.

The minimum-wage law focuses on decisions in factor markets. The wage and employment decisions that result, however, affect product markets as well. With labor less available and more expensive, firms are not so able or willing to produce. Hence the minimum-wage law effectively shifts the aggregate-supply curve to the left, as in Figure 13.7.

OCCUPATIONAL HEALTH AND SAFETY Government regulation of factor markets extends beyond minimum-wage laws. The government also sets standards for workplace safety and health. The Occupational Safety and Health Administration (OSHA), for example, sets limits on the noise levels at work sites. OSHA's Noise Exposure Standard limits the average sound level to 90 decibels for eight hours, 92 decibels for six hours, 95 decibels for three hours, and so forth, up to a maximum of 115 decibels for 15 minutes or less. If noise levels exceed these limits the employer is required to adopt administrative or engineering controls to reduce the noise level. Personal protection of workers (e.g., earplugs or earmuffs), though much less costly, will suffice only if source controls are not feasible. All such regulations are intended to improve the welfare of workers. In the process, however, such regulations tend to raise the costs of production and inhibit supply responses.

Regulation of product markets

The government's regulation of factor markets tends to raise production costs and inhibit supply. The same is true of regulations imposed directly on product markets. A few examples illustrate the impact.

TRANSPORTATION COSTS   At the federal level, a variety of agencies regulates the output and prices of transportation services. For years the Civil Aeronautics Board (CAB) determined which routes airlines could fly and how much they could charge. The Interstate Commerce Commission (ICC) has had the same kind of power over trucking, interstate bus lines, and railroads. The routes, services, and prices for ships (in U.S. coastal waters and foreign commerce) have been established by the Federal Maritime Commission. In all these cases, the regulations have constrained the ability of producers to respond to increases in demand. Existing producers have not been able to increase output at will and new producers have been excluded from the market. Hence the rate of output has been kept too low and prices too high. In other words, the effect of route and rate regulation has been a leftward shift of the aggregate-supply curve. Some of the more absurd manifestations of this shift are described in the news story on the next page by a former governor of Arizona.

FOOD AND DRUG STANDARDS   The Food and Drug Administration (FDA) has a broad mandate to protect consumers from dangerous

FIGURE 13.7   LEFTWARD SHIFTS OF AGGREGATE SUPPLY

Leftward shifts of the aggregate-supply curve result from higher marginal tax rates, government regulation, structural bottlenecks, excessive wage and price demands, and other forces. All such shifts tend to worsen stagflation, by increasing both inflation and unemployment. Compare equilibrium points E_1 and E_2.

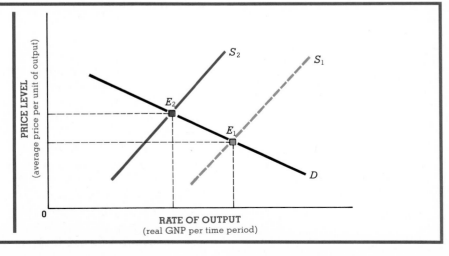

A regulatory ride in Arizona

In Arizona, as in many other states, bus and trucking companies are required to have public service certificates granting them monopolies on particular intrastate routes. The regulatory agency then maintains a rate-setting bureaucracy in order to prevent abuse of the monopoly power that the agency created in the first place.

These monopoly operating certificates are bought and sold for enormous sums at both the state and federal levels—one good measure of the added costs that this type of regulatory scheme imposes on the public. It is governmental regulation pure and simple that creates "value" for an otherwise worthless piece of paper and, in turn, artificially inflates the cost of transportation. For example, several years ago a Tucson firm acquired from the Arizona Corporation Commission a common-carrier certifi-

cate allowing it to operate heavy trucks and machinery. But the company never purchased so much as a single truck. It simply leased its certificate to another operator. At the end of the lease period, the certificate holder—still with absolutely no tangible holdings, goodwill, or operating history—sold its "assets" to yet another company for $150,000. All it really had to sell, of course, was that original state-granted monopoly, whose purchase price will be amortized (as was the lease) by higher rates to consumers. Unhappily, this Arizona experience is much the same as that at the federal level where, for example, one company holds certificates from the Interstate Commerce Commission (ICC) to operate in twenty-two states, although it owns no trucks and no terminals. The company leased all of its licenses to actual operators and skimmed $7.7 million off the top.

State-granted monopolies are so valuable that their holders—like all good monopolists—fight hard to keep them. Again, it is the public that suffers. An Arizona monopoly carrier

whose vans are specially equipped for serving the handicapped is actually suing one charitable organization for daring to provide free transportation to needy handicapped persons.

Moreover, monopoly privileges can lead to utterly absurd results. For example, riders who board one major company's buses in Phoenix can be carried *through* but not *to* Flagstaff. The buses stop there to pick up passengers headed out of state, but passengers boarding in Phoenix cannot be allowed to disembark because the company does not have service rights between Phoenix and Flagstaff. For a similar crazy reason, passengers cannot travel from Phoenix to Tucson on the buses of another major carrier, even though the buses stop in Tucson to discharge travelers from out of state. The innocent passenger confronting such no-no's is sometimes amused, often puzzled—and always frustrated.

From Bruce E. Babbitt, "The 'State' of Regulatory Reform," *Regulation*, September–October 1980.

products. In fulfilling this responsibility, the FDA sets health standards for the content of specific foods. A hot dog, for example, can be labeled as such only if it contains specific mixtures of skeletal meat, pig lips, snouts, and ears. By the same token, a milk-chocolate bar is a milk-chocolate bar, according to the FDA, only if it:

contains not less than 3.66 percent by weight of milk fat, not less than 12 percent by weight of milk solids, and not less than 10 percent by weight of chocolate liquor as calculated by subtracting from the weight of chocolate liquor used the weight of cacao fat therein and the weights therein of alkali and seasoning ingredients, if any, multiplying the remainder by 2.2, dividing the result by the weight of the finished milk chocolate, and multiplying the quotient by 100.

In addition, the FDA requires that chocolate bars must contain no more than 60 microscopic insect fragments (including rat feces) per 100 grams of chocolate. The FDA also sets standards for the testing of new drugs and evaluates the test results. In all three cases, the goal of regulation is to minimize health risks to consumers.

Like all regulation, however, the FDA standards entail real costs. The tests required for new drugs are very expensive and time-consuming. Getting a new drug approved for sale can take years of effort and require a huge investment. The net results are that (1) fewer new drugs are brought to market and (2) those that make it to the market are more expensive than they would be in the absence of regulation. In other words, the aggregate supply of goods is shifted to the left.

Other examples of government regulation are commonplace. The Environmental Protection Agency (EPA) regulates auto emissions, the discharges of industry, and water pollution. The U.S. Congress restricts foreign imports and raises their prices. The Federal Trade Commission (FTC) limits the freedom of firms to increase their output or advertise their products.

Deregulating

Many—perhaps most—of these regulatory activities are beneficial. In fact, all were originally designed to serve specific public purposes. As a result of such regulation, we do get safer drugs, cleaner air, and less deceptive advertising. We must also consider the costs involved, however. All regulatory activities impose direct and indirect costs. These costs must be compared to the benefits received. ***The basic contention of supply-side economists is that regulatory costs are now too high.*** To improve our economic performance, we must "deregulate" the production process, thereby shifting the aggregate-supply curve to the right again.

During the last few years, serious efforts to deregulate sectors of the private economy have taken place. As we noted in Chapter 11, the Monetary Control Act of 1980 permitted much greater flexibility in the prices and services offered by domestic banks. Before that the Securities and Exchange Commission had granted stockbrokers the same kind of flexibility. But the most noteworthy deregulation occurred in the airline industry. The accompanying story of World Airways' long-delayed first flight illustrates the high costs of airline regulation. The Airline Deregulation Act of 1978 put an end to such regulation as of 1983. The trucking and oil and gas industries have also been substantially deregulated in the last few years.[4]

[4] Deregulation of the oil and gas industry is discussed in Chapter 16.

THE DELAYED FLIGHT OF WORLD AIRWAYS: A LESSON IN REGULATION

For decades the Civil Aeronautics Board (CAB) regulated all airline service and fares between California and the East Coast. Only three major airlines were permitted to fly these transcontinental routes, and their fares were quite high. In 1967 World Airways asked the CAB for permission to fly these routes. World Airways wanted to offer transcontinental flights for only $75 one way, less than half the lowest fare then being charged. World figured the lower fares would greatly increase passenger traffic and bring in substantial profits.

For 11 years the CAB continued to deny World Airways the necessary route approval. During all this time, transcontinental air fares were kept artificially high and the rate of air-transport "output" was kept unnecessarily low. Finally, in September 1978, the CAB relented and gave World Airways permission to introduce a few low-priced transcontinental flights (at off-hours and secondary airports!). Other airlines quickly followed suit, and air fares plummeted while passenger traffic increased greatly. Shortly thereafter, President Carter signed the Airline Deregulation Act, which set a time limit on the CAB's authority. The CAB's route controls were eliminated in 1982 and its control of prices was abolished in 1983. The CAB itself is scheduled for elimination in 1985.

ELIMINATING STRUCTURAL BOTTLENECKS

It is tempting to blame the government for all of our stagflation problems. And most Americans apparently do. A 1980 Gallup survey asked people who was to blame for our continuing inflation. Eighty-four percent of the respondents singled out the government, either by itself (33 percent) or in conjunction with business, labor, and consumers (51 percent).

This tendency to blame the government for all our stagflation problems not only is unfair, but also focuses all our attention on tax rates and deregulation. There are other supply-side causes of stagflation and other policy options as well.

Structural unemployment

Another major cause of stagflation originates in a mismatch between available workers and the requirements of production. When aggregate demand ($M \times V$) increases, we want output (Q) to increase, not prices (P). For this to happen, the required factors of production must be available at the right time and place. If they are not, we will not be able to increase output (Q) as we desire, but will instead end up watching prices (P) rise.

A decision to stimulate aggregate demand is usually prompted by excessive unemployment, so it seems reasonable to assume that labor will be available. But we can't be sure that the right kind of labor will be available at the right price (wage rate), or that it will be in the locations where it is needed. Recall our earlier discussion of structural unemployment (Chapter 5). The essential message of **structural unemployment** is that the workers we demand may not be there when we need them. If they are not, output (Q) cannot expand; instead, prices will rise as demand increases.

Table 13.1 provides some evidence on structural unemployment. The aggregate rate of unemployment of 8.5 percent that prevailed in early 1982 was not representative of all workers. Unemployed managers, administrators, and technicians were very hard to find. Nonfarm laborers were readily available, however, and even

structural unemployment: Unemployment caused by a mismatch between the skills (or location) of job seekers and the requirements (or location) of available jobs.

TABLE 13.1 UNEMPLOYMENT RATES BY OCCUPATION

Unemployment rates vary markedly across occupations. As a result, a shortage of more skilled workers (e.g., professional and technical workers) may emerge long before other occupational groups are fully employed.

Occupational category	Unemployment rate (percent)
Professional and technical	2.9
Managers and administrators	2.7
Sales workers	4.5
Clerical workers	6.3
Craftsmen	9.0
Operatives	15.4
Nonfarm laborers	16.9
Service workers	9.2
Farmers and farm workers	6.9
All occupations	8.5

Source: *Monthly Labor Review*, March 1982 (January rates, seasonally adjusted).

operators (people who operate production machinery) and service workers were not hard to locate. Unemployment also varied greatly across industries. Unemployment in the auto, construction, and lumber industries approached the level of the Great Depression in 1981–82. At the same time, relatively few people were unemployed in the office-machines industry, financial services, or even government. Accordingly, some groups were in a position to secure wage increases while other groups remained unemployed.

Experience is also an important determinant of employability. The more experience a worker has had, the higher his or her productivity is likely to be. Hence employers will prefer such workers. This preference is often expressed in terms of age, particularly in a reluctance to hire teenagers and other younger workers. Once again, the impact of this barrier is evident in unemployment statistics. In early 1982 the unemployment rate for teenagers was over 22 percent, nearly three times higher than for the rest of the **labor force.** Had employers been more willing and able to fill their job vacancies with younger workers, more employment might have been attained with less inflation than actually occurred. During the 1970s a far greater proportion of women also began entering the labor force, many with little job experience. They too, contributed to structural unemployment.

As a result, it became more difficult to reach full employment before prices started to rise. In other words, ***the aggregate-supply curve shifted to the left as the labor force became less skilled.***

labor force: All persons over age 16 who are either working for pay or actively seeking paid employment.

EMPLOYMENT AND TRAINING   Two possibilities for overcoming structural unemployment problems are fairly obvious. First, the government could provide or encourage training for those unemployed people whose skills fail to match available job openings. Such training would reduce the mismatch of skills and job openings that characterizes structural unemployment and would thus speed the flow of unemployed workers into jobs.

Training takes time, however, and does not guarantee a job. For this reason, it is often desirable to attack structural unemployment from the other side of the mismatch as well. Public policy can just as readily focus on job openings as on the skills of the unemployed. We may find that the fastest way to put unemployed people to work is to hire them for newly created jobs, either in the public sector or in subsidized private employment.

JOB-SEARCH ASSISTANCE   Another component of public labor-market policy concentrates on bringing job seekers and jobs together more efficiently. Want ads in the newspapers list only a fraction of all potential job openings. As a consequence, people with the required skills may remain unemployed simply because they don't know about available jobs. They don't find jobs because they don't know where to look.

The most important public agency for bringing employers and job seekers together is the U.S. Employment Service, more commonly referred to as the "state unemployment office," because it also has the responsibility for disbursing unemployment-insurance checks. The Employment Service acts as a clearinghouse for job vacancies and job seekers, conveying information from one to the other. The government can also provide less direct job-search assistance. Tax credits for job relocation and other job-search expenses reduce the costs of finding and accepting new jobs, and so speed up the matching of job seekers with jobs.

Discrimination

Lack of skills and experience are not the only reason it's sometimes hard to find the "right" workers. The mismatch between unemployed workers and jobs is often a matter less of skills than of race, sex, or age. In other words, discrimination can create an artificial barrier between job seekers and available job openings. Employers (and unions) who are convinced that women, blacks, or other minority groups are inherently less capable are unlikely to look at these groups when job vacancies occur. As a consequence, they are likely to overlook many qualified workers. In overlooking such workers, producers create an artificial shortage of skilled labor and push production costs up.[5] The consequences are by now predictable—a leftward shift of the aggregate-supply curve.

EQUAL OPPORTUNITY PROGRAMS If discrimination tends to shift the aggregate-supply curve leftward, then reducing discriminatory barriers should shift it to the right. Equal opportunity programs are thus a natural extension of a supply-side approach to macro policy. However, Supply-Siders are also quick to point out the risks inherent in government regulation of hiring decisions. From a supply-side perspective, laws that forbid discrimination are welcome and should be enforced. But aggressive "affirmative action" programs that require employers to hire specific numbers of women or minority workers limit productive capabilities and can lead to excessive costs.

WAGE-PRICE CONTROLS

Suppose the supply side of the economy contained no structural bottlenecks, was unfettered by government regulations, and confronted low marginal tax rates. In such a supply-side utopia, producers could respond quickly and fully to increases in aggregate demand. But what assurance do we have that they would? *Producers might find it more profitable to raise prices rather than output when aggregate demand increased. Likewise, workers might respond to increased demand by increasing wages rather than employment.* In either case, we could end up with more inflation rather than more output when demand increases.

Profit-push inflation

The option of increasing prices rather than output when demand increases looks very tempting. If production costs don't rise, higher prices imply more profits for any given rate of production. Surely

[5] A longer discussion of the nature and impact of discrimination is provided in Chapter 32.

profit-push inflation: An increase in the price level initiated by attempts of producers to raise profit margins.

there are more than a few producers who would want to increase their profits in this way. By demanding higher prices and profits for a given rate of output, however, they would shift the aggregate-supply curve to the left. This process is referred to as **profit-push inflation.**

MARKET POWER As tempting as profit-push inflation might look, not all producers can do it. The extent to which a producer can increase prices and profits unilaterally depends on the amount of market power he possesses. The essence of **market power** is the ability to change market prices without suffering a substantial decline in unit sales. Individual fishermen, for example, seldom have the power to change the market price of fish: they have no market power. General Motors, however, can directly alter the price at which Chevrolets are sold: GM has market power. In this case, market power exists because GM produces over half of the cars made in the United States. As a result, GM can exercise significant control over the market-supply curve (and therewith the market price). By contrast, our lone fisherman accounts for a tiny fraction of all the fish brought to market and has no significant control over the market supply curve.[6]

market power: The ability to alter the market price of a good or service.

Producers who have significant market power are in a unique position to determine whether P or Q responds to an increase in aggregate demand. Should those producers decide to increase their prices and profit margins, they will contribute to inflation while slowing progress toward full employment. In other words, the exercise of market power can cause stagflation.

The potential of market power to aggravate a stagflation problem is equally apparent when the government is trying to close an inflationary gap. The objective of restrictive fiscal and monetary policies is to reduce the rate of inflation (changes in P) while maintaining output (Q). But it is producers who must ultimately decide to cut back on P or Q. Should producers decide to cut back output rather than prices, we could end up with both high unemployment and high inflation, that is, stagflation.

Inflationary wage demands

Profit-push is not, of course, the source of all price increases, even in a supply-side utopia. We must take care to avoid what Reuben Kessel of the University of Chicago calls "the simplicity of an old Western," in which the bad guys (the big corporations) are responsible for all price increases.[7] Prices may go up simply because costs have risen. If producers are to maintain (not increase) their profit margins, they must raise product prices when the costs of production increase. In these cases, however, it is a change in costs, not profit margins, that fuels **cost-push inflation.**

cost-push inflation: An increase in the price level initiated by an increase in the cost of production.

Costs may be forced up by any number of events. A drought in the Midwest, for example, can sharply reduce agricultural output (Q) and drive up prices (P), thereby contributing to stagflation. Like-

---

[6] The nature and use of market power is discussed at much greater length in Chapters 21—24.
[7] Reuben A. Kessel, "Inflation and Controls," *American Economic Review,* September 1972, p. 528.

TABLE 13.2 PRODUCTIVITY, WAGES, AND PROFITS

While profits increase most when wage rates do not rise, profits also increase when wages rise in line with productivity improvements. In fact, when wage increases equal to productivity improvements are allowed, both wages and profits rise by the same percentage (without price increases). In this sense, stable prices and productivity-based wage-rate increases fix the income shares of capital and labor.

Suppose we are producing 50 art posters and selling them for $2 each. Our revenues and costs initially consist of:

A. Gross revenues:

50 posters @ $2.00 each =		$100.00
Costs:		
Labor: 10 labor-hours @ $6.00 an hour		
or $1.20 per poster=	$60	
Materials: $0.40 per poster × 50 =	$20	— 80.00
Profits:		$ 20.00

Owing to increased experience, our artists become more productive and can now turn out 20 percent more posters; that is, *productivity* increases by 20 percent. If we did *not* increase wage rates, profits would become:

B. Gross revenues:

60 posters @ $2.00 each =		$120.00
Costs:		
Labor: 10 labor-hours @ $6.00 an hour		
or $1.00 per poster =	$60	
Materials: $0.40 per poster × 60 =	$24	— 84.00
Profits:		$ 36.00

On the other hand, if we increase wage rates in line with productivity improvements—that is, by 20 percent, from $6.00 to $7.20 an hour—profits would be:

C. Gross revenues:

60 posters @ $2.00 each =		$120.00
Costs:		
Labor: 10 labor-hours @ $7.20 an hour		
or $1.20 per poster =	$72	
Materials: $0.40 per poster × 60 =	$24	— 96.00
Profits:		$ 24.00

wise, a decision by foreign oil producers (who have market power) to cut off oil supplies can curtail domestic production and set off an inflationary spiral at the same time. These kinds of events, which suddenly and unexpectedly reduce aggregate supply, played major roles in the stagflations of the 1970s.[8]

LABOR COSTS Costs may also go up because workers demand and receive wage increases. The labor cost of producing a product depends on two things: the wage rate paid and the worker's productivity—**labor productivity.**

Not all wage increases are inflationary. On the contrary, ***only wage increases that exceed productivity improvements are truly inflationary.*** When wages increase faster than output per hour, **unit labor costs** rise. As unit labor costs go up, producers respond by increasing prices, and a cost-push inflation is under way.

The relationship between wage rates, productivity, and unit labor cost is illustrated in Table 13.2. If workers become more productive—produce more output per hour—and wage rates are unchanged, unit labor costs will fall. The employer ends up getting

labor productivity: Amount of output produced by a worker in a given period of time; output per hour (or day, etc.).

unit labor cost: Hourly wage rate divided by output per labor-hour.

[8] The impact of the oil crisis on output and prices is discussed in Chapter 16.

more output for the same wage. Such a drop in unit labor costs would enhance profits, of course, and be welcomed by an employer. The important point here, though, is that wage increases equal to productivity gains simply maintain unit labor costs; they do not increase them. Such wage increases do not cut into profits or contribute to cost-push inflation. Indeed, were wages to keep pace with productivity improvements, both employers and workers would benefit (by the same percentage) from productivity advances (see Table 13.2).

LABOR UNIONS One force that might drive wage rates up faster than productivity gains is labor unions. To the extent that a labor union controls the supply of a particular type of labor (bricklayers, say, or firefighters), it has power in that labor market. With such market power, a union can push market wage rates up, just as corporations with market power can push up product prices. Indeed, a major objective of labor unions is to increase the wage rates of their members (see Chapter 27).

Limits on wages and prices

wage-price controls: Direct governmental restraints on the wage and price decisions of market participants.

To the extent that powerful producers and unions can shift the aggregate-supply curve to the left, they aggravate our stagflation problems. For this reason, many economists have advocated explicit limits on wage and price increases. The essence of **wage-price controls** is some form of direct governmental restraint on the wage and price decisions of market participants.

The wage-price "guideposts" issued by President John F. Kennedy in 1961 illustrate one form of wage-price controls. When Kennedy assumed office, the unemployment rate was 6.6 percent and rising. Kennedy had vowed to get the country "moving again," and wanted to lower the rate of unemployment. But he feared that the rate of inflation would increase if he stimulated aggregate demand. Accordingly, he started down the road to wage-price controls in 1961 by writing a letter to the heads of the 12 largest steel corporations. He advised them that "steel is a bellwether as well as a major element in industrial costs. A rise in steel prices would force price

"I blame government, labor, business, and my ex-wife."

Drawing by C. Barsotti; © 1978 The New Yorker Magazine, Inc.

increases in many industries and invite price increases in others." In the light of these facts, the president underscored "the urgency of preventing inflationary movements." He suggested that price restraint on the part of the steel companies would strengthen their "moral position" in collective bargaining and the industry's "claim to the support of public opinion." To ensure that price restraint on the part of the steel companies would not be compromised by cost pressures, the president addressed a similar letter to the United Steelworkers of America in October 1961. He urged restraint in wage demands so as to achieve "a labor settlement within the limits of advances in productivity and price stability." The message was loud and clear. The president had taken an active interest in wage and price determination and was prepared to intervene if necessary to maintain stable prices.

THE KENNEDY GUIDEPOSTS Early in 1962, the Council of Economic Advisers explained in greater detail what the president regarded as "appropriate" price and wage behavior. In general, the council argued, wage rates should not rise faster than productivity improvements. If output per labor-hour increased by 3.2 percent—as it had been doing over the preceding five years—wage rates could also increase by 3.2 percent without fueling inflation. The reasoning was identical to that which we employed earlier. If wages increased no faster than productivity, unit labor costs would not rise and there would be no cost-push pressure on prices.

Although the president suggested that average productivity gains for the economy as a whole serve as "guideposts" for wage increases in particular industries,[9] he had no explicit means to enforce their use. He noted that "the Nation must rely on the good sense and public spirit of our business and labor leaders to hold the line on the price level."

JAWBONING President Lyndon Johnson continued to enunciate the wage and price guideposts, perhaps even more vigorously than his predecessor. The combination of rapidly expanding aggregate demand and relatively low unemployment in the Johnson years constituted a serious threat to price stability. Nevertheless, President Johnson felt that full employment and price stability could be maintained simultaneously if only big business and big labor would cooperate with the administration. Accordingly, the Johnson administration offered an increasing quantity of advice on prices and wages. The art of "jawboning" was perfected as the president "reasoned together" with business and labor leaders and suggested "acceptable" wage and price decisions.

THE NIXON FREEZE The Nixon administration introduced more explicit controls on wage and price behavior. In 1971 President Rich-

---

[9] There is great variation among firms and industries in their respective productivity improvements, of course. Thus a firm with a higher-than-average rate of productivity improvement would reap substantial profit if it were obliged to increase wages by no more than the national average rate of productivity advance. To limit such possibilities, President Kennedy requested that such firms *lower* their product prices. Few firms heeded that request, however.

ard Nixon proclaimed a general wage and price freeze—a prohibition of *any* wage or price increases. The freeze lasted 90 days and was succeeded by a comprehensive set of wage and price controls.

A unique feature of the Nixon wage-price program was its explicit recognition of market power. Rather than trying to police millions of individual firms, the administration classified all businesses and labor unions in three tiers, on the basis of size. The 1,500 largest firms were watched most closely and were required to get prior approval for any price increase. They were also required to submit quarterly price, cost, and profit reports.

THE CARTER WAGE-PRICE STANDARDS President Gerald Ford did not ask Congress to renew the power to impose wage-price controls, and President Jimmy Carter likewise disavowed their use. Instead, President Carter outlined a voluntary wage and price program designed to slow the rate of inflation. According to these guideposts, wage rates (including fringe benefits) should not rise by more than 7 percent per year and prices should not increase by more than 5.75 percent.[10] In explaining these standards, the president noted the need for collective action. When wages and prices are rising rapidly, no single individual or group can risk the loss of real income implied by a more modest wage or price demand. "It is like a crowd standing at a football stadium," he noted. "No one is willing to be the first one to sit down" and miss the action.

Do controls work?

In view of the varied and repeated experiences we have had with wage-price controls, it seems fair to ask whether or not they have been effective. Is there any evidence that wage-price controls have improved the inflation-unemployment trade-off? The answer is a clear and resounding "Maybe."

Assessment of the impact of wage and price controls is difficult. It requires us to compare actual wage and price behavior with the behavior that would have occurred in the absence of controls. We know, for example, that the price level rose hardly at all during Nixon's wage-price freeze. We also know that the price level increased by less than 3 percent during the subsequent period of controls. Since we don't know how fast prices would have risen during the period without controls, however, we can't be sure how effective the controls were in *reducing* the rate of inflation. We do know, though, that prices increased more rapidly (by over 5 percent) right after controls were eliminated. Hence it is possible that controls only *postponed* price increases rather than prevented them.

We should not conclude that wage-price controls have been ineffective in reducing inflation; all we are saying is that their effectiveness is difficult to measure. In fact, most economists who have tried to measure the effectiveness of wage and price controls have concluded that controls were at least somewhat successful in reducing the rate of inflation.

[10] The actual price guidelines asked firms to "decelerate" the rate of inflation by limiting price increases to one-half of a percentage point below the firm's average annual rate of price increase during 1976–77. On average, this increase would have amounted to 5.75 percent.

Wage-Price Panel Concludes Guidelines Were a 'Dismal Failure' but Helped a Bit

WASHINGTON—The Carter administration issued a humble post-mortem on its two-year experiment with wage and price guidelines.

The Council on Wage and Price Stability, which administered the program, said in a final evaluation that the guidelines were largely overwhelmed by events and thus appeared to be a "dismal failure" at controlling the blistering inflation of the past two years. Still, the council argued, the program "merits some commendation for preventing a bad situation from becoming even worse."

The council noted, however, that the guidelines created one economic distortion that may diminish whatever success was achieved. The guidelines, it said, enabled workers with cost-of-living-adjustment clauses in their labor contracts to realize significantly greater gains than workers without such inflation pro-

tection. As a result, the council warned, there may be a round of catch-up wage increases by workers without such clauses that may partly offset the small anti-inflation gains made during the two years of the guideline program.

The council's evaluation appears to be the agency's last crack at the history books. President-elect Ronald Reagan has scoffed at incomes policies such as the guidelines program, and he has promised to abolish the council on the first day of his presidency.

The guidelines set overall limits for wage and price increases beginning in October 1978. There were various alternative rules and exceptions, however, for companies with "uncontrollable" cost increases. The guidelines were "voluntary," although the administration threatened to deny violators the right to bid on government contracts. During the two years of the program, though, no company was denied a contract because it exceeded the guidelines.

The council said the guidelines suffered from the onset because during the past two years the economy proved to be stronger than expected. The guidelines were designed, according to the council, to complement restrained fiscal and monetary policies that would keep markets slack to

reduce upward price pressures. Instead, there was a "world-wide boom" until 1980 that produced "excess aggregate demand and a worldwide surge in commodity prices," the council said.

The council concluded that "the environment in which the (guidelines) program was intended to work never existed, and the job the program was called upon to do was one it was never intended to perform."

The council estimates that wage and price inflation each were reduced an average of one or 1.5 percentage points during the two years of the program as a result of the guidelines.

The council estimated that companies had to spend $300 million to comply with the program, compared with a negligible $10 million cost to the government. The council argued that the expense was worth it, however, because trying to achieve a similar one percentage point reduction in inflation through tight fiscal and monetary policy would have required raising the unemployment rate one percentage point, thus reducing the nation's economic output by 2%, or $47 billion.

—Christopher Conte

THE COSTS OF CONTROLS Those who regard wage-price controls as failures are less concerned with their impact on the rate of inflation than with their impact on market efficiency. Indeed, many economists argue that the apparent effectiveness of wage-price controls is proof of their failure! Because such controls—"voluntary" or mandated—suspend normal market functioning to some degree, they tend to distort resource allocation over time. Market prices, it will be recalled, operate as signals to direct product distribution and resource allocation. If demand shifts from product X to product Y, the resulting increase in Y's relative price constitutes a signal and incentive for resources to move in the same direction. Changes in wage rates (the price of labor) perform the same function, motivating workers to enter industries or companies that offer higher relative wages. The changing structure of (relative) prices is thus a basic motivating force in a market economy and a primary determinant of general economic efficiency.

Wage-price controls constitute a threat to economic efficiency to the extent that they constrain movements in relative prices. A general price freeze freezes not only the *level* of prices but the *structure* of prices as well. If demand were to shift from product X to product Y during a price freeze, prices would not be allowed to emit the required signals to producers and workers. Although the mix of output might still respond to changes in demand, the response would be less certain and less timely. These kinds of inefficiencies grow in importance the longer wage-price controls are continued and the more broadly and severely they are applied. Such inefficiencies have the effect of shifting the aggregate-supply curve in the wrong direction.

POLICY IMPLICATIONS: A TWO-FISTED BATTLE AGAINST STAGFLATION

Stagflation has been the most vexing macro problem of the last ten years or so. That experience has taught us the futility of trying to beat stagflation with demand-side policies alone. By focusing exclusively on only one side of the market, we have effectively tied one hand behind our backs. That handicap has not left us helpless, but it has turned out to be costly. The basic implication of supply-side economics is that we would fare much better if we attacked stagflation from *both* sides of the marketplace—demand *and* supply.

The costs of demand-side dependence

The costs of fighting stagflation with demand-side policies alone are illustrated by the Phillips curve. Basically, such policies encourage a trade-off between unemployment and inflation. To reduce inflation, for example, restrictive monetary and fiscal policies discourage aggregate demand. But those same policies tend to increase unemployment.

The costs of this demand-side dependence can be high. In 1979 the Congressional Budget Office (CBO) evaluated the prospects for reducing the rate of inflation in the 1980s with restrictive monetary and fiscal policies. The CBO assumed a goal of 4 percent inflation, to be reached in 1984. To reach this goal, the CBO figured the unemployment rate would have to stay up around 7 percent for five years. This persistently high rate of unemployment would reduce GNP in 1984 by roughly $250 billion. That works out to roughly $1,000 less GNP per person. The cost of fighting inflation would not be distributed equally, of course. Much of the impact would fall on the additional 1.5 million workers who would be without jobs in 1984 as a result of reduced output.[11]

Supply-side options improve the trade-off

It should be apparent from our review of supply-side options that we need not pay such a high cost to control inflation. To the extent that demand-side policies cannot cope with stagflation, we may employ supply-side policies that directly influence prices and output. This does not mean that full employment and price stability are assured,

[11] A more recent study computed the cumulative costs of fighting inflation in terms of one year's output. The conclusion: that the restrictive demand policies required to reduce the long-run inflation rate by 5 percent would cost the equivalent of 29 percent of a year's GNP. See Robert J. Gordon and Stephen R. King, "The Output Cost of Disinflation in Traditional Vector Autoregressive Models," *The Brookings Papers on Economic Activity* 1 (1982).

only that no particular combination of inflation and unemployment is inevitable. We have observed that policy makers have a variety of options for improving our economic performance, and thus for shifting the Phillips curve to the left. Indeed, some observers have suggested that policy mistakes in the 1970s confirm this conclusion—policy choices helped shift the Phillips curve to the right! Our challenge now is to improve on previous performance, and shift the Phillips curve to the left again. The specific supply-side initiatives of the Reagan administration are reviewed in Chapter 15.

SUMMARY

▪ Fiscal and monetary policies seek to attain full employment and price stability by altering the level of aggregate demand. Their success, however, depends on microeconomic responses, as reflected in the price and output decisions of market participants.

▪ The market's response to shifts in demand are reflected in the shape and position of the aggregate-supply curve. If the curve slopes upward, a trade-off between unemployment and inflation exists. This trade-off is illustrated by the Phillips curve.

▪ If the aggregate-supply curve shifts to the left, the trade-off between unemployment and inflation worsens. Stagflation—a combination of substantial inflation and unemployment—results. This is illustrated by rightward shifts of the Phillips curve.

▪ Supply-side policies attempt to alter price and output decisions directly. If successful, they will shift the aggregate-supply curve to the right. Such a shift implies less inflation *and* less unemployment.

▪ Marginal tax rates are a major concern of supply-side economists. High tax rates discourage extra work, investment, and saving. A reduction in marginal tax rates should shift aggregate supply to the right.

▪ Deregulation is intended to reduce costly restrictions on price and output behavior. Again the goal is to shift aggregate supply to the right.

▪ Structural bottlenecks also contribute to sluggish and costly output responses. To alleviate such bottlenecks, the government can facilitate training, job search, and more equal opportunity in labor markets.

▪ Wage-price controls represent an attempt to limit inflationary abuses of market power. Large firms and unions often have considerable discretion to raise wages and prices. Wage-price controls are often viewed as a mechanism for limiting such supply decisions. Controls also foster inefficiency, however, by constraining relative prices.

Terms to remember | Define the following terms:

supply   derived demand
equation of exchange   structural unemployment
stagflation   labor force
Phillips curve   profit-push inflation
aggregate supply   market power
natural rate of unemployment   cost-push inflation
marginal tax rate   labor productivity
investment   unit labor cost
tax rebate   wage-price controls
saving

Questions for discussion

1. What were the rates of unemployment and inflation last year? Where would they lie on Figure 13.2? Can you explain the implied shift from curve PC_4?

2. If you were suddenly to start earning $20,000 per year, how much of that income would you have to pay in taxes? Include not only federal income taxes but social security and any state and local taxes as well. At what tax rate would you stop working?

3. Can you give specific examples of government regulations that significantly increase production costs?

4. What has happened to prices and output in industries that have been deregulated (e.g., stockbrokers, banks, airlines, oil and gas, trucking)?

5. How can job vacancies exist when people are unemployed (that is, looking for work)? What forces in the labor market contribute to this apparent inconsistency?

Problem

The following table depicts the rate of output people would be willing and able to produce at different price levels, under different tax structures. The first, Tax System A, imposes high marginal tax rates on work and investment. Tax System B imposes low marginal tax rates. Graph the relevant aggregate-supply curves and explain the difference between them.

Price level	100	110	120	130	140	150	160
Rate of output							
Tax System A	100	125	150	175	200	225	250
Tax System B	120	150	180	210	240	270	300

CURRENT
POLICIES

CHAPTER 14
THEORY
AND
REALITY

In his 1978 Economic Report, President Jimmy Carter hinted at some of the frustrations of formulating economic policy:

> We cannot concentrate just on inflation, or just on unemployment or just on deficits in the Federal budget or our international payments. Nor can we act in isolation from other countries. We must deal with all of these problems simultaneously and on a worldwide basis.

As if the burdens of a continuously changing world were not enough, the president must also contend with sharply differing economic theories and advice, a slow and frequently belligerent Congress, a massive and often unresponsive bureaucracy, and a wholesale lack of knowledge about future economic events. In view of these obstacles, it is not too surprising that Professor Paul McCracken has concluded that with few exceptions, "economic policy has been a loser politically for the nation's leader."[1] President Carter's own reelection hopes were dealt a crushing blow by the 1980 recession and continuing high rates of inflation.

The purpose of this chapter is to confront the discrepancies between economic theory and economic performance. The economic theories reviewed in Chapters 7 through 13 provide an impressive collection of policy tools. Taken together, those policy tools seem capable of making any necessary repairs to the economy. While there might be some disagreements about which tool to use in any

[1]Paul W. McCracken, "The Risk of Making Policies in a Stampede," *Wall Street Journal*, October 22, 1981, p. 26.

specific situation, a little experimentation should quickly get the economy functioning well again.

Unfortunately, these expectations have not been fulfilled. Our economic performance has not been as good as our economic theory. Something is wrong. Our experience with unemployment and inflation suggests that either our theories are not as good as they appear or they are difficult to implement. Accordingly, a major purpose of this chapter is to identify real-world constraints on policy design and implementation. In so doing, we may be able to answer the question asked by many people: "If economists are so smart, why is the economy always in such a mess?" As you might expect, economists put most of the blame on the real world, not on their theories.

POLICY TOOLS

The economic policy tools available to the president and Congress are summarized in Table 14.1. Although the list is brief, we hardly need a reminder at this point of how powerful each instrument can be. Every one of these major policy instruments can significantly alter the dimensions of the economy. Their use not only may alter inflation and unemployment rates, but also may change our answers to the basic economic questions of WHAT to produce, HOW, and FOR WHOM.

A change in Federal Reserve requirements, while it is likely to go unnoticed by most people, illustrates the potential of this list. A reduction of half a percentage point in reserve requirements can significantly affect employment (by stimulating demand), the mix of output (by encouraging housing), and the level and distribution of income (in both ways). It can also affect price stability (by increasing spending) and growth (by altering the level and content of output).

Tax cuts, a staple of both fiscal and supply-side policies, may have similarly broad impact. The across-the-board tax cuts of 1981 and 1982 stimulated demand, increased the incentives for work and production, shifted resources from the public to the private sector, altered production processes, and redistributed income.

The desired synthesis

opportunity costs: The most desired goods or services that are forgone in order to obtain something else.

Although the tools listed in Table 14.1 are powerful, they cannot fulfill all our wishes. Since we still live in a world of scarce resources, all policy decisions will entail **opportunity costs.** In everyday language, this means that we will always be confronted with trade-offs. The *best* we can hope for is a set of compromises that yields *optimal* outcomes, not ideal ones. This means getting as much collective satisfaction as possible from our available resources.

In principle, we can achieve optimal outcomes by pulling the right set of policy levers. Suppose, for example, that we want to reduce unemployment, increase investment (for growth), and redistribute more income to the poor. Several policy options are available to help us achieve this set of goals. We could use monetary policy to expand the money supply and to lower interest rates (thus encourag-

TABLE 14.1 THE POLICY ARSENAL	Type of policy	Policy instruments
Economic policy makers have access to a variety of policy instruments. The challenge is to choose the right tools at the right time. The mix of tools required may vary from problem to problem.	Fiscal	Changes in government spending
		Tax cuts and increases
	Monetary	Open-market operations
		Reserve requirements
		Discount rates
	Supply-side	Tax incentives
		Deregulation
		Skill training and other labor-market aid
		Wage-price controls

ing investment and employment). We could use fiscal policy to provide tax incentives for hiring low-income workers (to ensure that they get some of the newly created jobs). We could buttress these actions by using government purchasing powers to expand demand for the goods and services that can be produced in areas or industries most accessible to the poor and unemployed. Such a combination, or *synthesis,* of policy tools would very likely produce the desired results. The number of possible policy combinations available to achieve these goals approaches infinity.

In practice, the desired synthesis does not come so easily. To begin with, there are usually profound disagreements about the underlying goals of economic policy. Moreover, many people and institutions formulate policy decisions. This fragmented approach can produce absurd results. As we observed in earlier chapters, if the president thinks only of full employment, he may strive to increase aggregate demand by cutting taxes or expanding government purchases. At the same time, the Federal Reserve Board may be seeking to restrain demand by reducing the money supply and raising interest rates because it is thinking only of price stability. The outcome of these contradictory policies will probably not satisfy anyone, and will leave both goals unfulfilled. That is not to say that fiscal and monetary authorities are always in conflict, only that single-mindedness with respect to any goal can frustrate policy intentions. The policy synthesis required to fulfill our economic goals requires:

□ Consensus on economic goals
□ Coordinated and timely policy initiatives

The challenge of economic policy is to devise and implement that synthesis.

IDEALIZED USES

To see how a policy synthesis might work, we may consider three distinct macroeconomic problems.

Case 1: depression or serious recession When output and employment levels are seriously short of the economy's full-employment potential, the mandate for public policy is clear. Aggregate demand must be expanded and the recessionary gap closed. At such times the most urgent need is to put people to work, and relatively little concern is expressed for other, possibly conflicting economic goals.

We have already discussed a variety of ways to stimulate aggregate demand, including tax cuts, increases in government spending, increases in the money supply, and even improved consumer and investor confidence. It is important to emphasize at this juncture that all of these actions can be taken simultaneously. To give the economy a really powerful stimulus, we might want to cut taxes, increase government expenditure, and expand the money supply all at the same time. By taking such convincing action, we might also increase consumer confidence, raise investor expectations, and induce still greater spending and output.

The demand-stimulating actions we take to push the economy out of a slump can also help fulfill our other economic goals. If we want the full-employment economy we are striving for to reflect an improved distribution of income or a different mix of output, we can choose fiscal, monetary, and supply-side actions more selectively. We could, for example, stimulate consumer spending either by eliminating federal excise (sales) taxes on alcoholic beverages or by cutting payroll (social security) taxes. In the former case, we would probably end up having a lot more fun, but the latter kind of stimulus is more likely to promote a mix of output that is both healthier and more productive. Recall also the choice we confront between stimulating the private sector and expanding public employment and output.

The policy choices are never easy, but they must be made, deliberately or by default. The range of possible policies and outcomes is limited only by our imaginations and the amount of effort we want to devote to policy design and implementation.

Case 2: excessive demand and inflation

An overheated economy provides as clear a mandate to public policy as does a sluggish one. In this case, the task of policy is to restrain aggregate demand until the rate of total expenditure is compatible with the productive capacity of the economy. Here again the major thrust of required policy is clear. On the one hand, reductions in the money supply will help to reduce the amount of purchasing power available and discourage borrowing. On the other hand, reductions in government spending and increases in tax rates will directly diminish expenditure levels. We might also want to provide increased tax incentives for saving. Together these actions will serve to restrain demand, close the inflationary gap, and restore price stability. In the past these actions have also been reinforced with wage-price control programs designed to quell inflationary expectations. Such controls could play no more than a supporting role in this context, however. The basic imbalance between the rate of spending and the rate of full-employment output requires more fundamental correction.

In restraining aggregate demand, the government also influences other dimensions of our economic welfare. Cutbacks in government spending shrink the size of the public sector, while tax increases tend to have the opposite effect; either action will cut aggregate demand. Likewise, the government may choose to raise everyone's taxes equally, thus maintaining the current distribution of income. Or it might choose to increase taxes on the rich only, making the distribution of income more equal. Here again, the essential message is that *any* action taken to alter the rate of total spending will influence other economic outcomes as well.

Case 3: stagflation

Although serious inflations and depressions provide very clear mandates for economic policy, simultaneous inflation and unemployment complicate policy decisions. If aggregate demand were stimulated to reduce unemployment, the resultant pressure on prices might fuel the existing inflation. And if fiscal and monetary restraints were introduced to alleviate inflationary pressures, the unemployment problem might worsen. In such a situation—the most familiar one for modern economies—the achievement of our economic goals requires considerably more finesse, and no simple solutions can be given. More often than not, a variety of forces created stagflation, and policy actions to combat it have to be equally complex.

When prices are rising despite the presence of unemployed resources, some degree of structural unemployment is likely to be present. Prices may be rising in the telecommunications industry, for example, while unemployed workers are abundant in the housing industry. The higher prices and wages in telecommunications function as a signal to transfer resources from the housing industry into telecommunications. Such resource shifts, however, may not occur smoothly or quickly. In the interim, public policy can be developed to alter the structure of supply or demand.

On the demand side, the government could decrease the demand for telecommunications by increasing excise taxes on phone and other transmission services, buying fewer terminals for government use, or raising installment-loan interest rates. It could increase the demand for houses by providing housing subsidies to poor people, greater home-related tax deductions for everyone, or lower interest rates in the mortgage market. On the supply side, the government could offer tax credits for housing construction, teach construction workers how to install and operate telecommunications equipment, or speed up the job-search process.

More general barriers to production may emanate from high tax rates or costly regulations. If either of these constraints exists, high prices (inflation) may not be a sufficient incentive for increased output. In this case, reductions in tax rates and regulation might help reduce both unemployment and inflation. This is the basic goal of supply-side policies.

Finally, we have noted that stagflation may be aggravated by noncompetitive market structures. As we saw in Chapter 13, powerful corporations may respond to increasing product demand with higher prices, even if they have excess production capacity. In competitive markets, output would increase faster and prices more slowly in response to an expansion of demand that occurred at a

Wage Freeze

France will freeze wages and prices for four months to help curb its 14% inflation rate and reinforce this weekend's devaluation of the franc.

Fine-tuning

fine-tuning: Adjustments in economic policy designed to counteract small changes in economic outcomes; continuous responses to changing economic conditions.

time of significant unemployment and excess capacity. The same is true in labor markets; the less competitive they are, the more wages will rise as demand expands. Accordingly, the simultaneous reduction of both unemployment and inflation in an economy with concentrations of market power may require more than conventional fiscal, monetary, and supply-side policies. Some form of wage-price controls may be appropriate as well.[2]

Stagflation may also arise from a temporary contraction of aggregate supply that both reduces output and drives up prices. In this case, neither structural unemployment nor excessive demand is the culprit. Rather, something like a drought, a freeze, or an oil embargo is likely to be the root cause of the policy dilemma. Accordingly, none of our familiar policy tools is likely to provide a complete "cure." In most cases, the economy simply has to adjust to a temporary setback. In the short run, economic policy must educate the public about the nature of the sudden dislocation and thereby restrain unfounded inflationary fears. In the long run, policy makers may also try to avoid a repetition of the events that caused the dislocation, thus reducing the chances of future stagflation.

The apparently inexhaustible potential of public policy to alter the economy's performance has often generated optimistic expectations about the efficacy of fiscal, monetary, and supply-side tools. In the early 1960s, such optimism pervaded even the highest levels of government policy making. People frequently spoke of the ability of economic policy not only to solve major economic problems, but also to fulfill a broad spectrum of lesser objectives. Those were the days when prices were relatively stable, unemployment rates were falling, the economy was growing rapidly, and preparations were being made for man's first trip into space. The potential of economic policy looked great indeed. It was also during the 1960s that a lot of people (mostly economists) spoke of the potential for **fine-tuning,** or

[2] It might also be appropriate to break up concentrations of market power, but this is a much slower process; such antitrust activities are discussed in Chapter 22.

THE COMPLEXITIES OF FIGHTING INFLATION

I believe that the most damaging thing for us to do is to get fixed on any one factor as being the cause of inflation. If that were true, the task of fighting inflation would be infinitely simpler than it is. If that were true, many countries, like the United States, would have found the way of dealing with inflation.

There is no one solution. It isn't just a question of the budget. It isn't just the question of inflationary labor rates. It isn't just the question of sticky prices. It isn't just the question of what the Government does to keep prices up or to make regulations that tend to be inflationary. It isn't just the weather or just the drought.

It is all of these things. The interaction of these various factors is what is so terribly difficult for us to understand and, of course, what is so terribly difficult for us to deal with.

—Former Secretary of the Treasury W. Michael Blumenthal, April 13, 1977

altering economic outcomes to fit very exacting specifications. Flexible responses to changing market conditions, it was argued, could ensure fulfillment of our economic goals. As far as stabilization was concerned, the prescription was simple. When unemployment is the problem, simply give the economy a jolt of fiscal or monetary stimulus; when inflation is worrisome, simply put on the fiscal or monetary brakes. To fulfill our goals for content and distribution, we simply pick the right target for stimulus or restraint. With a little attention and experience, the right speed could be found and the economy directed successfully down the road to prosperity.

THE ECONOMIC RECORD

In view of the much-heralded potential of economic policy to fulfill our goals, the actual record is disappointing. To be sure, we have continued to grow and have attained an impressive standard of living. We cannot lose sight of the fact that our per capita income greatly exceeds the realities and even the expectations in most other countries of the world. Nevertheless, we must also recognize that our economic history is punctuated by periods of recession, high unemployment, inflation, and recurring concern for the distribution of income and mix of output. We have witnessed a significant gap between the potential and the reality of economic policy.

The graphs in Figure 14.1 provide a quick summary of our experiences since 1946, the year the Employment Act committed the federal government to macro stability. It is evident that we have not successfully fulfilled our major economic goals during this period. In recent years, we have rarely come close. The goal of 4 percent unemployment looks like a distant mirage, as does the goal of 3 percent inflation.

In terms of real economic growth, the record is equally dismal, output having actually declined in eight years and grown by less than 3 percent in another nine. Moreover, the distribution of income in 1982 looked virtually identical to that of 1946, and nearly 25 million people were still officially counted as poor in the later year.[3] Accordingly, we must acknowledge that the potential of economic policy to fulfill our goals has not yet been fully realized.

When one looks at the specific policy initiatives of various administrations, the gap between theory and practice looks even larger. The decision of the Federal Reserve System to reduce the money supply on repeated occasions during the Great Depression was colossally perverse. Only slightly less so was the Fed's decision to expand the money supply rapidly in 1978, despite evidence that inflationary pressures were already building up. In 1980–81 the Fed slowed money-supply growth much more and far longer than was justified. As a consequence, the economy suffered two consecutive recessions (1980 and 1981–82).

On the fiscal side of the ledger, we must note President Roosevelt's timid efforts to expand aggregate demand during the Great

[3] See Chapter 31.

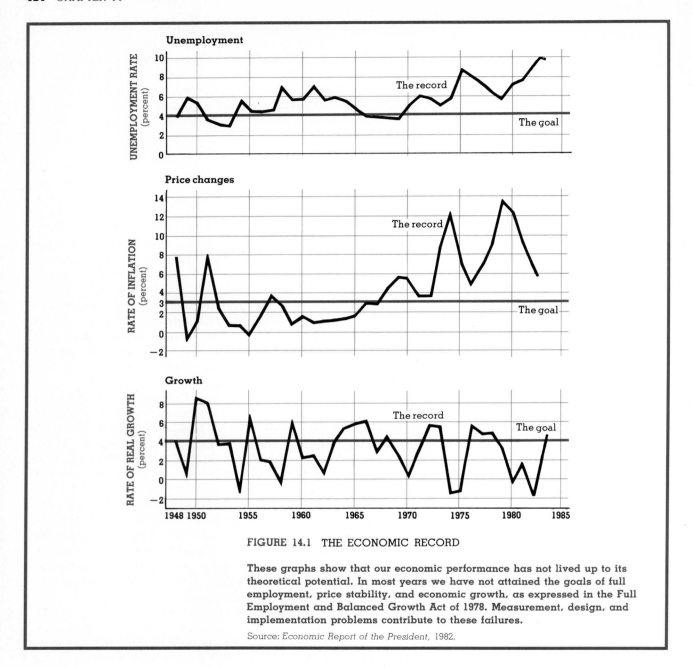

FIGURE 14.1 THE ECONOMIC RECORD

These graphs show that our economic performance has not lived up to its theoretical potential. In most years we have not attained the goals of full employment, price stability, and economic growth, as expressed in the Full Employment and Balanced Growth Act of 1978. Measurement, design, and implementation problems contribute to these failures.

Source: *Economic Report of the President, 1982.*

Depression. Also worth remembering is President Johnson's refusal to "pay" for the Vietnam War by either raising taxes or cutting non-military expenditures. The resulting strain on the economy's capacity kindled inflationary pressures that lasted for years. For his part, President Carter increased labor costs (higher payroll taxes and minimum wages), farm prices, and government spending at a time when inflation was a foremost policy concern. President Reagan has made his share of mistakes, too, including the pursuit of deep budget cuts in the early stages of a recession.

In view of our overall record and the occasional but salient blunders of policy makers, it is necessary to ask why the gap between promise and performance persists. Why don't we do a better job of fulfilling our economic goals? Are our theories incomplete? Are our policy makers incompetent? Or have we failed to note some important constraints on policy design and implementation?

WHY THINGS DON'T ALWAYS WORK

It is tempting to blame policy makers, especially the president and his advisers, for our economic disappointments, particularly since they are so quick to take credit for good economic news. It is more important, however, to discern the reasons why economic policies often fail. In this regard, we can distinguish three kinds of problems: design, measurement, and implementation.

Measurement problems

The measurement problems that plague economic policy have little to do with economic theory. Although our theoretical perspectives are by no means complete, they are adequately developed to deal with most economic situations. As long as we can diagnose the major dimensions of a problem, economic theory is equipped to provide a fairly reliable set of policy guidelines.

A good many of our problems arise in the diagnosis stage, however. One reason fire fighters are pretty successful in putting out fires before whole cities burn down is that fires are highly visible phenomena. Such visibility is not characteristic of economic problems, at least not in their more moderate manifestations. An increase in the unemployment rate from 4 to 5 percent, for example, is not the kind of thing you notice while crossing the street. Unless you work in the unemployment-insurance office or lose your own job, the increased unemployment rate is unlikely to attract your attention. The same is true of prices; small increases in product prices are unlikely to ring many alarms. Hence both inflation and unemployment may worsen considerably before anyone takes serious notice. Were we as slow and ill equipped to notice fires, whole neighborhoods would burn before someone rang the alarm.

Measurement problems, then, are an initial constraint on the formulation of public policy. To formulate appropriate economic policy, we must first determine the nature of our problems. To do so we must measure employment changes, output changes, price changes, and other dimensions of the marketplace. The old adage that governments are willing and able to solve only those problems they can measure is relevant here. Indeed, before the Great Depression, one of the fundamental impediments to public policy was the absolute dearth of statistics on what was happening in the economy. One of the lasting benefits of that experience is that we now try to keep informed on changing economic conditions.

The massive data collections we now maintain—in the Bureau of Labor Statistics, the Census Bureau, the National Center for Social Statistics, the Federal Reserve Board, and elsewhere—have substan-

FORECASTING: WHAT'S IN THE BLACK BOX?

Typically, economic forecasts are generated by complex computer models. The computer itself is not responsible for the forecasts that result, however. All the computer does is solve some mathematical equations fed to it by an economist. The economist is the person who limits the range of possible solutions and therefore the nature of the forecast.

An economist "feeds" the computer two essential inputs. One is a model of how the economy allegedly works. Such models are quantitative summaries of one or more macro theories. A Keynesian model, for example, will include equations that show multiplier spending responses to tax cuts. A Monetarist model will show that tax cuts raise interest rates ("crowding out"), not total spending. And a Supply-Siders' model stipulates labor-supply and production responses. The computer can't tell which theory is right; it just predicts what it is programmed to see. In other words, the computer sees the world through the eyes of its economic master.

The second essential input in a computer forecast is the assumed values for critical economic variables. A Keynesian model, for example, must specify how large a multiplier to expect. All the computer does is carry out the required mathematical routines, once it is told that the multiplier is relevant and what its value is. It cannot discern the true multiplier any better than it can pick the right theory.

Given the dependence of computers on the theories and perceptions of their economic masters, it is not surprising that computer forecasts often differ greatly. It's also not surprising that they are often wrong. To generate an accurate forecast, the computer's economic masters must not only hold the right theories of how the

tially improved the basis for policy formulation. The information at hand, however, is always dated and incomplete. *At best, we know what was happening in the economy last month or last week.* The processes of data collection, assembly, and presentation take time, even in the age of high-speed computers. In the absence of current information, policy prescriptions are by necessity based on yesterday's perceptions. Even those perceptions may be faulty, since yesterday's data are often later revised.

FORECASTS   In an ideal world, policy makers would not only respond to economic problems that occur, but also anticipate their occurrence and act to avoid them. If we foresee an inflationary gap emerging, for example, we want to take immediate action to keep aggregate demand from increasing. That is to say, the successful fire fighter not only responds to fires, he also looks for hazards that might start one.

Unfortunately, economic policy makers are again at a disadvantage. Their knowledge of future problems is even worse than their knowledge of current problems. *In designing policy, policy makers must depend on economic forecasts,* that is, informed guesses about what the economy will look like in future periods under different economic policies. As you might suspect, the future does not always

world works, but also be able to foresee changes in all the critical variables that drive the model. Despite frequent claims to the contrary, few economists possess such clairvoyance.

In view of the fragile foundations and spotty record of computer forecasts, many people shun them altogether. In a 1981 Gallup survey of corporate chief executives, most respondents said economists' forecasts had little or no influence on company plans or policies. The head of one large company said, "I go out of my way to ignore them." Donald Regan, secretary of the Treasury in the Reagan administration, echoed his feelings in testimony to the U.S. Congress. Regan blasted "the obsession that people have with economic forecasts in spite of their consistent failure." These failed forecasts, he noted, have contributed greatly to failed economic policies.

Economic forecasters defend themselves in two ways. First, they note that economic policy decisions are inevitably based on anticipated changes in the economy's performance. The decision to stimulate or restrain the economy cannot be made by a flip of a coin; someone must try to foresee the future course of the economy. Second, forecasters claim that their quantitative approach is the only honest one. Because forecasting models require specific behavioral assumptions and estimates, they force people to spell out their versions of the future. Less rigorous ("gut feeling") approaches are too ambiguous and often inconsistent.

These are valid arguments. Still, one must be careful to distinguish the precision of a computer from the inevitable uncertainties of their spoon-fed models. The basic law of the computer is GIGO: garbage in, garbage out. If the underlying models and assumptions are no good, the computer's forecasts won't be any better.

look like the forecasts, and many policies therefore end up being misdirected.

Some of the difficulties of measuring economic outcomes and forecasting their future direction were superbly illustrated in the early months of the Reagan administration. One of the principal themes of Ronald Reagan's election campaign was the need to balance the federal budget. When he took office, his plan for balancing the budget included big cuts in both taxes and government spending (see Chapter 15). Congress resisted this approach, however, for fear that the tax cuts would aggravate inflation. The Congressional Budget Office and others foresaw a strong economy in 1981 and urged Congress to reject massive tax cuts.

By the time Congress finally approved a scaled-down tax cut and the spending cuts, the economy had actually entered a recession. No one knew it, though. Indeed, President Reagan was still demanding further spending cuts in November 1981, in an effort to restrain aggregate demand. Only a few weeks later the president and Congress belatedly realized that the country was in a deep recession that had begun many months earlier. They then began talking about the need to postpone further spending cuts and accelerate planned tax reductions.

The saga of the 1981 budget debate illustrates two major points

WHO WAS RIGHT?

Successful policy design depends on accurate forecasts of future economic performance. But forecasts vary widely—and all of them may be wrong. Notice in particular the different forecasts of the president, Congress, and the Federal Reserve, each of whom formulates economic policy. Did anyone forecast 1982 performance correctly?

ECONOMIC FORECASTS FOR 1982

	Real growth in GNP (percent)	Price increase (percent)	Average unemployment (percent)
Private forecasts			
U.S. Chamber of Commerce	5.2	6.8	8.1
New York Stock Exchange	2.3	7.5	8.7
Chase Econometrics	2.9	8.3	8.6
Georgia State University	2.0	7.8	8.4
University of California, L.A.	0.8	6.2	8.9
Wharton Econometrics	1.9	8.2	8.9
National Association of Business Economists	2.5	8.2	7.4
Public forecasts			
Reagan administration	3.0	6.6	8.9
Congressional Budget Office	−0.1	7.5	8.9
Federal Reserve Board	1.8	7.1	8.9
The actual record	?	?	?

Source: Forecasts published in late 1981 or January/February 1982; Federal Reserve forecast is midpoint of FOMC projections.

about fine-tuning. First, it may be possible to fine-tune an economy if we know what problems exist and how serious they are likely to become. Second, it reminds us that we seldom have such good information and are thus likely to fail as often as we succeed. Moreover, our fine-tuning mistakes are not always so easily remedied. The "mistakes" of 1981 turned out to be well timed. But what if the economy had overheated? Could the president have gone on TV and asked people not to spend their tax cuts? Could he have quickly raised taxes again, as some of his advisers actually suggested?

Design problems

Once the existence of a problem is clearly established, the design of policy initiatives can proceed. We still confront significant obstacles, however. What action should we take? Which theory of macro behavior should guide us? How will the marketplace respond to any specific action we take?

Suppose, for example, that we adopt a Keynesian approach to ending a recession. Specifically, we cut income taxes to stimulate consumer spending, with the hope of closing a recessionary gap. How do we know that consumers will respond as anticipated? Perhaps the marginal propensity to consume has changed. Or the veloc-

rational expectations: Hypothesis that people's spending decisions are influenced by anticipated government policy, itself presumed to be like previous policies.

ity of money has slowed. Maybe the level of consumer confidence has dropped. Any of these changes could frustrate even the best-intentioned policy. Thorough familiarity with economic theory and past experience is necessary for successful policy design, but it is not sufficient. The policy maker also needs a sense of the way market participants are going to respond to any specific actions taken. The successful policy maker needs a very good crystal ball.

RATIONAL EXPECTATIONS   Recently some economists have suggested that no crystal ball will work well enough. The market will simply not respond as expected to policy actions. Over time, consumers and investors have witnessed repeated changes in economic policy. First the government stimulates the economy, then it reverses direction and steps on the economic brakes. This kind of erratic stop-and-go policy has tended to make people skeptical of government promises to pursue specific anti-inflation or antirecession policies. The perennial promise to "balance the budget" typifies the problem: after decades of continual deficits, the oft-repeated promise to "restore balance" falls on deaf ears. The government's promises simply are not credible. A rational consumer or investor will not believe them.

If market participants do not believe that the government will implement or maintain a specific policy, they will not adapt their behavior to that policy. As a consequence, the Congress and the administration will have to "prove" their seriousness with bigger efforts, maintained over longer time periods. Only then will people believe the policy and begin to adapt their behavior in desired ways.

This credibility problem can limit the effectiveness of specific policy initiatives. Suppose the administration announced its intention to slow inflation by curbing government spending and urging slower growth of the money supply. Ideally, people would see in such policies the potential to keep prices from rising further. People would feel less need to demand higher wages and prices or to buy things quickly ("before prices go any higher"). By changing people's expectations and behavior in these ways, the government's anti-inflation initiatives would have immediate impact. Inflation would moderate, with only a modest slowdown in economic activity.

But what if no one believed the government's anti-inflation proclamations? In that case, the administration's vows to curb spending and the money supply would be ignored. People with **rational expectations** would continue to seek protection from inflation via higher wages and prices and faster purchases. Only a prolonged spell of fiscal and monetary restraint would alter people's expectations. By that time, however, aggregate demand might have slowed so much that the economy fell into recession. In that case, a lack of basic credibility would force the economy into an unnecessarily severe stagflation. The news story on the next page illustrates how this credibility problem constrained President Carter's efforts to stop inflation. By contrast, many people have argued that President Reagan's greatest policy asset was the widespread belief that he would "stick to his guns" in fighting inflation.

Anti-Inflation Program Faces More Problems

When President Carter unveiled his new budget-balancing plan on March 14, there was widespread skepticism about whether he ultimately would be able to get Congress to approve his proposed $13 billion to $14 billion in budget cuts.

It was doubtless the most sweeping anti-inflation package the president had proposed since taking office. But like other major Carter inflation-fighting efforts, it came late and at a price.

There were these points:

■ For all the current attention to the breadth of the new measures Carter has announced, the policy turnabout raises serious questions in the minds of some analysts about the administration's judgment on economic issues.

On Jan. 28, the president announced a fiscal 1981 budget calling for a deficit of $15.8 billion. The White House pronounced it appropriate both for the economic situation and the nation's political mood.

Barely four weeks later, however, Carter and his advisers already were moving to tear up that January plan and draft new budget-cutting measures that would reverse their earlier policy.

Indeed, critics contend with some accuracy that Carter has been dragged kicking and screaming into virtually every serious anti-inflation program he has proposed. . . .

Moreover—incredibly to many Budget Committee members who were in the front trenches—Carter politicos already tried to weaken the package by seeking $700 million in new aid to cities to "mitigate" the impact of the cuts on cities.

Indeed, less than a week since Carter's new announcement, Budget panel members already are complaining they've been receiving conflicting signals from the White House on precisely what Carter wants cut or kept intact.

—Art Pine

Implementation problems

Measurement and design problems can break the spirit of even the best-intentioned and most diligent public official (or his economic advisers). Yet measurement and design problems are only part of the story. A good idea is of little value unless someone puts it to use. Accordingly, to understand how things often go wrong, we must also consider the difficulties of implementing a well-designed (and believed) policy initiative.

CONGRESSIONAL DELIBERATIONS   Suppose that the president and his Council of Economic Advisers (perhaps in conjunction with the secretary of the Treasury and the director of the Office of Management and Budget) decide that the rate of aggregate spending is slowing down. A tax cut, they believe, is necessary to stimulate demand for goods and services. Can they simply go ahead and cut tax rates? No, because all tax changes must be legislated by Congress. Once the president decides on the appropriate policy initiative, he must ask Congress for authority to take the required action. This means a delay in implementing policy, and possibly no policy at all.

At a minimum, the president must convince Congress of the accuracy of his own perspectives and the appropriateness of his suggested action. The tax proposal must work its way through separate committees of both the House of Representatives and the Senate, get on the congressional calendar, and be approved in each chamber. If there are important differences in Senate and House versions of the tax-cut legislation, they must be compromised in a joint conference. The modified proposal must then be returned to each chamber for approval.

This description of congressional activity is not just an outline for a civics course; rather it is an important explanation of why economic policy is not fully effective. *Even if the right policy is formulated to solve an emerging economic problem, there is no assurance that it will be implemented. And if it is implemented, there is no assurance that it will take effect at the right time.* One of the most frightening prospects for economic policy is that a policy design intended to serve a specific problem will be implemented much later, when economic conditions have changed. The policy's effect on the economy may then be the opposite of what was intended. We have already noted how close President Reagan's budget-cutting proposals came to realizing this nightmare.

Figure 14.2 provides a schematic view of why things don't always work out as well as economic theory suggests they might. There are always delays between the time a problem emerges and the time it is recognized, between recognition and response design, between design and implementation, and finally between implementation and impact. Not only may mistakes be made at each juncture, but even correct decisions may be overcome by changing economic conditions.

We can illustrate the processes of Figure 14.2 by considering how the income surtax of 1968 came about. The expansion of the Vietnam War in July 1965 added something like $15 billion to aggregate demand.[4] At that time the economy was already buoyant and the unemployment rate was moving down to 4 percent. To offset resulting inflationary pressures, the president and Congress took limited fiscal action, including the restoration of excise taxes on cars and telephones. Much stronger action was necessary, however, if the higher rate of Vietnam spending was to be maintained. But President Johnson insisted that the escalation of the war was temporary and that hostilities would soon end. From his perspective, the imposition of stronger fiscal restraints was tantamount to an admission that the war would not be won quickly. Only after the expanded war effort continued for 18 months did the administration propose further action. In January 1967 President Johnson called for a 6 percent surtax to correct the "imbalances created by the special pressures of Vietnam procurement."[5] Thus the problem that emerged in July 1965 was not recognized until 1966, and a response was not formulated until January 1967. Compounding these delays was the reluctance of Congress to help finance an undeclared war. Congress did not take the requested action until June 1968. Thus there was a three-year lag between the time the problem emerged and the implementation of a responsive action. In the interim, of course, inflationary pressures worsened.

[4] This figure includes multiplier effects through the first quarter of 1966.
[5] *Economic Report of the President*, 1967, pp. 5 and 9.

FIGURE 14.2 POLICY RESPONSE:
A SERIES OF TIME LAGS

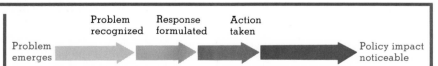

Even the best-intentioned economic policy can be frustrated by time lags. It takes time for a problem to be recognized, time to formulate a policy response, and still more time to implement that policy. By the time the policy begins to affect the economy, the underlying problem may have changed.

The Politics of Fighting Unemployment and Inflation

"I can't think of anything you can do to keep inflation down that is popular," lamented one frustrated Cabinet official. "It's completely different from fighting unemployment. There, you pump money into programs and people feel they benefit. When you fight inflation, people feel you're taking something away from them. You are always goring somebody's ox."
—Hedrick Smith

New York Times, March 8, 1978. © 1978 by The New York Times Company. Reprinted by permission.

POLITICS VS. ECONOMICS The delayed fiscal response to accelerated Vietnam expenditures also illustrates another basic impediment to policy implementation: *goal conflicts.* Just as the design of policy is compromised by conflicting interests and objectives, so, too, is the implementation of those designs. Especially noteworthy in this regard is the potential conflict of economic policy with political objectives. The conflict that existed between President Johnson's war objectives and his economic objectives is obvious. More generally, observers have noted that the president and Congress are reluctant to impose fiscal restraints (tax increases or budget cutbacks) in election years, regardless of economic circumstances. Indeed, some argue that the business cycle has been replaced with the political cycle: the economy is stimulated in the year before an election, then restrained in the postelection year. The conflict between the urgent need to get reelected and the necessity to manage the economy results in a seesaw kind of instability.

In theory, the political independence of the Federal Reserve's Board of Governors provides some protection from ill-advised but politically advantageous policy initiatives. In practice, however, the Fed's relative obscurity and independence may backfire. The president and the Congress know that if they don't take effective action against inflation—by raising taxes or cutting government spending—the Fed can and will take stronger action to restrain aggregate demand. This is a classic case of having one's cake and eating it too. Elected officials win votes for not raising taxes or cutting some constituent's favorite spending program and take credit for any reduction in the rate of inflation brought about by Federal Reserve policies. To top it off, Congress and the president can also castigate the Fed for driving up interest rates or starting a recession if monetary policy becomes too restrictive!

The conflict between political reality and economic reality often arises out of ignorance. For example, nearly 90 percent of the people in this country believe a balanced federal budget is "important," regardless of economic circumstances. As we noted in Chapter 9, there is even a growing call for a constitutional amendment that would require balanced federal budgets. Yet economic theory suggests that budget deficits or surpluses are typically required to achieve our economic goals. Under such circumstances, should a president promise to balance the budget—thereby winning votes but risking greater economic instability—or unbalance it, as economic conditions require?[6]

Finally, we must recognize that policy design is obstructed by a certain lack of will. Neither the man in the street nor the elected public official is constantly attuned to economic goals and activities. Even students enrolled in economics courses have a hard time keeping their minds on the economy and its problems. For their part, the executive and legislative branches of government are likely to focus on economic concerns only when economic problems become serious or voters demand action. Otherwise, policy makers are apt to be

---

[6] A successful politician might do both, of course—that is, *promise* to balance the budget, but unbalance it at the same time. President Reagan had some success with this approach.

SEARCHING FOR A POLICY SYNTHESIS: THE 1980 EXPERIENCE

In his January 1980 Economic Message to Congress, President Carter proclaimed his "strong conviction that inflation remains the Nation's number one economic problem." With a presidential election approaching, Carter had good reason for concern. During the first three years of his presidency the nation's inflation rate had *tripled*, to nearly 14 percent annually. Although his economic policies had substantially reduced the unemployment rate (to 5.8 percent), it was evident that taxpayers would no longer tolerate rapid price increases. The search for restrictive economic policies was on. President Carter proposed an anti-inflation package that included:

□ Reduced government spending
□ No tax reductions
□ Tight monetary policy
□ Strengthened wage and price guidelines

President Carter took note of the fact that "a mild recession is widely forecast," but dismissed those concerns with the observation that "forecasts are necessarily uncertain." He persuaded Congress to pursue a more austere fiscal policy, while the Fed kept money-supply growth to a minimum.

As late as March 1980 Carter pledged: "I will not consider any reduction in taxes until I am convinced that the 1981 budget will be balanced." He even proposed *raising* taxes to ensure a balanced budget. Through the early part of the summer he continued to hold this position.

By midyear Congress was getting nervous. Inflation was still running at a double-digit pace, and the unemployment rate was increasing rapidly. Taxpayers were also protesting continuing increases in social security and income-tax rates. With the 1980 elections approaching, congressional Democrats threatened to jump off of Carter's anti-inflation bandwagon and cut taxes. Candidate Ronald Reagan had already proposed massive tax cuts and appeared to be winning voter sentiment.

Despite evidence of spreading recession, President Carter initially rejected appeals for a tax cut. But the economic and political pressures for a policy reversal grew. Unemployment rates had risen from 6.2 percent in January to 7.6 percent in August. Worse still, Reagan had pulled far ahead of Carter in voter surveys. Since the Fed was continuing to restrain money-supply growth, the only hope for quick recovery lay in a tax cut. On August 28 Carter relented and proposed a $28 billion tax cut. He urged Congress to wait until early 1981 before implementing it, however, so that the tax cut would not be influenced by "election-year politics."

complacent about economic policy as long as economic performance is within a "tolerable" range of desired outcomes.

POLICY IMPLICATIONS: RULES VS. DISCRETION

In view of the lengthy list of measurement, design, and implementation problems, it is less surprising that things sometimes go wrong than that things often work out right. The maze of obstacles through

The Political Nature of the Budget Impasse

. . . Two decades of accommodating new constituencies have bloated the budget to levels well beyond what taxpayers traditionally have supported. Persisting deficits are the result, but focusing on them obscures the political nature of the impasse: an unwillingness to abandon past spending commitments colliding with an equal unwillingness to pay new taxes.

The gap is huge. Even at lower levels of unemployment—say 6.5 percent, which would mean more tax receipts and less unemployment and welfare spending—spending commitments in 1985 would exceed revenues by between 3 and 4 percent of gross national product. With GNP at roughly $3 trillion, that implies an underlying budget deficit between $90 billion and $120 billion in current dollars.

The arithmetic easily explains to-day's political stalemate. Nothing the White House and Congress do—including doing nothing—can bridge that gap without causing considerable political pain. Taxes have to be raised sharply, programs have to be cut sizably or large deficits will persist. The arithmetic is unyielding, and the magnitude of the numbers means that changes can't be cosmetic. . . .

In a political vacuum, finding budget and tax changes to bridge the gap isn't difficult. Some possible choices include abandoning the B1 bomber, taxing Social Security payments and eliminating the special double exemption for the elderly, limiting or eliminating the deductibility of interest on mortgages and personal loans, and limiting or eliminating tax preferences for medical expenses and health insurance.

But for every good economic argument, there's a bad political one. For example, it's difficult to justify excluding Social Security payments from income taxes. There's no good reason why a couple of 67-year-olds with income of, say, $25,000 should pay less income tax than a couple of 63-year-olds or 36-year-olds with the same income. But the privilege exists (at a current cost of about $12 billion), and groups of the elderly would resist its removal fiercely.

The trouble is that future budget gaps are so large that they can be narrowed only by invading such politically sacrosanct areas. Failure to do so perpetuates large deficits. The burden of higher federal spending then falls on the economy's credit-sensitive sectors: housing, autos and business investment. . . .

The greatest hurt may be political and psychological. "The mandate of the 1980 election was not really to make government more conservative," Senate Budget Committee Chairman Pete V. Domenici (R-N.M.) recently observed. "It was to make government behave properly." The large deficits symbolize bad behavior; they represent political irresponsibility and indecisiveness—the inability to make difficult choices.

—Robert J. Samuelson

which theoretical prescriptions must pass before they become actual public policy explains a great many of our collective shortcomings. ***Consistent fine-tuning of the economy is not compatible with either our design capabilities or our institutional decision-making procedures.*** We have exhibited a strong capability of avoiding major economic disruptions in the last three decades. We have not, however, been able to make all the minor adjustments necessary to fulfill our goals completely. As Arthur Burns, former chairman of the Fed's Board of Governors, said:

There has been much loose talk of "fine-tuning" when the state of knowledge permits us to predict only within a fairly broad level the course of economic development and the results of policy actions.[7]

Some critics of economic policy take this argument a few steps further. If fine-tuning isn't really possible, they say, we should abandon discretionary policies altogether. As it is now, policy makers continue to seek minor adjustments in interest rates, unemployment, inflation, and growth. The pressure to "do something" is particularly irresistible in election years. In so doing, however, policy makers are as likely to worsen the economic situation as to improve it. Moreover, the potential for such short-term discretion undermines people's confidence in the economy's future.

Critics of discretionary policies say we would be better off with fixed policy rules. With respect to monetary policy, such a rule

[7] *Newsweek*, August 27, 1973, p. 4.

would require the Fed to increase the money supply at a constant rate. Fiscal policy would be required to maintain balanced budgets, or at least to ensure a budget that was balanced over the business cycle. Such rules would prevent policy makers from over- or understimulating the economy, and the risks of economic instability would be reduced.

Milton Friedman has been one of the most persistent advocates of fixed policy rules instead of discretionary policies. With discretionary authority, Friedman argues,

the wrong decision is likely to be made in a large fraction of cases because the decision-makers are examining only a limited area and not taking into account the cumulative consequences of the policy as a whole. On the other hand, if a general rule is adopted for a group of cases as a bundle, the existence of that rule has favorable effects on people's attitudes and beliefs and expectations that would not follow even from the discretionary adoption of precisely the same policy on a series of separate occasions.[8]

Thus the case for nondiscretionary monetary authority is based on practical, not theoretical, arguments. Everyone agrees that flexible, discretionary policies *could* result in better economic performance. But Friedman and others argue that the practical requirements of monetary and fiscal management are too demanding and thus prone to failure. Moreover, required policies may be compromised by political pressures.

Defenders of discretionary policies argue that flexibility is an essential ingredient of sound economic policy. They acknowledge occasional policy blunders, but emphasize that the historical record of prices, employment, and growth has improved since active fiscal and monetary policies were adopted. Without flexibility in the money supply and the budget, they argue, the economy would be less stable and our economic goals would remain unfulfilled.

When we assess the arguments for and against discretionary policy, it is important to note that historical evidence is ambiguous at best. No one really knows whether the economy would have been better or worse off during the last fifty years—or even the last two—if policy options had been more limited. It is easy to observe what actually happened, but almost impossible to determine what would have occurred in other circumstances. It is also evident that there have been noteworthy occasions—World War II, for example—when something more than fixed rules for monetary and fiscal policy was called for, a contingency even Professor Friedman acknowledges. Thus occasional flexibility is required, even if a nondiscretionary policy is appropriate in most situations.

Finally, one must contend with the difficulties inherent in adhering to any fixed rules. How is the Fed, for example, supposed to maintain a steady rate of growth in $M1$? As we observed in Chapter 10, people move their funds back and forth between different kinds of "money." Also, the demand for money is subject to unpredictable shifts. To maintain a steady rate of $M1$ growth in this environment would require superhuman foresight and responses.

---

[8] Milton Friedman, *Capitalism and Freedom* (Chicago: University of Chicago Press, 1962), p. 53.

automatic stabilizer: Federal expenditure or revenue item that automatically responds countercyclically to changes in national income; for example, unemployment benefits, income taxes.

The same is true of fiscal policy. Government spending and taxes are directly influenced by changes in unemployment, inflation, interest rates, and growth. These **automatic stabilizers** make it virtually impossible to maintain any fixed rule for budget balancing. Were we to eliminate the automatic stabilizers, moreover, we would risk greater instability. Without them, we would have to anticipate and correct for any changes in macroeconomic activity.

Modest expectations

The clamor for fixed policy rules is more a rebuke of past policy than a viable policy alternative. We really have no choice but to pursue discretionary policies. Recognition of measurement, design, and implementation problems is important for an understanding of the way the economy functions. But even though it is difficult or even impossible to reach all our goals, we cannot abandon conscientious attempts to get as close as possible to goal fulfillment. If public policy can create a few more jobs, a better mix of output, a little more growth and price stability, or an improved distribution of income, those initiatives are significant and worthwhile. Modest improvements in our economic performance are important even if perfection is not attained. More restrained expectations about the potential of public policy need not and should not constrain our efforts to improve economic performance.

SUMMARY

- The basic principles of economics engender optimism about the potential of policy to fulfill our economic goals. The government possesses an array of policy tools, each of which can significantly alter economic outcomes. To expand aggregate demand in a period of unemployment, we can cut taxes, expand the money supply, or increase government spending. To restrain aggregate demand in an inflationary period, we can reverse each of these policy weapons. To overcome stagflation, we can combine fiscal and monetary weapons with improved production incentives, labor-market policies, and deregulation to regain price stability and full employment.

- Although the potential of economic theory seems impressive, the economic record does not look so good. Persistent unemployment, recurring economic slowdowns, and nagging inflation suggest that the realities of policy making are more difficult than theory implies.

- To a large extent, the "failures" of economic policy are a reflection of scarce resources and competing goals. Even when consensus exists, however, serious obstacles to effective economic policy remain. These obstacles include:

    (a) Measurement problems. Our knowledge of economic performance is always dated and incomplete. We must rely on forecasts of future problems.

    (b) Design problems. We don't know exactly how the economy will respond to specific policies. Moreover, "rational expectations" may constrain market responses.

(c) Implementation problems. It takes time for Congress and the president to agree on an appropriate plan of action. Moreover, the agreements reached may respond more to political needs than to economic needs.

For all these reasons, the fine-tuning of economic performance rarely lives up to its theoretical potential.

Terms to remember	Define the following term:

opportunity costs   **rational expectations**
fine-tuning   **automatic stabilizer**

Questions for discussion

1. Should economic policies respond immediately to any changes in reported unemployment or inflation rates? When should a response be undertaken?

2. Suppose that it is an election year and that aggregate demand is growing so fast that it threatens to set off an inflationary movement. Why might Congress and the president hesitate to cut back on government spending or raise taxes, as economic theory suggests is appropriate?

3. The Defense Department argued that its fiscal 1975 budget should be increased by $5 billion to help boost aggregate demand. Although such reasoning might have been good economics at the time, is it likely that military expenditures are dictated by the level of aggregate demand? What programs should be expanded or contracted to bring about needed changes in G? Is this feasible?

4. Suppose that the president proposes mandatory wage-price controls to slow the rate of inflation. What is likely to happen to wages and prices in the interval between the time the proposal is made and the time Congress acts to impose controls?

5. Suppose the government proposes to cut taxes while maintaining the current level of government expenditures. To finance this deficit, it may either (1) sell bonds to the public or (2) print new money (via Federal Reserve cooperation). What are the effects of each of these alternatives on each of the following?

(a) Interest rates
(b) Consumer spending
(c) Business investment
(d) Aggregate demand

CHAPTER 15
REAGAN ECONOMICS

The election of Ronald Reagan in 1980 was widely interpreted as a mandate for new economic policies. In poll after poll, taxpayers had expressed their anguish over continuing inflation (see p. 122). They were also convinced that the federal government was "wasting" taxpayers' income and fueling inflation. President Carter's own warnings about continuing economic distress, coupled with the economic record of his administration, hardly calmed these concerns. Just before the election only 25 percent of the American people believed the U.S. economy would improve if Carter were reelected.[1]

In his election campaign Ronald Reagan promised a dramatic reversal of our economic fortunes. Inflation would be reduced, economic growth would accelerate, and employment would increase. These promises would be kept with a whole new set of economic policies, with an emphasis on supply-side tax cuts.

The public evidently believed Reagan could deliver on his promises. In September 1980, 36 percent of the U.S. public thought the U.S. economy would improve if Reagan were elected. By the time he was sworn in as president, confidence was even higher: 46 percent of the public felt Reagan would cut both inflation and unemployment in his first year.[2]

Reagan's initial economic program did not fulfill its early promises. Inflation did decline in 1981, but unemployment increased sharply. Instead of growing rapidly, the U.S. economy fell into a deep recession in 1981–82.

[1] CBS–*New York Times* poll, September 1980.
[2] Gallup Poll reported in *U.S. News & World Report*, January 26, 1981, p. 23.

"ROLL 'EM"

© Liederman/Rothco.

The early years of the Reagan administration provide a case study in the difficulties of formulating, implementing, and maintaining a successful economic policy. In this chapter we shall examine that experience. We shall look first at Reagan's initial economic proposals and the assumptions that motivated them. We shall then look at the obstacles, both theoretical and institutional, that limited their success. The chapter concludes with a look at Reagan's FY 1983 budget and its changed economic assumptions. As we shall see, "Reagan economics" has incorporated a changing mix of Supply-side, Keynesian, and Monetarist perspectives.

REAGAN'S TAX-CUT PROPOSAL

The centerpiece of Reagan's economic program was a supply-side tax cut. Following the advice of Professor Arthur Laffer of the University of Southern California and other advisers, Reagan proposed a three-year program of substantial tax cuts. In the 1980 presidential campaign, Reagan urged that tax rates for consumers be cut by 10 percent in each of three consecutive years, beginning in January 1981. This would amount to a cumulative cut of nearly 30 percent in individual tax rates. Businesses, too, would enjoy lower tax rates, largely because of increased tax deductions (accelerated depreciation).

The idea for large, multiyear tax cuts did not originate with Reagan. The basic idea had been proposed several years earlier, by Congressman Jack Kemp and Senator William Roth. In fact, the Kemp-Roth bill, providing for large-scale tax cuts, had been debated for many years. But President Carter and Congress had consistently opposed that bill. President Reagan adopted its essential elements and molded them into his own program.

A checklist of Reagan's promises

□ **Tax cuts.** Slash tax rates on personal income 10 percent across the board in each of the next three years, followed by indexing of tax code to prevent inflation from pushing taxpayers into higher brackets. Exempt from taxes at least part of the interest earned on savings and abolish federal estate taxes. Accelerate depreciation allowances for businesses.

□ **Spending.** Balance the budget by 1983. Increase defense spending, but cut the growth of the budget over all by 7 percent over five years, largely by reducing waste and fraud in government programs.

□ **Defense.** Shelve the draft-registration system started by President Carter and avoid a draft in peacetime. Boost military pay and benefits to match private-sector jobs. Spur plans for production of the MX-missile system, the neutron bomb and an advanced bomber similar to the B-1.

□ **Arms control.** Scrap SALT II and negotiate with the Soviet Union a new arms-limitation treaty that would place tighter limits on Moscow.

□ **Business.** Stimulate productivity by lessening the burden of government regulations and paper work. Eliminate the minimum wage outright or provide a lower minimum for teen-age workers. Abolish wage-price guidelines.

□ **Farmers.** End President Carter's embargo on American grain shipments to the Soviet Union.

□ **Women.** Appoint a woman to the Supreme Court and other women to high positions in government.

□ **Government reorganization.** Abolish the Department of Energy and the Department of Education. Restore the influence of cabinet members, especially the Secretary of State, while paring the staffs of such White House bodies as the National Security Council.

□ **Energy.** Encourage private industry to develop new energy sources but avoid costly government "schemes" such as the Synthetic Fuels Corporation. Remove all remaining price controls from the oil and natural-gas industries.

□ **Cities.** Provide tax breaks for businesses that agree to locate in blighted urban areas.

□ **Welfare.** Consolidate present aid programs into broad, flexible grants administered by states and localities. Loosen federal strings generally, while helping states reduce costs, case loads and fraud.

□ **Social Security.** Remove the limit on earned income—$5,500 in 1981—for retirees age 65 to 71 receiving Social Security, while putting the Social Security system on a sounder financial footing.

□ **Parochial schools.** Provide tuition tax credits for parents of students attending private schools.

Reprinted from *U.S. News & World Report,* December 8, 1980. Copyright © 1980, U.S. News & World Report, Inc.

Tax-cut motives

bracket creep: The movement of taxpayers into higher tax brackets (rates) as nominal incomes grow.

There were several good reasons for proposing tax cuts in 1981 and beyond. First, the size of the federal government had grown significantly in the 1960s and 1970s. As Table 15.1 shows, the government's share of GNP had increased from 18.5 percent in 1960 to 22.5 percent in 1980. Government revenues and the federal deficit had grown as well. By cutting taxes, Reagan could stop this growth, thereby giving consumers and investors a larger share of GNP.

The second motive for cutting taxes was the fear of further **bracket creep.** In the U.S. income-tax system, higher incomes are taxed at higher tax *rates* (see Chapter 29). The intent of this progres-

TABLE 15.1 THE GROWING FEDERAL SHARE

Between 1960 and 1980 the federal government's share of GNP increased significantly. Had federal outlays remained at 18.5 percent of GNP (as in 1960), the government would have spent $100 billion less in 1980. This relative growth of federal outlays, receipts, and the deficit led to demands for cutbacks in federal taxes and expenditures.

	Percent of GNP				
	1960	1965	1970	1975	1980
Outlays	18.5	17.9	20.3	22.0	22.5
Receipts	18.5	17.7	20.0	19.0	20.3
Surplus or deficit	0.1	−0.2	−0.3	−3.0	−2.3

Source: Robert W. Hartman, "The Budget Outlook," in *Setting National Priorities: The 1982 Budget,* ed. Joseph Pechman (Washington, D.C.: Brookings Institution, 1981).

marginal tax rate: The tax rate imposed on the last (marginal) dollar of income.

sive tax structure is to redistribute income from the rich to the poor. But inflation increases everyone's nominal income. As a result, people "creep" into higher tax brackets when prices (and incomes) rise. In the process, consumers confront steadily increasing tax *rates*. Between 1970 and 1980 the **marginal tax rate** for the average household rose from 18.2 percent to 21.6 percent. Individuals with higher incomes experienced even faster bracket creep: households with real incomes of $50,000 to $100,000 in 1980 confronted marginal tax rates of 46.8 percent, versus only 32.5 percent in 1970. Worse still, continuing inflation was pushing these tax rates even higher.

Bracket creep not only was fueling the government's growth, but was also weakening work and investment incentives. High tax rates were also encouraging more "underground" activity (Chapter 4). To reverse these trends, marginal tax rates had to be cut.

Finally, there was growing realization that the economy was falling into another recession. Even President Carter had recognized that a 1981 tax cut might be necessary to stimulate aggregate demand (see p. 333). Some kind of tax cut was both desirable and inevitable.

The controversy

Despite these many good reasons for a tax cut, Reagan's tax-cut proposals were fiercely debated, both before and after the election. People were especially worried about the *timing* of the tax cuts. The economy was still experiencing substantial inflation in early 1981. Any fiscal stimulus might push prices still higher. Under these conditions, could taxes be cut immediately? Or would tax cuts have to await offsetting reductions in government expenditures?

Others questioned the *size* of the tax cuts. Over a three-year period, Reagan's proposed income-tax cuts would total nearly $200 billion. This much fiscal stimulus might overwhelm our production capacity. Finally, there were questions about the *structure* of the tax cuts. Were consumers getting too large a share of the tax cut, relative to investors? Were high-income families getting most of the tax breaks?

The timing of the tax cut generated the most intense debates, even within the circle of Reagan advisers. Supply-Siders urged Reagan to push his tax cut immediately, without waiting for offsetting budget cuts. Politically, Congressman Jack Kemp feared that any proposal for massive cuts in fiscal 1981 spending was doomed to fail in Congress. Kemp warned Reagan that if budget cutting was "the primary or exclusive focus of the initial fiscal package, the ball game will be lost." Such economists as Arthur Laffer also sought to convince Reagan that budget cuts were not even necessary. The benefits of a tax cut would be so large, they argued, that corresponding reductions in government spending were not necessary. They advocated cutting taxes immediately, even if expenditure cuts could not be legislated at the same time. More traditional, demand-side economists argued that it would be highly inflationary to cut taxes without corresponding budget cuts. They urged Reagan to postpone tax cuts until a balanced budget was ensured.

The demand-side argument

The essential logic of traditional demand-side economics has been described in Chapters 7–12. Both Keynesians and Monetarists assert that *demand management* is the primary concern of macro policy. Within that context, both Monetarists and Keynesians also agree that a tax cut tends to stimulate spending—although for very different reasons.

disposable income (DI): After-tax income of consumers; personal income less personal taxes.

Keynesians argue that a tax cut directly increases **disposable income.** Consumers use this additional income to buy more goods and services, in accordance with their (high) marginal propensity to consume. This added spending has a multiplied impact on aggregate demand, pushing the economy toward its potential **full-employment GNP.**

full-employment GNP: The total market value of final goods and services that could be produced in a given time period at full employment; potential GNP.

Monetarists also accept the possibility of a tax-cut stimulus, but argue that the stimulus originates in the money supply (M). A tax cut without corresponding budget cuts widens the budget deficit. To maintain this enlarged deficit, the U.S. Treasury must borrow more funds. If the money supply is not increased, the additional borrowing by the Treasury will push interest rates higher and "crowd out" private investors and consumers who also desire loans. In this case, aggregate demand may *not* increase. Typically, however, the additional borrowing requirements of the Treasury are "accommodated" by the Federal Reserve. The Fed is usually under intense political and economic pressure to avoid high interest rates and excessive **crowding out.** The Fed typically responds to this pressure by increasing the money supply. Indeed, **rational expectations,** based on such previous experience, lead one to anticipate that a tax cut will be followed by increased growth of the money supply. This new money feeds aggregate demand.

crowding out: A reduction in private-sector borrowing (and spending) necessitated by increased government borrowing.

rational expectations: Hypothesis that people's spending decisions are influenced by anticipated government policy, itself presumed to be like previous policies.

From a Monetarist perspective, the increased demand (M × V) will result in higher prices. Recall that Monetarists expect the rate of output to hover around the "natural" rate of unemployment. Hence an increase in M primarily affects prices (P), not output (Q).

Even Keynesians expect the increase in demand to push prices up. As the economy nears "full" employment, inflationary pressures increase. These inflationary pressures result from a variety of factors, especially supply bottlenecks (e.g., shortages of skilled labor or essential resources). In the face of such pressures, demand-side economists are reluctant to stimulate demand when the economy is near capacity. This leaves us in the unsatisfactory state of **stagflation,** with both unemployment and inflation.

stagflation: Simultaneous presence of substantial unemployment and inflation.

From this traditional Keynesian/Monetarist perspective, tax cuts in an inflationary environment should be accompanied by reductions in expenditures. In this way, income can be transferred from the public to the private sector (as voters demanded in 1980) without stimulating aggregate demand too much. Meaningful improvements in stagflation will have to come from structural changes in the economy. Chapter 13 provided a checklist of such possibilities, including deregulation, increased competition, reduced discrimination, improved training programs, and so on.

The supply-side argument

Reagan's Supply-Siders thought this approach to tax cutting was unnecessarily inhibited. Much better results could be obtained much faster. The "capacity" of the economy is not fixed, they argued. Instead, our potential to produce is directly affected by tax rates, particularly *marginal tax rates*. When marginal tax rates are too high, people are less willing to work. They also have less incentive to save or invest. As a result, the "capacity" (or "full-employment GNP") of the economy appears smaller than it really is. If marginal tax rates were reduced, observed capacity would increase, because people would work and invest more in response to higher "take-home" (after-tax) pay. These ***tax-induced increases in supply were the essential foundation of Reagan's supply-side tax-cut proposals.***

From this supply-side perspective, a tax cut need not generate inflationary pressures. True, aggregate demand will increase, as traditional economists assert. But the emphasis on cuts in marginal tax rates will ensure an expansion in output (Q). Thus more of the demand stimulus that comes from the left-hand side of the **equation of exchange** will be reflected in Q than in P. As a result, we will achieve greater output (real GNP) and employment without any increase in inflation. In these circumstances, budget cuts to offset tax-cut pressures are unnecessary; taxes can safely be cut without corresponding reductions in government expenditures.

In Chapter 13 we illustrated these different perspectives with aggregate-supply and -demand curves. Figure 15.1 repeats that illus-

equation of exchange: Money supply (M) times velocity of circulation (V) equals level of aggregate demand ($P \times Q$).

FIGURE 15.1 MUST BUDGET CUTS ACCOMPANY TAX CUTS?

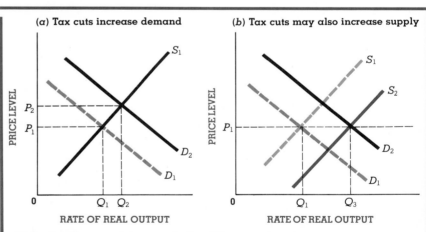

(a) Tax cuts increase demand

(b) Tax cuts may also increase supply

Virtually all economists concede (for different reasons) that tax cuts will shift the aggregate-demand curve to the right (from D_1 to D_2 in Figure *a*). If supply behavior is unchanged, this will cause both prices (P_2) and output (Q_2) to rise. From this perspective, taxes cannot be cut in an inflationary environment unless government expenditures are cut at the same time.

Reagan's supply-side advisers rejected this view by emphasizing the potential of reduced marginal tax rates to shift aggregate supply (from S_1 to S_2 in Figure *b*). This supply shift makes possible still more output (Q_3) *without* higher prices (P_1), *despite* increased demand (D_2). From this perspective, tax cuts need not be accompanied by budget cuts, even in an inflationary environment.

tration. Note again how a rightward shift of aggregate demand leads to both higher output and higher prices if aggregate supply is unchanged (S_1). But if aggregate supply responds (shifts) to marginal tax cuts, it is at least *possible* to get more output without higher prices. It is this possibility that encouraged Reagan's supply-side advisers.

TAX ELASTICITY OF SUPPLY

The optimistic predictions of the Supply-Siders depend on the response of labor and capital supplies to a tax cut. As we saw in Chapter 13, reductions in marginal tax rates tend to shift labor-supply and investment curves outward. *The policy issue is how large a supply shift will occur.* Will the increase in work effort and investment be so large that it offsets the stimulus to aggregate demand?

A second issue relates to the federal deficit. If tax rates are cut, tax revenues will normally be expected to fall. If government spending is not curbed at the same time, a larger budget deficit will seem to be inevitable. But Reagan's Supply-Siders rejected this conclusion. Recall that they wanted an immediate tax cut *without* offsetting budget cuts. They argued that the supply-side response to a tax cut would be so large that tax revenues would actually *rise,* not fall, after taxes were reduced. Hence they expected an extremely large supply-side response to tax cuts.

The Laffer curve

Laffer curve: A graph depicting the relationship of tax rates to total tax revenues.

The high expectations of the more ardent Supply-Siders were illustrated by Professor Arthur Laffer. The **Laffer curve,** as it has come to be known, begins with a very simple proposition. If tax rates are zero, no tax revenues will be collected. Similarly, if the tax rate is 100 percent, no one will want to work or report his or her income. Hence there are two very different tax *rates* (0 and 100 percent) that generate the same *level* of total tax revenues (zero). These two possibilities are illustrated by points *A* and *B* in Figure 15.2.

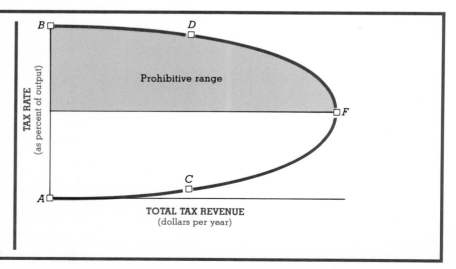

FIGURE 15.2 THE LAFFER CURVE

The Laffer curve illustrates the relationship between tax rates and total tax revenues. High tax rates (e.g., point *B*) discourage output and yield minimal tax revenue. As tax rates are reduced (point *D*), work effort increases so much that tax revenues actually increase. This response continues until point *F*, where total revenue is maximized. Below that point, further tax cuts lower tax revenues. Because *two* different tax rates will generate any desired level of tax revenue, rates above *F* are regarded as "prohibitive."

Prohibitive range

TAX RATE
(as percent of output)

TOTAL TAX REVENUE
(dollars per year)

Points A and B also imply very different rates of output. At point B, output of goods and services is at a minimum, since all (reported) output is confiscated by the tax authorities. Output at point A is much greater, since no taxes are collected. However, the absence of a public sector at point A (no taxes to support it) also implies minimal law enforcement, transportation, communication, and other services that facilitate business growth.

The focus of the Laffer curve is on the response of output and tax revenues to changes in tax *rates*. Suppose, for example, that the tax rate was lowered from 100 percent (point B) to something less (point D). How would workers and investors respond? With a 100 percent tax rate, there was no incentive to work or invest because all output was confiscated. At lower rates, people are permitted to keep some part of what they produce. Hence there is a greater incentive to work and invest at point D than at point B. We therefore expect more output to be produced at D. In this case, a *reduction* in tax rates leads to an *increase* in output. Tax revenues rise, too, since the increase in output is larger than the decline in tax rates.

ELASTICITY OF SUPPLY   The expected response of labor and capital to a change in tax rates is summarized by the elasticity of supply. Like other elasticities, this one measures the proportional response of supplies to a change in price (in this case, a tax rate). Specifically, the **tax elasticity of supply** is the percentage change in quantity supplied divided by the percentage change in tax rates, that is,

$$E = \frac{\text{percentage change in quantity supplied}}{\text{percentage change in tax rate}}$$

Normally we expect quantity supplied to go up when tax rates go down. E is therefore negative, although it is usually expressed in absolute terms (without the minus sign).[3] The (absolute) value of E is typically greater than zero, since we expect *some* response to a tax cut. (A zero value for E would imply no increase in quantity supplied—look at the formula for E again.) The policy issue boils down to the question of how large E actually is.

The top half of the Laffer curve assumes very high tax elasticities. As we lower tax rates from point B (100 percent) to point D, tax revenues actually increase in Figure 15.2. *A reduction in tax rates will yield larger tax revenues only if the tax elasticity of supply is greater than 1.* If E is greater than 1 ("relatively elastic"), the loss in tax revenues implied by a lower tax rate will be more than made up by increases in taxable output.[4] This expectation is illustrated by the move from point B to D and again from D to F.

The lower half of the Laffer curve is constructed on different

tax elasticity of supply: The percentage change in quantity supplied divided by the percentage change in tax rates.

---

[3] The value of E could also be *positive*. A reduction in quantity supplied in response to a tax cut would produce a positive E. This possibility is illustrated by the backward-bending supply curve discussed in Chapter 25.

[4] This is analogous to the pricing decision of a noncompetitive producer. Lower prices increase the quantity sold if price elasticity is greater than zero. Total revenue rises, however, only if price elasticity is greater than 1. See pp. 429–30.

How the tax system is discouraging work

One key element in the debate over supply-side economics is the effect of a change in taxes on the amount of time people are willing to work. The orthodox view is that the amount of work is insensitive to taxes and that there may even be a "backward-bending supply curve" in which, faced with rising tax rates, employees put in longer hours to maintain aftertax incomes.

The supply-siders, of course, have another view. University of Southern California economist Arthur B. Laffer has become famous for arguing that workers would greet a tax cut with such a tremendous outpouring of vocational enthusiasm that the initial revenue loss would eventually be made up. But even most supply-side-oriented econometricians have heretofore found that taxes mainly affect the behavior of secondary workers rather than that of the primary labor force, largely married men.

Now J.D. Hausman of the Massachusetts Institute of Technology has come up with new econometric evidence indicating that the work behavior of prime-age males also is affected by taxes. His study, scheduled to be published next year by the Brookings Institution, finds that the progressive tax system has reduced the man-hours supplied by married men by some 8% below what they would be under a proportional tax system. Because Hausman's figures ended with 1975 and the "bracket creep" effect of inflation has made the tax system even more progressive than it had been (chart), the effect is probably even greater.

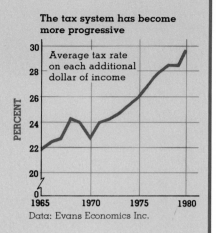

The tax system has become more progressive

Average tax rate on each additional dollar of income

Data: Evans Economics Inc.

assumptions. At point *A* the tax rate and total tax revenues are both equal to zero. To increase tax revenues, the tax rate must be raised. The question again is: How do labor and capital supplies respond to a change in tax rates? In this case, the tax rate is being *increased*.

The Supply-Siders argue that the initial response of capital and labor to an increased tax rate will be positive. When there were no taxes (point *A*) there were also no essential government services (transportation, law enforcement, etc.). With the introduction of taxes, these essential services can be provided by government. Because such services facilitate and encourage market transactions, the quantity of output should increase. Hence the move from point *A* to point *C* implies both more output and greater tax revenues, despite rising tax rates.

Once essential public services have been provided, the response of labor and capital to further tax increases is more complicated. Now we must deal with the possibility that the productivity of the economy will *shrink* as tax rates continue to rise beyond point *C*. In other words, beyond point *C* the tax elasticity of supply is expected to be *negative*, as it was in our earlier analysis. In this case, an *increase* in tax rates leads to a *decrease* in the quantity of labor and capital supplied.

A reduction in supply does not necessarily lead to lower tax revenues, however. Notice that total revenues continue to increase as we move from *C* to *F* in Figure 15.2, despite rising tax rates. This happens because the reduction in supply is proportionately less than the increase in tax rates. In other words, the tax elasticity of supply is evidently less than 1 (in absolute value) between points *C* and *F*. Output falls, but by less than taxes rise; that is, supply is relatively *inelastic* in the range from *C* to *F*.

REVENUE MAXIMIZATION   The lower and upper portions of the Laffer curve converge at point F. Point F has a special significance. At this tax rate, total tax revenues are *maximized* (there are no points to the right of F). A government that sought to maximize its own revenues would choose this tax rate.[5]

Another feature of point F is that it clearly separates "good" tax rates from "bad" ones. All rates above F are undesirable because some lower rate would generate just as much tax revenue and more output. (If the high tax rate at D generates no more revenue than the low rate at C, then less output must be produced [and taxed] at D.) Because of this, Laffer regards all tax rates above F as "prohibitive." No government would want to depress total output unnecessarily.

No one seems to know exactly where point F is. Jude Wanniski, who popularized the Laffer curve, suggests that F "is the point at which the electorate desires to be taxed."[6] But the Supply-Siders' argument for a tax cut required a stronger assumption. They were asserting that a tax cut would increase output without additional pressure on prices. This assumes that 1981 tax rates were in the prohibitive range, above F. Only in this range does output (supply) increase faster than tax rates fall. Below F, output continues to increase, but at a slower pace than tax rates fall.

If we were actually at point F or lower in 1981, a tax cut would reduce tax revenues. This is a potential problem, particularly if government spending is not reduced at the same time. In the absence of compensating budget cuts, a tax cut below point F will increase the federal **budget deficit.** An enlarged deficit could in turn intensify inflationary pressures, owing to either greater velocity of money or accommodating increases in the money supply.

budget deficit: The amount by which government expenditures exceed government revenues.

The critique

The general nature of the objections to the Supply-Siders' tax-cut argument should be evident. Critics pointed out that there is simply no evidence that tax rates are or ever were in the "prohibitive range" of the Laffer curve. Voter demands for a tax cut are not sufficient evidence that we are at point F. Tax cuts below F are presumably welcomed, too.

The Achilles heel in the Supply-Siders' argument is the assumed size of the tax elasticity of supply. The absolute value of E must be larger than 1 if we are actually in the prohibitive range. Yet accumulated evidence on supply elasticities falls far short of such estimates. Indeed, no study of either labor or capital has found such a large response. Typically the supply-side increase is only a fraction of the percentage cut in taxes. In a recent survey of empirical studies, Professor Don Fullerton of Princeton University argued that 0.15 is a reasonable estimate of labor-supply elasticity in the United States.[7]

[5] Some Supply-Siders have claimed that total output (GNP) is also maximized at F. Total output and tax revenues cannot be maximized simultaneously, however, so long as output tends to increase when tax rates fall. At point F the tax-rate elasticity of output must be equal to -1 if revenues are at a maximum. Below F the absolute value of elasticity is smaller than 1 but still greater than zero. In other words, output continues to increase below point F, even though revenues fall.

[6] Jude Wanniski, "Taxes, Revenues, and the 'Laffer Curve,'" *Public Interest*, Winter 1978, p. 4.

[7] Don Fullerton, "Can Tax Revenues Go Up When Tax Rates Go Down?," Office of Tax Analysis, U.S. Department of the Treasury, September 1980.

The expectation of a strong supply response was further weakened by one of the basic motives for the tax cut. The proposed three-year tax cut would not really reduce marginal tax rates very much. Inflation would still be pushing people into higher tax brackets. In large part, the Reagan proposal would just offset this bracket creep. In fact, lower- and middle-income households would not see their marginal tax rates drop at all: bracket creep would offset all of a three-year 30 percent tax cut. Only households with incomes of $50,000 or more would enjoy actual tax-rate reductions. Hence any positive supply-side effects would have to come from this relatively small segment of the population. For the *average* tax elasticity of supply to exceed 1, an enormous quantity of additional production would have to come from these high-income households.

Another problem relates to *timing*. Even if the tax elasticity of supply were higher, the increase in productive capacity would not appear overnight. More labor can be employed rather quickly. But time is needed to build new factories, modernize old ones, or acquire additional machinery. Hence supply expansion, however large it may ultimately be, may not occur quickly enough to reduce the inflationary pressures of a tax cut.

THE INITIAL BUDGET COMPROMISE

During the course of the 1981 budget debate, the Supply-Siders were forced to concede the improbability of high supply elasticities. They also conceded that the supply response to tax cuts might be delayed. David Stockman, director of Reagan's Office of Management and Budget, later went so far as to suggest that the across-the-board tax cuts were a "Trojan horse." The true intent of the proposal, he said, was to reduce taxes on high-income households. Hence the economic argument for "balanced" tax and budget cuts looked persuasive.

The political arguments for coordinated tax and spending cuts were also important. Taxpayers had sent a very clear message to Washington: they wanted to see some budget cuts. Reagan's credibility as well as the success of his economic program depended on his ability to deliver promised budget cuts. Reagan also had to reckon with Congress. There were enough Demand-Siders, budget cutters, and plain skeptics in Congress to prevent any one-sided tax cuts.

One final consideration was compelling. No Supply-Sider had ever argued that budget cuts were undesirable. The debate was whether such cuts were *necessary* or not. The Supply-Siders had argued that compensating budget cuts weren't necessary. Because tax cuts are easier and faster to implement than budget cuts, the Supply-Siders urged Reagan to proceed immediately with Kemp-Roth tax cuts. They also argued that immediate tax cuts would force faster congressional action on budget cuts. But Reagan wasn't persuaded. Ultimately he recognized that

☐ Budget cuts were politically desired

    □ Budget cuts might be necessary to offset the inflationary impact of tax cuts

    □ Budget cuts certainly couldn't worsen inflation

In the end, Reagan's tax-cut decision was relatively simple.

Reagan's budget package

On February 18, 1981, President Reagan proposed to Congress a fiscal policy of "balanced" tax cuts and spending cuts. He stuck with the Kemp-Roth idea of three-year 30 percent cuts in personal income-tax rates. He conceded to Congress that "some will argue, I know, that reducing tax rates now will be inflationary." But he cited a "solid body of economic experts" who had shown that large tax cuts would provide "incentive to increase productivity for both workers and industry" and would therefore "expand our national prosperity." The three-year tax-cut horizon would also provide an environment "in which private individuals can confidently plan and make appropriate decisions." In response to demand-side critics, Reagan offered to delay the first cuts until July, so as to minimize any initial inflationary pressures.

    The greatest gesture to demand-side economics occurred on the outlays side of the budget. In response to the inflationary threat of his tax cuts, Reagan proposed massive cuts in projected government expenditures. Projected FY 1982 spending was to be cut $41 billion, with further cuts of $80 billion in FY 1983 and $104 billion in FY 1984. These cuts, Reagan claimed, not only would restrain inflation but also would help eliminate the government's budget deficit.

Congressional action

Like all tax and spending proposals, Reagan's fiscal package had to be approved by Congress. The House of Representatives was still controlled by Democrats, and they were not about to accede to all of the president's wishes too easily or too fast. Many Republican members of Congress also had their own ideas of what taxes and spending items to cut, and in what amounts. In addition, most traditional demand-side economists kept issuing dire forecasts about the inflationary impact of Reagan's three-year tax-cut proposals.

    The congressional debate continued for nearly five months. Finally, on July 31, 1981, Congress passed the Economic Recovery Tax Act of 1981. The act included Reagan's major proposals, although with significant changes. The three-year tax cut was approved, but its initial installment was delayed to October 1, 1981, and reduced. The 1981 tax cut amounted to only 1¼ percent, to be followed by 10 percent cuts in July 1982 and July 1983. By 1984 these cuts would amount to a 23 percent tax cut for consumers. Income-tax rates were also to be indexed to inflation beginning in 1985, thus eliminating future bracket creep. In addition, Congress reduced business taxes more than Reagan had originally proposed, and provided new tax incentives for consumer saving (e.g., liberalized individual retirement accounts).

    As Table 15.2 indicates, the tax cuts passed by Congress in 1981 were expected to have substantial impact. In its first full year (1982),

TABLE 15.2   THE REAGAN TAX CUTS

The Economic Recovery Tax Act of 1981 provided substantial tax cuts for consumers and business. The figures here indicate the size of the cuts, relative to what would have been paid under earlier tax law. The size of the annual cuts increases because of economic growth (higher real incomes) and continuing inflation (higher nominal incomes).

Provision	Estimated revenue loss (billions of dollars)				
	1981	1982	1983	1984	1985
Personal tax cuts	$0.4	$26.9	$71.1	$114.7	$148.2
Business tax cuts	1.6	10.7	18.6	28.3	39.3
Savings incentives	—	0.2	1.8	4.2	5.7
Miscellaneous	−0.4	−0.1	1.2	2.8	6.1
Total tax cut	$1.6	$37.7	$92.7	$150.0	$199.3

the tax cuts would total nearly $38 billion. By 1984 the tax cuts would equal $150 billion per year. These estimates refer to forgone tax revenues only. If these tax cuts had a multiplier effect on demand or an incentive effect on supply, their impact would be larger still.

To offset the potential stimulus of such large tax cuts, Congress also cut the growth in federal spending. First year spending cuts were limited to $35 billion, however, rather than the $41 billion Reagan had requested.

MONETARY RESTRAINT

As important as the fiscal package was, it was only part of the president's economic plan. In his initial proposals to Congress, Reagan had also urged a more restrictive monetary policy. "To curb inflation," he argued, "we need to slow the growth in our money supply."

Reagan's call for monetary restraint was generally welcomed by Monetarists and Supply-Siders. Both regard monetary restraint as the ultimate bulwark against inflation. The essence of their faith has been illustrated by the equation of exchange:

$$M \times V = P \times Q$$

As discussed in Chapters 12 and 13, M is the basic lever of monetary policy; V is the basic lever of fiscal policy. P and Q are the principal targets of either policy.

A tax cut has the potential to increase the **income velocity of money** (V) and therewith the demand for goods and services. If structured correctly, it may also increase incentives for producing more output. If supply-side responses are not adequate, however, Q will not rise sufficiently. Any "excess" demand will then spill over into P, increasing the rate of inflation.

This spillover can be avoided, however, if M is reduced. A smaller (growth of) money supply will "choke off" excess demand and keep prices from rising. Hence Supply-Siders argued that a one-sided tax cut *combined with monetary restraint* would ensure noninflationary growth. Traditional Monetarists also liked this proposal, for slightly different reasons. From a strict Monetarist perspective, monetary restraint is the *only* way to stop inflation. Accompanying tax cuts are pretty much irrelevant, even though they

income velocity of money: The number of times per year, on average, a dollar is used to purchase final goods and services; $PQ \div M$.

may encourage some output growth and shift resources from the public to the private sector.

Not everyone liked this policy package. Although sufficient monetary restraint can surely stop inflation, it can also retard growth. Indeed, a truly noninflationary monetary policy can easily result in a recession. Recall that monetary restraint only limits the growth of aggregate demand (PQ). By itself, it exercises no direct control over either P or Q separately. Output rather than prices may fall when the monetary brakes are applied. This is the essence of the stagflation problem discussed in Chapter 13.

Monetary restraint is especially threatening in the short run. At the time Reagan became president, interest rates were extremely high. These high interest rates had virtually halted the construction and sales of houses, sharply reduced auto sales, and generally increased consumption and production costs. They had also persuaded many voters to elect Reagan rather than Carter. Greater monetary restraint in the Reagan administration threatened to push interest rates still higher. Higher interest rates might, in turn, obliterate the supply-side incentives created by Reagan's tax cuts.

Despite these potential problems, the Federal Reserve followed the restrictive path Reagan had charted. The money supply (M1) had increased by 10.8 percent in 1980. In the first quarter of 1981 the Fed cut this growth rate in half and kept money "tight" throughout the year.

DEREGULATION

Another important component of Reagan's economic package was its commitment to deregulation. Reagan and his advisers were convinced that excessive federal interference in the marketplace was a major constraint on private-sector initiative. Unnecessary federal rules and regulations also raised production costs and contributed to higher inflation. Professor Murray Weidenbaum, first chairman of Reagan's Council of Economic Advisers, had estimated that government regulation was costing U.S. consumers more than $100 billion per year. By cutting government red tape, Reagan believed, he could foster growth and efficiency while reducing inflation.

The move toward deregulation was started during the Carter administration. The airline, transportation, communications, and securities industries had already undergone significant deregulation by the time Reagan took office. But Reagan vowed to broaden and accelerate the pace of deregulation. He started by imposing a 60-day freeze on all new federal regulations. He then moved to dismantle existing regulations. Reagan abolished the program of wage-price guidelines established by Carter and vowed not to interfere further with those market outcomes. He also accelerated deregulation of oil prices and allocations. Later targets of his deregulaton program became workplace rules (especially Occupational Safety and Health Administration regulations) and "unnecessary" environmental safeguards. By the end of 1981 the administration claimed to have substantially reversed the momentum of federal regulation.

TABLE 15.3 REAGAN'S ECONOMIC PROJECTIONS
(February 1981)

Reagan's promise of a balanced budget by 1984 was based on his economic assumptions. At the heart of these assumptions was the expectation that aggregate supply would shift to the right in response to reduced marginal tax rates. If this happened, real growth would accelerate and both inflation and unemployment would subside.

	Budget projections (billions of dollars)			
	FY/1981	FY/1982	FY/1983	FY/1984
Spending	$654.7	$695.5	$733.1	$771.6
Revenues	600.2	650.5	710.2	772.1
Deficit	−$ 54.5	−$ 45.0	−$ 22.9	+$ 0.5
	Economic assumptions (percent)			
	1981	1982	1983	1984
Real growth	1.1	4.2	5.0	4.5
Inflation	11.1	8.3	6.2	5.5
Unemployment	6.6	6.4	6.0	5.6

THE ECONOMY

The expected response

The administration expected the economy to respond well to its fiscal, monetary, and supply-side policies. In his initial (February 1981) economic address to Congress, Reagan unveiled his expectations. He foresaw a vigorous expansion of the economy beginning in late 1981. As Table 15.3 reveals, the administration anticipated the rate of real economic growth to accelerate to 4.2 percent in 1982, after a modest turnaround in 1981 (in 1980 total output had actually declined by 0.1 percent). This vigorous expansion of output would:

□ Increase government revenues
□ Help reduce the deficit
□ Slow inflation
□ Reduce unemployment

By 1984, Reagan predicted, the economy would achieve a balanced budget, a much lower (5.5 percent) rate of inflation, and a significant decline in unemployment (5.6 percent).

INFLATIONARY EXPECTATIONS A key element in the administration's projection was an assumed change in inflationary expectations. The president shared the belief that rising interest rates and prices were in large part an expression of inflationary expectations. In late 1980 virtually all Americans expected inflation to continue at high rates. Lenders demanded extraordinarily high rates of interest to protect their assets against future inflation. Consumers and businesses continued to borrow at these high rates in an effort to "beat inflation." For their part, workers demanded large pay increases, and businesses raised prices to cover expected cost increases. As everyone sought to stay ahead of rising prices, inflation accelerated.

Of crucial importance in this process was people's perceptions of the causes of inflation. Right or wrong, the American people were convinced that runaway government spending was the primary cause of inflation. From this perspective, Ronald Reagan looked like the last great hope. He promised to reduce government "waste and abuse." In place of the on-again, off-again economic stimulus undertaken by his predecessors, he offered a *predictable* economic policy. Specifically, he offered to initiate and maintain a long-term economic program of tax and spending cuts that would ultimately reduce inflationary pressures.

The administration argued that in view of the election outcome, inflationary expectations would subside. With greater confidence in the country's economic future, people would reduce their wage, price, and interest-rate demands. They might also begin to save and invest more of their income, rather than spend it immediately.

The potential of changed inflationary expectations to alter the economic outlook is immense. Look at the equation of exchange again. The problem faced by the administration was that P might rise instead of Q when taxes were cut. If inflationary expectations actually improved (fell), this need not happen. Better expectations would directly reduce (the growth of) P. Greater savings and investment could also contribute directly to higher Q. Hence the expansionary effects of increased aggregate demand could be funneled to real output rather than to higher prices. A greater willingness to hold money would also allow the Fed to ease up on monetary restraints.

The prediction of improved inflationary expectations became an essential element in the president's economic program. The president himself made repeated predictions of an improving economy, hoping thereby to alter market perceptions and behavior. The administration realized that if expectations improved enough, almost any outcome was possible. From this perspective, their predictions of noninflationary growth didn't look completely impossible. There was no denying, however, that reliance on improved expectations was a substantial gamble. As Senator Howard Baker put it, shortly after Congress approved Reagan's economic plan: "What we are doing is really a river-boat gamble."

The 1981–82 recession

As it turned out, the economy did not respond as vigorously as Reagan anticipated. Interest rates stayed high through most of 1981 and the stock market actually declined 150 points shortly after Reagan's fiscal package was approved by Congress. In fact, the reaction of the bond and stock markets to Reagan's initiatives was so bad that the president and members of his cabinet began to wonder publicly whether the financial markets weren't too "short-sighted." Pessimism was not confined to financial markets. In September 1981 only 21 percent of the public expected inflation to slow down in 1982.[8] The rate of business investment had also failed to accelerate in 1981 despite the availability of new and substantial supply-side incentives. These anemic responses raised serious doubts about the very foundations of Reagan's economic program.

In the face of continuing economic stagnation, the administration went on the defensive. The president first attempted to dismiss

[8] Time-Yankelovich poll of September 15–17, as reported in *Time*, October 5, 1981.

any suggestions of failure by arguing that his economic program had not really begun until October 1981. That was the date of the first installment of his personal income-tax reductions. But the business-tax deductions were retroactive to January 1, 1981. Moreover, the administration had itself predicted a much earlier effect as a result of altered expectations.

In September the administration took further defensive moves. It began "jawboning" the Fed to ease up on monetary restraint, with the hope that this would reduce interest rates. In response to forecasts of increasingly large deficits, Reagan proposed another $16 billion in spending cuts. The administration even began to discuss the possibility of delaying or even rescinding the supply-side tax cuts Congress had approved.

Ultimately the president acknowledged that the U.S. economy had slipped into recession. According to the National Bureau of Economic Research, the recession had actually begun in July, just about the time Reagan's fiscal package was approved by Congress. It then gained significant downward momentum, depressing output far below almost everyone's predictions. Instead of falling to 6.4 percent, as the president had predicted (Table 15.3), unemployment jumped to 10 percent in 1982. Instead of diminishing, the federal deficit began to grow enormously. The only good news in 1981–82 was the drop in inflation. The rate of inflation fell from 12.4 percent in 1980 to 8.9 percent in 1981, and fell still further in 1982.

The post-mortem

The 1981–82 recession looked like a classic Phillips-curve problem. Reagan had succeeded in reducing inflation, but only at the cost of substantially greater unemployment. This is exactly the kind of trade-off traditional demand-side economists had always envisioned (see Figure 13.2, p. 290). The claims of supply-side economists that they could shift the aggregate-supply curve (Figure 15.1)—and with it the Phillips curve—seemed to be discredited. Traditional Keynesian and Monetarist economists were quick to say "I told you so."

The 1981–82 recession could not be blamed entirely on supply-side economics, however. Indeed, the seeds of the 1981–82 recession were sown much earlier. Tight monetary policies begun in late 1980, together with President Carter's final attempt at restrictive fiscal policies, were the primary causes of the recession. By the time Reagan took office, aggregate demand was already beginning to slow down. Reagan accelerated that slowdown, but not by his supply-side tax cuts. On the contrary, fiscal policy was actually restrictive in 1981 and early 1982. By cutting government spending early in 1981 and agreeing to a delay of the initial tax cuts, Reagan restrained aggregate demand.[9] In large part, this was a classic measurement problem (failure to foresee the recession) compounded by design compromises and delays in implementation.

The Federal Reserve also restrained aggregate demand. As noted earlier, the Fed cut the growth rate of $M1$ in half in 1981. In the third quarter of 1981 there was virtually no growth at all in the money supply. ***The combination of monetary and fiscal restraint in 1981 pushed the economy deeper into recession.***

To the extent that Supply-Siders bore any blame for the 1981–82 recession, it was for their excessively optimistic projections. Although they foresaw a slowdown in 1981, they expected a much stronger investment response to the early tax cuts. They concluded that the economy would achieve sustained, noninflationary growth in a relatively short time. They also pinned their hopes for increased

[9] The full-employment budget balance moved from a deficit of roughly $17 billion in FY 1980 to a *surplus* of $7 billion in FY 1981. This reduction in the full-employment deficit reflected the true impact of Reagan's initial fiscal policies (see Chapter 9, Appendix).

The Washington Post/ABC News Poll

Public expresses doubts on Reagan's economic program

Q. Should Reagan stick with his economic program of cuts in domestic social spending and cuts in taxes, or should Reagan try some other program to help the economy?

STICK WITH THE PROGRAM	35%
TRY SOME OTHER PROGRAM	61%
NO OPINION	4%

Q. Do you approve or disapprove of the way Reagan is handling the nation's economy?

	FEB. 17–18	JAN. 22–30	OCT. 16–20
APPROVE	38%	46%	54%
DISAPPROVE	57%	46%	39%
NO OPINION	5%	8%	7%

Q. Do you think majority of the people will be helped by Reagan's economic program if the program does what Reagan really wants it to do?

A MAJORITY WILL BE HELPED	48%
LESS THAN A MAJORITY WILL BE HELPED	46%
NO OPINION	6%

Figures are from a Washington Post-ABC News poll of 1,004 people interviewed by telephone nationwide Wednesday and Thursday, and from earlier Post–ABC News polls.

The Washington Post, Washington, D.C., February 20, 1982.

consumer and investor confidence on early indications of such a recovery. When the recovery failed to materialize, public confidence in Reagan economics faltered. This made the job of stimulating the economy that much harder.

THE FY 1983 BUDGET

Given the depth and duration of the 1981–82 recession, it might seem that everyone would have advocated a quick injection of fiscal/monetary stimulus. But this was not the case. The debate over the FY 1983 budget, which began in January 1982, was essentially a replay of Reagan's first budget debate.

Once again Keynesian economists warned of excessive fiscal stimulus when additional tax cuts took effect (in July 1982). The budget deficit was projected to soar to over $100 billion when the cuts were implemented. This fiscal stimulus might reduce unemployment, but it would also accelerate inflation.

Monetarists emphasized that the projected deficits would drive up interest rates and "crowd out" any hope of an investment boom, at least so long as the money supply was help in check. As for the money supply itself, Fed Chairman Paul Volcker repeatedly emphasized his determination to continue a restrictive monetary policy. This set the stage for a classic clash between fiscal and monetary policy. Interest rates would fall, Volcker warned, only if the budget deficit was cut. Indeed, the *anticipation* of tight money and excessive crowding out was a major force keeping interest rates high. Virtually all demand-side economists thus called for greater fiscal restraint in 1983, to be achieved by larger spending cuts or tax increases.

The administration again tried to defend its program on supply-side grounds. It argued that the tax cuts still coming would in-

Volcker Blasts Huge Deficit

Federal Reserve Chairman Paul Volcker yesterday told Congress he would rather have higher taxes in 1983 than accept the $91.5 billion deficit proposed in President Reagan's budget.

In his first congressional appearance since a meeting with Reagan last week, Volcker spoke out even more strongly against large budget deficits than before.

Volcker has blamed present high interest rates on the huge budget deficits projected for 1983 and beyond, while administration officials previously argued that volatile money policy had kept rates up. Volcker yesterday said "short-term fluctuations (in the money supply) should have no important implication for economic activity or inflation."

The president reaffirmed his support for the Fed's tight money policy at a press conference last week, after several weeks of administration sniping at the Federal Reserve.

But Volcker warned Congress yesterday that large budget deficits now threaten economic recovery, and called on legislators to go beyond President Reagan's proposed budget savings to bring down the projected deficits.

He dismissed the argument advanced by some administration officials, particularly Treasury Secretary Donald Regan, that U.S. savings are going to rise so much under the impact of the new tax laws that large deficits will be financed easily. "To count on a dramatically large increase in savings to bail us out of the budgetary problem would be to miss the point, at best," he told the House Ways and Means Committee.

Even assuming an increase in savings in the future and some further deep budget cuts, the federal government will be absorbing a disproportionate amount of available credit in 1983 and beyond to finance its budget deficit, the Fed chairman said.

—Caroline Atkinson

The Washington Post, Washington, D.C., February 24, 1982. Copyright © 1982 The Washington Post.

crease output more than anticipated. Reagan also argued that consumer savings would increase greatly, in response to new tax incentives and lower inflation. These added savings would enlarge the pool of loanable funds and therefore reduce the risk of "crowding out." With a vastly larger pool of savings, both higher federal deficits *and* increased investment were possible.

Reagan also emphasized again the importance of consistent, predictable fiscal and monetary policies. To abandon the tax cuts in 1982 or 1983 would be to adopt "the stop-go policies of the past which, with their short-term focus, only added to our long-run economic ills."

To a large extent, the FY 1983 budget debate was again a clash of competing forecasts. The Reagan administration was predicting faster growth and lower deficits than everyone else. This time around, however, the administration's forecasts had much less credibility. Indeed, even the administration's own deficit projections were so high that Reagan had to abandon his oft-repeated promise of a balanced budget by 1984. In a complete reversal of his earlier positions, he embraced the concept of the "full-employment" (or "high-employment") budget. The actual deficit, he said, was a result of recession, not excessive fiscal stimulus. It would disappear, although much more slowly than he had originally anticipated.

To close the budget more quickly, Reagan urged Congress to cut spending further. But he initially refused to accept cuts in either defense spending or social security benefits. Since these two items accounted for over half of total federal expenditures, Reagan left Congress with little room to maneuver. To achieve any semblance of fiscal balance, sharp cuts in nondefense spending would have to be made. This created a conflict between the economic goal of reduced spending and the political goal of preserving specific public programs.

Ultimately Reagan had to strike a compromise with Congress and the Fed. In exchange for keeping his 10 percent income-tax cut in the budget, Reagan had to agree to raise other taxes. The compromise was contained in the Tax Equity and Fiscal Responsibility Act of 1982. That act essentially revoked about one-third of the business tax cuts voted one year earlier. It also tightened some consumer "loopholes" and made provision for tighter enforcement of tax laws. The net effect of the 1982 act was to increase taxes by roughly $90 billion for the years 1983 to 1985.

Taken together, the 1981 and 1982 tax acts reflected an eclectic pragmatism that combined the essential ingredients of Keynesians, Monetarists, and Supply-Siders. In the process, however, much of the uniqueness of Reagan economics was lost. By the end of 1982 most of Reagan's original Supply-Siders had left government, to be replaced by more traditional economists. Treasury Secretary Donald Regan acknowledged the existence of a short-term trade-off between unemployment and inflation, while the second chairman of Reagan's Council of Economic Advisers, Martin Feldstein, publicly disavowed "extreme" supply-side propositions. As for the economy, it did not begin to recover until late 1982 with the help of lowered inflationary expectations, faster money-supply growth, lower interest rates, and improved tax incentives.

**Interview with
Arthur B. Laffer, Economist**

What went wrong with "supply side" economics

Q Professor Laffer, the economic picture now is far worse than President Reagan predicted when he came into office a year ago. What went wrong?

A The administration and Congress postponed the tax cuts. I put much of the blame on David Stockman, director of the Office of Management and Budget. This is the Stockman recession and the Stockman deficit. He was too concerned about budget deficits and watered down the tax cuts, which has slowed the economy. Stockman, with his talk of huge deficits, tax increases and more budget cuts, is fighting to bring back the days of Herbert Hoover. He's trying to scare people.

Deficits aren't the cause of bad economics; deficits are the consequence of bad economics. You never balance the budget when you have slow growth, high unemployment, high inflation and high interest rates, as we do now.

Q But Reagan's business-tax cut was not postponed, and the personal-tax cut was postponed for only a short period of time. Is the mechanism of "supply side"

economics so delicate that even small changes upset it?

A I'll answer with an illustration. Suppose you have to go back to school and won't earn any income for a year. You have to decide whether to go this year when income-tax rates are high or next year when they are low. So which year do you go to school? This year, of course.

Now, apply that to the tax structure. We have had a cut in personal income taxes so far of 1.25 percent in 1981. In 1982, we'll have a 10 percent cumulative cut. In 1983, it will be a 20 percent cumulative cut. The whole economy works on incentives like these. What's happening is that people are putting off investments and income-producing work now to wait for a more favorable tax situation. . . .

Q With the economic policies now in place, when is the recession going to end?

A Nineteen eighty-two will probably be sluggish, but not as bad as 1981. Then 1983 will be great, and 1984 will be phenomenal. Once the incentives to postpone taxes are gone, people will make production decisions immediately instead of waiting.

Q If 1983 and 1984 turn out as well as you are predicting, will the federal-budget deficit be shrinking, rather than ballooning as some estimates suggest?

A Yes. The deficit in and of itself is not a problem. It's a barometer of what's going on. Right now, it's an indicator that our economy is sicker

than a dog. But the way you solve a deficit is to create economic growth and low inflation. These huge estimates are sabotaging Reagan's Presidency. It's strictly scare tactics. If you look back at estmates OMB has made in the past, they are never anywhere close to the later reality. Whoever is putting out these wild numbers is trying to unelect Reagan, the same way that Hoover was unelected.

Q What should be President Reagan's strategy in the 1983 budget that will be unveiled later this month?

A The President should do all he can to spur economic growth. No. 1, he should make all the tax cuts effective retroactive to Jan. 1, 1982. No. 2, he should go back to convertibility—that is, a version of the gold standard—as fast as possible. He should restore some of the funds that have been cut for social programs. Finally, he should pressure the Federal reserve to bring interest rates down. High rates won't solve our inflation problem.

Q If the President were to do all that, when would we begin to see results?

A You would see the benefits right away. It may take a long time to offset the total damage to the economy, but you wouldn't have hard times.

SUMMARY

■ The core of Reagan economics was constructed from supply-side theories of economic behavior. These theories emphasize the negative effects of higher marginal tax rates on people's willingness to work, save, and invest. To reverse these disincentives, Reagan called for large three-year tax cuts, as originally proposed in the Kemp-Roth bill.

■ The central issue in the formulation of Reagan's policy was whether to "offset" the tax cuts with comparable spending cuts. Supply-Siders said budget cuts were not necessary; traditional demand-side economists argued that "one-sided" tax cuts would be inflationary.

■ The Laffer curve illustrates the relationship of tax rates to total tax revenues. It raises the possibility that lower tax rates might yield at least as much tax revenue as high rates, and more GNP. To do so, the tax elasticity of supply must be greater than 1.

Interview with James Tobin, Nobel Laureate in Economics

Reaganomics "never was a consistent policy"

Q Professor Tobin, can Reaganomics work?

A The problem with Reaganomics is that it never was a consistent policy from the start. The Federal Reserve Board's restrictive monetary policy to fight inflation is at odds with the President's expansionary fiscal policy to promote economic growth.

It's like attaching to a train in New Haven station a locomotive at one end headed east and another one at the other end headed west. The station-master announces that the train will leave for both Boston and New York. But, under the circumstances, it's doubtful the train will reach either destination. That's what happened to Reaganomics.

One locomotive was Mr. Reagan's tax-reduction bill; the other locomotive was the Fed's tight-money policy. The result of this tug of war was that the President's train stalled, interest rates rose, and we ended up with the deep recession we now have.

Q What should the President do now to get his economic "train" going in the right direction?

A He must tighten fiscal policy, and the Fed must ease up on monetary policy. And he should use his great powers of persuasion to bring an "incomes"—or wage-price—policy to bear in the flight against inflation.

Q How do you think fiscal policy should be tightened?

A It's universally recognized, even by the administration itself, that the President overdid the tax cut. The 1982 deficit, largely the result of the recession itself, is no problem. Large deficits loom for fiscal 1983 and 1984, even if the economy were then operating at reasonably prosperous levels. These deficits should be reduced. I would postpone the third installment of the tax cuts for individuals— scheduled for July of 1983—and the indexing of brackets. . . .

Q What do you mean by the term "incomes policy"?

A My version of an incomes policy would couple a transitional schedule of declining guideposts for wage and price increases with tax incentives for companies and workers to obey them. Those who voluntarily hold down price and wage increases would be rewarded with tax rebates or credits so they would not be penalized by their cooperation with the anti-inflation effort.

The government's job would be to manage fiscal and monetary policy to bring about a recovery from the recession. An incomes policy would make it easier to control inflation and, by promoting a quicker recovery, would benefit everybody. . . .

Q What should Reagan have done?

A As I said, I favor an incomes policy. But if the President was going to mount a purely monetary attack on inflation—and this is what his policy has turned out to be—he should have had, like Mrs. Thatcher, the guts to say so plainly. He could have told the American people, on national television, that he intends to support a tight-money policy to get rid of inflation, even if it takes two or three years and damages output and employment. That would have been the courageous thing to do, so that businessmen, union leaders and everybody would have known that unless they moderated wage and price increases fast, they were in for rough times.

- Advocates of "balanced" tax and budget cuts argue that (*a*) actual tax elasticities of supply are much smaller than Supply-Siders assert, (*b*) the demand-side stimulus of a tax cut will outpace supply growth and accelerate inflation.

- Reagan's initial fiscal policy was a compromise of supply- and demand-side theories. The tax and budget cuts were accompanied by substantial monetary restraint and a commitment to deregulation. The administration felt this three-pronged attack on stagflation would also dampen inflationary expectations.

- The 1981–82 recession was not anticipated by the Reagan administration. By increasing unemployment and reducing inflation, it dramatically increased the federal deficit. This turn of events compelled Reagan to accept the concept of a full-employment budget and forsake quick attainment of a balanced budget.

- The FY 1983 budget reflected further compromises in Reagan's supply-side orientation. Many of the earlier (1981) business tax cuts were effectively revoked, and new spending cuts were initiated.

Terms to remember

Define the following terms:

bracket creep
marginal tax rate
disposable income (DI)
full-employment GNP
crowding out
rational expectations

stagflation
equation of exchange
Laffer curve
tax elasticity of supply
budget deficit
income velocity of money

Questions for discussion

1. What measurement, design, or implementation problems were evident in the creation of Reagan's economic program?

2. What significant policy changes (fiscal, monetary, or supply-side) have taken place in the last year?

3. How has the economy's performance changed in the last year? Can any of these changes be attributed to Reagan's economic policies?

4. Describe four specific ways in which improved inflationary expectations reduce inflationary pressures.

5. Suppose taxes and government spending were cut equally. What effect would this "balanced-budget" tax cut have on (a) the economy, (b) the budget deficit? Contrast the views of traditional Demand-Siders with those of Supply-Siders. (Hint: see pp. 212–13.)

Problem

The following table depicts the quantity of labor that would be supplied at different tax rates. Calculate the tax elasticities of supply for tax cuts from A to B, B to C, C to D, and D to E. (Note: use the midpoint elasticity formula provided in Chapter 18, p. 427).

	A	B	C	D	E
Marginal tax rate (percent of income)	70	60	50	40	30
Quantity of labor supplied (units per year)	300	382	458	502	548

CHAPTER 16

ENERGY SHOCKS

I n 1973 and again in 1979 the Organization of Petroleum Exporting Countries (OPEC) sharply increased oil prices. The price of oil quadrupled in 1973 and doubled again in 1979. These sudden "oil shocks" pushed the U.S. and other Western economies into recessions and accelerated the rate of inflation.

Although oil prices declined significantly in the early 1980s, many people foresee additional oil shocks in the years ahead. The Congressional Budget Office (CBO), for example, projects a worldwide shortage of over 4 million barrels of oil per day in 1985, even at prices near $50 per barrel. The CBO projects a far larger shortage by 1990. If these projections prove to be correct, we can expect sharply higher oil prices in the coming years.

The purpose of this chapter is to describe how an oil shock affects the U.S. economy. As we shall see, the initial shock is as much a problem of leakage from the circular flow (income spent on imports) as it is an actual shortage of oil. We shall also consider what fiscal and monetary policies might be appropriate in such a crisis, and which ones were actually followed in 1973 and 1979. Finally, we shall consider how and why oil prices have fallen since the last oil shock and how future shocks may be avoided.

U.S. ENERGY CONSUMPTION

To appreciate the significance of an energy shock, we must first recognize that the United States uses an enormous amount of energy. At present we consume more than 75 quadrillion (75,000,000,000,000,000)

TABLE 16.1 U.S. ENERGY CONSUMPTION

One-fourth of U.S. energy consumption goes into transportation—primarily gasoline. Manufacturing and other industries use another 41 percent in production processes. Most residential and commercial energy is consumed for space heating.

Sector and end use	Percent of total consumption
Transportation	25.2
Residential use	19.2
Heating	13.9
Cooling	1.8
Other	3.5
Commercial use	14.4
Heating	8.0
Cooling	2.9
Other	3.5
Industrial use	41.2
Direct heat	11.5
Process steam	16.7
Electric drive	7.9
Other	5.1

Source: U.S. Department of Energy.

Btu's of energy every year, or about one-third of the world's total energy output.[1] To put this consumption more tangibly, imagine a string of railroad hopper cars stretching from here to the moon, each filled with 100 tons of coal. It would take that much coal to produce the energy consumed in the United States in just one year.

Although electric toothbrushes and hair dryers epitomize our dependence on nonhuman energy, such uses account for only a small fraction of our energy consumption. Most U.S. energy is consumed in transportation (gasoline for vehicles) and in industrial production. We use much of the rest to heat our homes, classrooms, and offices (see Table 16.1).

One reason we consume so much energy is that we produce so much output. Energy consumption has, in fact, increased along with total output (GNP). This is illustrated in Figure 16.1. Also shown in Figure 16.1 is our population growth. Notice that the energy-use curve lies below GNP growth and above the population-growth curve. Taken together, the three growth lines indicate that

☐ Energy use *per capita* has increased substantially over time
☐ Energy use *per dollar of GNP* has declined somewhat

In other words, we are consuming more goods and services per person than we did in earlier years, but those goods and services require, on average, less energy use. This trend is a reflection of the continuing change in the mix of output toward more services (e.g., education, medicine, law) and fewer goods. Nevertheless, energy use per dollar of GNP is still much higher in the United States than in other countries (see Table 16.2).

[1] A Btu (British thermal unit), a common measure of energy, is the amount of heat necessary to raise the temperature of one pound of water one degree Fahrenheit. More important, it is a convenient measure for comparing the energy contained in various fuel sources and for contrasting energy-use patterns. There are, for example, 5,000 Btu's in a pound of wood, 13,000 in a pound of coal, and 125,000 in a gallon of gasoline. It takes about 30,000 Btu's to run a clothes dryer for less than an hour.

FIGURE 16.1 GROWTH IN U.S. POPULATION, GNP, AND ENERGY USE

As we continue to produce more goods and services each year, our consumption of energy increases. However, energy consumption has not increased as fast as GNP. This indicates that we are using less energy per unit of output.

Source: *Statistical Abstract*, 1982; *Economic Report of the President*, 1982.

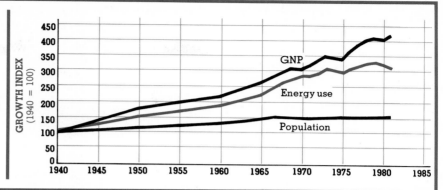

U.S. ENERGY SOURCES

The continued availability of the energy required to fuel our affluence was taken for granted before the 1973 oil crisis. People now realize, however, that energy supplies not only are subject to sudden disruption but are also exhaustible. Where do we get the energy to fuel our cars, homes, and factories?

The largest single source of energy for the United States is oil. As Figure 16.2 illustrates, oil accounts for nearly 50 percent of all energy consumed in the United States. This heavy dependence on oil is largely explained by our extensive use of automobiles and the difficulty of using alternative fuels to drive them. By contrast, other industrial countries use automobiles less extensively and also drive smaller, more fuel-efficient cars. This helps explain why other countries use less oil per dollar of GNP (see Table 16.2).

Natural gas is the second largest source of U.S. energy, followed at some distance by coal. Hydroelectric dams (mostly in the West)

TABLE 16.2 OIL CONSUMPTION PER DOLLAR OF GNP IN VARIOUS COUNTRIES

The United States is the world's largest consumer of energy. Our heavy use of energy reflects two characteristics of the U.S. economy: (1) we produce more goods and services than any other country; (2) we use more energy to produce each good.

Country	Petroleum consumption (millions of barrels per year)	Gross national product (billions of dollars)	Petroleum consumption per dollar of GNP (barrels per thousand dollars of GNP)
United States	6,242	$2,582.5	2.42
Japan	1,834	1,152.9	1.59
Germany	1,001	827.8	1.21
France	840	627.7	1.34
United Kingdom	613	442.8	1.38
Italy	727	368.9	1.97
Canada	679	242.5	2.80

Sources: International Monetary Fund and American Petroleum Institute (1980 data).

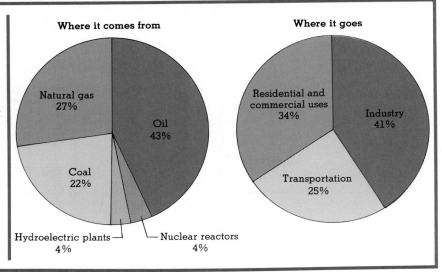

FIGURE 16.2 U.S. ENERGY SOURCES

Oil is the source of nearly half of all U.S. energy consumption. This heavy dependence on oil is due largely to our transportation choices. Industrial and commercial energy needs can be met more easily by sources other than oil. Newer energy sources (e.g., nuclear and solar) still account for very small fractions of our energy supply.

Source: U.S. Energy Information Agency (1981 figures).

Where it comes from

Natural gas 27%
Oil 43%
Coal 22%
Hydroelectric plants 4%
Nuclear reactors 4%

Where it goes

Residential and commercial uses 34%
Industry 41%
Transportation 25%

and nuclear power plants each provide a small fraction of total U.S. energy, while solar converters, windmills, and the like are of no consequence at present.

Oil imports

In the fall of 1973, just before the first OPEC oil shock, the United States was importing 6 million barrels of oil per day. In 1979, just before the second oil shock, we were importing 8 million barrels per day. In both years imports accounted for close to half of all the oil consumed in the United States. Accordingly, continued enjoyment of our consumption patterns depended in large part on access to imports. The OPEC countries threatened to cut off that access on October 14, 1973. The 1979 revolution in Iran led to an actual cutoff of imports from that country.

Market equilibrium

law of demand: The quantity of a good demanded in a given time period increases as its price falls (*ceteris paribus*).

Although it is tempting to think of energy consumption as a basic "need," ***our consumption of energy, like all other goods and services, reflects a response to market prices.*** That is to say, there is a demand for energy, and that demand obeys the **law of demand.** This is illustrated in the downward-sloping demand curve of Figure 16.3.

The energy market also resembles other markets on the supply side: at higher prices, a greater quantity is typically supplied. In other words, the market-supply curve slopes upward.

Both supply and demand conditions are subject to basic change, however. In the energy markets of 1973 and 1979 the OPEC countries announced that they were no longer willing to sell oil at the same prices as before. In each instance they insisted on being paid higher prices for any given quantity of oil. The OPEC price decisions amounted to a leftward **shift** of the world oil supply, as illustrated in Figure 16.3.[2] The world energy supply curve shifted in similar fashion, because oil is a major source of world energy.

shift of supply: A change in the quantity supplied at any (every) given price.

[2] A changed willingness to supply reflects a violation of the *ceteris paribus* assumption and is expressed by a supply-curve shift (see Chapter 2).

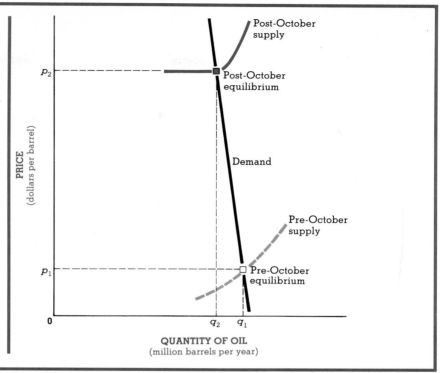

FIGURE 16.3 THE WORLD OIL MARKET, 1973

The refusal of OPEC countries to continue selling oil at lower prices (p_1) can be expressed as a shift of the oil supply curve. This shift resulted in substantially higher prices (p_2) and slightly less consumption (q_2).

The immediate effects of the changed OPEC supply behavior on energy prices and consumption are evident in Figure 16.3. In mid-1973 the world price of OPEC oil was approximately $3.30 per barrel, as indicated by p_1 in Figure 16.3. The leftward shift of the supply curve in October 1973 soon pushed the market price up to $12 a barrel ($p_2$). Consumers responded to this higher price by reducing their oil consumption. Few substitute sources of energy were immediately available, however, and the total quantity of oil demanded fell only slightly. Accordingly, consumers ended up by buying only slightly less oil (q_2) at a much higher price (p_2). The same thing happened in 1979.

MACRO IMPACT: THE SHORT RUN

The new equilibrium in the world oil market affected the U.S. economy in several ways. In the short run, the new equilibrium contributed to both inflation and unemployment.

Inflationary impact

The increase in the price of oil set the stage for **cost-push inflation.**[3] Industries using oil to fuel their machines or heat their furnaces

cost-push inflation: An increase in the price level initiated by an increase in the cost of production.

[3] The cost increases originated, however, in the profit-push behavior of OPEC countries. Hence from a worldwide perspective, it might be more appropriate to view the price rise as a profit-push inflation, even though cost-push phenomena prevailed in the United States.

were hit with an increase in production costs. To maintain profits, they had to increase their product prices, thus contributing to inflation. Because oil was used in so many industries, the inflationary impact was large.

The inflationary impact of the increased oil prices was aggravated by demands for wage increases. As first gasoline prices, then an increasing number of other product prices rose, the **real income** of workers fell. In order to maintain their standard of living, workers bargained for higher wages, thereby further increasing production costs. These higher unit labor costs in turn pushed prices still higher. Largely as a consequence of these developments, the Consumer Price Index rose by more than 11 percent from November 1973 to November 1974, the worst inflation since 1947. The rate of inflation jumped even higher in 1979 (to over 13 percent), when the second round of abrupt oil price increases was initiated.

real income: Income in constant dollars; nominal income adjusted for inflation.

Shortages and shutdowns

The OPEC action not only raised oil prices but also contributed to outright shortages and plant shutdowns. These consequences came about in one of two ways. Many producers could neither raise the prices of the products they produced nor afford to absorb higher production costs. In such cases, producers chose simply to shut down their factories rather than incur losses. A more frequent reason for plant shutdowns, however, was an outright shortage of available oil.

The shortage was only partly the fault of OPEC, however. The prices of domestic oil and other fuels were subject to price controls in 1973 (and 1979 as well). Thus when OPEC prices went up, U.S. consumers shifted their demand to domestic producers. But the resultant quantity demanded far exceeded the quantity supplied at the controlled price. A classic **market shortage** developed. In the absence of domestic price controls, U.S. oil producers would have increased their prices and produced more oil. The controls prevented this response, however. Indeed, some domestic oil producers actually reduced their output, hoping to sell their oil later when price controls were eliminated or price ceilings raised. As a consequence, many manufacturers were forced to shut down because they could not get the oil they were willing and able to purchase.

market shortage: The amount by which the quantity demanded exceeds the quantity supplied at a given price; excess demand.

Unemployment

Although the most visible effects of the 1973 and 1979 oil shocks were inflation and shortages, the greatest threats lay on the demand side of product and factor markets. The OPEC price boosts forced consumers to spend more of their income on gasoline and other oil-related products. As a consequence, ***consumers had less income to spend on nonoil products.*** The resultant fall in aggregate demand for domestic goods created a **recessionary gap,** into which the economy soon fell.

recessionary gap: The amount by which the rate of desired expenditure at full employment falls short of full-employment output.

OIL LEAKAGE The recessionary effects of an oil shock on aggregate demand can be illustrated by the familiar circular flow. As we observed in earlier chapters, the maintenance of full employment depends on the continued flow of purchasing power between product and factor markets. Should leaks develop in the flow, aggregate demand will drop, thereby setting off a chain of multiplier effects that will ultimately lead to recession. This is exactly what happened when oil prices rose so suddenly in 1973 and 1979.

Figure 16.4 illustrates the basic **leakage** problem. As we first observed in Chapter 7, the income consumers spend on imported goods and services represents a form of leakage in the circular flow. Those dollars end up in foreign product markets rather than in our own. Should foreign consumers decide to use their dollars to buy American goods (exports), the import leakage will be balanced by the foreign inflow, leaving the circular flow intact. But we have no guarantee that such a balance will be struck. On the contrary, the oil crisis demonstrated that our trade balance can be thrown far out of kilter. In both 1973 and 1979, import leakage increased abruptly while exports remained unchanged.

In 1973 we were spending approximately $10 billion on imported oil. After the OPEC price increase, however, our annual import bill suddenly jumped by $15 billion. In the absence of an oil shock, most of this $15 billion would have been spent on domestic output. As it was, the $15 billion leaked out, leaving unsold goods here at home. This accumulation of unsold goods soon led to production cutbacks and layoffs, resulting in rising unemployment.

U.S. EXPORTS The increased oil leakage could have been offset by increased exports. If the OPEC countries had used their increased incomes to buy American-made goods, our exports would have risen along with our imports, and no net leakage from the circular flow would have occurred. In that case, the $15 billion would have returned to the circular flow (after a slight detour) and the domestic product markets would not have been disrupted.

Unfortunately, this happy sequence of events did not occur. The OPEC countries were slow to spend their added income. U.S. export sales to the OPEC countries increased by only $2.6 billion in 1974, and

leakage: Income not spent directly on domestic output, but instead diverted from the circular flow; e.g., saving, imports, taxes.

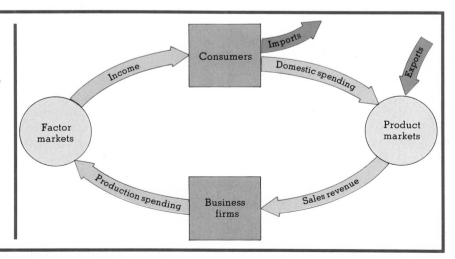

FIGURE 16.4 IMPORT LEAKAGE

Income spent on imports represents leakage from the domestic circular flow of income. This leakage may be offset by increased exports. In the aftermath of the 1973 and 1979 oil shocks, however, oil leakage increased much faster than did exports.

TABLE 16.3 INITIAL IMPACT OF THE 1973 OIL SHOCK ON U.S. AGGREGATE DEMAND
(in billions of 1974 dollars)

Higher OPEC prices raised the cost of imported oil. This additional leakage from the circular flow was aggravated by reduced exports to other oil-importing countries. Increased exports to OPEC countries helped offset the oil leakage, however.

	1974	1975	1976	1977
Increased cost of oil imports	− $15.0	− $13.0	− $15.5	− $18.7
Reduced exports to oil-importing developing countries	− 0.4	− 2.1	− 2.9	− 3.2
Increased exports to oil-exporting countries	− 2.6	+ 5.1	+ 8.1	+ 10.1
Net impact on aggregate demand	− 12.8	− 10.0	− 10.3	− 11.8

Source: Edward R. Fried and Charles L. Schultz, eds., *Higher Oil Prices and the World Economy* (Washington, D.C.: Brookings Institution, 1975), Table 1–5. Copyright © 1975 by The Brookings Institution.

multiplier: The multiple by which an initial change in spending will alter aggregate demand after an infinite number of spending cycles; $1/(1 − MPC)$.

continued to lag behind the continuing oil leakage (see Table 16.3). At the same time, our exports to the rest of the world were actually *falling*. Most of the other countries in the world were also suffering from the increased oil prices. As a consequence, they had to *reduce* their expenditures on other goods and services, including American exports. Thus export sales to the rest of the oil-consuming countries began to fall at the same time that our oil leakage was increasing. This only made matters worse.

NET LEAKAGE The net effect of these import and export changes on aggregate demand is summarized in Table 16.3. The initial leakage of $15 billion grew by another $0.4 billion as export sales to other oil-importing countries fell. But it was offset in part by $2.6 billion in increased exports to the oil-exporting countries, leaving us with a *net loss* of $12.8 billion from the circular flow in 1974. Similar losses were experienced in subsequent years.

MULTIPLIER EFFECTS The initial net leakage of $12.8 billion in 1974 (Table 16.3) grossly underestimates the full impact of the 1973 oil crisis, of course. Those American producers who ended up with unsold goods and services cut back on the rate of production, thereby leading the economy down the familiar **multiplier** trail. At the end of that trail lay a depressed economy, experiencing high unemployment.

In the two years following the October 1973 oil crisis, real GNP in the United States fell by $44 billion and unemployment increased from 4.8 percent to a high of 9 percent. But the impact of the oil shock was even larger than that. In the absence of such a shock, GNP would have *risen*. Hence the true impact of the oil shock equals the difference between the rate of GNP that *would have* occurred in the absence of an oil shock and the rate of GNP that actually did occur. Using a computer model of the U.S. economy, Lawrence Kumins of the Library of Congress estimated that the oil shock reduced GNP by $100 billion in 1975 and raised unemployment by 3.8 percentage points. In terms of people, this meant that over 3.5 million American workers joined the ranks of the unemployed as a result of the OPEC oil-price increase.

Consumer confidence

The fall in GNP that followed the 1973 oil crisis was aggravated by a breakdown of consumer and investor confidence. Consumer and investor spending depends on *expectations* as well as on income, prices, and interest rates. In the face of gasoline shortages, rising prices, and growing unemployment, consumers were not given to rosy expectations. On the contrary, fear and pessimism were rampant. At the beginning of 1973, 40 percent of all Americans anticipated economic prosperity in that year. At the beginning of 1974— after the OPEC price increases—only 7 percent of all Americans foresaw good times ahead. This loss of consumer confidence shifted the entire consumption function downward (see Figure 7.5), further decreasing aggregate demand. Because investors' confidence was also shaken, the investment function (Figure 7.8) experienced a similarly depressing shift.

**Stagflation:
the combined impact**

stagflation: The simultaneous
presence of substantial
unemployment and inflation.

The macroeconomic consequences of the OPEC oil crisis were thus twofold. On the one hand, the higher oil prices set off a cost-push inflation. On the other hand, the increased expenditures on imported oil reduced the rate of domestic spending and contributed to high unemployment. Thus we ended up in the worst of all macroeconomic worlds, **stagflation**.

MACRO IMPACT: THE LONG RUN

The short-run impact of the shift in OPEC oil supplies was so sudden and severe that it inspired fears of a steadily worsening economy. It was widely anticipated that the rate of leakage from the circular flow would not only continue but probably increase as OPEC continued to raise prices. Looming still farther out on the horizon was the threat of an extended cutoff of oil supplies, which would throw the industrialized economies into a severe and prolonged depression. The fears raised by this possibility were so widespread that the Ford administration hinted publicly at the possibility of "armed intervention" to maintain oil supplies. When OPEC again raised prices sharply in 1979, the Central Intelligence Agency predicted a real crisis. By 1982, the CIA predicted, the United States would be getting 3.2 to 7.7 million fewer barrels of oil per day than it needed.

The dire fears and predictions that accompanied the 1973 and 1979 oil shocks were prompted in part by an inadequate understanding of the way markets work. There was a basic confusion between the "need" and the "demand" for oil, on the one hand, and the relationship of imports to exports, on the other.

**Adjustments in
consumption**

In the short run, there is little that consumers can do to reduce the quantity of oil demanded. We still have to drive to work, heat the furnace, and cool the refrigerator, even if the price of oil quadruples. Business firms confront the same dilemma; in the short run, they cannot alter production processes significantly. With more time,

FIGURE 16.5 LONG-TERM ADJUSTMENTS IN OIL DEMAND AND SUPPLY

With more time to adjust, consumers are able to reduce the quantity demanded at the price p_2. This is expressed by the long-run demand for oil. As time passes, alternative supplies also reach the market, as reflected in the long-run supply curve. In the period 1974–78, the real price of oil actually fell (from p_2 to p_3) largely in response to these adjustments. After the 1979 oil shock, the adjustment was even faster, and oil prices again declined in 1981–82.

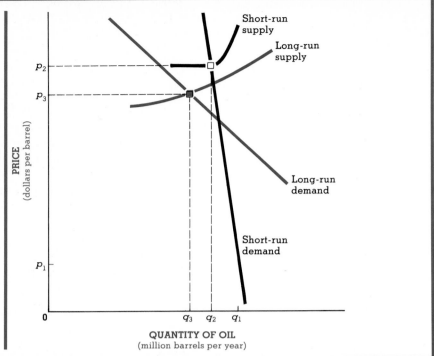

however, both consumers and business firms can reduce their consumption of oil. Hence the long-run demand curve for oil is likely to be more sloped, as in Figure 16.5.

The long-run reduction in quantity demanded at P_2 actually came about in a variety of ways, including;

□ As gasoline prices rose, people demanded smaller and more fuel-efficient cars. In 1973 new cars averaged only 14 miles per gallon; by 1982 they were getting over 25 miles to the gallon.

□ As home-heating and air-conditioning bills rose, consumers demanded more insulation. New homes built today contain twice as much insulation as homes built before 1973. Owners of older homes added storm windows, weatherstripping, and attic insulation.

□ Producers greatly increased their energy efficiency by reducing their energy use per unit of output.

□ An increasing number of manufacturing firms and utility companies switched their fuel source from oil to coal.

Taken together, these and other adjustments reduced oil consumption per dollar of GNP in Western economies by almost 28 percent between 1973 and 1981. Just in the few years between 1978 and 1981, per capita energy use in the United States fell by 20 percent.

Adjustments in supply

The supply side of the energy market also responded to the higher price of oil. Indeed, the OPEC-initiated price increase set off a world-wide surge in oil exploration and development. Potential oil fields

CONSERVATION: A LONG-RUN ADJUSTMENT

Some of the most impressive reductions in energy use have originated in industry. Some examples:

□ Energy consumption in the ten most energy-intensive industries has declined 2.2 percent since 1972, while production has increased an average of 20 percent.

□ Motor-vehicle manufacturers have achieved a 20.5 percent increase in energy savings since 1972, surpassing the government's goal of 16 percent.

□ The chemical industry has cut consumption by 22.1 percent since 1972, well on the way toward the 1985 goal of a 30 percent reduction.

□ Exxon Chemical Company has saved the equivalent of 35 million barrels of oil since 1974—enough to heat 1.3 million homes in the Northeast for a year.

□ The Maytag Company, a major appliance manufacturer, reports that the energy required to produce each appliance was 22 percent lower in 1980 than in 1972.

□ The B. F. Goodrich Company reduced fuel purchases for lighting, heating and power from 79 trillion British thermal units in 1972 to 51 trillion Btu's last year, a figure that would have been more impressive except for a 15 percent drop in production.

□ Airlines, in an effort to strip weight from planes, are going to such extremes as putting less water in drinking fountains, carrying fewer magazines, installing thinner carpets.

□ Boeing, an aircraft manufacturer, rewards employes who come up with weight-reducing ideas. Example: a new insulation for wiring in its planes, saving 385 pounds on a 727. "In each plane, we're saving 3,000 gallons of fuel a year because of the reduced weight of the wiring insulation," a spokesman said.

□ Result of these improvements: Airlines today use one-third less fuel per passenger-mile than they did in 1973.

Source: Information from *U.S. News & World Report*, July 27, 1981.

---

market surplus: The amount by which the quantity supplied exceeds the quantity demanded at a given price; excess supply.

that had not seemed profitable enough to explore or develop suddenly looked very attractive. In the ensuing wave of exploration, vast oil fields were opened up in Alaska, the North Sea, Canada, and Mexico, and new exploration activity was initiated in China. In the United States, the number of new wells increased by 51 percent between 1972 and 1976, reversing an earlier trend.[4]

As a result of all this exploration activity, the world's proven oil reserves increased substantially. These additional reserves served to weaken OPEC's market power, restraining further price increases and supply restrictions. This restraint is illustrated by the reduced slope of the long-run supply curve in Figure 16.5.

Notice that in Figure 16.5 the long-run quantity supplied at price p_2 exceeds the long-run quantity demanded. This indicates that the eventual adjustments in demand and supply will lead to a **market surplus.** This is exactly what happened in the years after the 1973 and 1979 oil shocks. The real (inflation-adjusted) price of oil declined between 1974 and 1978, and fell even more sharply in 1981–82. In fact, OPEC has been able to avert drastic reductions in oil

---

[4] New wells were not subject to the domestic price controls discussed earlier.

prices only by sharply curtailing its own production. Total OPEC production fell from 31 million barrels per day in 1973 to only 18 million barrels per day in 1982. Hence the short-run price increases greatly overstated the ultimate impact of the oil shocks.

Trade adjustments

Another major form of long-term adjustment occurred in international trade. As we noted earlier, the major cause of increased domestic unemployment was the increase in import prices for OPEC oil. In the short run, this income was not recycled to any great extent. As their incomes grew, however, the OPEC countries did begin to buy more goods and services from the industrialized countries. OPEC merchandise imports grew from only $20 billion in 1973 to $136 billion in 1980. U.S. exports to the OPEC countries increased by nearly $0.50 for each additional $1.00 of oil imports. Hence the initial leakage caused by costlier oil imports was substantially offset by injections of new OPEC spending. Table 16.4 shows that the net worldwide leakage declined from $82 billion in 1974 to only $42 billion in 1978. The OPEC surplus jumped to over $100 billion again after the 1979 oil shock. But by the end of 1981 the OPEC countries were actually spending more on imports than they were taking in from oil exports. Hence, the oil leakage was stopped, at least temporarily.

Increased real cost of oil

The initial impact of the 1973 and 1979 OPEC price increases was substantially alleviated by subsequent adjustments in consumption, supply, and trade patterns. Nevertheless, the real price of oil was still much higher in 1983 than it was in 1973. After adjustments for inflation, the price of oil in early 1983 was four times higher than in 1973. Thus **the long-run effect of the oil shocks is a permanent increase in the real cost of energy.** The higher oil price demanded by the OPEC countries means that we have to give up more goods and services in order to acquire a barrel of oil. In other words, the higher money price of oil enabled OPEC countries (and other oil producers

TABLE 16.4 NET WORLDWIDE OIL LEAKAGE
(in billions of dollars)

Oil-importing countries were beset by dramatically higher rates of income leakage after 1973. Increased OPEC spending offset much of this leakage, however. By 1978 net worldwide oil leakage was only $42 billion, compared with $82 billion in 1974.

Year	Cost of imports from OPEC countries	OPEC spending on imported goods and services	Net worldwide leakage (OPEC exports − OPEC imports)
1972	$ 16	$ 14	$ 2
1973	29	20	9
1974	115	33	82
1975	106	57	49
1976	130	64	66
1977	144	85	59
1978	143	101	42
1979	203	102	101
1980	286	136	150

Source: International Monetary Fund.

as well) to buy more of our goods and services with a barrel of oil.[5] Thus we can continue to use as much oil as before only if we are willing to sacrifice more of our output to pay for it.

The increased real price of oil is not very significant to the United States, because our economy is immense and is not very dependent on imports. Other countries, however, are not so well able to pay the higher price. Japan, for example, imports nearly all of its energy supplies. Hence the OPEC price increase had a greater effect on its economy; the real loss to Japan has been estimated to be at least 4 percent of total output. Countries of Western Europe experienced losses less severe than Japan's, but still significantly higher than those of the United States.

The countries most damaged by the OPEC price increases were the less-developed countries of Asia, Africa, and Latin America. Those countries—which include four-fifths of the world's population—are simply too poor to be able to pay such high prices. Yet they cannot develop without energy, so they must continue to import oil. But to do so, they have to sacrifice goods and services that they desperately need for domestic investment and consumption.

POLICY OPTIONS

From a policy perspective, oil shocks create two distinct problems: (1) short-term increases in inflation and unemployment and (2) long-run increases in real energy costs. What kinds of policies are appropriate for combating these two problems?

Anti-inflation policies

In theory, the inflationary effects of an oil shock can be avoided. Recall that inflation is an increase in the *average* level of prices. Hence if prices of other goods were to drop enough to offset the increase in oil prices, no inflation would be recorded. In reality, however, such an outcome is unlikely. The oil price increase raised the costs of production. Hence producers' profits were already being squeezed at constant (unchanged) prices; any lowering of their prices would have meant outright losses in many cases. Even producers who did not use oil-related products in their production processes—and thus did not incur higher costs—had no incentive to lower *their* prices.

equation of exchange: Money supply (*M*) times velocity of circulation (*V*) equals level of aggregate demand (*P* × *Q*).

Incentives notwithstanding, monetary policy could force a reduction in the prices of goods other than oil. The **equation of exchange** ($MV = PQ$) indicates what would happen if the money supply were held constant. With velocity unchanged, either *Q* would have to drop or the prices of goods other than oil would have to come down to hold *P* constant. If domestic producers were slow to reduce those prices, the forced reduction in sales (*Q*) would ultimately cause them to do so. For this reason, Monetarists often assert that inflation cannot be blamed on oil shocks, since average prices will rise only if the money supply is expanded.

[5] This phenomenon is referred to as a shift in the *terms of trade* against the United States. International trade is discussed further in Chapter 33.

Unfortunately, the same restrictive monetary policies that might prevent inflation are also likely to cause a severe recession. Recall that the mechanism that pushes down the prices of goods other than oil is a recession (a drop in Q). This can turn out to be a very expensive way to stop inflation.

This does not mean that policy makers were helpless to fight inflation, however. The severity of an oil-shock inflation depends not only on the amount of the increase in the price of oil but also on people's responses to it. Consumers and producers who viewed the 1973 and 1979 oil price increases as harbingers of doom tended to overreact. Particularly alarming was the sudden kindling of inflationary expectations, which stimulated demands for higher wages and prices. Under such circumstances, a basic objective of policy might be to calm inflationary jitters. In the short run, the government could do that by providing a realistic assessment of the OPEC action and its consequences for the American economy. With more time, the government could also pursue long-run energy policies that would bolster confidence in the future and directly reduce inflationary pressures originating in oil prices.

Antirecession policies

Although some inflation following an oil shock is inevitable, policy makers can try to minimize the unemployment effects. Recall that the primary problem here is leakage from the circular flow. If that leakage can be offset by new spending inflows ("injections"), no shortfall in aggregate demand will occur. In other words, the potential unemployment problem can be averted by skillful management of aggregate demand.

The fiscal and monetary possibilities for stimulating aggregate demand should be familiar from earlier chapters. The oil leakage problem we are concerned with here is no different in principle from other macroeconomic leakage problems (e.g., consumer saving). The trick is to replace lost demand with new spending. In terms of fiscal policy, this means increasing government spending or cutting taxes so that consumers and investors can spend more. Monetary responses could include an increase in the money supply, perhaps engineered through open-market purchases of government securities.[6]

By expanding aggregate domestic demand, then, we could avoid at least half of our stagflation problem. To clarify the principles at work here, we may refer to the equation of exchange once again:

$$MV = PQ$$

If P rises as a result of oil price increases and attendant inflation, Q *must* drop unless something on the left side of the equaton increases. That is to say, production cutbacks and unemployment will occur unless the money supply (M) is increased by the Federal Reserve or the velocity of money (V) is increased by expansionary fiscal policy.

---

[6] Note that the OPEC countries could (and did) buy U.S. government securities as well, thus effectively returning some of the oil leakage to the domestic economy.

Reducing real energy costs

In addition to combating stagflation, economic policy can also be used to reduce the real costs of energy. In the long run, we can think about alternative sources of energy and even more efficient uses of the energy we already consume. In pursuit of such objectives, policy makers could use tax incentives to encourage energy conservation and energy research. Increased incentives for domestic energy production would also reduce our dependence on imports, thereby reducing both real macroeconomic costs and the threat of further disruptions in energy supplies.

THE POLICY EXPERIENCE

How did the federal government actually respond to the oil shocks? In view of the fact that the economy suffered high inflation *and* excessive unemployment in 1974–75 and again in 1979–80, it should be apparent that the above guidelines were not followed.

Short-term policies

full-employment budget: The federal revenues and expenditures that would exist at full employment, under prevailing fiscal policy.

In the aftermath of the 1973 oil price increase, the immediate concern of the Nixon administration was to combat inflation. Hence it sought to *reduce* domestic expenditure by curtailing government expenditure and even proposed an increase in taxes. In pursuit of such policies, it allowed the **full-employment budget** balance to grow from near zero in mid-1973 to a surplus of $30 billion by the fall of 1974. As discussed in Chapter 9, such an increase in the full-employment budget balance is a reflection of restrictive fiscal policies.

These restrictive fiscal policies were accompanied by tight monetary policies. The Federal Reserve kept a lid on the growth of the money supply after the initial OPEC price increases. From November 1973 to August 1974 the supply of money rose by only 5.5 percent, even though prices rose by 11 percent. As a consequence, the *real* stock of money fell, and there was not enough money around to buy the available (and higher-priced) goods.

The cumulative impact of these restrictive monetary and fiscal policies was predictable. The basic principle remains

$$MV = PQ$$

With V falling as a result of restrictive fiscal policies, M growing only slightly, and P increasing significantly, Q had to fall. And it did. As we noted earlier, Q fell by over $100 billion, and more than 3.5 million people joined the ranks of the unemployed.

Long-term policies

Although it is evident that the increase in unemployment that followed the OPEC price increase would have been less severe with more expansionary economic policies, we still would have suffered an income loss. As Professors Robert Hall (Stanford) and Robert Pindyck (MIT) have noted: "When foreign energy producers receive more for their products in real terms, the real incomes of energy consumers must fall, and even the best economic policy cannot change this."[7]

The question remains, however, whether this real income loss can be minimized. Were any policies implemented to reduce long-term losses? At this juncture, our previous discussion of policy lags (Chapter 14) is most relevant. It took over five *years* for Congress to respond to the 1973 oil crisis with new energy legislation. Moreover, that response (the National Energy Act of 1978) was widely criticized as inadequate. Only after a second crisis hit (in 1979) did Congress and the president begin to formulate more effective long-term policies, including the development of alternative energy sources and incentives for increased production and conservation.

PRICE CONTROLS Among the most notable features of the long-term policy response was the insistence on maintaining price controls on domestic oil and gas. Although the world price of crude oil rose to nearly $12 per barrel in 1974, the price of "old" domestic oil (from existing wells) was not allowed to rise above $5.17 per barrel. Price controls were also imposed on "new" oil (new or deeper wells) and maintained on interstate shipments of natural gas.

The objective of these oil and gas price controls was twofold. First, the federal government wanted to shelter consumers from the inflationary impact of higher energy prices. By controlling domestic energy prices, they could reduce *average* energy costs in the short run. And by increasing allowable prices over time, they could facilitate a more gradual adjustment to higher energy costs. Second, the policy makers wanted to avoid a substantial redistribution of income from consumers to oil producers, a redistribution widely regarded as unfair.

Unfortunately, oil and gas price controls also had adverse effects. The low prices for domestic oil and gas reduced production incentives. They also discouraged development of alternative fuel sources that might replace oil and gas in the long run. As we noted earlier, the price controls created serious market shortages as well. These shortages, in turn, led to complex and inefficient regulations on the allocation of domestic oil. In addition, by restraining domestic alternatives, the price controls effectively subsidized the demand for imported oil.

Congress sought to alleviate these problems in 1978 by permitting gradual deregulation of energy prices.[8] But the decontrol and deregulation features of the legislation were quite timid. Consequently, the U.S. economy was not much better prepared for the second oil shock, in 1979.

The 1979 experience

When OPEC again raised oil prices in 1979, the U.S. was importing more oil than ever. Moreover, domestic oil prices were still under federal controls, because President Carter chose not to use the de-

---

[7] Robert E. Hall and Robert S. Pindyck, "What to Do When Energy Prices Rise Again," *Public Interest*, Fall 1981, p. 60.

[8] The question of how high a price is required to ensure the desired quantity is discussed in Chapter 28, under "Economic Rent."

control power Congress had given him in 1978. No significant new energy policies had been implemented to stave off another crisis. As a consequence, the new oil price increases—to over $20 per barrel—fueled inflation and increased leakage from the circular flow. At first President Carter responded to the new oil crisis by asking Americans not to use their cars one day a week and to take other modest fuel-saving steps. As gasoline shortages spread, however, the president called for stronger action, including a limit on oil imports and massive subsidies for the development of alternative energy sources. He refused to decontrol domestic energy prices, however, unless Congress agreed to impose a steep tax on additional oil-company profits. Congress did not pass the "windfall profits" tax until March 1980.[9] Even after that, decontrol and deregulation were implemented only gradually. Carter's energy program was widely criticized for this, as well as for its neglect of potential energy-conservation possibilities. As the Harvard Energy Project observed, conservation is "a source of energy that produces no radioactive waste, nothing in the way of petrodollars, and very little pollution."[10] Conservation efforts can be encouraged by taxes on energy use and subsidies for fuel-saving innovations.

President Reagan completed decontrol of oil prices immediately after taking office. In 1981 Congress also reduced the windfall-profits tax, thereby providing greater production incentives. These actions increased the rate of domestic oil production, reduced demand for imports, and encouraged greater conservation. However, the Reagan administration failed to decontrol natural gas prices and cut funding for research on alternative fuel sources. These decisions slowed long-run adjustments. When world oil prices declined in 1982, the administration and Congress also failed to impose an oil-import tax. Such a tax would have provided a further incentive for domestic production and a barrier to OPEC imports.

SUMMARY

▪ The U.S. economy is the world's largest energy consumer. This distinction results from the fact that we produce more goods and services than any other country and use more energy per dollar of GNP produced.

▪ Energy-use patterns reflect a response to market forces. The amount of energy consumed or supplied is affected by energy prices.

▪ The short-run effects of oil shocks include a rise in both inflation and unemployment. This stagflation emerges from two distinct sources: (a) the oil price increase itself, which raises the costs of production and fuels cost-push inflation; and (b) the increased expenditure on oil imports, which represents a form of leakage from the circular flow.

[9] The windfall-profits tax is discussed at length in Chapter 28.
[10] See Robert Stobaugh and Daniel Yergin, eds., *Energy Future* (New York: Random House, 1979), p. 136.

▪ The long-term effect of an oil shock is a higher real cost of energy. This reduces real incomes.

▪ To minimize short-run problems, the government can try to maintain domestic aggregate demand by means of macroeconomic policies—either increased government expenditure and tax cuts (fiscal policy) or increases in the money supply (monetary policy). From the equation $MV = PQ$, it is apparent that when P increases, either M or V must rise if a fall in Q is to be avoided.

▪ In the long run, economic policies must focus on oil prices directly, by encouraging more efficient use of energy and the production of alternative fuels. Such policies would limit increases in the real cost of energy, particularly imported oil.

▪ The policy response to oil shocks has been both belated and inadequate. Restrictive monetary and fiscal policies worsened the short-term unemployment problem, while price controls on domestic oil and gas inhibited development of alternative energy sources and encouraged continued consumption.

Terms to remember

Define the following terms:

law of demand	**leakage**
shift of supply	**multiplier**
cost-push inflation	**stagflation**
real income	**market surplus**
market shortage	**equation of exchange**
recessionary gap	**full-employment budget**

Questions for discussion

1. What would happen to the U.S. economy if the OPEC countries started spending all their accumulated oil revenues on American goods and services? What fiscal and monetary policies should we pursue in this situation?

2. Why did the Nixon administration and the Federal Reserve Board choose to deflate the economy after OPEC raised oil prices? What good reasons might have motivated such policies?

3. Why did the quantity of oil demanded fall so little when oil prices quadrupled? Give four examples of oil use that are difficult to curtail in the short run.

4. What is the difference between the *nominal* price of oil and its *real* price? How might we lower the real price?

5. Why doesn't OPEC double the price of oil every year?

Problem

Suppose that the expenditure patterns of a country are as follows:

C = $60 billion per year + 0.8Y
I = $100 billion per year
G = 0 (no taxes either)
Exports = imports = $10 billion per year

As a result of higher oil prices, this country must now spend an additional $10 billion per year on imported oil. Assuming that prices of other goods do not change, what impact will the higher oil prices have on equilibrium GNP?

GROWTH AND PRODUCTIVITY: SOURCES AND LIMITS

Economic growth has been the engine of mankind's ever-rising standard of living. Economic growth has brought us not only more material goods and services, but also better health, advanced educations, and even longer lives. Just in the relatively brief period since 1900, the average U.S. standard of living has more than *tripled*. Our life expectancy at birth has increased by over 20 years (to age 74). While many of us look back nostalgically to the simpler ways of the past, few people would give up today's standards and opportunities for those of an earlier era.

Although the engine of economic growth has pulled us a long way, its future progress is hotly debated. On the one hand, many people are worried that the engine is wearing out. They see the rate of growth declining and worry that our living standards will stagnate or even fall in the years ahead. This decline in growth is attributed to a variety of problems, including dwindling resources of one kind or another, lagging technology, the weakening of the work ethic, and excessive government interference in product and resource markets.

Other people express very different concerns. They fear that we *will* continue to grow rapidly. In the process, they fear, we will strip the world of its resources. Ultimately there will be nothing left to feed or clothe us. The process of industrial growth may even kill us off faster via excessive pollution, nuclear accidents, or deadly wars fought over dwindling resources. Such doomsday prophecies have a long tradition in economics. In fact, similar prophecies made over 100 years ago earned the profession its characterization as the "dismal science."

The purpose of this chapter is to examine the nature of economic growth. First we shall look to see what grows when we experience economic growth. Then we shall look at the sources of that growth, especially the magic of productivity improvements. Finally we shall examine the risks of growing too fast.

THE NATURE OF GROWTH

At first glance the concept of economic growth is simple. It refers to increases in the output of the economy. But there are two distinct ways in which output increases, and they have very different implications for our economic welfare.

Short-run changes in capacity utilization

production possibilities: The alternative combinations of final goods and services that could be produced in a given time period with all available resources and technology.

The easiest kind of growth comes from increased use of our productive capabilities. At any given moment there is a limit to an economy's potential output. This limit is determined by the quantity of resources available and our technological know-how. We have earlier illustrated these short-run limits with a **production-possibilities** curve, as in Figure 17.1a. By using all of our (institutionally) available resources and our best expertise, we can produce any combination of goods on or inside our production-possibilities curve.

We do not always take full advantage of our production possibilities, however. As we have observed, the U.S. economy often produces a mix of output that lies *inside* our production possibilities, like point A in Figure 17.1a. This failure to utilize our productive capacity results in unemployment, that is, the nonuse of some of our available factors of production.

A major short-run goal of macroeconomics is to achieve full employment. If successful, short-term macro policies will move us from point A to some point on the production-possibilities curve

FIGURE 17.1 TWO TYPES OF GROWTH

Increases in output may result from increased use of existing productive capacity or from increases in that capacity itself. In Figure a the initial mix of output at point A does not make full use of our production possibilities. Hence we can grow—get more output—by moving toward full employment, as illustrated by point B (or any other point on the curve). Once we are on the production-possibilities curve, we can increase our output further only by *increasing* our productive capacity. This is illustrated by the *shift* of the production-possibilities curve in Figure b.

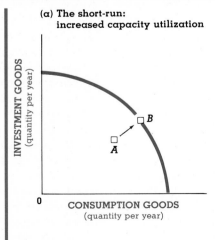

(a) The short-run: increased capacity utilization

INVESTMENT GOODS (quantity per year)

CONSUMPTION GOODS (quantity per year)

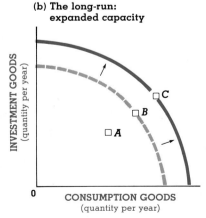

(b) The long-run: expanded capacity

INVESTMENT GOODS (quantity per year)

CONSUMPTION GOODS (quantity per year)

(e.g., point *B*). In the process, we will produce more output. This increase in GNP will be reflected in measures of our economic growth.

Long-run changes in capacity

As desirable as full employment is, there is an obvious limit to how much additional output we can obtain in this way. Once we achieve full employment—that is, some point on our production-possibilities curve—further short-run increases in output cannot be obtained by macro stabilization policies. Once we are fully utilizing our productive capacity, further increases in output are attainable only if we *expand* that capacity. To do so we have to *shift* the production possibilities outward, as in Figure 17.1*b*. Such shifts imply an increase in *potential* GNP, that is, our productive capacity.

Over time, increases in capacity are critical. Short-run increases in the utilization of existing capacity can generate only modest increases in output. Even "high" unemployment rates (e.g., 7 percent) leave little room for increased output. ***To achieve large and lasting increases in output we must push our production possibilities outward.*** For this reason, economists tend to define growth in terms of changes in *potential* GNP.

Despite the importance of distinguishing changes in actual and potential GNP, the distinction is rarely made in practice. The measures of economic growth cited in the press and elsewhere typically lump together all increases in output, regardless of their source. Accordingly, *measured* economic growth includes increases in output attained through either (1) increases in capacity utilization (movements toward our production-possibilities curve) or (2) increases in capacity itself (shifts of the curve). Over long periods of time, however, capacity expansion dominates, since short-run changes in utilization (unemployment rates) tend to wash out. For convenience, we shall simply state that **economic growth** refers to an increase in real output. We shall also note that *long-run* growth is synonymous with increases (shifts) of our production possibilities.

economic growth: An increase in output (real GNP); an expansion of production possibilities.

Nominal vs. real GNP

nominal GNP: The value of final output produced in a given period, measured in the prices of that period (current prices).

Notice that we refer to *real* GNP, not *nominal* GNP, in our concept of economic growth. **Nominal GNP** is the current dollar value of output, that is, the average price level (*P*) multiplied by the quantity of goods and services produced (*Q*). Accordingly, increases in nominal GNP can result from either increases in the price level or increases in the quantity of output. In fact, nominal GNP can rise even when the quantity of goods and services falls. This was the case in 1980, for example. The total quantity of goods and services produced in 1980 was less than the quantity produced in 1979. Nevertheless, prices rose so fast in 1980 (+ 12.4 percent in the Consumer Price Index) that nominal GNP grew.

real GNP: The value of final output produced in a given period, measured in the prices of another period (constant prices).

Real GNP refers to the actual quantity of goods and services produced. Real GNP avoids the distortions of inflation by valuing output in *constant* prices. By using 1972 prices as a standard, we observe that real GNP fell from $1,483.0 billion in 1979 to only $1,480.7 billion in 1980. This comparision, in constant dollars, clearly depicts the economic decline experienced in 1980.

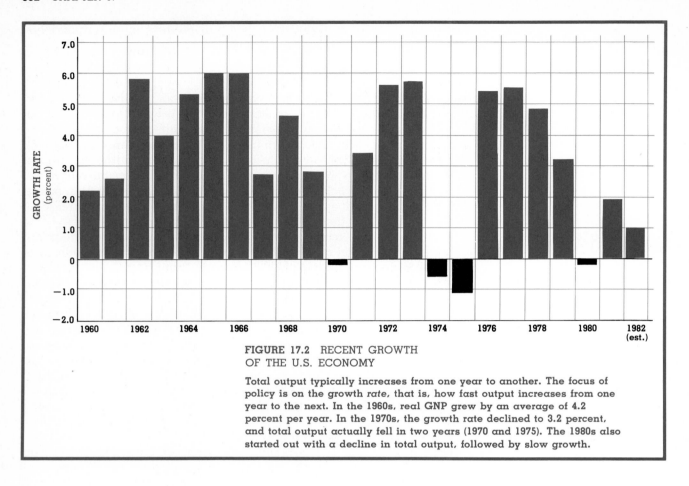

FIGURE 17.2 RECENT GROWTH
OF THE U.S. ECONOMY

Total output typically increases from one year to another. The focus of
policy is on the growth *rate*, that is, how fast output increases from one
year to the next. In the 1960s, real GNP grew by an average of 4.2
percent per year. In the 1970s, the growth rate declined to 3.2 percent,
and total output actually fell in two years (1970 and 1975). The 1980s also
started out with a decline in total output, followed by slow growth.

GROWTH INDEXES

The growth rate

growth rate: Percentage
change in real GNP from one
period to another.

Typically, changes in real GNP are expressed in percentage terms, as
a growth *rate*. The **growth rate** is simply the change in real output
between two periods divided by total output in the base period. The
percentage decline in real output during 1980 was thus

$2.3 billion ÷ $1,483.0 billion,

or 0.16 percent. By contrast, real output grew in 1981 by 1.9 percent.
　Figure 17.2 illustrates the recent growth experience of the U.S.
economy. Neither 1980 nor 1981 was a very good year. During the
1970s we enjoyed a growth rate that averaged 3.2 percent per year. In
the 1960s we did even better, averaging 4.2 percent per year. The
challenge of the 1980s is to resume the higher rates of economic
growth we have enjoyed in the past.

THE EXPONENTIAL PROCESS　At first blush, the "challenge" of raising
the growth rate from 1 or 2 percent to 3 percent may appear neither
difficult nor important. Indeed, the whole subject of economic
growth looks rather dull when you discover that "big" gains in economic growth are measured in fractions of a percent. However, this

initial impression is not fair. First of all, even one year's "low" growth implies lost output. If our output had grown by 3.0 percent instead of only 1.9 percent in 1981, we would have had $15 billion more worth of goods and services. Lots of people would have liked that extra output. Even those few people who felt they already had enough material goods might have gotten some satisfaction from seeing others better off.

Second, economic growth is a *continuing* process. Gains made in one year accumulate in future years. It's like interest you earn at the bank. If you leave your money in the bank for several years, you begin to earn interest on your interest. Eventually you accumulate a nice little bankroll.

The process of economic growth works the same way. Each little shift of the production-possibilities curve broadens the base for future GNP. As shifts accumulate over many years, the economy's productive capacity is greatly expanded. Ultimately we discover that those "little" differences in annual growth rates generate tremendous gains in GNP.

This cumulative process—whereby interest or growth is compounded from one year to the next—is called an "exponential process." To get a feel for its impact, consider the longer-run difference between annual growth rates of 1.9 and 3 percent. In 30 years, a 1.9 percent growth rate will raise our GNP to $5.9 trillion (in 1982 dollars). But a 3 percent growth rate would give us $8.3 trillion of goods and services in the same amount of time. From this longer-term perspective, the difference between 1.9 percent and 3 percent growth begins to look very meaningful.

GNP per capita: a measure of living standards

GNP per capita: Total GNP divided by total population; average GNP.

The exponential process might look even more meaningful if we translated it into *per capita* terms. We can do this by looking at *GNP per capita* rather than total GNP. **GNP per capita** is simply total output divided by total population. In 1981 the total output of the U.S. economy was $2.9 trillion. Since there were 230 million of us around to share that output, GNP per capita was

$$1981 \text{ GNP per capita} = \frac{\$2.9 \text{ trillion of output}}{230 \text{ million people}} = \$12,609$$

This does not mean that every man, woman, and child in the United States received $12,609 worth of goods and services in 1981. Rather, it simply indicates how much output was potentially available to the "average" person.

GNP per capita is often used as a basic measure of our standard of living. It tells us a lot about the material well-being of the population. The higher the GNP per capita, the greater the volume of goods and services likely to be available to the average citizen.

Growth in GNP per capita is attained only when the growth of output exceeds population growth. In the United States, this condition is usually achieved. In the 1970s our population grew by an average of only 1 percent a year. Hence our average economic growth rate of 3.2 percent (see Figure 17.3) was more than sufficient to ensure steadily rising living standards. Faster growth of GNP—or

FIGURE 17.3 U.S. OUTPUT AND
POPULATION GROWTH, 1900–80

Over time, the growth of output in the
United States has greatly exceeded
population growth. As a consequence,
GNP per capita has grown
tremendously. GNP per capita was
roughly three times higher in 1980
than in 1900.

Source: U.S. Department of Labor.

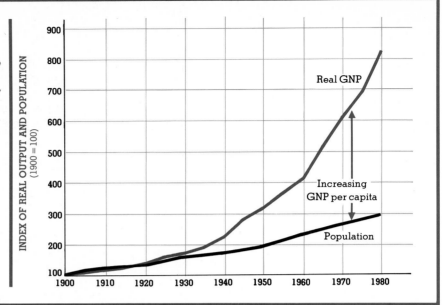

TABLE 17.1 THE DOUBLING OF
GNP PER CAPITA

Small differences in annual growth
rates cumulate into large differences
in GNP. Shown here are the number
of years it would take to double GNP
per capita at various net growth
rates. "Net" growth refers to GNP
growth rate minus the population
growth rate.

Net growth rate (percent)	Doubling time (years)
0.0	**Never**
0.5	140
1.0	70
1.5	47
2.0	35
2.5	30
3.0	24
3.5	20
4.0	18

slower population growth—would have generated even larger gains
in GNP per capita.

Less developed countries do not enjoy such rapid growth. Most
less developed countries suffer from both slower growth of GNP and
faster rates of population growth. Ethiopia, for example, is one of the
poorest countries in the world, with GNP per capita of less than
$200. Yet its population continues to grow rapidly (2.2 percent per
year), leaving little room for improvement in living standards. The
populations of Zimbabwe and Zambia grew by more than 3 percent
per year in the 1970s, while GNP grew at a slower rate. As a consequence, GNP per capita *declined* by almost 2 percent per year.[1]

By comparison with these countries, the United States has been
most fortunate. Our GNP per capita has more than doubled since
World War II. This means that the average person today has twice as
many goods and services as the average person had only 30 years
ago.

What about the future? Will we continue to enjoy substantial
gains in living standards? It all depends on how fast output continues to grow in relation to population. Table 17.1 indicates some of
the possibilities. If GNP per capita continues to grow at 2.2 percent
per year—as it did in the 1970s—our average income will double
again in 32 years. If GNP per capita grows by 3 percent, our standard
of living will rise even faster, doubling in only 24 years.

GNP per worker: a measure of productivity

The increases in living standards depicted in Table 17.1 will not
occur automatically, just because we wish them to. Someone is
going to have to produce more output if we want GNP per capita to

[1] The problems of less developed countries are examined in Chapter 35.

labor force: All persons over age 16 who are either working for pay or actively seeking paid employment.

rise. One reason our living standard rose in the 1970s is that the **labor force** grew faster than the population. Those in the World War II baby boom had reached maturity and were entering the labor force in droves. At the same time, more women began to take jobs outside the home. As a consequence, the number of workers grew faster than our population. This increase in the proportion of workers in the economy helped to increase GNP per capita.

The percentage of people who participate in the labor market cannot increase forever. At the limit, everyone would be in the labor market and no further workers could be found. Long before this point was reached, we would probably stop short of forcing young children, older people, and the sick and disabled into the labor market. Hence we have to look elsewhere for sustained increases in GNP per capita.

Sustained increases in GNP per capita are more likely to come from increases in output *per worker*. The total quantity of output produced depends not only on how many workers we employ but also on how productive each worker is. If **productivity** is increasing, then GNP per capita is likely to rise as well.

productivity: Output per unit of input; for example, output per labor-hour.

The most common measure of productivity is output per labor-hour. This is simply the ratio of total output to the number of hours worked. As we noted earlier, total GNP in 1981 was $2.9 trillion. In that same year the labor force was employed for a total of 180 billion hours. Hence the average worker's productivity was $16.11 of output per hour.

The spectacular rise of our GNP per capita in recent decades is directly related to the increased productivity of the average American worker. Since 1950, average output per worker has more than doubled, as Figure 17.4 reveals.

FIGURE 17.4 U.S. PRODUCTIVITY GAINS, 1950–81

Economic growth originates in an increased number of workers and increases in output per worker. In recent years, improvements in productivity have been the primary source of growth. Since 1950 productivity has more than doubled.

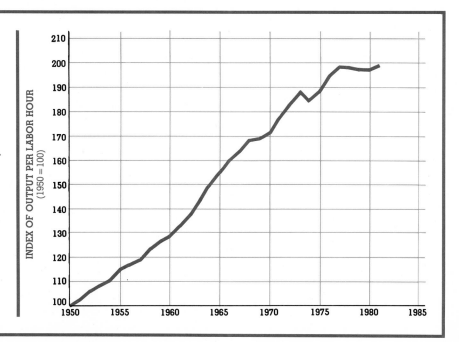

THE PRODUCTIVITY SLOWDOWN For economic growth to continue, the productivity of the average American worker must continue to rise. In recent years, however, productivity growth has slowed considerably (see Figure 17.4). The annual increase in productivity averaged 3.4 percent from 1947 to 1966, then fell to 2.15 percent for the years 1966–73. Since then, the growth of productivity has been even slower, averaging closer to 1 percent a year. This substantial decline in productivity growth has caused people to wonder if the "growth machine" is wearing out. In order to address this concern, we need to identify the sources of past productivity growth.

SOURCES OF PRODUCTIVITY GROWTH

Increases in output per labor-hour come about in many ways. The quality of labor itself may improve. The productivity of labor may be enhanced by new and better machines. Better management may contribute to higher output per worker. Government policies can also alter the efficiency of production and the incentives to work or produce.

Labor quality

The quality of labor changes over time. In general, continuing advances in education and skill training have increased the quality of labor. In 1950 less than 8 percent of all U.S. workers had completed college. Today nearly 20 percent of the workforce has completed four years of college. In addition to this advance in general education, there has been a substantial increase in vocational training, both in the public sector and by private firms. These improvements in labor quality have added 0.2 to 0.4 points to the annual productivity increase.[2]

Offsetting these improvements in the quality of individual workers has been a change in the composition of the labor force. As we observed in Chapters 5 and 13, the proportion of teenagers and women in the labor force grew tremendously in the 1960s and 1970s. These additional workers contributed to higher output. Because teenagers and women generally have less job experience than adult men, however, *average* productivity fell. This reduction in average labor quality reduced productivity growth by roughly 0.2 to 0.3 percent per year.

Capital investment

Any worker's productivity depends to a large extent on the quantity and quality of other inputs in the production process. A worker with no tools or equipment will not be very productive. Similarly, a worker with outmoded equipment will not produce as much as an equally capable worker who is equipped with the newest machines and the best technology. From this perspective, ***a primary determi-***

_____

[2] These estimates are based on a survey of empirical studies provided in Gregory B. Christiansen and Robert H. Haveman, "The Determinants of the Decline in Measured Productivity Growth: An Evaluation," in U.S. Congress, Joint Economic Committee, *Special Study on Economic Change,* vol. 10, December 29, 1980.

TABLE 17.2 AVERAGE ANNUAL GROWTH RATE OF LABOR, CAPITAL, AND PRODUCTIVITY, 1959–79 (percent)

In the 1970s the rate of capital growth slowed while the rate of labor growth increased. As a consequence, productivity gains declined.

Period	(1) Labor	(2) Capital	(3) Output per labor-hour
1959–65	0.9	3.8	3.3
1965–69	1.2	4.1	2.2
1969–73	0.4	3.5	2.6
1973–79	1.6	2.5	0.8

Source: *Economic Report of the President,* 1982.

nant of labor productivity is the rate of capital investment. In other words, improvements in output per labor hour depend in large part on increases in the quantity and quality of capital equipment.

While labor-force growth accelerated in the 1970s, the growth of capital slowed. As Table 17.2 indicates, the capital stock increased by 4.1 percent per year in the late 1960s. In the 1970s, however, the growth of capital slowed to only 2.5 percent per year. The stock of capital was still growing faster than the labor force (compare columns 1 and 2 in Table 17.2), but the difference was getting smaller. This means that the average worker was continuing to get more and better machines, but the rate of increase was slower. As a consequence, productivity growth declined (see column 3 of Table 17.2).

SAVINGS AND INVESTMENT RATES The dependence of productivity gains on capital investment shifts our perspective on consumption and saving. In the short run, the primary concern of macroeconomic policy is to balance aggregate demand and supply. To this end, fiscal and monetary policies seek to manipulate the rate of total spending. Success is measured by how close equilibrium GNP comes to full-employment GNP. In this context, savings are a form of leakage that requires offsetting injections of investment or government spending.

From the longer-run perspective of economic growth, savings and investment take on added importance. Savings are not just a form of leakage, but a basic source of investment financing. Within the confines of our production possibilities we have to choose among consumption, government spending, and investment. If we use all our resources to produce consumer and public-sector goods, there won't be any investment. In that case, we might not face a short-run stabilization problem—our productive capacity might be fully utilized—but we would confront a growth problem. By consuming everything we produced at full employment, we would be leaving nothing for investment and further growth. Indeed, if we consumed our entire output, our productive capacity would actually shrink, since we wouldn't even be replacing worn-out plant and equipment. We must have at least enough saving to finance **net investment.**

net investment: Gross investment less depreciation.

Actual saving and investment rates have been quite low in the United States. In 1981 consumers saved only 5.3 percent of their disposable income. This compares to saving rates of 6 to 8 percent in the 1960s and early 1970s. Business saving (depreciation plus re-

TABLE 17.3 INVESTMENT AND GROWTH RATES IN SELECTED COUNTRIES, 1974–81 (percent)

The United States has allocated a small proportion of GNP to investment. As a consequence, our total output has grown more slowly than the outputs of other countries.

	Investment ratio	Growth rate
United States	17	2.4
Japan	32	3.9
Canada	23	2.8
United Kingdom	19	0.5
Soviet Union	29	2.6
China	30	6.1

Source: U.S. Department of Commerce and *Economic Report of the President,* 1982.

tained earnings) was larger but grew slowly. As a consequence, the rate of investment was only 15.4 percent of GNP. In other words, we devoted 84.6 percent of our output to public and private consumption, leaving only 15.4 percent for investment. Most of this investment was needed just to replace worn-out plant and equipment. Accordingly, only 4.4 percent of GNP was allocated to net investment. Other countries allocated a much greater proportion of their output to investment and enjoyed faster rates of economic growth (see Table 17.3). To increase our own growth rate, we will have to invest more heavily.

Management

The quantity and quality of factor inputs do not completely determine the rate of economic growth, of course. On the contrary, resources, however good and abundant, must be organized into a production process and managed. Hence entrepreneurship and the quality of continuing management are major determinants of economic growth.

It is difficult to characterize differences in management techniques or to measure their effectiveness. However, much attention has been focused in recent years on the alleged shortsightedness of American managers. U.S. firms, it is said, focus too narrowly on short-term profits, to the neglect of long-term gains in productivity. They also emphasize quantity over quality of output. And they fail to include workers in key decisions, thus depriving themselves of important insights and good will. By contrast, firms in Japan and elsewhere concentrate on longer-term gains, quality control, and strong bonds between labor and mangement. As a consequence, Japanese firms enjoy remarkably good labor and customer relations, intense worker loyalty, and faster productivity gains.

No single management style can be characterized as "best." The recent critiques of traditional management styles, however, have led to some new approaches. American labor unions and managers have experimented with some new cooperative approaches. These include "quality-of-work" circles and other collective efforts to improve relationships and productivity. In some cases workers have even assumed a direct role in management or ownership. At the same time, U.S. firms have put renewed emphasis on product quality, as exemplified by the recent offering of multiyear warranties on American-made cars.

In many industries labor unions play a critical, if indirect, role in management. Unions bargain not only for wages but also for working conditions. Those conditions include the nature of the tasks to be performed on the job, the number of workers assigned to each task, the frequency and duration of breaks (e.g., lunch time), and even seniority rights to specific jobs. These union demands ultimately limit the discretion of management to alter production processes and increase productivity. Hence, increased productivity often requires explicit work-rule concessions by labor unions, and in all cases union–management cooperation.

Research and development

A fourth and vital source of productivity advance is research and development (R&D). R&D is a broad concept that includes scientific research, product development, innovations in production technique, and the development of management improvements. R&D activity may be a specific, identifiable activity (e.g., a research lab) or it may be part of the process of "learning by doing." In either case, the insights developed from R&D generally lead to new products and cheaper ways of producing them. Over time, R&D is credited with the greatest contributions to economic growth. In his study of U.S. growth during the period 1948–73, Edward Dennison concluded that 28.7 percent of *total* growth was due to "advances in knowledge" (see Table 19.5). The relative contribution of research and development to productivity (output per worker) was probably twice that much.

There is an important link between R&D and capital investment. As we noted earlier, part of each year's gross investment compensates for the depreciation of existing plant and equipment. However, new machines are rarely identical to the ones they replace. Instead, new capital equipment tends to embody improved technology. Indeed, the availability of improved technology is often a major motivation for new investment, long before old machines have literally worn out. From this perspective, R&D and capital investment make a joint contribution to productivity advance.

Government policy

A fifth major determinant of productivity growth is the government. Government policies affect virtually every dimension of the production process. Government spending on education and training greatly influences labor quality. Government support of research and development has also been a major source of R&D activity. Further, as we discussed in Chapter 13, tax policies affect basic decisions to supply labor, to save, to increase production, and to make new investments. In addition, more general monetary and fiscal policies can alter both the level and the content of GNP.

Government regulation of business is also relevant here. Indeed, many business executives blame excessive government regulation for most of their productivity problems. Although this charge is vastly exaggerated, government regulation undoubtedly has raised

An army of regulators—the tasks they perform

The Reagan administration is clamping down on federal rules, but an army of Uncle Sam's enforcers still polices the marketplace.

Some 324,000 government employes staff 54 regulatory agencies, despite the tighter budgets and personnel cuts of recent months. Among the major agencies:

Consumer Product Safety Commission. Issues and enforces performance and safety standards for more than 10,000 products, including toys, lawn mowers, tools and clothing.

Federal Trade Commission. Insures that firms compete fairly—without price fixing, deceptive advertising and other questionable practices.

Food and Drug Administration. Inspects and tests drugs, cosmetics and food products before they are offered to the public.

Environmental Protection Agency. Protects the nation's water and air by monitoring discharges and emissions from factories, sewer systems, other polluters.

Occupational Safety and Health Administration. Investigates on-the-job accidents and enforces rules for protecting employes in some 3.5 million workplaces.

Securities and Exchange Commission. Regulates trading in stocks and bonds and gathers financial information on firms.

National Labor Relations Board. Oversees elections to determine whether workers want union representation and investigates employer-worker disputes.

Equal Employment Opportunity Commission. Investigates complaints of discrimination in hiring or promotion of workers on the basis of race, sex, physical handicap or age.

Federal Communications Commission. Grants operating licenses for radio and TV stations and citizens'-band radio owners. It also oversees interstate telephone operations, including rates on long-distance calls, and sets standards for cable TV and communications satellites.

Drug Enforcement Administration. Controls legal distribution and sale of narcotics and dangerous drugs and hunts down traffickers in illicit drugs.

Federal Aviation Administration. Spells out what kinds of aircraft may be used for commercial and personal flying and sets standards for airline maintenance, air-traffic control and pilot fitness.

Federal Deposit Insurance Corporation. Insures the deposits held by banks belonging to the Federal Reserve System and establishes standards for the proper operation of financial institutions.

National Highway Traffic Safety Administration. Sets rules for fuel efficiency and safety standards for bumpers, seat belts, tires and other features.

Interstate Commerce Commission. Establishes railroad and truck rates, investigates complaints against carriers and oversees mergers of transportation companies.

Federal Home Loan Bank Board. Regulates the federally chartered savings and loan associations and insures the deposits held by member S&L's through its Federal Savings and Loan Insurance Corporation.

U.S. Forest Service. Regulates the cutting of timber on federal lands and provides national leadership in forestry.

Immigration and Naturalization Service. Controls the flow of newcomers into the U.S. and enforces rules for citizenship.

Civil Aeronautics Board. Soon to be abolished, it regulates commercial air routes and passenger and cargo rates, and grants air-shipping licenses.

Nuclear Regulatory Commission. Issues licenses for nuclear power plants, sets standards for plant construction and supervises the disposal of nuclear wastes.

Food Safety and Quality Service. Certifies the wholesomeness, grade, and quality of meats, poultry and fresh fruits and vegetables.

Patent and Trademark Office. Protects the rights of inventors and producers of new goods and services and prevents infringement upon established products.

costs and restrained innovation in many industries. From this perspective, deregulation may contribute to increased productivity and growth. The recent deregulation of the airline, trucking, oil, banking, and securities industries illustrates how deregulation can spur growth.

The goals of increased productivity and growth do not require abrupt rejections of all government intervention in product and factor markets. However, these goals do add an important consideration in evaluating public policy. Policies must be evaluated not only in terms of their own narrow objectives (e.g., cleaner air), but also in terms of their impact on productivity and growth.

THE LIMITS TO GROWTH

It is evident that continued economic growth is neither assured nor easy. At a minimum, further increases in our living standards will require more research and development, additional investment, continuing skill development, improved management, and supportive government policies. Even if all these things happen, however, success is not assured. On the contrary, some people assert that there are insurmountable limits to growth, and even our best efforts will ultimately prove futile. Sooner or later we will simply run out of the resources that feed the growth process. When our resources are exhausted, growth will come to a screeching halt. Even before that happens, we may so pollute the environment that further growth is undesired and even dangerous. From this perspective, zero economic growth (ZEG) is the optimal strategy.

The Malthusian formula for destruction

The ZEG strategy for survival originated in the eighteenth-century warnings of the Reverend Thomas Malthus. Malthus argued that continued economic growth was impossible because food production could not keep pace with population growth.

When Malthus first issued his dire warnings, in 1798, the population of England (including Wales) was on the order of 9 million people. Annual production of barley, oats, and related grains was approximately 162 million bushels, and wheat production was around 50 million bushels, just about enough to feed the English population (a little had to be imported from other countries). Although the relationship between food and population was satisfactory in 1798, Malthus reasoned that starvation was not far off. First of all, he observed that "population, when unchecked, goes on doubling itself every twenty-five years, or increases in a geometrical ratio."[3] Thus he foresaw the English population increasing to 36 million people by 1850, 144 million by 1900, and more than 1 billion by 1975, unless some social or natural restraints were imposed on population growth.

One natural population check that Malthus foresaw was a scarcity of food. England had only a limited amount of land available for cultivation and was already farming the most fertile tracts. Before long, all available land would be in use and only improvements in agricultural productivity (output per acre) could increase food supplies. Some productivity increases were possible, Malthus concluded, but "the means of subsistence, under circumstances the most favorable to human industry, could not possibly be made to increase faster than in an arithmetical ratio."[4] In particular, he concluded that barley and oats production could increase by only 162 million bushels and wheat production by 50 million bushels every 25 years.

With population increasing at a *geometric* rate and food supplies at an *arithmetic* rate, the eventual outcome is evident. Table 17.4 and Figure 17.5 illustrate Malthus' projections. In Figure 17.5*a* the difference between a **geometric growth** path and an **arithmetic growth** path is obvious.

Figure 17.5*b* simply translates this growing imbalance between population size and food supplies into per capita terms. From Malthus' time on, the amount of barley, oats, and wheat available to the

geometric growth: An increase in quantity by a constant proportion each year.

arithmetic growth: An increase in quantity by a constant amount each year.

[3] Thomas Malthus, *An Essay on the Principle of Population* (1798; reprint ed., Homewood, Ill.: Richard D. Irwin, 1963), p. 4.
[4] Ibid., p. 5.

TABLE 17.4 MALTHUSIAN PROJECTIONS, CIRCA 1798

In the nineteenth century, the English population appeared to be doubling every 25 years (geometric growth). Yet the output of food was growing by a constant amount each year (arithmetic growth). This implied a diminishing quantity of food per capita and, ultimately, starvation of the English population.

Year	English population (millions)	Output of barley and oats (millions of bushels)	Output of wheat (millions of bushels)	Barley and oats output per capita (bushels)	Wheat output per capita (bushels)
1800	9	162	50	18.0	5.5
1825	18	324	100	18.0	5.5
1850	36	486	150	13.5	4.2
1875	72	648	200	9.0	2.8
1900	144	810	250	5.6	1.7
1925	288	972	300	3.4	1.0
1950	576	1,134	350	2.0	0.6
1975	1,152	1,296	400	1.1	0.3
2000	2,304	1,458	450	0.6	0.2

Source: Malthus' arithmetic applied to actual data for 1800 (see text).

average Englishman declines rapidly. Even if we assume that the average Englishman was well fed in 1800 (an erroneous assumption, according to nutritional experts), he could have expected to experience hunger pains before 1850. He could have expected to die from starvation before 1900. According to Malthus' projections, either England died off about 100 years ago or it has been maintained at the brink of starvation for more than a century. Its continued survival

FIGURE 17.5 THE MALTHUSIAN DOOMSDAY

By projecting the growth rates of population and food output into the future, Malthus foresaw England's Doomsday. At that time, the amount of available food per capita would be too small to sustain human life. Fortunately, Malthus overestimated population growth and underestimated productivity growth.

Source: Malthus' arithmetic applied to actual data for 1800.

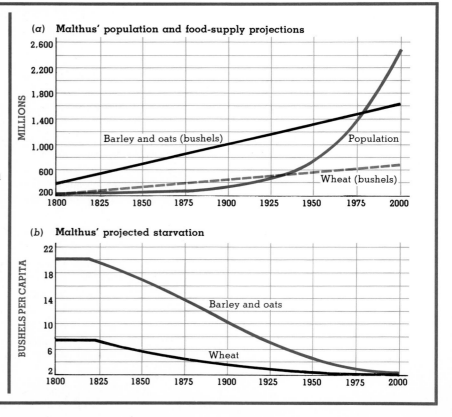

(a) Malthus' population and food-supply projections

(b) Malthus' projected starvation

can be explained only by recurrent plagues, wars, or the kind of "moral restraint" commonly associated with Victorian preachments.

Malthus' logic was impeccable. As long as population increased at a geometric rate while output increased at an arithmetic rate, England's doomsday was as certain as two plus two. Malthus' error was not in his logic but in his empirical assumptions. He did not know how fast output would increase over time any more than you know whether people will be wearing electronic wings in the year 2203. He had to make an educated guess about future productivity trends. He based his estimates on his own experiences at the very beginning of the Industrial Revolution. As it turned out (fortunately), he grossly underestimated the rate at which productivity would increase. ***Output, including agricultural products, has increased at a geometric rate, not the much slower arithmetic rate foreseen by Malthus.*** As we observed earlier, U.S. output has grown at a long-term rate of roughly 3 percent a year. This *geometric* growth has doubled output every 25 years or so. Even the productivity slowdown in the 1970s left us with geometric growth of 1 percent per year.

In addition to underestimating potential productivity growth, Malthus also underestimated the "moral restraint" of his fellow Britons. The United Kingdom's population numbered only 60 million in 1975, far short of the 1,152 million projected by Malthus.

The modern doomsday formula

In retrospect, Malthus' projections look absurd. The earth is still finite, however, and population is still growing. Hence we must *continue* to increase output at a geometric rate if we wish to maintain our standards of living. In particular, the rate of output growth must equal or exceed the rate of population growth. If output growth falls behind population growth, output per capita will decline. If that trend continues, doomsday is as certain as simple arithmetic.

Modern doomsday prophets suggest, of course, that we will not be able to sustain the required rate of economic growth. First of all, they are skeptical about our ability to duplicate *ad infinitum* the brilliant productivity increases we have already achieved. They say that you can't keep a good thing going forever.

Much of this modern pessimism is based on comprehensive, usually computerized, analyses of the future of our species. A vivid example of such analysis was undertaken at the Massachusetts Institute of Technology. Professor Jay Forrester constructed a computerized model of the way economic growth interacts with other components of our environment. Using this basic model, another team of M.I.T. scientists, directed by Professor Dennis Meadows, attempted to identify the limits to growth.[5] They noted that continued output depends on two ingredients: resource inputs and technological know-how. What concerned them was that we are persistently using up the stock of the world's material resources, leaving us no basis for further output, much less growth. On the basis of these resource

[5] Jay W. Forrester, *World Dynamics* (Cambridge, Mass.: Wright-Allen Press, 1971); and Dennis L. Meadows et al., *The Limits to Growth* (New York: Universe Books, 1972).

FIGURE 17.6 THE M.I.T. DOOMSDAY

Many modern projections of the limits to growth are based on a comparison of resource use and resource stocks. If the stock of resources is fixed, continued resource use appears impossible. Ultimately, output (including food) per capita declines. Such projections ignore possible adjustments in supply and demand, however.

Source: *The Limits to Growth: A Report for the Club of Rome's Project on the Predicament of Mankind*, by Donella H. Meadows, Dennis L. Meadows, Jørgen Randers, William W. Behrens III. A Potomac Associates book published by Universe Books, New York, 1972. Graphics by Potomac Associates.

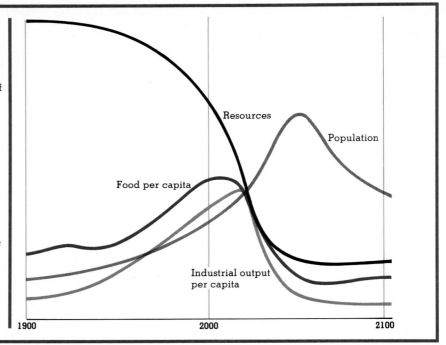

constraints, the M.I.T. scientists concluded that "under the assumption of no major change in the present system, population and industrial growth will certainly stop within the next century, at the latest."[6] Most of the M.I.T. calculations indicated that the world's growth would come to a halt around the year 2050 and be followed by rapidly deteriorating standards of living (see Figure 17.6).

RESOURCE CONSTRAINTS Like Malthus, the M.I.T. scientists were particularly worried about an ultimate shortage of land. The earth has only 7.86 billion acres of land potentially suitable for agriculture, and we are already farming half that total. We can boost agricultural production only by bringing the rest of the land into cultivation or by increasing the output per acre. Using these Malthusian observations as a benchmark, the M.I.T. scientists estimated how much land we would "require" to feed ourselves over time. Their results are presented in Figure 17.7. The basic cause of our increasing land requirements is population increase. The amount of land we actually need, however, will also depend on the amount of food we get per acre. With no improvements in productivity, we will run out of arable land around the year 2010 (see Figure 17.7).

The M.I.T. team recognized that we will probably increase agricultural productivity (output per acre) over time. Therefore, they also estimated our land requirements under the assumption that our productivity will double or even quadruple over the next 50 to 100 years. As is evident in Figure 17.7, even such large increases in productivity only postpone the day of reckoning a few years. The M.I.T.

[6] Meadows et al., *Limits to Growth*, p. 126.

FIGURE 17.7 THE LAND CONSTRAINT

The amount of arable land is limited. Hence increases in food output will depend on productivity advances. But how fast will productivity grow? The M.I.T. model projected low rates of productivity growth, and thus a foreseeable doomsday.

Source: Dennis L. Meadows et al., *The Limits to Growth* (New York: Universe Books, 1972), p. 50.

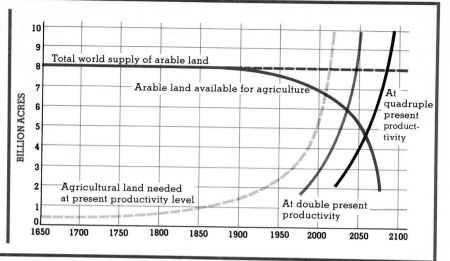

team's optimistic assumptions carry us only to the year 2070. More likely, they say, our demise will come sooner, since we are paving over arable land with highways and transforming farms into suburban housing projects.

As impressively detailed as the M.I.T. calculations are, they still suffer from the same flaw that upset Malthus' projections. They reflect good logic and arithmetic, but faulty assumptions. The M.I.T. team concedes that productivity increases are possible, but they still perceive such possibilities as being unduly limited. Note that their "most optimistic" projection calls for a quadrupling of current crop yields. Now, a fourfold increase in productivity may sound heroic, but it amounts to no more than a 3 percent annual productivity increase compounded over a period of 47 years. The United States and other countries have maintained even higher rates of productivity increase (see Chapter 21, Appendix), and less developed countries may soon exceed them. Thus the M.I.T. team's "most optimistic" productivity projections are unduly pessimistic.

Moreover, productivity changes are a *continuing* phenomenon. There is no reason to believe that productivity improvements will cease after we have achieved a modest quadrupling of present crop yields. Accordingly, it is difficult to accept the M.I.T. projections. It is equally difficult to accept the dire warnings of Stanford demographer Paul Ehrlich that "no conceivable increase in food supply can keep up with the current population growth rates over the long term."[7] It is actually quite conceivable, as long as the rate of productivity increase remains higher than the rate of population increase.

THE PRICE MECHANISM There are some good *economic* reasons for assuming that the relationship between productivity and population will remain favorable. If food production slows down significantly,

[7] Paul R. Ehrlich and Anne H. Ehrlich, *Population, Resources, Environment: Issues in Human Ecology*, 2nd ed. (San Francisco: W. H. Freeman, 1972), p. 138.

food prices will rise. The higher food prices will have two important effects. On the one hand, higher food prices will induce people to buy and consume less food. In view of our present consumption habits (see Chapter 18), this might not be a wholly undesirable consequence. Such a solution to the food problem has biologically limited potential, however. It could not even be applied in many areas of the world, where undernourishment (inadequate calorie intake) and malnutrition (inadequate intake of nutrients) are common.[8]

An increase in the price of food would have another, generally beneficial effect, however. Higher food prices would tend to create greater incentives for productivity research. Farmers and nonfarmers alike would begin to see the enhanced value of agricultural innovation and would increase their efforts to improve crop yields. Part of the basis for this expectation resides in the strength of the profit motive, the subject of Chapters 20 and 21. Suffice it to observe here that if potatoes were suddenly worth their weight in gold, everyone and his brother would be devising methods to grow potatoes faster and cheaper. Thus **the market mechanism helps both to signal impending shortages (via higher prices) and to alleviate them (via the profit motive).** In Chapter 16 we observed how the very same kind of price-induced supply and demand effects are capable of saving the world from an energy blackout. In addition, the government has consistently invested heavily in agricultural research, thereby greatly augmenting market incentives.

Even if we make the totally unfounded assumption that all agricultural productivity improvements will cease tomorrow, we need not starve to death as quickly as the M.I.T. computer predicts. Another essential economic phenomenon neglected by the computer is the potential for **substitution effects** in food consumption.

substitution effect: The replacement of one resource (or good) with another in response to changing relative prices.

The M.I.T. computer projected our current consumption habits 100 years into the future, thereby assuming that we would continue to eat the same foods we do today. That assumption, too, is unwarranted. One hundred years from today people may not even know what a hamburger is, much less a Big Mac. If land does become scarce, the price of those foods that require more land to produce will rise relative to those that require less. The Japanese, who have about as little land per person as anybody, learned this lesson long ago. The relative price of beef in Japan is about three times as high as it is in the United States, primarily because beef production requires a lot of land. The Japanese thus end up *substituting* fish and other foods for the red meat we tend to regard as essential. Were relative prices to change so drastically in the United States, we could expect to alter our consumption and land-use patterns accordingly. Chemists claim we may even be able to make do on entirely synthetic foods. Whether or not you regard these futuristic diets as a gourmet's nightmare is beside the point. The essential observation is that we *can* survive with less land per capita and a different diet. The price mechanism will encourage us to make the required adjustments.

Contrary to the computer printouts at M.I.T., then, we may confidently anticipate the maintenance of adequate food supplies well

[8] It has been estimated that one-third of the world's population is either undernourished or malnourished; see ibid., p. 82, and Chapter 35.

past the year 2100, and perhaps indefinitely. The computer erred because the people who programmed it were unduly pessimistic about the potential for productivity improvements. They totally neglected the production incentives and substitution effects that are part and parcel of the market mechanism.[9]

The same economic forces that tend to avert universal starvation also work to overcome other resource constraints. In future generations, we can expect to substitute more plentiful (and thus cheaper) resources for less plentiful (and thus more expensive) resources. We can thus expect to avert one resource "crisis" after another. In addition, we are already incorporating a basic law of physics into our production decisions and learning to recycle resources we "use up." Recycling becomes attractive from an economic perspective only as "new" resources become more difficult and expensive to obtain.[10]

Environmental destruction

Our demonstrated and potential ability to circumvent resource constraints would seem to augur well for our future. Still, the M.I.T. scientists and others warn that doomsday is imminent, even in a

[9] Nonmarket economies could achieve the same results with an appropriate system of quotas, allocations, and perhaps even nonpecuniary incentives. Thus they, too, will probably survive.
[10] For more details on recycling, see Chapter 30.

IS THE GREAT PLAINS DRYING UP?

Fifty years ago the Great Plains region was bone dry, and Depression-era farmers were leaving the area in droves. Today, however, the Great Plains is one of the richest agricultural areas in the world. Water is the resource that transformed the farmlands of Nebraska, South Dakota, Kansas, Oklahoma, and North Texas into such a fertile region. Below the ground in these states lies the Ogallala aquifer, a gigantic deposit of water-laden sand, silt, and gravel. The aquifer is 1,000 feet thick in parts of Nebraska, although only a few inches thick in parts of Texas. The Ogallala holds a quadrillion gallons of water, the equivalent of Lake Huron.

The Ogallala was first tapped in the 1930s. However, not until the 1950s were high-capacity pumps used to exploit it. Now the region's farmers use water extensively, oftentimes with the aid of massive sprinklers. In the process, however, the Ogallala water supply is being depleted. The annual net drainage (overdraft) is now almost equal to the annual flow of the Colorado River. Gradually built up over a period of millions of years, the Ogallala is being depleted in a few decades.

To irrigate their farms, many Great Plains farmers must dig new and deeper wells to replace those that have dried up. But this does not solve the problem. Ultimately, the water will become so expensive to pump that farmers will have to alter their production processes. This will require a change in crops (e.g., to wheat and sorghum from corn) as well as new water-saving technologies. The Great Plains will dry up only if the farmers who live there ignore economics completely and are willing to pay any price to get the last drop of the Ogallala's water.

FIGURE 17.8 THE POLLUTION DOOMSDAY

Pollution also threatens continued economic growth. If pollution grows as fast as output, the environment will be destroyed. Environmental destruction will retard further output growth and perhaps destroy humankind as well. The unsettled question is whether such a doomsday is inevitable.

Source: Dennis L. Meadows et al., *The Limits to Growth* (New York: Universe Books, 1972), p. 132.

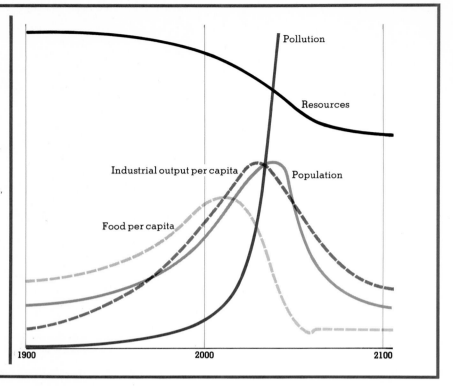

world of "unlimited" resources. The villain this time is pollution. As Professor Ehrlich sees it:

Attempts to increase food production further will tend to accelerate the deterioration of our environment, which in turn will eventually *reduce* the capacity of the Earth to produce food. It is not clear whether environmental decay has now gone so far as to be essentially irreversible; it is possible that the capacity of the planet to support human life has been permanently impaired. Such technological "successes" as automobiles, pesticides, and inorganic nitrogen fertilizers are major contributors to environmental deterioration.[11]

Because of the pollution problem, Professor G. Evelyn Hutchinson gauges the remaining time of habitable existence on earth "in decades." The M.I.T. scientists also reckon that pollution reinforces their conclusions about doomsday, whether or not we are able to circumvent a few more (or even all) resource constraints.[12] Figure 17.8 adds one more dimension to the doomsday model, this time a pollution line that rises up and chokes us off around the year 2030.

It is not difficult for anyone with the basic five senses to comprehend the problem that the M.I.T. scientists and others have addressed. Pollution is as close these days as the air we breathe. Moreover, we cannot fail to observe a distinct tendency for pollution levels to rise along with GNP and population expansion. As the

[11] Ehrlich and Ehrlich, *Population, Resources, Environment*, p. 442.
[12] G. Evelyn Hutchinson, "The Biosphere," *Scientific American*, September 1970, p. 53; Meadows et al., *Limits to Growth*, chap. 4.

"And so, extrapolating from the best figures available, we see that current trends, unless dramatically reversed, will inevitably lead to a situation in which the sky will fall."

Drawing by Lorenz; © 1972, The New Yorker Magazine, Inc.

M.I.T. computer has confirmed, many of the major pollutants—carbon dioxide, waste heat, nuclear wastes, lead, DDT, nitrogen, and mercury—have been growing geometrically.

If one projects such pollution trends into the future, things are bound to look pretty ugly. Moreover, ecologists tell us that the ability of the ecosystem to absorb wastes is limited. At some point, the threshold is passed and the ecosystem is unable to regenerate clean air and water; it is this *threshold effect* that will cause our sudden demise. Most doomsday prophets focus on one of three thresholds: the oxygen supply, the clean-water supply, or heat dissipation (the heat released by our energy-using economies, which, when it melts the polar ice caps, will drown us all).

Paul Ehrlich says:

Below a certain level of pollution, trees will survive in smog. But when a small increment in population produces a small increment in smog, living trees become dead trees. Five hundred people may be able to live around a lake and dump their raw sewage into it, and the natural systems of the lake will be able to break down the sewage and keep the lake from undergoing rapid ecological change. But 505 people may overload the system and result in a "polluted" or eutrophic lake.[13]

But although pollution in its many forms is universally acknowledged to be an important and annoying problem, we cannot assume that the *rate* of pollution will continue unabated. On the contrary, the growing awareness of the pollution problem has already led to significant abatement-policy efforts. The Environmental

[13] Paul R. Ehrlich and John P. Holdren, "Impact of Population Growth," in Commission on Population Growth and the American Future, *Population, Resources, and the Environment* (Washington, D.C., U.S. Government Printing Office, 1972), p. 372.

Protection Agency (EPA), for example, is unquestionably a force working for cleaner air and water. Indeed, active policies to curb pollution are as familiar as auto-exhaust controls and DDT bans. A computer programmed five or ten years ago to project present pollution levels would not have foreseen these abatement efforts and would thus have overestimated current pollution levels.

This is not to say that we have in any final way "solved" the pollution problem or that we are even doing the best job we possibly can. It simply says that continuing high rates of pollution are not inevitable. There is simply no compelling reason why we have to continue polluting the environment; if we stop, another doomsday can be averted.[14]

FUTURE GROWTH

The possibility of growth

Clearly we have the capability of altering productivity, resource-use patterns, production techniques, and consumption behavior. It therefore seems more reasonable to predict that the human race will survive many more centuries than to predict a doomsday in the next 50 years or so. Stated boldly and simply, there are no evident limits to growth, at least none emanating from resource constraints or pollution thresholds. As Professor Robert Solow (of M.I.T., no less!) has summed up the issue:

My real complaint about the Doomsday school [is that] it diverts attention from the really important things that can actually be done, step by step, to make things better. The end of the world *is* at hand—the earth, if you take the long view, will fall into the sun in a few billion years anyway, unless some other disaster happens first. In the meantime, I think we'd be better off passing a strong sulfur-emissions tax, or getting some Highway Trust Fund money allocated to mass transit, or building a humane and decent floor under family incomes, or overriding President Nixon's veto of a strong Water Quality Act, or reforming the tax system, or fending off starvation in Bengal—instead of worrying about the generalized "predicament of mankind."[15]

Karl Marx expressed these same thoughts nearly a century earlier. Marx chastised "the contemptible Malthus" for turning the attention of the working class away from what he regarded as the immediate problem of capitalistic exploitation to some distant and ill-founded anxiety about "natural" disaster.[16]

Finally, the Club of Rome, the group of eminent scientists that had supported and adopted the M.I.T. doomsday projections in 1972, later decided that perhaps growth was possible. In 1976, the Club of Rome concluded that the real issue was not whether the world economy would continue to grow, but how the benefits of growth would be distributed.[17]

---

[14] The econonomics of pollution control are discussed at length in Chapter 30.
[15] Robert M. Solow, "Is the End of the World at Hand?" *Challenge*, March 1973, p. 50.
[16] Cited by John Maddox in *The Doomsday Syndrome* (New York: McGraw-Hill, 1972), pp. 40 and 45.
[17] The revised Club of Rome position is described in Mihajlo Mesarovic and Eduard Pestel, *Mankind at the Turning Point* (New York: E. P. Dutton, 1974).

The desirability of growth

Let us concede, then, that continued, perhaps even "limitless" growth is *possible*. Can we also agree that it is *desirable*? Those of us who commute on congested highways, breathe foul air, and can't find a secluded camping site or drink the water may raise a loud chorus of no's. But before reaching a conclusion on this issue, let us at least determine what it is people don't like about the prospect of continued growth. Is it really economic growth per se that people object to, or instead the specific ways GNP has grown in the past? To state the question this way may provoke a few second thoughts.

First of all, let us distinguish very clearly between economic growth and population growth. Congested neighborhoods, dining halls, and highways are the consequence of too many people, not of too many goods and services. Indeed, if we had *more* goods and services—if we had more houses and transit systems, and if we traveled more—much of the population congestion we now experience might be relieved. Maybe if we had enough resources to meet our existing demands *and* to build a solar-generated "new town" in the middle of Montana, people might move out of the crowded neighborhoods of Chicago and St. Louis. Well, probably not, but at least one thing is certain: with fewer goods and services, more people will have to share any given quantity of output.

Which brings us back to the really essential measure of growth, GNP per capita. Are there any serious grounds for desiring less GNP per capita, a reduced standard of living? And don't say yes just because you think we already have too many cars on the road or calories in our bellies. That argument refers to the *mix* of output again and does not answer the question of whether or not we want *any* more goods or services per person. As we noted in Chapter 4, increasing GNP per capita can take a million forms, including the educational services you are now consuming. The rejection of economic growth per se implies that none of those forms is desirable.

We could, of course, acquire more of the goods and services we consider beneficial simply by cutting back on the production of the things we consider unnecessary. But who is to say which mix of output is "best," and how are we going to bring about the desired shift? The present mix of output may be considered bad because it is based on a maldistribution of income, deceptive advertising, or failure of the market mechanism to account for external costs. If so, it would seem more efficient (and politically more feasible) to address those problems directly rather than to attempt to lower our standards of living.

SUMMARY

▪ Economic growth refers to increases in real GNP. Short-run growth may result from increases in capacity utilization (less unemployment). In the long run, however, growth requires increases in capacity itself.

▪ GNP per capita is a basic measure of living standards. By contrast, GNP per worker gauges our productivity. Over time, increases in productivity have been the primary cause of rising living standards.

- Productivity gains can originate in a variety of ways. These sources include better labor quality, increased capital investment, research and development, improved management, and supportive government policies.

- The productivity slowdown of the late 1970s resulted from lower investment, a shift in the composition of the labor force, increases in government taxes and regulation, and other factors.

- The argument that there are identifiable and imminent limits to growth—perhaps even a cataclysmic doomsday—are founded on one of two concerns. First, we are depleting the reserve of resources required to sustain ourselves and the economy. Second, the processes of growth are so polluting the ecosystem that further growth will make life too unpleasant, perhaps biologically impossible.

- The general weakness of doomsday arguments is that they regard existing patterns of resource use or pollution as necessary for further growth. As a consequence, they consistently underestimate the possibilities for technological advance or adaptation. Even "optimistic" projections of technological possibilities turn out to be glumly pessimistic.

- Economic growth need not irreparably damage the environment. Public policy is capable of imposing incentives and regulations to reduce pollution.

- But is growth still desirable? Yes, as long as economic growth means a higher standard of living for people and an increased ability to invest in pollution-abatement equipment and other desirable social projects.

Terms to remember

Define the following terms:

production possibilities	labor force
economic growth	productivity
nominal GNP	net investment
real GNP	geometric growth
growth rate	arithmetic growth
GNP per capita	substitution effect

Questions for discussion

1. In what specific ways (if any) does a college education increase a worker's productivity?

2. Why don't we consume all of our current output instead of sacrificing some present consumption for investment?

3. In 1866 Stanley Jevons predicted that economic growth would come to a halt when England ran out of coal, a doomsday that he reckoned would occur in the mid-1970s. How have we managed to avert that projection?

4. Fertility rates in the United States have dropped so low that we are approaching zero population growth, a condition that France has maintained for decades. How will this affect our economic growth? Our standard of living?

5. Is limitless growth really possible? What forces do you think will be most important in slowing or halting economic growth?

Problems

1. What is the current rate of population growth in the United States? In the world? At these rates, how many years will it take for the United States and world populations to double?

2. How fast is productivity growing in the United States? In the world?

3. On the basis of 1 and 2, how fast is per capita output growing? How long will it be before it doubles?

4. What factors might improve the rate of productivity increase or lower the rate of population growth?

(*Note:* For information on population and productivity, you may want to consult an almanac, the *Economic Report of the President*, or *The Statistical Abstract of the United States.*)

MICROECONOMICS

Microeconomics is concerned with the little pieces of the economy—the individual consumers, workers, business firms, and unions that keep the economy moving. The basic objective of **microeconomics** is to explain the behavior of all these market participants. Why do consumers buy goods and services? What determines which goods they will buy and in what quantities?

microeconomics: The study of individual behavior in the economy, of the components of the larger economy.

With respect to business firms, microeconomics focuses on the specific decisions people make. These decisions include the choice of how much output to produce, how to produce it, and at what prices to sell it. In microeconomics we also study how decisions to buy, build, or lease factories and machinery are made by business people.

Virtually all of these issues discussed in microeconomics are also discussed in macroeconomics. The difference is the level of abstraction. In **macroeconomics,** we tend to view the economy from afar. We seek the "big picture" and don't really concern ourselves with all the messy details.

macroeconomics: The study of aggregate economic behavior, of the economy as a whole.

Microeconomics takes a much closer look. In microeconomics we want to know how things really work. Why is it that total investment tends to rise when interest rates drop? What business decisions are affected by interest rates and in what ways? Why does consumer spending tend to increase when incomes rise? In macroeconomics we satisfy ourselves with the observation that such responses are common and thus predictable. In microeconomics we want to know *why* these responses are typical. By examining the determinants of behavior, we also hope to be better prepared to predict *changes* in market behavior. Such information not only satisfies intellectual curiosity, but can be of great value to people who want to sell goods or, for that matter, to tax them.

One must also understand the origins of market behavior to assess the general desirability of having a market system in the first place. Most of us become familiar with only one economic system, namely, the U.S. economy. As a result, we learn to accept its virtual inevitability, without ever really understanding *how* it is different or what advantages or disadvantages it has. In microeconomics we take a closer look at how the **market mechanism** works. How is it that the basic economic questions of WHAT to produce, HOW, and FOR WHOM can be resolved without a finely detailed master plan? What do we gain or lose by letting market signals like prices and profits determine the basic outcomes of our economy? How are such decisions made in countries where central government planning dominates? Are countries like the Soviet Union and China, which rely heavily on central planning, more efficient or in any other way better off? To answer these questions we need to know how the market mechanism affects producer and consumer decisions, and what central planners would do instead. This requires a much closer inspection of market activity than macroeconomics undertakes.

market mechanism: The use of market prices and sales to signal desired outputs (or resource allocations).

Even if we satisfy ourselves that the market mechanism works best, we still have to worry about how well it works in different situations. In 1982 the U.S. Department of Justice acted to break up the largest private corporation in the United States, AT&T, but declined to take any action against another corporate giant, IBM. Why did the Justice Department feel the need to act against one corporation but not the other? In what ways were consumers affected by these decisions? To answer these questions—and to understand government antitrust activity—we need to know how market outcomes are affected by corporate size, power, and behavior. Microeconomics examines these questions.

A lot of attention in microeconomics is devoted to the welfare of the individual market participants. We want to know why some people are richly rewarded for their market activity while others receive little. We also want to know how the level and distribution of income would change with different economic circumstances or shifts in government policy.

The micro part of this book starts with a closer look at consumer behavior (Chapter 18), then proceeds to look at producer behavior. There is more than just theory in these pages.

The behavior of actual industries (e.g., electronic calculators) and firms are described. Chapter 24 provides a close look at the power and behavior of some of the largest U.S. corporations. Chapter 27 offers a similarly close view of specific labor unions.

Part C provides detailed discussions of three major microeconomic issues. These include pollution (Chapter 30), welfare and poverty (Chapter 31), and discrimination (Chapter 32). The final chapters examine our economic relationships with the rest of the world.

PRODUCT MARKETS

THE
DEMAND
FOR
GOODS

Americans love to go shopping. Consumer purchases of goods and services now exceed *$2 trillion* annually. This amounts to an *average*, or per capita, expenditure of nearly $8,000 for every man, woman, and child in the United States. On a per capita basis, this is five times as much as we consumed in 1929, and also about five times as much as the rest of the world spends today.

A major concern of microeconomics is to explain all of this activity. What drives us to department stores, grocery stores, and every Big Sale in town? How do we decide which goods to buy, and in what quantities? These are the kinds of questions that attract not only economists, but also sociologists, psychiatrists, advertisers, and just about everyone who owns or manages a business. Economists hope that their answers to such questions will both explain what is happening in product markets now and predict what will happen in the future.

In this chapter we shall briefly survey American consumption patterns, then try to develop explanations of consumer behavior. As we shall observe, the actual purchase of a good is the culmination of a series of decisions involving tastes, prices, income, expectations, and the availability of different goods. Once we have examined those decisions, we will be able to predict consumer responses to changes in the price of a good or other market influences. The emphasis here will be on the individual consumer, that is, on microeconomics.

PATTERNS OF CONSUMPTION

Figure 18.1 provides a quick summary of how the average consumer dollar is spent. Forty-six cents out of the typical consumer dollar is devoted to housing, including everything from rent and repair to utility bills and grass seed. Another seventeen cents out of every dollar is spent on food. Thus, nearly two-thirds of all consumer spending is for food and shelter.

The other large items in our shopping bag are transportation (car purchases and maintenance, gasoline, bus fares) and clothing. These items are followed by medical care, entertainment, and an assortment of other goods and services.

Table 18.1 provides an even closer look inside the average shopping bag. The average U.S. consumer purchases 298 eggs a year—slightly less than one per day. We also consume, on average, 220 pounds of meat each year, and 121 pounds of potatoes. Indeed, when all our food consumption is added up, it comes to 1,500 pounds of food per year for the average person! Small wonder that diet plans and health spas are so popular. In addition, we consume nearly 37 gallons of booze a year, while trying to maintain a sense of sobriety with 9.4 pounds of coffee. We also smoke an average of 3,104 cigarettes each year. (Think how many the smokers smoke!)

Not all our consumer expenditures are related to food, of course. Food expenditures account for less than one-fifth of our total purchases. The variety of consumer items ranges from the practical to the useless, from the familiar to the bizarre. The list of consumer goods also grows longer daily, with over 100 new products introduced each week.

FIGURE 18.1   HOW THE CONSUMER DOLLAR IS SPENT

Consumers spend their incomes on a vast array of goods and services. This figure summarizes those consumption decisions, by showing how the average consumer dollar is spent. The goal of economic theory is to explain and predict these consumption choices.

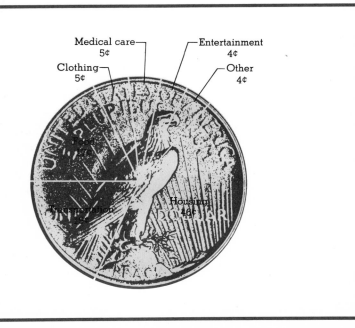

TABLE 18.1   THE ANNUAL SHOPPING LIST

This table shows the quantities of some familiar products consumed by the average American in a single year. What determines how much of each good consumers buy?

Item	Annual consumption per capita
Beer	32 gallons
Distilled spirits	2.0 gallons
Wine	2.5 gallons
Milk	28 gallons
Eggs	298
Beef and veal	130 pounds
Pork	62 pounds
Potatoes	121 pounds
Coffee	9.4 pounds
Cigarettes	3,104
Refrigerators	1 per 38 persons
Television sets	1 per 14 persons
Automobiles	1 per 17 persons
Gasoline	476 gallons

Source: U.S. Departments of Commerce and Agriculture.

DETERMINANTS OF DEMAND

Why do we buy and consume so many goods and services year in and year out? Do our materialistic appetites know any limits? What leads us to buy some goods while rejecting others?

The sociopsychiatric explanation

As one might expect, psychiatrists and psychologists have had a virtual field day formulating explanations of our behavior in the supermarket. Sigmund Freud was among the first to describe us poor mortals as bundles of subconscious (and unconscious) fears, complexes, and anxieties. From a Freudian perspective, we strive for ever higher levels of consumption to satisfy basic drives for security, sex, and ego gratification. Like the most primitive of people, we seek to clothe and adorn ourselves in ways that assert our identity and worth. We eat and smoke too much because we need the oral gratifications and security associated with mother's breast. Self-indulgence, in general, creates in our minds the safety and satisfactions of childhood. Oversized homes and cars provide us with a source of warmth and security remembered from the womb. On the other hand, we often buy and consume some things we expressly don't desire, just to assert our rebellious feelings against our parents (or parent substitutes). In Freud's view, it is the constant interplay of these id, ego, and superego drives that motivates us to buy, buy, buy.

Sociologists have provided still more explanations for our consumption behavior. Lloyd Warner and David Riesman, for example, have noted our yearning to stand above the crowd, to receive recognition from the masses. For those of truly exceptional talents, such recognition may come easily. But for the ordinary person, recognition may depend on conspicuous consumption. A larger car, a newer fashion, a more exotic vacation become expressions of identity that provoke recognition, even social acceptance. Thus, we strive for ever higher levels of consumption—so as to *surpass* the Joneses, not just to keep up with them.

Not *all* consumption is motivated by ego or status concerns, of course. Some food is consumed for the sake of self-preservation, some clothing for warmth, and some housing for shelter. Once our incomes exceed minimum subsistence levels, however, the potential for discretionary spending grows. Spending on nonnecessities is obviously more susceptible to the dictates of personality and social interaction. At current and ever rising levels of American affluence, the theories of psychiatrists and sociologists take on increasing relevance.

The economic explanation

As perceptive as sociopsychiatric theories of consumer behavior are, they tell only part of the story. They shed light on why consumers *desire* certain goods, but desire is only the first step in the consumption process. To acquire goods and services, one must be willing and able to *pay* for one's wants. Producers won't give you their goods just because you want to satisfy your Freudian desires. They want money in exchange for their goods. Hence prices and income are just as relevant to the consumption decision as are more basic desires and preferences.

In explaining consumer behavior, then, economists focus on the demand for goods and services. **Demand** entails the *willingness and ability to pay* for goods and services. Many people with a strong desire for a Rolls-Royce have neither the ability nor the willingness actually to buy it; they do not *demand* Rolls-Royces. Similarly, there are many rich people who are willing and able to buy goods they only remotely desire; they *demand* all kinds of goods and services.

demand: The ability and willingness to buy specific quantities of a good at alternative prices in a given time period (*ceteris paribus*).

To say that someone *demands* a particular good, then, means that he or she is able and willing to buy it at some price(s). As suggested above, **desire alone is not sufficient to create demand. Instead, an individual's demand for a specific product is determined by:**

- TASTES (desire for this and other goods)
- PRICE (of this particular good)
- INCOME (of the consumer)
- EXPECTATIONS (for income, prices, tastes)
- OTHER GOODS (their availability and prices)

In the remainder of this chapter we shall examine these determinants of demand. Our objective is not only to explain consumer behavior, but also to see (and predict) how consumption patterns change in response to *changes* in tastes, prices, income, the prices or availability of other goods, or expectations. Subsequent chapters will examine the nature of producer supply.

THE DEMAND CURVE

Tastes: the role of utility theory

The first determinant of demand is *taste*, or desire. Economists generally don't concern themselves with the origins of tastes; we leave

utility: The pleasure or satisfaction obtained from a good or service.

total utility: The amount of satisfaction obtained from entire consumption of a product.

marginal utility: The change in total utility obtained from an additional (marginal) unit of a good or service consumed.

law of diminishing marginal utility: The marginal utility of a good declines as more of it is consumed in a given time period.

that explanation to psychologists and sociologists. We simply assume that a person must have a taste for a good—must expect to derive some satisfaction from it—even to consider buying it. This is an eminently reasonable assumption.

It is also reasonable to assume that the more pleasure a product gives us, the higher the price we would be willing to pay for it. If the oral sensation of buttered popcorn at the movies really turns you on, you're likely to be willing to pay dearly for it. If you have no great taste or desire for popcorn, they might have to give it away before you'd eat it. Thus, there exists a positive relationship between our expected pleasure (tastes) and our willingness to pay for something. Economists focus on that relationship, leaving the question of why we desire certain goods and services to the explorations of other social scientists.

TOTAL VS. MARGINAL UTILITY   Economists use the term **utility** to refer to the expected pleasure, or satisfaction, obtained from goods and services. We also make an important distinction between total utility and marginal utility. **Total utility** refers to the amount of satisfaction obtained from your *entire* consumption of a product. By contrast, **marginal utility** refers to the amount of satisfaction you get from consuming the last (i.e., "marginal") unit of a product.

DIMINISHING MARGINAL UTILITY   The concepts of total and marginal utility explain not only why we buy popcorn at the movies, but also why we stop eating it at some point. Even people who love popcorn (i.e., derive great utility from it), and can afford it, don't eat endless quantities of popcorn. Why not? Presumably because the thrill diminishes with each mouthful. The first box of popcorn may bring sensual gratification, but the second or third box is likely to bring a stomachache. We express the phenomenon by noting that the marginal utility of the first box is higher than the additional or marginal utility derived from the second box of popcorn.

The behavior of popcorn connoisseurs is not abnormal. Generally speaking, the amount of additional utility we obtain from a product declines as we continue to consume it. The third pizza is not so desirable as the first, the sixth beer not so satisfying as the fifth, and so forth. Indeed, this phenomenon of diminishing marginal utility is so nearly universal that economists have fashioned a law around it. The **law of diminishing marginal utility** states that each successive unit of a good consumed yields less *additional* utility.

The law of diminishing marginal utility does *not* say that we won't like the third box of popcorn, the second pizza, or the sixth beer; it just says we won't like them as much as the ones we've already consumed.[1] This expectation is illustrated in Figure 18.2. Notice in Figure 18.2a that total utility continues to rise as we consume the first five boxes (ugh!) of popcorn. But total utility increases by smaller and smaller increments. Each successive step in Figure

[1] Note also that time is important here: if the first pizza was eaten last year, the second pizza may now taste just as good. The law of diminishing marginal utility is most relevant to short time periods.

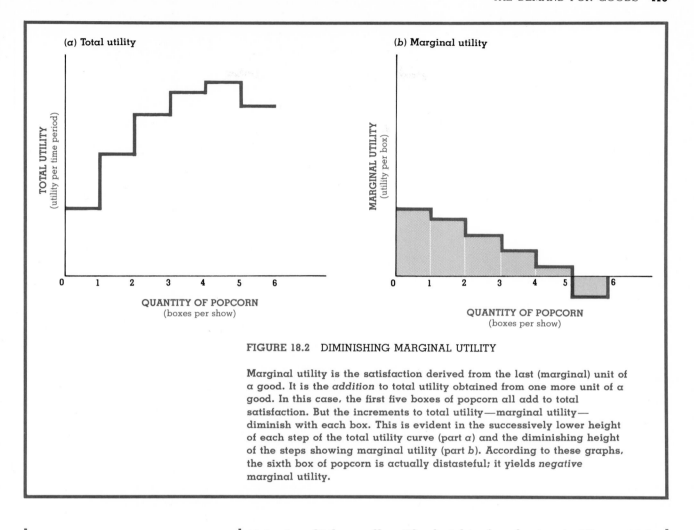

FIGURE 18.2   DIMINISHING MARGINAL UTILITY

Marginal utility is the satisfaction derived from the last (marginal) unit of
a good. It is the *addition* to total utility obtained from one more unit of a
good. In this case, the first five boxes of popcorn all add to total
satisfaction. But the increments to total utility—marginal utility—
diminish with each box. This is evident in the successively lower height
of each step of the total utility curve (part *a*) and the diminishing height
of the steps showing marginal utility (part *b*). According to these graphs,
the sixth box of popcorn is actually distasteful; it yields *negative*
marginal utility.

18.2*a* is a little smaller. The height of each step in Figure 18.2*a*
represents *marginal* utility—the increments to total utility. *Marginal* utility is clearly diminishing. Nevertheless, because marginal
utility is still positive, total utility must be increasing. The *total*
utility curve keeps rising.

The height of each step in Figure 18.2*a* is also illustrated in
Figure 18.2*b*. Here we show marginal utility only. Again we observe
that marginal utility is diminishing but still positive as we consume
the first five boxes of popcorn.

The situation changes with the sixth box of popcorn. According
to Figure 18.2, the good sensations associated with popcorn consumption are completely forgotten by the time the sixth box arrives.
Nausea and stomach cramps dominate. Indeed, the sixth box is absolutely *dis*tasteful, as reflected in the downturn of total utility (Figure
18.2*a*) and the negative value for marginal utility (Figure 18.2*b*).

Not every good ultimately gives off negative marginal utility.
And it's clear that people won't desire those increments of a good
that detract from total satisfaction. Yet the more general principle of
diminishing marginal utility is experienced daily. That is to say,

additional quantities of a good tend to yield increasingly smaller increments of satisfaction. Total utility continues to rise, but at an ever slower rate as more of a good is consumed. For our purposes, it does not matter whether marginal utility can be measured (it cannot), just so long as it declines with continued consumption of a good. There are exceptions to the law of diminishing marginal utility, but not many. (Can you think of any?)

Price: a constraint on desire

In product markets, no matter how much marginal utility a particular good or service promises, you won't get any unless you're willing to *buy* that product. In other words, we must distinguish our *desire* for a product from our *demand* for that product. Our demand for a good is an expression of our ability and willingness to buy it at some price(s).

How much of a certain good we are willing to buy at any particular price depends not only on its marginal utility (an expression of our "taste"), but also on our income, our expectations, and the prices of alternative goods and services. Rather than try to explain all these forces at once, however, let us focus on the relationship between the price of the good and the amount of it we are willing to buy. This simplification is common to economic analysis. If we want to focus on the relationship between any two phenomena (e.g., price and consumption), we momentarily ignore everything else. This doesn't mean that other forces are unimportant, just that we want to proceed one step at a time. In effect, we are assuming that everything else is constant, or unchanging. This assumption is typically referred to by its Latin term, *ceteris paribus*.

ceteris paribus: The assumption of "everything else being equal," of nothing else changing.

Notice how we used *ceteris paribus* in our definition of demand. Demand refers to a person's readiness to buy a good at some price(s), given that person's tastes and income, the person's expectations, and the prices of other goods. Were these other determinants of demand to change, we have no assurance that the person would continue to be willing to buy, at the old price(s) or any other.

We can explain the two-dimensional relationship between demand for a product and its price with the help of utility theory. In fact, it is an easy step from the law of diminishing marginal utility to the law of demand.

Recall our earlier observation that the willingness to pay is directly related to utility; the more utility a product delivers, the more a consumer will be willing to pay for it. But we have also noted that

KICKING THE COFFEE HABIT

In early 1976, the price of coffee more than doubled, to over $4 per pound, when a frost in Brazil destroyed most of the coffee crop. Consumers responded to this sudden and dramatic price increase by cutting back on coffee drinking, often switching to tea or other beverages. In other words, *the quantity of coffee demanded decreased when its price increased.* The coffee habit was not easy to kick, however: the quantity of coffee demanded fell by only 17 percent when the price of coffee doubled. This modest change in drinking habits did not reflect a reduced *desire* for coffee on the part of consumers, but instead an increase in the cost of satisfying that desire.

TABLE 18.2 THE DEMAND SCHEDULE OF A POPCORN CONSUMER

Consumers are generally willing to buy larger quantities of a good at lower prices. This demand schedule illustrates the specific quantities demanded at alternative prices. If popcorn sold for 25 cents per ounce, the typical consumer would buy 12 ounces per show (row *F*). At higher prices, less popcorn would be consumed.

	Price (per ounce)	Quantity demanded (ounces per show)
A	$0.50	1
B	0.45	2
C	0.40	4
D	0.35	6
E	0.30	9
F	0.25	12
G	0.20	16
H	0.15	20
I	0.10	25
J	0.05	30

quantity demanded: The amount of a product a consumer is willing and able to buy at a specific price in a given time period (*ceteris paribus*).

law of demand: The quantity of a good demanded in a given time period increases as its price falls (*ceteris paribus*).

demand schedule: A table showing the quantities of a good a consumer is willing and able to buy at alternative prices in a given time period (*ceteris paribus*).

marginal utility *diminishes* as increasing quantities of a product are consumed. This suggests that consumers will be willing to pay progressively less for additional quantities of a product. The moviegoer who is willing to pay 50 cents for that first mouth-watering ounce of buttered popcorn may not be willing to pay so much for a second or third ounce. The same is true for the second pizza, the sixth beer, and so forth. *With given income, taste, expectations, and prices of other goods and services,* **people are willing to buy additional quantities of a good only if its price falls.** In other words, as the marginal utility of a good diminishes, so does our willingness to pay. This inverse relationship between the **quantity demanded** of a good and its price is referred to as the **law of demand**.

The law of demand is illustrated by the **demand schedule** of Table 18.2 and the downward-sloping demand curve of Figure 18.3. Notice that in Table 18.2 the quantity demanded rises as price falls. When popcorn is selling for 50 cents an ounce (row *A*), the typical moviegoer buys only one ounce per show. At reduced prices, how-

FIGURE 18.3 THE DEMAND CURVE OF A POPCORN CONSUMER

A downward-sloping demand curve expresses the law of demand: the quantity of a good demanded increases as its price falls. People buy more popcorn at low prices than at high prices. Notice that points *A* through *J* on the curve correspond to the rows of the demand schedule (Table 18.2).

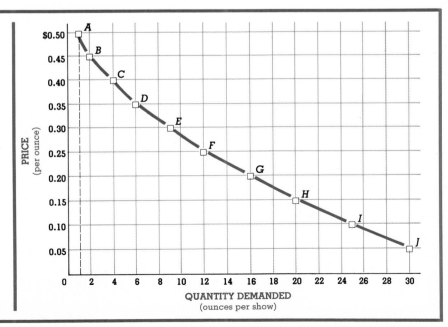

ever, the quantity demanded increases. At a price of 45 cents per ounce (row *B*), the average moviegoer demands two ounces per show; at 40 cents an ounce, the quantity demanded jumps to four ounces per show.

The tendency of quantity demanded to rise as price falls is also seen in Figure 18.3. According to the demand schedule (Table 18.2), the typical moviegoer is willing to buy only one ounce of popcorn per show when it sells for 50 cents per ounce; this is illustrated by point *A* on the **demand curve.** At 45 cents per ounce (point B), the quantity demanded increases to two ounces per show. The remainder of the demand curve expresses the law of demand, as detailed in Table 18.2. The most important characteristic of the demand curve is its downward slope. ***The demand curve slopes down to the right, in accordance with the law of demand.***

The law of demand and the law of diminishing marginal utility tell us nothing about why we crave popcorn or why our cravings subside. They do describe much of our behavior, however. Accordingly, the theory of demand can be used to predict our responses to changing prices: prediction of larger amounts of popcorn consumed at low prices than at high prices is a pretty safe bet. Moreover, such a prediction is easily tested, unlike most theories of motivation. How can we prove or reject the notion that we eat popcorn to satisfy needs for security or autoerotic titillation? To prove that prices influence consumer behavior, we need only raise or lower the price of popcorn.

SHIFTS OF THE DEMAND CURVE

A demand curve tells us how consumers respond to a change in the price of a particular good or service, *ceteris paribus*. But other things

Auto Makers Rethink Pricing Policies to Woo Still-Reluctant Buyers

They Brake on Rises Posted On '82 Models, Accelerate On Rebates and Freebies

DETROIT—The Big Three auto makers are in a tizzy over their pricing strategies.

At General Motors Corp., a high-level debate is raging over whether the company priced its 1982 models too high. At Ford Motor Co., executives are poring over the results of recent price experiments for clues on how to boost sales. And at Chrysler Corp., financial officials are hoping that their decision to trim back the size of their price increase won't backfire.

Slowly and painfully, the auto companies are reevaluating their price policies. They have begun to gamble on the heavy and repeated use of price-discount gimmicks. Customers showing up in showrooms this fall will be barraged by salesmen heralding $1,000 rebates, free options and cut-rate auto loans. They will even see some 1982 cars at 1981 prices.

Deterrent to Sales

Detroit is reacting to growing evidence that soaring sticker-prices, which have pushed the average price of a new car to $10,000, are primarily responsible for keeping car sales in the doldrums. So far in the young 1982 model year, sales are running 35% behind last year's depressed levels, and auto company financial results remain disastrous.

A recent University of Michigan survey found that "high price" is the main reason why more consumers than ever are simply deciding not to buy a new car. . . .

—John Koten and Amanda Bennett
Reprinted by permission of *The Wall Street Journal,* © Dow Jones & Company, Inc. (1981). All Rights Reserved.

don't remain equal forever: tastes, income, expectations, and the prices of other goods do change. When they do, the demand curve will change as well.

A change in tastes

Suppose for the moment that roasted pumpkin seeds became immensely popular. Perhaps pumpkin-seed roasters could convince consumers that pumpkin seeds fight tooth decay, thus eliminating the necessity of brushing your teeth. If roasted pumpkin seeds really caught on, how would popcorn sales be affected?

Before pumpkin seeds became popular, we saw that the average moviegoer was willing to buy six ounces of popcorn per show at a price of 35 cents per ounce. This relationship was illustrated by point D in Figure 18.3 and is illustrated again by point D on the "initial demand" curve in Figure 18.4. Now, however, we have to contend with a change in tastes. Once moviegoers start turning on to roasted pumpkin seeds and off popcorn, the willingness to buy popcorn will diminish. Specifically, we shall assume that after tastes change, the typical moviegoer will buy only two ounces of popcorn per show, rather than six, at a price of 35 cents per ounce. This new quantity demanded is represented by point P in Figure 18.4.

Similar reductions in quantity demanded occur at other prices. Before the pumpkin-seed craze, 12 ounces of popcorn were demanded at a price of 25 cents (point M). Now only 4 ounces are demanded at that price (point N). These and other changes cause a

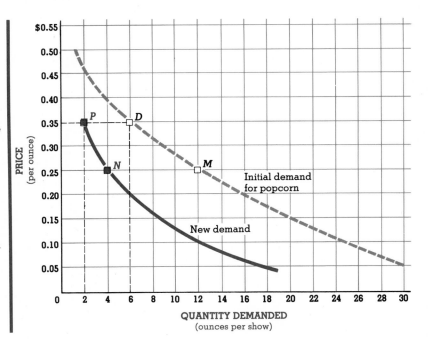

FIGURE 18.4 A SHIFT IN DEMAND

If consumer tastes turn from popcorn to pumpkin seeds, consumers will be less willing to pay for popcorn than they used to be. That is to say, the quantity of popcorn demanded at any particular price will decline. In such a case, the demand curve *shifts* to the left. Initially, consumers purchased six ounces of popcorn per show at 35 cents an ounce (point D). After tastes change, consumers buy only two ounces at that price (point P). Nevertheless, the demand curve still slopes downward because consumers can still be persuaded to buy a third or fourth ounce if the price of popcorn drops far enough.

shift in demand: A change in the quantity demanded at any (every) given price.

shift in demand—the popcorn demand curve shifts to the left. As a result of the change in tastes, people demand a smaller quantity of popcorn at each and every price.

An increased taste for popcorn would shift the demand curve to the right, indicating that moviegoers were willing and able to increase their purchases of popcorn at all prices. Such a favorable shift might occur if popcorn were discovered to be a cure for acne or if movie theaters started selling beer.

A change in income

Changes in a consumer's income have the same kind of effect on demand curves as do changes in taste. Poor people may have a great taste for popcorn at the movies but still consume little of it. By contrast, a rich person may be *willing and able to buy* lots of hot buttered popcorn even if he gets only minimal gratification from it. Hence, we may assert that *the shape and position of the demand curve depend on income as well as on taste.* Should a consumer's income change, the relevant demand curve will probably *shift.* Thus, the leftward shift of the demand curve depicted in Figure 18.4 could also express a fall in demand due to a reduction in the income of the average moviegoer.[2] (What would happen to the demand curve if income *increased?*)

A change in expectations

A demand curve may also shift if a consumer *expects* a change in income. College seniors, for example, often step up their spending for goods and services as soon as they are reasonably certain of obtaining a postgraduation job. Anticipating a rise in income in the near future, they increase the quantity they demand in the present. Whenever income expectations change, demand curves tend to shift.

Expectations also affect consumer responses to prices. If consumers expect prices to rise tomorrow, they may increase their purchases today (before the price goes up). That is to say, price expectations also influence consumer behavior.

A change in other goods

Finally, we note again that the demand for popcorn or any other product is influenced by the prices and availability of other goods and services. This was evident in our turn to pumpkin seeds. Before the appearance of pumpkin seeds, everyone ate popcorn. Similarly, people's demand for typewriters shifted significantly when word-processing machines were introduced. The demand for conventional typewriters shifted even further to the left when the price of word processors fell.

SUBSTITUTES AND COMPLEMENTS Changes in the prices of other goods can shift a demand curve in either direction. Once people have a taste for both roasted pumpkin seeds and popcorn, their consumption decisions will be influenced by the respective prices of the two

[2] In some cases, a reduction in income will cause an *increase* in demand. Such goods are called "inferior" goods (potatoes and plain white bread are examples).

FIGURE 18.5 A CHANGE IN THE PRICES OF OTHER GOODS

The curve D_1 represents the initial demand for popcorn, given the prices of other goods. Those other prices may change, however. If a reduction in the price of another good (pumpkin seeds) causes a reduction in the demand for this good (popcorn), the two goods are substitutes. In this case, popcorn demand shifts to the left, to D_2.

If a reduction in the price of another good (e.g., Pepsi) leads to an *increase* in the demand for this good (popcorn), the two goods are complements. In this case, popcorn demand shifts to the right, to D_3.

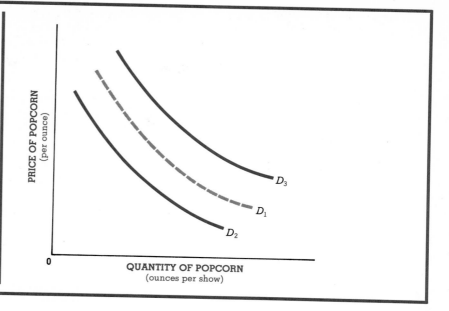

substitute goods: Goods that substitute for each other; when the price of good X rises, the quantity of good Y demanded increases (*ceteris paribus*).

complementary goods: Goods frequently consumed in combination; when the price of good X rises, the quantity of good Y demanded falls (*ceteris paribus*).

Movements vs. shifts

goods. If pumpkin seeds become cheaper, people will be less willing to buy popcorn. As a consequence, the demand curve for popcorn will shift to the left.

Popcorn and pumpkin seeds are called **substitute goods,** because a fall in the price of one leads to a decrease in the demand for the other. Substitute goods are used *instead* of each other.

Other goods are used *with* each other. Suppose the price of Pepsi fell at movie theaters. What would happen to the demand for popcorn? Would people demand larger or smaller quantities of popcorn at a given price? Experience suggests that the demand curve for popcorn would shift to the *right*. A reduction in Pepsi prices leads to an *increase* in the demand for popcorn. Pepsi and popcorn are **complementary goods.**

The distinction between substitute goods and complementary goods is illustrated in Figure 18.5. Note that the price of one good and the demand for the other move in the *same* direction for substitute goods. (A *decrease* in pumpkin-seed prices causes a *decrease* in popcorn demand.) In the case of complementary goods (e.g., Pepsi and popcorn, cream and coffee), the price of one good and the demand for the other move in opposite directions. This helps explain why American consumers cut back on car purchases when the price of gasoline jumped in 1979 and 1980.

To understand consumer behavior, it is essential to distinguish shifts of a demand curve from movements along that demand curve. A demand curve for a particular product is constructed on the basis of given tastes, income, expectations, and the prices of other goods. It tells us how a consumer will respond to a change in the price of that good, *ceteris paribus*. Thus ***consumer responses to changes in the price of a particular good are illustrated by movements along***

TABLE 18.3 THE TERMINOLOGY OF DEMAND	A change in:	implies:
	quantity demanded	a movement along a demand curve, in response to a change in price, *ceteris paribus.*
	demand	a shift of the demand curve, in response to a change in tastes, income, expectations, or the prices of other goods.

a given demand curve. But if the tastes, income, expectations, or other goods that underlie a particular demand curve change, the curve itself will be altered. That is to say, **consumer responses to changes in income, tastes, expectations, or the price or availability of other goods are illustrated by shifts of the demand curve.** These distinctions are summarized in Table 18.3.

Were all the determinants of demand changing repeatedly, an economist would be almost helpless in trying to predict consumer behavior. We would not be completely helpless, however, if we could at least identify some of the salient factors that give a demand curve its particular shape. As long as we know, for example, that the demand for popcorn depends to some extent on demand for pumpkin seeds, we can better predict when and how the popcorn demand curve will shift. Such knowledge still leaves us without a satisfactory theory of motivation, but it does enable us to keep up better with consumer expenditure patterns.

CHOOSING AMONG PRODUCTS

The dilemma of choosing between pumpkin seeds and popcorn is an example of a basic decision we make daily. As consumers, we are always choosing from among available products. It is not simply a question of how much popcorn to buy at alternative prices (the demand curve), but also whether to buy something else besides popcorn. In other words, the existence of other products gives us a *choice.* When we purchase popcorn, we are not only giving up income for popcorn but also relinquishing the opportunity to buy something else with that same income. In other words, consuming popcorn (or any other good) entails distinct **opportunity costs.** On what basis do we make such choices?

opportunity cost: The most desired goods and services that are forgone in order to obtain something else.

Marginal utility vs. price

The economic explanation for consumer choice builds on the theory of marginal utility and the law of demand. On the basis of utility theory, we expect people to prefer those products that give them greater utility to others (or at least those they think will give greater utility). Suppose you have a choice between buying a Coke and playing a video game. The first proposition of consumer choice simply states that if you think a Coke will be more satisfying than playing a video game, you will prefer to buy the Coke. Hardly a revolutionary proposition.

The second postulate of consumer-choice theory takes into account the market prices of the goods we desire. Although you may prefer to drink a Coke rather than play a video space game, one play of a video game is cheaper than a Coke. Under these circumstances, your budget may win out over your desires, and you may forgo the Coke. There is nothing irrational about playing a video game instead of buying a Coke when you have a limited amount of income to spend. On the contrary, **rational behavior requires one to compare the anticipated utility of each expenditure with its cost,** and to choose those products that promise to provide the most pleasure for the amount of income available.

Suppose your desire for a Coke is one and a half times as great as your desire to play a video game. In economic terms, this means that the marginal utility of the first Coke is 1.5 times as high as the marginal utility of the first space game. Which one should you consume? At first glance, the answer seems obvious. But what if a Coke costs 50 cents, while one play on a video game costs only 25 cents? In this case, you must pay *two* times as much for a Coke that gives only 1.5 times as much pleasure. This is not a good deal. You could get more utility per dollar by playing video games.

The same kind of principle explains why some rich people drive around in Fords rather than shiny new Mercedeses. The marginal utility (*MU*) of driving a Mercedes is substantially higher than the *MU* of driving a Ford. A nice Mercedes, however, costs about four times as much as a basic Ford. Hence Ford delivers more for the money. Specifically, Ford yields more *marginal utility per dollar spent*. The key to consumer choice is to compare the marginal utilities of different goods with their respective prices. In general, **the consumer should choose that good which delivers the most marginal utility per dollar.**

Utility maximization

This basic principle of consumer choice is easily illustrated. Suppose you have $1.50 to spend on a combination of Cokes and video games, the only consumer goods available. Your objective, as always, is to get the greatest satisfaction possible from this limited income. That is to say, you want to maximize the *total* utility attainable from the expenditure of your income. The question is how to do it. What combination of Cokes and games will maximize the utility you get from $1.50?

We have already assumed that the marginal utility of the first Coke is 1.5 times as high as the *MU* of the first video game. This is reflected in the second line of Table 18.4. The *MU* of the first video-game play has been set arbitrarily at 10 utils. We don't need to know whether 10 utils is a real thrill or just a bit of amusement. Indeed, the concept of "utils," or units of utility, has little meaning by itself; it is only a useful basis for comparison. In this case, we want to compare the *MU* of the first game with the *MU* of the first Coke. Hence we set the *MU* of the first game at 10 utils and the *MU* of the first Coke at 15 utils. The first Coke is 1.5 times as satisfying as the first video space game ($MU_{\text{Coke}} = 1.5\ MU_{\text{game}}$).

TABLE 18.4 MAXIMIZING UTILITY

Q: How can you get the most satisfaction (utility) from $1.50 if you must choose between buying Cokes that cost 50 cents and video games that cost 25 cents each?

A: By drinking one Coke and playing four video games. See text for explanation.

Quantity consumed	Amount of utility (in units of pleasure)			
	From Cokes		From video games	
	Total	Marginal	Total	Marginal
0	0	0	0	0
1	15	15	10	10
2	23	8	19	9
3	25	2	26	7
4	25	0	31	5
5	22	−3	34	3
6	12	−10	35	1

optimal consumption: The mix of consumer purchases that maximizes the utility attainable from available income.

The remainder of Table 18.4 indicates how marginal utility diminishes with increasing consumption of a product. Look at what happens to the good taste of Coke. The marginal utility of the first Coke is 15; but the *MU* of the second Coke is only 8 utils. Once you've quenched your initial thirst, a second Coke still tastes good but is not nearly so satisfying as the first one. A third Coke yields even less marginal utility, and a fourth one none at all (*MU* = 0). A fifth or sixth Coke would make your teeth rattle and cause other discomforts—its marginal utility is actually negative.

Video games also conform to the law of diminishing marginal utility. However, marginal utility doesn't decline quite so rapidly in the consumption of electronic space games. The second game is almost as much fun (*MU* = 9) as the first (*MU* = 10). It's not until you have played several games that you realize you don't stand a chance of breaking the previous high score. At that point you begin to feel the tension and enjoy the game less. By the sixth game, marginal utility is fast approaching zero.

With these psychological insights to guide us, we can now determine how best to spend $1.50. What we are looking for is that combination of Cokes and video games which *maximizes* the total utility attainable from an expenditure of $1.50. We call that combination **optimal consumption,** that is, the mix of goods that yields the most utility for the available income.

We can start looking for the optimal mix of consumer purchases by assessing the utility of spending the entire $1.50 on video games. At 25 cents per play, we could "buy" six games. This would give us *total* utility of 35 utils (see Table 18.4).

You might also want to consider spending all your income on Cokes. With $1.50 to spend, you could buy three Cokes. However, this would generate only 25 utils of total utility. Hence, if you were forced to choose between three Cokes and six games, you would pick the games.

Fortunately, we do not have to make such awful choices. In reality, we can buy a *combination* of Cokes and video games. This complicates our decision making (with more choices) but also permits us to attain still higher levels of total satisfaction.

To reach the peak of satisfaction, consider spending your $1.50 in three 50-cent increments. How should you spend the first 50 cents? If you spend it on a Coke, you will get 15 utils of satisfaction. On the other hand, 50 cents will buy your first *two* video games. The first game has a *MU* of 10 and the second game adds another 9 utils to your happiness. Hence by spending the first 50 cents on games, you reap 19 utils of total utility. This is superior to the pleasures of a first Coke and is therefore your first purchase.

Having played two space games, you now can spend the second 50 cents. How should it be spent? Your choice now is that first Coke or a third and fourth video game. That first unconsumed Coke still promises 15 utils of real pleasure. By contrast, the *MU* of a third video game is 7 and the *MU* of a fourth game only 5 utils. Together, then, the third and fourth games will increase your total utility by 12 utils while a first Coke will give you 15 utils. You should spend the second 50 cents on a Coke.

The decision on how to spend the remaining half dollar is made the same way. The final choice is either a second Coke (*MU* = 8) or the third (*MU* = 7) and fourth (*MU* = 5) video games. The two games together offer more marginal utility and are thus the correct decision.

After working your way through these calculations, you will end up drinking one Coke and playing four video games. Was it worth it? Do you end up with more total utility than you could have gotten from any other combination? The answer is yes. The *total* utility of one Coke (15 utils) and four games (31 utils) amounts to 46 units of utility. This is significantly better than the alternatives of spending your $1.50 on Cokes alone (total utility = 23) or games alone (total utility = 35). In fact, the combination of one Coke and four games is the *best* one you can find. Because this combination maximizes the total utility of your income ($1.50), it represents *optimal consumption*.

The essence of utility maximization, then, lies in comparisons of marginal utilities and prices. If a dollar spent on product X yields more marginal utility than a dollar spent on product Y, we should buy product X. To use this principle, of course, we have to know the amounts of utility obtainable from various goods and be able to perform a little arithmetic. By doing so, however, we can be assured of getting the greatest satisfaction from our limited income.

ELASTICITY

The dilemma posed by the choice between Coke and video games illustrates the complexity of the relationship between consumer choices and product prices. The decision to buy a particular product is not based solely on the pleasure or utility anticipated from its consumption—that is, on how much the consumer wants it. There are many products we greatly desire but do not buy. Nor is the decision to buy based on price alone; we pass up thousands of inexpensive products every day. To understand consumer choices fully, we have to consider not only the anticipated utility and price of a particular good, but also a consumer's income, expectations, and the util-

FINDING YOUR OPTIMAL CONSUMPTION

The basic rule for utility maximization is to purchase that good next which delivers the most *marginal utility per dollar*. Marginal utility per dollar is simply the *MU* of the good divided by its price: $MU \div P$.

From Table 18.4 we know that a first Coke has an *MU* of 15 and a price of 50 cents. It thus delivers a marginal utility per dollar of

$$\frac{MU_{\text{first Coke}}}{P_{\text{Coke}}} = \frac{15}{0.50} = 30$$

On the other hand, the first video game has a marginal utility of 10 and a price of 25 cents. It offers a marginal utility per price of

$$\frac{MU_{\text{first game}}}{P_{\text{game}}} = \frac{10}{0.25} = 40$$

From this perspective, the first video game is a better deal than the first Coke and should be purchased.

Optimal consumption implies that the utility-maximizing combination of goods has been found. If this is true, you cannot increase your total utility by trading one good for another. There is no unpurchased good that offers a higher marginal utility per dollar. Moreover, there is no good in your shopping bag that offers less *MU* per price. If there were, you would trade it in for a preferred good. Hence we conclude that all goods included in the optimal consumption mix yield the *same* marginal utility per dollar. We know we have reached maximum utility when

$$\frac{MU_x}{P_x} = \frac{MU_y}{P_y}$$

where x and y represent any two goods included in our consumption.

---

ity and prices of alternative goods. In other words, the *ceteris paribus* assumption that underlies demand curves covers a lot of potential influences on consumer choice.

Price elasticity of demand

Despite the multiple influences that shape consumption decisions, demand curves are useful tools. Over short periods of time, tastes, income, and expectations do not change much. As a consequence, the price of a good is likely to have the greatest immediate impact on the quantity demanded. For this reason, we often need to know quite precisely how consumers will respond to a change in a product's price.

By itself, the law of demand tells us that the quantity demanded will go down if price goes up. But it does not tell us by *how much* quantity demanded will fall when price rises. Yet this is the kind of information needed by a producer who is trying to decide whether to increase prices. Will an increase in the price of popcorn cause a big drop in sales or only a small decline? How high a price can the theater manager charge for popcorn without losing all of his gratification-seeking customers? What price will bring in the highest total receipts?

Such concerns are not unique to profit-hungry theater managers. In 1982 President Reagan's advisers urged him to raise excise taxes on cigarettes, liquor, and gasoline. The objective of the proposed tax increases was to raise government revenues. In the process, however, the prices of these products would have gone up and their sales would have declined. Reagan concluded that the resulting decline in sales, output, and employment would be too great and decided against such tax hikes.

Even Communists have to worry about the law of demand. In socialist economies such as the Soviet Union and China, the prices of goods are typically set by central planners. In setting prices, the central planners must consider how consumption will vary with different prices. If the price of wheat is set too low, the quantity demanded may exceed available supplies and consumer demand will not be met. On the other hand, if the price of wheat is raised too high, the quantity demanded may fall so far that the nutritional well-being of the population is threatened.

The central question in all these decisions is the response of quantity demanded to a change in price. The ***response of consumers to a change in price is measured by the price elasticity of demand.*** Specifically, the **price elasticity of demand** refers to the percentage change in quantity demanded divided by the percentage change in price, that is,

price elasticity of demand: The percentage change in quantity demanded divided by the percentage change in price.

$$\text{Price elasticity } (E) = \frac{\text{percentage change in quantity demanded}}{\text{percentage change in price}}$$

According to the law of demand, when price increases (decreases), the quantity demanded decreases (increases). Since price and quantity demanded always move in opposite directions, the price elasticity of demand (E) is always negative. However, E is typically expressed in absolute terms (without the minus sign).

A NUMERICAL EXAMPLE   To get a feel for the concept of elasticity, let us return to the popcorn counter at the movies. We have already observed that consumers respond to reductions in the price of popcorn by demanding larger quantities of it. At a price of 45 cents an ounce (point B in Figure 18.6), for example, the average moviegoer demands two ounces of popcorn per show. At the lower price of 40 cents per ounce (point C), the quantity demanded jumps to four ounces per show.

We can summarize this response with the price elasticity of demand. To do so, we have to calculate the *percentage* changes in quantity and price. Consider the percentage change in quantity first. In this case, the change in quantity demanded is 4 ounces − 2 ounces = 2 ounces. The *percentage* change in quantity is therefore:

$$\text{Percentage change in quantity} = \frac{2}{q}$$

The problem is to transform the denominator q into a number. Should we use the quantity of popcorn purchased *before* the price reduction, that is, $q_1 = 2$? Or should we use the quantity purchased *after* the price reduction, that is, $q_2 = 4$? To avoid confusion, econo-

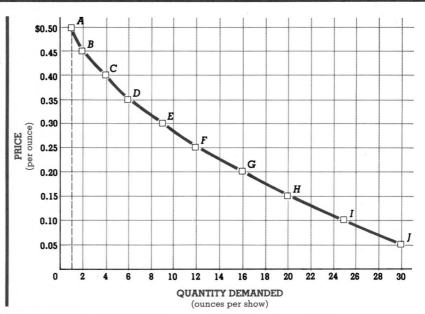

FIGURE 18.6   GAUGING ELASTICITY

From the downward-sloping demand curve, we know that a price reduction will lead to an increase in quantity demanded. The price *elasticity of demand* (E) is a *measure* of that response. In this case, demand for popcorn is elastic (E = 5.65) between points B and C: quantity demanded increases by a much larger *percentage* than price falls (see text for calculation).

mists prefer to use the *average* quantity in the denominator.[3] The average quantity is simply:

$$\text{Average quantity} = \frac{q_1 + q_2}{2} = \frac{2 + 4}{2} = 3 \text{ ounces}$$

We can now complete the calculation of the percentage change in quantity demanded. It is:

$$\text{Percentage change in quantity demanded} = \frac{q_1 - q_2}{\dfrac{q_1 + q_2}{2}} = \frac{2}{3} = 0.667$$

Popcorn sales increased by an average of 67 percent when the price of popcorn was reduced from 45 cents to 40 cents per ounce.

The computation of the percentage change in price is similar. We first note that the price of popcorn fell by 5 cents (45¢ − 40¢). We then compute the *average* price of popcorn as:

$$\text{Average price of popcorn} = \frac{p_1 - p_2}{2} = \frac{45 + 40}{2} = 42.5 \text{ cents}$$

This is our denominator in calculating the percentage price change. Using these numbers, we see that

$$\text{Percentage change in price} = \frac{p_1 - p_2}{\dfrac{p_1 + p_2}{2}} = \frac{5}{42.5} = 0.118$$

The price of popcorn fell by 11.8 percent.

Now we have all the information required to compute the price elasticity of demand. In this case,

$$E = \frac{\text{percentage change in quantity}}{\text{percentage change in price}} = \frac{q_1 - q_2}{\dfrac{q_1 + q_2}{2}} \div \frac{p_1 - p_2}{\dfrac{p_1 + p_2}{2}} = \frac{0.667}{0.118} = 5.65$$

What have we learned from all these calculations? Have we gotten anything useful? Fortunately, the answer is yes. The computed elasticity of demand is a very useful number. It says that the consumer response to a price reduction will be extremely large. Specifically, the quantity of popcorn consumed will increase 5.65 times as fast as price falls. A 1 percent reduction in price brings about a 5.65 percent increase in purchases. The theater manager can therefore boost popcorn sales greatly by lowering price a little. Central planners would view such a high elasticity of demand as signaling the need for great caution in abruptly changing the price of wheat.

ELASTIC VS. INELASTIC   In general, we categorize goods according to their relative elasticity—whether E is larger or smaller than 1. If E is larger than 1, demand is *relatively elastic* in the immediate price range. If E is less than 1, we say demand is relatively *inelastic*. In that

[3] This procedure is referred to as the *arc* (midpoint) elasticity of demand. If a single quantity and price are used in the denominator, we refer to the *point* elasticity of demand.

TABLE 18.5 ELASTICITY ESTIMATES

Price elasticities vary greatly. When the price of gasoline increases, consumers reduce their consumption only slightly. When the price of fish increases, however, consumers cut back their consumption substantially. These differences reflect the availability of immediate substitutes, the prices of the goods, and the amount of time available for changing behavior.

Type of elasticity	Estimate
Relatively elastic ($E > 1$)	
Airline travel, long run	2.4
Fresh fish	2.2
New cars, short run	1.2–1.5
Unitary elastic ($E = 1$)	
Private education	1.1
Radios and televisions	1.2
Shoes	0.9
Relatively inelastic ($E < 1$)	
Cigarettes	0.4
Coffee	0.3
Gasoline, short run	0.2

Source: Compiled from Hendrick S. Houthakker and Lester D. Taylor, *Consumer Demand in the United States, 1929–1970* (Cambridge: Harvard University Press, 1966); and F. W. Bell, "The Pope and Price of Fish," *American Economic Review*, December 1968.

case, the percentage change in quantity demanded is less than the percentage change in price; that is, consumers are not very responsive to price changes. Notice in Table 18.5, for example, the relatively low elasticity of demand for coffee and cigarettes. When the prices of these products increase, consumers don't reduce their consumption very much. In the extreme case, when quantity demanded does not respond at all to a change in price—people are willing and able to buy the same (unchanged) quantity of a good no matter how high its price goes—the price elasticity of demand is zero. Varying degrees of elasticity are illustrated in Figure 18.7.

FIGURE 18.7 DEGREES OF ELASTICITY

These various demand curves illustrate different responses to a price increase from p_1 to p_2. In each case, the initial quantity demanded at price p_1 is q_1. In part a when price rises to p_2, no output is sold (quantity demanded drops to zero); the demand curve is perfectly elastic. In part e quantity demanded does not change at all; people continue to buy the quantity q_1 even when price goes up. In that case, demand is completely inelastic. Between these two extremes consumer response may be relatively elastic (part b), unitary elastic (part c), or relatively inelastic (part d).

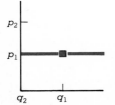

(a) Perfectly elastic
$E = \infty$

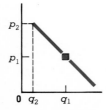

(b) Relatively elastic
$E > 1$

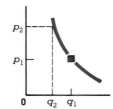

(c) Unitary elastic
$E = 1$

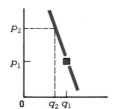

(d) Relatively inelastic
$E < 1$

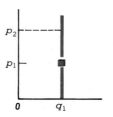

(e) Perfectly inelastic
$E = 0$

FIGURE 18.8 ELASTICITY AND
TOTAL REVENUE

Total revenue is equal to the price of
the product times the quantity sold. It
is illustrated by the area of the
rectangle formed by $p \times q$. The
shaded rectangle illustrates total
revenue ($1.60) at a price of 40 cents
and a quantity demanded of four.
When price is increased to 45 cents,
the rectangle and total revenue shrink
because demand is relatively elastic
in that price range.

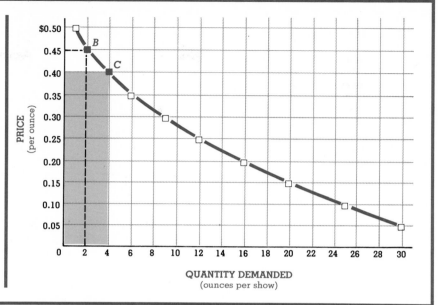

QUANTITY DEMANDED
(ounces per show)

Price elasticity and total revenue

total revenue: The price of a
product multiplied by the
quantity sold in a given time
period; $p \times q$.

The concept of price elasticity is useful for destroying the popular
misconception that producers often charge the "highest price possible." Except in the very rare case of completely inelastic demand, this
notion makes no sense. Indeed, higher prices may actually *lower*
total sales revenue.

The **total revenue** of a seller is the amount of money received
from product sales. It is determined by the quantity of the product
sold and the price at which it is sold. If the price of popcorn is 40
cents per ounce and only four ounces are sold, total revenue equals
$1.60 per show. This total revenue is illustrated by the shaded rec-
tangle in Figure 18.8. (Recall that the area of a rectangle is equal to
its height [p] times its width [q].)

Now consider what happens to total revenue when the price of
popcorn is increased. From the law of demand, we know that an
increase in price will lead to a decrease in quantity demanded.
Hence it is not apparent whether total revenue will rise or fall. The
change in total revenue depends on *how much* quantity demanded
falls when price goes up. This brings us back to the concept of elasticity.

Suppose we raised popcorn prices again, from 40 cents back to
45 cents. What happens to total revenue? At 40 cents per box, four
ounces are sold (see Figure 18.8) and total revenue equals $1.60. If
we increase the price to 45 cents, only two ounces are sold and total
revenue drops to 90 cents. In this case, an increase in price leads to a
decrease in total revenue. This new and smaller total revenue is illustrated by the dotted rectangle in Figure 18.8.

Price increases don't always lower total revenue, of course. If
demand were relatively *in*elastic ($E < 1$), a price increase would

TABLE 18.6 PRICE ELASTICITY OF DEMAND AND TOTAL REVENUE

The impact of higher prices on total revenue depends on the price elasticity of demand. Higher prices result in higher total revenue only if demand is relatively inelastic. If demand is relatively elastic, *lower* prices result in *higher* revenues.

If demand is:	and price increases, total revenue will:	If price decreases, total revenue will:
Elastic ($E > 1$)	decrease	increase
Inelastic ($E < 1$)	increase	decrease
Unit-elastic ($E = 1$)	not change	not change

lead to higher total revenue. The possible outcomes of a price change are summarized in Table 18.6.

Once we know the price elasticity of demand, we can predict quite accurately how consumers will respond to changing prices. By the same token, we can also predict what will happen to the total revenue of the seller. The elasticity of demand we calculate, however, applies to a specific range of prices only. The demand for popcorn or any other product may be highly elastic at one price level but relatively inelastic at much different prices, as Figure 18.9 illustrates.[4] Finally, elasticity, like the demand curve itself, is subject to the vagaries of changing tastes, changing incomes, and changes in the prices or availability of alternative goods. All of these potential changes are ignored when we calculate elasticity along a given demand curve.

Determinants of elasticity

The price elasticity of demand is influenced by all of the determinants of the demand curve. Table 18.5 indicated the actual price elasticity for a variety of familiar goods and services. These large differences in elasticity are explained by several factors. One of them is *price*. If the price of an item is very high in relation to one's income, then price changes will be important. Airline travel and new cars, for example, are quite expensive, so even a small percentage change in their prices could have a big impact on a consumer's budget (and consumption decisions). By contrast, coffee is so cheap

[4] Thus elasticity is not equal to the slope of the demand curve. A linear demand curve has a constant slope but a changing elasticity.

DELTA AIRLINES: PRICES DOWN, REVENUES UP

In 1978 major airlines offered fare discounts in order to boost traffic. The average fare on Delta flights was reduced by 4 percent in the fourth quarter of 1978 (some fares were reduced greatly, others not at all). In response, revenue passenger miles increased by 21 percent. In other words, the quantity demanded increased by a much larger percentage than average air fares fell. This high elasticity of demand led to a 16 percent increase in Delta's total revenue.

FIGURE 18.9 THE PRICE ELASTICITY OF DEMAND

The concept of price elasticity can be used to determine whether kids will spend more money on bubble gum when its price rises, an issue of continuing concern to bubble-gum producers. The answer to this question is yes and no, depending on how high the price goes.

Notice in the table and the graph that total revenue rises when the price of bubble gum increases from 1 cent to 2 cents, and again to 3 cents. At low prices, the demand for bubble gum is relatively inelastic: price and total revenue move in the same direction. As the price of bubble gum continues to increase, however, total revenue starts to fall. As the price is increased from 3 cents to 4 cents, total revenue drops. At higher prices, the demand for bubble gum is relatively elastic: price and total revenue move in opposite directions. Hence the price elasticity of demand depends on where one is on the demand curve; *that is,* at which price-and-quantity combination one starts.

Price of bubble gum	×	Quantity demanded	=	Total revenue	
$0.01		100		$1.00	Low elasticity (total revenue rising as price increases)
0.02		90		1.80	
0.03		70		2.10	
0.04		50		2.00	High elasticity (total revenue falling as price increases)
0.05		25		1.25	
0.06		10		0.60	
0.07		6		0.42	

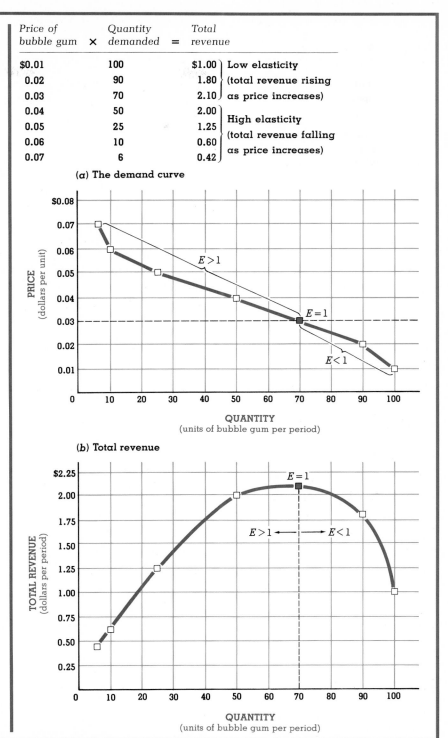

(a) The demand curve

(b) Total revenue

for most people that even a large percentage change in price is of little real significance.

A second determinant of elasticity is the *availability of substitutes.* The high elasticity of demand for fish reflects the fact that consumers can always eat chicken, beef, or pork if fish prices rise.

RAISING THE D.C. GAS TAX: A LESSON IN ELASTICITY

Like many local governments, the District of Columbia is perennially short of revenues. In an effort to raise additional revenue, Mayor Marion Barry of Washington, D.C., decided in early 1980 to increase the city's tax on gasoline. On August 6, 1980, the city government raised the gas tax to 18 cents per gallon, from the previous level of only 10 cents per gallon. The higher gas tax raised the retail price of gasoline by 8 cents, to $1.60 per gallon.

The mayor and city council thought the higher gas tax would be an easy way to increase city revenue. First of all, the difference of a few pennies a gallon would hardly be noticed, they reasoned, especially since gasoline prices were already so high. Second, much of the increased tax would be paid by tourists and suburbanites rather than city residents. Finally, a few pennies a gallon would generate lots of revenue, since District gas stations were then selling 16 million gallons a month.

The D.C. Department of Finance and Revenue had heard about the law of demand, of course. But it thought the reduction in quantity demanded (gasoline sales) would be very small in relation to the gas-tax increase. After all, U.S. motorists had reduced their gasoline consumption only slightly when OPEC had *tripled* the price of gasoline. Economists had consistently estimated the price elasticity of demand for gasoline to be very low (see Table 18.5).

Unfortunately, the District's projections were grossly in error. In August 1980, gasoline sales in the nation's capital fell from 16 million gallons per month to only 11 million. Ten gas stations closed down and more than 300 service-station workers were laid off. Realizing his mistake, Mayor Barry asked the city council to repeal the higher gas tax in November, just four months after it was introduced.

The price elasticity of demand for D.C. gasoline obviously turned out to be much higher than the city had thought. How did the city make such a mistake? Evidently the leaders forgot about the *price and availability of other goods.* True, the price elasticity for gasoline is generally quite low. But motorists in the D.C. area can buy gasoline in the District itself or in the neighboring states of Virginia and Maryland. Hence there are readily available substitutes for D.C. gasoline. By driving just another mile or so, a motorist can buy gasoline not subject to D.C. taxes. When the price of D.C. gasoline went up, motorists responded by doing just that. The ready availability and lower price of gasoline in Maryland and Virginia doomed the hopes of the D.C. government for increased revenues.

On the other hand, most cigarette smokers cannot imagine any other product that could substitute for a cigarette. As a consequence, when cigarette prices rise, smokers do not reduce their purchases very much at all. The price elasticity of demand for cigarettes is very low.

Finally, *time* affects the price elasticity of demand. Car owners cannot switch to coal-fired autos every time the price of gasoline goes up. In the short run, consumers are stuck with their gasoline-drinking automobiles and can only vary the amount of driving they do. Even that can't be varied much, however, unless one relocates one's home or job. Hence the quantity of gasoline demanded doesn't drop much immediately when gasoline prices increase. In the short run, the elasticity of demand for gasoline is quite low. With more time to adjust, however, consumers can buy more fuel-efficient cars, relocate homes or jobs, and even switch fuels. As a consequence, the long-run price elasticity of demand for gasoline is higher than the short-run elasticity.

POLICY IMPLICATIONS: CAVEAT EMPTOR

No discussion of consumer demand would be complete without consideration of the role that advertising plays in shaping our consumer behavior. As we noted earlier, psychiatrists see us as complex bundles of basic drives, anxieties, and layers of consciousness. They presume that we approach the market and all external things with confused senses of guilt, insecurity, and ambition. Economists, on the other hand, regard the consumer as the rational *homo economicus*, conversant with his or her wants and knowledgeable about how to satisfy them. In reality, however, we do not always know what we want or which products will satisfy us. This uncertainty creates a vacuum into which the advertising industry has eagerly stepped.

The efforts of producers to persuade us to buy, buy, buy are as close as the nearest television, radio, magazine, or billboard. Much advertising (including product labeling) is intended to provide information about existing products or to bring new products to our attention. A great deal of advertising, however, is also designed to exploit our senses and lack of knowledge. Recognizing that we are guilt-ridden, insecure, and sex-hungry, advertisers offer us pictures and promises of exoneration, recognition, and love; all we have to do is buy the right product. The attitude is summed up nicely by the preachments of a major perfume seller: "Promise her anything, but give her Arpège." To the extent that our social and psychological needs remain unsatisfied, the sales potential is unlimited.

One of the favorite targets of advertisers is our sense of insecurity. Thousands of products are marketed in ways that appeal to our need for identity, most often by creating a specific identity image for each product. Thousands of brand images are designed to help the consumer answer the nagging question "Who am I?" The answers, of course, vary. *Playboy* magazine says I'm a virile man of the world; Marlboro cigarettes say I'm a rugged individualist who enjoys "man-sized flavor." All users of Tide detergent are neat and worthy homemakers, whereas all Virginia Slims cigarette smokers are liberated women. The right bourbon or scotch is reserved for the successes among us, of either sex.

Other needs and drives are equally susceptible to the blandishments of promoters. Those who fear rejection can find solace and confidence in the right mouth freshener or deodorant; exhibitionist urges can be sublimated with the right bra (or no bra). A measure of immortality may be achieved through insurance plans that will exercise our wishes and control in our absence. On the other hand, eternal youth can be preserved with a proper mix of vitamin supplements, face lotions, and laxatives. Some products even appeal to a variety of needs simultaneously, such as the low-calorie ice cream sundae, which satisfies the craving for self-indulgence while allaying our sense of guilt.

Are wants created?

It does not appear reasonable to identify the blandishments of advertisers as the origin of our needs and desires. In the first place, the dynamics of personality structure and social interaction give rise to generalized drives and needs that operate in any economic context. Even members of the most primitive tribes, uncontaminated by the seductions of advertising, encrusted themselves with rings, bracelets, and pendants. These adornments demonstrated their worth and status, and alternately satisfied and denied the urges of Freud's id, ego, and superego. Second, advertising has grown to massive proportions only in the last three decades, but regular increases in consumption spending have taken place throughout recorded history. Accordingly, on both conceptual and historical grounds, it is a mistake to attribute the growth of consumption to the persuasions of advertisers.

This is not to say that advertising has necessarily made us happier or directed consumption into preferred channels. Although advertising cannot be charged with creating our needs, it does provide specific (if not necessarily correct) outlets for satisfaction of those needs. The objective of all advertising is to alter the choices we make. Just as product images are used to attract us to particular commodities, so are pictures of hungry, ill-clothed children used to persuade us to give money to charity. In the same way, public-relations gimmicks are employed to sway our votes for public servants. In the case of consumer products, advertising seeks to increase tastes for particular goods and services and therewith our willingness to pay. *A successful advertising campaign is one that shifts the demand curve to the right,* inducing consumers to increase their purchases of a product at every price (see Figure 18.10). Advertising may also

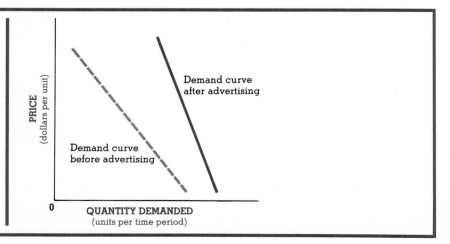

FIGURE 18.10   THE IMPACT OF ADVERTISING ON A DEMAND CURVE

Advertising seeks to increase our taste for a particular product. If our taste (the product's perceived utility) increases, so will our willingness to buy. The resulting change in demand is reflected in a rightward shift of the demand curve, often accompanied by diminished elasticity.

MILLER LITE: AN ADVERTISING SUCCESS

In January 1975 Miller Brewing Company set out to change the tastes of U.S. beer drinkers. It introduced Miller Lite, a low-calorie beer. Many other companies had produced low-calorie beers and failed. But Miller was convinced it could succeed. Other companies had directed their sales pitches to diet-conscious people and had ignored the mass of beer drinkers. In introducing its new beer, Miller emphasized that Lite tasted as good as regular beer but simply contained fewer calories. In its advertising, Miller used macho sports figures and other celebrities to emphasize that Lite was *real* beer, not a diet drink for sissies. As one analyst noted, "The typical beer drinker is not dietetically oriented, but when he sees a football player drinking this low-calorie beer, he figures he shouldn't be ashamed to drink it." Miller spent nearly $10 million per year to get this message across.

The results of the advertising campaign were phenomenal. Sales of Miller Lite skyrocketed and Miller Brewing moved up from fifth place to second place in total U.S. beer sales. In the wake of Miller's success, all other brewers were forced to introduce their own low-calorie beers to satisfy the new tastes of American drinkers. In the process, the demand for regular beer shifted to the left, while the demand for light beers shifted to the right.

make the demand curve less elastic, thus reducing consumer responses to price increases. By influencing our choices in this way, advertising alters the distribution of our consumption expenditures, if not their level.

SUMMARY

▪ In their role as consumers, Americans purchase roughly $2 trillion worth of goods and services each year. On a per capita basis, we consume nearly five times as much as the rest of the world.

▪ Our desires for goods and services originate in the structure of personality and social dynamics, and are not explained by economic theory. Economic theory focuses on *demand*, that is, our ability and willingness to *pay* for goods.

▪ The determinants of individual consumer demand include tastes, price, income, expectations, and the price and availability of other goods.

▪ Our demand for goods is dependent on the expectation of satisfaction, or *utility*. We will be willing to buy a product only if it increases our total utility.

▪ Marginal utility measures the additional satisfaction obtained from consuming one more unit of a good. The law of diminishing marginal utility says that the more of a product we consume, the smaller the increments of pleasure we tend to derive from additional units of it.

▪ The law of diminishing marginal utility translates readily into the law of demand, which asserts that we will buy increasing quantities of a product as its price falls. That is, an inverse relationship exists between quantity demanded and price. This law is graphically illustrated by a downward-sloping demand curve.

■ The shape and position of any particular demand curve depend on a consumer's income, tastes, expectations, and the price and number of substitute and complementary goods. Should any of these things change, the assumption of *ceteris paribus* will no longer hold and the demand curve will *shift*, indicating that a different quantity will be demanded at any given price.

■ In choosing among alternative goods and services, a consumer compares the prices and anticipated satisfactions that they offer. To maximize utility with one's available income—to achieve an optimal mix of goods and services—one has to get the most utility for every dollar spent. To do so one must compare relative prices and pleasures, and choose those goods that offer the most pleasure per dollar.

■ The price elasticity of demand is a numerical measure of consumer response to a change in price (*ceteris paribus*). It equals the percentage change in quantity demanded divided by the percentage change in price. Elasticity depends on the relative price of a good, the availability of substitutes, and time.

■ Advertising seeks to change consumer tastes, and thus the willingness to buy. If tastes do change, the demand curve will shift.

Terms to remember Define the following terms:

demand	demand curve
utility	shift in demand
total utility	substitute goods
marginal utility	complementary goods
law of diminishing marginal utility	opportunity cost
ceteris paribus	optimal consumption
quantity demanded	price elasticity of demand
law of demand	total revenue
demand schedule	

Questions for discussion 1. Is it possible to have a great taste for French cooking and still eat at McDonald's? What is the relationship of tastes, income, prices, and consumer behavior in this case?

2. If status anxieties create a need for a shiny new Statusmobile, will our car purchases still be affected by income or prices?

3. It has been suggested that a consumer can get the most satisfaction from expenditures by buying a mix of goods such that the marginal utility of the last dollar spent on each good is equal to the marginal utility of the last dollar spent on every other good. Is this suggestion correct? Can you prove it?

4. What is the effect of Schlitz beer advertisements on your total consumption of beer? Your demand for Budweiser?

5. What is the price elasticity of demand for gasoline in Washington, D.C. (see p. 432)? for Delta flights (see p. 430)? What accounts for these elasticities?

Problem

The following figures summarize someone's demand for ice cream:

Price per cone:	$0.50	$0.40	$0.30	$0.20	$0.10
Cones demanded per day:	1	2	4	6	9

Using this information,

(a) Draw the demand curve.

(b) Indicate the change in quantity demanded as the price of ice cream drops from 50 to 40 cents.

(c) Calculate the price elasticity of demand for this change.

(d) Calculate the price elasticity of demand for a change in price from 30 to 20 cents.

(e) Explain the difference in the price elasticities calculated for c and d.

THE COSTS OF PRODUCTION

supply: The ability and willingness to sell (produce) specific quantities of a good at alternative prices in a given time period (*ceteris paribus*).

Although consumers desire to buy a vast array of goods and services, and are willing to pay for that privilege, it is not so obvious how or why their desires can be fulfilled. If consumers are to buy digital watches, designer jeans, and video cassette players, somebody must agree to produce and sell these goods. Knowledge of consumer behavior will not in itself enable us to understand how product markets work. Like all markets, product markets have two sides, one of demand, the other of supply. **Supply** refers to the willingness and ability to sell (produce) goods and services at different prices.

In this chapter we shall begin to explore the supply side of product markets. Our inquiry begins with a quick survey of who's who on the supply side, then examines the nature of production costs. Our major objective in this chapter is to determine the costs of producing desired goods. In Chapter 20 we shall look at how producers' supply decisions are affected by these costs.

WHO'S WHO IN BUSINESS

We can begin our exploration of the supply side of product markets by observing who actually supplies goods and services in the United States. At the present time, more than *14 million* business firms produce and supply the goods and services we demand (see Table 19.1). Among these firms are more than 218,000 grocery stores, 216,000

TABLE 19.1 NUMBER AND TYPES OF BUSINESS FIRMS, BY INDUSTRY

Millions of business firms supply goods and services to U.S. product markets. They are organized as proprietorships, partnerships, or corporations. Most proprietorships are found in agriculture, services, and retail trade.

Industry	Proprietorship		Partnership		Corporation		Total	
	Number (thousands)	Percent of industry	Number (thousands)	Percent of industry	Number (thousands)	Percent of industry	Number (thousands)	Percent of industry
Agriculture, forestry, fishing	3,177	94	121	4	66	2	3,364	100
Mining	71	63	22	20	19	17	112	100
Construction	994	78	69	5	215	17	1,278	100
Manufacturing	224	46	28	6	231	48	483	100
Transportation, public utilities	385	79	17	3	85	18	487	100
Wholesale trade	307	53	29	5	238	42	574	100
Retail trade	1,862	76	164	7	433	17	2,459	100
Financial, insurance, real estate	895	50	476	26	433	24	1,804	100
Services	3,303	82	227	6	516	12	4,046	100
	11,346*	77	1,153	8	2,242*	15	14,741*	100

*Sums do not total because businesses not allocable to individual industries are included.

Source: U.S. Department of Commerce, *Statistical Abstract of the United States,* 1981.

gas stations, and 111,000 purveyors of alcoholic beverages. Among them also are a handful of giant computer firms that provide the machinery for counting and classifying the millions of other firms.

Most people think all U.S. business firms are corporations. This is far from the truth. Corporations account for only 15 percent of all business firms. Much more common are the other two forms of business enterprise, proprietorships and partnerships. The primary distinction among these three forms lies in their ownership characteristics. A single proprietorship is a firm owned by one individual. A partnership is owned by a small number of individuals. A corporation is typically owned by many individuals (stockholders)—even hundreds of thousands.

One consequence of different ownership structures is reflected in the disparate size of proprietorships, partnerships, and corporations. In general, the more people you can get to invest in a firm, the larger its potential size. As a rule, corporations tend to be much larger than the other two forms because they bring together the financial resources of more individuals. Single proprietorships are typically quite small, because few individuals have vast sources of wealth or credit. The typical proprietorship has less than $10,000 in assets, whereas the average corporation has assets in excess of $1

FIGURE 19.1   U.S. BUSINESS FIRMS: NUMBERS VS. SIZE

Proprietorships (individually owned companies) are the most common form of American business firm. Corporations are so large, however, that they account for most business sales and assets. Although only 15 percent of all firms are incorporated, corporations control 87 percent of all sales and 95 percent of all assets.

Source: U.S. Department of Commerce (1980 data).

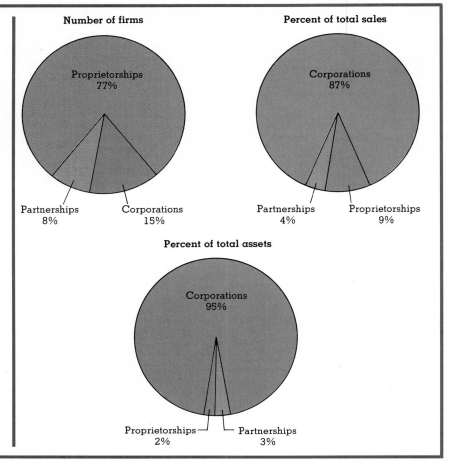

million. As a result of their size, corporations dominate market transactions, accounting for 87 percent of all business sales.

We can describe who's who in the business community, then, in two very different ways. In terms of numbers, the single proprietorship is the most common type of business firm in America. Proprietorships are particularly dominant in agriculture (the family farm), retail trade (the corner grocery store), and services (your dentist). In terms of size, however, the corporation is the dominant force in the economy (see Figure 19.1). The four largest nonfinancial corporations in the country (AT&T, Exxon, GM, Mobil) alone have more assets than *all* the 11 million proprietorships represented in Table 19.1. Just one of the four, General Motors, commands over $40 billion in assets and $60 billion in sales, and employs more than 600,000 workers (and pays its president four times as much as we pay the president of the country). Even in agriculture, where corporate entities are still comparatively rare, the few "agribusiness" corporations are so large as to dominate many thousands of small farms. Some of the consequences of corporate size, especially in regard to economic and political power, are discussed in Chapters 22–24.

THE PRODUCTION FUNCTION

No matter how large a business is or who owns it, all businesses confront one central fact: it costs something to produce goods. To produce corn, a farmer needs land, water, seed, equipment, and labor. To produce fillings, a dentist needs a chair, a drill, some space, and labor. Even the "production" of educational services (e.g., this economics class) requires the use of labor (your teacher), land (on which the school is built), and some capital (the building and blackboard). In short, unless you are producing unrefined, unpackaged air, you need some **factors of production,** that is, resources that can be used to produce a good or service.

factors of production: Resource inputs used to produce goods and services; for example, land, labor, capital.

Resource costs

The first inklings of what costs are should be evident already. If factors of production are needed to produce goods, then the amount needed of such factors must be a basic measure of cost. The costs of production are, in fact, measured in terms of the value of these factors. As always, *we gauge the value of the resources used in the production of one good by their opportunity costs,* that is, the other goods and services that could have been produced with the same resources. The costs of this class are thus measured in the first instance by the amount of land, labor, and capital it requires. The *value* of these resources is measured in terms of the goods and services forgone when we "produce" this class.

The essential question for production is how many resources are actually needed to produce a given product. The answer depends on our technological know-how and how we organize the production process. At any moment, however, there is sure to be some minimum amount of resources needed to produce a good. Or, to put it another way, there will always be some *maximum* amount of output attainable from a given quantity of resources. These limits to our production of any good are reflected in the **production function.** The production function tells us the maximum amount of good X producible from various combinations of factor inputs. With one chair and one drill, a dentist can fill a maximum of 32 cavities per day. With two chairs, a drill, and an assistant, a dentist can fill up to 55 cavities per day.

production function: A technological relation expressing the maximum quantity of a good attainable from different combinations of factor inputs.

A production function, then, is a technological summary of our ability to produce a particular good.[1] Table 19.2 provides a partial glimpse of one such function. In this case, the desired output is designer jeans, as produced by University Jeans Corporation. The essential inputs in the production of jeans are: land, labor (seamstresses), and capital (a factory and sewing machines). With these inputs, a person can buy denim by the yard, cut and sew it, and sell fancy jeans to status-conscious consumers.

As in all production endeavors, we want to know how many pairs of jeans we can produce with our available resources. We shall

---

[1] By contrast, the production-possibilities curve discussed in Chapter 1 expresses our ability to produce various *combinations* of goods, given the use of *all* our resources. The production-possibilities curve summarizes the output capacity of the entire economy. A production function describes the capacity of a single firm.

TABLE 19.2   THE PRODUCTION OF JEANS   (pairs per day)

A production function tells us the maximum amount of output attainable from alternative combinations of factor inputs. This particular function tells us how many pairs of jeans we can produce in a day with a given factory and varying quantities of capital and labor. With one sewing machine and one seamstress, we can produce a maximum of 15 pairs of jeans per day, as indicated in the second column of the second row. To produce more jeans, we need more labor and/or more capital.

Capital input (sewing machines per day)	Labor input (workers per day)							
	0	1	2	3	4	5	6	7
0	0	0	0	0	0	0	0	0
1	0	15	34	44	48	50	51	46
2	0	20	46	64	72	78	81	80
3	0	21	50	73	82	92	99	102

productivity: Output per unit of input; for example, output per labor-hour.

assume that the factory is already built, with fixed space dimensions. The only inputs we can vary are labor (the number of seamstresses per day) and additional capital (the number of sewing machines we lease per day).

As you would expect, the quantity of jeans we can produce depends on the amount of labor and capital we employ. The purpose of the production function in Table 19.2 is to tell us just *how much* output can increase as we employ more factors of production.

Consider the simplest option, that of employing no labor or capital (the upper left corner of Table 19.2). An empty factory cannot produce any jeans; maximum output is zero per day. The lesson here is quite simple: no inputs, no outputs. Even though land, capital (an empty factory), and even denim are available, some essential labor and capital inputs are missing, and jeans production is precluded.

Suppose now we employ some labor (a seamstress) but do not lease any sewing machines. Will output increase? Not according to the production function. The first row of Table 19.2 illustrates the consequences of employing labor without any additional capital equipment. Without sewing machines, the seamstresses cannot make jeans out of denim. Maximum output remains at zero, no matter how much labor is employed in this case.

The dilemma of seamstresses without sewing machines illustrates a more general principle of production. ***The productivity of any factor of production depends on the amount of other resources available to it.*** Industrious, hard-working seamstresses cannot make designer jeans successfully without sewing machines.

We can increase the productivity of seamstresses by providing them with machines. The production function again tells us by *how much* jeans output could increase if we leased some sewing machines. Suppose we leased just one machine per day. Now the second row of Table 19.2 is the relevant one. It says jeans output will remain at zero if we lease one machine but employ no labor. If we employ one machine *and* one worker, however, the jeans will start rolling out the front door. Maximum output under these circumstances (row 2, column 2) is 15 pairs of jeans per day. Now we're in business!

The remaining columns of row 2 tell us how many additional jeans we can produce if we hire more workers, still leasing only one sewing machine. Conversely, if we read down any column of Table 19.2 we can see how jeans output could increase if we leased more sewing machines, with a given number of seamstresses. For example, with one machine and two seamstresses, maximum output is 34 pairs per day. If we lease an additional machine but hire no additional workers, maximum output jumps to 46 pairs per day.

Efficiency

The production function summarized in Table 19.2 underscores the essential relationship between resource *inputs* and product *outputs*. It also provides a basic introduction to economic costs. To produce 46 pairs of jeans per day, we need two sewing machines, two seamstresses, a garage, and the denim itself. All of these inputs comprise the resource cost of producing that many jeans. Were we to produce 46 jeans with another combination of inputs—for example, one machine and slightly more than three workers per day—the value of those inputs would be our basic measure of cost.

Another essential feature of Table 19.2 is that it conveys the *maximum* output of jeans producible from particular input combinations. The standard seamstress and sewing machine, when brought together at University Jeans Corporation, can produce *at most* 15 pairs of jeans per day. They could also produce a lot less. Indeed, a careless cutter can waste a lot of denim. A lazy or inattentive one will not keep the sewing machines humming. As many a producer has learned, actual sales (output) can fall far short of the limits described in the production function. Indeed, jeans output will reach the levels of Table 19.2 only if the jeans factory operates with relative **efficiency**. This requires getting *maximum* output from the resources used in the production process.

efficiency: Maximum output of a good from the resources used in production.

We can always be inefficient, of course. This merely means getting less output than possible for the inputs we use. But this is not a desirable situation, however comfortable it might be for the seamstresses in question. To a factory manager, it means less output for a given amount of input (cost). To society as a whole, inefficiency implies a waste of resources. If seamstresses are not performing up to par, society is either (1) getting fewer jeans than it should for the resources devoted to jeans production or (2) giving up too many other goods and services in order to get a desired quantity of jeans. From a social (economy-wide) perspective, labor is one of our scarce resources. When we allocate some of it to sewing jeans, we are forsaking the opportunity to use it to produce something else. The seamstresses that represent a payroll cost to the University Jeans Corporation also represent an **opportunity cost** to society. If they don't function efficiently, we all end up with fewer goods than possible.[2]

opportunity cost: The most desired goods or services that are forgone in order to obtain something else.

[2] Inefficiency in the production of any good implies that the economy is operating *inside* our production-possibilities frontier, rather than on it; see pp. 14–15.

Although we can always do worse than the production function suggests, we cannot do better, at least in the short run. The production function represents the best we can do with our current technological know-how. For the moment, at least, there is no better way to produce a specific good. As our technological and managerial capabilities increase, however, we will attain higher levels of productivity. These advances in our productive capability will be represented by new production functions.[3] These new functions will then define the new and higher limits of efficiency, at least until new technologies are discovered.

MARGINAL PRODUCTIVITY

Let us step back from the threshold of scientific advance for a moment and return to University Jeans Corporation. Forget about possible technological breakthroughs in jeans production (e.g., electronic sewing machines, robot seamstresses) and concentrate on the economic realities of our modest endeavor. In the **short run,** we are stuck with existing technology. We are also encumbered with commitments to some factors of production. In particular, suppose we have already committed ourselves not only to the lease of the factory but also to the lease of only one sewing machine. Under these circumstances, there is only one input we can vary in order to get more jeans output. That variable input is labor. We need to focus, then, on the relationship between jeans output and additional quantities of labor.

As we noted before, a factory and sewing machine without seamstresses produce no jeans. This was observed in Table 19.2 (second row, first column) and is now illustrated by point A in Figure 19.2. Only after we employ a seamstress do jeans start appearing. By placing just one seamstress in the factory we can produce 15 pairs per day. This possibility is represented by point B. At this point, *total* output is 15 pairs per day.

Another way of viewing this situation is to note that total output has *increased* by 15 pairs when we employ the first seamstress. This is called the **marginal physical product** of that first seamstress, that is, the *increase* in total output that results from employment of one more unit of (labor) input. Without that first seamstress we get zero output; with her, we get 15 pairs of jeans per day.

Marginal physical product provides a basic measure of how desirable additional seamstresses are. Consider the impact of hiring more seamstresses. According to Table 19.2, with one seamstress we can get 15 pairs per day, with two seamstresses we can get 34 pairs. Potential output more than doubles! Whereas the *marginal* physical product of the first seamstress was only 15 pairs, a second seamstress increases total output by 19 pairs. This is represented by point c on the marginal physical product curve in Figure 19.2 and also by the rise in the total output curve (to point C).

short run: The period in which the quantity (and quality) of some inputs is fixed, that is, cannot be changed.

marginal physical product (MPP): The change in total output associated with one additional unit of input.

[3] From an economy-wide perspective, technological advances are illustrated by outward shifts of the production-possibilities curve; see p. 16.

FIGURE 19.2   MARGINAL PHYSICAL PRODUCT

Marginal physical product is the *increase* in total output that results from employing one more unit of input. The second unit of labor, for example, increases *total* output from 15 (point *B*) to 34 (point *C*). Hence the *marginal* output (*MPP*) of the second worker is 19 pairs of jeans (point *c*). What is the *MPP* of the third seamstress? What happens to *total* output when she is hired?

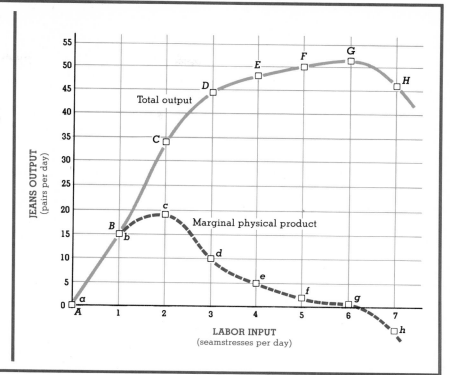

The higher *MPP* of the second seamstress raises a question about the first seamstress. Why was her *MPP* lower? Was she lazy? Is the second seamstress faster, less distracted, or harder working?

The higher *MPP* of the second seamstress is not explained by superior talents or effort. We assume, in fact, that all "units of labor" are equal, that is, one seamstress is just as good as another.[4] Their different marginal products are explained by the structure of the production process, not by their respective abilities. The first seamstress had not only to sew jeans but also to unfold bolts of denim, measure the jeans, sketch out the patterns, and cut them to approximate size. She spent a lot of time going from one task to another. Despite her best efforts (we're assuming she is working efficiently), she simply could not do everything at once.

A second seamstress greatly changes this situation. With two workers, less time is spent running from one task to another. While one seamstress is measuring and cutting, the other can continue sewing. This improved ratio of labor to other factors of production results in the large jump in total output. The superior *MPP* of the second seamstress is not unique to her; it would have occurred even if we had hired the seamstresses in the reverse order. What matters is the amount of other factors of production each unit of labor must work with.

[4] In reality, seamstresses do differ greatly in energy, talent, and diligence. These differences can be eliminated by measuring units of labor in *constant-quality* units. A seamstress who works twice as hard as everyone else would count as two *quality-adjusted* units of labor.

Diminishing returns

Unfortunately, these large increases in output cannot be maintained as still more workers are hired. Look what happens when a third seamstress is hired. Total jeans production continues to increase. But the increase from point C to point D in Figure 19.2 is only 10 pairs per day. Hence the *MPP* of the third seamstress (10 pairs) is *less* than that of the second (19 pairs). Marginal physical product is *diminishing*. This is illustrated by point *d* in Figure 19.2.

What accounts for this decline in *MPP*? The answer again lies in the ratio of labor to other factors of production. A third seamstress begins to crowd our facilities. We still have only one sewing machine. Two people cannot sew at the same time. As a result, some time is wasted as the seamstresses wait for their turns at the machine. Even if they split up the various jobs, there will still be some "downtime," since measuring and cutting are not so time-consuming as sewing. In this sense, we cannot make full use of a third worker. The relative scarcity of other inputs (capital and land) constrains the marginal physical product of labor.

Resource constraints are even more evident when a fourth seamstress is hired. Total output does increase again, but the increase this time is very small. With three workers, we got 44 pairs of jeans per day (point *D*); with four workers, we get a maximum of 48 pairs (point *E*). Thus the marginal physical product of the fourth seamstress is only 4 pairs of jeans. A fourth seamstress really begins to strain our productive capacity to the limit. There simply aren't enough machines to make productive use of so much labor.

The situation gets downright comical if a seventh seamstress is hired. Now the seamstresses are getting in each other's way, arguing, and wasting denim. Total output actually falls when a seventh seamstress is hired! In other words, the *MPP* of the seventh seamstress is *negative*, as reflected in point *h* of Figure 19.2 and the downturn in the total output curve (from 51 to 46 pairs of jeans).

LAW OF DIMINISHING RETURNS   The problem of crowded facilities applies to most production processes. In the short run, a production process is characterized by a fixed amount of available land and capital. Typically, the only factor that can be varied in the short run is labor. Yet **as more labor is hired, each unit of labor has less capital and land to work with.** This is simple division: the available facilities are being shared by more and more workers. At some point, this begins to matter. When it does, marginal physical product starts to decline. This eventuality is so common that it is the basis for another law: the **law of diminishing returns.** This law says that the marginal physical product of any factor of production (e.g., labor) will begin to diminish at some point as more of it is used in a given production setting.

law of diminishing returns: The marginal physical product of a variable factor declines as more of it is employed with a given quantity of other (fixed) inputs.

RESOURCE COSTS

The law of diminishing returns has important implications for the costs of production. The economic cost of a product is measured by the value of the resources needed to produce it. What we have seen here is that those resource requirements increase. Each additional seamstress produces fewer and fewer jeans. In effect, then, each additional pair of jeans produced uses more and more labor.

Suppose that we are employing one sewing machine and one seamstress again, for a total output of 15 pairs of jeans per day. How much labor are we using *per pair*? The answer is one-fifteenth of a seamstress' day, that is, 0.067 units of labor.

Marginal cost

marginal cost: The increase in total cost associated with a one-unit increase in production.

In order to increase total output, we need more labor, that is, a second seamstress. When we employ that second seamstress, output increases by 19 pairs. To get these additional 19 pairs, we did not lease more space or machines, but instead just hired one more unit of labor. Hence an increase in labor and denim costs is the only extra, or marginal, cost of those additional jeans. **Marginal cost** refers to the *increase* in total costs required to get one additional unit of output. In this case, we are only interested in labor and denim costs, since no additional land or capital is required to increase output. Since we need one more unit of labor to get 19 additional pairs of jeans, we can say that $1 \div 19$, or 0.053 units of labor, is the amount of labor input required to produce *one* more pair of jeans. That labor cost plus the price of the denim itself comprises the marginal cost of additional jeans.

Notice that the marginal labor cost of jeans production declines when the second seamstress is hired. Marginal cost falls from 0.067 units of labor (plus denim) per pair to only 0.053 units of labor per pair. It costs less labor *per pair* to use two seamstresses rather than only one. This is a reflection of the increased *MPP* of the second seamstress. ***Whenever MPP is increasing, the marginal cost of producing a good must be falling.*** This is illustrated in Figure 19.3.

Unfortunately, as we observed a moment ago, marginal physical product typically declines. As it does, the marginal costs of production rise. In this sense, each additional pair of jeans becomes more expensive—it uses up more and more labor per pair. This inverse relationship between *MPP* and marginal cost is illustrated in Figure 19.3. The third seamstress has an *MPP* of 10 pairs, as illustrated by point *d* in Figure 19.3a. The marginal labor input of these extra 10 pairs is thus $1 \div 10$, or 0.10 units of labor. In other words, one-tenth of a seamstress' daily effort goes into each pair of jeans. This additional labor cost *per unit* is illustrated by 1/*d* in Figure 19.3a.

Increasing marginal cost is as common as diminishing returns. Indeed, increasing marginal costs are typically caused by declining *MPP*. These increasing costs are not the fault of any person or factor, but simply a reflection of the resource constraints found in any established production setting (i.e., existing and limited plant and equipment). Nevertheless, they imply that increased output of any good from existing facilities will drive up the economic cost of that good. To keep costs from rising, we would have to discover new and improved production technologies or build better production facilities. These are *long-run* possibilities, however, and not available for short-run cost savings. In the *short run*, the quantity and quality of land and capital are fixed, and we can vary only their intensity

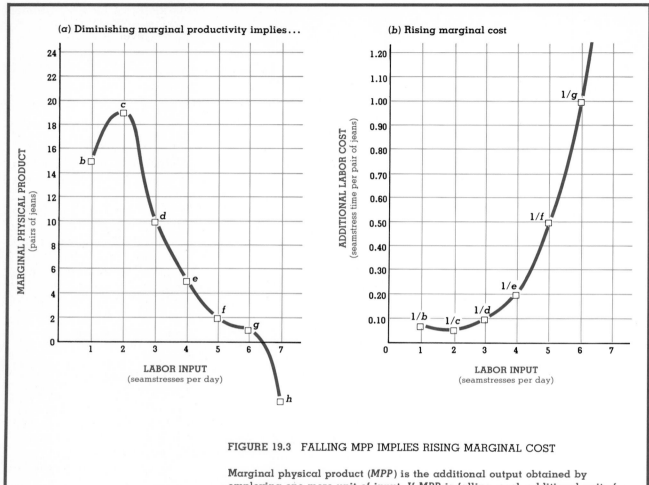

FIGURE 19.3 FALLING MPP IMPLIES RISING MARGINAL COST

Marginal physical product (*MPP*) is the additional output obtained by
employing one more unit of input. If *MPP* is falling, each additional unit of
input is producing less additional output. This means that the input cost of
each unit of output is rising. The *MPP* of the third seamstress is 10 pairs (point
d in part *a*. Therefore, the labor cost of these additional jeans is approximately
$^1/_{10}$ unit of labor per pair (point 1/*d* in part *b*).

of use (e.g., with more or fewer seamstresses). It is in this context
that we keep running into diminishing marginal returns and rising
marginal costs.

DOLLAR COSTS

This entire discussion of diminishing returns and marginal costs
may seem a bit alien. After all, we are interested in the costs of production, and costs are typically measured in *dollars*, not such technical notions as *MPP* or whatever. A jeans producer needs to know
how many dollars it costs to keep jeans flowing; he doesn't want a
lecture on marginal physical product. Can't we provide any useful
answers?

A jeans manufacturer need not study marginal physical products, or even the production function. He can confine his attention to dollar costs. The dollar costs he observes, however, are directly related to the underlying production function. To understand why his costs rise—and how they might be reduced—some understanding of the production function is necessary. In this section we shall translate production functions into dollar costs.

Total cost

total cost: The market value of all resources used to produce a good or service.

The **total cost** of producing a product includes the market value of all the resources used in its production. To determine these costs, we simply identify all the resources used in production and their value, then add everything up.

In the production of jeans, these resources included land, labor, and capital. Table 19.3 identifies these resources, their unit values, and the total costs associated with their use. This table is based on maximum output of 15 pairs of jeans per day, with the use of one seamstress and one sewing machine. The rent on the factory is $100 per day, a sewing machine costs $20 per day, the wages of a seamstress are $80 per day. We shall assume University Jeans Corporation can purchase bolts of denim for $30 apiece, each of which provides enough denim for 10 pairs of jeans. In other words, one-tenth of a bolt ($3 worth of material) is required for one pair of jeans. We shall ignore any other potential expenses.[5] With these assumptions, the total cost of producing 15 pairs of jeans per day amounts to $245.

fixed costs: Costs of production that do not change when the rate of output is altered; for example, the cost of basic plant and equipment.

Total costs will, of course, change as we alter the rate of production. But not all costs increase. On the contrary, some costs don't increase at all when output is increased. These are **fixed costs** in the sense that they do not vary with the rate of output. The factory lease is an example. Once you lease a factory, you are obligated to pay for it, whether you use it or not. The person who owns the factory wants $100 per day, whether you produce any jeans or not. Even if you produce no jeans, you are still going to have to pay the rent. That is the essence of fixed costs.

The leased sewing machine is another example of a fixed cost. When you rent a sewing machine, you must pay the rental charge. It doesn't matter whether you use it for a few minutes or all day long—the rental charge is fixed at $20 per day.

---

[5] One cost we are ignoring is profit. Traditionally, "normal" profits are counted as a cost of production. The concept of profit is explored in Chapter 20.

TABLE 19.3 THE TOTAL COSTS OF PRODUCTION
(total cost of producing 15 pairs of jeans per day)

The total cost of producing a good equals the market value of all the resources used in its production. In this case, we have assumed that the production of 15 pairs of jeans per day requires resources worth $245.

Resource	Price	Total cost
1 factory	$100 per day	$100
1 sewing machine	20 per day	20
1 seamstress	80 per day	80
1.5 bolts of denim	30 per bolt	45
Total		$245

FIGURE 19.4   THE COSTS OF JEANS PRODUCTION

Total costs include both fixed and variable costs. Fixed costs must be paid even if no output is produced (point *A*). Variable costs start at zero and increase with the rate of output. The total cost of producing 15 pairs of jeans (point *B*) includes $120 in fixed costs (rent on the factory and sewing machines) and $125 in variable costs (denim and wages). Total cost rises as output increases because additional variable costs must be incurred.

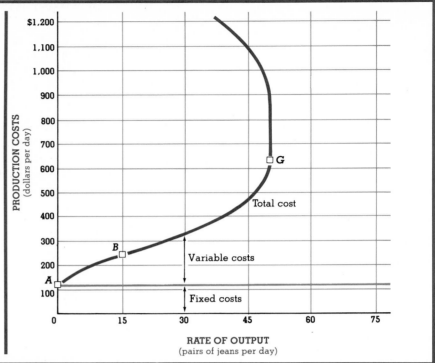

RATE OF OUTPUT
(pairs of jeans per day)

variable costs: Costs of production that change when the rate of output is altered; for example, labor and material costs.

Labor costs are another story altogether. The amount of labor employed in jeans production can be varied easily. If we decide not to open the factory tomorrow, we can just call Suzy Seamstress and tell her to take the day off. We will still have to pay rent, but we can cut back on wages. On the other hand, if we want to increase daily output, we can also get additional seamstresses easily and quickly. Labor, then, is regarded as a **variable cost** in this line of work, that is, a cost that varies with the rate of output.

The denim itself is another variable cost. Denim not used today can be saved for tomorrow. Hence, how much we "spend" on denim today is directly related to how many jeans we produce. In this sense, the cost of denim input varies with the rate of jeans output.

Figure 19.4 illustrates how these various costs are affected by the rate of production. On the vertical axis are the associated costs of production, in dollars per day. Notice that the total cost of producing 15 pairs per day is still $245, as indicated by point *B*. This figure consists of $120 of fixed costs (factory and sewing-machine rents) and $125 of variable costs ($80 in seamstress wages and $45 for denim). If we increase the rate of output, total costs will rise. ***How fast total costs rise depends on variable costs only,*** however, since fixed costs remain at $120 per day.

With one sewing machine and one factory, there is an absolute limit to daily jeans production. The capacity of a factory with one machine is roughly 51 pairs of jeans per day. If we try to produce more jeans than this by hiring additional seamstresses, our total costs will rise, but not our output. Recall that the seventh seamstress had a *negative* marginal physical product (Figure 19.2); she actually reduced total output. In fact, we could fill the factory with seamstresses and drive total costs sky-high. But the limits of space and one sewing machine do not permit output in excess of 51 pairs per day. This limit to productive capacity is represented by point G on the total-cost curve. Further expenditure on inputs will increase production costs but actually reduce output.

Although there is no upper limit to costs, there is a lower limit. If output is reduced to zero, total costs only fall to $120 per day, the level of fixed costs. This is illustrated by point A in Figure 19.4. As before, there is no way to avoid fixed costs in the short run.

Average costs

average total cost (ATC): Total cost divided by the quantity produced in a given time period.

average fixed cost (AFC): Total fixed cost divided by the quantity produced in a given time period.

average variable cost (AVC): Total variable cost divided by the quantity produced in a given time period.

Often there is an interest in the cost per pair of jeans, that is, in average total costs. **Average total cost (ATC)** is simply total cost divided by the rate of output. At an output of 15 pairs of jeans per day, total costs are $245. The average cost of production is thus $16.33 per pair ($245 ÷ 15).

Figure 19.5 shows the level and composition of average total costs for various rates of output. Row J of the table, for example, again indicates the fixed, variable, and total costs of producing 15 pairs of jeans per day. Fixed costs are still $120; variable costs are $125. Thus the total cost of producing fifteen pairs per day is $245.

The rest of row J shows the average costs of jeans production. These figures are obtained by dividing each total (columns 2, 3, and 4) by the rate of output (column 1). At an output rate of 15 pairs per day, **average fixed cost (AFC)** is $8 per pair, **average variable cost (AVC)** is $8.33, and *average* total cost (ATC) equals $16.33. ATC, then, is simply the sum of AFC and AVC, that is,

$$\text{ATC} = \text{AFC} + \text{AVC}$$

At this relatively low rate of output, fixed costs are a large portion of total costs. The rent paid for the factory and sewing machine works out to $8 per pair. This high average fixed cost accounts for nearly one-half of total average costs. This suggests that it is pretty expensive to lease a factory and sewing machine to produce only 15 pairs of jeans per day. To reduce average costs, we must make fuller use of our leased plant and equipment.

Notice what happens to average costs when the rate of output is increased to 20 pairs per day. Average fixed costs are cut by a third, to only $6 per pair. This sharp decline in AFC results from the fact that total fixed costs ($120) are now spread over much more output. Even though our rent has not dropped, the *average* fixed cost of producing jeans has.

As jeans output is increased from 15 to 20 pairs per day, AVC falls as well. AVC includes the price of denim purchased and labor costs. The price of denim is unchanged, at $3 per pair ($30 per bolt). But per-unit *labor* costs have fallen, from $5.33 to $4.50 per pair. Thus the reduction in AVC is completely due to the greater productivity of a second seamstress. To get 20 pairs of jeans, we had to employ a second seamstress part-time.[6] In the process, the marginal physical product of labor rose, and AVC fell.

---

[6] We are assuming a seamstress' time is divisible, that is, she can be hired for less than a full day.

FIGURE 19.5 AVERAGE COSTS

Average total costs (ATC) in column 7 equal total cost (column 4) divided by the rate of output (column 1). Since total costs include both fixed (column 2) and variable (column 3) costs, ATC equals AFC (column 5) plus AVC (column 6). This relationship is also illustrated in the graph below. The ATC of producing 15 pairs per day (point J) equals $16.33, the sum of AFC ($8.00) and AVC ($8.33).

	(1) Rate of output	(2) Fixed costs	+	(3) Variable costs	=	(4) Total costs	(5) Average fixed cost	(6) Average + variable cost	(7) Average = total cost
H	0	$120		$ 0		$120	—	—	—
I	10	120		85		205	$12.00	$ 8.50	$20.50
J	15	120		125		245	8.00	8.33	16.33
K	20	120		150		270	6.00	7.50	13.50
L	30	120		240		360	4.00	8.00	12.00
M	40	120		350		470	3.00	8.75	11.75
N	50	120		550		670	2.40	11.00	13.40
O	51	120		633		853	2.35	12.80	15.15

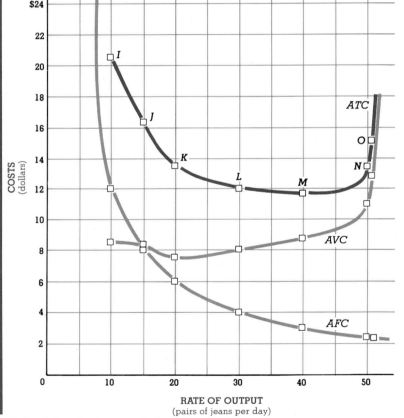

COSTS (dollars)

RATE OF OUTPUT
(pairs of jeans per day)

With both AFC and AVC falling, ATC must decline as well. In this case, *average* total costs fall from $16.33 per pair to $13.50. This is reflected in row K of the table as well as in point K on the ATC curve in Figure 19.5.

FALLING AFC   If we increase production beyond 20 pairs of jeans per day, AFC will continue to fall. Recall that

$$AFC = \frac{\text{total fixed cost}}{\text{total output}}$$

The numerator is fixed (at $120 in this case). Increases in output enlarge the denominator. Hence any increase in output will lower average fixed cost.

RISING *AVC*   The steady decline of *AFC* is not matched by declining *AVC*. On the contrary, *AVC* tends to start rising quite early in the expansion process. Look at column 6 of the table in Figure 19.5. After an initial decline, *AVC* starts to increase. At an output of 20 pairs, *AVC* is $7.50. At 30 pairs, *AVC* is $8.00. By the time the rate of output reaches 51 pairs per day, *AVC* is $12.80.

*The rise in **AVC** is another reflection of diminishing returns in the production process.* We have been through all this before. As output expands, each unit of labor has less land and capital to work with. Marginal physical product falls. As it does, labor costs *per pair of jeans* rise, pushing up *AVC*.

U-SHAPED *ATC*   The steady decline of *AFC*, when combined with the typical increase in *AVC*, results in a U-shaped pattern for average *total* costs. In the early stages of output expansion, the large declines in *AFC* tend to outweigh any increases in *AVC*. As a result, *ATC* tends to fall. Notice that *ATC* declines from $20.50 to $11.75 as output increases from 10 to 40 pairs per day. This is also illustrated in Figure 19.5 with the downward move from point *I* to point *M*.

The battle between falling *AFC* and rising *AVC* takes an irreversible turn soon thereafter. When output is increased from 40 to 50 pairs of jeans per day, *AFC* continues to fall (row *N* in the table). But the decline in *AFC* (− 60 cents) is overshadowed by the increase in *AVC* (+ $2.25). Once rising *AVC* dominates, *ATC* starts to increase as well. *ATC* increases from $11.75 to $13.40 when jeans production expands from 40 to 50 pairs per day.

This and further increases in average total costs cause the *ATC* curve in Figure 19.5 to start rising. The initial dominance of falling *AFC*, combined with the later resurgence of *AVC*, is what gives the *ATC* curve its characteristic U shape.

MINIMUM AVERAGE COST   The bottom of the U is an important point. Point *M* in Figure 19.5 represents *minimum* average total costs. This rate of production (40 pairs of jeans per day) represents the most efficient use of our sewing machines, factory, and labor. Any other rate of production alters the balance between *AFC* and *AVC* and increases average total costs. By producing exactly 40 pairs per day, we minimize the amount of land, labor, and capital used per pair of jeans. For University Jeans Corporation, point *M* represents least-cost production—the lowest-cost jeans. For society as a whole, point *M* also represents lowest possible opportunity cost, that is, we are minimizing the sacrifice of resources implied by the production of a pair of jeans. We are maximizing the amount of resources left over for the production of other goods and services.

As attractive as point *M* is, you should not conclude that it is everyone's dream. As we shall discuss at length in Chapter 20, the primary objective of producers is to maximize their *profits*. This is not necessarily the same thing as minimizing *costs*. In fact, the two objectives rarely coincide. Nevertheless, minimum average cost re-

TABLE 19.4 RESOURCE COMPUTATION OF MARGINAL COST	Resources used to produce 16th pair of jeans	Market value	Marginal cost
Marginal cost refers to the value of the additional inputs needed to produce *one* more unit of output. To increase daily jeans output from 15 to 16 pairs, we need 0.053 units of labor and one-tenth of a bolt of denim. These extra inputs cost $7.24.	0.053 units of labor	0.053 × $80/day	$4.24
	0.1 bolt of denim	0.1 × $30	3.00
			$7.24

mains an important economic objective for society. In subsequent chapters we shall see how these different objectives are reconciled.

Marginal cost

One final cost concept is important. Indeed, this last concept is probably the most important one for production. It is *marginal cost*. We have already encountered this concept in our discussion of resource costs. There we noted that marginal cost refers to the value of the resources needed to produce *one* more unit of a good. To produce *one* more pair of jeans, we need the denim itself and a very small amount of additional labor. These are the extra or added costs of increasing output by one pair of jeans per day. To compute the dollar value of these marginal costs, we could determine the market price of denim and labor, then add them up. Table 19.4 provides an example. In this case, we calculate that the additional or **marginal cost** of producing a sixteenth pair of jeans is $7.24. This is how much *total* costs will increase if we decide to expand jeans output by one pair per day (from 15 to 16).

marginal cost: The increase in total cost associated with a one-unit increase in production.

Table 19.4 emphasizes the links between resource costs and dollar costs. However, there is a much easier way to compute marginal cost. Marginal cost refers to the change in total costs associated with one more unit of output. Accordingly, we can simply observe *total* dollar costs before and after the rate of output is increased. The difference between the two totals equals the *marginal* cost of increasing the rate of output. This technique is obviously much easier for jeans manufacturers, who don't know much about marginal resource utilization but have a sharp eye for increases in total dollar costs. It's also a lot easier for economics students, of course. But they have an obligation to understand the resource origins of marginal costs and the potential causes of rising or falling marginal costs. As we noted before, diminishing returns in production cause marginal costs to increase as the rate of output is expanded. Hence the marginal cost curve generally slopes upward, as in Figure 19.6.

A cost summary

By now we have enough curves to put together a summary of production costs. This summary is provided in Figure 19.7. As before, we are concentrating on a short-run production process, with fixed quantities of land and capital. In this case, however, we have abandoned the University Jeans Corporation and provided hypothetical

FIGURE 19.6 THE MARGINAL COST CURVE

Marginal cost (*MC*) is the increase in *total* costs resulting from a one-unit increase in the rate of production. *MC* is the additional cost of producing one more unit. These hypothetical numbers indicate that total costs increase from $25 to $34 when a fifth unit is produced (compare rows *u* and *t*). Hence the *MC* of the fifth unit is $9, as illustrated by point *u* on the marginal cost curve. The *MC* curve generally rises (as a consequence of the law of diminishing returns).

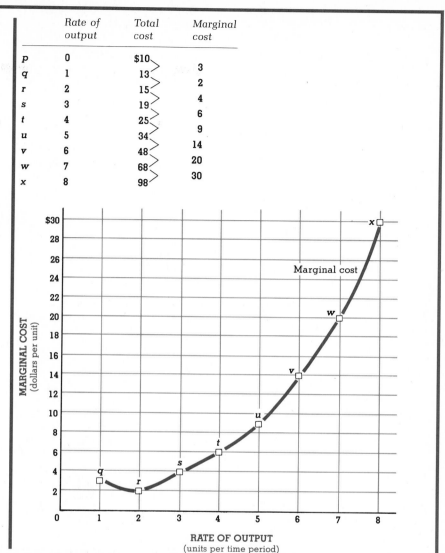

	Rate of output	Total cost	Marginal cost
p	0	$10	
q	1	13	3
r	2	15	2
s	3	19	4
t	4	25	6
u	5	34	9
v	6	48	14
w	7	68	20
x	8	98	30

costs for an idealized production process. The purpose of these figures is to provide a more general view of how the various cost concepts relate to each other. Note that *MC*, *ATC*, *AFC*, and *AVC* can all be computed from total costs. All we need, then, is the first two columns of the table and we can compute and graph all the rest of the cost figures.

The centerpiece of Figure 19.7 is the U-shaped *ATC* curve. What is of special significance is its relationship to marginal costs. Notice that ***the MC curve intersects the ATC curve at its lowest point*** (point *m*). This will always be the case. So long as the marginal cost of producing one more unit is less than the existing average cost, average costs must fall. Thus average costs decline as long as the marginal cost curve lies below the average cost curve, as to the left of point *m* in Figure 19.7.

FIGURE 19.7 BASIC COST CURVES

With total costs and the rate of output, all other cost concepts can be computed. The resulting cost curves have several distinct features. The *AFC* curve always slopes downward. The *MC* curve typically rises, sometimes after a brief decline. The *ATC* curve has a U shape. And the *MC* curve will always intersect both the *ATC* and *AVC* curves at their lowest points (*m* and *n*, respectively).

Rate of output	TC	MC	ATC	AFC	AVC
0	$10.00	—	—	—	—
1	13.00	$ 3.00	$13.00	$10.00	$ 3.00
2	15.00	2.00	7.50	5.00	2.50
3	19.00	4.00	6.33	3.33	3.00
4	25.00	6.00	6.25	2.50	3.75
5	34.00	9.00	6.80	2.00	4.80
6	48.00	14.00	8.00	1.67	6.33
7	68.00	20.00	9.71	1.43	8.28
8	98.00	30.00	12.25	1.25	11.00

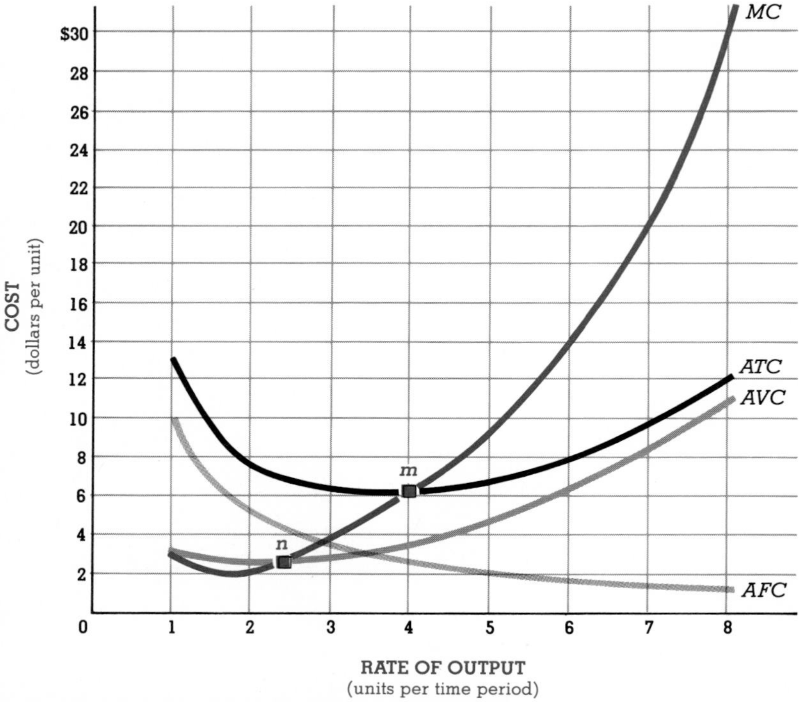

We have already observed, however, that marginal costs themselves tend to rise as output expands, largely because additional workers reduce the amount of land and capital available to each worker (in the short run, the size of plant and equipment is fixed). Consequently, at some point (*m* in Figure 19.7) marginal costs will rise to the level of average costs.

As marginal costs continue to rise beyond point *m*, they begin to pull average costs up, giving the average cost curve its U shape. Average costs increase whenever marginal costs exceed average costs. This is the case to the right of point *m*, since the marginal cost curve always lies above the average cost curve in that part of Figure 19.7.

To visualize the relationship between marginal cost and average cost, imagine computing the average height of people entering a room. If the first person who comes through the door is six feet tall, then the average height of people entering the room is six feet at that point. But what happens to average height if the second person entering the room is only three feet tall? *Average* height declines because the last (marginal) person entering the room is shorter than the previous average. Whenever the last entrant is shorter than the average, the average must fall.

The relationship between marginal costs and average costs is also similar to that between your grade in this course and your grade-point average. If your grade in economics is better (higher) than your other grades, then your overall grade-point average will rise. In other words, a high *marginal* grade in economics will pull your *average* grade up. If you don't understand this, your grade-point average is likely to fall.

ECONOMIC VS. ACCOUNTING COSTS

An essential characteristic of the cost curves we have observed is that they are based on *real* production relationships. The dollar costs we compute are a direct reflection of underlying resource costs, that is, the land, labor, and capital used in the production process. Not everyone counts this way. On the contrary, accountants and business people typically count dollar costs only and ignore any resource use that doesn't result in an explicit dollar cost.

Return to University Jeans Corporation for a moment to see the difference. When we computed the dollar cost of producing 15 pairs of jeans, we noted the following resource inputs:

1 factory rent	@	$100
1 machine rent	@	20
1 seamstress	@	80
1.5 bolts of denim	@	45
Total cost		$245

The total value of the resources used in the production of 15 pairs of jeans was thus $245. But this figure need not conform to *actual* dollar costs. Suppose the owner of University Jeans decided to sew jeans himself. Then he would not have to hire a seamstress or pay $80 per day in wages. *Dollar* costs would drop to $165 per day. This figure would be the focus of attention for the producer or his accountant. They would assert that the cost of producing jeans had fallen.

Economic cost

An economist would draw no such conclusions. The essential *economic* question is how many *resources* are used to produce jeans. This has not changed. One unit of labor is still being employed at the factory. That unit of labor is not available for the production of other goods and services. Hence society is still paying $245 for jeans, whether the owner of University Jeans writes checks in that amount or not. We really don't care *who* sews jeans—the essential point is that someone (i.e., a unit of labor) does.

economic cost: The value of all resources used to produce a good or service; opportunity cost.

The same would be true if University Jeans owned its own factory rather than rented it. If the factory was owned rather than rented, the owner probably would not write any rent checks. Hence accounting costs would drop by $100 per day. But society would not be saving any resources. The factory would still be in use for jeans production and therefore unavailable for the production of other goods and services. The economic (resource) cost of producing 15 pairs of jeans would still be $245.

The distinction between an economic cost and an accounting cost is essentially one between resource and dollar costs. *Dollar cost* refers to the actual dollar outlays of a producer; it is the lifeblood of accountants. **Economic cost,** in contrast, refers to the dollar value of all resources used in the production process; it is the lifeblood of economists. *Economic and accounting costs will diverge whenever any factor of production is not paid an explicit wage (or rent, etc.).*[7]

LONG-RUN COSTS

All of our discussion thus far has been confined to short-run production costs. The short run is characterized by a commitment to plant and equipment. A factory, an office building, or some other plant and equipment have been leased or purchased: we are stuck with *fixed* costs. In this context, our objective is to make the best use of those fixed costs by choosing the appropriate rate of production.

long run: A period of time long enough for all inputs to be varied (no fixed costs).

The long run opens up a whole new range of options. In the long run, we have no lease or purchase commitments. We are free to start all over again, with whatever scale of plant and equipment we desire. There are no fixed costs in the **long run.**

Long-run average costs

The opportunities available in the long run include building a plant of any desired size. Suppose we still wanted to go into the jeans business. In the long run, we could build or lease any size factory we wanted and could lease as many sewing machines as we desired. Figure 19.8 illustrates three choices: a small factory (ATC_1), a medium-sized factory (ATC_2), and a large factory (ATC_3). As we observed earlier, it is very expensive to produce lots of jeans with a small factory. The ATC curve for a small factory (ATC_1) starts to head straight up at relatively low rates of output. In the long run, we would lease or build such a factory only if we anticipated a continuing low rate of output.

The ATC_2 curve illustrates how costs might fall if we leased or built a medium-sized factory. With a small-sized factory, ATC becomes prohibitive at an output of 50 to 60 pairs of jeans per day. A medium-sized factory can produce these quantities at lower cost. Moreover, ATC continues to drop as jeans production increases in the medium-sized factory. At least for a while. Even a medium-sized

[7] The distinction between economic and accounting costs is also referred to as the difference between implicit costs (all costs) and explicit costs (only those paid).

FIGURE 19.8 LONG-RUN COSTS WITH THREE OPTIONS

Long-run cost possibilities are determined by all possible short-run options. In this case, there are three options of varying size (ATC_1, ATC_2, and ATC_3). In the long run we would choose that option which yielded the lowest average cost for any desired rate of output. The solid portion of the curves ($LATC$) represents these choices.

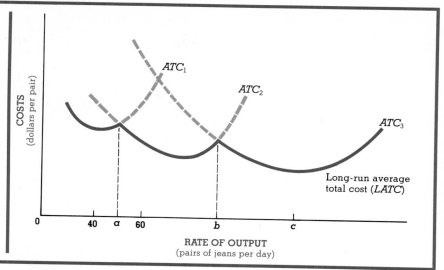

factory must contend with resource constraints and therefore rising average costs: its ATC curve is U-shaped also.

If we expected to sell really large quantities of jeans, we would want to build or lease a large factory. Beyond the rate of output b, the largest factory offers the lowest average total cost. There's a risk in leasing such a large factory, of course. If our sales don't live up to our high expectations, we will end up with very high fixed costs and thus very expensive jeans. Look at the high average cost of producing only 60 pairs of jeans per day with the large factory (ATC_3).

In choosing an appropriate factory, then, we need to know how many jeans we expect to sell. Once we know our expected output, we can easily pick the right-sized factory. It will be the one that offers the lowest ATC for that rate of output. In this case, the decision is pretty easy. If we expect to sell fewer jeans than a, we will choose the small factory. If we expect to sell jeans at a rate between a and b, we will select a medium-sized factory. Beyond rate b, we will want the largest factory. These choices are reflected in the solid part of the three ATC curves. The "curve" created by these three segments constitutes our long-run cost possibilities. ***The long-run cost curve is just a summary of our best short-run cost possibilities.***

We might confront more than three choices, of course. There is really no reason we couldn't build a factory to any desired size. In the long run we face an infinite number of scale choices, not just three. The effect of all these choices is to smooth out the long-run cost curve. Figure 19.9 depicts the long-run curve that results. Each rate of output is most efficiently produced by some size (scale) of plant. That sized plant indicates the minimum cost of producing a particular rate of output. Its corresponding short-run ATC curve provides one point on the long-run ATC curve.

Long-run marginal costs

Like all average cost curves, the long-run ($LATC$) curve has its own marginal cost curve. The long-run marginal cost (LMC) curve is not a composite of short-run marginal cost curves. Rather, it is computed

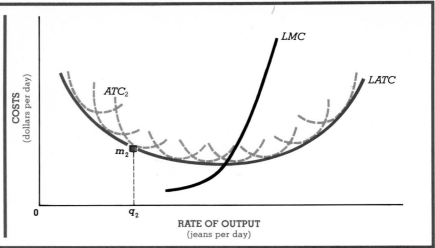

FIGURE 19.9 LONG-RUN COSTS WITH UNLIMITED OPTIONS

If plants of all sizes can be built, short-run options are infinite. In this case, the *LATC* curve becomes a smooth U-shaped curve. Each point on the curve represents lowest-cost production for a plant size best suited to one rate of output. The long-run *ATC* curve has its own *MC* curve.

on the basis of the costs reflected in the long-run *ATC* curve itself. We won't bother to compute those costs here. We will note, however, that the long-run *MC* curve—like all *MC* curves—intersects its associated average cost curve at its lowest point.

ECONOMIES OF SCALE

In reality, a producer is not confined to the choice of only *one* plant. A producer can use either one large plant or several smaller ones to produce the same output. Suppose the output level c was desired in Figure 19.8. The producer would never try to produce such a high rate of output with a single small plant (ATC_1). But it might be desirable to produce that rate of output with *several* small plants rather than one large one (ATC_3). In this case, the producer must compare the *minimum ATC* associated with different plant sizes.

Notice what happens to *minimum ATC* in Figure 19.8 when the size (scale) of the factory changes. When a medium-sized factory (ATC_2) replaces a small factory (ATC_1), minimum average cost drops (the bottom of ATC_2 is below the bottom of ATC_1). This implies that a jeans producer who wants to minimize costs should build one medium-sized factory rather than try to produce the same quantity with two small ones. In this situation, **economies of scale** exist: larger facilities reduce minimum average costs.

Larger production facilities do not always result in cost reductions. Suppose a firm has the choice of producing the quantity Q_m from several small factories or from one large, centralized facility. Centralization may have three different impacts on costs. These are illustrated in Figure 19.10. In each of the three illustrations, we see the average total cost (ATC) curve for a typical small firm or plant and the ATC curve for a much larger plant producing the same product. Figure 19.10a depicts a situation in which there is no economic advantage to centralization of manufacturing operations, because a large plant is no more efficient than a multitude of small plants. The critical focus here is on the *minimum* average costs attainable for a

economies of scale:
Reductions in average costs that come about through increases in the size (scale) of plant and equipment.

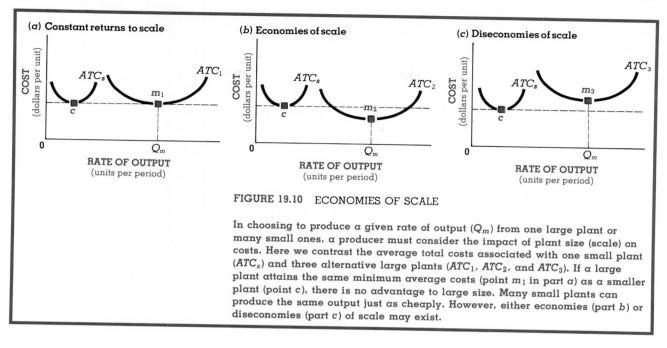

FIGURE 19.10 ECONOMIES OF SCALE

In choosing to produce a given rate of output (Q_m) from one large plant or many small ones, a producer must consider the impact of plant size (scale) on costs. Here we contrast the average total costs associated with one small plant (ATC_s) and three alternative large plants (ATC_1, ATC_2, and ATC_3). If a large plant attains the same minimum average costs (point m_1 in part a) as a smaller plant (point c), there is no advantage to large size. Many small plants can produce the same output just as cheaply. However, either economies (part b) or diseconomies (part c) of scale may exist.

constant returns to scale:
Increases in plant size do not affect minimum average cost; minimum per-unit costs are identical for small plants and large plants.

given rate of output. Note that the lowest point on the smaller plant's ATC curve (point c) is no higher or lower than the lowest point on the larger firms's ATC curve (point m). Hence it would be just as cheap to produce the quantity Q_m from a multitude of small plants as it would be to produce Q_m from one large plant. Thus increasing the size (or *scale*) of individual plants will not reduce minimum average costs: this is a situation of **constant returns to scale.**

Figure 19.10b illustrates the situation in which a larger plant is able to attain a lower minimum average cost than a smaller plant. That is, economies of scale (or "increasing returns to scale") exist. This is evident from the fact that the larger firm's ATC curve falls *below* the dotted line in the graph (m_2 is less than c). The greater efficiency of the large factory might come from any of several sources. A large factory, for example, might be able to enjoy greater specialization of labor, with each worker becoming expert in a particular skill. By contrast, a smaller establishment might have to use the same individual(s) to perform several functions, thereby reducing productivity at each task. Also, some kinds of machinery may be economical only if they are used to produce massive volumes,[8] an opportunity only very large factories have. Finally, a large plant might acquire a persistent cost advantage through the process of learning by doing. That is, its longer experience and greater volume of output may translate into improved organization and efficiency.

But even though large plants may be able to achieve greater efficiencies than smaller plants, there is no assurance that they actually will. In fact, increasing the size (scale) of a plant may actually *reduce* operating efficiency, as depicted in Figure 19.10c. Workers

[8] That is to say, the machinery itself may be subject to economies of scale.

Some Firms Fight Ills of Bigness by Keeping Employe Units Small

---

At 3M Plants, Workers Have Flexibility, Involvement —And Their Own Radios

ST. PAUL, Minn.—For a company with some 87,000 employes and annual sales in excess of $6 billion, Minnesota Mining & Manufacturing Co. spends a lot of time "thinking small."

"We are keenly aware of the disadvantages of large size," says Gordon W. Engdahl, the company's vice president for human resources and its top personnel officer. "We made a conscious effort to keep our units as small as possible because we think it helps keep them flexible and vital," he says. "When one gets too large, we break it apart. We like to say that our success in recent years amounts to multiplication by division."

Mr. Engdahl's comment is no conceit. 3M's average U.S. manufacturing plant employs just 270 people, and management groups as small as five guide the fortunes of the company's numerous household, industrial and scientific products. In the 1970s, its sales and earnings grew almost fourfold, while its U.S. work force increased by 40%.

3M's record stands in sharp contrast to a mostly overlooked trend developing over the past 15 years or so: the declining role of large companies in this country's employment picture. . . .

The Inefficiencies of Size

Not all of the mechanisms behind these developments are clear, and some surely are complex. Observers note that many of the biggest companies of the 1970s were manufactureres that suffered from heightened foreign competition and the related swing of the U.S. economy toward "service" functions. . . .

Increasingly, however, blame for the laggard performance of many large corporations is focusing on their structures and entrenched ways of doing things. A growing body of opinion has it that the "economies of scale" made possible by bigness often are more than nullified by organizational rigidities and bottlenecks.

"More companies seem to be showing concern that their neat organization charts don't always reflect reality and certainly don't, in themselves, overcome the tensions between autonomy and control that get worse with size," says Larry E. Grejner, a professor of organizational behavior at the University of Southern California's School of Business Administration.

—Frederick C. Klein

may feel alienated in a plant of massive proportions and feel little commitment to productivity. Moreover, a large plant may offer greater opportunities to slack off without getting caught. For these reasons and others, a large plant may require more intensive managerial supervision, which would raise production costs. Indeed, even a decentralized supercorporation may find that the managerial efforts required to coordinate a multitude of separate plants raise average costs above those of the smaller firm. These kinds of situations, wherein minimum average costs rise as the scale of operations increases, are referred to as "diseconomies of scale."

In evaluating long-run options, then, we must be careful to recognize that *efficiency and size do not necessarily go hand in hand.* Some firms and industries may be subject to economies of scale, but others will not be. Bigger is not always better.

POLICY IMPLICATIONS: PRODUCTIVITY IMPROVEMENTS

All of the cost concepts discussed in this chapter have been derived from the production function. That function, describing our productive capabilities, has been taken as a technological fact of life. It represents the *best* we can do, given our state of technological and managerial knowledge. In the real world, however, the best is always getting better. Science and technology are continuously advancing. So is our knowledge of how to organize and manage our

FIGURE 19.11   IMPROVEMENTS IN PRODUCTIVITY REDUCE COSTS

Advances in technological or managerial knowledge increase our productive capability. This is reflected in upward shifts of the production function (part *a*) and downward shifts of production cost curves (part *b*).

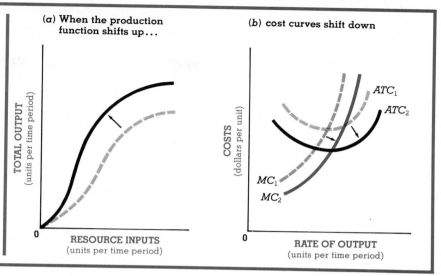

(a) When the production function shifts up...

TOTAL OUTPUT (units per time period)

RESOURCE INPUTS (units per time period)

(b) cost curves shift down

COSTS (dollars per unit)

ATC_1

ATC_2

MC_1

MC_2

RATE OF OUTPUT (units per time period)

resources. These advances keep *shifting* our production functions upward: more can be produced with any given quantity of inputs. In the process, the costs of production shift downward. This is illustrated in Figure 19.11 by the downward shifts of the *MC* and *ATC* curves. These downward shifts imply that we can get more of the goods and services we desire with available resources.

Table 19.5 indicates the historical importance of productivity improvements in the U.S. economy. From 1948 to 1973, total output grew at just less than 4 percent per year. Less than half of this growth was due to increased use of labor and capital, that is, more inputs. The rest of our growth came from improvements in technology, management, and the quality of our labor. Advances in knowledge

TABLE 19.5   THE SOURCES OF U.S. GROWTH, 1948–73

From 1948 to 1973 total output grew by 3.87 percent annually. More than half of this growth was due to improvements in our technological and managerial capabilities. These advances in productivity have made it possible to produce more output at less cost.

Source	Percentage contribution to output growth
More inputs	
additional labor	27.6
additional capital	18.3
	45.9
Productivity advances	
education of labor	10.6
advances in knowledge	28.7
improved resource allocation	7.8
economies of scale	8.3
	55.4
Miscellaneous	−1.3
	100.0

Source: Edward F. Denison, *Accounting for Slower Economic Growth: The United States in the 1970s* (Washington, D.C.: Brookings Institution, 1979).

are credited with over one-fourth of our economic growth. Greater education of the labor force (quality improvements) contributed another 10 percent. In addition, reallocation of resources from low-productivity industries to high-productivity industries boosted growth. Finally, economies of scale accounted for 8 percent of our greater productive capability.

The implication of this historical experience is that future reductions in growth and costs depend on further advances in productivity. Government policy can and does play an important role in this regard. At present, the federal government pays for 47 percent of all basic research. The public sector is also responsible for most of our educational system. Finally, the government helps establish the institutional climate (e.g., regulations, standards) for U.S. businesses. How fast productivity advances thus depends not only on the persistent inquiries of lone scientists and managers, but also on how well the public sector encourages or impedes research and development. Edward Denison, the source of Table 19.5, sees potential problems here. From 1973 to 1976, the rate of growth declined significantly. Denison and others attribute much of this slowdown in productivity to government regulation, particularly rules governing workplace safety and environmental protection.[9] Others point to the sharply higher costs of energy that occurred after 1973 and the resulting changes in investment and production behavior. For the most part, however, the causes of the productivity slowdown remain a mystery. Solving that mystery may provide insights for greater productivity improvements in the future.

SUMMARY

▪ A production function indicates the maximum amount of output that can be produced with different combinations of inputs. It is a technological relationship and changes (shifts) when new technology or management techniques are discovered.

▪ The contribution of an input to total output is measured by its marginal physical product (*MPP*). This is the amount by which *total* output increases when one more unit of the input is employed. The productivity of any input depends on technology and the amount of other resources it has to work with.

▪ The *MPP* of a factor tends to decline as more of it is employed in a given production facility. Diminishing returns are attributable to the declining ratio of other inputs to the one factor that is being used in greater quantity.

▪ Marginal cost is the increase in total cost that results when output is increased by one unit. Marginal cost increases whenever marginal physical product diminishes.

[9] The costs and benefits of environmental policies are discussed in Chapter 30.

■ Not all costs go up when the rate of output is increased. Fixed costs (e.g., space and equipment leases) do not vary with the rate of output. Only variable costs (e.g., labor and material) go up when output is increased.

■ Average total cost (ATC) equals total cost divided by the quantity of output produced. ATC declines whenever marginal cost (MC) is less than average cost and rises when MC exceeds it. The MC and ATC curves intersect at minimum ATC (the bottom of the U). That intersection represents least-cost production.

■ The economic costs of production include the value of *all* resources used. Accounting costs typically include only those dollar costs actually paid (explicit costs).

■ In the long run there are no fixed costs; the size (scale) of production facilities can be varied. The long-run ATC curve indicates the lowest cost of producing output with facilities of appropriate size.

■ Economies of scale refer to reductions in minimum average cost attained with larger plant size (scale). If minimum ATC rises with plant size, diseconomies exist.

■ Historically, advances in technology and the quality of our inputs have been the major source of economic growth. These advances have shifted production functions upward and pushed cost curves down.

Terms to remember

Define the following terms:

supply	total cost
factors of production	fixed costs
production function	variable costs
productivity	average total cost (*ATC*)
efficiency	average fixed cost (*AFC*)
opportunity cost	average variable cost (*AVC*)
short run	economic cost
marginal physical product	long run
law of diminishing returns	economies of scale
marginal cost	constant returns to scale

Questions for discussion

1. What is the marginal cost of enrolling one more student in your class? What are the fixed and variable costs associated with "production" of students?

2. Suppose all your friends offered to help wash your car. Would marginal physical product decline as more friends helped? Why, or why not?

3. Owner-operators of small gas stations rarely pay themselves an hourly wage. Does this practice reduce the economic cost of dispensing gasoline?

4. Supermarkets have replaced small grocery stores in many areas, in large part because of the lower costs they achieve. What kind of economies of scale exist in supermarkets? Why doesn't someone build one colossal supermarket and drive costs down further?

Problem | Complete the following table and graph the marginal cost and average total cost curves.

Rate of output	Total cost	Marginal cost	Average fixed cost	Average variable cost	Average total cost
0	$100				
1	110				
2	130				
3	165				
4	220				
5	300				

CHAPTER 20

PROFITS AND THE SUPPLY DECISION

supply: The ability and willingness to sell (produce) specific quantities of a good at alternative prices in a given time period (*ceteris paribus*).

The production of goods and services entails real costs. In view of these costs, we should not expect business firms simply to give us the goods and services we desire. At a minimum, they will want to be paid enough to recover the costs of production. Ideally, they would like to be paid something *more* than the costs of production, so as to benefit from their efforts. Such is the nature of a business. Like most of us, people who create and maintain production units are motivated by self-interest. Even though they *could* supply us with goods "at cost," they want more. In general, they will be *willing* to produce the goods and services we desire only when they get their "just rewards." The **supply** of goods requires both the ability and the willingness to produce.

In this chapter we shall examine the nature of the supply decision. The central motivator here is profits. We shall first look at the nature of profits and who gets them. We shall then look at how profits are earned and how the quest for profits influences supply decisions.

THE PROFIT MOTIVE

The market mechanism answers the basic question of FOR WHOM to produce by distributing goods and services on the basis of ability to pay. To the extent that people who own a business want a share of total output, they must acquire an income that can be used to buy the

profit: The difference between total revenue and total cost.

consumer goods they desire. *Owning* plant and equipment is not enough. To generate a current flow of income, one must *use* that plant and equipment to produce goods. When sold, those goods generate the income business owners need for their own consumption desires. ***The basic incentive to produce is the promise of income.***

Whereas the monetary incentives for motivating workers are usually expressed in terms of wages and salaries, returns to the efforts of a business are commonly referred to as profits. **Profit** is the difference between the total revenues of a firm and its total costs. It is the "residual" that is received by the owners of a business. The recipient of that residual may be the single owner of a corner grocery store or it may be the group of stockholders who collectively own a large corporation. In either case, it is the promise (hope?) of some residual profit that motivates people to own and operate a business.

Other motivations

Profit is not the only thing that motivates producers. Like the rest of us, producers also worry about social status and crave recognition. Hence they are most willing to take on production responsibilities for those products or services that command most acceptance or prestige. Producers will also be more willing to make the leisure and consumption sacrifices required by production if business people are generally held in high regard by the rest of society. That is to say, producers will work for less profit if we reward them with high status.[1]

Psychological influences are also important in motivating producers. People who have a need to feel important, to control others, or to demonstrate achievement are likely to be easily drafted for the job of producing goods. On the other hand, some people are lured into business by a relentless need to be "their own man," to confirm their independence and freedom. Owners of small businesses are especially prey to this motivation. Many small businesses are maintained by people who gave up 40-hour weeks, $20,000 incomes, and a sense of alienation in exchange for 80-hour weeks, $15,000 incomes, and a sense of identity.

Additional motivations for producing arise from the structure of many production units. The ownership of large corporations tends to be fragmented among thousands of individual stockholders, most of whom have never even seen corporate headquarters. At the same time, the people who manage the corporation's business on a day-to-day basis may have little or no stock in the company. As a consequence, the possibility arises that the self-interests of owners and of managers may conflict. Corporate managers who have little or no ownership rights are likely to be at least as interested in their own jobs, salaries, and self-preservation as in the profits that accrue to the owners. Such "technocrats," as John Kenneth Galbraith of Harvard has labeled them, may seek to mollify owners with a steady flow of profits rather than maximum profits at any given point in time. To

---

[1] The People's Republic of China has experimented with this trade-off between monetary and social incentives. A comparison of Chinese, Soviet, and American incentive systems is provided in Chapter 36.

FIGURE 20.1 U.S. BUSINESS
PROFITS, 1960–81

The level of corporate profits is highly
sensitive to economic conditions,
particularly the level of business
activity (total output). Total corporate
profits fell sharply in 1970, 1974, and
1980, all years of economic decline
(recession).

Source: U.S. Department of Commerce.

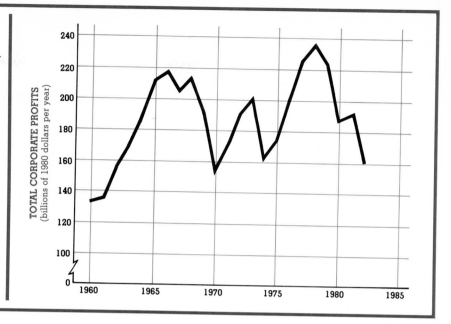

the extent that their salaries depend on corporate size or sales—as
they usually do—corporate managers may show more interest in
corporate growth than in corporate profits. If these efforts reduce the
flow of profits below some minimum acceptable to owners, however, the corporation may start looking for new managers. Hence the
level of profits must still be an object of concern.

PROFITS OF U.S. BUSINESS

Public perceptions
Although profits might be a necessary inducement for producers,
most consumers feel that profits are too high (see box). And they
may be in many cases. But most consumers do not have any idea
how much profit U.S. businesses receive or which firms get the
lion's share. We start, then, with a quick survey of profit experiences
in U.S. businesses.

Reported profits
U.S. corporations reported profits of $233 billion in 1981. As Figure
20.1 illustrates, 1981 was a fairly good year for U.S. corporations;
profits in 1980 had been much lower. Included in this total were the
profits of American Telephone & Telegraph, IBM, and some other
truly huge corporations, as well as substantial losses for a few major
firms (see Table 20.1).
 Figure 20.2 provides a glimpse of how profits are distributed
across U.S. industries. The emphasis here is not on total profits in
dollars but on the profit *rate*, in percentages. The profit rate is expressed in two ways: as a percentage of sales and as a percentage of
net worth. The first rate indicates how many cents of each sales dollar represents profits. This is the rate discussed in the public-opin-

TABLE 20.1 THE BIG MONEY MAKERS AND LOSERS

U.S. corporations reported total profits of $233 billion in 1981. Included in this total were the huge profits of some corporations and sizable losses of others. Some of the largest winners and losers are shown here.

Big winners	Profits
AT&T	$7,026,390,000
Exxon	5,567,481,000
IBM	3,308,000,000
Mobil	2,433,000,000
Standard Oil of California	2,380,000,000

Big losers	Losses
Ford	$1,060,100,000
Chrysler	475,600,000
Kaiser Steel	437,455,000
International Harvester	393,128,000
Lockheed	288,800,000

Source: *Fortune Magazine.*

CORPORATE PROFITS: PUBLIC OPINION VS. REALITY

Most consumers—including college students—think profits are far higher than they really are. This misperception is revealed in public-opinion surveys that ask what percentage of each sales dollar represents after-tax profits. The average responses in recent years are noted below. They reveal that the American public thinks profits are six or seven times higher than they really are. The perceptions of college students are even more exaggerated: the average college student thinks 45 cents out of each sales dollar goes to profits!

	1971	1973	1975	1976	1979	1981
Mean public estimate of profit per sales dollar:	28.0¢	28.0¢	33.0¢	29.0¢	32.0¢	31.0¢
Actual after-tax profit per sales dollar:	4.5¢	5.1¢	5.2¢	4.4¢	5.2¢	4.8¢

In view of these misperceptions, it is hardly surprising that most Americans think business profits are too high. In a series of public-opinion polls about the level of profits, more and more consumers have said business profits are too high. Fewer than 10 percent of the public has ever thought profits were too low. The question and responses are noted below:

Q: Do you think business as a whole is making too much profit, a reasonable profit, or not enough profit?

A:	1965	1969	1973	1976	1979	1981
Too much profit	24%	38%	35%	50%	51%	51%
Reasonable profit	58	47	50	37	38	37
Not enough profit	6	4	3	9	8	8
No opinion	12	11	12	4	3	4

Source: Opinion Research Corporation and Gallup.

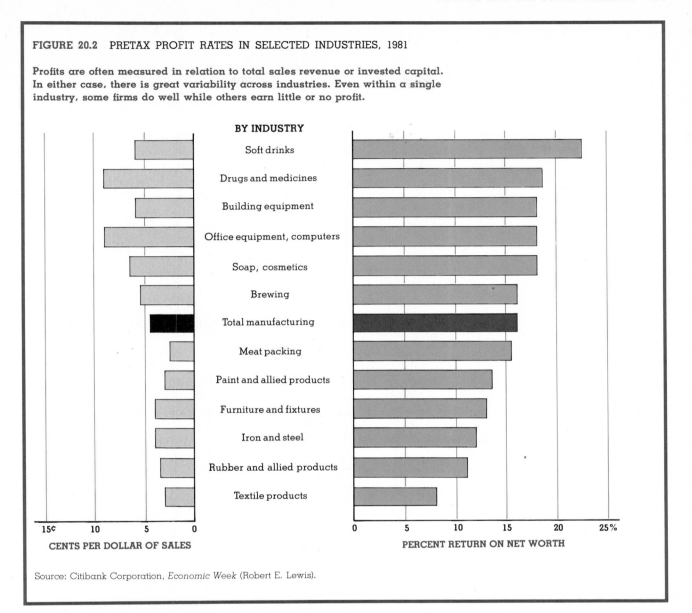

FIGURE 20.2   PRETAX PROFIT RATES IN SELECTED INDUSTRIES, 1981

Profits are often measured in relation to total sales revenue or invested capital.
In either case, there is great variability across industries. Even within a single
industry, some firms do well while others earn little or no profit.

BY INDUSTRY

Soft drinks
Drugs and medicines
Building equipment
Office equipment, computers
Soap, cosmetics
Brewing
Total manufacturing
Meat packing
Paint and allied products
Furniture and fixtures
Iron and steel
Rubber and allied products
Textile products

15¢   10   5   0
CENTS PER DOLLAR OF SALES

0   5   10   15   20   25%
PERCENT RETURN ON NET WORTH

Source: Citibank Corporation, *Economic Week* (Robert E. Lewis).

ion surveys noted on the previous page. The second rate expresses
profits as a percentage of the value of the firm's net assets, that is, its
"investment" in the business. On either measure, the soft drink,
computer, and office equipment industries score quite well.

ECONOMIC VS. ACCOUNTING PROFITS

Public perceptions of profits and reported corporate profits are
clearly very different. Ironically, economists' computations of profits coincide with neither. Economists calculate profits differently
from the way everyone else does.

Economic profits

economic cost: The value of all resources used to produce a good or service; opportunity cost.

economic profit: The difference between total revenues and total economic costs.

The basic concept of profits concerns the difference between total revenues and total costs. What distinguishes economists' calculations of profits is their treatment of costs. Recall from Chapter 19 how economists compute costs. **Economic cost** refers to the value of *all* resources used in production, whether or not they are paid an explicit wage. By contrast, most businesses count only explicit costs, that is, those they actually write out checks for.

Because economists and business people compute costs differently, their calculations of profits must differ as well. If businesses (and their accountants) count only *paid* (explicit) costs, they will understate true costs. This incomplete accounting of costs leads to an *over*statement of profits. Part of the accounting "profit" will really be compensation to unpaid land, labor, or capital used in the production process. ***Whenever economic costs exceed explicit costs, observed (accounting) profits will exceed true (economic) profits.*** To determine the **economic profit** of a business, we must subtract all implicit factor returns from observed "net returns"; profits, if any, are the residual.

Suppose, for example, that Table 20.2 accurately summarizes the revenues and costs associated with a local drugstore. Monthly sales revenues amount to $27,000. Explicit costs paid by the owner-manager include the cost of merchandise bought from producers for resale to consumers ($17,000), wages to the employees of the drugstore, "rent" and utilities paid to the landlord, and local sales and business taxes. When all of these explicit costs are subtracted from total revenue, we are left with a *net revenue* of $6,000 per month.

The owner-manager of the drugstore may be quite pleased with a net revenue of $6,000 per month. He is working hard for this income, however. To keep his store running, the owner-manager is working ten hours per day, seven days a week. This adds up to 300 hours of labor per month. Were he to work this hard for someone else, his labor would be compensated explicitly, with a paycheck. Although he doesn't choose to pay himself in this way, part of the

---

TABLE 20.2 THE COMPUTATION OF ECONOMIC PROFIT (per month)

To calculate economic profit, we must take account of *all* costs of production. The economic costs of production include the implicit (opportunity) costs of the labor and capital a producer contributes to the production process. The net revenues of a business take into account only explicit costs paid by the owner.

Total (gross) revenues	$27,000
less explicit costs:	
Cost of merchandise sold	$17,000
Wages to cashier, stock, and delivery help	2,500
Rent and utilities	800
Taxes	700
Total explicit costs	$21,000
Net revenue	$ 6,000
less implicit costs:	
Wages of owner-manager, 300 hrs. @ $10 per hour	$ 3,000
Return on inventory investment, 10% per year on $120,000	1,000
Total implicit costs	$ 4,000
Economic profit	$ 2,000

net returns of the drugstore nevertheless represent a return for his labor. Hence we compute his implicit wages by noting that he would earn $10 per hour in the best alternative job. Multiplying this wage rate ($10) by the number of hours he works in the drugstore (300), we see that the implicit return for his labor is $3,000 per month.

We also observe that he has used his savings to purchase inventory for the store. He purchased the goods on his shelves for $120,000, and they represent his capital investment in the business. If he had invested his savings in some other business, he could have earned a return of 10 percent per year. This opportunity cost is used to determine the implicit return to his capital investment. In this case, the implicit return amounts to $12,000 per year (10 percent × $120,000), or $1,000 per month.

To calculate the "economic profit" generated by the corner drugstore, we subtract all implicit factor payments (costs) from net revenue. The residual in this case amounts to $2,000 per month. That is the drugstore's economic profit.

"Normal" profits are an economic cost. Note that when we compute the drugstore's economic profits, we include a measure of the opportunity costs of the owner's capital. Specifically, we assumed that his funds would have reaped a 10 percent return somewhere else. In effect, we have assumed that a standard, or "normal," rate of return is 10 percent. Rather than investing in a drugstore, the owner could have earned a 10 percent return on his funds by investing in a fast-food franchise, video games, a steel plant, or some other production activity. By choosing to invest in a drugstore instead, the owner was seeking a *higher* return on his funds—an *above-average* return. Had he not succeeded, he would have had no *economic* profits. In other words, economic profits represent an above-average return— something over and above "normal profits."

Our treatment of "normal" returns as an economic cost leads to a startling conclusion: on average, economic profits are zero. Only firms that reap *above-average* returns can claim economic profits. If some firms are above the average, other firms must be below the average. In other words, the economic profits (above-average returns) of some firms are offset by the economic losses (below-average returns) of other firms. This seemingly strange perspective on profits emphasizes the opportunity costs of all economic activities. ***A productive activity is "profitable" only if it earns more than its opportunity cost.***

Sources of profit

Naturally, everyone in business wants to earn an economic profit. But relatively few people can stay ahead of the pack. To earn economic profits, a business must see opportunities that others have missed, discover new products, find new and better methods of production, or take above-average risks. In fact, economic profits are often regarded as a reward to entrepreneurship, the ability and willingness to take risks, to organize factors of production, and to produce something society desires. From this perspective, profit represents a return to an intangible but vitally important "fourth factor of production."

Cubist profits

Ideal Toy rebounds with Rubik

Lionel A. Weintraub, 61, chairman of Ideal Toy Corp., has yet to figure out the solution to Rubik's cube. But he's having no trouble figuring out the bottom-line effect of the cube, which has put his company squarely in the black. Ideal Toy, headquar-tered in Hollis, New York, expects to sell more than ten million cubes in the fiscal year that ends on January 29, 1982, boosting revenues by $40 million to an estimated $210 million. Earnings will reach an all-time high of at least $9 million, a wide swing from a net loss of $15.5 million in the previous fiscal year.

Ideal Toy stumbled onto its salvation. Weintraub picked up the U.S. rights to manufacture Rubik's cube (named for its inventor, Ernö Rubik, a Hungarian architecture professor) two years ago, after several big American toy makers turned it down. He hasn't always been so lucky. His company's Evel Knievel line of toys bombed when the stuntman was jailed for beating a former press agent with a baseball bat. But the cube, Weintraub says, "is like Frisbee. It will be around forever."

Consider the local drugstore again. People in the neighborhood clearly desire such a drugstore, as evidenced by its substantial sales revenue. But why should anyone go to the trouble and risk of starting and maintaining one? In calculating the profits of the drugstore, we noted that the owner-manager *could* earn $3,000 in wages by accepting a regular job plus $1,000 per month in returns on capital by investing in an "average" business. Why should he take on the added responsibilities and risks of owning and operating his own drugstore?

The inducement to take on the added responsibilities of owning and operating a business is the potential for profit, the "extra" income over and above nominal factor payments. In the absence of such additional compensation, few people would want to make the extra effort required. From this perspective, the potential for profit is a major source of economic activity and growth.

Although entrepreneurship is an important source of economic profits—and economic losses!—it is not the only explanation for above-average returns. Some firms command above-average returns through their control of specific processes, products, or markets. The most familiar situation is a monopoly, exclusive production of a particular product by one firm. In such cases, a firm may continue to earn economic profits simply because no other firms are allowed to produce the same good or sell it at lower prices. In this case, profits are less a reward to entrepreneurship than a tribute to market power.

In the chapters that follow, we shall examine the origins of profits more closely. We shall be especially concerned with assessing the potential for profits in markets dominated by market power (e.g., monopolies) and those in which competition thrives. First, however, we shall look more carefully at how profits are actually determined.

PROFITS, PRICES, AND COSTS

Prices and profits

Profits are directly related to the prices producers charge for their output. But the relationship is not as simple as most people think. High prices do not necessarily mean high *profits*. If this isn't immediately obvious to you, try selling ice cream cones at $4 apiece outside the student union. You're apt to find that you have the highest

law of demand: The quantity of a good demanded in a given time period increases as its price falls (*ceteris paribus*).

price in town and the lowest profit. Remember the **law of demand?** It says that ice cream lovers buy fewer cones at high prices than at low prices. Even if you are the only ice cream seller in sight, you are not likely to sell many cones at $4 apiece. If there are other ice cream vendors around, the situation will be even worse. Indeed, you may not sell *any* ice cream if your price is higher than theirs.

The first thing a producer has to consider, then, is how the price charged will affect sales. Is the firm the only producer of the good, or are many other firms selling the same good? Does the firm have to charge the "prevailing" price? Or can the price be raised or lowered? What impact would a different price have on unit sales?

Prices and total revenue

total revenue: The price of a product multiplied by the quantity sold in a given time period; $p \times q$.

Your brief introduction to the ice cream market should provide convincing evidence that the quantity sold rarely increases when price rises. But it is still possible for **total revenue** to rise when price is increased. As we observed in Chapter 18, the critical question is not whether the demand curve slopes downward—as it almost always does—but rather *how much* the quantity demanded increases when the price falls. In particular, the impact of a change in price on total revenue depends on the price elasticity of demand (see Table 20.3).

Consider the case of meat prices and sales. When the Safeway store prices its sirloin steaks at $3.95 per pound, it is able to sell 200 pounds of steak per day. Total revenue—price times quantity sold—equals $790 ($3.95 × 200) in this case.

What would happen to total revenue if Safeway Stores were to raise the price of steak to $4.40 a pound? Would consumers continue to buy 200 pounds of steak a day? If they did, total revenue would rise to $880 a day (200 pounds × $4.40 per pound). But this outcome is most unlikely, because it suggests a completely vertical (perfectly inelastic) demand curve. A more likely result is that consumers will reduce their steak purchases as the price of steak rises, switching instead to other meats, poultry, or fish. Sales volume will drop below 200 pounds per day, and total revenue will be less than $880. How far sales drop depends on the **price elasticity of demand** for steak. Total revenue will actually fall below the original $790 if demand is elastic in this price range. *Total revenue will rise when price is increased only if demand is relatively inelastic.*

The dependence of total revenues on the price elasticity of de-

price elasticity of demand: The percentage change in quantity demanded divided by the percentage change in price.

TABLE 20.3 PRICE, ELASTICITY AND TOTAL REVENUE	Response to price increase		Response to price reduction	
Degree of elasticity	Quantity demanded	Total revenue	Quantity demanded	Total revenue
$E = 0$	no change	rises	no change	falls
$E < 1$	falls	rises	rises	falls
$E = 1$	falls	no change	rises	no change
$E > 1$	falls	falls	rises	rises
$E = \infty$	falls	falls to zero	rises	infinite

Higher prices do not necessarily lead to higher profits. In fact, higher prices do not even ensure increased revenues. The response of total revenue to a change in price depends on the price elasticity of demand. If demand is perfectly elastic ($E = \infty$), the firm can sell all it produces at the current price.

Apple Computer Sets Expansion of Facility

CUPERTINO, Calif.—Apple Computer Inc. said it will spend $25 million to expand its manufacturing and test plant in Singapore.

The maker of personal computers said the plant, which opened in July, would be increased to 273,000 square feet from 133,000 square feet.

The project is expected to begin in about four months and the company said it hopes to have it completed in 1½ to two years.

Reprinted by permission of *The Wall Street Journal,* © Dow Jones & Company, Inc. (1982). All Rights Reserved.

mand came as a shock to many airlines. During the early 1960s, airline traffic was growing rapidly and profits were high. Then some wild-eyed airline executive got the idea of increasing output (and revenue) by enlarging the planes. The Boeing 707, with a capacity of 189 passengers, was replaced by the 747, with a capacity of 490. Did sales keep pace? No. The airlines had erroneously assumed that they could sell a far greater number of seats at the existing (high) fares. What they got was a lot of empty seats, tremendous losses, and a lesson in the price elasticity of demand. It took at least five years for the airlines to recover, and then only with the help of reduced-rate fares. And it was not until 1978, when bargain fares became commonplace, that jumbo planes began to fill up. Unfortunately, the airlines started raising prices significantly shortly after that. Once again they got stuck with empty seats and had to reintroduce "bargain" fares. The price elasticity of demand for air travel remained high.

We should also note, however, that in some situations additional output *can* be sold at virtually unchanged prices. You can sell another 100 shares of IBM stock, another 1,000 textbooks, or another 100,000 bushels of wheat with very little effect on prices. In these cases, the additional quantity offered for sale is so small in relation to total sales that the demand curve may be characterized as *completely* elastic (horizontal) in the relevant price range. Increased sales in these cases contribute directly to increased revenues. Even in these cases, however, a point will be reached where additional sales can be made only at lower prices. How far away that point is depends on the size of the added output in relation to total sales or consumption. With 600 million shares of IBM available, 750,000 copies of introductory economics texts for sale, and 1½ billion bushels of wheat produced annually, the added sales contemplated here will hardly affect prices at all.

These interactions of product prices and sales lead to a few simple observations. *A producer who seeks to improve total revenues by increasing the price of his product must consider the impact of the price change on sales.* By the same reasoning, *a producer who wishes to improve total revenues by expanding output must take into account the effect of increased output on product prices.* What is required in both cases is some knowledge of the price elasticity of consumer demand.

Sales and costs

Just as sales vary with price (or price with output), so too do costs vary with sales. This relationship is perhaps the most obvious of all. Unless you are selling unrefined, unpackaged air, anything you sell is going to cost something to produce. Each textbook produced costs a certain amount for paper, printing, binding, and labor; each bushel of wheat uses up a certain amount of land, fertilizer, harvesting, and packaging. Even another passenger on an airplane costs something for additional fuel, food, and service. In general, then, we may conclude that ***additional output is obtainable only at greater cost,*** and profitability depends in part on how fast costs rise with output.

In Chapter 19 we examined how costs vary with the rate of output. The central force in production decisions is **marginal cost.**

marginal cost: The increase in total cost associated with a one-unit increase in production.

total cost: The market value of all resources used to produce a good or service.

Marginal cost measures the *change* in **total cost** asociated with a change in output. It is the *added* cost of producing one more unit of a good. In deciding whether to expand the rate of output, a producer needs to consider what will happen to costs. Even if additional units of output could be sold, the marginal cost of producing them may be too high.

LONG-RUN VS. SHORT-RUN DECISIONS

It may be evident by now that the road to profits is not an easy one. Successful producers must be able to juggle prices, sales, revenues, and costs. They must know how these concepts relate to each other and what will happen to profits in the process. In the remainder of this chapter we shall examine the techniques of successful profit maximizers. To simplify matters, we shall concentrate on **short-run** decisions.

short run: The period in which the quantity (and quality) of some inputs is fixed, that is, cannot be changed.

The short-run production decision

In the short run, producers are saddled with fixed costs. They have already bought or leased basic plant and equipment. This was the situation of the Universal Jeans Corporation in Chapter 19. Its problem was to make the best possible use of fixed facilities (leased factory and sewing machines). In this short-run context, the primary concern is to operate the plant at its most profitable rate of output. Choosing the short-run rate of output is called the **production decision.** The right production decision is the one that maximizes the profits attainable with the firm's available plant and equipment.

production decision: The selection of the short-run rate of output (with existing plant and equipment).

The long-run investment decision

Producers without any fixed-cost commitments have a broader range of options. They are not confined to selecting a single rate of output for existing facilities. Instead, they have the option of selecting different facilities, or even none at all. In the **long run,** there are no fixed commitments and thus no fixed costs. In this context, firms can make a fundamental **investment decision,** that is, a decision about whether to build, buy, or lease basic plant and equipment. The news clipping on the preceding page summarizes a recent investment decision made by Apple Computer. By expanding its production facilities, Apple incurred larger fixed costs. It did so because it anticipates continued growth of demand for personal computers. In the following analysis of supply behavior, we shall first discuss a firm's production decision, then look at these less frequent but very basic investment decisions.[2]

long run: A period of time long enough for all inputs to be varied (no fixed costs).

investment decision: The decision to build, buy, or lease plant and equipment to start or expand a business.

MAXIMIZING SHORT-RUN PROFITS

The best single rule for maximizing profits in the short run is this: never produce anything that costs you more than it brings in. By

[2] In Chapters 21 and 26 we shall also examine the *efficiency decision,* involving the long-term choice of production processes and related cost curves.

following this simple rule, a producer is likely to make the right production decision. We shall see how this rule works, first by looking at the revenue side of production ("what it brings in"), then at the cost side ("what it costs").

The horizontal demand curve

The first thing a producer must determine is whether a change in the rate of output will affect the price of the good sold. In other words, does the producer have the power to change the product's price? To most people, the obvious answer would seem to be yes. But our brief experience trying to sell $4 ice cream cones should raise some doubts. A producer can, of course, put higher price tags on his output. But there is no assurance that those goods can be sold. Two kinds of situations might preclude sales at higher prices.

Government regulation could preclude sales at higher prices. A utility company, for example, cannot charge prices above those approved by the state utility commission. The telephone company, many railroads, and international airlines also confront price ceilings that limit their power to change prices. In this context, the firm need not worry about what price to charge; the primary concern is to find that rate of output which maximizes profits at the regulated price.

Short-run prices are effectively constant in other contexts as well. Recall the ice cream dilemma. If the student union is surrounded by ice cream vendors charging $2 per cone, you cannot sell much ice cream at $4 per cone. The presence of other vendors pretty much precludes sales at higher prices. In fact, if your ice cream is no different from anyone else's and there are lots of other vendors nearby, you will be compelled to charge the prevailing price of $2 per cone (or sell no ice cream). From this perspective, price is constant; producers can only adapt their rate of output to that price. This kind of situation is characteristic of **competitive firms.** They have no power to raise the price of their output. Moreover, such firms can sell their entire output at the prevailing market price, so they have no incentive to charge a lower price. For competitive firms, the demand curve appears to be *horizontal,* as in Figure 20.3. The demand curve is *perfectly elastic* over the relevant range of output.

In Chapter 21 we shall take a closer look at the nature of compet-

competitive firm: A firm without market power, with no ability to alter the market price of the goods it produces.

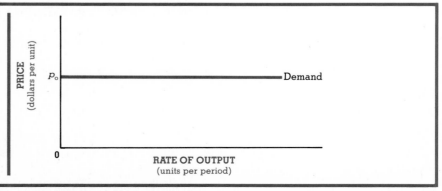

FIGURE 20.3 HORIZONTAL DEMAND

A single firm often cannot raise the price of its product and continue to sell its output. On the other hand, it may be able to sell its entire output at the prevailing price. In the short run, such firms confront a constant price. This is illustrated by the horizontal demand curve at the price p_0. An individual firms objective is to find the rate of output that maximizes profits at this price.

itive firms. We shall also examine the behavior of firms that are non-competitive, in the sense that they *can* raise their prices and continue to sell their output. For the moment, however, we shall focus on a trait common to both: the quest for maximum profit.

Marginal revenue

In making a production decision, we are searching for the most profitable rate of output from existing plant and equipment. This implies looking at all possible short-run rates of output. In each case, we want to know if *one more* unit of output would increase our profits. In making this decision, we need to know what that additional unit of output will bring in, that is, how much it adds to the total revenue of the firm. *Total revenue* is the sum of money a firm takes in from *all* of its production. It is equal to the average price of output multiplied by the quantity sold:

Total revenue = price × quantity
   (*TR*)   (*p*)   (*q*)

The contribution to total revenue of an additional unit of output is called **marginal revenue.** Marginal revenue is the *change* in total revenue that occurs when the rate of output is increased by one unit. To calculate marginal revenue, we can just compare the total revenues received before and after a one-unit increase in the rate of production: the *difference* between the two totals equals marginal revenue.

marginal revenue: The change in total revenue that results from a one-unit increase in the quantity sold.

When the price of a product is constant, the computation of marginal revenue is even simpler. Suppose we are actually selling ice cream cones at a constant price of $2 apiece. In this case, a one-unit increase in sales (one more cone) increases total revenue by $2. This is illustrated in Table 20.4. Notice that **as long as the price of a product is constant, price and marginal revenue are one and the same thing.**

This is not always the case. Often additional output can be sold only if price is reduced. In these situations, price is not constant and marginal revenue and price are no longer equal. We shall look at these situations a bit later.

Marginal cost

Knowing what marginal revenue is leaves us just one step away from applying the simple rule for profit maximization: never produce anything that costs more than it brings in. We already know what

---

TABLE 20.4   TOTAL AND MARGINAL REVENUE

Marginal revenue (MR) is the *change* in total revenue associated with the sale of one more unit of output. A third ice cream cone increases total revenue from $4 to $6; *MR* equals $2. If the price is constant (at $2 here), marginal revenue equals price.

Quantity sold		Price per unit		Total revenue	Marginal revenue
0	×	$2	=	$ 0	
1	×	2	=	2	$2
2	×	2	=	4	2
3	×	2	=	6	2
4	×	2	=	8	2
5	×	2	=	10	2

one more unit brings in; all we need to do now is look at its cost.

The added cost of producing one more unit of a good is its *marginal* cost. Figure 20.4 summarizes the marginal costs associated with the production of brass doorknobs.

The production of brass doorknobs requires a certain set of tools and equipment that can be leased for $10 a day on a long-term basis. Once leased, these tools and equipment become part of fixed costs; they must be paid for no matter how many doorknobs are produced.[3] In addition, labor and material (primarily brass) must be purchased to produce the doorknobs. Obviously, the quantity of labor and brass varies with the number of doorknobs produced. These are *variable costs. Marginal costs* in this case are the cost of the added labor and brass needed to produce *each* additional doorknob.

According to Figure 20.4, marginal costs tend to increase when doorknob production is increased. Like most production processes, doorknob manufacture takes place in an existing plant that is equipped with a certain amount of tools and machinery. To increase output in the short run, more labor is hired to use that (fixed) plant and equipment. As the number of workers increases, however, each worker has fewer tools and machines to work with. In other words, the existing (fixed) plant and equipment must be shared by an ever

[3] Whether one should lease this equipment in the first place is an investment decision.

FIGURE 20.4   THE COSTS OF BRASS DOORKNOB PRODUCTION

Marginal cost is the increase in total cost associated with a one-unit increase in production. When the production of brass doorknobs expands from two to three per day, total costs increase by $9 (from $22 to $31 per day). The marginal cost of the third knob is therefore $9, as illustrated by point *D* in the graph below.

	Rate of output (knobs per day)	Total cost (per day)	Marginal cost (per unit)	Average cost (per unit)
A	0	$10	—	—
B	1	15	$ 5	$15.00
C	2	22	7	11.00
D	3	31	9	10.33
E	4	44	13	11.00
F	5	61	17	12.20

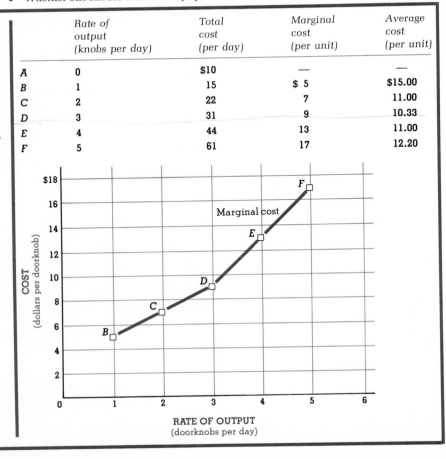

law of diminishing returns: The marginal physical product of a variable factor declines as more of it is employed with a given quantity of other (fixed) inputs.

The production decision

profit-maximization rule: Produce at that rate of output where marginal revenue equals marginal cost.

larger (variable) number of workers. Eventually, this situation reflects the **law of diminishing returns.** As marginal product diminishes, marginal cost increases. The upward-sloping MC curve of Figure 20.4 illustrates this phenomenon.

We are now in a position to make a production decision. The rule about never producing anything that costs more than it brings in can now be stated in more technical terms. What an additional unit of output brings in is its marginal revenue (MR); what it costs is its marginal cost (MC). Therefore, we do not want to produce an additional unit of output if its MC exceeds MR. If MC exceeds MR, we are spending more to produce that extra unit than we are getting back: total profits will decline if we produce it.

The opposite is true when MR exceeds MC. If an extra unit brings in more revenue than it costs to produce, it is adding to total profit. Total profits must increase in this case. Hence we want to expand the rate of production whenever MR exceeds MC.

Since we want to expand output when MR exceeds MC and contract output if MR is less than MC, the profit-maximizing rate of output is easily found. ***Short-run profits are maximized at that rate of output where*** **MR = MC.** The **profit-maximization rule** is summarized in Table 20.5.

Figure 20.5 illustrates the application of our profit-maximization rule in the production of brass doorknobs. We shall assume that the prevailing price of brass doorknobs is $13 apiece. At this price we can sell all the knobs we can produce, up to our short-run capacity. Knobs cannot be sold at a higher price, because lots of producers make doorknobs and sell them for $13. If we try to charge a higher price, consumers will buy their knobs from other producers. Hence the demand curve facing this one firm is horizontal at the price of $13. ***Whenever the price of a firm's product is constant in the short run, marginal revenue and price are identical.*** Thus the horizontal demand curve confronting this producer of doorknobs also represents marginal revenues.

The costs of producing brass doorknobs were already examined in Figure 20.4. The key concept illustrated here is marginal cost. The MC curve slopes upward, in conventional fashion.

Also depicted in Figure 20.5 are the total revenues, costs, and profits of alternative production rates. Study the table first. Notice first of all that the firm loses $10 per day if it produces no doorknobs (row A). At zero output, total revenue is zero ($p \times q = 0$). However,

---

TABLE 20.5 SHORT-RUN PROFIT-MAXIMIZATION RULES

The relationship between marginal revenue and marginal cost dictates short-run production decisions. Profits are maximized at that rate of output where $MR = MC$.

If	Then
$MR > MC$	increase output rate
$MR = MC$	maintain output rate (profits maximized)
$MR < MC$	decrease output rate

FIGURE 20.5 MAXIMIZATION OF PROFITS WITH CONSTANT PRICES

Knowing the marginal cost and marginal revenue associated with each doorknob, we can easily determine the most profitable rate of output. The table and graph show the desired rate of brass doorknob production. Profits are at a maximum at that rate of output where marginal revenue equals marginal cost. In this case, profit maximization occurs at an output of four doorknobs per day.

	(1) Number of doorknobs (per day)	(2) Price	(3) Total revenue	(4) Total cost	(5) Total profit	(6) Marginal revenue	(7) Marginal cost
A	0	—	0	$10.00	−$10.00	—	—
B	1	$13.00	$13.00	15.00	− 2.00	$13.00	$ 5.00
C	2	13.00	26.00	22.00	+ 4.00	13.00	7.00
D	3	13.00	39.00	31.00	+ 8.00	13.00	9.00
E	4	13.00	52.00	44.00	+ 8.00	13.00	13.00
F	5	13.00	65.00	61.00	+ 4.00	13.00	17.00

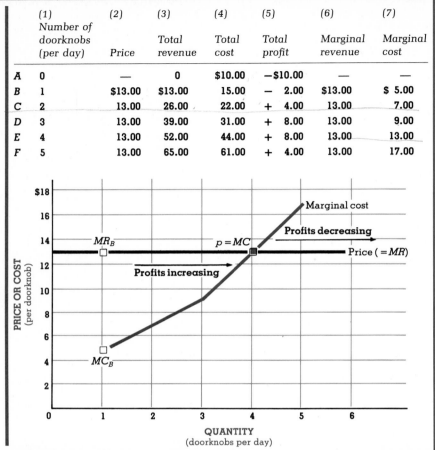

the firm must still contend with fixed costs of $10 per day. Total profit—total revenue minus total cost—is therefore *minus* $10; the firm incurs a loss.

Row B of the table shows how this loss is reduced when one doorknob is produced per day. The production and sale of one doorknob per day brings in $13 of total revenue (column 3). The total cost of producing one knob per day is $15 (column 4). Hence the total loss associated with an output rate of one knob per day is $2 (column 5). This may not be what we hoped for, but it is certainly better than the $10 loss incurred at zero output.

The superiority of producing one knob per day rather than zero is also evident in columns 6 and 7 of row B. The first doorknob produced has a *marginal revenue* of $13. Its *marginal cost* is only $5. Hence it brings in more added revenue than it costs to produce. Under these circumstances—whenever MR exceeds MC—output should definitely be expanded.

The excess of MR over MC for the first unit of output is also illustrated by the graph in Figure 20.5. Point MR_B ($13) lies above MC_B ($5); the *difference* between these two points measures the contribution that first doorknob makes to the total profits of the firm. In this case, that contribution equals $13 − $5 = $8; and production losses are reduced by that amount when the rate of output is increased from zero to one knob per day.

So long as* MR *exceeds* MC, *further increases in the rate of output are desirable. Notice what happens to profits when the rate of output is increased from one to two doorknobs per day (row *C*). The *MR* of the second knob is $13; its *MC* is $7. Therefore it *adds* $6 to total profits. Instead of losing $2 per day, the firm is now making a profit of $4 per day. The second unit of daily output has improved the situation considerably.

The firm can make even more profits by expanding the rate of output further. Look what happens when the rate of output reaches three doorknobs per day (row *D* of the table). The marginal revenue of the third knob is $13; its marginal cost is $9. Therefore the third knob makes a $4 contribution to profits. By increasing its rate of output to three doorknobs per day, the firm doubles its total profits.

This firm will never make huge profits. The fourth unit of output has a *MR* of $13 and a *MC* of $13 as well. It does not contribute to total profits, nor does it subtract from them. The fourth unit of output represents the highest rate of output the firm desires. At the rate of output where *MR* = *MC,* total profits of the firm are maximized.[4]

Notice what happens if we expand output beyond four doorknobs per day. The *MR* of the fifth doorknob is $13; its *MC* is $17. The fifth knob costs more than it brings in. If we produce that fifth doorknob, total profit will decline by $4. The fifth unit of output makes us worse off. This eventuality is evident in the graph of Figure 20.5; at the output rate of five knobs per day, the *MC* curve lies above the *MR* curve. The lesson here is clear: ***output should not be increased if* MC *exceeds* MR.**

The outcome of the production decision is illustrated in Figure 20.5 by the intersection of the *MR* and *MC* curves. At this intersection, *MR* equals *MC* and profits are maximized. If we produced less, we would be giving up potential profits. If we produced more, total profits would also fall.

Adding up profits

To reach the right production decision, we have relied on *marginal* revenues and costs. Having found the desired rate of output, however, we may want to take a closer look at the profits we are accumulating. We could, of course, content ourselves with the statistics in the table of Figure 20.5. But a picture would be nice, too, especially if it reflected our success in production. To draw that picture, we can use either *total* revenue and cost curves or *average* revenue and cost curves. Figure 20.6 illustrates both approaches.

Figure 20.6*a* depicts *total* revenues and costs at various rates of

---

[4] In this case, profits are the same at output levels of three and four. Given the choice between the two levels, most firms will choose the higher level. By producing the extra unit of output, the firm increases its customer base. This not only denies rival firms an additional sale but also provides some additional "cushion" when the economy slumps. Also, corporate size may connote both prestige and power (more on this later). In any case, the higher output level defines the limit to maximum-profit production.

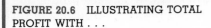

FIGURE 20.6 ILLUSTRATING TOTAL PROFIT WITH . . .

Total profits can be computed as $TR - TC$, as in part a. Or they can be computed as profit *per unit* ($p - ATC$) multiplied by the quantity sold. This is illustrated in part b by the shaded rectangle. To find the profit-maximizing rate of output, we could use either of these graphs or the MR and MC curves of Figure 20.5.

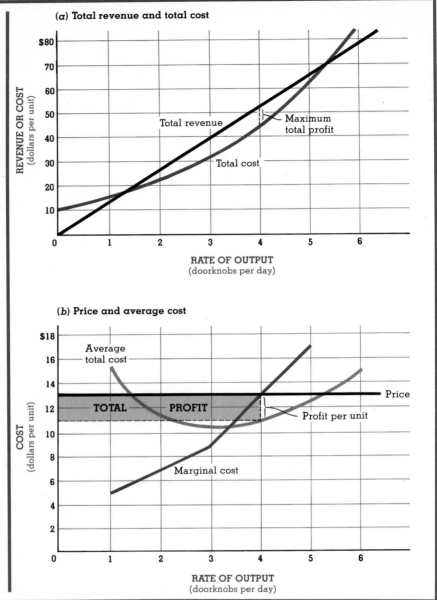

output. Recall that all brass doorknobs are sold at the prevailing price of $13 each. Hence total revenue equals $q \times \$13$. The resulting TR curve is a straight line. The total cost (TC) curve in Figure 20.6a starts above the total revenue line, dips below it, then rapidly overtakes it again. This is a reflection of the fact that marginal costs are initially low but rise quite rapidly as output expands.

Total profits are represented in Figure 20.6a by the vertical distance between the total revenue and total cost curves. This is a straightforward interpretation of our definition of total profits, that is, total profits $= TR - TC$. The vertical distance between the TR and TC curves is maximized at the output of four doorknobs per day.

Our success in producing brass doorknobs can also be illustrated by *average* revenue and costs. Total profit is equal to *average* profit per unit multiplied by the number of units produced. Profit *per unit*, in turn, is equal to price *minus* average total cost, that is,

Profit per unit $= p - ATC$

The price of brass doorknobs is illustrated in Figure 20.6*b* by the price line at $13. The average cost of producing brass doorknobs is illustrated by the *ATC* curve. Like the *ATC* curve we encountered in Chapter 19, this one has a U shape. Therefore, the *difference* between price and average cost—profit per unit—is illustrated by the vertical distance between the price and *ATC* curves. At four doorknobs per day, for example, profit per unit equals $13 - $11 = $2.

To compute *total* profits, we note that

Total profits $=$ profit per unit $\times$ quantity
$$= (p - ATC) \times q$$

In this case, the four doorknobs generate a profit of $2 each, for a *total* profit of $8 per day. *Total* profits are illustrated in Figure 20.6*b* by the shaded rectangle. (Recall that the area of a rectangle is equal to its height [profit per unit] multiplied by its width [quantity sold].)

Profit per unit not only is used to compute total profits but is often of interest in its own right. Business people like to cite statistics on "markups," which are a crude index to per-unit profits. However, **the profit-maximizing producer never seeks to maximize per-unit profits.** What counts is *total* profits, not the amount of profit per unit. This is the old $4 ice cream problem again. You might be able to maximize profit per unit if you could sell one cone for $4, but you would probably make a lot more money if you sold 100 cones at a per-unit profit of only 50 cents each.

Similarly, **the profit-maximizing producer has no desire to produce at that rate of output where ATC is at a minimum.** Minimum *ATC* does represent least-cost production. But additional units of output, even though they raise average costs, will increase total profits. This is evident in Figure 20.6; *MR* exceeds *MC* for some output to the right of minimum *ATC* (the bottom of the U). Therefore, profits are increasing as we increase the rate of output beyond the point of minimum average costs. *until reach MR*

THE SHUTDOWN DECISION

The rule established for short-run profit maximization makes no reference to the costs of building a plant or equipping it with the necessary tools and machines. It speaks only of *marginal* costs and revenues. To determine the most profitable level of doorknob production, for example, we never really worried about the costs of the basic plant and equipment. The fixed costs of production were $10 per day and we accepted them as a fact of life. Yet we surely would have been better off if we could have leased the necessary facilities for only $5 per day. Shouldn't the level of fixed costs have some effect on our output decision?

To understand the influence of fixed costs on supply behavior, we must recall the distinction between the production decision and the investment decision. The *investment decision* requires a potential producer to decide whether he wants to build, buy, or lease a production plant, or to acquire the machinery needed to produce a particular product. That is to say, he must first decide whether he wants to go into business, thereby incurring fixed costs. This is an investment decision. Once in business, the producer must then determine how much to produce in any given day, week, or month. This is a *production decision*. The short-run profit-maximizing rule we have discussed relates only to this second decision; it assumes that a production unit exists.

To producers, of course, the investment decision is of enormous concern. The fixed costs that we have ignored in the production decision represent the producers' (or the stockholders') investment in the business. If they are going to avoid an economic loss, they have to generate at least enough revenue to recoup their investment. Thus it is not enough to generate marginal revenues in excess of marginal costs. To be successful, producers must generate enough income to cover the cost of (fixed) plant and equipment. Failure to do so will result in a net loss, despite allegiance to our profit-maximizing rule.

Even when total revenue does not cover all fixed costs, producers may keep producing. In this case they will be trying to recover as much of their original investment as possible. To do that, they will seek to collect as much revenue from production as they can, even though they know they will never recoup their entire investment. In other words, they must accept the fact that they made one bad decision—the decision to go into business—and seek to minimize the consequences.

They still have the choice of being big losers or small losers, and the rules of profit maximization can guide that choice. Once the plant is built and the tools are acquired, only **variable costs** and revenues count.

The role of costs in investment and production decisions is summarized in Figure 20.7. The curves in Figure 20.7 represent the short-run costs and potential demand curves associated with production of brass doorknobs. As long as the price of brass doorknobs is $13, the typical firm will produce four doorknobs a day, as determined by the intersection of the *MC* and *MR* (= price) curves (point *X*). In this case, price ($13) exceeds average total cost ($11) and doorknob production is profitable; the decision to go into business was a good one.

The investment decision would not look so good, however, if the market price of brass doorknobs fell to $9. Following the short-run rule for profit maximization, the firm would be led to point *Y*, where *MC* intersects the new demand (*MR*) curve. At this intersection, the firm would produce three doorknobs per day. But total revenues no longer cover total costs, as can be seen from the fact that the *ATC* curve now lies above the demand curve. The *ATC* of producing three knobs is $10.33 (Figure 20.4); price is $9. Hence the firm is incurring a loss of $4 per day (three doorknobs at a loss of $1.33 each).

variable costs: Costs of production that change when the rate of output is altered; for example, labor and material costs.

FIGURE 20.7 THE FIRM'S SHUTDOWN POINT

A firm should cease production only if total revenue is less than total variable cost. The shutdown decision may be based on the *MC*, price, and *AVC* curves. If the price of standard doorknobs were $13, a firm would want to produce at point *X*. At that rate of output, price exceeds average variable cost and production should continue. The same is true when price equals $9 (point *Y*). At point *Y*, the firm is losing money (*p* is less than *ATC*) but more than covering all variable costs (*p* is greater than *AVC*). If the price falls to $4 per doorknob, output should cease.

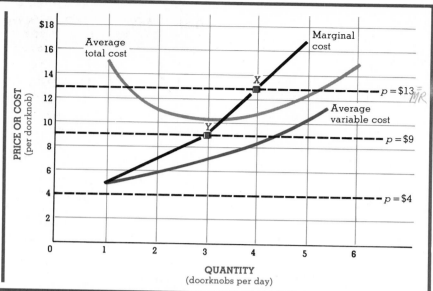

Should the firm stay in business under the circumstances? The answer is yes. Recall that the producer has already leased the plant and equipment required for doorknob production, at a (fixed) cost of $10 per day. The producer will have to pay these fixed costs whether the machinery is used or not. Stopping production of doorknobs would result in a loss amounting to $10 per day. Staying in business, even when doorknob prices fall to $9 each, generates a loss of only $4 a day. In this case, **where price exceeds average variable costs but not average total costs, the profit-maximization rule minimizes losses.** The investment decision turns out badly, but at least part of the initial investment is recovered. This was the situation for Ford Motor Company and other auto producers in the early 1980s.

The shutdown point

If the price of doorknobs falls far enough, however, the producer may be better off to cease production altogether. Suppose the price of brass doorknobs fell to $4 each (Figure 20.7). A price this low does

Ford Loses a Record $1.5 Billion in 1980

Ford Motor Co. said its losses for 1980 totaled $1.5 billion after a $316 million loss in the fourth quarter.

Ford's 1980 losses—which were in line with expectations—are, at this point, the largest ever by an American corporation, although it will lose that distinction soon, when Chrysler Corp. reports its 1980 losses—

expected to total $1.7 billion. Chrysler lost $1.1 billion in 1979, the previous record.

All three companies were licking their wounds from the impact of high interest rates on their markets. Ford's 1980 after-tax loss of $1.5 billion resulted from declines of 33 percent in domestic sales and 26 percent in worldwide sales from 1979. . . .

Ford Chairman Philip Caldwell said the company had weathered the disastrous year "without basic damage to its operations or a reduction in the scope of its plans for future products."

Ford also was cheered by the

showing of its new line of front-wheel-drive subcompacts, the Ford Escort and Mercury Lynx, which thus far has outsold all of the 70 imported car lines in the United States, according to Ford.

But Ford and its chief American competitors, Chrysler and General Motors Co., have had to curtail plant operations to conserve cash and give up hundreds of dollars per car in rebates to stimulate sales.

—Peter Behr

The Washington Post, Washington, D.C., February 20, 1981, p. D1. Copyright © 1981 The Washington Post.

Copper Company Shuts Down

NEW YORK—Phelps Dodge Corp., citing the lowest prices for copper in more than 30 years, said today it will suspend production at all its U.S. copper mines and concentrators and at its three Arizona smelters, effective Saturday, April 17.

The nation's second-largest copper producer said the suspension will last at least until June 1 and will result in the layoff of approximately 3,800 employes. . . .

Phelps Dodge Chairman George B. Munroe said, "the current recession has driven copper prices to their lowest levels in real terms in more than 30 years, and for the past several months we have been selling our copper for less than it costs us to produce it."

Munroe added that "by suspending operations we will conserve our ore reserves, reduce our inventories and cash outflows and thereby serve the long-term best interest of the company."

Phelps Dodge has an annual production of 350,000 short tons of copper, under normal operating condi-

tions, including some 50,000 tons from leaching operations. Since the first of the year, however, operating rates have been curtailed to 80 percent of capacity.

The company said it may continue the cutback beyond June 1 if the copper market remained depressed.

Munroe said the company would resume operations "when conditions warrant."

The Washington Post, Washington, D.C., April 8, 1982. Reprinted by permission of United Press International.

---

shutdown point: That rate of output where *AVC* equals price.

not even cover the marginal cost of producing one doorknob per day ($5). Continued production of even one doorknob per day would imply a total loss of $11 per day ($10 of fixed costs plus $1 of variable costs). Higher rates of output would lead to still greater losses. Hence the firm would be well advised to shut down production, even though that action implies a loss of $10 per day. The initial investment decision was awful. In all cases **where price does not cover average variable costs at any rate of output, production should cease.** Thus, the **shutdown point** occurs where price is equal to average variable cost. Any lower price will result in losses that are larger than fixed costs.

Whether or not fixed costs count, then, depends on the decision being made. For producers trying to decide how best to utilize the resources they have purchased or leased, fixed costs no longer enter the decision-making process. For producers deciding whether to enter business, sign a lease, or replace existing machinery and plant, fixed costs count very much. Business people will proceed with an investment only if the anticipated profits are adequate to compensate for the effort and risk undertaken.

Long-run costs

In contemplating an investment decision, business people confront not one set of cost figures, but many. A plant not yet built can be designed for various rates of production. Producers expecting to sell large quantities of a good may want to build a large plant. In making long-run decisions a given producer is not bound to one size of plant or to a particular mix of tools and machinery. In the long run, one can be flexible. In general, *a producer will want to build, buy, or lease a plant that is most efficient for the anticipated rate of output.*[5] Once such a plant is selected, the producer may proceed with the problem of short-run profit maximization. Once production is started, he can only hope that his choice was a good one and that a shutdown can be avoided.

[5] The choice of long-run plant size (and related cost curves) was illustrated in Chapter 19.

DETERMINANTS OF SUPPLY

Whether the time frame is the short run or the long run, the one central force in production decisions is the quest for profits. Producers will go into production—incur fixed costs—only if they see the potential for economic profits (above-average returns). Once in business, they will continue to expand the rate of output so long as profits are increasing. They will get out of business—cease production—when economic losses exceed the fixed costs of production.

Nearly anyone could make money with these principles if he or she had complete information on costs and revenues. What renders the road to fortune less congested is the general absence of such complete information. In the real world, production decisions involve considerably more risk, since business people often don't know how much profit or loss they will incur until it's too late to alter production decisions. Consequently, business people are compelled to make a reasoned guess about the shape of demand and cost curves and then proceed, trusting to their market researchers, production specialists, and hunches. By way of summary, we can identify the major influences that will shape their short- and long-run decisions on how much output to supply to the market.

Short-run determinants

Since short-run production decisions are dominated by marginal revenues and marginal costs, the quantity of a good supplied will be affected by all forces that alter either *MR* or *MC*. Specifically, *the **quantity of output a producer is able and willing to supply will depend on:***

□ The price of factor inputs
□ The price of the product
□ Technology (the available production function)
□ Expectations (for prices, costs, sales, technology)

The costs that count in the short run are marginal costs. The lower they are, the greater the willingness and ability to produce. The price of the good is important because it determines the marginal revenue of the firm—the other half of the profit-maximization equation. Technology is important because it can change production costs (see Chapter 19). And finally, expectations are critical because they express producers' perceptions of what future costs, prices, sales, and profits are likely to be.

ceteris paribus: The assumption of "everything else being equal," of nothing else changing.

quantity supplied: The amount of a product offered for sale at a specific price during a given time period (*ceteris paribus*).

THE SHORT-RUN SUPPLY CURVE   By using the familiar **ceteris paribus** assumption, we can predict quite accurately how the **quantity supplied** in the short run will respond to a change in price. In other words, we can draw a short-run supply curve in the same way that we earlier constructed consumer demand curves. In this case, the forces we assume to be constant are input prices, technology, and expectations. The only thing we allow to change is the price of the product itself. Under these circumstances, how will the quantity supplied change when the price of the product rises or falls?

Figure 20.8 illustrates the response of quantity supplied to a

FIGURE 20.8 THE SHORT-RUN SUPPLY CURVE

A profit-maximizing producer will not supply additional quantities of output unless marginal revenue at least equals marginal cost. For competitive firms, price and marginal revenue are identical. Hence marginal cost defines the lowest price a firm will accept for a given quantity of output. In this sense, the marginal cost curve *is* the supply curve: it tells us how quantity supplied will respond to price. At $p = \$13$, the quantity supplied is four. At $p = \$9$, the quantity supplied is three.

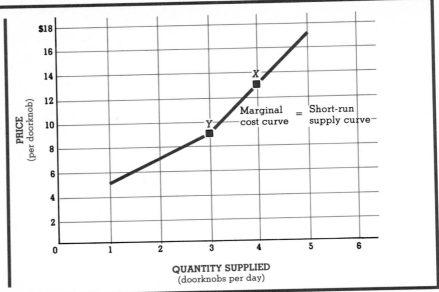

supply curve: A curve describing the quantities of a good a producer is willing and able to sell (produce) at alternative prices in a given time period (*ceteris paribus*).

change in price. Notice the critical role of marginal costs: *the marginal cost curve is the short-run supply curve for a competitive firm.* Recall our basic profit-maximization rule. A competitive producer wants to supply a good only if its price exceeds its marginal cost. Hence marginal cost defines the lower limit for an "acceptable" price. A producer of doorknobs is willing and able to produce four doorknobs per day only if the price of doorknobs is \$13 (point *X*). If the price of doorknobs dropped to \$9, the *quantity supplied* would fall to three (point *Y*). The marginal cost curve tells us what the quantity supplied would be at all other prices as well.[6] Hence the *MC* curve summarizes the response of a producer to price changes: it is the short-run supply curve.[7]

Long-run determinants

All of the forces that shape short-run production decisions are relevant in the long run as well. In the long run, however, the other determinants of supply are more likely to change. New technologies, for example, may reduce both the fixed costs of production and the marginal costs of production. Over time, an increase in the number of producers (sellers) may reduce the price of the good or increase the price of required inputs. Hence, even though the list of supply determinants looks the same, it takes on a new dimension in the long run. That dimension includes a greater potential for *change* in the underlying determinants of supply.

[6] There is an exception to this rule: if price is less than *minimum* average variable cost, no output will be supplied. This is the shutdown contingency we just examined.
[7] In noncompetitive situations—where the demand curve facing the firm is downward sloping rather than horizontal—the marginal cost curve does *not* represent the short-run supply curve. Such firms will be discussed in Chapters 22–24.

POLICY IMPLICATIONS: SUPPLY-SIDE TAX INCENTIVES

The motivating force in business supply decisions is the quest for profits. Because the amount of profit a producer can keep depends on taxes, government policy directly affects the incentives for producing goods and services. To the extent that taxes reduce the amount of profit a producer can make or keep, they discourage investment and production. Conversely, policies that reduce net costs or increase after-tax profits encourage additional investment and production. These observations were the basis for the "supply-side" tax reductions implemented by President Reagan in 1981. Some of the major business tax cuts included in the Economic Recovery Tax Act of 1981 are noted below.[8]

Lower corporate profits tax

The profits of U.S. corporations are taxed by the federal government. In 1980 the standard corporate tax rate was 46 percent for profits in excess of $50,000 per year. Forty-six cents out of every profit dollar was turned over to the U.S. Treasury. Firms with less than $50,000 in annual profits paid taxes at lower rates.

The corporate tax does not directly alter either the marginal revenues or marginal costs of a firm.[9] In this sense, *the corporate profits tax does not affect the short-run production decision.* Whatever rate of output maximizes short-run profits in the absence of a profits tax will also maximize profits after the tax is levied. The basic difference is that the corporation gets to keep less of the profit it earns.

Although the corporate tax will not alter short-run production decisions, it will affect investment decisions. Decisions to enter or expand a business are based on expected profits. What counts are "after-tax profits," that is, the amount of profit a producer gets to keep. This is the income producers/owners can spend on their own consumption or use for further investment.

To improve the incentives for investment, the Reagan administration proposed a cut in the tax rate for corporate profits. The tax legislation passed by Congress in August 1981 reduced the tax rate on the first $25,000 of annual profit from 17 percent in 1981 to 15 percent in 1983. The tax rate on profits between $25,000 and $50,000 was reduced from 20 percent to 18 percent. But the rate on profits in excess of $50,000 was left unchanged, at 46 percent. Accordingly, the tax reductions were far more significant for smaller corporations than for larger ones.

Faster depreciation

Both large and small corporations received greater tax relief from enlarged tax deductions. A firm pays taxes on its "taxable" income, not its economic profit. In computing taxable income, a firm may

---

[8] The provisions of the act, and its macroeconomic effects, are discussed in Chapter 15.

[9] If corporations are able to "pass on" the corporate tax by raising consumer prices, marginal revenues may change. Our short-run analysis ignores this possibility.

depreciation (tax): The tax deduction allowed for the cost of using capital and equipment in production.

deduct the costs of labor and material (variable costs) as well as some portion of its capital (fixed) costs. The critical question in tax accounting is what fraction of fixed costs can be deducted from revenues in any year. The amount of that deduction is referred to as **(tax) depreciation.**

The more depreciation a firm is permitted to deduct from its revenues, the less taxable income it will have. Hence a firm's tax payment can be reduced either by (1) reducing the tax rate on taxable income, as we discussed above, or (2) allowing larger deductions for depreciation, which reduce the amount of income subject to taxation. Faster (larger) depreciation was preferred by the Reagan administration and Congress because depreciation is directly linked to investment. To get a larger tax deduction, a firm must have plant and equipment to depreciate. Hence faster depreciation encourages firms to build new factories and expand or modernize old ones. A reduction in corporate tax rates also encourages investment but is less focused.

The 1981 tax bill severed whatever links existed between depreciation and the actual "wearing out" of capital. Instead of trying to figure out how fast their assets are being "used up" in production, corporations may now depreciate their capital assets according to fixed schedules. According to this new Accelerated Cost Recovery (ACR) system, equipment and machinery may be "written off" in five years. This means that corporations can deduct one-fifth of the cost of machinery and equipment from their annual revenues in any year. Previously the deduction varied from one-fifth to as little as one-fifteenth. Similarly, all buildings can now be depreciated in 15 years, rather than the previous range of 20 to 40 years. These faster depreciation (cost recovery) schedules will reduce the tax bill of U.S. businesses by billions of dollars each year. These tax savings, it is hoped, will encourage still more investment in machinery, equipment, and buildings.

Larger investment tax credits

A third incentive for increased investment was provided by larger investment tax credits. A tax credit directly reduces a firm's tax bill. First a firm calculates its taxable income, based on actual revenues, expenses, and depreciation. Then it applies the corporate tax rate to this taxable income. The result is the firm's tax liability. It need not pay this amount, however. Uncle Sam allows "credits" for various activities, including new investment. The Economic Recovery Tax Act of 1981 permits a tax credit equal to 10 percent of the cost of new investment. Hence a firm that buys $10,000 of new machinery gets a tax credit of $1,000. That credit reduces its tax bill.

Research and development tax credits

Faster depreciation and larger investment tax credits both reduce the dollar cost of plant and equipment. In this sense, they lower the fixed costs of production. They have no direct effect on marginal costs or revenues, however, and so no impact on short-run production decisions. They are designed to increase investment, that is, long-run supply.

Tax credits for research and development expenses are another story. They reduce the dollar cost of using variable inputs. A firm that increases its spending on research and development gets a tax credit equal to 25 percent of that added spending. Suppose a firm hires one new engineer at a salary of $24,000 per year. The firm will get a tax credit of $6,000 (0.25 × $24,000). Hence the *marginal* cost of employing labor is effectively reduced. These reduced marginal costs should encourage the firm to make a new short-run production decision, at a higher rate of output.

The combined incentives

Altogether, these various tax reductions imply a tremendous incentive for increased investment and production. The impact of these tax reductions on a small firm are illustrated in Table 20.6. The figures in the table depict a firm with total revenues of $500,000 per year and operating costs of $350,000. Before the tax cuts, this firm was able to deduct $80,000 in annual depreciation, leaving it with $70,000 in taxable profits. At the old tax rates and without tax credits, the firm paid $14,350 in taxes.

The second column of Table 20.6 shows how the 1981 tax legislation reduced this firm's taxes. Revenues and operating costs are unchanged. But the firm can now deduct $100,000 for depreciation. Its taxable income therefore falls from $70,000 to $50,000. Lower tax rates further reduce its tax liability, to $8,250. It need not pay Uncle Sam this much, however. It gets an investment tax credit of $1,000 for buying $10,000 worth of new machinery. It gets another $6,000 credit for hiring a new engineer. As a result, it pays only $1,250 in taxes, rather than $14,750. This tax reduction directly increases after-tax profits and encourages more production and investment. For the U.S. business community as a whole, the 1981 tax cuts will increase after-tax profits by roughly $160 *billion* during the period 1981–86. Whether these incentives will be sufficient to increase the overall rate of U.S. investment will depend on the condition of the larger economy.[10]

---

[10] The relationships of aggregate (total) investment to economic activity (GNP) are discussed in Chapters 7–15.

TABLE 20.6 THE IMPACT OF THE "SUPPLY-SIDE" TAX CUTS ON A FIRM'S TAX BILL

The Economic Recovery Tax Act of 1981 tax cuts reduced business taxes in several ways. Firms are allowed faster depreciation (line 4), pay lower tax rates (line 6), and can get tax credits for new investment (line 7) and expanded research and development (line 8). The "bottom line" is lower taxes. The firm gets to keep more of its net revenues. See text for explanations.

Item	Before tax reductions	After tax reductions
1. Total revenue	$500,000	$500,000
2. Operating expenses (paid costs)	350,000	350,000
3. Revenue less expense	$150,000	$150,000
4. Depreciation	(80,000)	(100,000)
5. Taxable profit	$ 70,000	$ 50,000
6. Corporate tax	14,750	8,250
7. Investment tax credit	—	1,000
8. R&D credit	—	6,000
9. Taxes due	$14,750	$1,250

SUMMARY

■ The public, the business community, and economists all have different ideas about the nature and level of profits. *Economic* profit is the difference between total revenue and total cost. Total economic cost includes the value of *all* inputs used in the production, not just those paid an explicit payment.

■ In seeking economic profits (above-average returns), firms make both short-run and long-run decisions. The short-run producton decision concerns the rate of output to produce from existing (fixed) facilities. The long-run investment decision concerns the choice of whether to acquire or expand production facilities.

■ Because profits are the difference between total revenues and total costs, a profit-maximizing firm must consider how revenues and costs change as levels of production change. On the cost side, we distinguish three kinds of cost: *fixed, variable,* and *marginal.*

■ Only marginal costs (the cost of producing one additional unit of output) influence the short-run production decision. The profit-maximizing producer compares marginal cost to marginal revenue. As long as marginal revenues exceed marginal costs, profits are growing and the producer has an incentive to increase output.

■ Output expansion is limited by the tendency of marginal costs to rise and of marginal revenues to remain constant or decline as output increases. Marginal costs will typically catch up to marginal revenues at some point, thereby bringing to a halt profitable output expansion. At the point at which marginal revenue equals marginal cost, total profits are at a maximum.

■ A firm will continue to produce in the short run so long as total revenue exceeds variable costs. The firm will shut down when price falls below average variable cost.

■ The determinants of supply include all forces that affect costs or revenue. These forces include the price of the product, the price of inputs, technology, and expectations. In the long run all these forces may change significantly.

■ Taxes affect the amount of profit a producer can keep. Business tax cuts increase after-tax profits and encourage additional investment and production.

Terms to remember | Define the following terms:

supply	investment decision
profit	competitive firm
economic cost	marginal revenue
economic profit	law of diminishing returns
law of demand	profit-maximization rule
total revenue	variable costs
price elasticity of demand	shutdown point
marginal cost	*ceteris paribus*
total cost	quantity supplied
short run	supply curve
production decision	depreciation (tax)
long run	

Questions for discussion

1. Besides profits, do firms have any other incentive to produce the goods and services we demand?

2. What economic costs is a large corporation likely to overlook when computing its "profits"? How about the owner of a family-run business or farm?

3. If a firm is incurring an economic loss, would society be better off if the firm shut down? Would the firm want to shut down? Explain.

4. Why wouldn't a profit-maximizing firm want to produce at the rate of output that minimizes average total cost? Illustrate your answer with graphs.

5. If new technology or management techniques succeeded in lowering fixed costs but not marginal costs, would production decisions be affected? How about innovations that reduced marginal costs but not fixed costs?

Problem

A firm has leased plant and equipment to produce video-game cartridges, which can be sold in unlimited quantities at $21 each. The figures below describe the associated costs of production:

Rate of output (per day)	0	1	2	3	4	5	6	7	8
Total cost	$50	$55	$62	$75	$96	$125	$162	$203	$248

Using these figures:

(a) Draw total revenue and total cost curves on the same graph. How much are fixed costs?

(b) On a separate graph, draw the average total cost (ATC), marginal cost (MC), and marginal revenue (MR) curves.

(c) What is the profit-maximizing rate of output?

(d) Should the producer stay in business? Why or why not?

CHAPTER 21

COMPETITIVE MARKETS

Millions of individuals and firms participate in product markets daily, buying and selling specific goods and services. Individual consumers enter product markets to purchase goods and services they desire, seeking to get as much utility as they can for the lowest price possible. Producers participate in product markets with the thought of maximizing profits, and so they welcome the chance to sell as many goods as possible for the highest possible price. In view of these disparate interests, what kind of outcome is likely? In particular, how will prices be determined, and how much output will be produced and sold? Are consumer interests likely to prevail in the market, or will all price and production decisions be made by producers?

To answer these kinds of questions, we have to abstract from individual behavior and think in terms of *markets*. As we first observed in Chapter 2, individual consumer demands can be combined to formulate *market* demands for particular goods and services. In the same way, individual firm decisions can be combined to construct *market* supply possibilities. The interaction of these market forces yields the array of goods and services we confront daily and the prices attached to them.

Although the mechanics of supply and demand are fairly simple, we cannot conclude that all markets function alike. Quite the contrary. As we shall discover in this and the following chapters, market outcomes are significantly influenced by the number, the size, and the power of producers. In this chapter we shall observe how markets work when all producers are relatively small and without market power. Chapters 22 and 23 will focus on markets dominated by a small number of powerful firms.

MARKET POWER: A FIRST LOOK

When asked to identify "powerful" firms, most people respond in terms of corporate size. And it is true that most of the really large corporations—General Motors, IBM, AT&T, and the like—do have market power. But small firms can have power, too, at least according to the concept of market power we are going to use. From an economist's viewpoint, *market power is gauged by a firm's ability to control the market price of the goods it sells.* If a firm can alter the market price of its goods, it is said to have **market power.**

market power: The ability to alter the market price of a good or service.

Firms without market power

This definition of market power may appear to render all firms powerful, but it doesn't. The important concept here is *market* price, that is, the price at which goods are actually sold. Remember our experience trying to sell ice cream cones at $4 apiece (Chapter 20)? In that episode, we were able to raise the *asking* price for our ice cream. But we didn't *sell* any, because the market price—the price at which other firms' cones were being sold—was much lower. In other words, we had no market power—we could not raise the market price of ice cream cones. To sell our cones, we would have had to lower our prices to the level at which other ice cream vendors were selling them.

The same kind of powerlessness is characteristic of the small wheat farmer. Like any producer, the lone wheat farmer can increase or reduce his rate of output by making alternative production decisions. But his decision will not affect the market price of wheat.

Even a large farmer who can alter his harvest by as much as 10,000 bushels of wheat per year will not influence the market price of wheat. Why not? Because nearly *2 billion* bushels of wheat are brought to market every year, and another 10,000 bushels simply isn't going to be noticed. In other words, *the output of the lone farmer is so small relative to the* **market supply** *that it has no significant effect on the total quantity or price in the market.*

market supply: The total quantities of a good that sellers are willing and able to sell at alternative prices in a given time period (*ceteris paribus***); the combined willingness of all market suppliers to sell.**

A distinguishing characteristic of *powerless* firms is that, individually, they can sell as much output as they can produce at the prevailing market price. We call all such producers **competitive firms;** they have no independent influence on market prices. In effect, *a competitive (powerless) producer confronts a horizontal (perfectly elastic) demand curve for his own output,* as in the case of our doorknob maker (Chapter 20).[1] When an entire market is com-

competitive firm: A firm without market power, with no ability to alter the market price of the goods it produces.

---

[1] Notice that a distinction is made between the market demand curve and the demand curve facing a particular firm. Even though the market demand curve for wheat is negatively sloped, the part of market demand satisfied by one farmer is so small that he effectively faces a horizontal demand curve. One can visualize this latter demand as residing in the *width* of the market demand curve. We shall return to this distinction.

perfectly competitive market: A market in which no buyer or seller has market power.

Firms with market power

monopoly: A firm that produces the entire market supply of a particular good or service.

posed of competitive firms (and powerless consumers as well), we call it a **perfectly competitive market.**[2]

A perfectly competitive market can be contrasted with another extreme case, that of monopoly. A **monopoly** exists when one firm is the sole supplier of a particular product. Because such a firm represents the entire supply side of the market, its output decisions are obviously significant for market supply and price; it has market power. Should a monopoly wish to raise the market price of its product, it can simply withhold the product. We might have been successful in our ice cream venture, for example, if we had managed to eliminate all other sellers from the market. As a monopolist, we could have forced people to pay $4 per cone or do without ice cream.

A monopolist's pricing decision is not directly constrained by the behavior of other firms. A monopolist's price decision is limited only by the shape and position of the market demand curve. A monopolist confronts a downward-sloping demand curve and must worry about the impact of its production (output) decision on the market price of its goods.

Degrees of market power

There is, of course, a whole range of market structures between the extremes of perfect competition and monopoly. There are *degrees* of market power. General Motors, for example, does have the power to change the market price of automobiles but is not a monopolist. The amount of power a particular firm has depends on its size, the number of other producers, the number of *potential* producers, the price and availability of similar (substitute) goods, and a number of other factors that we shall discuss in Chapter 24. For the time being, however, we shall focus on the extremes of perfect competition and monopoly, hoping thereby to discover the impact of market power on the behavior of the economy.

THE NATURE OF COMPETITION

Before we look at the behavior of a highly competitive market—the electronic calculator market—it will be useful to preview the primary characteristics of competitive behavior. As we have noted, *a firm without market power is one whose output is so small in relation to market volume that its output decisions have no perceptible impact on price.* The complete and sudden demise of such a firm would not be noticed in the market. By contrast, the demise of a large and powerful firm would visibly reduce market supplies and disrupt the previous market equilibrium. One can visualize the difference between these two situations by considering what would happen to U.S. egg supplies and prices if Farmer Kitt's 37 hens were to die, and what would happen to U.S. auto supplies and prices if the Ford Motor Company were to close down suddenly. The one

---

[2] The potential for power on the demand side of markets is discussed in Chapter 27.

event would go unnoticed; the impact of the other would be dramatic.

The same kind of contrast is evident when an expansion of output is contemplated. Were Farmer Kitt to double his production capacity (breed another 37 hens), the added output would not even show up in commerce statistics, because U.S. egg production is calibrated in the billions. Were Ford, on the other hand, to double its production, the added output not only would be noted, but would tend to depress automobile prices as Ford tried to unload heavy inventories.

The critical distinction between Ford and Farmer Kitt is not in their motivation but in their ability to alter market outcomes. Both are out to make a buck and thus seek to produce the rate of output that maximizes profit. What makes Farmer Kitt's situation different is the fact that his output decisions do not influence egg prices. In this sense, he has one less problem to worry about. Like the door-knob producer of Chapter 20, Farmer Kitt confronts a horizontal demand curve, the level of which is determined by much larger market forces. However much he stimulates his hens to produce, he will have no influence on the price of eggs. In seeking to maximize his profits, Farmer Kitt strives to run an efficient operation, producing up to the point where his marginal cost of production equals the going market price for eggs. In this sense, he is a *price taker*, taking the market price of eggs as a fact of life and doing the best he can within that constraint. Were he to attempt to enlarge his profits by raising his egg prices above market levels, he would find himself without customers, because the consumers would go elsewhere to buy their eggs.

Ford Motor Company, on the other hand, can behave like a *price setter*. Instead of waiting to find out what the market price is and making appropriate output adjustments, Ford has the discretion to "announce" prices at the beginning of every model year. Ford knows that sales will not fall to zero if its car prices are set a little higher than those of other car manufacturers. This, of course, is a consequence of the fact that Ford confronts a downward-sloping rather than a perfectly horizontal demand curve. Accordingly, Ford has some identifiable impact on market prices and seeks to maximize profits by finding the price and output *combination* that equates marginal revenue and marginal cost.

Market demand curves vs. firm demand curves

It is important to distinguish between the market demand curve and the demand curve confronting a particular firm. Farmer Kitt's little operation does not contradict the law of demand. The quantity of eggs purchased in the supermarket still depends on egg prices. That is to say, the *market* demand curve for eggs is still downward-sloping, just as the market demand curve for cars is negatively inclined. Farmer Kitt himself faces a horizontal demand curve only because his share of the market is so infinitesimal that changes in his output do not disturb the market equilibrium.

Were 10,000 competitive farmers to expand their egg production at the same time as Farmer Kitt, the market equilibrium would

FIGURE 21.1   THE COMPETITIVE EGG MARKET

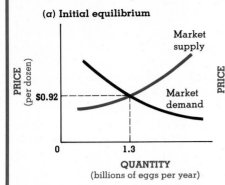

(a) Initial equilibrium

(b) Equilibrium after Farmer Kitt doubles his production

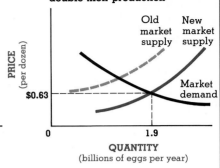

(c) Equilibrium after 10,000 farmers double their production

(a) The market price of eggs is determined by the collective behavior of all farmers and consumers. The market demand curve slopes downward; the market supply curve slopes upward. The intersection of these two curves establishes the market equilibrium.

(b) One farmer's decision to double egg output has no significant impact on the market supply or price of eggs. In effect, a single farmer can sell as many eggs as he wishes to at the equilibrium price.

(c) When many competitive egg farmers simultaneously attempt to increase their sales at existing prices, their collective action *shifts* the market supply curve to the right and lowers the equilibrium price.

be disturbed, of course. That is to say, a market composed of 10,000 individually powerless producers still sees a lot of action. The power here resides in the collective action of all the producers, however, and not in the individual action of any one. Were egg production to increase so markedly, the eggs could be sold only at lower prices, in accordance with the downward-sloping nature of the *market* demand curve. The distinction between the actions of a single producer and those of the market are illustrated in Figure 21.1.[3]

The tendency toward zero profits

Whether or not 10,000 farmers will actually double their egg production depends on the profit outlook they perceive. If the price and cost relationship is favorable enough, egg production can be quite profitable. When it is, individual farmers will seek to expand production, and will continue to do so until rising marginal costs catch up with the high price of eggs. If the profit outlook is alluring enough, even city folk will be tempted to get into egg production. This surge of egg production will disturb the market equilibrium, however. As farmers add to market supplies, their collective efforts will begin to depress egg prices. As egg prices slide down the market demand curve (Figure 21.1c), the profitability of egg production will begin to decline somewhere along the line. At some point, further expansion of egg production will cease. Farmers and city folk alike will decide that **economic profit** has disappeared. At that point other pursuits may begin to look more attractive. When that happens, egg

economic profit: The difference between total revenues and total economic costs.

[3] Chapter 2 demonstrates how a market's supply curve is derived from the supply curves of individual firms.

New Video-Game Makers Jump into Fight for a Share of the Booming Home Market

The market for home video games is starting to resemble a Space Invaders combat zone.

More than half-a-dozen companies plan to introduce video-game products in 1982, and sales are expected to more than double from last year to $3 billion. Players haven't deserted the arcades. Parents across the country are still battling to outlaw video-game parlors in their towns, and their kids—and others—are still feeding millions of quarters into arcade machines. But the home market is where the rapid growth is expected. . . .

Eighty million households in the U.S. have televisions, but only 8.5% have bought video games. By 1985, some industry analysts predict, 50% of the households with TVs will have video games. And the overseas market has just opened, with a million consoles sold so far in Europe.

Atari's Big Share

Despite the expanding market, the newcomers won't have an easy job. According to industry estimates, Atari controls 75% of the market. Mattel and the Odyssey game marketed by North American Philips Corp.'s Magnavox division dominate the other 25%. All three companies plan new products of their own for 1982. And Atari is expected to double its ad budget to $75 million.

But the newcomers say the risk is worthwhile. One successful cartridge, like Atari's Space Invaders, can generate $100 million to $150 million in sales, with margins of about 20%. And when Atari sells a lot of consoles, the cartridge makers benefit because their market expands.

—Laura Landro

---

prices will tend to stabilize at a new equilibrium, at least until significant changes occur in technology or market demand.

Egg producers would be happier, or course, if the price of eggs did not decline to the point where profits began to disappear. But how are they going to prevent it? Farmer Kitt knows all about the law of demand and would like to get other farmers to slow production a little before all the profits disappear. But he himself cannot afford to initiate or join such an effort. Were he to reduce his own egg production, nobody would notice the difference in market supplies, and egg prices would continue to slide. The only one affected would be Farmer Kitt, who would be denying himself the opportunity to share in the good fortunes of the egg market while they lasted. As long as others are willing and able to expand production, Farmer Kitt must do likewise or deny himself even a small share of the available profits. Others will be willing to expand egg production so long as eggs breed economic profits—that is, so long as the rate of return in egg production is superior to that available elsewhere. They will be able to do so as long as it is easy to get into egg production.

Farmer Kitt's dilemma goes a long way toward explaining why egg production is not terribly profitable. Every time the profit picture looks good, somebody tries to get in on the action, a phenomenon that keeps egg prices down close to the costs of production. This kind of pressure on prices and profits is a fundamental characteristic of competitive markets. As long as it is easy for existing producers to expand production or for new firms to enter an industry, high profits will attract profit maximizers. Output will expand, market prices will fall, and rates of profit will diminish. Thus the rate of profits in egg production is kept down by the fact that anyone with a good rooster, a couple of hens, and a vacant lot can get into the business fairly easily. People will be tempted to enter the egg business whenever profits are attractive.

We can formulate a few general observations, then, about the structure, behavior, and outcomes of a competitive market:

After Lucrative Run, Atlantic City's Casinos Brace for Profit-Dampening Competition

The long-lived Atlantic City casino boom hasn't gone bust, but the easy-come, easy-go days are fading with the autumn weather.

"The days of just opening your doors and the crowds stampeding in are over," says Stephen Hyde, executive vice president of the Boardwalk Regency, the second casino to open in Atlantic City.

Although the recession spared the casino business, competition and higher costs may not. The opening of a fourth casino in August and the scheduled openings of three more by early 1981 will have created competition that could cut into each casino's revenue. At the same time labor costs are rising as the larger number of casinos compete for pit bosses, croupiers, and other employes. New Jersey's cumbersome regulatory bureaucracy, is also slicing the houses' edge.

September Win Is Off

That's not to say that the house is going broke. With a market of 37 million adults in their territory, the casinos managed to win $193.3 million more than they lost to players in June, July and August. But analysts say the three established casinos won an average of only $17 million each in

September, down from $23 million to $25 million each in August. In September 1979, the two then-established outfits, Resorts International and Caesars World Inc.'s Boardwalk Regency, reported gross winnings of $19.6 million and $16.7 million.

If the official September gross win figures to be released today or tomorrow decline as expected, analysts will blame seasonal factors and the effect of an extra weekend in August. Even so, Marvin Roffman, an analyst at Janney Montgomery Scott Inc., calls the September win "horrendous," and he says it spells trouble for casino profits. "There is definitely an erosion of profit margins, and it will continue as more casinos come on stream," he says.

—Ronald Alsop

- A competitive market will include a great many firms, none of which has a significant share of total output.
- All competitive firms will seek to expand output until marginal costs are equal to price, inasmuch as price and marginal revenue are identical for such firms.
- If significant economic profit is available, increasing numbers of producers will enter the industry and participate in the high profit.
- The tendency of production and market supplies to expand when profit is high puts heavy pressure on prices and profits in competitive industries. Economic profit will approach zero as prices are driven down to the level of average production costs.

No barriers to entry

barriers to entry: Obstacles that make it difficult or impossible for would-be producers to enter a particular market; for example, patents.

New producers will be able to enter a profitable industry and help drive down prices and profits as long as there are no significant **barriers to entry.** Such barriers may include patents, control of essential factors of production, long-established consumer acceptance, and various forms of price control. All such barriers make it expensive, risky, or impossible for new firms to enter into production. In the absence of such barriers, new firms can enter an industry more readily and at less risk. Not surprisingly, firms already entrenched in a profitable industry do their best to keep newcomers out, by erecting barriers to entry.

COMPETITION AT WORK: THE POCKET-CALCULATOR MARKET

Although few factor or product markets are completely devoid of market power, many function much like the competitive model we have sketched out. In addition to egg production, most other agricultural product markets are characterized by highly competitive supply conditions, with hundreds of thousands of producers supplying the market.[4] Other highly competitive, and hence not very profitable, businesses are retail food stores, printing, clothing manufacturing and retailing, dry-cleaning establishments, and furniture. Other markets exhibit competitive structures as well, and even more behave as the competitive model suggests. In these markets, prices and profits are always under the threat of expanded supplies brought to market by existing or new producers. Insight into the workings of a particularly interesting competitive market may be gleaned from a look at the electronic calculator market, especially the market for the small pocket calculators.[5]

Electronic calculators consist of a very few components. Their driving force is a set of electronic circuits that are designed to handle specific addition, subtraction, division, and multiplication problems; these circuits are the calculator's "brain." The circuits themselves—referred to as MOS/LSI (or metal oxide semiconductor/large-scale integrated) circuits—take the place of thousands of transistors and are etched onto tiny chips of silicon only one-quarter-inch square and 8/1,000ths-inch thick. The MOS/LSI chips were developed in the course of missile guidance system research and are in common use as the "brains" for Touch-Tone telephones, home computers, video games, and other electronic products.

To signal the electronic brain of a calculator to go to work, all one has to do is press the appropriate keys on the keyboard. Once the problem is entered through the keyboard, the electric impulses go through their programmed motions and flash an answer on the viewing screen. The whole operation is driven by electricity, usually supplied by a rechargeable battery, and takes but a fraction of a second. The only components required other than the chips, keyboard, viewing screen, and battery are a baseboard to hold the pieces together and an exterior shell.

Given the small number and basic simplicity of calculator parts, it is fairly easy to get into the calculator industry. Indeed, quite a few of today's firms got started in their owners' garages. Thus we may characterize the industry as having *minimal barriers to entry*, because anyone with a little capital, a place to work, and a very modest knowledge of electronic circuitry can set up shop.

The initial conditions

The electronic calculator industry really got started in March 1969, when a Japanese electronics corporation, Sharp, introduced the Sharp "Micro-Compet QT-8D," the first commercial calculator to use advanced electronic circuitry. The retail price of the Micro-

---

[4] In some of these markets, the independent producers may try to exercise market power by forming some form of producer association that can influence market supplies (e.g., the dairy associations); more on this subject in Chapter 24.
[5] The following description of the U.S. calculator market is based on articles in *Barron's, Electronic News, Business Week, Consumer Reports,* and *Popular Science,* on confidential industry reports prepared by investment advisory services, and on annual reports of calculator companies; all figures are approximations. The calculator market was not perfectly competitive in the 1970s, but it did exhibit all of the tendencies described here.

equilibrium price: The price at which the quantity of a good demanded in a given time period equals the quantity supplied.

Compet was $395. Within a very brief time, other companies—primarily Japanese firms, such as Ricoh, Canon, and Casio—introduced similar machines, and the price of calculators fell while the size of the market expanded. By the beginning of 1972, the standard pocket calculator was selling for $200 and industry sales were around 17,000 a month (or 200,000 a year).

Figure 21.2 depicts the initial (1972) equilibrium in the calculator market and the approximate costs of production for the typical calculator manufacturer at that time. Note that the market *demand* curve (Figure 21.2a) slopes downward just as the law of demand requires. Note also that the market *supply* curve intersects the demand curve at a price of $200, which thereby becomes the market **equilibrium price.** That same intersection tells us that 17,000 calculators a month will be bought and sold at that price.

Individual producers never see these market curves, of course. All they see are their own cost curves and the price at which calculators are selling. That price ($200) has been determined by market forces.

FIGURE 21.2 INITIAL EQUILIBRIUM IN THE CALCULATOR MARKET

In 1972, the market price of calculators was $200. This price was established by the intersection of the market supply and demand curves as shown in part a. Each competitive producer in the market sought to produce calculators at that rate (800 per month) where marginal cost equaled price (point C in part b). Profit per calculator was equal to price (point C) minus average total cost (point D). Total profits for the typical firm are indicated by the shaded rectangle.

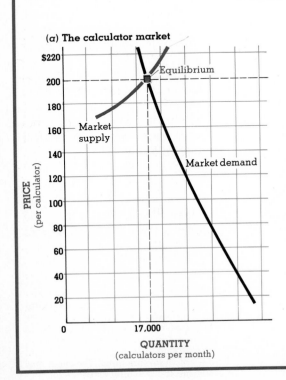

(a) The calculator market

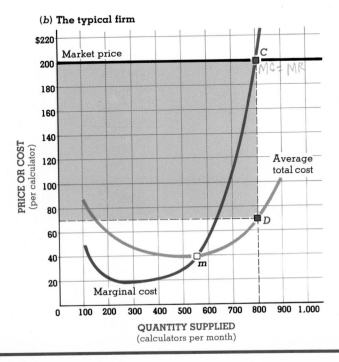

(b) The typical firm

The production decision

production decision: The selection of the short-run rate of output (with existing plant and equipment).

marginal cost: The increase in total cost associated with a one-unit increase in production.

Profit calculations

average total cost: Total cost divided by the quantity produced in a given time period.

What the individual firm must do in the short run is choose the rate of output that maximizes profits. In the long run, a producer can decide to enter or leave the calculator industry, or alter the firm's scale of operation. In this analysis, however, we shall assume that affirmative investment decisions have been made, and we shall focus on the **production decision.** In this short-run context, each firm seeks the rate of output at which marginal cost equals marginal revenue. For the competitive firm, this means finding the point at which marginal cost equals price.

Figure 21.2b illustrates the cost and price (marginal revenue) curves the typical calculator producer confronted in 1972. As in most lines of production, the marginal costs of calculator production tend to rise with the rate of output, as reflected in the rising MC curve. Marginal costs rose in part because output could be increased in the short run (with existing plant and equipment) only by crowding additional workers onto the assembly line. As each worker got less capital and land to work with, marginal physical product fell. The law of diminishing returns thus pushed marginal costs up. Moreover, additional labor could be obtained only by paying overtime wages, and even the price of integrated circuits and other materials tended to rise as increased quantities were ordered.

For all of these reasons, marginal costs rose quite sharply, intersecting the price line at an output level of 800 calculators per month (point C in Figure 21.2b).[6] That rate of output was the most profitable (MC = p), of course, and was chosen by the typical manufacturer. Were the producer to manufacture any more calculators, the excess of **marginal costs** over price beyond the output level of 800 per month would reduce earlier profits. To manufacture less would be to pass up an opportunity to make another buck.

To figure out how much *profit* a typical calculator manufacturer was making at the output rate of 800 per month, we need to look at something besides marginal cost and price. Profits are, of course, the difference between total revenues and total costs (including the cost of the owner's time and an "average" return on investment). We can calculate those profits quickly (even more quickly if we use a pocket calculator!) by looking at Table 21.1. As the profit column indicates, the calculating calculator manufacturer makes a real killing in the calculator market, reaping a monthly profit of $104,680 by producing and selling 800 calculators.

We could also calculate the calculator manufacturer's profits by asking how much he makes on *each* calculator and multiplying that figure by his total output. Clearly, the average profit per calculator times the number of calculators sold must be equal to total profits. We can compute these profits by studying the first and last columns of Table 21.1 or by using a little geometry on Figure 21.2b. In the figure, average costs (total costs divided by the rate of output) are portrayed by the **average total cost** (ATC) curve. At the output rate of

---

[6] The marginal cost curves depicted here rise more steeply than they did in reality; but the general shape of the curves is our primary concern at this point.

TABLE 21.1 CALCULATOR REVENUES, COSTS, AND PROFITS

The competitive producer seeks to produce at that rate of output where total profit is maximized. This table illustrates the alternatives the typical calculator producer faced in 1972. The profit-maximizing rate of output occurred at 800 calculators per month. At that rate of output, marginal cost was equal to price ($200) and profits were $104,680 per month.

Output per month	Price	Total revenue	Total cost	Profit	Marginal revenue*	Marginal cost*	Average cost	Profit per unit (price minus average cost)
0	—	—	$ 2,000	−$ 2,000	—	—	—	—
100	$200	$ 20,000	8,661	11,335	$200	$ 66.65	$86.65	$113.35
200	200	40,000	10,330	29,670	200	16.65	51.65	148.35
300	200	60,000	12,330	47,670	200	20.00	41.10	158.90
400	200	80,000	15,330	64,670	200	30.00	38.33	161.67
500	200	100,000	18,660	81,340	200	33.30	37.32	162.68
600	200	120,000	23,991	96,009	200	53.31	39.99	160.01
700	200	140,000	35,320	104,680	200	113.29	50.46	149.54
800	200	160,000	55,320	104,680	200	200.00	69.15	130.85
900	200	180,000	85,000	95,000	200	296.80	94.44	105.56

*Note that output levels are calibrated in hundreds in this example; therefore, we have divided the *change* in total costs and revenues from one output level to another by 100 to calculate marginal revenue and marginal cost. Very few manufacturers deal in units of one. The additional revenue associated with a multiple-unit increase in sales is often called "incremental revenue" to distinguish it from the *marginal* revenue generated by *one* additional sale; we ignore this distinction here.

profit per unit: Total profit divided by the quantity produced in a given time period; price minus average total cost.

800 (the row in color in Table 21.1), the distance between the price line ($200 at point C) and the *ATC* curve ($69.15 at point D) is $130.85. This represents the average **profit per unit.** Multiplying this figure by the number of units sold (800 per month) gives us *total* profit per month. Total profits are represented by the shaded rectangle in Figure 21.2b and are equal, of course, to our earlier profit figure of $104,680.

While gaping at the calculator manufacturer's enormous profits, we should note two things about the average cost curve. First is its familiar shape. Note that average costs first decline, then bottom out and rise, giving the curve a distinct U shape. The tendency of average costs to fall initially as output is expanded can be attributed to two phenomena: (1) the spreading out of fixed costs over an increasingly large number of calculators,[7] and (2) the tendency for marginal costs to be lower than average costs at low rates of output. At some point, however, marginal costs begin to exceed average costs and exert an upward pull on the *ATC* curve. Thus beyond point m, the minimum average cost point, the higher marginal costs begin to raise average costs. There is nothing very tricky about these relationships; they only reflect a little arithmetic.

A more interesting observation about the *ATC* curve depicted in

[7] That is, the tendency for $2,000/x to get smaller as x gets larger. (As Table 21.1 confirms, $2,000 is the *fixed cost* of calculator production, as that much expense is incurred even when output is zero. In this case, fixed costs are the costs of rent, utilities, and equipment leases.

Figure 21.2b is the fact that the calculator's maximum profits are not attained at the point where average costs are at a minimum (point m). On the contrary, the most profitable rate of output is considerably to the right of point m. In general, we may observe that *a profit-maximizing producer seeks to maximize total profits, and this is not necessarily or even very frequently the same thing as maximizing profits per unit.* As we observed long ago, it's better to make a nickel on each of 300 ice cream cones than to make 50 cents a cone and sell only four.

The lure of profits

We could discuss the calculator manufacturer's profits at length, but we should not lose sight of the fundamental fact that they are enormous. Indeed, the more quick-witted among us will already have seen and heard enough to know they've discovered a good thing. And in fact, the kind of profits attained by the early calculator manufacturers attracted a lot of entrepreneurial interest. Within a very short time, a whole crowd of profit maximizers entered the calculator industry in hot pursuit of its fabulous profits. As we observed earlier, there were no significant barriers to entry into that industry and thus no mechanism for preventing others from elbowing in to share the spoils.

A SHIFT OF MARKET SUPPLY   Figure 21.3 shows what happened to the calculator market and the profits of the typical firm once the word got out. As more and more entrepreneurs heard how profitable calculator manufacturing could be, they grabbed a book on electronic circuitry, rushed to the bank, got a little financing, and set up shop. Before many months had passed, the supply of pocket calculators was much larger, as reflected in a **shift of** the **supply** curve from S_1 to S_2 (Figure 21.3a). Almost as fast as a calculator can compute a profit (loss) statement, the willingness to supply increased abruptly.

shift of supply: A change in the quantity supplied at any (every) given price.

The new calculator enthusiasts were in for a bit of disappointment, however, as Figure 21.3b suggests. With so many new firms hawking calculators, it became increasingly difficult to make a fast buck. The downward-sloping market demand curve confirms that a greater quantity of calculators could be sold only if the price of calculators dropped. And drop it did. The price slide began as calculator manufacturers found their inventories growing and so offered price discounts to maintain sales volume. The price fell rapidly in 1972 from $200 to $113.

The lower market price changed the profit picture and production decisions for the typical firm. The sliding market price squeezed the profits of each firm, causing the profit rectangle to shrink (compare Figure 21.2b to Figure 21.3b). Although the typical firm's cost structure hadn't changed, its sales opportunities had been drastically reduced. It now found that marginal cost was equal to marginal revenue (the new price) at an output of 700 calculators per month. As Table 21.1 confirms, the typical firm could produce 700 calculators a month at a marginal cost of $113.29 and an average cost of $50.46. Unfortunately, the prices, revenues, and profits depicted in Table 21.1 no longer applied at the end of 1972, owing to the

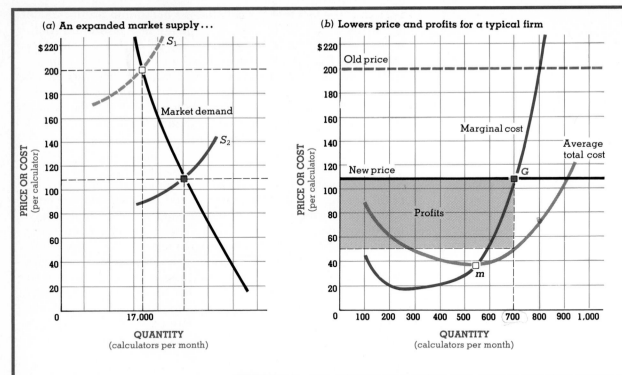

FIGURE 21.3   THE COMPETITIVE PRICE AND PROFIT SQUEEZE UNDER WAY

The availability of substantial economic profits in the calculator industry
encouraged new firms to enter the industry. As they did so, the market supply
curve in part *a* shifted from S_1 to S_2. This rightward shift of the supply curve
lowered the equilibrium price of calculators. The lower price, in turn, forced
the typical producer to cut back the rate of output to the point where *MC* and
price were equal again (point *G* in part *b*). At this reduced rate of output, the
typical firm earned less total profit than it had earned before.

changed market situation. At that time, the typical firm could earn
only $43,778 a month (700 × [price of $113 − average total cost of
$50.46]); not a paltry sum, to be sure, but nothing like the fantastic
fortunes pocketed earlier.

As long as an economic profit is available it will continue to
attract would-be suppliers. Those entrepreneurs who were a little
slow to digest the implications of Figure 21.2 eventually perceived
what was going on and tried to get in on the action, too. Even though
they were a little late, they did not wish to bypass the opportunity to
make the $43,778 in monthly profits still available to the typical
firm. Hence the market supply curve continued to shift and calculator prices slid further, as in Figure 21.4. This process squeezed the
profits of the typical firm still more, further shrinking the profit rectangle.

The competitive pressure on market supplies, prices, and profits
will continue as long as the rate of profit obtainable in calculator
production is higher than that available in other industries. Profit-
maximizing entrepreneurs have a special place in their hearts not for

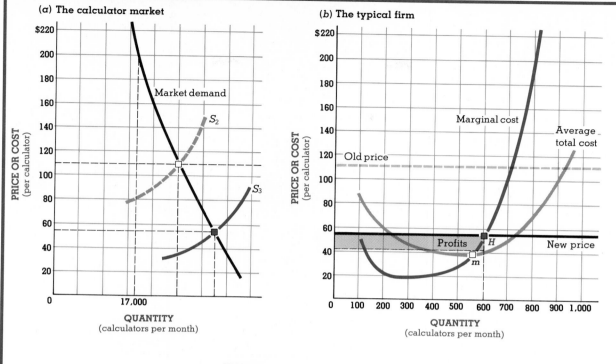

FIGURE 21.4 THE COMPETITIVE SQUEEZE APPROACHING ITS LIMIT

Further shifts of market supply drove down price and profits. Even at a price of $113 per calculator, economic profit was available in the calculator industry. Such profit attracted still more entrepreneurs, shifting the market supply curve further (S_3). The resultant equilibrium occurred at a price of $53 per calculator. At this reduced price, the typical manufacturer wanted to supply only 600 calculators per month (point H in part b). Total profits were much less than they had been earlier, with fewer producers and higher prices.

Electric calculators contain very few parts and are easily assembled. Hence, entry into the industry is fairly easy.

Courtesy of Commodore International, Inc.

calculators but for the economic profit they can produce. When that profit looks no better than the profit obtainable elsewhere, calculator manufacturers may move on to other ventures, and would-be suppliers will lose their fervor. The absolute *limit* to the price and profit decline will occur when the price of calculators is equal to the *minimum* average cost of production (point m), at which point there is no longer any economic profit to be squeezed. Further profit (and price competition) will then occur only if market demand shifts outward or technological progress reduces the cost of calculator production. In fact, both of these things happened in the calculator market.

THE COST BREAKTHROUGH

As profit margins narrowed to the levels shown in Figure 21.4, quick-thinking entrepreneurs realized that future profits would have to come from cost reductions rather than from expanded sales. With

Calculator Makers Add Features and Cut Prices to Find a Niche in a Crowded Market

Casio Inc. sells an electronic pocket calculator that lets its owner conduct boxing matches between calculations. Canon Inc.'s U.S. unit plans to sell a calculator next year for $7.95, its lowest price ever. And today, Hewlett-Packard Co. plans to introduce new products it claims will turn its top calculators into powerful hand-held computers.

These products indicate a few of the ways calculator makers are moving these days to develop niches for their products in a domestic market that is now, or soon will be, saturated. "Everyone owns a calculator," says Bonnie Digruis, an electronics industry analyst for Creative Strategies International, a research concern in San Jose.

At the high-priced end of the market, companies are looking toward—or already producing—products that can compete in the newly formed hand-held computer market, born within the past two years when Tandy Corp., Casio Inc. and others introduced their pocket computers. At the low, or consumer, end, dominated by Japanese producers like Casio, Sharp Corp., and Canon, calculator makers are fighting to produce ever more clever gimmicks and specialties to meet the demands of customers buying replacement calculators. . . .

At the lower end of the calculator market, the big Japanese producers are aiming gimmicks and games at customers who have lost or worn out their old four-function calculators, the so-called replacement market. Casio, for example, is producing and further developing solar calculators that can run by candlelight. It also plans to introduce its MG-777, a calculator with several games including an electronic cube puzzle. "We're probably going to be the Atari of the calculator industry," says Mr. Gordon.

Fit in Shirt Pocket

Canon is trying to get more of the market by driving prices lower still. It was "very successful" at selling one of its calculators for $9.50 in drug stores and other general merchandise outlets, so the company decided to lower the prices once again to $7.95 for its LX-30, says Mitsuru Tamai, vice president, calculator and systems division. It and Casio also are offering low-cost printer calculators that can fit in a shirt pocket. . . .

—Eric Larson and
Brenton R. Schlender

prices continually sliding, the only way to make an extra buck would be to push the cost curve down. A few companies pursued such possibilities and sent costs and calculator prices down to previously unheard-of levels. Indeed, all the way down to $6.95 (which is a long way down from $395 in only a few years' time).

As we noted earlier, an electronic calculator has very few parts, the most important of which are the MOS/LSI chips that function as its brain. The basic determinant of calculator manufacturing costs is the number of chips required to make the calculator work. Fewer chips not only mean a reduction in direct materials costs, but, more important, significantly reduce the amount of labor required for calculator assembly. Indeed, when a lot of chips are required, the labor costs associated with the assembly process dominate cost structures. During the early phases of the calculator boom, it was most economical to buy chips in the United States, send them to Japan for assembly, then reimport them as part of a finished calculator. The method in this madness was the availability of cheap labor in Japan.[8] Thus such firms as Canon, Sharp, Casio, and Commodore were major marketers of pocket calculators in the price range of $80–$160.

What changed the relative position of foreign and domestic manufacturers and brought about another steep decline in calculator prices was the introduction of more sophisticated chips in 1972. Texas Instruments and a few other companies learned how to

---

[8] Labor is cheaper in Japan than in the United States only if it produces more output per dollar of wages—that is, if it is more cost-*efficient*. Wage comparisons alone convey no information. In the calculator case, the conditions for greater cost efficiency were met. Cost efficiency is discussed in Chapter 26.

miniaturize the chips even further, packaging more functions and circuits in a single chip. This meant that a standard four-function (addition, subtraction, multiplication, and division) calculator could be produced with only one chip, rather than the four or five that had been customary up to that time. This technological breakthrough had dramatic effects on production costs. As the cost of materials for the calculator's "brain" dropped, the amount of labor time required for basic assembly fell from four hours to less than one hour. The size of the calculators shrank, too; some recent models fit into wristwatches.

Further supply shifts

The impact of the miniaturized chips on calculator production costs and profits is illustrated in Figure 21.5, which takes over where Figure 21.4 left off. Recall that the market price of calculators had been driven down to $53 by the beginning of 1972. At this price, the typical firm maximized profits by producing 600 calculators per month, as determined by the intersection of the prevailing *MR* and *MC* curves (point *H* in Figure 21.5).

Technological improvements are illustrated by a downward shift of the ATC and MC curves. Notice, for example, that the new technology permits 600 calculators to be produced for a *lower* marginal cost (about $35) than previously (point *H*).

The lower cost structure increases the profitability of calculator production and stimulates a further increase in production. Note in particular that the new *MC* curve intersects the price ($53) line at an output of 700 calculators per month (point *N*). By contrast, the old, higher *MC* curve dictated a production rate of only 600 calculators per month for the typical firm (point *H*) at that price.

While many Japanese firms saw the desirability of expanding

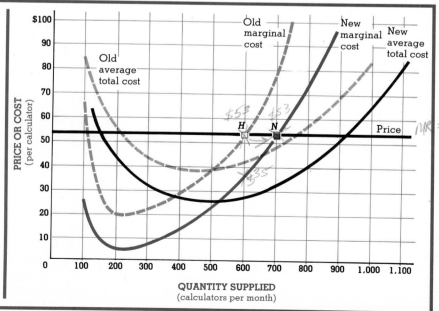

FIGURE 21.5 A DOWNWARD SHIFT OF COSTS IMPROVES PROFITS AND STIMULATES OUTPUT

The quest for profits encouraged producers to discover cheaper ways to manufacture calculators. The resultant improvements lowered costs and encouraged further increases in the rate of output. The typical calculator producer increased output from point *H* to point *N*.

Technology, Competition Cut Price of Electronics Gear as Quality Rises

NEW YORK—Five years ago, a cumbersome Technics tape cassette deck cost about $350. A "needle," now old-fashioned, metered recording levels. The deck required finger pressure to rewind and advance the recording tape. The 50-watt receiver that went with the deck had manual radio control and so-so high fidelity at a cost of $500.

Today, the comparable Technics tape deck is quiet and streamlined with soft-touch controls. A fluorescent light warns of distortions in recording. A dbx device eliminates electronic background "noise." The deck costs just about what it cost five years ago. The receiver costs even less, about $350, although it comes with a new, superaccurate digital tuning mechanism.

Other manufacturers tell the same story: Prices have fallen on just about every product in the world of electronic sound and sight, while quality has increased. "Electronics is the only product group in existence that has undergone reverse inflation," says Richard Ekstract, editor of Consumer Electronics, a monthly trade publication. Says Ray Boggs, head of consumer electronics research at Venture Development Corp.: "If General Motors built cars the way Pioneer builds stereos, you'd have a $200 car and get 1,900 miles to the gallon."

Technological advances have made possible the low-cost production of high-quality electronics gear, but competition has translated those advances into low retail prices. It's fairly easy to get into electronics retailing; manufacturers often help finance newcomers, usually by carrying inventories for retailers who stock only floor samples.

But if the competition makes things nice for shoppers, it's tough on the retailers. Twice as many electronics retailers fold as other retailers, Mr. Boggs says. "Today," he says, "retailers have to compete with the guy who opens on 42nd Street,"—a commercial New York City thoroughfare—"sells for $10 over cost, and then goes bankrupt." Mr. Ekstract says, "There's so much competition to get into the one business where there are a million new products a year that people are willing to sell under the table and steal the sales tax."

Initial High Price Sought

Price-cutting extends to the top of the line in electronics. The manufacturer's "suggested," or retail list, price has become meaningless in most places, even in department stores and at old-line dealerships. . . .

If the product does sell at its initial high prices, the maker recovers some of his research and development costs and can afford to produce in quantity at lower unit costs. Competitors meanwhile also rush to the market. "Whatever we make, once it is on the market, someone can duplicate it at a lower price," Mr. Martin says. "In order to stay ahead, the next time you are able to change models, you have to introduce a more innovative product, or find a way to produce the same thing at a lower price."

The process is expected to occur again next year in the case of digital audio disk players. A number of manufacturers plan to introduce such players, which use a laser to detect audio signals on a palm-size high-fidelity disk, in 1982. The players are expected to go on the market at $2,000 or so. But people in the business think the price could fall to half that in a short time.

—Laura Landro

production, many domestic entrepreneurs perceived that the simplicity of the chips assembly more than offset higher domestic labor costs. The great rush into calculator production was on again.

The market implications of another entrepreneurial stampede should now be obvious. As more and more firms tried to get in on the action, the market supply curve again shifted to the right, and calculator prices slid further down the market demand curve. This shift diminished the profitability of calculator production, squeezing the profit rectangle once again. As prices dropped below $40, foreign manufacturers found that the transportation costs of supplying a market over 6,000 miles away were cutting profits to a minimum. Domestic producers acquired a clear advantage. Indeed, a few, such as Commodore Business Machines, abandoned foreign assembly plants and concentrated production in the United States. At the same time, a whole new crop of companies entered the market: Olympus, Corvus, Columbia, Craig, Bowmar, Eldorado, Master, Rapid Data Systems, and many more. Calculator prices ventured into the under-$30 range, and unit sales reached over 6 million in 1973–74. Those firms that didn't keep up a fast technological pace

SHORT-RUN VS. LONG-RUN EQUILIBRIUM

short-run competitive equilibrium: $p = MC$.

Profit-maximizing competitive firms always strive for the rate of output at which marginal cost (MC) equals price (p). When they achieve that rate of output, they are in **short-run equilibrium,** in the sense that they have no incentive to alter the rate of output produced with existing (fixed) plant and equipment.

But if the short-run equilibrium is profitable (price [p] greater than average total cost [ATC]), existing firms will want to acquire additional plant and equipment, and other firms will want to enter the industry. As they do so, market price will fall until it reaches the level of minimum average total costs, and profits are eliminated. In this **long-run equilibrium,** there is no further incentive to enter the industry or increase the scale of production until technology or market demand improve.

long-run competitive equilibrium: $p = MC = $ minimum ATC.

Hence, in both the short and long run, a competitive industry's marginal cost pricing ($p = MC$) generates reliable signals to consumers about the opportunity cost of producing specific goods and services. In the long run, as profits are driven to a minimum, competitive industries also ensure that goods will be produced for the least opportunity cost (minimum $p = MC = $ minimum ATC).

soon found that their average costs were higher than the market price, and had to cease production. But cost reductions continued, as other profit-hungry firms sought to keep ahead of a rapidly expanding market. By 1982, annual world production of pocket calculators exceeded 20 *million* machines and the price of a basic four-function calculator fell below $7. Those figures can be compared to the 1972 situation, in which a standard calculator cost close to $200, and fewer than 200,000 were sold.[9]

REFLECTIONS ON THE COMPETITIVE PROCESS

That consumers reaped substantial benefit from competition in the calculator market is by now evident. A lot of consumers have found that pocket calculators make life a little easier, especially when it comes time to balance the checkbook, do lengthy problem sets, or figure out how much they owe Uncle Sam in income taxes. Perhaps it is true that an abundance of inexpensive calculators would have been produced in other market (or nonmarket) situations as well. But we cannot ignore the fact that competitive market pressures were a driving force in the developments we have reviewed.

The relentless profit squeeze

The unrelenting squeeze on prices and profits which we have observed in the calculator market is a fundamental characteristic of the competitive process. Indeed, the **market mechanism** works best

market mechanism: The use of market prices and sales to signal desired outputs (or resource allocations).

[9] The dramatic drop in calculator prices was due not only to technological breakthroughs, but also to the increased efficiency of calculator companies. As output increased, firms gained experience and learned how to reduce production costs. This phenomenon of "learning by doing" is common in many industries (see Chapter 22).

We've come a long way Baby

To maintain high profits in the calculator industry, firms must continually lower production costs. A series of technological breakthroughs reduced the size and cost of calculators dramatically in only a few years.

Source: Courtesy of *Washingtonian* and Leon Office Machines.

under such circumstances. The existence of economic profits is an indication that consumers place a high value on a particular product and are willing to pay a comparatively high price to get it. The high price and profits signal this information to profit-hungry entrepreneurs, who eagerly come forward to satisfy consumer demands. Thus **high profits in a particular industry indicate that consumers want a different mix of output** (more of that industry's goods). The competitive squeeze on those same profits indicates that resources are being reallocated to produce that desired mix. In a competitive market, consumers get more of the goods they desire, and at a lower price.

When the competitive pressure on prices is carried to the limit, the products in question are also produced at the least possible cost, another dimension of economic efficiency. This was illustrated by the tendency of calculator prices to be driven down to the level of minimum average costs. In this sense, society is getting the most it can from its available (scarce) resources.

Thus society in general benefits from competition in product markets, and the producers who participate in the competitive process come out well, too. At the limit, of course, all economic profit is eliminated. But the limit is rarely if ever reached, because new products are continually being introduced, consumer demands change, and more efficient production processes are discovered. In fact, the competitive process creates strong pressures to pursue product and technological innovation. In a competitive market, the adage about the early bird getting the worm is particularly apt. As we observed in the calculator market, the first ones to perceive and respond to the potential profitability of calculator production were the ones who made the greatest profits. Latecomers did well but never so well as the early entrants. Hence the pressure of competition stimulates a high degree of production responsiveness and a relatively rapid pace of innovation.[10]

[10] The incentives of larger, less competitive firms to pursue or suppress product innovation are discussed in Chapter 22.

Apple's morning after: Lots of competition

Apple Computer Inc.'s $96.8 million initial public offering on Dec. 12 added another chapter to the company's textbook success story. In just four years, the Cupertino (Calif.) concern has evolved from a garage workshop to a leading force in the fast-moving market for personal computers, with annual sales topping $100 million. But as the fanfare of the public offering recedes, Apple faces an onslaught of new high-powered competitors.

Within the next year as many as a dozen large companies are expected to join the battle, offering personal computers costing less than $10,000. International Business Machines, Xerox, and Digital Equipment are all working on personal computers in their laboratories, and each is opening a string of company-owned retail stores as a possible means of distribution. . . . Meanwhile, at least eight Japanese companies—including Nippon Electric, Casio, and Sharp—have introduced personal computers. And some are preparing to come to the U.S. market. "Looking out a few years, the competition will be very rough," notes George P. Elling, industry analyst at Bear, Stearns & Co.

Taking aim

Many of the newcomers are aiming to eat away at Apple's business. At Xerox Corp., in fact, members of the personal computer development team refer to their machine as "the worm." Other manufacturers are elbowing in on Apple's distribution network. Just a week before the Apple offering, Commodore International Ltd., a key Apple competitor, signed a deal with ComputerLand Corp., the independent chain of retail computer stores that sells 15% of all Apple computers.

The sequence of events common to a competitive market situation includes:

- High prices and profits signal consumers' demand for more output.
- Economic profit attracts new suppliers.
- The market supply curve shifts to the right.
- Prices slide down the demand curve.
- A new equilibrium is reached at which increased quantities of the desired product are produced and its price is lower. Average costs of production are at or near a minimum, much more of the product is supplied and consumed, and economic profit approaches zero.
- Throughout the process producers experience great pressure to keep ahead of the profit squeeze by reducing costs, a pressure that frequently results in product and technological innovation.

What is essential to note about the competitive process is that the potential threat of other firms' expanding production or new firms' entering the marketplace keeps existing firms on their toes. In seeking to keep ahead of the game, competitive firms collectively move closer to society's goals, producing the level and mix of output consumers desire with the most efficient combination of resources. In this sense, a market composed of hundreds or even thousands of individually powerless firms is capable of maximizing consumer welfare.

Competitive efficiency

Two specific dimensions of competitive efficiency are worthy of note. First, because competitive pressures continue to squeeze profit margins, the price of a competitively produced good is driven down to its minimum average cost of production. This result can be interpreted in two ways. On the one hand, it means that society is devoting the minimal amount of resources necessary to produce that good. On the other hand, it also means that society is able to get the greatest quantity of goods from a given amount of productive resources. Although these two implications are equivalent, the latter formulation relates directly to the production-possibilities curve we first encountered in Chapter 1. As we observed then, there is a limit to our **production possibilities**—the amount of output we can produce in any time period. That limit is determined by the amount of resources at our disposal and our knowledge of how to use them. This limit is reflected in the production-possibilities curve, which depicts the quantity of various goods and services we are capable of producing.

production possibilities: The alternative combinations of final goods and services that could be produced in a given time period with all available resources and technology.

efficiency: Maximum output of a good from the resources used in production.

It is important to emphasize here that competitive pressures tend to stimulate maximum economic **efficiency.** *Production is pushed to the point of minimum average cost*—thus moving us *closer* to our production possibilities. Moreover, to the extent that competitive forces stimulate new technology, they also serve to *expand* our production possibilities, shifting the production-possibilities curve outward. These phenomena are illustrated in Figure 21.6.

FIGURE 21.6 THE IMPACT OF COMPETITION ON GNP

Competitive market forces tend to bring us closer to the existing production-possibilities curve and may even shift it outward. In the calculator illustration, competitive forces tended to improve technology and expand output, moving us from point A to point B. This increased the level of GNP while changing its composition.

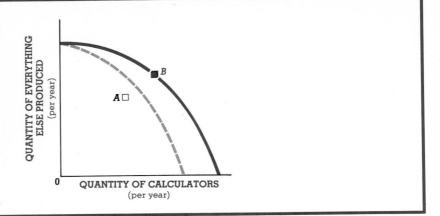

opportunity cost: The most desired goods or services that are forgone in order to obtain something else.

MARGINAL COST PRICING   The second dimension of competitive efficiency relates to the mix of output we produce rather than the specific level. A basic economic question we must collectively answer is WHAT goods to produce—specifically, how much of one and how much of another. In making such choices, we know that the production of one good must be cut back if we are to get more of another good, at least as long as we are operating on or near the production-possibilities curve. The goods given up are, of course, the **opportunity cost** of getting what we want. We can restate this problem by saying that society must choose some point on the production-possibilities curve. That point represents the desired mix of output.

It would be to our advantage, of course, to know what we have to give up in order to get more of a particular product. Such vital information is a prerequisite to rational choice. In economic terms, what we give up to get more of a particular good is the best alternative use of the resources used in that good's production. The labor and materials used up in the production of calculators cannot be used to produce harmonicas. Accordingly, rational choices about the mix of output require that we know how many resources are required to get one more calculator (or anything else). The amount of resources used to produce one more calculator is its marginal cost. Thus rational decision-making requires that we be able to choose among alternative goods and services on the basis of our desires and each good's marginal cost.

The beautiful thing about a competitive market is that it provides us with the necessary information on which to make such choices. Why? Because competitive firms offer their goods for sale at the level of marginal costs. That is, they always strive to produce at the rate of output at which price equals marginal cost. Hence the price signal the consumer gets in the marketplace is an accurate and reliable basis for making choices about the mix of output and attendant allocation of resources. In this sense, the **marginal cost pricing** characteristic of competitive markets permits society to fulfill its economic goals. The amount consumers are willing to pay for a good (its price) equals its opportunity cost (marginal cost).

marginal cost pricing: The offer (supply) of goods at prices equal to their marginal cost.

MR   =   MC

POLICY IMPLICATIONS: COMPETITIVE MARKET EFFICIENCY

In Chapter 2 we noted that there is a comparatively strong case to be made for the market mechanism. In particular, we observed that the market mechanism permits individual consumers and producers to express their views about WHAT to produce, HOW to produce, and FOR WHOM to produce by "voting" for particular goods and services by way of market purchases and sales. If a great many people want and are willing to pay for a particular good, the market mechanism will assist in bringing about more of the desired production. If little of a particular good or service is desired, the market mechanism will signal this fact to producers and stimulate a reallocation of the economy's resources in another direction.

We also observed, however, that there are several important qualifications to this laissez faire view of the world. The appropriateness or fairness of consumer "voting" patterns depends on how equitably voting power is distributed. If some consumers have little opportunity to acquire income or wealth, they will be unable to participate fully in the collective decision making in resource and product markets. We also noted that some goods and services cannot be peddled efficiently in the market because their consumption cannot be confined to those who pay for them. These *public goods* are an important exception to laissez faire economics. Finally, we have observed that the concept of public goods applies more generally to externalities—benefits or harm that cannot be communicated efficiently through the marketplace.

In view of these three major qualifications to market efficiency, the argument for a completely laissez faire policy must be met with some skepticism. Nevertheless, we cannot disregard the fact that the market mechanism is an efficient tool for communicating and fulfilling society's wishes when the three qualifications we have noted are compensated for. In this regard, it is particularly important to note that markets tend to be most efficient when competitive forces are at work. As we observed in the calculator illustration, competitive firms and industries tend to respond quickly and efficiently to consumer desires. In this sense, competitive markets do best what markets are supposed to do, and it is in society's interest to maintain competitive market structures. In the following chapters we shall look more closely at our successes and failures in this regard.

SUMMARY

- A firm that has market power can alter the market price of the goods it sells. A monopoly, for example, as the only supplier of a particular good, can raise the market price of that good by reducing the total quantity supplied. In contrast, a competitive firm, one without any market power, has no visible effect on total market supply, and therefore no effect on market price.

- The difference between competitive (powerless) firms and non-competitive (powerful) firms is reflected in the distinction between the market demand curve and the demand curve facing an individual firm. If a firm is very small in relation to the size of the market, it can produce up to its capacity without altering the market price of the good it sells. In this sense, the perfectly competitive firm confronts a horizontal demand curve for its own output even though the relevant market demand curve is negatively sloped.

■ The competitive firm translates the basic profit-maximization rule about equating marginal revenue and marginal cost into the simpler rule of equating marginal cost and price. This translation is made possible by the fact that marginal revenue is identical to price for the perfectly competitive (powerless) firm.

■ When economic (above-normal) profit is available in a competitive industry, new firms will enter the market. The resulting shift of supply will drive down market prices in accordance with the downward slope of the market demand curve. As prices fall, the profit of the industry and its constituent firms will be squeezed.

■ The limit to the competitive price and profit squeeze is reached when price is driven down to the level of minimum average cost. At this point (long-run equilibrium) additional output and profit will be attained only if technology is improved (lowering costs) or if demand increases.

■ The most distinctive thing about competitive markets is the persistent pressure they exert on prices and profits. The threat of competition tends to act as a tremendous incentive for producers to respond quickly to consumer demands and to seek more efficient means of production. In this sense, competitive markets do best what markets are supposed to do—efficiently allocate resources.

Terms to remember

Define the following terms:

market power	average total cost
market supply	profit per unit
competitive firm	shift of supply
perfectly competitive market	short-run competitive equilibrium
monopoly	long-run competitive equilibrium
economic profit	market mechanism
barriers to entry	production possibilities
equilibrium price	efficiency
production decision	opportunity cost
marginal cost	marginal cost pricing

Questions for discussion

1. Why would anyone want to enter a profitable industry knowing that profits would eventually be eliminated by competition?

2. Why wouldn't producers necessarily want to produce output at the least average cost? Under what conditions would they end up doing so?

3. If profit-maximizing producers do not generally seek to produce their output at the level where average costs are at a minimum, what sense can be made of the typical plant manager's instructions to "reduce costs to a minimum"?

4. What industries do you regard as being highly competitive? Can you identify any barriers to entry in those industries?

Problem | Suppose that the market demand schedule for frisbees is:

Price	$8	$7	$6	$5	$4	$3	$2	$1
Quantity demanded (per month)	1,000	2,000	4,000	8,000	16,000	32,000	64,000	150,000

Suppose further that the marginal and average costs of frisbee production for every competitive firm are:

Rate of output (per month)	100	200	300	400	500	600
Marginal cost	$2.00	$3.00	$4.00	$5.00	$6.00	$7.00
Average cost	2.00	2.50	3.00	3.50	4.00	4.50

Finally, assume that the equilibrium market price is $6 per frisbee.

(a) Draw the cost curves of the typical firm and identify its profit-maximizing rate of output and its total profits.

(b) Draw the market demand curve and identify market equilibrium.

(c) How many (identical) firms are initially producing frisbees?

(d) In view of the profits being made, more firms will want to get into frisbee production. In the long run, these new firms will shift the market supply curve to the right and price down to average total cost, thereby eliminating profits. At what equilibrium price are all profits eliminated? How many firms will be producing frisbees at this price?

THE FARM PROBLEM

Competition in agriculture

In 1980, 1981, and again in 1982 the net income of U.S. farmers fell to near-Depression levels. The real income of U.S. farmers in 1982 was only a third of what it had been in 1973—and only a couple of billion dollars higher than the level of 1933. Thousands of farmers were forced to sell their farms and machinery; still more were forced to deplete their savings and go deeply into debt.

This mini-depression in the early 1980s was symptomatic of recurring farm problems. Farmers have to contend with intense competition, abrupt changes in weather, low price elasticity of demand, and sudden shifts in both demand and supply. As a consequence, the agricultural industry is prone to recurring "booms" and "busts." In this appendix, we shall look more closely at these forces that make farm prices, output, and income inherently unstable. We shall also examine the nature and impact of government policies designed to foster greater stability in agricultural markets. As will be seen, those policies have helped stabilize agricultural markets, but at a substantial cost.

DESTABILIZING FORCES

The agricultural industry is one of the most competitive of all U.S. industries. To begin with, there are over 2 million farms in the United States. Although some of these farms are immense in size—with thousands of acres—no single farm has the power to affect the market supply or price of farm products. That is to say, individual farmers have no market power.

Competition in the agricultural industry is also maintained by relatively low barriers to entry. Although farming is becoming increasingly mechanized and scientific, the rudiments of farming are easily mastered. Even most city dwellers learn how to grow vegetables in their backyards or window boxes. Moreover, the investment required to start a farm is relatively modest. A few acres of land, a good plow, and a lot of energy are enough to start a working farm. By contrast, entry into most other industries requires substantial capital investment or technological expertise. This does not imply that it is easy to succeed in farming, but only that it is easy to become a farmer.

Given the competitive structure of U.S. agriculture, **_individual farmers tend to behave like perfect competitors._**[1] Individual farmers seek to expand their rate of output until marginal cost equals price. By following this rule, each farmer makes as much profit as possible from existing resources, prices, and technology.

Like other competitive firms, U.S. farmers can maintain economic profits only if they achieve continuing cost reductions. Above-normal profits obtained from current production techniques and prices are not likely to last. Such profits will entice more people into agriculture and stimulate greater output from existing farmers. This is exactly the kind of dilemma that confronted the early producers of electronic calculators. To stay ahead, individual firms (farms) must continue to improve their productivity.

---

[1] There are exceptions, including a variety of production and marketing associations. These are discussed in Chapter 24.

Technological advance

The rate of technological advance in agriculture has, in fact, been spectacular. Less land is used for farming today than was used 100 years ago. Yet, farm output today is far larger. Just in the period since 1950 farm output per acre has doubled. Farm output per labor hour has grown even faster, having increased by 700 percent in the same time period. Such high rates of productivity advance rival those of our most "technological" industries. These technological advances have come about in countless ways, including development of higher yielding seeds (the "green revolution"), advanced machinery (e.g., mechanical feeders and milkers), improved animal breeding (e.g., crossbreeding), improved plants (e.g., rust-resistant wheat), better land-use practices (e.g., rotations and fertilizers), and computer-based management systems. These many improvements have been discovered and developed by individual farmers, the companies that sell products to them, and by research supported by the U.S. Department of Agriculture.

Inelastic demand

In most industries, continuous increases in technology and output would be most welcome. The agricultural industry, however, confronts a long-term problem. Simply put, there is a limit to the amount of food people want to eat. Hence, more and more output threatens to satiate our collective hunger.

This constraint on the demand for agricultural output is reflected in the relatively inelastic demand for food. Typically, consumers do not increase their food purchases very much when farm prices fall. The **price elasticity** of food demand is low. As a consequence, abundant harvests (rightward shifts of the supply curve) can lead to sharply lower prices and a *decline* in total revenue.

The **income elasticity** of food demand is also low. As incomes increase, people tend to buy more of many goods and services. But they do not buy much more food. Hence, neither lower prices nor higher incomes significantly increase the quantity of food demanded.

In the long run, then, the increasing ability of U.S. agriculture to produce food must be reconciled with very slow growth of U.S. demand for food. Over time, this implies that farm prices will fall, relative to nonfarm prices. And they have. Between the years 1910–14 and 1980, the ratio of farm prices to nonfarm prices fell by 24 percent. In the absence of government price-support programs and foreign demand for our farm products, farm prices would have fallen still further.

price elasticity of demand:
The percentage change in quantity demanded divided by the percentage change in price.

income elasticity of demand:
The percentage change in quantity demanded divided by the percentage change in income.

Abrupt shifts of supply

The long-term downtrend in (relative) farm prices is only one of the major problems confronting U.S. agriculture. The second major problem is short run in nature. Prices of farm products are subject to abrupt short-term swings. If the weather is good, harvests are abundant. Abundant harvests imply a severe drop in prices, however, particularly when food demand is relatively inelastic. On the other hand, a late or early freeze, a drought, or an infestation can reduce harvests substantially and push prices sharply higher. So long as agricultural harvests are subject to the whims of nature, farm prices will be highly unstable from year to year. These natural price swings are illustrated in Figure A.1.

FIGURE A.1 SHORT-TERM INSTABILITY

Changes in weather cause abrupt shifts of the food supply curve. When combined with the relatively inelastic demand for food, these supply shifts result in wide price swings. Notice how the price of grain jumps from p_1 to p_2 when bad weather reduces the harvest. If good weather follows, prices may fall to p_3.

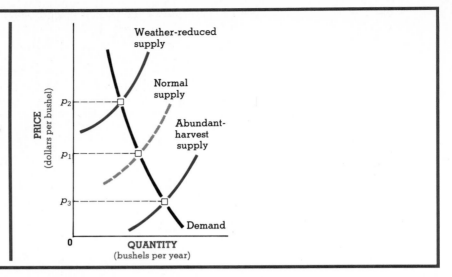

Natural forces are not the only cause of short-term price instability. Time lags between the production decision and the resultant harvest also contribute to price instability. If prices are high one year, farmers have an incentive to increase their rate of output. In this sense, prices serve the same signaling function in agriculture as they do in nonfarm industries. What distinguishes the farmers' response is the lack of inventories and the fixed duration of the production process. In the auto and electronics industries, a larger quantity of output can be supplied to the market fairly quickly. Some additional supplies can be marketed immediately by reducing available inventories. A further increase in the quantity supplied can be obtained by increasing the rate of output, perhaps with periods of overtime. In farming, however, supply cannot respond so quickly. First of all, little inventory is available, because most farm products are highly perishable. Second, overtime efforts won't speed up the growing or breeding cycles. In the very short run, the farmer can only till more land, plant additional seed, or breed more livestock. No additional food supplies will be available until a new crop or herd grows. Hence, the agricultural supply response to a change in prices is always one harvest (or breeding period) later.

The natural lag in responses of agricultural supplies intensifies short-term price swings. Suppose corn prices are exceptionally high at the end of a year, due to a reduced harvest. High prices will make corn farming appear unusually profitable. Hence, farmers will want to expand their rate of output—plant more corn acreage—to share in these high profits. But the corn will not appear on the market until the following year. By that time, there is likely to be an abundance of corn on the market, as a result of both better weather and increased corn acreage. Hence corn prices are likely to plummet (see Figure A.1 again).

No single farmer can avoid the boom-or-bust movement of prices. Even a corn farmer who has mastered the principles of economics has little choice but to plant more corn when prices are high. If he does not plant additional corn, prices will fall anyway, because his own production decisions do not affect market prices. By not planting additional corn, he only denies himself a share of corn market sales. In a highly competitive market, each producer must act independently.

The historical instability of corn prices is illustrated in Figure A.2. Notice how corn prices repeatedly rise, then abruptly fall. This kind of price swing is particularly evident in 1915–20, 1935–37, 1946–48, and 1973–76.

THE CRISIS YEARS

The U.S. agricultural industry operated without substantial government intervention until the 1930s. In earlier decades, an expanding population, recurrent wars, and less advanced technology had helped to maintain a favorable supply-demand relationship for farm products. There were frequent short-term swings in farm prices, but these were absorbed by a generally sound farm sector. The period 1910–19 was particularly prosperous for farmers, largely because of the expanded foreign demand for U.S. farm products by countries engaged in World War I.

The two basic problems of U.S. agriculture grew to crisis proportions after 1920. In 1919, most farm prices were at historical

FIGURE A.2 UNSTABLE CORN PRICES

Most agricultural prices are subject to abrupt short-term changes. Notice how corn prices rose dramatically during World Wars I and II, then fell sharply. Poor harvests in the rest of the world increased demand for U.S. food in 1973–74.

Source: U.S. Department of Agriculture, *Agricultural Statistics*, 1978.

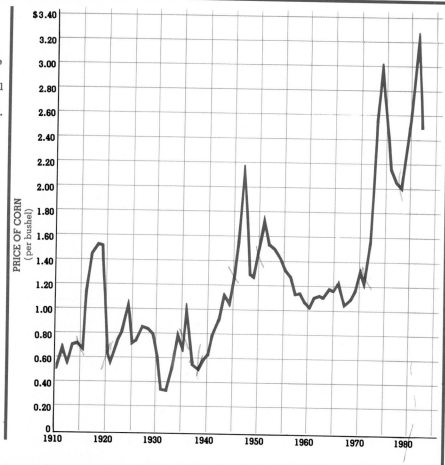

FIGURE A.3 FARM PRICES, 1910–40
(1910–14 = 100)

Farm prices are less stable than nonfarm prices. During the 1930s, relative farm prices fell by 50 percent. This experience was the catalyst for government price supports and other agricultural assistance programs.

Source: U.S. Department of Agriculture, *Agricultural Statistics*, 1950.

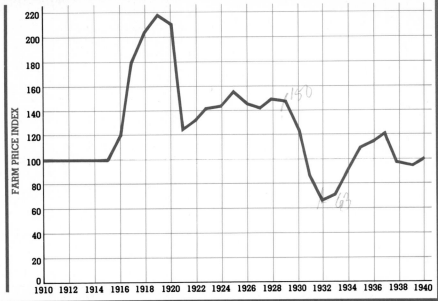

highs (see Figure A.2). After World War I ended, however, European countries no longer demanded as much American food. U.S. exports of farm products fell from nearly $4 billion in 1919 to $1.9 billion in 1921. Farm exports were further reduced in the following years by increasing restrictions on international trade. At home, the end of the war implied an increased availability of factors of production and continuing technological improvement.

The impact of reduced demand and steadily increasing supply is evident in Figure A.3. In 1919, farm prices were more than double their levels of the period 1910–14. Prices then fell abruptly, however. In 1921 alone, average farm prices fell by nearly 40 percent.

Farm prices rose somewhat in the mid-1920s, but resumed a steep decline in 1930. In 1932, average farm prices were 75 percent lower than they had been in 1919, and were only 65 percent of their prewar levels. At the same time, the average income per farmer from farming fell from $2,651 in 1919 to $855 in 1932.

The depression hit smaller farmers particularly hard. They had fewer resources to withstand consecutive years of declining prices and income. Even in good times, small farmers must continually expand output and reduce costs just to maintain their incomes. Hence, the Great Depression accelerated an exodus of small farmers from agriculture, a trend that continues today.

Table A.1 shows that the number of small farms has declined dramatically. In 1910 there were 3.7 million farms under 100 acres in size. Today, there are barely 1 million small farms. During the same period, the number of large farms (500 acres or more) has increased by over 200,000. This loss of small farmers, together with the increased mechanization of larger farms, has reduced the farm population by 23 million people since 1910.[2]

[2] The Census Bureau defines farms as property that produces at least $1,000 worth of agricultural products for the market in a year.

TABLE A.1 SIZE DISTRIBUTION OF U.S. FARMS, 1910 AND 1978

Size of farm	Number, 1910	Percent	Number, 1978	Percent
Under 100 acres	3,691,611	58.0	1,077,000	43.4
100–499 acres	2,494,461	39.2	1,024,000	41.3
500–999 acres	125,295	2.0	215,000	8.7
1,000 acres and over	50,135	0.8	163,000	6.6
Total	6,361,502	100.0	2,479,000	100.0

Inelastic food demand, combined with increasing agricultural productivity, implies a declining number of farmers. Small farmers are particularly vulnerable because they do not have the resources to maintain a high rate of technological improvement. As a result, the number of small farms has declined dramatically, while the number of large farms has grown.

Source: U.S. Department of Commerce, *Statistical Abstract of the United States*, 1933, 1981.

U.S. FARM POLICY

The U.S. Congress has responded to these agricultural problems with a variety of programs. Most seek to raise and stabilize the price of farm products. Other programs seek to reduce the costs of production. More recently, the federal government has also provided direct income support to farmers.

Price supports

market surplus: The amount by which the quantity supplied exceeds the quantity demanded at a given price; excess supply.

Price supports have always been the primary focus of U.S. farm policy. As early as 1926, Congress decreed that farm products should sell at a "fair" price. By "fair," Congress meant a price higher than the market equilibrium. Unfortunately, an above-equilibrium price would create a **market surplus** of food (see Figure A.4). Congress proposed to get rid of this surplus by selling it abroad at world market prices. President Calvin Coolidge vetoed this legislation both times Congress passed it.

The basic notion of "fair" prices resurfaced in the Agricultural Adjustment Act of 1933. The basic objective of the act was to restore the purchasing power of farm products to the 1909–14 level. The farm-nonfarm price relationships of 1909–14 were regarded by Con-

FIGURE A.4 "FAIR" PRICES AND MARKET SURPLUS

The interaction of market supply and demand establish an equilibrium price (p_e) for any product, including food. If a higher price (p_f) is set, the quantity of food supplied (q_s) will be larger than the quantity demanded (q_d). Hence, attempts to establish a "fair" (higher) price for farm products must cope with resultant market surpluses.

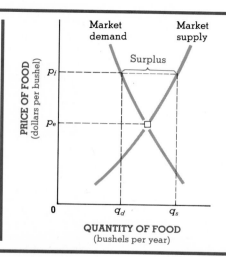

FIGURE A.5 THE IMPACT OF PRICE SUPPORTS

In the absence of price supports, the price of farm products would be determined by the intersection of market supply and demand. In this case, the equilibrium price would be P_1, as shown in part b. All individual farmers would confront this price and produce up to the point where $MC = p_1$, as in part a.

Government price supports raise the price to p_2. By offering to buy (or "loan") unlimited quantities at this price, the government shifts the demand curve facing each farmer upward. Individual farmers respond by increasing their output to q_2. As farmers increase their output, a market surplus develops (part b).

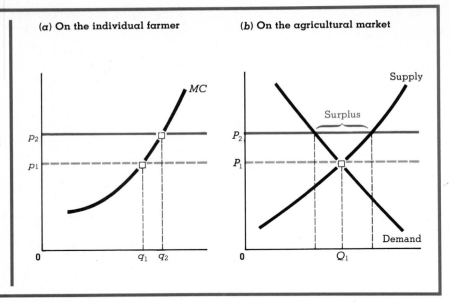

(a) On the individual farmer

(b) On the agricultural market

gress as "fair" and came to be known as "parity" prices. The objective of the 1933 act was to restore that parity by raising farm prices. To do so, Congress this time proposed to reduce market supplies (shift the market supply curve to the left), thereby avoiding a market surplus. This reduction in supply would come about by paying farmers for voluntary reductions in crop acreage.

In January 1936 the U.S. Supreme Court ruled that Congress did not have authority to pay farmers not to produce. Congress responded to this decision quickly. In February Congress passed the Soil and Conservation and Domestic Allotment Act. That act authorized payments to farmers for growing soil-conserving legumes and grasses. Hence, farmers were paid for shifting acreage from the production of soil-depleting surplus crops to soil-conserving uses. The effect, of course, was to limit production, thereby increasing market prices. Such acreage "set-asides" are still part of U.S. farm policy.

A second mechanism for reducing market supply was introduced by an executive order of President Franklin Roosevelt. In October 1933 he established the Commodity Credit Corporation (CCC). Its function is ostensibly to lend money to farmers. But farmers may use their crops as collateral. The effect of such loans is to establish a minimum ("floor") price for farm products. If a farmer does not repay the loan, the CCC simply keeps the crops held as collateral. Hence, the farmer effectively "sells" his crops to the CCC whenever he defaults on a loan. The "price" for these crops is equal to the crop loan rate, that is, the amount of money lent for each bushel of grain. Whenever market prices exceed CCC loan rates, the farmer can repay his loan, retrieve his crops, and sell them in the open market.

The effect of CCC price supports on individual farmers and the agricultural market is illustrated in Figure A.5. In the absence of price supports, competitive farmers would confront a horizontal demand curve at price p_1, itself determined by the intersection of market supply and demand (in part b). The CCC's offer to buy ("loan") unlimited quantities at a higher price shifts the demand curve facing each farmer upward, to the guaranteed price p_2. This

A mess however it's sliced

One way to unload 30 million lbs. of processed cheddar cheese

Free the cheese! Consumer groups have been beaming that message at the White House in petitions and telegrams for a month, and last week Ronald Reagan agreed to do just that. In an Oval Office ceremony, during which he signed an $11 billion farm price-support bill, the President announced that the Government will give away 30 million lbs. of surplus cheese to states for distribution to the needy. Explained Reagan: "At a time when American families are under increasing financial pressure, their Government cannot sit by and watch millions of pounds of food turn to waste."

As a present to the poor, the free cheese has its drawbacks. Needy recipients will have to scrape mold off some of the cheese, which has been stored in 150 warehouses or limestone caves in 35 states for as long as 18 months. But, insists Merritt Sprague, a commodity supervisor for the Department of Agriculture, "mold does not produce toxin that is harmful." Not much variety in the menu, either: the cheese, stored in 5-lb. loaves, is all processed cheddar, the kind sold in grocery stores as "American cheese." . . .

The giveaway still leaves the Government holding some 530 million lbs. of cheese—more than 2 lbs. for every man, woman and child in the country—plus 848 million lbs. of nonfat dry milk stored in 50-lb. sacks and 212 million lbs. of butter frozen at 0° F in 68-lb. blocks. Annual storage and handling cost: $43 million. As Reagan noted in signing the farm bill last week, "surpluses will continue to pile up" because the Government must keep on buying dairy products at prices ($1.4375 per lb. for processed cheddar) that are currently higher than commercial buyers will pay. Processed cheese presents the biggest storage problem, because it spoils if held too long—beyond a maximum of two years. Secretary of Agriculture John R. Block has taken to waving pieces of moldy cheese during speeches to dramatize the scandal, which has led to the telegrams urging the White House to give cheese to the poor.

Other suggestions for disposing of the surplus range from dumping the cheese in the sea to staging bring-your-own-wine-and-crackers parties at warehouses. Reagan hinted last week that more might be given to the needy, and some of the cheese might be sold abroad, at a loss to the Government. The all-too-obvious solution, of course, would be to lower price-support levels until dairy farmers are no longer tempted to produce more cheese than they can sell commercially. But that would be a lot to ask of politicians. The new farm bill actually increases present price-support levels over four years. Meanwhile, the Government is left with a stockpile that is a mess . . . oh, all right, no matter how you slice it.

higher price induces each farmer to increase his rate of output, from q_1 to q_2.

As all farmers respond to price supports, the agricultural market is pushed out of equilibrium. At the support level p_2, more output is supplied than demanded. The surplus ends up in storage. Since 1977, farmers have been permitted to store their own surplus and bill the federal government for storage costs. Thus farmers get paid to produce output that consumers don't want and are then paid again to store the unsold crops.

The federal government also buys some farm products outright. The most important purchases are for milk products. The Agriculture and Food Act of 1981, like its predecessors, required the U.S. Department of Agriculture to purchase all surplus milk, in the form of butter, cheese, and dry milk. The act also specified what prices were to be paid for this milk. For the years 1982−84, the act set minimum prices of $13.25, $14.00, and $14.60 per hundred weight of milk. The avowed purpose of these prices is to guarantee prices equal to at least 70 percent of parity (the price of milk in 1910−14). Their effect is to raise market prices, reduce consumption, and increase output. The net result is a growing market surplus. In 1981 alone, the federal government purchased nearly $2 *billion* worth of cheese, butter, and nonfat dry milk. Just *storing* this surplus costs over $1 million a day. In fact, inventories of surplus milk products grew so large that in 1981 President Reagan ordered the Agriculture Department to give away 30 million pounds of cheese at Christmas!

FIGURE A.6   THE IMPACT OF COST SUBSIDIES

Cost subsidies lower the marginal cost of producing at any given rate of output, thereby shifting the marginal cost curve downward. The lower marginal costs make higher rates of output more profitable and thus increase output. At price p_2, lower marginal costs increase the desired rate of output from q_2 to q_3.

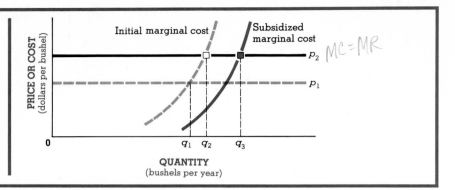

Cost subsidies

To encourage output further, the government also subsidizes various costs of farm production, thereby slowing the rise of marginal costs. Irrigation water, for example, is delivered to many farmers by federally funded reclamation projects. The price paid by farmers for the water is substantially below the cost of delivering it; the difference amounts to a subsidy. Other forms of subsidy have been conveyed by the Department of Agriculture's Rural Environmental Assistance Program (REAP). REAP has distributed something like $150–$200 million a year to farmers to help defray the costs of certain production factors (such as fertilizers and drainage).

The federal government has also provided basic research, insurance, marketing, grading, and inspection services to farmers at subsidized prices. All of these subsidies serve to lower fixed or variable costs. Their net impact is to stimulate additional output, as illustrated in Figure A.6.

Direct income support

Price supports and cost subsidies are designed to stabilize agricultural markets and assure farmers an adequate income. As we have seen, however, they entail significant distortions of market outcomes. The Congressional Budget Office estimates that the milk price supports alone have increased retail dairy prices by 3 to 6 percent, reduced consumption by 1 to 5 percent, and encouraged excessive dairy production. Because of such distortions, direct income supports were authorized by the Agriculture and Consumer Protection Act of 1973. The advantage of direct income supports is that they achieve the goal of income security without distortions of market prices and output.

The principal form of direct income support are so-called deficiency payments. Producers of wheat, feed grains, rice, cotton, and other commodities receive direct payments from the federal government when crop prices are low (below stipulated "target prices"). These payments are designed to make up the deficiency in income that results from low prices. Deficiency payments are also made to farmers who agree to reduce their output (acreage) of certain crops.

In principle, direct income payments are a more efficient mechanism for subsidizing farm incomes. But farmers don't like them. In fact, 5,000 angry farmers drove their tractors to Washington, D.C., in February 1979 to protest this policy approach. Their rallying cry was "parity, not charity." They wanted higher price supports (an indirect subsidy) rather than more deficiency payments (a direct subsidy).

CHAPTER 22

MONOPOLY

The price, the quantity, even the quality of the goods and services we buy are determined in product markets by the interaction of supply and demand forces. As we have seen, every potential buyer translates his or her tastes and income into a single denominator—price—and indicates a willingness to buy certain products at various prices. Individual sellers do much the same thing, in their case transforming sales, cost, and profit expectations into a willingness to sell various quantities at particular prices. The interaction of all these individual decisions in the marketplace yields the prices and product flows we observe daily.

The dependence of prices and product flows on the interaction of market supply and demand underscores the importance of market structures and behavior. As we observed in Chapter 21, competitive market structures create a unique kind of pressure on producers. Under the threat of competition, producers are motivated to adapt quickly to changing consumer demands, to improve product quality, and to reduce costs.

Such pressures are less evident in a market characterized by concentrations of **market power**. A firm with market power has some direct influence over market prices. Its own production decisions have an independent impact on the price at which its product may be sold. A firm with market power may find it more profitable to maintain high prices in a particular market than to increase the rate of output, improve product quality, or experiment with new cost structures. Moreover, a firm with significant market power will be

market power: The ability to alter the market price of a good or service.

able to keep prices high as a consequence of its control over market supplies. A powerless (or perfectly competitive) firm has no such option, as it is unable to alter market supplies or prices.

The power to influence prices and product flows may have far-reaching consequences for our economic welfare. Changes in prices and product flows directly influence the level and composition of GNP, employment and resource allocation, the level and distribution of income, and, of course, the level and structure of prices. Hence firms that wield significant market power affect all dimensions of economic welfare.

Market power is not the only kind of power wielded in society, of course. Political power, for example, is obviously a different kind of power and important in its own right. Indeed, the power to influence an election or to sway a Senate committee vote may ultimately be more important than the power to increase the price of laundry soap. Nevertheless, market power is a force that influences the way we live, the incomes we earn, and our relationships with other countries. Moreover, market power may provide the basis for other forms of power. The individual or firm with considerable market power is likely to have the necessary resources to influence an election or sway a vote on a congressional committee. Hence market power is a critical dimension of both economic and social welfare.

In light of the potential impact of market power on the way we live and the way the economy functions, we need to determine whether market power exists in the United States. If it does exist, how is it used, and what effects has it had? This chapter begins to answer these questions by examining the way market power may be used to alter market outcomes.

MARKET POWER

The essence of market power is the ability to alter the price of a product. The doorknob producers and calculator manufacturers of Chapters 20 and 21 had no such power. Because many other firms were producing and selling the same good, each doorknob or calculator producer had to act as a *price taker*. Each firm could sell all it wanted at the prevailing price but would lose all of its customers if it tried to charge a higher price. This inability to raise the price of their own output is what we refer to when we say competitive firms have no market power.

The absence of market power is illustrated by a horizontal demand curve. Although the demand for the product itself always slopes downward, the demand curve confronting a single competitive firm is horizontal. ***Horizontal demand curves are the hallmark of perfectly competitive firms.***

The downward-sloping demand curve

Firms that have market power *can* alter the price of their output without losing all their customers. Sales volume may drop when price is increased, but the quantity demanded will not drop to zero.

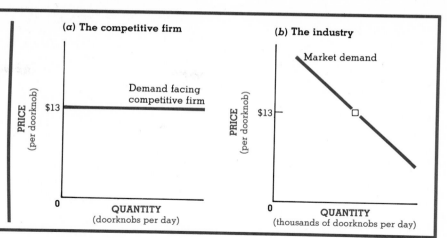

FIGURE 22.1   FIRM VS. INDUSTRY DEMAND

A competitive firm can sell its entire output at the prevailing market price. In this sense, the firm confronts a horizontal demand curve, as in part *a*. Nevertheless, market demand for the product still slopes downward. The demand curve confronting the industry is illustrated in part *b*. Note the difference in the units of measurement (single doorknobs vs. thousands).

In other words, ***firms with market power confront downward-sloping demand curves.***

The distinction between competitive (powerless) and noncompetitive (powerful) firms is illustrated in Figure 22.1. Figure 22.1*a* recreates the market situation that confronts a single producer of doorknobs. In Chapter 20 we assumed that the prevailing price of brass doorknobs was $13 and that a small, competitive firm could sell its entire output at this price. Hence each individual firm effectively confronted a horizontal demand curve.

We also noted earlier that brass doorknobs are not in violation of the law of demand. As nice as brass doorknobs are, people are not willing to buy unlimited quantities of them at $13 each. The marginal utility of extra doorknobs, in fact, diminishes very rapidly. To induce consumers to buy more doorknobs, the price of doorknobs must be reduced.

This seeming contradiction between the law of demand and the situation of the competitive firm is resolved in Figure 22.1. There are *two* relevant demand curves. The one on the left, which appears to contradict the law of demand, refers to a single competitive producer. The one on the right refers to the entire *industry*, of which the competitive producer is one very tiny part. The industry or market demand curve *does* slope downward, even though individual competitive firms are able to sell their entire output at the going price.

Monopoly

monopoly: A firm that produces the entire market supply of a particular good or service.

An industry need not be composed of many small firms, however. Indeed, the entire output of doorknobs could be produced by a single large producer. Such a firm would be a **monopoly,** that is, a single firm that produces the entire market supply of a good.

The emergence of a monopoly obliterates the distinction between industry demand and the demand curve facing the firm. A monopoly *is* the industry. Hence there is only *one* demand curve to worry about and that is the market (industry) demand curve, as illustrated in Figure 22.1*b*. ***In monopoly situations the demand curve facing the firm is identical to the market demand curve for the product.***

FIGURE 22.2 PRICE EXCEEDS MARGINAL REVENUE

If a firm must lower its price to sell additional output, marginal revenue is less than price. If the firm wants to increase its sales from one to two doorknobs per day, for example, price must be reduced from $13 to $12. The marginal revenue of the second doorknob is therefore only $11. This is indicated in row *B* of the table and by point *b* on the graph.

DOORKNOB SALES AND REVENUES

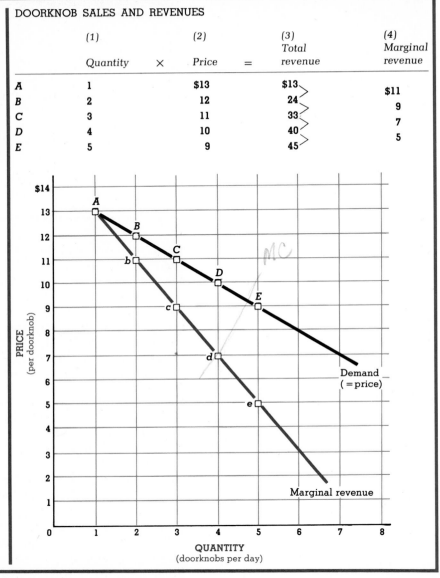

	(1) Quantity	×	(2) Price	=	(3) Total revenue	(4) Marginal revenue
A	1		$13		$13	
B	2		12		24	$11
C	3		11		33	9
D	4		10		40	7
E	5		9		45	5

QUANTITY
(doorknobs per day)

Price and marginal revenue

profit-maximization rule:
Produce at that rate of output where marginal revenue equals marginal cost.

Although monopolies simplify the geometry, they complicate the arithmetic of **profit maximization.** The beautiful thing about a horizontal demand curve is that it makes price and marginal revenue equal. Hence a competitive firm can maximize profits by selling that rate of output where price equals marginal cost.

A monopolist also seeks to maximize profits. He, too, seeks that rate of output where marginal revenue equals marginal cost. But that rate of output is not quite so obvious for the monopolist. Because the demand curve slopes downward, price and marginal revenue are not identical. In fact, *marginal revenue is always less than price for a monopolist.* This makes it just a bit more difficult to find the profit-maximizing rate of output.

Figure 22.2 provides a simple illustration of the relationship between price and marginal revenue. The monopolist can sell one doorknob per day at a price of $13. If he wants to sell a larger quantity of doorknobs, however, he has to reduce his price. According to the demand curve depicted here, the price must be lowered to $12 to sell two doorknobs per day. This reduction in price is shown by a movement along the demand curve from point *A* to point *B*.

Our primary interest here is marginal revenue. We want to show what happens to total revenue when sales increase by one doorknob per day. To do this, we simply compute the total revenue associated with each rate of output. **Marginal revenue** represents the *change* in total revenue that results from a one-unit increase in the rate of output.

The necessary calculations are summarized in Figure 22.2. Row *A* of the table indicates that the total revenue resulting from one sale per day is $13. To increase sales, price must be reduced. Hence row *B* indicates that total revenues rise to only $24 per day when doorknob sales double. The *increase* in total revenues resulting from the added sales is thus $11. The marginal revenue of the second doorknob is therefore $11. This is illustrated in the last column of the table and by point *b* on the marginal revenue curve. Notice that the *MR* of the second doorknob ($11) is *less* than its price ($12). This is because *both* doorknobs are being sold for $12 apiece. In effect, the firm is giving up the opportunity to sell only one doorknob per day at $13 in order to sell a larger quantity at a lower price. In this sense, the firm is sacrificing $1 of potential revenue on the first doorknob in order to increase *total* revenue. Marginal revenue measures the change in total revenue that results.

So long as the demand curve is downward-sloping, *MR* will be less than price. Compare columns 2 and 4 of the table in Figure 22.2. At each rate of output in excess of one doorknob, marginal revenue is less than price. This is also evident in the graph: ***the MR curve lies below the demand (price) curve at every point but the first.***

Profit maximization

The most immediate consequence of market power, then, is an extra curve—one for marginal revenue. The rules of profit maximization remain the same, however. Now instead of looking for an intersection of marginal cost and price, we look for the intersection of marginal cost and marginal revenue. This is illustrated in Figure 22.3 by the intersection of the *MR* and *MC* curves (point *d*). Looking down from that intersection, we see that the associated rate of output is four doorknobs per day. Looking upward from that intersection, we see (point *D*) that consumers are willing to pay $10 each for that many doorknobs.

Also illustrated in Figure 22.3 are the total profits of the doorknob monopoly. To compute total profits we can first calculate profit per unit, that is, price minus *average* total cost. In this case, profit per unit is $2. Multiplying profit per unit by the quantity sold (4) gives us total profits of $8 per day, as illustrated by the shaded rectangle.

marginal revenue: The change in total revenue that results from a one-unit increase in the quantity sold.

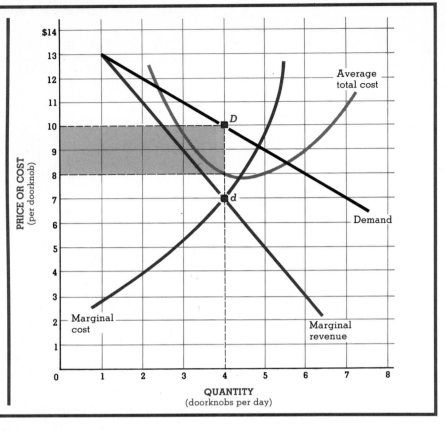

FIGURE 22.3 PROFIT MAXIMIZATION

The most profitable rate of output is indicated by the intersection of marginal revenue and marginal cost (point *d*). In this case, marginal revenue and marginal cost intersect at an output of four doorknobs per day. Point *D* indicates that consumers will pay $10 per knob for this much output. Total profits equal price ($10) minus average total cost ($8), multiplied by the quantity sold (4).

barriers to entry: Obstacles that make it difficult or impossible for would-be producers to enter a particular market (e.g., patents).

MARKET POWER AT WORK: THE CALCULATOR MARKET REVISITED

To develop a keener appreciation for the nature of market power, we can return to the pocket-calculator market of Chapter 21. This time we will make some different assumptions about market structure. In particular, assume that a single firm, Universal Electronics, acquires an exclusive patent on the production of the MOS/LSI chips that run pocket calculators.[1] This one firm is now in a position to deny potential competitors access to the basic ingredient of calculators. The patent thus functions as a significant **barrier to entry**, to be erected or set aside at the will of Universal Electronics.[2]

The management of Universal is familiar enough with the principles of economics (including W. C. Fields's advice about never giving a sucker an even break) to know when it's onto a good thing. It is not about to let every would-be Horatio Alger have a slice of the profit pie. So we shall assume that Universal decides not to sell or give away any rights to its patent or the chips it produces, and thus

[1] In actuality, several firms attempted to obtain such patents, but their applications were rejected by the U.S. Patent Office on the grounds that the chips did not constitute a new technological process.
[2] At least as long as the patent is valid; patents expire at the end of 17 years (although they can usually be extended with product improvements). Other barriers to entry are discussed in Chapter 24.

STATUE OF LIBERTY BAKE SALE
ONE DAY ONLY!!!
MONDAY, MAY 6

BUY A DESSERT FOR YOUR LUNCH
EVERYTHING IS ONLY $.25

- -

SM COOKIES	3/25 CENTS
LG. COOKIES	2/25 CENTS
CUPCAKES	25 CENTS
SM. BROWNIES	2/25 CENTS
LG BROWNIES	25 CENTS
SM. CHOC. CHIP SQ.	2/25 CENTS
LG. CHOC. CHIP SQ.	25 CENTS

BRING AN EXTRA QUARTER MONDAY AND
SUPPORT THE RESTORATION OF THE
STATUE OF LIBERTY111

establishes itself as the sole producer of calculators. That is to say, Universal Electronics sets itself up as a calculator monopoly.

Let us also assume that Universal has a multitude of manufacturing plants, each of which is identical to the typical competitive firm of Chapter 21. This is an unlikely situation, because a monopolist would probably be able to achieve **economies of scale** by closing at least a few plants and consolidating production in larger plants. Universal would maintain a multitude of small plants only if constant returns to scale or actual diseconomies of scale were rampant. This is not likely to be the case. By assuming that multiple plants are maintained, however, we can compare monopoly behavior with competitive behavior on the basis of identical cost structures. In particular, if Universal continues to operate the many plants that once comprised the competitive calculator industry, it will confront the same short-run marginal and average cost curves already encountered in Chapter 21. Later in this chapter we shall relax this assumption of multiplant operations to determine whether, in the long run, a monopolist may actually lower the costs of production below those attained by a competitive industry.

Figure 22.4a recreates the marginal costs faced by the typical competitive firm in the early stages of the calculator boom (from Figure 21.2 and Table 21.1). We now assume that this MC curve expresses the costs of operating one of Universal's many (identical) plants. Thus the extension of monopoly control is assumed to have no immediate effect on production costs.

The market demand for calculators is also assumed to be unchanged. There is no obvious reason why people should be more or less willing to buy calculators now than they were when the market was competitive. Even if we assumed that consumers were reluctant to purchase the products of a monopolist, Universal could easily camouflage its market position by giving each of its plants a different name. Consumers would then be less likely to know that they were dealing with a monopoly, if that was considered an issue. Thus, Figure 22.4b expresses an unchanged demand for calculators.

Our immediate concern is to determine how Universal Electronics, as a monopolist, will respond to these demand and cost curves. Will it produce as many calculators as a competitive industry in the same situation? Can it squeeze out more profits? Will it achieve comparable cost reductions?

economies of scale: Reductions in average costs that come about through increases in the size (scale) of plant and equipment.

The production decision

production decision: The selection of the short-run rate of output (with existing plant and equipment).

Like any producer, Universal Electronics will strive to produce its output at the rate that maximizes total profits. But unlike competitive firms, Universal will take explicit account of the fact that an expansion of its output will put pressure on calculator prices and thereby threaten corporate profits.

The implications of Universal's market position for the **production decision** of its many plants can be seen clearly in the new price and marginal revenue curves imposed on each of its manufacturing plants. Universal cannot afford to let each of its plants compete with the others, expanding output and driving down prices. That is the kind of folly reserved for truly competitive firms. Instead,

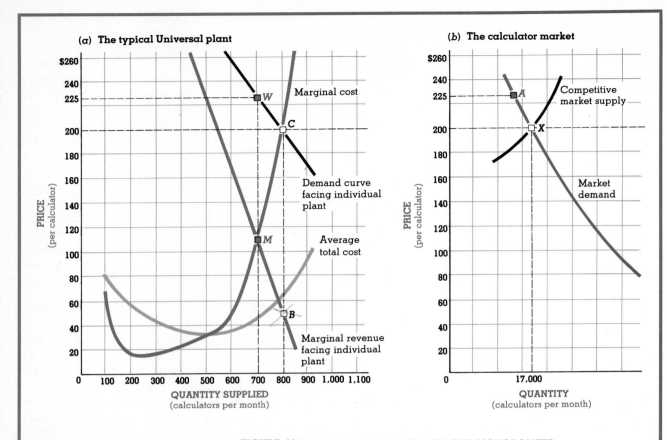

(a) The typical Universal plant

(b) The calculator market

FIGURE 22.4 INITIAL CONDITIONS IN THE MONOPOLIZED CALCULATOR MARKET

We assume that a monopoly firm (Universal Electronics) would confront the same costs (*MC* and *ATC*) and demand as would the competitive industry of Chapter 21. However, the monopolist is not bound by the competitive market price (*p_c* = $200). Indeed, if each monopoly plant produced where *MC* = $200 (point *C* in part *a*), marginal cost (point *C*) would exceed marginal revenue (point *B*). Instead, the monopolist must contend with downward-sloping demand and marginal revenue curves. He will maximize profits at that rate of output where *MC* = *MR* (point *M* in part *a*). That rate of output can be sold at the monopoly price of $225 (point *W* in part *a*). Part *b* illustrates the market implications of the monopolist's production decision: a reduced quantity is sold at a higher price (point *A*).

Universal will seek to *coordinate* the production decisions of its plants, instructing all plant managers to expand or contract output simultaneously, to achieve the corporate goal of profit maximization.

A simultaneous reduction of output by each Universal plant will lead to a significant reduction in the quantity of calculators supplied to the market. This reduced supply will cause a move up the market demand curve to higher prices. By the same token, an expansion of output by all Universal plants will lead to an increase in the quantity supplied to the market and a slide down the market demand curve. As a consequence, each of the monopolist's plants effectively confronts a downward-sloping demand curve. These downward-sloping demand curves are illustrated in Figure 22.4a.[3]

Notice that in Figure 22.4b the market demand for calculators is unchanged; only the demand curve confronting each plant (firm) has changed. A competitive *industry*, like a monopoly, also must obey the law of demand. But the individual firms that comprise a competitive industry all act independently, *as if* they could sell unlimited quantities at the prevailing price. That is, they all act as if they confronted a horizontal demand curve at the market price of $200. A competitive firm that doesn't behave in this fashion will simpy lose sales to other firms. In contrast, a monopolist not only foresees the impact of increased production on market price, but can also act to stop such production increases by its separate plants.

MARGINAL REVENUE The downward-sloping demand curve now confronting each Universal plant implies that marginal revenue no longer equals price. Marginal revenue will fall faster than price because the additional revenues generated by increased calculator sales are offset by the price reductions necessary to increase sales volume.

Notice that the marginal revenue curve in Figure 22.4a lies *below* the demand curve at every rate of output. Because marginal revenue is less than price for a monopoly, Universal's plants would no longer wish to produce up to the point where marginal cost equals price. ***Only firms that confront a horizontal demand curve (perfect competitors) equate marginal cost and price.*** Universal's plants must stick to the more basic profit-maximizing rule about equating marginal revenue and marginal cost. Should the individual plant managers forget this rule, Universal's central management will be quick to remind them.

The output and price implications of Universal's monopoly position become apparent as we examine the new revenue and cost relationships of Figure 22.4. Recall that the equilibrium price of calculators in the early stages of the calculator boom was $200. This equilibrium price is indicated in Figure 22.4b by the intersection of the competitive market supply curve with the market demand curve (point X). Each competitive *firm* produced up to the point where marginal cost (MC) equaled that price. This rate of output is indicated by the intersection of the firm's MC curve and the industry's price line (point C in Figure 22.4a). At that point, each competitive firm was producing 800 calculators a month.

The emergence of Universal as a monopolist alters these production decisions. Now each plant has to recognize that marginal revenue is less than price. Each Universal plant *does* have an impact on market price because its behavior is imitated simultaneously by all Universal plants. In fact, the marginal revenue associated with the 800th calculator is only $70, as indicated by point B in Figure

[3] The demand and marginal revenue curves in Figure 22.4a are illustrative; they are not derived from earlier tables. As discussed above, we are assuming that the central management of Universal determines the profit-maximizing rate of output, then instructs all individual plants to produce equal shares of that output.

22.4*a*. Hence, at this rate of output, the typical Universal plant would be operating with marginal costs ($200) far in excess of marginal revenues ($70). Such behavior is inconsistent with profit maximization and requires another look at the production decision.

The enlightened Universal plant manager will soon discover that the profit-maximizing rate of output is less than 800 calculators per month. In Figure 22.4*a* we see that the marginal revenue and marginal cost curves intersect at point *M*. This intersection, which identifies the profit-maximizing rate of output, occurs at an output level of only 700 calculators per month. Accordingly, the typical Universal plant will want to produce fewer calculators than were produced by the typical competitive firm in the early stages of the calculator boom. Individual competitive firms, you will recall, had no incentive to engage in such production cutbacks. They could not alter the market supply curve or price on their own and were not coordinated by a central management. Thus the first consequence of Universal's monopoly position is a reduction in the rate of industry output.

The monopoly price

The reduction in output at each of Universal's plants translates automatically into a decrease in the *quantity supplied* to the market. As consumers compete for this reduced market supply, they will bid calculator prices up. We can observe the increased prices in Figure 22.4 by looking at either the typical Universal plant or the calculator market. Notice that in Figure 22.4*a* the price is determined by moving directly up from point *M* to the demand curve confronting the typical Universal plant. The demand curve always tells how much consumers are willing to pay for any given quantity. Hence, once we have determined the quantity that is going to be supplied (700 calculators per month), we can look at the demand curve to determine the price ($225 at point *W*) that consumers will pay for these calculators. That is to say, ***the intersection of the marginal revenue and marginal cost curves (point M) establishes the profit-maximizing rate of output. The demand curve tells us how much consumers are willing to pay for that quantity of output.***

Figure 22.4*a* thus confirms that Universal's monopoly position results in both reduced output and increased prices. This result is also evident in Figure 22.4*b*. Here we see that a smaller quantity supplied to the market will force a move up the demand curve to the higher price of $225 per calculator (point *A*).

Monopoly profits

Universal is not going through all this effort to establish a new market equilibrium simply to exercise our minds, of course. Its objective was and remains the maximization of profits. That it has succeeded in its effort can be confirmed by a scrutiny of Figure 22.5. As you can see, the typical Universal plant ends up selling 700 calculators a month at a price of $225 each (point *W*). The **average total cost** of production at this rate of output is only $50.46 (point *K*), as we can see also in Table 21.1.

average total cost *(ATC)*: Total cost divided by the quantity produced in a given time period.

As always, profit per unit equals price ($225) minus average

FIGURE 22.5 MONOPOLY PROFITS: THE TYPICAL UNIVERSAL PLANT

The profit-maximizing rate of output occurs where the marginal cost and marginal revenue curves intersect (point *M*). The demand curve indicates the price (point *W*) that consumers will pay for this output. Total profit equals price (*W*) minus average total cost (*K*) multiplied by the quantity sold (700). Total profits are represented by the shaded rectangle.

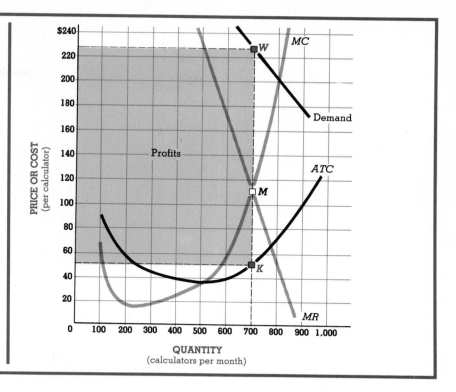

total cost ($50.46) or, in this case, $174.54 per calculator. Multiplying this profit per unit by the number of calculators produced (700 per month), we can see that the typical Universal plant makes a profit of 700 × ($225 − $50.46), or $122,178 a month.[4] This figure may be compared with the monthly profit of $104,680 earned by the typical competitive firm in the early stages of the calculator boom (see Table 21.1).

It is apparent from these profit figures that Universal management has learned its economic principles well. By reducing the output of each plant and raising prices a little, it has managed to enlarge the size of the profit pie, while keeping it all to itself, of course. This can be seen again in Figure 22.6, which is an enlarged illustration of the *market* situations for the calculator industry. The figure translates the economics of our single-plant and competitive-firm comparison into the dimensions of the whole industry. We can see that the competitive industry of Chapter 21 initially produces the quantity q_c and sells it at a price of $200 each. Its profits are denoted by the rectangle formed by the points R, X, T, U. The monopolist, on the other hand, produces the smaller quantity q_m and charges a higher price, $225. The monopoly firm's profits are indicated by the larger profit rectangle that is shaded in the figure. We see that **_a monopoly receives larger profits than a comparable competitive industry by reducing the quantity supplied and pushing prices up._** The larger profits make Universal very happy and make consumers a little sad-

---

[4] These profit calculations were performed on a pocket calculator.

FIGURE 22.6 MONOPOLY PROFIT: THE ENTIRE COMPANY

Total profits of the monopolist (including all plants) are illustrated by the shaded rectangle. The monopolist's total output (q_m) is determined by the intersection of the (industry) MR and MC curves. The price of his output is determined by the market demand curve (point A). In contrast, a competitive industry would initially produce q_c calculators and sell them at a lower price (X) and profit per unit ($X - U$).

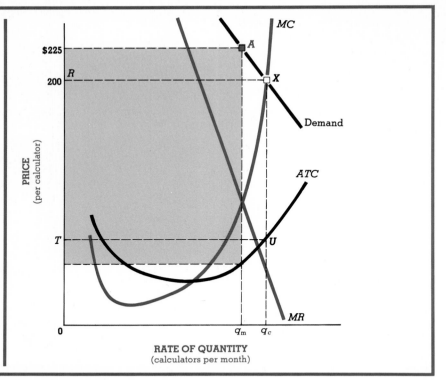

der and wiser. Consumers are now paying more and getting less, in effect, transferring additional income to Universal. Indeed, this kind of income redistribution is the primary objective of those who seek to establish and exploit market power.

Barriers to entry

The higher profits attained by Universal Electronics as a result of its monopoly position are not the end of the story. As we observed earlier, the existence of economic profit tends to bring profit-hungry entrepreneurs swarming like locusts. Indeed, in the competitive calculator industry of Chapter 21, the lure of high profits brought about an enormous expansion of calculator output, a steep decline in calculator prices, and significant technological innovation. What, then, can we expect to happen in the calculator market now that Universal has a monopoly position and is enjoying huge profits?

Remember that Universal is now assumed to have an exclusive patent on MOS/LSI chips and can use this patent as an impassable barrier to entry. Consequently, would-be competitors can swarm around Universal's profits until their wings drop off; Universal is not about to let them in on the spoils. Hence the competitive forces that earlier led to such a dramatic boom in calculator sales are prohibited from going to work. As long as Universal is able to keep the competition out, only the more affluent consumers will be able to use calculators. Universal may discover ways to reduce the costs of production and thus lower prices, but there is no *pressure* on it to do so, as there was in the competitive situation.

A COMPARATIVE PERSPECTIVE ON MARKET POWER

It may be useful to formulate an interim comparison of the workings of markets under competitive and monopoly conditions. Building on our examination of the electronic calculator market, we may summarize the sequence of events that occurs in each as follows:

Competitive industry	Monopoly industry
1. High prices and profits signal consumers' demand for more output.	1. High prices and profits signal consumers' demand for more output.
2. The high profits attract new suppliers.	2. Barriers to entry are erected to exclude potential competition.
3. Production and supplies expand.	3. Production and supplies are cut back.
4. Prices slide down the market demand curve.	4. Prices move up the market demand curve.
5. A new equilibrium is established wherein more of the desired product is produced, its price falls, average costs of production approach their minimum, and economic profits approach zero.	5. A new equilibrium is established wherein less of the desired product is produced, its price rises, average costs are not necessarily at or near a minimum, and economic profits are at a maximum.
6. Price equals marginal cost throughout the process.	6. Price exceeds marginal cost at all times.
7. Throughout the process, there is great pressure to keep ahead of the profit squeeze by reducing costs or improving product quality.	7. There is no squeeze on profits and thus no pressure to reduce costs or improve product quality.

In our discussion, we have assumed that both the competitive industry and the monopolist adjust their production schedules from some given point of departure—a fixed equilibrium in which the price of calculators is $200. In reality, of course, an industry may manifest concentrations of market power *before* such an equilibrium is established. That is to say, the sequence of events we have depicted may be altered (with step 3 occurring first, for example). Nevertheless, the basic distinctions between competitive and monopolistic market behavior are evident.

To the extent that monopolies behave as we have discussed, they alter our output of goods and services in two specific ways. You remember that competitive industries tend, in the long run, to produce at minimum average costs and encourage cost reductions, thereby expanding our production possibilities. No such forces are at work in the monopoly we have discussed here. Hence there is a basic tendency for monopolies to inhibit economic growth.

Another important feature of competitive markets is their tendency toward **marginal cost pricing.** Marginal cost pricing is important to consumers because it permits rational choices among alterna-

marginal cost pricing: The offer (supply) of goods at prices equal to their marginal cost.

tive goods and services. In particular, it informs consumers of the true opportunity costs of various goods, thereby allowing them to choose the *mix* of output (GNP) that delivers the most utility with available resources. In our monopoly example, however, consumers end up getting fewer calculators than they would like, while the economy continues to produce other goods that are less desired. Thus the mix of output shifted away from calculators when Universal took over the industry.

In general, we may observe that market power is economically undesirable because it can be used to alter the mix of output, misallocate resources, constrain society's production possibilities, and redistribute income. Not all of these things will necessarily happen, but they may. In addition, the possession of such power can lead to the acquisition of substantial political power, with adverse consequences for other institutions.

The limits to power

Even though market power does permit a producer or supplier to manipulate market outcomes, there is a clear limit to the exercise of power. Even a monopolist cannot get everything he wants. Universal, for example, would really like to sell q_m calculators at a price of $500 each, because that kind of price would bring it even greater profits. Yet, despite its monopoly position, Universal is constrained to sell that quantity of calculators at the much lower price of $225 each. Even monopolists have their little disappointments.

The limitations to a monopolist's exercise of power are evident in Figure 22.6. Universal's attainment of a monopoly position allows it only one prerogative: the ability to alter the quantity of output *supplied* to the market. This is no small prerogative, but it is far from absolute power. Universal, and every other monopolist, must still contend with the market *demand* curve. Note again that the new equilibrium in Figure 22.6 occurs at a point on the *unchanged* demand curve. In effect, a monopolist has the opportunity to pick any point on the market demand curve and designate it as the new market equilibrium. The point it selects will depend on its own perceptions of effort, profit, and risk (in this case point A, determined by the intersection of marginal revenue and marginal cost).

The limitation to monopoly power arises from the fact that the monopolist has no direct control over consumer behavior. As a supplier, the monopolist can alter the choices available to consumers, but he cannot force them to pick any combination he desires. Universal could set the price of calculators at $500 each, for example, but it could not compel consumers to purchase the number of calculators it wished to sell at that price. Were the company to set such an exorbitant price, even the more affluent among us would go back to counting on their fingers.

The ultimate constraint on the exercise of market power, then, resides in the market demand curve.[5] The greater the **price elasticity of demand** by consumers, the more a monopolist will be frustrated

price elasticity of demand: The percentage change in quantity demanded divided by the percentage change in price.

[5] Government regulation can also be used to constrain monopolistic behavior, but we are concerned here with market constraints.

PRICE DISCRIMINATION: ANOTHER PREROGATIVE OF POWER

price discrimination: The sale of an identical good at different prices to different consumers by a single seller.

A monopolist has the power not only to raise the market price of a good (by reducing the quantity supplied), but also to charge various prices for the same good. Recall that the market demand curve reflects the combined willingness to buy of many individuals. Some of those individuals are willing to buy the good at prices higher than the market price, just as other individuals will buy only at lower prices. A monopolist may be able to increase total profits by selling each unit of the good separately, at a price each *individual* consumer is willing to pay. This practice is called **price discrimination.**

The airline industry has practiced price discrimination for many years. Basically, there are two distinct groups of travelers, business and nonbusiness travelers. Business executives generally must fly from one city to another on a certain day and at a particular time. They typically must make flight arrangements on short notice and may have no other way to get to their destination. Nonbusiness travelers (for example, people on vacation and students going home during semester break) usually have more flexible schedules. They may plan their trips weeks or months in advance and often have the option of traveling by car, bus, or train.

The different travel needs and opportunities of business and vacation travelers are reflected in their respective demand curves. Business demand for air travel tends to be less price elastic at any given price than the demand of nonbusiness travelers for the same service. Few business executives would stop flying if air fares increased. Higher air fares would, however, discourage air travel by nonbusiness travelers.

What should airlines do in this case? Should they *raise* air fares to take advantage of the relative price inelasticity of business demand, or should they *lower* air fares to attract more nonbusiness travelers?

They should do both. In fact, they have done both. The airlines offer a "full fare" ride, available at any time, and a "discount fare" ride, available only by purchasing one's ticket in advance and agreeing to some restrictions on time of departure. The advance-purchase and other restrictions on discount fares effectively exclude most business travelers, who end up paying full fare. The higher "full" fare does not, however, discourage most nonbusiness travelers, who can fly at a discount. Consequently, the airlines are able to sell essentially identical units of the same good (an airplane ride) at substantially different prices to different customers. Indeed, by experimenting with various discount fares and travel restrictions, airlines can discriminate even more thoroughly among passengers, thereby reaping the highest possible average price for the quantity supplied. The same type of price discrimination is commonly practiced by doctors, lawyers, and new- and used-car dealers. In all of these cases, the seller may "adjust" the price to the income and taste of each individual consumer.

in his attempts to establish both high prices and high volume. Consumers will simply reduce their purchases if price is increased. If, however, consumer demand is highly inelastic—if consumers need or want that product badly and few viable substitutes are available—the monopolist can reap tremendous profit from market power.

PROS AND CONS OF MARKET POWER

Despite the strong and general case to be made against market power, it is conceivable that it could also yield some benefit to society. One of the arguments made for concentrations of market power is that monopolies have greater ability to pursue research and development. Another is that the promise of market power creates a tremendous incentive for invention and innovation and that large companies can produce goods more efficiently than smaller firms. We must pause to reflect, then, on whether and how such benefits flow from market power.

Research and development

The argument that monopolies or other holders of market power are in a position to undertake valuable research and development rests on two facts. First, such firms are sheltered from the constant pressure of competition. Second, they have the resources (monopoly profits) with which to carry out expensive R&D functions. The manager of a perfectly competitive firm, by contrast, has to worry about day-to-day production decisions and profit margins. As a result, he is unable to take the longer view necessary for significant research and development, and could not afford to pursue such a view even if he could see it. Thus, it is contended, market power is desirable because of the research and development opportunities it creates.

The basic problem with the R&D argument is that it says nothing about *incentives*. Although a monopolist has a clear advantage in pursuing research and development activities, he has no clear incentive to do so. He can continue to make substantial profits just by maintaining his market power. Research and development are not necessarily required for profitable survival. In fact, research and development that tend to make his existing plant and equipment technologically obsolete run counter to his vested interest and so may actually be suppressed.[6] In contrast, a perfectly competitive firm cannot continue to make significant profits unless it stays ahead of the competition. This pressure constitutes a significant incentive to discover new products or new and cheaper ways of producing old products.

A very limited but suggestive perspective on the R&D efforts of highly competitive industries can be gained by comparing different industries. The highly competitive semiconductor industry spends less on research and development than the much less competitive automobile industry. But the semiconductor industry is also much

---

[6] We shall examine this issue further in Chapter 24, especially as it relates to the U.S. auto industry.

smaller. When relative size is considered, the semiconductor industry spends twice as much on R&D as the automobile industry does. In 1981, the semiconductor industry spent 7.1 percent of sales on R&D efforts; the auto industry spent only 3.7 percent.

The commitment of electronics firms to R&D has had dramatic effects on consumer products and prices. Cheap pocket calculators are just one example of the benefits of that competitive R&D. Had technology in the auto industry advanced as rapidly—and had prices fallen as costs were reduced—the 1983 Cadillac would have been priced at less than $100 rather than over $15,000.

It is also important to observe that the R&D efforts that a monopolist does pursue will tend to serve his own interests and probably enhance his market power. The result will be greater redistribution of income and welfare in his direction. Accordingly, if we wish to create research opportunities unattainable by the typical competitive firm, we need not embrace monopolies. A stronger case can be made for directly subsidizing R&D efforts (for instance, through tax credits or research grants) than for indirectly subsidizing them through the mechanism of monopoly profits. In that way, we could achieve our goals of innovation and growth without sacrificing our income-distribution goals.

To some extent, of course, all firms are capable of improving their productive efficiency as they acquire experience. That is to say, firms can develop improved techniques via the process of "learning by doing," a process that may not necessitate any research expenditures. Hence large firms may learn to cut costs as they grow larger. Small firms, too, however, can profit from experience and thus increase their efficiency as well. The critical question is whether experience-based efficiency improvements are intrinsically related to output volume. If so, a case for monopoly can be built on this phenomenon. We shall return to this argument—and potential economies of scale—in a moment.

Entrepreneurial incentives

The second argument proffered in favor of market power is that the potential for monopoly profits acts as a tremendous incentive for entrepreneurial activity. As we observed in Chapter 20, every business is out to make a buck, and it is the quest for profits that keeps industries running. Thus, it is argued, even greater profit prizes will stimulate more entrepreneurial activity. Little Horatio Algers will work harder and longer if they can dream of one day possessing a whole monopoly.

The incentive argument for market power is interesting, but it must be approached cautiously. After all, an innovator can make substantial profits in a competitive market, as it typically takes a considerable amount of time for the competition to catch up. Recall that the early birds still got the worm in the competitive calculator industry of Chapter 21, even though profit margins were later squeezed. Hence it is not evident that the profit incentives available in a competitive industry are at all inadequate.

We must also recall the arguments about research and development efforts. A monopolist has little incentive to pursue R&D and

The new case for monopolists

Monopoly is losing its bad name in court.

For 90 years the antitrust movement has ridden a wave of outrage at the dominance of industries by single companies, a wave that led Congress, in the Sherman Antitrust Act, to make it a federal crime to garner too big a portion of any market. . . . As enunciated by the Supreme Court in 1948, the law was that "monopoly power, whether lawfully or unlawfully acquired, may itself constitute an evil and stand condemned."

But a string of recent court decisions shows that the old outrage at the mere fact of monopoly has cooled, especially if the monopolist champions innovation. . . .

In September, for instance, U.S. District Judge Malcolm M. Lucas in Los Angeles threw out a monopolization charge that a small auto-parts maker brought against W. R. Grace & Co. Even though Grace once had 100% of the market involved—a decorative wheel for sports cars—Lucas ruled that the later entrance of others into the field proved that Grace had no monopoly power.

The most significant indicator of the new attitude toward monopoly came in October, when the Federal Trade Commission dismissed an attempt by its staff to undo Du Pont Co.'s rapid extension of its capacity to produce titanium dioxide, a chemical brightener used in paint and paper. Du Pont's expansion was tied to a cheaper process that the giant chemical manufacturer developed. Explaining the unanimous decision, Commissioner David A. Clanton wrote that "the essence of the competitive process is to induce firms to become more efficient and to pass the benefits of the efficiency along to consumers. That process would be ill-served by using antitrust to block hard, aggressive competition that is solidly based on efficiencies and growth opportunities, even if monopoly is a possible result."

The changed judicial attitude toward monopolies stems from growing concern that innovation is lagging in the U.S. and that clamping down on risk-taking companies will stifle technological experimentation. Du Pont Chairman Irving S. Shapiro made the point repeatedly in lashing out at the FTC titanium dioxide case. In one private suit against IBM, the U.S. Court of Appeals in Denver said that "technical attainments were not intended to be inhibited or penalized" by the Sherman Act. And last year, in overturning much of a monopolization ruling against Eastman Kodak Co., the U.S. Court of Appeals in New York insisted that "innovativeness" is a marketing route open to a monopolist.

Burden of proof

In fact, Boston attorney Thayer Fremont-Smith noted at last month's annual New England Antitrust Conference that so much concern is developing for spurring new products and processes that, he predicts, courts will begin to presume legal any conduct that monopolists could argue would encourage innovation. The burden would then be on plaintiffs to prove that the conduct in question does not benefit the public.

Such a standard would most aid companies in new markets or those in which the technology is changing rapidly. These are the markets where one company is likely to dominate. "The Xerox machine created a short-term monopolist," says Donald I. Baker, former Justice Dept. antitrust chief, "but it has now been caught up with."

may have a vested interest in discouraging such efforts. Furthermore, those who might engage in product innovation or technological improvements for a particular industry may be dissuaded by their inability to penetrate the market. That is to say, the barriers to entry that surround market power may not only keep out potential competitors but also lock out promising ideas. These impediments to entrepreneurship must be balanced against any unique incentives flowing from the promise of market power.

Economies of scale

A third argument for market power is by far the most convincing. The argument is simple. A large firm can produce goods at a lower unit (average) cost than that attainable by a small firm. That is, there are economies of scale. Thus, if we desire to produce goods in the most efficient way—with the least amount of resources per unit of output—we should encourage and maintain large firms. By increasing efficiency through economies of scale, large firms expand society's production possibilities.

Consider once again the comparison we made earlier between Universal Electronics and the competitive calculator industry of

Chapter 21. We explicitly assumed that Universal confronted the same production costs as the competitive industry. We simply converted each typical competitive firm into a separate plant owned and operated by Universal. Thus Universal was not able to produce pocket calculators any more cheaply than the competitive counterpart, and we concerned ourselves only with the different production decisions made by competitive and monopolistic firms.

Over time, however, firms have an opportunity to make different **investment decisions** as well. In this long-run context, there is no compelling reason why we should assume that Universal will construct or maintain a multitude of separate plants. Why wouldn't it instead construct one large plant and centralize its manufacturing operations? One potential advantage to centralization would be an increase in efficiency and an attendant reduction in unit costs.

Even though large firms may be able to achieve greater efficiencies than smaller firms, there is no assurance that they actually will. As we observed in Chapter 19, increasing the size (scale) of a plant may actually reduce operating efficiency (see Figure 19.10). In evaluating the economies of scale for market power, then, we must be careful to recognize that efficiency and size do not necessarily go hand in hand. Some firms and industries may be subject to economies of scale, but others will not be. Therefore, each market-power situation must be examined separately.

NATURAL MONOPOLIES Industries that exhibit economies of scale over the entire range of market output are often referred to as **natural monopolies.** In these cases, one single firm can produce the entire market supply more efficiently than any larger number of (smaller) firms. As the size (scale) of the one firm increases, its minimum average costs continue to fall. These economies of scale give the one large producer a decided advantage over would-be rivals. Hence economies of scale act as a "natural" barrier to entry.

Telephone and utility services are classic examples of natural monopoly. A single telephone or utility company can supply the market more efficiently than a large number of competing firms.

Although natural monopolies are economically desirable, they may be abused. We must ask whether and to what extent consumers are reaping some benefit from the efficiency a natural monopoly makes possible. Do consumers end up with lower prices, expanded output, and better service? Or does the monopoly tend to keep much of the benefits for itself, in the form of higher profits, wages, and more comfortable offices? Typically, federal, state, and local governments are responsible for regulating natural monopolies to ensure that the benefits of increased efficiency are shared with consumers.

POLICY IMPLICATIONS: IBM AND AT&T

Monopolies may have adverse effects on prices, output, technological advance, and the distribution of income. For this reason, federal, state, and even local governments have been empowered to prevent or regulate concentrations of market power. The cornerstone of these

investment decision: The decision to build, buy, or lease plant and equipment, to start or expand a business.

natural monopoly: An industry in which one firm can achieve economies of scale over the entire range of market supply.

Monopoly pays off in the business of sports

When the New York Giants football team opened its 1980 home season against the Washington Redskins on Sept. 13, two sounds were clearly audible at Giants Stadium in New Jersey: the roar of 73,000 fans and the ringing of owner Wellington Mara's cash register. Had the vast stadium been entirely devoid of spectators—who paid roughly $700,000 for the privilege of seeing the Giants lose—Mara's money counter would have slowed somewhat, but the national television contract he shares in equally with other National Football League owners provides about the same amount of revenues as do paid admissions. On that Sunday, for example, the Giants' take for national television rights to the game totaled $620,000.

While football is the blue chip of professional sports, Mara's experiences are not dissimilar from those of many owners of professional baseball, basketball, and hockey teams, for the $700 million-a-year business of professional sports today is a highly charged enterprise capable of producing heavy profits for its owners. . . .

Snowball Effect

Moreover, professional sports is spinning off several times that amount of money to the plethora of businesses that it touches—television, radio, brewing, retailing, and even gambling, where as much as $75 million a year is wagered on sporting events. In fact, given professional sports' monopoly status and self-regulating characteristics, the business can only become bigger. "Americans are affected every day by two cartels—OPEC and professional sports," says one insider. "People just don't realize how powerful the latter one is."

Owning a professional sports franchise is a popular daily double: Huge profits are available both through the ongoing-business side of the venture as well as via the sale of a franchise. Indeed, in becoming America's home-grown cartel, the business of professional sports has undergone a remarkable metamorphosis: Disappearing, for the most part, are the mom-and-pop and family-run operations motivated by civic pride and public relations, replaced instead by savvy broadcasting- and entertainment-sensitive businessmen eager to reap the riches that only a monopoly enterprise can ensure. . . .

Profit is the name of the game. The average National Football League franchise earns a profit of about $1.2 million a year on revenues of $11 million regardless of whether it wins the Super Bowl or winds up the season losing all 16 games. . . .

At the foundation of the boom is an antitrust exemption that has guarded professional sports for many years. Yet the exemption is sketchy at best.

Based on a 1922 decision by the Supreme Court, baseball, in fact, is the only sport actually ruled to be exempt. But the same ruling has provided hockey, football, and basketball with de facto exemptions. Sports management bristles at the suggestion that they are getting away with something, however. Baseball Commissioner Bowie Kuhn, for example, has a difficult time admitting that baseball is a business. And Pete Rozelle, commissioner of the NFL, says that football has been scrutinized repeatedly and comes up clean each time. "We've been investigated by the FCC, FTC, Justice Dept., NLRB, and IRS, plus a multitude of state and local bodies," he says. "We are not an unregulated monopoly. We are constantly challenged. What we are is a natural monopoly."

Dividing the Spoils

Natural or not, the monopoly allows baseball to operate with a financial structure under which about 30% of total revenues of about $310 million goes to player salaries, bonuses, and pension costs—which owners constantly cite as the most onerous expense of the business. In football, the figure rises to 40%, and in basketball to some 55%. The remainder, then, is available for other expenses and profits.

"trust-busting" powers is the Sherman Act of 1890, which permits the federal government to penalize and even dismember a corporation that engages in monopoly practices (see the accompanying box). With this act as its principal weapon, the U.S. Department of Justice has blocked attempted mergers and acquisitions, forced changes in price or output behavior, required large companies to sell some of their assets, and even sent corporate executives to jail for "conspiracies in restraint of trade."

Despite all this trust-busting, however, two questions always linger. First, what constitutes a "monopoly" in the real world? Second, what kind of monopoly practices should be prohibited? The

THE LEGAL FOUNDATIONS OF ANTITRUST ACTIONS

The Sherman Act (1890) — The Sherman Act prohibits "conspiracies in restraint of trade," including mergers, contracts, or acquisitions that threaten to monopolize an industry. Firms that violate the Sherman Act are subject to fines of up to $1 million, and their executives may be subject to imprisonment. In addition, consumers who are damaged—for example, via high prices—by a "conspiracy in restraint of trade" may recover treble damages.

The Clayton Act (1914) — The Clayton Act of 1914 was passed to outlaw specific antitrust behavior not covered by the Sherman Act. The principal aim of the act was to prevent the development of monopolies. To this end, the Clayton Act prohibited price discrimination, exclusive dealing agreements, certain types of mergers, and interlocking boards of directors among competing firms.

The Federal Trade Commission Act (1914) — The increased antitrust responsibilities of the federal government created the need for an agency that could study industry structures and behavior so as to identify anticompetitive practices. The Federal Trade Commission was created for this purpose in 1914.

---

first question relates to the *structure* of markets, the second to their *behavior*. Both questions were the center of attention in two historic cases—against IBM and AT&T. The two cases were ended on the same day (January 8, 1982) but for very different reasons. Together they illustrate the central concerns of public antitrust policy.

AT&T: extending a natural monopoly

The American Telephone and Telegraph (AT&T) Corporation has long held a virtual monopoly on domestic phone service. As recently as 1981, AT&T provided 96 percent of all long-distance phone service and over 80 percent of local phone service. AT&T had total revenues of roughly $60 billion in 1981 (equal to 2 percent of GNP!) and profits of roughly $7 billion.

The dominant position of AT&T in the telephone industry was widely viewed as inevitable. As we noted earlier, telephone service tends to be a *natural monopoly*. One large firm can supply the market more cheaply than a multitude of small, competitive firms. The source of this natural monopoly lies in the economies of scale associated with transmission networks. Once the networks are in place, the marginal costs of increasing output are negligible. In recognition of this situation, the government permitted development of a monopolistic structure in the telephone industry.

While permitting monopoly structure, the government has regulated AT&T's behavior. In particular, state utility commissions and the Federal Communications Commission (FCC) have regulated the price and quantity of phone service while setting a limit on AT&T's

AT&T Divestiture

□ AT&T must divest itself of the local telephone services of its 23 Bell System operating companies.

□ Western Electric, Bell Laboratories and the long-distance division of AT&T will be retained by AT&T. All intrastate long-distance service will be turned over to AT&T by the local companies.

□ AT&T no longer will be barred from offering unregulated nontelephone service, thereby opening the way for the corporation to enter the computer processing and information service business.

□ Local telephone companies divested by AT&T will be required to share their facilities with all long-distance telephone companies on the same terms.

□ Local companies will be barred from discriminating against AT&T competitors in buying equipment and planning new facilities.

□ AT&T shareholders will retain stock in AT&T and will be issued proportionate values of shares in the local exchange companies.

□ The Justice Department will have visiting rights at the local operating companies to interview employes and review the books.

The Washington Post, Washington, D.C., January 8, 1982, p. 1.

---

monopoly profits. The objective of this regulation was to ensure that consumers reaped the advantages of a natural monopoly.

What got AT&T into trouble was its attempt to extend its monopoly over its "natural" limits. AT&T established a subsidiary, Western Electric, to manufacture phones and other equipment that can be connected to the transmission network. Because it controlled all telephone service, AT&T could effectively dictate whose phones would be used. By establishing Western Electric, AT&T was essentially proclaiming a monopoly in phone manufacturing and sales, as well as in telephone service. Unfortunately, there are no inherent economies of scale in phones themselves, so AT&T's move could not be defended as a "natural" extension of telephone service. Instead, the creation of Western Electric looked like a mechanism for transferring monopoly profits out of a regulated market (phone service) into an unregulated one (phone manufacture).

As the electronics revolution progressed, other firms wanted to produce and sell not only telephones but also more sophisticated services, including satellite transmissions. To do so, however, they had to have access to AT&T transmission networks (including the users' phones). AT&T resisted all such attempts, arguing that the hooking up of non-AT&T equipment would harm the transmission network. When pressed by lawsuits or regulatory actions to permit such hookups, AT&T required costly and cumbersome connection devices.

As a result of such behavior, the U.S. Department of Justice filed suit against AT&T in 1978, arguing that AT&T and "their co-conspirators have used their positions of dominance in long-distance transmission, equipment manufacturing, and local franchise monopolies, and the leverage derived therefrom, to suppress this new competition and to maintain and enhance their monopoly power."[7]

---

[7] This was the third major antitrust case filed by the Justice Department against AT&T; the second one was settled by consent decree in 1956. That consent decree required AT&T to stay out of all new unregulated markets.

As the federal suit against AT&T made its way through the courts, some of AT&T's competitors filed antitrust suits of their own. Two of these suits, by MCI, Inc., and Litton Industries, ended with huge fines against AT&T. The Federal Trade Commission and the U.S. Congress also increased the pace of their own investigations. By 1982 it was fairly clear that AT&T would not be able to defend itself successfully against the Justice Department's charges. Accordingly, AT&T agreed—without admitting to monopoly practices—to give up its monopoly position in local phone service. Local phone service will be provided instead by new and independent local telephone-service companies ("Baby Bells"), all of which will remain under government regulation. The rest of AT&T ("Ma Bell"), including Western Electric and other subsidiaries (see news clipping), will keep out of local telephone service and thus be free to compete on an equal and unregulated basis in all other segments of the communications industry. In this way, the public can reap the advantages of enhanced competition in markets not subject to natural monopoly while continuing to enjoy the advantages of a natural monopoly in transmission networks. The Justice Department gave AT&T six months to devise a divestiture plan that would satisfy these objectives and another year to implement the plan after court approval.

IBM: big is not necessarily bad

The federal government's antitrust case against IBM was very different. Like AT&T, IBM dominated its industry. At the time the suit was filed in 1969, IBM was producing roughly 70 percent of all computers. The Justice Department argued that there was no "natural" basis for such dominance and thus that the structure of the computer market was anticompetitive.

It was further asserted that IBM's *behavior* stifled increased competition. Three specific practices were cited. First, it was alleged that IBM intimidated customers who wanted to connect non-IBM equipment (e.g., disc drives, add-on memories) to IBM systems (a charge like the one leveled at AT&T). Second, IBM was said to discourage prospective buyers of competing computers by "pre-announcing" new IBM models. By hinting that a newer and better IBM computer was just around the corner, IBM could persuade customers to withhold orders from competitors. Finally, IBM was alleged to engage in aggressive price cutting whenever competition increased.

The IBM suit dragged on for 13 years. During that time, over 66 *million* pages of documents were filed. Both the structure of the industry and IBM's behavior were contested. With respect to structure, IBM claimed the computer market was larger than the government alleged and growing enormously. Although IBM was dominant in one segment of the industry (large main-frame computers), it was a relatively small force in other segments (see Figure 22.7). Furthermore, IBM had to contend with aggressive competitors even in the one market segment it dominated. Hence, IBM argued, the charge of monopoly was baseless.

IBM also denied engaging in monopolistic behavior. IBM

FIGURE 22.7 IBM's SHARE OF THE MARKET (percentage of dollar value of units installed)

The computer market includes several different kinds of products. IBM has always dominated the market for large, general-purpose computers. In the production of small computers, however, IBM confronts intense competition.

Reprinted by permission from TIME, The Weekly Newsmagazine; copyright © Time Inc., 1982.

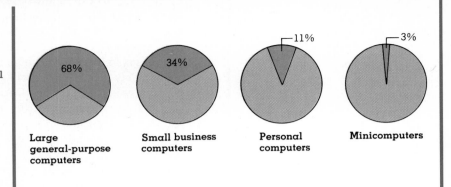

68%
Large general-purpose computers

34%
Small business computers

11%
Personal computers

3%
Minicomputers

pointed out that it had no barriers to entry (unlike AT&T) and therefore had no power to create or maintain a monopoly. On the contrary, competitors were continually swarming like flies into the computer industry. All IBM was "guilty" of, it argued, was reducing prices, improving its products, and competing aggressively. In the process, consumers had benefited enormously from dramatic technological improvements in computer design and service and markedly lower prices.

On January 8, 1982, the Justice Department accepted these arguments and dropped the antitrust suit against IBM. In explaining his decision, Assistant Attorney General William Baxter said: "What we learned today is that a company that is large and has a large market share should be allowed to compete aggressively. Period." With those remarks, the government acknowledged that monopoly powers can either harm (AT&T) or benefit (IBM) consumers, depending on how that power is obtained and used.

SUMMARY

■ Market power is the ability to influence significantly the market price of goods and services. In product markets, such power usually resides on the supply side of the market, as consumers are too numerous and too independent to have any individual influence on the shape of the market demand curve.

■ The extreme case of market power is monopoly, a situation in which only one firm produces the entire supply of a particular product, and thus has an immediate impact on the quantity supplied to the market and the market price.

■ The distinguishing feature of any firm with market power is the fact that the demand curve it faces is downward-sloping. In the case of monopoly, the demand curve facing the firm and the market demand curve are identical.

■ The downward-sloping demand curve facing a monopolist creates a divergence between marginal revenue and price. To sell larger quantities of output, the monopolist must lower product prices. A firm without market power has no such problem.

■ Like other producers, a monopolist will produce at the rate of output at which marginal revenue equals marginal cost. Because marginal revenue is always less than price for a noncompetitive firm, the monopolist will produce less output than will a competitive industry confronting the same market demand and cost opportunities. That reduced rate of output will be sold at higher prices, in accordance with the (downward-sloping) market demand curve.

■ A monopoly will attain a higher level of profit than a competitive industry because of its ability to equate industry (its own) marginal revenues and costs. By contrast, a competitive industry ends up equating marginal costs and price, because its individual firms have no control over the market supply curve.

■ Because the higher profits attained by a monopoly will attract envious entrepreneurs, barriers to entry are needed to prohibit other firms from expanding market supplies. Patents are one such barrier to entry.

■ The principal arguments for market power focus on (1) the alleged ability of large firms to pursue long-term research and development, (2) the incentives implicit in the chance to attain market power, and (3) the efficiency that larger firms may attain. The first two arguments are weakened by the fact that competitive firms are under much greater pressure to innovate and can stay ahead of the profit game if they do so.

■ A natural monopoly exists when one firm can produce the output of the entire industry more efficiently than can a number of smaller firms. This advantage is attained from economies of scale. Large firms are not necessarily more efficient, however, because either constant returns to scale or diseconomies of scale may prevail.

Terms to remember

Define the following terms:

market power	**average total cost**
monopoly	**marginal cost pricing**
profit-maximization rule	**price elasticity of demand**
marginal revenue	**price discrimination**
barriers to entry	**investment decision**
economies of scale	**natural monopoly**
production decision	

Questions for discussion

1. The objective in the game of Monopoly is to get all the property and then raise the rents. Can this power be explained with market supply and demand curves?

2. Is single ownership of a whole industry necessary to exercise monopoly power? How might an industry with many firms achieve the same result? Can you think of any examples?

3. In addition to higher profits, what other benefits accrue to a firm with market power?

4. Why don't monopolists try to establish "the highest price possible," as many people allege? What would happen to sales? to profits?

5. Do consumers have any market power?

Problem | The following table summarizes the sales and cost situation confronting a monopolist:

Price (per unit)	Quantity demanded (per week)	Total revenue (per week)	Marginal revenue	Total cost	Marginal cost	Average total cost
$40.00	20			$510		
40.50	19			466		
41.00	18			424		
41.50	17			384		
42.00	16			346		
42.50	15			310		
43.00	14			276		
43.50	13			244		
44.00	12	$528.00	$38.50	214	$28.00	$17.83
44.50	11			186		
45.00	10			160		

Use the figures provided in the table to:

(a) Complete the table (start from the bottom).
(b) Graph the demand, *MR*, *MC*, and *ATC* curves.
(c) Calculate the maximum total profits obtainable.

CHAPTER 23

IMPERFECT COMPETITION

Although it is convenient to think of the economy as composed of the powerful and the powerless, market realities do not always provide such clear distinctions. There are very few perfectly competitive markets in the world, and few monopolies. But market power is an important phenomenon, nonetheless. It's just that it is typically shared by several firms rather than monopolized by one. In the automobile industry, for example, General Motors, Ford, and Chrysler share tremendous market power, even though none qualifies as a pure monopolist. The same kind of power is shared by Coca-Cola, Pepsi, and Dr Pepper in the soft-drink market, and by Kellogg, General Mills, and General Foods in the breakfast-cereals market.

These kinds of situations, which fall between the extremes of perfect competition and pure monopoly, fall into the category of "imperfect competition." They contain some elements of competitive rivalry, but also exhibit vestiges of monopoly. Indeed, in many cases, imperfect competitors behave much like a monopoly, generally restricting output, charging higher prices, and reaping greater profits than firms in a competitive market. But behavior in imperfectly competitive markets is more complicated than in a monopoly, because it involves a number of decision makers (firms) rather than only one.

In this chapter we shall focus on two major forms of imperfect competition: *oligopoly* and *monopolistic competition*. We shall examine the nature of decision making in each of these market structures and the likely impacts on prices, production, and profits. In Chapter 24 we shall look at the actual behavior of some familiar firms that possess market power.

DEGREES OF POWER

Some individuals and firms have virtually no influence over the prices of the products they buy and sell, and thus no market power. They are constrained to reacting to market prices and are unable to change them by withholding production or purchases. Other individuals and firms do have some influence over prices, and thus some degree of market power. The degree of power they possess, however, varies tremendously. As we saw in Chapter 22, AT&T has been the sole supplier of telephone services in most urban areas of the United States. As a result, it has had tremendous market power. The corner grocery store, on the other hand, must compete with other stores and has less control over prices. But even the corner grocery is not completely powerless. If it is the only grocery within walking distance— or the only one open on Sunday—it, too, may exert *some* influence on prices and product flows. The amount of power it possesses depends on the proximity and convenience of alternative retail outlets.

The same kind of gradations in power can be seen in thousands of products and market situations. Take the case of Coca-Cola. The Coca-Cola Company has an exclusive license to use that particular brand name. As a result, it is the sole supplier of Coca-Cola, and can exert considerable influence on the price of that product. Coca-Cola's market power is diluted considerably, however, by the availability and price of other thirst-quenching alternatives. If Coca-Cola's price rises too far, more and more people will switch to Pepsi, cold beer, or, as a last resort, water. Consequently, the ability of the Coca-Cola Company to alter prices—its market power—is far from absolute.

Market structures

In accordance with the many gradations of market power, each market situation is separately defined. The case of absolute powerlessness is referred to as *perfect competition*. **Perfect competition is perfect in the sense that no buyer or seller of a particular product has any direct influence on the market price of that good.** Of course, the interactions of all buyers and sellers together still determine the market price. Each buyer and seller functions independently, however, and with no discernible effect on price determination. Were any single buyer or seller to change his or her behavior, the market price would remain the same. Such a situation, seen in the competitive calculator illustration of Chapter 21, exists when I sell my two shares of IBM stock or when Farmer Evans decides not to harvest his thirty acres of wheat. In each case, the dimensions of individual action are so small in relation to the size of the market that the action has no impact.

At the other extreme of market power is *perfect monopoly*. A perfect monopoly exists when only one individual or firm is the exclusive supplier of a particular product. In such a case, any change in the quantity supplied to the market by the monopolist is immediately reflected in the price and quantity sold of that good. Our illustration of Universal Electronics exemplifies such a firm. The amount of power a "perfect" monopoly can wield still depends on the availability of substitute goods, however. Even as perfect a monopoly as AT&T must take into consideration the prices of alternative communications media: Western Union, communications satellites, and the mail.

Between the two extremes of perfect competition and perfect monopoly lies most of the real world, which is imperfectly competitive. ***In imperfect competition, individual firms have some power in a particular product market.*** Two forms of imperfect competition are particularly noteworthy: oligopoly and monopolistic competition.

Oligopoly is a situation in which only a few firms have a great deal of power in a product market. An oligopoly may exist because only a few firms produce a particular product or because a few firms account for most, though not all, of a product's output. In either case, firms in an oligopoly are highly *interdependent*, because of their very small number. Changes in the price or output of one oligopolist immediately affect the other oligopolists.

A more limited degree of market power is possessed by firms in **monopolistic competition.** In this case, there are many firms supplying the market, not just a few. Because of the larger number of sell-

oligopoly: A market in which a few firms produce all or most of the market supply of a particular good or service.

monopolistic competition: A market in which many firms produce similar goods or services, but each maintains some independent control of its own price.

MARKET STRUCTURES

- **PERFECT COMPETITION** A market comprised of many powerless firms. The production decisions of any single firm have no effect on other firms or the market price of the product it sells. Individual farmers are classic examples of perfect competitors.

- **MONOPOLISTIC COMPETITION** A situation in which many firms sell similar products, each of which is perceived by consumers as being in some way unique. Although each firm has some influence over the price at which its own output (brand) is sold, the production decisions of any single firm do not directly affect the sales or selling price of other firms (brands). Examples include fast-food chains (McDonald's, Ponderosa, Burger King), supermarkets, and most apparel manufacturers.

- **OLIGOPOLY** A market in which a few firms control such a large share of total industry output that they can influence market price. In *pure (perfect) oligopoly*, all firms produce an identical good (for example, cement, steel rods, paper clips). In a *differentiated (imperfect) oligopoly*, each firm's product has a unique identity (for example, cigarettes, breakfast cereals), although all are basically the same. In either kind of oligopoly, the production decisions of any single firm affect all other firms and the market price of the product sold.

- **DUOPOLY** A market in which two firms produce the entire market supply.

- **MONOPOLY** A market with only one supplier, who therefore controls the quantity supplied to the market and its price.

ers, the individual firms are less interdependent than oligopolistic firms. An individual firm can alter its own price or output without directly affecting the other firms in the industry. At the same time, each firm has its own identity (brand name and image) in the market, and can therefore increase the price of its own output without losing most of its customers to its rivals.

Determinants of market power

The amount of market power that exists in any given situation depends on several factors, including:

□ Number of producers
□ Size of each firm
□ Barriers to entry
□ Availability of substitute goods

The most obvious determinant of power is the number of producers or sellers. When only one or a few producers or suppliers exist, market power is automatically conferred. In addition to the number of producers, however, the size of each firm is also important. One large producer competing with 17 small ones may possess more market power than he would if he had to compete with only six relatively large firms. Other firms of comparable size at least have some ability to withstand pressures and threats to change prices or product flows.

A third and critical determinant of market power is the extent of barriers to entry for potential competitors. A highly successful monopoly or oligopoly will tend to arouse the envy of other profit maximizers. They will seek to enter that particular product market in order to share in the spoils. Should they succeed, the power of the former monopolist or oligopolists would be reduced. Accordingly, the ease of entry into an industry is an important dimension of the ability to influence prices and product flow for any substantial period of time. In Chapter 22 we observed how a patent can be used to block entry. In Chapter 24 we shall examine other barriers to entry employed by powerful firms.

Finally, we may note that a fourth factor defining the dimensions of market power is the availability of substitute products. If a monopolist or other power baron sets the price of his product too high, consumers may decide to switch to other products. Thus the price of Coors is kept in check by the price of Coke, and the price of sirloin steak is restrained by the price of chicken and pork. By the same token, a lack of available substitute products may confer very great market power, as reflected in a very low price elasticity of demand for the product in question. Those who possess market power frequently attempt to extend and reinforce it by using advertising to create the impression that their product has no substitutes. If 10 million beer drinkers refuse to quench their thirst with anything but Coors beer, then the Adolph Coors Company will possess considerable market power. For loyal Coors drinkers, it simply doesn't matter how many other beer producers exist or how large they are. The same is true for Tide detergent, Maxwell House coffee, Coca-Cola,

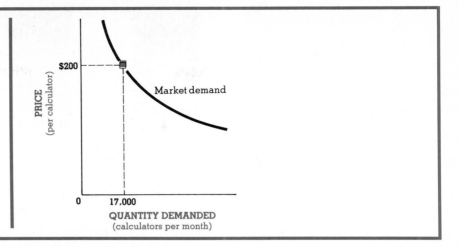

FIGURE 23.1 INITIAL CONDITIONS IN THE CALCULATOR MARKET

As in Chapters 21 and 22, we assume that the initial equilibrium in the calculator market occurs at a price of $200 and a quantity of 17,000 calculators per month. How will an oligopoly alter these outcomes?

and Zig-Zag cigarette papers. As long as each consumer identifies with and purchases only one brand, it doesn't matter how many other firms produce basically identical products; each consumer will have effectively imposed a monopoly on himself or herself.

OLIGOPOLY BEHAVIOR

We can illustrate the behavior of a typical oligopoly by assuming a different market structure for the electronic calculator market. In Chapter 21 we observed that in the absence of barriers to entry the pocket calculator market was highly competitive. In Chapter 22 we created an impassable barrier to entry (a patent on the electronic brain of the calculator) that transformed the calculator industry into a monopoly of Universal Electronics. Now we shall transform the industry again, this time assuming that three separate firms (Universal, World, and International) all possess patent rights. The patent rights permit each firm to produce and sell all the calculators it desires and to exclude all other would-be producers from the market.

The initial equilibrium

market share: The percentage of total market output produced by a single firm.

As before, we shall assume that the initial conditions in the calculator market are represented by a market price of $200 and market sales of 17,000 calculators per month, as illustrated in Figure 23.1.

We shall also assume that the **market share** of each producer is accurately depicted in Table 23.1. Thus Universal Electronics is as-

TABLE 23.1 INITIAL MARKET SHARES OF CALCULATOR PRODUCERS

The market share of a firm is the percentage of total market output it produces. These are hypothetical market shares of three fictional oligopolists.

Producer	Output (calculators per month)	Market share (percent)
Universal Electronics	8,000	47.1
World Calculators	5,000	29.4
International Semiconductor	4,000	23.5
Total industry output	17,000	100.0

sumed to be producing 8,000 calculators per month, or 47.1 percent of total market supply. World Calculators has a market share of 29.4 percent, while International Semiconductor has only a 23.5 percent share.

The battle for market shares

The first thing to note about the calculator oligopoly is that it is likely to exhibit great internal tension. Neither World Calculators nor International Semiconductor is really happy playing second or third fiddle to Universal Electronics. Each company would like to be Number One in this market. On the other hand, Universal, too, would like a larger market share, particularly in view of the huge profits being made on calculators. As we observed in Chapter 21, the initial equilibrium in the calculator industry yielded an *average* profit of $130.85 per calculator, and total *industry* profits of $2.2 million per month (17,000 × $130.85). Hence Universal would be very happy to take over the market shares of its fellow oligopolists, thereby increasing its own profits.

The problem here is how to gain a larger market share. In a truly competitive market, a single producer could expand production at will, with no discernible impact on market supply. But ***in an oligopoly, increased sales on the part of one firm will be noticed immediately by the other firms.***

How do we know that increased sales will be noticed so quickly? Because increased sales by one firm will have to take place either at the existing market price ($200) or at a lower price. Either of these two events will ring an alarm at the corporate headquarters of the other two firms.

INCREASED SALES AT THE PREVAILING MARKET PRICE Consider first the possibility of Universal Electronics' increasing its sales at the going price of $200 per calculator. We know from the demand curve of Figure 23.1 that consumers are *willing to buy* only 17,000 calculators per month at that price. Hence any increase in calculator sales by Universal must be immediately reflected in *lower* sales by World or International. That is to say, increases in the market share of one oligopolist necessarily reduce the shares of the remaining oligopolists. If Universal were to increase its sales from 8,000 to 10,000 calculators per month, the combined monthly sales of World and International would have to fall from 9,000 to 7,000 (see Table 23.1). The **quantity demanded** at $200 per calculator remains 17,000 calculators per month (see Figure 23.1).

quantity demanded: The amount of a product a consumer is willing and able to buy at a specific price in a given time period (*ceteris paribus*).

This interaction between the market shares of the three oligopolists assures us that Universal's sales success will be noticed. Moreover, it won't be necessary for World Calculators or International Semiconductor to engage in industrial espionage to acquire the necessary information about Universal. These firms can quickly figure out what Universal is doing simply by looking at their own (declining) sales figures.

INCREASED SALES AT REDUCED PRICES Universal could pursue a different strategy, of course, and attempt to increase its sales by lowering

law of demand: The quantity of a good demanded in a given time period increases as its price falls (*ceteris paribus*).

the price of its calculators. Following the **law of demand,** reduced prices would expand total market sales, as demonstrated by the downward-sloping market demand curve of Figure 23.1. Hence price reductions could enable Universal to increase its sales without directly reducing the sales of either World or International.

But this outcome is most unlikely. If Universal lowered its calculator price from $200 to, say, $190, all consumers would flock to Universal calculators and the sales of World and International would plummet. After all, we have always assumed that consumers are rational enough to want to pay the lowest possible price for any particular good. It is unlikely that consumers would continue to pay $200 for a World or International machine when they could get basically the same calculator from Universal for only $190. If there were no difference, either perceived or real, in the calculators of the three firms, a *pure* oligopoly would exist. In that case, Universal would capture the *entire* market if it lowered its price below that of its rivals. More often, consumers perceive differences in the products of individual oligopolists, creating a *differentiated* oligopoly. In this case, Universal would gain many but not all customers if it reduced its price for its calculators.[1] In either case, there simply isn't any way that Universal can increase its sales at reduced prices without causing all the alarms to go off at World and International.

Retaliation

So what if all the alarms go off at World Calculators and International Semiconductor? As long as Universal Electronics is able to enlarge its share of the market and take in increased profits, why should it care if World and International find out? Indeed, Universal may even get some additional satisfaction out of the fact that World and International are upset by its marketing success.

Universal does have something to worry about, though. World and International may not be content to stand by and watch their market shares and profits diminish. On the contrary, World and International are likely to take some action of their own once they discover what is going on.

There are two things World and International can do once they decide to act. In the first case, where Universal is expanding its market share at prevailing prices ($200), World and International can retaliate by:

□ Stepping up their own marketing efforts
□ Cutting prices on their calculators

product differentiation:
Features that make one product appear different from competing products in the same market.

To step up their marketing efforts, World and International might increase their advertising expenditures, repackage their calculators, put more sales representatives on the street, or sponsor a college homecoming week. All such efforts at **product differentiation** are designed to make World and International calculators appear different and superior to the one produced by Universal Electronics. If successful, such marketing efforts will increase the sales and market shares of World and International, or at least stop Universal from

---

[1] In this example, we are assuming a differentiated oligopoly.

Marketing: Cold Cures Spread Like Flu as Companies Fight for Sales

Everyone knows the standard prescription for a bad cold: Take two aspirins and go to bed. That's still as good a remedy as most, but it hasn't deterred drug companies from bringing out product after product to stop sniffles, quiet coughs and dry runny noses.

Competition this year is fiercer than ever: More than a dozen new cold cures have hit pharmacy and supermarket shelves, with more on the way. The prize is a piece of the $1.2 billion cold-remedy market, among the largest in the nonprescription drug industry. The problem: Unit sales of cold medicines have been growing only about 3% a year.

"Because the market isn't very dynamic, brands succeed at the expense of others," says Emma W. Hill, a securities analyst with Wertheim & Co. "Companies therefore must maintain a steady flow of new products, enter new segments of the market, do anything to increase their shelf space."

Coming out with new products isn't easy. The ingredients available and levels that can be used are strictly limited by the Food and Drug Administration. A product's success often depends on a company's inventiveness in using these limited ingredients and on its marketing ability. . . .

The company to beat in this business is Richardson-Vicks, which markets 20 different lozenges, syrups, ointments, nasal sprays and other products for the treatment of coughs and colds. It claims to have 30% of the entire market "because we know the cold-remedy consumer and we gear our messages to get a response," according to Ronald A. Ahrens, president of the company's health-care division. "Frankly, our products are no better or worse than anybody else's."

—Michael Waldholz

grabbing a larger share for itself. In either case, Universal's initial sales initiative will fail and may end up requiring increased outlays for advertising or other marketing efforts to combat the efforts of World and International.

An even quicker way to stop Universal from enlarging its market share is for World and International to lower the price of their calculators. Such price reductions will destroy Universal's hopes of increasing its market share. In fact, this is the other side of a story we have already told. If the price of World and International calculators drops to, say, $190, it is preposterous to assume that Universal will be able to expand its market share at a price of $200. Instead, we assume that Universal's market share will drop substantially if it maintains a price of $200 per calculator after World and International drop their prices to $190 per calculator. Hence the threat to Universal's market-share grab is that the other two oligopolists will retaliate by reducing their prices. Should they carry out this threat, Universal would be forced to cut calculator prices, too, or accept a greatly reduced market share.

The same kind of threat exists in the second case, where we assumed that Universal Electronics expands its sales by initiating a price reduction. As we noted earlier, World and International are not going to just sit by and applaud Universal's marketing success. They will have to respond with price cuts of their own. Hence **an attempt by one oligopolist to increase its market share by cutting prices will lead to a general reduction in the market price** of calculators. The three oligopolists will end up using price reductions as weapons in the battle for market shares, the kind of behavior normally associated with competitive firms. Should this behavior continue, not only will oligopoly become less fun, but it will also become less profitable as prices slide down the market demand curve (Figure 23.2).

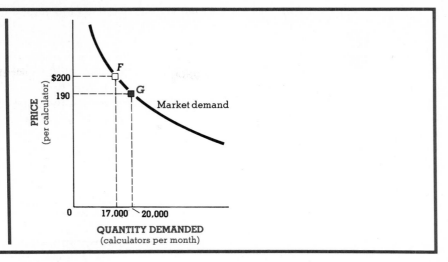

FIGURE 23.2 RIVALRY FOR MARKET SHARES THREATENS AN OLIGOPOLY

If oligopolists start cutting prices to capture larger market shares, they will be behaving much like truly competitive firms. The result will be a slide down the market demand curve to lower prices, increased output, and smaller profits. In this case, the market price and quantity would move from point *F* to point *G* if rival oligopolists cut prices to gain market shares.

THE KINKED DEMAND CURVE

The close interdependence of oligopolists—and the limitations it imposes on individual price and output decisions—is the principal moral of this story about Universal Electronics, World Calculators, and International Semiconductor. We can summarize this story with the aid of the kinked demand curve in Figure 23.3.

Recall that at the beginning of this oligopoly story Universal Electronics had a market share of 47.1 percent and was selling 8,000 calculators per month at a price of $200 each. This output is represented by point *A* in Figure 23.3. The rest of the demand curve illustrates what would happen to Universal's sales if it changed its selling price. What we have to figure out is why this particular demand curve has such a strange, "kinked" shape.

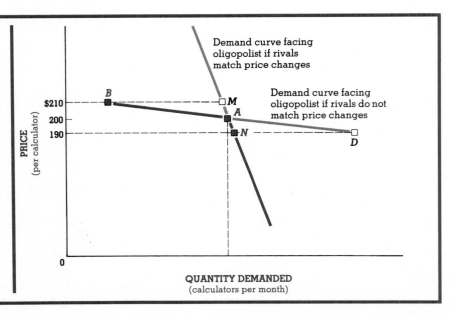

FIGURE 23.3 THE KINKED DEMAND CURVE CONFRONTING AN OLIGOPOLIST

The shape of the demand curve facing an oligopolist depends on the responses of its rivals to its price and output decisions. If rival oligopolists match price reductions but not price increases, the demand curve will be kinked. Initially, the oligopolist is at point *A*. If he raises his price to $210 and his rivals do not raise their prices, he will be driven to point *B*. If his rivals match a price reduction (to $190), the oligopolist will end up at point *N*.

Price reductions

Consider first what would happen to Universal's sales if it lowered the price of its calculators to $190. In general, we expect a price reduction to increase sales. However, *the degree to which sales increase when the price is reduced depends on the response of rival oligopolists.* Suppose World and International did not match Universal's price reduction. In this case, Universal would have the only low-priced calculator in the market. Consumers would flock to Universal and sales would increase dramatically, to point D. But point D is little more than a dream, as we have observed. World and International are sure to cut their prices to $190, too, in order to maintain their market shares. As a consequence, Universal's sales will expand to point N (not much), rather than to point D. Universal's increased sales at point N reflect the fact that the total quantity demanded in the market has risen as the market price has fallen to $190 (see Figure 23.2). Thus, although Universal's *market share* may not have increased, its monthly sales have.

The section of the demand curve that runs from point A to point D is unlikely to exist in an oligopolistic market. Instead, *we expect rival oligopolists to match any price reductions* that Universal initiates, forcing Universal to accept the demand curve that runs from point A through point N. The accompanying news clipping indicates the consequences of such rivalry.

Price increases

What about price increases? How will World and International respond if Universal raises the price of its calculators to $210?

Recall that the demand for calculators is assumed to be price elastic in the neighborhood of $200 and that all calculators are basically similar. Accordingly, if Universal raises its price and neither World nor International follows suit, Universal will be out there alone with a higher price and reduced sales. Hence *rival oligopolists may not match price increases.* In terms of Figure 23.3, a price increase that is not matched by rival oligopolists will drive Universal from point A to point B. At point B, Universal is selling very few calculators at its price of $210 each.[2]

[2] Notice again that we are assuming that Universal is able to sell some calculators at a higher price (point B) than its rivals'. The kinked demand curve applies only to differentiated oligopolies. As we shall discuss later, such differentiation may result from slight product variations, advertising, customer habits, location, friendly service, or any number of other factors. Most oligopolies exhibit some differentiation.

Candy War

Snickers Jacks Up Price by 5¢; Hershey Vows to Hold the Line

There's a candy bar war going on between Hershey and Snickers.

The fight is over prices: Snickers, the No. 1-selling candy bar in the country, went to 30 cents last month, up a nickel, while Hershey says it is "holding the line on candy bar prices."

Trouble is, some retailers decided to raise prices for all of their candies—including those of the two other big candy manufacturers, Hershey Foods Corp. and Nabisco Brands, makers of Baby Ruth and Butterfinger. . . .

Hershey was so upset by all this that it launched an advertising campaign to tell consumers that it wasn't responsible for the higher prices that some stores now charge. "We want you to know that Hershey is not raising the price of any of its candy bars," said the ad that appeared in 70 publications around the country in recent days.

—Molly Sinclair

The Washington Post, Washington, D.C., October 17, 1981.

Is this a likely outcome? Suffice it to say that World Calculators and International Semiconductor would not be unhappy about enlarging their own market shares. Therefore they are not likely to come to Universal's rescue with price increases.

Anything is possible, however, and World and International might match Universal's price increase. In this case, the *market* price would rise to $210 and the total quantity of calculators demanded would diminish. Under such circumstances Universal's sales would diminish, too, in accordance with its (constant) share of a smaller market. This would lead us to point *M* in Figure 23.3.

Gamesmanship

We may draw two conclusions from Figure 23.3:

- The shape of the demand curve facing an oligopolist depends on the responses of its rivals to a change in the price of its own output.
- That demand curve will be kinked if rival oligopolists match price reductions but not price increases.

An interesting thing about oligopolies is the potential they create for gamesmanship. The appropriateness of an oligopolist's pricing decision depends on the expected response of one's rivals. But this response is normally not known in advance; it must be guessed. For example, Universal *would* want to lower its prices *if it* thought its rivals would not retaliate with similar price cuts. It probably won't lower its prices, however, since it fears retaliation. Universal might be tempted to experiment a bit, though. It might offer a few large customers a discount, hoping World and International would not notice or would not react to modest reductions of their market shares.

The potential cost of such experimentation is high, however. Selective price cutting may lead to an all-out price war over market shares. In this sense, oligopolistic behavior is not unlike the kind of

---

United Airlines to Raise Fares on Many Flights

Price War Called 'Ruinous'; American and TWA Plan to Match Most Increases

United Airlines said it will increase transcontinental and midcontinental fares Nov. 1 in an effort to stop a costly fare war with its competitors. Some rivals said they would match at least some of United's increases.

The move comes only nine days after the UAL Inc. subsidiary slashed fares to defend its market share on coast-to-coast routes. United's major transcontinental competition comes from American Airlines, Continental Airlines and Trans World Airlines.

"We didn't start it. We want to stop it," a United spokesman in Chicago said, referring to the fare war that has sent prices tumbling in recent weeks. "It's ruinous for everyone," he said. . . .

In Dallas, a spokesman for American Airlines welcomed the fare increases and said American would match the higher fare on its transcontinental flights, starting Nov. 1.

"United's action is an encouraging sign for the industry," the spokesman said. "It supports the concept of restoring these fares to a more reasonable level." But he said American is still "studying the question" of whether to raise its fares, as United did, for midcontinental flights.

In Los Angeles, Continental Airlines' senior director for pricing, Sandy Rederer, said, "Our reaction is that United's action seems very reasonable.

"What we expect to do is wait to see what TWA and American do," he said, "If they match that, I assume we would adjust our fares as well."

Cold War games that the world's great powers play. Neither side is certain of the enemy's next move but knows it could bring total destruction. As a consequence, the United States and the Soviet Union are continually probing each other's responses but are quick to retreat from the brink whenever all-out retaliation is imminent. Oligopolists play the same kind of game on a much smaller scale, using price discounts and advertising rather than nuclear warheads as their principal weapons. The reward they receive for coexistence is the oligopoly profits that they continue to share. This reward, together with the threat of mutual destruction, leads oligopolists to limit their price rivalry.

Sticky prices

The kinked demand curve confronting the typical oligopolist leads to an even stranger-looking marginal revenue curve. ***The kinked demand curve is really a composite of two separate demand curves*** (Figure 23.4). One curve is predicated on the assumption that rival oligopolists do not respond to price increases (d_1). The other curve is predicated on the assumption that rivals do respond to price cuts (d_2). Each of these curves has its own marginal revenue curve, as illustrated in Figure 23.4. The demand curve d_1, for example, has **marginal revenue** curve mr_1, while demand curve d_2 has marginal revenue curve mr_2.

marginal revenue: The change in total revenue that results from a one-unit increase in the quantity sold.

To the extent that oligopolists behave in accordance with the kinked demand curve, each firm confronts the possibility of starting down the demand curve d_1, and switching to d_2 at point A. Hence from point S to point A the curve mr_1 depicts the relevant marginal revenues. At point A (the quantity of 8,000 calculators per month), however, we suddenly switch demand curves (to d_2). Hence we must seek out a new marginal revenue curve corresponding to d_2. To the right of point A, the marginal revenue curve mr_2 is operational.

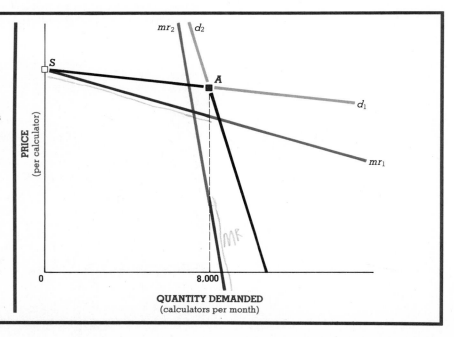

FIGURE 23.4 AN OLIGOPOLIST'S MARGINAL REVENUE CURVE

A kinked demand curve incorporates portions of two different demand curves (d_1 and d_2). Hence a kinked demand curve also has portions of two distinct marginal revenue curves (mr_1 and mr_2). Below the kink in the demand curve (point A) a gap exists between the two marginal revenue curves.

PRICE (per calculator)

QUANTITY DEMANDED (calculators per month)

FIGURE 23.5 THE MARGINAL REVENUE GAP

The kinked demand curve confronting an oligopolist creates a gap in his marginal revenue curve. As a consequence, a change in price or cost may not have any impact on the production decision. In this case, higher (MC_2) or lower (MC_3) marginal costs do not change the profit-maximizing rate of output.

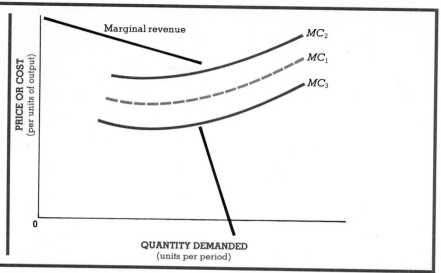

The oligopolist's marginal revenue curve thus contains two distinct segments. Figure 23.4 shows that *there is a gap in an oligopolist's marginal revenue curve, a gap that occurs just below the kink in the demand curve.* This gap turns out to be an important explanation of an oligopolist's behavior.

Recall that *all* producers **maximize profits** by producing at the rate of output at which marginal revenue equals marginal cost. As a consequence, most producers alter their production decision when the costs of production change. In general, a reduction in production costs (a downward shift of the marginal cost curve) will lead to an increase in the rate of output. An upward shift of the marginal cost curve will lead to a cutback in production.

These expectations are not always fulfilled in an oligopoly, however. Look at the marginal cost curves in Figure 23.5. If the marginal cost curve passes through the gap in the marginal revenue curve, *modest shifts of the cost curve will have no impact on the production decision of an oligopolist.* That is to say, an oligopolist need not reduce his rate of output when costs rise somewhat, or increase his rate of output when costs fall. As a consequence, an oligopolist's output does not fluctuate as much as either a competitive firm's or a profit-maximizing monopolist's. An oligopolist has a cost cushion around his production decision. Among other things, this cushion allows him to maintain a given price for longer periods and to incur higher marketing costs (such as advertising) if the need arises. In other words, the kinked demand curve results in "sticky" prices.

profit-maximization rule: Produce at that rate of output where marginal revenue equals marginal cost.

OLIGOPOLY VS. COMPETITION

Our examination of the demand and marginal revenue curves confronting an oligopolist reveals the close interdependence of rival oligopolists. Specifically, we have seen that *an individual oligopolist must consider rivals' responses before altering his own rate of output or price.* Now it is time to take a broader view of an oligopoly and compare its behavior with that of a competitive market.

Price rigidity

A basic lesson to be learned from the kinked demand curve is that *oligopoly prices will tend to be "sticky"; they will not fluctuate much.* This stickiness arises from the fact that individual oligopolists cannot lower their prices without inviting retaliation and cannot raise them without risking sales losses.

The price behavior of an oligopoly stands in vivid contrast to that of a firm in a competitive market. A competitive market typically has thousands of individual producers. The survival of any individual firm depends on its ability to hold down costs. To increase profits, individual firms must reduce costs. Consequently, competitive firms are under constant pressure to lower their costs (and prices), knowing that some other firm is going to do so eventually. Competitive firms are not restrained by fears of "retaliation"; on the contrary, they are constantly being pushed toward price reductions.

The tendency toward price rigidity in oligopolistic markets is reinforced by the nature of the marginal revenue curves facing individual oligopolists. The gap we saw in oligopoly marginal revenue curves allows oligopolists to withstand modest changes in costs. No such flexibility exists in a competitive industry. Should a competitive firm experience a cost reduction, it will expand production to the point where marginal cost again matches marginal revenue (price). As other firms react in the same way, an increased market supply will drive prices downward. By the same token, a competitive firm cannot afford to absorb cost increases; it will have to cut back output until marginal cost again matches marginal revenue (price). As all firms respond similarly to cost increases, the market supply will diminish and prices will rise. Thus market prices will tend to rise and fall with costs in a competitive market, but may not respond to cost changes in an oligopoly.

The greater size of the typical oligopolist also permits it to withstand changes in costs or demand. An oligopolist with profits in excess of $100 million a year is obviously in a better position to ignore small changes in costs or sales than the competitive firm with typical profits of less than $100,000.

Price and output

Although the kinked demand curve suggests that oligopoly prices will be relatively rigid, it says nothing about the way the market price is established. In our calculator example, we assumed an initial market price of $200, then demonstrated why that price was unlikely to change. But what establishes the (sticky) market price?

The objective of an oligopoly is to establish a price that maximizes total industry profits. A distinguishing feature of oligopolies is that they tend to be more successful in attaining this objective. Clearly, both competitive industries and oligopolies desire to make as much profit as consumer demand and production costs will allow. But competitive industries experience relentless pressure on profits as individual firms expand output, reduce costs, and lower prices. To maximize *industry* profits, competitive firms would have to band together and agree to restrict output and raise prices. If they did, though, the industry would no longer be competitive.

The potential for maximizing *industry* profits is clearly greater in an oligopoly, because very few firms are involved, and each is aware of its dependence on the behavior of the others. In fact, **an oligopoly will want to behave like a monopoly, choosing a rate of industry output that maximizes total industry profit.** If successful, the oligopolists will have more total profit to split up among themselves.

Coordination

The problem oligopolists confront is how to coordinate their production decisions. Recall that each firm desires as large a market share as possible, at prevailing prices. But encroachments on the market shares of rival oligopolists threaten to bring retaliation, price reductions, and reduced industry profits. Hence the oligopolists have a mutual interest in coordinating their production decisions so that:

- Industry profits are maximized.
- Each oligopolistic firm is content with its market share.

To bring about this happy outcome, the rival oligopolists could discuss their common interests and attempt to iron out an agreement on both issues. Identifying the profit-maximizing rate of industry output would be comparatively simple, as Figure 23.6 illustrates. The difficult issue would be the division of this output among the oligopolists, that is, the assignment of market shares. The outcome would depend on the relative strength of each firm and its negotiating skills.

Unfortunately for oligopolists, the kind of explicit discussions

---

FIGURE 23.6 MAXIMIZING OLIGOPOLY PROFITS

An oligopoly strives to behave like a monopoly, maximizing total industry profits. Industry profits are maximized at the rate of output at which the industry's marginal cost equals its marginal revenue (point *J*). In a monopoly, this profit all goes to one firm; in an oligopoly, it must be shared among a few firms.

In an oligopoly, the *MC* and *ATC* curves represent the combined production capabilities of several firms, rather than only one. The industry *MC* curve is derived by horizontally summing the *MC* curves of the individual firms.

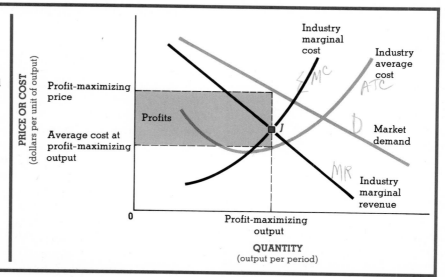

collusion: Explicit agreements among producers to limit competition among them.

price leadership: An oligopolistic pricing pattern that allows one firm to establish the (market) price for all firms in the industry.

or **collusion** we have described are illegal. According to the Sherman Act of 1890, all such discussions are "conspiracies in restraint of trade" and thus illegal. Corporations found to have colluded in this way are subject to stiff financial penalties and their executives may be sent to jail.

Because collusion is illegal (although not extinct, as we shall see in Chapter 24), oligopolistic firms must reach a consensus on total output and market shares in less explicit ways. One firm may "signal" its desire to reduce total output and raise prices by publicly announcing that it is studying the need for a price increase. This announcement gives rival oligopolists the opportunity to assess the implications of a move up the market demand curve. Should they agree that such a move is desirable, they may themselves announce similar "studies" of potential price increases, or simply increase their prices. This process, by which one oligopolistic firm "leads" its rivals to a change in price, is referred to as **price leadership.**

The firm that first expresses concern about potential price increases may be called the *price leader,* although leadership may also be retained by the firm that casts the decisive vote on the size of the ultimate price increase. Typically, the firm with the greatest market share will have the most influence on the oligopoly's final price decision, even if it is not the first one to announce a price increase. Hence price leadership is a matter less of who raises prices first than of whose decision has the greatest influence on the oligopoly.

Some form of industry-wide coordination—be it explicit price fixing, price leadership, or informal experimentation—is required to establish the profit-maximizing price and rate of output for the industry. Once this price is established, the dynamics of the kinked demand curve ensure that it will be maintained—for a while, anyway. When the market demand or the cost curve shifts substantially, or when the rival oligopolists become dissatisfied with their respective market shares, a new price will be established.

MONOPOLISTIC COMPETITION

However harmoniously an oligopoly may function, its existence is always threatened. On the inside, there is always the worry that one of the oligopolists will become dissatisfied with its profits or market share, and take action that ultimately reduces total industry profits. From the outside, there is the persistent threat that high profits will attract new firms into the industry. If the barriers to entry are not formidable enough, sooner or later the oligopoly will be destroyed.

The demise of an oligopoly does not necessarily lead to perfect competition, however. On the contrary, it is at least as likely that each of the many firms that enter the industry will establish its own identity ("brand image"), giving it some modest amount of market power. In this case, the industry will manifest *monopolistic competition.* Note that product differentiation ("brand image") exists in either a differentiated oligopoly or monopolistic competition. The difference here is the number of producers; there are many firms in monopolistic competition, but only a few in oligopoly.

OPEC Agrees to Cut Output

VIENNA, March 20—Fighting to regain control over the world oil market, ministers of the Organization of Petroleum Exporting Countries today agreed to set their first formal production limits, establishing an overall ceiling of 18 million barrels a day while pledging to hold firm on prices.

In a separate action, Saudi Arabia, OPEC's dominant producer, announced an additional unilateral cut in its production of a half-million barrels per day, fixing its daily production for April at 7 million barrels. It was the Arab kingdom's third reduction in five months.

The combined result of today's moves at the conclusion of a two-day emergency conference represents a production drop to 17.5 million barrels a day. That level is about 1.5 million barrels less than what the cartel says it supplied during the first quarter of the year and slightly more than half the 32 million barrels OPEC pumped daily at the peak of its production just three years ago.

OPEC members also called on major oil exporters outside the organization, such as Britain, Norway and Mexico, to reduce their production rather than cut prices further. OPEC's president, United Arab Emirates Oil Minister Mana Said Oteiba, declared the organization's determination to protect prices, saying, "We are ready to go to 10 million barrels a day if necessary." . . .

The oil ministers heralded their decision as a demonstration that OPEC, facing what many regard as the cartel's most serious challenge in its 20-year history, can coordinate production and pricing among its 13 members to save itself from panic and disintegration.

Significantly, today's action marked the first time that organization members formally agreed to honor production quotas. Two previous attempts at drafting OPEC production schedules, in 1978 and 1981, were cast as informal gentlemen's agreements.

To help ensure that OPEC's members hold to their new commitment, the conference decided to establish a special committee, made up of ministers from the United Arab Emirates, Venezuela, Indonesia and Algeria, to monitor compliance. While no sanctions for violators were spelled out, the establishment of a self-policing group was seen as reinforcing the image of OPEC as a traditional cartel actively managing production.

—Bradley Graham

The Washington Post, Washington, D.C., March 21, 1982.

How will a monopolistically competitive industry behave? Will each firm act like an oligopolist? Or will the many firms that comprise the industry behave more competitively?

Independent production decisions

Once many firms enter an industry, each firm's market share will decline. Ultimately, there may be 25 firms in the industry, each with a market share of close to 4 percent. ***In monopolistic competition, modest changes in the output or price of any single firm will have no perceptible influence on the sales of any other firm.*** This relative independence results from the fact that the effects of any one firm's behavior will be spread over 24 other firms (rather than only two or three other firms, as in an oligopoly).

The relative independence of monopolistic competitors means that they don't have to worry about retaliatory responses to every price or output change. As a result, they confront more traditional demand curves, with no kinks. The kink in the oligopolist's curve resulted from the likelihood that rival oligopolists would match any price reduction (to preserve market shares), but not a price increase (to increase their shares). In monopolistic competition, the market shares of rival firms are not perceptibly altered by one firm's price changes.

Product differentiation

A monopolistically competitive firm is distinguished from a purely competitive firm by its downward-sloping demand curve. Individual firms in a perfectly competitive market confront horizontal demand curves because consumers view their respective products as

Those Little Alligators on Clothes Sell Big, Breed Imitators, Impostors and Detractors

What is an inch and a quarter long, three-fourths of an inch high, and oozes snob appeal? Clues: It usually is green or blue; it can be found on practically any piece of apparel except underwear; it is expensive, and it has been imitated endlessly.

The answer, as every proper preppy knows, is the Izod-Lacoste alligator.

In a world smitten by designer emblems, the alligator is everywhere. Mothers send their toddlers to the sandbox, their older children to school and their husbands to the club in alligator wear. President Reagan wore an alligator shirt to a news conference. . . .

Inevitable Reaction

The alligator movement is so advanced that it has spawned an anti-alligator movement. The anti-Izod crown struts around in anti-alligator T-shirts or the Croc O' Shirt, which features an upside-down, dead crocodile. . . .

Going Hog Wild

Then there is the pig shirt, and accessories, offered by Hog Wild!, a Boston retailer. "It's a good way of poking fun at all the fancy designer emblems," says David Mercer, the owner. The original pig shirt has done so well that Hog Wild! introduced another line—the Pork Avenue Collection, featuring designs by Calvin Swine. It is, he adds, the height of hog couture.

Actually, it took quite a while for the alligator to catch on big in the U.S. The emblem dates back to 1926, when French tennis star Rene Lacoste, nicknamed "le Crocodile," wore a polo shirt with a crocodile on it. He began marketing it commercially in 1933 in France.

In 1951, the Izod division of David Crystal Inc. apparel company started importing Lacoste shirts and selling them here, and later it got the license to sell Lacoste-label clothing in the U.S., Canada and the Caribbean. Somewhere along the way, Americans got the idea that the crocodile was really an alligator, and the wrong name stuck. . . .

Then came General Mills Inc., which bought David Crystal in 1969 and began selling alligator wear like breakfast cereal. A boys' line of alligator clothing was added around 1975, a girls' line in 1978 and a line for infants and toddlers in 1979. "We take them from cradle to grave in Izod-Lacoste," says Jane Evans, an executive vice president of General Mills. In 1969, alligator apparel sales were about $15 million; sales now are some $450 million a year. . . .

Still, one shouldn't get carried away with discretion. After all, letting others know that one can afford the alligator is a reason why many people buy it. At $25, the alligator polo shirt sells for $5 to $10 more than most of its rivals (and other alligator apparel is priced accordingly). "It gives you status in the eyes of others. People wouldn't admit it, including myself, but that carries a lot of weight," says Gilbert Perry, a 34-year-old St. Paul, Minn., stockbroker.

"A lot of people aren't confident of their own taste," says William Hull, a Chicago marketing consultant. "With the alligator shirt, you've got some assurance you're not a boob."

Not all alligators are *the* alligator. General Mills attorneys are kept busy fending off impostors. Outright counterfeiters copy Izod-Lacoste clothing stitch for stitch, right down to the label. Other companies have put their own version of the alligator on stationery, wrapping paper, napkins, coasters, shoelaces, checkbook covers, laundry bags, even ice buckets.

Saurian Claims

General Mills, which claims that its license gives it the rights to the trademark of all saurian reptiles (anything resembling a lizard), dashes off nasty notes to infringers. Most back off, and those that don't generally are sued. . . .

—Lawrence Ingrassia

interchangeable ("homogeneous"). As a result, an attempt by one firm to raise its price will drive its customers to other firms. In monopolistic competition, each firm has a distinct identity. Its output is perceived by consumers as being somewhat different from the output of all other firms in the industry. As a consequence, a monopolistically competitive firm can raise its own price without losing all of its customers to rival firms.

In the electronic calculator industry, product differentiation can be (and has been) achieved in a variety of ways. The particular mix of functions performed on any calculator can be varied, as can its appearance ("packaging"). Effective advertising can convince consumers that one calculator is "smarter" than another, even if all calculators have identical "brains." Also, a single firm may differentiate itself by providing faster or more courteous repair service. If

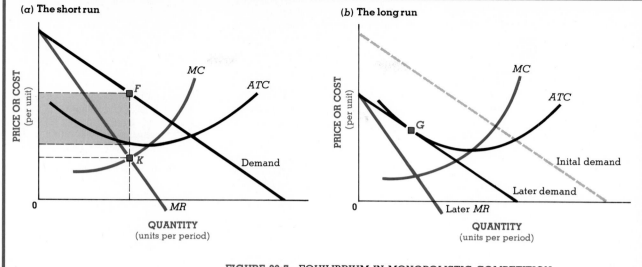

FIGURE 23.7 EQUILIBRIUM IN MONOPOLISTIC COMPETITION

(*a*) In the short run, a monopolistically competitive firm equates marginal revenue and marginal cost (point *K*). It sells the resulting output at a price (point *F*) above marginal cost. Total profits are represented by the shaded rectangle.

(*b*) In the long run, more firms enter the industry. As they do so, the demand curve facing each firm *shifts* to the left, as all market shares decline. Ultimately, the demand curve will be tangent to the *ATC* curve (point *G*), at which point price equals average total cost and no economic profits exist.

successful in any of these efforts, ***each monopolistically competitive firm will establish some consumer loyalty.*** Thus it is able to alter its own price somewhat, without fear of great changes in unit sales (quantity demanded). In other words, the demand curve facing each firm will slope downward, as in Figure 23.7*a*.

Inefficiency

marginal cost pricing: The offer (supply) of goods at prices equal to their marginal cost.

Because the demand curve facing a firm in monopolistic competition slopes downward, such a firm will violate the principle of **marginal cost pricing.** Specifically, it will always price its output *above* the level of marginal costs, just like firms in an oligopoly or monopoly (see Figure 23.7*a*). As a consequence, monopolistically competitive industries will tend to restrict output and misallocate society's resources.

In the long run, the profits of a monopolistically competitive industry will be eliminated. In oligopoly or monopoly, an above-normal rate of profit can be maintained indefinitely, because only one or a few firms ever participate in the market. In monopolistic competition, however, new firms can and do enter the market, depressing average prices and profits. In fact, in the absence of significant barriers to entry, new firms will continue to enter a monopolistically competitive industry until its profit potential is no higher than that of alternative pursuits. Point *G* in Figure 23.7*b* illustrates the absence of **economic profit** in long-run equilibrium.

economic profit: The difference between total revenues and total economic costs.

Warring Toothpaste Makers Spend Millions Luring Buyers to Slightly Altered Products

Proctor & Gamble Co. and Colgate-Palmolive Co. are about to spend $75 million or more touting new toothpastes that are most noteworthy for what they *won't* do.

They won't make teeth whiter than those manufacturers' current offerings. They won't prevent cavities any better. They won't even have new names; P&G's product will wear the Crest banner and Colgate-Palmolive's will be called Colgate.

What the new toothpastes will do is taste different. And they will have a new color; both are translucent blue gels instead of the familiar opaque white and aqua pastes.

New Weaponry

Such are the weapons of war in the $675 million dentifrice industry. The fight is typical of the rivalries becoming increasingly common among manufacturers of everyday personal-care, household-cleaning and food items sold by supermarkets and drug stores. Consumer demand for those products is growing slowly. Most competing brands are pretty much alike, and so is their advertising. Significant technological improvements are hard to come by.

The result is that marketers are pegging their hopes on minor changes in product appearances, packaging, scents or flavors. And the companies are spending tens of million of dollars to advertise those changes and to lure consumers with free samples, price discounts, coupons and other promotions.

"The price of entry into the packaged-goods market has become colossal," says Stanley Canter, a New York marketing consultant. "Companies are attempting to break in by dint of dollars, rather than by the unique features of a product."

Lucrative Margins

Still, rewards often can be great. "In very large categories, small changes in market share are worth a lot of money; that justifies spending a lot to make something happen," says Edward Tauber, chairman of the marketing department at the University of Southern California in Los Angeles. "Whether the consumer reaches to the left or right on the store shelf often depends on very trivial things." . . .

Trade sources indicate that Colgate-Palmolive has budgeted $10 million for the first three months of Colgate gel's introduction and could spend up to $40 million in the first year. Mr. Meade says P&G may well spend $15 to $25 million in Crest gel's first year. Others say the company may spend even more to match Colgate.

Leading National Advertisers Inc., which measures ad spending, estimates that last year $17.9 million was spent on Colgate's television and magazine advertising and $28.6 million was spent on Crest's. Aim was backed by $16 million. Mr. Segalas says an additional 25% or more typically is spent on discounts, coupons and other incentives. . . .

Fluctuating Shares

Since then, Colgate's share has climbed a point or two to 20%. Crest's share, helped by strong shipments in July and August, is near 40%, compared to 36% a year ago. Still, analysts caution, Crest's share may drop back a point or two.

There is no indication what effect the new gels will have on the market. They could take away shares from the other gels or from the regular forms of Crest or Colgate.

—Bill Abrams

The long-run equilibrium of firms in monopolistic competition, as illustrated in Figure 23.7b, differs from the perfectly competitive equilibrium. In the long run, a competitive industry produces at the *lowest* point on the average total cost (ATC) curve, and thus maximizes efficiency. In monopolistic competition, however, the downward slope of the demand curve facing each firm implies that profits will be eliminated *before* minimum average cost is achieved (see Figure 23.7b). As a consequence, an industry characterized by monopolistic competition tends to be less efficient in the long run than a perfectly competitive industry.

POLICY IMPLICATIONS: NONPRICE COMPETITION

A distinguishing feature of competitive markets is that individual firms compete on the basis of price. Through cost and price reductions, competitive firms hope to increase sales and profits. Price competition is not so prevalent in noncompetitive markets. Indeed, in oligopolies, the kink commonly found in the demand curve facing each firm inhibits price reductions, even when cost reductions might otherwise justify a lower price. In monopolistic competition, there is also a tendency toward reduced price competition. Because each firm has its own "captive" market—consumers who prefer its particular brand over competing brands—price reductions by one firm will not induce many consumers to switch brands. Thus *price reductions are not a very effective way to increase sales or market share in monopolistic competition.*

If imperfectly competitive firms do not compete on the basis of price, do they really compete at all? The answer is evident to anyone who listens to the radio, watches television, reads magazines or newspapers, or drives on the highway. A prominent form of *nonprice competition* is advertising. An imperfectly competitive firm typically uses advertising to enhance its own product's image, thereby increasing the size of its "captive market" (consumers who identify with a particular brand). Through advertising, an imperfectly competitive firm begins to shift its own demand curve to the right, while perhaps making it less price elastic as well (see Figure 18.10). By contrast, competitive firms have no incentive to advertise because they can individually sell their entire output at the current market price.

Advertising is not the only form of nonprice competition. Before the airline industry was deregulated (1978), individual airlines were compelled to charge the same price for any given trip; hence price competition was prohibited. But airlines did compete—not only by advertising, but also by offering "special" meals, movies, more frequent or convenient departures, and "faster" ticketing and baggage services.

Is there anything wrong with nonprice competition? Surely airline passengers enjoyed their "special" meals, "extra" services, and "more convenient" departure times. But these services were not free. As always, there were opportunity costs. From an air traveler's perspective, the "special" services stimulated by nonprice competition substituted for cheaper fares. With more price competition, customers could have chosen to travel more cheaply *or* in greater comfort. From society's perspective, the resources used in advertising (see Table 23.2) and other forms of nonprice competition could be used

TABLE 23.2 ADVERTISING EXPENDITURES	Medium	Amount (in millions)
Imperfectly competitive firms tend to engage in nonprice (rather than price) competition. Advertising is a primary form of nonprice competition. In 1980, $54 billion was spent on advertising.	Newspapers	$15,541
	Radio	3,827
	Magazines	3,149
	Direct mail	7,596
	Business papers	1,674
	Outdoor	610
	Television	11,295
	Miscellaneous	10,898
	Total	$54,590

Source: U.S. Department of Commerce, *Statistical Abstract of the United States*, 1981.

instead to produce larger quantities of desired goods and services (including airplane trips). Unless consumers are given the chance to *choose* between "more" service and lower prices, there is a presumption that nonprice competition leads to an undesirable use of our scarce resources.

SUMMARY

■ Imperfect competition refers to markets in which individual suppliers (firms) have some independent influence on the price at which their output is sold. Two prominent forms of imperfect competition are oligopoly and monopolistic competition.

■ An oligopoly is a market structure in which a few firms produce all or most of a particular good or service; it is essentially a shared monopoly. Because oligopolies involve several firms rather than only one, each firm must consider the effect of its price and output decisions on the behavior of its rivals. Such firms are highly interdependent.

■ A basic conflict exists between the desire of each individual oligopolist to expand its market share and the *mutual* interest of all the oligopolists in restricting total output so as to maximize profits. This conflict must be resolved in some way, via either collusion or some less explicit form of agreement (e.g., price leadership).

■ Once a common oligopoly price is established, it tends to be fairly rigid, as illustrated by the kinked demand curve. The kink results from the threat of rival oligopolists to match price reductions but not price increases.

■ The basic "stickiness" of oligopoly output and prices is reinforced by the gap that occurs in an oligopolist's marginal revenue curve. The gap itself occurs just below the kink in the demand curve and results from the switch from one marginal revenue (and demand) curve to another. Because marginal cost may not equal marginal revenue in this gap, small changes in cost need not alter the production decision.

■ In monopolistic competition, many producers supply the market but each retains some independent control of its own price. The demand curve facing each firm is downward-sloping, but not kinked. Firms in monopolistic competition engage in product differentiation, seeking to maintain and expand "captive" markets.

■ In the long run, economic profits are eliminated in monopolistic competition by the entry of additional firms, even though minimum average costs are never attained.

■ Oligopoly and monopolistic competition encourage nonprice competition instead of price competition. The resources used in nonprice competition (e.g., advertising, packaging, service) may have more desirable uses, and thus such forms of competition represent a form of resource misallocation.

Terms to remember | Define the following terms:

oligopoly

monopolistic competition

market share

quantity demanded

law of demand

product differentiation

marginal revenue

profit-maximization rule

collusion

price leadership

marginal cost pricing

economic profit

Questions for discussion

1. Can an oligopolist ever increase its market share? How?

2. What is the function of advertising in monopolistic competition? Provide specific examples.

3. What prevents other firms from entering an oligopolistic industry and sharing in the profits? Give some examples.

4. In addition to outright collusion and price leadership, how might oligopolists communicate their desire for a change in price or output?

Problem

Suppose that the following schedule summarizes the sales (demand) situation confronting an oligopolist.

Price (per unit)	$8	$10	$12	$14	$16	$17	$18	$19	$20
Quantity demanded (units per period)	9	8	7	6	5	4	3	2	1

Using the figures provided:

(a) Draw the demand and marginal revenue curves facing the firm.

(b) Identify the profit-maximizing rate of output in a situation where marginal cost is constant at $10 per unit.

MARKET POWER IN THE U.S. ECONOMY

Chapters 21, 22, and 23 have examined the potential of market power to restrict output, raise prices, and command above-normal profits. But we have not yet demonstrated how much market power actually exists in American product markets or how it is used. In this chapter we shall attempt to measure the extent of market power in U.S. product markets and assess its impact on the economy. In so doing, we will be mindful of the warning given by Adam Smith in 1776: "People of the same trade seldom meet together, but the conversation ends in a conspiracy against the public, or in some diversion to raise prices."

MEASURING MARKET POWER

The degree of market power possessed by any single firm is determined by several factors:

- The number of producers in the market
- Their relative size
- The extent of barriers to entry
- The availability of substitute products

All of these factors are important in both theory and fact. Nevertheless, it is useful—and far simpler—to focus on just one measure of market power to attain some perspective on the structure of U.S. product markets.

Concentration ratio

concentration ratio: The proportion of total industry output produced by the largest firms (usually the four largest).

oligopoly: A market in which a few firms produce all or most of the market supply of a particular good or service.

The standard measure of market power is the **concentration ratio.** This ratio tells the share of output (or combined market share) accounted for by a small number of firms. Using this ratio, one can readily distinguish between an industry composed of hundreds of small, relatively powerless firms and another industry also composed of hundreds of firms but dominated by a few that are large and powerful. Thus *the concentration ratio is a measure of market power that relates the size of firms to the size of the product market.*

Table 24.1 gives the concentration ratios for selected products in the United States. The standard measure used here depicts the proportion of domestic production accounted for by the largest firms, usually the four largest. In some cases, however, the concentration ratio refers to the combined market share of even fewer firms—for example, the tennis-ball market, which is controlled by only three firms.

As is apparent from the table, the supply of some of the most familiar consumer products is dominated by a very few firms. In most of the examples cited here, producer concentration is so great as to be tantamount to a monopoly shared among a few corporations. Thus the supply side of these product markets can be described as **oligopolies.** Indeed, in some markets, one single firm is so large that an outright monopoly is nearly attained. Eighty percent of all canned soup, for example, is produced by Campbell. IBM supplies 70 percent of all large computers. Western Electric produces 85 percent of all telephone equipment. Eastman Kodak supplies two-thirds of all still cameras and film. Procter & Gamble makes 75 percent of this country's disposable diapers. All of those firms that have a market share of at least 40 percent are printed in boldface type in the table.

Any one of the firms listed in Table 24.1 has considerable potential for influencing the quantity of a particular good supplied to the market and thus its market price. If William Wrigley decides to supply Spearmint gum only at prices higher than those of its competitors, a lot of gum chewers will have to pay more for Spearmint or switch to another brand. If Wrigley, Squibb (Beech-Nut), and Warner-Lambert (Chiclets) all raise their prices at the same time, gum chewers will have to choose between paying higher prices and chewing their nails. This is the essential feature of market power. In

Wm. Wrigley Boosts Gum Prices in U.S. Except Orbit Brand

CHICAGO—Wm. Wrigley Jr. Co. said it increased the wholesale price of all its chewing gum brands in the U.S. except the recently introduced Orbit sugar-free brand. The new schedule brings the price for a regular 20-package box to $2.25, up from $1.72. Wrigley had held the line at $1.72 since December 1974. In that year, the company raised prices three times. . . .

Graham Morgan, Wrigley's vice president, sales, said a factor in the price move was a recent similar increase by American Chicle Co., a Morristown, N.J.-based division of Warner-Lambert Co. He added the effect at the retail level will probably be that a package of seven sticks will sell for 20 cents, up from the current 15 cents.

TABLE 24.1 POWER IN U.S. PRODUCT MARKETS

The domestic production of many familiar products is concentrated among a
few firms. These firms have substantial control over the quantity supplied to
the market, and thus over market price. The concentration ratio measures the
share of total market output produced by the largest producers in a given market.

Product	Largest firms	Concentration ratio (percent)
Automobiles	**General Motors,** Ford, Chrysler, American Motors	98
Telephone service	**American Telephone & Telegraph,** General Telephone & Electronics, United Telecommunications, Continental Telephone	98
Chewing gum	**Wm. Wrigley,** Warner-Lambert, Squibb, Philip Morris	97
Toothpaste	**Procter & Gamble,** Colgate-Palmolive, Lever Bros., Beecham	85
Tennis balls	**General Tire,** Spalding, Dunlop	100
Breakfast cereals	**Kellogg,** General Mills, General Foods, Quaker Oats	91
Cigarettes	**R. J. Reynolds,** Philip Morris, Brown & Williamson, American Brands	88
Razor blades	**Gillette,** Warner-Lambert (Schick), Procter & Gamble (Wilkinson), Philip Morris (American Safety)	98
Electric razors	**Norelco,** Remington, Warner-Lambert, Sunbeam	96
Sanitary napkins	**Johnson & Johnson** (Modess, etc.), Kimberly-Clark (Kotex)	98
Handguns	**Smith & Wesson,** Sturm, Ruger, Colt, Harrington & Richardson	76

Sources: Data from Federal Trade Commission, *The Wall Street Journal, Advertising Age, Financial World, Standard & Poor's, Fortune,* and industry sources.

a more competitive market, with a large number of small firms, the likelihood of an across-the-board price increase would be much smaller, as we observed in the calculator example of Chapter 21.

Firm size We noted before that market power is not necessarily associated with firm size—in other words, a small firm could possess a lot of power in a relatively small market. Table 24.1, however, should be convincing testimony that we are not talking about small product markets here. Every one of the products listed enjoys a broad-based market. Annual sales for these products range from approximately $300 million (for men's hair grooming) to over $60 billion (for telephone service). Accordingly, for most of the firms listed in the table, market power and firm size go hand in hand. Indeed, the largest of

Product	Largest firms	Concentration ratio (percent)
Canned soup	**Campbell,** Heinz	90
Cameras and film	**Eastman Kodak,** Polaroid, Bell & Howell, Berkey Photo	98
Disposable diapers	**Procter & Gamble** (Pampers), Kimberly-Clark, Curity, Romar Tissue Mills	99
Detergents	**Procter & Gamble,** Lever Bros., Colgate-Palmolive	86
Soft drinks	**Coca-Cola,** PepsiCo, Philip Morris (Seven-Up), Dr Pepper	65
Office typewriters	**IBM,** Royal, SCM, Olivetti	85
Portable typewriters	**SCM,** Royal, Brother, Olivetti	86
Records and tapes	Warner Bros., CBS, Capitol, RCA	54
Tires and tubes	Goodyear, Firestone, Uniroyal, B. F. Goodrich	85
Coffee	General Foods, Procter & Gamble, Hills Bros., Standard Brands	64
Chocolate candy	**Hershey,** Peter Paul, Russell Stover, Fanny Farmer	79
Beer	Anheuser-Busch, Miller, Stroh (Schlitz), Pabst	72
Large computers	**IBM,** Honeywell, Sperry-Rand, Burroughs	89
Personal computers	**Apple,** Tandy, Commodore, IBM	60
Photocopiers	**Xerox,** Minnesota Mining & Mfg., SCM, Addresso-Multigraph	90
Telephones	**Western Electric,** General Telephone, United Telecommunications, Continental Telephone	95
Men's hair grooming	Bristol-Myers, Gillette, Beecham, Mennen	62
Air travel	United Air Lines, TWA, American, Delta	61
Bicycles	**Huffy,** Murray Ohio, Schwinn, AMF	67

Note: Individual corporations with a market share of at least 40 percent are designated in boldface type. Market shares based on sales for selected years, 1970–82.

the firms listed here (AT&T and General Motors) enjoy sales volumes that exceed the entire output of most of the *countries* in the world (see Table 24.2). That kind of size and market concentration constitutes undeniable power.

Although concentration ratios are a neat summary of power in a particular product market, they do not fully convey the extent to which particular firms can influence the production and consumption of goods and services. The vast size of the corporations listed in Tables 24.1 and 24.2 creates the potential for extending market power beyond the confines of a particular product market. Firms with sales and assets measured in billions of dollars have the power to extend their influence into other production areas. The most striking example of such an extension is AT&T, which until recently not only supplied nearly all telephone services, but also owned the firm

TABLE 24.2 CORPORATE SALES AND WORLD GNP, BY RANK, 1980 (in billions of dollars)

The dominant firms in U.S. product markets sell as much output each year as most countries produce.

Rank	Country or corporation	Sales or GNP	Rank	Country or corporation	Sales or GNP
1	United States	$2,582	26	**Mobil**	$69
2	USSR	1,212	27	South Africa	67
3	Japan	1,153	28	Argentina	66
4	West Germany	828	29	Denmark	66
5	France	628	30	Turkey	66
6	United Kingdom	443	31	**General Motors**	63
7	Italy	369	32	Indonesia	62
8	China	283	33	**Texaco**	59
9	Brazil	243	34	Yugoslavia	59
10	Canada	223	35	**AT&T**	57
11	Spain	200	36	Venezuela	54
12	The Netherlands	161	37	Romania	52
13	Iran	159	38	Norway	52
14	Australia	142	39	Finland	47
15	Poland	140	40	**Standard Oil (Calif.)**	47
16	Mexico	123	41	Hungary	45
17	East Germany	121	42	Greece	42
18	Belgium	120	43	Iraq	40
19	**Exxon**	115	44	**Ford Motor Co.**	38
20	Sweden	112	45	Bulgaria	37
21	Switzerland	106	46	Algeria	36
22	Saudi Arabia	101	47	Philippines	34
23	Czechoslovakia	89	48	**Standard Oil (Indiana)**	32
24	Nigeria	86	49	Colombia	32
25	Austria	77	50	Thailand	31

Source: *World Bank Atlas*, 1981, and *Fortune*, March 1982.

(Western Electric) that manufactures most telephone hardware. Thus the sixth largest corporation in the country owned the tenth largest manufacturing corporation.[1]

Other corporations, too, have considerable power in more than one product market. Procter & Gamble, for example, shows up in 5 of the 29 markets listed in Table 24.1, producing not only 75 percent of all disposable diapers, but also 50 percent of all detergents, 40 percent of all toothpaste, 10 percent of all razor blades, and 20 percent of all coffee. Warner-Lambert, IBM, and Philip Morris also appear in many of the product markets listed here.

Table 24.1 indicates the market power possessed by corporations in specific product markets. But because concentration ratios refer to only one product or industry, they tend to understate the power of many corporations to influence economic outcomes. Obviously, a firm that can affect the supplies (and prices) of many products may have at least as much power as those that wield control

[1] As noted in Chapter 22, the U.S. Department of Justice ordered AT&T to divest its local phone service by the end of 1983.

conglomerate: A firm that produces significant quantities of output in several industries.

over a single product. Procter & Gamble, Warner-Lambert, and Philip Morris are clear examples. In fact, many other corporations control some of the action in many product markets, although not necessarily a large share of the action in any single market. Such heterogeneous firms even have a special name: **conglomerates.**

Although rarely observed in concentration ratio lists, conglomerates (such as ITT, LTV, Litton Industries, Tenneco, Textron, Rockwell International) are among the largest corporations in the country. International Telephone & Telegraph, for example, with annual sales in excess of $23 billion, has supplied such familiar products as Avis Rent-A-Cars, Levitt housing, Sheraton hotels, Hartford Life Insurance, and Hostess Twinkies.[2] Litton Industries, with sales in the $5 billion range, has supplied S&H Green Stamps, Stouffer foods, missile guidance systems, and nuclear attack submarines. At the same time, Litton has participated in domestic social programs and foreign economic development planning. Such conglomerate firms enjoy many of the prerogatives otherwise reserved for those with extensive power in a single market.

Other measures of market power

It is also important to note that a high concentration ratio is not the only way to achieve market power. The supply and price of a product can be altered by the actions of many firms acting in unison. Even if a thousand producers supply one product and none of them has a strikingly large share of total output, they may still band together to change the quantity supplied to the market, thus exercising market power. Recall how Universal Electronics exercised market power by coordinating the production decisions of its many separate plants. Clearly those plants could have attempted such coordination on their own even if they had not all been owned by the same corporation. Lawyers and doctors possess and exercise this kind of power by maintaining uniform fee schedules for members of the American Bar Association (ABA) and the American Medical Association (AMA).[3] Dairy farmers exercise the same kind of power by acting jointly through three large cooperatives (the American Milk Producers, Mid-America Dairies, and Dairymen, Inc.), which together control 50 percent of all milk production.

Finally, all the figures and corporations cited here refer to *national* markets. They do not convey the extent to which market power may be concentrated in a *local* market. Yet local concentrations of market power are of immediate concern to every consumer, even if the firms and stores that possess such power have little national impact. In fact, many industries with low concentration ratios nationally tend to be represented by just one or a few firms locally. Prime examples include milk, newspapers, and transportation companies (both public and private). For example, of the 35,000 cities in the United States, fewer than 60 have two or more independently

---

[2] ITT was forced to sell Avis and Levitt after threat of antitrust action.

[3] In recent years, the courts have ruled that uniform fee schedules are illegal and that individual lawyers and doctors have the right to advertise their prices (fees). Nevertheless, a combination of inertia and self-interest has effectively maintained high fee schedules and inhibited advertising.

owned daily newspapers, and nearly all rely on only two news services (Associated Press and United Press International).

We may conclude, then, that market power is real and pervasive in the U.S. economy. The corporations listed in Table 24.1 only suggest the dimensions of that power. Other elements of power are discussed in later chapters, but note here that these firms have combined sales of well over $300 billion and employ nearly 7 million people. The 200 largest manufacturing companies—only 0.06 percent of the total—account for almost one-half of all manufacturing output, assets, and employment. Accordingly, although many product markets can also be characterized as highly competitive (furniture, fashions, computer software, printing, motels, produce), concentration and market power characterize a broad spectrum of American industry. As Professors Carl Kaysen and Donald Turner concluded in 1959, "There are more concentrated than unconcentrated industries in manufacturing and mining, they are larger in aggregate size, and they tend to occupy a more important position in the economy."[4] More recent studies have estimated that market power pervades something like two-thirds of American industry; in most instances, product markets are dominated by oligopolies.

POWER AT WORK

With so much market power concentrated in so few hands, evidence of power at work should be easy to find. Indeed, it would be surprising to find many product markets unaffected by the concentration ratios we have surveyed. As we review examples of market power at work in some of these markets, the ultimate objective of those who wield the power must be kept in view. Power in product markets is sought and exercised for the primary purpose of increasing the profits of those who wield the power.[5] In pursuit of higher profits, monopolies and oligopolies may seek to restrict market supplies, raise product prices, lower product quality, or reduce direct costs. In all of these cases, they rely on their ability to control market supply. Where possible, they attempt to extend such power by influencing market demand as well.

Successful use of market power will, of course, attract the interest and envy of other profit maximizers and can thus lead to its own destruction. Hence a monopoly or oligopoly with extensive control of a particular market must take steps to protect its position by erecting **barriers to entry**. *Above-normal profits cannot be maintained over the long run unless barriers to entry exist.* In the following pages we will focus on both the exercise of market power and the kinds of barriers to entry that establish and preserve such power.

barriers to entry: Obstacles that make it difficult or impossible for would-be producers to enter a particular market; for example, patents.

[4] Carl Kaysen and Donald Turner, *Antitrust Policy* (Cambridge: Harvard University Press, 1959).

[5] The profits accrue not just to the faceless corporations, of course, but also to the stockholders who own them. In this regard, it is well to remember that 5 percent of the population owns 83 percent of all corporate stock. See Frank Ackerman et al., "Income Distribution in the United States," *Review of Radical Political Economics,* Summer 1971, p. 23. In addition, the executives and employees of powerful corporations are themselves paid above-average wages.

Control of prices

A basic focus of market power is the price at which particular goods and services are sold. In general, we expect firms with market power to raise prices whenever it is profitable to do so and to maintain prices at levels higher than a more competitive market would sustain.

PRICE FIXING   In oligopolies, the establishment and maintenance of a high market price requires some form of coordination among the rival firms. The most explicit form of coordination among oligopolists involves **price fixing:** the oligopolists explicitly agree to charge a uniformly high price. Consumers are compelled to pay that high price or do without.

price fixing: Explicit agreements among producers regarding the price(s) at which a good is to be sold.

Price-fixing agreements are particularly successful when market demand for the product is highly inelastic, as high prices will not significantly reduce the quantity demanded. Although price fixing is outlawed by the Sherman Antitrust Act—and therefore often difficult to document—a few examples may serve to convey the nature of such agreements:

□ In 1961, General Electric, Westinghouse, and a group of other producers in the electrical-products industry were convicted of criminally conspiring to fix prices on turbine generators, transformers, and several other kinds of electrical equipment that they had been selling to the Tennessee Valley Authority and commercial customers. Available evidence suggested that the price-fixing conspiracy had significantly raised product prices on sales totaling nearly $2 billion per year. As a result of their participation in the conspiracy, seven corporate executives went to jail and twenty-three others were put on probation. In addition, the companies were fined a total of $1.8 million and compelled to pay triple damages in excess of $500 million to their victimized customers. Nevertheless, another suit was filed against General Electric and Westinghouse in 1972, charging these same companies—still the only two U.S. manufacturers of turbine generators—with continued price fixing.

□ In January 1982, three major dairies in Arkansas pleaded no contest to federal charges of price fixing. State officials had discovered that the three firms (Borden, Inc.; Coleman Dairy, Inc.; and Dean Foods) had been submitting identical bids to provide milk for schools in Little Rock and other cities in central Arkansas. They were also said to be fixing the price of milk sold to the public. The state attorney general estimated that the price fixing, which had begun as far back as 1963, had boosted prices by $3 million per year. Two salesmen were sent to jail and the companies were fined $2.4 million.

□ In 1981 the three largest supermarket operators in Cleveland agreed to give consumers $21.5 million worth of free groceries to settle price-fixing charges. Suits against the companies (Fisher Foods, First National Supermarkets, and Association of Stop-N-Shop Supermarkets) asserted that officers of the three supermarkets had secretly met in parking lots, hotels, and an apartment to fix meat and grocery prices.

□ Control of the supply of quinine was achieved by a group of international firms in the early 1960s. The firms then raised the

Levi Strauss Agrees to Pay $3.5 Million to Settle Price Case

SAN FRANCISCO—Levi Strauss & Co. said it agreed to a $3.5 million settlement of a court action by the California Attorney General.

The action, filed in superior court here, charged illegal price maintenance between 1972 and 1975. It alleged that jeans purchasers had been overcharged by retailers as a result of Levi's alleged efforts to maintain suggested retail prices.

A company spokesman said the company agreed to the settlement to avoid costly and time-consuming litigation. The spokesman also said the company stopped suggesting retail prices a year and a half ago. The settlement doesn't involve any admission by the company that it violated any law or that consumers were overcharged, he said.

price of quinine from $0.37 an ounce to $2.13. The demand for quinine (in the form of the drug quinidine), it may be noted, is highly inelastic; the drug is taken primarily by the elderly to restore natural heart rhythm. Profits of the quinine suppliers and their distributors skyrocketed, the profits of one company quintupling in a period of six months.

□ The price of tetracycline (a common antibiotic) was allegedly inflated by an illegal conspiracy involving five leading drug companies (American Cyanamid, Pfizer, Bristol-Myers, Upjohn, and Squibb Beech-Nut). Although the drug cost only $1.52 (per 100 capsules) to manufacture, the companies sold it to druggists at a price of $30.60. The druggists, in turn, sold it to the public at $51. After the government began to prosecute the companies for a price-fixing conspiracy, the retail price fell to $6. The five companies agreed to pay over $120 million to settle claims resulting from their pricing behavior.

□ The price of bread in the state of Washington was raised to artificially high levels as a result of price fixing among major bakers (including ITT's Wonder Bread and Safeway's Mrs. Wright's). The price-fixing conspiracy lasted over ten years (1954–64) and ended up costing Washington residents over $35 million in excessive bread prices. After the conspiracy was uncovered, bread prices in the state fell by nearly 6 cents a loaf.

Similar price-fixing agreements have been discovered in a variety of product markets, including plumbing fixtures, cigarettes, drugs, and newspaper advertising. Even the pocket-calculator industry, discussed in Chapters 21–23, was the target of price fixing. According to *Electronic News* (August 7, 1972), leading Japanese firms were able to fix calculator prices until technological innovations facilitated competition by American producers.

PRICE LEADERSHIP   Although price-fixing agreements are undoubtedly still a reality in many product markets, oligopolies have discovered that they do not necessarily need *explicit* agreements to arrive at uniform prices. If all oligopolists in a particular product market

Adolph Coors Co. Gets FTC Order to Stop Fixing Its Beer Prices

Agency Says Charges Controlled at Wholesale, Retail Levels, Selling Restrictions Imposed

WASHINGTON—The Federal Trade Commission ordered Adolph Coors Co. to stop fixing prices of its Coors beer.

The FTC ruled that Coors "has pursued a policy of fixing, controlling and maintaining prices" at both the wholesale and retail levels. The commission said Coors specifically threatened to refuse to deal with some concerns that sold Coors beer at prices below those suggested by the company.

The FTC also found that Coors imposed illegal territorial and other selling restrictions on distributors or retailers. The commission's order also prohibits such restrictions.

Coors, a privately owned brewery based in Golden, Colo., sells beer in 11 states, the FTC said. Coors is the top-selling beer in 10 of those states, according to the agency. The company is the nation's fourth largest beer producer, and had sales of about $350 million in 1971. All the company's beer is produced from a single plant in Golden, the FTC said.

In Golden, an Adolph Coors spokesman said it wouldn't have comment at this time on the FTC action.

follow the lead of one firm in raising prices, the result is the same as if they had all agreed to raise prices simultaneously. Instead of conspiring in motel rooms (as in the electrical-products case), the firms can achieve their objective simply by reading *The Wall Street Journal* or other industry publications and responding appropriately. Such **price leadership** is exercised annually in the automobile industry and frequently characterizes other product markets (television, cigarettes, detergents).

What happens in these cases is that one firm announces a price increase of x percent. In a highly competitive market, other companies would exploit this price differential by continuing to sell their products at lower prices. The more expensive firm would thus be driven out of business or forced to rescind its price increases. In a highly concentrated industry, however, the remaining oligopolists may raise their prices in accordance with the price increases initiated by the price leader. Often the price followers raise their prices a bit less than x percent, compelling the price leader to reduce its price increases and giving the impression of intense competition. These little "adjustments," however, do not alter the fact that in highly concentrated industries a price increase by one firm usually signals price increases by all firms.[6]

Allocation of market shares

Whenever oligopolists successfully raise the price of a product, the quantity of that good sold in a particular period decreases, in accordance with the law of demand. Even in markets with highy inelastic demand curves (such as those for tetracycline and quinine), *some* decrease in sales always accompanies an increase in price. When this happens in a monopolistic industry, the monopolist simply cuts back his rate of output to adjust to the reduced sales. In an oligopolistic industry, however, it is not obvious which of the oligopoly firms will confront diminished sales. A reduction in sales and output will occur; how will that reduction be spread around? Clearly, no single firm will wish to incur the whole weight of that cutback while the other oligopolists maintain their previous output; some form of accommodation is required.

The adjustment to the reduced sales volume can take many forms. Once again, the firms may engage in an explicit agreement on dividing up the sales reduction. If market sales drop by 10 percent, each firm may agree to reduce its rate of output by that same proportion. Such an agreement would preserve the **market share** previously enjoyed by the separate companies.

A particularly novel and ingenious method of allocating market shares occurred in the price-fixing case involving General Electric and Westinghouse. Agreeing to establish high prices on electrical equipment was not particularly difficult; but how would the companies decide who was to get the sales? In a competitive market, sales would be distributed according to prices, with the firm charging the

price leadership: An oligopolistic pricing pattern that allows one firm to establish the (market) price for all firms in the industry.

market share: The percentage of total market output produced by a single firm.

[6] As the kinked demand curve of Chapter 23 illustrated, no single oligopolistic firm will raise its price unless it is convinced that rivals will follow suit. When they do, a new market price is established from which the rival firms are not expected to deviate.

Toilet Seat Makers Said to Fix Prices

A federal grand jury yesterday charged four leading makers of toilet seats with a decade-long conspiracy to fix prices.

The indictment was handed down in Detroit at the same time the Justice Department filed a civil suit against the companies asking for an injunction to bar such collaboration in the future.

The indictment and civil action named the Beatrice Foods Co. of Chicago, which markets seats through its Beneke Division; the Olsonite Corp. of Detroit; the Bemis Manufacturing Co. of Sheboygan Falls, Wis., and the Standard Tank and Seat Co. of Camden, N.J.

Reuters dispatch reprinted from *The Washington Post*, Washington, D.C., June 20, 1974.

predatory price cutting: Temporary price reductions designed to alter market shares or drive out competition.

lowest price getting most of the business. But in this case, General Electric, Westinghouse, Allis-Chalmers, and a few other companies had agreed that low prices would be unseemly (and less profitable). Accordingly, they needed another mechanism for allocating sales. They agreed that each firm would be designated as the "low" bidder for a particular phase of the moon. The "low" bidder would charge the previously agreed-upon (high) price, with the other firms offering their products for sale at a higher price. The "low" bidder would naturally get the sale. Each time the moon entered a new phase, the order of "low" and "high" bidders would change. Hence each firm got a share of the business, and the price-fixing scheme was hidden behind a facade of "competitive" bidding.[7]

Such intricate plans for allocating market shares are probably more the exception than the rule. More often the oligopolists let the sales and output reduction be divided up according to consumer demands, intervening only when market shares are thrown markedly out of balance. At such times an oligopolist may take drastic action. A popular mode of action is **predatory price cutting**. Predatory price cuts are temporary price reductions that are intended to drive out new competition or reestablish market shares. The sophisticated use of price cutting can function as a significant barrier to entry, inhibiting potential competitors from trying to gain a foothold in the price cutter's market.

Gasoline station "price wars" were once a familiar manifestation of the price-cutting technique, although other examples abound. In the 1930s, for example, the cigarette oligopoly successfully raised cigarette prices (in the middle of the depression!). It was soon threatened, however, by new competitors, who managed to achieve 23 percent of total market sales. In early 1933 the oligopolists decided to reestablish their previous market shares and dropped cigarette prices from $6.04 per thousand to $4.85. Some brands were actually sold below cost, a practice the small competitors could not afford. The effect was to reduce the market share of the new competitors to less than 10 percent. Their objective attained, the oligopolists increased the price of cigarettes again in January 1934.

A more recent example of price cutting occurred in the supermarket (retail food) industry. Although the industry is a comparatively competitive one, a few giant chains (A&P, Safeway, Kroger,

[7] For a detailed description of this price-fixing arrangement, see Richard Austin Smith, "The Incredible Electrical Conspiracy," *Fortune*, May 1961.

Predatory bread prices

ITT Continental Baking Co., one of the world's largest bakers, has for decades been illegally snuffing out competition, often by charging too little for its Wonder, Home Pride, and other brands of white bread, a Federal Trade Commission administrative law judge ruled. The decision, which can be reviewed by the entire commission, handed a major victory to the FTC's antitrust staff, which brought the case in 1974 against Continental and its parent, International Telephone & Telegraph Corp. Judge Miles J. Brown told Continental it cannot win new business by offering prices below fully allocated costs or attack competition by lowering prices in selective markets. Brown also suggested that the commission consider forcing ITT to sell off Continental.

Reprinted from the May 25, 1981, issue of *Business Week* by special permission. © 1978 by McGraw-Hill, Inc., New York, N.Y. 10020. All rights reserved.

Food Fair) still possess significant market power. Unhappily, the largest chain grocer, A&P, found its market share declining in the late 1960s. It decided to stop that erosion of power with price cuts so drastic that smaller competitors would be driven out of business. According to *Fortune* magazine and the Federal Trade Commission, A&P initiated price cuts in 1972 that brought some prices below costs and led to huge losses in the industry. A&P was able to increase its market share, however, and later raise prices to their "normal" level.

One last example of price cutting to enforce market power suggests elements of both collusion and price fixing. The automobile manufacturers sell a substantial number of cars to fleet owners— firms or agencies that purchase at least ten vehicles. General Motors and Ford had always dominated fleet sales. Chrysler's share of the market, however, grew from 4 to 25 percent after it refused to maintain high prices and introduced price reductions. As a result, Ford and GM were compelled to lower their prices in order to maintain sales. The price reductions, however, lowered profits, a most unwelcome result. According to government complaints, GM and Ford then conspired to cut prices so low that they actually fell below cost, thus forcing losses and a change of attitude on Chrysler. Chrysler apparently took the hint. When GM and Ford eliminated all price concessions on 1971 models, Chrysler followed suit the following week. As *Business Week* reported, "GM let it be known that it planned to retaliate, presumably by further price cutting, if Chrysler did not go along."[8]

Control of supply

Price cutting, either real or threatened, can be an effective weapon for excluding competition. It is by no means the only available weapon, however. Patents, control of distribution outlets, acquisitions, and product differentiation can also be used to limit competition.

PATENTS Patents prohibit potential competitors from using developed technology, since a patent endows the holder with exclusive use of his technology for seventeen years. A potential competitor cannot set up shop until he either develops an alternative method for producing a product or receives permission from the patent holder to use the patented process. Such permission, when given, will cost something, of course. Moreover, the larger, more powerful firm will always have more resources available to pursue further research and development, thus increasing the comparative disadvantage of the would-be rival. Patents were the primary source of market power for the hypothetical Universal Electronics case of Chapter 21. In the real world, they also provide a substantial explanation for the market power of such firms as Xerox and Polaroid.

Even tennis rackets are now patented. In 1976 the Prince Manufacturing Company convinced the U.S. Patent Office that its over-

[8] *Business Week,* January 27, 1973, p. 24. In December 1973 GM and Ford were acquitted of criminal charges by a federal district court in Detroit; civil suits against these companies were dismissed in 1977 on the basis of inadequate evidence of collusion.

sized rackets were a unique product. The racket's design, it was claimed, provided more power and stability than conventionally sized (70-square-inch) rackets. The Patent Office agreed and gave Prince the exclusive right to produce rackets with surface areas of 85 to 130 square inches. With that patent, Prince has been able to monopolize sales of oversized rackets and reap extraordinary economic profits.[9]

DISTRIBUTION CONTROL   Another way to control the supply of a product is to take control of distribution outlets. A firm will usually sell wares in a variety of retail outlets. If it can persuade those outlets not to peddle anyone else's competitive wares, it will further solidified its market position. This control of distribution outlets can be accomplished through many means, including price concessions, long-term supply contracts, and expensive gifts at Christmas. The automobile industry provides an even more effective option.

Nearly all new cars in the United States are sold through dealerships franchised by car manufacturers. The individual dealers are beholden to the manufacturer for the "right" to buy and sell cars. As a condition of their franchises, dealers are prohibited from selling cars produced by a competitor. Although the clause detailing this prohibition was ruled illegal by the Supreme Court in 1949, few dealers have taken it upon themselves to defy the wishes of GM, Ford, and Chrysler. As a result, the supply of new cars sold to the public is effectively governed by a few manufacturers who exercise control over approximately 26,000 dealerships (GM alone has over 12,000).

To tighten their control over distribution networks, auto manufacturers have also entered the financing and parts-replacement industries. Nearly all new cars purchased are "financed" (paid for in part by a loan). Thus a firm that can gain control of the financing mechanisms can tighten its control over sales. As early as 1919 — and shortly after buying out Buick, Cadillac, Oldsmobile, and a score of other producers — General Motors organized the General Motors Acceptance Corporation (GMAC) for that very purpose. Ob-

---

[9] Prince sold Wilson a license to manufacture oversized rackets through 1983; such licenses do not alter Prince's primary monopoly.

Transamerica Unit, 3 Car-Rental Firms Agree to Settle Suit

NEW YORK—The nation's three largest rent-a-car companies—Hertz Corp., Avis Inc. and National Car Rental System Inc.—have privately agreed to settle a lawsuit filed against them by Budget Rent-A-Car Systems Inc. in 1977.

It's understood that the three larger companies have agreed to pay Budget more than $9 million under terms of the tentative agreement. . . .

Budget filed suit against the three larger companies after they consented in 1976 to Federal Trade Commission orders barring them from conspiring to monopolize the car-rental industry and from participating in other anticompetitive practices including monopolizing car-rental concessions at airports. The three big companies consented to the FTC order without admitting to the practices.

Since 1976 the number of airport counters operated by Budget and smaller companies has increased significantly, with Budget increasing its total to 159 from 94 just three years ago.

—Priscilla S. Meyer

viously, the consumer who wishes to purchase a competitor's car would have difficulty obtaining financing from GMAC. Accordingly, the convenience and financial resources of GMAC serve to reduce potential competition.

The control that the auto manufacturers exert over parts and services is as familiar as your car warranty or neighborhood dealership. Although most auto parts could easily be designed to be interchangeable, only "authorized" parts and services, provided by franchised dealers, may be used to maintain the warranty. Hence the Big Three effectively fragment the independent parts and service market. They force auto purchasers to pay higher prices for such services, and compel would-be entrants to the auto industry to establish their own parts and service networks. As a result of these many barriers to entry, it has been estimated that a potential competitor would need at least $1 *billion* to establish a foothold in the automobile industry. Few entrepreneurs are prepared for that kind of investment.

Similar control of distribution outlets can be found in many industries—photocopying, beer, telephones, computers, and cameras, for example. One particular industry, breakfast cereals, is especially noteworthy in this regard for its direct and simple approach to control of sales. Sales of breakfast cereals are heavily influenced not only by product advertising but also by shelf displays at the local supermarket. The package with the most prominent display (shelf height, space, and position) is most likely to catch the attention of the shopper (or child-in-tow). One might think that the grocer took responsibility for such displays, but the Federal Trade Commission claimed that is often not the case. In particular, the FTC discovered that

Kellogg is the principal supplier of shelf space services for the RTE [ready-to-eat] cereal sections of retail grocery outlets. Such services include the selection, placement and removal of RTE cereals to each respondent and to other RTE cereal producers.

Through such services respondents have interfered with and now interfere with the marketing efforts of other producers of RTE and other breakfast cereals and producers of other breakfast foods. Through such services respondents restrict the shelf positions and the number of facings for Nabisco and Ralston RTE cereals, and remove the RTE cereals of small regional producers.

All respondents [Kellogg, General Mills, General Food, Quaker Oats] acquiesce in and benefit from the Kellogg shelf space program which protects and perpetuates their respective market shares through the removal or controlled exposure of other breakfast food products including, but not limited to, RTE cereal products.[10]

According to the FTC complaint, this control over shelf space gave the cereal makers control of the market supply curve, and cost consumers $1.2 billion in higher grocery prices between 1958 and 1972.

ACQUISITION Large and powerful firms can restrain competition and attain control of product supply by a number of means, but none

---

[10] Complaint, *Kellogg Company et al.,* FTC Dkt. 8883 (1972). The FTC dropped the case in 1982 after ten years of litigation.

"With our latest merger, gentlemen, we've passed from a conglomerate to a world power!"

GRIN AND BEAR IT by Lichty and Wagner. Copyright Field Enterprises, Inc., 1978. Courtesy Field Newspaper Syndicate.

quite so direct as outright *acquisition*. When one firm buys another, the effect on its market share, and thus its market power, is fairly obvious. A *merger* between two firms amounts to the same thing, although mergers often entail the creation of new corporate identities. The new identity, however, does not alter the fact that a single firm has attained increased market power.

Perhaps the single most dramatic case of acquisition for this purpose occurred in the breakfast cereal industry. In 1946 General Foods acquired the cereal manufacturing facilities of Campbell Cereal Company, a substantial competitor. Following this acquisition, General Foods dismantled the production facilities of Campbell Cereal and shipped them off to South Africa!

Although the General Foods acquisition was more dramatic than most, acquisitions have been the most popular route to increased market power. General Motors, for example, attained a dominant share of the auto market largely by its success in merging with and acquiring two dozen independent manufacturers. In the cigarette industry, the American Tobacco Company attained monopoly powers by absorbing some 250 independent companies. Each acquisition increased the company's market control and ability to acquire additional companies. Later antitrust action (1911) split up the resultant tobacco monopoly into an oligopoly consisting of four companies (R. J. Reynolds, Liggett & Myers, Lorillard, and American Tobacco), which continued to dominate the cigarette market. Other companies that came to dominate their product markets through mergers and acquisitions include U.S. Steel, U.S. Rubber, General Electric, United Fruit, National Biscuit Company, and International Salt. In addition, all the conglomerates discussed earlier attained their size and power via the acquisition route. ITT alone purchased an average of ten companies per year in the period 1964–69.

Nonprice competition

Producers who have control over market supply, as we have seen, are in a position to alter prices and thereby increase their share of economic welfare. They can expand their power and share of income even further by establishing some influence over market demand.

The means for acquiring some degree of control over the market demand curve are familiar from Chapters 18 and 23. The primary mechanism of control is *advertising*. To the extent that a firm can

Christmas Tree Makers Sued by Justice

The government asked a federal court yesterday to hold the nation's two largest producers of artificial Christmas trees in contempt for violating a 1975 agreement prohibiting anticompetitive mergers in the industry.

Named in a petition filed by the Justice Department in U.S. District Court in Harrisburg, Pa., were American Technical Industries Inc. (ATI) of Pittsburgh and Marathon Manufacturing Co. of Houston.

ATI is the country's No. 1 producer of artificial Christmas trees and Marathon Manufacturing ranks second.

The 1975 agreement had settled a 1973 civil suit against ATI and had prohibited the firm from acquiring the assets of any company engaged in the manufacture or sale of artificial Christmas trees in the United States.

—Ranjit de Silva

Reuters dispatch reprinted from *The Washington Post*, Washington, D.C., March 23, 1982.

product differentiation:
Features that make one product appear different from competing products in the same market.

convince you that its product is essential to your well-being and happiness, it has effectively shifted your demand curve. If the firm can convince millions of other consumers in the same way, it will have acquired some degree of direct control over the *market* demand curve. With such control, the producer can attain a still more profitable price-quantity equilibrium. Accordingly, we may anticipate that firms with large amounts of market power will tend to advertise most heavily.[11]

Advertising deepens the attachment of consumers to particular brands (thus rendering their demand curves less elastic). It also makes it expensive for new producers to enter the market, because a new entrant must buy not only production facilities but advertising outlets as well. In addition, the proliferation of brand names—all produced by a few companies—tends to mask the concentration of power that exists. Thus **product differentiation** both increases profits (and prices) and camouflages the true extent of market power.

The cigarette industry is a classic case of high concentration and product differentiation. As Table 24.1 shows, the top four cigarette companies produce 88 percent of all domestic output; two more firms (Lorillard and Liggett & Myers) produce the rest. Yet you would never guess that such high concentration exists in the industry if you were merely to survey the cigarette shelves at the local supermarket. Together, the six cigarette companies produced well over a 100 brands in 1982. Confronted with such a diversity of choices, how many consumers would even imagine that Marlboro, Benson & Hedges, Parliament, Virginia Slims, Philip Morris, Alpine, Galaxy, English Ovals, Merit, Saratoga, Players', and Cambridge are all produced by a single company (Philip Morris)? To maintain the

[11] Next time you watch television, note who sponsors the commercials. Then check to see if they, or their parent corporations, are included in our list of powerful firms (Table 24.1).

DESIGNER JEANS: PRODUCT DIFFERENTIATION IS EVERYTHING

The Levi Strauss Company first produced jeans in the 1850s and has dominated the industry ever since. In the late 1970s, however, a whole new mini-industry evolved: the "designer jeans" market. It all started when Puritan Corporation came up with the idea of selling jeans emblazoned with the label of fashion designer Calvin Klein. Calvin Klein jeans sold like hot cakes, at about twice the price of traditional jeans. Within only a few years' time, Puritan was selling over $30 million worth of Calvin Klein jeans.

Other companies were quick to follow Puritan's lead. Murjani Industries was the next big success story. In 1978 Murjani put the Gloria Vanderbilt label on its jeans and started advertising heavily. Sales in 1979 reached $150 million. Jordache came next, also in 1978. In its second year sales of Jordache jeans reached $75 million.

By 1981 the status jeans industry looked like a classic case of monopolistic competition. There were over 200 different labels available. Yet all of the jeans were basically identical, their only difference residing in the designer's name and the color or pattern of the stitching. To make their own jeans seem different, the designer-jeans makers advertise extensively.

appearance of competition in the industry and to intensify consumer loyalties, the cigarette industry spent over $700 million in 1982 for advertisements in newspapers, magazines, and on radio (television ads were banned after 1971).

Another highly concentrated industry that spends great amounts of money on advertising is the breakfast cereal industry. Although the Federal Trade Commission has suggested that "a corn flake is a corn flake no matter who makes it," the four firms (Kellogg, General Foods, General Mills, Quaker Oats) that supply more than 90 percent of all ready-to-eat breakfast cereals spend over $200 million a year to convince consumers otherwise. During the last 20 years, more than 150 brands of cereals have been marketed by these companies. As the FTC has documented, the four companies "produce basically similar RTE [ready-to-eat] cereals, and then emphasize and exaggerate trivial variations such as color and shape. . . . [They] employ trademarks to conceal such basic similarities and to differentiate cereal brands."[12] Most cereal advertising, the commission noted, is aimed at children. Here again the diversity of brands creates the impression of intense competition, and the attendant advertising leads consumers (especially children) to purchase a particular brand with which they can identify (as athletes, outer-space heros, or cowboys).

One final example of market power manifested in product differentiation is the detergent industry. Only three firms (Procter & Gamble, Lever Brothers, and Colgate-Palmolive) account for 86 percent of all detergent output. These firms, however, package detergents under 20 trademarked brands and a host of private labels for supermarket chains. Procter & Gamble alone, with over 50 percent of the market, produces nine trademarked brands (including Tide, which accounts for nearly one-fourth of all detergent sales). It is not completely coincidental that Procter & Gamble spends more on advertising than any other company in the world (see Table 24.3).

[12] Complaint, *Kellogg Company et al.*, FTC Dkt. 8883 (1972).

Sears' Dishwasher Claims Ruled False

Sears, Roebuck and Co. falsely claimed its dishwashers make prior rinsing or scraping of dishes unnecessary, the Federal Trade Commission ruled yesterday.

Sears, the nation's largest retailer and biggest marketer of household dishwashers, sells them under its Kenmore and Lady Kenmore brands.

The $8 million broadcast and print ad campaign made such claims as "now's the time to really clean up during Sears' gigantic dishwasher sale. With a Kenmore you'll never have to scrape or rinse again" and "Sears Lady Kenmore. The do-it-yourself dishwasher. No scraping. No prerinsing."

The opinion by Commissioner Paul Rand Dixon said the campaign lasted three to four years and that "even at the time that the no-scrape, prerinse claim was first disseminated, Sears lacked substantiation or a reasonable basis for making it.

"Indeed, if anything, the tests purportedly relied upon by Sears at the time that it made its claim demonstrated precisely the reverse—that the Lady Kenmore could not ensure the consumer 'would never have to scrape or rinse again,' the commission said.

In Chicago, Sears said it will appeal the decision to a federal appeals court.

—Jeffrey Mills

The Washington Post, Washington, D.C., May 17, 1980. Reprinted by permission of the Associated Press.

TABLE 24.3 ADVERTISING EXPENDITURES OF THE TOP TEN ADVERTISERS

Firms with market power attempt to preserve and extend that power through advertising. A successful advertising campaign alters the demand curve facing the firm, thus increasing potential profits.

Company	Advertising expenditure (millions of dollars)
Procter & Gamble	$650
Sears Roebuck	600
General Foods	410
Philip Morris	365
K-Mart	319
General Motors	316
R. J. Reynolds Industries	299
Ford Motor	280
AT&T	259
Warner-Lambert	235
Total	$3,733

Source: *Advertising Age*, September 10, 1981.

Other barriers to entry

Predatory price cutting, patents, control of distribution outlets, acquisitions, and product differentiation are all effective barriers to entry. Individually and collectively, they enable powerful producers to maintain high prices and profits without fear of attracting too much competition. As important as these barriers are, however, they do not exhaust the supply of weapons available to a successful oligopoly. Market power may be solidified in other ways as well.

The very size of a powerful oligopoly may preclude effective competition. Once a firm or group of firms attains tremendous size, potential competitors may be kept at bay by the capital-investment requirements necessary to attain competitive status. In the pocket-calculator market, at which we looked earlier, initial capital-investment requirements were minimal. In heavy manufacturing industries, however, the initial outlay for plant and equipment may be colossal. Even in disposable diapers, initial capital investment and advertising expenses were so high that only one new entrant—Johnson & Johnson, already a large corporation—joined this highly concentrated industry in the 1970s, despite the rash of profits available. Smaller firms were reluctant to enter, for fear that the existing firms could use their control over prices, supply, and demand to destroy competitive possibilities. Johnson & Johnson itself pulled out of the industry after only a few years.

A single firm or group of firms with considerable market power can also extend and solidify that power by exacting concessions from resource suppliers. Powerful firms can erect protective entry barriers by winning price concessions or distribution guarantees from those who supply them with labor, capital, or other productive inputs.

Finally, we must confront the potential that oligopolists possess to influence government regulation. As we saw in Chapter 3, government activities reach into all sectors of the economy. What is of particular interest here is the role of government in restricting competition. Government restricts competition through various

Topps Gum Strikes Out on Baseball Card Game

PHILADELPHIA (UPI)—Topps Chewing Gum Inc. lost its 14-year monopoly of the bubblegum baseball card industry this week and was ordered to pay triple damages of $3 to a Philadelphia competitor.

Fleer Corp. of Philadelphia filed a lawsuit in 1975 against Topps of Brooklyn, which since 1966 signed exclusive contracts with virtually every major and minor league baseball player to appear on 2½-by-3½ cards tucked in with a sheet of pink bubble gum.

U.S. District Judge Clarence Newcomer ruled that Topps and the Major League Baseball Players' Association unfairly edged Fleer out of the market.

But he balked at what he called "guesswork" at determining the extent of Fleer's loses. Newcomer awarded Fleer a nominal $1 damage award, which under antitrust laws is tripled to $3. . . .

Topps is the nation's largest manufacturer and seller of baseball cards, selling $6.6 million worth in 1978.

The Washington Post, Washington, D.C., July 5, 1980. Reprinted by permission of United Press International.

---

proscriptions, licensing arrangements, differential taxes, import quotas and tariffs, and an all-too-frequent tendency to award contracts to the largest firms. Patents, too, could be included in this category, because they are issued and enforced by the federal government. What makes government regulation particularly hazardous for would-be rivals is the potential for influence possessed by large and powerful firms. It is worthwhile to recall the words of Senator Russell Long, chairman of the powerful Senate Finance Committee:

Most campaign money comes from businessmen. Labor contributions have been greatly exaggerated. It would be my guess that about 95 percent of campaign funds at the congressional level are derived from businessmen. At least 80 percent of this comes from men who could sign a net worth statement exceeding a quarter of a million dollars. Businessmen contribute because the Federal Corrupt Practices Act prohibits businesses from contributing. . . .

A great number of businessmen contribute to legislators who have voted for laws to reduce the power of labor unions. . . .

Many businessmen contribute to legislators who have fought against taxes that would have been burdensome to their businesses, whether the tax increase was proposed as a so-called reform, a loophole closer, or just an effort to balance the Federal budget.

Power company officials contribute to legislators who vote against public power. . . .

Bankers, insurance company executives, big moneylenders generally contribute to legislators who vote for policies that lead to high interest rates.

Many large companies benefit from research and development contracts which carry a guaranteed profit, a so-called fixed fee of about 7 percent of the amount of the contract. Executives of such companies contribute to those who help them get the contracts or who help make the money available. . . . Research contractors contribute to legislators who vote to permit them to have private patent rights on government research expenditures.

Drug companies are often able to sell brand-name drug products at anywhere from twice to 50 times the price of identical nonbranded products for welfare and Medicare patients if the companies can prevail upon government to permit their drugs to be prescribed and dispensed by their private brand names rather than by the official or generic name of the product. Executives of drug companies will contribute to legislators who vote to permit or bring about such a result.

Many industries are regulated. This includes the railroads, the truckers, the airlines, the power companies, the pipelines, to name but a few. Executives of regulated companies contribute to legislators who vote to go easy on the regulation, and ask no more questions than are necessary about their rates.

Companies facing threat of ruinous competition from foreign sources have executives who contribute to those who help protect them from competition by means of tariffs and quotas.

Many industries are subsidized . . . the merchant marine, the shipbuilders, the sugar producers, the copper producers and a host of others. Executives in such industries contribute to those who help keep them in business.

This list is merely illustrative. . . . Merely by assiduously tending to the problems of business interests located in one's own state, a legislator can generally assure himself of enough financial support to campaign effectively for re-election.[13]

POLICY IMPLICATIONS: ANTITRUST LIMITATIONS

Examples of market power at work in U.S. product markets could be extended to the closing pages of this book. The few cases cited here, however, are testimony enough to the fact that market power has some influence on our lives. Market power *does* exist; market power *is* used. It is not possible to summarize briefly all the ways in which seller concentrations influence market outcomes. In general, power in U.S. product markets has contributed to resource misallocations, higher prices, restricted output, higher levels of unemployment, and greater inequality of income and wealth. A staff study by the Federal Trade Commission has suggested that product prices in oligopolistic industries are at least 25 percent higher than they would be in the absence of such market power. Economists have estimated that oligopolies have constrained GNP—that is, restricted output—by approximately 6 percent. Neither of these estimates is beyond dispute (indeed, they are often disputed), but they are suggestive.

The demonstrated potential and use of market power to transform the dimensions of our economic welfare make the subject of power in product markets a basic issue for economic policy. Do we want to delegate so much authority to determine prices, incomes, employment, and output to a relatively small number of corporations with extensive market power? As we have seen, that authority has often been used to the marked disadvantage of consumers and society as a whole. If we choose to regain authority over economic outcomes, we must decide the appropriate focus of public policy and the most appropriate kinds of policy intervention.

Industry behavior

Our primary concern in product markets is the *behavior* of those who buy and sell goods and services. We have an interest in the way goods and services are priced, in collusion (explicit or otherwise) among producers, and in the erection of barriers to new competition.

[13] *Congressional Record*, April 4, 1967, cited in Morton Mintz and Jerry S. Cohen, *America, Inc.: Who Owns and Operates the United States* (New York: Dial Press, 1971), pp. 203–205.

All of these elements of industry behavior will directly affect economic outcomes.

A variety of policy options are available to influence the behavior of oligopolists and thereby assure a more desirable set of economic outcomes. We could, for example, explicitly outlaw collusive agreements and cast a jaundiced eye on industries that regularly exhibit price leadership. We could also prohibit oligopolists from extending their market power via such mechanisms as acquisitions, excessive or deceptive advertising, and, alas, the financing of political campaigns. In fact, we have established mechanisms for each of these kinds of control. Such agencies as the Justice Department, the Federal Trade Commission, and the Food and Drug Administration have authority to assess and control market behavior.

Two limitations to the behavioral orientation of public policy should be noted, however. First, public resources to control market behavior have always been and continue to be extremely limited. Indeed, the advertising expenditures of just one oligopolist, Procter & Gamble, are more than ten times as large as the *combined* budgets of both the Justice Department's Antitrust Division and the Federal Trade Commission. As Ralph Nader has suggested, "The posture of two agencies with a combined budget of $20 million and 550 lawyers and economists trying to deal with anticompetitive abuses in a trillion-dollar economy, not to mention an economy where the 200 largest corporations control two-thirds of all manufacturing assets, is truly a charade."[14] The dimensions of this charade were poignantly demonstrated in 1969, when the Justice Department filed suit against IBM for monopoly practices. In the subsequent 13 years, IBM submitted 66 million pages of documents in its own defense, effectively stymieing the prosecution. By the time the case was dropped (see Chapter 22), all of the Antitrust Division lawyers who had originally prepared the IBM case had left the Justice Department.

There are many reasons why efforts to control market behavior are so limited. For one thing, consumers are generally insensitive to the relationship between market structure and their own economic welfare. They (and you) rarely think about the connection between market power and the price of the goods they buy, the wages they receive, or the way they live. Furthermore, as Ralph Nader sadly discovered, "Antitrust violations are part of a phenomenon which, to the public, is too complex, too abstract, and supremely dull."[15] As a result, there is little public pressure for a more concerted effort to regulate market behavior. Moreover, the direct and vested interest of oligopolists in behavioral freedom creates an active lobby to constrain regulation efforts. Accordingly, the first requirement of effective antitrust efforts is public knowledge and concern. The second is the mobilization of that concern in the form of pressure for antitrust resources.

Industry structure

Another reason why regulatory efforts have not yielded greater success is their focus on market behavior. Such exclusive focus on behavior ignores the relationship between market structure and behav-

[14] Mark J. Green et al., *The Closed Enterprise System: The Report on Antitrust Enforcement* (New York: Grossman, 1972), p. x.
[15] Ibid., p. ix.

ior. As former Supreme Court Chief Justice Earl Warren observed, "An industry which does not have a competitive structure will not have competitive behavior."[16] To expect an oligopolist to disavow profit opportunities or to ignore the potential effect of its actions on its fellow oligopolists (and vice versa) is naive. It also violates the basic motivations imputed to a market economy. As long as markets are highly concentrated, we must expect to observe oligopolistic behavior.

Public efforts to alter market structure have been even less frequent than efforts to alter market behavior. With the exception of the AT&T case (Chapter 22), the few really concerted efforts to break up market concentration occurred at the beginning of the century, when Standard Oil and the Tobacco Trust were partially dismantled. The prevalent feeling today, even among antitrust practitioners, is that the oligopolies are too big and too powerful to make deconcentration a viable policy alternative. There is also a feeling that big firms are needed to maintain America's competitive position in international markets (which are themselves often dominated by foreign monopolies and oligopolies).

In addition to explicit antitrust efforts, two other mechanisms are available to alter market structure and behavior. First, there is the force of market demand. Consumers do have the power to reject shoddy products, exaggerated advertising claims, and high prices. The exercise of such power depends on consumer willpower, the extent of market and product information, and the availability of substitute products. Consumers' persistent demands for smaller, cheaper cars, for example, coupled with the availability of foreign substitutes, finally prodded the U.S. auto industry in that direction. Typically, however, determined consumer action can only moderate prices, profits, and power enjoyed by oligopolists. Movements of the market demand curve will not by themselves significantly alter the concentration of supply.

Another mechanism to influence market behavior and structure is international trade. To the extent that foreign producers are allowed to sell their products in the American market, the impact of domestic concentration can be contained. When foreign producers are permitted to compete in domestic markets, oligopolists must contend with their reactions when formulating price and output decisions. Thus international trade may serve to broaden market structure and render market behavior more competitive.[17] Indeed, the increased competition that international trade promises has led many oligopolies to seek strengthened barriers to trade (in the form of tariffs and quotas) and increased control of foreign supplies (through mergers, acquisitions, and supply agreements).

SUMMARY

■ The concentration ratio is a measure of the extent of market power in a particular product market. It equals the share of total industry output accounted for by the largest firms, usually the top four.

---

[16] Ibid., p. 7.

[17] International economic relations are discussed in Chapters 33 and 34.

■ Market power, particularly *oligopoly*, characterizes many of the product markets in the United States. As much as two-thirds of all manufacturing output is produced by firms with market power.

■ In addition to those firms with a large *market share* in one product market, many others have large market shares in several markets. Also, *conglomerates* have a little power in each of many markets. Finally, regional and local markets create still further opportunities for market power.

■ The primary mechanism for the exercise of market power is control over prices, particularly price fixing and price leadership.

■ In order to maintain and exercise market power, firms must be sheltered from potential competition by barriers to entry. Patents are one form of barrier, but others abound as well. Occasional predatory price cutting ("price wars"), control of distribution outlets, high capital-investment requirements, advertising and product differentiation, and resource control constitute important and frequent barriers to entry. Outright acquisition or merger offer additional means to eliminate competition.

■ The effects of market power include increased prices, reduced output, and a transfer of income from the consuming public to a relatively few powerful corporations and the people who own them.

■ Among the policy alternatives available to combat oligopolistic structure or behavior are antitrust action, government regulation, consumer action, and international trade.

Terms to remember

Define the following terms:

concentration ratio	price leadership
oligopoly	market share
conglomerate	predatory price cutting
barriers to entry	product differentiation
price fixing	

Questions for discussion

1. Market power usually results in high profits. Why, then, don't more firms enter an oligopolistic industry to share in the high profits, and thereby increase competition? Why don't more firms enter the auto industry? the photocopying industry?

2. In 1977 Laker Airways, then a three-plane airline, introduced a "Skytrain" air fare between New York and London that was less than half the fare previously charged by TWA, Pan Am, and other large airlines. Why didn't some other firm lower the fare sooner? Why did Laker eventually go bankrupt (in 1982)?

3. On what grounds is price fixing distinguished from price leadership?

4. What would be the advantages of breaking up the market power depicted in Table 24.1? What problems would such "trust busting" create?

FACTOR MARKETS AND INCOME DISTRIBUTION

THE SUPPLY OF LABOR

The following two ads recently appeared in the campus newspaper of a well-known university:

Will do ANYTHING for money: able-bodied liberal-minded male needs money, will work to get it. Have car. Call Tom 765-3210.

Computer Programmer: Computer sciences graduate, fluent in FORTRAN, COBOL, APL; experience with UNI-VAC, IBM and CDC systems. Looking for part-time position on or off campus. Please call Judy, ext. 4120, 9–5.

Although placed by individuals of very different talents, the ads clearly expressed Tom's and Judy's willingness to work. While we don't know how much money they were asking for their respective talents, or whether they ever found jobs, we can be sure that they were prepared to take a job at some wage rate. Otherwise, they never would have paid for the ads in the "Jobs Wanted" column of the campus newspaper.

LABOR SUPPLY: A FIRST LOOK

The advertised willingness to work expressed by Tom and Judy represents a **supply of labor.** They are offering to sell their time and talents to anyone who is willing to pay the right price.

The explicit offers of Tom and Judy are similar to that of anyone who looks for a job. Job seekers who check the current job openings at the student employment office or send résumés to potential em-

labor supply: The willingness and ability to work specific amounts of time at alternative wage rates in a given time period; the quantities of labor that would be supplied at specific wage rates (*ceteris paribus*).

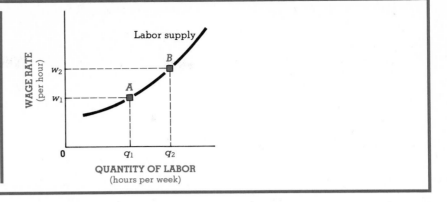

FIGURE 25.1   THE SUPPLY OF LABOR

The quantity of any good or service offered for sale typically increases as its price rises. Labor supply responds in the same way. At the wage rate w_1, the quantity of labor supplied is q_1 (point A). At the higher wage w_2, workers are willing to work more hours per week, that is, to supply a larger quantity of labor (q_2).

ployers are demonstrating a *willingness* to accept employment, that is, to supply labor. Whether they accept an available job or not will depend on the nature of the job and the wage it pays. Thus we can say that the decision to work will depend at least in part on the pay that is offered. ***The quantity of labor supplied depends on the wage rate.*** In general, we anticipate that the quantity of labor supplied—the number of hours people are willing to work—will increase as wage rates rise (see Figure 25.1).

Labor supply is analogous to the supply of any other good or service. As we observed in our discussion of product markets, would-be sellers of calculators participate in the calculator market by offering to sell calculators at specific prices. We also observed that the quantity of calculators supplied tends to increase as prices rise.

People and calculators obviously differ considerably, however, and some of their differences are important in explaining the particular shape of the labor-supply curve. The motivation for supplying calculators is the maximization of profits. But why do people supply labor? And how do these motivations affect the quantity of labor supplied at various wage rates? Our primary concern in this chapter is to answer these questions. We begin by looking at the motivations for working, then examine the actual labor-supply decisions that result.

150,000 Line Up for Postal Jobs

MIAMI—Approximately 150,000 jobseekers rushed to south Florida post offices this week to fill out applications for 700 letter carrier and postal clerk positions that will become available in south Florida over the next few years.

"We're still trying to absorb it all," said Steve Korker, postal public information officer. "We've had it going on all week, but it's still unbelievable."

The jobs are for postal workers in 60 outlets in Dade and Broward counties.

About 90,000 applicants waited hours in line Monday, Tuesday and Wednesday to get applications for the 700 positions expected to open up through attrition in the next two to three years. Another 25,000 grabbed applications Thursday and yesterday's total was estimated at 35,000.

"I guess given the economy today, that's what's happening," Korker said.

"You can see how serious people are about this by looking at who is waiting in line. We've had a lawyer, an accountant. These are very insecure times and people are looking for a little more security. The Postal Service is historically secure."

The last time the Postal Service advertised in Miami for letter carrier and clerk positions was in 1978. "Then, we gave out only 17,000 applications," Korker said. "Some difference, huh? It's the times."

San Francisco Chronicle, February 27, 1982. Reprinted by permission.

THE MOTIVATION TO WORK

From the comfortable perspective of an overstuffed chair or a blanket on the beach, the notion of supplying labor often seems quite alien. It reminds one of the bees, whose only function in life is to work, work, work. They spend every available moment of their short lives gathering pollen and producing honey. They rarely, if ever, get or take the opportunity to enjoy the fruits of their labor. Yet one imagines the bees might be a whole lot happier by producing less and consuming more.

The lesson of the bees has not been lost on all of nature's creatures. The bears, for example, have adopted a very different life-style. Generally contemptuous of hard labor, the bears prefer to let the bees do all the work. The bears themselves choose to hibernate half the year, later stealing and consuming the honey produced by the bees. This particular life-style seems most compatible to the bears, who have a life expectancy 600 times as long as that of the bees.[1]

Two distinctive elements in the bear's life-style are worthy of note. Its preference for leisure over material consumption frees the bear from most of the agonies associated with production. By hibernating half the year, it drastically reduces its needs and demands. Thus it attains substantial contentment with very little effort, by substituting leisure for other forms of satisfaction that require material support.

The second distinctive element in the bear's life-style is its tendency to satisfy its remaining few needs through plunder. This particular habit is easier to admire than to replicate in a civilized world, yet it unquestionably increases the bear's total satisfaction. It satisfies its consumption needs without great expenditure of time and effort. Were the bee's sting mightier or the honey yield smaller, the bear would not be so well off.

The distinctive life-styles of the bees and bears have not escaped human notice. The ancient Greeks, for example, were quick to perceive the relative desirability of the bear's status. They put great emphasis on leisure and eschewed both excessive consumption and manual labor. As Aristotle put it, "All paid employments absorb and degrade the mind." Like the bears, the Greeks took long naps and relied on others (primarily slaves) to produce their modest consumption needs.

The commitment to work

Given the apparent satisfaction of the bears and the ancient Greeks, how can we explain our own demonstrated willingness to work? Most people confront the prospect of eight hours of work per day, five days a week, for most of their adult lives. Yet most of us could enjoy standards of living unimagined by the ancient Greeks by working only a few hours a day. Why do we choose to work more? Have our material needs and wants expanded? Have we discovered new virtues and satisfactions in the act of producing?

---

[1] Lest the bees feel unfairly ridiculed here, let it stand as a matter of record that the male members of the bee colony, the drones, behave very much like bears, although they are later severely penalized.

To some extent, the present commitment to work can be explained by various forms of sanctions. In the first place, plundering and slavery have come to be regarded as antisocial activities. As a result, we are largely dependent on our own productive resources for the staples and frills of consumption. St. Paul, an early convert to the work ethic, put it succinctly: "If any one will not work, let him not eat."

Although the proscription of slavery and theft helps explain our commitment to work, it is hardly a complete explanation. Recall that there are two distinctive features in the life-styles of the bears and Greeks, and that only one of these has been denied us. The bears and Greeks also learned how to get by on relatively little. Surely we, too, could reduce our consumption, and thereby eliminate the necessity for so much work.

Sociopsychological forces

Our commitment to work beyond the provision of basic necessities can be explained by two complementary forces. On the one side, we have been persuaded to regard work as an end in itself. With the advent of Christianity, work came to be regarded as a form of worship. The Benedictine monks set the tone for many of us with their maxim, "Laborare est orare"—to work is to pray. Later sects, especially the Calvinists, carried forth this message, equating work with righteousness, worthiness, and chastity. Building on this tradition, the Puritans enshrined work as a form of salvation, and proclaimed that the devil would find work for idle hands. Much of the satisfaction derived from leisure became tarnished.

Sociological factors have also enhanced our attachment to work. Just as some people find their identity in conspicuous consumption, so do others find their identity in work. To be a banker, a salesperson, or a plumber is to have a distinct identity, to *belong*. Many people look to jobs for self-identification and a definition of their role in society. As Elliot Liebow has observed, "no man can live with the terrible knowledge that he is not needed," and work may make a person feel needed.[2] Co-workers also provide a small community of friends and acquaintances. These sociological aspects of working help explain why the vast majority of working Americans report that they like their jobs (see box). It also may explain why millions of people do volunteer work or continue working even when they don't need the income.

Economic forces

Reinforcing these religious and sociopsychological pushes toward work effort is the pull of materialist appetites. As we saw in Chapter 18, producers, their advertising agents, and our next-door neighbors are continually urging us to buy, buy, buy. As we seek to increase our consumption, we find ourselves needing more income. Even our leisure time often ends up being expensive. We currently spend nearly $244 billion on "leisure time" pursuits each year (see Table 25.1). To pay for all this activity, we often find ourselves in need of a job.

[2] Elliot Liebow, "No Man Can Live with the Terrible Knowledge That He Is Not Needed," *New York Times Magazine*, April 5, 1970.

DO AMERICANS LIKE THEIR JOBS?

Question or statement	Response category	Percent
All in all, how satisfied would you say you are with your job—very satisfied, somewhat satisfied, not too satisfied, or not at all satisfied?	Very satisfied	46.7
	Somewhat satisfied	41.7
	Not too satisfied	8.9
	Not at all satisfied	2.7
The work is interesting	Very true	57.2
	Somewhat true	28.3
	Not too true	12.1
	Not at all true	6.9
The pay is good	Very true	27.2
	Somewhat true	38.0
	Not too true	20.2
	Not at all true	14.6

Source: *The 1977 Quality of Employment Survey*, University of Michigan Institute for Social Research, Ann Arbor, Michigan, 1979.

THE LABOR VS. LEISURE TRADE-OFF

The psychological and economic forces that motivate us to work are only part of the story, of course. We do not work *all* of the time, but instead choose to devote some of our time to nonwork activities (leisure). That is to say, *not* working obviously has some value, too. In part, we need some nonwork time just to recuperate from working. But we also want some time to watch TV, go to a soccer game, or otherwise enjoy the goods and services we have purchased.

The more time we spend working, the less time we have to enjoy our incomes, or simply to relax. Accordingly, we recognize that working, like all activities, involves an opportunity cost. Generally, we say that **the opportunity cost of working is the amount of leisure time that must be given up in the process.**

The conflicting desires for work and leisure create an obvious dilemma: we can't increase one without decreasing the other. The

TABLE 25.1 LEISURE EXPENDITURES, 1980

The demise of philosophical contemplation as a form of leisure has been accompanied by a rise in more expensive pursuits. It now costs a lot more to relax, as these figures confirm. Can we afford not to work?

Item	Amount (in billions of dollars)
Vacation travel	$130.0
Recreation/sports equipment	33.0
TV sets, records, etc.	21.6
Admission tickets	6.4
Books, magazines, etc.	14.8
Gardens	4.5
Miscellaneous	33.7
Total	$244.0

Source: *U.S. News & World Report*, August 1981.

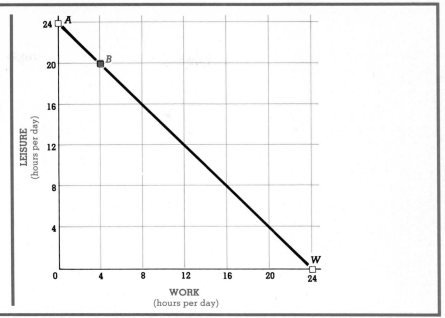

FIGURE 25.2   THE LEISURE VS. WORK CHOICE

There are only 24 hours in a day and we must allocate them between work and nonwork (leisure). The choices available are represented by the line stretching from point *A* (all leisure) to point *W* (all work). The actual choice of a particular labor-leisure combination (e.g., point *B*) is based on the satisfaction one obtains from either activity.

question we must decide is how to allocate our available time between these two competing activities. To see how this conflict is resolved—and the kind of labor-supply curve that emerges—we may examine the labor-supply decision of a single worker. For this purpose, we may study the behavior of Freddie, a fictional freshman economics major whose great ambition is to spend the rest of his life sleeping, listening to his stereo, and playing video games.

Unfortunately for Freddie, at least two of his life's goals require payment of money, and his parents cut off his allowance when he got three F's in his first semester. Even his continued sleeping in a warm bed is contingent upon payment of rent. As a consequence, Freddie, who has never felt a strong religious or sociopsychological attachment to work, now confronts the awful prospect of getting a job. The question becomes: How much is he willing to work?

The time constraint

Like everyone else, Freddie has only 24 hours in a day, so his work decision can be formulated in terms of the number of hours per day he is willing to give up for a job. Figure 25.2 illustrates the choices he confronts. At present, Freddie is not working at all, but is devoting all 24 hours per day to leisure (nonwork). This choice is represented by point *A* in Figure 25.2. Now that Freddie's allowance has been cut off, the question becomes: How much leisure will he give up? That is, how far will he proceed down the curve toward point *W*, which represents the extreme case of "all work and no play"?

Marginal utility of leisure

In order to make a rational work vs. leisure decision, Freddie must compare the relative values of labor and leisure. What is an hour of leisure worth to him? What is an hour of labor worth? By comparing

utility: The pleasure or satisfaction obtained from a good or service.

law of diminishing marginal utility: The *marginal* utility of a good declines as more of it is consumed in a given time period.

Marginal utility of labor

marginal utility of labor: The change in total utility derived from another hour's work.

Changes in marginal utility

these two values, Freddie can make a rational, utility-maximizing decision about the number of hours he will work.

On the leisure side, we can presume that giving up a few hours of leisure each day would not represent a great loss of **utility** to Freddie. He already has a lot of free time. And we expect that the value of another hour's leisure depends in part on the amount of leisure one already has. That is to say, leisure is subject to the **law of diminishing marginal utility:** additional hours of leisure tend to yield increasingly smaller amounts of satisfaction. From this perspective, the relative loss to Freddie would not be great if he were to get out of bed and work a few hours a day.

On the work side, similar considerations apply. Work has some utility, too. By working, Freddie can earn income to pay rent, buy food, and play video games. From this perspective, ***the marginal utility of labor is measured by the utility of the goods and services that can be purchased with an additional hour's wages.*** If Freddie *liked* working, the marginal utility of labor would be higher still. But since Freddie gets no *direct* satisfaction from working, only the wages are of value to him.

Since working is now Freddie's only source of income, the marginal utility of labor is presumably very high. The first few hours of work represent the difference between sleeping in a warm bed (paying rent) and getting thrown out in the cold. Under the circumstances, the *MU* of labor at point *A* in Figure 25.2 is sure to exceed the *MU* of leisure. As an economics major, Freddie realizes that he will be better off giving up some hours of leisure for paid employment. Accordingly, he goes to work, thereupon beginning the long descent from point *A*.

The calculation of marginal utility that drove Freddie from the idle comforts of point *A* will also determine the number of hours per day he works. The decisive factor will again be the law of diminishing marginal utility. On the leisure side, the law of diminishing marginal utility begins to work in reverse. As Freddie spends more time working each day, his leisure hours become increasingly precious. That is to say, the marginal utility of an hour's leisure is high when one has few such hours.

The law of diminishing marginal utility is illustrated in Figure 25.3. At point *A*, where Freddie is not working at all, the marginal utility of leisure is very small. In other words, that twenty-fourth hour of leisure is of relatively little value to Freddie, inasmuch as he has spent the last 23 hours relaxing. As Freddie begins working — substituting labor for leisure — he moves up the marginal-utility-of-leisure curve. In the process, each hour of leisure given up becomes increasingly valuable.

Suppose that Freddie's initial job involves four hours of work per day. This amount of work is represented by a move from point *A* to point *B* in Figures 25.2 and 25.3. From Figure 25.2 all we learn is that Freddie has gone to work. From Figure 25.3 we learn that

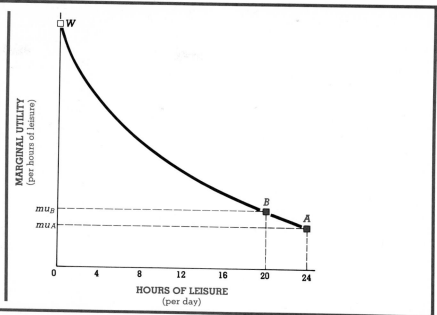

FIGURE 25.3 DIMINISHING MARGINAL UTILITY OF LEISURE

The amount of utility derived from an additional hour's leisure depends on the amount of leisure a person *time* already has. If a person worked all of the time (point *W*), leisure would have a high marginal utility. However, the last four hours of leisure (point *B* to *A*) are not as satisfying as the first four hours. In general, the marginal utility of leisure diminishes as leisure time is increased. Would you agree?

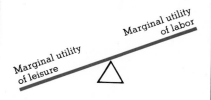

FIGURE 25.4 BALANCING THE MARGINAL UTILITIES OF WORK AND LEISURE

The marginal utility of labor is very high when one is not working at all and needs some income, while the marginal utility of leisure is quite low. As we substitute labor for leisure (go to work), however, the marginal utility of labor starts to fall while the marginal utility of leisure rises. Our objective is to balance the marginal utilities of labor and leisure. At that point, our work effort is optimal.

optimal work effort: The amount of work at which the marginal utility of an hour's labor is just equal to the marginal utility of another hour's leisure.

Freddie's marginal utility of leisure has *risen* as a consequence. We don't know how marginal utility is measured, but we do know that Freddie's perceived value of leisure has gone up.

When labor is substituted for leisure, the marginal value of leisure increases and the marginal utility of work declines. Recall that the value of work to Freddie is simply the goods and services he can buy with his paycheck (he gets no intrinsic satisfaction from work). Those first few dollars were precious to him, as they enabled him to pay the rent, eat, and even play a few video games. But the marginal utility of additional dollars quickly diminishes. Because Freddie is a person of simple tastes, the pleasures he can buy with an additional hour's wages are of relatively little value to him.

Freddie was driven from complete idleness (point *A* in Figure 25.2) to four hours of work per day (point *B*). The marginal utility of an hour's work exceeded the marginal utility of another hour's leisure at that point. But as Freddie descends from point *A*, the marginal utility of an hour's work falls, while the marginal utility of leisure rises. Sooner or later the marginal utility of an hour's work will no longer exceed the marginal utility of an hour's leisure. At that point, Freddie will no longer be willing to substitute labor for leisure. His descent toward point *W* in Figure 25.2 will come to a screeching halt. At that point, where the marginal utility of an hour's work is equal to the marginal utility of an hour's leisure, Freddie will have no further incentive to alter his life-style. He will be getting as much satisfaction as his talents, wages, and tastes allow. At this point, we say that Freddie has achieved an **optimal work effort** (see Figure 25.4). *Optimal work effort is the combination of work and leisure that yields the greatest total utility available from given tastes and wages.*

We can assure ourselves that a balance of the marginal utilities

TABLE 25.2 THE MARGINAL UTILITY OF LEISURE AND LABOR

The table depicts the marginal utility of each hour of labor or leisure, as perceived by Freddie. Initially (point *A*), Freddie isn't working at all. Yet the table confirms that he would be better off (happier) if he *substituted* one hour of labor (*MU* = 432) for the twenty-fourth hour of leisure (*MU* = 2). He should continue to substitute labor for leisure until he is working six hours a day. The *MU* of a seventh hour of labor (*MU* = 196) does not exceed the *MU* of the additional (eighteenth) leisure hour that would be given up (*MU* = 196).

	Total hours		Marginal utility (in utils)	
	Leisure	Labor	Leisure	Labor
Point A	24	0	2	—
	23	1	11	432
	22	2	39	421
	21	3	68	408
Point B	20	4	104	386
	19	5	153	360
	18	6	196	329
	17	7	213	196
	16	8	232	172
	15	9	247	140
	14	10	291	113
	13	11	339	96
	12	12	367	88
	11	13	392	73
	10	14	450	61
	9	15	473	50
	8	16	499	42
	7	17	531	25
	6	18	586	3
	5	19	644	−2
	4	20	721	−29
	3	21	805	−61
	2	22	911	−105
	1	23	962	−167
Point W	0	24	—	−349

represents an optimal situation by considering the implications of an imbalance. Suppose that the marginal utility (*MU*) of labor is greater than the marginal utility of leisure, that is,

$$MU_{labor} > MU_{leisure}$$

when Freddie is working five hours a day. Could Freddie be better off with another mix of work and play? Clearly, yes. If another hour's labor is worth more than another hour's leisure, a person should trade in one hour of leisure for one hour of labor. That is to say, Freddie should work another hour each day. By so doing, he will increase his *total* utility, that is, the satisfaction he gets out of life. Optimal work effort occurs when the marginal utilities of labor and leisure are equal.

Once the *MU* of labor equals the *MU* of leisure, there is no incentive to substitute one activity for the other. Further changes in the leisure vs. labor decision will not increase total utility (see Table 25.2).

ALTERNATIVE WAGE RATES

wage rate: The amount of money paid for an hour's work; the price of labor.

So far we have said nothing about the **wage rate** Freddie is receiving, because the hourly wage was not really relevant to our analysis.

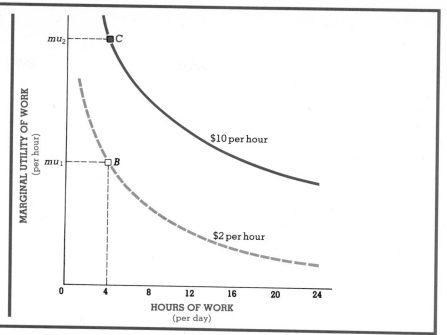

FIGURE 25.5 THE EFFECT OF WAGE RATES ON THE MARGINAL UTILITY OF LABOR

Higher wage rates imply more goods and services for every hour worked. Hence the marginal utility of labor increases when wage rates rise. The marginal utility of the fourth work hour increases from mu_1 (point B) to mu_2 (point C) when the wage rate increases from $2 to $10 per hour.

Whether Freddie is paid $2 an hour or $10 an hour, the law of diminishing marginal utility still applies. That is to say, the *marginal utility of an hour's work will decline as Freddie works longer hours.* Thus no matter how great the initial imbalance between the marginal utilities of labor and leisure, we still expect them to balance before Freddie is working 24 hours a day.

The wage rate will help Freddie to decide how much he will work, however. A wage of $10 an hour is clearly superior to a wage of $2 an hour, because it enables Freddie to buy more goods and services for any given amount of work. Thus **as wage rates rise, the marginal utility of work tends to increase.** We can see this effect in Figure 25.5. The lower curve represents the marginal utility associated with work when the wage rate is $2 an hour. Were Freddie to work four hours a day at this wage rate, the marginal utility of another hour's labor would be equal to the value mu_1 (point B in Figure 25.5).

If by some miracle Freddie's wage rate were suddenly increased to $10 an hour, a new and higher marginal utility curve would apply. Each hour of work would provide more income and thus greater utility. Note that the entire marginal utility curve in Figure 25.5 shifts upward. At the wage of $10 an hour, Freddie would enjoy a marginal utility of mu_2 by working four hours a day (point C) rather than only mu_1.

Suppose for the moment that point B initially represented Freddie's *optimal work effort.* That is, at point B the marginal utility of an hour's labor equaled the marginal utility of an hour's leisure. Were Freddie's wage rate really to increase, this equality would be thrown out of balance. The higher wage rate would not affect the value of leisure, but it would increase the value (marginal utility) of

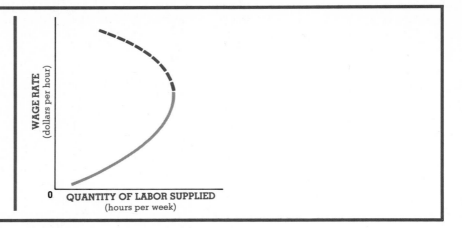

FIGURE 25.6 THE BACKWARD-BENDING SUPPLY CURVE

Increases in wage rates make additional hours of work more valuable, but also less necessary. Higher wage rates increase the quantity of labor supplied as long as substitution effects outweigh income effects. At the point where income effects begin to outweigh substitution effects, the labor-supply curve starts to bend backward.

---

labor-supply curve: A curve depicting the quantities of labor supplied (offered) in a given time period at alternative wage rates (*ceteris paribus*).

The backward bend

substitution effect of wages: An increased wage rate raises the marginal utility of an hour's labor, thereby encouraging people to work more hours (to substitute labor for leisure).

labor. Thus an increase in the wage rate raises the marginal utility of labor.

We can induce Freddie to work more, then, by raising his hourly wage rate. Thus the quantity of labor supplied tends to increase as the wage rate rises. This kind of labor-supply response is illustrated by the solid portion of the **labor-supply curve** in Figure 25.6.

The solid portion of the labor-supply curve illustrated in Figure 25.6 should look familiar. In fact, it looks very much like the supply curve for *any* product or resource, with the quantity supplied increasing as prices rise. What we have demonstrated here is that this kind of supply curve applies to labor as well.

The supply curve in Figure 25.6 does not look exactly like other supply curves we have studied. As wage rates continue to rise, the supply curve appears to *bend backward,* as indicated by the dashed portion of the curve. How does this strange result come about?

The force that drives people up the labor-supply curve is the marginal utility of labor, as represented by the goods and services that wages can buy. Higher wages represent more goods and services and thus induce people to **substitute** labor for leisure.

At some point, however, additional goods and services will be of little value. Individuals whose incomes are already extremely high have a multitude of goods and services to enjoy. More income is of relatively little value to them. If they are offered a wage rate higher still, they are likely to respond by *reducing* the number of hours they work, thereby maintaining a high income *and* increasing their leisure. While you might do cartwheels for $4 an hour, a Rockefeller or Du Pont might not lift an eyelash for such a paltry sum. Muhammad Ali once announced that he would not spend an hour in the ring for less than $1 million, and would box *less,* not more, as the pay for his fights exceeded $3 million. For him, the added income obtainable from one championship fight was so great that he felt he did not have to fight more to satisfy his income and consumption desires. Many entertainers and other high-income earners respond in the same way to high wage offers. In such cases, we may say that

income effect of wages: An increased wage rate allows a person to reduce hours worked without losing income.

the higher income made possible by increased wage rates induces a *negative* supply reaction, a reduced willingness to work. This negative response to increased wage rates is referred to as the **income effect** of a rise in wages. This kind of reaction is illustrated by the backward-bending portion of the supply curve in Figure 25.6.[3]

A worker's decision to work more or less at higher wages depends on the way the conflict between income effects and substitution effects is resolved. As long as substitution effects outweigh income effects—that is, as long as the lure of increased income outweighs the sense of sufficiency—the labor-supply curve will have its more conventional upward slope.

NONMONETARY INCENTIVES

Some people work for reasons other than money alone, of course. As we observed earlier, millions of individuals find some status or salvation in their jobs. As a consequence, each hour of labor yields more satisfaction than just a paycheck.

Were Freddie to start enjoying his job, his marginal utility calculations would change, too. In Figure 25.7a, the curve MU_1 represents Freddie's marginal-utility-of-labor curve before he found salvation in work. After he finds out that people like him more when he has a job, the marginal utility of each hour's labor increases. This change is represented by an upward *shift* of Freddie's marginal utility curve to MU_2. The resultant increase in marginal utilities will also shift Freddie's labor-supply curve to the right, as in Figure 25.7b. All we are saying here is that if Freddie likes his job, he will be willing to work more hours per day for any given wage rate.

Like Freddie, workers on the assembly line or in offices are also influenced by nonmonetary incentives. Pleasant surroundings, piped-in music, and colorful walls are often used to make employees

[3] Income effects are relevant at low incomes also. A person paid very low wage rates (e.g., migrant workers, baby sitters, household workers) may end up working more hours at low wages in order to maintain some minimum level of income. The higher income made possible by higher wage rates may induce some cutback in hours of work. These are the kinds of situations Karl Marx had in mind when he said that capitalists would strive to keep wage rates low to induce people to work. The modern version of this problem is discussed in Chapter 31, where the welfare system is considered.

FIGURE 25.7 THE EFFECT OF
INCREASED JOB SATISFACTION

A given labor-supply curve is based
on the assumption that the "taste" for
work is constant. If work becomes
more enjoyable, however, its
marginal utility increases and the
assumption is no longer valid. An
increase in job satisfaction is
illustrated in part *a* by an upward
shift of the marginal utility curve.
When job satisfaction increases, the
labor-supply curve shifts to the right,
as in part *b*. People are willing to
work more hours at any given wage
rate when they enjoy their work.

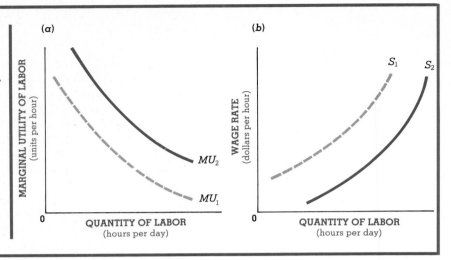

*"Leave it to good old G.M. to break the monotony
of the assembly line!"*

Drawing by Alan Dunn: © 1972 The New
Yorker Magazine, Inc.

feel they are on some tropical beach, and help make the trade-off
between work and leisure less apparent.

High wages and superficial changes in the work environment
are not the only relevant incentives, of course. Worker behavior is
also affected by the nature of the work to be performed and the sense
of attachment the worker associates with the job. If people can identify with their work and feel their efforts are important, they are
likely to perform not only more work but better work for a given rate
of pay. When they perceive little interest or significance in their
efforts, the willingness to work declines. Industrial research has suggested that the problem of worker alienation is particularly acute in
jobs that are exceedingly specialized and routine. It is difficult to
sustain interest in a job that requires one to tighten bolts on the left
rear wheel of every car moving down the assembly line or punch
holes in IBM computer cards. Wage increases may not be sufficient
to improve worker motivation in such cases.

Finally, willingness to work may be affected by more general
perceptions of the significance of work. The women's liberation
movement, for example, has allayed the guilt feelings formerly associated by many wives and mothers with work performed outside the
home. As a consequence, more women are willing to work at existing wage rates (that is, their supply curves have shifted to the right).
Other forms of persuasion have been used to motivate entire countries, such as patriotic appeals in Cuba and China during the 1960s
and 1970s to produce more sugar and wheat.[4] In each case, the objective of policy was to raise workers' perception of the value of work,
to make them feel that they gave up less than they got when they
sacrificed leisure for work.

---

[4] The extensive use of nonmonetary incentives in the People's Republic of China is
discussed in Chapter 36. Of particular interest in this regard is the way socialist countries rely on various combinations of monetary and nonmonetary incentives.

INSTITUTIONAL CONSTRAINTS

Both the monetary and the nonmonetary incentives offered to workers are intended to alter their work patterns, the amount of labor they supply. We must recognize, however, that people seldom have the opportunity to adjust their hours of employment in accordance with their desired trade-off between work and leisure. True, Sugar Ray Leonard, Devo, Richard Pryor, Chris Evert Lloyd, the Rolling Stones, and many others may alter their labor supply almost at will. Most workers, however, face more rigid choices. They must usually choose to work at a regular eight-hour-day, five-day-week job or not to work at all. Very few firms are flexible or interested enough to accommodate a desire to work only between the hours of 11 A.M. and 3 P.M. on alternate Thursdays. As a consequence, relatively few people are able to achieve the optimum balance between work and leisure suggested by their labor-supply curves (see box). Adjustments in work hours are more commonly confined to choices about overtime work or secondary jobs ("moonlighting") and vacation and retirement decisions. Insofar as families make collective decisions about the labor they supply, adjustments in work effort may also be reflected in decisions about the number of family members to send into the labor force at any given time.

POLICY IMPLICATIONS: A VOLUNTEER ARMY

The desire of consumers for income and status creates the conditions for altered patterns of work effort. As we have seen, people can be induced to increase or reduce their work effort simply by changes in the monetary or nonmonetary incentives they confront. If workers

---

MISSING THE OPTIMUM: INFLEXIBLE WORK SCHEDULES

The U.S. Department of Labor recently surveyed American workers to determine whether they were satisfied with their present mix of labor and leisure. Specifically, workers were asked if they would prefer a bit more leisure in exchange for a bit less income. Would they, in other words, substitute more leisure for a few hours of work if they had the opportunity? The added leisure could take the form of fewer hours per day or week, longer vacations, occasional sabbaticals, or earlier retirement. The "cost" of the added leisure would be a reduction in income.

The responses were overwhelming. Eighty-five percent of all workers said they would gladly give up a raise (marginal income) for added leisure. Sixty percent said they would give up some of their *current* income for added leisure. In other words, the vast majority of American workers feel they have not achieved their optimal work effort. Inflexible work schedules prevent them from achieving the most satisfying combination of labor and leisure.

market mechanism: The use of market prices and sales to signal desired outputs (or resource allocations).

can be persuaded to work long or little, they may also be induced to move from one occupation to another with appropriate encouragement. Suppose that prospective wage earners would rather be social workers than accountants but that we need more accountants. Are we helpless to change people's occupational choices? Certainly not. Recognizing the various incentives that shape occupational choices, we can offer higher pay for accountants than for social workers. As the relative pay of accountants rises, more and more people will choose that occupation. As a result, we will have more accountants and fewer social workers. In general, we can alter people's occupational choices by changing the structure of employment rewards.

In a completely totalitarian regime, we could impose the same kind of results by fiat. The theory of labor supply explains how various work patterns can be induced by the **market mechanism.** A classic example of labor-supply theory at work was the conversion from a draft army to an all-volunteer army.

The hope has long existed that we could fill our armies with dedicated volunteers serving at low pay, but those expectations have usually remained unfulfilled. We have found that the willingness to do battle with the enemy varies considerably from one person to another and from one war to the next. Generally, however, the total number of people volunteering to serve in the armed forces has been below the number required. As a result, we have had to go to war without a sufficient army, increase the willingness to serve, or compel people to serve against their will. Each solution has been tried at one time or another.

In the early years of the Republic, there was widespread hostility to the notion of military conscription. Although local conscription laws did exist, they were rarely enforced. For the most part, local defenses consisted of militia volunteers who rallied to repel outside attacks. Even the Revolutionary War was fought almost entirely by volunteers, who were encouraged by patriotism and financial bounties to join the state militias or the Continental Army. In effect, the supply of labor shifted to the right when independence was declared (see Figure 25.8), and military service was encouraged by higher wages.

Soon after the Revolutionary War, both the need for armed forces and the willingness to serve declined. The standing army of the United States was reduced to a mere 80 men. To enlarge our defenses, Secretary of War Henry Knox proposed in 1790 to create a universal draft, compelling military service. Congress, however, rejected his proposal. As a result, when the United States entered the less popular War of 1812, we found ourselves seriously short of military manpower. This shortage led to an almost unbroken series of defeats, including the humiliating burning of the nation's capital in 1814.

The Civil War, too, was fought primarily by volunteers on both sides. When war was declared, the Union Army had fewer than 16,000 officers and men. Within the first two years, however, more than 1 million men voluntarily answered the call to arms, reflecting another shift in the supply curve. Nevertheless, at the outset of the war, President Abraham Lincoln had proposed a national draft to

FIGURE 25.8 THE WILLINGNESS TO SERVE

A person's willingness to serve in the military depends on both attitudes and pay scales. Suppose an individual's perceptions of national defense are expressed by supply curve A. Clearly, this person is more likely to serve, or voluntarily to serve more time, if military wage rates are increased (say, from w_1 to w_2). If the army's image improves or a particularly righteous war commences, however, the general commitment to national defense will increase, as reflected by supply curve B. If the popularity of war falls, the commitment to defense will decline, as expressed by supply curve C.

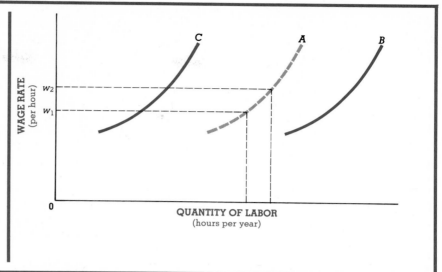

ensure an adequate supply of manpower. When the draft was enacted in March 1863, widespread resistance erupted, reaching a bloody climax in the New York draft riots, in which more than 1,000 people were killed. During the course of the war, the new powers of conscription were used sparingly, with draftees accounting for only 2.3 percent of the North's military manpower and about 14 percent of the South's.

In 1917 a comprehensive draft law was passed immediately after the United States entered World War I. Because of extensive opposition to the war, Congress felt compelled to forgo reliance on voluntary enlistments. Congress felt that compulsory service was cheaper than the pay increases and enlistment bonuses that had been used to recruit volunteers in earlier crises. Evasion of the draft replaced open resistance during World War I, with more than 250,000 draftees failing to appear for induction. The draft law expired after the end of the war.

With the onset of World War II, we were again faced with the problem of recruiting additional manpower. The Selective Service Act of 1940 created the authority by which the government could compel men to join the army, regardless of their willingness to serve. The act not only gave the government new authority, but also permitted it to keep military pay at levels significantly lower than comparable civilian pay. More than 10 million men were drafted for service in World War II.

The unpopularity of the Vietnam War aroused resistance to the draft once again. As a result, Congress debated the possibility of returning to the concept of an all-volunteer army. In accordance with the theory of labor supply, Congress concluded that such an army was possible only if a war were particularly popular or if military pay and status were considerably increased. The first condition was clearly not met. The President's Commission on an All-Volunteer Armed Force estimated in 1970 that basic military pay would

Reagan on draft—why he changed

Ronald Reagan's decision to continue Jimmy Carter's draft-registration system demonstrated that issues can look different when seen from the White House instead of the campaign trail.

The crackdown in Poland, tensions in the Mideast, uprisings by Soviet surrogates in Central America—all prompted Reagan on January 7 to abandon his 1980 campaign claim that registration is a meaningless gesture that "destroys the very values that our society is committed to defending."

Carter reinstated registration for a possible draft in July, 1980, in response to the Soviet invasion of Afghanistan. Reagan now believes, aides said, that dropping registration would send a wrong signal to Moscow. "We live in a dangerous world," he said.

Advisers hoped Reagan's action will reverse a falloff in draft registrations, a slump that accelerated after Reagan took office. At last check, 1 of every 4 youths had declined to sign up within 30 days of his 18th birthday as required by law. During the Vietnam War, the level of noncompliance did not exceed 2 percent.

The Justice Department moved to establish a grace period of 30 to 60 days for late registrations. After that, officials warned, laggards may be hit by penalties ranging up to five years in prison and a $10,000 fine.

Reagan changed his mind on registration, aides said, after a military task force concluded that the system would save up to six weeks in mobilization time—virtually the same conclusion as in a study done for Carter two years ago.

Reprinted from *U.S. News & World Report*, January 18, 1982. Copyright © 1982 U.S. News & World Report, Inc.

---

have to rise from $180 to $315 a month to attract an additional 100,000 men per year. In the light of these facts, Congress opted to study and debate the subject for two years. Congress finally allowed the authority for conscription to expire only at the war's end in 1973.

Our experiences with an all-volunteer army have demonstrated the principles of labor-supply theory. Willingness to serve is directly affected not only by one's perception of patriotism and danger, but also by military wage rates and status. Since 1973 we have placed increased reliance on higher pay scales, early retirement benefits, and advertising to induce a steady flow of volunteers. While military wages have skyrocketed, the old, drab army has become "Today's Army," with spruced-up and tailor-fitted uniforms and more amenities. In addition, the Army, Navy, and Air Force have vastly enlarged the pool of potential volunteers by actively recruiting women and providing them with more equal status and benefits.

Although we have generally succeeded in "buying" an all-volunteer armed force, several problems remain. Critics claim that the all-volunteer army is most attractive to low-income and minority people, who have fewer civilian job opportunities (and thus lower opportunity costs). Also, the armed forces have not been very successful in retaining experienced personnel or in maintaining a pool of reservists. The armed services have tried to remedy the first problem by substantial reenlistment bonuses (up to $15,000), but even this "wage" has not been adequate. To help overcome the lack of reservists, Congress reinstated Selective Service registration in July 1980. All men must register at the age of 18 and provide their permanent address. Registration will enable the Selective Service to find and recruit military personnel more quickly in the event of a war. In the meantime, however, the armed forces must recruit more than one out of every five 18-year olds (roughly 2 million personnel) just to keep our peacetime forces at full strength.

SUMMARY

■ The motivation to work arises from a variety of social, psychological, and economic forces. People need income to pay their bills, but they also need to feel they have a role in society's efforts, and to attain a sense of achievement. As a consequence, people are *willing to work—to supply labor.*

■ There is an opportunity cost involved in working; namely, the amount of leisure one sacrifices. By the same token, the opportunity cost of not working (leisure) is the income and related consumption possibilities thereby forgone. Thus each person confronts a trade-off between leisure and income.

■ People choose between labor and leisure according to the perceived rewards of each. The marginal utility of labor reflects the satisfaction to be gained from added income, as well as any direct pleasure a job may provide. A worker compares these satisfactions with those of leisure and chooses the one that yields greater marginal utility.

■ An individual's work effort is optimal when the marginal utility of labor equals the marginal utility of leisure. This particular combination of labor and leisure yields the greatest utility for available time and wage rates.

■ Increases in wage rates raise the marginal utility of labor and tend to induce people to increase their hours of work, that is, to substitute labor for leisure. But this substitution effect may be offset by an income effect. That is, increased wage rates also enable a person to work fewer hours with no loss of income. When income effects outweigh substitution effects, the labor-supply curve begins to bend backward.

■ The choice between labor and leisure is also affected by nonmonetary incentives and institutional constraints. Inflexibility of working hours may preclude the attainment of an optimal labor-leisure combination.

Terms to remember

Define the following terms:

labor supply	wage rate
utility	labor-supply curve
law of diminishing marginal utility	substitution effect of wages
marginal utility of labor	income effect of wages
optimal work effort	market mechanism

Questions for discussion

1. Would you continue to work after winning a lottery prize of $50,000 a year for life? Would you change schools, jobs, or career objectives? What factors besides income influence work decisions?

2. If garbagemen were paid twice as much as doctors, how would this reversal affect people's occupational or educational plans?

3. Will a doubling of wage rates stimulate people to work twice as long? Why, or why not?

4. If daytime television were to improve dramatically, would labor supplies be affected?

Problem | Use the following schedules of individual labor supply to construct a market labor-supply curve.

Hourly wage rate	Number of hours supplied per week			
	Adam	Susan	Linda	David
$ 1	6	0	28	0
2	14	0	25	0
3	18	5	20	0
4	22	8	16	10
5	27	18	12	15
6	35	27	10	20
7	40	35	8	25
8	46	35	7	30
9	40	35	6	30
10	28	35	6	40

What wage rate is required to enlist at least 100 hours of help per week?

THE DEMAND FOR LABOR

In 1982 the president of General Motors was paid over half a million dollars for his services. The president of the United States was paid $200,000. And the secretary who typed the manuscript of this book was paid $8,000. What accounts for these tremendous disparities in earnings?

And why is it that the average college graduate was earning over $20,000 in 1982 while the average high school graduate earned only $12,000? Do such disparities simply reflect a reward earned by those who endured the rigors of four years of college, or do they reflect real differences in talent? Are you really learning anything that makes you that much more valuable than a high school graduate?

Surely we cannot hope to explain these earnings disparities on the basis of the willingness to work. After all, my secretary would be more than willing to work day and night for $500,000 per year. For that matter, so would I. Accordingly, the earnings disparities cannot be attributed to differences in the quantity of labor supplied. If we are to explain why some people earn a great deal of income while others earn very little, we will have to consider also the *demand* for labor. What determines the wage rate employers are *willing to pay*, and why do they pay individual workers such disparate wage rates? These are the primary concerns of this chapter.

DERIVED DEMAND

Employers tend to be profit maximizers. That is to say, their primary motivation in going into business is to make as much income as

derived demand: The demand for labor and other factors of production results from (depends on) the demand for final goods and services produced by these factors.

possible. In their quest for maximum profits, firms attempt to identify the rate of output at which marginal revenue equals marginal cost. Once they have identified the profit-maximizing rate of output, firms enter factor markets to purchase the required amounts of labor, equipment, and other resources. The quantity of resources purchased by business firms depends, then, on the firm's expected sales and output. In this sense, we say that the demand for factors of production, including labor, is a **derived demand;** it is derived from the demand for goods and services.

Consider the plight of strawberry pickers. Strawberry pickers are paid very low wages and are employed only part of the year. But their plight cannot be blamed on the greed of the strawberry growers. Strawberry growers, like most producers, would love to sell more strawberries at higher prices. If they did, there is a strong possibility that the growers would hire more pickers and even pay them at a higher wage rate. But the growers must contend with the market demand for strawberries. Growers have discovered that consumers are not willing to buy more strawberries at higher prices. As a consequence, the growers cannot afford to hire more pickers or pay them higher wages. In contrast, producers of computers are always looking for more workers and offer very high wages to get them (see news clipping).

The principle of derived demand suggests that if consumers

SHIFTING DEMANDS FOR LABOR

Wages and job prospects in future years will depend on changes in the demand for labor. The U.S. Department of Labor foresees major increases in the demand for computer technicians and paralegals as consumer demands for computer and legal services continue to increase. Conversely, an actual decline in the demand for college professors is anticipated as college enrollments decline. Things look even worse for shoemakers and farm workers. These figures show projected growth in employment for the fastest- and slowest-growing occupations.

Occupations in high demand	Projected growth of jobs, 1978–1990
Computer technicians	148%
Paralegal aides	132
Office machine technicians	81
Computer programmers	74
Food-service workers (including fast-food outlets)	69
Tax preparers	65
Correction officials and jailers	60
Architects	60
Dental assistants	57
Veterinarians	56
Travel agents	56
Nurse's aides	55
Occupations in low demand	
College and university teachers	−10%
Textile weavers	−11
Secondary school teachers	−13
Taxi drivers	−13
Private household workers	−15
Railroad car repairers	−19
Shoemaking machine operators	−20
Farm laborers	−25

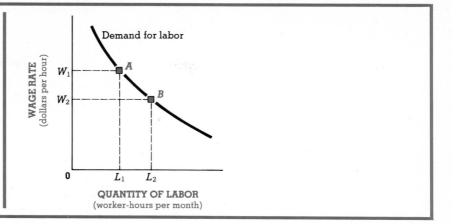

FIGURE 26.1   THE DEMAND FOR LABOR

The higher the wage rate, the smaller the quantity of labor demanded (ceteris paribus). At the wage rate W_1, only L_1 of labor is demanded. If the wage rate falls to W_2, a larger quantity of labor (L_2) will be demanded. The labor-demand curve obeys the law of demand.

really want to improve the lot of strawberry pickers, they should eat more strawberries. An increase in the demand for strawberries will motivate growers to plant more berries and hire more labor to pick them. Until then, the plight of the pickers is not likely to improve.

THE DEMAND FOR LABOR

demand for labor: The quantities of labor employers are willing and able to hire at alternative wage rates in a given time period (ceteris paribus).

The number of strawberry pickers hired by the growers is not completely determined by the demand for strawberries, of course. On the contrary, the number of pickers will also depend on the wage rate of pickers. That is to say, ***the quantity of labor demanded will depend on its price (the wage rate).*** In general, we expect that strawberry growers will be *willing to hire* more pickers at low wages than at high wages. Hence the **demand for labor** looks very much like the demand for any good or service (see Figure 26.1).

Marginal physical product

marginal physical product (MPP): The change in total output associated with one additional unit of input. *of factor of production*

The fact that the demand curve for labor slopes downward does not tell us very much about the quantity of labor that will be hired, of course. Nor does it tell us the wage rate that will be paid. To answer such questions, we need to know what determines the particular shape and position of the labor-demand curve.

A strawberry grower will be willing to hire another picker only if that picker contributes more to output than he costs. Growers, as rational business people, recognize that *every* sale, *every* expenditure has some impact on total profits. Hence the truly profit-maximizing grower will want to evaluate each picker's job application in terms of the applicant's potential contribution to profits.

Fortunately, a strawberry picker's contribution to output is easy to measure; it is the number of boxes of strawberries he or she picks. Suppose for the moment that Sunshine, a college dropout with three summers of experience as a canoe instructor, can pick five boxes per hour. These five boxes represent Sunshine's **marginal physical product (MPP)**, that is, the *addition* to total output that will occur if the grower hires Sunshine for an hour.

The concept of marginal physical product is extremely useful in determining how much Sunshine might make as a strawberry picker. Clearly the grower can't afford to pay Sunshine more than five boxes of strawberries for an hour's work; to do so would imply a net loss. Thus Sunshine's marginal physical product establishes an *upper limit* to the grower's willingness to pay. The grower will not pay Sunshine more than he produces.

Marginal revenue product

Most strawberry pickers don't want to be paid in strawberries, of course. At the end of a day in the fields, the last thing a picker wants to see is another strawberry. Sunshine, like the rest of the pickers, wants to be paid in cash. Fortunately, the conversion of productivity from physical units to monetary units is straightforward. All we need to know is what a box of strawberries is worth. The market value of a box of strawberries is simply the price at which the grower can sell it. Thus Sunshine's contribution to output can be measured in either marginal physical product (five boxes per hour) or the dollar value of that product. The latter is called Sunshine's **marginal revenue product.** If the grower can sell strawberries for $2 a box, Sunshine's marginal revenue product is easily calculated; it is simply 5 boxes per hour × $2 per box, or $10 per hour. In compliance with the rule about not paying anybody more than he or she contributes, the profit-maximizing grower should be willing to pay Sunshine up to $10 an hour. Thus *marginal revenue product sets an upper limit to the wage rate an employer will pay.*

But what about a lower limit? Suppose that the pickers aren't organized and are desperate for money. Under such circumstances, they might be willing to work—to supply labor—for only $3 an hour.

Should the grower hire Sunshine for such a low wage? The profit-maximizing answer is obvious. If Sunshine's marginal revenue product is $10 an hour and his wages are only $3 an hour, the grower will be eager to hire him. Obviously Sunshine promises to contribute to profits at the rate of $7 an hour. In fact, the grower will be so elated by the economics of this situation that he will want to hire everybody he can find who is willing to work for $3 an hour. After all, if the grower can make $7 an hour by hiring Sunshine, why not hire 1,000 pickers and accumulate profits at an even faster rate?

THE LAW OF DIMINISHING RETURNS

The exploitive possibilities suggested by Sunshine's picking are clearly attractive; however, they merit some careful consideration. It isn't at all clear, for example, how the grower could squeeze 1,000 workers onto one acre of land and have any room left over for strawberry plants. There must be some limit to the profit-making potential of this situation.

A few moments' reflection on the absurdity of trying to employ 1,000 people to pick one acre of strawberries should be convincing evidence of the limits to profits here. You don't need two years of

marginal revenue product (MRP): The change in total revenue associated with one additional unit of input.

business school to recognize this. But some economics may help explain exactly why the grower's eagerness to hire additional pickers will begin to fade long before 1,000 are hired. The magic concept here is *marginal productivity*.

Diminishing marginal physical product

The decision to hire Sunshine originated in his marginal physical product, that is, the five boxes of strawberries he can pick in an hour's time. To assess the profitability of hiring additional pickers, we again have to consider what will happen to total output as additional labor is employed. To do so we will need to keep track of marginal physical product.

Table 26.1 provides a summary of the increases in strawberry output as additional pickers are hired. We start with Sunshine, who picks five boxes of strawberries per hour. Total output and his marginal physical product are identical, because he is initially the only picker employed. When the grower hires Moon, Sunshine's old college roommate, we observe that total output increases to ten boxes per hour. This figure represents another increase of five boxes per hour. Accordingly, we may conclude that Moon's *marginal physical product* is five boxes per hour, the same as Sunshine's. Naturally, the grower will want to hire Moon and continue looking for more pickers.

Sara is also willing to work for $3 an hour, so the grower agrees to employ her as well. But the output statistics don't look quite so good this time. Total output rises from ten boxes an hour to fourteen, indicating that Sara's marginal physical product is only four boxes per hour. But Sara is working just as hard as Sunshine and Moon and is at least as capable. What accounts for this decline in marginal physical product?

If the observed decline in *MPP* can't be blamed on Sara herself, then it must be attributable to the production process. After careful investigation, the grower discovers that Sunshine and Moon have been picking the largest strawberries first, leaving the smaller ones for someone else. As a consequence, further picking yields smaller strawberries and thus fewer boxes. The decline in *MPP* therefore has nothing to do with Sara's abilities; any other picker would have ex-

TABLE 26.1 MARGINAL PHYSICAL PRODUCT

Marginal physical product *(MPP)* measures the change in total output that occurs when one additional worker is hired. When the second worker (Moon) is hired, total output increases from five to ten boxes per hour. Hence the second worker's *MPP* equals five boxes per hour.

Number of pickers (per hour)	Total strawberry output (boxes per hour)	Marginal physical product (boxes per hour)
1 (Sunshine)	5	5
2 (Moon)	10	5
3 (Sara)	14	4
4 (Eddy)	17	3
5	19	2
6	20	1
7	20	0
8	18	−2
9	15	−3

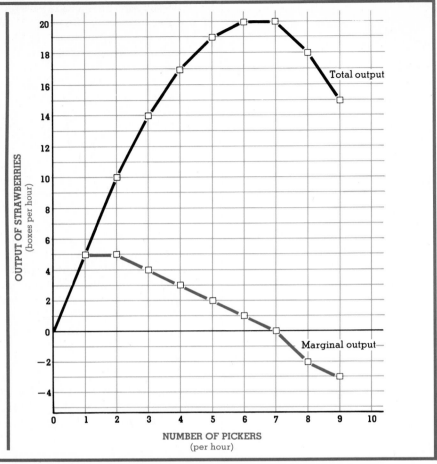

FIGURE 26.2 DIMINISHING MARGINAL PHYSICAL PRODUCT

The marginal physical product of labor is the increase in total production that results when one additional worker is hired. Marginal physical product tends to fall as additional workers are hired in any given production process. This decline occurs because each worker has increasingly less of other factors (e.g., land) with which to work. (Note that these curves correspond to the last two columns in Table 26.1.)

perienced the same problem. There simply aren't that many large berries.

When the grower hires Eddy, still another decline in marginal physical product occurs. Total output rises from fourteen boxes an hour to only seventeen, yielding an *MPP* of three boxes per hour. Again the problem appears to have nothing to do with Eddy personally, because he has been picking strawberries over eight years. The problem, it appears, is the number of boxes. There are only a dozen boxes, and the four pickers often have to wait for an empty box. The time spent waiting lowers output and thus drives down marginal physical product.

As the grower continues to hire pickers, still more problems arise. The worst problem is space: as additional workers are crowded onto the one-acre patch, they begin to get in each other's way. The picking process is slowed and marginal physical product is further depressed. Note that the *MPP* of the fifth picker is two boxes per hour, while the *MPP* of the sixth picker is only one box per hour. By the time we get to the seventh picker, marginal physical product actually falls to zero, as no further increases in total strawberry output take place.

Things get even worse if the grower tries to hire still more pickers. If eight pickers are employed, total output actually *declines*, because the pickers can no longer work efficiently under such crowded conditions. Hence the *MPP* of the eighth worker is *negative*, no matter how ambitious or hard-working this person may be. Figure 26.2 illustrates this decline in marginal physical product.

Our observations on strawberry production are similar to those made in most industries. In general, ***the marginal physical product of labor declines as the quantity of labor employed increases.*** This is the **law of diminishing returns** we first encountered in Chapter 19. It is based on the simple observation that an increasing number of workers leaves each worker with less land and capital to work with.

law of diminishing returns: The marginal physical product of a variable factor declines as more of it is employed with a given quantity of other (fixed) inputs.

Diminishing marginal revenue product

As marginal *physical* product diminishes, so does marginal revenue product *(MRP)*. As we noted earlier, marginal revenue product is the increase in the *value* of total output associated with an added unit of labor (or other input). In our example, it refers to the increase in strawberry revenues associated with one additional picker.

The decline in marginal revenue product mirrors the drop in marginal physical product. Recall that a box of strawberries sells for $2. With this price and the output statistics of Table 26.1, we can readily calculate marginal revenue product, as summarized in Table 26.2. As the growth of output diminishes, so does marginal revenue product. Sunshine's marginal revenue product of $10 an hour has fallen to $4 by the time four pickers are employed and reaches zero when seven pickers are employed.[1]

---

[1] Marginal revenue product would fall even faster if the price of strawberries declined as increasing quantities were supplied. We are assuming that the grower's output does not influence the market price of strawberries, and hence that the grower is a competitive producer.

TABLE 26.2 DIMINISHING MARGINAL REVENUE PRODUCT

Marginal revenue product (*MRP*) measures the change in total revenue that occurs when one additional worker is hired. At constant product prices, *MRP* equals *MPP* × price. Hence, *MRP* declines along with *MPP*.

Numbers of pickers (per hour)	Total strawberry output (in boxes per hour)	×	Price of strawberries (per box)	=	Total strawberry revenue (per hour)	Marginal revenue product
0	0		$2		0	—
1 (Sunshine)	5		2		$10	$10
2 (Moon)	10		2		20	10
3 (Sara)	14		2		28	8
4 (Eddy)	17		2		34	6
5	19		2		38	4
6	20		2		40	2
7	20		2		40	0
8	18		2		36	−4
9	15		2		30	−6

FIGURE 26.3 THE MARGINAL REVENUE PRODUCT CURVE IS THE LABOR-DEMAND CURVE

The *MRP* curve tells us how many workers an employer would want to hire at various wage rates. An employer is willing to pay a worker no more than his or her marginal revenue product. In this case, a grower would gladly hire a second worker, because that worker's *MRP* (point *B*) exceeds the wage rate ($3). The sixth worker will not be hired at that wage rate, however, since his *MRP* (at point *D*) is less than $3. The *MRP* curve is the labor-demand curve.

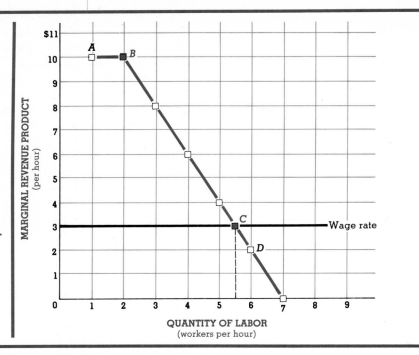

THE HIRING DECISION

The tendency of marginal revenue product to diminish will clearly cool the grower's eagerness to hire 1,000 more pickers like Sunshine. As we observed earlier, marginal revenue product establishes a *limit* to the wage rate an employer is willing to pay for hired labor.

The labor-demand curve

Consider Figure 26.3, which provides a graphic illustration of the decline in marginal revenue product indicated in Table 26.2. With this curve, we can quickly determine the quantity of labor that the grower will be *willing* to hire at any particular wage rate. That is to say, we can readily determine his *demand for labor.*

Let us continue to assume that an unlimited number of strawberry pickers are willing to work for $3 an hour. The grower must then decide how many pickers to hire at this wage. Figure 26.3 provides the answer. We already know that the grower is eager to hire at least one worker at that wage, because the *MRP* of the first picker is $10 an hour (point *A* in Figure 26.3). A second worker will be hired as well, because that picker's *MRP* (point *B* in Figure 26.3) also exceeds the going wage rate. In fact, **the grower will continue hiring pickers until the MRP has declined to the level of the market wage rate.** Figure 26.3 indicates that this intersection (point *C*) occurs after five pickers are employed. Hence we can conclude that the grower will be willing to hire—will *demand*—five pickers if wages are $3 an hour.

The folly of hiring more than five pickers is also apparent in

Figure 26.3. The marginal revenue product of the sixth worker is only $2 an hour (point D). Hiring a sixth picker will cost more in wages than the picker brings in as revenue. The *maximum* number of pickers the grower will employ at prevailing wages is five and one-half (point C).

The law of diminishing returns also implies that all of the five pickers will be paid the same wage. Once five pickers are employed, we cannot say that any single picker is responsible for the observed decline in marginal revenue product. Marginal revenue product of labor diminishes because each worker has less capital and land to work with, not because the last worker hired is less able than the others. Accordingly, the "fifth" picker cannot be identified as any particular individual. Once five pickers are hired, Sunshine's MRP is no higher than Eddy's or any other picker's. Thus each (identical) worker is worth no more than the marginal revenue product of the last worker hired, and all workers are paid the same wage rate.

Changes in wage rates

law of demand: The quantity of a good demanded in a given time period increases as its price falls *(ceteris paribus).*

The grower's decision to hire only five pickers is not unalterable. If the wage rate were to drop, more pickers would be hired. Suppose for the moment that the pickers agree to work for only $2 an hour. The grower will now be able to hire a sixth worker without sacrificing any profits. Figure 26.4 illustrates the effect of a reduction in wage rates. When wages drop, the employer moves down the labor-demand curve to a larger quantity of labor. Hence the labor-demand curve obeys the ancient **law of demand.**

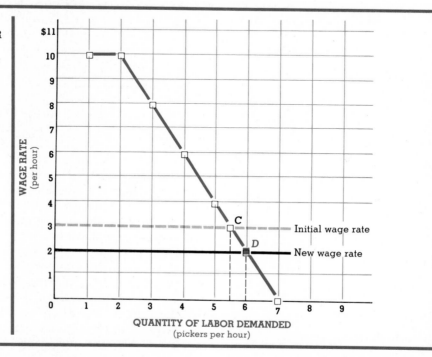

FIGURE 26.4 LOWER WAGE RATES INCREASE THE QUANTITY OF LABOR DEMANDED

If the wage rate drops, an employer will be willing to hire additional workers *(ceteris paribus).* At $3 an hour, only 5½ pickers per hour would be demanded (point C). If the wage rate dropped to $2 an hour, 6 pickers per hour would be demanded (point D).

THE MINIMUM WAGE AND EMPLOYMENT

The Fair Labor Standards Act of 1938 decreed that workers had to be paid a wage of at least 25 cents per hour. Since that time, Congress has repeatedly raised the minimum wage, up to its current level of $3.35 per hour. The objective of the minimum wage law is to ensure workers a decent standard of living. But the rules for profit maximization create a problem. An employer will not hire a worker unless marginal revenue product exceeds the wage rate. Accordingly, higher minimum wages tend to reduce the quantity of labor demanded. This is illustrated on the graph below; note the drop in quantity demanded, from q_1 to q_2, when the minimum wage is introduced.

When the minimum wage was increased to $3.35 in 1981, over 5 million workers were earning less than that amount. Most of them probably got a raise, but others may have lost their jobs. Still others, particularly teenagers looking for their first jobs, found employers less willing to hire them. In other words, some workers gain but others lose when the minimum wage is increased. The actual distribution of gains and losses is hotly debated. The negative impact of a higher minimum wage will be smaller if (1) the minimum wage is close to the equilibrium wage; (2) the demand for labor is relatively inelastic; and (3) wage rates are not directly related to marginal revenue product.

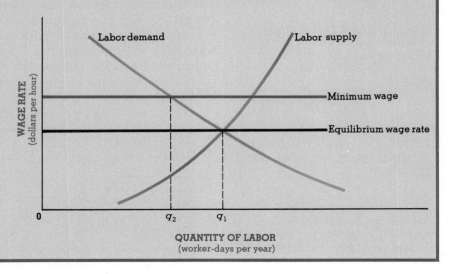

Changes in productivity

Reductions in wages are not the only path to increased employment of strawberry pickers. The hiring decision involves a comparison of marginal revenue product and the wage rate. Accordingly, an increase in *MRP* can be just as effective as a wage *(W)* reduction in increasing employment.

Suppose that Sunshine and his friends all enroll in the local agricultural extension course on strawberry-picking techniques and learn new methods of picking. With these new methods, the marginal physical product of each picker increases by one box per hour. With the price of strawberries still at $2 a box, this productivity improvement implies an increase in marginal *revenue* product of $2 per worker. This change causes a rightward **shift** of the labor-demand *(MRP)* curve, as in Figure 26.5.

shift in demand: A change in the quantity demanded at any (every) given price.

FIGURE 26.5 A SHIFT IN LABOR DEMAND

The willingness of an employer to hire labor at any specific wage rate is based on labor's marginal revenue product. If the marginal revenue product of labor improves, the employer will be willing to hire a greater quantity of labor at any given wage rate. The labor-demand curve will shift to the right (e.g., from D_1 to D_2). In this case, an increase in *MRP* leads the employer to hire 6 workers (point *E*) rather than only 5½ workers (point *C*) at $3 per hour.

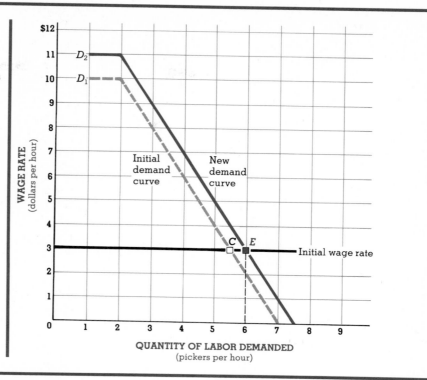

Notice that the old wage rate of $3 an hour, when combined with the new labor-demand curve, leads to the employment of a sixth picker. Hence *either an increase in productivity or a fall in wage rates can bring about an increase in the quantity of labor demanded.* Naturally, the pickers are happier when the additional employment comes about through increased productivity, because in that case they don't suffer a wage reduction.

CHOOSING AMONG INPUTS

The principles determining the shape and position of the demand curve for labor can be extended to rationalize the choice among various factors of production. Suppose that someone invents a mechanical strawberry picker that can pick berries twice as fast as Sunshine. Who will the grower hire, Sunshine or the mechanical picker?

At first it would seem that the grower would choose the mechanical picker. But the choice isn't so obvious. So far, all we know is that the mechanical picker's *MPP* is twice as large as Sunshine's. But we haven't said anything about the *cost* of the mechanical picker.

Cost efficiency

Suppose that a mechanical picker can be rented for $10 an hour, while Sunshine is still willing to work for $3 an hour. Will this difference in hourly cost change the grower's input choice?

cost efficiency: The amount of output associated with an additional dollar spent on input; the *MPP* of an input divided by its price (cost).

To determine the relative desirability of hiring Sunshine or renting the mechanical picker, the grower must compare the ratio of their marginal physical products to their cost.[2] Sunshine's *MPP* is five boxes of strawberries per hour and his cost (wage) is $3. Thus the return on each dollar of wages paid to Sunshine is:

$$\text{Cost efficiency of labor} = \frac{MPP_{labor}}{cost_{labor}} = \frac{5 \text{ boxes}}{\$3} = 1.67 \text{ boxes per \$1 of cost}$$

By contrast, the mechanical picker has an *MPP* of ten boxes per hour and costs $10 an hour, yielding a return per dollar of:

$$\text{Cost efficiency of mechanical picker} = \frac{MPP \text{ of mechanical picker}}{\text{cost of mechanical picker}} = \frac{10 \text{ boxes}}{\$10} = \frac{1 \text{ box per}}{\text{dollar of cost}}$$

These calculations indicate that Sunshine is more cost-effective than the mechanical picker. From this perspective, the grower's money will be put to best use by the hiring of Sunshine rather than by the rental of a mechanical picker.

From the perspective of **cost efficiency,** the "cheapness" of a productive input is measured not by its price but by the amount of

---

[2] Note that it doesn't matter whether we are dealing with marginal physical product or marginal revenue product, because we are only comparing the productivity of two inputs used to produce the same good.

output it delivers for that price. Thus ***the most cost-efficient factor of production is the one that produces the most output per dollar.***

The concept of cost efficiency helps to explain why American firms don't move en masse to Haiti, where peasants are willing to work for as little as 10 cents an hour. Although this wage rate is far below the minimum wage in the United States, the marginal physical product of Haitian peasants is even further below American standards. Hence American workers remain more cost-efficient than the "cheap" labor available in Haiti and other less developed countries.

ALTERNATIVE PRODUCTION PROCESSES

production process: A specific combination of resources used to produce a good or service.

Typically a producer does not choose between individual inputs, but rather between alternative production processes. General Motors, for example, cannot afford to compare the cost efficiency of each job applicant with the cost efficiency of mechanical tire mounters. Instead, GM compares the relative desirability of a **production process** that is labor-intensive (uses a lot of labor) with others that are less labor-intensive. GM ignores individual differences in marginal revenue product. Nevertheless, the same principles of cost efficiency guide the decision.

The efficiency decision

Let us return to the strawberry patch to see how the choice of an entire production process is made. We shall again assume that strawberries can be picked by either human or mechanical hands. Now, however, we shall assume that one ton of strawberries can be produced by only one of the three production processes described in Table 26.3. Process *A* uses the most labor and thus keeps more human pickers employed. By contrast, process *C* uses many mechanical pickers and provides less employment to human pickers. Process *B* falls in between these two extremes.

Which of these three production processes should the grower use? If he used process *A*, he would demand the largest quantity of labor, and in this sense do the pickers a real favor. But his goal is to maximize profits, so we assume he will choose the production process that best serves this objective. That is to say, he will choose the *least-cost* process to produce one ton of strawberries.

TABLE 26.3 ALTERNATIVE PRODUCTION PROCESSES

One ton of strawberries can be produced with varying input combinations. Which process is most efficient? What information is missing?

Input	Alternative processes for producing one ton of strawberries		
	Process A	Process B	Process C
Labor (hours)	400	270	220
Machinery (hours)	13	15	18
Land (acres)	1	1	1

But which of the production processes in Table 26.3 is least expensive? We really can't tell on the basis of the information provided. To determine the relative cost of each process—and thus to understand the producer's choice—we have to know something more about costs. In particular, we have to know how much an hour of mechanical picking costs and how much an hour of human picking (labor) costs. Then we can determine which combination of inputs is least expensive in producing one ton of strawberries, that is, which is most *cost-efficient*. Note that we don't have to know how much the land costs, because the same amount of land is used in all three production processes. Thus land costs will not affect our efficiency decision.

Suppose that strawberry pickers are still paid $3 an hour and that mechanical pickers can be rented for $10 an hour. The acre of land rents for $500 per year. With this information we can now calculate the total dollar cost of each production process and quickly determine the most cost-efficient. Table 26.4 summarizes the required calculations.

The calculations performed in Table 26.4 clearly identify production process *C* as the least expensive way of producing one ton of strawberries. Process *A* entails a total cost of $1,830 while process *C* costs only $1,340 to produce the same quantity of output. As a profit-maximizer, the grower will choose process *C*, even though it implies less employment for strawberry pickers.

The choice of an appropriate production process is called the **efficiency decision.** As we have suggested, a producer seeks to employ the combination of resources that produces a given rate of output for the least cost. The efficiency decision requires the producer to find that particular least-cost combination.

efficiency decision: The choice of a production process for any given rate of output.

The three profit-maximizing decisions

Given the input choices faced by a producer, can we still make sense of our earlier ground rules for profit maximization, especially the one about equating marginal revenues and marginal costs? If many

---

TABLE 26.4 THE LEAST-COST COMBINATION

A producer wants to produce a given rate of output for the least cost. Choosing the least expensive production process is the efficiency decision. In this case, process C represents the most cost-efficient production process for producing one ton of strawberries.

Input	Cost calculation	
PROCESS A		
Labor	400 hours at $3 per hour	= $1,200
Machinery	13 hours at $10 per hour	= 130
Land	1 acre at $500	= 500
	Total cost	$1,830
PROCESS B		
Labor	270 hours at $3 per hour	= $ 810
Machinery	15 hours at $10 per hour	= 150
Land	1 acre at $500	= 500
	Total cost	$1,460
PROCESS C		
Labor	220 hours at $3 per hour	= 660
Machinery	18 hours at $10 per hour	= 180
Land	1 acre at $500	= 500
	Total cost	$1,340

ROBOTICS: THE ROLE OF TECHNOLOGY

In 1982, 4,000 robots were at work in U.S. factories. According to a Carnegie-Mellon study, over 4 million factory jobs may be performed by robots in the year 2000. Robots, which have arms, hands, and independent "brains," are going to become increasingly important in production processes. Is this robotics revolution a threat to American workers?

Mechanical strawberry pickers illustrate the kind of dilemma robotics poses. Strawberry-picking robots are a direct threat to the livelihood of human pickers and will actually replace them as either the price of robots falls or their marginal productivity rises. That is to say, the demand for human pickers will fall when robot pickers become more cost-efficient.

Although the mechanization of strawberry patches will reduce the employment and income of human pickers, it will benefit many other groups in society. The people who manufacture robots will obviously benefit from increasing automation; their employment and earnings will rise. Strawberry consumers will also benefit as the price of strawberries is reduced by the greater cost efficiency of the robots.

The fact that many individuals benefit from robotics while a few are harmed raises difficult questions for society. In essence, we have an income-distribution problem. How can the benefits of robotics (of increased cost efficiency) be shared by those who, like the strawberry pickers, are threatened by advancing technology? Our answers to date have taken the form of unemployment benefits, retraining programs, and relocation assistance. All of these programs are intended to help workers who are displaced by robots to find new jobs and maintain their incomes.

---

possible input combinations are available for the production of every product—and thus a number of cost alternatives—how can we determine when marginal revenue exceeds marginal cost?

Recall that we used only one set of cost estimates in our earlier analysis of short-run production decisions (Chapters 19–23). This simplification was possible because we assumed that the producer based his output decision on a comparison of revenues and the *least expensive* set of production costs. Thus we assumed he was contemplating producing only in the most economical or *cost-efficient* way. The focus of attention then settled on the question of how much output to produce with existing plant and equipment.

Hard-nosed, calculated, profit-maximizing behavior thus involves three distinct steps. The first step, the *efficiency decision*, requires the producer to determine the most efficient way of organizing the production process for some particular rate of output. This determination is based on the technical requirements of production and the costs of various factors of production. As a result of this inquiry, the producer will have a single set of production costs (or cost curves, if graphs are preferred). These costs will represent a particular plant size and related equipment.

The second step involves the comparison of potential sales revenues with the set of costs already identified as most efficient and the selection of the optimal rate of output. We have already identified this step as the **production decision.**

After completing the first two steps, the producer can decide

production decision: The selection of the short-run rate of output (with existing plant and equipment).

investment decision: The decision to build, buy, or lease plant and equipment to start or expand a business.

whether to go into business or, if he is already in business, whether to expand. This is the **investment decision.**

POLICY IMPLICATIONS: UNEQUAL WAGES

The concepts of marginal productivity and cost efficiency can be used to help explain the very disparate wages paid to individuals in our economy. The theory of labor demand suggests that workers are evaluated in terms of their *marginal revenue product*. Individuals who contribute the most to the revenues of a firm will be paid the highest wage rates, those whose *MRP* is low will be paid little. As we observed at the beginning of this chapter, the president of General Motors is paid over half a million a year. Why are GM's stockholders willing to pay him so much? The only rational explanation is that his marginal revenue product exceeds $500,000. Presumably his managerial skills and knowledge of the automobile market are considered to be so vast that GM's total revenues might fall by at least $500,000 a year if he departed. While this might sound extraordinary, it is certainly not impossible in the case of a firm with over $60 *billion* in annual revenues.

GM does not pay all its employees so handsomely, of course. The worker who tightens the bolts on the left rear wheel of every Chevette rolling down the assembly line earns only $11.67 an hour, a far cry from the $250 an hour GM's president is paid. This difference in wage rates is explained in part by their respective marginal revenue products. GM has discovered that tight rear wheel bolts aren't an essential determinant of car sales and represent a very small proportion of total cost. No matter how hard the bolt tighteners work, they have very little influence on GM's total revenues. Thus both the marginal revenue product and the wage rate of bolt tighteners are comparatively low.

The fantastic incomes of top entertainers and athletes can also be explained in terms of marginal revenue product. Muhammad Ali was paid $3.5 million in 1978 for one boxing match (one he lost, no less!). This wage reflected the fact that fight fans were *willing to pay* relatively high prices to see Ali fight. In fact, the fight promoters (the people who paid Ali) figured that thousands of people would buy high-priced tickets to see the fight at ringside. Millions of others would watch the fight on television. The total revenues generated by the fight included the ticket sales and the sale of TV advertising time. If a pair of nobodies were fighting, total revenue might equal only a few hundred dollars, but with Ali in the ring total revenues might soar into the millions. This increased revenue represented Ali's *MRP* and thus set the limit to the amount of money the fight promoters were *willing to pay* for Ali's labor.

The same considerations induced Texas A&M to pay its new football coach $287,000 per year (see news clipping). Texas A&M has a football stadium that will seat 70,016 fans. But attendance in 1980–81 averaged only 63,833 persons. If a new coach could create a winning team, the stadium might fill up. An additional 6,183 paying fans would bring in more than enough (marginal) revenue to pay the coach's salary.

Campus millionaire—the football coach

Educators across the country looked on in anger and dismay in late January at a bidding war that produced some 1.7 million dollars in pay and benefits for a collegiate-football coach.

Jackie Sherrill, coach at the University of Pittsburgh for the last five seasons, agreed to become coach and athletic director at Texas A&M for six years at $287,000 a year—$95,000 in base salary and the rest in fringe benefits and television earnings.

Robert Atwell, vice president of the American Council on Education, called it a "terrible distortion of values when the compensation of coaches exceeds that of Nobel laureates."

Sherill's $95,000 base salary will be more than triple the $31,649 average pay of university professors in the U.S. and double the $47,610 median salary of university presidents.

Texas A&M officials quickly pointed out that Sherrill will be paid not by the university but by donations to the athletic department. This, too, worried some critics, who said it gave A&M's "boosters" a strong voice in the running of a university program.

Sherrill is not the only college coach with six-figure pay. The University of Kentucky in December hired Jerry Claiborne from the University of Maryland for a package estimated at $200,000 a year. Frank Broyles, athletic director at the University of Arkansas, said he was offered 1.2 million dollars over several years to coach Georgia Tech.

Some defended high pay for coaches. Said Dick Dull, athletic director at the University of Maryland: "A winning football program gives institutions exposure on radio, television and print that they couldn't afford to buy."

Others agreed with Howard Swearer, president of Brown University, who contended: "When schools are paying these kinds of salaries to coaches, you begin to wonder whether there is a clear demarcation between college and professional sports."

Reprinted from *U.S. News & World Report,* February 1, 1982. Copyright © 1982 U.S. News & World Report, Inc.

The value of a college education

The higher earnings of college graduates also reflect differences in marginal revenue product. Recent estimates by the Census Bureau suggest that the average male college graduate will earn $1.4 million during his lifetime, while the average high school graduate will earn only $960,000 (see Table 26.5). This difference of $440,000 presumably reflects the higher marginal productivity of college-educated labor. Apparently people do learn some skills in four years of college.

Unmeasurable MRP

We cannot hope to explain all wages on the basis of marginal revenue product, however. We noted earlier that the president of the United States is paid $200,000. Can we argue that this salary represents his marginal revenue product? For that matter, how would one begin to measure the *MRP* of the president? The wage we pay the president of the United States is less a reflection of his contribution to total output than a matter of custom. His salary also reflects the

---

TABLE 26.5 INDIVIDUAL LIFETIME EARNINGS, BY YEARS OF EDUCATION

Additional years of schooling translate into increased earnings in the labor market. Over a lifetime, these differences in earnings accumulate into tremendous disparities. College graduation, for example, increases average lifetime earnings by $300,000 over those of college dropouts.

Years of school completed	Lifetime earnings
8 or less	$ 600,000
9–11 (high school dropout)	780,000
12 (high school graduate)	960,000
13–15 (college dropout)	1,100,000
16 (college graduate)	1,400,000
17 or more (some graduate school)	1,600,000

Source: U.S. Department of Commerce, Bureau of the Census, *Consumer Income,* March 1974; updated to 1982 wages by author.

opportunity wage: The highest wage an individual would earn in his or her best alternative job.

price voters believe is required to induce competent individuals to forsake private-sector jobs and assume the responsibilities of the presidency. In this sense, the wage paid to the president and other public officials is determined by their **opportunity wage,** that is, the wage they could earn in private industry.

The same kinds of considerations influence the wages of college professors. The marginal revenue product of a college professor is not easy to measure. Is it the number of students he or she teaches, the amount of knowledge conveyed, or something else? Confronted with such problems, most universities tend to pay college professors according to their opportunity wage, that is, the amount they could earn elsewhere.

Opportunity wages also help explain the difference between the wage rate paid to GM's president and that paid to its rear-wheel bolt tighteners. The low wage of bolt tighteners reflects not only their marginal revenue product at General Motors, but also the fact that they are not trained for many other jobs. That is to say, their opportunity wages are low. By contrast, GM's president has impressive managerial skills that are in demand by many corporations; his opportunity wages are high.

Market power and segmentation

Although marginal productivity theory and opportunity costs explain much inequality, they do not fully account for all wage differentials. Two individuals of equal productivity may command very different wages simply because of race or sex, or because of membership in a powerful labor union. That is to say, not all workers engage in perfect wage competition. Some workers are sheltered from wage competition by market power (e.g., labor unions) or discriminatory employment practices. Indeed, many economists argue that the U.S. labor market is highly segmented, with each segment defined by race, sex, or institutional barriers. Once assigned to a particular segment of the labor market, workers have little or no chance to acquire the skills or wage rates available in other segments. These arguments, which represent major qualifications to marginal productivity theory, are discussed at length in Chapters 27 and 32.

SUMMARY

▪ The rate of output a firm produces, and therefore the amount of resources it uses, depends on the extent of consumer demand. The demand for labor and other resources is a derived demand.

▪ The demand for labor is a direct reflection of labor's marginal revenue product. The greater the marginal revenue product of labor, the larger the quantity of labor a firm is willing to hire at any given wage.

▪ The marginal revenue product of labor also establishes a limit to the wage rate that firms willingly pay. A profit-maximizing employer will not pay a worker more than the worker produces.

▪ The marginal revenue product of labor tends to diminish as additional workers are employed on a particular job (the law of diminishing returns). This decline occurs because additional workers have to share existing land and capital, leaving each worker with less land and capital to work with.

▪ A producer seeks to get the most output for every dollar spent on inputs. This means getting the highest ratio of marginal product to input price. Accordingly, a profit-maximizing producer will always choose the most cost-efficient input (not necessarily the one with the cheapest price).

▪ The efficiency decision involves the choice of the least-cost production process and is also made on the basis of cost efficiency. A producer seeks the least expensive process to produce a given rate of output.

▪ Differences in marginal revenue product offer an important explanation for existing wage inequalities. But the difficulty of measuring MRP in many instances leaves many wage rates to be determined by custom, power, discrimination, or opportunity wages.

Terms to remember

Define the following terms:

derived demand	cost efficiency
demand for labor	production process
marginal physical product *(MPP)*	efficiency decision
marginal revenue product *(MRP)*	production decision
law of diminishing returns	investment decision
law of demand	opportunity wage
shift in demand	

Questions for discussion

1. Is this course increasing your marginal productivity? If so, in what way?

2. Suppose George is making $13 an hour installing transistorized digital chips in electronic calculators. Would your offer to work for $8 an hour get you the job? Why might a profit-maximizing employer turn down your generous offer?

3. What do you think happened to the marginal productivity of painters when the paint roller was invented? Did it improve their wages?

4. Explain why marginal physical product would diminish as
(a) More secretaries are hired in an office
(b) More professors are hired in the economics department
(c) More construction workers are hired to build a school

5. How is the wage of a judge determined?

Problem

The following table depicts the number of grapes that can be picked in an hour with varying amounts of labor.

Number of pickers (per hour)	1	2	3	4	5	6	7	8
Output of grapes (in flats)	20	38	53	64	71	74	74	70

Using these data, determine how many pickers will be hired if the wage rate is $10.00 per hour and a flat of grapes sells for $1.25. Illustrate graphically.

CHAPTER 27

POWER IN LABOR MARKETS

market power: The ability to alter the market price of a good or service.

Labor markets are no different in concept from other markets. Market supply and market demand interact to determine the quantity of labor hired and its price (the wage rate). Like all markets, also, labor markets can be distorted by market power. Power may reside on the supply side of the market (labor unions) or on the demand side (large employers). In either case, the objective of those who hold market power is to alter wages and employment conditions. This chapter focuses on the extent of **market power** in the U.S. labor market, the kinds of confrontations that occur, and the impact of labor-market power on our economic welfare.

THE LABOR MARKET

To gauge the impact of labor-market power on wages and employment, we can review the nature of a competitive labor market. On the supply side, we have all those individuals who are willing to work—to supply labor—at various wage rates. By counting the number of individuals who are willing to work at each and every wage rate, we can construct a *market* **labor-supply** curve, as in Figure 27.1.[1]

The willingness of producers (firms) to hire labor is reflected in

labor supply: The willingness and ability to work specific amounts of time at alternative wage rates in a given time period; the quantities of labor that would be supplied at alternative wage rates (*ceteris paribus*).

---

[1] The *market* supply curve may slope upward even if individual workers have backward-bending supply curves (Chapter 25) as long as additional workers are attracted into the labor force by high wages.

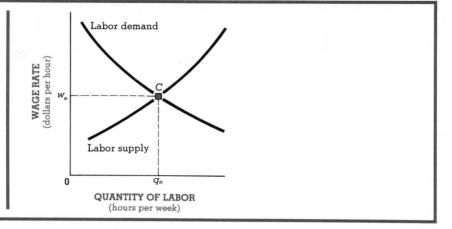

FIGURE 27.1 COMPETITIVE EQUILIBRIUM IN THE LABOR MARKET

In a competitive market, the intersection of the labor-supply and labor-demand curves (point C) determines the equilibrium wage rate (w_e) and the amount of employment (q_e).

---

demand for labor: The quantities of labor employers are willing and able to hire at alternative wage rates in a given time period (*ceteris paribus*).

Competitive equilibrium

equilibrium wage: The wage rate at which the quantity of labor supplied in a given time period equals the quantity of labor demanded.

Local labor markets

the market labor-demand curve. The curve itself is constructed by simply counting the number of workers each firm says it is willing and able to hire at each and every wage rate. The curve illustrates the market **demand for labor.**

The intersection of the market supply and demand curves (point C in Figure 27.1) reveals the **equilibrium wage** rate (w_e): the wage rate at which the quantity of labor supplied equals the quantity demanded. At this wage rate, every job seeker who is willing and able to work for the wage w_e is employed. In addition, firms are able to acquire all the labor they are willing and able to hire at that wage. Not everyone is employed, of course; workers who demand wages in excess of w_e are unable to find jobs. By the same token, employers who refuse to pay a wage as high as w_e are unable to attract workers.

Figure 27.1 appears to suggest that there is only *one* labor market, and thus only one equilibrium wage. But we already know this is a gross simplification. Although the concept of a national labor market is important and useful, it is more appropriate to think in terms of localized labor markets. If you were looking for a job in Tulsa, Oklahoma, you would have little interest in employment prospects or power configurations in New York City. You would be more likely to be concerned about the number of job openings and job seekers in Tulsa—that is, the condition of the *local* labor market.

Even within the confines of a particular geographical area, interest usually focuses on particular classes of jobs and workers rather than on all the people supplying labor. If you were looking for work as a disco dancer, you would have little interest in the employment situation for carpenters or dentists. Rather, you would want to know how many discos or nightclubs had job vacancies and what wages and working conditions they offered. By the same token, people in the construction industry or in dentistry would probably have no more than a passing interest in the job market for disco dancers. Accordingly, we can focus not only on geographically defined labor markets, but also on labor markets for particular industries or occupations.

The distinction among various geographical, occupational, and industrial labor markets provides a more meaningful basis for analyzing labor-market power. The tremendous size of the national labor market, with over 100 million workers, precludes anyone from acquiring control of the entire market. The largest private employer in the United States (General Motors) employs less than 1 percent of the labor force. The top 500 industrial corporations employ only 20 percent of all workers. The situation on the supply side is similar. The largest labor union (the Teamsters) represents just slightly more than 2 percent of all workers in the country. *All* unions together represent only one-fifth of the labor force. This does not mean that the actions of particular employers or unions have no important effects on our general economic welfare. It does, however, show that power in labor markets is likely to be more apparent and effective in particular areas, occupations, and industries than in others.

LABOR UNIONS

Types of unions

The immediate objective of labor unions is to alter the equilibrium wage and employment conditions in specific labor markets. To be successful, unions must be able to exert control over the market-supply curve. For this purpose, workers have organized themselves along either industry or occupational craft lines. *Industrial unions* include workers in a particular industry (the United Auto Workers, for example). *Craft unions* represent workers with a particular skill (e.g., the International Brotherhood of Electrical Workers), regardless of the industry in which they work.

The purpose of both types of labor union is to coordinate the actions of thousands of individual workers, thereby achieving control of market supply. If a union is able to control the supply of workers in a particular industry or occupation, the union acquires a monopoly in that market. Like most monopolies, unions attempt to use their market power to increase their incomes.

Union objectives

A primary objective of unions is to raise the wages of union members. But union objectives also include improved working conditions, job security, and other forms of compensation, such as retirement (pension) benefits, vacation time, and health insurance. The Players' Association and the National Football League have bargained about the use of artificial turf, early retirement, player fines, and the revenues derived from closed-circuit television broadcasts. In 1981 the Major League Baseball Players Association stopped all games for 49 days while the players and team owners bargained over the rules for "free agents." In that same year the Professional Air Traffic Controllers Organization (PATCO) struck for shorter workweeks and earlier retirement. A few years earlier the Air Line Pilots Association had worried about weight restrictions for flight attendants (United Airlines required that a female flight attendant five feet,

Auto workers take a wage cut

American auto companies and their employees have been caught for months in a quandary. As car sales dragged along at their lowest level in 21 years, more and more workers lost their jobs. Some 240,000 United Auto Workers members are on indefinite layoff. Auto companies claimed that high salaries and benefits helped push up the price of American cars and made it hard to compete against Japanese imports. Although worried about further layoffs, workers were reluctant to accept substantial wage reductions. But last week Ford and the U.A.W. agreed to a new 2½-year contract that cuts workers' benefits in return for guarantees of job security. . . .

Indeed, the union won a surprising two-year moratorium on closing plants because of outside suppliers and an agreement in principle that future labor reductions would come only as a result of attrition. In addition, Ford promised to replace all union jobs lost because of out-sourcing. In exchange, the union will give up its 3% pay increase this year and in 1983, ten paid personal holidays and cost of living increases for the next nine months.

four inches tall weigh no more than 125 pounds). In the United Farm Workers' grape strike of 1965–70, the primary issue was the growers' recognition of the UFW as the legitimate spokesman for the grape pickers. The UFW was striking to force the growers into bilateral negotiations—to discuss employment issues with the workers' representatives.

Although union objectives tend to be as broad as the concerns of union members, we shall focus here on just one objective, wage rates. This is not too great a simplification, because most nonwage issues can be translated into their effective impact on wage rates. In 1979, for example, the Teamsters secured a wage increase of 80 cents per hour. Additional benefits (cost-of-living allowance, increased pension and health benefits, additional days off, etc.) cost employers another 70 cents an hour. Hence the increase in total wage costs was

WHAT MINE WORKERS WON IN THE 1981 COAL STRIKE

In 1981 a 71-day coal strike cost the industry an estimated $1 billion in lost sales and over $100 million in vanished profits. The miners lost over $50 million in wages while on strike. When the United Mine Workers (UMW) and the Bituminous Coal Operators Association finally signed a new 40-month contract, it included:

WAGES An increase in average wages from $10.10 an hour in 1981 to $13.70 an hour in 1984.

ROYALTY PAYMENTS An increase in the royalty paid by producers to the UMW for coal mined from non-UMW mines from $1.90 to $2.23 per ton.

SUNDAYS OFF Continuation of a ban on Sunday work.

NONUNION LABOR Agreement by the producers to use nonunion subcontractors only when UMW members are unavailable.

ARBITRATION Abolition of the arbitration review board, which had previously acted as the judge of grievances.

WORKING VACATIONS Authorization for UMW members to work through their scheduled 1981 vacations, thereby drawing double pay.

CLOTHING ALLOWANCE An increase from $125 to $150.

HEALTH BENEFITS An increase in payments for sickness and injury from $150 to $185 per week.

HOLIDAYS One additional paid holiday per year.

BACK-TO-WORK BONUS A $150 bonus for miners who reported for work on the first poststrike shift.

$1.50 per hour. Accordingly, our simple two-dimensional illustration of union objectives can be used to convey the nature and substance of most collective-bargaining situations. What we seek to determine is whether and how unions can raise wage rates in a specific labor market by altering the competitive equilibrium depicted in Figure 27.1.

THE POTENTIAL USE OF POWER

In a competitive labor market, each worker makes a labor-supply decision on the basis of his or her own perceptions of the relative values of labor and leisure (Chapter 25). Whatever decision is made, it will not alter the market wage. One worker simply isn't that significant in a market composed of thousands of workers. Once a market is unionized, however, these conditions no longer hold. A union must evaluate job offers on the basis of the *collective* interests of its members. In particular, it must be concerned with the effects of increased employment on the wage rate paid to its members. ***Like all monopolists, unions have to worry about the downward slope of the demand curve.*** In the case of labor markets, a larger quantity of labor can be "sold" only at lower wage rates.

The marginal wage

Suppose that the workers in a particular labor market confront the market labor-demand schedule depicted in Table 27.1. This schedule tells us that employers are not willing to hire any workers at a wage rate of $6 per hour (row S) but will hire one worker per hour if the wage rate is $5 (row T). At still lower wage rates, the quantity of labor demanded increases; five workers per hour are demanded at a wage of $1 per hour.

An individual worker offered a wage of $1 an hour would have to decide whether such wages merited the sacrifice of an hour's leisure. But a union would evaluate the offer differently. Notice that when four workers are hired at a wage rate of $2 an hour (row W), total wages are $8 per hour. In order for a fifth worker to be employed, however, the wage rate must drop to $1 an hour (row X), whereupon *total* wages paid amount to only $5 per hour. Thus total

---

TABLE 27.1 THE MARGINAL WAGE

The *marginal wage* is the change in *total* wages (paid to all workers) associated with the employment of an additional worker. If the wage rate is $4 per hour, only two workers are hired. The wage rate must fall to $3 per hour if three workers are to be hired. In the process, *total* wages paid rise from $8 ($4 × 2 workers) to $9 ($3 × 3 workers). The *marginal wage* of the third worker is only $1.

	Wage rate (per hour)	×	Number of workers demanded (per hour)	=	Total wages paid (per hour)	Marginal wage (per labor-hour)
S	$6		0		$0	$0
T	5		1		5	5
U	4		2		8	3
V	3		3		9	1
W	2		4		8	−1
X	1		5		5	−3

FIGURE 27.2 THE MARGINAL WAGE

Additional workers will be hired only if the wage rate drops (*ceteris paribus*). Hence the wages of an additional worker are offset by reduced wage rates for all other workers already employed. In this case, a second worker will be employed only if the wage rate drops from $5 (point *T*) to $4 (point *U*). Total wages increase from $5 ($5 × 1 worker) to $8 ($4 × 2 workers). The *marginal* wage is therefore $3 (point *u*).

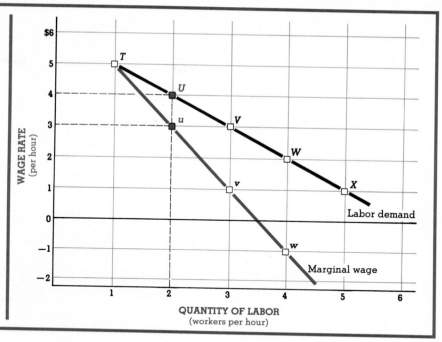

MRC = MCL =

marginal wage: The change in total wages paid associated with a one-unit increase in the quantity of labor employed.

wages paid to the workers actually *fall* when a fifth worker is employed. Collectively, then, the workers would be better off sending only four workers to work at the higher wage of $2 an hour and paying the fifth worker $1 an hour to stay home!

The basic mandate of a labor union is to evaluate wage and employment offers from this collective perspective. To do so, *a union must distinguish the marginal wage from the market wage.* The market wage is simply the current wage rate paid by the employer; it is the wage received by individual workers. The **marginal wage,** on the other hand, is the change in *total* wages paid (to all workers) when an additional worker is hired.

The distinction between marginal wages and market wages arises from the downward slope of the labor-demand curve. It is analogous to the distinction we made between marginal revenue and price for monopolists in product markets. The distinction simply reflects the law of demand: as wages fall, the number of workers hired increases.

The impact of increased employment on marginal wages is also illustrated in Figure 27.2. According to the labor-demand curve, one worker will be hired at a wage rate of $5 an hour (point *T*). Two workers will be hired only if the market wage falls to $4 an hour (point *U*). At this point, the first and second workers are each getting $4 an hour.[2] Thus the increased wages of the second worker (from zero to $4) are partially offset by the reduction in the wage rate paid to the first worker (from $5 to $4). *Total* wages paid increase by only $3; this is the *marginal* wage (point *u*). The marginal wage actually

[2] Recall that the decline in wage rates reflects the law of diminishing marginal productivity and is not caused by any particular worker (see Chapter 26).

FIGURE 27.3   THE UNION WAGE OBJECTIVE

The intersection of the marginal wage and labor-supply curves (point *u*) determines the union's desired employment. Employers are willing to pay a wage rate of $4 per hour for that many workers, as revealed by point *U*.

More workers (*N*) are willing to work at $4 per hour than employers demand (*U*). To maintain that wage rate, the union must exclude some workers from the market. In the absence of such power, wages would fall to the competitive equilibrium (point *C*).

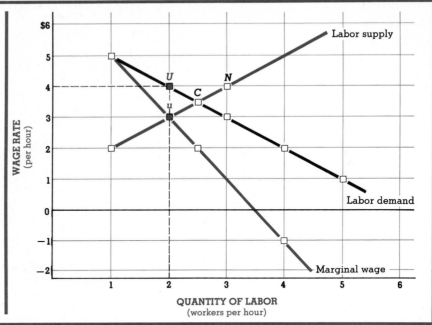

becomes negative at some point, when the implied wage loss to workers already on the job begins to exceed the wages of a newly hired worker.

Monopolistic equilibrium

A union never wants to accept a negative marginal wage, of course. At such a point, union members would be better off paying someone to stay home. The question, then, is what level of (positive) marginal wage the union should accept.

We can answer this question by looking at the labor-supply curve. The labor-supply curve tells us how much labor workers are *willing to supply* at various wage rates. In Figure 27.3, ***the intersection of the marginal wage curve with the labor-supply curve identifies the optimal level of employment for the union.*** In Figure 27.3 this intersection occurs at point *u*, yielding total employment of two workers per hour.

Notice that the union-imposed wage rate is $4 per hour. Graphically, we locate this wage rate by moving straight upward from point *u* to the labor-demand curve. Point *U* on the demand curve tells us that employers are *willing to pay* a wage rate of $4 an hour to employ two workers per hour. Hence $4 becomes the union wage.

What the union is doing here is choosing a point on the labor-demand curve that the union regards as the optimal combination of wages and employment. In a competitive market, point *C* would represent the equilibrium combination of wages and employment. But the union forces employers to point *U*, thereby attaining a higher wage rate and reducing employment. The union's motivation for moving to point U arises from its recognition of the *marginal wage,* that is, the impact of increased employment on the total wages of its members.

Exclusion

The union's ability to maintain a wage rate of $4 an hour depends on its ability to exclude some workers from the market. Figure 27.3 suggests that three workers are willing and able to work at the union wage of $4 an hour (point N), whereas only two are hired (point U). If the additional worker were to offer his or her services, the wage rate would be pushed down the labor-demand curve (to $3 per hour). Hence *to maintain a noncompetitive wage, the union must be able to exercise some control over the labor-supply decisions of individual workers.* The essential force here is union solidarity. Once unionized, the individual workers in an industry or occupation must agree not to compete among themselves by offering their labor at nonunion wage rates. Instead, the workers must agree to withhold labor—to strike, if necessary—if wage rates are too low, and to supply labor only if a specified wage rate is offered.

union shop: An employment setting in which all workers must join the union within 30 days after being employed.

Unions attempt to solidify their control of the labor supply by establishing **union shops,** workplaces where workers must join the union within 30 days after being employed. In this way, the unions gain control of all the workers employed in a particular company or industry and thereby reduce the number of workers available for employment during a strike. Stiff penalties (such as loss of seniority or pension rights) and general union solidarity ensure that only nonunion workers will "fink" or "scab"—take the job of a worker on strike. When the United Auto Workers (UAW) threatens a strike, the Big Three auto makers know that nonunion automotive workers will be hard to find and thus take the UAW threat seriously. But the grape growers in California ignored the UFW strike for five years because unionization among farm workers was minimal and substitute labor (including Mexican *braceros*) was readily available.

Union shops help to increase the degree of unionization within an industry, but they are not so effective as the closed shop. A closed shop permits only union members to be hired by an employer. Under a closed-shop arrangement, a worker must first be accepted by the union, whereas in a union shop, the employer makes the initial employment decision. Although closed shops are illegal under the provisions of the Taft-Hartley Act, they still operate under the guise of union shops coupled with union hiring halls (union-run employment referrals). In many states, however, even union shops may be prohibited by the provisions of "right-to-work" laws that make union membership completely voluntary.

Another mechanism for restricting the use of substitute labor is union control of training facilities. Union-controlled apprenticeship programs offer skill training for persons found acceptable for union membership. Thus nonunion workers will have less chance of acquiring the necessary skills and hence will be less available to substitute in case of a strike. Apprenticeship programs are particularly effective when linked to certification programs, which grant people the right to practice a particular craft or trade or to affirm their vocational skills. For example, individuals are required to undertake a four-year apprenticeship program before they can be certified as union plumbers.

THE EXTENT OF UNION POWER

Early growth

The first labor unions in America were organized as early as the 1780s and the first worker protests as early as 1636. Union power was not a significant force in labor markets, however, until the 1900s, when heavily populated commercial centers and large-scale manufacturing became common. Only then did large numbers of workers begin to view their employment situations from a common perspective.

The period 1916–20 was one of particularly fast growth for labor unions, largely because of the high demand for labor resulting from World War I. All of these membership gains were lost, however, when the Great Depression threw millions of people out of work. By 1933, union membership had dwindled to the levels of 1915.

As the depression lingered on, public attitudes and government policy toward the relationship between labor and business began to reflect a new perspective. No longer was the public willing to let the business community render all economic decisions. Too many people had learned the meaning of layoffs, wage cuts, and prolonged unemployment. Moreover, the notion was growing that layoffs and wage cuts were not appropriate solutions to economic recessions. Accordingly, as the country began to work its way out of the depression, the labor union movement was infused with renewed vigor. In 1933 the National Industrial Recovery Act (NIRA) was passed, including provisions that established the right of employees to bargain collectively with their employers. When the NIRA was declared unconstitutional by the Supreme Court in 1935, its labor provisions were incorporated into a new law, the Wagner Act. With the encouragement of these legislative developments, union membership doubled between 1933 and 1937. It continued to grow markedly during the subsequent eight years, as the production needs of World War II enhanced the marginal revenue product and bargaining strength of labor. The tremendous spurt of union activity between the depths of the depression and the height of World War II is reflected in Figure 27.4.

Union power today

Since World War II, union membership has continued to grow, but not as fast as the labor force. As a consequence, union power, expressed as the percentage of workers belonging to labor unions, has fallen. Today roughly 21 percent of the labor force is enrolled in labor unions for a combined membership of over 22 million workers.[3]

[3] These and the following figures include membership in the professional associations (such as the National Educational Association), which function much like unions.

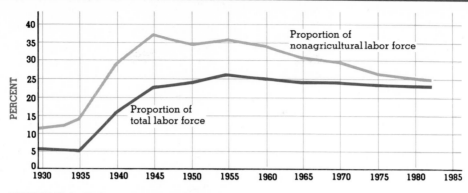

FIGURE 27.4   UNIONIZATION OF THE LABOR FORCE

Unions grew most rapidly during the decade 1935–45. Since that time, the growth of unions has not kept pace with the growth of the U.S. labor force.

Source: U.S. Department of Labor, Bureau of Labor Statistics.

unionization ratio: The percentage of the labor force belonging to a union.

Although a **unionization ratio** of 21 percent is an impressive basis for market (and political) power, union strength varies greatly from labor market to labor market. As we noted before, the national labor market is really a mix of thousands of distinguishable labor markets, each defined by geographical, industrial, or occupational characteristics. Concentrations of union power in any of these localized labor markets can be far greater than the national average. Moreover, these local concentrations can have tremendous influence on related economic outcomes. This situation is analogous to concentration among producers. As we noted in Chapter 24, concentration in particular product markets is much higher and of more immediate consequence than national averages sometimes suggest.

Table 27.2 provides an overview of union power in various industries. As is apparent, there is tremendous variation in labor-supply concentration among industries. In group *A*, labor-supply concentration is so high (75–100 percent) as to confer monopoly powers on particular unions. The Teamsters, Longshoremen, and United Mine Workers stand out in this regard. The unions in group *B* also have great market power, because they represent over half the workers in each industry. Many of the unions are familiar from their many confrontations with business over the exercise of market power (the United Auto Workers, the garment unions, the communications unions, and the printers stand out).

Although Table 27.2 provides a convenient index to who's who on the supply side of the labor market, some additional observations are in order. Each industry classification depicted in the table represents a broad assortment of firms and products. Accordingly, a low degree of unionization for an industry may mask very high levels of supply concentration in particular labor markets. The "service industry" (group *D*), for example, has a relatively low level of unionization but includes such disparate workers as professional football players, laundry workers, barbers, and broadcasters. Obviously, the

TABLE 27.2 UNION POWER

A union's power may be measured by the percentage of the related work force that it controls. The Teamsters, for example, have substantial market power because most truck drivers belong to that union.

Degree of unionization	Industry	Principal unions
A: 75–100 percent	Transportation	Teamsters
		Longshoremen
		Maintenance of Way
		Maritime
		Railway unions
	Contract construction	Carpenters
		Painters
		Plumbers
		Laborers
	Mining	United Mine Workers
B: 50–75 percent	Transportation equipment	United Auto Workers
		Marine and Shipbuilding
	Primary metals	Steelworkers
	Apparel	Amalgamated Clothing Workers
		Garment Workers
		Ladies' Garment Workers
	Tobacco manufactures	Cigar
		Tobacco Workers
	Electrical machinery	International Brotherhood of Electrical Workers (IBEW)
		International Union of Electrical Workers
	Federal government	Government Employees (AFGE)
		Letter Carriers
		Post Office Clerks
	Paper	Papermakers
		Pulp, Sulphite
C: 25–50 percent	Rubber	Rubber Workers
	Machinery	Automobile
		United Electrical Workers
	Lumber	Coopers
		Woodworkers
	Leather	Shoe Workers

low level of unionization reflected in the industry average is of little relevance to you when you go to get a haircut. It certainly offers no comfort to the owners of NFL football teams when they have to negotiate playing conditions or retirement benefits. Even relatively small unions may have great market power if they control labor supply for a particular area, company, product, or occupation.

One union noticeably missing from the table is the AFL-CIO (the American Federation of Labor–Congress of Industrial Organizations). To comprehend this omission, we must refer back to the structure of labor organizations, especially the need for intercompany and interindustry affiliations. The AFL-CIO is not a separate union, but a representational body of 120 national unions. It does not represent or negotiate for any particular group of workers, but instead focuses on issues of general labor interest. Thus to a large

Degree of unionization	Industry	Principal unions
C: 25–50 percent	Electric, gas, utilities	Electrical (IBEW)
	Furniture	Furniture Workers
	Government (state and local)	Teachers
		Fire Fighters
	Telephone and telegraph	Communications Workers
		Electrical (IBEW)
	Petroleum	Oil, Chemical
		Operating Engineers
	Food and kindred products	Bakery Workers
		Brewery
		Meat Cutters
	Stone, clay, and glass products	Glass Cutters
	Fabricated metals	Boilermakers
		Steelworkers
		Iron Workers
D: Less than 25 percent	Chemicals	Chemical
		District 50
	Textiles	Textile Workers
	Instruments	Machinists
	Service	Hotel
		Laundry Workers
		Watchmen
	Finance	Insurance Agents
	Agriculture and fishing	Teamsters
		United Farm Workers
	Trade	Retail Clerks
	Printing, publishing	Newspaper Guild
		Printing Pressmen
		Typographers

Source: U.S. Department of Labor, Bureau of Labor Statistics, *Directory of National Unions and Employee Associations*, 1979.

extent its role is to act as a spokesman for the labor movement and represent labor's interest in legislative areas. It is the primary vehicle for political action. In addition, the AFL-CIO may render economic assistance to member unions or to groups of workers who wish to organize into an AFL-CIO affiliate. Not all national or local unions belong to the AFL-CIO—the Teamsters, United Mine Workers, and United Auto Workers being notable (and powerful) exceptions—but three out of four union members are affiliated with it.

EMPLOYER POWER

The impressive power possessed by labor unions in various areas and industries seldom exists in a power vacuum. On the contrary, tremendous power exists on the demand side of labor markets, too. The United Auto Workers confront GM, Ford, and Chrysler; the Steelworkers confront U.S. Steel, Bethlehem, Republic, and Armco; the Teamsters confront the Truckers' Association; the Communications Workers confront AT&T; and so on. An imbalance of power often exists on one side of the market or the other (as with, say, the Carpenters versus individual construction contractors). Labor markets with significant power on both sides, however, are common. To understand how wage rates and employment are determined in such markets, we have to consider the nature and potential of market power possessed by employers.

Monopsony

Power on the demand side of a market is analogous to power on the supply side. Such power belongs to a *buyer* who is able to influence the market price of a good. With respect to labor markets, market power on the demand side implies the ability of a single employer to alter the market wage rate. The extreme case of such power is called a **monopsony,** a situation in which one employer is the only buyer in a particular market. The classic example of a monopsony is a company town, that is, a town that depends for its livelihood on the decisions of a single large employer.

monopsony: A market in which there is only one buyer.

There are many degrees of market power, of course, and they can be defined in terms of *buyer concentration*, the converse of the seller concentration we have discussed. When buyers are many and of limited market power, the demand for resources is likely to be competitive. When only one buyer has access to a particular resource market, a monopsony exists. In between the two extremes lie the various degrees of imperfect competition, including the awkward-sounding but empirically important case of oligopsony. In an oligopsony only a few buyers account for most of the purchases of a particular resource. The similarity of these definitions to those used to characterize power on the supply side of markets should be obvious.

The potential use of power

Firms with power in labor markets generally have the same objective as all other firms; to maximize profits. What distinguishes them from competitive (powerless) firms is their ability to attain great profits. Firms with monopsony power can exploit the market supply curve, and end up using fewer resources and paying less for them than competitive firms would. In labor markets, this means using fewer workers and paying them lower wages than a firm in a competitive market would have to do.

The distinguishing characteristic of labor-market monopsonies is the fact that their hiring decisions influence the market wage rate. In a competitive labor market, no single employer has any direct influence on the market wage rate. Each firm can hire as much labor as it needs at the prevailing wage. But a monopsonist recognizes that an increase in the quantity of labor demanded will force him to climb up the labor-supply curve in search of additional workers. In

TABLE 27.3 MARGINAL COST OF LABOR

An additional worker can be attracted only if the wage rate increases. As it rises, all workers must be paid the higher wage. Consequently, the change in *total* wage costs exceeds the actual wage paid to the last worker. Notice that in row *I*, for example, the marginal wage of the fourth worker ($8) exceeds the wage actually paid to that worker ($5).

	Wage rate (per hour)	×	Quantity of labor supplied (workers per hour)	=	Total wage cost (per hour)	Marginal cost of labor (per labor-hour)
D	$0		0		$ 0	$0
E	1		0		0	0
F	2		1		2	2
G	3		2		6	4
H	4		3		12	6
I	5		4		20	8
J	6		5		30	10

marginal cost of labor: The change in total wage costs that results from a one-unit increase in the quantity of labor employed.

marginal revenue product (MRP): The change in total revenue associated with one additional unit of input.

other words, *a monopsonist can hire additional workers only if he offers a higher wage rate.*

MARGINAL COST OF LABOR   Any time the price of a resource (or product) changes as a result of a firm's purchases, a distinction between marginal cost and price (average cost) must be made. Making this distinction is one of the little headaches—and potential sources of profit—of a monopsonist. In the case of labor, the distinction to be made is between the **marginal cost of labor** and its wage rate.

Suppose for the moment that Table 27.3 accurately describes the labor-supply schedule confronting a monopsonist. It is evident that the monopsonist will have to pay a wage of at least $2 an hour if he wants any labor. But even at that wage rate only one worker is willing to work. If the firm wants more labor, it will have to pay higher wages.

Two things happen when the firm raises its wage offer to $3 an hour (row *G*). First, the quantity of labor supplied increases (to two workers per hour). Second, the total wages paid rise by $4. This high *marginal* cost of labor is attributable to the fact that the first worker's wages rise when the wage rate is increased to attract additional workers. If all the workers perform the same job, the first worker will demand to be paid the new (higher) wage rate. Thus the marginal cost of labor exceeds the wage rate because additional workers can be hired only if the wage rate for all workers is increased.

MONOPSONISTIC EQUILIBRIUM   The marginal-cost-of-labor curve confronting this monopsonist is shown in Figure 27.5. It starts at the bottom of the labor-supply curve and rises above it. The monopsonist must now decide how many workers to hire, given the impact of his hiring decisions on the market wage rate.

Recall from Chapter 26 that the labor-demand curve reflects labor's **marginal revenue product,** that is, the increase in total revenue attributable to the employment of one additional worker.

As we have seen before, the profit-maximizing producer always seeks to equalize marginal revenue and marginal cost. Accordingly, the monopsonistic employer will seek to hire the amount of labor at which the marginal revenue product of labor equals its marginal

FIGURE 27.5 THE MONOPSONIST'S DESIRED EQUILIBRIUM

The intersection of the marginal cost of labor and labor-demand curves (point U) indicates the quantity of labor a monopsonist will want to hire. The labor-supply curve (at point G) indicates the wage rate that must be paid to attract the desired number of workers. This is the monopsonist's desired wage ($3). In the absence of market power, an employer would end up at point C (the competitive equilibrium), paying a higher wage and employing more workers.

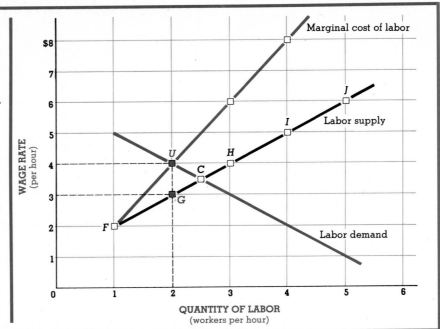

cost. In Figure 27.5, this objective is illustrated by the intersection of the marginal cost and labor-demand curves, at point U.

At point U the monopsonist is *willing to hire* two workers per hour at a wage rate of $4. But he doesn't have to pay this much. The labor-supply curve informs us that two workers are *willing to work* for only $3 an hour. Hence the firm first decides how many workers it wants to hire (at point U), then looks at the labor-supply curve (point G) to see what it has to pay them. As we suspected, a monopsonistic employer ends up hiring fewer workers at a lower wage rate than would prevail in a competitive market (point C).

COLLECTIVE BARGAINING: A CLASH OF POWER

The potential for conflict between a powerful employer and a labor union should be evident. The objective of a labor union (Figure 27.3) is to establish a wage rate that is *higher* than the competitive wage. A monopsonistic employer, on the other hand, seeks to establish a wage rate that is *lower* than competitive standards (Figure 27.5). The resultant clash is often exciting.

The confrontation of power on both sides of the labor market is referred to as **bilateral monopoly.** In such a market, wages and employment are not determined simply by supply and demand. Rather, economic outcomes must be determined by deliberate negotiations between buyers and sellers. Such negotiations in the labor market have acquired a unique name and status: collective bargaining. **Collective bargaining** consists of negotiations between employers and labor unions for the purpose of determining wages, employment, working conditions, and related issues.

bilateral monopoly: A market with only one buyer (a monopsonist) and one seller (a monopolist).

collective bargaining: Direct negotiations between employers and unions to determine labor-market outcomes.

Possible agreements

In a typical labor-business confrontation, the two sides begin by stating their preferences for equilibrium wages and employment. The *demands* laid down by the union are likely to revolve around point *U* in Figure 27.6; the *offer* enunciated by management is likely to be at point *G*.[4] Thus the boundaries of a potential settlement—a negotiated final equilibrium—are usually established at the outset of collective bargaining.

The interesting part of collective bargaining is not the initial bargaining positions but the negotiation of the final settlement. The speed with which a settlement is reached and the nature of the compromise it embodies depend on the patience, tactics, and resources of the negotiating parties. The fundamental source of negotiating power for either side is its ability to withhold employment or jobs. The union can threaten to strike, thereby cutting off the flow of union labor to the employer. In a strike, union members simply refuse to work under existing conditions and force a cutback or cessation of production activities. The employer can impose a lockout, thereby cutting off jobs and paychecks previously available to union members. In practice, each weapon constitutes an ultimate threat to the other side of the collective-bargaining negotiations. The effectiveness of those threats depends on the availability of alternative workers or jobs and the credibility of the strike or lockout threat.

The pressure to settle

The essential strength of both labor and management in collective bargaining emanates from their ability to cut off the flow of revenues (in the form of sales or wages). But both sides suffer from either a strike or a lockout, no matter who initiates the work stoppage. The strike benefits paid to workers are rarely comparable to wages they would otherwise have received, and the payment of those benefits

[4] Even though points *U* and *G* may not be identical to the initial bargaining positions, they represent the positions of maximum attainable benefit for both sides. Points outside the demand or supply curve will be rejected out of hand by one side or the other.

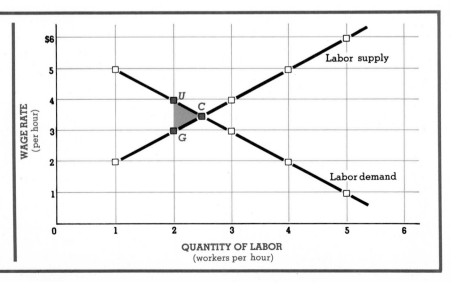

FIGURE 27.6   THE BOUNDARIES OF COLLECTIVE BARGAINING

Firms with power in the labor market seek to establish wages and employment levels corresponding to point *G*. Unions, on the other hand, seek to establish an equilibrium at point *U*. The competitive equilibrium is at point *C*. The function of collective bargaining is to identify a compromise between these points, that is, to locate an equilibrium somewhere in the shaded area.

The Baseball Strike Is a Monopolists' Slugfest

So you think the baseball strike is a classic struggle between greedy owners and embattled players. Or perhaps you see greedy players preying on sports-loving owners.

Before you cast Tom Seaver as Luke Skywalker and George Steinbrenner as Darth Vader, consider another view: This strike is just a tiresome squabble between greedy owners and greedy players for slices of a pie baked by embattled, sports-loving fans. Baseball is, as an economist would put it, a textbook illustration of a bilateral monopoly. And the strike is no more than the owners' monopsony power (that means a monopoly-buyer-of-labor, and I promise not to use the word again) pitted against the monopoly power of the players for the possession of the "scarcity rents" accruing from the teams themselves. To explain:

As a group, the owners are the sole employers of major-league baseball players; they could, and did, collude to limit the salaries and job mobility of those players. What were the hired hands to do? If they wanted to hit homers and be memorialized in candy bars (i.e., keep their jobs), they had to settle for a less-than-competitive wage. The hapless sluggers were faced with a take-it-or-leave-it wage, and from the days of Abner Doubleday till a few years ago, they took it.

But the players have a monopoly, too: Their organization, the Players Association, is a genteel name for a labor union that is the sole supplier of major-league-quality baseball players. And now that monopoly is refusing to supply the owners with sluggers or hurlers or fielders until the owners come to terms. In short, the players want the owners' monopoly to compete within itself for the players' services.

Back in 1976, the owners took the players' terms—sort of—and free-agent status got underway. Players whose contracts expired were free to sell their hitting or hurling to the highest bidder. Star players started shining in different cities in different uniforms—and salaries shot up. Indeed, average salaries zoomed 175% over the past five years, from the low $50 Ks in 1976 to the high $140 Ks last year.

The owners, feeling the squeeze from a monopoly other than their own, squawked about restoring "competitive balance." The players, enjoying the fruits of their own monopoly power, jawed about finally being paid a "just and reasonable wage." . . .

Until 1976, the monopolistic owners ate the full share of those big, juicy pies made from fans' ticket receipts, broadcasting rights and so forth. After 1976 and free agency, however, the players' monopoly started grabbing slices of the money pie. This strike, then, is just a tug-of-war between monopolists—and it is every bit as unseemly as these fights are.

—Susan Lee

depletes the union treasury.[5] By the same token, the reduction in labor costs and other expenses rarely compensates the employer for lost profits. In the 67-day auto strike of 1970, General Motors lost $90 million a day in sales, while the United Auto Workers spent $160 million in strike benefits. The 49-day baseball strike of 1981 cost the players $600,000 in salaries for every game canceled and the owners an estimated $1.25 million. These kinds of losses create pressure to reach a settlement.[6]

Because potential income losses are usually high, both labor and management try to avoid a strike or lockout if they can. In fact, over 90 percent of all collective-bargaining agreements are concluded without recourse to a strike, and often without even the explicit threat of one.

The final settlement

The built-in pressures for avoidance or quick termination of a work stoppage help to ensure the successful resolution of collective bargaining. They do not tell us, however, what the dimensions of that final settlement will be. All we know is that the settlement will be

[5] A wage increase of 5 cents an hour works out to only $100 per year for the average worker. A one-month strike over such an increase would cost union members more than they would recoup in six to eight years.

[6] Interestingly, the baseball owners had insurance to cover $50 million of strike-related losses. A settlement was reached shortly after losses exceeded this amount.

located within the boundaries established in Figure 27.6, and that the relative pressures on each side will determine whether the final equilibrium is closer to the union or the management position.

The final settlement reached will almost always necessitate hard choices on both sides. The union will usually have to choose between a slight increase in job security or slightly higher pay. In other words, higher wage rates may be acceptable to management only if the labor force is reduced somewhat. For the union, this would mean a cutback in employment and possibly even union membership, a potentially stiff price to pay. A union must also consider how management will react in the long run to higher wages. That is, the union must consider the likelihood that management will introduce new technology that reduces its dependence on labor.

POLICY IMPLICATIONS: THE IMPACT OF UNIONS

Stepping back from the negotiations that take place between individual unions and companies, we may ask whether the presence of unions has altered economic outcomes in general. We do know that unions tend to raise wage rates in individual companies, industries, and occupations. That, after all, is one of their basic objectives. But can we be equally sure that unions have raised wages in general? If the UAW is successful in raising wages in the automobile industry, what, if anything, happens to wages in the breakfast cereal industry? Or what, for that matter, happens to the price of automobiles when auto workers' wages go up? If car prices rise in step with UAW wage rates, labor and management in the auto industry will get proportionally larger slices of the economic pie. At the same time, workers in other industries are burdened with higher car prices.

Relative wages | One measure of union impact is *relative* wages, the wages of union members in comparison with those of nonunion workers. As we have noted, unions seek to control the supply of labor in a particular industry or occupation and thereby increase union wages. In their efforts to control labor supply, they restrict the number of people who can compete for available jobs, forcing those workers who are excluded to seek work elsewhere. Accordingly, unions reduce the supply of labor available to unionized industries and increase the supply of labor available to nonunion industries. As a result of this imbalance, wages tend to be higher in union industries than in nonunion industries. Figure 27.7 illustrates this effect.

Although the theoretical impact of union exclusionism on relative wages is clear, empirical estimates of the extent of that impact are fairly rare. We do know that union wages in general are significantly higher than nonunion wages ($3.20 versus $2.78 per week in 1980). But part of this differential is due to the fact that unions are more common in industries that have always been more capital-intensive and paid relatively high wages. When comparisons are made within particular industries or sectors, the differential narrows considerably. Nevertheless, there is a general consensus, based on

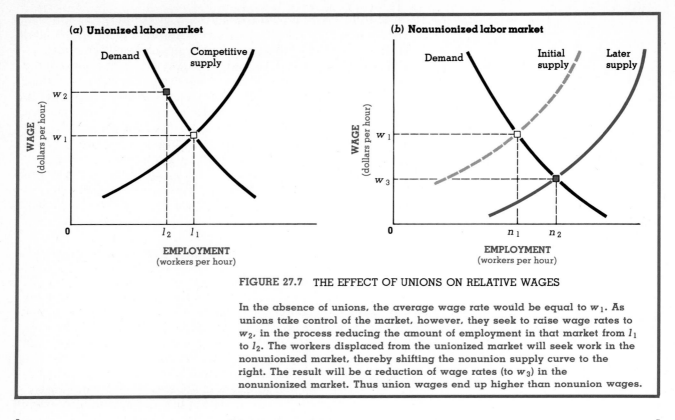

(a) Unionized labor market

WAGE (dollars per hour)

Demand

Competitive supply

w_2

w_1

0   l_2 l_1

EMPLOYMENT (workers per hour)

(b) Nonunionized labor market

WAGE (dollars per hour)

Demand

Initial supply

Later supply

w_1

w_3

0   n_1 n_2

EMPLOYMENT (workers per hour)

FIGURE 27.7   THE EFFECT OF UNIONS ON RELATIVE WAGES

In the absence of unions, the average wage rate would be equal to w_1. As unions take control of the market, however, they seek to raise wage rates to w_2, in the process reducing the amount of employment in that market from l_1 to l_2. The workers displaced from the unionized market will seek work in the nonunionized market, thereby shifting the nonunion supply curve to the right. The result will be a reduction of wage rates (to w_3) in the nonunionized market. Thus union wages end up higher than nonunion wages.

limited studies, that unions have managed to increase their relative wages by anywhere from 15 to 20 percent. Some unions, of course, have been markedly more successful than others, as a comparison of the wages received by Teamsters and United Farm Workers attests.

Labor's share of total income

Even though unions have been successful in redistributing some income from nonunion to union workers, the question still remains as to whether they have increased labor's share of *total* income. The labor share of total income is the proportion of income received by all workers, in contrast to the share of income received by owners of capital (the capital share). If unions are effective in excluding non-union workers from highly productive industries and also in increasing their share of income in those industries, the total labor share will grow. In this case, unions redistribute from capital owners to workers. Thus the increase in relative union wages is the result of two factors: redistribution from capital to labor and union exclusion of nonunion workers.

Evidence of unions' impact on labor's share is almost as difficult to assemble as evidence on relative wages, and for much the same reasons. Labor's share has risen dramatically, from only 56 percent in 1919 to over 76 percent in 1982.[7] But there have been tremendous changes in the mix of output during that same period. The proportion of output composed of personal services (accountants, teachers,

[7] The functional distribution of income is discussed in Chapter 29.

electricians) is much larger now than it was in 1919. The labor share of income derived from personal services is and always was close to 100 percent. Accordingly, most of the rise in labor's share of total income is due to changes in the structure of the economy rather than to unionization.

Prices Closely related to the issue of the labor share is the question of union impact on product prices. If all union wage increases were reflected in the prices of related products, the ability of unions to increase the labor share of income would be limited severely. In such a case, the additional money firms needed to pay their workers would come out of increased prices, not out of profits. Accordingly, the ability of firms to "pass on" wage increases to consumers is a major determinant of their ability to maintain their capital share. If they are successful, they may contribute to cost-push inflation, a subject of Chapters 6 and 13. At this juncture, we may note that the cause of price increases, especially in oligopolistic market situations, is usually very difficult to identify. Undoubtedly, however, unions have provided an incentive for firms to increase product prices faster than they otherwise would have done.

Political impact Perhaps more important than any of these specific union effects is the general impact the union movement has had on our economic, social, and political institutions. Unions are a major political force in the United States. They not only have provided critical electoral and financial support for selected political candidates (mostly Democrats), but have also fought hard for important legislation. Unions have succeeded in establishing minimum-wage laws, work and safety rules, and retirement benefits. They have also actively lobbied for such things as civil rights legislation and health and education programs. Whatever one thinks of any particular union or specific union action, it is clear that our institutions and welfare would be very different in their absence.

SUMMARY

- Power in labor markets is the ability to alter market wage rates. Most often, such power is evident in local labor markets defined by geographical, occupational, or industrial boundaries.
- Power on the supply side of labor markets is typically manifested by labor unions, organized along either industry or craft lines. The basic function of a union is to evaluate employment offers in the light of the *collective* interest of its members.
- The downward slope of the labor-demand curve creates a distinction between the marginal wage and the market wage. The marginal wage is the change in *total* wages occasioned by employment of one additional worker and is less than the market wage.
- Unions seek to establish that rate of employment at which the mar-

ginal wage curve intersects the labor-supply curve. The desired union wage is then found by following the labor-*demand* curve to the wage that employers are willing to pay for that number of workers.

■ Power on the demand side of labor markets is manifested in buyer concentrations such as monopsony and oligopsony. Such power is usually found among the same firms that exercise market power in product markets.

■ Be definition, power on the demand side implies some direct influence on market wage rates: additional hiring by a monopsonist will force up the market wage rate. Hence a monopsonist must recognize a distinction between the marginal cost of labor and its (lower) market wage rate.

■ The goal of a monopsonistic employer is to hire the number of workers indicated by the point at which the marginal cost of labor equals its marginal revenue product. The employer then looks at the labor-supply curve to determine the wage rate that must be paid for that number of workers.

■ The desire of unions to establish a wage rate that is *higher* than competitive wages directly opposes the desire of powerful employers to establish *lower* wage rates. In bilateral monopolies, in which power exists on both sides of the labor market, unions and employers engage in collective bargaining to negotiate a final settlement.

■ The impact of unions on the economy is difficult to measure. It appears, however, that they have increased their own relative wages and contributed to rising prices. They have also had substantial political impact.

Terms to remember

Define the following terms:

market power
labor supply
demand for labor
equilibrium wage
marginal wage
union shop

unionization ratio
monopsony
marginal cost of labor
marginal revenue product
bilateral monopoly
collective bargaining

Questions for discussion

1. Collective-bargaining sessions often start out with "unreasonable" demands and "categorical" rejections. Why do unions and employers tend to begin bargaining from extreme positions?

2. Does a strike for a 5-cent-an-hour raise make any sense? What kinds of long-term benefits might a union gain from such a strike?

3. Are large and powerful firms easier targets for union organization than small firms? Why, or why not?

4. Nonunion firms tend to offer wage rates that are close to rates paid by unionized firms in the same industry. How do you explain this?

5. In 1973 a group of priests in Milwaukee sought to establish a union to bargain over wages and retirement benefits. Whom would the priests negotiate with, and what kinds of tactics could they use to achieve their demands?

Problem

Suppose that the following supply and demand schedules apply in a particular labor market.

Wage rate (per hour)	$4	$5	$6	$7	$8	$9	$10
Quantity of labor supplied (workers per hour)	2	3	4	5	6	7	8
Quantity of labor demanded (workers per hour)	6	5	4	3	2	1	0

Graph the relevant curves and identify:

(a) The competitive wage rate

(b) The union wage rate

(c) The monopsonist's wage rate

RENT, INTEREST, AND PROFIT

Chapters 25—27 have focused on only one factor of production—labor. The emphasis on labor reflects the fact that wages and salaries account for three-fourths of total national income. Hence any forces that influence the level and distribution of wages and salaries largely determine FOR WHOM our output is produced. Nevertheless, the share of income received by capital (25 percent) is not negligible, and its distribution significantly affects our collective answer to the basic question of FOR WHOM to produce.

The basic purpose of this chapter is to examine the nature of the income commonly included in the capital share of total income. What is the nature of rent, interest, and profit, and what forces determine their market value? How are **factor shares** determined?

factor share: The proportion of total income received by a factor of production.

RENT

In the national-income accounts (Chapter 4) "rent" is one of the payments included in the capital share (see Table 28.1). Yet the term "rent," as used by economists, does not necessarily refer to returns to "capital." Nor does it even refer to the monthly payments made by tenants to landlords. In other words, *economists use the term "rent" differently from the way it is used by almost everyone else in the world.*

The origins of this confusion go back to nineteenth-century England. At that time, there was great concern about the rapidly increas-

TABLE 28.1 THE FUNCTIONAL DISTRIBUTION OF INCOME

Wages and salaries account for 75 percent of all income; this is the labor share. The capital share is divided among farmers, small businesses, landlords, corporations, and lenders.

Source of income	Capital share (percent)	Labor share (percent)
Agriculture	1.1	
Nonfarm business	4.7	
Rents	1.4	
Corporate profits	8.2	
Interest	9.3	
Wages and salaries		75.3
Total	24.7	75.3

Source: *Economic Report of the President*, 1982.

ing price of "corn" (actually all grains), the staple of English diets. In looking for an explanation for the rising price of corn, many Englishmen (including quite a few economists) pointed to the escalating prices being demanded and paid for agricultural land. The landlords, it appeared, were the villains responsible for the plight of the working masses. By raising land rents, they were driving up the price of corn and driving the population of England into poverty.[1]

Not so, argued David Ricardo, one of the great classical economists: "Corn is not high because a rent is paid, but a rent is paid because corn is high." Were landlords to reduce their rents, Ricardo noted, this action would only increase the incomes of tenant farmers: the price of corn itself would not drop.

Ricardo's view of land rents as *price-determined* rather than *price-determining* can be explained in terms of either the corn market or the land market.

The price of corn

The market price of corn, like that of any other product, is determined by the intersection of market supply and demand curves. In Figure 28.1, the price p_1 prevails as long as D_1 and S_1 represent the market demand and supply curves.

[1] Chapter 17 provides more detail on nineteenth-century agricultural output and living standards.

FIGURE 28.1 THE PRICE OF CORN

The market price of corn is established by the intersection of market supply and demand. The corn controversy in nineteenth-century England was based on the assumption that rising land rents shifted the corn supply curve upward (to S_2). They did not. Rising corn prices led to rising land prices, not vice versa.

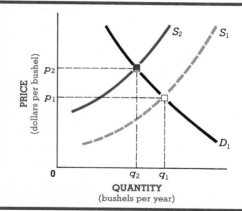

marginal cost: The increase in total cost associated with a one-unit increase in production.

fixed costs: Costs of production that do not change when the rate of output is altered; for example, the cost of basic plant and equipment.

price elasticity of supply: The percentage change in quantity supplied divided by the percentage change in price.

The price of land

In essence, the nineteenth-century debate over corn prices focused on the effect of rising land prices on the market supply of corn. Those who blamed landlords for rising corn prices were implicitly arguing that increases in land rents would cause an upward *shift* of the corn supply curve, to S_2. The increased costs associated with S_2, they argued, led to a reduction in the quantity of corn supplied (q_2) and a higher corn price (p_2).

But Ricardo argued that rising land rents would *not* shift the corn supply curve. His argument was based on the concept of marginal cost. In his own words, "The reason why raw produce rises in comparative value (price) is because more labor is employed in the production of the last portion obtained, and not because a rent is paid to the landlord." In other words, **marginal costs** determine the supply price of competitively produced goods.

We saw in Chapter 20 that producers will be willing to produce and sell goods in competitive markets as long as price exceeds marginal cost. In fact, the short-run supply curve of a competitive firm is identical to its marginal cost curve. Hence the market supply curve for corn (a competitively produced good) will shift upward only if the marginal cost of producing a given quantity of output changes. Thus an increase in land rent will not alter the market supply or price of corn, because land rent is a **fixed cost** for farmers.

As Ricardo himself concluded, an increase in land rent only served to redistribute income from farmers to landlords. In his own words again, "No reduction would take place in the price of corn, although [even if] landlords should forgo the whole of their rent. Such a measure would only enable some farmers to live like gentlemen, but would not diminish the quantity of labor necessary to raise raw produce on the least productive land in cultivation."[2]

Landlords do not have the power to raise rents indiscriminately. Land rents, too, are determined by market supply and demand. As Figure 28.2 reveals, however, the supply curve of land has an unconventional shape: it is vertical.

Typically, we expect producers to respond positively to increased prices. That is, we expect the **price elasticity of supply** to be greater than zero; the quantity supplied increases as prices rise, as in Figure 28.1. In the case of land, however, few such possibilities exist. Although some possibilities exist for increasing the amount of cultivable land through swamp drainage or filling in tidal areas, the quantity of land available is basically fixed. As a consequence, the quantity of land supplied *cannot* increase in response to rising prices. The supply of land is perfectly price inelastic, as illustrated by the vertical supply curve of Figure 28.2.

Because the supply of land is price inelastic—does not change as prices rise and fall—changes in the price of land must be completely determined by market demand. Notice that the initial price of land in Figure 28.2 is R_1, as determined by the intersection of D_1

---

[2] Ricardo blamed the high price of English corn on the Corn Laws of 1815, which placed high tariffs (taxes) on imported corn (grains), forcing domestic farmers to expand output into the range of substantially higher marginal cost. The impact of international trade restrictions on domestic prices is discussed in Chapter 33.

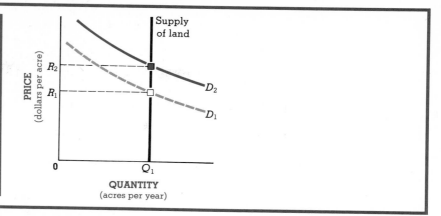

FIGURE 28.2   THE PRICE OF LAND

The quantity of land available to the market is essentially fixed (Q_1). Hence changes in the price of land will be determined by market demand. In this case, land rents increase from R_1 to R_2 as a result of an upward shift of the demand curve from D_1 to D_2.

Economic rent

rent: Payments to a factor of production in excess of the amount required to call forth a given quantity of the factor.

and the land supply curve. If the demand for land were to shift upward, to D_2, the price of land would rise to R_2. But no additional land would be supplied, and no less. This is exactly the kind of situation that occurred in Ricardo's time, when the demand for corn rose, increasing the (derived) demand for agricultural land.

Normally the function of price increases is to signal consumers' desire for more of a particular good or service. Indeed, price signals are the basic characteristic of the market mechanism. In the case of land, however, the price signals have no effect: the quantity of land is unchanged. In this sense, rising prices for land exceed the amount required to call forth the available quantity of land. In fact, the land would be available even if no price were paid for it! Hence any rent paid for the use of land exceeds the price required to call forth the available supply; in this sense, all rent is "surplus" payment.

The term "economic rent" is used to refer to such surplus payments, whether they are paid for land or for any other factor of production. Specifically, *economic rent is a factor payment above the minimum necessary to attract a given quantity of an input.* In the case of "pure," unimproved land, all payments made are regarded as economic rent.

U.S. FARM INCOMES AND LAND PRICES

In 1972–73 the demand for U.S. farm output increased substantially as a consequence of poor harvests elsewhere in the world. U.S. farm output could not expand fast enough to keep pace with demand. As a result, the price of farm products increased dramatically; the average price of farm output rose by nearly 40 percent in one year.

The rising prices of farm goods sharply increased farm incomes. They also made farmland more valuable. The resultant competition for farmland pushed land prices up by more than 25 percent in 1973–74. The rest of the 1970s continued to be good for farmland. Crop prices generally increased faster than inflation, and the value of farmland more than tripled.

The 1980s have not been so good for farm prices. The prices of major agricultural products started falling in 1980, as a consequence of huge harvests and generally weak demand. The price of farmland started falling as well. In 1981–82 farmland prices fell sharply, along with the price of farm products.

Clearly, "pure" rent, as defined by economists, is not the same thing as the rent people pay for their homes or apartments. Rental payments made to landlords typically include compensation for the use of capital (the building structure) and labor (building maintenance and management), and for the use of utility services (water, electricity, gas). In most cases, a very small fraction of the rental payment represents pure economic rent, as defined here.

Even in Ricardo's time, a distinction was drawn between "pure," "natural" land and land that had been improved through cultivation, irrigation, or fencing. Land improvements entail resource costs and will not be made unless a sufficient compensation (price) is offered. Only the land itself will be there at any price. Hence the rental payments made by nineteenth-century farmers included economic rent as well as compensation for the use of labor and capital in improving the land.

The concept of pure rent applies to other factors of production besides land. The demand for the services of Devo, The Police, the Rolling Stones, and Dave Winfield is very high, because these performers can generate substantial revenues for an athletic or musical event. In other words, their **marginal revenue product** is high in certain situations. As a result, sports and music promoters are willing to pay very high prices for performances by such individuals.

Marginal revenue product only establishes a *limit* to a factor's price, however. To determine the market price of the factor, we have to examine the supply curve as well. We find that the supply curves of individual performers are relatively vertical, much like that in Figure 28.2. They can perform only a limited number of times in a given time period. Consequently, these performers are getting eco-

marginal revenue product (MRP): The change in total revenue associated with one additional unit of input.

The man with the golden bat

Just as you knew there would be, there are two points of view about the latest big deal in baseball. First, there is the view that it is ridiculous for Yankee owner George Steinbrenner to give a reported $25-million contract to outfielder Dave Winfield. Among those in the ridiculosity camp is Edward Bennett Williams, the well-known mouthpiece and sports investor—he has interests in both the Washington Redskins and Baltimore Orioles. Said Williams of the Winfield deal: "It's just another example of economic madness. If this irrational spending continues, it's going to destroy the industry."

The other point of view, expressed by Winfield himself, derives from classical economics. "There's a market value for everything," Dave observed genially.

Our own instinct is, of course, to side with Dave here and to maintain that the only ridiculous prices in this world are the ones that don't get paid. We will go further: multiyear contracts with star athletes can be viewed as another of those "collectibles" that give wealthy investors like Steinbrenner some protection against galloping inflation. Winfield will look cheap if inflation is bad enough. His deal actually provides $1 million for signing and then $1.5 million annually for ten years, plus cost-of-living increases capped at 10%. (Those who are putting a $25 million total on the payment assume that there will in fact be a 10% increase each year.) If the inflation rate started galloping again, and averaged, say, 25% over the decade, then by 1990 Winfield would be earning a mere $380,000 in today's prices.

It's true that, like many other collectibles, Dave could begin to look rather expensive if inflation does not accelerate. If the rate stays below

10%, he really would be collecting 1.5 million 1980 dollars every year between now and 1990. Even on the optimistic assumption that he will average 150 hits a year during this decade, which ends when he's 39— 150 being roughly his average for the seven full years he has been in the major leagues thus far—the deal would leave him collecting 10,000 1980 dollars per hit, which does seem on the high side.

There was a time, within the memory of persons still breathing, when baseball's best hitters got $10,000 for a whole season's work. That is, in fact, what Napoleon Lajoie boasted of collecting in 1906, a year in which he generated 214 hits. But, of course, prices were lower then, players' earnings were depressed by the reserve clause, and Lajoie knew little about classical economics.

nomic rent, that is, payments in excess of the amount required to call forth their services. If all performers' wages were cut in half, Rick Springfield, for example, would probably continue to sing just as well and just as often. Whatever he is being paid in excess of the amount required to get him to sing is economic rent.

RENTS AS AN ALLOCATION MECHANISM Although rising economic rents do not increase the quantity of a factor supplied, they do serve an economic function. Why have all the farmers left Manhattan, where much of the land was once used for pasture and crops? The answer is simple. The rising price of land drove the fixed costs of farming so high that farmers could no longer earn a profit in New York City. Hence, in the long run, as they made new investment decisions, the farmers migrated to less expensive land in the Midwest.

The farmers were initially replaced by modest homes, rooming houses, and factories, and ultimately by skyscraping office buildings. Each step in the evolutionary process was propelled in part by increasing rents. Firms and individuals with more valuable uses for the scarce land offered increasingly high prices for its use. In turn, the high rents forced others to move their firms or households to other locations. Accordingly, *rents serve to allocate a scarce factor among competing uses. The most valuable use will determine the market rent.* People seeking to make less valuable use of the scarce factor will not be able to pay the price and will therefore not acquire it. In this way, the market mechanism determines who will use society's scarce resources.

Rent control

In many cities apartment rents are "controlled" by the city government. Rent control generally places a limit on the amount of rent or annual rent increases a landlord can charge. Although apartment rents and economic rents are not the same thing, the theory behind rent control is related to the concept of economic rent.

In cities such as New York there isn't much room for new apartment buildings. Yet the city's population keeps growing. This implies that apartment rents will keep escalating in the manner of Figure 28.2. Upward shifts of demand, together with an inelastic supply of apartments, will drive apartment prices up. In the process, landlords will reap extraordinary gains (economic rents).

Rent control is imposed to prevent apartment rents from becoming economic rents. They are based on the assumption that the supply of apartments is highly inelastic. This is not a valid assumption. The supply of apartments *can* change over time, as new and larger buildings replace old, smaller ones. In the short run, the supply of habitable apartments also depends on continued maintenance. If landlords earn below-average incomes as a consequence of rent control, they will not build new apartments or maintain old ones. (Landlords will also want to convert rent-controlled apartments into uncontrolled condominiums.) Over time, the quantity of apartments will fall, thereby aggravating the market shortage.

Rent control also implies a windfall gain for people who already occupy rent-controlled apartments. If rents are kept below their

Panel's Plan Would End Rent Control

Local rent controls such as those in the District [of Columbia] would effectively be prohibited by federal law under a recommendation approved last night by the President's Commission on Housing. . . .

The commission's regulations panel said that rent controls in some 200 cities throughout the country prevent landlords from getting a fair return on their investment and therefore prevent new construction of rental housing. This is one of the main arguments used by developers and lenders in the District in opposing the controls that affect around 120,000 apartments in Washington.

New York City has had an "emergency" rent control law in effect since 1943.

In calling for a prohibition, and in justifying it in the face of the Reagan administration's dedication to federalism, the commission took circuitous routes.

The mechanism recommended for ending controls was denial of federal assistance, direct or indirect, for housing for any state that did not agree to remove controls in its jurisdiction. This would force a ban throughout the country, as it would include such widespread housing programs as FHA- and VA-insured loans or mortgages from any federally insured lending institution. The states would have five years to end rent controls or lose all such assistance.

—Sandra Evans Teeley

The Washington Post, Washington, D.C., February 25, 1982. Copyright © 1982 The Washington Post.

equilibrium price, the quantity demanded will exceed the quantity available. People who are lucky enough to live in rent-controlled apartments will be able to "sell" their leases to others. The "price" of occupancy rights will be determined by market forces. Those consumers most able and willing to "buy" occupancy will get the scarce apartments. In this case, the initial occupants, rather than the landlord, get the *economic* rent. New occupants still pay higher (equilibrium) rents; only the form and direction of the payments are changed.

INTEREST

Interest payments are a second major form of property income and are also included in the capital share of income. In its purest form, interest is simply the amount of money paid for using someone else's money; typically, it is expressed in percentage terms, as the **interest rate.** An interest rate of 9 percent means that the borrower must pay $9 yearly for every $100 borrowed until the loan is repaid.

interest rate: The price paid for the use of money.

The loanable funds market

The rate of interest may be determined through a study of supply and demand forces in the loanable funds market. Some people and firms (particularly banks) are willing and able to lend money at alternative interest rates. From a consumer's point of view, lending money entails the sacrifice of some immediate consumption possibilities and thus real **opportunity costs.** As interest rates climb, however, the trade-off between future consumption and present consumption tilts in the direction of future consumption. In other words, high interest rates make it appealing to sacrifice some consumption now for more consumption later. As a consequence, the quantity of loanable funds *supplied* increases as interest rates rise, as indicated by the upward slope of the supply curve in Figure 28.3. (This situation contrasts with that of land, which entailed a vertical supply curve. Higher interest rates *do* call forth larger quantities of loanable funds.)

opportunity cost: The most desired goods or services that are forgone in order to obtain something else.

The quantity of loanable funds *demanded* has the familiar downward slope, as Figure 28.3 illustrates. From an individual consumer's perspective, borrowing money at high interest rates implies sacrificing a relatively large amount of future consumption possibilities (when the loan must be paid back) for a smaller increase in present consumption. As the implied cost of borrowing diminishes, the quantity of loanable funds demanded increases.

From a potential investor's point of view, increases in interest rates represent an increase in investment costs. Hence high interest rates reduce the net revenues of any potential investment. Here again we anticipate an increase in the quantity of loanable funds demanded as interest rates decline (*ceteris paribus*).

The rate of return to capital

Although we can readily determine the equilibrium rate of interest by studying the supply and demand for loanable funds,[3] the significance of the interest rate for factor prices is not always apparent. After all, money is not a factor of production; it cannot produce anything. Instead, money is a medium of exchange that can be used to acquire goods and services. When people lend or borrow money, they are really lending or borrowing access to goods and services.

People who use their own or someone else's money to build an apartment house or factory are making the same kind of sacrifice a lender makes. They are giving up the opportunity to spend their money on consumer goods, choosing instead to build, buy, or lease plant and equipment. As compensation for this use of funds, an investor expects increased consumption opportunities in the future. Essentially, the investor expects to be paid interest on his investment. In this case, however, the resultant payments represent *returns to capital*, that is, payments for the use of real plant and equipment.

Typically, an investment is made for many years. A person who builds a factory does not begin to receive any income back until the factory is constructed and in use. The same is true of an apartment

[3] In Chapters 10–12, the equilibrium rate of interest is analyzed in terms of the supply and demand for *money*, not just loanable funds; the results are identical.

FIGURE 28.3   THE LOANABLE FUNDS MARKET

The market rate of interest (r_e) is determined by the intersection of the curves representing supply of and demand for loanable funds. The rate of interest represents the price paid for the use of money.

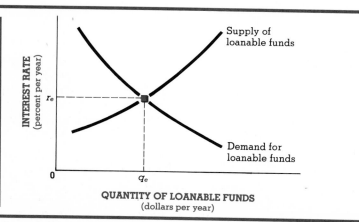

INTEREST RATE (percent per year)

Supply of loanable funds

r_e

Demand for loanable funds

0

q_e

QUANTITY OF LOANABLE FUNDS
(dollars per year)

building. It may take a year to construct an apartment building and years more before rent payments equal the owner's original investment. Such investments return a *flow* of income over time. To compute the rate of return to capital in these situations, that future flow of income must be summarized in a meaningful way.

Suppose that the cost of constructing an apartment building is $1 million. After completion, the apartments will generate net rent payments (after expenses) of $100,000 per year, forever. Is this a good investment?

One way to answer this question is to calculate the implicit rate of return. Rent payments of $100,000 per year represent a 10 percent return on a million-dollar investment. This is a "good" investment so long as money can be borrowed for less than 10 percent. If, for example, $1 million could be borrowed at 9 percent, the landlord would have to make annual interest payments of $90,000. But he would get back $100,000 in annual rent payments. He could pocket the difference of $10,000 per year. Hence *it pays to invest so long as the return on capital exceeds the cost of money.*

Present discounted value

Another way of evaluating the attractiveness of an investment is to *discount* the future stream of rental income to a lump-sum figure. If the rate of interest is 9 percent, $100,000 received one year from today is worth only $91,743 today. This is because money earns interest. If we had $91,743 today, we could deposit it and earn interest. If the interest rate were 9 percent, our $91,743 deposit would be worth $100,000 at year's end. Hence "discounting" involves adjusting future income receipts for forgone interest. By discounting, we translate future receipts into *present* values.

Our apartment building generates $100,000 in income every year, not just the first. Hence we need to discount the *entire* future stream of rent payments, not just the first year's. This is done with the formula:

$$\begin{array}{l} \text{Present discounted} \\ \text{value} \end{array} = \frac{\$100,000}{1.09} + \frac{\$100,000}{(1.09)^2}$$
$$+ \frac{\$100,000}{(1.09)^3} + \ldots \frac{\$100,000}{(1.09)^n}$$
$$= \$91,743 + \$84,168 + \$77,218 + \ldots$$

All this formula does is discount each future year's rent back to today's value, then add the values up. The second year's income of $100,000 must be discounted back two years; therefore, the interest rate in the denominator is squared. If the investment income stretches far into the future (n is large), this sum equals $1,111,111.

Fortunately, the formula for computing present discounted values can be simplified to a much shorter expression. If the same income is received every year into the indefinite future, the formula becomes

$$\begin{array}{l} \text{Present} \\ \text{discounted} \\ \text{value} \end{array} = \frac{\text{annual income}}{\text{interest rate}} = \frac{\$100,000}{0.09} = \$1,111,111$$

This is the same answer we got above. What it means is that the future stream of rental payments is worth $1.11 million when it is discounted at 9 percent. Since the cost of the investment is only $1 million, the investment is attractive.

In equilibrium, the rate of return to capital will be equal to the rate of interest. Likewise, the present discounted value of future income will be equal to the cost of the investment. This is evident when you think what would happen if an inequality existed. So long as the rate of interest is less than the rate of return to capital, people will continue to borrow and invest. This will drive up interest rates and lower the rate of return to capital. On the other hand, if the rate of interest were higher than the rate of return to capital, investors would simply lend out funds rather than purchase plant and equipment. By doing so, they would increase their future incomes. As the quantity of loanable funds increased, the market rate of interest would fall. At the same time, the rate of investment would slow, because investors were lending their funds rather than buying plant and equipment. With less new investment, marginal revenue product and thus the returns to capital would increase. Ultimately the rate of interest and the rate of return to capital would converge, eliminating motives for any further changes in investor behavior.

PROFIT

economic profit: The difference between total revenues and total economic costs.

economic cost: The value of all resources used to produce a good or service; opportunity cost.

The last major form of income is profit. Like rent, its economic definition differs from common perceptions of the term. As we saw in Chapter 20, **economic profit** is the difference between total revenues and all factor payments, whether explicitly made or not. It is the residual that remains after all **economic costs** have been subtracted.

Entrepreneurship

In view of the fact that profit is a residual that remains after all factors of production have been paid, the question arises as to what profit "buys" in the market. Wages, for example, buy the use of labor, interest rates buy the use of money and capital, and rent buys the use of land. But what does society get in return for profits paid to business?

One of the most prevalent theories of profit regards profit as the reward for entrepreneurship, the ability and willingness to take risks, to organize factors of production, and to produce something society desires. From this perspective, profit represents a return to an intangible but vitally important "fourth factor of production." Profit represents the payoff for making an "extra" effort, over and above "normal" factor payments. In the absence of such additional compensation, few people would want to make the extra effort required.

Risk

It is also important to observe that the *potential* for profit is not a *guarantee* of profit. Quite the contrary. Substantial risks are attached to starting and operating a business. In fact, thousands of businesses

The Top 10 New Products

The top 10 new products of all time, according to 350 research and development executives polled by New Product Development newsletter, are, in order: the wheel, bow and arrow, telegraph, electric light, plow, steam engine, vaccine, telephone, paper, flush toilet.

fail every year, and still more suffer economic losses. From this perspective, profit represents compensation for risks incurred.

The risks associated with a new business are particularly high when new products or processes are being developed. The electronic calculator industry, discussed in Chapters 21–23, for example, was developed on the basis of repeated technological improvements, each of which required substantial investments of labor and capital. Who would have risked such investments without some potential for high profits?

Monopoly profits

Although profits serve an important function in stimulating economic activity, not all profits can be justified on that basis. In many situations, profits may result from the exercise of market power that inhibits rather than encourages economic progress. Monopolies provide a classic example. As we observed in Chapter 22, a monopoly can maintain economic profits by limiting the market output of a good or service. Such profits take on the appearance of economic rent, as high prices and profit do not necessarily call forth a greater quantity supplied. The same kind of quasi-rent is obtained by other firms and unions that possess market power.

POLICY IMPLICATIONS: EXCESS-PROFITS TAX

In a market economy, profits do perform an important economic function. In particular, the potential for profits creates an incentive for entrepreneurs to mobilize society's resources to satisfy consumer demands. The question remains, however, as to how much profit is required to bring about the desired response. As we have observed, any profits in excess of the amount required to elicit desired entrepreneurial responses represent economic rent and do not contribute to increased output. Hence such *"excess" profits could be taxed away with no impairment of economic goals.* In fact, taxation of excess profits might improve the distribution of income without impairing economic efficiency, thereby improving total social welfare.

Unfortunately, it is far easier to state the general case for excess-profits taxes than it is to identify excess profits in the real world. We may, however, point to monopolies or other concentrations of economic power as likely sources of excess profit.[4] Excess profits may also emerge when external events abruptly alter market supply or demand forces. When World War II broke out, for example, there was

---

[4] Public regulation of monopoly behavior (e.g., utility rates) is designed to minimize economic rent.

THE CRUDE OIL WINDFALL PROFIT TAX ACT OF 1980

Tier	Oil covered	Maximum tax rate on windfall profit*
1	Lower- and upper-tier oil under previous price controls	70%
2	Stripper well oil	60
3	Newly discovered (since 1978) oil, certain "heavy" oil, and incremental tertiary oil	30

*"Windfall profit" is the difference between the selling price and an "adjusted base price." Average adjusted base prices per barrel are $13.06 for Tier 1, $15.50 for Tier 2, and $16.96 for Tier 3. This windfall profit is limited to 90 percent of net income per barrel.

a dramatic increase in the demand for U.S. armaments but little change in our production possibilities. Hence armaments producers suddenly found themselves confronting a market shortage that they could not satisfy. Under such circumstances, the potential for reaping high economic rents was enormous. To prevent U.S. producers from profiting excessively from the war, Congress enacted an excess-profits tax.

The same kind of dilemma has inhibited U.S. energy policies. If we truly want to curb U.S. consumption of energy (particularly imported oil), we have to raise domestic energy prices. As prices rise, the quantity of energy demanded will fall, and U.S. producers will increase their domestic exploration and production activities. Higher energy prices, however, will also bestow a "windfall" profit on the owners of existing oil and gas wells. Wells already in production require no further incentives. Higher energy prices represent a "surplus" over the amount required to attract the quantity of oil or gas supplied from "old" wells. Unless this redistribution of income is desired on grounds of equity, the windfall profits serve no function.

To achieve our energy goals without generating windfall profits, Congress tried to distinguish between "old" oil (from established wells) and "new" oil (from new wells) and established separate prices for each.[5] Unfortunately, old oil looks exactly like new oil, and this policy generated high administrative costs and reduced production efficiency. By contrast, a direct excess-profits tax looks more appealing. In 1979 President Carter moved to dismantle the distinction between "old" and "new" oil prices by partially decontrolling the price of domestic oil and establishing a timetable for complete decontrol. President Reagan speeded up the process by eliminating all controls on crude oil prices in February 1981. To limit the economic rent producers might receive, Congress enacted the Crude Oil Windfall Profit Tax Act of 1980. The act established tax rates of 30 percent (on "new oil") to 70 percent (on "old oil") on the windfall profits producers would reap from higher oil prices.

[5] The actual definitions of "old" and "new" oil were more complex; in 1978 the Carter administration also proposed a third category of oil, called "new new oil." New new oil consists of "oil which is located more than 2½ miles from any onshore domestic well in existence on April 20, 1977, or more than 1,000 feet deeper than any well within the 2½ mile radius, or from an offshore lease entered into after April 20, 1977."

SUMMARY

- Total income in the economy includes payments for labor, capital, land, and entrepreneurship. Each form of compensation has some unique characteristics.

- Economic rent is defined as payments for a factor of production in excess of the amount required to call forth the desired supply. Because the quantity of "pure," unimproved land is fixed—cannot respond to increases in prices—all payments for the use of unimproved land represent economic rent. Rents are also paid for the use of other factors whose supply is essentially fixed.

- Economic rent does not attract a larger quantity of the fixed factor for which it is paid. The "surplus" factor payments, however, do serve to allocate the fixed resource among competing uses.

- Interest payments are the price paid for the use of money. Interest rates measure the opportunity cost of investing one's funds in plant and equipment. The payments made for the use of such capital are the returns to capital. In equilibrium, the returns to capital will equal the market rate of interest.

- Economic profits are the income that remains after all economic costs have been accounted for. These above-normal profits represent a reward for entrepreneurship and compensation for its risks. When market power or other institutional barriers inhibit economic activity, however, profits may take on the appearance of economic rent.

- Profits in excess of those needed to call forth increased supply represent a "windfall" that can be taxed away without reducing market supplies.

Terms to remember

Define the following terms:

factor share	marginal revenue product
marginal cost	interest rate
fixed costs	opportunity cost
price elasticity of supply	economic profit
rent	economic cost

Questions for discussion

1. Dave Winfield, the former San Diego outfielder, was hired by the New York Yankees in 1981 for a contract worth over $25 million. How much of this payment represents economic rent?

2. A 1981 Rand Corporation study of rent control in Los Angeles concluded that "rent control confers its benefits early and exacts its costs late." What is meant by this statement?

3. What functions, if any, do economic profits perform? Do they help allocate any scarce resources?

4. Henry George, a nineteenth-century printer, author, and politician, advocated adoption of a single property tax that would replace all other taxes. What economic arguments might be used to defend or reject such a tax?

5. Why do lenders charge interest on loans? Why are borrowers willing to pay it?

Problem Suppose that the following figures summarize the annual revenues and costs of operating a Baskin-Robbins ice cream store.

(a) Investment in store equipment and franchise $100,000

(b) Annual sales

    Ice creams 180,000

    Other confections 32,000

(c) Cost of goods 134,000

(d) Lease expenses ($600 per month) _____

(e) Employee wages (4 workers @ $8,000 per year each) _____

(f) The owner-manager works in the store 50 hours
    per week except for a two-week vacation;
    his opportunity wage ($8 per hour) _____

(g) Interest (9 percent) _____

Using these figures, determine the net revenue and economic profit of the store's owner-operator. Assume that half of the initial investment is borrowed.

CHAPTER 29

THE DISTRIBUTION OF INCOME

The outcomes of individual factor markets consist of wage levels, profit rates, interest rates, and rents. Taken together, they add up to the distribution of income. The distribution of income, in turn, represents our collective response to the basic FOR WHOM question, that is, who gets to consume the goods and services that are produced. People who participate more extensively in factor markets, or whose efforts are rewarded more generously, get more income. With that income, they have a greater claim on the goods and services produced.

The issue of FOR WHOM we produce is not entirely resolved by market forces, of course. The government plays a major role in redistributing incomes. The government takes income from some people (via taxes) and gives it to others (via income transfers). In the process, it reshapes the distribution of income and changes our answer to the FOR WHOM question.

In this chapter we shall examine the actual distribution of income. Who gets the most income from factor markets? How much do taxes and transfers alter the income distribution?

WHAT IS "INCOME"?

Before examining the distribution of income in the United States, we have to decide what to include in our concept of "income" and what to leave out. There are several possibilities. In the national-income

personal income *(PI)*: Income received by households before payment of personal taxes.

accounts (Chapter 4) we typically focus on **personal income**—the flow of annual income received by households before payment of personal income taxes. Personal income includes wages and salaries, corporate dividends, rent, interest, social security benefits, welfare payments, and any other form of money income.

Personal income is not a completely satisfactory basis for measuring the distribution of income, however. Measures of the distribution of income should tell us FOR WHOM our output is produced. The distribution of personal income does not fully answer this question. Many goods and services are distributed directly ("in kind"), rather than through market purchases. Many poor people, for example, live in public housing and pay no (or little) rent. As a consequence, they receive a larger share of total output than their money incomes imply. People with low incomes also receive food stamps that allow them to purchase more food than their money incomes would allow. In this sense, food-stamp recipients are better off than the distribution of personal income (which does not include food stamps) implies.

The distinction between the distribution of money incomes and the distribution of real output is not confined to welfare recipients. Students who attend public schools and colleges consume more goods and services than they directly pay for; public education is subsidized by all taxpayers. As a consequence, the distribution of money income understates the share of output received by students in public schools.

So long as some goods and services need not be purchased in the market, *the distribution of money income is not synonymous with the distribution of goods and services.* Accordingly, the distribution of money receipts is not a complete answer to the question of FOR WHOM we produce. This measurement problem is particularly important when comparisons are made over time. For example, the federal government officially classifies people as "poor" if their money income is below a certain threshold. By this standard, the number of poor people in America has been roughly constant for more than 15 years. In that time, however, we have provided a vastly increased amount of in-kind benefits to low-income people. Hence their *real* incomes have risen much more than the *money* statistics indicate. In this case, money statistics give a misleading picture of the changing income distribution.[1]

The distinction between money incomes and real incomes also affects international comparisons. Many people in less-developed countries rely more on home production than on market participation for essential goods and services. As a consequence, the measured distribution of money income may look more unequal than it really is. This overstatement affects comparisons between the United States and such countries as Sweden and Great Britain, although for different reasons. In those countries, the governments provide more direct goods and services (e.g., housing, medical care) than the U.S. government does. Hence *real* income is more evenly distributed in those countries than money incomes imply.

[1] The poverty problem is discussed in more detail in Chapter 31.

Wealth and happiness

Concentration on money incomes raises still other problems. If our real concern is access to goods and services, the distribution of wealth is also important. "Wealth" refers to the market value of the assets (e.g., houses, bank accounts) people own. Hence wealth represents a stock of potential purchasing power. Income statistics tell us only how *this* year's flow of purchasing power (income) is being distributed. Yet goods and services can be purchased with income saved in previous years (or generations, through inheritance). That is to say, ownership of wealth implies greater access to goods and services than income alone permits. Accordingly, to provide a complete answer to the FOR WHOM question, we have to know how wealth, as well as income, is distributed. In general, wealth tends to be distributed much less equally than income.[2]

Finally, we have to confront a very basic question about the importance of income and wealth. By focusing on access to goods and services, we are implicitly asserting that material things are primary determinants of individual well-being. Does money really buy happiness? Apparently so. In a study of attitudes and income in 19 countries, Richard Easterlin of the University of Pennsylvania came to the following conclusion:

> Does greater happiness go with higher income? The answer is, quite clearly, yes. This does not mean there are no unhappy people among the rich and no happy people among the poor. On the average, however, higher-income people are happier than the poor.[3]

Professor Easterlin also noted, however, that entire societies don't become happier as their abundance grows. What matters to people is their *relative* position in society, not the absolute quantity of goods and services they consume. Hence a "rich" fisherman in Sri Lanka might feel better off than a "poor" American, even though the American has access to far more goods and services.

THE FUNCTIONAL DISTRIBUTION OF INCOME

There are a variety of ways to measure the distribution of money income, and thus to gauge relative economic position. Karl Marx believed that the most meaningful way was to focus on the shares of total income received by the two primary factors of production, labor and capital. He recognized that incomes varied *within* the capitalist and proletariat (laboring) classes. He believed, however, that the distinction between those who owned the means of production (the capitalists) and those whose labor was exploited (the proletariat) overwhelmed all other differences. He predicted that the capitalists would continue to accumulate wealth, power, and income, steadily increasing their share of total output. Ultimately, those who had little would vastly outnumber those who had much and would come to resent them. This resentment at inequality would lead to a proletarian revolution.

[2] Recent estimates indicate that 1 percent of the U.S. population owns more than one-fifth of all wealth in the United States (see Anthony Atkinson, "The Concentration of Wealth in Britain," *Challenge*, July–August 1978).
[3] Richard A. Easterlin, "Does Money Buy Happiness?" *Public Interest*, Winter 1973.

TABLE 29.1   THE FUNCTIONAL DISTRIBUTION OF INCOME, 1929–1981

Labor's share of total income has risen substantially in the last fifty years. Much of this increase is due to the shift away from manufacturing to more labor-intensive service industries. Increased capital investment, education, skill training, and labor organization have also contributed to a rising labor share of income.

Year	Total labor share (percent)	Capital share (percent)*					
		Total	Farmers	Nonfarm proprietors	Rental income	Corporate profits	Interest income
1929	60.3	39.7	7.3	10.4	5.8	10.8	5.5
1933	73.9	26.1	6.5	8.0	5.5	− 4.3†	10.3
1943	64.8	35.2	6.9	10.2	2.6	13.9	1.6
1953	69.9	30.1	4.3	9.5	3.3	11.8	1.1
1963	71.0	29.9	2.4	8.0	3.3	12.3	3.0
1973	75.1	24.9	3.0	5.7	2.0	9.3	4.9
1981	75.6	24.4	1.0	4.8	1.4	8.1	9.1

*Includes income of farmers, landowners, and landlords, as well as those who own plant and equipment.
†In 1933, corporate profits were negative, as was net investment.
Source: *Economic Report of the President*, 1982.

functional distribution of income: The division of income among factors of production, especially between capital and labor.

factor share: The proportion of total income received by a factor of production.

The division of income between labor and capital is now called the **functional distribution of income.** No one is quite sure what the functional distribution looked like in the mid-nineteenth century (when Marx was writing). Recent estimates suggest, however, that wage and salary workers were getting less than 40 percent of total output. This low labor share was explained largely by the prevalence of small farmers, whose income was derived primarily from their own labor, and was not paid in wages and salaries. More recent statistics, as provided in Table 29.1, may be more representative of basic trends in the functional distribution of income.

Since 1929, labor's share of total income has increased substantially and now accounts for three-fourths of total income. In part, this trend is explained by the substantial shift in our GNP away from heavy manufacturing (which is capital-intensive) to labor-intensive services (including government services and education). As the mix of output continues to shift toward goods and services that use little capital and much labor, labor's share of total income—its **factor share**—may be expected to rise.

Another force that has helped to boost labor's share of total income is labor unionism. Unions have reduced the size of the labor force (by demanding earlier retirements, longer school attendance, and tougher immigration restrictions) and have shortened the working day. These actions have served to make labor a scarcer commodity and thus more valuable.

Finally, we may note that the supply of capital has expanded much more quickly than the supply of labor. While the labor force has grown at a rate of something like 1 percent a year, the stock of capital has grown by 3 to 4 percent a year. This disparity has the effect of making capital relatively abundant and thus cheaper, while making labor relatively scarce and thus expensive.[4]

[4] Also, by making more capital available to the average worker, this trend raises the productivity of labor. The concept of marginal productivity and its determinants are discussed in Chapter 26.

THE SIZE DISTRIBUTION OF INCOME

size distribution of income: The way total personal income is divided up among households or income classes.

In view of the fact that labor's share of income is already so large, the functional distribution of income no longer arouses much interest. People are now more concerned about the distribution of income among *individuals* than about its distribution among anonymous factors of production. To address this concern, we need to know what the distribution of personal income looks like *within* functional classes (labor and capital), as well as between them.

The most common measure of the income shares received by individuals is the **size distribution of income.** This measure tells us how large a share of total personal income is received by various households, grouped by income class. Imagine for the moment that the entire population is lined up in order of income, with lowest-income recipients in front and highest-income recipients at the end of the line. What we want to know is how much income the people in front get, in comparison with those at the back. Table 29.2 provides the answer.

The figures in Table 29.2 indicate that no household in the first (lowest) fifth of the line received more than $10,286 in 1980; thus $10,286 was the upper boundary for the lowest income class. Note also that this class received only 5.1 percent of total income, despite the fact that it included 20 percent of the population (the lowest *fifth*). Thus the **income share** of the people in the lowest group was much smaller than their proportion in the total population.

income share: The proportion of total income received by a particular group.

Moving back to the end of the line, we observe that a family needed only $35,000 in annual income to make it into the highest income class in 1980. Naturally, many families in that class made much more than $35,000, some even millions of dollars. But $35,000 was at least enough to get into the top fifth (or quintile).

The top fifth of all families obviously fared much better than everyone else. The extent of their prosperity is indicated by their relative income share. They got 41.5 percent of total income and, by implication, that much of total output. This was eight times as much income as the lowest class received.

The Lorenz curve

The size distribution of income provides the kind of information we need to determine how total personal income is distributed. A more convenient summary of that same information is often desired, how-

---

TABLE 29.2   SIZE DISTRIBUTION OF PERSONAL INCOME, 1980

The size distribution of income indicates how total income is distributed among income classes. That fifth of our population with the lowest incomes received only 5.1 percent of total income. The highest-income class (fifth) received over 41 percent of total income.

Household income group	1980 income	Aggregate income (billions of dollars)	Share of total income (percent)
Lowest fifth	$ 0–10,286	$ 73.7	5.1
Second fifth	10,287–17,390	167.7	11.6
Third fifth	17,391–24,630	253.0	17.5
Fourth fifth	24,631–34,534	351.3	24.3
Highest fifth	above 34,534	601.4	41.5

Source: U.S. Department of Commerce, Bureau of the Census.

Reprinted by permission of the *San Francisco Chronicle*. Artist: Robert Graysmith.

ever. For this purpose we can draw a Lorenz curve, first suggested by an American statistician, Max Otto Lorenz, in 1905.

A Lorenz curve for the United States is illustrated in Figure 29.1. Our line-up of individuals is on the horizontal axis, with the lowest income earners on the left. On the vertical axis we depict the cumulative share of income received by people in our income line. Consider the lowest fifth of the distribution again, that is, the people in front of our income line. They are represented on the horizontal axis at 20 percent. What we want to know is how large a share of income they receive. If their share of income was identical to their share of population, they would get 20 percent of total income. This

FIGURE 29.1 THE LORENZ CURVE

The Lorenz curve illustrates the extent of income inequality. If all incomes were equal, each fifth of the population would receive one-fifth of total income. In this case, the diagonal line through point C would represent the cumulative size distribution of income. In reality, incomes are not distributed equally. Lower-income groups receive smaller income shares. Point A, for example, indicates that 20 percent of the population with the lowest income receives only 5.1 percent of total income.

Source: Table 29.2.

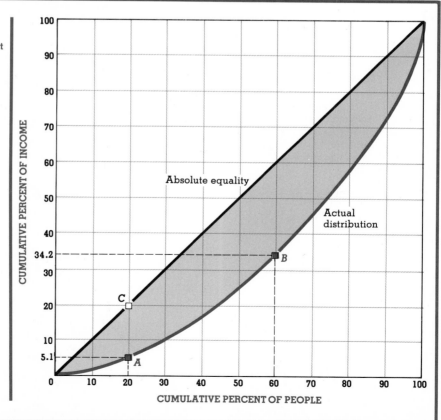

Lorenz curve: A graphic illustration of the cumulative size distribution of income; contrasts complete equality with the actual distribution of income.

would be represented by point C in the figure. In fact, the lowest quintile gets much less than 20 percent of total income. They get only 5.1 percent, as indicated by point A. We already knew this from Table 29.2, of course.

Past point A, the **Lorenz curve** starts to provide a bit more information. Point B, for example, tells us that the *cumulative* share of income received by the lowest three-fifths of the population was 34.2 percent. We could have gotten this information from Table 29.2 as well, but it would have required a little addition.

The really handy feature of the Lorenz curve is the way it contrasts the actual distribution of income with an absolutely equal one. If incomes were distributed equally, all income shares would be identical. In that case, the first 20 percent of the people in line would be getting exactly 20 percent of all income and the Lorenz curve would run through point C. Indeed, the Lorenz "curve" would be a straight line along the diagonal. The fact that the actual Lorenz curve lies below the diagonal indicates that our national income is not distributed equally. In fact, the area between the diagonal and the actual Lorenz curve (the shaded area in Figure 29.1) is a convenient measure of the degree of inequality. ***The greater the area between the Lorenz curve and the diagonal, the more inequality exists.***[5]

[5] The ratio of the shaded area to the area of the triangle formed by the diagonal and the axes is often used as a numerical summary of the Lorenz curve. This ratio, called the "Gini coefficient," was 0.359 in 1972.

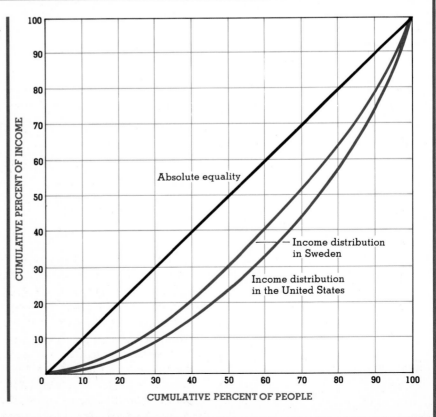

FIGURE 29.2 INCOME INEQUALITY IN THE UNITED STATES AND SWEDEN

These Lorenz curves illustrate the distribution of *after-tax* money incomes in the United States and Sweden for standardized household size. The greater equality of Swedish incomes is apparent from the fact that the Swedish Lorenz curve is closer to the diagonal.

Source: Organization for Economic Cooperation and Development, 1976.

FIGURE 29.3 THE IMPACT OF TAXES ON INEQUALITY

These Lorenz curves depict distributions of adjusted family income before and after federal, state, and local taxes. The tax system does not substantially reduce income inequality.

Source: Joseph A. Pechman and Benjamin A. Okner, *Who Bears the Tax Burden?* Fig. 1-3, p. 7. Copyright © 1974 by the Brookings Institution, Washington, D.C.

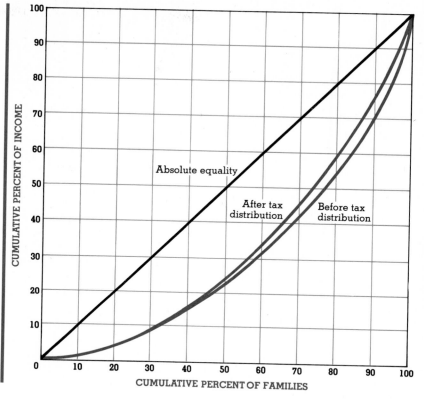

The Lorenz curve is a particularly useful tool for comparing the income distributions of countries or of the same country at two or more points in time. Figure 29.2, for example, provides a quick comparison of income inequalities in the United States and Sweden. The Lorenz curve for Sweden lies closer to the diagonal, indicating that money incomes are distributed more equally in Sweden than in the United States. Other countries, including West Germany, France, and most less developed nations, exhibit less equality than the United States.

The impact of taxes

progressive tax: A tax system in which tax rates rise as incomes rise.

marginal tax rate: The tax rate imposed on the last (marginal) dollar of income.

A particularly interesting Lorenz curve comparison is illustrated in Figure 29.3. It shows the reduction in inequality brought about by federal, state, and local taxes. Many people regard the tax system as a major tool for equalizing incomes, particularly for reducing the very high incomes of the wealthiest classes. In fact, the federal income tax is designed to be **progressive,** that is, to impose higher tax *rates* on high incomes than on low ones. As Table 29.3 illustrates, the **marginal tax rate** for single taxpayers increases from zero on incomes under $3,400 to 26 percent on incomes over $30,000. For extremely high incomes—those above $150,000—the marginal tax rate is 50 percent.

TABLE 29.3 FEDERAL INCOME TAX RATES FOR SINGLE TAXPAYERS, 1983

Federal income taxes are progressive: tax rates rise as income increases. However, many high-income individuals avoid high tax rates by taking advantage of available exemptions and deductions ("loopholes"). The progressivity of the federal tax system is further offset by the regressivity of state and local taxes.

Total income	Marginal tax rate (percent)	Total income	Marginal tax rate (percent)
$0 – 3,400	0	$ 30,000	26
5,000	11	60,000	40
10,000	15	100,000	48
20,000	19	150,000 or more	50

Note: The tax rates given here assume all income is fully taxable (as it would be if it were derived solely from wages and salaries) and that the standard deduction is used at incomes below $20,000. Actual tax rates vary with the sources of income, the number of dependents, and the availability of additional deductions and credits.
Source: Internal Revenue Service.

regressive tax: A tax system in which tax rates fall as incomes rise.

But the progressive nature of our federal income tax is significantly reduced by a variety of special provisions, including various tax deductions, exemptions, and credits, that benefit higher income groups. Moreover, most state and local taxes—on income, property, and sales—are actually **regressive.** That is, they impose higher tax rates on *lower* incomes. Indeed, state and local taxes are so regressive that they offset the progressivity of the federal income tax, thereby rendering our total tax system ineffective as a leveler of incomes. This is evident in Figure 29.3, where the before-tax and after-tax Lorenz curves are compared. The tax system does reduce inequality somewhat—the after-tax Lorenz curve is closer to the diagonal—but the reduction is slight.

The impact of transfers

The tax system tells only half the redistribution story. It tells whose income was taken away. Equally important is who gets the income the government collects. The government completes the redistribution process by *transferring* income to consumers. The transfers may be explicit, as in the case of welfare benefits, social security payments, and unemployment insurance. Or the transfers may be indirect, as in the case of public schools, farm subsidies, and student loans. The direct transfers are more likely to be progressive, that is, to increase the income share of lower-income households. This

Reagans Made $418,826 in '81, Paid U.S. 40%

President Reagan and his wife, Nancy, made $418,826 in 1981 and paid nearly 40 percent of it in federal income taxes, according to returns made public at the White House without comment yesterday.

The Reagans' joint return shows that they paid income taxes of $165,305 and claimed charitable deductions of $11,895. Nearly half of this ($5,930) was in clothes donated by Mrs. Reagan to two museums two weeks before her husband was inaugurated president. . . .

Reagan earns $200,000 a year as president. His presidential salary in 1981, however, was $189,167, because he did not take office until Jan. 20.

The president's other income in-

cluded $42,635 in royalties and payments for past writings, radio or acting performances, $66,558 from investments made by his blind trust and $51,482 for a past property sale.

Reagan also receives a pension of $22,197 from the state of California, where he was governor for eight years.

—Lou Cannon

The Washington Post, Washington, D.C., April 17, 1982. Copyright © 1982 The Washington Post.

CBO Says Benefit Cuts, Tax Rises Hit Hardest at Under-$10,000 Households

More than half of all the benefit cuts and individual tax increases proposed by President Reagan for fiscal 1983 would fall on households with less than $10,000 annual income, according to a Congressional Budget Office study sent to Congress yesterday.

The CBO said the average loss as a result of Reagan's proposals would be about $320 for households with income less than $10,000, about triple the figure for families earning more than $10,000.

The study, requested by Sen. Ernest F. Hollings (D-S.C.) and other members of Congress, estimated that Reagan's request for cash and in-kind benefit program cuts directly affecting individuals would total $10.8 billion in fiscal 1983 if enacted. The cuts would come largely from reductions in food stamps and Medicare, but also include housing, Medicaid, welfare, education benefits, civil service, veterans' and military benefits.

The individual tax increases, totaling $830 million, would result from Reagan's request for imposition of the federal Medicare tax on civil servants.

Of the $11.6 billion total from the cuts and tax increases, the CBO said $6.2 billion would come from households with less than $10,000 income a year; about $2.3 billion from those in the $10,000 to $20,000 category; about $2.1 billion from the $20,000 to $40,000 group, and about $950 million from those with incomes of more than $40,000.

The CBO figures show that the same general pattern would hold for 1984 and 1985 as well.

—Spencer Rich

The Washington Post, Washington, D.C., April 15, 1982. Copyright © 1982 The Washington Post.

progressiveness results from the fact that low-income status is often a requirement for a direct income transfer. By contrast, most indirect transfers are ostensibly designed to fulfill other purposes (e.g., education, agricultural stability). As a consequence, they are less likely to be progressive, and may even be regressive in some cases. A recent study of "social welfare" expenditures (including all direct transfers, housing, and education) attempted to assess the share of such transfers going to the poor. It found that only half of federal transfers and even a smaller proportion (30 percent) of state and local transfers go to the poor.[6] Were indirect transfers included, the proportions would be smaller yet.

WHAT IS "FAIR"?

It is evident that incomes are distributed unequally in the United States, even after all taxes and transfers are considered. It is not at all clear, however, in which direction we should go from here. Should we make the tax system more progressive? Do we really want greater equality? Or are the existing inequalities sufficiently justified to preclude further efforts at redistribution?

Nearly everyone has an answer to these questions, but the answers vary widely. "Fairness" is a subjective concept that is often indistinguishable from self-interest. Rich people, for example, can rattle off as many good reasons for preserving income inequalities as poor people can recite for eliminating them. People in the middle income brackets tend to be ambivalent.

Economists are not uniquely qualified to overcome self-interest, much less to divine what a fair distribution of income might look

[6] Robert Plotnick and Felicity Skidmore, *Progress against Poverty* (New York: Academic Press, 1975).

like. But economists are in a position to assess some of the costs and benefits of altering the distribution of income, and such assessments can facilitate policy decisions.

The costs of greater equality

The greatest potential cost of a move toward greater equality is the reduced incentives it might leave in its wake. People *are* motivated by income. In factor markets, higher wages call forth more workers and may induce them to work longer hours. Indeed, in fields where earnings are exceptionally high, as in the medical and legal professions, people are willing to spend years of their lives and many thousands of dollars acquiring the skills such earnings require. Could we really expect people to make such sacrifices in a market that paid everyone the same wage?

The same problem exists in product markets. The willingness of producers to supply us with goods and services depends on their expectation of profits. Why should they work hard and take risks to produce goods and services if their efforts will not make them any better off? If incomes were in fact distributed equally, producers might just as well sit back and enjoy the fruits of someone else's labor.

The essential economic problem that absolute income equality poses is that it breaks the market link between effort and reward. If all incomes were equal, it would no longer pay to make an above-average effort. If people stopped making such efforts, total output would decline and we would have less income to share. Not that all high incomes are attributable to great skill or effort. Such factors as luck, market power, and family connections also influence incomes. It remains true, however, that the promise of higher income encourages work effort. Moreover, we can reach our production-possibilities curve only if we are efficient, highly motivated producers. Absolute income equality threatens those conditions.

The argument for preserving income inequalities is thus anchored in a concern for productivity. From this perspective, income inequalities are the driving force behind much of our production. By preserving such inequalities, we not only enrich the fortunate few but also, by providing incentives to increase total output, make more goods and services available to lower income groups. Thus everyone is potentially better off, even if only a few end up "rich."

The benefits of greater equality

Although the potential benefits of inequality are impressive, *there is a trade-off between efficiency and equality.* Moreover, many people are convinced that the terms of the trade-off are exaggerated and the benefits of greater equality are ignored. These rebuttals are both economic and noneconomic.

The economic arguments for greater equality also focus on incentives. The first argument is that the present degree of inequality is more than necessary to maintain work incentives. Upper-class incomes need not be eight times as large as those of the lowest income classes; perhaps *five* times as large would do as well.

The second argument is that low-income earners might actually

Fame drain

Over the years Great Britain has produced countless men of fame—scientists, artists, entertainers of every stripe.

Now it is in danger of losing its current crop of star achievers.

The income tax rates are largely to blame. They range up to 83 percent on earned income and up to 98 percent on investment income. After a certain point such rates become confiscatory.

As a result the Bay City Rollers, the No. 1 pop group, will probably leave Britain and join the growing number of tax exiles seeking refuge in the United States, France, Switzerland, and other countries.

Mick Jagger and the Rolling Stones left England in 1971. "If the maximum tax was reduced to 50 percent," says Jagger, "which is what it is in America, it's more than likely that the Rolling Stones would return to England."

Former Beatle Ringo Starr, living in California, says, "I'd love to live in Britain again. But it seems terribly unfair that so much of what we earn should be taken away from us in taxes."

Another recent tax exile, singer Rod Stewart, also living in California, joins in with, "Let the government reduce that awful tax rate, and I'll be back in London in the morning."

Richard Burton, David Niven, Rex Harrison, Elizabeth Taylor, Charlotte Rampling—the cream of the British entertainment world—have all escaped from the oppression of British taxes by living abroad. Nor are tax exiles limited to entertainers. The loss of eminent scientists and highly qualified doctors is now arousing governmental concern. An estimated 1500 physicians are reportedly leaving Great Britain each year, largely because no senior doctor or surgeon on the National Health Service earning $20,000 or more a year is allowed an increase in salary.

—Lloyd Shearer

Parade, 1977. Reprinted by permission.

---

work harder if incomes were distributed more fairly. As matters now stand, the low-income worker sees little chance of making it big. Extremely low income can also inhibit workers' ability to work, by subjecting them to poor health, malnourishment, or inadequate educational opportunities. Accordingly, some redistribution of income to the poor might improve the productivity of low-income workers and compensate for reduced productivity among the rich. Together, these two arguments suggest that greater equality could be attained with little loss of total output.

There are noneconomic arguments for greater equality as well. To the extent that high incomes go hand in hand with political power, an unequal distribution of income weakens the democratic process. Inequalities may also tend to distort our values by their very emphasis on material reward. By the same token, the anxieties and frustrations created by the quest for upper-income positions may actually make us less happy as a society, even if somewhat richer.

The compromises

There are strong arguments both for and against greater income equality. In the absence of hard facts about the effect of income inequalities on work incentives, it is difficult to tell who is right. By how much would output drop if we actually raised taxes on the rich and distributed incomes more equally? By how much, if at all, would the productivity of low-income workers increase? Without such answers, we cannot claim that any income-redistribution plan represents the "right" compromise of equality and efficiency. Instead, we are virtually compelled to proceed in piecemeal fashion, altering our tax and transfer systems slightly and observing the impact of such changes. The alternative approach—a wholesale restructuring of the tax and transfer system—risks a severe reduction in total output and income.[7]

[7] "Radical" economists are quick to point out that this approach amounts to a defense of the status quo and existing income and wealth distributions, whether so intended or not. They are right.

SUMMARY

▪ The distribution of income is a vital economic issue because money incomes largely determine access to the goods and services we produce. Wealth distributions are also important, for the same reason.

▪ The functional distribution of income tells us how incomes are divided up between capital and labor. Over time, labor has received an increasing income share.

▪ The size distribution of income tells us how incomes are divided up among individuals. The Lorenz curve provides a graphic summary of the cumulative size distribution of income.

▪ Personal incomes are distributed quite unevenly in the United States. At present, the highest income group (the top 20 percent) gets eight times as much income as the lowest income group.

▪ Our tax system has had little impact on the distribution of personal income. Mildly progressive federal income taxes are offset by regressive state and local taxes. Income transfers may be more progressive, but their net effect is not certain.

▪ There is a trade-off between efficiency and equality. If all incomes are equal, there is no economic reward for superior productivity. On the other hand, a more equal distribution of incomes might increase the productivity of lower income groups and serve important noneconomic goals as well. The actual terms of this trade-off between equality and efficiency are not known, however, and the debate on the appropriate distribution of our income continues.

Terms to remember | Define the following terms:

personal income

functional distribution of income

factor share

size distribution of income

income share

Lorenz curve

progressive tax

marginal tax rate

regressive tax

Questions for discussion | 1. What goods or services does the average American receive without directly paying for them? How do these goods affect the distribution of economic welfare?

2. Why are incomes distributed so unevenly? Identify and explain three major causes of inequality.

3. Do inequalities stimulate productivity? In what ways? Provide two specific examples.

4. Should parents have the right to bequeath their assets to their children, without inheritance taxes? Is productivity a relevant concern here? Explain.

Problem | Using the numbers in Table 29.2 as a base, calculate the average tax rates that would have to be imposed on each income class to bring about absolute equality across income classes.

MICROECONOMIC ISSUES

CHAPTER 30
POLLUTION

Progress in environmental problems is impossible without a clear understanding of how the economic system works in the environment and what alternatives are available to take away the many roadblocks to environmental quality.

—COUNCIL ON ENVIRONMENTAL QUALITY,
FIRST ANNUAL REPORT

What good is a clean river if you've got no jobs?

—STEELWORKER UNION OFFICIAL IN
YOUNGSTOWN, OHIO (1977)

According to the President's Council on Environmental Quality, 1970 marked "a turning point, a year when the quality of life [became] more than a phrase; environment and pollution [became] everyday words; and ecology [became] almost a religion to some of the young." That is not to say that pollution was never a problem before 1970. As early as A.D. 61, the statesman and philosopher Seneca was complaining about the smoky air emitted from household chimneys in Rome. And historians are quick to remind us that open sewers running down the street were once the principal mode of urban waste disposal and that typhoid epidemics were a recurrent penalty for water pollution. So we cannot say that pollution is a new phenomenon, or that it is now worse than ever before.

But we do know more about the sources of pollution than our ancestors and can better afford to do something about them. After all, it was centuries before people discovered the scientific relationship between open sewers and periodic epidemics. And it took just about as long for us to discern the chemical link between auto exhaust and air pollution.

Our understanding of the economics of pollution has increased as well. On the one hand, we have come to recognize that pollution imposes direct costs on the economy. Pollution impairs health and thus reduces labor-force activity and output. Pollution also destroys capital (e.g., the effects of air pollution on steel structures) and diverts resources to undesired activities (e.g., car washes, laundry, and cleaning). Not least of all, pollution directly reduces our social welfare by denying us access to clean air, water, and beaches.

On the other hand, we have also learned that *controlling* pollution is costly, too. To clean up sewage, car exhausts, and smoke stains, we have to employ scarce factors of production to build, install, and maintain antipollution equipment. These factors of production could be used elsewhere. Hence there is an *opportunity cost* associated with pollution control. Much of the recent debate over pollution policy has focused on balancing these costs against the benefits of a cleaner environment.

Finally, we now recognize that much pollution is actually *encouraged* by the market system. People and industries typically pollute because they have no financial incentive to do otherwise. Accordingly, public antipollution policy has placed increasing emphasis on the profitability of not polluting. In this chapter we shall first review the nature and origins of pollution, then examine the market incentives for polluting. We conclude with a look at recent attempts to balance the costs and benefits of pollution control.

WHO POLLUTES WHAT?

Everyone seems to have his or her own idea of what pollution is and who causes it. Typically one particular pollutant comes to mind most quickly or is regarded as most annoying. Usually associated with that pollutant is an image—say, of an automobile—identified as the culprit. Such personal perspectives, however, tend to be incomplete. Accordingly, before we consider the alternatives available to eliminate pollution, we shall review the nature and sources of three major forms of pollution: air, water, and solid waste.

Air pollution | Air pollution is as familiar as a smoggy horizon. But smog is only one form of air pollution, as Table 30.1 indicates. There are five major air pollutants: carbon monoxide (CO), total suspended particulates (TSP), sulfur dioxide (SO_2), hydrocarbons (HC), and nitrogen oxides (NO_x). Each comes from a variety of sources.

Carbon monoxide (CO) is the colorless, odorless, and poisonous gas that is produced by incomplete burning of the carbon in fuels. In general, carbon monoxide slows reaction speeds and contributes to a wide variety of heart and lung problems. As is apparent from Table 30.1, the primary source of CO pollution is the automobile. Automobiles accounted for two-thirds of all CO emissions in 1977 (nine years after federal auto-emission controls were initiated). Another familiar source of carbon monoxide is cigarette smoking, which ac-

Source	CO	TSP	SO$_2$	HC	NO$_x$
Transportation	85.7	1.1	0.8	11.5	9.2
Fuel combustion in stationary sources	1.2	4.8	22.4	1.5	13.0
Industrial processes	8.3	5.4	4.2	10.1	0.7
Solid-waste disposal	2.6	0.4	0	0.7	0.1
Miscellaneous	4.9	0.7	0	4.5	0.1
Total	102.7	12.4	27.4	28.3	23.1

TABLE 30.1 ESTIMATED EMISSIONS OF AIR POLLUTANTS BY WEIGHT (in millions tons per year)

There are five major air pollutants. Automobiles account for most carbon monoxide (CO) emissions, but utilities and industrial plants are prime sources of other air pollutants.

Source: Environmental Protection Agency (1977 data).

counts for a tiny fraction of total air pollution but for most of the CO in the lungs of smokers.

The second major air pollutant depicted in Table 30.1, particulates (TSP), includes such visible annoyances as soot and smoke. These, too, are products of combustion, especially from industrial plants and power-generating plants. Particulates contribute to respiratory problems and are a major factor in the reduction of visibility. Some specific particulates, such as asbestos (from construction materials and brake linings) and lead (from car exhausts), have been identified as particularly dangerous to health.

Sulfur dioxide (SO$_2$), an acrid, corrosive, and poisonous gas, also comes from combustion, whenever fuels containing high levels of sulfur are burned. Electric utilities and industrial plants that burn high-sulfur coal or fuel oil are the prime sources of SO$_2$. Coal burning alone accounts for about 60 percent of all emissions of sulfur oxides. Sulfur oxides have been identified as the primary cause of the deaths and respiratory ailments accompanying air-pollution disasters. During one such disaster, in Donora, Pennsylvania, in 1948, half of the town's 14,000 inhabitants fell ill and twenty died. In 1952 a "killer smog" in London accounted for 1,600 deaths. Sulfur dioxide emissions also play a major role in the creation of acid rain.

Hydrocarbons (HC), like carbon monoxide, represent unburned and wasted fuel. Hydrocarbons are not normally toxic, but they are still regarded as a major pollutant because they contribute to the chemical formation of smog. Most HC emissions come from automobiles.

The other principal source of smog is nitrogen oxides (NO$_x$), which are produced when fuel is burned at very high temperatures, especially when the exhaust gases are cooled too quickly. Automobiles again are among the prime polluters, but electric power plants and industrial boilers account for most NO$_x$ pollution.

The seriousness of a pollution problem is not adequately conveyed by emission measures alone. In particular, one should not use Table 30.1 to compare the significance of various pollutants. Some pollutants (such as CO) are considerably more dangerous than others, pound for pound. Weight measures are simply a convenient and common frame of reference. More important, national emissions data combine the very distinct environments of all cities, states, and regions. Thus the data tell us nothing about how the air around Chi-

TABLE 30.2   THE POLLUTED CITIES

Most large cities suffer from air pollution. Cars are the principal source of most urban air pollution, but industrial plants and utilities also pollute the air.

City	Number of "unhealthful" days in 1980[a]	City	Number of "unhealthful" days in 1980[a]
Los Angeles	243	Salt Lake City	81
New York	224	Birmingham	75
Pittsburgh	168	Portland	75
San Bernardino	167	Houston	69
Cleveland	145	Detroit	65
St. Louis	136	Jersey City	65
Chicago	124	Baltimore	60
Washington, D.C.	97	San Diego	50
Phoenix	84	Cincinnati	45
Philadelphia	82	Dayton	45
Seattle	82	San Francisco	30

Source: Council on Environmental Quality.

[a] Number of days the Pollutant Standards Index (PSI) exceeded 100. The PSI measures exposure to sulfur oxides, particulates, carbon monoxide, photochemical oxidants, and nitrogen dioxide.

cago compares to the air around Fossil, Oregon.[1] Table 30.2 indicates the extent of air pollution in some of our largest cities.

Water pollution

Water pollution is the second major category of pollution. Its effects are apparent in the contamination of drinking water, restrictions on swimming and boating, foul-smelling waterways, and swarms of dead fish and floating debris. Statistics on water pollution, like those on air pollution, are still fragmentary. The Environmental Protection Agency (EPA) estimates, however, that one-third of U.S. water characteristically is polluted, in the sense that it violates federal water-quality standards. Nearly 80 percent of all water basins suffer measurable pollution, though not necessarily enough to make the water unsafe. Table 30.3 provides a rough impression of annual discharges into U.S. waterways.

[1] You've probably never heard of Fossil, Oregon, which is one reason the air is so clean there.

TABLE 30.3   WATER POLLUTANTS

Enormous volumes of material are discharged into U.S. waterways each year. Most discharges come from so-called nonpoint sources—namely, agricultural runoff, urban runoff, and solid-waste-disposal sites. The rest come from point sources, particularly industrial and municipal discharge pipes.

Pollutant	Annual discharge (millions of pounds)
Suspended solids	3,436,596
Dissolved solids	1,707,594
Biochemical oxygen demand	25,722
Nitrogen	13,743
Phosphorus	3,181
Dissolved heavy metals	98

Source: Council on Environmental Quality, *Environmental Trends* (Washington, D.C.: Government Printing Office, 1981).

ORGANIC POLLUTION   The most common form of water pollution occurs in the disposal of organic wastes. They not only are unsightly and foul-smelling, but also strain the biological capacity of water to sustain life. Organic wastes are decomposed in water by natural processes, but the decomposition process reduces the amount of oxygen available in the water to support aquatic life.[2]

The most familiar sources of organic waste are the bathroom toilet and the kitchen garbage disposal. The wastes that originate there are collected in sewer systems and ultimately discharged into the nearest waterway. The key question is whether the wastes are treated (separated and decomposed) before ultimate discharge. Sophisticated waste-treatment plants can reduce organic pollution by up to 99 percent.[3] Unfortunately, as recently as 1978 only one-half of the U.S. population was served by a system of sewers and adequate (secondary) treatment plants.

In addition to household wastes, our waterways must also contend with industrial wastes. Over half the volume of industrial discharge comes from just a few industries—principally paper, organic chemicals, petroleum, and steel. And within these industries, a relatively small number of very large firms account for most of the discharge. In a study of industrial pollution in the Southeast, the EPA found that only 1 percent of the 1,920 operating plants were responsible for more than 50 percent of the total untreated waste discharged.

Finally, there are all those herds of cattle and other farm animals that are being raised to provide us with food. Naturally, livestock contribute a little organic waste, too. Much of this waste enters waterways directly, particularly after heavy rains. Animal wastes don't cause too great a problem in such places as Boston and New York, but they can work havoc on the water supplies of towns in California, Texas, and Kansas.

THERMAL POLLUTION   *Thermal pollution* is an increase in the temperature of waterways brought about by the discharge of steam or heated water. Among other consequences, heat discharges can kill fish, upset marine reproductive cycles, and accelerate biological and chemical processes in water, thereby reducing its ability to retain oxygen.

The sources of thermal pollution are very few and quite specific. In general, the heat discharge is the result of using water to cool an industrial process, just as radiator water is used to cool a car's engine. In the United States, electric power plants account for over 80 percent of all such discharges, with primary metal, chemical, and petroleum-refining plants accounting for nearly all the rest.

---

[2] The standard measure of such pollution is *biochemical oxygen demand* (BOD), the amount of oxygen used in five days to decompose organic wastes. Waste-treatment plants help reduce BOD by separating out and decomposing some of the waste before it is discharged into the water.

[3] But that doesn't mean that all our pollution problems will be solved. On the contrary, the treatment of sewage creates new disposal problems, as we shall discuss shortly.

EUTROPHICATION   Another common form of water pollution results from the discharge of sediments and nutrients into waterways. The sediments tend to make the water shallower while the nutrients increase algae growth. During the process, called "eutrophication," the character of the waterway is altered, with fish populations changing and eventually disappearing. If eutrophication continues long enough, a lake will "die," ultimately turning into marshland and swamp. The Great Lakes, particularly Lake Erie, are typical examples of bodies of water undergoing the eutrophication process.

Although the causes of eutrophication are not completely known, phosphates and nitrogens have been identified as major factors in the process. Phosphates in household detergents, which reach waterways via municipal sewage systems, account for approximately half the phosphate volume. Chemical fertilizers, which are used to increase agricultural output, reach waterways via the runoff from rain and natural drainage and are another major source of eutrophication.

Litter: solid-waste pollution

The third major form of pollution is solid waste. Solid-waste pollution is apparent everywhere, from the garbage can to litter on the streets and beaches, to debris in the water, to open dumps. Although we tend to think of consumption as the end of the line for economic activity, a great deal of solid waste is generated in the process of consumption. Indeed, from a physical point of view, all we do in production and consumption is change the form of the earth's fixed stock of resources. Our world environment contains as many atoms now as it did ten thousand years ago. During those years, however, we (and nature) have continually changed the physical form of our resources. Virgin timber is converted into pulp, the pulp into newsprint, the newsprint into a newspaper; the newspaper is read (thereby "consumed") and discarded; the discarded newspaper ends up at the dump. No material is lost, it just takes on several different forms. This is what environmentalists refer to as the "materials-balance problem." Resources will not disappear once we have used them but must instead be shuffled around into a new use or hidden from view.[4]

Empty cans and bottles, discarded packaging, paper bags, old tires, and steak bones are sufficient reminders of the materials-balance problem. According to EPA estimates, we generate over 5 billion tons of solid waste each year (see Table 30.4). This figure includes more than 30 billion bottles (!), 60 billion cans, 100 million tires, and millions of discarded automobiles and major appliances. Where do you think all this refuse goes?

As Table 30.4 indicates, most solid wastes originate in agriculture (slaughter wastes, orchard prunings, harvest residues) and mining (slag heaps, mill tailings). The much smaller amount of solid waste originating in residential and commercial use is considered

---

[4] This is true even of wastes that are treated in an attempt to eliminate water pollution. The treated (removed) wastes are referred to as "sludge," which, alas, transforms the water-pollution problem into a waste-disposal problem. If we choose to burn the solid waste, we create an air-pollution problem.

TABLE 30.4 WHAT MAKES SOLID WASTES	Source	Tonnage (millions)
Over 5 billion tons of solid waste (paper, glass, scraps, etc.) are generated each year. Where does it all go?	Municipal trash and garbage	173
	Sewage sludge	5
	Industrial wastes	340
	Mineral wastes	2,100
	Agricultural wastes	2,600
	Total	5,218

Source: Environmental Protection Agency.

more dangerous, however, simply because it accumulates where people live. Refuse collected in urban areas, for example, increased from 2.75 pounds per person per day in 1920 to nearly 4 pounds in 1980.

THE COST OF POLLUTION

Enough has been said at this point to convey the seriousness of our pollution problems. Pollution of the air, the water, and the land-scape is pervasive, originates from a variety of specific sources, and is damaging our social welfare. The EPA estimates that air pollution costs us over $30 billion a year in health, property, and vegetation damage, not to mention aesthetic costs. Total damages inflicted by water pollution, particularly in the form of foreclosed recreational opportunities, may be greater still. As one indication of water-pollution damages, the EPA says 482 million fish were *reported* killed between 1961 and 1976 as a direct result of pollution. These reports account for only a fraction of the total kill. More than one-fifth of the nation's shellfish beds have been closed for the same reason. Although all estimates of pollution damages are necessarily inexact, it is clearly in the public interest to avoid such damages and to improve our enviroment.

Cleanup possibilities

Not only is the reduction of pollution in the public interest, but the means for reducing it are readily at hand. The EPA estimates that 95 percent of current air and water pollution could be eliminated by known and available technology. Nothing very exotic; just simple things like auto-emission controls, smokestack cleaners, improved sewage and waste-treatment facilities, and cooling towers for electric power plants. Even solid-waste pollution could be reduced by comparable proportions if we made the necessary effort. Approximately half of our municipal and commercial wastes represent salvageable materials (paper, glass, metal) that can readily be recycled for further use. Or we could compact and burn the whole mess under controlled conditions, thereby transforming our garbage into a useful (relatively low-polluting) energy source. That would still leave us with some noncombustible residuals and hydrocarbons to con-

New York City Is Looking to Its Garbage As Source of Methane Gas, Steam Power

NEW YORK —This city has decided to prospect for energy in its mountains of garbage. And it hopes to mine a few royalties along the way.

Plans call for tapping the decayed debris in landfills for methane gas, and for burning fresh garbage to make steam. The developers of the projects will pay royalties to the city while helping it reduce its dependence on oil.

UOP Inc., a Des Plaines, Ill., subsidiary of Signal Cos., will build and operate a plant designed to burn 3,000 tons of fresh garbage a day—or about 15% of the 20,000 tons of refuse the city produces daily. The steam generated at the plant, to be built at the Brooklyn Navy Yard and operating in 1986, will be used by Consolidated Edison Co., the city's electricity supplier.

And on the other front, the city has moved to utilize the hidden energy in Fresh Kills, the sprawling, 3,000-acre Staten Island landfill reputed to be the world's largest. In a joint venture, Getty Oil Co. and Brooklyn Union Gas Co. are building a $20 million plant capable of producing four million cubic feet of methane gas a day for 15 years. The city hopes the plant will be producing enough gas this summer to meet the needs of about 10,000 homes in the borough.
—Raymond A. Joseph

tend with, but we would at least be getting some cheap energy in the form of heat. The EPA estimates that if we converted all our solid wastes into energy, we could save over 200 million barrels of oil per year.

During the last decade, public policy has been increasingly forceful in combating pollution. In many cases (as in that of auto emissions), the results have been dramatic. The question remains, however, why we continue to pollute so much. Why do individual consumers and business firms pollute the air, water, and land?

THE ROLE OF MARKET INCENTIVES

Previous chapters have laid great stress on the market forces that influence the economic behavior of individual consumers, firms, and even government agencies. A persistent theme running through those discussions was the role that various kinds of incentives can play in altering behavior. As we have noted, incentives in the form of price reductions can be used to change consumer buying habits. Incentives in the form of high profit margins serve to encourage production of desired consumer goods and services. And market incentives in the form of cost differentials help to allocate resources efficiently. Accordingly, we should not be too surprised to learn that market incentives play a major role in pollution behavior and can be used as a tool of abatement policies.

The production decision

Imagine that you are the majority stockholder and manager of an electric power plant. As we have observed, such plants are responsible for a significant amount of air pollution (especially sulfur dioxide and particulates) and nearly all thermal water pollution. Hence your position immediately puts you on the most-wanted list of pollution offenders. But suppose you bear society no grudges and would truly like to help to eliminate pollution. Let's consider the alternatives.

As the owner-manager of an electric power plant, you will strive to make a profit-maximizing **production decision.** That is to say, you will seek the rate of output at which marginal revenue equals marginal cost. We shall assume that the electric power industry is regulated by the state power commission so that the price of electricity is fixed, at least in the short run. The effect of this assumption is to render marginal revenue equal to price, thus giving us a horizontal price line, as in Figure 30.1a.

production decision: The selection of the short-run rate of output (with existing plant and equipment).

Figure 30.1a also depicts the marginal and average total costs (MC and ATC) associated with the production of electricity. By equating marginal cost (MC) to price (marginal revenue, MR), we observe (point A) that profit maximization occurs at an output of 1,000 kilowatt hours per day. Total profits are illustrated by the shaded rectangle between the price line and the average total cost (ATC) curve.

The efficiency decision

efficiency decision: The choice of a production process for any given rate of output.

The profits illustrated in Figure 30.1a are achieved in part by use of the cheapest available fuel under the boilers (which create the steam that rotates the generators). Recall that the construction of a marginal cost curve presumes some knowledge of alternative production processes. Recall, too, that the **efficiency decision** requires a producer to choose that production process (and its associated cost curve) that minimizes costs for any particular rate of output.

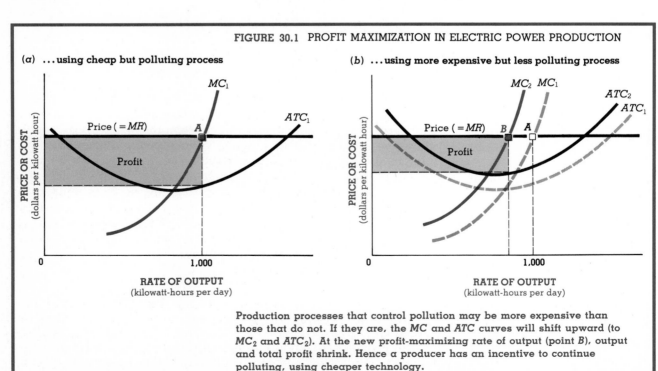

FIGURE 30.1 PROFIT MAXIMIZATION IN ELECTRIC POWER PRODUCTION

Production processes that control pollution may be more expensive than those that do not. If they are, the MC and ATC curves will shift upward (to MC_2 and ATC_2). At the new profit-maximizing rate of output (point B), output and total profit shrink. Hence a producer has an incentive to continue polluting, using cheaper technology.

Unfortunately, the efficiency decision in this case leads to the use of high-sulfur coal, the prime villain in SO_2 and particulate pollution. Other fuels, such as low-sulfur coal, fuel oil, and nuclear reactors, cost considerably more. Were you to switch to one of them, both the *ATC* and *MC* curves would shift upward, as in Figure 30.1*b*. Under these conditions, the most profitable rate of output would be less than before (point *B*), and total profits would decline (note the smaller profit rectangle in Figure 30.1*b*. Thus pollution abatement can be achieved, but only at significant cost to the plant.

The same kind of cost considerations lead the plant to engage in thermal pollution of adjacent waterways. Cool water must be run through an electric utility plant to keep the turbines from overheating. And once the water runs through the plant, it is too hot to recirculate. Hence it must be either dumped back into the adjacent river or cooled off by being circulated through cooling towers. As you might expect, it is cheaper simply to dump the hot water in the river. The fish don't like it, but they don't have to pay the construction costs associated with cooling towers. Were you to get on the antipollution bandwagon and build those towers, your production costs would rise, just as they did in Figure 30.1*b*. The fish would benefit, but at your expense.

The big question here is whether you and your fellow stockholders would be willing to incur higher costs in order to cut down on pollution. Eliminating either the air pollution or the water pollution emanating from the electric plant will cost a lot of money; eliminating both will cost much more. And to whose benefit? To the people who live downstream and downwind? We don't expect profit-maximizing producers to take such concerns into account. The behavior of profit-maximizers is guided by comparisons of revenues and costs, not by aesthetic concerns or the welfare of fish.

EXTERNALITIES: SOCIAL VS. PRIVATE COSTS

The moral of this story—and the critical factor in pollution behavior—is that people tend to maximize their personal welfare, balancing private benefits against private costs. For the electric power plant, this means making production decisions on the basis of revenues received and costs incurred. The fact that the power plant imposes costs on others, in the form of air and water pollution, is irrelevant to its profit-maximizing decision. Those costs are *external* to the firm and do not appear on its profit-and-loss statement. Those **external costs** are no less real, but they are incurred by society at large rather than by the firm itself.

externalities: Costs (or benefits) of a market activity borne by a third party; the difference between the social and private costs (benefits) of a market activity.

Externalities in production

Whenever external costs exist, a private firm will not allocate its resources and operate its plant in such a way as to maximize social welfare. In effect, society is permitting the power plant the free use of valued resources—clean air and clean water. Thus the power plant has a tremendous incentive to substitute those resources for others (such as high-priced fuel or cooling towers) in the production

"Gentlemen, we have polluted the environment of this community long enough. It's time we moved our plant to a new location."

Reproduced by special permission of *Playboy* Magazine, © 1973 by Playboy.

social costs: The full resource costs of an economic activity, including externalities.

private costs: The costs of an economic activity directly borne by the immediate producer or consumer (excluding externalities).

process. The inefficiency of such an arrangement is obvious when we recall that the function of markets is to allocate scarce resources in accordance with consumers' expressed demands. Yet here we are, proclaiming a high value for clean air and clean water and encouraging the power plant to use up both resources by offering them at zero cost to the firm.

The inefficiency of this market arrangement can be expressed in terms of a distinction between social costs and private costs. **Social costs** are the total costs of all the resources used in a particular production activity. They are to be distinguished from **private costs,** which are the resource costs incurred by the specific producer.

Ideally, a producer's private costs will encompass all the attendant social costs, and his production decisions will be consistent with our social welfare. Unfortunately, this happy identity does not always exist, as our experience with the power plant illustrates. When social costs differ from private costs, external costs exist, and are, in fact, equal to the difference between them.[5] In such cases, the market mechanism will lead us to an undesirable allocation of resources, and thus to less social welfare than might otherwise be obtained.

The distinction between social and private costs is illustrated in Figure 30.2, which again depicts the cost situation confronting the electric power plant. Notice that we use two different marginal cost curves this time. The lower one, the *private MC* curve, reflects the private costs incurred by the power plant when it operates on a profit-maximization basis, using high-sulfur coal and no cooling towers. It is identical to the *MC* curve of Figure 30.1*a*. We now know, however, that such operations impose external costs on others in the

[5] The term "externality" may be used to refer to either external costs or external benefits; here we are dealing only with external costs.

FIGURE 30.2 SOCIAL VS. PRIVATE COSTS

Social costs exceed private costs by the amount of external costs (externalities). Production decisions based on private costs alone will lead to more output (q_p) of a good than is socially desired (q_s).

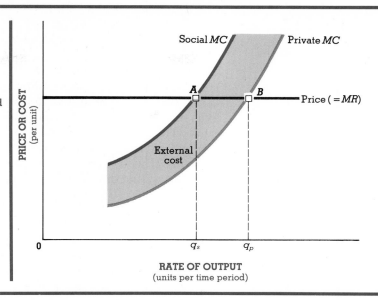

form of air and water pollution. Hence social costs are higher than private costs, as reflected in the *social MC* curve. Were we to maximize social welfare, we would equate social marginal costs with marginal revenue (point *A* in Figure 30.2) and thus produce at the output level q_s. The private profit maximizer, however, equates *private* marginal costs and marginal revenue (point *B*) and thus ends up producing at q_p, making more profit but also causing more pollution. As a general rule, ***if pollution costs are external, firms will produce too much of a polluting good.***

Externalities in consumption

The divergence between private and social costs that is apparent in the case of electric power plants can also be observed in many consumption activities. A consumer, like a producer, tends to maximize personal welfare. Among other things, we buy and use more of those goods and services that yield the highest satisfaction (marginal utility) per dollar expended. By implication (and the law of demand), we tend to use more of a product if we can get it at a discount—that is, pay less than the full price. Unfortunately, the "discount" often takes the form of an external cost imposed on neighbors and friends.

One familiar illustration of such a discount is automobile driving. The amount of driving one does is influenced by the price of a car and the marginal costs of driving it. As was convincingly illustrated during the energy crisis of the 1970s, people buy smaller cars and drive less when the attendant marginal costs (for instance, gasoline prices) increase substantially. But automobile use involves not only *private costs* but *external costs* as well. As observed earlier, auto emissions (carbon monoxide, hydrocarbons, and nitrogen oxides) have long been a principal cause of air pollution. In effect, automobile drivers have been able to use a valued resource, clean air, at no cost to themselves. Naturally, they tended to use more of that resource than they otherwise would, thus lowering their private marginal costs and driving and polluting more. Few motorists saw any personal benefit in installing exhaust-control devices, because the quality of the air they breathed would be little affected by their efforts. Hence private cost structures led to excessive pollution when social cost structures were dictating cleaner air.

A divergence between social and private costs can be observed even in the simplest of consumer activities, such as throwing an empty beer can out the window of your car. To hang onto the beer can and later dispose of it in a trash barrel involves personal effort and thus private marginal costs. To throw it out the window not only is more exciting but effectively transfers the burden of disposal costs to someone else. Thus private costs can be distinguished from social costs. The resulting externality ends up as roadside litter.

The same kind of divergence between private and social costs helps to explain why people abandon old cars in the street rather than haul them to scrapyards. It also explains why people use vacant lots as open dumps. In all of these cases, **the polluter benefits by substituting external costs for private costs.** In other words, market incentives encourage pollution.

SOME POLICY OPTIONS

In view of the strong market incentives that encourage pollution, we are lucky that our pollution problems are not worse than they are. Fortunately, only a handful of industries confront significant opportunities to substitute social costs for private costs in the production process, at least with respect to our air and water resources. On the consumer side of the market, such substitution possibilities are more widespread, but are held in check somewhat by social consciousness and frequent legal sanction. Nevertheless, our pollution problems are serious enough to require a public policy response. What can be done?

To begin with, we should realize that people will continue to respond to market incentives whenever they can. This suggests two general approaches for pollution-abatement policy:

- Alter market incentives in such a way that they discourage pollution.
- Bypass market incentives with some form of regulatory intervention.

Altering market incentives

Insofar as market incentives are concerned, the key to pollution abatement is to eliminate the divergence between private costs and social costs. As we have observed, it is the opportunity to shift some costs onto others that lies at the heart of the pollution problem. If we could somehow compel producers to *internalize* all costs—to pay for both private and previously external costs—the divergence would disappear, along with the incentive to pollute. Thus we have to find a way to make polluters pay for their pollution.

emission charge: A fee imposed on polluters, based on the quantity of pollution.

EMISSION CHARGES   One possibility is to establish a system of **emission** (or effluent) **charges,** direct costs attached to the act of polluting. Suppose that we let you keep your power plant and permit you to operate it as your profit-maximizing calculations dictate. The only difference is that we no longer agree to supply you with clean air and cool water at zero cost. From now on, we will charge you in accordance with the amount of these scarce resources that you use. We might, say, charge you 2 cents for every gram of noxious emission you discharge into the air. In addition, we might charge you 3 cents for every gallon of water you use, heat, and discharge back into the river.

Confronted with such emission charges, you would surely be motivated to reconsider your efficiency and production decisions. Consider again the choice of fuels. We earlier chose high-sulfur coal, for the very good reason that it was the cheapest available fuel. Now, however, there is an additional cost attached to burning such fuel, in the form of an emission charge on noxious pollutants. This cost may change the efficiency decision in one of two ways. The increased cost of using high-sulfur coal may encourage you to switch to other, cleaner sources of energy. Or it may prove more economical to install "scrubbers" and other smokestack controls that reduce the volume of emissions from the burning of high-sulfur coal. This would entail additional capital outlays for the necessary abatement equipment, but would leave operating margins unchanged. The choice between these two options will depend on the relative costs involved. Of course, if emission charges are too low, neither option may be as profitable as continuing to burn and pollute with high-sulfur coal and simply paying a nominal fee. It is evident, however, that we could impose emission charges high enough to make the less polluting production alternatives appear more profitable.

The same kind of relative cost considerations would apply to the thermal pollution associated with the power plant. The choice heretofore has been between building expensive cooling towers (and not polluting) and not incurring such capital costs (and simply discharging the heated water into the river). The profit-maximizing choice was fairly obvious. Now, however, when the choice is between building cooling towers and paying out a steady flow of emission charges, the profit-maximizing decision is not so evident. The decisive factor will be how high we set the emission charges. If the emission charges are set high enough, the producer will find it unprofitable to pollute.

What works on producers will also sway consumers. Surely you've heard of deposits on returnable bottles. At one time the deposits were imposed by the beverage producer to encourage you to bring the bottle back so it could be used again. But producers discovered that such deposits discouraged sales and yielded very little cost savings. The economics of returnable bottles were further undermined by the advent of metal cans and, later, plastic bottles. Thirty years ago, virtually all soft drinks and most beer came in returnable bottles. Today, returnable bottles are rarely used. One result is the inclusion of over 30 billion bottles and 60 billion cans in our solid-waste-disposal problem.

We could reduce this solid-waste problem by imposing a deposit on all beverage containers. This would internalize pollution costs for the consumer and render the throwing of a beer can out the window equivalent to throwing away money. Some people would still find the thrill worthwhile, but they would be followed around by others who attached more value to money. The state of Oregon imposed a five-cent deposit on beverage containers in 1972 and soon thereafter discovered that beverage-container litter in Oregon declined by 81 percent! Since that time, several states and many communities have also imposed mandatory deposits as a mechanism for eliminating the distinction between social and private costs.

RECYCLING MATERIALS   An important bonus that emission charges offer is an increased incentive for the recycling of materials, and thus a reduction in our solid-waste problem. The glass and metal in used bottles and cans can be recycled to produce new bottles and cans. Such recycling not only eliminates a lot of unsightly litter, but also diminishes the need to mine new resources from the earth, a process that often involves its own environmental problems. The critical issue is once again relative costs and market incentives. A container producer has no incentive to use recycled materials unless they offer superior cost efficiency and thus greater profits. The largest component in the costs of recycled materials is usually the associated costs of collection and transportation. In this regard, an emission charge such as the 5-cent container deposit lowers collection costs because it motivates consumers to return all their bottles and cans to a central location.

POLLUTION FINES   Not far removed from the concept of emission charges is the use of fines or the imposition of cleanup costs. In some

EPA Ponders Letting Concerns Buy and Sell 'Right' to Pollute Air

---

Agency Studies Novel Ways to Clean Up Atmosphere But Hold Down the Costs

WASHINGTON —Douglas Costle, administrator of the Environmental Protection Agency, is looking into ways to peddle real filth.

The EPA chief talks about creating auctions and futures markets in which companies would buy and sell the "right" to spew pollutants into the air. His thesis: As long as all the companies in a specified area don't exceed strict emissions limits for that entire area, they could bid against one another to determine how much each could emit individually within the area. Mr. Costle even looks approvingly on the idea of private brokers arranging such deals.

Dirty-air transactions are among several novel, market-style ideas the EPA is seriously considering to help control pollution from industrial plants. Another notion is to allow companies to "bank," for future use, part of pollution savings they can achieve in an area. And the agency plans to test a "bubble concept" that would give manufacturers more leeway in deciding how best to reduce overall emissions from a single plant.

A Chance for Flexibility

The new approaches would be tested as possible alternatives to EPA antipollution regulations that tell companies how they must reduce plant emissions. Such rules frequently are sharply criticized both by industry and by government inflation-fighters as too rigid and too costly. "It may be that if you give (businessmen) some flexibility," Mr. Costle says, "they can find a more efficient way to control pollution than I could by coming in and doing the engineering for them."

—Douglas Martin

situations, such as an oil spill, the pollution is so sudden and concentrated that society has little choice but to clean it up quickly. The costs for such cleanup can be imposed on the polluter, however, through appropriate fines. Such fines would place the cost burden where it belongs. In addition, they would serve as an incentive for greater safety, for such things as double-hulled oil tankers and more efficient safety mechanisms on offshore oil wells. In the absence of pollution penalties, a producer has an incentive to avoid safety costs and take greater risks. The Water Quality Improvement Act of 1970 established financial liability for the cleanup costs involved in oil spills. It also required the producer to notify the government whenever such spills occurred.

The EPA acquired still greater authority to control oil and chemical spills with passage of the Comprehensive Environmental Response, Compensation, and Liability Act of 1980. That act establishes a tax on crude oil and an assortment of chemical products. The resulting revenues have created a "superfund" to be used to monitor and clean up hazardous oil and chemical spills. The act also allows the EPA to recoup *treble* damages from a firm that causes a spill but fails to help clean it up.

Bypassing market incentives

Although the potential benefits to be gained by using market incentives to encourage pollution abatement are substantial, they are not the only or always the best approach to the task. Consider again the case of automobile emissions. Were we to rely on emission charges as a mechanism for abating auto pollution, we might have to measure the amount of pollutants discharged by each vehicle and levy appropriate charges. But such a program would require tremendous effort and cost, because there are over 100 million cars on the road. In this case, the costs of monitoring emissions and levying charges might outweigh the benefits of reduced pollution. Certainly they would at least constitute a strong argument for seeking an alternative control mechanism.

In point of fact, public policy has relied almost exclusively on regulatory prohibitions. The federal government began regulating auto emissions in 1968 and got really serious under the provisions of the Clean Air Act of 1970. The act required auto manufacturers to reduce hydrocarbon, carbon monoxide, and nitrogen oxide emissions by 90 percent within six years of the act's passage. Although the timetable for reducing pollutants was later extended, the act did stimulate auto manufacturers to reduce auto emissions by 67 percent in a period of only five years.

Even stronger direct action against industrial polluters was initiated by the Environmental Protection Agency in 1977. For several years the EPA and the courts have been imposing fines on major polluters. In 1977, however, the EPA took advantage of a provision in the Clean Air Act that allows it to "blacklist" major polluters. A blacklisted firm is barred from doing business with the federal government. The first firm threatened with blacklisting was Kaiser Steel Corporation, which sells 20 percent of its output to the federal government. Once threatened with a loss of so much business, Kaiser stepped up its pollution-abatement efforts.

Public-sector behavior has also been affected by regulation. As we observed earlier (Chapter 3), most public-sector activity involves the production of goods and services with extensive externalities (both external benefits and external costs), and is not dictated by market prices and costs. Accordingly, changing market incentives would do little to reduce the pollution associated with public-sector activity (for example, highway construction). To remedy this situation, the National Environmental Policy Act of 1970 requires public agencies to give explicit consideration to environmental concerns in all major public actions. In particular, public agencies are required to formulate an environmental impact statement that discusses the environmental consequences of any contemplated action. Government agencies must also explore the environmental effects of alternative actions. In this way, the act provides some assurance that environmental considerations will become a routine feature of public-sector decision making.

THE ECONOMIC IMPACT OF POLLUTION CONTROL

If producers and consumers respond fully to altered incentives and regulations, the environment can be cleaned up dramatically. But such an antipollution effort will involve considerable cost. The EPA estimates that we shall have to spend an additional $518 billion in the period 1979–88 to achieve national air and water standards, while significantly reducing other forms of pollution (see Table 30.5). Such a huge outlay of resources will not only clean up the

TABLE 30.5 ESTIMATED MARGINAL POLLUTION-CONTROL EXPENDITURES, 1979–88 (billions of 1979 dollars)

The marginal cost of cleaning up pollution is substantial. This expense must be assessed in terms of its opportunity cost. Is a cleaner environment worth more than the goods and services forgone when resources are used to clean up pollution?

Kinds of pollution	Costs	
Air pollution		
Public	$ 19.5	
Private	279.6	
All air pollution		$299.1
Water pollution		
Public	$ 84.3	
Private	85.4	
All water pollution		$169.7
Solid-waste pollution		
Public	$ 4.6	
Private	$ 10.8	
All solid-waste pollution		$ 15.4
Noise pollution		$ 6.9
Land reclamation		$ 15.3
Toxic substances		$ 8.2
Drinking water		$ 2.7
Pesticides		$ 1.2
All forms of pollution		$518.5

Source: Council on Environmental Quality.

**REVISING THE
CLEAN AIR ACT:
STANDARDS VS. CHARGES**

The Clean Air Act of 1970 requires the EPA to set uniform standards for several air pollutants. "Primary" standards are intended to protect the public health; "secondary" standards are to protect property and general welfare.

In 1981 the Clean Air Act was scheduled for revision. As in earlier years, most of the debate was over the use of standards or charges as the mechanism for attaining cleaner air. Should the EPA require all producers (and consumers) to attain a uniform standard? Or should the EPA instead impose fines or other incentives to reach the same objective? Finally, should the EPA take greater account of the costs of meeting specific pollution controls and modify their enforcement accordingly?

The Reagan administration urged Congress to abandon the use of uniform national standards. It also urged the EPA to rely more on economic incentives (e.g., emission fees) than on the imposition of specific and uniform pollution-control standards and techniques. In this way, individual firms could operate more efficiently. Specifically, firms that could control their pollution at less cost would do so and avoid paying emission fees. By contrast, firms that faced high pollution-abatement costs would opt for less pollution control and higher fines. In the process, society would achieve the desired level of *average* pollution control at less total cost.

Opponents of the incentive approach offered several arguments. First, there is a strong ideological resistance to providing a "license to pollute." Environmentalists argue that everyone has a social obligation to control pollution. Second, it would be difficult to identify that fee which would exactly induce the desired level of pollution control. Even if it could be found, it would be politically tempting to raise or lower it as election circumstances dictated. Third, the use of pollution fines would necessitate high administrative and enforcement costs.

A survey of congressional, industry, and environmentalist participants in the Clean Air Act debate indicated that their views were worlds apart. Few understood the economic arguments for emission fees rather than uniform standards—and even fewer accepted them.* Ultimately Congress ducked the whole issue by simply extending the act another year (rather than explicitly renewing it).

* See Steven Kelman, "Economists and the Environmental Muddle," *Public Interest*, Summer 1981.

---

environment, but also affect more familiar economic outcomes. In this section we shall review a few of the anticipated effects.

Opportunity costs

Obviously, $518 billion is a lot of money, and the sum reflects enormous command over our productive resources. Although cleaning up the environment is a universally acknowledged goal, we must remind ourselves that those resources could be used to fulfill other goals as well. The $518 billion would buy a lot of subways and parks, or build decent homes for the poor. If we choose to devote those resources instead to environmental efforts, we shall have to forgo some other goods and services. This is not to say that environmental goals don't deserve that kind of priority, but simply to re-

opportunity cost: The most desired goods or services that are forgone in order to obtain something else.

mind us that any use of our scarce resources involves an **opportunity cost.**

Fortunately, the amount of additional resources required to clean up the environment is relatively modest in comparison to our productive capacity. GNP is expected to total nearly $30 trillion (in 1979 dollars) during the period 1979–88. On this basis, the environmental expenditures contemplated in Table 30.5 represent only 1.7 percent of total output.

The optimal rate of pollution

optimal rate of pollution: The rate of pollution that occurs when the marginal social benefit of pollution control equals its marginal social cost.

Whether 1.7 percent of GNP is too much or too little to spend on pollution control depends on the value we assign to other goods and services and to a cleaner environment. That is to say, the **optimal rate of pollution** occurs at the point at which the opportunity costs of further pollution control equal the benefits of further reductions in pollution. *To determine the optimal rate of pollution, we need to compare the marginal social benefits of additional pollution control with the marginal social costs of additional pollution-control expenditure.* If another dollar spent on pollution control yields no more than a dollar of social benefits, then additional pollution-control expenditure is not desirable. In such a situation, the goods and services that would be forsaken for additional pollution control are more valued than the environmental improvements that would result.

Who will pay?

Because clean air, water, and land are not market goods, the calculation of the marginal social benefits of pollution control is a formidable task. It is far easier to determine who will pay for the associated costs. Pollution-abatement efforts will not affect all producers and consumers equally. A relatively small number of economic activities account for the bulk of emissions and effluents. These activities will clearly have to bear a disproportionate share of the cleanup burden.

To ascertain how the burden of environmental protection will be distributed, consider first the electric power plant we discussed earlier. As we observed (Fig. 30.2), the plant's output will be reduced if production decisions are based on social rather than private marginal costs; that is, if environmental consequences are considered. If the plant itself is compelled to pay full social costs, in the form of either compulsory investment or emission charges, its profits will be reduced. Were no other changes to take place, the burden of environmental improvements would be borne primarily by the producer.

Such a scenario is unlikely, however. Rather than absorb all of the costs of pollution controls themselves, producers will seek to pass some of this burden on to their customers in the form of higher prices. Their ability to do so will depend on the extent of competition in their industry, their relative cost position in it, and the price elasticity of consumer demand. In reality, the electric power industry is not very competitive and its prices are subject to government regulation. In addition, consumer demand is relatively price inelastic. Accordingly, the profit-maximizing producer will appeal to the state or local power commission for an increase in electricity prices based on the costs of pollution control. Electric power consumers are likely to end up footing part or all of the environmental bill. This distribution of costs may be regarded as equitable because the increased prices will more fully reflect the social costs associated with electricity use.

In addition to the electric power industry, the automobile, paper, steel, and chemical industries will be adversely affected by pollution controls. In all of these cases, the prices of the related products will increase, in some instances by significant percentages. These price increases will help to reduce pollution in two ways. First, they will help to pay for pollution-control equipment. Second, they will encourage consumers to change their expenditure patterns in the direction of less polluting goods.

The same kinds of arguments apply to public-sector expenditures for pollution control. If a municipality wants to clean up the water, it will have to invest in better sewage and treatment facilities. If it finances these investments out of its existing budget, it will have to cut back on expenditures in other areas—schools, roads, public welfare. If it wants to maintain existing levels of those services, it will have to finance its pollution-control investments out of increased taxes, higher emission charges, or aid from Washington. Higher emission charges are the most efficient and equitable means of finance, especially if the pollution problem is localized and its sources easily monitored. Grants from the federal government are obviously the easiest method of local finance. They represent some equity to the extent that the beneficiaries of pollution control extend across state and local jurisdictions. In recent years, the federal government has assumed a large responsibility for such expenditures. In fiscal 1982, the federal government gave over $3 billion to state and local governments for pollution control.

TRANSITIONAL DISLOCATIONS Even though the resource requirements for environmental protection are relatively modest and the means for allocating them known, we should not conclude that our cleanup efforts will proceed painlessly. As we have already noted, some producers and consumers will end up paying a disproportionate share of the costs. Even though those large shares may be justified on the basis of pollution activity, they will inflict economic losses on specific individuals. Indeed, in some cases, the added costs of environmental protection may be so great as to force a plant to shut down. According to surveys by the EPA and the U.S. Department of Commerce, 107 plants were closed in the period 1971—77 as a result of pollution-control regulations and costs. Over 20,000 workers lost their jobs. Although these plant closings involved a very tiny proportion of the labor force, the affected workers and producers hardly welcomed their role in environmental progress. In general, affected firms and workers seek to postpone or avoid their losses through legal and political action. To reduce political friction and ease the transition to a cleaner environment, public policy has to respond to such microeconomic costs. The response may entail phasing out plants, retraining and relocating workers, or rebuilding a community's economic base.

SUMMARY

▪ Air, water, and solid-waste pollution impose social and economic costs. The costs of pollution include the direct damages inflicted on our health and resources, the expense of cleaning up, and the general aesthetic deterioration of the environment.

▪ Pollution is an externality, a cost of a market activity imposed on someone (a third party) other than the immediate producer or consumer.

▪ Producers and consumers generally operate on the basis of private benefits and costs. Accordingly, a private producer or consumer has an incentive to minimize his own costs by transforming private costs into external costs. One way of making such a substitution is to pollute—to use "free" air and water rather than install pollution-control equipment, or to leave the job of waste disposal to others.

▪ Social costs are the total amount of resources used in a production or consumption process. When social costs are greater than private costs, there are external costs. In this case, individuals will be motivated to produce and consume more of a product than is socially desirable, because they are not compelled to pay its full (social) cost. This motivation is readily illustrated with marginal cost curves and profit-maximizing production and efficiency decisions.

▪ One way to correct the market inefficiency created by externalities would be to compel producers and consumers to internalize all (social) costs. This result could be attained by the imposition of emission charges. Such charges would create an incentive to invest in pollution-abatement equipment, recycle reusable materials, or otherwise control pollution.

▪ An alternative approach to cleaning up the environment is to require specific pollution controls or to prohibit specific kinds of activities. The appropriate choice between the market and regulatory approaches depends on the feasibility and cost of monitoring pollution activity, as well as on ideological and political considerations.

▪ The opportunity costs of pollution control are the most desired goods and services given up when factors of production are used to control pollution. The optimal rate of pollution is reached when the marginal social benefits of further pollution control equal associated marginal social costs.

▪ In addition to diverting resources, pollution-control efforts alter relative prices, change the mix of output, and redistribute incomes. These effects are salutary from the perspective of environmental protection but cause losses for particular groups and thus require special economic or political attention.

Terms to remember

Define the following terms:

production decision	**private costs**
efficiency decision	**emission charge**
externalities	**opportunity cost**
social costs	**optimal rate of pollution**

Questions for discussion

1. Should we try to eliminate *all* pollution? What economic considerations might favor permitting some pollution?

2. Why would auto manufacturers resist exhaust-control devices? How would their costs, sales, and profits be affected?

3. Does anyone have an incentive to maintain auto-exhaust control devices in good working order? How can we ensure that they will be maintained?

4. Suppose we established a $10,000 fine for water pollution. Would some companies still find that polluting was economical? Under what conditions?

Problem

The following cost schedule depicts the private and social costs associated with the production of apacum, a highly toxic fertilizer. The sales price of apacum is $18 per ton.

Output (in tons)	0	1	2	3	4	5	6	7	8
Total private cost	5	7	13	23	37	55	77	103	133
Total social cost	7	13	31	61	103	157	223	301	391

Using the schedule:

(a) Graph the private and social marginal costs associated with apacum production.

(b) Identify the profit-maximizing private and social outputs and associated profits.

(c) On the basis of these curves, identify the pollution fee (fine) we would have to charge per unit in order to persuade the producer to produce the socially optimal rate of output.

CHAPTER 31
WORK AND WELFARE

The war on poverty is not a struggle simply to support people, to make them dependent on the generosity of others. It is a struggle to give people a chance. It is an effort to allow them to develop and use their capacities, as we have been allowed to develop and use ours, so that they can share, as others share, in the promise of this nation.

—LYNDON B. JOHNSON, 1964

[Welfare is] a cancer that is destroying those it should succor and threatening society itself.

—RONALD REAGAN, 1971

Public policy toward the poor has been plagued by a persistent dilemma. Should we provide poor people with enough income to buy "adequate" nutrition, housing, and clothing? Or should we instead provide them with improved opportunities to earn their own incomes? Quite simply, should we offer welfare or work to low-income families?

It is tempting to respond that *both* welfare and work are needed. In practice, however, the two policy options often conflict. The availability of welfare benefits reduces the need to work. All too often, welfare also lessens the *incentives* to work. On the other hand, not everyone who is poor has the ability or opportunity to earn an adequate income.

The trade-off between work and welfare is examined in this chapter. We start by looking at the scope of poverty in America. The "welfare system" is then described, with an emphasis on its work-inhibiting features. As we shall discover, there is no easy solution to the "welfare mess."

THE EXTENT OF POVERTY

To be counted as poor in America, an individual or family must be unable to provide for the essential needs of food, shelter, and clothing. Naturally, there is not going to be universal agreement about how little is not enough. Much effort has been expended in trying to establish an acceptable standard of poverty. Large families clearly have greater needs than do smaller families and thus could be regarded as poor even if they had slightly more income than a smaller, nonpoor family. A man and wife with six children and an annual income of $7,000 are demonstrably in greater financial straits than a childless couple earning $6,000 a year or a college student earning $5,000. In recognition of these differences in need, ***the official poverty index is based on a comparison of cash income and family size.***

Table 31.1 presents the official poverty standards for 1981. A single person was counted as poor in 1981 if he or she received less than $4,620 in cash income. A family of four, on the other hand, could have received up to $9,287 in 1981 (approximately $10,000 in 1983 dollars) and still been counted among the poor. A family of six with as much as $12,449 was included in the poverty count. Although there is some degree of arbitrariness in these "poverty lines," they are based on the costs of providing a subsistence food budget and other needs. They serve as a convenient yardstick for measuring the dimensions of poverty in the United States.

According to the Census Bureau, approximately 32 million Americans—nearly one in every seven people in the country—had cash incomes in 1981 that were smaller than the minimum standards shown in Table 31.1. Figure 31.1 indicates who all of these poor people were. In terms of sheer numbers, the poverty population is dominated by younger families with children. Indeed, the poverty population includes over 12 million children living either with two parents (6 million) or only their mother (6 million). Nearly one-third of all the poor are black, and a substantial proportion of the poor are over the age of 65. In general, these groups of the poor are located in all areas of the country, although the percentage of poor people in the South and in urban ghettos is slightly higher than elsewhere.

An exaggerated count These official statistics on the extent of poverty in America paint a grim picture. Not only do they imply that one out of eight Americans is poor, but they also suggest that the number of poor people is growing. The number of people officially counted as poor in 1981 was

---

TABLE 31.1 FEDERAL POVERTY STANDARDS, BY FAMILY SIZE, 1981

The official definition of poverty relates current income to the "minimal" needs of a family. The poverty standard varies with family size and source of income (farm vs. nonfarm).

Number of family members	Family income
1	$ 4,620
2	5,917
3	7,250
4	9,287
5	11,007
6	12,449
7	14,110

Source: U.S. Department of Commerce, Bureau of the Census.

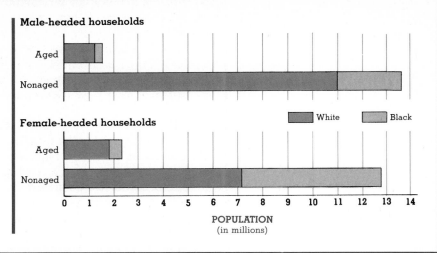

FIGURE 31.1 AGE AND FAMILY STATUS OF THE POOR, 1981

The poverty population is composed of three distinct groups: aged persons, two-parent families, and single-parent families. Almost all of the latter are headed by women.

Source: U.S. Department of Commerce, Bureau of the Census.

---

in-kind transfers: Direct transfers of goods and services rather than cash; for example, food stamps and Medicaid.

larger than in any year since 1966. Yet in that span of time a massive War on Poverty had been undertaken, and hundreds of billions of dollars had been paid out in income transfers.

One reason the official poverty count remains so high is that it neglects in-kind transfers. As we first noted in Chapter 29, the government not only provides *cash* transfers but **in-kind transfers** as well. These transfers include food stamps, Medicaid, and housing assistance.

FOOD STAMPS   Food stamps are simply coupons ("stamps") that may be used to purchase food. Food stamps are given to poor families, who use them like regular money at the grocery store. The grocer, in turn, cashes the stamps in at a local bank, which redeems them at face value from the government. Thus food stamps increase the *real* income of poor families by increasing the amount of goods and services they can consume at any given level of *cash* income. In 1982 a poor family of four could receive a food-stamp allotment of up to $233 a month ($2,796 a year). The actual value of the stamps a family gets depends on its needs, as measured by family size and cash income.

MEDICAID   Even larger than the food-stamp program is Medicaid, a program that provides medical services to the poor. Under Medicaid, an eligible person can use the services of a doctor or hospital just like anyone else. The difference is that the Medicaid patient simply passes the bill on to the government, rather than paying for it himself or submitting it to a private insurance company. Obviously, the amount of benefit a poor family gets from Medicaid depends on the amount of medical treatment it requires. In 1982 nearly all public-welfare recipients made some use of Medicaid, as did many others who had incomes just above the poverty standard. The average value of the services received exceeded $1,000 per family.

HOUSING ASSISTANCE In addition to food and medical services, a poor family can receive housing assistance. For the most part, such assistance is provided in the form of public housing, usually large housing projects owned and operated by the government. In a public housing project, the tenants enjoy cheap (subsidized) rents, although not a great deal more. Nevertheless, the fact that they are paying less than the market value of their apartments means that they are effectively receiving an income transfer. Although fewer than 3 million families receive such transfers every year, the average transfer works out to something like $1,000 a year. In addition to the public housing projects, there are housing assistance programs for low-income people who are renting or even buying their apartments and homes in the private market. In these programs, the rent or mortgage payment is reduced, with the government (the Department of Housing and Urban Development, or HUD) making up the difference.

Table 31.2 provides a summary of these major in-kind transfers. In 1981 alone, nearly $40 billion was spent on such in-kind transfers. None of this income was counted by the Census Bureau in determining who was poor. The Census Bureau counted only *cash* transfers and ignored *in-kind* transfers when computing people's incomes.

One reason the Census Bureau has ignored in-kind benefits is that their value is difficult to compute. Consider Medicaid, for example. The amount of Medicaid a person receives depends on how sick he or she is. If the full value of Medicaid services were counted as income, a serious illness would greatly increase a person's imputed income. By this measure, people would climb out of poverty by becoming ill or disabled!

Although there are difficulties in assessing the market value of in-kind transfers, such transfers clearly increase the real incomes of recipients. As a consequence, **the official poverty count, based on cash incomes only, exaggerates the extent of poverty.** The true count of poor people is probably 20 to 40 percent less than official estimates.

TABLE 31.2 IN-KIND TRANSFERS, 1981

The government transfers billions of dollars to the poor in the form of in-kind benefits. None of these benefits are counted, however, in census surveys of the poverty population. Hence the official count of poverty is too high.

Program	Number of recipients (millions)	Average benefit per household (per month)	Total annual (billions of dollars)
Food stamps	23.0	$ 85	$11.3
Medicaid	22.0	100	16.8
Housing assistance	3.4	90	6.8
Nutrition programs (including school lunches)	25.7	20	5.0
Total	74.1		$39.9

Source: Congressional Budget Office.

POLICY OPTIONS

Even after adjustments for in-kind transfers, there are still lots of poor people in the United States. Moreover, there appears to be a persistent public desire to aid the poor. The question is: What form should that assistance take? Should we encourage poor people to *earn* more income? Or should we simply provide them with income transfers?

More work

Encouraging poor people to work is a generally acceptable policy option. There are limits, however, to the effectiveness of this approach. Many poor people are too old or too sick to participate in the labor market. Others have full-time child-care responsibilities that make it difficult to hold a steady job. As Figure 31.1 indicates, 3.9 million poor people are over age 65 and another 12.8 million live in single-parent households.

We must also be careful to note that labor-force participation itself is no ticket out of poverty. In 1981 approximately 50 percent of the families in poverty participated in the labor force at some point during the year. Among poor families whose head was 25 to 64 years old, over 60 percent participated. Over a million of those families were headed by individuals who held full-time jobs all year long.

labor-force participant: Someone who is either employed for pay or actively seeking paid employment.

One reason even **labor-force participants** remain poor is that they have inadequate *human capital*. **Human capital** is the bundle of skills and abilities that a person carries into the labor market. Such capital may include specialized vocational skills, a high level of general education, or simply raw talent. The impact of human capital on employment prospects is evident from our earlier discussion (Chapter 26) of marginal productivity. The more human capital an individual has to offer, the greater will be his or her **marginal productivity** in any given production process. By the same token, individuals with little human capital offer less productivity and are more likely to experience low wages and unemployment.

human capital: The bundle of skills an individual possesses.

marginal productivity: The change in total output that results from employment of one additional unit of input (e.g., one more worker).

Having the "right" amount of human capital is itself no guarantee of job success, however. Such assets as education merely define the characteristics of the supply of labor. It is equally important to examine the nature of the *demand* for labor. Of particular concern in this regard is **cyclical unemployment.** When the demand for labor is inadequate, there aren't enough jobs to go around. Hence even people with "adequate" human capital discover that their earnings are too low.

cyclical unemployment: Unemployment attributable to a lack of job vacancies; unemployment that results from an inadequate level of aggregate demand.

Discrimination also precludes full use of human capital. Minority groups, women, and the offspring of the poor are generally not given an equal chance to acquire the "right" set of human-capital characteristics. Nor do they have an equal chance to use those characteristics in the labor market.[1] Hence race, sex, and class discrimination have significant impact on both the distribution and the extent of poverty. Even in a relatively prosperous economy, discrimination tends to create artificial barriers between workers and jobs.

[1] The nature and impact of discrimination are discussed in Chapter 32.

An Oversupply of College Graduates Forces Some into Lower-Level Jobs

In 1974, Anne Harbut went to Pennsylvania State University, at the age of 33, to earn a graduate degree because she wanted to run a social-services program. Today she is doing routine office work, and she is bitter.

"Basically, I shuffle a lot of papers across my desk, I fill out forms and interview people for low-level jobs," she complains. Unable to find a suitable post in her profession, she has worked since last summer as a personnel assistant at Philadelphia's Metropolitan Hospital.

"It's boring and at times it seems pointless," she says. "Once I had a job working on a construction gang in the Swiss Alps. It was more satisfying than this. At least we were accomplishing something. At the end of the day, we could see the road getting built."

Like Mrs. Harbut, large numbers of Americans are working at jobs for which their training has made them overqualified. They are the products of the nation's education binge over the last two decades, when colleges were churning out graduates at a far faster rate than the economy required. Government statistics show that while the proportion of college-educated members of the work force nearly doubled over that period, to 17.6% in 1979, there was more demand for service jobs than for general white-collar skills. This mismatch is exacerbated by the current recession.

Higher Education Oversold

As a result, the Labor Department predicts that during this decade one in four college graduates will take jobs in occupations that don't require a four-year college education. This is in sharp contrast to the booming 1960s, when "persons with college degrees could generally find the kind of professional, technical or managerial jobs they wanted," says Michael Pilot, who heads the department's occupation outlook program.

"In short, we've oversold the value of higher education," concludes Sar Levitan, an economist who specializes in employment problems. "It's a further tattering of the American dream."

—Robert S. Greenberger

The objective of "more work," then, entails several distinct policy approaches. First and foremost, it requires the attainment of full employment. Professor Harry Johnson summarized the point well: "In the absence of a policy of raising the demand for labor . . . , ad hoc policies for remedying poverty by piecemeal assaults on particular poverty-associated characteristics are likely to prove both ineffective and expensive. The most effective way to attack poverty is to attack unemployment, not the symptoms of it."[2]

If people are to work themselves out of poverty, they also need to acquire more human capital. The government, then, can further reduce poverty by providing increased education and training opportunities, particularly for low-income families.

More welfare

Although the work options for reducing poverty are straightforward, their success is not assured. Moreover, the work approach strikes many observers as unnecessarily roundabout and uncertain. If we really want to eliminate poverty, why not simply give people more money? Among others, economist Milton Friedman and urbanologist Irving Kristol have wondered aloud whether our public commitment to end poverty is sincere in the light of our failure to provide this obvious remedy.

income transfers: Payments to individuals for which no current goods or services are exchanged; e.g., social security, welfare, and unemployment benefits.

But the apparent simplicity of **income-transfer** solutions to poverty is deceptive. We could, of course, provide enough income transfers to close the poverty gap—the difference between what the poor now have and what they need to maintain minimum living standards. In 1981 that gap was only $37 billion, or just over 1 percent of

[2] Harry G. Johnson, "Poverty and Unemployment," in *The Economics of Poverty*, ed. Burton Weisbrod (Englewood Cliffs, N.J.: Prentice-Hall, 1965), p. 170.

total GNP. An expansion of income transfers to fill this gap, however, might create significant problems.

First of all, exclusive reliance on income transfers as a "solution" to poverty serves to perpetuate the poverty problem. Simply transferring income to the needy does little to improve their opportunities for employment and upward mobility. The added income makes life easier for the poor, of course, but otherwise leaves their circumstances unchanged. Thus income transfers are best viewed as an interim form of support, especially for those who are in a position to benefit from increased education or employment opportunities.[3]

Even on an interim basis, however, income transfers give rise to problems. Suppose we guaranteed everyone an income equal to the 1983 poverty standard of $10,000 for a nonfarm family of four. Any family earning less than this amount would receive an income-transfer payment to make up the difference, thus eliminating all existing poverty.

Unfortunately, this kind of program creates a strong incentive for persons just above the poverty line to leave the labor market. If offered an income transfer, people working at dead-end, low-paying jobs may abandon employment and join the ranks of the nonworking poor. Recall (from Chapter 25) that the decision to work is largely a response to the financial and psychological rewards associated with employment. People in dull, dirty, low-paying jobs get little of either. Hence by quitting their jobs, declaring themselves poor, and accepting a guaranteed income transfer, they would gain much more leisure at little financial or psychological cost.

People already counted as poor would have a similar incentive. By substituting public transfers for the meager employment income they already possessed, they would work less while still maintaining their incomes. Accordingly, **the provision of income transfers may conflict with established work incentives.** Hence both the size of the poverty population and the "need" for income transfers may be sensitive to the particular form our income-transfer policies take. The following section highlights this work–welfare dilemma.

THE WORK–WELFARE DILEMMA

The welfare system   Although many people tend to think of welfare as one big, centrally administered program, the realities of welfare are quite otherwise. As we noted earlier, the welfare system is composed of two distinct kinds of assistance. Some programs provide cash assistance to the poor. Other programs provide in-kind assistance—such things as housing, food, and medical services. Within each classification, there are a variety of programs, each with its own characteristics, regulations, and objectives. The programs are designed and administered by a changing mix of state, local, and federal governments.

Table 31.3 provides a summary of the major programs that pro-

---

[3] If the education and employment opportunities are slow in coming, however, the "interim" support may have to continue for a long time. In the interim, the children of the poor will at least benefit from improved nutrition and shelter.

TABLE 31.3 CASH-ASSISTANCE PROGRAMS, 1981

AFDC, the largest welfare program, provides cash assistance to families with children. SSI helps the aged and disabled. GA assists those poor people who aren't eligible for other cash-assistance programs.

Program	Number of recipients	Average benefit per household (per month)	Total annual payments (billions of dollars)
Supplemental security income (SSI)	4 million	$185	$ 7.2
Aid to families with dependent children (AFDC)	11 million	300	13.2
General assistance (GA)	1 million	165	1.6
Total	16 million		$22.0

Source: U.S. Department of Health and Human Services.

vide cash assistance to the poor. Each of the three programs listed in the table is directed toward a distinct population group. The federal supplemental security income (SSI) program aids the aged, the blind, and the permanently disabled. In 1981 it provided cash assistance to 4 million people at an estimated annual cost of approximately $7 billion. By contrast, the federal-state aid to families with dependent children (AFDC) program served 11 million people at an annual cost of roughly $13 billion. The third program, general assistance (GA), is operated solely under state and local auspices to provide help to those who are poor but do not fit one of the other two categories.

Who gets welfare

Although the cash assistance programs clearly help many people and cost a lot of money, they do not fully meet the needs of the poor. First, not all of the poor are helped. Of the 32 million people counted as poor in 1981, only 16 million received cash assistance. Second, even those who were helped did not receive enough income to stave off poverty. The typical AFDC family (mother and two or three children), for example, received less than half the cash income the government estimated it needed. Moreover, the amount of cash assistance provided varies tremendously from state to state. In 1981, average AFDC payments for a welfare family ranged from $1,000 a year in Mississippi to over $5,000 in California.

Conspicuously missing from the welfare rolls in nearly every state, regardless of the amount of cash assistance provided, are male-headed poor families. Being poor and in a family with children is not sufficient qualification for AFDC support. The presence of an able-bodied male adult in the home is taken as prima facie evidence that the family is capable of its own support. AFDC payments are largely reserved for fatherless homes. Male-headed poor families rarely receive welfare benefits, regardless of the needs such families may have.[4]

[4] An exception to this rule is the AFDC-UF program, which provides benefits to poor families with unemployed fathers. But the program is too small and restrictive to merit attention here. In early 1981 only 920,000 persons were receiving AFDC-UF benefits in 27 states.

Breaking Through the Welfare Myths

From remarks by Secretary of Health, Education and Welfare Joseph A. Califano Jr. before the Washington Press Club April 27:

Past debates about welfare have too often focused on pernicious myths about the poor in America. These myths have been perpetrated and perpetuated by ignorance, by incoherent and demagogic discussion by public officials, and inadequate reporting by the media. It is imperative that the forthcoming national debate on welfare not focus on phony issues, false choices or unrealistic expectations that have so clouded past discussions. . . .

Five myths have come to distort public understanding of the poor and welfare.

Myth No. 1—the most pernicious and most widespread—is that people are poor because they don't work and don't want to work, that the welfare rolls are replete with lazy loafers.

The facts are quite different.

Nearly 71 per cent of the 26 million poor Americans are people that we do not normally ask to work: children and young people under 16, the aged, the severely disabled, students or mothers with children under six. Another 19 per cent of the poor population works either full-time or part-time. Thus, 90 per cent of poor Americans either work full-or-part-time or are people no civilized society would force to work. . . .

Only 2 per cent of the 26 million poor people even resemble the mythical welfare stereotype—non-aged, non-disabled males who do not work. But census figures indicate that most of this group is between 62 and 64, ill, or looking for work. . . .

Myth No. 2 is that most of the poor are poor for life—that they represent a permanent stagnant group.

The fact is that the poverty population is extremely fluid—with sizable numbers of people moving in and out of poverty with remarkable frequency. Each year about 7.5 to 10 million people move above the poverty line, and a like number become poor.

Over the period 1967 through 1972, only 3 per cent of the American population was poor in every one of those 6 years. More than one-fifth—21 per cent—of the American population was poor in at least one of those 6 years. . . .

Most of the poor are poor, not because of some inherent character flaw or personal failing, but because of events they cannot control. And many of them do, in fact, regain higher incomes and climb back out of poverty.

Myth No. 3 is that the poor are mostly black and non-white. The fact is that 69 per cent of the American poor are white.

Myth No. 4 is that the poor don't know how to spend their money. The evidence we have shows that low-income people spend a somewhat greater proportion—about 88 per cent—of their income on food, clothing, housing, medical care and transportation than do people with higher incomes.

Myth No. 5 is that many welfare families receive payments that are far too high. The fact is that in 24 states, the combined benefits of Aid for Families with Dependent Children and food stamps total less than three-fourths of the official poverty-income level. And that poverty level was only $5,500 for a family of four in 1975. . . .

Our failure to provide welfare payments to male-headed families and our provision of very low benefits to eligible families is due in part to the fear that poor people wouldn't work if welfare benefits were higher. This is the work-incentive problem we noted earlier. We can see the problem in more detail by examining the way AFDC benefits are calculated.

The work-incentive problem

Until 1967, a family receiving AFDC payments had very little financial incentive to seek employment. This was not because welfare represented the "good life," however. Welfare benefits have always been below poverty standards. Rather, welfare regulations prohibited a family from improving its standard of living by working. Such a regulation might appear absurd, but it was simply the consequence of the way in which the amount of a family's benefits was calculated.

When a family applies for welfare, it is obliged to report any income at its disposal. A woman with small children, for example, might earn $50 a month by baby sitting and ironing for neighbors. Until 1967, the welfare authorities subtracted any such income from the family's needs (as determined by the local welfare department) and provided the difference. Suppose the welfare authorities concluded that Mrs. Jones and her three children needed $300 a month. They paid her only $250, knowing that Mrs. Jones herself could provide the rest. This procedure may have distributed welfare funds equitably among needy recipients, but it destroyed all motivation for self-improvement.

Imagine that Mrs. Jones was offered regular part-time employment as a nurse's aide at $4 an hour for ten hours per week. Now, Mrs. Jones may have been reluctant to leave her small children in the care of others, but she could certainly use the money. So she would have been inclined to accept the job, especially if transportation problems (she had no car) and child-care arrangements could be worked out. But what would have happened to her actual income if she had taken this step toward self-improvement? Absolutely nothing. The welfare authorities would simply have noted that she was now earning $160 a month and would have reduced her welfare payment to $140. Her family's income would have remained at $300 whether or not Mrs. Jones found employment and no matter how hard she strove for self-improvement.

The pre-1967 method of calculating benefits is illustrated in Figure 31.2. If she doesn't work at all, Mrs. Jones remains at point A, with $3,600 per year in welfare benefits and no wages. Now watch what happens when she takes a part-time job. If she works 500 hours a year (10 hours a week) she moves to point W on the wage line, with $2,000 of wages. But her gross income doesn't change. The welfare department cuts her benefits to $1,600 (point X) when she earns $2,000 on her own. Hence her gross income moves from point A to

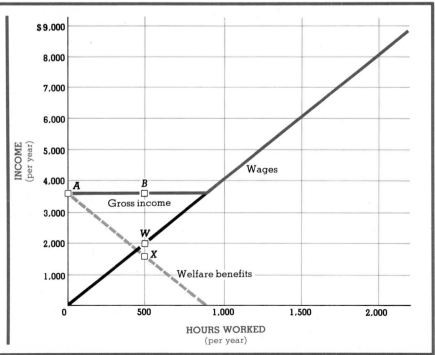

FIGURE 31.2 WORK AND WELFARE: PRE-1967 OPTIONS

Before 1967, a welfare family's cash benefit was equal to the difference between state-determined needs and other income. As a result, benefits fell when other income increased. Gross income was thus unchanged. In this case, $2,000 of wages (point W) reduced welfare benefits to $1,600 (point X), leaving the family with its initial income of $3,600 (point B). A family stayed on welfare until its other income exceeded $3,600.

marginal tax rate: The tax rate imposed on the last (marginal) dollar of income.

marginal utility of labor: The change in total utility derived from another hour's work; includes the utility associated with the extra goods and services that can be purchased with another hour's wages, as well as any intrinsic satisfaction derived from additional labor.

point *B*. She has no more money to spend after working 500 hours per year than she had when she stayed at home.

The "old" AFDC system clearly provided very little financial incentive to go out and find a job. In effect, any income earned was simply turned over to the welfare department through the mechanism of reduced cash assistance. The method of calculating welfare benefits on a residual basis—on the basis of the difference between needs and income—imposed a 100 percent tax on any wages a welfare recipient might earn.

Clearly, not many people would be eager to work if they confronted a **marginal tax rate** of 100 percent. As we saw in Chapter 25, the decision to work is based on a comparison of the marginal utility of labor with the marginal utility of leisure. The **marginal utility of labor** consists of the satisfaction obtainable from the goods and services that can be purchased with one's wages plus any enjoyment derived from the job itself. In this case, labor provides no net increase in income. Thus a person would have no incentive to work unless leisure were actually burdensome (yielded *negative* marginal utility) or the job provided a lot of personal satisfaction.

IMPROVED INCENTIVES   This glaring failure of the AFDC program to reinforce work incentives prompted some improvements in the welfare system. In 1967 Congress adopted a new procedure for calculating benefits.

Take again the case of Mrs. Jones. In the absence of any work effort, Mrs. Jones again starts out with $3,600 in welfare benefits. This is illustrated by point *A* in Figure 31.3. Now suppose she decides to accept the job as a nurse's aide, working 500 hours a year (10 hours per week). Under the old AFDC system, she would move from point *A* to point *B*, working more but with no change in total income. Under the revised system, however, she moves to point *C* and increases her income by working. Point *C* is obviously a more desirable place to be than point *B*, because it represents more income for the same amount of effort. Hence, whatever Mrs. Jones' feelings about work, she is more likely to take a job under the new system than under the old one. In this sense, the new system provides a greater incentive to work.

How does Mrs. Jones get to point *C* under the new system? First of all, the welfare authorities now recognize that there are certain costs associated with working—transportation expenses, additional child care, clothes, added meal costs, and so on. To ensure that Mrs. Jones' spendable income is not reduced by the amount of these work-related expenses, the welfare department "disregards" that much income in calculating her welfare benefits. Hence her welfare benefits are not reduced until she is earning at least enough income to cover her work expenses. To give Mrs. Jones still greater incentive to work, the 1967 amendments also required welfare authorities to disregard an *additional* $30 per month, *plus* one-third of any remaining income.

Suppose that Mrs. Jones' work expenses total $170 per month ($2,040 per year). She can now earn this much income without los-

**FIGURE 31.3 WORK AND WELFARE:
1967–81 CASH OPTIONS**

To encourage more work effort,
welfare authorities have disregarded
some income in computing a family's
benefits. Until 1981 a welfare mother
could earn $30 per month plus enough
income to cover work expenses before
her benefits were reduced. In this
case, wages of $2,000 (point W) do not
reduce welfare benefits at all, so
gross income rises to $5,600 (point C).
The family stays on welfare until its
income exceeds $7,800.

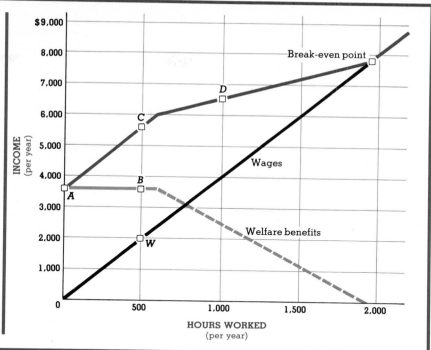

ing any welfare benefits. She can also earn an additional $360 per
year without losing any welfare benefits, thanks to the $30-per-
month "disregard." Hence Mrs. Jones can now earn as much as
$2,400 per year without losing any welfare benefits. In other words,
the marginal tax rate on her first $2,400 of earnings is zero. By work-
ing 500 hours per year, Mrs. Jones now moves from point A to point
C, keeping $3,600 in welfare benefits *and* $2,000 in wages. This contrasts sharply with the pre-1967 system, which left Mrs. Jones at
point B, with only $1,600 in welfare benefits and $2,000 in wages.

The welfare department begins to "tax" Mrs. Jones' earnings
(reduce her welfare benefits) only after her wages exceed the "disregard" of $360 per year plus work expenses. Even at that point,
however, the marginal tax rate is "only" 67 percent, rather than 100
percent. Hence Mrs. Jones has an economic incentive to work more
than 500 hours per year. She will get to keep 33 cents out of every
additional dollar she earns. The incentive is still modest, to be sure,
but nevertheless greater than the one (nothing) that existed earlier.

Suppose now that Mrs. Jones wants to increase her work effort
to 20 hours per week. If she worked 1,000 hours per year she could
earn $4,000. What would happen to her welfare benefits? The for-
mula for calculating her benefit is:

Welfare benefits
$$= \$3,600 - \tfrac{2}{3} \text{ (wages in excess of work expenses and disregard)}$$
$$= \$3,600 - \tfrac{2}{3} \, [\$4,000 - (\$2,040 + \$360)]$$
$$= \$3,600 - \$1,067$$
$$= \$2,533$$

Hence by doubling her work effort, Mrs. Jones would move from point *C* to point *D* in Figure 31.3. At point *D* she receives $4,000 in wages plus $2,533 in welfare benefits. By her own efforts, then, Mrs. Jones is able to increase her family's income.

CONFLICTING WELFARE GOALS

It is comforting to know that Mrs. Jones can increase her family's income from $3,600 to $6,533 a year by working as a nurse's aid 20 hours a week. It might be nicer still if the welfare department would let her keep a little more of the money she earns from making beds, emptying bedpans, and sterilizing bandages. After all, the life of a nurse's aide is not exactly glamorous, and Mrs. Jones obviously needs the money. So why not lower the marginal tax rate from 67 percent to, say, 25 percent, or even zero? Such a reduction in the marginal tax rate would solve two problems. First, it would give Mrs. Jones an even greater incentive to work (see Figure 31.4). Second, it would enable Mrs. Jones to achieve a higher standard of living.

Incentives vs. costs

Unfortunately, a reduction in the marginal tax rate would also increase welfare costs. Suppose that we actually eliminated the marginal tax rate on Mrs. Jones' earnings, thus allowing her to keep everything she earned. Her total income would then rise to $7,600 ($3,600 in benefits plus $4,000 in wages). Terrific. But should we

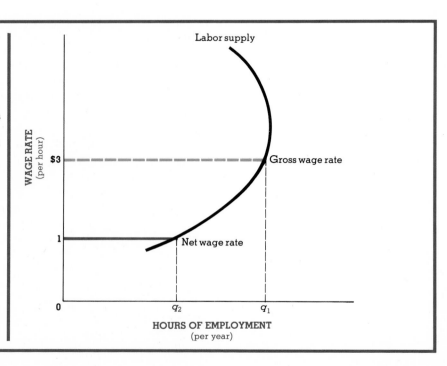

FIGURE 31.4 THE EFFECT OF WELFARE BENEFITS ON LABOR SUPPLY

The reduction in welfare benefits that accompanies an increase in earnings effectively reduces net wage rates. As a consequence, we expect the quantity of labor supplied to diminish when high marginal tax rates are imposed. A marginal tax rate of 67 percent implies that a worker gets to keep only $1 (net wage) out of every $3 earned (the gross wage). At the lower net wage, fewer hours of labor (q_2 vs. q_1) are supplied.

still be providing $3,600 in welfare payments to someone who earns $4,000 on her own? How about someone earning $8,000? $10,000? To make a long story short, where should we draw the line? Clearly, *if we don't impose a marginal tax rate at some point, everyone will be eligible for full welfare benefits.*

While the thought of giving everyone a welfare check might sound like a great idea, it would turn out to be incredibly expensive. In the end, we would have to take those checks back in the form of increased taxes in order to pay for the vastly expanded program. We must recognize, then, a basic dilemma:

- Low marginal tax rates encourage more work effort but make more people eligible for welfare.

- High marginal tax rates discourage work effort but make fewer people eligible for welfare.

The conflict between work incentives and the desire to limit welfare costs and eligibility can be summarized in a neat little equation:

$$\frac{\text{Break-even level}}{\text{of income}} = \frac{\text{basic benefits}}{\text{marginal tax rate}} + \text{earnings disregards}$$

The break-even level of income is the amount of income a person can earn before losing all welfare benefits. In Mrs. Jones' case, the annual income disregard was $2,400 ($2,040 for work expenses plus $30 per month) and the basic welfare benefit was $3,600 per year. Hence she could earn as much as $7,800 per year before losing all her welfare benefits. In other words, she could virtually hold a full-time job and still collect some welfare benefits. In this case, we encouraged work but made it difficult for Mrs. Jones to work her way off of welfare.

If the marginal tax rate were 100 percent, as under the pre-1967 system, the break-even point would be $3,600 ($3,600 ÷ 1.00). In that case, people who earned $3,600 on their own would get no assistance from welfare. Fewer people would be eligible for welfare, but those who drew benefits would have no incentive to work. Under our aborted proposal to lower marginal tax rates to zero, the break-even point would rise to infinity ($3,600 ÷ 0), and we would all be on welfare.

As this arithmetic makes apparent, *we can achieve a lower break-even level of income only by sacrificing a high income floor, earnings disregards, or low marginal tax rates.* Hence welfare costs can be minimized only if we sacrifice income provision or work incentives.

In-kind benefits   The conflict between work incentives and welfare costs was further intensified by the provision of in-kind benefits. People on welfare are also eligible for food stamps, Medicaid, housing assistance, and other direct benefits. Moreover, cash benefits are not reduced by the value of in-kind benefits. Hence *real* incomes of welfare recipients are typically higher than their cash incomes imply.

DO WORK INCENTIVES MATTER?

The potential disincentives associated with cash and in-kind welfare benefits are substantial. Debate continues, however, on just how large an impact these disincentives actually have on the labor supply of poor people. Do welfare recipients work less as a result of high marginal tax rates and income guarantees? If so, by how much?

To answer these questions, the U.S. Department of Health and Human Services funded several income-maintenance experiments. In these experiments, one group of poor people was provided with income guarantees and high marginal tax rates, while another group received nothing. The behavior of both groups was then observed for several years to determine whether the "welfare" group worked less than the "nonwelfare" group.

Income-maintenance experiments were conducted in New Jersey, North Carolina, Gary, Indiana, Denver, and Seattle. In general, the results indicate that high marginal tax rates *do* reduce the quantity of labor supplied, just as our theory predicts. In one experiment (Denver and Seattle) the labor supply of husbands declined by 5 percent as a result of income transfers. The labor supply of wives fell by 22 percent.

The implications of in-kind benefits for the work–welfare dilemma are illustrated in Figure 31.5. AFDC cash benefits still start out at $3,600 (point *A*). But now Mrs. Jones gets $1,000 in food stamps, $1,000 in housing assistance, and $1,000 worth of Medicaid services. Her *real* income jumps to $6,600 (point *A**), even if she doesn't work at all.

Once Mrs. Jones starts working, she will begin to lose some food stamps, since their value is based on family income. But she will keep her full Medicaid benefits so long as she is on welfare, and probably her housing assistance as well. Hence a *real* break-even level of income will be $2,000 higher than it was before. As Figure 31.5 reveals, Mrs. Jones can now enjoy a real income of $9,799.99 and still be on welfare! This level of income not only exceeds her family's poverty standard, but also surpasses the income of many working families not on welfare. Hence Mrs. Jones is not likely to leave the welfare rolls.

Figure 31.5 highlights another barrier to Mrs. Jones' exodus from welfare. Notice the drop in real income that occurs at the break-even point. If Mrs. Jones earned $7,800 or more in wages, she would lose all cash welfare benefits. At the same time, she might lose her Medicaid eligibility. Hence the last dollar earned at the break-even level results in a $1,000 loss of real income. Clearly there is a tremendous incentive *not* to earn that last dollar.

THE REAGAN REFORMS

President Reagan, among others, felt that the welfare system depicted in Figure 31.5 was far too generous. The combination of high disregards and "low" tax rates permitted too many people to receive

FIGURE 31.5 WORK AND WELFARE: 1967–81 REAL OPTIONS

The provision of in-kind benefits to welfare families increases their *real* incomes above their cash incomes. With food stamps, Medicaid, and housing assistance, plus AFDC benefits, Mrs. Jones would have $6,600 of real income (point *A**) without working. By working 500 hours per year, she would increase her income to $8,000 (point *C**). In this case, a welfare family could command a real income of nearly $9,800 before losing welfare eligibility. There would be a strong disincentive to earn that last dollar, however, since the family might then lose Medicaid benefits.

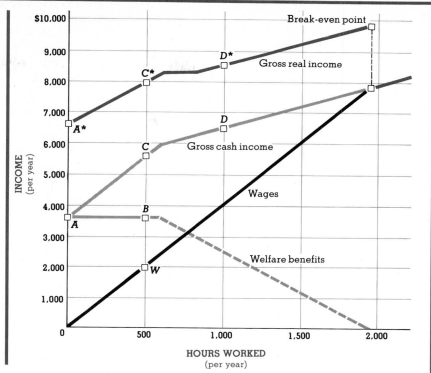

welfare. Moreover, once on welfare, a family was likely to stay on for years, because the break-even level was too high. Also, the discretionary nature of "work expenses" invited fraud and abuse. In the example we have studied, the real break-even level of income was $9,800. If Mrs. Jones had claimed more work expenses, her break-even level of income would have been still higher.

President Reagan felt that these income limits were far too high. A person on welfare could easily end up with more income than a person who was working. Moreover, the welfare recipient could enjoy an income in excess of the poverty standard. Reagan argued that this was inequitable and wasteful. He proposed to focus the welfare system more narrowly on the "truly needy." He also sought to encourage people to move off of welfare and into jobs.

In 1981 the Reagan administration succeeded in changing the rules for welfare eligibility and benefits. The major changes were:

□ *Limit on gross income.* A family can receive welfare benefits only if its total income is less than 150 percent of the state's standard of need (itself usually less than the federal poverty standard). This rule sets an upper limit on the break-even level of income.

□ *Limit on work expenses.* Recipients can no longer itemize work-related expenses. Uniform deductions of $75 per month for work expenses and $160 for child care are now to be used.

□ *Time limit on work incentives.* The "30 and a third" rule for computing welfare benefits applies only to the first four months of welfare receipt. After four months, the recipient confronts a 100 percent tax rate on all earnings in excess of standardized work and child-care expenses.

□ *Asset limitation.* Poor families are eligible for AFDC benefits only if the value of their assets is less than $1,000, exclusive of home and car.

The most severe of these changes is the income ceiling. In the case we have been examining, the state standard of need was $3,600.[5] Hence the Reagan-imposed ceiling on cash income is $5,400 per year (150 percent of $3,600). The cash ceiling also implies a ceiling on *real* income. Hence **the immediate impact of the income ceiling is to restrict welfare eligibility more tightly to families with low incomes.** This restriction is consistent with Reagan's objective of serving only the "truly needy." The restriction also implies a smaller welfare population and therefore lower costs.

The gross-income ceiling also lessens work incentives, however. If Mrs. Jones were to work 500 hours per year, as before, she would earn $2,000. Theoretically, this amount of wages would not reduce her welfare benefits, since it does not cover all her work expenses (including child care). However, the $2,000 in wages, when combined with $3,600 in welfare benefits, exceeds the new income ceiling. Hence Mrs. Jones cannot keep both $2,000 in wages and $3,600 in welfare benefits. Any wages in excess of $1,800 will be "taxed" at 100 percent. This means that Mrs. Jones will not enjoy a higher cash income until she is able to work at least 1,351 hours a year. By working that much, she would earn $5,404 in wages (at $4 per hour), just above the welfare ceiling. Hence Mrs. Jones has no incentive to take a job that pays between $1,800 and $5,400 in wages. Indeed, were she to earn $5,400 or more and move off of welfare, she might lose Medicaid and thus suffer a real income loss.

The net effect of the Reagan reforms is to discourage welfare recipients from taking part-time jobs, or even full-time jobs. In this sense, the reforms again reflect the basic conflict between holding down welfare costs and providing work incentives. The 1981 rule changes reduced the size of the potential welfare population but discouraged recipients from seeking employment.

Workfare

To overcome the disincentive features of the new welfare rules, President Reagan proposed that the "carrot" of low marginal tax rates be replaced by the "stick" of compulsory employment. The administration proposed that welfare recipients be required to "work off" their benefits by doing community-service work. With such compulsory "workfare," a welfare recipient could not choose between some work and no work. Rather, the choice would be between a public "work-experience" job (at the minimum wage) and any private-sector job that was available. In this case, the issue of work incentives, as measured by marginal tax rates, would be secondary.

---

[5] In many states the maximum welfare benefit is less than the need standard. In Mrs. Jones' case, we have assumed they are equal.

Governor Approves Welfare Cuts, Workfare Project in Pennsylvania

HARRISBURG, PA.—Republican Gov. Richard L. Thornburgh yesterday signed into law his proposal to cut off welfare checks to at least 64,000 Pennsylvanians, about one-third of those receiving cash grants from the state.

The legislation, approved by the Republican-controlled legislature last week, halts maximum $172-a-month state grants to childless, "able-bodied" recipients between the ages of 18 and 45, effective Jan. 1.

It also establishes Pennsylvania's first "workfare" program, under which an estimated 140,000 welfare recipients will be required to work at community service jobs to earn cash grants.

Thornburgh proposed the cuts in October, 1979, contending that Pennsylvania had become "a welfare haven" that burdened taxpayers.

"With 5.2 percent of the nation's population, Pennsylvania has nearly 20 percent of the nation's general assistance welfare recipients," he said. "This has placed an increasing burden on Pennsylvania taxpayers over the past decade."

He said savings from the cutoff would be used to provide a 5 percent increase in the cash grants for welfare families of three or more. For a family of three, that would amount to $16 more a month.

The Washington Post, Washington, D.C., April 9, 1982. Copyright © 1982 The Washington Post.

Welfare, Workfare, Warfare

Some welfare recipients in Siskiyou County, Calif., will be required to try to join the military, the AP reports. The county's board of supervisors unanimously adopted a policy that both men and women between the ages of 18 and 35 who receive general welfare assistance would be required to try to enlist on the theory that the military is a job like any other. Those who actually go to the recruiting office and get turned down can continue on welfare. Those who don't want to take the chance—well, we assume that's the idea.

Reprinted by permission of *The Wall Street Journal*, © Dow Jones & Company, Inc. (1981). All Rights Reserved.

Congress refused to adopt a national workfare plan but did allow states to experiment with their own versions of workfare. The primary objections to workfare were that many recipients simply could not work, that such jobs were nonproductive and costly to supervise, and that they obstructed welfare recipients' efforts to find regular jobs.

SUMMARY

▪ On the basis of cash incomes, 29 million people are officially counted as poor. In-kind transfers, however, substantially reduce the true poverty count.

▪ Welfare benefits are provided to many, but not all, poor people. Cash benefits are largely restricted to female-headed families with children.

▪ A reduction in welfare benefits that occurs when a recipient takes a job is an implicit tax. The rate at which welfare benefits are reduced when recipients earn wages represents the marginal tax rate.

▪ Marginal tax rates illustrate the work–welfare dilemma. High tax rates discourage work but restrict welfare eligibility. Low tax rates encourage work but enlarge the potential welfare population.

▪ The 1981 welfare reforms restricted welfare eligibility but also lessened work incentives. Compulsory jobs were proposed as a substitute for incentives.

Terms to remember

Define the following terms:

in-kind transfers	**cyclical unemployment**
labor-force participant	**income transfers**
human capital	**marginal tax rate**
marginal productivity	**marginal utility of labor**

Questions for discussion

1. Negative income tax (NIT) plans are distinguished by their promise of universal eligibility, based only on income standards (without regard for "employability" or other demographic factors). How would such plans differ from our current welfare system?

2. What compromise of the three welfare goals do you regard as most appropriate? How high would you set marginal tax rates?

3. What incentives would a father have under the AFDC system to desert his family if he were unable to find and retain a job that provided enough money to support them? How should we correct this situation?

Problem

Using the rules of the post-1981 (Reagan) welfare system, complete the following table relating income to hours worked. Assume the welfare recipient can earn $6 per hour and receives $1,000 each of Medicaid, food stamps, and housing aid so long as she is on welfare. She loses Medicaid when welfare benefits cease.

Hours worked	Wages	Welfare benefits	Total cash income	Total real income
0				
500				
1,000				
2,000				

CHAPTER 32

DISCRIMINATION

I have a dream that one day this nation will rise up and live out the true meaning of its creed: "We hold these truths to be self-evident, that all men are created equal."

—MARTIN LUTHER KING, JR., 1963

Discrimination has been identified as the source of substantial disparities in socioeconomic status. Blacks, Hispanics, and other minorities suffer from poor housing, limited educational opportunities, and lack of access to good jobs. The disadvantages imposed on women are less apparent, owing to the fact that they commonly share in the socioeconomic status of their mates. Nevertheless, women participate in the labor force much less extensively than men. When women do work, they usually command jobs and incomes markedly inferior to those available to men. These status disparities, plus a more general denial of opportunities for self-fulfillment, help to explain why the charges of racism and sexism persist and why they are important.

To understand how racism and sexism operate to create status disparities, we shall focus primarily on the labor market. We shall ask how and why minorities and women tend to get fewer rewards for their labor-force participation than do white men.

DIFFERENCES IN JOBS AND INCOMES

That minority groups and women generally occupy less attractive jobs and receive lower incomes in the labor market than do white males is beyond dispute. In 1980, the average white male worker earned an income of $16,657. By contrast, the average black male worker earned $10,979 and the average female worker received only about $8,500 (see Figure 32.1). Contributing to these enormous ine-

FIGURE 32.1 EARNINGS INEQUALITIES IN THE UNITED STATES

White males command much higher earnings than do minority males or women. Many, perhaps most, of these differences are due to discrimination, in both educational and employment opportunities.

Source: U.S. Department of Labor.

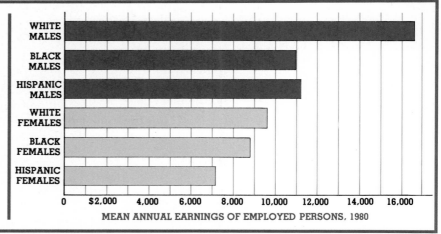

MEAN ANNUAL EARNINGS OF EMPLOYED PERSONS, 1980

qualities in earnings is the fact that white males tend to hold jobs markedly different from those held by minorities and women. White males are far more likely to be employed as doctors, engineers, and college professors than are women or minority males. White males are seldom secretaries, file clerks, or private household workers. Minority males, on the other hand, are heavily concentrated in blue-collar occupations, particularly as operative and unskilled laborers. Women tend to hold jobs as clerks and secretaries but are also predominant in the ranks of schoolteachers (noncollege) and private service workers (maids, for instance).

Not only do white males tend to hold different kinds of jobs from those of either minority males or females; they also have a much easier time finding work. In early 1982 7.3 percent of adult white males were officially counted as "unemployed"—that is, seeking work. By contrast, the unemployment rate among minority males was a staggering 16.9 percent. Unemployment rates for women in 1982 fell between these two extremes, at 8.3 percent.

How much inequality is due to discrimination?

discrimination: Inequality of treatment; denial of opportunity on the basis of characteristics unrelated to performance.

The arguments about racism and sexism are not over the existence of these status disparities, but over their causes. To what extent are the job and income disparities due to underlying differences in talent or personal aspiration? And to what extent do they arise from an inequality of opportunity—from **discrimination** based on race or sex?

What makes the controversy so intense is that it is seldom easy to determine why a particular person did or did not get a particular job. Consider a situation in which a white worker and a black worker apply for the same job. The white applicant is accepted and the black applicant claims that he was unfairly discriminated against. What grounds do we have for accepting the charge of discrimination as opposed to, say, the charge that the black applicant is simply a poor loser?

The easiest cases of discrimination to prove are those that involve blatant discrepancies in treatment. In the example above, if only the black applicant had been required to take special tests or had possessed identifiably superior qualifications, the issue is readily resolved. The same kind of simplicity exists when black children are confined to dilapidated schools. Or when a prospective black home buyer is turned down after offering to pay the full retail value of a house. But the practice of discrimination is not always so apparent. Indeed, with the public eye focused on discrimination, those who engage in discriminatory practices are likely to develop great subtlety. Accordingly, evidence of discriminatory treatment may have to rest on the observation of end results. If a company has 4,000 employees, none of whom is black, a strong presumption exists that its hiring procedures are not impartial. So it is with the schools. If blacks and whites go into the educational system comparatively equal but come out with gross disparities in ability, it may be concluded that they were treated differently somewhere along the line. In other words, evidence of discriminatory treatment may be gathered by direct observation of treatment or by inference from results. Both types of evidence are used in formulating public policy and deciding court cases.

The acquisition and use of human capital

human capital: The bundle of skills that an individual possesses.

To identify more clearly the nature and impact of discrimination, we may return to the concept of marginal productivity. As we have noted in earlier chapters (particularly Chapter 26), a worker's employment opportunities and wages are directly related to his or her marginal productivity. In particular, we noted that a person's stock of **human capital**—one's skills and abilities—are a basic determinant of the contribution a person can make to output.

The level of marginal productivity actually attained will depend on one's human capital and the way it is employed. The amount of other resources (such as plant and equipment) that one has to work

OPINIONS ON DISCRIMINATION

A Harris poll taken in 1977 asked Americans about the extent of discrimination in schools, jobs, and housing. The responses revealed sharply different perspectives between whites and blacks. For example,

□ *Schools:* 61 percent of all blacks believe there is racial discrimination in public schools. Only 19 percent of all whites agree.

□ *Jobs:* 73 percent of all blacks feel they are discriminated against in access to white-collar jobs. Whites don't agree; 68 percent see no discrimination.

□ *Wages:* 66 percent of blacks feel they are unfairly paid lower wages; 72 percent of whites disagree.

□ *Housing:* 74 percent of blacks believe they lack equal access to decent housing; 61 percent of whites see no racial discrimination in housing.

A 1981 *Washington Post*/ABC News poll revealed much the same pattern. Sixty-seven percent of all blacks attributed their lower economic status to discrimination, but only 38 percent of all whites saw discrimination as the main cause of disparities in jobs, income, and housing.

marginal revenue product (MRP): The change in total revenue associated with one additional unit of input.

with are important determinants of marginal productivity. Finally, the *value* of a worker's output, **marginal revenue product,** will depend on the market worth of the goods and services produced. Thus discrimination can reduce an individual's income by:

- Denying a person the opportunity to acquire human capital.
- Denying a person the opportunity to use all of the human capital he or she has acquired.

The distinction between the acquisition and the use of human capital is important in measuring the full impact of discrimination. Suppose we found that the black worker who was denied a job had actually been rejected because he was unqualified; that is, on the basis of a human capital deficiency. Can we then conclude that he has not been the target of discrimination? No, at least not in any comprehensive sense. All we would know is that there appeared to be no discrimination *in the labor market* with respect to the utilization of human capital. The black job applicant might still have been denied an equal opportunity to acquire needed human capital, and in that respect he suffered economically from discrimination.

Many black workers, for example, are excluded from high-paying union jobs because they have been denied access to union apprenticeship programs that develop the required skills and experience. In such cases, the control over human-capital acquisition effectively translates into control over who gets which jobs. The same kind of relationship exists between acceptance at medical school and doctors' jobs, between admission to business school and corporate management, and between college admission and a broad assortment of highly paid jobs. One reason there are so few women in business management and professional positions is that business and professional schools have historically denied them admission. Hence to evaluate the full force of discrimination, we must ask two related questions: (1) Does everyone have an equal opportunity to acquire human capital? (2) Does everyone have an equal opportunity to employ it?

DISCRIMINATION IN EDUCATION

Much of the human capital that people bring to the labor market is developed in school. In effect, going to school represents an investment in one's own human capital. Such an investment is typically rewarded with more interesting jobs and higher pay. Hence we can begin to gauge the impact of discrimination by looking at the way educational opportunities are distributed in the United States.

Racial discrimination

The history of racial and other minority discrimination in education is well known. For most of our history, black and other minority children have confronted a situation of separate and unequal education. It was not until 1954 that the Supreme Court unanimously decided (*Brown* v. *Board of Education*) that separate schools are inherently unequal. Before that decision, little was done to upgrade

TABLE 32.1 SCHOOL INTEGRATION, 1980

Segregation is still prevalent in American schools. Most minority children attend schools in which at least half of the students are members of minority groups. Only one-third of minority children attend schools in which (Anglo) whites outnumber minority pupils.

Region	Percentage of minority students in schools where minority enrollment is:		
	80–100 percent	50–79 percent	Less than 50 percent
U.S. total	41	24	35
Northeast	57	19	24
Midwest	45	20	35
South	36	25	39
West	37	29	34

Source: U.S. Department of Health and Human Services.

the quality of black schools, much less to bring white and black children together in the same schools. It was not until the Civil Rights Act of 1964 that the 1954 Supreme Court decision began to be enforced with any sense of urgency. And it was not until the court-ordered busing plans of the early 1970s that black and white children began to approach equality of educational opportunity. That equality has still not been achieved but is considerably closer than it was two decades ago.

Table 32.1 summarizes the extent of racial integration in U.S. schools. In 1980 41 percent of all minority pupils (in elementary and secondary grades) were still attending schools in which nearly all the students were minority members. Only one-third of all minority pupils attended schools that were predominantly nonminority. Although there were large variations across regions—and interestingly enough, less segregation in the South than elsewhere—it is fair to conclude that segregated educational facilities prevailed everywhere. Whether in the North or in the South, in a city or on a farm, a minority child is very unlikely to attend a truly integrated school. Racial isolation in the schools is still a distinguishable feature of American educational systems.

INEQUALITY OF FACILITIES The statistics of Table 32.1 provide a sobering view of our efforts to furnish equal opportunity "with all deliberate speed." In the light of that background, we may argue that many minorities and whites still attend school separately. How equal, then, are their separate opportunities?

In the only comprehensive survey of our educational facilities ever undertaken, the U.S. Office of Education employed 67 separate measures of school quality, ranging from the number of books in the school library to the education of a teacher's mother. The Office of Education discovered that minority and white schools differed on a multitude of separate measures, but that such individual differences were relatively small. Only one clear pattern emerged from the mountain of statistics: minority schools tended to be most deficient in those facilities that were primarily academic in nature (science labs, textbooks, debate clubs).

In assessing these results, the Office of Education recognized many limitations in their approach. They reported:

EQUAL OPPORTUNITY?

A Harris survey asked a national cross-section of 1,497 adults: "As a matter of principle, do you favor or oppose desegregation of the public school system in the United States?"

DESEGREGATION OF PUBLIC SCHOOLS

	Favor (percent)	Oppose (percent)	Not sure (percent)
Nationwide	56	35	9
By region			
East	57	33	10
Midwest	48	41	11
South	58	32	10
West	64	32	4

In every region of the country desegregation of public education is favored in principle—but by only a slight majority.

The Harris survey then asked: "Would you favor or oppose busing school children to achieve racial balance?"

BUSING TO ACHIEVE RACIAL BALANCE

	Favor (percent)	Oppose (percent)	Not sure (percent)
Nationwide	20	74	6
By region			
East	20	70	10
Midwest	19	74	7
South	18	77	5
West	27	70	3

Although a slight majority of people in every region favor desegregation of schools in principle, they adamantly oppose busing as a means of achieving it.

Source: Harris survey, October 2, 1975.

The school environment of a child consists of many things, ranging from the desk he sits at to the child who sits next to him, and including the teacher who stands in front of his class. Any statistical survey gives only the most meager evidence of these environments, for two reasons. First, the reduction of the various aspects of the environment to quantitative measures must inherently miss many elements, tangible and more subtle, that are relevant to the child. . . .

Second, the child experiences his environment as a whole, while the statistical measures necessarily fragment it. Having a teacher without a college degree may indicate an element of disadvantage; but in the concrete situation, a schoolchild may be taught by a teacher who is not only without a college degree, but who has grown up and received his schooling in the local community, who has never been out of the State, who has a 10th-grade vocabulary, and who shares the local community's attitudes.

For both these reasons, the statistical examination of difference in school environments for minority and majority children will give an impression of lesser differences than actually exist.[1]

[1] U.S. Office of Education, *Equality of Educational Opportunity* (Washington, D.C.: U.S. Government Printing Office, 1966), p. 37.

We are left, then, with a very incomplete assessment of the school facilities available to whites and minorities. All we can say with certainty is that both everyday observation and the government survey lead one to conclude that tangible differences exist in the educational facilities available to minorities and whites. We have no summary measure, however, of the extent or the significance of those differences.

INHERENT INEQUALITIES The Supreme Court provided a way out of this statistical ambiguity when it determined in 1954 that segregated facilities were *inherently* unequal. The Court declared that "to separate [black children] from others of similar age and qualifications solely because of their race generates a feeling of inferiority as to their status in the community that may affect their hearts and minds in a way unlikely ever to be undone." The Court thus relegated the issue of tangible facilities to one of distinctly secondary importance. Even ostensibly "equal" schools for blacks and whites could never generate equal educational opportunity.

The Supreme Court justices were led to their landmark decision by several specific considerations. They recognized that black pupils in segregated schools would have low self-esteem, derived from the knowledge that they were surrounded by failures and in schools regarded as inferior. Moreover, they would acquire a personal sense of futility. They would know that regardless of their individual attainments, they would always be identified as members of a group viewed as less able, less successful, and less acceptable than whites. Hence individual black children would perceive little incentive to develop their individual talents. Community views would affect the attitudes of teachers also. Aware of (and probably sharing) the white community's low regard for blacks, teachers attached to black schools would tend to accept and transmit low expectations. They would not teach as much or as well to children deemed less teachable.

COLLEGE COMPLETION The disadvantages of a minority education accumulate. In general, minority students drop out of school earlier than whites. The cumulative disadvantage may be gauged by the low rate of college completion among minority groups. As Table 32.2 reveals, one-fourth of all white males aged 25 to 29 has completed four years of college. By contrast, the college graduation rate among minority males averaged only about 10 percent. A similar discrepancy exists between white and minority women. The implication of these statistics is that **minority groups enter the labor market with much less human capital than whites.**

Sex discrimination

The educational handicaps of black and other minority groups are reasonably easy to document. The disadvantages that women confront in the educational system are more subtle, at least in the early grades. For the most part, the sex barriers that characterize primary and secondary educational systems consist of the sex-typing of certain kinds of curricula. Girls are encouraged to take home economics, foreign languages, and typing. They are gently discouraged from

TABLE 32.2 COLLEGE COMPLETION BY RACIAL OR ETHNIC GROUPS

Relatively few minority-group members complete four years of college. As a consequence, minority groups enter the labor market with less human capital than whites.

Racial or ethnic group	Persons aged 25–29 who have completed at least 4 years of college (percent)
Men	
White	24.3
Black	12.1
Hispanic	8.6
Women	
White	20.5
Black	11.1
Hispanic	6.5

Source: The National Center for Education Statistics.

taking manual crafts, business courses, and science. Some barriers are erected by school counselors who want to be "realistic" about occupational goals. Even higher barriers are erected by parents and peers, who are attuned to certain kinds of expectations with respect to male and female roles in society. As the Carnegie Commission on Higher Education has noted:

Almost from the moment of birth, boys and girls are subject to a wide variety of cultural influences that tend to prepare them for differentiated roles in life. Little girls are typically given dolls or miniature cooking utensils for toys; boys are generally given trucks and electric trains and mechanical toys. School readers show pictures of father going off to work and mother waving good-bye at the window, or of father playing baseball with his sons while mother bakes cookies. Girls play jump rope or tag on the school playground, while boys play ball. At about the seventh or eighth grade, boys take a course in manual training, while girls are taught cooking and sewing.

We are not suggesting that matters ought to be reversed, or that little girls should be forbidden to play with dolls, but rather that there ought to be more freedom of choice. Girls who show signs of a mechanical bent should be given an opportunity to play with mechanical toys and to enter the course on manual training. Boys should not be barred from courses on cooking and sewing if they are interested.[2]

This kind of acculturation tends to restrict the educational aspirations of female students and to frustrate them when they challenge those restrictions.

More explicit manifestations of sex discrimination in education have been apparent at the postcollege level. As suggested earlier, female college graduates have had a difficult time gaining access to the professional schools that confer the necessary credentials for many desirable jobs. Secretarial schools have always been easy to get into, but law schools, medical schools, and business schools have often been a different story. Figure 32.2 depicts the proportion of various academic degrees awarded to women.

[2] Carnegie Commission on Higher Education, *Opportunities for Women in Higher Education* (New York: McGraw-Hill, 1973), pp. 42–43.

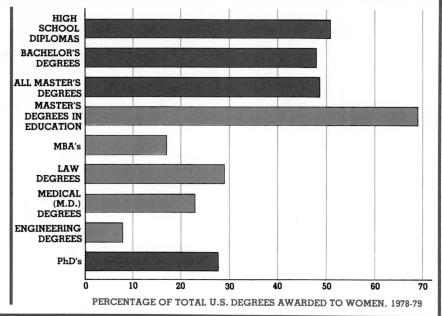

FIGURE 32.2   WOMEN IN EDUCATION

Men and women graduate from high school in equal numbers. Thereafter, their educational experiences vary considerably. While relatively few women go on to law, medical, or engineering schools, women receive a preponderance of graduate degrees in education.

Source: National Center for Education Statistics.

PERCENTAGE OF TOTAL U.S. DEGREES AWARDED TO WOMEN, 1978-79

DISCRIMINATION IN THE LABOR MARKET

The discrimination confronting minorities, low-income children, and women obviously constrains their ability to acquire human capital and thus puts them at a disadvantage in the competition for jobs. The handicaps imposed in the educational system are only part of a continuing story, however. Once these groups enter the labor market, they cannot even anticipate the opportunity to employ fully the human capital that they have managed to acquire.

Racial discrimination

That minority workers are not treated equally in the labor market is now generally recognized. One needn't go back to the days of slavery to observe that black workers are undervalued and underutilized in the labor market. Nor need one go back to 1927, when a clothing manufacturer in New York advertised for help with the following wage offer: "White Workers $24; Colored Workers $20."[3] Such examples are not only outdated, but far too blatant and unsophisticated for labor markets that are monitored by government agencies and the courts.

Racial discrimination today rarely takes the form of paying unequal wages for equal work. More commonly, minority workers are simply denied access to a variety of occupations, jobs, and industries that happen to offer higher pay and better working conditions. Garbage collection and bus driving are regarded as appropriate occupations for minority workers. Retail salesmanship, management, and

[3] Cited by Orley Ashenfelter, "Changes in Labor Market Discrimination over Time," *Journal of Human Resources*, Fall 1970.

TABLE 32.3 OCCUPATIONAL STATUS, BY RACE AND SEX, 1981

Minority workers of either sex are underrepresented in white-collar occupations and overrepresented in blue-collar and service occupations. White males enjoy the greatest advantage in managerial-administrative and skilled-craft jobs.

Occupation	Male workers		Female workers	
	White (percent)	Minority (percent)	White (percent)	Minority (percent)
White collar				
Professional and technical	16.3	11.7	17.3	15.4
Managers and administrators	15.5	7.0	7.8	4.1
Sales workers	6.5	2.7	7.3	3.2
Clerical workers	6.1	8.2	35.5	29.5
Total	44.4	29.6	67.9	52.2
Blue collar				
Craft workers	21.2	16.4	1.9	1.5
Operatives	10.6	15.0	9.1	14.2
Transport drivers	5.2	8.5	0.7	0.7
Nonfarm laborers	6.5	11.5	1.2	1.3
Total	43.5	51.4	12.9	17.7
Service workers	8.0	16.4	17.9	29.6
Farm workers	4.1	2.6	1.2	0.5

Source: U.S. Department of Labor, Bureau of Labor Statistics.

even teaching are not regarded by whites as equally appropriate. And only in the most dire of circumstances could most whites imagine trusting themselves to the services of a black doctor or lawyer. Accordingly, blacks and other minorities are largely excluded from more pleasant and remunerative employment. Table 32.3 indicates the general nature of existing occupational patterns.

The professional, managerial, clerical, and craft occupations embrace most of the better-paying and pleasant jobs in the economy. Two-thirds of all white workers are in those positions now. Yet only 50 percent of all minority workers has gained access to these occupations. The situation is further aggravated by the fact that minority workers who do gain access to the better occupations often end up in the lowest and least desirable jobs *within* each occupational group. Within the professional, technical, and managerial class, for example, white workers tend to be lawyers, doctors, engineers, and accountants. Minority workers, on the other hand, are more likely to be recreation directors, welfare workers, and teachers in segregated schools. The same situation exists in the other occupational categories, sometimes in even more extreme form.

At the bottom of the occupational ladder, the respective concentrations of blacks and whites are, of course, reversed. As Table 32.3 reveals, one-half of all minority workers are concentrated in the lower occupational categories. And again, the disparities in actual jobs are great. Minority women are more likely to be maids in private homes, hotels, and office buildings. Minority men are more likely to be porters and janitors. The better service and laboring jobs (fire fighters, police officers, bartenders, and teamsters) are still largely reserved for whites.

THE ROLE OF EDUCATIONAL DIFFERENCES To some extent, of course, the occupational disparities between whites and minorities are attributable to the human-capital differences that they bring with them into the labor market. Very few universities, for example, are prepared to hire Hispanic high-school dropouts as professors, however "liberal" their claims for an equal-employment-opportunity policy. Hence Hispanics are underrepresented in that occupational category partly as a result of prior discrimination in the educational system. Thus we would be remiss if we blamed the entire occupational disparity on discriminatory employment practices.

The interesting question, then, is what kinds of employment differences persist *after* we take into account the initial handicaps imposed by human-capital differentials. Table 32.4 provides a tentative answer to this question by showing the comparative earnings of blacks and whites with equal educations. If there were no racial discrimination in the labor market, blacks and whites with equal education should command approximately equal wages. When this adjustment is actually made, however, the gap in wages between whites and blacks is only partially closed. The wages of black males are generally only 80 to 90 percent of the amount earned by white males with equivalent years of schooling.

The same kind of earnings differential applies to other minority groups. In 1981 the median wage of male Mexican-American high-school graduates was only $7.54 per hour. By contrast, white high-school graduates earned a median wage of $8.61 per hour.

These earnings differentials underscore the fact that **the human capital of minority groups is generally undervalued in the labor market relative to white capital.** Much but not all of this difference is due to discrimination. The 10 to 20 percent earnings differential that persists between minority and white workers with equal schooling overstates the degree of labor-market discrimination. It does not adjust for the *quality* of minority and majority schools. As we have already observed, a year of school for a minority student does not have the same educational value as a year of school for a white student. Minority educations are generally inferior. Hence comparisons of years of schooling, like those in Table 32.4, overstate the relative human capital possessed by black workers. On the other hand, we

TABLE 32.4 HOURLY WAGES, BY RACE, SEX, AND EDUCATION, 1981

The human capital of minority groups is generally undervalued in the labor market. Black males, for example, earn 10 to 20 percent less than white males with equal years of schooling. Part of this difference reflects disparities in the quality of education of blacks and whites. But some of this difference also reflects continuing discrimination in the labor market.

Years of schooling	Male White	Male Black	Male Hispanic	Female White	Female Black	Female Hispanic
High-school dropout	7.65	6.16	6.59	4.24	3.98	3.92
High-school graduate	8.61	7.05	7.54	4.71	4.71	4.46
Some college	8.78	7.74	8.48	5.47	5.70	4.73
College graduate	8.21	7.58	—	5.92	6.22	—

Source: U.S. Department of Labor, Bureau of Labor Statistics.

GPO Women Win $16 Million in Sex Bias Suit

A U.S. District Court judge yesterday ordered the federal government to pay an estimated $16 million to 324 women who successfully charged the Government Printing Office with sex discrimination—one of the largest awards ever made in a bias case brought against an employer, public or private.

Judge Charles R. Richey, who set the amount yesterday, had ruled last October that the GPO paid men higher wages then women for the same jobs in its bindery and that the agency deliberately maintained a job classification system that perpetuated sex discrimination. . . .

The judge's award yesterday means that [28] women who operated sewing machines at the bindery in May 1973 will each receive up to $110,000 in back pay, based on Richey's ruling that they were deliberately paid less than men for jobs that required the "same skill, effort (and) responsibility. . . ."

In his ruling last October, Richey also said that the GPO bindery's job classification system kept women . . . out of better "craft" jobs as bookbinders. Those jobs, Richey said, paid higher salaries and provided promotion opportunities. A four-year apprenticeship program, required for employes who wanted to become bookbinders, was virtually closed to 324 women who . . . were classified as "journeymen bindery workers," Richey said.

Those actions, Richey said, amounted to a pattern of sex discrimination, violating Title VII of the Civil Rights Act of 1964.

As a result, Richey yesterday ordered that the government pay 296 other women, working in other low-paying jobs at the bindery, about $3 million in back wages.

Moreover, Richey said, the GPO must continue to pay the women additional money until 50 percent of all bookbinder and supervisory jobs are filled by women. —Laura A. Kiernan

must recognize that minority educational achievements are themselves influenced by labor-market discrimination. That is to say, minority students will have less incentive to remain in school if they foresee little reward for their efforts. This kind of negative feedback makes labor-market discrimination that much more oppressive.

Sex discrimination

The same forces that tend to constrain the earnings of minority men also limit the employment and income opportunities of women. Here again, of course, we must take into account the fact that women enter the labor market with less human capital than men do, especially when measured in terms of advanced degrees. And they tend to be trained for different kinds of work, as a result of both social pressures and overt discrimination in the educational system. The consequence, as might be expected, is less labor-force participation, inferior occupations, and lower pay.

The tendency of women to work in different occupations from those of men has already been illustrated in Table 32.3. Those statistics are only a crude index to the actual disadvantage of women in the labor market, however. The occupation categories depicted in Table 32.3 are extremely broad and summarize an incredible variety of job experiences. The U.S. Department of Labor itself claims to have identified over 40,000 separate occupations. As we noted in our discussion of racial employment patterns, occupational statistics sometimes mask more differences than they reveal.

Table 32.5 attempts to provide a bit more insight into the segregation by sex that exists in the labor market. Within each of the major occupational categories of Table 32.3, there are thousands of more detailed occupations and literally millions of jobs. The statistics in Table 32.5 provide a clue as to the height that sex barriers reach when one begins to examine the labor market in some detail. Within the "professional and technical" occupational category, for

TABLE 32.5 A NONLIBERATED LABOR FORCE

There are still "women's jobs" and "men's jobs." Even within the same occupational category, men and women tend to perform different jobs. Among professional workers, for example, 84 percent of all elementary school teachers but only 4 percent of all engineers are women.

Occupational categories	The jobs that women hold	Proportion of jobs held by women (percent)	The jobs that women don't hold	Proportion of jobs held by women (percent)
Professional and technical	Librarians	86	Engineers	4
	Registered nurses	97	Lawyers and judges	13
	Elementary teachers	84	Dentists	2
	Dieticians	94	Clergy	5
Managers and administrators	Food service	39	Public agencies	6
Sales workers	Demonstrators	95	Sales representatives	13
Clerical and kindred workers	Secretaries	99	Mail carriers	16
	Bank tellers	94	Shipping clerks	22
	Telephone operators	93	Dispatchers	38
Craftworkers	Bookbinders	56	Electricians	2
	Decorators	72	Telephone line and service workers	5
Operatives	Dressmakers	97	Taxicab drivers	9
	Laundry and dry cleaning	66	Truck drivers	3
Service	Waiters and waitresses	90	Police officers	6
	Household service	98	Bartenders	47

Source: U.S. Department of Labor (1981 data).

example, we discover that there are clearly "female jobs" and "male jobs." Ninety-seven percent of all registered nurses are women, while only 2 percent of dentists are women. The same kind of imbalance is evident throughout the list.

Nor is this the end of the story. Even within the more detailed occupations of Table 32.5, men and women tend to be employed at different kinds of jobs, in different industries, and in different work settings. Consider just one example, that of waiters and waitresses. Women comprise a whopping 90 percent of that category, but how many of them are employed in the best restaurants (where prices and tips are highest)? Very few. Is it because they don't speak French as well?

BUT WOMEN HAVE BABIES! Perhaps it is because they have babies. Not on the job, of course, but 84 percent of all women do bear children at

"COMPARABLE WORTH":
A NEW AND
PERPLEXING MEASURE
OF DISCRIMINATION

The Equal Pay Act of 1963 requires employers to pay men and women equal wages for equal work. In recent years, however, many women have argued that this measure of equality is too restrictive. Most women, after all, do not hold jobs identical to men's (see Table 32.5). Hence, there is seldom a basis for assessing "equal" pay.

To remedy this situation, it has been argued that women should get "comparable" pay, that is, equal pay for jobs *comparable* to men's in importance, skill, and responsibility. This concept has been the basis for a rash of new discrimination suits. In San Jose, California, comparable worth was a major demand in a 1981 strike by municipal workers. The strike was settled after the city agreed to pay $1.4 million in bonuses to "undervalued" female-dominated positions.

Although the concept of comparable worth has obvious appeal, it suggests a radical departure from market economics. In a competitive market, the "worth" of a job is measured by the prevailing wage. To assess "comparable worth," someone has to assign nonmarket values to each job, based on subjective judgements of "importance, skill, and responsibility." In the San Jose case, a consulting firm was hired to make these judgments. But many critics questioned the qualifications of that firm—or anyone—to substitute their judgments for those of the market.

The ultimate proof of sex discrimination

For years economists have been documenting the case that women have been discriminated against in the work place. The most direct decisive evidence yet of systematic sex discrimination in labor markets emerges not from an economic study but from a survey by Dr. Norman M. Fisk, a Stanford University psychiatrist. His questionnaire, sent to 170 people involved in sex-change operations, showed "that each person who changed from female to male earned more after the change."

some time in their lives. The job interruption that typically accompanies childbirth translates into lost job experience and thus less human-capital development, at least from a labor-market point of view. Can't this "natural" barrier to female productivity explain occupational and income differentials?

Partially, but only partially. As the president's Council of Economic Advisers has observed:

One important factor influencing the [earnings] differential is experience. The lack of continuity in women's attachment to the labor force means that they will not have accumulated as much experience as men at a given age. The relatively steeper rise of men's income with age has been attributed to their greater accumulation of experience, of "human capital" acquired on the job. . . .

. . . [But] a differential, perhaps on the order of 20 percent, between the earnings of men and women remains after adjusting for factors such as education, work experience during the year, and even lifelong work experience.[4]

Accordingly, we cannot dismiss occupational and earnings differentials between men and women on the basis of "natural" responsibilities of motherhood. Discrimination is clearly at work here. Moreover, we must take care to note that the same kind of negative feedback that constrains the human-capital development of minority men affects women, too. Why should a woman postpone childbirth or pursue a lengthy and difficult course of study if it appears that she will not receive commensurate rewards in the labor market? Role differentiation and labor-market discrimination tend to reinforce each other.

[4] *Economic Report of the President*, 1973, pp. 104–06.

THE IMPACT OF DISCRIMINATION

That discrimination continues to exist both in the educational system and in labor markets is beyond doubt. Rather obvious, too, is the fact that minority men and all women suffer real and tangible losses from such discrimination. But who gains? And what kinds of benefits do they reap? How are our principal economic outcomes affected?

Micro gains and losses

It is tempting to conclude that the prime beneficiaries of discrimination are white males, particularly those of the white, Anglo-Saxon, Protestant (WASP) type. And such a conclusion would not be entirely wrong. We should also recognize, however, that not all males, or even all WASP males, benefit from discrimination and, more important, that we all suffer in the aggregate.

With respect to educational facilities, there is a clear economic gain to whites. If minority students are relegated to inferior schools, then the better schools end up being white preserves. In a world where resources are limited—and the supply of good teachers is definitely limited—whites gain by expropriating a larger share of those resources. White children of lesser ability are also released from the necessity of competing with more able minority children in the quest for admissions. These are clear economic gains. Unfortunately, not all whites share in the spoils. Indeed, many whites suffer from racial discrimination. Not all whites can flee the inner city. Those left behind, primarily the poorest, are trapped in increasingly inferior educational systems, unable to enjoy the white monopolies held elsewhere, typically in the suburbs. They, like their minority neighbors, find their human-capital potential underdeveloped. Thus some whites gain while others lose.

The same kind of benefit distribution is apparent in the labor market. In general, racial discrimination in the labor market takes the form of confining minority workers to particular kinds of occupations, industries, and jobs. Two distinct groups of whites gain from this racial segregation of the labor market. White workers gain by being immunized against competition from blacks and other minorities in "white only" jobs. Employers (for instance, operators of laundries and hotels) who actually hire black workers in "black only" jobs gain by getting higher quality labor than they are in fact paying for. These economic gains are illustrated in Figure 32.3.

Not all whites gain directly, however, from such discrimination. Some, in fact, actually lose. White workers who cannot escape menial occupations suffer from increased competition from minority workers. The wages of white laundry and hotel workers, for example, are held down by the large number of blacks and other minority workers who are excluded from other occupations. These are the workers trapped in Market B of Figure 32.3, either by skill deficiencies or by geographical location. Some employers, too, suffer losses. In a segregated labor market, some employers often have to incur high labor costs through the use of poorly qualified whites. Some employers may even be driven out of business because they cannot afford to pay the higher wage, W_W.

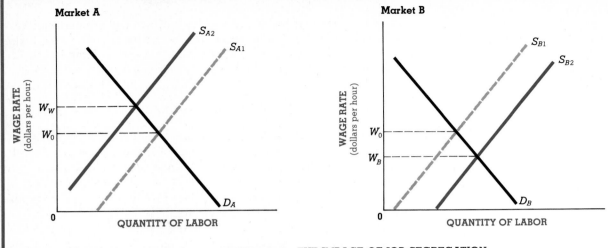

FIGURE 32.3 THE IMPACT OF JOB SEGREGATION

Suppose there are only two kinds of jobs, those in Market A and those in Market B. If everyone is allowed to move freely from one market to another, the equilibrium wage will end up at W_0 in both markets. Why? Because if wages were higher in A than in B, people would move out of B and into A. Such movements would lower the marginal revenue productivity in A while raising it in B. Hence freedom of movement between Markets A and B ensures an equality of average wage rates.

But now suppose black workers in Market A are kicked out and sent to Market B, making A a "whites-only" preserve. This has the effect of shifting the labor-supply curve in A to the left (to S_{A2}) and the labor-supply curve in B to the right (to S_{B2}). The net result, indicated by the new supply and demand intersections, is an increase in wages in Market A (to W_W) and a reduction of wages in Market B (to W_B).

Market incentives

cost efficiency: The amount of output associated with an additional dollar spent on input; the *MPP* of an input divided by its price (cost).

The fact that some whites lose as a consequence of racial discrimination is especially noteworthy because it suggests the existence of market forces that seek to eliminate discrimination. Consider an employer in Market A of Figure 32.3. As we have observed, racial discrimination ends up raising his costs of production by requiring him to pay higher wage rates. Were he a true profit-maximizer, he would strive to break the racial barrier and hire more cost-effective workers. He could then attain greater **cost efficiency**, expand production, and increase his profits.

Although the financial incentive for the producer in Market A to break the racial barrier is evident, it may be held in check by a variety of forces. He may himself harbor racial prejudices and be willing to subvert the profit motive for the sake of dissociating himself from blacks. As Professor Gary Becker has shown, such a posture may satisfy him psychologically, even if it costs him financially. Or he may fear reprisals from his white employees, fellow producers, or customers if he were to hire blacks. Professor Duran Bell has suggested that the white employees may turn out to be especially troublesome, because they are the prime beneficiaries of existing racial segregation. They may respond to integration of the workplace by

REVERSE DISCRIMINATION: THE UNSETTLED ISSUE

The patterns of discrimination practiced against minorities and women have inflicted significant economic losses on these groups. To compensate in part for these losses, the federal government and the courts have required schools and employers to take "affirmative action" to end discrimination. Schools and employers are required to make special efforts to recruit, admit, employ, train, and promote minorities and women. In almost all cases, affirmative action has meant some form of preferential treatment for minorities and women. In the more extreme cases, it has meant outright quotas for the admission or employment of these groups.

The preferential treatment associated with affirmative action implies discriminatory treatment of previously favored groups, particularly white males. This charge of "reverse discrimination" reached the U.S. Supreme Court in 1978 on the basis of a complaint by Allan Bakke. Bakke, a white male, argued that he had been denied admission to the University of California (Davis) medical school at the same time that less qualified minority applicants were being admitted. The Court agreed with Bakke, and ruled that rigid minority quotas were unconstitutional, although race could be considered as one of many factors in admissions decisions.

In essence, the courts have recognized a fundamental conflict between the desire to compensate the victims of past discrimination and the desire to uphold the principle of equal opportunity. Without affirmative action, the legacy of past discrimination will persist for decades. With affirmative action, however, white males and others will suffer some discrimination. Not surprisingly, over 80 percent of the public favor "selection on the basis of ability" but only 11 percent favor "preferential treatment." Congress and the courts have been attempting to strike an acceptable compromise between these two principles.

reducing their own productivity or impeding the efforts of minority workers.

"Radical" economists take an even dimmer view of the prospects of achieving equality through the market mechanism. From a Marxian perspective, discrimination against black workers functions to "divide and conquer" the laboring class. By dissipating energy and power on the maintenance of segregated job opportunities, the laboring class weakens its bargaining position. As a consequence, capitalists become the primary beneficiaries of continued discrimination.

Macro losses

Because some whites gain while other whites lose as a direct result of discrimination, it is difficult to calculate the net gain or loss to the white community on a microeconomic level. The same may be said of sex discrimination. Those men who want to be college professors or accountants clearly gain, while those who want to be elementary school teachers or bank tellers lose.

No such ambiguity attaches to the indirect losses that are incurred on an aggregate or macroeconomic level, however. When discrimination against minorities is pervasive, society as a whole loses potential human capital. The abilities and creativity of minority

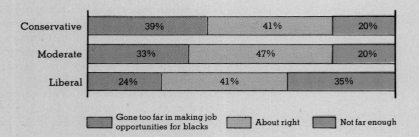

HAVE WE GONE TOO FAR?: VIEWS ON AFFIRMATIVE ACTION

Question: A number of efforts have been made to help certain groups in this country improve their opportunities. . . . What about blacks and job opportunities—do you think that we in this country have gone too far, not far enough, or have done about the right amount in making job opportunities for blacks?

	Gone too far	About right	Not far enough
Conservative	39%	41%	20%
Moderate	33%	47%	20%
Liberal	24%	41%	35%

☐ Gone too far in making job opportunities for blacks   ☐ About right   ☐ Not far enough

Answer: In the national sample, 33% said "gone too far . . . ," 43% said "about right," and 24% "not far enough."

Source: Survey by the Roper Organization (Roper Report 80-3), February 9–23, 1980, as reported in *Public Opinion*, February/March 1981.

workers remain underdeveloped and underemployed. The same may be said of discrimination against women or low-income families. ***Discrimination serves to shrink society's production possibilities and reduce total output.*** Estimates of the size of this loss in GNP run as high as $30 billion a year. In addition, much of the output we do produce is directed to such relatively unattractive uses as the surveillance of homes, streets, jails, and welfare case loads. This is clearly an undesirable shift in the mix of output. Finally, the practice of discrimination—the erection of artificial race, sex, or class barriers—undermines the efficiency of labor markets, thereby making prices higher than they would otherwise be (see Chapter 13). Thus any direct gains or losses to individual whites, males, or upper-income persons are overwhelmed by the very large indirect losses suffered by the economy as a whole.

SUMMARY

▪ Discrimination is still a fact of life in both the educational system and the labor market. The effect of such discrimination is to deny people an opportunity to develop their human capital and to utilize fully the human capital they possess.

▪ Within the educational system, discrimination takes many forms. For minority students, discrimination frequently means segregated and inferior schools. For women, it means both subtle and overt pressures to pursue distinctive kinds of curricula and to constrain educational aspirations. For all those discriminated against, discrimination means less human capital with which to enter the labor market.

■ In the labor market itself, minority groups and women do not have an equal opportunity to make the best of their restricted human-capital investments. Prejudice and institutional employment practices combine to handicap them still further. Thus blacks and whites with equal educational attainment end up getting different incomes. The same is true of men and women, even after we adjust for the fact that women typically interrupt their careers to bear children.

■ Discrimination in the labor market may take many forms, but the most common is segregation by occupation, industry, or specific job responsibilities. A broad assortment of jobs tends to be "white only" or "male only," just as a great many jobs are filled largely by minorities or women. This segregation of jobs tends to depress the wages of those discriminated against and raise the wages of those who are in favored jobs.

■ Although those discriminated against clearly lose in the quest for status, not all others gain. In particular, many employers are burdened with higher wage rates than would otherwise prevail as a result of job segregation. This situation creates an important market incentive for employers to break down race and sex barriers, thereby increasing both efficiency and profit.

■ On a microeconomic level, discrimination translates into lower incomes for those discriminated against. On a macroeconomic level, discrimination results in reduced output, a less desirable mix of output, greater unemployment, and higher prices.

Terms to remember

Define the following terms:

discrimination	**marginal revenue product**
human capital	**cost efficiency**

Questions for discussion

1. Suppose a man gets a job in a steel plant while another man with identical abilities (human capital) ends up working in a textile mill. The man in the steel plant earns twice as much as the man in the textile mill, although both work the same number of hours. How can you explain this difference?

2. In the example above, the steel worker obviously has a good thing going. What would happen to his wages if everyone suddenly wanted to work in steel plants? How could he prevent that from happening?

3. Continuing the same illustration, suppose the owners of the steel mill decided that more competition for available jobs would increase their profits. What risks would they be taking in hiring new workers?

4. What basis does an employer have for evaluating the potential productivity of a job applicant? Why might employers, especially large ones, adopt rigid hiring criteria, even if those criteria discriminated against minorities and women? How could public policy overcome such obstacles?

Problem

Suppose that the initial demand and supply for labor are identical in two industries, construction and bus driving. In each of these industries the initial conditions are:

Wage rate (per hour)	$1	$2	$3	$4	$5	$6	$7	$8
Quantity of labor demanded (workers per week)	19	18	17	16	15	14	13	12
Quantity of labor supplied (workers per week)	11	12	13	14	15	16	17	18

(a) Graph the market conditions in each industry.

(b) What is the equilibrium wage in each industry?

(c) Illustrate what happens to supply conditions when four workers are excluded from the construction industry (at all wage rates) and forced to become bus drivers.

(d) What is the resultant equilibrium wage rate in each industry?

(e) Who gained and who lost as a result of this discrimination?

INTERNATIONAL ECONOMICS AND COMPARATIVE SYSTEMS

CHAPTER 33

INTERNATIONAL TRADE

The 1982 World Series between the Milwaukee Brewers and the St. Louis Cardinals was played with Japanese gloves, Korean baseballs, and Mexican bats, making baseball something less than the "all-American" game. In that same year, consumers spent a lot of their income on French racing bikes, Japanese stereo equipment, Italian sweaters, Swiss chocolates, Colombian coffee, Scotch whiskey, and Venezuelan oil. Most of these goods could have been produced in the United States, and many were. Why did we purchase them from other countries? For that matter, why did the rest of the world buy computers, tractors, electronic calculators, airplanes, and wheat from us rather than produce such products for themselves? Is there some advantage to be gained from international trade? If so, what is the nature of that advantage, and who reaps the benefits?

In this chapter we shall first survey the nature of international trade patterns, then examine the motivation for such trade. We shall also explore potential restrictions on trade and consider who might gain or lose from them.

U.S. TRADE PATTERNS

exports: Goods and services sold to foreign buyers.

imports: Goods and services purchased from foreign sources.

The United States is becoming increasingly dependent on international trade. In 1981 our merchandise **exports** totaled over $236 billion. This represented nearly 8 percent of total output. In addition, we had service exports (e.g., tourism, investment income) of nearly $100 billion. Our **imports** of goods and services were comparable.

FIGURE 33.1 EXPORTS IN RELATION TO GNP

Merchandise exports account for 7.8 percent of total U.S. output. Although substantial, this trade dependence is relatively low by international standards. Germany, for example, exports 26 percent of its total output.

Source: U.S. Department of Commerce, 1981.

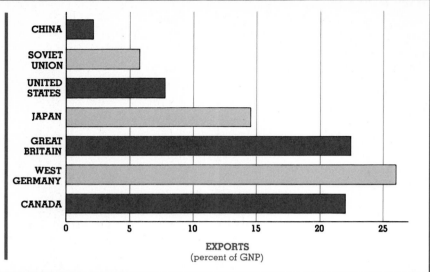

EXPORTS
(percent of GNP)

Although we depend on international trade much less than other countries (see Figure 33.1), our exports and imports are extremely important. Exports, for example, are part of the *aggregate demand* for goods and services. Hence an increase in exports reflects more demand for domestic goods and services. On the other hand, imports represent a form of leakage from the circular flow of income. A change in the volume of exports or imports will directly affect domestic production, employment, and prices. Moreover, the effects will tend to be *multiplied* as the initial change in trade makes its way around the circular flow.

The importance of trade for the domestic economy is even more apparent when specific goods are considered. True, there probably would have been a World Series in 1981 even without imported equipment. But Americans might have been asleep if we hadn't imported coffee (or tea). Likewise, there would have been no aluminum if we hadn't imported bauxite, no chrome bumpers if we hadn't imported chromium, no tin cans without imported tin. Just how vital imports of basic resources can be to our accustomed patterns of economic activity was dramatized when the OPEC countries reduced oil sales to us in 1973 and 1979. These supply interruptions and later price increases caused significant inflation and unemployment in the United States (see Chapter 16).

The export situation is similar: the relatively low ratio of exports to total sales disguises our heavy dependence on exports in specific industries. Over 60 percent of our rice, corn, and wheat production was exported in 1981, as was half of our soybeans. Clearly, a decision by foreigners to stop eating American agricultural products could have devastated a lot of American farmers. Such companies as Boeing (planes), Caterpiller Tractor (construction equipment), Weyerhauser (logs, lumber), and Hewlett-Packard (electronics) sell over one-fourth of their output in foreign markets. Pepsi and Coke

FIGURE 33.2 U.S. TRADE PATTERNS

Most U.S. merchandise exports and imports consist of manufactured goods. However, agricultural exports and oil imports are growing rapidly. About 40 percent of all U.S. trade is with developing countries, including OPEC (oil-exporting) nations.

Source: U.S. Department of Commerce.

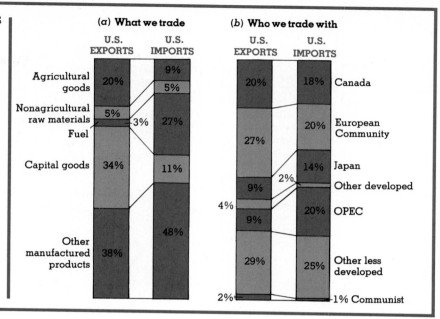

(a) **What we trade**

	U.S. EXPORTS	U.S. IMPORTS
Agricultural goods	20%	9%
		5%
Nonagricultural raw materials	5%	27%
Fuel	3%	
Capital goods	34%	11%
Other manufactured products	38%	48%

(b) **Who we trade with**

	U.S. EXPORTS	U.S. IMPORTS	
	20%	18%	Canada
	27%	20%	European Community
		14%	Japan
	9%	2%	Other developed
	4%	20%	OPEC
	9%		
	29%	25%	Other less developed
	2%	1%	Communist

trade deficit: The amount by which the value of imports exceeds the value of exports in a given time period.

trade surplus: The amount by which the value of exports exceeds the value of imports in a given time period.

are battling it out in the soft-drink markets of such unlikely places as Egypt, Abu Dhabi, and the Soviet Union.

Figure 33.2 provides a quick summary of the trading we do in goods, and with whom. In 1981 we imported over $264 billion worth of merchandise. We exported a smaller amount ($236 billion), giving us a **trade deficit** of $28 billion. Had we exported more than we imported we would have had a **trade surplus.**[1]

Most of our imports came from Europe and Canada, although oil imports have accounted for an increasing share of our total imports. Trade with such planned economies as China and the Soviet Union is currently very small, but growing rapidly.

MOTIVATION TO TRADE

Our extensive trade with other countries of the world is motivated by the recognition that *specialization increases total output.* In other words, our decision to trade with other countries arises from the same considerations that motivate individuals to specialize in production, satisfying their remaining needs in the marketplace. Why don't you become self-sufficient, growing all your own food, building your own shelter, recording your own songs? Presumably because you have found that you can enjoy a much higher standard of living (and better music) by producing only a few goods and buy-

[1] Traditionally the trade deficit (surplus) refers to merchandise only. Imports and exports of services are added to compute the "current account" balance. In 1981 the current account was in surplus, since service exports (e.g., air travel) exceeded service imports by $41 billion.

FIGURE 33.3 CONSUMPTION POSSIBILITIES WITHOUT TRADE

In the absence of trade, a country's consumption possibilities are identical to its production possibilities. The assumed production possibilities of the United States and France are illustrated in the graphs and the corresponding schedules. Before entering into trade, the United States chose to produce and consume at point *D*, with 40 zillion loaves of bread and 30 zillion barrels of wine. France chose point *I* on its own production-possibilities curve. By trading, each country hopes to increase its consumption beyond these levels.

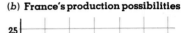

U.S. production possibilities				French production possibilities		
	Bread	+	Wine		Bread	+	Wine
A	100	+	0	*G*	15	+	0
B	80	+	10	*H*	12	+	12
C	60	+	20	*I*	9	+	24
D	40	+	30	*J*	6	+	36
E	20	+	40	*K*	3	+	48
F	0	+	50	*L*	0	+	60

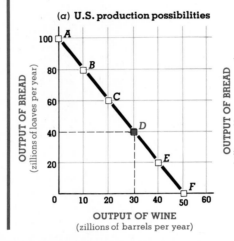
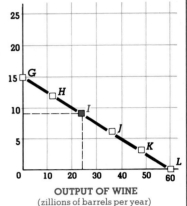

(a) U.S. production possibilities

(b) France's production possibilities

Production and consumption without trade

production possibilities: The alternative combinations of final goods and services that could be produced in a given time period with all available resources and technology.

ing the rest in the marketplace. When countries engage in international trade, they are expressing the same kind of commitment to specialization, and for the same reasons.

To demonstrate the economic gains obtainable from international trade, we may examine the production-possibilities curves of two countries. We want to demonstrate that two countries that trade can together produce more output than they could in the absence of trade. If they can, *the gain from trade will be increased world output and thus higher standards of living in both countries.*

Consider the production and consumption possibilities of just two countries—say, the United States and France. For the sake of illustration, we shall assume that both countries produce only two goods, bread and wine. We shall also set aside worries about the law of diminishing returns and the substitutability of resources, thus transforming the familiar **production-possibilities** curve into a straight line, as in Figure 33.3.

The "curves" in Figure 33.3 and our own intuition suggest that the United States is capable of producing much more bread than France is. After all, we have a greater abundance of labor, land, and other factors of production than France does. We shall assume that the United States is capable of producing up to 100 zillion loaves of bread per year, if we devoted all of our resources to that purpose. This capability is indicated by point *A* in Figure 33.3*a* and the accompanying production-possibilities schedule. France (Figure 33.3*b*), on the other hand, confronts a *maximum* bread production of only 15 zillion loaves per year (point *G*) because it has little land available, less fuel, and fewer potential workers.

The capacities of the two countries for wine production are 50 zillion barrels for us (point *F*) and 60 zillion for France (point *L*), largely reflecting France's greater experience in tending vines. Both countries are also capable of producing alternative *combinations* of bread and wine, as evidenced by their respective production-possibilities curves (points *B–E* for the United States and *H–K* for France).

In the absence of contact with the outside world, the production-possibilities curve for each country also defines its **consumption possibilities,** because neither country can consume more than it produces.[2] Thus the burning issue in each country is which mix of output to choose—WHAT to produce—out of the infinite number of choices available.

Assume that Americans choose point *D* on their production-possibilities curve. At point *D* we would produce and consume 40 zillion loaves of bread and 30 zillion barrels of wine each year. The French, on the other hand, prefer the mix of output represented by point *I* on their production-possibilities curve. At that point they produce and consume 9 zillion loaves of bread and 24 zillion barrels of wine.

Our primary interest here is in the combined annual output of the United States and France. In this case (points *D* and *I*), total world output comes to 49 zillion loaves of bread and 54 zillion barrels of wine. What we want to know is whether world output would increase if France and the United States abandoned their isolation and started trading. Could either country, or both, be made better off by engaging in a little trade?

consumption possibilities:
The alternative combinations of goods and services that a country could consume in a given time period.

Production and consumption with trade

In view of the fact that both countries are saddled with limited production possibilities, trying to eke out a little extra wine and bread from this situation might not appear very promising. Such a conclusion is unwarranted, however. Take another look at the production possibilities confronting the United States, as reproduced in Figure 33.4. Suppose that the United States were to produce at point *C* rather than point *D*. At point *C* we could produce 60 zillion loaves of bread and 20 zillion barrels of wine. That combination is clearly possible, even if less desirable (as evidenced by the fact that the United States earlier chose point *D*). Suppose further that the French were to move to point *K*, producing 48 zillion barrels of wine and only 3 zillion loaves of bread.

Two observations are now called for. The first is simply that output mixes have changed in each country. The second, and more

[2] If a country has inventories of consumer goods, consumption can exceed production for a brief period. The option is short-lived, however.

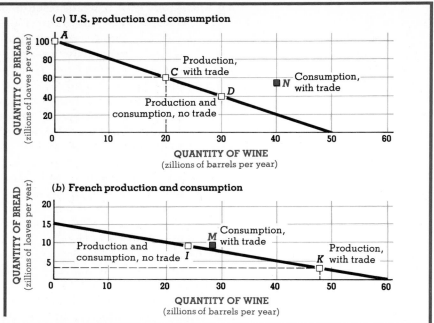

interesting, is that total world output has increased. When the
United States and France were at points D and I, their *combined*
annual output consisted of:

	Bread (zillions of loaves)	Wine (zillions of barrels)
U.S. (at point D)	40	30
France (at point I)	9	24
Total	49	54

Now world output includes:

	Bread (zillions of loaves)	Wine (zillions of barrels)
U.S. (at point C)	60	20
France (at point K)	3	48
Total	63	68

Total world output has increased by 14 zillion loaves of bread and 14
zillion barrels of wine. Clearly there is the potential here for making
both countries better off than they were in the absence of trade.

The reason the United States and France weren't producing at
points C and K before is that they simply didn't want to consume
those particular combinations of output. The United States wanted a
slightly more liquid combination than that represented by point C
and the French could not survive long at point K. Hence they chose
points D and I. Nevertheless, our discovery that points C and K result
in greater total output suggests that everybody can be happier if we
all cooperate. The obvious thing to do is to trade, to start exchanging
wine for bread and vice versa.

Suppose that we are the first to discover the potential benefits
that result from trade. Using Figure 33.4 as our guide, we suggest to

the French that they move their mix of output from point *I* to point *K*. As an incentive for making such a move, we promise to give them 6 zillion loaves of bread in exchange for 20 zillion barrels of wine. This would leave them at point *M*, with as much bread to consume as they used to have, plus an extra 4 zillion barrels of wine. At point *I* they had 9 zillion loaves of bread and 24 zillion barrels of wine. At point *M* they can have 9 zillion loaves of bread and 28 zillion barrels of wine. Thus by altering their mix of output (from point *I* to point *K*) and then trading (point *K* to point *M*), the French end up with more goods and services than they had in the beginning. Notice in particular that the new consumption possibility made available through international trade (point *M*) lies outside the domestic production-possibilities curve.

The French will obviously be quite pleased with their limited trading experience, but where does this leave us? Do we gain from trade as well? The answer is yes. By trading, we, too, end up consuming a mix of output that lies outside our production-possibilities curve.

Note that at point *C* we produce 60 zillion loaves of bread per year and 20 zillion barrels of wine. We then give up 6 zillion loaves to get 20 zillion barrels of wine from the French. Hence we end up consuming at point *N*, enjoying 54 zillion loaves of bread and 40 zillion barrels of wine. Thus by first changing our mix of output (from point *D* to point *C*), then trading (point *C* to point *N*), we end up with 14 zillion more loaves of bread and 10 zillion more barrels of wine than we started with! Clearly international trade has made us better off.

There is no sleight of hand going on here. Rather, the gains from trade are due to the specialization that occurs when countries begin to exchange goods and services. When each country goes it alone, it is a prisoner of its own production-possibilities curve and must makes its production decisions on the basis of its own consumption desires. When international trade is permitted, however, each country can concentrate on the exploitation of its production capabilities. Each country then trades to acquire the goods it desires to consume. In other words, international trade allows each country to focus on what it does best, with the resultant specialization increasing total world output. In this way each country is able to escape the confines of its own production-possibilities curve, to reach beyond it for a larger basket of consumption goods. ***When a country engages in international trade, its consumption possibilities always exceed its production possibilities.*** This excess of consumption possibilities is demonstrated by the fact that points *N* and *M* lie outside the production-possibilities curves in Figure 33.4. If it were not possible for countries to increase their consumption by trading, there would be no incentive for trading, and thus no trade.

PURSUIT OF COMPARATIVE ADVANTAGE

Although international trade can make everyone better off, it is not so obvious what goods should be traded, or on what terms. In our previous illustration, the United States ended up trading loaves of

opportunity cost: The most desired goods or services that are forgone in order to obtain something else.

comparative advantage: The ability of a country to produce a specific good at a lower opportunity cost than its trading partners.

bread for wine on terms that were decidedly favorable to us. Why did we choose to export bread rather than wine, and how did we end up getting such a good deal?

The basis for our decision to export bread lies in our comparative advantage in producing bread rather than wine. Recall that we can produce a maximum of 100 zillion loaves of bread per year or 50 zillion barrels of wine. Thus the domestic opportunity cost of producing 100 zillion loaves of bread is the 50 zillion barrels of wine we forsake in order to devote our resources to bread production. In fact, at every point on the U.S. production-possibilities curve of Figure 33.4a, the **opportunity cost** of a loaf of bread is one-half barrel of wine. That is to say, we are effectively paying half a barrel of wine to get a loaf of bread.

Although the opportunity costs of bread production in the United States might appear outrageous, note the even higher opportunity costs that prevail in France. According to Figure 33.4b, the opportunity cost of producing an additional loaf of bread in France is a staggering four barrels of wine. The production of additional bread entails giving up too much wine.

A comparison of the opportunity costs prevailing in each country unveils the nature of what we call comparative advantage. The United States has a **comparative advantage** in bread production because less wine has to be given up to produce bread in the United States than in France. In other words, the opportunity costs of bread production are lower here than in France. *Comparative advantage refers to the relative (opportunity) costs of producing particular goods.*

Naturally, a country should specialize in what it is relatively efficient at producing, as reflected in the opportunity costs of production. Were you the production manager for the whole world, you would certainly want each country to exploit its relative abilities, thus maximizing world output. Each country can arrive at that same decision itself by comparing its own opportunity costs to those prevailing elsewhere and offering to trade to mutual advantage. World output, and thus the potential gains from trade, will be maximized when each country pursues its comparative advantage. It does so by exporting goods that entail relatively low domestic opportunity costs and importing goods that involve relatively high (domestic) opportunity costs.

Absolute costs don't count

absolute advantage: The ability of a country to produce a specific good with fewer resources (per unit of output) than other countries.

In assessing the nature of comparative advantage, notice that we needn't know anything about the actual costs involved in production. Have you seen any data suggesting how much labor, land, or capital is required to produce a loaf of bread in either France or the United States? For all you and I know, the French may be able to produce both a loaf of bread and a barrel of wine with fewer resources than we are using. Such an **absolute advantage** in production might exist because of their much longer experience in cultivating both grapes and wheat, or simply because they have more talent.

We can envy such productivity, and even try to emulate it, but it should not alter our production and international trade decisions. All we really care about are *opportunity costs*—what we have to give

REALLOCATING LABOR: COMPARATIVE ADVANTAGE AT WORK

Labor moved out of these industries:	*Jobs Lost*
Apparel	− 103,363
Motor vehicles and parts	− 76,195
Furnaces, steel products	− 46,502
Shoes	− 37,745
Motorcycles, bicycles, and parts	− 22,667
Radio and television sets	− 20,405

And into these industries:	*Jobs gained*
Aircraft	+ 54,050
Aircraft equipment	+ 45,296
Computing machines	+ 38,483
Logging	+ 26,245
Oil field machinery	+ 20,505
Construction machinery	+ 17,626

Source: C. Michael Aho and James A. Orr, "Trade-Sensitive Employment: Who Are the Affected Workers?" *Monthly Labor Review*, February 1981.

Between 1964 and 1975, imports displaced workers from some industries while growing exports created new jobs elsewhere. These figures depict some of the major trade-related job losses and gains. By reallocating our labor in this way, we altered the mix of output in the direction of comparative advantage.

up in order to get more of a desired good. If we can get a barrel of imported wine for less bread than we have to give up to produce that wine ourselves, we have a comparative advantage in producing bread. In other words, as long as we have a comparative advantage in bread production, as reflected in relative opportunity costs, we should exploit it. It doesn't matter to us whether France could produce either good with fewer resources. For that matter, even if we had an absolute advantage in both goods, our comparative advantage would still be in wheat, as we have already confirmed. The absolute costs of production were omitted from the previous illustration because they were irrelevant.

To clarify the distinction between absolute advantage and comparative advantage, consider this example. When Charlie Osgood joined the Willamette Warriors' football team, he was the fastest runner ever to play football in Willamette. He could also throw the ball farther than most people could see. In other words, he had an *absolute advantage* in both throwing and running that made all other football players look like second-string water boys. Without extolling Charlie's prowess any further, let it stand that Charlie would have made the greatest quarterback *or* the greatest end ever to play football. *Would have.* The problem was that he could play only one position at a time, just as our resources can be used to produce only one good at a time. Thus the Willamette coach had to play Charlie either as a quarterback or as an end. He reasoned that Charlie could throw only a bit farther than some of the other top quarterbacks but could far outdistance all the other ends. In other words, Charlie had a *comparative advantage* in running and was assigned to play as an end.

TERMS OF TRADE

It is clear that it pays to pursue one's comparative advantage and trade with the rest of the world on that basis. It may not yet be clear, however, why we got such a good deal with France. We are clever traders, to be sure. But beyond that, is there any way to determine the **terms of trade,** the quantity of good *A* that must be given up in exchange for good *B*? In our previous illustration, the terms of trade were very favorable to us, as we exchanged only 6 zillion loaves of bread for 20 zillion barrels of wine. The terms of trade were thus 6 loaves = 20 barrels.

terms of trade: The rate at which goods are exchanged; the amount of good *A* given up for good *B* in trade.

The limits to the terms of trade

The terms of trade with France were determined by our offer and France's ready acceptance. France was willing to accept our offer because the attendant terms of trade permitted France to increase its wine consumption without giving up any bread consumption. In other words, our offer to trade 6 loaves for 20 barrels was an improvement over France's domestic opportunity costs. France's domestic possibilities required her to give up 24 barrels of wine in order to produce 6 loaves of bread (see Figure 33.4*b*).[3] Getting bread via trade was simply cheaper for France than producing bread at home, as evidenced by the fact that France ended up with an extra 4 zillion barrels of wine.

Our first clue to the terms of trade, then, lies in each country's domestic opportunity costs. A country will not trade unless the terms of trade are superior to domestic opportunities. As Figure 33.4*a* illustrates, the opportunity cost of wine in the United States is 2 loaves of bread. Accordingly, we will not export bread unless we get at least one barrel of wine in exchange for every 2 loaves of bread we ship overseas. In other words, we will not play the game unless the terms of trade are superior to our own opportunity costs, thus providing us with some benefit.

We can confidently predict that ***the terms of trade between any two countries will lie somewhere between their respective opportunity costs in production.*** That is to say, a loaf of bread in international trade will be worth at least ½ barrel of wine (the U.S. opportunity cost) but no more than 4 barrels (the French opportunity cost). In point of fact, the terms of trade ended up at 1 loaf = 3.34 barrels (that is, at 6 loaves = 20 barrels). This represented a very large gain for the United States and a small gain for France. This outcome and several other possibilities are illustrated in Figure 33.5.

The role of markets and prices

Relatively little trade is subject to such direct negotiations between countries. More often than not, the decision on whether to import or export a particular good is left up to the market decisions of individual consumers and producers. There are exceptions, as is illustrated by much of our trade with centrally planned economies and frequent

[3] People sometimes use the term "domestic terms of trade" to refer to opportunity costs in production. In this case, we would say that France will trade only if the international terms of trade are superior to the domestic terms of trade.

FIGURE 33.5 SEARCHING FOR THE TERMS OF TRADE

Trade creates the conditions for increasing our consumption possibilities. Note in *a* that the United States is capable of producing 100 zillion loaves of bread per year (point *A*). If we reduce bread production to only 85 zillion loaves of bread per year, we could move down the production-possibilities curve to point *X*. At point *X* we could produce and consume 7.5 zillion barrels of wine per year and 85 zillion loaves of bread. On the other hand, if we continued to produce 100 zillion loaves of bread, we might be able to trade 15 zillion loaves to France in exchange for as much as 60 zillion barrels of wine. This would leave us producing at point *A* but consuming at point *Y*. At point *Y* we have more wine and no less bread than we had at point *X*. Hence consumption possibilities with trade exceed our production possibilities.

A country will end up on the consumption-possibilities curve only if it gets all of the gains from trade. It will remain on its own production-possibilities curve only if it gets *none* of the gains from trade. In reality, the terms of trade determine how the gains from trade are distributed, and thus at what point in the shaded area each country ends up.

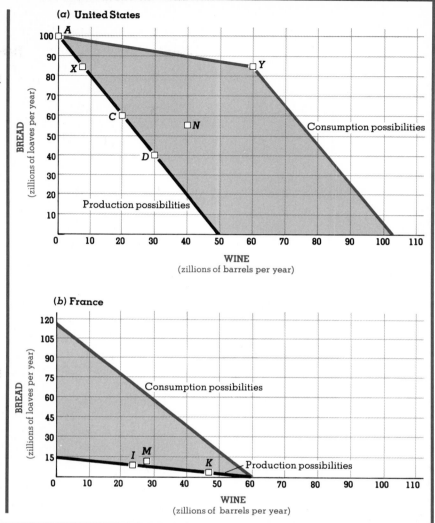

(a) United States

(b) France

trade intervention by government agencies. But before we look at those exceptions, it is important to note the role that individual consumers and producers play in trade decisions.

Individual consumers and producers are not much impressed by such abstractions as comparative advantage and the gains from trade. Individual market participants tend to focus on market prices, always trying to allocate their resources in order to maximize profits or personal satisfaction. As a result, consumers tend to buy the products that deliver the most utility per dollar of expenditure, while producers try to get the most output per dollar of cost. Everybody's looking for a bargain.

So what does this have to do with international trade? Well, suppose that Henri, an enterprising Frenchman, visited the United States before the advent of international trade and observed our market behavior. He noticed that bread was relatively cheap while wine was relatively expensive, the opposite of the price relationship prevailing in France. These price comparisons brought to his mind the opportunity for making a fast buck. All he had to do was bring over some French wine and trade it in the United States for a large quantity of bread. Then he could return to France and exchange the bread for a greater quantity of wine. *Alors!* Were he to do this a few times, he would amass substantial profits.

Our French entrepreneur's exploits will not only enrich him but will also move each country in the direction of its comparative advantage. The United States ends up exporting bread to France and France ends up exporting wine to the United States, exactly as the theory of comparative advantage suggests. The activating agent is not the Ministry of Trade and its 620 trained economists, however, but simply one enterprising French trader. He is aided and encouraged, of course, by the consumers and producers in each country. The American consumers are happy to trade bread for his wines. They thereby end up paying less for wine (in terms of bread) than they would otherwise have to. In other words, the terms of trade Henri offers are more attractive than the prevailing (domestic) relative prices. On the French side of the Atlantic, Henri's welcome is equally warm. French consumers are able to get a better deal by trading their wine for his imported bread than by trading with the local bakers.

Even some producers are happy. The wheat farmers and bakers in America are pleased and eager to deal with Henri. He is willing to buy a lot of bread and even to pay a premium price for it. Indeed, bread production has become so profitable in the United States that a lot of people who used to grow and mash grapes are now starting to grow wheat and knead dough. This alters the mix of U.S. output in the direction of more bread, exactly as suggested earlier in Figure 33.4*a*. In France the opposite kind of production shift is taking place. French wheat farmers start to plant grapes so they can take advantage of Henri's generous purchases. Thus Henri is able to lead each country in the direction of its comparative advantage, while raking in a substantial profit for himself along the way.

Where the terms of trade and the volume of exports and imports end up depends in part on how good a trader Henri is. It will also depend on the behavior of the thousands of individual consumers and producers who participate in the market exchanges. In other words, trade flows depend on both the supply and the demand for bread and wine in each country. ***The terms of trade, like the price of any good, will depend on the willingness of market participants to buy or sell at various prices.***

PRESSURES FOR TRADE RESTRICTIONS

Although the potential gains from world trade are perhaps clear, we should not conclude that everyone will be smiling at the Franco-American trade celebration. On the contrary, some people will be very upset about the trade routes that Henri has established. They will not only boycott the celebration but actively seek to discourage us from continuing to trade with France.

Microeconomic pressures

Consider, for example, the winegrowers in upstate New York. Do you think they are going to be very happy about Henri's entrepreneurship? Recall that Americans can now buy wine more cheaply from France than they can from New York. New York winegrowers are apt to be outraged at some foreigner cutting into their market. Before long we may hear talk about unfair foreign competition or about the greater nutritional value of American grapes (which, incidentally, came originally from France).[4] The New York winegrowers may also emphasize the importance of maintaining an adequate grape supply and a strong wine industry at home, just in case of nuclear war.

Joining with the growers will be the farm workers and all of the other workers, producers, and merchants whose livelihood depends on the New York wine industry. If they are aggressive and clever enough, the growers will also get the governor of the state to join their demonstration. After all, the governor must recognize the needs of his people, and his people definitely don't include the wheat farmers in Kansas who are making a bundle from international trade. New York consumers are, of course, benefiting from lower wine prices, but they are unlikely to demonstrate over a few cents a bottle. On the other hand, those few extra pennies translate into millions of dollars for domestic wine producers.

The winegrowers in upstate New York (not to mention those in California) will gather additional support from abroad. The wheat farmers in France are no happier about international trade than are the winegrowers in the United States. They would dearly love to sink all those boats bringing wheat from America, thereby protecting their own market position.

If we are to make sense of international trade patterns and policies, then, we must recognize one central fact of life. There will always exist identifiable producer groups who have a direct and tangible interest in restricting or eliminating international trade. In particular, *workers and producers who must compete with imported products—who work in import-competing industries—have an economic interest in restricting trade.* Which helps to explain why GM, Ford, and Chrysler are unhappy about trade in Toyotas and Mercedes and why workers in Massachusetts want to end the importation of Italian shoes. It also explains why the textile producers in South Carolina think Taiwan and Korea are behaving irresponsibly when they sell cotton shirts and dresses in the United States.

Microeconomic resistance to international trade, then, arises from the fact that imports typically mean fewer jobs and less income for some part of the domestic population. At the same time, however, exports represent increased jobs and incomes for another part of the population. Producers and workers who are associated with export industries gain from trade. Thus on a microeconomic level, there are identifiable gainers and losers from international trade. *Trade not only alters the mix of output but also redistributes in-*

Wine War

The European Common Market ordered an urgent explanation from France yesterday in an effort to head off a new flareup in the "wine war" which has soured relations with Italy.

The Executive Commission of the European Economic Community said it asked the French government why it imposed a temporary ban during the weekend on imports of Italian wine.

The wine war broke out last August when French winegrowers spoiled the cargo of an Italian wine tanker, protesting that the massive imports spoiled their market.

The Washington Post, Washington, D.C., February 2, 1982. Copyright © 1982 The Washington Post.

---

[4] In fact, the French had to re-import vines earlier sent to California after a grape blight destroyed the French vineyards in the late nineteenth century.

come from import-competing industries to export industries. This potential redistribution is the source of political and economic friction.

We must be careful to note, however, that the microeconomic gains from trade are greater than the microeconomic losses. It's not simply a question of robbing Peter to enrich Paul. On the contrary, we must remind ourselves that consumers in general are able to enjoy a higher standard of living as a result of international trade. As we saw earlier, trade increases world efficiency and total output. Accordingly, we end up slicing up a larger pie rather than just reslicing the same old smaller pie. Although this may be little consolation to the producer or worker who ends up getting a smaller slice than before, it does point up an essential fact. The gains from trade are large enough to make everybody better off if we so choose. Whether we actually choose to undertake such a distribution of the gains from trade is a separate question, to which we shall return shortly. We may note here, however, that restrictions on international trade designed to protect specific microeconomic interests have the effect of reducing the gains from trade. Trade restrictions leave us with a smaller pie to split up.

Additional pressures

Import-competing industries are the principal obstacle to expanded international trade. Selfish micro interests are not the only source of trade restrictions, however. Other arguments are also used to restrict trade.

NATIONAL SECURITY   The national-security argument for trade restrictions is twofold. On the one hand, it is argued that we cannot depend on foreign suppliers to provide us with essential defense-related goods, because that would leave us vulnerable in time of war. The argument has some obvious merit, although it is easily subject to abuse. The oil industry, for example, used the national-security argument to persuade President Dwight Eisenhower to curtail oil imports. The result was that we used up our "essential" reserves faster than we would have in the context of unrestricted trade. The domestic oil industry, of course, reaped enormous benefit from Eisenhower's decision to protect our national security.[5]

The second part of the national-security argument relates to our export of defense-related goods. There is some doubt about the wisdom of shipping nuclear submarines or long-range missiles to a potential enemy, even for a high price. The case for limited trade restriction is again evident. But here also the argument can be overextended, as when we forbade the export to the Soviet Union of sugar-coated cereals and of machinery for making pantyhose.

DUMPING   Another set of arguments against trade arises from the practice of dumping. Foreign producers "dump" their goods when they sell them in the United States at prices lower than those pre-

[5] The Mandatory Oil Import Program was terminated in 1973, when our domestic oil production could no longer satisfy domestic demand (see Chapter 16).

A LITANY OF LOSERS

Some excerpts from the Congressional Hearings on the Trade Reform Act of 1973:

In the past few years, sales of imported table wines . . . have soared at an alarming rate. . . . Unless this trend is halted immediately, the domestic wine industry will face economic ruin. . . . Foreign wine imports must be limited.
—Wine Institute

The apparel industry's workers have few other alternative job opportunities. They do want to work and earn a living at their work. Little wonder therefore that they want their jobs safeguarded against the erosion caused by the increasing penetration of apparel imports.
—International Ladies' Garment Workers' Union

We are never going to strengthen the dollar, cure our balance of payments problem, lick our high unemployment, eliminate an ever-worsening inflation, as long as the U.S. sits idly by as a dumping ground for shoes, TV sets, apparel, steel and automobiles, etc. It is about time that we told the Japanese, the Spanish, the Italians, the Brazilians, and the Argentinians, and others who insist on flooding our country with imported shoes that enough is enough.
—United Shoe Workers of America

We want to be friends with Mexico and Canada. . . . We would like to be put in the same ball game with them. . . . We are not trying to hinder foreign trade . . . [but] plants in Texas go out of business (17 in the last 7 years) because of the continued threat of fly-by-night creek bed, river bank Mexican brick operations implemented overnight.
—Brick Institute of America

vailing in their own country, perhaps even below the costs of production. Should the foreign producers continue this practice indefinitely, dumping would represent a great gain for us, because we would be getting foreign products on decidedly favorable terms. The problems over dumping arise from the fear that low prices will prevail only until the domestic import-competing industry is driven out of business. At that time we will be compelled to pay the foreign producer higher prices for his products. The fear of dumping, then, is analogous to the fear of predatory price cutting by powerful corporations, a practice we observed in Chapter 24.

The potential costs of dumping are serious and merit some policy response, but it is not always easy to prove dumping when it occurs. Those who must compete with imports have an uncanny ability to associate any and all low prices with predatory dumping. Thus responsible policy makers must take special care to confirm that dumping has occurred before attempting to restrict trade.

INFANT INDUSTRIES Dumping threatens to damage already established domestic industries. Even normal import prices, however, may make it difficult or impossible for a new domestic industry to develop. Infant industries are often burdened with abnormally high start-up costs. These high costs may arise from the need to train a whole work force and the expenses of establishing new marketing channels. With time to grow, however, an infant industry might experience substantial cost reductions and establish a new comparative advantage. In such cases, trade restrictions are sought to nurture an industry in its infancy. Trade restrictions are justified, however, only if there is tangible evidence that the industry can develop reasonably quickly and expand the gains from trade.

IMPROVING THE TERMS OF TRADE   One final argument for restricting trade rests on our earlier discussion of the way the gains from trade are distributed. As we observed, the distribution of the gains from trade depends on the terms of trade. That is, it depends on the quantity of exports that must be given up in order to get a given quantity of imports. If we buy fewer imports, foreign producers may lower their prices. If they do, the terms of trade will move in our favor, and we will end up with a larger share of the gains from trade.

One way to bring this sequence of events about is to put restrictions on imports, making it more difficult or expensive for Americans to buy foreign products. This kind of intervention will tend to cut down on import purchases, thereby inducing foreign producers to lower their prices. Unfortunately, this kind of strategem is available to everyone. Accordingly, our trading partners are likely to follow suit if we pursue such a course of action. Retaliatory restrictions on imports, each designed to improve the terms of trade, will ultimately eliminate all trade and therewith all of the gains people were competing for in the first place.

BARRIERS TO TRADE

The microeconomic losses associated with imports give rise to a constant clamor for trade restrictions. People whose jobs and incomes are threatened by international trade tend to organize quickly and air their grievances. Moreover, they are assured of a reasonably receptive hearing, both because of the political implications of good, well-financed organization and because the gains from trade are widely diffused. If successful, such efforts can lead to a variety of trade restrictions.

Embargoes

embargo: A prohibition on exports or imports.

The sure-fire way to restrict trade is simply to eliminate it. To do so, a country need only impose an embargo on exports, imports, or both. An **embargo** is nothing more than a prohibition against trading particular goods.

In 1973, for example, the Arab countries imposed an export embargo on oil destined for the United States in an effort to alter America's position on Israeli–Arab conflicts. And in 1959, when Fidel Castro became the prime minister of Cuba, the United States imposed an import embargo on Cuban goods. This embargo caused severe damage to Cuba's sugar industry and deprived American smokers of the famed Havana cigars.

Tariffs

tariff: A tax (duty) imposed on imported goods.

One of the most popular and visible restrictions on trade is the **tariff**, a special tax imposed on imported goods. Tariffs, also called "customs duties," were once the principal source of revenue for governments. In the eighteenth century, tariffs on tea, glass, wine, lead, and paper were imposed on the American colonies to provide extra revenue for the British government. The tariff on tea led to the Boston Tea Party in 1773 and gave added momentum to the independence movement. In modern times, tariffs have been used primarily as a means of import protection to satisfy specific microeconomic or macroeconomic interests. In 1982 U.S. tariffs added approximately 5 percent to the price of imported goods.

The attraction of tariffs to import-competing industries should be obvious. *A tariff on imported goods makes them more expensive to domestic consumers, and thus less competitive with domestically produced goods.* Among familiar tariffs in effect in 1982 were $0.51 per gallon on Scotch whiskey, $0.62 per gallon on Canadian whiskey, and $1.17 per gallon on imported champagne. All of these tariffs made American-produced spirits look like relatively good buys and thus contributed to higher sales and profits for domestic distillers and grape growers. In the same manner, imported-car prices are higher as a result of a 2.9 percent tariff, and Japanese stereos are burdened with tariffs ranging from 6.5 to 7.5 percent. In each of these cases, domestic producers in import-competing industries gain. The losers are domestic consumers, who end up paying higher prices; foreign producers, who lose business; and world efficiency, as trade is reduced.

Microeconomic interests are not the only source of pressure for tariff protection. As we have observed, imports represent leakage from the domestic circular flow and a potential loss of jobs at home. In the same way, exports represent increased aggregate demand and more jobs. From this perspective, the curtailment of imports looks like an easy solution to the problem of domestic unemployment. Just get people to "buy American" instead of buying imported products, it is argued, and domestic output and employment will expand. Congressman Willis Hawley used this argument in 1930. He assured his colleagues that higher tariffs would "bring about the growth and development in this country that has followed every other tariff bill, bringing as it does a new prosperity in which all people, in all sections, will increase their comforts, their enjoyment, and their happiness."[6] Congress responded by passing the Hawley-Smoot Tariff Act of 1930, which raised tariffs to an average of nearly 60 percent. The Hawley-Smoot Tariff effectively cut off most imports and contributed to the Great Depression.

Tariffs designed to expand domestic employment are more likely to fail than to succeed. If a tariff is successful in cutting down on imports, it effectively transfers the unemployment problem to other countries, a phenomenon often referred to as "beggar-my-neighbor." The resultant loss of business in other countries leaves them less able to purchase our exports and creates intense economic

[6] *New York Times*, June 15, 1930, p. 25.

and political pressures for retaliatory action. That is exactly what happened in the 1930s, as other countries erected barriers to trade to compensate for the effects of the Hawley-Smoot Tariff. World trade subsequently fell from $60 billion in 1928 to a mere $25 billion in 1938. In the process, all countries suffered from reduced demand (aggravated, of course, by foreign trade multipliers).

Quotas

quota: A limit on the quantity of a good that may be imported in a given time period.

Tariffs help to reduce the flow of imports by raising import prices. As an alternative barrier to trade, a country can impose import **quotas,** restrictions on the quantity of a particular good that may be imported. The United States maintained a quota on imported petroleum for a period of 14 years. Other goods that have been (and most of which still are) subject to import quotas in the United States are sugar, meat, dairy products, textiles, cotton, peanuts, and steel. According to the U.S. Department of State, approximately 12 percent of our imports are subject to import quotas.

Quotas, like all barriers to trade, reduce world efficiency and invite retaliatory action. Moreover, quotas are especially pernicious because of their impact on competition and the distribution of income. To see this impact, we may compare the market outcomes that result from no trade, free trade, tariff-restricted trade, and quota-restricted trade.

Figure 33.6a depicts the supply-and-demand relationships that would prevail in an economy that imposed a trade embargo on textiles. In this situation, the **equilibrium price** of textiles is completely determined by domestic demand and supply curves. The equilibrium price is p_1 and the quantity of textiles consumed is q_1.

equilibrium price: The price at which the quantity of a good demanded in a given time period equals the quantity supplied.

Suppose now that the embargo is lifted and foreign producers are allowed to sell textiles in the American market. The immediate effect of this decision will be a rightward shift of the market supply curve, as foreign supplies are added to domestic supplies (Figure 33.6b). If an unlimited quantity of textiles can be bought in world markets at a price of p_2, the new supply curve will look like S_2 (infinitely elastic at p_2). The new supply curve (S_2) intersects the old demand curve (D_1) at a new equilibrium price of p_2 and an expanded consumption of q_2. At this new equilibrium, domestic producers are supplying the quantity q_d while foreign producers are supplying the rest ($q_2 - q_d$). Comparing the new equilibrium to the old one, we see that the initiation of trade results in reduced prices and increased consumption.

Domestic textile producers are unhappy, of course, with their foreign competition. In the absence of trade, the domestic market equilibrium would provide more sales and higher prices to domestic companies. Once trade is opened up, the willingness of foreign producers to sell unlimited quantities of textiles at the price p_2 puts a limit on the price behavior of domestic producers. Accordingly, we can anticipate some lobbying for trade restrictions.

Figure 33.6c illustrates what would happen to prices and sales if the United Textile Producers were successful in persuading the government to impose a tariff. Let us assume that the tariff has the effect

FIGURE 33.6 THE IMPACT OF TRADE RESTRICTIONS

In the absence of trade, the domestic price and sales of a good will be determined by domestic supply and demand curves (point *A* in part *a*). Once trade is permitted, the market supply curve will be altered by the availability of imports. With free trade and unlimited availability of imports at price *p₂*, a new market equilibrium will be established at world prices (point *B*). Tariffs raise domestic prices and reduce the quantity sold (point *C*). Quotas put an absolute limit on imported sales, and thus give domestic producers a great opportunity to raise the market price (point *D*).

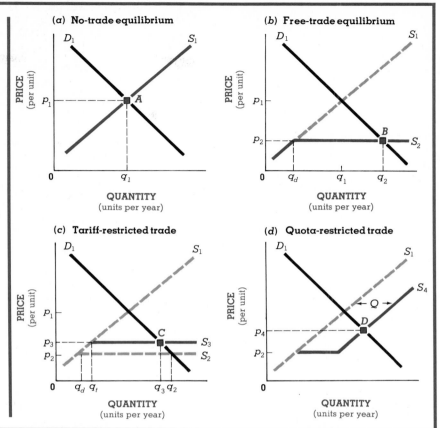

(*a*) **No-trade equilibrium**

(*b*) **Free-trade equilibrium**

(*c*) **Tariff-restricted trade**

(*d*) **Quota-restricted trade**

of raising imported textile prices from p_2 to p_3,[7] making it more difficult for foreign producers to undersell so many domestic producers. Domestic production expands from q_d to q_t, imports are reduced from $q_2 - q_d$ to $q_3 - q_t$, and the market price of textiles rises. Domestic textile producers are clearly better off, whereas domestic consumers and foreign producers are worse off. In addition, the U.S. Treasury will be better off as a result of increased tariff revenues.

Now consider the impact of a textile quota. Suppose that we eliminate tariffs but decree that imports cannot exceed the quantity Q. Because the quantity of imports can never exceed Q, the supply curve is effectively shifted to the right by that amount. The new curve S_4 (Figure 33.6d) indicates that no imports will occur below the world price p_2, and that above that price the quantity Q will be imported. Thus the *domestic* demand curve determines subsequent prices. Foreign producers are precluded from selling greater quantities as prices rise further. This outcome is in marked contrast to that of tariff-restricted trade (Figure 33.6c), which at least permits foreign

---

[7] Import prices will not necessarily rise by the full amount of a tariff, as foreign producers may lower their export prices somewhat to maintain sales. Thus the impact of a tariff on import prices depends in part on the price elasticity of foreign supply. In this case, we have assumed that foreign supplies are perfectly elastic, so that the difference $p_3 - p_2$ measures both the tariff and the ultimate price change.

U.S. Clothespin Industry Squeezed by Imports

The four major American manufacturers of wood spring clothespins want the government to stem the flow of rising imports from China, Romania, Poland and Czechoslovakia.

In case you believed the wood spring clothespin had been sent to oblivion by the gas and electric clothes dryer, consider these figures:

Last year, the United States imported 446.1 million clothespins with a total value of $2.8 million. . . .

The big gainers in sales were China, which rose from zero in 1974 to $447,000 worth in 1977, and Romania, which climbed from $11,000 in 1973 to $167,000 last year. Poland, always ahead of the rest on clothespins sales, remained the leader last year at $513,000.

As these countries were gaining, the four U.S. firms—three with plants in Maine, one in Vermont—were falling behind in holding their share of the market, according to statistics they gave the U.S. International Trade Commission, which is investigating the firms' complaints. . . .

"The money figures and the number of people are not fantastic, compared to what the American public hears every day. But if you stop the U.S. industry, you've ruined the economy of small towns and cut off workers' incomes," said Frederick C. McAlpin III, whose Washington law firm is handling the companies' petition. —Ward Sinclair

The Washington Post, Washington, D.C., June 3, 1978. Copyright © 1978 The Washington Post.

---

producers to respond to rising prices. Accordingly, **quotas are a much greater threat to competition than tariffs, because quotas preclude sales increases (of imported goods) at any price.**

Orderly marketing agreements

orderly marketing agreement (OMA): An agreement to reduce the volume of trade in a specific good; a "voluntary" quota.

A slight variant of quotas has been used in recent years. The worldwide economic slump of the mid-1970s had two important effects on world trade. First, falling incomes reduced both export and domestic sales. Second, producers became more aggressive in foreign markets, trying to make up for their domestic losses. In the American shoe, textile, and color television industries, these developments were further aggravated by a lack of comparative advantage. As a consequence, sales in these industries slumped significantly, and industry spokesmen clamored for trade restrictions. President Carter responded by negotiating **orderly marketing agreements** (OMAs) with foreign governments (Japan, South Korea, Taiwan). The essence of these agreements was a promise by those governments to reduce the volume of television, shoe, and textile exports to the United States. Korea, for example, agreed to reduce its annual shoe exports to the United States from 44 million pairs to 33 million pairs. Taiwan reduced its shoe exports from 156 million pairs to 122 million pairs per year. For their part, the Japanese agreed to reduce sales of color television sets in the United States from 2.8 million to 1.75 million per year. All of these agreements represented an informal type of quota. The only differences were that they were negotiated rather than imposed, and they made provisions for later increases in sales. But these differences were lost on consumers, who ended up paying higher prices for these goods.

Other barriers

Embargoes, export controls, tariffs, and quotas are the most visible barriers to trade, but they are far from being the only ones. Indeed, the variety of protectionist measures that have been devised is testimony to the ingenuity of the human mind. At the turn of the century, the Germans were committed to a most-favored-nation policy, a policy of extending equal treatment to all trading partners. The Germans, however, wanted to lower the tariff on cattle imports from Denmark without extending the same break to other countries, particularly Switzerland. But such a preferential tariff would have violated the most-favored-nation policy. Accordingly, the Germans created a new and higher tariff on "brown and dappled cows reared at a level of at least 300 meters above sea level and passing at least one month in every summer at an altitude of at least 800 meters." The new tariff was, of course, applied equally to all countries. But Danish cows never climbed that high, so they were not burdened with the new tariff.

Today most industrialized countries are likewise committed to a most-favored-nation policy, according to the General Agreement on Tariffs and Trade (GATT). That agreement, first signed in 1947, commits the world's trading partners to pursue free-trade policies. In pursuit of that objective, GATT signatories have negotiated agreements to lower tariffs and broaden quotas. In 1979, after six years of negotiation, the GATT countries agreed to reduce tariffs an average of 30 to 35 percent and to eliminate many of the 900 nontariff barriers to trade that exist. However, nontariff barriers to trade continued to grow. Italy, for example, has long discouraged auto imports by imposing a road tax based on weight and axle width. Not surprisingly, the tax resulted in increased levies on imported cars. The Japanese use complex and time-consuming licensing regulations and standards to keep out imports, thus sheltering domestic producers from competition. The United States is no less imaginative than most of its trading partners when it comes to nontariff barriers to trade. For example, we tax all distilled spirits entering this country as though they were 100 proof, thus effectively raising the tariff on an 86-proof bottle of Scotch. Domestic producers are thereby sheltered a bit from competition while the rest of us pay more for a drink.

Bat Men Strike Out in Japan

It may be a brand new baseball season, but they're still playing the same old game in the Japanese leagues.

U.S. bat manufacturers continue to strike out in Japan where they are pitched curves and sinkers by Japanese baseball groups preventing them from getting a handle on that big league baseball bat market.

After futilely slugging away, U.S. bat makers are calling a foul on the Japanese baseball leagues for refusing to certify foreign baseball equipment for use in their highly popular games.

The issue has been discussed by the Reagan administration and the Japa-

nese government for several months. When the Japanese government announced this year that it was taking 99 steps to open its markets to foreign goods, the Japanese Ministry of Education issued guidance to all of the private sports associations to approve foreign products, according to the U.S. Trade Representative's Office.

But the U.S. sporting goods manufacturers said they have yet to make it to first base because they haven't made a single sale. The Japanese are balking and using delaying tactics such as sending certification papers to the American firms written in Japanese. . . .

What's at stake is scoring in the $30 million Japanese baseball bat market, which consists mostly of aluminum bats used to hit rubber balls in the Japanese-style game. . . .

Several years ago, American bat manufacturers such as Hillerich & Bradsby Co. Inc., which produces the Louisville Slugger and which has annual sales of $38 million, started making the lightweight bats, which retail from $18 to $40. About six months later, the Japanese began manufacturing their own aluminum bats.

A Japanese Embassy spokesman said the certification process was started after a spectator at one of the games was injured by a metal bat that broke during play. However, [a U.S. industry spokesperson] said the bat was Japanese-made. The embassy spokesman said he didn't know what kind of bat it was.

—Jane Seaberry

The Washington Post, Washington, D.C., April 15, 1982. Copyright © 1982 The Washington Post.

THE NUT WARS

The U.S. Department of Agriculture is responsible for establishing quality standards for filberts (hazelnuts) sold in U.S. markets. Typically, however, the federal agency has simply adopted the standards developed by the state of Oregon, the nation's number one filbert-producing state. On August 1, 1980, Oregon tightened its standards for shelled filberts. The new standards reduce permissible "decay" to 1 percent of volume from the earlier standard of 5 percent. The new standard had no effect on Oregon filberts, which are uniformly machine-dried. But it effectively eliminated imported filberts (most of which come from Turkey), which are air-dried in the traditional way. Turkey protested the new rule, as did American candy manufacturers, consumer groups, and even the Office of Management and Budget. Domestic growers, however, led by the Filbert Control Board, argued that "decayed" nuts were both unpleasant and potentially toxic.

The GATT countries started a new round of discussions on trade barriers in November 1982. The focus of this round is on trade in services (e.g., air transport, insurance, banking), which is particularly sensitive to nontariff barriers.

POLICY IMPLICATIONS: TRADE ADJUSTMENT

The microeconomic pressures for trade barriers arise from the economic losses inflicted on import-competing industries. If those losses could be avoided or compensated for, no such pressures would arise. The strategy to pursue in this case is some form of **adjustment assistance.**

adjustment assistance: Compensation to market participants for losses imposed by international trade.

The objective of trade, we should remember, is to reallocate resources in such a way as to increase world output and domestic consumption. To this end, each country is expected to shuffle its capital and labor from one industry to another, in the direction of comparative advantage. As we observed in Figures 33.4 and 33.5, this simply entails a move from one point on the production-possibilities curve to another point. Unfortunately, such shuffling from one industry to another is more difficult in practice than it is along the dimensions of a textbook graph.

In our previous illustration of Franco-American trade, vineyards were transformed instantaneously into wheat fields, vats into ovens, and grape pickers into wheat threshers. A nice trick if you can manage it, but few people can. Indeed, were such instantaneous resource reallocations possible, there would be no microeconomic resistance to international trade. Everyone would be able to share in the jobs and profits associated with comparative advantage. *The resistance to trade arises from the fact that resource reallocations are difficult and costly in practice,* both in human and in financial terms. The nature of resistance to trade is evident in a few grim statistics. In a recent survey of workers who lost their jobs as a result of import competition, it was found that 26 percent had gone for at least a year without work. Those who had found jobs had worked, on the average, only 50 percent of the time.

Worker assistance

The objective of adjustment assistance is to speed up the reallocation of resources and to make the transition less painful for affected workers. For this purpose, workers may be taught new skills, assisted in finding new jobs, aided in moving to new areas, and provided with interim income maintenance. In the case of older workers whose skills are not easily transferred, early retirement and pension benefits may be the most efficient kind of adjustment assistance.

All such assistance is expensive, of course. The Trade Expansion Act of 1962 permits displaced workers to receive 70 percent of their previous wages for a period of up to 18 months, plus training and relocation allowances. Between 1975 and 1981 over 1 million workers received nearly $3 billion in such assistance. Nevertheless, many labor unions have dismissed the program as "burial insurance." They argue that benefits are too low, and that in any case many workers can neither retrain nor relocate without considerable hardship. As John Mara, head of the Boot and Shoe Workers' Union, put it after seeing ninety shoe factories shut down in Massachusetts in the early 1970s: "Retraining for what? I want the economists to tell me what alternatives are available. Picking tomatoes in California?" ***The critical issue in trade adjustment is whether alternative jobs do exist and whether we are prepared to help workers get them.***

Industry subsidies

Not only workers but employers as well are adversely affected by import competition. When the competition from abroad is too great, a plant may have to shut down and its owners absorb a loss on their investment. Even though the owners may not need adjustment assistance as badly as do the displaced workers, they are going to be a source of protectionist pressure. Furthermore, their loss may leave an entire community without a major source of economic support. For both of these reasons, some adjustment assistance may be necessary or appropriate.

"Don't be childish, man! Kicking Toyotas is no answer to our balance-of-trade gap."

Drawing by Donald Reilly; © 1971 The New Yorker Magazine, Inc.

INDUSTRIES WORRIED BY GROWING IMPORTS

	Percent of total industry sales	
Imported products	1960	1979
Shoes	2	37
Autos	5	21
Steel	4	14
Textile machinery	7	45
Apparel	2	10
Consumer electronics	16	51
Machine tools	3	26
Industrial chemicals	2	19
Farm machinery	7	15

Source: Data from *Business Week*, June 30, 1980, p. 60.

The most common form of adjustment assistance to import-competing firms is a subsidy, a direct payment from the public treasury to the affected firm. Ideally, such a subsidy will be provided for the purpose of converting a plant to more profitable lines of production. When the plant cannot be easily converted, the subsidy should be temporary, with the explicit intent of simply slowing, not obstructing, the process of adjustment to comparative advantage. The Trade Act of 1974 provided for loans of up to $1 million for affected companies and another $3 million in loan guarantees, but few companies accepted such aid. They argued that it was both inadequate and too encumbered with red tape.

The Reagan administration, too, concluded that trade-adjustment assistance was not effective, but for different reasons. The administration concluded that special benefits to trade-impacted workers and industries slow the adjustment process more often than they facilitate it. It proposed to treat trade-displaced workers just like other unemployed workers. Only after regular unemployment benefits were exhausted would trade-displaced workers get explicit "adjustment assistance." Even then, their assistance would be no more generous than regular unemployment benefits. Firms, too, would have a more difficult time obtaining special trade-adjustment assistance. In this way, the Reagan administration hoped to encourage greater competition in domestic markets and to speed the move toward comparative advantage.

SUMMARY

■ International trade permits each country to concentrate its resources on those goods it can produce relatively efficiently. This kind of productive specialization increases world output. For each country, the gains from trade are reflected in the fact that its consumption possibilities exceed its production possibilities.

■ In determining what to produce and offer in trade, each country will exploit its comparative advantage—its *relative* efficiency in producing various goods. One way to determine where comparative advantage lies is to compare the quantity of good *A* that must be given up in order to get a given quantity of good *B* from domestic production. If the same quantity of *B* can be obtained for less *A* by engaging in world trade, we have a comparative advantage in the production of good *A*. Comparative advantage rests on a comparison of relative opportunity costs.

■ The terms of trade—the rate at which goods are exchanged—are subject to the forces of international supply and demand. All we can say with certainty is that the terms of trade will lie somewhere between the opportunity costs of the trading partners. Once established, the terms of trade will help to determine the share of the gains from trade received by each trading partner.

■ Resistance to trade emanates from workers and firms that must compete with cheap imports. Even though the country as a whole stands to benefit from trade, these individuals and companies may lose jobs and incomes in the process.

■ The means of restricting trade are many and diverse. Embargoes are outright prohibitions against import or export of particular goods. Quotas merely limit the quantity of a good imported or exported. Tariffs, on the other hand, discourage imports by making them more expensive. Other nontariff barriers make trade too costly or time-consuming.

■ Trade-adjustment assistance is a mechanism for compensating people who incur economic losses as a result of international trade, and thus represents an alternative to trade restrictions.

Terms to remember

Define the following terms:

exports   absolute advantage
imports   terms of trade
trade deficit   embargo
trade surplus   tariff
production possibilities   quota
consumption possibilities   equilibrium price
opportunity cost   orderly marketing agreement (OMA)
comparative advantage   adjustment assistance

Questions for discussion

1. Suppose a lawyer can type faster than any secretary. Should the lawyer do her own typing? Can you demonstrate the validity of your answer?

2. How much adjustment assistance should a displaced worker receive? For how long?

3. In what sense does international trade restrain the exercise of domestic market power?

4. Suppose we refused to sell goods to any country that reduced or halted its exports to us. Who would benefit and who would lose from such retaliation? Can you suggest alternative ways of ensuring import supplies?

5. Domestic producers often base their claim for import protection on the fact that workers in country X are paid substandard wages. Is this a valid argument for protection?

Problem

Alpha and Beta, two tiny islands off the east coast of Tricoli, produce pigs and pineapples. The following production-possibilities schedules describe their potential output in tons per year:

Alpha		Beta	
Pork	Pineapples	Pork	Pineapples
0	30	0	20
2	25	10	16
4	20	20	12
6	15	30	8
8	10	40	4
10	5	45	2
12	0	50	0

(a) Graph the production and consumption possibilities confronting each island.

(b) What is the opportunity cost of pineapples in each island (before trade)?

(c) Which island has a comparative advantage in pork production?

(d) Demonstrate that both islands will be better off by trading.

CHAPTER 34

INTERNATIONAL FINANCE

The essential role of money, whatever its appearance, is to provide a generally accepted unit of exchange and standard of value. Money enables markets to function with some reasonable degree of efficiency. Where money is widely used and accepted, people are willing to exchange their goods and services for paper currency. They know that they can later use that paper to acquire desired products. It doesn't really matter what kind of paper is used or whose picture is on it. As long as everyone is in agreement that the paper has a distinct value in the market, it will serve its essential function.

Money is important for international economic relations as well, and for many of the same reasons. Imagine that you are wandering through the ancient village of Layopia and come upon a solid quartz statue of Homo economicus, the god of economics. Overcome with desire, you offer $400 in U.S. currency to the Layopian monk who owns the statue. But the monk merely smiles a quizzical smile and declines your offer. He points out that although he thinks the pictures of George Washington framed in green are very pretty indeed, he has no use for such paper. Obviously, the monk has never seen American money and doesn't know its worth. American Express travelers' checks, maybe? No, no success with that either. Either you have to offer the monk something that is of value to him or you go home without Homo economicus. As it turns out, Layopians do have a monetary system, denominated in the wisdom teeth of porpoises. This won't help you, however, unless you have some porpoise teeth with you or can convince him that your own money is even more valuable than his.

Imagine that you are now in France, trying to cut into the wine and bread trade that Henri demonstrated (in Chapter 33) could be so profitable. As you recall, all you have to do is buy some wine in France, bring it back to the United States for sale, and use the proceeds to buy bread. Then you take the bread back to France for sale and add up your handsome profits. Easy enough. But you will discover a possible flaw in your plans to exploit comparative advantage as soon as you reach the vineyards. The French winegrowers are just as unreceptive to your dollars and travelers' checks as were the Layopian monks. As one grower explains, "*Je regrette, monsieur, but what use have I of American dollars? I buy my meats and vegetables from Monsieur Pedot, and he accepts only French francs. Monsieur Sordoux, the cheese man, behaves the same way. So what am I to do with your dollars? I cannot buy groceries with them. Nonsense! Come back when you have groceries or French francs and we shall make a deal. Until then, au revoir.*"

A few experiences like this and you will quickly perceive the importance of money for international trade. Unless trade is to be confined to clumsy and inefficient barter deals, some unit of exchange that is accepted as a standard of value in all trading countries is necessary. With such a medium of exchange, you would have no problem buying wine in France or quartz statues in Layopia. The problems of international finance generally revolve around this basic requirement of formulating an international standard of value. The difficulties of formulating such a standard arise from the fact that each country has created and maintains its own units of exchange—its own money.

EXCHANGE RATES: THE CRITICAL LINK

We do in fact buy Japanese cars, French wines, and other goods from abroad. That we can do so suggests that some international unit of exchange has been established, that some common form of money exists. But we also know that the French still use francs, the Japanese use yen, and we use dollars in everyday market transactions. How is it, then, that extensive international trade is possible?

What makes international trade so easy is that we are able to exchange dollars for francs, for yen, or for any other national currency we may desire. If you want to buy French wines from the growers, you can exchange your dollars for francs at the Bank of France or almost any commercial bank in France. With your newly acquired francs, you can proceed to the vineyards. There you may dicker with the growers over the price of their Beaujolais and buy as much wine as your income permits.

In fact, if you have no great desire to visit the vineyards but still enjoy Beaujolais, you can stay in the United States and simply go to the local liquor store. In this case, you pay for the wine in dollars. The person who imported the wine attends to the problems of exchanging your dollars for French francs and dickering with the growers.

No matter who actually haggles with the growers or brings the

exchange rate: The price of one country's currency expressed in terms of another's; the domestic price of a foreign currency.

wine back to the United States, however, someone is going to have to exchange dollars for francs. The critical question for everybody concerned is how many francs we can get for our dollars—that is, what the **exchange rate** is. If we can get five francs for every dollar, the exchange rate is 5 francs = 1 dollar. Or to express the whole thing in another way, we could note that the price of a French franc is 20 cents when the exchange rate is 5 to 1. Thus an exchange rate is simply the price of one currency in terms of another.

FOREIGN-EXCHANGE MARKETS

Most exchange rates are determined in foreign-exchange markets. Stop thinking of money as some sort of magical substance and view it instead as a useful commodity that can facilitate market exchanges. From that perspective, an exchange rate—the price of money—is subject to the same influences that determine all market prices: demand and supply.

The demand for foreign currency

With the possible exception of coin collectors and speculators, few people have much demand for foreign currencies per se. Foreign currencies, including French francs and Layopian porpoise teeth, are demanded not for their intrinsic value but for what they can buy. Hence *the demand for foreign currency is primarily an expression of the demand for foreign goods and services.*

The demand for foreign currency originates in many ways. First and foremost, there is a demand for imported products, such as French wines, German cars, and Japanese stereo equipment. To acquire these things, we need foreign money. Table 34.1 indicates that we demanded over $264 billion worth of foreign currency for this purpose in 1981.

Foreign travel by Americans also generates a demand for foreign currency ($27 billion in 1981). When you are traveling, you need foreign currency to pay for transportation, hotel rooms, food, and anything else you wish to buy and can afford. Even if you are able to use U.S. dollars or travelers' checks on occasion, the recipients of such money will ultimately exchange them for local money, thereby reflecting your demand for foreign currency.

TABLE 34.1 U.S. DEMANDS FOR FOREIGN CURRENCY, 1981 (billions of dollars)

Our demand for foreign currency originates in our demand for foreign goods and services. Foreign producers want to be paid in their own currency. Hence to buy imported goods or services (including travel), we must first buy foreign currency.

Item	Value
Merchandise imports	$264.1
Travel expenditures	27.6
U.S. direct investment	8.7
Return on foreigners' investments	7.8
Private remittances and miscellaneous services	5.8
Military expenditures	11.3
Foreign aid, net	6.6

Source: U.S. Department of Commerce.

U.S. corporations demand foreign exchange, too. General Motors builds cars in Germany, Coca-Cola produces Coke in China, Exxon produces and refines oil all over the world. In nearly every such case, the U.S. firm must first build or buy some plant and equipment, using another country's factors of production. This activity requires foreign currency, and thus becomes another component of our demand for foreign currency.

Investment opportunities work both ways. Foreign producers often make direct investments in the United States. Shell and BP gas stations are a familiar example of direct foreign investment here, as are foreign auto plants, such as Volkswagen in Pennsylvania and Volvo in Virginia. In making such investments, foreign firms must first demand U.S. currency that can be used to buy our factors of production. Sooner or later, however, the foreign firms will want to reverse the flow of money, taking some of their profits back to their own banks and stockholders. In doing so, they create a demand for foreign currency as they convert the dollars they have earned in the United States into the currencies their stockholders and creditors can spend at home.

The other sources of the U.S. demand for foreign currency include transfers (typically by foreign workers who send home some of their U.S. income), U.S. military installations abroad (which are fed and housed with foreign goods and services), and foreign aid (which is often used to buy foreign goods).

The supply of foreign currency

Foreigners have the same kind of demand for U.S. dollars that we have for foreign currencies. They buy our merchandise (our exports, their imports), travel in the United States, and invest in productive resources located within our borders. Such **demands for U.S. dollars also represent a supply of foreign currencies.** That is to say, foreigners offer to exchange (supply) foreign currency when they desire (demand) U.S. dollars. The supply of foreign currencies generated by these foreign demands for U.S. dollars is summarized in Table 34.2.

Of particular note in Table 34.2 is the large amount of money involved in repatriated profits from direct American investments abroad. As we observed earlier, a company that invests in a foreign country wants to get some of its profits out sooner or later. U.S. firms have accumulated a tremendous investment in foreign countries,

TABLE 34.2 SUPPLIES OF FOREIGN CURRENCY, 1981
(billions of dollars)

The supply of foreign currency reflects a demand for American goods and services. To buy American goods and services, foreigners need U.S. currency. They offer to buy U.S. dollars with foreign currency. Such offers comprise the supply of foreign currency.

Item	Value
U.S. merchandise exports	$263.3
Travel income	27.4
Foreign direct investment in U.S.	21.3
Foreign purchases of U.S. securities, net	5.0
Return on U.S. foreign investments	31.9
Military exports	9.7

Source: U.S. Department of Commerce.

over $133 billion in book value by 1978.[1] These investments now generate a steady flow of profits and dividends back to the United States. This flow requires the conversion of foreign currencies into U.S. dollars (supply of foreign currencies, demand for U.S. dollars). Indeed, the current flow of profits exceeds the flow of new investments, as a comparison of Tables 34.1 and 34.2 will confirm.

Also noteworthy in Table 34.2 is the relatively large volume of net foreign purchases of U.S. securities. Foreign investors have tended to acquire limited participation in U.S. corporations by purchasing shares of stock rather than buying or building whole companies.[2]

Supply and demand curves

supply of foreign exchange: The quantities of foreign currency supplied (offered) in a given time period at alternative exchange rates (*ceteris paribus*).

demand for foreign exchange: The quantities of foreign currency demanded in a given time period at alternative exchange rates (*ceteris paribus*).

Tables 34.1 and 34.2 provide a reasonably complete view of the quantity of money that flowed through foreign-exchange markets in 1981. But such summary statistics can be misleading, because they don't convey how much those flows would have changed had exchange rates been different. Americans surely would have bought more imported goods in 1981 if foreign currencies had been less expensive. In other words, we should anticipate that the quantity of foreign currency demanded or supplied, like the quantity of any good traded in markets, depends on its price.

What this means is that both the demand for and **supply of foreign exchange** (foreign currencies) should be represented as curves, not as single points. In particular, we should recognize that the **demand for foreign exchange** is likely to have the familiar downward slope, while the supply of foreign exchange will have the usual upward slope. These two curves are illustrated in Figure 34.1.

THE DEMAND CURVE The explanations for the shape of the curves in Figure 34.1 should sound familiar. Consider the U.S. demand for any foreign product—say, Volkswagens.[3] Even people who have

---

[1] That is, the original cost less accumulated depreciation. Actual market values would be substantially higher, as a result of inflation.
[2] Whenever a foreign investor owns less than 25 percent of a U.S. company's stock, the investment is considered a *portfolio* investment rather than a *direct* investment.
[3] Two-thirds of all Volkswagens sold in the United States are now manufactured here. This decision was motivated in part by changing exchange rates, as we shall see.

FIGURE 34.1 THE FOREIGN-EXCHANGE MARKET

The foreign-exchange market operates like other markets. In this case, the "good" bought and sold is money (foreign exchange). The price and quantity of foreign exchange are determined by market supply and demand.

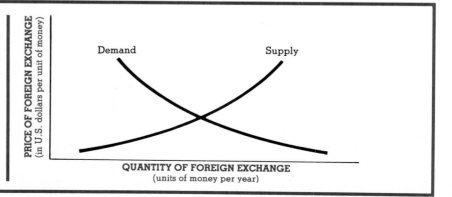

law of demand: The quantity
of a good demanded in a
given time period increases
as its price falls (ceteris
paribus).

never heard of foreign-exchange markets, or haven't the vaguest idea of what a deutsche mark is, buy VWs. All they know and care about is that they are willing to pay so many dollars for a Volkswagen and will buy something else when VWs are too expensive. Hence the U.S. demand curve for VWs will slope downward, reflecting **the law of demand**—the fact that the number of people willing and eager to buy a VW increases as VW prices drop.

Once we know the U.S. sales price for VWs, we can use the demand curve to determine how many VWs will be purchased and thus how much foreign exchange will be demanded. Two factors influence the U.S. price of VWs. The first is the willingness of the Volkswagen company to sell VWs for various amounts of deutsche marks. Remember that the VW producer and his workers want to be paid in their own currency—in deutsche marks (DM), the German monetary unit. The second factor is the number of deutsche marks that can be purchased for a dollar; that is, the *exchange rate* between deutsche marks and dollars. Hence the U.S. price of VWs is:

$$\text{Dollar price of VW} = \text{mark price of VW} \times \text{dollar price of German mark}$$

Suppose that the Volkswagen company (Volkswagenwerk) is prepared to sell a VW for DM10,000, and that the current exchange rate is DM2 = $1. At these rates, a VW will cost you $5,000. If you are willing to pay this much for a shiny new Volkswagen, you may do so at current exchange rates.

Now suppose that the exchange rate changes from DM2 = $1 to DM1 = $1. *A higher dollar price for German marks will raise the dollar costs of German goods.* In this case, the dollar price of a mark increases from $0.50 to $1. At this new exchange rate, the Volkswagen company is still willing to sell VWs at DM10,000 apiece. And German consumers continue to buy VWs at that price. But this constant mark price now translates into a higher *dollar* price. Thus a VW now costs you $10,000.

As the U.S. price of a VW rises, the number of VWs sold in the United States will decline. As VW sales decline, the quantity of German marks may decline as well. Thus the quantity of foreign currency demanded declines when the exchange rate rises because

U.S. Prices of Most Volkswagens Boosted for the Second Time Since Last October

ENGLEWOOD CLIFFS, N.J.—For the second time in two months, the prices of most Volkswagens sold in the U.S. are being raised. The latest increases average out to $155 a car, or 3.1%, and follow a $145-a-car boost last October.

The announcement of the latest increases by Volkswagen of America Inc., importer of German-made Volkswagens, Audis and Porsches, extends an almost nonstop string of price increases being made recently on foreign autos in the U.S. The flurry of price increases is being caused by the continued decline of the value of the U.S. dollar in comparison with overseas currencies. . . .

It isn't clear whether these latest increases, as they start to show up on cars currently being shipped to dealers, will dampen buyer enthusiasm for imports. Some Detroit auto men predict that foreign-car shoppers soon will begin to flinch at the sharply higher price tags.

Stronger Dollar

The stronger dollar prompts more Americans to travel abroad.

Advance bookings for European travel are up about 20% from a year ago for Mid-South Travel Service,

Memphis, Tenn., which cites recent gains in the dollar's buying power. In Tyler, Texas, Jackson Tours says business is up more than 15% from last year, largely because of increased travel to Mexico, which devalued its peso 30% in February. And in the Cleveland area, Berea Travel

Bureau is seeing more college students. "Now they can afford to take vacations in Europe," says a Berea manager.

---

equilibrium price: The price at which the quantity of a good demanded in a given time period equals the quantity supplied.

shift in demand: A change in the quantity demanded at any (every) given price.

foreign goods become more expensive and imports decline.[4] When the dollar price of the German mark actually increased in 1978, the Volkswagen company expressed considerable alarm.

THE SUPPLY CURVE The supply of foreign exchange can be explained in similar terms. Remember that the supply of foreign exchange arises from the foreign demand for dollars. If the exchange rate moves from DM2 = $1 to DM1 = $1, the mark price of dollars will fall. As dollars become cheaper for Germans, all American exports effectively fall in price. Thus we anticipate that Germans will want to buy more American products and therefore demand a greater quantity of dollars. In addition, foreign investors will perceive in a cheaper dollar the opportunity to buy American stocks, businesses, and property at fire-sale prices. Accordingly, they join foreign consumers in demanding more dollars and supplying more marks. Not all of these behavioral responses will occur overnight, but they are reasonably predictable over a brief period of time.[5]

MARKET DYNAMICS

Given a neat and orderly demand curve and an equally neat and orderly supply curve, we can predict the **equilibrium price** of any commodity; that is, the price at which the quantity demanded will equal the quantity supplied. This prediction requires very little effort, since nearly anyone can figure out where the two curves cross in Figure 34.1.

The interesting thing about markets is not their character in equilibrium but the fact that prices and quantities are always changing in response to shifts in demand and supply. The American demand for Volkswagens shifted overnight when Japan introduced a new line of competitively priced cars (Datsun, Honda, Toyota, Mazda). This **shift in demand** threw the demand curve in Figure 34.1 out of place and sent foreign-exchange specialists, GM executives, and worried VW managers back to the drawing boards. When wheat harvests in China and elsewhere turned out poorly in 1978,

---

[4] The extent to which imports decline as the cost of foreign currency rises depends on the *price elasticity of demand* (see Chapter 18).

[5] If the demand for our exports is relatively price inelastic, the percentage change in quantity demanded will be smaller than the percentage change in price. In this case, the quantity of foreign exchange supplied may actually decline as the dollar becomes cheaper. In such a case, the supply curve in Figure 34.1 would bend backward at higher exchange rates.

FIGURE 34.2 SHIFTS IN FOREIGN-EXCHANGE MARKETS

When Japan started selling Hondas, Toyotas, and Datsuns in the United States, the demand for Volkswagens shifted to the left (from D_1^* to D_2^* in b), while the demand for Japanese yen shifted to the right (from D_1 to D_2 in a). The dollar price of marks fell from p_1^* to p_2^* in b; the dollar price of yen rose from p_1 to p_2 in a.

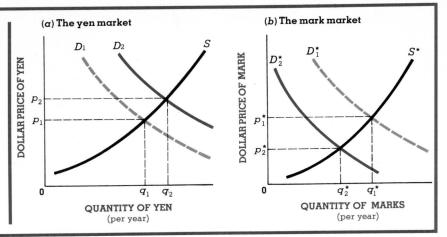

the demand for American wheat increased significantly. This increased demand shifted the supply of foreign exchange to the right (the demand for U.S. dollars to the left). Such shocks to the foreign-exchange market are illustrated in Figure 34.2.

Depreciation and appreciation

depreciation: A fall in the price of one currency relative to another.

appreciation: A rise in the price of one currency relative to another.

Exchange-rate changes have their own terminology. **Depreciation** of a currency refers to the fact that one currency has become cheaper in terms of another currency. In our earlier discussion of exchange rates, for example, we assumed that the exchange rate between deutsche marks and dollars changed from DM2 = $1 to DM1 = $1, making the price of a dollar cheaper. In this case the dollar depreciated with respect to the mark.

The other side of depreciation is **appreciation,** an increase in value of one currency as expressed in another country's currency. ***Whenever one currency depreciates, another currency must appreciate.*** When the exchange rate changed from DM2 = $1 to DM1 = $1, not only did the mark price of a dollar fall, but the dollar price of a mark rose. Hence the mark appreciated as the dollar depreciated.

Figure 34.3 illustrates actual changes in exchange rates since 1973. During the 1970s the German mark and Japanese yen appreciated substantially relative to the U.S. dollar. At the same time, the British pound depreciated. Hence German and Japanese goods got more expensive, while the dollar price of British goods fell. These trends were reversed in the early 1980s.

Also shown in Figure 34.3 is the trade-adjusted value of the U.S. dollar. This is the (weighted) average of all exchange rates for the dollar. In general, the dollar lost value in the late 1970s, but recovered in the early 1980s.

Market forces

Exchange rates change for the same reasons that any market price changes: either the underlying supply or demand (or both) has shifted. Among the more important sources of such shifts are:

■ Relative income changes. If incomes are increasing faster in country A than in country B, consumers in A will tend to spend

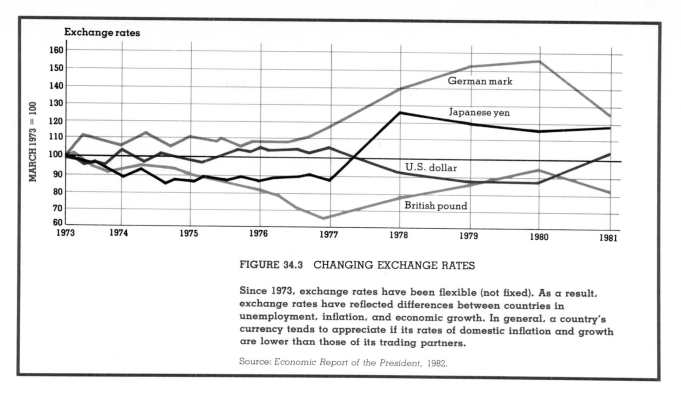

FIGURE 34.3   CHANGING EXCHANGE RATES

Since 1973, exchange rates have been flexible (not fixed). As a result, exchange rates have reflected differences between countries in unemployment, inflation, and economic growth. In general, a country's currency tends to appreciate if its rates of domestic inflation and growth are lower than those of its trading partners.

Source: *Economic Report of the President*, 1982.

more, thus increasing the demand for *B*'s exports and currency. *B*'s currency will appreciate.

■ Relative price changes. If domestic prices are rising rapidly in country *A*, consumers will seek out lower-priced imports. The demand for *B*'s exports and currency will increase. *B*'s currency will appreciate.

■ Changes in product availability. If country *A* experiences a disastrous wheat-crop failure, it will have to increase its food imports. *B*'s currency will appreciate.

■ Relative interest-rate changes. If interest rates rise in country *A*, people in country *B* will want to move their deposits to *A*. Demand for *A*'s currency will rise and it will appreciate.

■ Speculation. If speculators anticipate an increase in the price of *A*'s currency, for the above reasons or any other, they will begin buying it, thus pushing its price up. *A*'s currency will appreciate.

All of these kinds of changes are taking place every minute of every day, thus keeping **foreign-exchange markets** active. Significant changes occur in currency values, however, only when several of these forces are moving in the same direction at the same time.

RESISTANCE TO EXCHANGE-RATE CHANGES

Exchange-rate changes are resisted by a broad assortment of micro-economic and macroeconomic interests. This resistance to exchange-rate changes is analogous to the resistance to trade flows

foreign-exchange markets:
Places where foreign currencies are bought and sold.

based on comparative advantage and, in fact, typically derives from the same concerns (see Chapter 33).

Micro interests

The microeconomic resistance to foreign-exchange-rate changes arises from two general concerns. First, people who engage in international investment and trade flows like to have some basis for forecasting future costs, prices, and profits. Forecasts are always uncertain, but they are even less dependable when the value of money is subject to change. An American firm that invests $20 million in a tire factory in Brazil expects not only to make a profit on the production there, but also to return that profit to the United States. If the Brazilian cruzeiro depreciates sharply in the interim, however, the profits amassed in Brazil may dwindle to a mere trickle, or even a loss, when the cruzeiros are exchanged back into dollars. From this perspective, the uncertainty associated with fluctuating exchange rates is an unwanted and unnecessary burden.

Even when the direction of an exchange-rate move is certain, those who stand to lose from the change are prone to resist. *A change in the price of a country's money automatically alters the price of all of its exports and imports.* When the United States dollar appreciated in 1982, for example, the foreign price of all U.S. exports rose and the domestic price of all U.S. imports fell. U.S. importers were pleased, but U.S. exporters were upset.

In general, exporters are hostile to appreciations of their domestic currency, that is, exchange-rate movements that make their products more expensive in export markets. The workers associated with such exports are equally hostile to such exchange-rate movements, because their very jobs are at stake.

Even in the country whose currency becomes cheaper, there will be opposition to exchange-rate movements. When the U.S. dollar appreciates, Americans buy more foreign products. This increased U.S. demand for imports may drive up prices in other countries. In addition, foreign firms may take advantage of the reduced

The mighty dollar slams U.S. trade

Hobbled by an overvalued dollar, U.S. manufacturers and farmers are taking one of the worst drubbings they have ever suffered in world markets. Price-conscious foreign customers, battered by a business slowdown that is virtually worldwide, are turning elsewhere for the kind of manufactured goods—petrochemicals, aircraft, and computers, for example— that are the traditional source of U.S. competitive strength. And growers in countries with cheaper currencies are

"just cutting us to pieces" in agricultural export markets, according to Burton M. Joseph, chairman of I.S. Joseph Co., a Minneapolis grain and agricultural-byproducts trader.

The declining ability of U.S. producers to compete was reflected in last year's U.S. trade deficit of $27 billion, the biggest since 1978. This year the deficit is expected to balloon to a record $35 billion, despite a sharp drop in the volume and cost of oil imports. Much of the trade erosion has occurred in manufactured goods, expected to show a surplus of only $8 billion this year, down from $19 billion in 1980.

The U.S. predicament is the mirror

image of strong performances by West Germany and Japan, the chief industrial competitors of the U.S. Both have depressed currencies: The Deutschemark is currently worth 42¢, down from a 1978 peak of 58¢, and the yen is trading at 0.41¢, down from 0.56¢ in 1978. The competitive advantage of a cheap currency is spurring export booms in both nations. For Germany, a dramatic upswing in exports is expected to yield a trade surplus of $21 billion this year, up from $12 billion in 1981.

American competition by raising their prices. In either case, some inflation will result. The consumer's insistence that the government "do something" about rising prices may turn into a political force for "correcting" foreign-exchange rates.

Macro interests

Any microeconomic problem that becomes widespread enough can turn into a macroeconomic problem that requires major changes in domestic economic policies. Consider the problems confronting German industries after the 1978 appreciation of the deutsche mark. As we noted in Chapter 33 (Figure 33.1), West Germany exports a staggering 26 percent of the goods it produces. When German export industries are in trouble, the whole country is in trouble. Thus upward movements in the foreign price of German money threaten German economic planners and politicians with increasing unemployment. It is the kind of problem they could happily do without.

On the other side of foreign-exchange markets, a very different problem arises. As we have observed, a fall in the value of the U.S. dollar increases import prices, as well as the foreign demand for American products. Both of these factors contribute to inflationary pressures at home. That could present an awkward dilemma, especially if the administration is seeking to achieve full employment in a context of price stability.

In general, then, a country whose currency rises in value (appreciates) will have to contend with reduced aggregate demand and the threat of increased unemployment. On the other hand, a country whose currency falls in value (depreciates) will have to contend with increased aggregate demand and the threat of greater inflation. These problems are the core of macroeconomic (and political) resistance to exchange-rate movements.

POLICY ALTERNATIVES

Given the potential opposition to exchange-rate movements, governments may welcome institutional arrangements that can eliminate or restrain exchange-rate fluctuations. Governments have in fact embraced an assortment of measures to ensure exchange-rate stability. But such stability may itself give rise to undersirable micro- and macroeconomic effects, may even compound rather than solve economic problems. We will explore these issues as we review the major policy alternatives that countries confront.

Fixed exchange rates

gold standard: An agreement by countries to fix the price of their currencies in terms of gold; a mechanism for fixing exchange rates.

One way to eliminate fluctuations in exchange rates is to fix their value. To fix exchange rates, each country may simply proclaim that its currency is "worth" so much vis-à-vis that of other countries. The easiest way to do this is for each country to define the worth of its currency in terms of some common standard. The standard that has been most popular is gold. Under a **gold standard**, each country determines that its currency is worth so much gold. In so doing, it implicitly defines the worth of its currency in terms of all other currencies, which also have a fixed gold value. In 1944, for example, the major trading nations met at Bretton Woods, New Hampshire, and agreed that each currency was worth so much gold. The value of the U.S. dollar was defined as being equal to 0.0294 ounces of gold, while the British pound was defined as being worth 0.0823 ounces of gold. Thus the exchange rate between British pounds and U.S. dollars was effectively fixed at $1 = 0.357 pounds, or 1 pound = $2.80 (or $2.80/0.0823 = $1/0.0294).

BALANCE-OF-PAYMENTS PROBLEMS   It is one thing to proclaim the worth of a country's currency; it is quite another to maintain the fixed rate of exchange. As we have observed, foreign-exchange rates are subject to continual and often unpredictable changes in supply and demand. Hence two countries that seek to stabilize their exchange rate at some fixed value are going to find it necessary either to eliminate or to compensate for such foreign-exchange market pressures.

Suppose that the exchange rate established by the United States and Great Britain is equal to e_1, as illustrated in Figure 34.4. As is apparent, that particular exchange rate is consistent with the then-prevailing demand and supply conditions in the foreign-exchange market (as indicated by curves D_1 and S_1).

Now suppose that Americans suddenly acquire a great taste for British ale and song and start spending more income on imported brew and records. As U.S. purchases of British goods increase, a U.S. **trade deficit** is likely to emerge: we will be spending more on their goods than they are spending on ours.

The emergence of a trade deficit implies a net increase in our demand for British currency, as reflected in the *shift* from D_1 to D_2 in Figure 34.4. Were exchange rates allowed to respond to market influences, the dollar price of a British pound would clearly rise, in this case to the value of e_2. But we have already noted that it is official policy to maintain the exchange rate at e_1. Unfortunately, at e_1 American consumers want to buy more pounds (q_D) than the British are willing to supply (q_S). The difference between the quantity de-

trade deficit: The amount by which the value of imports exceeds the value of exports in a given time period.

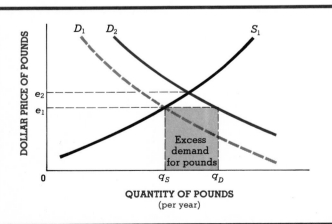

FIGURE 34.4   FIXED RATES AND MARKET IMBALANCE

If exchange rates are fixed, they cannot adjust to changes in market supply and demand. Suppose the exchange rate is initially fixed at e_1. When the demand for British pounds increases (shifts to the right), an excess demand for pounds emerges. More pounds are demanded (q_D) at the rate e_1 than are supplied (q_S).

market shortage: The amount by which the quantity demanded exceeds the quantity supplied at a given price; excess demand.

balance-of-payments deficit: An excess demand for foreign currency at current exchange rates.

balance-of-payments surplus: An excess demand for domestic currency at current exchange rates.

foreign-exchange reserves: Holdings of foreign exchange by official government agencies, usually the central bank or treasury.

manded and that supplied in the market at the rate e_1 represents a **market shortage** of British pounds.

The excess demand for pounds represents, first, a potential **balance-of-payments deficit** for the United States, because it implies that more dollars are flowing out of the country than into it. Second, it represents a **balance-of-payments surplus** for England, because its outward flow of pounds is less than its incoming flow. Both kinds of imbalance can cause real problems for policy makers.

Basically, there are only two solutions to balance-of-payments problems brought about by the attempt to fix exchange rates:

- Allow exchange rates to rise to e_2 (Figure 34.4), thereby eliminating the excess demand for pounds.
- Alter market supply or demand so that they intersect at the fixed rate e_1.

Since fixed exchange rates were the initial objective of policy, only the second alternative is of immediate interest.

THE NEED FOR RESERVES   One way to alter market conditions would be for someone simply to supply British pounds to American consumers. The U.S. Treasury could have accumulated a reserve of foreign exchange at times when market conditions resulted in an excess supply of rather than an excess demand for British pounds. As we have noted, the market supply of and demand for foreign exchange are subject to frequent shifts. Although there is an excess demand for pounds today, there may have been an excess supply yesterday. Such a surplus would have enabled the U.S. Treasury to accumulate reserves. By selling some of those reserves now, the Treasury could help to stabilize market conditions at the officially established exchange rate. The sale of accumulated British pounds **(foreign-exchange reserves)** by the U.S. Treasury is illustrated in Figure 34.5 by the rightward shift of the pound supply curve.

Although foreign-exchange reserves can be used to fix exchange rates, such reserves may not be adequate when they are needed. Indeed, Figure 34.6 should be testimony enough to the fact that today's deficit is not always offset by tomorrow's surplus. One of the princi-

---

FIGURE 34.5   THE IMPACT OF MONETARY INTERVENTION

If the U.S. Treasury holds reserves of British pounds, it can use them to buy U.S. dollars in foreign-exchange markets. As it does so, the supply of pounds will shift to the right, to S_2, thereby maintaining the desired exchange rate, e_1. The Bank of England could bring about the same result by offering to buy U.S. dollars with pounds.

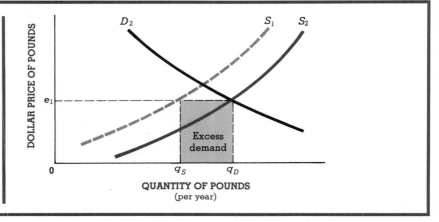

FIGURE 34.6 THE U.S. BALANCE
OF PAYMENTS, 1950–73

The United States had a balance-of-
payments deficit for 22 consecutive
years. During this period, the
foreign-exchange reserves of the U.S.
Treasury were sharply reduced. Fixed
exchange rates were maintained by
the willingness of foreign countries to
accumulate large reserves of U.S.
dollars. However, neither the
Treasury's reserves nor foreigners'
willingness to accumulate dollars
were unlimited. In 1973, fixed
exchange rates were abandoned.

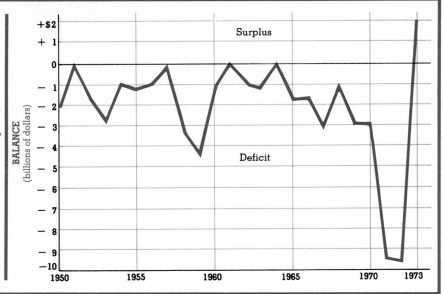

gold reserves: Stocks of gold
held by a government to
purchase foreign exchange.

pal reasons that fixed exchange rates have not lived up to their expectations is that the United States had balance-of-payments deficits
for 22 consecutive years. This long-term deficit overwhelmed our
stock of foreign-exchange reserves and led to a search for other
measures to balance foreign-exchange markets at officially fixed
rates.

THE ROLE OF GOLD   Gold reserves represent a potential substitute for
foreign-exchange reserves. As long as each country's money has a
value defined in terms of gold and is available at that price, we can
use gold to buy British pounds, thereby restocking our foreign-
exchange reserves. Or we can simply use the gold to purchase U.S.
dollars in foreign-exchange markets. In either case, the exchange
value of the dollar will tend to rise. However, we must have **gold
reserves** available for this purpose. Unfortunately, the continuing
U.S. balance-of-payments deficits recorded in Figure 34.6 exceeded
even the hoards of gold buried under Fort Knox. As a consequence,
our gold reserves lost their credibility as a potential "guarantee" of
fixed exchange rates.

DOMESTIC ADJUSTMENTS   The supply and demand for foreign exchange can also be shifted by changes in basic fiscal, monetary, or
trade policies. We could eliminate the excess demand for pounds
(Figure 34.4), for example, by imposing quotas and tariffs on British
goods. Such trade restrictions would reduce British imports to the
United States and thus the demand for British pounds. Such restrictions on international trade, however, violate the principle of comparative advantage and thus reduce total world output.

Fiscal policy provides another way out of the imbalance. An
increase in U.S. income-tax rates will reduce disposable income and
have a negative effect on the demand for all goods, including im-

ports. A reduction in government spending will have similar effects. In general, deflationary (or restrictive) fiscal policies can help correct a balance-of-payments deficit by lowering domestic incomes and thus import demands.

Monetary policies in a deficit country could follow the same restrictive course. A reduction in the money supply will tend to raise interest rates and slow aggregate spending. The balance of payments will be benefited in two ways. The slowdown in spending will help to reduce import demands and may induce domestic producers to focus more attention on export possibilities. In addition, the higher

BALANCE-OF-PAYMENTS ACCOUNTING

Most foreign-exchange transactions are related to imports and exports of goods and services. But foreign-exchange demands and supplies arise from a variety of other transactions as well. As a result, several different "balances" are computed for foreign-exchange markets.

TRADE BALANCE
equals merchandise exports minus merchandise imports.
CURRENT-ACCOUNT BALANCE
equals trade balance,
plus receipts from foreign travelers in the U.S. and receipts from U.S. investments abroad
less travel expenditures abroad and income payments to foreigners for their investments in the U.S.
CAPITAL-ACCOUNT BALANCE
equals foreign investment in the U.S. and other private capital inflow
less U.S. direct investment abroad and other private capital outflow.

Under a system of fixed exchange rates, the "balance of payments" equaled the sum of the current- and capital-account balances. If current and capital outflows exceeded inflows, a "deficit" existed in the balance of payments. This deficit (imbalance) between the quantities of foreign exchange demanded and supplied was "paid" for with official foreign-exchange reserves. The deficit country would transfer foreign exchange or gold to surplus countries.

Flexible exchange rates eliminate any residual "balance of payments." If foreigners demand more dollars than we supply, the price of dollars will rise. As a result of such exchange-rate movements, the quantity of dollars supplied and demanded is brought into equality. No overall residual "balance" remains; official "payments" are not required.

In fact, most countries still intervene in foreign-exchange markets to limit exchange-rate movements. The value of such official purchases and sales of foreign exchange are often regarded as an approximation to the "balance of payments." The "official-settlements balance" equals the change in foreign-exchange reserves held by the government.

interest rates may induce international investors to move some of their funds out of other countries into the deficit country. Such moves will provide immediate relief to the payments imbalance.

A surplus country wishing to help in solving the balance-of-payments problem could pursue expansionary—even inflationary—fiscal and monetary policies. By putting more money into the hands of its consumers, a surplus country could stimulate the demand for imports. As prices rose at home, the relative attractiveness of imports would be increased. Moreover, any inflation at home would reduce the competitiveness of exports, thereby helping to restrain the inflow of foreign demand. Taken together, such efforts would clearly help to reverse an international-payments imbalance.[6]

Even though domestic economic adjustments are capable of improving balance-of-payments problems, there are obvious costs involved, particularly in terms of full employment and price stability. In effect, **domestic adjustments to payments imbalances require a deficit country to forsake full employment and a surplus country to forsake price stability.** These are sacrifices few countries are willing to make. Accordingly, balance-of-payments problems typically lead to protracted arguments about who should adjust, repeated hopes that the imbalances will go away, and frequent "crises" ending in exchange-rate adjustments. It is important to realize that foreign-exchange imbalances brought about by fixed exchange rates must be overcome with either abundant supplies of foreign-exchange reserves or deliberate changes in fiscal, monetary, or trade policies. The accompanying news clipping on Mexico's

---

[6] Before 1930, not only were foreign-exchange rates fixed, but domestic monetary supplies were tied to gold stocks as well. Countries experiencing a balance-of-payments deficit were thus forced to contract their money supply and countries experiencing a payments surplus were forced to expand their money supply by a set amount. Monetary authorities were powerless to control domestic money supplies except by erecting barriers to trade. The system was abandoned when the world economy collapsed into the Great Depression.

Mexican Peso Plunges 28% Against Dollar

Nation's Economic Troubles Touch Off the Decision to Let Currency Float

MEXICO CITY—The Mexican peso dropped 28% against the U.S. dollar yesterday following the Mexican government's decision late Wednesday to let the currency float.

Shortly before the devaluation, the peso traded at about 27 to the dollar, and by late trading yesterday it had fallen to about 37.70 to the dollar, or about 2.6 cents. Economists said it was too early to tell where the peso would eventually settle. . . .

Apparently, capital flight forced the government to act, as Mexicans are flocking to the U.S. to travel and invest. The government has tried to stop the wave—by exhorting Mexicans to invest at home, raising passport fees, and prohibiting advertisements by U.S. real estate developers—but it wasn't enough.

Last year, Mexico had an $11.5 billion deficit in its current international payments account, which includes trade in goods and services as well as certain unilateral transfers. That was almost twice as wide as the $6.6 billion deficit of 1980.

"The government had little choice," said a Mexican banker. "Its reserves were getting low."

The peso float should bring down Mexican interest rates. To keep money in pesos, the government has kept interest rates at more than 20 percentage points above the interest on dollar accounts. But that policy was beginning to choke investment. The devaluation should allow the government to bring interest rates down to a level that will spur local investment.

—Lawrence Rout

1982 devaluation indicates what happens when these domestic adjustments are exhausted.

Flexible exchange rates

flexible exchange rates: A system in which exchange rates are permitted to vary with market supply and demand conditions.

Balance-of-payments problems would not arise in the first place, of course, if exchange rates were allowed to respond to market forces. Under a system of **flexible exchange rates** (often called "floating" exchange rates), the exchange rate moves up or down to choke off any excess supply of or demand for foreign exchange. Notice again in Figure 34.4 that the exchange-rate move from e_1 to e_2 prevents any excess demand from emerging. With flexible exchange rates, the quantity of foreign exchange demanded always equals the quantity supplied, and there is no imbalance. For the same reason, there is no need for foreign-exchange reserves.

Although flexible exchange rates eliminate balance-of-payments and foreign-exchange-reserves problems, they do not solve all of a country's international trade problems. *Exchange-rate movements associated with flexible rates alter relative prices and may disrupt import and export flows.* As we noted before, depreciation of the dollar raises the price of all imported goods. The price increases may contribute to domestic, cost-push inflation. Also, domestic businesses that sell imported goods or use them as production inputs may suffer sales losses. On the other hand, appreciation of the dollar raises the foreign price of U.S. goods and reduces the sales of American exporters. Hence someone is always hurt (and others are helped) by exchange-rate movements. The resistance to flexible exchange rates originates in these potential losses. Such resistance creates pressure for some form of official intervention in foreign-exchange markets.

"Damn it! How can I relax, knowing that out there, somewhere, somehow, someone's attacking the dollar?"

Drawing by Lorenz; © 1973 The New Yorker Magazine, Inc.

The United States and its major trading partners abandoned fixed exchange rates in 1973. Although exchange rates are now able to fluctuate freely, it should not be assumed that they necessarily go through wild gyrations. On the contrary, experience with flexible rates since 1973 suggests that some semblance of stability is possible even when exchange rates are free to change in response to market forces. In 1979 the Council of Economic Advisers concluded that the first five years of flexible exchange rates had worked reasonably well. Flexible rates had been particularly successful "in permitting the industrial economies to absorb shocks that were unprecedented in the post-war period."[7]

SPECULATION   One force that often helps to maintain stability in a flexible-exchange-rate system is speculation. Speculators often counteract short-term changes in foreign-exchange supply and demand. If an exchange rate temporarily rises above its long-term equilibrium, speculators will move in to sell foreign exchange. By selling at high prices and later buying at lower prices, speculators hope to make a profit. In the process, they also help to stabilize foreign-exchange rates.

Speculation is not always stabilizing, however. Speculators may not correctly gauge the long-term equilibrium. Instead, they may move "with the market" and help push exchange rates far out of kilter. This kind of destabilizing speculation sharply lowered the international value of the U.S. dollar in 1978, forcing the Carter administration to intervene in foreign-exchange markets, borrowing foreign currencies to buy U.S. dollars.

Managed exchange rates

managed exchange rates: A system in which governments intervene in foreign-exchange markets to limit but not eliminate exchange-rate fluctuations; "dirty floats."

Governments can intervene in foreign-exchange markets without completely fixing exchange rates. That is to say, they may buy and sell foreign exchange for the purpose of narrowing rather than eliminating exchange-rate movements. Such limited intervention in foreign-exchange rates is referred to as **managed exchange rates,** or, more popularly, "dirty floats."

The basic objective of exchange-rate management is to provide the stabilizing force that some people hope private speculators will provide. In this regard, governments use their foreign-exchange reserves to buy domestic currency when it is depreciating too much. Or they will buy foreign exchange if domestic currency is appreciating too much. From this perspective, exchange-rate management appears as a fail-safe system for the private market. Unfortunately, the motivation for official intervention is sometimes suspect. Private speculators buy and sell foreign exchange for the sole purpose of making money. But government sales and purchases may be motivated by other considerations. A falling exchange rate increases the competitive advantage of a country's exports. A rising exchange rate makes international investment less expensive. Hence a country's efforts to "manage" exchange-rate movements may arouse suspicion and outright hostility in its trading partners.

[7] *Economic Report of the President,* 1979, p. 149.

Accordingly, although managed exchange rates would seem to be an ideal compromise between fixed rates and flexible rates, they can work only when some acceptable "rules of the game" and a condition of mutual trust have been established. As Sherman Maisel, a former governor of the Federal Reserve Board, has put it: "Monetary systems are based on credit and faith: if these are lacking a . . . crisis occurs."[8]

SUMMARY

▪ Money serves the same purposes in international trade as it does in the domestic economy—namely, to facilitate productive specialization and market exchanges. The basic problem of international finance is to create acceptable standards of value from the various currencies maintained by separate countries.

▪ Exchange rates are the basic mechanism for translating the value of one national currency into the equivalent value of another. Thus an exchange rate of $1 = DM3 means that one dollar is worth three German marks and can be purchased at that price in foreign-exchange markets.

▪ Foreign currencies have value because they can be used to acquire goods and resources from other countries. Accordingly, the supply of and demand for foreign currency reflect the demands for imports and exports, for international investment, and for overseas activities of governments.

▪ The equilibrium exchange rate is subject to any and all shifts of supply and demand for foreign exchange. If the relative incomes, relative prices, or relative interest rates of two countries change, their respective demands for foreign exchange will be affected. A depreciation is a change in market exchange rates that makes one country's currency cheaper in terms of another currency. An appreciation is the opposite kind of change.

▪ Changes in exchange rates are often resisted. Producers of export goods do not want their currencies to rise in value (appreciate), because the foreign price of exports will then rise and sales will fall. Importers and people who travel dislike it when their currencies fall in value (depreciate) because imports and foreign travel become more expensive.

▪ Under a system of fixed exchange rates, changes in the supply and demand for foreign exchange cannot be expressed in exchange-rate movements. Instead, such shifts will be reflected in excess demand for or excess supply of foreign exchange. Such market imbalances are referred to as balance-of-payments deficits or surpluses.

▪ To maintain fixed exchange rates, monetary authorities must enter the market to buy and sell foreign exchange. In order to do so, deficit countries must have foreign-exchange reserves. In the absence of sufficient reserves, a country can maintain fixed exchange rates only if it is willing to alter basic fiscal, monetary, or trade policies.

[8] Sherman Maisel, *Managing the Dollar* (New York: W. W. Norton, 1973), p. 196.

■ Flexible exchange rates eliminate balance-of-payments problems and the crises that accompany them. But complete flexibility can lead to excessive changes. To avoid this contingency, many countries prefer to adopt managed exchange rates—that is, rates determined by the market but subject to government intervention.

Terms to remember

Define the following terms:

exchange rate	gold standard
supply of foreign exchange	trade deficit
demand for foreign exchange	market shortage
law of demand	balance-of-payments deficit
equilibrium price	balance-of-payments surplus
shift in demand	foreign-exchange reserves
depreciation	gold reserves
appreciation	flexible exchange rates
foreign-exchange markets	managed exchange rates

Questions for discussion

1. How would rapid inflation in Mexico alter our demands for travel to Mexico and for Mexican imports? Does it make any difference whether the exchange rate between pesos and dollars is fixed or flexible?

2. Under what conditions would a country welcome a balance-of-payments deficit? When would it *not* want a deficit?

3. In what sense do fixed exchange rates permit a country to "export its inflation"?

4. In 1979 U.S. exports rose significantly while the value of imports rose slowly. How did the dollar depreciation contribute to this development?

5. Under a managed exchange-rate system, exchange rates can vary by small degrees. When should more significant rate changes be permitted or encouraged?

Problem

The following schedules summarize the supply and demand for trifflings, the national currency of Tricoli.

Triffling price (in U.S. dollars)	0	$4	$8	$12	$16	$20	$24
Quantity demanded (per year)	40	38	36	34	32	30	28
Quantity supplied (per year)	1	11	21	31	41	51	61

Using the above schedules:

(a) Graph the supply and demand curves.

(b) Determine the equilibrium exchange rate.

(c) Determine the size of the excess supply or excess demand that would exist if the Tricolian government fixed the exchange rate at $22 = 1 triffling.

(d) How might this imbalance be remedied?

CHAPTER 35

INTERNATIONAL DEVELOPMENT

In 1950 the per capita income of Haiti was $260 (in 1982 dollars), or about one-sixteenth the per capita income of the United States. Thirty years later, U.S. per capita income had doubled. But incomes in Haiti were not much higher in 1980 than they had been in 1950. Haiti remained poor while the gap between rich and poor countries widened.

The economic stagnation of Haiti is an extreme case of underdevelopment. But most less developed countries (LDCs) of the world share two problems: (1) a low per capita income and (2) a slow growth rate. Because of their shared poverty and relative political independence, these countries are often referred to as "Third World" countries. They are also sometimes called "developing" countries, but this term tends to express more hope than progress.

This chapter provides a brief glimpse of the Third World. We shall first examine the variety of economic conditions that characterize the Third World, then try to explain their persistence. Our ambitions must of necessity be modest, however. As Professor Theodore Schultz has written, "Being rich makes it hard to comprehend the economic behavior of poor people."[1] It is also difficult to comprehend their abject poverty itself.

THIRD WORLD INCOMES

GNP per capita

The common denominator of all Third World countries is low incomes. As Table 35.1 reminds us, the United States enjoyed a per capita income of $10,610 in 1979. Most of the people in the world

[1] Theodore Schultz, "Knowledge Is Power in Agriculture," *Challenge*, September–October 1981, p. 6.

TABLE 35.1 INCOMES AROUND THE WORLD
(in 1979 U.S. dollars)

The primary distinction between "developed" countries and "less developed" ones is reflected in average incomes. However, there is great variety in living standards within each of these broad groupings. Here the countries of the world are classified in five groups, on the basis of per capita GNP.

Country	GNP per capita	Country	GNP per capita
Rich countries		Soviet Union	4,040
Kuwait	$20,250	Trinidad and Tobago	3,910
Switzerland	15,360	Hungary	3,780
Sweden	12,250	Poland	3,770
Germany, Federal		Singapore	3,770
Republic of	12,200	Hong Kong	3,640
Denmark	12,030	Bulgaria	3,630
Norway	11,230	Venezuela	3,440
Belgium	11,020	Puerto Rico	2,840
France	10,650	Iraq	2,710
United States	10,610		
Netherlands, The	10,490	**Low-income countries**	
Saudi Arabia	9,960	Uruguay	$2,500
Canada	9,410	Yugoslavia	2,370
Austria	9,130	Argentina	2,210
Australia	8,870	Romania	2,100
Japan	8,730	Portugal	2,060
Finland	8,520	South Africa	2,000
Libya	8,480	Chile	1,890
United Kingdom	7,390	Mexico	1,880
New Zealand	6,400	Algeria	1,770
German Democratic		Brazil	1,770
Republic	6,310	Costa Rica	1,630
Italy	5,730	Panama	1,550
		Korea, Republic of	1,510
Moderate-income countries		Malaysia	1,450
Czechoslovakia	$5,190	Turkey	1,380
Spain	4,920	Jordan	1,200
Ireland	4,480	Syrian Arab	
Israel	4,230	Republic	1,170
Greece	4,140	Tunisia	1,160

could not begin to fathom the meaning of such affluence. Nearly half of the people in the world subsist on incomes of less than $350 per year. Another one-fourth of the world's population struggles along with less than $1,000 of per capita GNP. Even in some of the seemingly "rich" Third World countries (e.g., Saudia Arabia, Kuwait) most of the population lives in relative poverty.

Statistics on per capita income are a fundamental measure of a country's economic development. The figures themselves, however,

Country	GNP per capita	Country	GNP per capita
Paraguay	1,140	Togo	400
Ecuador	1,110	Kenya	390
Jamaica	1,110	Indonesia	370
Ivory Coast	1,070	Lesotho	370
Colombia	1,060	Yemen, People's	
Dominican Republic	1,030	Democratic	
Guatemala	1,010	Republic of	370
		Madagascar	330
Poor countries		Mauritania	300
Nigeria	$910	Niger	300
Peru	850	Uganda	290
Morocco	780	Central African	
Papua New Guinea	760	Republic	280
Congo, People's		Benin	270
Republic of the	670	Guinea	270
El Salvador	640	Pakistan	270
Philippines	640	China	260
Nicaragua	610	Mozambique	250
Thailand	600	Sierra Leone	250
Cameroon	590	Tanzania	250
Bolivia	550	Haiti	230
Zimbabwe	550	Sri Lanka	230
Zambia	540	Malawi	220
Honduras	520	India	210
Liberia	520	Zaire	210
Egypt, Arab		Burundi	190
Republic of	500	Rwanda	190
		Mali	180
Extremely poor countries		Upper Volta	180
Senegal	$450	Burma	150
Sudan	450	Nepal	130
Angola	430	Chad	120
Yemen Arab		Ethiopia	120
Republic	420	Bangladesh	110
Ghana	400	Bhutan	80

Source: *World Bank Atlas*, 1981.

can never convey the dimensions of poverty experienced in many of these countries. Can you really imagine living with only one-*fiftieth* of your income, as do the people in the bottom section of Table 35.1?[2]

[2] Many economists emphasize that foreign exchange rates (Chapter 34) distort international GNP comparisons. They are right. The distortions are minor, however, relative to the pervasive poverty that exists in these countries.

Basic human needs

The reality of Third World poverty is also reflected in statistics on life expectancy, literacy, and social conditions. In Haiti, life expectancy at birth is 53 years; in Ethiopia, it is only 46 years. By contrast, babies born in the United States have a life expectancy of nearly 74 years. Hence a fundamental consequence of underdevelopment is shortened life.

One reason people live such short lives in less developed countries is that they have so little to eat. The World Health Organization estimates that an average person requires a minimum intake of 2,600 calories per day for basic nutrition. People in the United States are well above this threshold, consuming an average of 3,400 calories per day. But people in Haiti try to survive on only 1,730 calories per day. The World Bank estimates that 80 other countries of the world also suffer from inadequate food consumption. Moreover, the water in most LDCs is unsafe to drink. In Ethiopia, only 6 percent of the population has access to safe drinking water. In Haiti, only 14 percent of the people can find safe water.

When people in LDCs get sick, they are not likely to find a doctor, a hospital, or even medicine. Haiti has only one doctor for every 13,000 people; Ethiopia has only one doctor for every 73,000 people. By comparision, the United States has one doctor for every 600 people. As for hospitals, the United States has one hospital bed for every 152 people. Haiti has one bed for every 1,169 people and Ethiopia has one for every 3,081. Medical care may be expensive in the United States, but at least you can get it when you need it.

Life expectancy, food consumption, the availability of doctors, access to safe water, and literacy are all indicators of the extent to which *basic human needs* are being fulfilled. The gap between rich and poor countries is enormous, even on this basis. The gap grows larger still when more conventional measures of development are considered. Perhaps the most telling measure of economic development is energy consumption. Although Americans are learning to use energy more efficiently, we still rely on nonhuman energy to do much of the work entailed in consumption and production. In LDCs, virtually all of the work is done by people, using their own energy. This is evident in statistics on *per capita* energy consumption. The average Haitian uses only 66 kilograms of (coal-equivalent) energy per year; the average American uses 12,350 kilograms.

GNP growth

The kind of poverty that most of the Third World endures is not unknown in the history of countries that are now affluent. On the contrary, all of the "rich" countries of the world were once poor themselves. What distinguishes today's developed countries is their past ability to *grow*—in particular, to increase output faster than population growth. Even the growth of developed countries, however, is a fairly recent phenomenon. For centuries, per capita incomes grew imperceptibly in Europe. It was not until the Industrial Revolution that Europe really began to grow. In this historical context, the LDCs are not very far behind. Hence the basic issue today is whether the LDCs are just late starters with good growth prospects. Can they expect to grow out of poverty, and perhaps even catch up with today's developed countries? Or are growth prospects in the LDCs so fundamentally different that poverty is a permanent condition?

Table 35.2 provides a quick summary of recent growth experiences around the world. The table classifies countries according to the categories of Table 35.1 and indicates their respective GNP and population growth rates. A number of observations can be made. First, it is evident that developed countries are still growing. GNP per capita in rich countries is growing at a rate of 2 to 3 percent per year. This growth rate is the result of moderate growth of output combined with very slow population growth.

At the other end of the income spectrum GNP per capita is almost stagnant. The output of the poorest countries is increasing by 2 to 3 percent per year. But their populations are increasing just as fast. Hence GNP per capita is barely growing. If these trends continued, the poorest LDCs would never develop, much less catch up with the rest of the world.

Between the extremes of rich and poor are many LDCs with low incomes but better growth records. People in South Korea, Brazil, Ecuador, and Romania still confront low GNP per capita. But their incomes are growing rapidly, creating some hope for substantial improvement in living standards. Even if such rapid growth rates were maintained, however, it would take another century or so for these countries to catch up to the ever-increasing income levels of the rich countries.

BARRIERS TO GROWTH

The statistics in Tables 35.1 and 35.2 virtually preclude the possibility that LDCs may catch up with the rich countries of the world. Nevertheless, their growth prospects are still of great concern. Growth in Third World GNP per capita implies rising standards of living, even if it doesn't lead to equality with the most developed economies. Hence there is still great interest in accelerating the growth process. Before growth can accelerate, the present barriers to growth must be identified and overcome.

Labor resources

One constraint on faster growth of per capita GNP is already evident from Table 35.2: LDC populations are increasing so rapidly that it is difficult to raise average incomes. The problem here entails more than simple arithmetic. With relatively little land or capital available, a growing population soon presses against its productive capacity. Additional workers simply don't have enough resources to work with.[3] As a consequence, there is widespread disguised unemployment in LDCs, especially in subsistence agriculture. **Disguised unemployment** is a situation in which people are employed but contribute little or nothing to total output. This situation contrasts with conventional unemployment, in which people simply cannot find acceptable jobs.

disguised unemployment: People are employed but contribute little or nothing to total output.

[3] This is a generalization of the law of diminishing returns (see Chapters 1 and 26).

TABLE 35.2 GROWTH RATES IN
SELECTED COUNTRIES (1970–1979)

Most countries of the world continue
to experience economic growth. But
the relationship between GNP growth
and population growth is very
different in rich and poor countries.
The populations of rich countries are
growing very slowly, and gains in per
capita GNP are easily achieved. In
the poorest countries, population is
still increasing rapidly, making it
difficult to raise living standards.

Country	GNP growth	Population growth	Per capita growth
Rich Countries			
Sweden	1.4	0.3	1.1
Germany	2.6	0.0	2.6
France	3.6	0.6	3.0
United States	3.1	0.9	2.2
Japan	5.1	1.2	3.9
United Kingdom	2.0	0.1	1.9
Moderate-income countries			
Spain	4.1	1.1	3.0
Israel	4.3	2.7	1.6
Greece	4.7	0.6	4.1
Hungary	5.2	0.4	4.8
Hong Kong	9.3	2.6	6.5
Venezuela	6.2	3.4	2.7
Low-income countries			
Brazil	8.3	2.3	6.1
South Africa	2.6	2.0	0.6
Chile	2.5	1.7	0.8
Korea, Republic of	10.2	1.9	8.1
Turkey	6.1	2.5	3.5
Ivory Coast	7.1	5.7	1.3
Dominican Republic	6.8	3.0	3.7
Poor countries			
El Salvador	4.3	2.9	1.4
Philippines	6.7	2.7	3.9
Thailand	7.0	2.5	4.4
Zimbabwe	1.5	3.3	−1.7
Zambia	1.1	3.1	−1.9
Honduras	4.0	3.4	0.6
Egypt	7.4	2.0	5.3
Extremely poor countries			
Senegal	2.7	2.6	0.1
Uganda	−0.6	3.0	−3.5
China	4.7	1.9	2.8
Tanzania	3.8	3.0	0.8
Haiti	3.5	1.7	1.8
India	3.7	2.1	1.6
Ethiopia	2.5	2.2	0.3

Source: World Bank.

China to Levy Tax as Birth Check

PEKING—China, a land of almost 1 billion people, will begin taxing families who have too many children, a top government official said Saturday. The goal is to achieve zero population growth by the year 2000.

Vice Premier Chen Muhua, in an article in the Communist Party newspaper People's Daily, said birth control was an "urgent problem" in China.

She said the population plan has two stages: lowering the birth rate from 12 per thousand to five per thousand by 1985, then lowering it further to achieve a balance between births and deaths—zero population growth —by the end of the century.

One birth per couple will be encouraged, she said. She said the government would "resolutely check three births."

The government will adopt a family planning law that will provide "a series of economic measures to check the birth rate," the vice premier said. "People who refuse to be persuaded and insist on having more children will be taxed."

—Victoria Graham

The Oregonian, August 12, 1979. Reprinted by permission of The Associated Press.

High fertility rates and large families also restrict opportunities for work, saving, and investment. Every dollar of available income must be spent on immediate consumption, just to keep families fed. As a consequence, there are no resources left over for savings or investment. Nor is there enough income to permit extended schooling or any other significant investments in human capital. In other words, people in abject poverty tend to be caught in a vicious circle of deprivation.

The problems of rapid population growth are often compounded by cultural and social values. Additional children are viewed as economic assets in many LDCs, especially among the vast majority of families that subsist in agriculture. More children mean more hands to till the soil and harvest the crop. And those little hands are sent to the fields at a very early age. Children are also viewed as a form of income security for old age, since extended families are still the norm in most LDCs. Unfortunately, those same children restrict income-earning opportunities and ultimately growth of per capita incomes.

Rapid population growth is only one dimension of the labor problem. Ironically, the other dimension consists of a labor shortage. In LDCs there is typically a severe shortage of *skilled* labor and managers. This is partially a consequence of the problems noted above. Relatively few children in the poorest LDCs stay in school very long. In Haiti, less than 10 percent of children attend secondary school. There are few schools or teachers available, little educational material, and the children are needed to help produce income. The lack of trained labor also reflects a paucity of public support for vocational education, owing to insufficient resources and a frequent disdain for "commercial" education. In addition, many LDCs have discovered that the first thing newly skilled labor does is leave the country for better opportunities elsewhere. This "brain drain" poses a persistent threat to both the public and private human capital investment.

Capital resources

productivity: Output per unit of input; for example, output per labor hour.

INTERNAL SAVINGS A lack of capital resources poses a second major barrier to growth. The LDCs are desperate for plant and equipment that will raise the **productivity** of labor. But their average incomes are so low that they can rarely afford to save enough to finance the

In Third-World India, College Students Study Humanities, Not Skills

CALCUTTA—At 102 Amherst St. there is a sagging old school, grimy from Calcutta's appalling pollution, scarred by years of overuse.

From 6:15 to 10:45 a.m. this is Rammohan College for 3,280 girls. From 10:45 to 5:15 p.m. it's City College for 2,500 boys. And from 5:15 to 9 p.m. it is Anandamohan College for 1,300 night students.

All three are part of the University of Calcutta, the biggest university in the world. There are 200,000 students at Calcutta and 257 colleges stretched over three states; 75,000 undergraduates sit for degree exams every year, and there are 13,000 students in graduate school.

In a country as poor as India, a university might be expected to offer the flicker of possibility, the intellectual means to move the nation ahead. So why is it that with its colleges working triple shifts, India still labors among the most backward countries in the world? . . .

Out of Focus

The British founded the University of Calcutta, the first in India, 125 years ago because they needed a few educated Indians to help them administer this huge back yard of their empire. Rich rajahs built the first campus, but the British wrote the curriculum, which was heavy on humanities, light on science and completely in English—perfect for turning out clerks, the Indians say.

But 34 years after independence, the University of Calcutta hasn't done much to change. The education ministry says a million Indians are studying the humanities; another half-million are going to college to become clerks.

"A poor country can't afford the luxury of an education in the humanities," argues J. D. Sethi, a New Delhi professor and former government education planner. Adds Barun De, the head of a social-science research center in Calcutta, "Our people are fairly well educated but totally unemployable."

What They Want

Jobs are scarce in India: Only 23 million of the country's 680 million people hold paying jobs (two-thirds of the population live on subsistence farms). So there's a spurt in interest in college courses that teach skills. At Presidency College, the most prestigious of Calcutta's colleges, 300 students a year apply for admission to the chemistry and physics departments.

But change comes at a hobbled march here. Presidency has room for only 36 chemistry students and 36 physics students. It had the same number in 1938 when B. S. Basak, Presidency's principal, was a student there himself. And even when chemistry applications climbed to 750 one year, Presidency wouldn't expand the department because "our requirements might change again some day," Prof. Basak says. . . .

Glacial Pace

It's a ponderous system. Calcutta's economics syllabus hasn't changed since 1975. . . .

India, ancient as civilization itself, is suspicious of change, and its smothering bureaucracy is resistant to it. Many students, too, oppose a shift to more practical studies. "Withdraw job-oriented education," demands a sign plastered in a Presidency College stairway.

So in this developing country, Calcutta doesn't have a program in rural development. There isn't a course in small-business administration, even though small businesses turn out countless products from fabric to steel. . . .

—June Kronholz

---

required investments. Most of the population lives at the subsistence level, struggling to survive until the next harvest. There is little margin for saving. As a consequence, the question of WHAT to produce is determined largely by subsistence needs. Figure 35.1 illustrates the resulting mix of output.

Even the meager saving that does occur is not effectively mobilized. Peasant farmers have a traditional distrust of banks and even paper money. In Haiti, for example, the most valuable crop is coffee. In years of good harvest and high prices, the peasant farmers often have more income than they need for immediate consumption. But they rarely convert that surplus income into money. Instead, they simply store the extra coffee beans. In this way they avoid the risks associated with both paper money and the local banks, and avoid potential taxes as well. Moreover, they can use the beans themselves to **barter** for desired goods. By holding their savings in this form, however, the peasants also prevent conventional investment financ-

barter: The direct exchange of one good for another, without the use of money.

FIGURE 35.1   HUNGER LIMITS INVESTMENT

In most LDCs the productive capacity of the country is barely sufficient to feed, clothe, and house the population. As a consequence, most available resources must be allocated to basic consumption. Very few resources are available for investment. Hence the mix of output tends to gravitate toward point *A*, a very low level of investment.

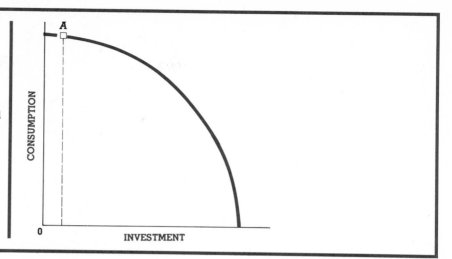

production possibilities: The alternative combinations of final goods and services that could be produced in a given time period with all available resources and technology.

ing, whereby savings held in banks are used to finance loans to investors.

In the absence of conventional financing mechanisms, LDCs must often resort to other saving mechanisms. In centrally planned economies the government may force high saving rates via taxes or controlled prices and wages. The Soviet Union and China have been extraordinarily successful with these techniques, having achieved investment ratios of 30 percent even at low levels of per capita income (see Chapter 36).

Another mechanism for financing investment is inflation. In general, inflation tends to redistribute income and wealth. LDC governments use this redistributive feature to transfer a larger share of income into the hands of investors (e.g., via loans at low real rates of interest and preferential tax treatment). In the process, the real incomes of consumers are reduced. This forced saving effectively alters the mix of output. Latin American countries have financed much of their investment in this way, with substantial success. Notice in Tables 35.1 and 35.2, for example, the relatively high per capita income and growth rates of Brazil, which had an average inflation rate of 60 percent per year in the 1970s.

EXTERNAL FINANCING LDCs are not completely dependent on internal savings for new investment. They can also draw on external sources. Foreign investors are one such source. Foreign investors typically provide not only skilled management and labor, but also scarce plant and capital equipment. By encouraging such investments, an LDC can significantly increase its investment rate without reducing current consumption. In other words, foreign investment represents an immediate outward shift of the **production-possibilites** curve (see Figure 35.2). The shift results not only from the increased availability of capital, but also from the improvements in management, technology, and labor training that typically accompany foreign investment.

Despite its substantial benefits, foreign investment is often dis-

FIGURE 35.2 EXTERNAL FINANCING
OF INVESTMENT

An inflow of capital, skilled labor, or
technology from abroad expands an
LDC's production possibilities. Such
an inflow permits an LDC to increase
its rate of investment (from I_1 to I_2)
without reducing its consumption
level (C_1). Foreign investment, loans,
and foreign aid are all sources of
external financing.

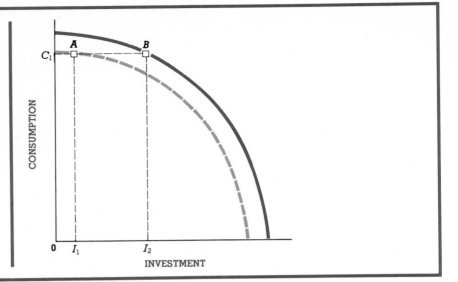

couraged by LDC governments. In part, this resistance reflects a fear
of becoming too dependent on foreign investors for continuing
growth. Such dependence has often entailed political risks, both
domestically and internationally. Also, the citizens of LDCs are frequently hostile to the notion of permitting foreigners to own key
resources or industries. On top of all this, there is often a widespread
conviction that foreign investors take out (in profits) more than they
put in (in investment capital), leaving the country worse off than
before. This perspective ignores, of course, all the other income generated in the production process. It also suggests that sound investments should reap no profits.

Even when profits are recognized as a legitimate reward to risk
and entrepreneurship, the resulting outflow of income is often re-
sented. LDCs need "hard" (internationally traded) currencies to buy
new capital and other imported resources. But foreign investors also
expect to take their profits home in hard currency. Hence the outward flow of profits is viewed as a direct constraint on new investment opportunities. Here again, however, the perspective tends to
by myopic, since the foreign investments are often the source of the
hard-currency earnings.

The myopic view many LDCs have of foreign investment often
results in severe limitations on the extent and form of foreign investment and on the return ("repatriation") of profits. Popular hostility
to foreign investment also leads on occasion to outright expropria-
tion of foreign-owned assets, with or without compensation. The
threat of such actions impedes increased foreign investment.

LOANS A second source of external financing for domestic investment is loans. Private banks, national governments, and international organizations all make loans to LDCs. Like foreign investment, loans represent an opportunity to increase current investment
without sacrificing current consumption.

The most prominent lending agency is the World Bank. Through its several organizations, the World Bank makes loans to LDCs for specific development projects. The World Bank group also provides technical assistance to help ensure the success of the projects it finances. The other multinational banks provide similar financial and technical assistance, although on a smaller scale. As a group, the multinational development banks provided $17 billion in new loans in 1980.

In addition to multilateral loans, the LDCs also have access to bilateral loans. In fact, the dollar volume of bilateral loans greatly exceeds the volume of multilateral loans. Bilateral loans are made directly from one country to another. The U.S. Agency for International Development (AID) is the principal agent for official U.S. bilateral loans.

LDCs have often professed a preference for multilateral loans over bilateral ones. Bilateral loans, it is argued, often are extended with too many economic and political strings attached. The lending country may insist on changes in basic trade, monetary, or tax policies. The loan may also be tied to projects or specific purchases of greater priority to the lending country than to the borrowing country. The LDC is forced to make a suboptimal "take it or leave it" decision. LDCs also feel that there is an implicit political agenda attached to bilateral loans and aid. Polish authorities, for example, claimed that Western countries (and banks) were unfairly using their financial leverage in 1982 to coerce the government into altering its internal policies.

Multilateral loans have similar strings attached, however. The World Bank and International Monetary Fund often insist on "responsible" fiscal and monetary policies as a condition for their development and foreign-exchange loans. These policies typically are more restrictive than the borrowing country desires and can cause political problems domestically. In one sensational case, the IMF refused to extend a loan to Zaire until that country agreed to let the IMF install its own experts at Zaire's national bank, so that it could monitor Zaire's finances (and corruption). In 1982 Peru was able to secure a $975 million IMF loan only after the Peruvian government agreed to cut government spending, reduce imports, and limit public debt.

In addition to official multilateral and bilateral loans, LDCs can also borrow from private banks. LDCs have in fact taken out so many private loans that private banks have become the biggest single source of LDC foreign capital. However, private banks are least likely to lend money to the poorest LDCs.

DEBT SERVICING Even in the best of political and economic situations there is a limit to the ability of LDCs to borrow. By definition, a loan requires repayment. Hence LDCs that borrow to finance domestic investment must have the capability of "servicing" (repaying) that debt. At a minimum, the economy of the LDC will have to grow at least enough to generate a surplus for debt servicing. Otherwise, debt servicing will require cutbacks in consumption, a contingency the loans were originally intended to avoid.

MULTINATIONAL DEVELOPMENT BANKS
World Bank Group

There are several multilateral development banks that provide loans, grants, and technical assistance to less developed countries.

The World Bank was created at the Bretton Woods Conference in 1944. Its principal aim was to facilitate the resurrection of world trade and the economic development of LDCs. There are three separate agencies within the World Bank Group:

- *International Bank for Reconstruction and Development (IBRD).* The IBRD is a profit-making institution that makes "hard" loans to LDCs for specific development projects. The loans are referred to as "hard" because they are made at rates close to market rates. LDC borrowers are expected to repay the loans within 20 years, as scheduled. The IBRD raises capital for the loans by borrowing funds in private money markets. In 1980 the IBRD lent approximately $9 billion to LDCs. In addition, the IBRD provides technical assistance on specific projects and consultation on general economic policies.

- *International Development Association (IDA).* The IDA makes "soft" loans to the poorest LDCs. The loans are "soft" in the sense that no interest is charged, and they may be repaid over a period of 50 years. IDA funds are obtained through contributions ("quotas") from developed countries and the earnings of the IBRD. In 1980 the IDA lent $3 billion to poor LDCs.

- *International Finance Corporation (IFC).* The IFC makes equity investments as well as loans. It encourages the development of the private sector and often manages private co-financing of specific projects. The IFC attempts to provide a mix of financial, technical, and management assistance. In 1980 the IFC lent over $1 billion.

Inter-American Development Bank (IDB)

The IDB focuses its efforts on Latin American countries. Forty-three nations provide contributions to promote public and private investments in Latin America. Additional funds are raised in private money markets (via bonds). Like the other multilateral banks, the IDB also provides technical assistance on specific development projects. In 1980 the IDB made over $2 billion in loans.

Asian Development Bank (ADB)

The ADB provides loans to LDCs in Asia. Because the loans are at market rates, most ADB loans go to the more developed LDCs. In 1980 the ADB lent nearly $1.5 billion.

African Development Bank (AFDB)

The AFDB focuses on Africa, and attaches a high priority to agricultural development. In 1980 it lent $0.3 billion.

International Monetary Fund (IMF)

Strictly speaking, the IMF is not a development bank. The IMF's function is to lend money to countries that are having short-term balance-of-payments problems. However, balance-of-payments problems are often a consequence of structural difficulties and slow growth of exports. In any case, IMF loans represent a source of foreign capital that can accelerate the development process. The IMF typically makes conditional loans requiring debtor countries to implement macroeconomic policies that will alleviate balance-of-payments problems. In 1980 the IMF had $60 billion in contributed funds.

IMF Cures Can Kill As Well As They Heal

WASHINGTON—Ignored by most Americans, the International Monetary Fund runs out of this city like some underground river, bringing aid, and often, turbulence when it breaks to the surface in foreign nations thousands of miles away.

In Egypt, riots left scores dead and President Anwar Sadat weakened in 1977 when food subsidies were cut briefly as part of an IMF plan to cope with the Egyptian government's debt. The Sudanese capital of Khartoum was the scene of disturbances and strikes last year when prices of basic commodities, including sugar and flour, were raised as a result of pressures from the IMF.

In Jamaica, the leftist administration of Prime Minister Michael Manley fell in a bitter election in Oc-

tober that turned on Manley's economic policies and battles with the Fund. In Turkey, former Prime Minister Bulent Ecvit was voted out of office last October after taking unpopular measures as part of the IMF stabilization program.

To its friends, the IMF is the good but mortal doctor forcing nations to swallow medicine they need to grow stronger. To its critics, the Fund is the rich man's club of Western powers, the enforcer and protector of the world's wealthiest banks.

"The IMF is not God," said former Treasury undersecretary Anthony Solomon before Congress. "Nobody will let it be God, and it does not have the wisdom to be God."

A Maryknoll missionary from Peru sees it another way: "The IMF shows a great sensitivity to the banks and a lack of sensitivity to people," he said. "A great sensitivity to balancing the budget, but a lack of sensitivity to bread on the table. . . . That is the gut issue."

Today nearly a quarter of the Fund's 141 members have signed

"standby" agreements allowing them to borrow well beyond their own quota in the IMF's reserves. All came looking for help, but most waited until other sources of credit had begun to dry up. They knew they would get less money than they thought they needed and more advice and strong-arming than they wanted.

"By definition, it is a situation where there's going to be a fair amount of light and heat and political difficulty," said an IMF executive.

But the agreement also is manipulated by both sides for their own purposes. Peru and Egypt can complain loudly about cuts in IMF subsidies, diverting attention from their failure to cut military expenditures instead. Powerful banks use the Fund to protect their loans. In recent years, the IMF has become the "Good Housekeeping Seal of Approval," the Standard & Poor's of international finance.

—David Rogers

Reprinted courtesy of The Boston Globe.

Even rapid economic growth, however, does not guarantee adequate debt-service capability. Most loans to LDCs are made in hard currencies, such as U.S. dollars, and creditors expect to be paid back in the same way. As a consequence, *the ability of LDCs to borrow money depends on their capacity to earn hard currency.* They earn foreign currency by selling exports. Hence debt servicing requires an LDC to increase its export potential. Export-related projects (e.g., a new harbor or factory) must take precedence over more domestic projects (e.g., new schools, improved sewage systems).

In 1980 the LDCs as a group had over $400 billion in outstanding debt. Annual debt servicing on these loans amounted to $75 billion. This was well within the payment capacity of the LDCs. As a group, they had over $400 billion in export earning in 1980; hence debt service claimed only 19 percent of hard-currency earnings. Averages are very misleading in this case, however. Some of the poorest LDCs had the greatest credit needs and the least export capacity.

FOREIGN AID The last source of external financing is foreign aid. Developed countries simply give money and resources to LDCs, either bilaterally or through multinational agencies (e.g., the United Nations). The distinction here is that no repayment is expected. The LDCs complain, however, that foreign aid has all the usual strings attached. Nevertheless, the LDCs were willing recipients of over $13 billion of aid in 1980. Nearly one-third of this amount was provided by the United States.

TABLE 35.3 FOREIGN AID IN RELATION TO GNP, 1981

Although the United States provides more development assistance (bilaterally and multilaterally) than any other country, its contribution is modest in relation to its GNP. In 1974 the United Nations set an aid goal equal to 0.7 percent of GNP. Few developed countries have attained that goal.

Country	Official development assistance	
	(Millions of U.S. dollars)	(As percent of GNP)
Australia	$ 649	0.41
Austria	317	0.48
Belgium	574	0.59
Canada	1,187	0.43
Denmark	405	0.73
Finland	135	0.28
France	4,022	0.71
Germany	3,182	0.46
Italy	670	0.19
Japan	3,170	0.28
Netherlands	1,510	1.08
New Zealand	67	0.29
Norway	467	0.82
Sweden	916	0.83
Switzerland	236	0.24
United Kingdom	2,194	0.43
United States	5,760	0.20
Total	$25,461	Average 0.41

Source: Organization for Economic Cooperation and Development.

Although developed countries have transferred substantial capital to the LDCs in the form of loans and aid, those transfers are relatively small fractions of GNP. In 1981 the United States allocated only 0.20 percent of total GNP to official development assistance. This was below the norm for most other developed countries (see Table 35.3) and much less than the goal of 0.7 percent established by the United Nations in 1974.

Foreign aid also represented a modest fraction of recipients' GNP, or even of their total investment. Because of this and the perceived problems of all external financing, the LDCs have petitioned for "trade, not aid." They assert that if we would simply buy more of the goods they produce, the LDCs could increase their export earnings and finance more investment themselves. We shall examine trade problems shortly.

Technology

Capital and labor are basic factors of production. However, technology is also a primary determinant of production possibilities. Indeed, as we saw in Chapter 17, technological advances have been the primary source of rising GNP per capita in the United States. LDCs, too, could greatly increase their growth with improved technology.

In principle, technological advances should be relatively easy in LDCs. The rich countries of the world have already developed advanced technology. LDCs can increase their own productivity simply by utilizing available research and innovation. Many LDCs have in fact benefited greatly from such transfers of technology. South Korea, Taiwan, and Singapore have all learned to copy and adapt American electronics technology. Japan, too, fueled much of its rapid growth with borrowed technology. Even the oil-exporting LDCs have benefited directly from American technological advances in oil exploration, production, and refining.

Technology transfers have also transformed agricultural productivity in much of the Third World. The "green revolution" of the 1950s and 1960s spread high-yielding, disease-resistant seeds all over the world. Improved fertilizers and irrigation techniques also generated substantial increases in output.

Although technology transfers have had enormous impact on the growth of LDCs, many observers feel we have only scratched the surface of potential growth. Theodore Schultz, who won a Nobel Prize for his agricultural studies, is one such observer. As he sees it, a major barrier to the growth of LDCs is their failure to disseminate and adapt new technologies in the agricultural sector (where the vast majority of LDC populations live and work). There is too much emphasis on capital improvements (physical technology) and too little on education and training of farmers (human capital). There is also a tendency to focus on big, glamorous industrial projects rather than small but cumulative improvements in organization and technology. China epitomized this problem with its "Great Leap Forward" in the mid-1970s (see Chapter 36).

Institutional structure

Another pervasive problem in LDCs is a lack of infrastructure. Infrastructure consists of the physical and institutional features that facilitate economic activity. Roads, telephones, schools, hospitals, and electricity are all essential ingredients of a viable economy. Yet most of these bare essentials are simply nonexistent in much of the Third World. As a consequence, productive regions of the country remain isolated and underutilized. The lack of infrastructure is also a serious impediment to foreign investment. Foreign investors want to be assured not only of electricity, water, and roads, but also of housing, schools, and other amenities for their workers, especially for the skilled employees they import from home.

The institutional structure also encompasses the legal and political structure of an economy. In many LDCs legal protection is a luxury and government corruption is pervasive. Political unrest is common, and governments are frequently overthrown. Under these circumstances, there are substantial risks attached to any long-term investments.

market mechanism: The use of market prices and sales to signal desired outputs (or resource allocations).

Finally, many LDCs are reluctant to rely on the **market mechanism** to allocate resources and distribute incomes. They prefer to use nonmarket prices to pursue specific economic or political objectives. This strategy is seen most commonly in the maintenance of low prices on agricultural products. By regulating prices and distribution, LDC governments often try to keep food prices low. The low prices raise the real incomes of consumers, particularly those in urban areas. At the same time, however, low food prices reduce farmers' incentives to produce. Hence, the quantity demanded in-

SENEGAL: A SUBSISTENCE STRUGGLE

According to World Bank estimates, Senegal is one of the world's poorest countries, with a per capita income of roughly $450. Even this low figure, however, greatly exaggerates the living standard of most Senegalese. In the small, urbanized area around the capital, Dakar, average incomes are $850. But in rural areas—where 70 percent of the population lives—average incomes are $150 per year. Rapid population growth (officially 2.6 percent a year, but unofficially estimated to be 3.3 percent) combined with minimal economic growth has kept the economy at subsistence levels. Most Senegalese are constantly at the brink of starvation, in mortal fear of recurrent droughts that will reduce their subsistence harvests. Average life expectancy is only 43 years.

Senegal is a resource-poor country, with extremely fragile and depleted soil. It is located in the Sahel, where droughts are a recurrent phenomenon. Although it is crossed by two great rivers, Senegal has never built a substantial irrigation system. It has no significant mineral deposits and little known oil. There are iron-ore deposits in the southeastern region, but no roads to get there. Since French colonial times, Senegal's principal export crop has been peanuts.

Although a lack of resources constrains Senegal's production possibilities, its growth has been further retarded by government policies. The first president of Senegal, Leopold-Sedar Senghor, enjoyed broad political support for 20 years. But this support was based in part on policies that curtailed economic growth. One of Senghor's first goals after independence was achieved in 1960 was to reduce foreign ownership and control of Senegal's crops, industry, and exports. The Senegalese government bought out most foreign investors and assumed control of their investments. In the process, however, the government overextended its management resources and skills, and business activity declined. The government's socialist stance also discouraged new inflows of foreign capital.

Another popular but ultimately self-defeating policy was the government's commitment to cheap food for the cities. The government

market shortage: The amount by which the quantity demanded exceeds the quantity supplied at a given price; excess demand.

creases while the quantity supplied falls. The end result is a **market shortage,** often accompanied by government rationing of basic foods. This distortion of market processes and outcomes is a barrier to growth in countries as diverse as China, Poland, Algeria, and Senegal.

GROWTH STRATEGIES

The array of barriers confronting LDCs looks formidable enough to stop any growth strategy. Indeed, many economists have concluded that the LDCs will not be able to achieve sustained economic growth until they can muster enough resources to overcome all of these barriers simultaneously. Walter W. Rostow popularized this notion by identifying five stages of economic development:

□ Stage 1. *Traditional society.* Rigid institutions, low productivity, little infrastructure, dependence on subsistence agriculture

imposed price and marketing controls on the agriculture sector. The aim of the controls was to hold urban food prices down. However, the low prices so discouraged farmers that they stopped marketing their output. Millet and rice are the principal food crops. But the farmers brought only 2 percent of their rice crop to the government-run markets in the late 1970s. As a consequence, Senegal had to import increasing quantities of food to feed its urban population.

Although Senegal desperately needed investment, the government tried to maintain consumption levels even when the economy was declining. In 1979 consumption absorbed 97 percent of gross domestic product. To further buttress consumption, the government increased the money supply rapidly and allowed consumer-goods imports to increase.

In 1979–80 an economic crisis developed. Senegal's trade deficit had reached alarming proportions as a result of a poor peanut harvest, higher oil prices, and increased consumer imports. The government was unable to meet its own payroll in June 1980 without emergency outside assistance.

In response to this crisis, a new economic strategy was adopted in the sixth Five-Year Plan (1981–85). The new president, Abdou Diouf, vowed to curtail consumption and stimulate agricultural production. To this end, he raised tariffs on imported goods an average of 50 percent, raised food prices (e.g., the price of bread increased 60 percent), increased farm prices for peanuts and cotton, expanded agricultural training and extension services, and provided greater incentives for food exports. Diouf also cut government employment and spending, restricted money and credit growth, and reduced government intervention in product markets.

The World Bank, the IMF, and several developed countries helped Diouf formulate the *Plan de Redressement* embodied in the sixth Five-Year Plan. In recognition of Diouf's commitment to economic development, these institutions granted Senegal extraordinary new assistance. Senegal is still desperately poor, but it now has some prospect of economic growth.

□ Stage 2. *Preconditions for takeoff.* Improved institutional structure, increased agricultural productivity, emergence of an entrepreneurial class

□ Stage 3. *Takeoff into sustained growth.* Increased saving and investment, rapid industrialization, growth-enhancing policies

□ Stage 4. *Drive to maturity.* Spread of growth process to lagging industrial sectors

□ Stage 5. *High mass consumption.* High per capita GNP attained and accessible to most of population.

The critical stage in this conception is Stage 2, which develops the essential preconditions for takeoff. The implication is that some minimum set of circumstances must exist before the economy can take off.

Although the need for some preconditions is plausible, their exact nature is usually not evident until the growth process is already under way. In the meantime, LDCs must decide what growth strategies to pursue, so as to maximize the probabilities of a takeoff and sustained growth. These strategic questions entail a variety of choices and difficult trade-offs.

Agriculture vs. industry

Ultimately the LDCs want to develop industrialized economies with high per capita GNP. It isn't clear, however, whether an early emphasis on industrialization is the fastest route to that objective. Industrialization cannot occur until an adequate flow of food and labor from the agricultural sector is assured. This flow cannot begin until agricultural productivity increases enough to generate a marketable surplus that will feed urban populations and permit some saving in rural communities. Agricultural productivity must rise even further if a surplus is to be maintained once farm workers migrate to urban industries. From this perspective, increased agricultural productivity looks like a precondition for an industrial takeoff. If it is, LDC governments should focus their limited managerial and capital resources on agricultural development rather than on early industrialization.

The massive concentration of LDC populations in the agricultural sector is another reason to give agriculture a higher priority than industry. Upwards of 80 percent of the people in LDCs work in agriculture. Accordingly, agricultural development has the potential to spread the benefits of growth broadly in a short span of time.

Agricultural development also has the potential to improve the balance of trade. Increased agricultural productivity lessens the need for food imports and also creates the potential for additional exports. By contrast, industrialization typically requires an early inflow of foreign resources and may not generate exportable output.

Balanced vs. unbalanced growth

The choice between agriculture and industry is a reflection of a broader question about "balanced" growth. Should an LDC pursue growth in many sectors simultaneously? Or should the growth effort be focused on only one or more "leading" sectors?

Ideally, a country would develop its agriculture, its industry, and all of its other component sectors at the same time. But that ideal is generally unattainable. We must remember the limited capacity most LDCs have for any growth effort. A country that pursued balanced growth would end up allocating a minuscule amount of resources to each of many industries. Moreover, it would find that it did not have the management capacity to keep track of these diverse investments. As a consequence, a truly balanced growth strategy is likely to generate no growth. Moreover, the failure of such a strategy is apt to disillusion consumers, savers, and investors, making subsequent growth policies less credible and therefore more difficult.

The pursuit of unbalanced growth, then, is a virtual necessity. That is to say, an LDC must concentrate the limited human and physical resources available for growth on only a few industries. In choosing an appropriate target for growth, an LDC must consider a variety of factors. Among the most important are bottlenecks and linkages. The industries selected must be ones that are not subject to overwhelming bottlenecks caused by shortages of skilled labor, essential inputs, or technology. That is to say, they must have some reasonable capacity to grow.

The second criterion for targeting unbalanced growth relates to the cumulative effects on an industry's development. Does the industry have significant linkages to other industries and sectors? If so, the growth of the target industry will stimulate the growth of other industries, thus ultimately promoting more balanced growth. Growth of the agricultural sector, for example, typically stimulates demand for fertilizer and farm equipment.

External vs. domestic markets

Another general criterion for targeting growth entails a choice between external markets and internal ones. Should an LDC rely on export markets for the growth of leading sectors? Or should it promote industries that primarily serve the domestic market? There are significant risks associated with either choice.

The advantage of focusing on export markets is twofold. First, every LDC needs foreign exchange (hard currency), and exports are the way to earn it. By promoting exports, an LDC effectively trades domestic resources for the capital and technology of other countries. The second advantage of exports is that they tap a ready market. World export markets are vastly larger than domestic ones, particularly those in poor LDCs. Hence exports confront a market with high levels of purchasing power.

Relying on exports for growth, however, is not a riskless strategy. The manufactured goods an LDC produces are likely to be of inferior quality and higher cost, given the scarcity of skilled labor, capital, modern technology, and experience. Hence an LDC may find that its manufactured exports are not competitive with goods produced in developed countries. To get a foothold in the export market, an LDC may need preferential treatment (purchases) from developed countries.

Even if an LDC is able to produce quality export goods at competitive prices, it may not be able to sell them. Producers in other countries will resist the added competition from LDC exports. Particularly successful LDC export campaigns are likely to result in trade restrictions of one kind or another (e.g., **quotas** and tariffs). The most notable example of such restrictions is probably the multination quotas on textiles. Many LDCs developed a **comparative advantage** in textile manufacturing and expected to accelerate their economic growth with earnings from the exportation of their textiles. But the higher-cost textile manufacturers in the United States and elsewhere have successfully limited textile imports from LDCs, thus constraining their growth potential. The same kinds of restrictions are common on shoes, steel, and an assortment of other manufactured goods. These kinds of restrictions are the primary motivation for the LDCs' demand for "trade, not aid."

Agricultural exports entail substantial risks also. Here again, the threat of trade restrictions is always present. The U.S. quotas on imported sugar exemplify the problem. In 1982 the Reagan administration reimposed quotas on sugar. The primary goal of the sugar quo-

quota: A limit on the quantity of a good that may be imported in a given time period.

comparative advantage: The ability of a country to produce a specific good at a lower opportunity cost than its trading partners.

price elasticity of demand: The percentage change in quantity demanded divided by the percentage change in price.

tas is to raise the income of domestic sugar producers. In the process, however, U.S. consumers are denied access to cheaper imported sugar and LDCs are shut out of a critical export market. The new restrictions severely limited the export earnings of Australia, Brazil, the Philippines, and several Caribbean countries.

Another risk associated with agricultural exports is their inherent instability. As we discussed in the appendix to Chapter 21, farm incomes are unstable. The quantity of food supplied in any year is as erratic as the weather. Yet the demand for food is relatively **price inelastic.** As a consequence, farm prices and incomes tend to fluctuate greatly. Haiti again provides a convenient illustration. Coffee is Haiti's most important product, and accounts for over 70 percent of its total export earnings. In 1977 the world price of coffee more than doubled when a frost in Brazil greatly reduced the quantity of coffee supplied in world markets. Haitian export earnings increased 50 percent and it looked as though a takeoff into growth might be possible. Two years later, however, coffee prices fell abruptly, and Haiti's export earnings declined to their previous levels. Virtually every LDC has had a similiar experience—even those LDCs that export oil (e.g., Nigeria).

Many LDCs have tried to stabilize their export earnings by organizing producer cartels. In theory, the cartels could limit exports in years of excess supply or reduced demand, thereby maintaining a mutually agreeable price (and income). However, all such cartels tend to be fragile. Each member country is confronted by an all but irresistible temptation to underprice the cartel when a market surplus develops. And importing countries confront an all but irresistible temptation to disavow any "gentleman's agreement" to maintain prices in such circumstances. Even OPEC was weakened by these market pressures.

DOMESTIC MARKETS Given the risks of international trade, many LDCs have assigned greater priority to domestic markets. Of particular interest here are import-competing industries, that is, industries that produce goods that are being imported by the LDC. The attraction here is twofold. First of all, a market for the product already exists, as evidenced by the imports. Second, by producing rather than importing the goods in question, an LDC can reduce its outflow of precious foreign exchange. Rather than trying to earn additional export income to pay for imports, the strategy here is to reduce the need for imports directly.

As alluring as the import-substitution strategy is, it, too, entails significant costs. Newly developed domestic industries are not likeky to be competitive with imported goods. To get started, they will probably need some protection, in the form of trade restrictions. This is the classic *infant industry* argument we encountered in Chapter 33. As is always the case, however, the nurture of infant industries implies higher costs to domestic consumers. These higher costs may in turn make other domestic industries less competitive in their own export markets. There is also the risk that the infant industry may never grow up, thus requiring perpetual subsidies and trade protection.

Should an LDC decide to promote a domestic industry that doesn't compete with imports, the problem of inadequate demand reemerges. Markets in LDCs tend to be very small and very poor. Accordingly, a growth strategy built on a leading domestic industry may flounder for lack of demand.

More aid

With all the problems inherent in any growth strategy, the prospects for development of poor LDCs hardly look good. One wonders, however, how awful the growth prospects of today's developed countries looked a couple of hundred years ago. Growth certainly is still possible, despite the substantial barriers that impede the process. At the same time, however, it is evident that some of the poorest LDCs are going to flounder for a very long time if they don't receive more aid. Other LDCs could likewise accelerate their growth with greater access to foreign capital and technology. During the last decade such access has been limited by the high cost of oil and the resultant diversion of scarce foreign exchange to pay for oil imports. For these reasons, the LDCs have petitioned for more foreign aid from both the industrialized countries and OPEC. In the United Nations' "Development Decade" of the 1970s the LDCs had asked industrialized countries to give 1 percent of their GNP in foreign aid. This goal was later reduced to 0.7 percent in the 1974 call for a New International Economic Order (NIEO). Even that more modest goal has largely remained unfulfilled, however.

SUMMARY

▪ GNP per capita provides a summary index of economic development. Most LDCs are characterized by both low GNP per capita and slow income growth. They are also far less able to satisfy basic human needs (e.g., life expectancy, health, literacy).

▪ High birth rates limit a country's ability to raise GNP per capita. Rapid population growth also tends to retard education, saving, and investment.

▪ LDCs are chronically short of skilled labor, management, capital, and technology. Although domestic saving can finance some of these inputs, external financing is usually required. Foreign investment, loans, and aid are all sources of external financing.

▪ In the short run, most LDCs must choose between agricultural development and industrialization. Agricultural development typically promises a greater payoff because the vast majority of the population works in agriculture, at low productivity. Improved farm productivity can create food, labor, and capital surpluses for industrialization.

▪ LDCs generally have no choice but to pursue unbalanced growth, that is, the concerted development of only a few leading industries.

▪ In seeking a leading industry, LDCs must choose between export promotion and domestic markets. Exports have the potential to earn needed foreign exchange, but may also confront unstable and protectionist markets. On the other hand, production for domestic markets may entail high costs or limited demand.

■ There is no single "correct" strategy for economic development. Each country confronts a unique set of barriers and growth possibilities. All LDCs, however, could benefit from more foreign aid.

Terms to remember

Define the following terms:

disguised unemployment   market shortage
productivity   quota
barter   comparative advantage
production possibilities   price elasticity of demand
market mechanism

Questions for discussion

1. Why do LDCs prefer trade over aid? Why don't developed countries buy more products from LDCs?

2. Should LDCs restrict the profits of foreign investors? What are the gains and costs of such restrictions?

3. Identify an LDC and discuss its recent growth experience. What explains its growth rate?

4. Did the United States experience "balanced" growth, or were there notable "leading sectors" in our early development?

5. How did the United States finance its early investments when its production possibilities were very limited?

SOCIALIST PLANNING

> One cannot work without a plan designed for the long run.
>
> —LENIN

Working with his good friend and later benefactor Friedrich Engels, Karl Marx described how capitalist systems would be destroyed. From his perspective, all history was a sequence of class strife, with class identities based on economic relationships. In the words of the *Communist Manifesto*, "The history of all existing society is the history of class struggles. Freeman and slave, patrician and plebeian, lord and serf, guildmaster and journeyman, in a word, oppressor and oppressed." **Capitalist** systems, Marx claimed, followed the same pattern; only the class identities were changed. In this case, the oppressors—the capitalists—owned the means of production, and the oppressed—the proletariat—were their modern-day serfs. The "natural" antagonism between these two classes arose out of the capitalist's unrelenting quest for profits and the attendant desire to pay workers as little as possible. This continued exploitation would eventually drive the working class to revolt and would come to an end with a "spontaneous" revolution.

Once the capitalists were sent packing (if they were so fortunate), the working class itself, the proletariat, would take over the means of production. There would be no more class strife, because there would be only one class, with everyone sharing equally in access to the means of production and the output it yielded. The abolition of private property would mean that nobody would have any means of exploiting anybody else. The motivating principle of the **communism** Marx envisioned would be "from each according to his ability, to each according to his need." In that idealized society, there would be no central authority—no state—because the only

capitalism: An economy in which the factors of production (e.g., land, capital) are owned by individuals; basic allocation decisions are made by market forces.

communism: A stateless, classless economy in which there is no private property and everyone shares in production and consumption according to individual abilities and needs.

function of a state was to express and pursue the interests of the dominant class. Since only one class would exist, in Marx's vision, no state would be necessary.

THE SOCIALIST TRANSITION

Marx was not very specific about exactly how a classless, stateless, communist society and economy would function. His immediate concern was with the continuing exploitation of the working class, the widespread poverty, sickness, and degradation that he himself had experienced in the early stages of the Industrial Revolution. Hence he focused on the need to raise the class consciousness of the working class. Marx sought to explain how workers could unite and throw off the shackles of capitalism, how they could speed up the "evolutionary" end of capitalism. Marx died some 25 years before the first successful communist revolution, and before he was able to complete *Das Kapital,* his voluminous study of the way capitalist systems functioned.[1]

While concentrated on the internal flaws of capitalism and the awakening of working-class interests, Marx also provided some sketches of the kind of society that would follow the revolution. In particular, he foresaw that a central government (the state) would be required for some time to give direction to the new society. The proletariat would not be prepared to embrace fully the basic tenets of communism, nor would it have the technical expertise required to organize the means of production. In the interim period, a central authority, a *socialist* state, would have to solidify class consciousness, reorganize property and production rights, expand output, and plan the transition to a truly communist society. As society moved along in that direction, the state would become increasingly unnecessary and would gradually wither away.

From Marx's perspective, then, the demise of capitalism would be succeeded by two further stages, **socialism** and communism. In both stages of development, the means of production would be publicly owned. Under socialism, however, the state would play an important role in allocating resources, and goods would be distributed in part according to each person's work effort. The economy would enter the final stage of development, communism, only after goods were in such abundance that everyone's needs could be satisfied. A striking characteristic of the communist ideal is that people work for the common good and need not be prodded with the promise of personal gain.

The communist revolutions that have taken place—in Russia in 1917, in China in 1949, and elsewhere—have not followed Marx's scenario in every respect. Indeed, Marx would have been surprised to see the revolutions occur in countries as underdeveloped as Rus-

socialism: An economy in which all nonlabor means of production are owned by the state, which exercises control over resource allocation.

---

[1] Marx never forgave capitalism for driving him into the relentless research (most of it undertaken in the British Museum) and political activism that exhausted his finances and health. Upon publication of the first volume of *Das Kapital,* he wrote to Engels, "I hope that the bourgeoisie as long as they live will have cause to remember my carbuncles" (cited in *Fortune,* May 1946, p. 146).

sia was in 1917 and China in 1949. Nevertheless, most "communist" countries have heeded Marx's admonition to exert strong central authority, to use the state as an instrument for developing and reforming society. Indeed, most "communist" countries refer to themselves as "socialist" countries, with communism expressed as a goal, not a description. Marx obviously would have understood such a response, and he would have encouraged them to plan for the classless, stateless society he idealized.[2]

THE CHALLENGE OF PLANNING

Outlining ideals and carrying them out, however, are very different tasks. Imagine that you have led a successful revolution and must now organize the economy to fulfill the revolution's goals. This is the kind of dilemma Nikolai Lenin and his comrades confronted in 1917 and Mao Tse-tung faced in 1949.

In general, you want to ensure greater equality for all the people, because that was a motivating force behind the revolution. And you want to improve the standard of living, both to satisfy revolutionary aspirations and to reassure the proletariat that they have bet on the right horse. Finally, you want to build up the country's defenses to protect yourself against counterrevolution from within and aggression from without.

How are you going to attain these goals, and what do you have to work with? The capitalists have all been sent packing, so you can't ask them for any help. What you've got is all capital stock left over from earlier investments (and now owned by the state). In addition you have the country's land and mineral resources (also owned by the state) and a proud but currently agitated labor force. Let's hope you haven't forgotten your basic economics!

Production possibilities

production possibilities: The alternative combinations of final goods and services that could be produced in a given time period with all available resources and technology.

One thing that may come to mind rather quickly is the concept of **production possibilities.** The notion that there are limits to output will become painfully clear as you are pressed to satisfy the revolutionary promise of improved living standards. The factory workers, the farmers, and the soldiers all want more food, better housing, and even a few luxuries. Will you be able to deliver?

By adding up all of society's productive resources and surveying available technology, you could conceivably determine what production possibilities exist. The solid line in Figure 36.1 might be an adequate description of those possibilities. Here we assume that all goods can be lumped into two major categories, here referred to as "consumption goods" and "investment goods." The variety of goods producible is, of course, infinitely larger, but some sort of summary is useful, not to mention more manageable.

[2] How long one must wait for the stateless society is the subject of considerable debate. Lenin emphasized the need for the state to guard against "capitalist encirclement," implying some form of eternal vigilance. Echoing these thoughts, Joseph Stalin declared in 1939 that Russians could expect to achieve a stateless society only when socialism had been established all over the world and "there is no more danger of attack." This question is more political than economic.

FIGURE 36.1 POSTREVOLUTIONARY PRODUCTION POSSIBILITIES

All countries confront limited production possibilities. A revolution may even destroy capital, land, or labor, thus reducing immediate production possibilities (to the solid curve). Deciding what to produce with available resources and technology is a basic planning issue. More consumption goods (point B) may be an immediate necessity even though that implies a cutback in investment.

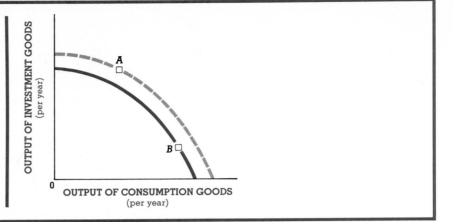

The first dilemma we have to confront is the fact that our production possibilities are probably no larger immediately after the revolution than they were just before it. In fact, they are probably smaller. A lot of buildings and equipment were destroyed in the revolt, many workers have been wounded, and most of the capitalists and their lackeys are either dead or fled.[3] Moreover, we have promised not only to improve living standards, but also to work everybody a little bit less than did their capitalist oppressors. Accordingly, our immediate production possibilities probably look more like the solid curve in Figure 36.1 than the larger, dotted one that prevailed earlier.

In the face of unchanged or even smaller production possibilities, it is evident that we are going to have a difficult time delivering on the revolution's promises. Any immediate improvement of living standards for the masses will have to come about through *redistribution* of output rather than from *added* output. Our hope for delivering more goods to the workers is going to depend largely on the chance that the capitalists had been eating, wasting, or hoarding a substantial proportion of output. If they did, that share of output can now be spread around. A most unlikely prospect, however, especially if one is thinking in terms of such basic goods as food, housing, and clothing.[4]

WHAT to produce

Fortunately, there are other possibilities for increasing living standards, and they reside in another basic economic outcome, the *mix of output*. The greedy capitalists were probably devoting a large share

[3] At the time (1949) the Communists took control of China, industrial output was one-half its prewar peak. Agricultural output was similarly depressed. In addition, the transportation system was partially destroyed, many skilled technicians and managers had fled, and the government's foreign-exchange reserves had been moved to Taiwan.

[4] Following the Bolshevik revolution of 1917, the mansions of many Russian aristocrats and affluent capitalists were converted into multifamily dwellings; but the number of mansions is obviously limited. Redistribution possibilities may have been slightly greater in China, where the landlord-gentry class had diverted a lot of output to personal consumption, including reserves of rice and other food.

investment: Expenditures on (production of) new plant and equipment (capital) in a given time period, plus changes in business inventories.

economic growth: An increase in output (real GNP); an expansion of production possibilities.

of the economy's productive resources to the output of **investment** goods. By building more machinery, more plants, and more transportation facilities, they were increasing their wealth and control, while starving the masses. By altering the mix of output in favor of more consumption goods, we could deliver an immediate improvement of living standards. Such a change in the output mix is illustrated by the move from point A to point B in Figure 36.1.

Although this move might satisfy the need to deliver quickly on revolutionary promises, it is fraught with difficulties for the years ahead. Remember the concept of **economic growth?** To provide higher living standards in the years ahead, or even just to maintain present living standards for a growing population, we will have to expand our production possibilities.

But economic growth, especially if it is to exceed population growth, requires additional investment. Some investment will be needed simply to maintain and replace existing plant and equipment. Additional, *net* investment will be required to *expand* our productive capacity. Accordingly, cutting back on investment goods in order to produce more consumption goods may be tantamount to eating tomorrow's dinner today. Tomorrow that decision may be regretted.

Consequently, ***one of the most basic decisions planners must confront is what proportion of resources to devote to investment and future consumption and what proportion to devote to present consumption.*** The trade-off is clearly a difficult one, especially in a country where living standards are abnormally low and we need to increase *both* consumption and investment. In the Soviet Union, the decision was made—first by Lenin and even more forcefully by Joseph Stalin—to shift the mix of output in favor of investment. Both men were well aware that this decision implied reduced living standards in the short run. Influencing that decision were persistent fears of capitalist attack and the attendant desire to build up strong defenses and a self-contained economy. As a consequence, investment goods have accounted for as much as one-third of Russian output, approximately double the investment ratio that has prevailed in the United States.

One consequence of this emphasis has been a faster rate of economic growth in the Soviet Union than in the United States. Only recently, however, has this growth been reflected in the volume and variety of consumer goods. Indeed, the level of agricultural production in the mid-1950s was no larger than it had been in 1928, and per capita output of food was actually smaller. It was not until the ninth Five-Year Plan (1971–75) that "the main task" was expressed as the need "to ensure a significant increase in the people's material and cultural standard of living."[5] That goal was submerged by defense needs in the tenth plan, however, and consumers did not again get priority until the current (eleventh) plan.

The political leaders of China decided that they could not afford such high rates of investment, even though they needed it even more

[5] *Pravda*, December 19, 1972, cited by Keith Bush in *Soviet Economic Prospects for the Seventies*, a compendium of papers submitted to the Joint Economic Committee of Congress, June 27, 1973.

than did the Soviets. In 1949 the Chinese people were on the brink of starvation. GNP per capita was around $140 (in 1982 U.S. dollars). Accordingly, the Chinese leaders had to devote a larger share of total output to consumption goods, especially such basic foodstuffs as wheat, rice, and cooking oil. Less than 10 percent of total output was devoted to investment in the early postrevolutionary years. Only after minimal consumption standards were ensured did the share of output devoted to investment increase (to as high as 25 percent in the early 1970s).

HOW to produce

Once we have decided on the most desirable mix of output, the question of resource allocation is quite straightforward. Obviously we want to allocate our human, land, and capital resources in such a way as to produce the desired mix of output.

Although the general dimensions of resource allocation may be evident, the details can get sticky. Now we have to pay some attention to the specific components of "consumption goods" and "investment goods" and ask just what kind of resource effort is required for each product. In other words, we must abandon the simplicity of a two-dimensional production-possibilities curve and start thinking about widgets and ball bearings, plows and threshers. Even in a socialist economy, the production of goods entails the coordination and completion of several distinct steps. Neither swords nor plowshares will appear out of thin air just because we specify a particular mix of output as being desirable.

Recall that just about any good can be produced in a variety of alternative ways. Such alternative **production processes** burden us with increasingly difficult decisions. We must decide first how many of each output we want, then which combination of inputs is most efficient for producing that quantity. Finally, we must be sure that the input requirements we derive from these calculations do not exceed the quantity of resources we have available.

production process: A specific combination of resources used to produce a good or service.

The kind of calculations required for efficient resource allocation would give you an unbelievable headache, even if you were equipped with pocket calculators and high-speed computers. A sense of how painful such an effort might be is only suggested by Table 36.1, on pp. 828–829, which indicates a few input—output relationships for the Soviet economy. Input—output coefficients, as displayed in the table, indicate how much output from one industry will be required to provide inputs for another industry.

You can discover by reading down the column marked "Automobiles," for example, that the production of 1 ruble's worth of automobiles requires 0.08503 ruble's worth of ferrous ores and metals, 0.02649 ruble's worth of nonferrous ores and metals, and so forth. Incredibly boring statistics, to be sure. But if you're in charge of allocating the people's resources, you'd better be certain that you allocate the right amount of resources to the production of such inputs. Otherwise you won't get the quantity of automobiles that has been promised. Come up short with those nonferrous ores and metals, and you could find yourself reassigned to some fairly unpleasant chores in eastern Siberia!

Soviets Find Job for Every College Grad

MOSCOW—"It's like their wedding day," the university rector said happily.

A graduating senior disagreed. "It's terrible," he said. "Everyone is taking tranquilizers."

The occasion was the Day of Distribution, which is far more emotional than Graduation Day at the 900 or so institutions of higher learning in the Soviet Union. On the Day of Distribution, graduates get their first job assignments.

By the end of June, virtually all of the 800,000 young men and women graduating from universities and other university-level institutions will have met with a placement commission and will know which job is waiting for them.

The system is a creature of this country's planned economy.

In the United States, collegians choose their specialties and take their chances in the job market after graduation. In the Soviet Union, the system cranks out cars, bombs and paper clips according to government decree, and it produces diplomas the same way.

"They give us money, we give them specialists," Arnold Koop, rector of Tartu University in Soviet Estonia, summed up.

Most Soviet students, even though they would probably balk at trading their security for what they see as the chaotic rough-and-tumble of the American job market, are not entirely happy with their system.

Eager to begin enjoying the good life that a college degree virtually assures in this society, many see the first job assignment as a way station at best.

When they scrawl "I consent" at the bottom of the placement commission's decision, Soviet graduates technically commit themselves to work at their first job for at least three years, repaying the state for a free education.

But they resent the fact that many assigned jobs are far from home, in the provinces, where life is often primitive and their talents are sometimes not appreciated. And many wind up with jobs only remotely related to their studies.

—Dan Fisher

Prices You might be thinking that markets and prices could help solve some of these problems, thereby relieving you and your planners of an immense burden. But such thoughts merely demonstrate that you have not yet cleansed your mind of its bourgeois capitalist prejudices. It is of course true that ***a basic function of prices in a market economy is to signal to producers and consumers that some products are relatively scarce or plentiful.*** These signals are expected to call forth appropriate supply and demand responses. Thus one way to solve the resource-allocation problem might be to let prices respond to shortages. If somebody in the Administration for Tires and Rubber Products messed up his homework and left us without enough tires, tire prices would rise. This price increase would provide an early warning of trouble and give tire producers a strong incentive to increase production. In this way, the tire shortage might be alleviated before it got too serious.

But such "efficiency" is not welcome in a planned socialist economy, especially not in the Soviet Union or the People's Republic of China.[6] The market mechanism has been rejected for three principal reasons. First, were prices allowed to function as market signals and help distribute goods and resources accordingly, we could no longer be assured that out planning goals would be achieved. Don't forget that a primary motivation for planning in the first place was a distaste for the outcomes generated in the marketplace. If prices were allowed to respond to market forces, we would be unlikely to devote so large a percentage of our resources to invest-

[6] But it is welcome in such countries as Yugoslavia. Indeed, a sharp theoretical distinction is made between *market socialism* (like that in Yugoslavia) and *planned socialism* (like that in the Soviet Union and China). In practice, the distinction is often blurred at the edges, as we shall note. Our focus in this chapter is on the planned (some call them "command") economies only.

TABLE 36.1 SOVIET INPUT–OUTPUT RELATIONSHIPS

No product can be produced unless the required inputs are available in the correct
quantities. An input–output table such as this describes the production
requirements of various goods. The production of one automobile, for example,
requires inputs of 0.08503 unit of ferrous ores and metals, 0.02649 unit of
nonferrous ores, and so on. Central planning agencies use such tables to
determine what goods and services can be produced with available resources and
technology.

Sector no.	Inputs	Input requirement per unit of:			
		Automobiles	Tractors and agricultural machinery	Bread, flour, and confections	Electric and thermal power
1	Ferrous ores and metals	0.08503	0.13637	0.00024	0.00137
2	Nonferrous ores and metals	0.02649	0.01685	0.00018	0.00000
3	Coke products and refractory materials	0.00173	0.00382	0.00002	0.00024
4	Industrial metal products	0.00954	0.00828	0.00015	0.00089
5	Coal	0.00216	0.00187	0.00238	0.20491
6	Oil extraction and refining	0.00524	0.00475	0.00065	0.06132
7	Gas	0.00332	0.00303	0.00083	0.05900
8	Peat and oil shales	0.00019	0.00011	0.00014	0.02763
9	Electric and thermal power	0.01171	0.01935	0.00284	0.00153
10	Energy and power machinery	0.00021	0.00065	0.00001	0.00174
11	Eltech machinery and cable products	0.01705	0.01571	0.00026	0.00153
12	Metalworking machinery	0.00155	0.00229	0.00000	0.00000
13	Tools and dies	0.00272	0.00506	0.00009	0.00013
14	Precision instruments	0.00080	0.00147	0.00004	0.00048
15	Mining and metallurgical machinery	0.00000	0.00000	0.00000	0.00000
16	Pumps and compressors	0.00123	0.00122	0.00001	0.00012
17	Specialized machinery	0.00000	0.00004	0.00054	0.00000
18	Hoist-transportation and construction equipment	0.00043	0.00006	0.00003	0.00004
19	Transportation equipment	0.00006	0.00006	0.00000	0.00003
20	Automobiles	0.17937	0.01088	0.00003	0.00016
21	Tractors and agricultural machinery	0.00026	0.18826	0.00001	0.00008
22	Bearings	0.00841	0.01723	0.00002	0.00009
23	Other machine-building	0.02052	0.02061	0.00041	0.00307
24	Other metalworking	0.00585	0.01013	0.00061	0.00035
25	Metal structures	0.00000	0.00000	0.00001	0.00000

ment and defense. Instead, the working class would keep the prices
of consumer goods high. Producers would than have an incentive to
close down truck and missile plants and start producing cars and
television sets. That clearly wouldn't do.

We could allow markets to function, of course, and still attain
our production goals by the adroit use of fiscal and monetary weapons. They do that in the United States and elsewhere, with considerable success. If the U.S. government, for example, wants to devote a
larger proportion of output to military hardware, it has the power to
do so. The U.S. government can use its taxing and expenditure powers to outbid private consumers for available resources. But that kind

Sector no.	Inputs	Input requirement per unit of:			
		Automobiles	Tractors and agricultural machinery	Bread, flour, and confections	Electric and thermal power
26	Repair of machinery	0.00101	0.00153	0.00053	0.00533
27	Abrasives	0.00106	0.00195	0.00001	0.00007
28	Mineral chemistry products	0.00004	0.00002	0.00001	0.00007
29	Basic and other chemistry products	0.00209	0.00187	0.00014	0.00186
30	Aniline dye products	0.00004	0.00076	0.00001	0.00001
31	Synthetic resins and plastics	0.00240	0.00065	0.00004	0.00040
32	Synthetic fibers	0.00004	0.00000	0.00000	0.00000
33	Organic synthetic products	0.00112	0.00086	0.00002	0.00008
34	Paints and lacquers	0.00703	0.00626	0.00012	0.00029
35	Rubber and asbestos products	0.08596	0.03779	0.00017	0.00040
36	Logging	0.00073	0.00057	0.00013	0.00011
37	Woodworking	0.00677	0.01067	0.00401	0.00039
38	Paper and pulp	0.00173	0.00107	0.00225	0.00009
39	Construction materials	0.00136	0.00084	0.00023	0.00044
40	Glass and porcelain	0.00393	0.00074	0.00004	0.00016
41	Textiles	0.00621	0.00296	0.00083	0.00037
42	Other light industry products	0.00574	0.00445	0.00164	0.00085
43	Fish products	0.00000	0.00000	0.00040	0.00000
44	Meat and dairy products	0.00048	0.00130	0.01258	0.00028
45	Sugar	0.00000	0.00006	0.05334	0.00000
46	Bread, flour, and confections	0.00000	0.00000	0.23885	0.00000
47	Other foods	0.00058	0.00036	0.03644	0.00044
48	Industry (all other)	0.00567	0.00542	0.00157	0.00247
49	Construction	0.00000	0.00000	0.00000	0.00000
50	Crops	0.00002	0.00002	0.31794	0.00000
51	Animal husbandry	0.00000	0.00002	0.00278	0.00000
52	Forestry	0.00000	0.00000	0.00000	0.00000
53	Transportation & communications	0.05446	0.06347	0.01214	0.00054
54	Trade and distribution	0.02239	0.00761	0.07199	0.00005
55	Other branches of material products	0.00125	0.00347	0.00007	0.00011

Source: U.S. Congress, *Soviet Economic Prospects for the Seventies*, a compendium of papers submitted to the Joint Economic Committee, June 27, 1973 (Washington, D.C.: U.S. Government Printing Office, 1973).

of fiscal camouflage not only is unseemly, it also violates other principles of the revolution. If prices are free to respond to market forces and producers are free to react accordingly, some people are going to make a lot of money. Producers will profit from market imbalances and their efforts to correct them. That kind of market efficiency threatens to unbalance our distribution of income, a very serious matter. After all, the elimination of income disparities was a motivating force behind the revolution and is now enshrined as one of our guiding principles. Hence to suggest that market prices could help to solve our allocation problems is tantamount to condoning profiteering.

Someone might object, however, that any excesses of profit could be taxed away, thereby fulfilling the allocation objective without disturbing the income distribution. But that idea only demonstrates an incomplete uunderstanding of capitalist economics. We simply can't have it both ways. If we enshrine the profit motive as an acceptable means of solving allocation problems, we violate the principle of "from each according to his ability, to each according to his need." Private gain, not communal effort, becomes the motivating force. If we try to correct these excesses by steeply progressive income and profit taxes, we will sanction selfish motives. We will also reduce marginal profits so much that they will lose their effectiveness as motivating forces. (Remember all those squabbles the capitalists had about marginal tax rates and work incentives?)

THE FUNCTION OF PRICES IN A PLANNED ECONOMY   Shall we completely abolish prices, then? No. Unless we are prepared to ration everything from basic resources to final consumer goods, prices will have to be an essential ingredient of our plans. But we will not use prices the same way the capitalists do. Instead, we will first determine the appropriate mix of output, and therewith the quantity of all goods to be produced. Some goods—especially such amenities as radios, television sets, cars, wristwatches, silk shirts, and steaks—will, of course, be in short supply. We can use the price mechanism to help distribute these goods. More specifically, we can attach high prices to such goods in order to keep the quantity demanded in line with our production plans. This course will have the further advantage of inspiring the people to tighten their belts, work harder, and save enough income for a few luxuries.

Are we not back in the camp of the capitalist pigs, then? No. Prices serve very different functions in market and planned economies. ***In a planned economy, prices are used to reconcile the mix of goods demanded to the planned supply.*** The mix of goods supplied is itself determined by the state plan. Prices are not permitted to have an independent influence on resource allocation. Specifically, central planners do not permit the high prices attached to some consumer goods to act as an incentive for increased production. Instead, those prices are maintained with high retail taxes, while producers are paid very little for their output of consumer goods. This strategy effectively dampens both consumer demand and producer incentives.

In some cases, however, we will want to maintain relatively low consumer prices, either to encourage certain kinds of consumer behavior or to ensure that everyone can afford basic staples. In China and Russia, for example, the prices of food, housing, and health services are kept very low (see Table 36.2). Rent on a two-room apartment in China costs something like $50 a year, a visit to the doctor 10 cents, and an abortion only $1.00.[7]

---

[7] The low price of an abortion is consistent with China's growing anxiety about its burgeoning population—estimated at 1 billion in 1980 and growing by 16 million or so people a year! It is also hoped that pervasive indoctrination and social counseling, including a prohibition against premarital sex, will restrain the demand for such services.

	Price in labor hours	
TABLE 36.2 RELATIVE PRICES IN THE U.S. AND THE SOVIET UNION		
Item	United States	Soviet Union
Rent	149	28
Utilities	12	3
Dentist	5	free
Jeans	3	33
Color TV	106	813
New car	928	7,428
Vodka (liter)	1	8

TABLE 36.2 RELATIVE PRICES IN THE U.S. AND THE SOVIET UNION

In the United States, the average factory worker must work 149 hours to earn enough to pay rent on a three-bedroom apartment. A Soviet worker needs to work only 28 hours. Soviet planners keep prices of basic goods (e.g., rent, utilities, dentist) low to ensure equal access to "necessities." By contrast, such "luxuries" as jeans, television sets, new cars, and even vodka are priced relatively high. These high prices discourage consumption, and thus free resources for other production priorities.

Source: *Time*, June 28, 1980.

We must also remember that prices can serve as a convenient measure of efficiency. How are we going to know whether the People's Bicycle Factory at Tientsin is producing as many bicycles as it can with the resources available to it? It would be a horrendous task to inventory all the separate inputs used, then to compare those input–output relationships with those of the People's Bicycle Factory at Kwangchow. And how do you know which factory is better serving the people if you can do no more than observe basic inputs and outputs? Say that the Tientsin factory produced 27 bikes last month and used 18 pounds of aluminum, 7 pounds of rubber, 1½ gallons of lacquer, and 13 pounds of steel. At the same time the Kwangchow factory produced 33 bikes, using 21 pounds of aluminum, 6½ pounds of rubber, 4 gallons of lacquer, and 12 pounds of steel. Some summary sort of measure is clearly necessary. Far better if we attach prices to all those inputs and simply see how much total cost goes into the production of so many bicycles. Prices will allow us to measure performance. We can also use relative prices to discourage use of relatively scarce inputs such as aluminum and rubber, or whatever resources we desire to ration carefully.[8]

FOR WHOM to produce

Insofar as planning objectives are concerned, the question of *distribution of income* is readily resolved. We want all our people to be equal after the revolution. In material terms, this means that we want to move closer to a situation wherein all people enjoy the same standard of living, whatever their respective abilities. Disparities in income serve to create jealousies, anxieties, and social friction. If such disparities are large enough, they can lead to conspicuous social stratification—that is to say, to socioeconomic *classes*. That is clearly inconsistent with the stateless, classless society for which we have fought. Hence we shall strive to ensure that everyone receives a more equal share of total income. To ensure further that people do

[8] Many luxury goods and basic commodities are explicitly rationed in China. Rationing further reduces the use of such goods.

not use their income for purposes of indulgent consumption, we will limit the availability of basic commodities and ration them equally among the people. And we shall price conspicuous consumption goods like automobiles so high that there is little chance of anyone's acquiring them.

PROBLEMS OF IMPLEMENTATION

At this point, we may have mixed feelings about the revolution. On the one hand, we have rid ourselves of capitalist oppression and demonstrated that a better society is possible. On the other hand, after discarding our shackles, manning the barricades, and overcoming our capitalist oppressors, the challenge of planning a new society may look like a real chore. Let's face it; the intricacies of planning are hardly exciting.

But as complex as our planning responsibilities may appear, we mustn't lose sight of Marx's dictum that economics is everything. If we can restructure productive relationships and economic outcomes, then we can build a new and better society on the ashes of bourgeois capitalism. Such thoughts may help strengthen our motivation to carry on the planning task.

We can reduce our burden, of course, by turning over to something like Gosplan (the Soviet planning agency) the task of filling in all the details. That is to say, we could simply issue a small set of general directives (say, more steel plants and an equal distribution of income). Then we could leave it up to the planners to translate those guidelines into specific inputs and outputs. But we should not fool ourselves about the difficulty of that assignment. ***The more completely planners seek to fashion economic outcomes in the name of the stateless society, the more complex the planning task will be.*** An especially difficult and onerous responsibility will be the task of confirming that all the planning details are *consistent*—that all inputs and outputs match up in the style of Table 36.1. If we push our planners too hard, they may start thinking revisionist thoughts.

Taking our chances, let us dismiss problems of planning detail and give some thought to the problems of implementation. How are we going to communicate our plans to the masses? What assurances do we have that our plans will be carried out? We're going to look pretty foolish if we advertise grandiose goals and nobody pays any attention to them. The bourgeois press will naturally try to exploit such a situation. They will claim that we have lost the support of the people, that we are out of touch, and that we have started moving our personal fortunes into Swiss bank accounts.

Incentives

The critical question is how to motivate the workers, the farmers, and the managers of our plants to fulfill the specific objectives of our plans. They may not possess the same revolutionary zeal and farsightedness that we do, and may thus have a difficult time understanding and accepting their roles in the master plan. And we can be certain that input–output coefficients will mean as little to them as they do to economics students in capitalist societies. How, then, can we get the masses to contribute to output in the form and quantity we desire?

One way to ensure compliance with our plans is to strike terror into the hearts of the workers. Such heavy-handedness has been used on occasion, most notably in the early stages of development in the Soviet Union under Stalin. It was also used in the early land reforms of Mao Tse-tung in China. Such an approach, however, is not only inconsistent with the concept of "a workers' state" but also unlikely to stimulate the kind of commitment and efficiency that is desired. Besides, more conventional and effective mechanisms are available for getting people to work.

As we noted in Chapter 25, people's willingness to supply labor, to work, is predicated on a variety of psychological, sociological, and economic considerations. In capitalist market economies, the greatest emphasis is placed on economic considerations. Material rewards in the form of higher wages, prices, or profits are used as carrots to call forth the desired supply responses. But such an emphasis is clearly less appropriate for a socialist state. As we have emphasized, **material incentives lead to income inequalities** and nurture selfish interests rather than social interests. Hence we must rely more heavily on nonmaterial incentives.

Another way to get people to work is to imbue them with a sense of involvement, to make them feel that their efforts are important. We must convince workers that the goals of the revolution are of paramount significance and that their role in the production process is critical to goal fulfillment. This attempt may, of course, entail fairly extensive public-relations, or educational, effort. If it is successful, however, **the communal spirit may be an effective substitute for material incentives.**

Most socialist countries have, in fact, put great stress on reeducation and what Western observers like to call "indoctrination." Socialist countries have achieved considerable success in this regard, especially China and Cuba. But the subordination of personal aspirations has been far from complete, and some appeals to private interest have been necessary. In the Soviet Union, for example, economic planners have come to depend heavily on material incentives for plan fulfillment. Workers are coaxed into "fullfilling and overfulfilling" plan targets by a variety of bonuses. In the industrial sector, such bonuses may be direct supplements to wages and account for as much as 30 percent of take-home pay. In addition, bonus funds for plan fulfillment are made available for improved housing and education ("cultural funds"), as well as for additional investment.

In the agricultural sector, the Soviet appeal to private gain takes two forms. On collective farms (*kolkhozy*), all workers are expected to contribute to the fulfillment of output targets. If actual output exceeds those targets, the surplus may be distributed to the workers, much like an industrial bonus. In addition, agricultural workers are allowed to cultivate their own private "garden plots." The output from such plots may be consumed directly or sold in farmers' markets, as in capitalist market economies. The incentive to produce from such plots has been strikingly effective. Farm workers can

Soviets Outline Dramatic Farm Deficiencies

MOSCOW—A confidential study prepared for the top Soviet leadership has outlined a nearly disastrous decline in the Soviet Union's ability to feed itself, demonstrating a compelling need for agricultural and other economic reforms.

The study, made available here, provided figures that showed a tenfold increase in Soviet food imports during the past decade, staggering levels of mishandling of agricultural equipment and "direct losses" of harvested crops due to negligence and lack of storage or drying facilities.

The document, prepared by a special government commission during the past year, said one-fifth of the grain harvest is lost because it is harvested late or left to rot.

The study said one-third of the country's potato crop is left to rot, and experts who took part in drafting the document put the losses even higher. They said about half of potato production—or the equivalent of the annual American production—is lost each year because of a chaotic distribution system and lack of storage facilities.

As a result, the study said, an average Soviet citizen is poorly fed, consuming 54 pounds of meat per year less than required by medical standards.

The commission, which prepared the study in cooperation with the state planning commission and 38 ministries and scientific institutes, concluded that "the existing economic mechanism does not provide necessary economic incentives for production increases and fuller use of the potentially available land." . . .

—Dusko Doder

"own" no more than 1½ acres, and the sum of all garden plots accounts for only 3 percent of all cultivated land. Nevertheless, in 1981 the output from garden plots accounted for 30 percent of Soviet meat, milk, and vegetable output. In fact, the Soviet planners, in recognition of such productivity, recently offered such incentives as increased fertilizer and free use of collective farm machinery for garden plots.

ECONOMICS VS. IDEOLOGY   The extensive use of private economic incentives in the Soviet Union obviously smacks of bourgeois materialism and threatens the goals of the revolution, particularly the goal of equality. For this reason, the Soviet leaders have tried to keep the resulting income differences within a narrow range. But in China, Mao Tse-tung repeatedly denounced such "revisionism," such dependence on material incentives. Mao made a much greater effort to rely exclusively on nonmaterial incentives. For over two decades, Chinese workers were urged to "develop the socialist economy, carry the revolution through to the end," by banners hung in every office and factory (together with photographs of Marx, Lenin, and Mao). Thoughts of personal gain were regarded as counterrevolutionary.

Such dedication was difficult to maintain, however. Over time, the Chinese leaders permitted limited use of material incentives (including private "garden plots"). But this was inconsistent with Mao's basic dictum that "politics must come before economics." This tension led to the Great Proletarian Cultural Revolution (1966–69), a widespread and sometimes violent reaction to "creeping materialism." The Cultural Revolution was designed to reassert revolutionary ideals and communal aspirations.

Since Mao's death in 1976, the Chinese leaders have placed greater emphasis on rapid development. The eight-year plan drawn up in 1978 calls for a "new long march" that will make China a major industrial power by the year 2000. This will entail Four

Modernizations—of agriculture, industry, technology, and defense. To achieve these ambitious goals, the Chinese reintroduced material incentives (bonuses) for urban workers and put greater emphasis on merit than on politics in universities and scientific research. They also permitted firms a limited degree of "self-management" (e.g., borrowing money directly from banks, determining production processes, selling some products independently, retaining some "profits"). However, even these moves in the direction of market incentives have been strictly limited and at times reversed.

The choice between ideological imperatives and economic pragmatism remains one of the most difficult ones a planned socialist economy must face. As long as people are motivated in part by private gain, material incentives hold out the promise of greater output. The increase in output comes from both increased work effort and more efficient utilization of existing effort. Hence material incentives can be an effective mechanism for fulfilling economic goals. The problem, of course, is that they threaten to compromise other goals in the process—particularly those of income distribution and communal orientation.

Feasibility

Neither the Soviet bonus system nor the Chinese appeal to communal spirit will be very effective if planning goals and targets are set unrealistically high. What good is the promise of a bonus for "fulfilling and overfulfilling" an output target if that target is totally beyond reach? How can workers feel that they are making an important contribution to the communal effort if their farm or factory consistently fails to fulfill its output goals? Being on a losing team year in and year out can really dampen one's revolutionary spirit.

The feasibility of output goals depends on the accuracy of the input–output calculations we outlined earlier. But it is important for us to realize that those calculations involve not only *economic* risks, but *political* ones as well. Mistakes in national goals, industry projections, and enterprise targets involve a potential loss of efficiency and the threat of dissatisfaction and alienation on the part of the working class. How can we expect workers in a bicycle factory to maintain confidence in our leadership if we urge them to produce 4,000 bikes while supplying them with only 6,000 wheels? The resultant loss of output is inconsequential compared to the potential loss of ideological commitment and political support. Of course, really gross miscalculations threaten serious losses, both economic and political. The Polish upheaval of 1982, for example, was in large part a consumer response to inept planning, especially price-induced shortages.

These questions of feasibility give rise to another potential goal conflict. On the one hand, we want to keep a firm grip on the economy, directing society's resources into those channels that will hasten fulfillment of our revolutionary goals. On the other hand, we want to maintain and extend the revolutionary commitment of the working class as we proceed down the path to the Marxian utopia. This latter goal implies that we must be realistic in our output goals and take great care to avoid mistakes in our input–output calculations.

POLISH PRICES

Socialist countries traditionally keep prices of basic commodities low so that all consumers can afford them. The low prices, however, both increase the quantity demanded and reduce the quantity supplied. The end result is typically a market shortage, as illustrated below at price p_1.

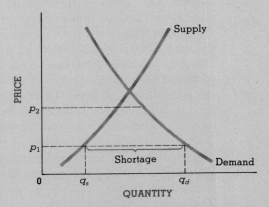

The symptoms of market shortages are empty shelves and long lines of consumers waiting for a chance to buy scarce goods. Such lines are commonplace in the Soviet Union and China. In 1981, however, they grew to epidemic proportions in Poland. The government itself estimated that the average Pole was spending four hours a day standing in food lines!

The Polish government first hoped to solve this problem by increasing food supplies. They did this by offering subsidies to farmers, then by prohibiting "free" markets in scarce goods. The first strategy proved to be too expensive, however, and the second one too difficult to enforce. The government also tried to limit the quantity of goods demanded by imposing severe rationing. In the fall of 1981 the average Pole was allowed an allotment of only $6\frac{1}{2}$ pounds of meat per month, 2 pounds of sugar, 2 pounds of flour, 12 packs of cigarettes, and a pint of vodka. Even rationing, however, could not ensure "adequate" quantities supplied.

Ultimately the frustrations caused by persistent food shortages helped to spark a workers' strike and political confrontation in Poland. After declaring martial law and disbanding the workers' union (Solidarity), the Polish government abruptly raised consumer prices. On February 1, 1982, the following price increases (in dollars) were implemented:

	Old price	New price		Old price	New price
Beef (lb.)	$0.52	$1.74	Gasoline (gal.)	$1.02	$1.55
Bread (lb.)	0.09	0.20	Milk (gal.)	0.11	0.49
Butter (lb.)	0.35	1.39	Salt (lb.)	0.01	0.04
Coal (ton)	8.29	28.06	Sugar (lb.)	0.06	0.27
Sausage (lb.)	0.51	2.42			

These sharply higher prices, illustrated by price p_2 in the graph above, both diminished the quantity demanded and increased the quantity supplied. This greatly alleviated the market shortages. The inefficiency of the initial prices, however, had cost the Poles dearly in both economic and political terms.

THE SOVIET RESPONSE One way to resolve the implied goal conflict is to maintain some flexibility in the goals we formulate. We can express output goals in somewhat general terms—such as calling for a "large" increase in widget output rather than for a 14.7 percent increase. We can also make the planning period long enough to permit some flexibility on a short-term basis. Both approaches are used in the Soviet Union, but the basic five-year planning period is most significant.

The first Five-Year Plan was for the period October 1928–32, and the eleventh Five-Year Plan covers the period 1981–85. Every such plan has focused on the general parameters of the economy and has emphasized basic priorities more than specific production details. On the basis of such plans, the Soviet planners issue directives for various sectors of the economy and attempt to formulate a specific annual target for each sector. Thus the five-year plans are designed to chart the directions for economic advance, and the one-year plans (directives) contain the nuts-and-bolts details.

The one-year plans are all-important. To ensure their workability, the central planners (Gosplan) engage in a lot of give-and-take with the bureaus, industries, firms, and farms they are assigned to orchestrate. Draft plans and outlines are sent down the bureaucratic channels for review. At that juncture, individual firms and industries may argue that the planned output targets are unfeasible and suggest more attainable targets in their place. This kind of feedback—often called **counterplanning,** or "planning from below"—is critical to the success of the plan.

The people down the line, of course, have a vested interest in minimizing output targets. Their bonuses depend on "fulfilling and overfulfilling" plan targets. Conversely, the planners at the top of the bureaucratic hierarchy have a vested interest in raising the targets. Higher targets may help to achieve more quickly the goals and projections enunciated in the five-year plan. Thus the final set of annual targets reflects compromises between vested interests and between the goals of central direction and assured feasibility.

THE CHINESE RESPONSE In many respects the Chinese planning system appears similar to the Soviet one, with ten-year plans, one-year plans, and extensive counterplanning. But in operational terms, the Chinese planning system is much more decentralized. Detailed planning targets are formulated and enunciated at the provincial or local level.

The reasons for this decentralization are many. The successful experience of the Chinese leadership in guerrilla warfare, with its attendant reliance on local organization, convinced the Chinese of the feasibility of "self-reliance." Perhaps an even more important argument for self-reliance emerges from the sheer dimensions of the Chinese economy. China is simply immense. Each of its 25 provinces rivals a modest-sized country in population and land area. Moreover, the transportation and communications systems are still underdeveloped. Accordingly, it would take a Herculean effort to control all production decisions from a central location. From this perspective, decentralization appears to be a very pragmatic approach.

counterplanning: The "bargaining" over plan targets between the central planning agency and local production managers.

A third motivation for decentralization is that it helps ensure that workers will identify with communal goals. The psychological rewards of self-realization are all-important. As Professor Wassily Leontief of Harvard (a Nobel Prize–winning developer of input–output analysis) has observed, the success of the Chinese planning system can be attributed to a "steady stream of propaganda that tries to whip up enthusiasm for efforts on behalf of the common good." It also owes much to "the powerful reinforcing action of fulfilled promises themselves."[9]

A COMPARATIVE ASSESSMENT

That socialist planning can work is undeniable. Planning and public ownership are salient features of economic reality in the Soviet Union, the People's Republic of China, and elsewhere.[10] Moreover, planned economies have recorded impressive economic achievements. Still, there is an irresistible urge to ask which system is better, the socialist planned economy or the capitalist market economy. Accordingly, some attempt at a comparative assessment may be appropriate.

Such an assessment is made difficult, however, by the necessity of choosing a criterion for evaluation. Suppose the criterion used were consumer sovereignty, the extent to which individual preferences fashion economic outcomes. Were we to compare the Soviet Union and China to the United States on this basis, the United States would win hands down. But the criterion of consumer sovereignty is clearly biased in favor of capitalistic market economies and may, in fact, be inconsistent with the long-term goals of socialist plans. On the other hand, comparisons of economic growth rates favor planned economies, because they have attached high priority to investment and the rapid buildup of a military-industrial base. Therefore, we must recognize that any comparative assessment of socialist and capitalist countries involves an implicit acceptance of certain values. In the final analysis, we may prove little more than that one set of values and priorities appeals to us more than another.

GNP comparisons

Figure 36.2 provides a summary perspective on the relative dimensions of the U.S., Soviet, and Chinese economies. As is evident, the U.S. economy is far larger than either of the others. In per capita terms the differences are even more striking, because the U.S. population is roughly the same size as the Soviet Union's but only one-fourth as large as China's. GNP comparisons can be very misleading, however, especially when economic structures vary widely, and in-

[9] Wassily Leontief, "Socialism in China," *Atlantic Monthly*, March 1973, p. 81.
[10] Neither the Soviet nor the Chinese planning process proceeded in the logical and orderly way we have illustrated. Development of plans has evolved sporadically, and only in recent years have the more formal techniques of planning (e.g., input–output analysis) been employed to a significant extent.

FIGURE 36.2 U.S., SOVIET, AND CHINESE GNPs, 1980

The U.S. economy produces a much greater quantity of goods and services than either the Soviet or Chinese economy. In per capita terms the differences are even more striking. Per capita GNP in the United States is double that of the Soviet Union and at least ten times that of China.

Source: World Bank.

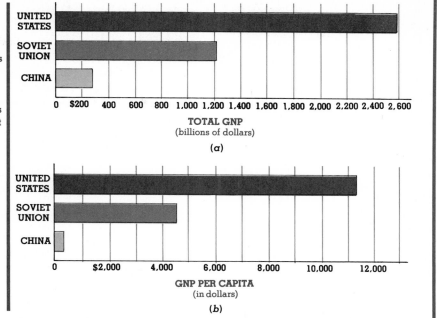

TOTAL GNP
(billions of dollars)

(a)

GNP PER CAPITA
(in dollars)

(b)

ternational exchange rates may not fully reflect relative prices and outputs.[11]

For example, per capita GNP in China is estimated at $290 per year. What meaning does this have? Could anyone really survive on $290 per year? In part, the unbelievably low GNP statistics for China are explained by our different economic systems. In China, urban workers are provided with government-subsidized apartments. Monthly rents are only $5 to $10. Cloth, rice, and a few other essential consumer goods are rationed. Hence everyone is ensured a minimal supply of basic essentials. As a result, the average monthly income of an urban worker is sufficient to provide an adequate if somewhat spartan standard of living. Professor Lloyd Reynolds of Yale has suggested that adjustments based on differences in diet, monetary values, and public-goods provision raise substantially the apparent value of Chinese incomes. After such adjustments, the urban Chinese family's standard of living in 1980 approximates that of an American family earning $8,000 a year (equal to the U.S. poverty standard; see Chapter 31). That figure is probably optimistic, but at least closer to the mark than a figure of $290.[12]

In comparing per capita GNP in China and the United States, it is also important to note that most Chinese families live on farms,

[11] Recall from Chapter 34 that the international value of a country's currency is subject to change. Accordingly, a rise in the exchange rate of the ruble or yuan would lead to an increase in GNP, as measured in dollars. This problem is particularly troublesome for comparisons between capitalist market economies and socialist planned ones because prices in the latter are not determined by market forces. Hence GNP comparisons should be regarded as approximations, particularly in the case of China.

[12] Lloyd G. Reynolds, "China as a Less-Developed Country," *American Economic Review*, June 1975; estimates adjusted for recent growth and inflation.

TABLE 36.3 OUTPUT OF SELECTED PRODUCTS IN THE UNITED STATES, THE SOVIET UNION, AND CHINA

Chinese output is far below either American or Soviet production. The greatest continuing problem for China is its low rate of grain output. The Soviet Union has caught up to the United States in many basic industries, but still lags far behind in consumer goods.

Product	United States	Soviet Union	China
Grain (kilograms per capita)	1,206	755	288
Meat (kilograms per capita)	117	57	n.a.
Automobiles (millions per year)	9.2	1.3	n.a.
Washing machines in use (per thousand persons)	263	200	negligible
Television sets in use (per thousand persons)	650	230	negligible
Radios in use (per thousand persons)	202	24	n.a.
Crude steel (million metric tons)	113	147	24
Pig iron (million metric tons)	74	107	32
Electricity (billion kilowatt-hours)	2,267	1,150	141
Nitrogen fertilizer (million metric tons)	24	9	24

Source: Central Intelligence Agency, 1977.

not in cities. Over 75 percent of the Chinese population is rural. By contrast, only 20 percent of the U.S. population lives in rural areas and fewer than 5 percent are farmers.

In general, it is safe to conclude that living standards in China are far below those prevailing in the United States (where urban family incomes averaged over $20,000 in 1980). Soviet standards of living fall somewhere in between, perhaps at half the level of U.S. standards. Table 36.3 provides some specific comparisons of recent production and consumption.

Alternative criteria Although comparisons of aggregate output, economic growth, and standards of living are important, the socialist states emphasize their accomplishments in two other areas: the distribution of income and economic stability. Recall that a basic motivation behind socialist revolutions has been hostility to income disparities and the poverty of the lowest classes, injustices that they explain on the basis of capital ownership. As Sir Arthur Lewis has written, "Socialism is about equality. A passion for equality is the one thing that links all socialists; on all other things they are divided.[13]

THE DISTRIBUTION OF INCOME Unfortunately, very little information is available on the distribution of income in the Soviet Union and virtually none on the distribution in China. Accordingly, income-distribution comparisons rely heavily on travelers' observations and select data for individual factories, communes, and cities. On this basis, however, it is reasonably clear that the Chinese distribution of income is most egalitarian, with the lowest income groups very close to the average. In individual enterprises, the wages of the highest-paid manager appear to be no more than three or four times the wages of the lowest-paid worker. On agricultural communes, disparities are even smaller. Earnings differentials in U.S. enterprises are,

[13] W. Arthur Lewis, *The Principles of Economic Planning*, 2d. ed. (London: Allen & Unwin, 1952), p. 10.

of course, much larger, as epitomized by General Motors Corporation, where the highest-paid executive gets in excess of 100 times the earnings of the lowest-paid worker. Income differentials are greater in the Soviet Union than in China, largely because the Soviets offer larger bonuses for successful enterprises, artists, scientists, and athletes. But there, too, income disparities are much smaller than in the United States, and wealth is, of course, not concentrated in the hands of a private minority. Hence if one is to compare the Soviet and Chinese economies to the United States on the basis of the degree of income equality, the socialist countries come out ahead.

ECONOMIC STABILITY   Another criterion that socialist economies emphasize is the degree of economic stability. In a planned, centrally controlled economy, there is no worry about unemployment resulting from a deficiency of aggregate demand. The basic level and structure of demand are determined by the central planners and are tightly controlled. Of course, the planners strive to keep their demands in line with society's production possibilities. In addition, however, firms and farms are not constrained by profit calculations in hiring additional workers and are, in fact, explicitly directed to find a job for everyone. Thus **unemployment,** in the conventional sense of people seeking employment without success, never occurs. As the socialist governments point out, this is far superior to the situation in capitalist market economies. There, fluctuations in aggregate demand lead to insecurity, poverty, low output, and potential alienation.

unemployment: Labor-force participants are unable to find jobs; people actively seeking paid employment.

On the other hand, capitalist-oriented economists emphasize that central control of aggregate demand may serve only to disguise the problem of unemployment. The fact that 100 people pass through a factory's entrance doesn't mean that 100 people are gainfully employed. As we noted earlier, centrally directed plans are subject to miscalculation. At the factory level, such miscalculations may mean that there is not enough machinery or other inputs to keep everyone employed. Worse still, the plant manager may be holding output levels down so as to minimize future planning targets (thereby assuring himself and his co-workers of bonuses every year). In either case, some of the workers will be **underemployed**—that is to say, at work but not performing up to (or even near) their potential.

underemployment: People work part time although they seek full-time jobs or are employed at jobs below their capability.

PRODUCTIVE EFFICIENCY   The problem of underemployment is part of the larger issue of economic efficiency that Western observers like to emphasize when comparing economic systems. Economic efficiency involves getting the greatest amount of output for a given quantity of input, a desirable outcome in any economic system. In the U.S. economy, the profit-maximizing aspirations of individual producers help to ensure productive efficiency, because greater efficiency in production translates into higher profits. Where markets are reasonably competitive, the quest for profits also stimulates product innovation and new technology. Thus the capitalist market system contains forces that tend to keep society pressing against its production-possibilities curve and, perhaps even more significant, pushing that curve outward.

Can we say the same thing of the Soviet and Chinese economies? No, because there is no explicit profit motive, no significant reward for productive efficiency, and more risk than reward attached to innovation. Recall that firms in the Soviet Union and China are directed to respond to specific planning targets and are rewarded, if at all, in terms of target fulfillment. When those targets are expressed in terms of output quantity alone, there is obviously no incentive to worry about the combination of inputs that is used to achieve it. Indeed, there may not even be any concern for the quality of output, as long as the quantity delivered is in accord with planning targets. Under such circumstances, there is also no incentive to experiment with new technology. Failure will mean unfulfilled targets, while success will be rewarded with higher targets for next year.

Soviet and Chinese leaders have not been impervious to these criticisms. In 1965, for example, former Soviet Premier Aleksei Kosygin publicly admitted that "our economic scholars have not busied themselves greatly with analysis of the effectiveness of social production and the elaboration of proposals for increasing it"—that is to say, with productive efficiency.[14] Since that time, the response of the central planners has been to increase the number of specific targets assigned to each firm. Thus a Soviet plant manager now has targets for output volume, for the use of specific inputs, for output per worker, and for what Gosplan calls a set of "uniform and interrelated indices." But the problems remain. No aggregate measure of

[14] *Pravda*, September 28, 1965, cited by Gertrude E. Schroeder in *Soviet Economic Prospects for the Seventies* (Washington, D.C.: U.S. Government Printing Office, 1973), p. 18.

JEEPS IN CHINA: A GLIMPSE OF PRODUCTIVITY DIFFERENCES

The Peking Auto Factory produces a stripped-down version of the American Motors Jeep. The Chinese Jeep comes in only one model (a standard-shift, four-wheel drive) and color (olive green). The Peking Auto Factory produced 15,000 of these Jeeps in 1979, using a work force of 9,400. The average employee worked 48 hours per week and was paid 50–60 yuan ($77–92) a month.

At the AMC plant in Toledo, Ohio, 7,100 employees produced 170,000 Jeeps in 1979, in seven models and fourteen colors. Production workers were paid from $960 to $1,040 a month, for the standard 40-hour week. Thus in Toledo, 24 percent fewer people, working 17 percent fewer hours, produced 10 times as many Jeeps (in greater variety and quality) than those produced in Peking.

What accounts for this huge difference in productivity? Do American workers toil harder than their Chinese counterparts? A more likely explanation is that Toledo workers have modern machines (capital) with which to work, while Chinese workers must cope with less-advanced machinery (and little of it). Profit incentives help explain why the American worker is so well endowed with capital equipment.

productive efficiency is stipulated, and there is a predisposition to favor those targets to which bonus payments are attached.

An alternative approach to productive efficiency was suggested by the Soviet economist Yevsei Liberman. He argued that firms should strive to maximize their "profits"—that is, the difference between the value of their output and the value of their inputs. The profits, of course, would be turned over to the state, with some allowance for bonus payments to the firm's employees. The Liberman proposal would allow firms greater flexibility in their production and efficiency decisions. There is still a problem, however. Both input and output prices are rigidly controlled by the central planners. Hence the attainment of efficiency, even with the introduction of a quasi-profit motive, would depend on the rationality of the price structure the central planners dictate. As long as relative prices fail to reflect the relative value of various inputs and outputs, any "profitability" may be entirely spurious. Thus the problem of efficiency takes us back to all the problems inherent in central planning.

Which is better?

Obviously, the U.S. economy fares better than the Soviet or Chinese economy on the basis of productive efficiency. But where does this leave our comparative assessment? What we end up with is a mixed bag of wins and losses. The Soviet and Chinese economies rank higher in terms of economic growth, the distribution of income, and economic stability. The U.S. economy rates higher in terms of living standards, consumer sovereignty, and productive efficiency. For those who place a higher value on equality and stability than on economic freedom and individualism, the planned socialist economies must look superior. On the other hand, those who value individualism and consumer sovereignty will prefer the capitalist market system. Thus the answer to the question of which system is better depends largely on the values we embrace, and no clear, objective response can be offered. What is important is that we understand how each system works and the priorities each attaches to various goals and values.

It is interesting to note that both the capitalist market economies and the planned socialist economies are improving their performance in areas where they are theoretically weakest. We have already noted that the Soviet planners have tried to increase productive efficiency with more incentives and targets, and that the Chinese planners are also experimenting with material incentives (bonuses). We should also recognize that U.S. policy makers devote considerable attention to the problems of economic instability (the basic focus of fiscal and monetary policy) and of income distribution (the thrust of welfare and many tax programs). Thus each system is striving to shore up it weak spots while maintaining its basic value orientation.

SUMMARY

■ All economic systems must address the three basic questions of WHAT to produce, HOW to produce it, and FOR WHOM. However, there are important differences in the ways in which market and planned economies resolve these questions. In market economies, the basic dimensions of the economy are largely determined by individual consumer and producer decisions. In planned economies, the basic dimensions of the economy reflect decisions of a central authority.

▪ The Soviet Union and China rely heavily on central planning. These economies are referred to as socialist, as the means of production are publicly owned and the state exerts broad authority. From a Marxian point of view, they represent a stage of economic development that will evolve ultimately into communism, a stateless, classless society in which goods are so abundant that everyone's needs can be fully satisfied.

▪ The objective of socialist planning is to fashion economic outcomes in accordance with specific goals, particularly those of income equality and a strong military-industrial base. To fulfill this objective, central planners must review resource supplies and examine the nature of production processes. Of particular importance in this regard are input–output coefficients, which reflect the amount of specific inputs required to produce a given quantity of a desired product.

▪ Planned socialist economies use prices, but not in the same way that market economies do. In planned systems, high prices help to distribute scarce goods, particularly consumer luxuries. Thus they keep demand at the level of planned supply. Since prices are not allowed to act as incentives for increased supply, however, the function of the market mechanism is constrained.

▪ Because the market mechanism is prevented from stimulating supply responses, other incentives to produce and work must be found. Soviet planners use material bonuses to create incentives for fulfilling plan targets. The Chinese also use incentives somewhat, but rely more heavily on ideological and patriotic appeals.

▪ In comparing capitalist market economies to socialist planned economies, one must recognize that they have different priorities. Hence any assessment will be biased by the specific criterion chosen. In general, socialist planned economies have achieved more equal distribution of income, greater stability, and somewhat faster growth. On the other hand, capitalist market economies have achieved higher standards of living, consumer sovereignty, and greater efficiency.

Terms to remember Define the following terms:

capitalism	economic growth
communism	production process
socialism	counterplanning
production possibilities	unemployment
investment	underemployment

Questions for discussion 1. Suppose that an increase in agricultural output were a major objective of economic policy. What policy tools would the U.S. Congress use to bring about this result? What tools would the Soviet Gosplan use?

2. Why is "counterplanning" regarded as essential to the success of plans in the Soviet Union and the People's Republic of China?

3. What are the advantages of consumer sovereignty? The disadvantages?

4. The unavailability of consumer luxury items in the Soviet Union has helped to equalize living standards. How will the recent expansion of Soviet automobile production affect equality? The incentive to work?

5. Would you plan to work less or choose to enter a different occupation if everyone were paid equal wages? What would be the incentive to work under such circumstances?

GLOSSARY

Numbers in parentheses indicate the chapters in which the definitions appear.

absolute advantage: The ability of a country to produce a specific good with fewer resources (per unit of output) than other countries. (33)

adjustment assistance: Compensation to market participants for losses imposed by international trade. (33)

aggregate demand: The total value of all final goods and services demanded in a given time period at alternative income levels; total spending. (7)

aggregate supply: The total quantity of final goods and services supplied to the market at alternative price levels in a given time period (*ceteris paribus*); total output. (13)

appreciation: A rise in the price of one currency relative to another. (34)

arithmetic growth: An increase in quantity by a constant amount each year. (17)

automatic stabilizer: Federal expenditure or revenue item that automatically responds countercyclically to changes in national income: for example, unemployment benefits, income taxes. (9) (14)

average fixed cost (AFC): Total fixed cost divided by the quantity produced in a given time period. (19)

average propensity to consume (APC): Total consumption in a given period divided by total disposable income. (7)

average total cost (ATC): Total cost divided by the quantity produced in a given time period. (19) (21) (22)

average variable cost (AVC): Total variable cost divided by the quantity produced in a given time period. (19)

balance-of-payments deficit: An excess demand for foreign currency at current exchange rates (34)

balance-of-payments surplus: An excess demand for domestic currency at current exchange rates. (34)

barriers to entry: Obstacles that make it difficult or impossible for would-be producers to enter a particular market (e.g., patents). (21) (22) (24)

barter: The direct exchange of one good for another, without the use of money. (10) (35)

bilateral monopoly: A market with only one buyer (a monopsonist) and one seller (a monopolist). (27)

bond: A certificate acknowledging a debt and the amount of interest to be paid each year until repayment; an IOU. (11)

bracket creep: The movement of taxpayers into higher tax brackets (rates) as nominal incomes grow. (3) (6) (15)

budget deficit: The amount by which government expenditures exceed government revenues. (15)

budget surplus: An excess of government revenues over government expenditures. (9)

capitalism: An economy in which the factors of production (e.g., land, capital) are owned by individuals: basic allocation decisions are made by market forces. (36)

categorical grants: Federal grants to state and local governments for specific expenditure purposes. (3)

ceteris paribus: The assumption of "everything else being equal," of nothing else changing. (1) (2) (18) (20)

collective bargaining: Direct negotiations between employers and unions to determine labor-market outcomes. (27)

collusion: Explicit agreements among producers to limit competition among them. (23)

communism: A stateless, classless economy in which there is no private property and everyone shares in production and consumption according to individual abilities and needs. (36)

comparative advantage: The ability of a country to produce a specific good at a lower opportunity cost than its trading partners. (33) (35)

competitive firm: A firm without market power, with no ability to alter the market price of the goods it produces. (20) (21)

complementary goods: Goods frequently consumed in combination; when the price of good X rises, the quantity of good Y demanded falls (*ceteris paribus*). (18)

concentration ratio: The proportion of total industry output produced by the largest firms (usually the four largest). (24)

conglomerate: A firm that produces significant quantities of output in several industries. (24)

constant returns to scale: Increases in plant size do not affect minimum average cost; minimum per unit costs are identical for small plants and large plants. (19)

Consumer Price Index (CPI): A measure (index) of changes in the average price of consumer goods and services. (6)

consumption: Expenditure by consumers on final goods and services. (7)

consumption function: A mathematical relationship indicating the rate of consumer spending that will take place in a given time period at various income levels. (7) (8)

consumption possibilities: The alternative combinations of goods and services that a country could consume in a given time period. (33)

cost efficiency: The amount of output associated with an additional dollar spent on input; the *MPP* of an input divided by its price (cost). (26) (32)

cost-of-living adjustment (COLA): Automatic adjustments of nominal income to the rate of inflation. (6)

cost-push inflation: An increase in the price level initiated by an increase in the cost of production. (6) (13) (16)

counterplanning: The "bargaining" over plan targets between the central planning agency and local production managers. (36)

crowding out: A reduction in private-sector borrowing (and spending) necessitated by increased government borrowing. (12) (15)

cyclical unemployment: Unemployment attributable to a lack of job vacancies; unemployment that results from an inadequate level of aggregate demand. (5) (7) (8) (31)

deficit spending: A situation wherein government expenditures exceed government revenues. (9)

deflation: A decrease in the average level of prices of goods and services. (6)

demand: The ability and willingness to buy specific quantities of a good at alternative prices in a given time period (*ceteris paribus*). (2) (18)

demand curve: A curve describing the quantities of a good a consumer is willing and able to buy at alternative prices in a given time period (*ceteris paribus*). (2) (18)

demand deposit: Checking-account balance. (10)

demand for foreign exchange: The quantities of foreign currency demanded in a given time period at alternative exchange rates (*ceteris paribus*). (34)

demand for labor: The quantities of labor employers are willing and able to hire at alternative wage rates in a given time period (*ceteris paribus*). (26) (27)

demand for money: The quantities of money people are willing and able to hold at alternative interest rates (*ceteris paribus*). (12)

demand-pull inflation: An increase in the price level initiated by excessive aggregate demand. (6) (7) (8)

demand schedule: A table showing the quantities of a good a consumer is willing and able to buy at alternative prices in a given time period (*ceteris paribus*). (2) (18)

deposit creation: The creation of transactions deposits by bank lending. (10)

depreciation: The consumption of capital in the production process; the wearing out of plant and equipment. (4)

depreciation (tax): The tax deduction allowed for the cost of using capital and equipment in production. (20)

depreciation (currency): A fall in the price of one currency relative to another. (34)

derived demand: The demand for labor and other factors of production results from (depends on) the demand for final goods and services produced by these factors. (7) (8) (13) (26)

discount rate: The rate of interest charged by the Federal Reserve banks for lending reserves to private banks. (11)

discounting: Federal Reserve lending of reserves to private banks. (11)

discouraged worker: An individual who is not actively seeking employment, but would look for or accept a job if one were available. (5)

discretionary fiscal spending: Those elements of the annual federal budget that are not determined by past legislative or executive commitments. (9)

discrimination: Inequality of treatment; denial of opportunity on the basis of characteristics unrelated to performance. (32)

disguised unemployment: People are employed but contributing little or nothing to total output. (35)

disposable income (DI): After-tax income of consumers; personal income less personal taxes. (4) (7) (9) (15)

dissaving: Consumption expenditure in excess of disposable income; a negative saving flow. (7)

economic cost: The value of all resources used to produce a good or service; opportunity cost. (19) (20) (28)

economic growth: An increase in output (real GNP); an expansion of production possibilities. (1) (17) (36)

economic profit: The difference between total revenues and total economic costs. (20) (21) (23) (28)

economics: The study of how best to allocate scarce resources among competing uses. (1)

economies of scale: Reductions in average costs that come about through increases in the size (scale) of plant and equipment. (19) (22)

efficiency: Maximum output of a good from the resources used in production. (19) (21)

efficiency decision: The choice of a production process for any given rate of output. (26) (30)

embargo: A prohibition on exports or imports. (33)

emission charge: A fee imposed on polluters, based on the quantity of pollution. (30)

equation of exchange: Money supply (M) times velocity of circulation (V) equals level of aggregate demand ($P \times Q$). (12) (13) (15) (16)

equilibrium GNP: The rate of output at which the rate of desired expenditure (aggregate demand) equals the rate of production (aggregate supply). (8) (9)

equilibrium price: The price at which the quantity of a good demanded in a given time period equals the quantity supplied. (2) (21) (33) (34)

equilibrium rate of interest: The interest rate at which the quantity of money demanded in a given period equals the quantity of money supplied. (12)

equilibrium wage: The wage rate at which the quantity of labor supplied in a given time period equals the quantity of labor demanded. (27)

excess reserves: Bank reserves in excess of required reserves. (10) (11)

exchange rate: The price of one country's currency, expressed in terms of another's; the domestic price of a foreign currency. (34)

exports: Goods and services sold to foreign buyers. (4) (33)

externalities: Costs (or benefits) of a market activity borne by a third party; the difference between the social and private costs (benefits) of a market activity. (1) (3) (30)

factor market: Any place where factors of production (e.g., land, labor, capital) are bought and sold. (2)

factor share: The proportion of total income received by a factor of production. (28) (29)

factors of production: Resource inputs used to produce goods and services; for example, land, labor, capital. (1) (19)

fine-tuning: Adjustments in economic policy designed to counteract small changes in economic outcomes; continuous responses to changing economic conditions. (14)

fiscal policy: The use of government taxes and spending to alter macroeconomic outcomes. (9)

fiscal year (FY): The twelve-month period used for government accounting purposes; begins October 1 and ends September 30. (3) (9)

fixed costs: Costs of production that do not change when the rate of output is altered; for example, the cost of basic plant and equipment. (19) (28)

flexible exchange rates: A system in which exchange rates are permitted to vary with market supply and demand conditions. (34)

foreign-exchange markets: Places where foreign currencies are bought and sold. (34)

foreign-exchange reserves: Holdings of foreign exchange by official government agencies, usually the central bank or treasury. (34)

free rider: An individual who reaps direct benefits from someone else's purchase (consumption) of a public good. (3)

frictional unemployment: Brief periods of unemployment experienced by people moving between jobs or into the labor market; not related to basic demand or supply inadequacies. (5)

full employment: The lowest rate of unemployment compatible with price stability; variously estimated at between 4 and 6 percent unemployment. (5) (7)

full-employment budget: The federal revenues and expenditures that would exist at full employment under prevailing fiscal policy. (9) (16)

full-employment GNP: The total market value of final goods and services that could be produced in a given time period at full employment; potential GNP. (5) (7) (15)

functional distribution of income: The division of income among factors of production, especially between capital and labor. (29)

geometric growth: An increase in quantity by a constant proportion each year. (17)

GNP gap: The difference between full-employment GNP and actual GNP. (5)

GNP per capita: Total GNP divided by total population; average GNP. (4) (17)

gold reserves: Stocks of gold held by a government to purchase foreign exchange. (34)

gold standard: An agreement by countries to fix the price of their currencies in terms of gold; a mechanism for fixing exchange rates. (34)

gross investment: Total investment expenditure in a given time period. (4)

gross national product (GNP): The total market value of all final goods and services produced in a given time period. (4)

growth rate: Percentage change in real GNP from one period to another. (17)

human capital: The bundle of skills an individual possesses. (31) (32)

imports: Goods and services purchased from foreign sources. (4) (33)

income effect of wages: An increased wage rate allows a person to reduce hours worked without losing income. (25)

income elasticity of demand: The percentage change in quantity demanded divided by the percentage change in income. (21)

income share: The proportion of total income received by a particular group. (29)

income transfers: Payments to individuals for which no current goods or services are exchanged; for example, social security, welfare, and unemployment benefits. (3) (31)

income velocity of money (V): The number of times per year, on average, a dollar is used to purchase final goods and services; $PQ \div M$. (12) (15)

inflation: An increase in the average level of prices of goods and services. (4) (II) (6)

inflation rate: The annual rate of increase in the average price level. (6)

inflationary gap: The amount by which the desired rate of expenditure at full employment exceeds full-employment output. (7) (8) (9)

in-kind transfers: Direct transfers of goods and services rather than cash; for example, food stamps and Medicaid. (31)

institutional production possibilities: The alternative combinations of final goods and services that could be produced in a given time period within the limits imposed by resources, technology, and social constraints on their use. (5)

interest: Payments made for the use of borrowed money. (3)

interest rate: The price paid for the use of money. (12) (28)

intermediate goods: Goods or services purchased for use as input in the production of final goods or services. (3) (4)

investment: Expenditures on (production of) new plant and equipment (capital) in a given time period, plus changes in business inventories. (4) (7) (13) (36)

investment decision: The decision to build, buy, or lease plant and equipment to start or expand a business. (20) (22) (26)

labor force: All persons over age 16 who are either working for pay or actively seeking paid employment. (5) (13) (17)

labor-force participant: Someone who is either employed for pay or actively seeking paid employment. (31)

labor productivity: Amount of output produced by a worker in a given period of time; output per hour (or day, etc.). (13)

labor supply: The willingness and ability to work specific amounts of time at alternative wage rates in a given time period; the quantities of labor that would be supplied at alternative wage rates (*ceteris paribus*). (25) (27)

labor-supply curve: A curve depicting the quantities of labor supplied (offered) in a given time period at alternative wage rates (*ceteris paribus*). (25)

Laffer curve: A graph depicting the relationship of tax rates to total tax revenues. (15)

laissez faire: The doctrine of "leave it alone," of nonintervention by governments in the market mechanism. (2)

law of demand: The quantity of a good demanded in a given time period increases as its price falls (*ceteris paribus*). (16) (18) (20) (23) (26) (34)

law of diminishing marginal utility: The marginal utility of a good declines as more of it is consumed in a given time period. (18) (25)

law of diminishing returns: The marginal physical product of a variable factor declines as more of it is employed with a given quantity of other (fixed) inputs. (19) (20) (26)

law of increasing opportunity costs: In order to get more of any good in a given time period, society must sacrifice ever-increasing amounts of other goods. (1)

leakage: Income not spent directly on domestic output, but instead diverted from the circular flow; for example, saving, imports, taxes. (7) (16)

liquidity trap: The portion of the money-demand curve that is horizontal; people are willing to hold unlimited amounts of money at some (low) interest rate. (12)

long run: A period of time long enough for all inputs to be varied (no fixed costs). (19) (20)

long-run competitive equilibrium: $p = MC = $ minimum ATC. (21)

Lorenz curve: A graphic illustration of the cumulative size distribution of income; contrasts complete equality with the actual distribution of income. (29)

macroeconomics: The study of aggregate economic behavior, of the economy as a whole. (1) (II)

managed exchange rates: A system in which governments intervene in foreign-exchange markets to limit but not eliminate exchange-rate fluctuations; "dirty floats." (34)

marginal cost: The increase in total cost associated with a one-unit increase in production. (19) (20) (21) (28)

marginal cost of labor: The change in total wage costs that results from a one-unit increase in the quantity of labor employed. (27)

marginal cost pricing: The offer (supply) of goods at prices equal to their marginal cost. (21) (22) (23)

marginal physical product (*MPP*): The change in total output associated with one additional unit of input. (19) (26)

marginal productivity: The change in total output that results from employment of one additional unit of input (e.g., one more worker). (31)

marginal propensity to consume (*MPC*): The fraction of each additional (marginal) dollar of disposable income spent on consumption; the change in consumption divided by the change in disposable income. (7) (8) (9)

marginal revenue: The change in total revenue that results from a one-unit increase in the quantity sold. (20) (22) (23)

marginal revenue product (*MRP*): The change in total revenue associated with one additional unit of input. (26) (27) (28) (32)

marginal tax rate: The tax rate imposed on the last (marginal) dollar of income. (13) (15) (29) (31)

marginal utility: The change in total utility obtained from an additional (marginal) unit of a good or service consumed. (18)

marginal utility of labor: The change in total utility derived from another hour's work; includes the utility associated with the extra goods and services that can be purchased with another hour's wages as well as any intrinsic satisfaction derived from additional labor. (25) (31)

marginal wage: The change in total wages paid associated with a one-unit increase in the quantity of labor employed. (27)

market: Any place where individuals buy or sell resources or products. (2)

market demand: The total quantities of a good or service people are willing and able to buy at alternative prices in a given time period; the sum of individual demands. (2)

market economy: An economy that relies on markets for basic decisions about WHAT to produce, HOW to produce it, and FOR WHOM to produce. (2)

market mechanism: The use of market prices and sales to signal desired outputs (or resource allocations). (1) (2) (3) (21) (25) (35)

market power: The ability to alter the market price of a good or service. (13) (21) (22) (27)

market share: The percentage of total market output produced by a single firm. (23) (24)

market shortage: The amount by which the quantity demanded exceeds the quantity supplied at a given price; excess demand. (2) (16) (34) (35)

market supply: The total quantities of a good that sellers are willing and able to sell at alternative prices in a given time period (*ceteris paribus*); the combined willingness of all market suppliers to sell. (2) (21)

market surplus: The amount by which the quantity supplied exceeds the quantity demanded at a given price; excess supply. (2) (16) (21)

microeconomics: The study of individual behavior in the economy, of the components of the larger economy. (1)

mixed economy: An economy that uses both market and nonmarket signals to allocate goods and resources. (1)

monetary policy: The use of money and credit controls to influence macroeconomic activity. (11) (12)

money: Anything generally accepted as a medium of exchange. (10)

money illusion: The use of nominal dollars rather than real dollars to gauge changes in one's income or wealth. (6)

money multiplier: The maximum multiple by which transactions deposits (money) can be created from any given level of excess reserves; equal to $1 \div$ required reserve ratio. (10) (11)

money supply (M1): Currency held by the public, plus balances in transactions accounts. (10) (11)

monopolistic competition: A market in which many firms produce similar goods or services, but each maintains some independent control of its own price. (23)

monopoly: A firm that produces the entire market supply of a particular good or service. (21) (22)

monopsony: A market in which there is only one buyer. (27)

multiplier: The multiple by which an initial change in spending will alter aggregate demand after an infinite number of spending cycles; $1/(1 - MPC)$. (8) (9) (16)

national income (NI): Total income earned by current factors of production; GNP less depreciation and indirect business taxes. (4)

national-income accounting: The measurement of aggregate economic activity, particularly national income and its components. (4)

natural monopoly: An industry in which one firm can achieve economies of scale over the entire range of market supply. (22)

natural rate of unemployment: Long-term rate of unemployment determined by structural forces in labor and product markets. (13)

net investment: Gross investment less depreciation. (4) (17)

net national product (NNP): GNP less depreciation. (4)

nominal GNP: The value of final output produced in a given period, measured in the prices of that period (current prices). (4) (17)

nominal income: The amount of money income received in a given time period, measured in current dollars. (6)

oligopoly: A market in which a few firms produce all or most of the market supply of a particular good or service. (23) (24)

open-market operations: Federal Reserve purchases and sales of government bonds for the purpose of altering bank reserves. (11)

opportunity cost: The most desired goods or services that are forgone in order to obtain something else. (1) (2) (3) (14) (18) (19) (21) (28) (30) (33)

opportunity wage: The highest wage an individual would earn in his or her best alternative job. (26)

optimal consumption: The mix of consumer purchases that maximizes the utility attainable from available income. (18)

optimal rate of pollution: The rate of pollution that occurs when the marginal social benefit of pollution control equals its marginal social cost. (30)

optimal work effort: That amount of work at which the marginal utility of an hour's labor is just equal to the marginal utility of another hour's leisure. (25)

orderly marketing agreement (OMA): An agreement to reduce the volume of trade in a specific good; a ''voluntary'' quota. (33)

perfectly competitive market: A market in which no buyer or seller has market power. (21)

personal income (*PI*): Income received by households before payment of personal taxes. (4) (29)

Phillips curve. A historical (inverse) relationship between the rate of unemployment and the rate of inflation; commonly expresses a trade-off between the two. (13)

physical production possibilities: The alternative combinations of final goods and services that could be produced in a given time period within the limits imposed by resources and technology. (5)

portfolio decision: The choice of how (where) to hold idle funds. (11) (12)

precautionary demand for money: Money held for unexpected market transactions or for emergencies. (12)

predatory price cutting: Temporary price reductions designed to alter market shares or drive out competition. (24)

price discrimination: The sale of an identical good at different prices to different consumers by a single seller. (22)

price elasticity of demand: The percentage change in quantity demanded divided by the percentage change in price. (18) (20) (21) (22) (35)

price elasticity of supply: The percentage change in quantity supplied divided by the percentage change in price. (28)

price fixing: Explicit agreements among producers regarding the price(s) at which a good is to be sold. (24)

price leadership: An oligopolistic pricing pattern that allows one firm to establish the (market) price for all firms in the industry. (23) (24)

price stability: The absence of significant changes in the average price level; officially defined as a rate of inflation of less than 3 percent. (6)

private costs: The costs of an economic activity directly borne by the immediate producer or consumer (excluding externalities). (30)

product differentiation: Features that make one product appear different from competing products in the same market. (23) (24)

product market: Any place where finished goods and services (products) are bought and sold. (2)

production decision: The selection of the short-run rate of output (with existing plant and equipment). (20) (21) (22) (26) (30)

production function: A technological relation expressing the maximum quantity of a good attainable from different combinations of factor inputs. (19)

production possibilities: The alternative combinations of final goods and services that could be produced in a given time period with all available resources and technology. (1) (3) (4) (17) (21) (33) (35) (36)

production process: A specific combination of resources used to produce a good or service. (26) (36)

productivity: Output per unit of input; for example, output per labor hour. (17) (19) (35)

profit: The difference between total revenue and total cost. (20) (See also economic profit.)

profit-maximization rule: Produce at that rate of output where marginal revenue equals marginal cost. (20) (22) (23)

profit per unit: Total profit divided by the quantity produced in a given time period; price minus average total cost. (21)

profit-push inflation: An increase in the price level initiated by attempts of producers to raise profit margins. (6) (13)

progressive tax: A tax system in which tax rates rise as incomes rise. (3) (29)

public good: A good or service whose consumption by one person does not exclude consumption by others. (3)

quantity demanded: The amount of a product a consumer is willing and able to buy at a specific price in a given time period (*ceteris paribus*). (18) (23)

quantity supplied: The amount of a product offered for sale at a specific price during a given time period (*ceteris paribus*). (20)

quota: A limit on the quantity of a good that may be imported in given time period. (33) (35)

rational expectation: Hypothesis that people's spending decisions are influenced by anticipated government policy, itself presumed to be like previous policies. (14) (15)

real GNP: The value of final output produced in a given period, measured in the prices of another period (constant prices). (4) (17)

real income: Income in constant dollars; nominal income adjusted for inflation. (6) (16)

real rate of interest: The nominal rate of interest minus anticipated inflation rate. (12)

recession: A decline in total output (real GNP) for two or more consecutive quarters. (II)

recessionary gap: The amount by which the rate of desired expenditure at full employment falls short of full-employment output. (7) (8) (9) (16)

regressive tax: A tax system in which tax rates fall as incomes rise. (3) (29)

relative price: The price of one good in comparison with the price of other goods. (6)

rent: Payments to a factor of production in excess of the amount required to call forth a given quantity of the factor. (28)

required reserves: The minimum amount of reserves a bank is required to hold by government regulation; equal to required reserve ratio times transactions deposits. (10) (11)

reserve ratio: The ratio of a bank's reserves to its total transactions deposits. (10)

revenue sharing: Federal aid to state and local governments without stringent restrictions on its use. (3)

saving: That part of disposable income not spent on current consumption; disposable income less consumption. (7) (13)

Say's Law: Supply creates its own demand. (8)

seasonal unemployment: Unemployment due to seasonal changes in employment or labor supply. (5)

shift in demand: A change in the quantity demanded at any (every) given price. (2) (18) (26) (34)

shift of supply: A change in the quantity supplied at any (every) given price. (16) (21)

short run: The period in which the quantity (and quality) of some inputs is fixed, that is, cannot be changed. (19) (20)

short-run competitive equilibrium: $p = $ MC. (21)

shutdown point: That rate of output where AVC equals price. (20)

size distribution of income: The way total personal income is divided up among households or income classes. (29)

social costs: The full resource costs of an economic activity, including externalities. (30)

socialism: An economy in which all nonlabor means of production are owned by the state, which exercises control over resource allocation. (36)

speculative demand for money: Money held for speculative purpose, for later financial opportunities. (12)

stagflation: Simultaneous presence of substantial unemployment and inflation. (13) (15) (16)

structural unemployment: Unemployment caused by a mismatch between the skills (or location) of job seekers and the requirements (or location) of available jobs. (5) (13)

substitute goods: Goods that substitute for each other; when the price of good X rises, the quantity of good Y demanded increases (*ceteris paribus*). (18)

substitution effect: The replacement of one resource (or good) with another in response to changing relative prices. (17)

substitution effect of wages: An increased wage rate raises the marginal utility of an hour's labor, thereby encouraging people to work more hours (to substitute labor for leisure). (25)

supply: The ability and willingness to sell (produce) specific quantities of a good at alternative prices in a given time period (*ceteris paribus*). (2) (13) (19) (20)

supply curve: A curve describing the quantities of a good a producer is willing and able to sell (produce) at alternative prices in a given time period (*ceteris paribus*). (20)

supply of foreign exchange: The quantities of foreign currency supplied (offered) in a given time period at alternative exchange rates (*ceteris paribus*). (34)

tariff: A tax (duty) imposed on imported goods. (33)

tax elasticity of supply: The percentage change in quantity supplied divided by the percentage change in tax rates. (15)

tax rebate: A lump-sum refund of taxes paid. (13)

terms of trade: The rate at which goods are exchanged; the amount of good A given up for good B in trade. (33)

total cost: The market value of all resources used to produce a good or service. (19) (20)

total revenue: The price of a product multiplied by the quantity sold in a given time period; $p \times q$. (18) (20)

total utility: The amount of satisfaction obtained from entire consumption of a product. (18)

trade deficit: The amount by which the value of imports exceeds the value of exports in a given time period. (33) (34)

trade surplus: The amount by which the value of exports exceeds the value of imports in a given time period. (33)

transactions account: A bank account that permits direct payment to a third party (e.g., with a check). (10)

transactions demand for money: Money held for the purpose of making everyday market purchases. (12)

underemployment: People work part-time although they seek full-time jobs or are employed at jobs below their capability. (5) (36)

unemployment: Labor-force participants are unable to find jobs; people are actively seeking paid employment. (5) (36)

unemployment rate: The proportion of the labor force that is unemployed. (5)

union shop: An employment setting in which all workers must join the union within 30 days after being employed. (27)

unionization ratio: The percentage of the labor force belonging to a union. (27)

union labor cost: Hourly wage rate divided by output per labor hour. (13)

user charge: Fee paid for the use of a public-sector good or service. (3)

utility: The pleasure or satisfaction obtained from a good or service. (18) (25)

value added: The increase in the market value of a product that takes place at each stage of the production process. (4)

variable costs: Costs of production that change when the rate of output is altered; for example, labor and material costs. (19) (20)

velocity of money (V): See Income velocity of money.

wage-price controls: Direct governmental restraints on the wage and price decisions of market participants. (13)

wage rate: The amount of money paid for an hour's work; the price of labor. (25)

yield: The rate of return on a bond; the annual interest payment divided by the purchase price. (11)

INDEX

ABOUT THE AUTHOR

Dr. Bradley Schiller has over a decade's experience teaching introductory economics, at American University, the University of California (Berkeley and Santa Cruz), and the University of Maryland. Dr. Schiller's unique contribution to teaching is his ability to relate basic principles to current socioeconomic problems, institutions, and public policy decisions. This perspective is evident throughout *The Economy Today*.

Dr. Schiller derives this policy focus from his extensive experience as a Washington consultant. He has been a consultant to most major federal agencies, many congressional committees, and political candidates. In addition, he has evaluated scores of government programs and helped design others. His studies of discrimination, employment and training programs, reindustrialization, pensions, welfare, and Social Security have appeared and been cited in both professional journals and popular media. In addition, Dr. Schiller has explained and evaluated "Reagan Economics" at numerous seminars and on radio shows.

Dr. Schiller received his Ph.D. from Harvard in 1969. His B.A. degree, with great distinction, was completed at the University of California (Berkeley) in 1965. He is now a professor of economics in the School of Government and Public Administration at The American University. In that capacity he is teaching basic economics to government workers, a job he hopes will have some visible impact one day.

FEDERAL BUDGET RECEIPTS AND OUTLAYS, FISCAL YEARS 1929–83 (Millions of dollars)

Fiscal year	Receipts	Outlays	Surplus or deficit (−)
1929	3,862	3,127	734
1933	1,997	4,598	−2,602
1939	4,979	8,841	−3,862
1940	6,361	9,456	−3,095
1941	8,621	13,634	−5,013
1942	14,350	35,114	−20,764
1943	23,649	78,533	−54,884
1944	44,276	91,280	−47,004
1945	45,216	92,690	−47,474
1946	39,327	55,183	−15,856
1947	38,394	34,532	3,862
1948	41,774	29,773	12,001
1949	39,437	38,834	603
1950	39,485	42,597	−3,112
1951	51,646	45,546	6,100
1952	66,204	67,721	−1,517
1953	69,574	76,107	−6,533
1954	69,719	70,890	−1,170
1955	65,469	68,509	−3,041
1956	74,547	70,460	4,087
1957	79,990	76,741	3,249
1958	79,636	82,575	−2,939
1959	79,249	92,104	−12,855
1960	92,492	92,223	269
1961	94,389	97,795	−3,406
1962	99,676	106,813	−7,137
1963	106,560	111,311	−4,751
1964	112,662	118,584	−5,922
1965	116,833	118,430	−1,596
1966	130,856	134,652	−3,796
1967	148,906	157,608	−8,702
1968	152,973	178,134	−25,161
1969	186,882	183,645	3,236
1970	192,807	195,652	−2,845
1971	187,139	210,172	−23,033
1972	207,309	230,681	−23,373
1973	230,799	245,647	−14,849
1974	263,224	267,912	−4,688
1975	279,090	324,245	−45,154
1976	298,060	364,473	−66,413
Transition quarter	81,232	94,188	−12,956
1977	355,559	400,506	−44,948
1978	399,561	448,368	−48,807
1979	463,302	490,997	−27,694
1980	517,112	576,675	−59,563
1981	599,272	657,204	−57,932
1982[1]	626,753	725,331	−98,578
1983[1]	666,118	757,638	−91,520

[1] Estimates.

Sources: Department of the Treasury and Office of Management and Budget.